#1X34.18

The Marriage and
Family Experience

Third Edition

The Marriage and Family Experience

Third Edition

Bryan Strong
UNIVERSITY OF CALIFORNIA, SANTA CRUZ

Christine DeVault

West Publishing Company
St. Paul   New York   Los Angeles   San Francisco

Copy editing:	Elaine Linden
Artwork:	Ben Turner Graphics (graphic illustrations)
	Susan Tannehill (unit opening art work)
Composition:	Janet Hansen & Associates
Cover:	Saybrook Institute and Research Center

Library of Congress Cataloging-in-Publication Data

Strong, Bryan.
   The marriage and family experience.

   Rev. ed. of: The marriage and family experience /
Bryan Strong . . . [et al.] 2nd ed. c1983.
   Bibliography: p.
   Includes index.
   1. Marriage.   2. Family.   I. DeVault, Christine.
II. Marriage and family experience.   III. Title.
HQ734.S9738   1986   306.8   85–26567
ISBN 0–314–95455–4

A Student Study Guide

A study guide has been developed to assist students in mastering the concepts presented in this text. It reinforces chapter material presenting it in a concise format with review questions. An examination copy is available to instructors by contacting West Publishing Company. Students can purchase the study guide from the local bookstore under the title *Study Guide to Accompany the Marriage and Family Experience*, Third Edition, prepared by Linda Green.

Acknowledgments

Cover   The quilt represented on the cover is called the San Francisco Peace Quilt and depicts the world's family, young and old, male and female, united in peace. It includes the work of over 100 people with the center design based on a drawing by Jonnie Vance and was made especially for the people of Leningrad, USSR. For more information, please contact Saybrook Institute and Research Center, 1772 Vallejo Street, San Francisco, CA 94123;   **19**   Drawing by Koren; © 1981 The New Yorker Magazine, Inc.;   **22**   Reprinted from *U.S. News & World Report*, Issue of 6/20/83. Copyright, 1983, U.S. News & World Report, Inc.;   **26**   From *The Nature of the Child* by Jerome Kagan. © 1984 by Basic Books, Inc., Publishers. Reprinted by permission of the publisher.;   **28**   Copyright © 1984 by The New York Times Company. Reprinted by permission.;   **35**   Drawing by D. Frandon; © 1969 The New Yorker Magazine, Inc.;   **50**   Copyright 1985 Time, Inc. All rights reserved. Reprinted by permission from *Time*.;   **51**   "Dating Behaviors of University Students," *Family Relations*, April, 1981, David Knox and Kenneth Wilson. Reprinted by permission of National Council on Family Relations.;   **55**   William J. Goode, *The Family*, © 1982, pp. 10–11. Reprinted by permission of Prentice-Hall, Inc., Englewood Cliffs, New Jersey.;   **56**   "The Dyadic Adjustment Scale," *Journal of Marriage and the Family*, February, 1976, Graham B. Spanier. Reprinted by permission of National Council on Family Relations.;   **79**   © Keith Reinhart;   **82**   From *The Rise of David Levinsky* by Abraham Cahan. Copyright 1917 by Harper & Row, Publishers, Inc.; renewed 1945 by Abraham Cahan. Reprinted by permission of Harper & Row, Publishers, Inc.;   **111**   "The Inexpressive Male: A Tragedy of American Society," *The Family Coordinator*, October, 1971, Jack Balswick and Charles Peek. Reprinted by permission of National Council on Family Relations.;   **113**   Copyright © 1983 by Susan Brownmiller. Reprinted by permission of Linden Press, a division of Simon & Schuster, Inc.;   **114**   Copyright 1984, by

(continued following index)

To the memory of Charlie Braun, a dedicated teacher and friend

If you have built castles in the air, your work need not be lost; that is where they should be. Now put the foundations under them.

HENRY DAVID THOREAU

Contents in Brief

Contents

Feature
Conventionality   38

Understanding Yourself
Using Theory to Understand
Yourself   46

CHAPTER 3

History of Marriage and the Family   59

Understanding Yourself
Discovering Your Family's
Past   70

Feature
Childhood Under
Slavery   77

PART TWO

Getting Together   85

PART THREE

Sexuality   181

CHAPTER 7

Sexual Learning and Behavior   183

CHAPTER 8

Sexuality and Relationships   213

Understanding Yourself
Styles of Miscom-
munication   430

CHAPTER 15

Family Dysfunctions: Violence and Abuse   451

Feature
The Mythology of Wife
Battering   455

Feature
Perspectives on the Abuse of
Children   462

Preface

It's been almost a decade since we began writing the first edition of *The Marriage and Family Experience*. It has always been a pleasure working on this textbook. As we worked on this third edition, rather than finding the research and writing repetitive and tedious, we found ourselves experiencing the same high level of interest and curiosity in exploring marriage and the family as we did in writing the previous editions. Once again we had the opportunity to reflect on both the nature of marriage and the family in America today and on our own relationships.

Revising the text was both pleasurable and challenging. We felt challenged to try new ways of making the text more valuable and interesting to students and professors alike. We strongly believe that academically-oriented courses can encourage personal knowledge and that functionally-oriented courses can encourage reflection and intellectual insight. We wanted to write a text that both pursued academic excellence and also gave students insights into their own personal lives and relationships. The new pedagogy in this edition reflects our attempts to unify functionally-oriented and academically-oriented approaches to the study of marriage and the family.

Additionally, working on this book is pleasurable because of the inherent nature of the field: to understand marriage and the family is to understand what it means to be human. In our marriages and families (or their alternatives) much of our humanness is formed, developed, and challenged. The relationships are as complex as any found in literature and drama: in our intimate relationships, whether they are family or family-like, we have the potential for experiencing the fullest range of human activities, feelings, and emotions: love, birth, intimacy, hatred, growth, illness, fear, courage, destruction, death, and sacrifice. Our family relationships may take strikingly diverse forms: traditional nuclear families, single-parent families, stepfamilies, families without children, dual-worker marriages, cohabitation, and so on. The significance and complexities of our relationships make work in marriage and the family both enormously challenging and rewarding.

Approaching marriage and the family from the perspective of only a single discipline such as sociology or psychology would leave us much as the blind men who tried to describe the nature of the elephant, each mistook a part for the whole. We have tried to extend our understanding by incorporating work not only from sociology and psychology but also from history, economics, and literature.

Our belief in the interconnectedness of the academic and the personal has led us to include a new chapter entitled "Studying Marriage and the Family." We show how theory enables us to better understand the everyday workings of our own lives. We also discuss the significance of methodology, as we are bombarded daily with radio and television psychologists, countless "pop surveys" and "studies" about "how to make love last," and so on. How can we evaluate them? This new chapter tries to answer that question.

We have also written another new chapter entitled "Marriage and Family Strengths" reflecting the growing interest in discovering what makes marriages and families successful. The chapter provides students with tools to strengthen their personal, marital, and familial relationships. As the last chapter, it summarizes the textbook's major themes and concludes it on a positive note.

Each chapter has been substantially revised or rewritten. About a third of the text is new material. A majority of the readings are new and contemporary.

A good textbook must be accessible to its students. To accomplish this, we have carefully thought out and planned its pedagogy. The textbook features questions at the beginning of each chapter to allow students to test their own preconceptions and knowledge. Each chapter begins with an outline and ends with a summary to assist students' comprehension of the material. Each chapter includes an "Understanding Yourself" feature that consists of values-clarification questions, exercises, and projects to encourage students to relate the chapter's concepts to their own lives. Along the margins of the text are numerous aphorisms, epigrams, sayings, and quotes that encourage reflection about the material and are often valuable starting points for discussions. Finally, each chapter ends with readings. These readings provide a different pace, give students various points of view, and are useful for classroom discussions. Students often treat the readings as a reward for finishing a chapter. As in the previous editions, we have maintained a reading level in the text appropriate to most college undergraduates.

In doing our research, we took full advantage of the computer technology available to scholars. To supplement traditional bibliographic research, we extensively used the Family Resources Data Base which allowed us to access over 60,000 citations in moments. We also utilized MELVYL which uses the statewide holdings of the University of California's library system as its data base. The result is a comprehensively researched textbook containing the latest research in the field. Our bibliography consists of almost 1300 citations, of which about a third are new to this edition.

Academic writing depends on the exchange of ideas, criticism, and help of other scholars and professors. We were especially fortunate to have a number of professors read the manuscript for this new edition. They include, alphabetically, Gwenn Carr, San Diego Mesa College; Paul Dail, University of Northern Iowa; Ann Goetting, Western Kentucky University; Allan Kirkpatrick, Riverside Community College; Amselyn Marshall, San Antonio College; Sandi Schrader, University of Connecticut; and Richard Stanville, Normandale Community College. Linda Green (Normandale Community College) has written an exceptional and innovative study guide, while Bob Turley (San Bernardino Valley College), who has used our textbook since its first publication, prepared a fine instructors' manual for this edition, as he did for the previous one.

Our research was greatly enhanced by the help of our friend Terrence Crowley, Professor of Library and Information Science at San Jose State University. He helped us with difficult reference questions relating to government documents and, with the assistance of a graduate student class, updated many of the statistics from our second edition. We would especially like to thank one of his graduate students, Libby Westie, for her bibliographic work.

We also received invaluable assistance from the reference staff and government documents staff at the Dean McHenry Library at the University of California at Santa

Cruz. Al Eickhorn spent many hours working on our data base searches; Alan Ritch worked with great perseverence tracking down elusive statistics and data. Judy Steen, Jacquelyn Marie, Jan Mandeville, and Rex Beckham all provided great assistance to us. The reference staff at the Stanford University Library and the Lane Library at the Stanford Medical School also provided us with courteous assistance.

Mary Nelson, the editor of *The Family Life Educator*, and Kay Clark, her editorial assistant, were extremely helpful in allowing us to use the National Family Life Education Network's library facilities and in locating material for us.

We would like to thank West Publishing Company for its support of this book and its encouragement of our participation in the development of the design and art program. We would like to thank our editor Carole Grumney for her considerable work and dedication to this new edition. We would also like to thank our designer, Kristen Weber, for her sensitivity, creativity, and unflagging energy. The constant and open exchange of ideas between the designer, editor, and ourselves has given the book a unity of written text, visual design, and underlying spirit. Thanks are also due to Janet Hansen who typeset all three editions of this textbook and who has become one of its biggest fans (she reads it as she typesets).

Nikoletta Bolas entered much of this text into the computer. She worked with us for many months, often under great pressure, and maintained a cheerful presence. Jolinda Letiere also worked on the manuscript.

The senior author would like to express his appreciation to the University of California, Santa Cruz, for the opportunity of teaching courses in marriage and the family and human sexuality and for providing office space during the writing of this textbook. In particular, he would like to thank Professor David Marlowe for his early and consistent support of these courses in the Psychology Board of Studies.

Bryan Strong
Christine DeVault

PART ONE

Marriage and the Family
in Perspective

CHAPTER 1

The Meaning of
Marriage and the Family

PREVIEW

To gain a sense of what you already know about the material in this chapter, answer "true" or "false" to the statements below. You will find the answers as you read the chapter.

1. The traditional nuclear family is the healthiest form of the family. True or false?
2. The majority of American families are traditional nuclear families in which the husband works and the wife remains at home caring for the children. True or false?
3. Because of technological advances, the family is no longer the sole agent of reproduction. True or false?
4. All cultures traditionally divide work into male and female work. True or false?
5. Because of industrialization, families are no longer important as productive units. True or false?
6. If women were paid for their household and homemaking responsibilities, they would make approximately $20,000 a year. True or false?
7. The majority of cultures throughout the world prefer polygyny (the practice of having several wives). True or false?
8. The higher the educational level for males, the higher the divorce rate. True or false?
9. Because of a return to traditional values, the number of unmarried couples who live together has been decreasing. True or false?
10. One out of ten children lives in poverty. True or false?

Outline

. . . if one advances confidently in the direction of his dreams, and endeavors to live the life which he has imagined, he will meet with a success unexpected in his common hours.

HENRY DAVID THOREAU

We generally take the family in which we grow up for granted. It is part of the natural backdrop of our lives. At various times, we may like or dislike our parents or siblings, fight with them, love them, ignore them; but the roles they play in our lives are generally invisible. We are usually not aware of them. This taken-for-granted quality of families is important. It exists when a family is more or less performing its functions. Only during a crisis—a severe illness, a sudden conflict, unemployment, divorce, or some other incapacitating event—do we notice the roles each person plays and recognize how vital our family and its members are to us.

The family dates back to prehistoric times when our hominid ancestors developed the original family unit. Although the family has evolved, it has maintained many of its original functions. It produces and socializes children, acts as a unit of economic cooperation, gives us significant roles as children, husbands, wives, and parents, and provides a source of intimacy. Modern society, however, is altering many of these functions, taking over some of them from the family and making others more difficult to perform. Many of the most recent changes in marriage and the family—divorce, single-parent families, working mothers—are adjustments to our contemporary society. However, our culture tends to idealize the nuclear family—the two-parent family with children. Any variation on it is seen as a decline, instead of as an alternative family form. Furthermore, because we think in terms of the nuclear family, we fail to appreciate the rich network of kin—aunts, uncles, cousins, grandparents—that most of us have. It is within the complex web of family life that we gain our identities. Whatever our feelings about them, our families are responsible for much of who we are and who we will be.

The main characteristics of the family were developed in prehistoric times. The males hunted and defended territories while the women remained near home. Males and females bonded in love relationships and shared the same hearth. This pattern seems very familiar. Some males still like to think of themselves as hunters as they set forth to "bring home the bacon" in the form of a paycheck. These characteristics have endured for millenia.

Neither man nor nation can exist without a sublime idea.

FYODOR DOSTOEVSKY (1821–1881)

Now, however, the family unit is undergoing fundamental alterations. The traditional nuclear family has become a minority family in contemporary America. Women no longer remain at home; they too go out to bring home the bacon, blurring the sexual division of labor and creating the dual-worker marriage. Similarly, women defer childbearing or choose not to have children, creating the childless marriage and giving themselves greater autonomy. Divorce rates are high. The single-parent

The family dates back thousands of years. This American family performs the same functions that families in Asia, Latin America, Europe, and Africa perform. Families give birth to and socialize children, cooperate economically, assign social roles, and provide intimacy.

family, usually headed by a woman, is common. Yet these changes do not signify the end of the family. Rather, they are signs of its resiliency in the face of sweeping changes in American society. Families continue to carry out their functions. (For a discussion of contemporary American marriages and families, see the reading, "Marriage: It's Back in Style" on pages 22–26.)

☐ THE FUNCTIONS OF THE FAMILY

Definitions

Marriage is a union between a man and a woman: they perform a public ritual (which means that their union is socially recognized), they are united sexually, and they cooperate in economic matters. The union is assumed to be more or less permanent. If they have children, their children will have certain legal rights. *Cohabitation* ("living together") may be similar to marriage in many of its functions and roles, but it does not have equivalent legal sanctions or rights.

A *family* has traditionally been defined as a married couple or group of adult kin who cooperate and divide labor along sex lines, rear children, and share a common dwelling place. A variety of family forms are emerging to challenge this definition: the single-parent family, egalitarian marriage, dual-worker marriage, and childless marriage, for example. (For a discussion of the unique features of Western marriage, see the reading by Jerome Kagan, "The Individual as the Basic Social Unit," on pages 26–28.)

The family performs four important functions. First, it produces and socializes children. Second, it acts as a unit of economic cooperation. Third, it assigns status

The family is a society limited in numbers, but nevertheless a true society, anterior to every state or nation, with rights and duties of its own, wholly independent of the commonwealth.

POPE LEO XIII (1810–1903)

and social roles to individuals. Fourth, it provides a source of intimate relationships. Technology, industrialization, mobility, and other factors are altering the way the family performs its functions. While these are the basic functions that families are "supposed" to fulfill, families do not necessarily fulfill them all nor always fulfill them well.

Reproduction and Socialization

The family makes society possible by producing and rearing children to replace the older members of society as they die off. In the past reproduction resulted only through sexual intercourse between a man and a woman. Through marriage it became an essential function of the family. But even this domain has not remained immune to technological change. The development of techniques for artificial insemination has separated reproduction from sexual intercourse. In addition to permitting infertile couples to give birth, such techniques have also made it possible for homosexuals to become parents. In 1978 the first "test-tube" baby was born after an ovum was fertilized by sperm in a glass dish and then implanted in the mother's uterus to follow the normal course of gestation. Although such procedures are relatively rare, they may nevertheless become more widespread, driving a wedge into the previously inviolate connection between sex and reproduction.

Children are helpless and dependent for years following birth. They must learn how to walk and talk, how to take care of themselves, how to act, how to love, how to touch and be touched. Teaching the child how to be human and how to fit into his or her particular culture is one of the family's most important tasks. It is socialization, or what Virginia Satir (1972) calls "peoplemaking."

Traditionally, the family has been responsible for socialization. This role, however, is dramatically shifting away from the family. One researcher (Guidubaldi, 1980) believes that the increasing lack of commitment to childrearing may be one of the most significant societal changes in our lifetime. With the rise of compulsory education, the state has become responsible for a large share of socialization after a child reaches the age of five. The increase in working mothers has placed many infants, toddlers, and small children in day-care centers, reducing the family's role in socialization. As many as half of the children between the ages of three and five may be in nursery school, day care, or kindergarten. Even while children are at home, television rather than their family may be mainly rearing them. Watching television is the most important activity for most children up to age fourteen. So strong is the role of television in young children's lives that, according to one study of four- to six-year-olds, 44 percent said they preferred television to "daddy" (Federal Trade Commission, 1978).

Economic Cooperation

The family is also a unit of economic cooperation. It divides its labor along sex lines. This division of labor along sex lines is universal and, according to anthropologist Claude Lévi-Strauss (1956), is what makes marriage necessary. Although sexual division of labor is characteristic of virtually all cultures, the work each sex performs (apart from childbearing and making war) varies from culture to culture. Among the Nambikwara in Africa, for example, the fathers take care of the babies and clean them when they soil themselves; the concubines of the chief prefer hunting over domestic activities. In American society, men traditionally have worked away from home while women have remained at home caring for the children and house. There is no reason, however, that these roles cannot be reversed. Such tasks are assigned by culture, not biology.

Regardless of what activities men and women do, traditionally work has been divided into "man's work" and "woman's work." The division of work along sex lines makes the sexes interdependent, cementing their need for each other (Lévi-Strauss, 1956). In primitive societies, where the family is the basic producing unit, it is impossible to imagine a man or woman remaining unmarried. It would be impossible to survive. In contemporary America, however, interdependence between the sexes has greatly lessened. In earlier times, a man needed a wife to cook his food; today he can make his own dinner or eat out. A woman once needed a husband for economic support; today she can support herself, thanks partly to an expanded job market, although most women have difficulty supporting children single-handedly. One result of reduced female dependence on males is that women who work are more likely to divorce than those who remain at home.

The family is still an important producing unit, although its productive activities are less apparent than formerly. Modern families no longer raise their own food entirely, weave their own cloth, or spin their own yarn. (Burns, 1972). We usually do not view the family as a productive unit because of its relative unimportance in the money economy as a whole. The family, for example, pays no wages for its work, nor does it call its members employees. The husband does not get paid for building a shelf or attending to the children; the wife is not paid for rewiring the house or cooking. Although children contribute to the household economy by cleaning house or helping prepare meals (Cogle and Tasker, 1982), they generally are not paid for cooking, cleaning their rooms, or watching their younger brothers or sisters. Yet they are all engaged in productive labor (see Hefferan, 1982a).

Recently, economists have begun to reexamine the family as a productive unit (see *Family Economics Review*, 1982, [3] for a special issue on "Household Production"). If the work done by men and women in their households were compensated monetarily, the total would be equal to the entire amount paid out in wages by every corporation in the United States. In 1980 unpaid household work by women was worth about $825 billion; such work by men was worth $375 billion. Similarly, the assets of households—the homes, cars, appliances, lawnmowers, tools, vacuum cleaners, and so on—produce an annual return equal to the net profits of all U.S. corporations (Burns, 1972). The household as a productive unit is very much alive. When work outside the home becomes less meaningful and prices increase because of inflation, family members produce more goods. In 1981, for example, families produced approximately $16 billion worth or vegetables and fruits from their home gardens (Adler et al., 1982). About 34 percent of the nation's families have a garden, and gardening is the fifth most popular hobby in America. Yet gardening is rarely seen as one of the family's productive activities because families don't produce a cash crop.

Although the family no longer produces as many goods as it did in the past, it still provides valuable services for its members. As a service unit, it is dominated by women. Because men are paid wages for their work outside the home and women's work at home is not paid, the productive contributions of homemakers have been overlooked. Yet women's household work is equal to about 44 percent of the gross national product (GNP), and the value of such work is double the reported earnings of women. Burns (1972) wrote:

The invisible household economy might also be called the matriarchal economy, because it is dominated by women. They perform most of the labor, make most of the household decisions, and are employed as managers for the labor and assets of the household. More than a few observers have noted that the household economy is invisible precisely because it is controlled by women and that present accounting conventions have the effect of demeaning the work and value of women.

If a woman were paid wages for her labor as mother and housewife according to the wage scale for chauffeurs, nurses, baby sitters, cooks, therapists, and so on, today her services would have been worth more than $40,000 a year. Many women would make more for their work in the home than men do for their jobs outside the home. Since family power is partly a function of who earns the money, paying women for their household work might have a significant impact on husband-wife relations.

You can see for yourself how your work at home can be translated into monetary terms by simply comparing how much it costs to make a dinner with the cost of the same meal out. Next time you have dinner at your favorite restaurant (this could be a good excuse to go out), keep track of how much you spend (including the tip) and for what. Then make the identical meal at home or at a friend's house. Tabulate how much the ingredients cost. Keep track of how long it takes you to shop, prepare he meal, and wash the dishes afterward. Subtract the cost of the ingredients from how much you spent at the restaurant. Then divide the balance by the amount of time it took you to shop, prepare the meal, and clean up. That figure will give you a rough idea of your hourly wage. You can do the same computations for plumbing, automobile repair, yard work, cleaning, and so on.

Assignment of Status and Social Roles

Assignment of Status. The status or place we are given in society is acquired in large part through our families. Our families place us in a certain social class, such as blue collar (working class), middle class, or upper class. We learn the ways of our class through identifying with our families. In blue-collar families, for example, we probably learn that work is merely a means of earning a living; work does not necessarily bring fulfillment, but is often drudgery done for the sake of family. Family is an escape from work (Rubin, 1976). In middle-class families, we are probably taught that work gives a person a sense of success or failure as an individual; it is a source of pleasure and fulfillment. Work and family may compete for loyalties. Our families also give us our racial or ethnic identities as white, black, Hispanic, Italian-American, Jewish, Japanese-American, and so forth. They provide us with a religious tradition as Protestant, Catholic, Jewish, Greek Orthodox, agnostic, atheist, and so on. These identities help form our cultural values and expectations. Their significance in our lives can be grasped if we imagine ourselves growing up in a different social class, racial or ethnic group, or religion. How would we feel about work? What would we expect from life? How would we be treated differently by society? Much of what

This "family tree" represents three generations of contemporary Americans. The family here includes both families of orientation and families of procreation. American families are often diverse in their ethnic heritage. These grandparents, at the base of the tree, were born in Austria and Czechoslovakia; their children and their partners in Switzerland, Denmark, Sweden, Australia, and the United States. The grandchildren's ancestral roots are both European and African; one was born in England, one in the United States.

we believe to be our own individual values and preferences is the result of the assignment of a certain status through our family.

Assignment of Social Roles.   Equally as important as the status we inherit from our families are the various roles we fulfill as family members. During our lifetimes, most of us will belong to two families. The *family of orientation* (also called *family of origin*) is the family in which we grow up, the family that orients us to the world. The *family of procreation* is the family we form if we have children. Although increasing numbers of Americans are choosing singlehood, cohabitation, or childless marriages, most Americans will form families of procreation sometime in their lives. Much of our identity is formed in the crucibles of these two families.

In our family of orientation, we are given the roles of child, son or daughter, brother or sister. We internalize these roles until they become a part of our being. In each of these roles we are expected to act in certain ways: for example, children obey their parents, sons roughhouse with their fathers, daughters imitate their mothers, siblings help each other. Sometimes our feelings fit the expectations of our roles. Other times they do not.

The family roles of offspring and sibling are most important when we are living with our parents and siblings in our family of orientation. After we leave home, they gradually diminish in importance, although they continue throughout our lives. In relation to our parents, we never cease being children; in relation to our siblings, we never cease being brothers or sisters. The roles change as we grow older. They begin the moment we are born and end only when we die.

As we leave our family of orientation, we usually are also leaving adolescence and entering adulthood. Being an adult in our society is defined in part by entering new family roles: husband or wife, father or mother. These roles are given to us by our family of procreation. They take priority over the roles we had in our family of orientation. When we marry, we transfer our primary loyalties from our parents and siblings to our husbands and wives; later, if we have children, we form additional bonds with them. When we assume the role of a husband or wife, we assume an entire new social identity linked with responsibility, work, and parenting. In earlier times these roles were considered to be lifelong in duration. That assumption is questioned now.

It is principally in roles as parents that we assume a lifelong obligation. We can divorce our spouse but we cannot divorce our children. Our roles as parents change dramatically, depending on whether our children are infants, young children, adolescents, or adults, but these roles are among the most enduring we will experience. They may be second only to our gender identity as male or female.

Intimate Relationships

Intimacy is a primary human need. According to Aristotle, "Only an animal or a god can live alone." He appears to be right. One study discovered that in most health categories, divorced and single persons appeared the least healthy (Verbrugge, 1979), and in other studies loneliness is correlated with disease and suicide (see also Haring-Hidore et al., 1985; Weingarten, 1985).

> Unlike all other organizations, families incorporate new members only by birth, adoption, or marriage, and members can leave only by death, if then.
>
> MONICA McGOLDRICK
> and ELIZABETH CARTER

The fact is that social isolation, the lack of human companionship . . . and chronic human loneliness are significant contributors to premature death. . . . Cancer, tuberculosis, suicide, accidents, mental disease—all are significantly influenced by human companionship. Nature uses many weapons to shorten the lives of lonely people.

Animals may give us intimacy if we do not find it with humans. Studies on the role of pets in human relationships suggest that the most prized aspects of pets, especially dogs and cats, is their attentiveness to their owners, their welcoming and greeting behaviors, and their role as confidants—qualities valued in our intimate relationships with humans as well (Arehart-Treichel, 1982). One study found that 98 percent of dog owners spent time talking to their pets, 75 percent thought their dogs were sensitive to their moods and feelings, and 28 percent even confided in their pets. Pets give children an opportunity to nurture, a best friend, someone to love. For adults, especially men, they are an outlet for touching; they act as companions and as social catalysts. Dog owners are more likely to interact with strangers when they are with their dogs than when they are without them (also see Brody, 1983).

The need for intimate relationships, whether they are satisfactory or not, may hold unhappy marriages together indefinitely. Loneliness may be a terrible specter. Among the newly divorced, it may be the worst aspect of marital breakup (Weiss, 1976).

Marriage and the family furnish emotional security and support. This has probably been true from earliest times. The book of Ecclesiastes, written thousands of years ago, suggests the significance of companionship (Ecclesiastes 4:9–12):

Two are better than one, because they have a good reward for their toil. For if they fall, one will lift up his fellow; but woe to him who is alone when he falls and has not another to lift him up. Again if two lie together, they are warm; but how can one be warm alone? And though a man might prevail against one, two will withstand him. A three-fold cord is not quickly broken.

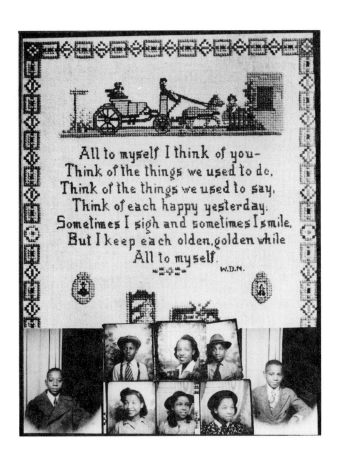

Families bring a sense of meaning and identity to their members. They are the crucible from which we are formed.

In our families we find our strongest bonds. These bonds can be forged from love, attachment, loyalty, or guilt. Whatever their source, they are extremely powerful.

Since the nineteenth century, marriage and the family have become important as the center of companionship and intimacy. They have become a "haven in a heartless world" (Lasch, 1978). As society has become more industrialized and bureaucratic, it is increasingly within the family that we expect to find intimacy and companionship. In the larger world around us we are generally perceived in terms of our roles. A professor sees us primarily as a student; a used car salesperson relates to us as a potential buyer; a politician views us as a voter. Only among our intimates are we seen on a personal level as John or Mary. Before marriage our friends are our intimates. After marriage our partner is expected to be the one with whom we are most intimate. With our partner we disclose ourselves most completely, share our hopes, rear our children, grow old.

The paradox of marriage, however, is that sometimes our families do not provide nurturance or intimacy. Wives commonly complain that their husbands don't talk to them. Husbands complain that their wives talk too much. Families may also breed conflict, anger, humiliation. Studies suggest that next to battlefields and scenes of large urban riots, families may be the most dangerous place to be (Lunde, 1976). One-fourth of all murders in the United States occur within the family. Half of these are husband-wife murders; the other half involve parents, children, or other close relatives. A quarter of all couples in the United States have had at least one fight

Home—the place where, when you have to go there, they have to let you in.

ROBERT FROST

Marriage is a great institution, but I'm not ready for an institution yet.

MAE WEST

including physical violence. More than 90 percent of parents in the United States physically punish their children.

☐ THE EXTENDED FAMILY

Most people throughout the world live in some form of extended family. Parents and children, the core of the nuclear family, combine in various ways to form extended families. Extended families may be formed in two ways: through marriage and through blood relationships. In the first form, conjugal extended families are created through polygamy, that is, plural marriages. The most common form of polygamy is polygyny, the practice of having several wives. One study of cultures throughout the world found that 75 percent of these cultures (representing, nevertheless, a minority of the world's population) preferred polygyny, and one percent preferred polyandry, the practice of having two or more husbands (Murdock, 1957). Plural marriages are in the minority primarily for simple economic reasons. They are generally a sign of status that relatively few people can afford. Problems of jealousy may arise in plural marriages—the Fula in Africa, for example, call the second wife "the jealous one"—but usually control mechanisms are built into the society to ease the problem. The wives may be related, especially as sisters; if they are unrelated, they usually have separate dwellings. Women often prefer that there be several wives: plural wives are a sign of status and, more important, ease the workload of individual wives.

The second form of extended family is based on consanguine relationships, that is, blood ties. In cultures that practice monogamous marriage—an exclusive relationship between a man and woman—extended families can be formed only along blood lines. The extended family may take the form of the nuclear family combined with grandparents, aunts or uncles, older siblings, cousins, or adult siblings.

According to Murdock (1957), 24 percent of the world's cultures, including our own, prefer monogamy as the primary marital form. With the high American divorce rate, monogamy may no longer be the best way of describing our marriage forms. Our marriage system might be called serial monogamy or modified polygamy because one person may have several spouses over his or her lifetime. With the rise of blended families (also called remarried or stepfamilies), which include children from a previous marriage, a new form of extended family is gaining significance in the United States. In the blended family a child is quite likely to have stepsiblings, and half-brothers or half-sisters living in the same household. If the child's other parent has formed another family, the other parent may have stepchildren and children by his or her new partner. Stepsiblings are created by marriage; half-siblings are formed by birth.

Although American families often exist as some form of extended family, we often don't recognize the fact because we uncritically accept the nuclear family model as a description of reality. We may even be blind to the reality of our own family structure. When someone asks us to name the members of our family, if we are unmarried we will probably name our parents, brothers, and sisters. If we are married, we will probably name our husband or wife and children. Only if questioned further may we include our grandparents, aunts or uncles, cousins, even friends or neighbors who are "like family." We may not name all our blood relatives, but we will probably name the ones with whom we feel emotionally close. Despite our habitual attitudes, the extended family is part of the reality of American family life. (For a discussion of non-Western marriages, see the reading "Marriage in India" on pages 28–30.)

Marriage enlarges the scene of our happiness and our miseries.

JOSEPH ADDISON (1672–1719)

☐ THE KINSHIP SYSTEM

Our families of origin and procreation provide us with some of the most important roles we will assume in life. These family roles combine with other family roles to form the *kinship system*. The kinship system is the social organization of the family. In American society the basic kinship system consists of parents and children, but it may include other relatives as well. Aunts, uncles, cousins, grandparents, and in-laws may also be part of an American family's kinship system. Each person in this system has certain rights and obligations as a result of his or her position in the family structure. Furthermore, a person may occupy several positions at the same time. For example, an eighteen-year-old female may simultaneously be a daughter, a sister, a cousin, an aunt, and a granddaughter. Each role entails different rights and obligations. As a daughter, she may have to defer to certain decisions of her parents; as a sister, to share her bedroom; as a cousin, to attend a wedding; as a granddaughter, to send a Christmas card. What are the different roles you have in your kinship system? What are the rights and obligations that accompany these roles?

The rights and obligations of relatives outside the basic kinship system are less strong and less clearly articulated. In other societies, by contrast, they may be very extensive. Among the Nayar of India, for example, men have a number of clearly defined obligations toward the children of their sisters and female cousins, although they have few obligations toward their own children (Gough, 1968). Nevertheless, our kin create a rich social network for us. Because we tend to think of our family as simply parents and children, we often fail to recognize the vital kinship system of which we are a part. Studies suggest that most people have a large number of kin living in their area (Gagnon and Greenblat, 1978). Interaction of adult children and parents is frequent and significant enough that some researchers believe the American family can be characterized as a *modified extended family* (Troll, 1971). This family form is characterized by adult children and parents living close to each other, making regular visits, and helping each other with child care, housework, maintenance, repairs, loans, and gifts. The relations between siblings are often strong throughout the life cycle.

Kinship ties ultimately depend more on feeling than on biology. A brother or sister can seem like a stranger; a grandmother can be more of a mother than one's biological mother; a parent can be like a brother or sister. The names we call our relatives or friends reflect degrees of feelings (Schneider, 1980). Psychologically, it is significant whether we call our mother "mom," "mother," "mummy," or by a nickname or her first name. The same is true for fathers. But an interesting variation can be seen in the case of fathers, according to Schneider (1980):

Informants who use "father" explained that they would seldom if ever use "pop" or "pa" because it was entirely too familiar and somehow did not imply the measure of respect that was required. Those who use "pop" or "pa" take the same position, but from the other side. They would seldom use "father," they say, because it implies authority and respect in greater measure than either they or their fathers deemed appropriate, and more formality and imper- sonal distance than was desirable. This is not to say that "pop" or "pa" or "dad" imply any lack of respect or any absence of authority. Quite the contrary. It is just that these qualities are not the salient ones in those terms.

Blood relationships do not define the type of feelings a person will have. Instead, they provide a framework to encourage brotherly feelings toward a brother, motherly feelings toward a child, and so on.

Children . . . have no choice about being born into a sys- tem; nor do parents have a choice, once children are born, as to the existence of the responsibilities of parenthood. . . . In fact, no family rela- tionships except marriage are entered into by choice.

MONICA McGOLDRICK
and ELIZABETH CARTER

*Most individuals and families
are not isolated, but exist in a
rich network of kin, friends,
and neighbors who give them
strength.*

Kinship ties symbolize love and trust, the willingness to give without question, to receive regardless of merit. In this manner, we transform good friends and neighbors into kin: "He is like a brother to me," "She's like my own sister," "We are like cousins." Because divorce and geographic mobility are breaking down our ability to interact with in-laws and biological kin, we are beginning to form new kinds of kin (Kempler, 1976; Lindsey, 1982). Single persons may attempt to create families from friends by sharing time, problems, meals, and houses with each other (Lindsey, 1982). They may create cooperative or communal living arrangements with each other. Single parents may form networks with other single parents for emotional support and exchange of child care (McLanahan, 1981). Family networks may be formed in which three or four families from the same neighborhood share problems, exchange services, and enjoy leisure together. In the *affiliated family*, another person, usually an older widow, widower, or single person, spends time with the family in a role similar to that of an aunt, uncle, or grandparent, joining in family activities, child care, work, meals, housework, or recreation. Often he or she is called by some family name such as "Auntie," "Gramps," or "Pop" (Kempler, 1976).

The rise of remarriage and blended families has made kinship ties between these family members more difficult. A major problem is that the kinship ties between stepparent and stepchild are initially based on law. The ties have not evolved; rather roles have been imposed. The role of stepparent is particularly difficult because more often than not, the stepparent is replacing an absent parent living elsewhere, rather than a parent who has died. Rivalries, feelings of loyalty to biological parents, questions about the legitimacy of a stepparent acting like a "real" parent, for example, often make the development of kin feelings difficult for the children. The older the children, the more unlikely such feelings are to develop (Visher and Visher, 1979).

Table 1-1   How Families Have Changed, 1970–1984

	1970	1980	1984	Percent Change 1970–1984	
Population	205,100,000	227,700,000	236,600,000	Up	15.4
Marriages performed	2,159,000	2,413,000	2,497,000	Up	15.7
Divorces granted	708,000	1,182,000	1,555,000	Up	219.6
Married couples	44,728,000	48,643,000	50,090,000	Up	12.0
Married couples with children	25,541,000	24,501,000	24,339,000	Down	1.0
Unmarried couples with children present	196,000	424,000	614,000	Up	313.3
Children living with two parents	58,926,000	48,295,000	46,555,000	Down	21.0
Children living with one parent	8,230,000	12,200,000	14,024,000	Up	60.0
Single-parent families	3,100,000	6,600,000	8,544,000	Up	275.6
Unmarried couples	523,000	1,600,000	1,988,000	Up	380.1
Births	3,731,000	3,598,000	3,697,000	Up	0.1
Births to unmarried women	398,000	600,000	850,000	Up	213.6

Sources: Bureau of the Census. *Current Population Reports.* "Population Characteristics." Series P-20, No. 391, 1984; *Current Population Reports.* "Population Characteristics." Series P-20, No. 398, 1984; *U.S. Statistical Abstract.* 1985; unpublished census data furnished by Marriage and Family Section, Bureau of the Census, September, 1985.

☐ THE CHANGING FAMILY

The Traditional Nuclear Family

The nuclear family dominates American thinking about the family. This family consists of a mother, father, and children, who live together and function as an economic group. When the children grow up, they leave home and establish their own families. According to some anthropologists, the nuclear family is universal, either in its basic form or as a building block for other family forms (Murdock, 1949). Only a fraction of American families, however, are traditional nuclear families. As a description of American family life, the nuclear family exists more as a cultural symbol or norm than as a reality; yet it has a powerful impact on us. We assume that the nuclear family with its 2.1 children is the "normal" family. The emphasis on the *normality* of the nuclear family results in two significant distortions.

First, other life styles are suspect: remaining single is immature, cohabitation is immoral, homosexual marriages are perverse, childless marriages are selfish, families with more than four children are irresponsible, single-parent families are "broken," blended families are unhappy. But as we shall see in future chapters, these family forms are adaptations to changes in society. Many of their problems and stresses are not necessarily inherent but are the result of society's failure to provide adequate support for them. Cohabitation, for example, tends to be unstable partly because there is little social support for it. Parents usually oppose it, banks often won't give credit to cohabitants, employers may fire them, and landlords may not rent to them. Single-parent families may be stressful for a mother, not because of the father's

As to marriage or celibacy, let a man take which course he will, he will be sure to repent it.

SOCRATES

(text continues on page 18)

FEATURE

Current Trends in Marriage and the Family

Census data provide us with considerable information about marriages, families, and households. (The data in this section, unless otherwise noted, are taken from Glick, 1984a; Glick, 1984b; U.S. Census, 1984a; U.S. Census, 1984b; U.S. Census, 1985.) Although statistical information may appear to be dry and boring, it contains critical information about the changing structure of our lives.

MARRIAGE LEVELS

About 95 percent of Americans above age forty-five have been married. Women tend to marry younger than men. The average age of marriage for men is twenty-four years, whereas for women it is twenty-two years. Among men, males educated beyond college represent the highest proportion who marry (93 percent), but female college graduates (as well as those with more education) represent the lowest proportion among women (83 percent). Probably as many as three times the number of today's generation of young adults will not marry as compared with their parents' generation. As many as 10 to 12 percent of today's young adults will never marry.

Why do you think increasing numbers of people are less likely to marry? Why are college-educated women the least likely group of women to marry?

DIVORCE

Data suggest that about half (49 percent) of all men and women between the ages of twenty-five to thirty-four years have either ended their marriages or will do so by the time they reach seventy-five years. This is about three times the divorce rate of their parents or grandparents. The higher the education level (except for women with education beyond college), the lower the divorce rate. Among men and women with some college edu-

cation, the divorce rate is around 60 percent; among those who completed college, the divorce rate falls to around 40 percent.

Why do you think divorce has increased so dramatically in the last generation? Why are different divorce rates associated with education?

FAMILY HOUSEHOLDS

Households are residences (owned or rented) in which one or more people live. Households may be divided into family and nonfamily households. In 1984 families accounted for 73 percent of all households; by contrast, in 1971 families accounted for 81 percent. In the family households, 50.1 million were married-couple households and 11.9 million were single-parent households. About 25 percent of new households formed since 1980 were single-parent households headed by women.

NONFAMILY HOUSEHOLDS

About 27 percent of all families were maintained by single adults, cohabitating couples, or other nonrelated adults. The rise of nonfamily households has been one of the major trends since 1970, when only 18.8 percent of the households were nonfamily. Most nonfamily households (85 percent) are composed of people living alone—twenty million in 1984. Ten percent of the nonfamily households were composed of unmarried couples.

In which type of household are you currently living? In which type were you raised? In which type do you expect to live in the next year? How does the type of household you live in affect you?

COHABITATION

Close to two million unmarried male-female couples lived together in 1984 (gay couples are not counted by the census). In 1980 this figure was 1.6 million and in 1970, only 523,000. Despite a 400 percent increase over the last fifteen years, unmarried couples account for less than 4 percent of American couples. About 31 percent of cohabiting couples have one or more children age fifteen or under living with them.

How many couples do you know that are cohabitating or have cohabitated? What are their age groups? Why do you think cohabitation has been increasing? What is the impact of cohabitation on children?

UNMARRIED MOTHERS

During the last two decades, the number of children born to unmarried women has more than tripled. In 1960 the proportion of births to unmarried women was about 5 percent; in 1980 it reached 18 percent. Unmarried mothers accounted for 11 percent of births among white women and 55 percent of births among black women.

Why do you think there has been a dramatic increase in births to unmarried women? Do you think it makes a difference whether a child is raised by an unmarried single parent or a divorced single parent? Why?

CHILDREN

Children are living in more diverse family units. Among children born in 1950–54, by age seventeen, 19 percent of the white children and 48 percent of the black children had lived with only one parent. Among white children born in 1980, by age seventeen, 70 percent may live with only one parent before they reach age eighteen; among black children, the figure may reach 94 percent (Hofferth, 1985). The white children who will live in a single-parent family will spend 25 percent of their childhood in such a family; among comparable black children, 44 percent of their childhood

will be spent in a single-parent family. As we have seen, 11 percent of births among white women and 55 percent of births among black women were to unmarried mothers.

Ninety percent of the children of divorced parents will live in a stepfamily; between 80 and 90 percent of these children, however, will experience separated again as the remarried family divorces or separates.

The poverty rate for children has been slowly rising since 1969, when 14 percent of America's children lived in poverty. Between 1979 and 1983, the poverty rate among children jumped dramatically, from 16 percent to 22 percent. Today children represent 40 percent of all poor people, and more than one child in five is poor. Fifty-five percent of the children living in single-parent families are poor—four times the rate of children living in two-parent families. Forty-seven percent of all black children and 38 percent of all Hispanic children are poor, compared with 15 percent of nonminority children (Congressional Budget Office, 1985).

Think about yourself or people that you know. How many have lived in single-parent or divorced families? What are their experiences in such families? Why is poverty increasing—especially among children—in the United States? Why do you think there are such striking differences according to race?

NEVER MARRIED

People are getting married later. The percentage of young adults in their twenties and early thirties that have never married was significantly higher in 1984 than in 1970. Among men between the ages of twenty and twenty-four, the percentage increased from 55 in 1970 to 75 in 1984. For women in the same age group, the figures are 36 and 57 percent, respectively. In 1984 for the age group twenty-five to twenty-nine years, 38 percent of the

FEATURE–*continued*

men and 26 percent of the women have never married; by contrast in 1970 the percentages were 19 and 10 for men and women, respectively. Both men and women are marrying later to complete education, to establish themselves in careers, or to pursue other goals that family responsibilities might curtail.

Are you married? If you are, at what age did you get married? Why did you marry at that age? If you are not married, at what age do you expect to marry? Why?

LIVING ALONE

The proportion of people choosing to live alone is increasing at a much swifter rate than the proportion of those choosing to live with a spouse. The number of people living alone increased by 173 percent between 1960 and 1983; the number of people living with a spouse increased by only 26 percent in the same time period. The largest number are older widowed women; but the rate of increase has been greatest among men and women age forty-five years and under. The rate of increase for this group has been 237 percent compared with 43 percent for those above forty-five years. In part, the increase in people less than forty-five years living alone is a result of the increasing divorce rate. When childless couples divorce, both tend to live alone; when children are involved, the husband tends to leave the house.

Do you live alone? If so, what are your reasons? What aspects of contemporary life make it possible for people to live alone?

---

absence per se, but because of the poverty in which she and her children are trapped.

Second, emphasizing the structure of the family tends to blind us to what goes on within it. We tend to assume that a family is happy simply because it is intact. But a nuclear family is not necessarily a happy family. Nuclear families may engage in small-scale nuclear warfare. Although they fit the structural norm on the outside, they may be hiding extensive conflict, alcoholism, incest, abuse, and hatred beneath the surface. We must look beneath its structure to see whether a family is performing its functions. Is it socializing its children healthily? Is it providing intimacy for its members? A blended family or single-parent family may perform the family functions discussed previously far better than an intact nuclear family.

America's Pluralistic Family Forms

Instead of using a family model that recognizes only the traditional nuclear family, we need a model that recognizes the diversity of our family forms. American marriages can take divergent paths:

1. *Dual-worker families.* More than half of America's families are dual-worker families; that is, both husband and wife work. Such families have tremendous impact on childrearing patterns as well as on husband-wife relations.
2. *Single-parent families.* Because of the tremendous rise in divorce rates and the numbers of unmarried women, the majority of children born in the United States today will spend part of their lives in single-parent families.

Fidelity is part of every human friendship. It is the strain toward permanence and toward public commitment to permanence that is involved in any relationship beyond the most superficial. Fidelity is a longing for love that does not end.

ANDREW GREELEY

"That's my mom and dad. They've just returned to traditional family values."

3. *Blended families*. Most single parents eventually marry or remarry. But the blended family (or stepfamily) has unique problems based on the roles and conflicts of stepparents and stepchildren.

As long as we look at these family forms as somehow deficient, abnormal, or bad, we will not understand them. Instead of labeling them as deviant, we need to understand them as adaptations to the changing problems confronting America's families.

☐ IDENTITY, THE FAMILY, AND THE LIFE CYCLE

Our identity, our sense of who we are, is not fixed or frozen. It changes as we mature. At different points in our lives we are confronted with different tasks. Our development as human beings depends on the way we resolve these problems. Erik Erikson (1963) describes the human life cycle as containing eight developmental stages. At each stage we have an important developmental task to accomplish, and each stage intimately involves the family. The way we deal with these stages, which are summarized here, is strongly influenced by our families and marriages. We cannot separate our identity from either.

Infancy: Trust versus Mistrust. In the first year of life, children are wholly dependent on their parenting figures for survival. It is then they learn to trust by having their needs satisfied, by being loved, held, caressed. Without loving care, the infant may develop a mistrusting attitude toward others and toward life in general.

Toddler: Autonomy versus Shame and Doubt. Between ages two and three children learn to walk and talk; they begin toilet training. At this stage they need to develop a sense of independence and of mastery over their environment and them-

UNDERSTANDING YOURSELF

Self and the Life Cycle

It is difficult to overestimate the impact that our families have had on us. As we look at Erik Erikson's theory of the life cycle, we see that each of us must resolve fundamental psychological crises if we are to develop our potential as human beings.

- *Infancy: trust versus mistrust*
- *Toddler: autonomy versus shame and doubt*
- *Early Childhood: initiative versus guilt*
- *School Age: industry versus inferiority*
- *Adolescence: identity versus role diffusion*
- *Young Adulthood: intimacy versus isolation*
- *Adulthood: generativity versus self-absorption*
- *Maturity: integrity versus despair*

Look at these crises and ask yourself these questions: Where am I currently in my life cycle? What is the psychological task that Erikson says I need to resolve? Is it an important issue for me? How am I resolving it?

These crises, or stages, are generally encountered in the family, since the family is the context for most of our lives. The first five or six stages take place in your family of orientation. What was your family's role in resolving these crises?

Erikson assumes that creating a family is an important task in resolving the crisis of generativity versus self-absorption. Do you think he is correct? How will your decision to marry or not marry affect the resolution of the later stages?

selves. Parents need to encourage independence and make toilet training a positive rather than a shameful experience.

Early Childhood: Initiative versus Guilt.   Ages four to five are years of increasing independence. The family must allow the child to develop initiative while at the same time directing the child's energy. The child must not be made to feel guilty about his or her desire to explore the world.

School Age: Industry versus Inferiority.   Between ages six and eleven children begin to learn that their activities pay off, that they can be creative. The family needs to encourage the child's sense of accomplishment. Failing to do so may lead to feelings of inferiority in the child.

Adolescence: Identity versus Role Diffusion.   The years of puberty between ages twelve and eighteen are a time of turmoil when children may try many roles. It is also the time when children are making the transition to adulthood. To make a successful transition, they need to develop goals, a philosophy of life, a sense of self. The family needs to be supportive amidst the turmoil. If the adolescent fails to establish a firm identity, he or she is likely to drift without purpose.

Young Adulthood: Intimacy versus Isolation.   These are the years when the adolescent leaves home and begins to establish intimate ties with other people through marriage, cohabitation, or other important intimate relationships. Without making other intimate connections, the young adult may be condemned to isolation and loneliness.

Adulthood: Generativity versus Self-Absorption.   Now the individual establishes his or her own family, has children, and finds satisfactions in family relationships. It is a time of creativity. Work becomes important as a creative act, perhaps as important as family or an alternative to it. The failure to be productive may lead to self-centeredness and a "what's-in-it-for-me" attitude toward life.

Maturity: Integrity versus Despair.   In old age the individual looks back on life to understand its meaning—to assess what has been accomplished and gauge the success or failure of his or her relationships. Those who can make a positive judgement, have a feeling of wholeness about their lives. The alternative is despair.

☐ SUMMARY

- *Marriage* is a socially recognized union between a woman and a man. Its main characteristics are (1) the performance of a *public ritual* to sanction the union, (2) *sexual unification*, and (3) *economic cooperation*.

- The traditional *family* is a married couple or group of adult kin who cooperate and divide labor along sex lines, rear children, and share a common dwelling. New family forms are emerging to challenge this definition.

- The four important family functions are (1) *childrearing*; (2) formation of a *co-operative economic unit*; (3) assignment of *status and social roles*, which are acquired both in our *family of orientation* (in which we grow up) and our *family of procreation* (which we form by having children); and (4) provision of *intimate relationships*.

- *The nuclear family* consists of a mother, a father, and their children. It exists more as a cultural symbol or norm than as a reality in our society.

- The *extended family* may be formed through marital ties (polygamy) or, in monogamous societies, through blood ties with grandparents, aunts, uncles, older siblings and so on. A modified type of extended family, based on both blood and marriage, is developing with the increase of remarriage and establishment of blended families.

- The *kinship system* is the social organization of the family. In American society it consists of parents and children but can also include other relatives, each of whom has specific rights and obligations within the family.

- The *modified extended family* includes parents and their adult children and is characterized by proximity of residence; regularity of visits; sharing of child care, housework, and home maintenance; and giving of loans and gifts.

- The *affiliated family* is one in which unrelated persons take on roles similar to those of relatives, joining in family work or recreation.

- By making the nuclear family the norm by which we judge families, we denigrate other family forms and are unable to look beneath the formal structure to see if a family—regardless of its form—is fulfilling its functions.

- Characteristics of American families that are changing significantly include age at marriage, divorce, family and nonfamily households, dual-worker marriages, cohabitation, unmarried mothers, children's living arrangements and economic status, never-married individuals, and living alone.

- The eight developmental stages of the life cycle described by Erik Erikson, include (1) infancy: trust versus mistrust, (2) toddler: autonomy versus shame and doubt, (3) early childhood: initiative versus guilt, (4) school age: industry versus inferiority, (5) adolescence: identity versus role diffusion, (6) young adulthood: intimacy versus isolation, (7) adulthood: generativity versus self-absorption, and (8) maturity: integrity versus despair.

READINGS

Marriage: It's Back in Style

ALVIN SANOFF, *U.S. NEWS & WORLD REPORT*

Marriage may be back in style, but it is different, more diverse than marriage a generation ago. What are some of the characteristics of contemporary marriages, according to Sanoff?

Wedding bells are ringing far and wide in this peak month for tying the knot, and everywhere the trappings that go with this happiest of ceremonies create the aura of an earlier, more innocent time.

Clearly, marriage is back in style after two decades during which men and women dabbled at alternative lifestyles. Last year, a record 2.5 million couples marched down the aisle, their ranks swelled by the large population in the prime marrying years of 18 to 26. With the economy improving, there could be even more weddings this year.

Many couples—even those marrying a second time—are staging old-fashioned, large weddings, the type of gatherings that lost favor in the late 1960s and 1970s when the counterculture reached its heyday. Says Joan Kaner, fashion director of Bergdorf Goodman in New York: "The younger generation is much more traditionally oriented, both in their work styles and lifestyles, and this is showing up in the way they choose to be married."

Something old, something new. While people are flocking to the altar again, the unions being forged today are a far cry from those of the past. With social barriers crumbling and women gaining more economic independence, matrimony is taking on a whole new look.

The traditional marriage in which the man works and the woman stays home to tend to youngsters is fast giving way to busy, dual-career alliances. Unions between people of similar backgrounds and values are being replaced increasingly by interfaith and interracial marriages. And many couples still experiment with living together before exchanging vows—a vestige of the sexual revolution.

People today wait longer to marry and expect far more of the marital relationship than their parents did. They demand more and put up with less. At the same time, many couples live far from family, old friends and others who might provide emotional support in trying times.

Such changes help explain why half of all new marriages are expected to end in divorce, a situation that is prompting an array of counseling programs to prepare couples for matrimony and help them iron out difficulties later on. "Marriage is the single most complex entity short of nuclear fusion—and nuclear fusion may be less complicated," observes Tom Clark, president of the American Association for Marriage and Family Therapy.

Despite the risks, Americans remain the marrying kind. Eventually, more than 90 percent of the population will marry. Even those who have endured the trauma of divorce usually make at least one more attempt to achieve wedded bliss. Says sociologist Jerry Talley of Stanford University: "People may be disappointed in a marriage partner, but they are not disappointed in marriage in general."

Indeed, a recent study by the National Opinion Research Center found that married people are happier than those without partners. Still, the road to self-fulfillment through marriage has grown far more confusing and treacherous as couples devise new methods to meet the uncertainties and demands of modern life.

Careers and Couples: The New Mix

No change has had more impact on married life than the flood of women into the workplace. As women moved away from the homemaker pattern, the number of dual-earner families increased by 500,000 a year during the 1970s. Today, they account for 52 percent of U.S. married couples.

David Mace, who helped establish the marriage-counseling profession over 40 years ago, sees matrimony changing from a one-vote system in which men made the decisions to a system in which couples sort out choices jointly.

Typical are John and Donna Williams of Manhattan, who have been married nearly five years and share household chores. Donna, a model and actress, normally does the grocery shopping and cooking, while John, a manager of a press-relations firm, does the pots and pans. But when she has had a hard day, he cooks, too. "She has no obligation to make dinner," he says.

Problems usually revolve around scheduling. Says John: "I may want to take a vacation and she can't because she's got a big job coming up. You learn to live with that."

For two-career couples with children, time demands can be even more intense. Jeff Justice and Jane Lynk, both 31-year-old lawyers, have few extra hours. "Our fathers could come home from work, have a drink and enjoy the children," says Jane. "But usually when we get home, we're starting dinner and taking care of Luke."

Ever since the child was born two years ago, the Sherman, Ill., couple has split child-care duties. Jane stayed home with the baby during his first two months, and Jeff did the honors in the third month so his wife could go back to work. They take turns picking Luke up from a sitter. Whoever gets home first cooks, and the other cleans up.

Any stresses that arise in the 9-year-old marriage are outweighed by the freedom and financial security that come from having two paychecks, but the couple agrees that juggling careers and family makes it necessary to have more certainty in other parts of their life. Says Jane: "Both of us are pretty committed to staying in one location for our sense of stability and Luke's."

The commuters. Other dual-career couples have been forced into long-distance marriages so that each can find job satisfaction. Joseph Duffey, 50, and Anne Wexler, 53, who both held top posts in the Carter administration, ended up in a commuting relationship last year after Duf-

fey became chancellor of the University of Massachusetts at Amherst. Says Wexler, who runs a political-consulting firm in Washington, D.C.: "We don't view this as the ideal way to live, but we have to if we want to pursue our careers."

Wexler travels to Massachusetts most weekends because her husband's commitments and social functions demand that he stay near the campus. Part of her routine is to scan the college newspaper just before seeing her husband so she'll be familiar with issues that he has been grappling with all week. Duffey adds that the couple, married for eight years before becoming commuters, must spend a good deal of Friday evening "just getting back on the same wavelength."

Whatever the problems, dual-career marriages, which now number nearly 30 million, often bring more satisfaction than traditional relationships. A survey by the National Opinion Research Center found that men with working wives are somewhat happier than other husbands. Adds sociologist Frank Furstenberg, Jr., of the University of Pennsylvania: "We as a culture are gradually rethinking what we want and expect of marriage."

Casting Convention to the Winds

The two-career relationship is by no means the only shift in marriage style. Education and increased mobility have greatly expanded the social circles of most people. "There is a greater mix in marriages as the religious and ethnic barriers come down," says Herbert Glieberman, a Chicago attorney and author of books on marriage and divorce.

For Heidi and Manbir Singh of Mar Vista, Calif., marriage means grappling with differences in religious rites and cultural practices. Heidi, 29, is a Roman Catholic. Manbir, 37, a native of India, is a Sikh, a member of a Hindu set that also believes in one God and rejects the Indian caste system.

Heidi recalls that the gap in culture created problems, especially at the start of their 12-year marriage: "I was very young, very emotional, from a volatile Irish Catholic home. He was from a serene Indian family and couldn't understand why I cried and had tantrums." For Manbir, who teaches nuclear medicine at the University of Southern California School of Medicine, marriage meant getting used to American ways, including overt displays of affection and saying "I love you." But the two have adjusted, while still practicing their different religions.

Adjustment is even tougher for couples who must overcome racial barriers, yet the number of interracial marriages in the U.S. climbed from an estimated 65,000 in

READINGS–*continued*

1970 to about 165,000 a decade later.

Walt Higginbotham, a white, 34-year-old sales representative in Houston, says that when he married a black schoolteacher two years ago, "we were making no social statement. We just cared a lot about each other." But as news of the wedding became public, he adds, "I found out who my real friends were, fast."

Since there is still strong objection to such marriages in some parts of the country, many interracial couples refuse to talk about their experiences publicly, fearing that they will be singled out by "cranks or kooks." Some are concerned, too, about how their children will fare. Says a white computer scientist in Virginia who married a black woman seven years ago: "Our daughter maybe wonders, 'Why couldn't you have married a white lady?' and perhaps asks herself, 'Should I be black or white?' "

Less controversial is divorce and remarriage, which even a generation ago often put men and women on the outs with family and friends. Now, about 75 to 80 percent of those who divorce eventually marry again, and about 45 percent of weddings involve at least one person who has been married before. Public attitudes have changed so much that a divorced and remarried man now occupies the White House.

Jeannie and Bruce Anderson of Dallas both had previous experience with marriage when they were wed eight years ago. Jeannie had three youngsters from her first marriage, and Bruce had a stepson with whom he kept close contact. The couple has since added a child of their own.

This "blended family" arrangement, which is becoming more common every day, can create all sorts of tensions. "It is hard to put a new person into a family," says Jeannie. "Sometimes the children resented my new husband. Sometimes he resented how much attention I paid to them. I was always in the middle and still am." But, she adds, most difficulties have been ironed out. "We still have our fusses and problems," she explains, "But basically we get along fairly well."

The couple planned their wedding with the children in mind and took two honeymoons, one without the youngsters and one with them. Says Jeannie: "It is a family marriage."

Also benefiting from the freer atmosphere of the 1980s: Senior citizens. Worried about "what the children would think," many older people lived out their lives alone after their spouses died. Now, they feel more comfortable about marrying again. Frequently spared the worries over children and finances that preoccupy young couples, people who marry during their "golden years" often are remarkably content. "It's like starting to live all over again," says Marcia Ballin of Houston, who married her husband Jack two years ago after both had lost their first spouses. "Marriage is a wonderful solution to a lonely life."

Marching to a Different Drummer

The new flexibility in marriage also makes it possible for more men and women to swap traditional roles. Nino and Tina Nannarone of Brooklyn are doing just that, with him staying home to care for their two young daughters while Tina, 34, works as an auto mechanic for the Port Authority of New York and New Jersey.

At first, Nino, 38, a community organizer, was reluctant to make the switch. "It was a double whammy because she was going into a nontraditional job," he recalls. "Being a man and taking care of my kids at home, I also worried about what friends would say." But for now, the couple seems happy with the arrangement, which has helped Tina succeed in her job. "I have a perfect attendance record because I don't have to worry about the kids," she says.

Others buck old mores by living together out of wedlock—in effect testing their compatibility before tying the knot. The Census Bureau estimates that the number of couples involved in such relationships soared from 523,000 in 1970 to 1.9 million last year.

Many of these couples eventually marry, and Bob Turgeon and Donna Riedinger of Denver, who have shared an apartment for almost five years, are grappling with just that decision right now. When they first got together, Bob, now 28, was on the road a lot selling encyclopedias. "Every time I came back I wanted to see Donna, so I decided we might as well live together," he says.

The relationship has worked, despite concerns about tensions in Donna's family, because each has retained a sense of independence. But now Donna, 34, who is a nurse, wants to make the arrangement formal and has given Bob until August to make up his mind. "I feel that at this point it's more or less a technicality that we ought to take care of," she says. "We're not married, but we're sure not single after five years. We're in limbo."

In the Old-Fashioned Way

Despite such changes, about one fourth of all married couples still opt for the old-style marriage in which the wife stays home to raise children while the husband works.

Susan Puckett, 40, of Rock Hill, Mo., has been a homemaker and mother to three daughters for the better

READINGS–*continued*

part of her married life. Susan was only 16 years old when she met her husband Gary. "We worked together in a dime store in St. Louis," she recalls. "He was a stock boy and I was a salesclerk."

They married five years later, after he got out of the military, and today Gary is a salesman for an oil company. Says Susan of her marriage: "I didn't want a career. I like the idea of having someone more or less take care of me."

Another throwback to an earlier time—teen marriages—also persists, even though most people today wait longer to wed. The median age for women at first marriage rose from 20.3 years in 1960 to 22.5 in 1982. Still, in 1979, the most recent year for which figures are available, nearly a third of women marrying for the first time were teenagers.

When Sandee and Eric Khloscz of San Francisco became man and wife last August, it was against the wishes of their parents. But the 18-year-old couple, who began dating when they were 15, reasoned that love would see them through. "Why wait if you know it's right?" asks Eric, who works at a gas station.

So far, they describe married life as "wonderful" despite financial problems that have forced them to sell Sandee's car and pare spending to the bone. "If anything, the money problem has brought us closer together," says Sandee, who will soon leave her job with a real-estate broker to have a baby. "We'll really have to scramble then," says Eric. Their parents, meanwhile, remain cool to the union. "The more they tell us we made a mistake," asserts Eric, "the more determined we are to prove them wrong."

Big Demands, Big Problems

No matter what type of marriage a couple has, they expect a great deal from it. Unlike in the past, men and women rarely join hands merely to have children and the necessities of life. Now, couples marry less for practical reasons than for emotional ones as they hunt for companionship and love. Lenore J. Weitzman, a sociologist at Stanford University, says that today "the marriage partner is supposed to be the be-all and end-all, an intellectual and sexual companion, a conversationalist and a good tennis player, but it is hard for one person to fulfill all these needs."

Analysts say that "the myth of romantic love" fosters unrealistic expectations. "That myth sells a lot of goods and merchandise, but it is not a particularly good criterion on which to select a partner," contends therapist Tom Clark of Winston-Salem, N.C. Experts warn that couples who put all their eggs in the basket of romance are likely to find

their marriages cracking.

Sociologists also trace breakups to the rise in marriages between people who have different backgrounds. "You have got to minimize potential areas of conflict, and that means similar social class, education, race, religion and the like," argues Clifton Barber, associate professor of human development and family stidies at Colorado State University. Others note the lack of commitment in many marriages. "As a society, we have come to embrace the obsolescence theory not only in material things, but in human relationships," observes Chicago attorney Glieberman.

Less stringent divorce laws aid couples in splitting up, and greater financial independence of working women keeps them from being locked into a bad marriage. "As the economic ability of women increases and their dependence decreases, they have a choice," says sociologist M. A. Najmi of the University of Colorado.

Yet many experts insist that the increase in failed marriages is not necessarily bad. They say that couples may be happier than in the past because those who stay together do so by choice, not necessity. "It is preferable to terminate an unhappy marriage than to live in holy deadlock," says Graham Spanier, a sociologist at the State University of New York at Stony Brook.

Still, there's enough concern about marital strains to generate an explosion in the field of marriage therapy. The American Association for Marriage and Family Therapy has increased tenfold over the past decade and today has a membership of 10,000 people who hold advanced degrees in such areas as sociology, social work and psychology.

Besides individual counseling, couples are signing up for marriage encounters, which bring husbands and wives together for a weekend and a series of subsequent meetings to discuss common concerns. An estimated 1 million couples have taken part in the program, which originated in the Roman Catholic Church but has spread to many denominations.

To get their unions off to a good start, more couples are taking marriage-preparation courses. Over 60 percent of the nation's Catholic dioceses require prospective newlyweds to participate in such programs, which often take the form of workshops dealing with such topics as sexuality and values. The approach also is attracting interest outside the church. The Denver Center for Marital and Family Studies offers a five-session course to increase awareness of potential problems and enhance communication.

Programs like this are viewed as long overdue. "There is nothing we do a worse job of than preparing kids for marriage," says Ray Fowler, a marriage and family counselor in

READINGS–*continued*

Claremont, Calif. "If kids graduating from high school knew a hundreth as much about marital interaction as they do about computers, marriage would be a lot more satisfactory experience."

Marriage experts say that the bedrock of a healthy union is compatibility, respect, intellectual curiosity and shared goals. "Balance of power" in a relationship also is important, says analysts, who warn against one partner becoming too dominant.

Veteran counselor David Mace offers this three-part prescription for achieving marital success: Both husband and wife must be committed to growth and change, have a system for regular communication and accept conflict as normal and inevitable and learn to use it creatively.

Marriage—It's Here to Stay

Where does all of this leave marriage?

Some experts say the institution is in trouble, that more people are waiting longer to marry and spending large parts of their lives in single and divorced states. They point out that the proportion of young women between ages 20 and 24 who remained unwed climbed from 36 percent in 1970 to 53 percent last year, reflecting society's growing acceptance of the singles lifestyle. "History shows us that when marriages are postponed they tend to be forgone," says James Weed, a Census Bureau specialist on marriage.

Still, most Americans believe strongly in marriage and regard it as an anchor in turbulent times. A study by the Institute of Social Research at the University of Michigan found that only 3 percent of 18-year-olds questioned in 1980 thought they would not marry. "The vast majority of Americans marry and will continue to do so," says the University of Pennsylvania's Furstenberg.

Indeed, even homosexual couples are seeking a degree of permanence to their relationships, although such unions are not legally recognized. Says one California man who had his union with another blessed by a sympathetic minister three years ago: "We consider ourselves married even though the law does not."

On a steady course. Sociologist Andrew Cherlin of Johns Hopkins University notes that the United States is in a period of stability in marriage after the great roller-coaster changes of recent years. But the divorce rate will remain high through this decade because of the huge number of people in the prime age group for divorce—25 to 39. Even so, most of these people are expected to marry again, adding to the growing complexity in family relationships and

making stepparents and stepchildren as much the norm as the exception.

Through all these changes, there remains the age-old search for self-fulfillment and a yearning for happiness that most people believe can still be found more easily by sharing one's life with another. Explains New Yorker John Williams of his marriage: "I like the feeling that we're growing together. It's exciting in every facet—emotionally, sexually and intellectually."

The Individual as the Basic Social Unit
JEROME KAGAN, EXCERPT FROM *THE NATURE OF THE CHILD*

Harvard psychologist Jerome Kagan argues that the individual has replaced the family as the basic social unit. What other significant characteristics affecting the family does he find in American society?

Among the nomadic Hebrews who herded sheep in the Sinai desert three thousand years ago, and for many contemporary African and Latin American communities, the basic social unit is composed of genetically related adults and children living together in a group to which loyalty is given and from which identity is derived. The fate of each person rests with the vitality, reputation, and success of the kinship group. Hence, the conception of self is dependent on the resources, status, and socially perceived qualities of the family group. Although the nuclear family existed in some early societies, it has replaced the larger kin group in many places and is, at the moment, the most common social unit for most of the world's communities. The future of the children in these societies is determined almost completely by each family's status, wealth, resouces, and practices.

But in the modern Western world, the individual, not the family, is slowly becoming the basic unit. The high divorce rate, the large number of single-parent families, and the public's willingness to work toward a more egalitarian society through interventions that abrogate the family's power make the person the central entity in the eyes of the law, the school, and the self. Additionally, early socialization practices that promote autonomy, and individual, rather than group, effort and responsibility, lead many adolescents to conclude that their future mood and material success depend upon their personal abilities and motivation. A divorced woman with only a high school education who was living with her three-year-old, said, "I must de-

READINGS—*continued*

velop myself, I can't be dependent on anyone but me." This attitude may be historically unique. Although historians argue about the form of the earliest families and when the nuclear structure emerged, no anthropologist or historian has ever suggested that the majority of adults living in older societies believed that their survival, personal reputation, and material success did not depend primarily on their family of rearing. Thus, each American adult must acquire a special state of mind which most families, consciously or unconsciously, train for from the earliest months of life. Few citizens of ancient Athens, Babylon, or Jerusalem, or of modern Tokyo, Jakarta, or Beijing (Peking) would understand this attitude. Thus, some of the qualities of the modern Western family are specific to this historical era.

A second significant characteristic of contemporary Western society is the dignity and respect awarded to women. Although women had high status in a few Polynesian societies and in polyandrous groups, for most cultures about which we have knowledge women had far less power than men, achieved status through marriage rather than through their own efforts, and were punished more severely than men for illicit sexuality. In some communities of Indians in Northwest Guatemala, for example, the most insulting accusation one man can level at another is to call him a woman.

The rise of women's status in Europe and North America over the past four centuries has been associated with an increasingly benevolent evaluation of romantic love. Carl Degler writes, "The growing acceptance of affection as the primary ground for family formation was an important stage in the evolution of women's place within the family and in our understanding of how the family has altered over time" . . . Although sexuality has never been unimportant in any culture, and is central to the romantic literature of the Middle East, romantic love is today regarded not just as a source of pleasure, but as an experience of great beauty and a major basis for feelings of vitality and self-enhancement.

Love is an intimate, spiritual experience in a world perceived to be impersonal and amoral. The deep anger toward pornography held by many Americans is based, in part, on the threat pornography poses to the idea of faithful romantic love, as distinct from sexual gratification. A love relation is regarded as such a vital part of adult life that families try to prepare their children for that function in ways that some cultures would not understand. Parents arrange parties for young children with boys and girls present, begin explanations of reproduction by noting how much the mother and father love each other, and accept

romantic attraction as the most reasonable basis for marital choice, despite differences in status, ethnicity, wealth, and religion.

A third relatively distinct quality of our society is its celebration of the freedom and selfhood of children. Although this attitude was enhanced in seventeenth-century Europe, it has become more pervasive with time. All societies, ancient and modern, love and value children, even though eleventh-century European fathers were not severely criticized for killing their newborn infant if he or she failed the test of fearfulness and cried after being put on a high branch of a tree. . . . The relation of child to parent in most societies is one of loyalty and obligation. In Chinese families, filial love defines the primary bond. The special ingredient in the American form of child-centeredness is its one-sidedness. Parents are supposed to sacrifice for their children, while the children are expected to grow increasingly independent of their parents. For many middle-class families, the child is a beautiful young bird to be cared for until it is ready to fly free in the forest.

Finally, . . . in contrast to many, but not all, contemporary societies, Americans place greater value on sincerity and personal honesty than on social harmony. But in many cultures—Java, Japan, and China, for example—the importance of maintaining harmonious social relationships, and of adopting a posture of respect for the feelings of elders and of authority, demands that each person not only suppress anger but, in addition, be ready to withhold complete honesty about personal feelings in order to avoid hurting another. This pragmatic view of honesty is regarded as a quality characteristic of the most mature adult and is not given the derogatory labels of insincerity or hypocrisy. The West derides the person who does not say what she thinks, who does not "call a spade a spade." People who are polite to someone whom they dislike, offer tea and cakes to a gossipy neighbor, and tell an incompetent employer how skilled he is are less admirable than those who "speak their mind." These "white lies" are supposed to reflect fear, timidity, and obsequiousness. But what American parents regard as obsequiousness, citizens of Java and Japan regard as appropriate respect.

With the exception of the celebration of romantic love, these qualities of modern American life award exaggerated value to the individual and less significance to the social groups in which each person acts.

In American families, the primary loyalty is to self—its values, autonomy, pleasure, virtue, and actualization. Most parents accept this criterion for maturity and try to arrange experiences that will make it easier for their children to

---

READINGS–*continued*

---

attain this ideal. Some societies tip the other way. In a popular book for parents written about twenty years before China became the People's Republic, the psychologist Chen Heqin listed the seven inborn qualities of children that parents should promote: active play, imitation of others, curiosity, mastery, mutually binding social relationships, pleasure in the outdoors, and seeking the praise of others. . . . Three of these ideals stress the social, not the individualistic, urges of children. I suspect that Professor Chen would have had some difficulty understanding John Dewey who wrote, at about the same time, that what men have esteemed and fought for is the "ability to carry out plans, the absence of cramping and thwarting obstacles, . . . the slave is the man who executes the wish of others.". . .

Marriage in India
WILLIAM STEVENS, *THE NEW YORK TIMES*

Prior to the 19th century in America, few people married for love as we think of it today. Throughout much of the world romantic love is of little significance in choosing a partner. Often marriages are arranged between families; the prospective partners may have little voice in such decisions except sometimes a veto power. In India we see a marriage system radically different from our own. How does it differ from our system?

The young women of India, some of them, may be wearing blue jeans these days or dancing the night away at discoteques, smoking in public, dating, eyeing strange men and defying Indian convention in other ways.

But when it comes to marriage, they and their parents still find themselves in the position, more or less, of C. L. Kanogia and his daughters, Usha Rani and Bimla.

Mr. Kanogia is a laundryman, and his daughters are 18 and 20 years old, ages at which convention decrees they should be married. In India, that can be a very difficult position for parents of modest means, and most parents in the country fall into that category.

The marrying of daughters is one of an Indian father's most important duties in this country, where boys are considered to be of greater account than girls, where anxious, hopeful parents routinely submit their daughters to formal inspection by a potential bridegroom's relatives, and where an especially desirable young man is often betrothed to the

daughter of the family that can provide the largest dowry.

Mr. Kanogia's problem was solved relatively easily. One night he was invited to dinner at a friend's house. There he met another father who happened to have two sons about the same ages as his daughters. An arrangement was struck on the spot: The older daughter would marry the older son, and the younger daughter the younger son.

It took Mr. Kanogia a year to get the 20,000 rupees, the equivalent of about $2,000, to pay for the wedding, to buy the gold jewelry that is de rigueur and to provide a small dowry of furniture for each bride. He did it by playing a special kind of lottery, organized by friends and neighbors. The rules of the game require him to pay his winnings back.

To a laundryman, 20,000 rupees is a fortune. Nevertheless, Bimla and Usha Rani were recently married in a gala double ceremony. Resplendent in elegant red organza saris and veils trimmed in gold thread, their eyes cast modestly down in a way that conveys not only virtue but submission, they placed the ritual garlands of flowers around their new husbands' necks, where strings of rupee notes already hung.

It was only the second time the brides and bridegrooms had ever laid eyes on each other. The first was at their engagement ceremony, six months before. Until after the wedding, neither bride had ever held a conversation with either bridegroom.

That, with many variations and permutations, is how most Indians get married, despite the widespread penetration of modern ways and modern thinking into this increasingly industrialied society.

The system is under considerable challenge for perpetuating the subservient status of women, for denying freedom to both men and women and for relying on a ritual that can literally bankrupt the bride's parents.

Periodically some horrible tragedy associated with traditional marriage is reported. A young woman hanged herself from a tree last month in a rural village. A despairing suicide note said that because her parents couldn't afford to marry her, she was marrying the tree.

The centuries-old system is, however, undergoing a decided metamorphosis. Some young, upper-middle-class Indians are kicking over the traces, sneaking out to meet potential mates in defiance of tradition and entering into "love marriages."

But for most—even the affluent, the highly educated and more modern urban crowd—the arranged marriage remains a tradition so solidly entrenched that breaking out of the mold is an act of courage. Not only is the traditional way generally accepted, it is widely defended as working at least as well as what is seen here as the West's chancy, unreliable system of courtship and marriage.

Several key assumptions, all of them growing out of a view of male-female relationships dating to antiquity, underlie the traditional Indian way of marriage—not of courtship, for essentially there is none. There is just marriage.

Affection is Secondary

Expectations that love will develop between bride and bridegroom are not terribly high. Companionship and affection are of secondary consideration in making a match, if they are considered at all. It is usually hoped that in time intimacy and attachment will develop, but later in life, after the other obligations of marriage have been fulfilled.

It is also typically assumed that in making a match, it is the responsibility of "the girl," as she is invariably called regardless of age, to pass the scrutiny of the family of "the boy."

Getting "looked at" becomes a moment of nervous drama in the life of many a young women. A match having been proposed on the basis of preliminary explorations by the two families, the prospective bridegroom and his family visit the home of the prospective bride, most likely for afternoon tea.

"The boy's side often brings every opinion leader in the family," says Asharani Mathur, a magazine editor who has been through it. In her case, the setting was what is called the tea-tray scene, a ritual so standard that it has become a staple of Hindi-language movies.

Considering the Assets

In making its decision, the boy's family may pose a number of questions: Is the girl properly subservient, or does she tend to talk back? Does she smoke or drink or go to night-clubs? Those are minuses. Can she earn money for the groom's family, with whom she would be expected to live? Physical defects are considered, and must by honor be declared.

Nine times out of 10, says a young New Delhi woman who has arranged a number of matches as go-between, if the boy's family accepts, the girl and her parents will go along.

Once a match is decided upon, a business discussion often ensues. Marriage is frequently a financial compact between families, often involving a major transfer of assets from the girl's side to the boy's. For this reason alone, the birth of a girl frequently is greeted with gloom: She is a financial liability.

The status and eligibility of the boy, and the financial condition of the girl's family, both bear on the amount of dowry. Dowries are illegal, but few pay any attention to the prohibition.

A graduate engineer, for example, will command a larger dowry than a lower-level civil servant. Just now, the biggest dowry-puller of all is possession by the prospective groom of a green card, the card that enables a foreigner to live and work in the United States.

Men holding green cards, it seems, are returning to India in a steady stream to seek wives in the traditional way, their newly adopted Western outlook notwithstanding. They frequently advertise for brides in the matrimonial advertisement section that runs in the English-language newspapers every Sunday.

One such advertisement recently invited correspondence from "beautiful, slim, tall, age 20–23" Indian girls for a "very handsome north Indian boy 25 years, green card holder," who had been living in the United States since 1962. It said that his family would be "visiting India May-June 1984 for marriage," and solicited applications with photographs.

Even in a love match, there may still be a dowry. Not long ago, an army officer's daughter fell in love with an aide to a high Government official. They decided to get married. Nothing doing, said the young man's parents, unless you give us a Fiat automobile and a few other things.

In northern India, the question of dowry often is not formally raised. However, the groom's family expects something, and if it isn't forthcoming, the bride and her parents may be hounded mercilessly. In an especially ugly turn, hundreds of brides are murdered each year because their husbands have gotten all the dowry possible and want to marry again for another try.

System Is Changing

The system in many ways is softening and evolving toward greater freedom and openness. Dowry is getting a bad name, and many young people reject the idea. "Girl's merit main consideration," said a far-from-rare matrimonial advertisement not long ago, marking an important shift away from tradition.

More and more, in the middle class, young men and women are asking for and getting more say in the matter of their marriages. They are meeting, talking with and even dating their prospective spouses before making up their minds.

This liberalized system, some Indians believe, represents the best of both worlds: You have the security of knowing that your parents are looking out for your interests, plus a ready mechanism for meeting a mate. At the same time, you have freedom to explore, to judge and, if necessary, to refuse.

CHAPTER 2

Studying Marriage
and the Family

PREVIEW

To gain a sense of what you already know about the material in this chapter, answer "true" or "false" to the statements below. You will find the answers as you read the chapter.

1. Many researchers believe that love and conflict can coexist. True or false?
2. Research in marriage and the family has little impact on how we understand the day-to-day interactions of our own and other families. True or false?
3. Since the beginning of the Reagan administration's "profamily" policy in 1981, the federal government has expanded the gathering and dissemination of statistics and other data, providing a wealth of information for family scholars. True or false?
4. In family research, the high incidence of "perfect" responses, such as "My mate never makes me feel miserable," indicates more "perfect" marriages exist than people ordinarily believe. True or false?
5. Sex role stereotypes do not necessarily reflect or predict actual behavior. True or false?
6. Loving relationships are always characterized by unselfish behavior. True or false?
7. Examining current marriage and family trends, researchers have concluded that the family as an institution is declining. True or false?
8. In most families, tasks are usually divided among family members according to skill and temperament. True or false?
9. According to some scholars, in love relationships we tend to weigh the costs against the benefits of the relationship. True or false?
10. When we interact with people, we *interpret* words or actions. True or false?

Outline

The universe is like a safe to which there is a combination. But the combination is locked up in the safe.

PETER DeVRIES

Nothing is so firmly believed as that which is least known.

MICHEL De MONTAIGNE
(1533–1592)

Enlightenment is man's release from his self-imposed tutelage. Tutelage is man's inability to make use of his understanding without direction from another. . . . Have courage to use your own reason.

IMMANUEL KANT (1724–1804),
WHAT IS ENLIGHTENMENT?

He who knows nothing doubts nothing.

FRENCH PROVERB

One of the first things we realize in studying marriage and the family is how little we really know. We even know very little about our own family. Is our family like other families or is it different? How do our parents really feel about each other? How did they meet? Why did they get married? What are their secret ambitions and desires? Do they harbor resentments toward each other? What do they talk about when they are alone?

We often know very little about ourselves in relationship to our families. Why were we born? What role have we played in our parents' lives? In what ways are we like our parents? How do our behavior patterns and values reflect those of our family? What part do we play in maintaining our families' interactional patterns and roles?

We hide much of our marital and family life from the outside world, other members of the family, and even ourselves. R. D. Laing (1972) wrote: "The first family to interest me was my own. I still know less about it than I know about many other families. This is typical. Children are the last to be told what was really going on."

A family may have a closetful of secrets that all family members know, even though each may pretend he or she knows nothing, such as a mother's alcoholism, a father's first marriage, and so on. We often have profound questions about our own marriages and families that we can't answer. How do our parents *really* feel about us? Our brothers? Our sisters? Who is their favorite? Many adolescent children complain that their parents never talk to them about their own feelings. Their parents are mysteries to them. Partners, too, may hide their feelings. They may act out their roles, but neither person may know what the other *really* thinks or feels. Many areas may be tabooed: feelings, sex, money, beliefs, politics. We are given the answers society expects to be given to our questions. But the conventional answer may not be the real answer.

Part of what research does is probe the unknown areas of marriage and family. It also studies the relationship of marriage and family to the larger society. In this chapter we examine the benefits of studying marriage and the family both for ourselves and society; then we look at the four primary methods used in such research: (1) surveys, (2) clinical studies, (3) direct observation, and (4) experimental research. Finally, we examine four theories underlying much of the current research: (1) structural functionalism, (2) conflict theory, (3) symbolic interaction, and (4) exchange or equity theory. As you examine these theories, you may find that they help explain much of what goes on in your own relationships and families.

☐ THE VALUE OF RESEARCH

Reflecting on Your Own Life

Researchers in marriage and the family have had an immense impact on our awareness of how families work and don't work. Their research affects us both personally and socially. As you study research findings, you'll discover yourself reflecting on your own relationships, marriages, or families because the questions researchers ask often touch on intensely personal issues in your own life. Researchers' questions and findings may give you new perspectives and insights into your relationships. As you study how people communicate (Chapter 14), for example, you will be able to use research findings to evaluate your own communication patterns, pinpoint difficulties, and discover possible solutions to them.

Understanding Changes in Marriage and the Family

Marriage and family research also helps us understand these institutions in relation to the larger society. Family scholars are charting the changing face of American families, allowing us to more fully understand what is happening to families in today's society (for example, see Adams, 1985).

In the last few decades, with the rise of cohabitation, divorce, single-parent families, and stepfamilies, the once dominant nuclear family has declined in significance. To many Americans, this decline represents the decline of *the* family itself.

Family scholars, however, offer a different perspective to the idea of the declining family. Instead, they look at contemporary families in terms of change rather than

Ignorance is like a delicate exotic fruit; touch it and the bloom is gone.

OSCAR WILDE

Contradictory adages such as "absence makes the heart grow fonder" and "out of sight, out of mind" are both part of the folk wisdom of our society. Which is true? Only the painstaking, careful accumulation of evidence on the effects of separation on marriage can answer this question. The answer is that both are true. Short separations make the heart grow fonder; prolonged and repeated separations wreck marriages. Societal myths, whatever their reason for being, crumble in the face of hard evidence and an open mind.

BETTY YORBURG, *FAMILIES AND SOCIETIES*

The "typical" American family is a middle-class, white family with two children; the husband works and the wife remains at home with the children. This type of family, however, is a minority. It represents only 17% of all American families. What types of families do you think are more representative of American families?

MARRIAGE AND FAMILY
PERIODICALS
The periodicals listed below
(adapted from Steinmetz and
Foulke, 1980) are of major interest to researchers, teachers,
and students of marriage and
the family.

- *The American Journal of
  Family Therapy* focuses on
  issues of particular interest
  to counselors and family
  therapists.
- *The American Journal of
  Orthopsychiatry* is a multi-
  disciplinary journal focusing
  on human development and
  mental health.
- *Cofo Memo* is a quarterly
  newsletter emphasizing marriage and family issues being
  acted upon in Washington,
  D.C.
- *Family Law Reporter* is a
  weekly newsletter dealing
  with the legal aspects of
  family life, such as rights,
  violence, divorce, abortion,
  and so on.
- *Family Process* focuses on
  family psychotherapy, especially from a general systems
  approach (see Chapter 13).
- *Family Planning Perspectives* deals with birth control, sex education, and
  other aspects of family
  planning.
- *Family Relations* is a major
  journal emphasizing the implications of research on
  family counseling and
  services.
- *Home Economics Research
  Journal* is published bi-
  monthly to encourage dialogue between home economists and scholars in related
  fields concerned with the
  well-being of the family and
  individuals.
- *Journal of Comparative
  Family Studies* is dedicated
  to the cross-cultural study of
  marriage and the family.

decline. This slight shift in perspective from "decline" to "change" allows researchers to achieve fresh insights into contemporary marriages and families. For example, researchers are viewing divorce as a process involving a reorganization and redefinition of the family instead of its destruction (Macklin, 1980). What emerge from divorce are different family forms, the single-parent family and the stepfamily. Both these family forms represent family adjustments in response to divorce.

Researchers are pointing out the differences between these emerging family forms and traditional nuclear families. The single parent and stepfamily carry on the traditional function of socializing children, but do it differently because their structures are different. By pointing out how the stepchild-stepparent relationship differs from the biological child-biological parent relationship, for example, researchers and therapists are able to help members of stepfamilies adjust to one another (see Nolan et al., 1984 for the treatment of stepfamilies in marriage and family textbooks).

Research and Social Issues

Family researchers also play an important role in the development of social issues and the formulation of public policy. Family scholars, for example, have documented the widespread incidence of violence and abuse in the family. National survey data analyzed by researchers reveal that violence is widespread in all social classes, not just occasionally in poor or psychologically disabled individuals as was formerly believed. By making surveys and examining statistics, scholars found that two million wives and about the same number of husbands are assaulted each year. More than 650,000 children are abused or neglected each year—almost 2,000 children a day. Fifteen children are killed daily. The federal government recognized the role of research in understanding the problem by establishing the Office of Domestic Violence and the National Center on Child Abuse and Neglect to support additional research.

Family scholars respond to the changing family and attempt to understand it (Berardo and Shehan, 1984). Their research arises out of major concerns and trends, as well as the researchers' own personal experiences and their interactions with teachers, social workers, lawyers, nurses, physicians, and other professionals involved in family matters. Marriage and family textbooks generally follow these research trends (Klein and Smith, 1985).

Feminist scholarship is also reexamining the family, utilizing three basic tenets of feminism: (1) a belief that women are exploited and devalued, (2) a commitment to changing the condition of women, and (3) a critique of the traditional social sciences as inherently biased against women. Feminist scholars are attempting to integrate their work into the general field of marriage and family studies (Walker and Thompson, 1984).

☐ RESEARCH METHODS

An enormous amount of research on marriage and the family is undertaken each year. The Family Resources Database (which we used extensively in the research for this textbook) annually adds 3,000 journal articles to its computerized data base of family studies. The data base includes 1,200 journals, books, government documents, directories, and audio-visual materials. In 1985 the data base contained more than 60,000 items. Of the journals, fifty are major publications in the general area of marriage and the family (see Steinmetz and Foulke, 1980, for an annotated bibliography of these journals). Two journals—*Marriage and Family Review* and *Sage Family Studies Abstracts*—are devoted to abstracting current research.

What researchers know about marriage and the family comes from four basic sources: (1) surveys, (2) clinical studies, (3) direct observation and (4) experimental research. (For a discussion of research methodology, see the special issue of *Journal of Marriage and the Family*, 44 [November, 1982]; in particular, see the articles by Brent C. Miller and Richard Galligan; also see LaRossa and Wolf, 1985.)

Surveys

The survey method, using questionnaires or interviews, is the most popular data gathering technique in marriage and family studies. From 1957 through 1976, for example, almost 65 percent of all research studies in marriage and the family relied *exclusively* on survey methods for gathering their data; the figure is about the same today (Galligan, 1982). These surveys may be conducted in person, over the telephone, or by written questionnaire. The purpose of a survey is to gather information

"How would you like me to answer that question? As a member of my ethnic group, educational class, income group, or religious category?"

Drawing by D. Fradon; © 1969 The New Yorker Magazine, Inc.

- *Journal of Divorce* focuses on divorce issues for counselors, therapists, lawyers, and family life professionals.
- *Journal of Family Issues* is a multi-disciplinary journal which alternates between general family issues and specific themes under a guest editor.
- *Journal of Home Economics* focuses on general home economic themes and devotes a portion of each issue to a specific topic.
- *Journal of Marital and Family Therapy* specializes in the understanding and treatment of marital and family dysfunctions.
- *Journal of Marriage and the Family* is a multi-disciplinary research journal devoted to the study of marriage and the family. The leading journal in the field, it contains theory, methodological studies, research interpretation, and book reviews.
- *Journal of Sex Research* is an interdisciplinary journal dedicated to sex research; contains original articles, commentary, and book reviews.
- *Marriage and Family Review* contains current abstracts and review articles of scholarly interest.
- *Sage Family Studies Abstracts* contains around 250 abstracts of recent literature grouped by topic.
- *Sex Roles: A Journal of Research* is an interdisciplinary journal on research and theory regarding gender-role socialization.
- *Signs: Journal of Women in Culture and Society* is devoted to original research, essays, reports, and commentaries about women.

from a small, representative group of people and to infer conclusions that are valid
for a larger population. Questionnaires offer anonymity, may be completed fairly
quickly, and are relatively inexpensive to administer. Questionnaires, however, usually
do not allow an in-depth response; a person must respond with a short answer, a yes,
a no, or a choice on a scale of 1 to 10. Unfortunately, marriage and family issues
are more complicated than questionnaires are able to probe. (See Graham Spanier's
"Dyadic Adjustment Scale" on pages 56–58 for an example of a questionnaire.)

Interview techniques avoid some of the shortcomings of questionnaires, as interviewers are able to probe in greater depth and follow paths suggested by the interviewee.
Interviewers, however, may allow their own preconceptions to bias their interpretation
of responses as well as the way in which they frame questions.

Whether done by questionnaires or interviews, surveys have certain inherent problems. First, how representative is the sample that volunteered to take the survey? Self-
selection tends to bias a sample. Second, how well do people understand their own
behavior? Third, people tend to underreport undesirable or unacceptable behavior.
A man may be reluctant to admit that he has extramarital affairs and a woman will
not quickly say that she is an alcoholic. (To compare popular surveys to scholarly
ones, see the readings "Ann Landers: Sex Researcher" [pages 50–51] and "Dating
Behaviors of College Students" [pages 51–55].)

Surveys are well suited for discovering the incidence of certain behaviors or traits
and trends. They are more commonly used by sociologists than by psychologists
because they tend to deal on a general or societal level rather than on a personal or
small group level. Surveys are not very well able to measure how people interact
with each other. For researchers and therapists interested in studying the dynamic
flow of relationships, surveys are not as useful as clinical, experimental, and observational studies.

Clinical Studies

Clinical studies or case studies are in-depth examinations of a person or small group
of people who come to a psychiatrist, psychologist, or social worker with psychological
or relationship problems. The people are interviewed individually. The case study
method is the traditional approach of all clinical research; it was, with few exceptions,
the sole method of clinical investigation through the first half of the twentieth century
(Runyan, 1982). The advantage of clinical approaches is that they offer long-term,
in-depth study of various aspects of marriage and family life. The primary disadvantage is that we cannot necessarily make inferences to the general population. People
who come into psychotherapy are not a representative sample. They may be more
motivated to solve their problems or have more intense problems than the general
population.

Clinical studies, however, have been very fruitful in developing insight into family
processes. Such studies have been instrumental in the development of general systems
theory, discussed in Chapter 13. By analyzing individuals and families in therapy,
psychiatrists, psychologists, and therapists, such as R. D. Laing, Salvador Minuchin,
and Virginia Satir have been able to understand how families create roles, patterns,
and rules which family members follow without being aware of them. A typical rule

that families have, for example, is not to be aware that it has rules, such as rules against discussing or expressing certain types of feelings (anger, love, aggression, and so on).

Direct Observation

Researchers may attempt to systematically study interpersonal behavior through direct observation while remaining as unobtrusive as possible. To measure power in a relationship, for example, an observer-researcher may sit in a home and note exchanges between husband and wife. The obvious disadvantage of this method is that couples may hide unacceptable ways of dealing with decisions, such as by threats of violence, while the observer is present.

Another problem with observational studies is that a low correlation often exists between what observers see and the self-reports of the people observed. This is especially true in observational studies of power (Cromwell and Olson, 1975). Interestingly, when there is a discrepancy, psychologists tend to distrust self-reports and sociologists tend to trust them too much, according to one researcher (Gottman, 1979). Another researcher (Olson, 1977) has suggested that self-reports and observations really measure two different views of the same thing: self-reports are an insider's view, whereas an observer's report is an outsider's view.

Experimental Research

Little experimental research is done in marriage and the family. Experimental findings can be very powerful since such research gives researchers control over many factors and enables them to isolate variables. Yet it is difficult to construct an experiment that not only controls all of the behaviors that make up real-world situations but that duplicates the situations as well. Measuring power in a laboratory situation is not the same as measuring it in the bedroom or the kitchen.

☐ FUTURE RESEARCH DIRECTIONS

Despite their limitations, surveys will probably be increasingly used. Phone interviews and mail questionnaires may very well become the dominant form of survey taking. The reason is simple: economics. Telephone interviews are considerably faster and cost only about one-fourth as much as face-to-face interviews. The response rate to telephone interviews is only slightly lower than to face-to-face interviews, and the results from the two methods are nearly identical (Miller et al., 1982). Studies of family processes and in-home observations will be limited because of declining funds for research (Hill, 1981). Much old data will be reevaluated. "Like scroungers working over the tailings of old gold mines," wrote Reuben Hill (1981), "family scholars are becoming adept at manipulating 'warmed-over family data' collected originally by economists, political scientists, and demographers for other purposes."

If the current trend continues, scholars will have less access to new data. Since 1981, when the Reagan administration first began restricting the collection and publication of statistics and other data, the amount of information available to both

Discovery consists of seeing what everybody has seen and thinking what nobody has thought.

ALBERT SZENT-GYORGYI

The most instructive experiences are those of everyday life.

FRIEDRICH NIETZCHE

Seeing is believing. I wouldn't have seen it if I hadn't believed it.

ASHLEIGH BRILLIANT

What really teaches a man is not experience but observation.

H. L. MENCKEN

Knowledge rests not upon truth alone, but on error also.

CARL JUNG

. . . men do not seek the truth. It is the truth that pursues men who run away and will not look around.

LINCOLN STEFFANS

Doubt everything at least once, even the statement that two times two makes four.

GEORG LICHTENBERG (1742–1799)

FEATURE

Conventionality

In studying people's responses to questions about their marriages, husbands and wives frequently give unusually positive responses. People report high degrees of marital satisfaction whether in truth they are happy or not. People often say what is socially acceptable or expected rather than express their real feelings. Their responses are *conventional* (Edmonds, 1967).

This conventionality has distorted research on satisfaction in marriage, one of the main areas of marriage and family research. Edmonds, on examining responses to questions about marital happiness, observed: "No one can be 'perfectly happy' and . . . any person thinking critically or answering honestly would have to indicate something less than this state of perfect bliss." In his study he found a number of "impossibly perfect" responses:

"None of my dealings with my mate are prompted by selfish motives" (69 percent responded yes). "If I had my life to live over, I wouldn't even think of marrying another person" (73 percent positive). "My mate has all the qualities I've ever wanted in a mate" (51 percent positive). "My mate never makes me feel miserable" (87 percent positive). "I never lie to my mate" (73 percent positive).

We do not see our marriages and families as they really are; we see idealized pictures of them, according to our culturally formed expectations

about marriage. For example, we expect the man to have the decision-making power in the family. But does he in reality have this power, despite how he and his wife perceive the decision-making process? Jessie Bernard (1972) described an experiment that tested whether men and women actually fulfilled their marital images. An experimenter asked husbands and wives to fill out a questionnaire to determine their relative decision-making power. Then he asked the young couples in a laboratory situation to make a number of decisions about their marriage and family. The results of the experiment were in striking contrast to the results of the questionnaire.

Husbands, according to their questionnaire responses, perceived they had more power than was actually shown in the laboratory situation; wives perceived they had less. Three-fourths of the husbands overestimated their power and almost as many wives underestimated theirs. Another experiment had similar results: both partners tended to believe that the partner who had the "right" to make the decisions had more power. Reality, however, failed to confirm their beliefs. Bernard (1972) concluded: "Their replies . . . conform to the model of marriage that has characterized civilized mankind for millenia. It is this model rather than their own actual behavior that husbands and wives tend to perceive."

scholars and the general public has declined. This trend is continuing. In 1985, for example, the federal government proposed that agencies would have to demonstrate that collecting data was "essential" to their mission, that it was not likely to be gathered or distributed by the private sector, and that the benefits of the gathered data were not outweighed by its costs. Not only is the federal government limiting the data collected but also, according to a Harvard University report, "Federal agencies have greatly expanded their demands to see academic research before it is published" (quoted in Tolchin, 1985).

As a result of these trends, family research will turn away from large-scale studies to small studies of neglected areas. More research will be conducted on single-parent families, gay relationships, and Mexican–American families, for example. These will

FEATURE–*continued*

We mistake the models of behavior for the actual behavior. We believe we act as we ought to act, not as we actually do. In this manner we keep ourselves from knowing how we are really behaving and acting. Reality is hidden.

In a similar fashion, sex roles obscure the reality of our behavior. Because a person is male or female, we assume that a close fit exists between a person and his or her sex role. So when we first meet a man or woman, we project an image onto them based on their sex, which tells us what they *ought* be like. A man who has just fallen in love with a woman, for example, may project onto her what he expects a woman to be like. He may adore her for being gentle and for expressing her feelings easily. She, however, may not be gentle at all but tough as nails; she may be closed and inexpressive of her feelings. But because her toughness and inexpressiveness do not fit his image of a woman, he either discounts them ("she's not acting herself today") or he does not see them ("she is quiet"). Conventionality blinds him from seeing her apart from her sex role.

Conventionality also serves a purpose. As we saw, when asked if they are happily married, people will usually respond "yes" unless something is radically wrong with their marriage. One researcher, Karen Renne (1970), explained this behavior in medical terms: People consider themselves healthy despite minor ailments—a cold, a deficiency in vision, the flu—but when they become

really ill, they no longer define themselves as healthy. This change in self-definition is a call to action. If they are not healthy, they must do something about it to change the situation. The same is true in marriages. Most marriages have minor complaints, or even major ones, but until people define themselves as unhappily married, they will not seek radical change.

Positive conventional responses support the status quo. When a person responds with negative conventionalism—"My spouse and I never agree," "My spouse has none of the qualities I value"—the marriage is defined as "unhealthy." Although these responses are exaggerations, they suggest that a person is going to take some action to alter the marital relationship. The danger of conventional responses is that the positive ones may encourage a person to overlook the negative aspects until these negative aspects grow to endanger a marriage.

Negative conventionality encourages a person to look at the weaknesses of a marriage rather than its strengths. As a result, conventional responses overlook or blur the many shades and variations of a marital relationship that give it depth and color. Furthermore, we may come to believe that our conventional responses are indeed our genuine feelings. In this situation, we end up deceiving ourselves as well as others.

be small, nonrepresentative, descriptive studies that will try to formulate new research questions rather than give definitive answers.

☐ THEORIES OF MARRIAGE AND THE FAMILY

We use surveys, clinical studies, observations, and experiments to gather data on marriages and families. We utilize theory to make sense of data. Theories provide frames of reference or viewpoints by which researchers interpret the data they collect. Theories also suggest directions for research because of the questions they raise.

The theories we discuss in this chapter are structural functionalism, conflict theory,

Every truth is true only up to a point. Beyond that, by way of counterpoint, it becomes untruth.

SOREN KIERKEGAARD (1813–1855)

Families are studied through surveys, clinical studies, observations, and experiments. If you wanted to study families, which method would you choose? Why? What kinds of things would you want to know about families? What theoretical framework would you use to interpret your data? Why?

There is no truth that a blockhead could not turn into an error.

LUC De VAUVENARGUES

Three blind men once stumbled upon an elephant that was blocking their path. Since they had never encountered an elephant before, each tried to describe it to the other. The first blind man, who had felt the elephant's tail, said an elephant was like a rope; the second blind man felt only the elephant's leg. He said an elephant was like a tree. The third blind man had felt only the trunk, and said an elephant was like a snake. As they quarreled among themselves about the nature of the elephant, the elephant walked away.

HINDU FOLKTALE

The effort to understand the universe is one of the very few things that lifts human life above the level of farce, and gives it some of the grace of tragedy.

STEVEN WEINBERG

symbolic interaction, and exchange theory. These theories are currently among the most influential ones used by sociologists and psychologists. The developmental framework, which studies the family life cycle, is discussed in Chapter 10, and the general systems theory, which is becoming increasingly important, is discussed in Chapter 13. (For a detailed discussion of the various theories, see Burr et al., 1979, and Nye and Berardo, 1981.)

As you study these different theories, notice how the choice of a theoretical perspective influences the way data is interpreted. As you read this textbook, ask yourself how a different theoretical perspective would lead to different conclusions about the same material.

Structural Functionalism

Structural functionalism is one of the leading theories used to explain how society works, how families work, and how families relate to the larger society and to their own members. The theory is used largely in sociology and anthropology, disciplines that focus on the study of society rather than individuals. When structural functionalists study the family, they look at three aspects of the family: (1) what functions the family serves for society, (2) what functional requirements are performed by its members for the family's survival, and (3) what needs the family meets for its individual members. (For a brief theoretical discussion of structural functionalism, see McIntyre, 1981.)

Society as a System. Structural functionalists look at society as if it were a living organism, like a human being, animal, or tree. In fact, they sometimes use the analogy of a tree in describing society. In a tree, there are many structures or parts, such as the trunk, branches, roots, leaves. Each structure has a function. The roots gather nutrients and water from the soil, the leaves gather sunlight, and so on. Society is like a tree insofar as it has different structures that perform functions for its survival. These structures are called subsystems. The subsystems are the major institutions, such as the family, religion, government, and the economy. Each of these structures has a function for maintaining society, just as the different parts of a tree serve a function in maintaining the tree. Religion, for example, gives spiritual and moral guidance, the government ensures order, and the economy produces goods. The family provides new members for society through procreation and socializes its members so that they fit into the society. In theory, all institutions work in harmony for the good of society and themselves.

The Family as a System. Not only is society a system but families themselves also may be regarded as systems. In looking at families, structural functionalists examine (1) how the family organizes itself for survival, and (2) what functions the family performs for its members. For the family to survive, its members must perform certain functions. Functions are usually divided along gender and age lines. Men and women have different tasks; these tasks differ according to age. The family must perform economic functions, for example, in order to survive. Someone must earn money by working outside the home and someone must work inside the home to maintain it. In fact, the division of labor along gender lines makes men and women interdependent. Until recently, it was expected that the man work outside the home and that the woman remain in the home, cooking, washing, cleaning, and caring for children. The man needed his wife to care for the home and to rear the children and the woman needed her husband to provide financial support. (See the reading by William Goode on pages 55–56 for an example of a structural functionalist interpretation of the theoretical advantages of the family.)

The family also functions to meet the emotional and developmental needs of its members. These needs include mutual companionship and support for husband and wife, the socialization of children, the development of personality and social skills, and so on.

According to structural functionalists, the family molds the kind of personalities it needs to carry out its functions. It encourages different character traits for men and women to ensure the family's survival. Men are given *instrumental* traits and women are given *expressive* ones. Instrumental traits encourage competitiveness, coolness, self-confidence, and rationality—qualities that will help men succeed in the outside world. In contrast, expressive traits encourage warmth, emotionality, nurturing, and sensitivity—qualities appropriate for a woman caring for a husband, children, and home.

Critique. Many people are structural functionalists without realizing it. Those who believe that social stability is in the best interests of society share this assumption with structural functionalists. Those who believe that families must be intact to fulfill their functions share a common view with structural functionalism. Those who feel that changes in sex roles, the increase in dual-worker families, single-parent families, and stepfamilies threaten the traditional nuclear family share the concerns of structural functionalists.

Although structural functionalism is an important theoretical approach to the family, it has some problems. First of all, because the theory cannot be empirically tested, we'll never know if it is "right" or "wrong." We can only discuss it theoretically, arguing whether it accounts for what we know about the family. Second, it is not

The fact will one day flower into a truth.

HENRY THOREAU (1817–1862)

We never really understand things. We just get used to them.

JOHN Von NEUMAN

always clear what function a particular structure serves. "The function of the nose," remarked Voltaire in the eighteenth century, "is to hold the pince-nez [eye-glasses] on the face." What is the function of the division of labor along gender lines? Efficiency, survival, or oppression? Also, how do we know what family functions are vital? For example, the family is supposed to socialize children, but much socialization has been taken over by the schools, peer groups, and television. Third, structural functionalism has a conservative bias. Aspects that encourage stability are called functional and those that encourage instability are called dysfunctional. Traditional roles are functional and nontraditional ones are dysfunctional. Mothers working outside the home are considered dysfunctional, for example, because they should be at home doing housework and caring for their children. But actually, working mothers could be considered functional because they contribute to the family's economic stability by earning money; their income often pushes their families above the poverty line. Similarly, divorce is considered a sign of family dysfunction. But is a family functional if the husband and wife are engaged in perpetual warfare? Finally, structural functionalism looks at the family from a distance; it looks at families as institutions and roles. If we are interested in how families actually interact in the everyday world, we must turn elsewhere. In fact, some of these conservative ideas may obscure the realities of family life. Claiming that men have instrumental character traits and that women have expressive ones, for example, may encourage us to look at people stereotypically. We may overlook the tenderness and sensitivity found in men and the logic and competitiveness found in women.

Conflict Theory

While structural functionalists tend to believe that what is, is good, conflict theorists believe that what is, is wrong. They see society not as basically cooperative but as divided, with individuals and groups in conflict with each other. Conflict theorists try to identify the competing forces.

We are familiar with the analysis of society in terms of competing interests: Republicans versus Democrats, rich versus poor, environmentalists versus developers, and so on. In these analyses, power is a critical element. The group with the greatest amount of power wins.

But how can we analyze marriages and families in terms of conflict and power? Marriages and families are based on love and affection, aren't they? Conflict theorists would agree that love and affection are important elements in marriages and families, but they believe that conflict and power are also fundamental. Marriages and families are composed of individuals with different personalities, ideas, values, tastes, and goals. Each person is not always in harmony with every other person in the family. Imagine you are living at home and want to do something your parents don't want you to do, such as spend the weekend with a friend they don't like. They forbid you to carry out your plan. "As long as you live in this house, you'll have to do what we say." You argue with them, but in the end you stay home. Why did your parents win the disagreement? They did so because they had power, according to conflict analysts.

Sources of Conflict.   Conflict theorists do not believe that conflict is bad. Instead, it is a natural part of family life. Families always have disagreements, from small ones like what movie to see to major ones such as how to rear children. Families

---

An idea that is not dangerous is unworthy of being called an idea at all.

OSCAR WILDE

All universal judgments are weak, loose, and dangerous.

MICHEL De MONTAIGNE
(1533–1595)

The modern individual family is founded on the open or concealed slavery of the wife. . . . Within the family [the husband] is the bourgeoise and his wife represents the proletariat.

FRIEDRICH ENGELS (1820–1895),
THE ORIGIN OF THE FAMILY

There are many truths of which the full meaning cannot be realized until personal experience has brought it home.

JOHN STUART MILL (1806–1873)

differ in the number of underlying conflicts of interest, the degree of underlying hostility, and the nature and extent of the expression of conflict. Conflict can take the form of competing goals, such as a husband wanting to start a law career in Tucson and a wife wanting to move to New York to attend medical school. Conflict can occur because of different role expectations: a wife wants to work but her husband wants her to remain at home caring for their small children.

Sources of Power.   When conflict occurs, who wins? Family members have different amounts of resources and power. Four important sources of power are legitimacy, money, physical coercion, and love. When arguments arise in a family, a man wants his way "because I'm the head of the house" or a parent "because I'm your mother." These appeals are based on legitimacy, that is, the belief that the person is entitled to prevail by right. Money is a powerful resource in marriages and families. "As long as you live in this house . . ." is a directive based on economics. Because men tend to earn more than women, they have greater economic power; this economic power translates to marital power. Physical coercion is a significant source of power. "If you don't do as I tell you, you'll get a spanking" is one of the most common forms of coercion. But physical abuse of a spouse is also common, as we see in Chapter 15. Finally, there is the power of love. Love can be used to emotionally coerce someone, as in, "If you really loved me, you'd do what I ask" or love can be a freely given gift, as in a person giving up something important, such as a plan, desire, or career to enhance a relationship.

Everyone in the family has power, although the power may be different and unequal. Adolescent children, for example, have few economic resources, so they must depend on their parents. This dependency gives the parents power. But adolescents also have power, through the exercise of personal charm, ingratiating habits, temper tantrums, wheedling, and so on.

Families cannot live with much open conflict. The problem for families, as for any group, is how to encourage cooperation amid differences. Since conflict is seen as normal, conflict theory seeks to channel it and to seek solutions through communication, bargaining, and negotiations. We return to these themes in Chapter 14, "Communication and Conflict Resolution."

Critique.   A number of difficulties arise in conflict theory. First, conflict theory derives from politics where self-interest, egotism, and competition are dominant elements. But is such a harsh judgment of human nature justified? People are also characterized by self-sacrifice and cooperation. Love is an important quality in relationships. Conflict theorists don't often talk about the power of love or bonding, yet the presence of love and bonding may distinguish the family from all other groups in society. We often will make sacrifices for the sake of those we love. We will defer our own wishes to another's desires; we may even sacrifice our lives for a loved one.

Second, conflict theorists assume that differences lead to conflict. Differences can also be accepted. Differences do not necessarily imply conflict.

Third, conflict in families is not easily measured or evaluated. Families live much of their lives privately, and outsiders are not always aware of whatever conflict exists or how pervasive it is. Also, much overt conflict is avoided because it is regulated through family and societal rules. Most children obey their parents, and most parents, although they may argue heatedly, do not employ violence.

Though women do not complain of the power of husbands, each complains of her own husband or of the husbands of her friends. It is the same in all other cases of servitude. . . .

JOHN STUART MILL, *ON THE SUBJECTION OF WOMEN*

Symbolic Interaction

Symbolic interactionists, like the rest of us, are concerned with relationships. And in certain ways their approach better reflects the everyday workings of human relationships than the approaches of structural functionalists and conflict theorists. When we complain that we can't relate to our spouse, that our partner doesn't understand us, that we can't communicate, we are complaining about matters that are at the heart of symbolic interaction.

Interpreting Meanings. Symbolic interaction is a theory that looks at how people interact. The key factor in these interactions is communication. We communicate with each other with more than words. We communicate through symbols, which include not only words but also intonations, gestures, movements, and so on. When we interact with people, we do more than simply react to them. We interpret or define their actions.

If someone we meet asks us to go to the movies, we interpret what he or she means. On one level, the invitation is simply a suggestion to share an entertainment, but the invitation also conveys symbolic meaning. In our culture, an invitation to the movies by someone we have just met is a "date"—and a date is a means by which people get to know each other; it is a part of American courtship. We react by being flattered or flustered, depending on whether we are unattached, whether we think it would be fun to spend time with the person, and so on.

In a relationship it is not always clear what words or actions mean. If we like the person with whom we went to the movies and we continue to see each other, what does this mean? Individuals often need to clarify a relationship. The way they do this is through communication. If they have good communication, then they can generally discover what each other thinks or feels. If they have poor communication, then they are left to guess what a particular symbolic act means. Does this continual dating mean love? Does it mean commitment? To find out, they may have to ask, and to ask is to communicate.

The Family as a Unity of Interacting Personalities. In the 1920s Ernest Burgess (1926) defined the family as a "unity of interacting personalities." This definition has been critical to symbolic interaction theory and in the development of marriage and family studies. Marriages and families consist of individuals who interact with one another over a period of time. The way each person interacts with others is partly defined by his or her social roles. A social role is an established pattern of behavior that exists independently of a person. For example, the role of a husband or wife exists independently of any particular husband or wife, just as your role as a student exists independently of you.

Each member in a marriage or family has a social role—husband, wife, mother, father, child, sibling, and so on. Three important processes in this world of social roles include role taking, role playing, and role making. *Role taking* refers to our tendency take on roles in different social situations and to modify our actions accordingly. When you enter school, you take on a student role, when you enter marriage, you take on a husband or wife role, and so on. If you feel you don't know how to act in a certain situation, it often means you don't know the appropriate role to take. It is fairly common for people to ask what role they are expected to play in a meeting, organization, or relationship. *Role playing* refers to our changing roles in response

We should be careful to get out of an experience only the wisdom that is in it—and stop there; lest we be like that cat that sits down on a hot stove-lid. She will never sit down on a hot stove-lid again—and that is well; but also she will never sit down on a cold one anymore.

MARK TWAIN

Motives are generally unknown.

SAMUEL JOHNSON (1709–1784)

to the roles of others. One moment we may be acting as a son or daughter in response to our parents. Another moment we may take on the role of a husband or wife in response to our partner. In a third moment we may play the role of a parent in response to the crying of a infant. *Role making* refers to our creation or modification of existing roles. Role making is particularly critical since the social roles we are given do not necessarily fit us particularly well. The role of male, for example, typically calls for an aggressive personality and the pursuit of worldly success, but a man may instead be cooperative and interested more in family life than in power or fame. Similarly, a female role traditionally calls for conciliatory behavior and family orientation, but a woman's temperament may lead her to politics or law. In both instances, the man and woman must modify their roles to fit their temperaments.

There is a constant interplay of roles, communication, and symbols as we play different roles and modifying them according to the expectations of others, the situation, and our own needs.

Symbolic interaction is used extensively in analyzing marital adjustment, dating, and mate selection. It has had a significant impact, not only on researchers but also on those interested in process and change—clinical psychologists, social workers, counselors, and therapists.

Critique. While symbolic interaction shifts the focus to the daily workings of the family, it suffers from several drawbacks. First, the theory tends to minimize the role of power in relationships. If a conflict exists, it may take more than simply communicating to resolve it. If one partner strongly wants to pursue his law career in Los Angeles and the other just as strongly wants to pursue hers in Boston, no amount of communication and role adjustment will resolve the conflict. Ultimately, the person with the greater power in the relationship will prevail.

Second, symbolic interaction doesn't fully account for the emotional aspects of human life, especially for unconscious processes. It sees us only as the sum of our roles. It neglects the "I"—the "self" or the "soul"—that exists independently of our roles. But limiting us to the sum of our parts is limiting our uniqueness as human beings.

Third, the theory emphasizes individualism. It encourages competence in interpersonal relationships and values individual happiness and fulfillment over stability, duty, responsibility and other familial values. As Jay Schvaneveldt (1981) observed, "The welfare and happiness of marital partners are held above the belief that the marital union or family union should stay intact. The happiness of the individual family members appears to be the dominant value."

Fourth, the theory does not place marriage or family within a larger social context and thereby disregards or minimizes the forces working on families from the outside, such as economic discrimination against minorities and women.

Social Exchange Theory

According to exchange theory, we measure our actions and relationships on a cost-benefit basis. In relationships we try to maximize our benefits and minimize our costs to obtain the most advantageous result. At first glance, exchange theory may be the least attractive theory we use to study marriage and the family. It seems more appropriate for accountants than lovers. But all of us use a cost-benefit analysis to

In all matters of opinion, our adversaries are insane.

MARK TWAIN

If I have a book which understands for me, a pastor who has a conscience for me, a physician who decides my diet . . . I need not trouble myself. I need not think if I can only pay . . . others will readily undertake the irksome work for me.

IMMANUEL KANT (1724–1804), *WHAT IS ENLIGHTENMENT?*

UNDERSTANDING YOURSELF

Using Theory to Understand Yourself

Theories often seem far removed from reality, but if a theory is at all valuable it gives you a tool to better understand reality. Reflect on the theories you studied in this chapter and see if they are able to give you insight into your own relationships, marriage, or family.

for you and other members? What kind of relations exist between your parents or yourself and your partner? Can you examine these relationships functionally? How did your family socialize you? What values were you taught? What personality characteristics did your family encourage?

STRUCTURAL FUNCTIONALISM

Using the structural functionalist approach, examine how your family works. How is labor divided in your family? Along gender lines? Along age lines? Who works outside the home; who works within the home? Who rears the children? Who fixes the plumbing? Who is expressive and who is instrumental?

What personal needs does your family meet

CONFLICT THEORY

What are the recurring conflicts in your relationship, marriage, or family? Who wins these various conflicts? What resources do the winners have? The losers? Do they differ according to the type of conflict? What are your resources in relationships? How do you use them?

---

some degree to measure our actions and relationships. Even the Beatles were caught up in exchange theory when they sang, "The love you take is equal to the love you make."

How Exchange Theory Works.   One of the reasons we don't recognize our use of this interpersonal accounting is that we do much of it unconsciously. If a friend is unhappy with a partner, you may ask, "What are you getting out of the relationship?" Your friend will start listing pluses and minuses: "On the plus side, I get company, a certain amount of security; on the minus side, I don't get someone who *really* understands me." When the emotional costs outweigh the benefits of the relationship, your friend will probably end it. This weighing of costs and benefits is exchange theory at work.

> A distinction that does not further understanding is no distinction.
>
> JOHANN GOETHE (1749–1832)

The fundamental ideas of exchange theory go back to the ancient Greek philosopher Epicurus, who founded the Epicurean or hedonic (from which the word "hedonism" is derived) school of philosophy. The basis of Epicurean thought is that people seek pleasure and avoid pain. The Epicureans developed a "hedonic calculus" by which people could determine whether an action was worthwhile based on the amount of pleasure minus the pain it brought. Exchange theorists are the heirs to ancient hedonic thought. According to exchange theorists, people maximize their rewards and minimize their costs by employing their resources to gain the most favorable

---

UNDERSTANDING YOURSELF–*continued*

SYMBOLIC INTERACTION

What are the different roles you play in your relationship, marriage, or family? How do you feel about these roles? How do you go about changing the contents of these roles? What encourages or discourages such changes?

EXCHANGE THEORY

Think about what benefits you are receiving from your current (or past) intimate, marital, or family relationships. What are the costs? Make a list to compare the benefits and costs. Assign a value from 1 to 10 for the various items on your list, 10 being the highest value and 1 being the lowest. Based on the equation reward − cost = outcome, how would you predict the ultimate outcome? Compare

how you value your items to how a friend or classmate would value your items. Is there a difference? Think about the last time you made a "trade-off" in a relationship. Was it fair? If it wasn't, how did you feel? How did the other person feel?

As you look over these various theories, which one makes the most sense to you for understanding your own relationships? Why? What are the problems with the other theories?

---

outcome. An outcome is basically figured with the equation *reward − cost = outcome.*

One problem many of us have in recognizing our own exchange activities is that we think of rewards and costs as tangible objects, like money. But in personal relationships, resources, rewards, and costs are more likely to be things such as love, companionship, status, power, fear, longing, and so on. As people enter into relationships, they have certain resources—either tangible or intangible—that others consider valuable, such as intelligence, warmth, good looks, high social status, and so on. People consciously or consciously use these resources, using their various resources to obtain what they want.

People continually use their resources and make trade-offs. Traditionally, a woman trades her career for a family but a man might also quit his job to stay at home. Most of us have had friends whose relationships are a mystery to us: we don't understand what our friend sees in his or her partner. Our friend is so much better looking and more intelligent than the partner. (Attractiveness and intelligence are typical resources in our society.) But it turns out that the partner has a good sense of humor, is considerate, and is an accomplished flutist, all of which our friend highly values.

Equity. A corollary to exchange is equity: exchanges that occur between people have to be fair, to balance out. In the everyday world, we are always exchanging favors. You do the dishes tonight and I'll take care of the kids. Often we don't even

> Facts do not cease to exist because they are ignored.
>
> ALDOUS HUXLEY (1894–1963)

articulate these exchanges. We have a general sense that they will ultimately be reciprocated. If in the end we feel that the exchange wasn't fair, we are likely to be resentful and angry. As Patterson (1971) observed:

There is an odd kind of equity which holds when people interact with each other. In effect, we get what we give, both in amount and in kind. Each of us seems to have his own bookkeeping system for love, and for pain. Over time, the books are balanced.

Some psychologists (Walster and Walster, 1978) suggest that people are most happy when they get what they feel they deserve in a relationship. Oddly enough, both partners feel uneasy in an inequitable relationship.

While it's not surprising that deprived partners (who are, after all, getting less than they deserve) should feel resentful and angry about their inequitable treatment, it's perhaps not so obvious why their *over*benefited mates (who are getting more than they deserve) feel uneasy too. But they do. They feel guilty and fearful of losing their favored position.

When partners recognize they are in an inequitable relationship, they generally feel uncomfortable, angry, or distressed. They try to restore equity in one of three ways:

- They attempt to restore *actual* equity in the relationship.
- They attempt to restore *psychological* equity by trying to convince themselves and others that an obviously inequitable relationship is actually equitable.
- They decide to end the relationship.

Society regards marriage as a permanent commitment (even if reality seems to contradict the assumption). Because marriages are expected to endure, exchanges take on a long-term character. Instead of being calculated on an individual exchange basis—one day the husband is the benefited partner, the next day the wife is the benefited one—outcomes are judged over time.

An important ingredient in these exchanges is whether the relationship is fundamentally cooperative or competitive. In cooperative exchanges, husbands and wives both try to maximize their "joint profit" (Scanzoni, 1979). These exchanges are characterized by mutual trust and commitment. Thus a man might choose to work part-time and also care for their infant so that his wife may pursue her education. In a competitive relationship, however, each is trying to maximize his or her own individual profit. If both spouses want the freedom to go out whenever or with whomever each wishes, despite opposition from the other, the relationship is likely to be unstable.

Critique. Exchange theory assumes that indivudals are rational, calculating animals, weighing the costs and rewards of their relationships. Sometimes we are rational, sometimes we are not. Sometimes we act altruistically without expecting any reward. This is often true of love relationships and parent-child interaction.

Exchange theory also has difficulty ascertaining the value of costs, rewards, and resources. If you want to buy eggs, you know they are $1.15 a dozen and you can compare buying a dozen eggs with spending the same amount on a notebook. But how does the value of an outgoing personality compare with the value of a compassionate personality? Is a pound of compassion equal to ten pounds of enthusiasm? Compassion may be the most valued trait by one person but not important to another. The value that we assign to costs, rewards, and resources are highly individualistic.

☐ SUMMARY

- Studying marriage and the family permits us to reflect on our own relationships since they are often the same ones researchers are exploring.

- Research has an impact on how we understand marriage and the family in society. Studies suggest that the family is not declining, but changing. Research also has an important role in the development of social issues and the formulation of public policy.

- Research data comes from: (1) surveys, (2) clinical studies, (3) direct observation, and (4) experiments.

- *Surveys* are the most important source of data. Their purpose is to gather information from a small, representative sample of the population and to infer conclusions that are valid for a larger group. Surveys are most useful for dealing with societal or general issues rather than personal or small group issues. Surveys use questionnaires and interviews. Inherent problems with the survey method include (1) volunteer bias, (2) individual's lack of self-knowledge, and (3) underreporting of undesirable or unconventional behavior.

- *Clinical studies* are in-depth examinations of individuals or small groups who have entered a clinical setting for the treatment of psychological or relationship problems. Their primary advantage is that they allow in-depth study; their primary disadvantage is that the people coming into the clinic are not representative of the general population.

- *Direct observation* studies refer to studies in which interpersonal behavior is studied in a natural setting, such as the home, by an unobtrusive observer.

- *Experimental studies* are of limited use in marriage and family research because of the difficulty of controlling behavior and duplicating real-life conditions.

- *Theories* attempt to provide frames of reference for the interpretation of data. Theories studied in this chapter are: (1) structural functionalism, (2) conflict theory, (3) symbolic interaction, and (4) exchange or equity theory.

- *Structural functionalism* looks at society and families as an organism containing different structures. Each structure has a function. Structural functionalists study three aspects of the family: (1) the functions the family serves for society, (2) the functional requirements performed by the family for its survival, and (3) the needs of individual members that are met by the family. Family functions are usually divided along gender and age lines. The family molds personalities to meet the needs of the family. Males are encouraged to develop instrumental traits and females expressive traits. Criticism of structural functionalism includes (1) difficulty in empirically testing it, (2) difficulty in ascertaining what function a particular structure serves, and (3) its conservative bias.

- *Conflict theory* assumes that individuals in marriages and families are in conflict with each other. Power is often used to resolve the conflict. Four important sources of power include (1) legitimacy, (2) money, (3) physical coercion, and (4) love. Criticism of conflict theory includes (1) its politically based view of human nature, (2) assumption that differences lead to conflict, (3) difficulty in measuring and evaluating.

- *Symbolic interaction* examines how people interact and how we interpret or define others' actions through the symbols they communicate—their words, gestures, acts, and so on. Within the family, each person is given various social roles: husband/father, wife/mother, son/brother, daughter/sister, and so on. Three important role processes include (1) role taking, (2) role playing, and (3) role making. The drawbacks of the symbolic interaction approach include (1) a tendency to minimize the role of power, (2) failure to fully account for the emotional aspects of human life, (3) emphasis on individualism and happiness at the expense of the marital or family unit, and (4) inadequate attention to the social context.

- *Social exchange theory* suggests that we measure our actions and relationships on a cost-benefit basis. People seek to maximize their rewards and to minimize their costs to gain the most favorable outcome. People have resources that others consider valuable; they use these resources in making exchanges with others. A corollary to exchange is equity: exchanges must balance out, otherwise hard feelings are likely to ensue. Exchanges in marriage can either be done in a cooperative or a competitive manner. In cooperative exchanges, both partners try to maximize their *joint* profit; in competitive exchanges, each tries to maximize his or her own *individual* profit. Criticism of exchange theory includes (1) the assumption that individuals are rational and calculating in relationships and (2) the belief that the value of costs, rewards, and resources can be gauged.

READINGS

Ann Landers: Sex Researcher
NATALIE ANGIER, TIME

Many of the "facts" we know about marriage and the family, sexuality, and human behavior come from "experts" in the media who conduct their own studies, polls, and surveys. Ann Landers is a "media expert" who conducted a poll of her female readers; she asked: "Would you be content to be held close and treated tenderly, and forget about the 'act?' ". The responses created a tempest in a teapot, as this reading suggests. How would you critique Ms. Lander's methodology? How do you think her use of "the 'act' " to describe sexual intercourse affected responses? What are the limitations of such media surveys? How else might such a study have been conducted? What impact do you think such "experts" have on people's lives? Who are some other "experts"? How do they differ from each other in their beliefs and audience?

Women have had access to the Pill for nearly 30 years, and many now unabashedly woo reluctant dates with phone calls and American Express gold cards. But they are still not sure what to make of sex. On the one hand, they want the freedom to express their sexual needs; on the other hand, they resent the idea that they should "express them-

selves" after every dutch treat at the Steak 'n' Ale. Calls for the Sensitive Man alternate with pleas for a few good neo-Neanderthals.

Now Ann Landers, 66, guru to the lovelorn, has concluded that despite all the talk of liberation, women have not changed much at all. According to a massive survey published in her daily column last week, almost three-quarters of the women in America would happily give up sexual intercourse for a little tenderness. That may sound like 1953, or maybe 1853, but Landers is convinced. Concludes the nation's most widely syndicated columnist (more than 1,000 papers): "Clearly, there's trouble in Paradise."

Because sex is one subject on which everybody is an expert, Landers' findings sparked cheers and sneers among sexologists, sex therapists, television commentators, newspaper columnists, and just about every red-blooded man and woman above the age of consent. Some called her survey biased, unscientific and even dangerous; others insisted it is right on target.

The impromptu poll was instigated six months ago when a male reader from Indiana wrote in extolling the virtues of his penile implant and how it changed his life. One irate female reader from Oregon shot back, "This man is totally ignorant of the workings of the female mind and heart. If you were to ask 100 women how they feel about sexual

READINGS–*continued*

intercourse, I'll bet 98% would say, 'Just hold me close and tender. Forget about the act.' " Taking up the challenge, Landers posed the query to her female fans: "Would you be content to be held close and treated tenderly, and forget about 'the act?' " She requested a simple yes or no response on a postcard, together with an indication whether the woman was over or under 40.

Almost immediately women began barraging Landers' office, and not just with postcards. Many sent four- and five-page letters discussing the most intimate details of their sex lives. Not since more than 100,000 readers sent anti-nuclear letters to President Reagan in response to a Landers column had the reaction been so fierce and voluminous. Says she: "Apparently I had touched a hot button."

Even after 30 years in the advice business, Landers was surprised by the verdict: of the more than 90,000 women who answered, 64,000 cried yes; one reader marked her yes on a 6-ft.-wide poster. More surprising still, 40% of the yea-sayers were under 40. "I'd expect that some women 50 to 70 had had enough sex," Landers observed. "But in this so-called enlightened age, with liberated womanhood—that's pretty startling."

By and large, the yes respondents combined disgruntlement over the mechanics of their mates' lovemaking with a desire for more human contact. A woman from Columbus wrote, "I am under 40 and would be delighted to settle for tender words and warm caresses. The rest of it is a bore. I am sure sex was designed for the pleasure of males." From Washington came the outburst: "Yes, yes, a million times yes! I would love to be spoken to tenderly. My boyfriend never says a word. If I say anything he says, 'Be quiet. You're spoiling things.' "

The 28% who answered no were equally impassioned in their replies. Among Landers' favorite responses was one from Eureka, Calif.: "I'm 62 and voting NO. As long as my old man is able to shake the walls and wake up the neighbors downstairs, I want to get in on the action. And I'll take an encore any time I can get it."

In analyzing her results, Landers gave her usual cross between philosophy and sermon. "This says something very unflattering about men in this country," she said. "It says men are selfish. They want theirs." Yet she was quick to distribute the blame. "Some women need the message: loosen up, be sexier." Above all, Landers cited the so-called sexual revolution as the root of many of the problems. "Women are anxious," she said. "They're reading in *Cosmopolitan* that if they don't have five orgasms a night they're undersexed or freaks."

The Landers survey appeared to have touched a hot but-

ton among sex therapists, who argued that the columnist's pile of letters should not be taken as definitive statements about sex in America. For one thing, argued the authorities, the groups tend to be self-selective, not the random respondents found in more scientifically conducted polls. Said San Francisco Psychologist Lonnie Barbach, author of *For Each Other, Sharing Sexual Intimacy* and several other books on human sexuality: "If you've got a problem you have more impetus to write in and share it."

No one was more miffed by what Landers had to say about the American male than the American man. Three male columnists hammered away at the survey in a single issue of the Washington *Post* last week. Writing in the Chicago *Tribune*, Columnist Mike Royko parodied the Landers poll by posing a question to the nation's newest oppressed class: "Given a choice, men, would you rather be having sex with your wife or out bowling with your buddies?" Royko continued with a more pointed observation: "Nobody ever asks us about *our* needs, *our* frustrations . . . It's always, 'Madam, do you have your quota of orgasms?' " One putative expert on that subject, *Cosmopolitan* Editor Helen Gurley Brown, had her own reaction to the hubbub. Hurried, "lackluster" sex is rotten for everybody, she concluded, while good sex is "pretty terrific"—second only, in her experienced opinion, to good food.

Dating Behaviors of College Students

DAVID KNOX AND KENNETH WILSON, *FAMILY RELATIONS*

This study was first published in Family Relations, *a scholarly journal. It is reprinted in its entirety. How does its methodology compare to Ann Landers'? What are the limitations to this particular study? What are the differences in a scholarly versus a popular approach, as exemplified by these readings?*

How do the behaviors discussed in this reading compare to your own and those of your friends? How do you account for the similarities or differences?

Data on 334 university students in a random sample revealed how students meet, where they go, and what they do on dates. Sexual behaviors of these students also indicate that men expect more sexual intimacy sooner in a fewer number of dates than women. Influences/involvements by their parents in their dating relationships are also discussed. Most students feel positive about limited parental involvement.

READINGS—*continued*

We stepped into the elevator on the way to our functional marriage course. Inside was a former student who said, "I really enjoyed that marriage class." We thanked her and asked what she liked about it. She replied, "I met my future husband."

If the number of women and men who go in their respective groups to campus movies is any indication, meeting partners of the opposite sex is a common problem among university students. "How do you meet people on this campus?" is a frequent question. As family life educators who talk about issues from bundling to test-tube conception we often have little data to answer some of the questions our students regard as most important. This study was designed to provide a series of answers to an array of questions including how to meet dating partners.

Previous studies on dating have focused on functions, types, desired characteristics of dating partners and premarital sexual behavior. Dating functions include recreation, companionship, socialization and mate selection (Winch, 1963; Skipper & Nass, 1966) whereas types of dating include playing the field, steady dating, and engagement (McDaniel, 1969). Specific dates may occur via the traditional method in which the man calls the woman or by meeting each other at a bar or party. The latter is referred to as "hanging around" (Libby, 1977).

What the partners look for in each other tends to be understanding, mutual affection, and emotional maturity (Melton & Thomas, 1976). Regarding their sexual behavior, depending on the study and the sample, between 50 and 80% of university students report engaging in intercourse during their premarital dating years (DeLamater & MacCorquodale, 1979; Bell & Coughey, 1980).

But this study focused on other aspects of dating. In addition to how students meet, we were concerned about where they go, what they talk about, and how much sex they expect how soon (or how late) in their dating experiences. We also asked about the degree to which their parents were involved in their dating relationships and how the students felt about such involvement.

David Knox and Kenneth Wilson are Professor and Assistant Professors of Sociology, East Carolina University, Greenville, North Carolina.

The authors would like to thank Christa Reiser, Linda Kraus, and the staff of the Brewster Social Science Lab for their help in collecting the data and Jo Ann Sutton for typing the manuscript.

Key concepts: dating, premarital attitudes, sexual attitudes, sexual behavior.

Sample

Five hundred and fifty-five questionnaires were distributed to students at East Carolina University in 29 randomly selected classes. They were asked to complete the questionnaire at home and to return it at one of the next two class periods. Three hundred and thirty-four students (227 women, 107 men) completed the questionnaires (a 60% return rate).

The questionnaire included 21 close-ended questions about dating, sexual, and parental behaviors. These questions were developed from the responses to similar open-ended questions in a previous pilot study of 100 women and 100 men students at the same university. Chi-square was used to analyze the data.

Meeting/Dating Event/Talking

How do university students meet the people they date? Most students reported that they came to know their current dating partner through a friend (Table 1). About a third met this way. Although other ways of meeting each other included "at a party," "at work" or "in class," no single way was mentioned as frequently as meeting someone through a friend. Those not meeting in these checked "other" which included "I grew up with him/her" and "we met on the school newspaper."

Going out to eat, to the football game (the data were collected during football season), to a party and back to his or her room was the typical agenda for an evening of dating. And for those who didn't do everything, eating out and going to his or her place seemed to be the most important.

But regardless of where they were, "our relationship" was the most frequent topic of conversation. About a third reported that this topic dominated what they talked about. Though less frequent, school and friends were other topics of conversation. Sex was discussed less than 5% of the time.

Table 1   **How 334 University Students Met Their Dating Partner**

Ways of Meeting	% Female n = 227	% Male n = 107
Through a friend	33	32
Party	22	13
At Work	12	5
Class	6	9
Other	27	41

READINGS–*continued*

Sexual Behaviors

The students revealed how many dates they felt they should have with a person before it would be appropriate to engage in kissing, petting, and intercourse (Table 2). Fourteen percent of both sexes felt that no dates were necessary for kissing to occur. Half of the women and 70% of the men felt that kissing on the first date was appropriate. And, by the fourth date, all but 3% of the women felt that kissing was o.k. Hence, kissing was viewed as appropriate within a short time.

But the responses about petting (hands anywhere) revealed more concern that this sexual behavior be delayed (Table 2). At least women felt that way. While over three fourths felt that petting should be delayed until after the fourth date, only one third of the men felt that way. Rather, almost one-third of the men felt that petting should occur on or before the *first* date.

Regarding intercourse, the tendency for men to want more sex quicker in the dating relationship than women was again evident. Almost half of the men felt that intercourse was appropriate by the fifth date in contrast to about 25 percent of the women.

Sexual Values

These women and men were aware of the discrepancies in how much sexual behavior how soon they and their partners wanted. Less than 15% of both sexes said that their dates always shared their understanding of how long people should wait before engaging in kissing, petting, and intercourse.

Since some of the students in the pilot study said that how much sex occurs how soon depends on the nature of the relationship and not on the number of dates, students in the present study were asked to specify the relationship conditions under which kissing, petting, and intercourse

would be appropriate. The various conditions included "feeling no particular affection," "feeling affection but not love," "being in love," "engaged," or "married." The results indicated that the more emotionally involved a person was in a relationship the more likely increasing levels of intimacy were regarded as appropriate. And, this was significantly ($p<.001$) more true for women than men. For example, intercourse with no particular affection was o.k. for about 1% of the women but for 10% of the men. That women are more concerned about the emotional context of a sexual relationship has been reported in earlier research (DeLamater & MacCorquodale, 1979; Reiss, 1967).

Encouraging Sexual Intimacy

What do university men and women do to encourage their partners to become more sexually intimate? Both say to be open about sex desires and expectations. "I get the sex issue up front," expressed one student; "I simply say that I want to make love." A quarter of the men and a third of the women encouraged sexual intimacy in this way. Other ways included "creating an atmosphere (music, candles, etc.)," "expressing love," "moving closer to," and "hinting." Women were more likely to use the latter two methods than men.

While alcohol and marijuana were not mentioned as being used on a frequent basis to encourage sexual intimacy, they were not uncommon on dates. Over half of the students said that they drank alcohol on their last date with fewer reporting use of marijuana. One-quarter of the men and 20% of the women said that they smoked marijuana on their last date.

Discouraging Sexual Intimacy

When partners disagree over whether or not to engage in increasing levels of sexual intimacy, the partner who does

Table 2 Percentage of 227 Women and 107 Men University Students Indicating Appropriateness of Various Sexual Behaviors by Number of Dates

Sexual Behaviors	Number of Dates						
	0	*1*	*2*	*3*	*4*	*5*	*6 or more*
Kissing	W = 14%	W = 55%	W = 73%	W = 6%			
	M = 14%	M = 69%	M = 14%	M = 1%			
Petting	W = 3%	W = 4%	W = 5%	W = 9%	W = 3%	W = 15%	W = 58%
	M = 12%	M = 19%	M = 13%	M = 7%	M = 11%	M = 15%	M = 22%
Intercourse	W = 8%	W = 4%	W = 1%	W = 1%	W = 1%	W = 8%	W = 69%
	M = 8%	M = 11%	M = 9%	M = 8%	M = 2%	M = 10%	M = 52%

READINGS–*continued*

not want sex must do something to stop it. "Telling the partner to stop" is the way a third of the men and half of the women said that they discouraged sexual intimacy. "Ignoring sexual advances" and "keeping my distance" were also mentioned.

Parents and Dating

Since our system of mate selection is "select your own" in contrast to arranged marriages in other cultures, the students were asked about their parents' involvement in their dating relationships. Women were significantly (p<.01) more likely than men to report that their parents tried to influence those they dated. Sixty percent of the women compared to 40 percent of the men said parental influence was involved. And, when asked, "To what degree have your parents interfered with your relationships?," the same pattern held—women were significantly (p<.001) more likely to say that their parents interfered.

Greater parental concern for the dating activities of the daughters over sons seemed to be what the respective sexes wanted. Women were much more likely to say that it was important to them that they dated the "kinds of people their parents would approve of." Twenty percent of the men said they didn't care what their parents thought in contrast to 10% of the women.

Discussion and Implications

Students often enroll in preparation for marriage classes to gain information they hope will be helpful in their own lives and relationships. One of their particular concerns is that they often have difficulty finding dating partners in a large university setting. Many look to parties, work, and classes as means of finding someone. But none of these ways (for these respondents) was as productive as meeting a partner through friends. Establishing relationships with *same* sex peers may be the best way to meet someone of the opposite sex. "When you don't have a date, go with a friend" is a suggestion family life educators might make to those seeking a partner.

Students might also be aware that (at least, on the basis of these data) discrepancies in what men and women expect on dates continues. Less than 15% felt that their dates always shared their understanding of how long they should wait before kissing, petting, and having intercourse. Men want to kiss, pet, and have intercourse in a shorter number of dates than women. And, since the result is potential conflict, students might be aware that other students encourage and discourage sexual intimacy in the same way— by being direct. To encourage sexual intimacy they tell their partner what they would like to do. Likewise, if they want to discourage sexual intimacy, they tell their partner to "stop."

Family life educators might help to prepare students for the potential conflict by making them aware of the discrepancies and encouraging in class communication exercises on such issues. One such teacher has developed such an exercise in which students verbalize what they expect from each other sexually (Britton, Note 1).

Differences also exist in reference to parental involvement in dating relationships. Parents exercise more influence/interference in the dating relationships of their daughters than sons (60 vs. 40%). Such parental involvement with the dating activities of their sons and daughters suggest that mate selection in America is not really "free." Individuals are not allowed to select their own partners. Rather, parents attempt to influence/interfere with the dating/mate selection of their offspring. Wanting their offspring to go with and marry "the right person with the right background" seems to be staple parental values in America. And in spite of the presumed "generation gap" most offspring regard their parents' involvement in positive terms. Only about 25% report that they feel "very negative" or "negative" about their parents' involvement in their dating relationships. Family life educators/counselors may suggest to disillusioned parents that in spite of the resistance they may get from their offspring about their involvement in their dating activities, most students seem to feel good about limited parental involvement.

Reference Note

1. Britton, T. Personal communication. Lenoir Community College, Kinston, North Carolina, September, 1980.

References

Bell, R. R., & Coughey, K. Premarital sexual experience among college females, 1958, 1968, and 1978. *Family Relations*, 1980, 29, 353–357.

DeLamater, J., & MacCorquodale, P. *Premarital sexuality*. Madison, WI: University of Wisconsin Press, 1979.

Libby, R. W. Creative singlehood as a sexual life-style: Beyond marriage as a rite of passage. In R. W. Libby & R. N. Whitehurst (Eds.), *Marriage and alternatives: Exploring intimate relationships*. Glenview, IL: Scott, Foresman, 1977.

McDaniel, C. O., Jr. Dating roles and reasons for dating. *Journal of Marriage and the Family*, 1969, 31, 97–07.

READINGS—*continued*

Melton, W., & Thomas, D. L. Instrumental and expressive values in mate selection of black and white college students. *Journal of Marriage and the Family*, 1976, 38, 509–17.

Reiss, I. L. *The social context of premarital sexual permissiveness.* New York: Holt, Rinehart & Winston, 1967.

Skipper, J. K., Jr., & Nass, G. Dating behavior: A framework for analysis and an illustration. *Journal of Marriage and the Family*, 1966, 28, 412–20.

Winch, R. F. *The modern family.* New York: Holt, Rinehart & Winston, 1963.

Theoretical Advantages of Families
WILLIAM GOODE, EXCERPT FROM *THE FAMILY*

This excerpt by Stanford sociologist William Goode is a theoretical discussion of why people live in families. Most of the functions of the family can be fulfilled outside the family, Goode argued earlier. After all, children can be raised communally, intimacy can be found among friends, sexual relations can be had outside of marriage, meals can be eaten at restaurants, and so on. Why then do people live in families? Goode suggests several advantages to family living. What are they? Do you find them true for your own family? How? Are there other advantages not mentioned? How would scholars test the validity of this theory?

We suppose that the most fundamental set of advantages is found in the division of labor and the resulting possibility of social exchanges between husband and wife (or members of a homosexual couple), as well as between children and parents. This includes not only economic goods, but help, nurturance, protection, and affection. It is often forgotten that the modern domestic household is very much an *economic* unit even if it is no longer a farming unit. People are actually producing goods and services for one another. They are buying objects in one place, and transporting them to the household. They are transforming food into meals. They are engaged in cleaning, mowing lawns, repairing, transporting, counseling—a wide array of services that would have to be paid for in money if some member of the family did not do them.

Families of all types also enjoy some small economies of scale. When there are two or more members of the household, various kinds of activities can be done almost as easily for everyone as for a single person; it is almost as easy to prepare one meal for three or four people as it is to prepare a similar meal for one person. Thus, the cost of a meal is less per person within a family. Families can cooperate to

achieve what an individual cannot, from building a mountain cabin to creating a certain style of life. Help from all members will make it much easier to achieve that goal than it would be for one person.

All the historic forms of the family that we know, including communal group marriages, are also attractive because they offer *continuity*. Thus, whatever the members produce together, they expect to be able to enjoy together later. Continuity has several implications. One is that members do not have to bear the costs of continually searching for new partners, or for new members who might be "better" at various family tasks. In addition, husband and wife, as well as children, enjoy a much longer line of social credit than they would have if they were making exchanges with people outside the family. This means that an individual can give more at one time to someone in the family, knowing that in the longer run this will not be a loss: the other person will remain long enough to reciprocate at some point, or perhaps still another member will offer help at a later time.

Next, the familistic mode of living offers several of the advantages of any informal group. It exhibits, for example, a very short line of communication; everyone is close by, and members need not communicate through intermediaries. Thus they can respond quickly in case of need. A short line of communication makes cooperation much easier. Second, everyone has many idiosyncratic needs and wishes. In day to day interaction with outsiders, we need not adjust to these very much, and they may be a nuisance; others, in turn, are likely not to adjust to our own idiosyncracies. However, within the familistic mode of social interaction, people learn what each other's idiosyncratic needs are. Learning such needs can and does make life together somewhat more attractive because adjusting to them may not be a great burden, but does give pleasure to the other. These include such trivia as how strong the tea or coffee should be, how much talk there will be at meals, sleep and work schedules, levels of noise, and so on. Of course with that knowledge we can more easily make others miserable, too, if we wish to do so.

Domestic tasks typically do not require high expertise, and as a consequence most members of the family can learn to do them eventually. Because they do learn, members derive many benefits from one another, without having to go outside the family unit. Again, this makes a familistic

*For further comparisons of bureaucracy and informal groups, see Eugene Litwak, "Technical Innovation and Theoretical Functions of Primary Groups and Bureaucratic Structures," *American Journal of Sociology*, 73(1968), 468–481.

mode of living more attractive than it would be otherwise. In addition, with reference to many such tasks, there are no outside experts anyway (throughout most of world history, there have been no experts in childrearing, taking care of small cuts or bruises, murmuring consoling words in response to some distress, and so on). That is, the tasks within a family setting are likely to be tasks at which insiders are at least as good as outsiders, and typically better.

No other social institutions offer this range of complementarities, sharing, and closely linked, interwoven advantages. The closest possible exception might be some ascribed, ritual friendships in a few societies, but even these do not offer the range of exchanges that are to be found in the familistic processes.

Measuring Marital Adjustment: The Dyadic Adjustment Scale

GRAHAM SPANIER, *JOURNAL OF MARRIAGE AND THE FAMILY*

The dyadic adjustment scale is an example of the type of questionnaire scholars use as they examine marital adjustment. What are the advantages of a questionnaire such as this? The disadvantages?

On a separate sheet of paper, answer the questions as best you can with regard to your own relationship with your intimate partners (past or present). At the end of this course, answer the questions again without referring to your first set of answers. Then compare your responses. What do you infer from this comparison?

For an exchange regarding the concept of adjustment, see Trost, 1985, and Spanier, 1985.

	Always Agree	Almost Always Agree	Occasionally Disagree	Frequently Disagree	Almost Always Disagree	Always Disagree
1. Handling family finances	5	4	3	2	1	0
2. Matters of recreation	5	4	3	2	1	0
3. Religious matters	5	4	3	2	1	0
4. Demonstrations of affection	5	4	3	2	1	0
5. Friends	5	4	3	2	1	0
6. Sex relations	5	4	3	2	1	0
7. Conventionality (correct or proper behavior)	5	4	3	2	1	0
8. Philosophy of life	5	4	3	2	1	0
9. Ways of dealing with parents or in-laws	5	4	3	2	1	0
10. Aims, goals, and things believed important	5	4	3	2	1	0
11. Amount of time spent together	5	4	3	2	1	0
12. Making major decisions	5	4	3	2	1	0
13. Household tasks	5	4	3	2	1	0
14. Leisure time interests and activities	5	4	3	2	1	0
15. Career decisions	5	4	3	2	1	0

READINGS–*continued*

	All the time	Most of the Time	More Often Than Not	Occasionally	Rarely	Never
16. How often do you discuss or have you considered divorce, separation, or terminating your relationship?	0	1	2	3	4	5
17. How often do you or your mate leave the house after a fight?	0	1	2	3	4	5
18. In general, how often do you think that things between you and your partner are going well?	5	4	3	2	1	0
19. Do you confide in your mate?	5	4	3	2	1	0
20. Do you ever regret that you married (or live together)?	0	1	2	3	4	5
21. How often do you and your partner quarrel?	0	1	2	3	4	5
22. How often do you and your mate "get on each other's nerves"?	0	1	2	3	4	5

	Every Day	Almost Every Day	Occasionally	Rarely	Never
23. Do you kiss your mate?	4	3	2	1	0

	All of Them	Most of Them	Some of Them	Very Few of Them	None of Them
24. Do you and your mate engage in outside interests together?	4	3	2	1	0

How often would you say the following events occur between you and your mate?

	Never	Less Than Once a Month	Once or Twice a Month	Once or Twice a Week	Once a Day	More Often
25. Have a stimulating exchange of ideas	0	1	2	3	4	5
26. Laugh together	0	1	2	3	4	5
27. Calmly discuss something	0	1	2	3	4	5
28. Work together on a project	0	1	2	3	4	5

These are some things about which couples sometimes agree and sometimes disagree. Indicate if either item below caused differences of opinions or were problems in your relationship during the past few weeks (Check yes or no)

Yes No

29. 0   1   Being too tired for sex.
30. 0   1   Not showing love.

31. The dots on the following line represent different degrees of happiness in your relationship. The middle point, "happy," represents the degree of happiness of most relationships. Please circle the dot which best describes the degree of happiness, all things considered, of your relationship.

0	1	2	3	4	5	6
●	●	●	●	●	●	●
EXTREMELY UNHAPPY	FAIRLY UNHAPPY	A LITTLE UNHAPPY	HAPPY	VERY HAPPY	EXTREMELY HAPPY	PERFECT

32. Which of the following statements best describes how you feel about the future of your relationship?

    5 ___ I want desperately for my relationship to succeed, and would go to almost any length to see that it does.

    4 ___ I want very much for my relationship to succeed, and will do all I can to see that it does.

    3 ___ I want very much for my relationship to succeed, and will do my fair share to see that it does.

    2 ___ It would be nice if my relationship succeeded, but I can't do much more than I am doing now to help it succeed.

    1 ___ It would be nice if it succeeded, but I refuse to do any more than I am doing now to keep the relationship going.

    0 ___ My relationship can never succeed, and there is no more that I can do to keep the relationship going.

CHAPTER 3

History of
Marriage and the Family

PREVIEW

To gain a sense of what you already know about the material in this chapter, answer "true" or "false" to the statements below. You will find the answers as you read the chapter.

1. Early Christian teachings maintained that chastity was better than marriage. True or false?
2. During the colonial period, women commonly had their last child around the same time that their first grandchild was born. True or false?
3. Despite the dour image of the Puritans, romantic love played a major role in their courtships and marriages. True or false?
4. The "housewife" was invented in the nineteenth century. True or false?
5. The idea of childhood as a unique period in life is a relatively modern concept. True or false?
6. During the colonial period, a law was passed providing the death penalty for disobedient children. True or false?
7. The Puritans believed that children were born in innocence but became corrupted by the world. True or false?
8. Under slavery, laws prohibited masters from selling the children of their slaves. True or false?
9. Throughout history, women have been financially dependent on their husband's wages. True or false?
10. During the colonial period, the rigorous puritanical code reduced the rate of premarital pregnancies to the lowest level in American history. True or false?

Outline

The past is never dead; it is not even past.

WILLIAM FAULKNER

If we could go back and live again in all of our two hundred and fifty million arithmetical ancestors of the eleventh century, we should find ourselves doing many surprising things, but among the rest we should certainly be ploughing most of the fields of the Cotentin and Calvados, going to mass in every parish church in Normandy [France]; rendering military service to every lord, spiritual or temporal, in all this region; and helping to build the Abbey Church at Mont-Saint-Michel.

HENRY ADAMS (1838–1918)

History is the ship carrying living memories to the future.

STEPHEN SPENDER

Blessed art Thou, oh Lord our God, King of the Universe, that I was not born a woman.

ORTHODOX JEWISH PRAYER

"Those who do not remember the past are condemned to repeat it," George Santayana observed. An understanding of our past places our lives and experiences in context. We are all part of an ever-moving stream of change; we cannot isolate ourselves from the flow of history. The family also evolves and changes. It changes as society changes, giving partnerships new forms and meanings. What follows is an examination of these changing forms and meanings. What we are today will be tomorrow's history.

In this chapter we first briefly describe Western culture's heritage from the early Christian and medieval periods. Then we look at the family in America from the colonial era through the nineteenth century, the "invention" of childhood, and the black family in slavery.

☐ EUROPEAN BACKGROUND

The Ancient Christian Heritage

The roots of the contemporary American family extend back thousands of years. The American family's form and content were significantly influenced by the Greek, Roman, and Christian family systems, which were patriarchal (dominated by the father). Descent was patrilineal: family lines were traced through the father; his wife and his children took his name and inherited his property.

Ironically, Christian ideas about marriage and the family were formulated by men who had rejected marriages and families in favor of celibacy. Fearing sexuality, they condemned it. Following the Judaic tradition, Jesus of Nazareth supported the institution of marriage; the early Christians who followed him did not. Jesus celebrated marriage, and his first miracle was to transform water into wine for a wedding feast. He urged people to "judge not lest ye be judged." But his apostle Paul looked on sexuality as an evil and urged all to follow his example of celibacy. "It is best," he wrote, "that all men were as me. But if they cannot, it is better to marry than to burn" (I Corinthians 7:10–12). The degree of a person's spirituality was measured by his or her celibacy. The denial of the world and flesh became as important as—sometimes more important than—Christian love and charity.

Celibacy was superior to marriage, and men were believed superior to women. Christian teaching required women to submit to their husbands in all matters. In church they were to remain silent, and if they had questions, they were to address them to their husbands at home. Women were not allowed to preach, a tradition that is still followed today in the Catholic church. In the sixth century, the Council of Macon debated whether women even possessed souls.

The Middle Ages

The Church, Marriage, and Celibacy.   During the Middle Ages the church extended its control over marriage. Traditionally, marriage had been an arrangement between families in which the father had the right to literally give his daughter away. Some marriages were simply an arrangement between a man and a woman, similar to common-law marriages today. Reacting against the power of families, the church initially maintained that couples could marry against the wishes of their fathers (Donahue, 1983). Then, as the church increased its own power, it began to describe marriage as a sacred union. Marriages now had to be performed in the presence of a priest. By the thirteenth century the ceremony was performed inside a church. It was then but a small step for the church to declare marriage a sacrament, that is, a divine creation. As a divine institution it could not be dissolved; thus ended the possibility of divorce, a position still held by the Catholic church today.

In the thirteenth century the question of celibacy within the priesthood was finally resolved. Until then many of the clergy married; others had mistresses or common-law wives. As late as the seventh century, a church council affirmed the right of the clergy to marry. It was only gradually that complete celibacy was required, despite resistance by the Eastern church, whose leaders considered celibacy unnatural. Their rejection of priestly celibacy was one of the chief reasons the Eastern church split off from Rome, forming the Orthodox church. By the thirteenth century celibacy had become a requirement for the Roman Catholic priesthood.

The Courtly Love Tradition.   While the Christian tradition placed marriage in opposition to the highest religious pursuit, a second tradition arose, the tradition of courtly love. Like Christianity, its attitude toward marriage was ambiguous. Christianity made marriage a sacrament while at the same time elevating celibacy to a higher plane. Courtly love introduced the idea of romantic love to Western culture. Beginning in the thirteenth century, knights and nobles became obsessed with the idea of serving a noble woman, who, however, was almost always married or given over to vows of chastity. Since the woman was unavailable sexually, love was manifested as a nonsexual ideal. As little contact existed between the noble and the lady, neither saw the other in ordinary, everyday light. Fantasy took over. In a parody of the courtly love ethic, Cervantes had his hero Don Quixote transform a homely peasant woman into the beautiful Dulcinea, in whose name he performed his heroic deeds. Don Quixote declared: "It is as right and proper for a knight-errant to be in love as the sky to have stars."

The ethic of courtly love gave women higher status. But this higher status was double-edged, for it obliged a woman to be pure, noble, and helpless, requiring a knight in shining armor to assist her. In the Middle Ages, however, romantic love remained outside of marriage; only in more recent times has romantic love become the ruling element in selecting a marriage partner. Medieval and Renaissance men and women were too practical to let the question of love enter into marriage. One of the earliest English uses of the word *love* in its present meaning was in an advice book, *Instructions to Christian Women,* published in 1592: "They that marry for love, shall lead their lives in sorrow" (*Oxford English Dictionary,* 1971). The romantic love tradition, however, survived more or less underground until it was resurrected as an ideal in the nineteenth century (Lantz, 1982).

> What is morality at any given time or place? It is what the majority then and there happened to like and immorality is what they dislike.
>
> ALFRED NORTH WHITEHEAD (1861–1947)

> Woman is defective, accidental . . . a male gone awry . . . the result of some weakness in the generative power.
>
> THOMAS AQUINAS (1225–1274)

☐ THE AMERICAN HERITAGE

The Colonial Family

To study the history of the American family is to conduct a rescue mission into the dreamland of our national self-concept. No subject is more closely bound up with our sense of a difficult present—and our nostalgia for a happier past.

JOHN DEMOS

The Puritans who established New England in the early seventeenth century found themselves in a wild, alien environment. William Bradford (1590–1657), looking at America for the first time, saw nothing but "a hideous and desolate wilderness, full of wild beasts and wild men" (Bradford, 1945). His wife, filled with despair, threw herself from the *Mayflower* and drowned. In this new land life was harsh and placed a considerable burden on both the individual and the family. But the family remained the center of life. It was, said Bradford, "a little commonwealth"; the well-being of the community depended on the well-being of the family.

Everyone was expected to be married once he or she reached adulthood. Marriage was, wrote one seventeenth-century writer, a "covenant of God, whereby all sorts of people may, of two, be made one flesh; for multiplying of an holy seed, avoiding fornication, and mutual comforting of each other" (quoted in Strong, 1972). In other words, marriage legitimized procreation, prevented sexual immorality, and provided companionship.

Marital Choice. Marriage was too important to be left to youthful indiscretion. Since marriage had profound economic and social consequences, parents often selected their children's mates, a custom still practiced throughout much of the world. Such choices, however, were not as arbitrary as it may seem. Parents tried to choose partners whom their children already knew and seemed compatible with. Children were expected to accept their parents' choices. One father wrote in his will that if his daughters did not accept the choices of the executor, "but of their own fantastical brain bestow themselves upon a light person," their inheritance would be cut in half (Miller, 1966). Romantic love was not a factor in choosing a partner; one practical seventeenth century marriage manual advised women that "this boiling affection is seldom worth anything . . ." (Fraser, 1984). Love came after marriage. It was a person's duty to love his or her spouse. Making a duty of love was consistent with the high self-expectations of the Puritans (Leites, 1982). If a person was unable to fulfill the duty to desire and love a marriage partner, it was a defect of character. Each was obliged to be kind and loving to the other, to treat the other with understanding and affection. For colonial Americans, love was companionate, not romantic.

Many a family tree needs trimming.

KIN HUBBARD (1868–1930)

The Governor of Hartford upon Connecticut came to Boston, and brought his wife with him (a godly young woman and of special parts) who was fallen into a sad infirmity, the loss of her understanding and reason which had been growing upon her divers years by occasion of her giving herself wholly to reading and writing, and had written many books. Her husband being very loving and tender of her, was loath to grieve her; but he saw his error when it was too late. For if she had attended her household affairs, and such things as belong to women, and not gone out of her way and calling to meddle in such things as are proper for men, whose minds are stronger, etc., she had kept her wits, and might have improved them usefully and honorably in the place God had set her.

JOHN WINTHROP (1588–1649)

Marriage and Sex. Although we think of the Puritans as being puritanical about sex, they were more liberal than their Victorian descendents. Their sexual ethic was basically Calvinistic; they accepted the power of human sexuality and the futility of trying to repress it. Sex, they believed, was legitimate in marriage; it was to be enjoyed by both husband and wife. The following advice, from a marriage manual published in 1712 (quoted in Scott and Wishy, 1982), indicates that sex was reciprocal between husband and wife:

Let the Husband render unto the Wife due benevolence, and likewise also the Wife to the Husband. The Wife hath not power of her own body, but the Husband; and likewise also the Husband hath not power of his own body, but the Wife.

Outside of marriage, however, sex was viewed as sinful and a threat to the social fabric. In the Puritan world, the two primary sexual offenses were adultery and illegitimacy, both of which threatened the family structure. Adultery threatened to break up marriages while illegitimacy lead to the rearing of children outside traditional family arrangements.

Although the Puritans prohibited premarital intercourse, they were not entirely successful. Bundling, the New England custom in which a young man and woman spent the night in bed together, separated by a wooden bundling board, was a consequence of harsh winters, the lack of fuel, and the difficulty of travelling—all of which made it difficult for the man to return home after an evening of courting. It provided a courting couple with privacy; it did not, however, encourage restraint. An estimated one-third of all marriages in the eighteenth century took place with the bride pregnant (Smith and Hindus, 1975). (Today about 20 percent of all brides are pregnant at the time of marriage.)

The Family as a Social Unit.   The family was the cornerstone of society. Everyone had to be a member of a family. As in many agrarian cultures today, in early America it was next to impossible to survive outside the family. The family planted and harvested the food, made the clothes, provided shelter, took care of the various necessities of life. Young, single men and women were not permitted to live alone or in pairs. Sixteen men were brought to trial in Massachusetts for not living with families. Maryland and Connecticut taxed bachelors. Single women were ridiculed as "spinsters," "old maids," or "ancient virgins." They generally lived with their families, which acted as the overseers of virtue. In 1790 fewer than 3 percent of the households were single-person households (Modell and Hareven, 1973); in 1980, by contrast, 23 percent of households were single-person households.

To enforce morality, New England towns appointed a "tithing man" to observe

Quiltmaking brought kin and friends together for talk and visits. Through childhood, girls traditionally made eleven quilts as part of their dowries; a twelfth quilt, the "bride's quilt," was made just before marriage, when the young woman and her friends came together for a quilting bee. When the young woman married, her husband gave her a "freedom quilt" that his mother, grandmother, or sister had made for him to celebrate his coming of age.

groups of ten families. These men supervised the children's behavior and the kind of education they received; they observed how husband and wife behaved toward each other and whether all attended church. If a couple fought excessively, they were brought to court. The court usually ordered them to quit fighting or be fined, whipped, or put in the stocks (Miller, 1975).

There was some cohabitation without marriage, but it was discouraged. One historian related how a magistrate was outraged when he saw a couple who called each other husband and wife (but had never been married) walking down the street (Calhoun, 1919). The magistrate called to the man: "John Rogers, do you persist in calling this woman, a servant, so much younger than yourself, your wife?"

"Yes, I do," retorted John.

"And do you, Mary," continued the magistrate gruffly, "wish such an old man as this to be your husband?"

"Indeed I do," she replied firmly.

"Then, by the laws of God and this commonwealth," said the magistrate, "I, as a magistrate, pronounce you man and wife."

A people without history is like wind on the buffalo grass.

TETON SIOUX PROVERB

The Status of Women.   Women were in a difficult position during colonial times. They were subordinate to men and had few legal rights independent of their husbands. But few people thought women were helpless creatures. Activities were not divided into male and female activities as they later were in the nineteenth century. One anthropologist noted that "prescribed roles for parents made no important distinctions on the basis of sex" (Margolis, 1984). In other activities too, men and women shared common tasks. A Virginia planter who went out to the frontier in the mid-eighteenth century met a "very civil woman . . . [who] shows nothing of ruggedness or immodesty in her carriage, yet she will carry a gun in the woods and kill deer, turkeys, etc., shoot down wild cattle, catch and tie hogs, knock down beeves with an ax and perform the most manful exercises as well as most men in those parts" (Pitt, 1976). Although women had low status in colonial America, no one doubted their worth. Most household goods had to be produced at home. Men had to marry for the simple reason that they could not live without a wife. The women usually raised the food for the family. They dried fruits and meats for the winter; they spun cloth, made clothes, produced candles; they worked the fields alongside their husbands, plowing, planting, weeding, and harvesting.

Women usually married in their early twenties and were mothers during most of their adult lives. Families were large, but many children died before reaching maturity. The mortality rate was about 25 percent for those twenty-one and under; today it is about 1 percent. A woman's first child was usually born about sixteen months after marriage; her last was not born until the woman was about forty years old. A woman's last child and first grandchild were often born during the same time period. As a consequence of their long child-bearing period, most women did not have any lengthy period in which children were not present in their households.

Childhood and Adolescence.   Although children were greatly desired, they were nevertheless believed to be evil by nature. The community accepted the traditional Christian doctrine that stated children were conceived and born in sin. Jonathan Edwards, the leading evangelist in colonial America, described unrepentant children as "young vipers and infinitely more hateful than vipers" (quoted in Wishy, 1968).

So parents saw the child's spontaneity not as a delight but as a sign of rebelliousness. This view of the child supported the stern authoritarianism that characterized child-rearing during this time.

The concept of childhood as a unique period of life, distinct from adulthood, is a modern concept according to Philippe Aries (1962) whose work *Centuries of Childhood* is a landmark in historical scholarship (also see Aries, 1982; Meckel, 1984; Vann, 1982). In colonial times children were regarded as simply small adults. When children were six or seven, childhood ended for them. From that time on, they began to be part of the adult world, participating in adult work and play. Most education took place in the home and was practical for both boys and girls. They learned the basic skills of house and field as well as basic reading, writing, and "figuring." Boys began with simple jobs such as hoeing, weeding, and fence mending. Girls started with domestic chores such as tending the garden, milking, and candle making. When children reached ten, they were often "bound out" for several years as apprentices or domestic servants. They lived in the home of a relative or stranger where they learned a trade or skill, were educated, and were properly disciplined (Morgan, 1966). By putting their children out, Puritan families avoided the conflict between independence and dependence as their children reached maturity.

Currently, a debate is taking place among historians about whether adolescence as we know it existed in colonial times (Fox, 1977; Thompson, 1984). Children after the age of twelve years or so did seem to form their own peer groups much as today's adolescents, and colonists complained about loud music, much as distraught parents do today. In 1658 one irritated colonist reported (in Thompson, 1984):

They were awakened out of their sleepe; his wife being awakened first was struck with great feare: Wee heard musick and dansing which was no smal disturbance to us: And they came harkeing unto our window where wee lay, which they did three times, between which the, danced and played with their musicke with much laughter.

But the time between puberty and maturity was not recognized as a separate state of development (Kett, 1977). As a rule, except for religious conversions, adolescent children did not experience any sudden period of awkwardness, stormy emotion, and uncertainty (see Greven, 1977). Since children were treated similarily to adults after about six years of age, there was no sudden change in their status during adolescence. They were introduced gradually into the adult world. Their lives were marked by continuity rather than discontinuity. They were never protected from the world because they participated in it.

The relationship between parents and children was based on both love and duty. Parents were expected to provide for their children; if they punished them excessively, they could be brought to court. Children also were expected to obey their parents. One Puritan community made disobedience punishable by death: "If any child or children over 16 years old of competent understanding shall curse or smite their natural father or mother, he or they shall be put to death" (Morgan, 1966).

Old Age. The condition of older people in colonial America was better in many ways than it is today. The old—especially men—were held in high esteem; they were venerated and cared for by their children. But this deferential treatment may not have been simply due to love. David Hacket Fischer (1978) suggests that the aged father was cared for because of the economic power he wielded. A colonial father often held on to his property until his death, his sons farming his land and building their homes on the property. The sons had no economic independence of their own. Fischer (1978) points out that "Land was an instrument of generation politics—a way of preserving both the power and the authority of the elderly. Sons were bound to their fathers by ties of economic dependency; youth was the hostage of age." In fact, it appears that the sons in many New England families remained living for five generations in the same vicinity as their fathers so they could inherit their fathers' lands (Adams and Kaskoff, 1984).

Elderly women, however, were not treated with the same respect and deference accorded to elderly men because, first, they generally lacked economic power and, second, they were women. To be poor, old, and female in colonial America was to be in a desperate situation. Children, whether well-off or poor, hesitated to take in their aged mothers. George Washington's mother repeatedly hinted to her son that she be invited to live at Mount Vernon. But Washington bought her a small house near his sister's home instead.

The Nineteenth-Century Family

The colonial family could trace its roots back thousands of years; its functions changed very little over that time. But in the nineteenth century the colonial type of family gradually vanished to be replaced by the modern family. This new family was radically different from any family system seen before in the world.

The Impact of Industrialization. Industrialization and urbanization shattered the old family. As individuals and families increasingly moved to cities, old patterns of family life had to change. Most significantly, the family stopped being a productive work unit. Families no longer worked together. Instead, in middle-class families the man went off to work in a factory or office. The woman remained home, tending the house and caring for the children. When children were old enough, they were sent to elementary school. Lower-class families remained a working unit but with great changes. Instead of being economically self-sufficient, they worked for pitifully low wages in factories, and entire families needed to work to support themselves. Thus husband, wife, and children only five or six years old would set out at dawn to the factories. Children now became an economic liability—more mouths to feed— whereas before they had been needed hands on the farm.

The effects of industrialization on family life and functions were enormous. First of all, industrialization created the idea of the man as sole provider for the family, since in most families he was the major wage earner. Because women either remained in the home or worked for substantially less pay than men, they became financially dependent on their husbands. In an urban, industrial society, it took money to buy the goods no longer made in the home, and it was the man rather than the woman who usually had access to work and money.

Furthermore, the new industrial economy encouraged objective, rational decision making and emotional detachment; feeling engendered suspicion (but see Finklestein and Clignet, 1981, for a critique of "dour" family historians who overlook nurture, warmth, and humor in the family). The ultimate objective of every management decision was profitability. If profits required firing hundreds of workers, leaving their families helpless, so it was. Severe competition encouraged business leaders to disregard the human impact of their decisions. The world of business was rational. Only in personal relations among family members and friends were feelings and emotions permitted sway. When the world of work centered on the home and the farm, family values had a significant impact on decisions. Life was not divided between what a person did to earn a living—work—and the rest of his or her existence.

The Status of Women. Industrialization also created the housewife, a nineteenth-century invention. Before that time, society regarded a woman's activities as economically important. The family could not survive without her. The woman's labor in the fields and her value as a producer of household necessities gave her status. But when the emphasis was placed on monetary rewards, the woman's contributions in terms of *unpaid* work and services were belittled. Previously, men and women were interdependent within the family unit. Now the woman, at least the middle-class woman, was dependent on her husband because he was the one who earned the wages to buy food, clothing, and other necessities. A woman became "only" a housewife, reflecting her diminished role. She was now isolated from her husband's sphere of work, which they had previously shared on the farm. (For a description of a woman's travel West in a covered wagon, see the reading by Arvazine Cooper, pages 79–80.)

Ironically, at the same time that women were losing economic stature as housewives, they began to be idealized. During the nineteenth century women were placed on pedestals and were considered warmer, finer, more emotional, and more delicate than men. Whereas women had traditionally been considered morally inferior to men (it was Eve, after all, who had tempted the "innocent" Adam), they were now judged morally superior—as long as they kept their place. The world in which men moved was now brutally harsh and fraught with struggle and competition. In order for women to be protected from the outside world, they had to stay home, where they were to cultivate the finer emotions. Resistance to women working was rooted in the feeling that the only true humanity left resided in their isolation from the rest of the world.

Childhood and Adolescence. The experience of childhood changed drastically during the nineteenth century. The concept of childhood innocence replaced the idea of childhood corruption (Aries, 1982). A new sentimentality surrounded the child, who was now viewed as born with a sweetness that must be nurtured. Wordsworth's (1770–1859) poem "Ode: Intimations of Immortality from Recollections of Early Childhood" was one of the turning points in the history of childhood. It both summed up and created the new view of the child:

> *Our birth is but a sleep and a forgetting:*
> *The soul that rises with us, our life's star,*
>   *Hath had elsewhere its setting,*
>   *And cometh from afar;*
>   *Not in entire forgetfulness,*
>   *And not in utter nakedness,*
> *But trailing clouds of glory do we come*
>   *From God, who is our home.*
> *Heaven lies about us in our infancy;*

Shades of the prison-house begin to close
  Upon the growing boy,
But he beholds the light, and whence it flows.
  He sees it in his joy;
The youth, who daily farther from the east
  Must travel, still is Nature's priest,
    And by the vision splendid
    Is on his way attended;
At length the man perceives it die away,
And fade into the light of common day.

The child no longer was born in sin, but had come from the bosom of God; as such, the child possessed angelic qualities. It was only contact with the world that the child's original goodness was corrupted.

Women, deprived of many of their earlier household functions, needed new roles to give meaning to their lives. They found that meaning in an increased commitment to childrearing and, more important, in "mothering" (Degler, 1980; Strong, 1972). Now children were being reared primarily by their mothers until they reached school age.

The mode of education changed. Children no longer learned by doing but by studying. They left behind the concrete world of hoes, plows, milking pails, and spinning wheels to enter a world of symbols. They studied only words and numbers now, not objects. With this trend, the family lost one of its basic functions: It no longer educated its own children for the world of work. This became the job of the state. The school did more than educate children. It socialized them as well, encroaching on still another traditional function of the family. Ideas and values were now transmitted by an impersonal institution over which the family had very little control. Conflicts between the beliefs of the family and those of the school were inevitable. At the school, the child's peer group increased in importance.

The nineteenth century not only saw the rise of the child but it also witnessed the beginning of "adolescence" (Kett, 1977). This term was not widely used until psychologist G. Stanley Hall wrote his classic *Adolescence* in 1909. By then it was clear that society had defined a new stage in life, characterized by immaturity, inexperience, and emotional turmoil. Adolescence was an outgrowth of nineteenth-century childhood, in which parents sheltered their children by protecting them against certain kinds of knowledge. The adolescent crisis had been virtually nonexistent in colonial times. But in the nineteenth century, the family did everything it could to protect its children from meeting the adult world. Feminist Charlotte Perkins Gilman (quoted in Kennedy, 1970) said it was the family's duty to ensure children "an even longer period of immaturity." Children and young adolescents were kept from knowledge of corruption, dishonesty, indifference, cruelty, and sex. They were only permitted to know about the good; they were cared for with love and isolated from unseemly sights and matters. Then suddenly they were thrust into the adult world. Their apprehension of assuming radically different (adult) roles led to adolescent conflicts, indecision, guilt, and despair.

The new concepts of childhood and adolescence, however, were primarily middle-class phenomena. Alongside the sentimentalization of childhood was the brutal fact of slavery and child labor. Working-class poverty was a significant feature of nineteenth-century industrial life. Families could not survive on the wages paid to working men. To relieve their desperate poverty, working-class families sent their children into factories and stores to supplement the starvation wages paid adult workers (Nasaw, 1985). In 1880, for example, more than 1 million children were working; by 1890 the number rose to 1.75 million. In the nineteenth- and early twentieth-century, the typical dual-worker family was not husband and wife but father and children. Wives remained at home caring for the smaller children. The older children worked in mines, factories, and mills, toiling ten to twelve hours a day, six days a week. They had no childhood. In fact, many had no adulthood either, for "child laborers in industry were so brutally exploited that many did not survive to adulthood" (Nasaw, 1985). Yet even for these working children, the new middle-class ideas were important, as the idealized visions of childhood provided fuel for reformers who sought to enact child labor laws to save childhood for the children. In the end, however, children were saved from the factories because industrialists could pay newly arrived immigrants even less than they paid children. (For a description of an immigrant's disorienting arrival in America at the turn of the century, see the reading by Abraham Cahan, pages 82–83.)

The New Family. These forces worked toward creating a new type of family. Without its central significance as a work unit, the family had a new burden placed on it. In earlier times, the grinding necessities of family-centered work gave marriage and family a strong center. Except in the most extreme cases, the emotional relationship between a couple did not matter as much as their working relationship. Each needed the other. In the emerging industrial society, the wife became economically dependent on her husband. At the same time, another momentous change was taking place: marriages became based on the relationship between husband and wife. Parental control over courtship declined to a mere veto power. Men and women chose their own partners on the basis of love; and love was supposed to bring personal happiness. Love as the basis of marriage represented the triumph of individual preference over family, social, or group considerations. It also gave women a new degree of power; they were now able to choose whom they would marry. As historian Carl Degler (1980) observed: "Simply because affection was a chief basis for marital choices, courtship in the 19th century was an important stage in family formation. At perhaps no other point in the course of a marriage was a woman's autonomy greater or more individualistically exercised." Women could rule out undesirable partners during courtship; they could choose mates with whom they believed they would be compatible.

Because of the affectionate bond, women had more power in influencing the marital relationship. For the first time, the American marriage bond was fused out of the mutual feelings of husband and wife. The success of their marriage depended on the success of their emotional relationship rather than on how well the family met its material needs. Happiness became an increasingly important criterion for measuring the quality of a marriage. Sociologist Arthur Calhoun (1919) observed early in this century that America had become the first civilization that had ever experimented with "placing the entire burden of securing the success of marriage and family life upon the characters and capacities of two persons. . . . American marriage is a union of two people and not an alliance between two families."

The family became more private (Jeffrey, 1972). Instead of being an integral part of the working world, it became a retreat—a refuge from a competitive, hostile, and

Probe the earth and see where your main roots run.

HENRY DAVID THOREAU

If history repeats itself, and the unexpected always happens, how incapable must man be of learning from experience.

GEORGE BERNARD SHAW

(text continues on page 74)

UNDERSTANDING YOURSELF

Discovering Your Family's Past

We are descendants of the past, yet our knowledge of our own family's past is often dim or nonexistent. But our parents, grandparents, and great grandparents—and their parents and grandparents—all have a story, and their stories are our family's history. The history of our family is part of the history of the family. The past is not so distant or abstract when we understand that its facts are the flesh from which we were born.

What do you know of your family's history? How did your parents meet? From where did their parents and their parents' parents come? Were they immigrants, slaves? You only need to go back a few generations to reach into the nineteenth century, when life was radically different from today. "Each of us is all the sums he has not counted: subtract us into nakedness and night again, and you shall see begin in Crete four thousand years ago the love that ended yesterday in Texas. . . ." Thomas Wolfe wrote in Look Homeward, Angel. "Every moment is a window on all time."

The authors' own grandparents and great-aunts and -uncles were born in the nineteenth century. They remember bells peeling at midnight to announce the arrival of the twentieth century. They remember the first automobile driving through town at a reckless fifteen miles an hour, and the first airplane flying overhead. They remember World War I and the movement for women's voting rights. And they remember their own grandparents who told stories of the Civil War, of fighting at Gettysburg or the wilderness. They relate hearing of a treadle sewing machine that was proudly displayed in their grandparents' parlor, a miraculous device admired by everyone as the greatest marvel of the 1840s. One elderly aunt was held as an infant by a great-grandparent who had been born in the 18th century. Through her living memory we can touch family history extending to the time of Thomas Jefferson.

Family histories are not lost. You can explore your own family history through photographs and family trees. Photographs are often used by psychologists as maps of family feelings and relationships. Gather together family photographs of your immediate family and your forebears—grandparents, great-grandparents, and so on. Identify who is in them. If you don't know, find out from someone who does. Look at their faces, the body language, the positions of the family members relative to one another. Are family members clustered closely together or far apart? Is someone standing off from the others? Is someone looking gloomy amidst others who are smiling? What family resemblances do you see? Do you look like a great-great grandparent, for example?

On separate sheets of paper, gather information about each of your pictured relatives. Then, after you read this chapter, find out what aspects of the family we have discussed apply to your early family members. Was a great-grandfather a child laborer? Was a great-grandmother a slave? How did they go about their daily tasks in the household? Did they make their bread or buy it?

On the facing page is a family tree. Fill it out. If you don't have information that you need, ask someone in your family who might know. After you fill out the names and dates, try to find out stories about the oldest family members. Where did they come from? What important historical events occurred during their lifetimes? In which ones did they actually participate? What were their own experiences of joy and sorrow? What did they pass down: love of learning, ambition, money, pride?

We ourselves are repositories of history. We are witnesses to it. In our time, we have wit-

UNDERSTANDING YOURSELF–*continued*

nessed the unleashing of nuclear energy, men walking on the moon, and the computer revolution. All of us have a story to tell our children and grandchildren: the times in which we have lived, the people we have loved, the dreams we have lost and found, our triumphs and our sorrows. What are the stories you will tell your grandchildren?

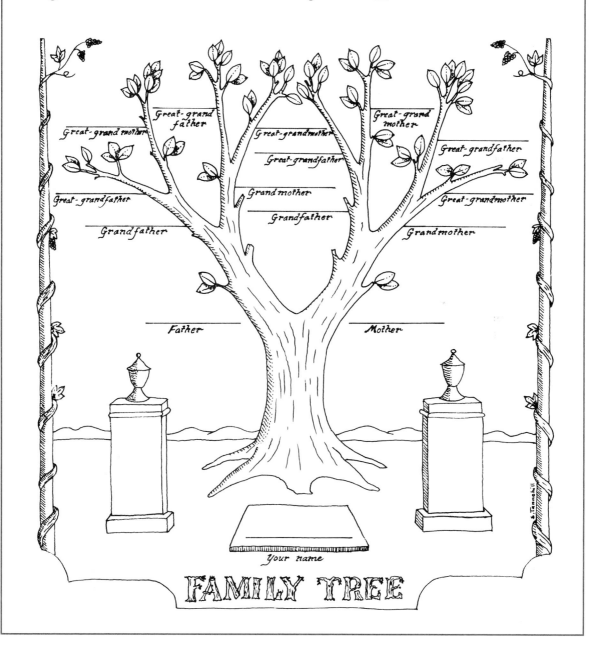

FAMILY TREE

Grandma Mary & her children
Baby is Lee's mother. 1910

Grandma Mary 1879, North Carolina

Dad   1944

Lee   1946

Mother 1935

Lee, Marie,
Gabriel, & Willie
1984

*Family albums help encourage
a sense of family continuity
and pride. Each photograph
captures a moment of family
history for future generations.*

Marie 1949

Grandma Mimi & Family
St. Paul 1901

Camping at Laguna Beach, 1923.
The baby is Marie's mother.

Marie with dad, mom,
and brother. 1946

Christmas with Mimi, 1982

Gabriel and Willie, 1978

brutal work environment. As geographic and social mobility increased, kin networks began to disintegrate. Friends were left behind. The family was increasingly isolated, and the resulting pressures on it were tremendous. Although homes were expected to be havens, historian Page Smith (1968) describes most nineteenth-century marriages as "minor disasters." Abraham Lincoln's domestic life, for example, was a succession of troubles originating in his melancholy temperament and the stubborn jealousy and ambition of his wife, Mary Todd. Abraham Lincoln and Mary Todd never really seemed to love each other; she always resented him for failing to appear at their first wedding. When Lincoln was a lawyer, a client came in seeking a divorce. He listed his marital grievances in great detail until finally Lincoln interrupted him, saying, "My friend, I regret to hear this; but let me ask you in all candor, can't you endure for a few moments what I have had as my daily portion for the last fifteen years?" (Herndon and Weik, 1920; but see Gallardo, 1984). He spoke with such sadness and dejection that the husband left without pursuing his divorce.

Society regarded marriage as a means of developing and maintaining good habits and character. It did not encourage the partners of a marriage to accept each other as they were but urged husband and wife to correct each other and make each other better persons. William Alcott (1849) advised that within marriage husband and wife were to "mutually correct and reform each other . . . because no friends have so good an opportunity of discovering each other's defect in the smaller matters." Married couples each had "the task of correcting one another's evil habits and manners. Let nothing to this end," Alcott continued, "pass unnoticed." Such a course probably increased rather than decreased the usual frictions in marriage. Alcott himself observed that there were "not a few husbands" who became "greatly agitated, and sometimes, for the moment, almost angry, when certain things were mentioned to them as faults."

Sexuality.   Sex was often a difficult problem for nineteenth-century men and women (see Vicinus, 1982, for a literature review). Generally, men felt guilty because they seemed to desire sex too much and women felt guilty if they desired it at all. Sex was legitimate only as a means of reproduction. As an expression of pleasure, it was considered abusive. Sexual relations were viewed as minor assaults, the woman yielding to her husband's "animal urges" and the husband feeling guilty because he was driven by "animal instinct." These sexual feelings had a negative impact on human relationships; mutual suspicion generally led to a cautious distancing between husband and wife (Strong, 1972).

Despite the Victorian emphasis on sex for reproduction, the nineteenth century witnessed the most dramatic decline in fertility in American history. Between 1800 and 1900, fertility dropped by 50 percent, falling from seven childen to about three and a half children per woman. Woman reduced their childbearing by insisting that they, not men, control the frequency of intercourse. In this sense, the Victorian belief in women's sexual purity worked toward women's emancipation (Degler, 1980). Abstinence, withdrawal, douching, and abortion were the most widely used methods of birth control. Abortion probably ended as many as 20 percent of all pregnancies (Mohr, 1978). Fewer children allowed women more freedom from childrearing responsibilities and opened the door to greater participation in the world outside the family.

Divorce. At the same time that marriage became increasingly based on emotional bonds, the divorce rate began to rise. In 1867 only 10,000 divorces were granted; by 1886 the number had risen to 25,000. By 1900 the divorce rate was increasing over three times as fast as the population. Four out of every 1,000 married couples divorced each year. The nation was rocked with debate concerning divorce and the breakdown of the family (Kennedy, 1970). Divorce continued to increase until 1920, when it leveled off at 8 divorces per every 1,000 marriages. Then it skyrocketed to 15.2 per 1,000 marriages in 1970, 20 per 1,000 marriages in 1980; since then the divorce rate has leveled off (U.S. Department of Commerce, 1985). Initially, this seems somewhat paradoxical: Why would divorce increase when love was becoming the most important reason for marriage? Divorce was, according to one historian, "the safety valve that makes the system workable" (O'Neil, 1967). When families become the center of society, "their intimacy can become too suffocating, their demands unbearable, and their expectations too high to be easily realizable." Divorce was actually an integral part of the new emotionally centered family. It was not a flaw but a device to make the new marriage system work. Divorce gave people a second chance.

The Black Family in the Nineteenth Century

In 1619 the first blacks came from Africa to colonial America aboard a Dutch man-of-war and were sold at Jamestown as indentured servants. Among them were a man and a woman who were called Antony and Isabella by the English. After being in Virginia several years, they married and Isabella gave birth to William Tucker, the first black child born in America. This was the beginning of the Afro-American family, a unique family system that grew out of the African adjustment to slavery in America.

Limits on the Slave Family. By the nineteenth century, the black slave family had already lost much of its African heritage under the severe regime of slavery. Under slavery the black family lacked several elements that helped give the free family stability. First, the black family lacked autonomy. Slave marriages were not recognized as legal. Final authority rested with the owner in all decisions about the lives of slaves. If the owner decided to break up a family by selling a husband, wife, or children, laws granted him that right. In the upper South, slave breeding was an important source of income for planters. The separation of families was a common occurrence, spreading grief and despair among thousands of slaves. One former slave (quoted in Botkin, 1945) remembered:

My mother told me that he [her master] owned a woman who was the mother of several children, and when her babies would get about a year or two of age he'd sell them, and it would break her heart. She never got to keep them. When her fourth baby was born and was about two years old, she just studied all the time about how she would have to give it up, and one day she said, "I just decided I'm not going to let Old Master sell this baby; he just ain't going to do it." She got up and give it something out of a bottle and pretty soon it was dead.

The slave owners understood their strength in relation to the slave family. They used the slave's affection for his or her family to ensure control. One slaveholder

Although marriage was not legally recognized under slavery, slaves formed strong family bonds. After freedom came, thousands of former slaves went searching for husbands, wives, and children who had been sold away.

Who I is, how old I is, and where I is born, I don't know. . . . The only thing I 'members 'bout all that am there am lots of crying when they tooks me 'way from my mammy. That something I never forgits.

SLAVE RECOLLECTION

(quoted in Genovese, 1976) wrote: "It is necessary that Negroes have wives, and you ought to know that nothing attaches them so much to a plantation as children." Although some slaveholders went to great lengths to hold families together even if it meant economic loss, the majority were willing to sacrifice the slaves' family where profits were at stake. Frederick Douglass (quoted in Stampp, 1956) referred to slaveholder control over the black family as "that painful uncertainty which in one form or another was ever obtruding itself in the pathway of the slave." (See the reading by Frederick Douglass, "A Slave Childhood" on pages 80–82 for a description of a slave child's life.)

The slave family also had little economic significance as a unit. Slave families worked for their masters, not themselves. Although many whites and free blacks worked in factories and fields they did not own, at least they received wages for their work. Slaves did not. Fundamentally, it was impossible for the slave husband to become the "provider" for his family. Yet the slave man did furnish an important part of their sustenance by hunting and trapping. If plantation food allowances had been the only source of nourishment for slave families, malnutrition would have been much more widespread. One slave (quoted in Genovese, 1976) recalled, "My dear old daddy partly raised his children on game. He caught rabbits, coons an' possums. He would work all day and hunt at night." Slave mothers would sing lullabies to their babies:

Bye baby buntin'
Daddy's gone a-huntin'
Ter fetch a little rabbit skin
Ter wrap de baby buntin' in.

FEATURE

Childhood Under Slavery

Under slavery a woman's owner determined her care during pregnancy and her relation to her infant after birth. During pregnancy a woman field slave continued her work; only in the last few weeks before birth were her duties relaxed. After birth she was generally given a few days off (or even weeks in some cases) before she had to return to her full duties. The new mother usually carried her baby to the fields with her or left the baby behind in the care of an elderly slave. The planters' desire to maximize a woman slave's productivity, despite her pregnancy, led to a decline in slave fertility and in increase in miscarriages during the final decades of slavery (Jones, 1985).

The age at which children recognized themselves as slaves depended on whether they were the children of field or house slaves. If their parents were field slaves, they would be subject to slave discipline from the beginning. One former slave (quoted in Blassingame, 1972) recalled: "I was born a slave. . . . I was made to feel, in my boyhood's first experience, that I was inferior and degraded and that I must pass through life in a dependent and suffering condition." But if the children were offspring of house slaves, they were often playmates of their master's children. They would play games together, hunt, fish, sometimes (although it was illegal) learn to read together. Only gradually would they learn that they were slaves. Lunsford Lane (quoted in Blassingame, 1972), a slave on a Carolina plantation, remembered his childhood: "I knew no difference between myself and the white children, nor did they seem to know any in turn. Sometimes my master would come out and give a biscuit to me and another of his white boys; but I did not perceive the difference between us." But the day would come when such a child would know that he was a slave, and that time would be filled with grieving, anger, and humiliation. This knowledge represented a deep crisis or turning point in the child's concept of self. This crisis occurred for Lunsford Land when he was ten years old. He remembered:

When I began to work, I discovered the difference between myself and my master's white children. They began to order me about, and were told to do so by my master and mistress. . . . Indeed all things now made me *feel* what I had before known only in words, that *I was a slave*. Deep was this feeling, and it preyed upon my heart like a never dying worm.

The slave women worked in the fields beside the men. Most did not work in houses. (The belief in female delicacy did not extend to black women. Although white middle- and upper-class men held this ideal, it never occurred to them to look at white women working in factories or black women working in fields and so to revise their opinions.) When the black woman returned home to her cabin, she worked her gardens to supplement the family's food supply. Then, working into the night, she prepared meals for her family and tended to her other household tasks. In this limited way the family worked as a productive unit. But its roles and functions were radically different from white middle-class families.

After Freedom. After freedom came, the black family already had strong emotional ties and traditions that emerged from slavery (Lantz, 1980). During Reconstruction the Freedman's Bureau registered informal slave marriages throughout the South. The bonds that existed between blacks surprised whites, who had believed slaves incapable of establishing strong family ties. Blacks filled out marriage affidavits such as the following to legalize their relationship (Guttman, 1976):

"I Elburt Williams & Marien Williams has been Livin together 18 years & We Both do affirm that We do want each other to Live as man & wife the balance of Life & being disable to walk & Marien being in the family way I will send this to you & you will please make it all Wright with us."

The black family in the South generally consisted of both parents and their children; only later did the father-absent black family become pervasive, especially after the Great Depression of the 1930s. Postslavery black families remained poor in the South, tied to the land by the sharecrop system, which kept them in a state of semislavery.

Our contemporary marriage and family forms did not spring up overnight. They have their roots in the nineteenth century when American society began to undergo the great transformation resulting from industrialization. It was during this time that the idea of romantic love took firm hold and the family became more an emotional unit than a productive one. The size of the family decreased and divorces began to rise, until by the turn of the century Americans believed the family to be in crisis. Today intimate relationships and social patterns continue to change, profoundly affecting the family. But what we are seeing may be simply the culmination of trends begun in the last century.

We are tomorrow's past.

MARY WEBB

☐ SUMMARY

- The early Christian tradition celebrated celibacy as a higher virtue than marriage; marriage was a concession to human frailty. The family continued to be patriarchal.

- In the Middle Ages the church made marriage a sacrament and prohibited priests from marrying. At the same time the rise of the courtly love ethic created the ideal of romantic love and raised the status of women. Romantic love, however, remained outside of marriage.

- In colonial America marriage was an economic arrangement and the marriage relationship was companionate. The family was self-sufficient. Women's economic contributions were recognized and children were economically important. From the age of about six or seven, they were regarded as small adults. The elderly, especially men, were treated with respect.

- In the nineteenth century industrialization revolutionized the family. The family was no longer economically self-sufficient. Men became wage earners and women, once they married, became housewives. In the middle class children lost their economic value and were sent to school. Children of the poor worked in shops and factories. Childhood was sentimentalized and adolescence was invented. Marriage was increasingly based on emotional bonds. Courtship was based on romance and marriages were supposed to be havens from the harsh world. Women were expected to be sexually pure, even in marriage, which may have contributed to the declining birthrate. Abstinence, withdrawal, douching, and abortion were frequently used as methods of birth control. Divorce began to rise in the 1870s.

- The stability of the black slave family suffered because it lacked autonomy. Slave families were broken up by slaveholders, and marriage between slaves was not legally recognized. Black families formed solid bonds nevertheless. Parents' relations with their children were influenced by the slaveholder. The children of field hands learned that they were slaves; the children of house slaves often did not realize they were slaves until they reached middle childhood.

READINGS

Traveling West in a Covered Wagon
ARVAZINE COOPER

In this excerpt from her diary, Arvazine Cooper describes her life in a wagon train as her family fled to Oregon from war-torn Missouri in 1862. How do you imagine the lives of the Western immigrants differed from those in the settled East and South? How does Arvazine Cooper's experience of relocating with her family compare with any experience you have had in changing your home? What differences and similarities do you see between your feelings and daily activities and hers?

All this time of preparation I was too bewildered to think much about the partings there would be for me, but when the day for starting came so quickly, I began to realize that little backwoodsy corner of Southwest Missouri was all the world to me, and I was not only leaving my native land, but every single tie of blood relations, for something so far away and vague that it seemed very unreal, and I had not the remotest idea that I would ever see any of my kindred again.

Very few of my kinfolks or neighbors came to bid me goodbye, for in that troublous time there was no knowing what the war fiend would do to their homes in their absence. In brooding over all this, I let a kind of wordless grief take possession of me, I kept it all to myself, and shed my tears when others were asleep, and kept up appearances so well that no one suspected I was not reasonably happy.

I was very inexperienced in every way, especially was it so about camping out, and the very first night was a very trying one. I was morbidly shy, and a strange man was traveling with us, and too my dear little baby Belle was just learning to walk, and would cling to my skirts, or if left to herself would get into things. Her favorite pursuit was washing the dish rag in the water bucket, which proved a rather

serious matter when we got farther on to where water was a very scarce article.

Somehow I got the supper ready and sprawled around on the ground among our pots and pans and dishes, and began our first meal of many that followed in uncomfortable circumstances. One good thing was that little Belle never cried and was supremely happy all the time. In fact, she was almost too self-assured, for she would go anywhere her little stumbling feet could carry her, and take anything her bright little eyes spied, provided it was not too cumbersome for her little hands. At this first meal, in her busy stumbling efforts, she put her foot into a big cup of thick sorghum molasses, and when I spied her she was making strenuous efforts to keep at her work with her foot in the cup. And thus ended our first day's travel. . . .

All the way over these lonely stretches, there had never been a single day that I can remember that we were not cheered by the music of the cheerful meadow larks. I say we, but in truth I must except myself, for I heard without heeding, though to outward appearances I was normal. Yet my inward gloom was so unnatural and morbid that nothing penetrated it to any ameliorating extent. . . .

. . . It became evident that I was in a poor fix to travel [because of being pregnant], so when our guide learned about that, he said that settled the matter as far as he was concerned, and anybody that insisted on a woman going on in the fix I was in ought to be hung, and that he would stay with Cooper if no one else did. . . .

So our train all decided to stay. . . . At two o'clock a little blue-eyed brother came to our wagon, to share the honors and favors with the little black-eyed Belle. . . .

[Editor's note: At this point in her narrative, the author temporarily shifts to writing in the third person.]

. . . There was little comfort or peace, though, for the mother of the new baby, for by this time he had the habit

READINGS—*continued*

firmly fixed of howling most of the time the wagon was stopped, and she was still unable to sleep when it was moving. Then, too, she took cold in her breast, and as all the remedies of all kinds, and all the delicacies of all the train, and all the patience and kindness of everybody had been severely taxed by a woman who had got a fish hook fast in her finger way back on Platte River and had it cut out, and the poor young mother had heard so much about her exactions, she did not ask for attentions, but mostly bore her sufferings in grim silence, and her ailment came to its own conclusion in its own way almost unaided. It was at the worst about Boise City, and her sufferings were so great that her recollections are not very distinct for quite a space along there. It all seems like a jumble and confusion of jolting wagon, crying baby, dust, sage-brush, and passing and being passed with friendly greetings by those we had traveled so far with, and the never ceasing pain and suffering which was not greatly diminished till we were way up Burnt River.

By this time we were meeting droves of people going to the mines around Boise. They told us wonderful tales about big red applies and all manner of other good things in the Willamette Valley. We thought it strange that they were getting away from there in such numbers, and that they would advise us to go to a land of such great plenty when provisions were so scarce and high along there. We soon concluded, though, that they were gold crazy. As we were not, we would get to this goodly land as soon as possible.

So we plodded on, meeting many freight teams, and pack trains, and bands of cattle. The folks we met all agreed about the terrible state of the road over the Cascade Mountains, which we found to our sorrow they did not exaggerate. But by dint of sticking to it, and tying logs to our wagons down hill, and digging footholds for our steers up hill, we arrived on the west side of the mountains, and oh! joy, we found the big red apples! and we found something else we had not expected. . . .

We found a welcome that a long lost brother might envy.

The people ministered to us personally, with the products of their own labor.

They did not wait for us to go to them and ask, but seeing us afar off, they ran with buckets, with baskets and pans, and failing these, ran with aprons and hats full of good things till we were threatened with overloading. Soon, seeng we were in such a hospitable land, and believing it would grieve their generous souls if we did not take all that was offered, we conceived the idea of putting what we could not eat in the brush by the road side, and so make

the people at the next house happy by finding us unsupplied.

And everywhere we went we were treated with such kindly consideration that we felt amply paid for our persistent struggle to reach this goodly land of peace and plenty.

A Slave Childhood
FREDERICK DOUGLASS, EXCERPT FROM *LIFE AND TIMES OF FREDERICK DOUGLASS*

Frederick Douglass, one of the leading black abolitionists, describes his early childhood in this excerpt from his autobiography. In what significant ways did the slave family differ from the non-slave family in the 19th century?

Whether because [my grandmother] was too old for field service, or because she had so faithfully discharged the duties of her station in early life, I know not, but she enjoyed the high privilege of living in a cabin separate from the quarters, having imposed upon her only the charge of the young children and the burden of her own support. She esteemed it great good fortune to live so, and took much comfort in having the children. The practice of separating mothers from their children and hiring them out at distances too great to admit of their meeting, save at long intervals, was a marked feature of the cruelty and barbarity of the slave system; but it was in harmony with the grand aim of that system, which always and everywhere sought to reduce man to a level with the brute. It had no interest in recognizing or preserving any of the ties that bind families together or to their homes.

My grandmother's five daughters were hired out in this way, and my only recollections of my own mother are of a few hasty visits made in the night on foot, after the daily tasks were over, and when she was under the necessity of returning in time to respond to the driver's call to the field in the early morning. These little glimpses of my mother, obtained under such circumstances and against such odds, meager as they were, are ineffaceably stamped upon my memory. She was tall and finely proportioned, of dark, glossy complexion, with regular features, and amongst the slaves was remarkably sedate and dignified.

Of my father I know nothing. Slavery had no recognition of fathers, as none of families. That the mother was a slave was enough for its deadly purpose. By its law the child followed the condition of its mother. The father might be a freeman and the child a slave. The father might be a white man, glorying in the purity of his Anglo-Saxon blood, and

READINGS–*continued*

the child ranked with the blackest slaves. Father he might be, and not be husband, and could sell his own child without incurring reproach, if in its veins coursed one drop of African blood.

Living thus with my grandmother, whose kindness and love stood in place of my mother's, it was some time before I knew myself to be a slave. I knew many other things before I knew that. Her little cabin had to me the attractions of a palace. Its fence-railed floor—which was equally floor and bedstead—upstairs, and its clay floor downstairs, its dirt and straw chimney, and windowless sides, and that most curious piece of workmanship, the ladder stairway, and the hole so strangely dug in front of the fireplace, beneath which grandmamma placed her sweet potatoes, to keep them from frost in winter, were full of interest to my childish observation. The squirrels, as they skipped the fences, climbed the trees, or gathered their nuts, were an unceasing delight to me. There, too, right at the side of the hut, stood the old well, with its stately and skyward-pointing beam, so aptly placed between the limbs of what had once been a tree, and so nicely balanced, that I could move it up and down with only one hand, and could get a drink myself without calling for help. Nor were these all the attractions of the place. At a little distance stood Mr. Lee's mill, where the people came in large numbers to get their corn ground. I can never tell the many things thought and felt, as I sat on the bank and watched that mill and the turning of its ponderous wheel. The millpond, too, had its charms, and with my pin-hook and threadline, I could get amusing nibbles if I could catch no fish.

It was not long, however, before I began to learn the sad fact that this house of my childhood belonged not to my dear old grandmother, but to some one I had never seen, and who lived a great distance off. I learned, too, the sadder fact, that not only the home and lot, but that grandmother herself and all the little children around her belonged to a mysterious personage, called by grandmother, with every mark of reverence, "Old Master." Thus early did clouds and shadows begin to fall upon my path.

I learned that this old master, whose name seemed ever to be mentioned with fear and shuddering, only allowed the little children to live with grandmother for a limited time, and that as soon as they were big enough they were promptly taken away to live with the said old master. These were distressing revelations, indeed. My grandmother was all the world to me, and the thought of being separated from her was a most unwelcome suggestion to my affections and hopes.

I wished that it was possible for me to remain small all my life, knowing that the sooner I grew large the shorter would be my time to remain with them. Everything about the cabin became doubly dear and I was sure that there could be no other spot on earth equal to it. But the time came when I must go, and my grandmother, knowing my fears, and in pity for them, kindly kept me ignorant of the dreaded moment up to the morning (a beautiful summer morning) when we were to start; and, indeed, during the whole journey, which, child as I was, I remember as well as if it were yesterday, she kept the unwelcome truth hidden from me.

The distance from Tuckahoe to Colonel Lloyd's, where my old master lived, was full twelve miles, and the walk was quite a severe test of the endurance of my young legs. The journey would have proved too severe for me, but that my dear old grandmother (blessings on her memory) afforded occasional relief by "toting" me on her shoulder. Advanced in years as she was, as was evident from the more than one gray hair which peeped from between the ample and graceful folds of her newly and smoothly-ironed bandana turban, grandmother was yet a woman of power and spirit. She was remarkably straight in figure, and elastic and muscular in movement. I seemed hardly to be a burden to her. She would have "toted" me farther, but I felt myself too much of a man to allow it. Yet while I walked I was not independent of her. She often found me holding her skirts lest something should come out of the woods and eat me up. Several old logs and stumps imposed upon me, and got themselves taken for enormous animals. I could plainly see their legs, eyes, ears, and teeth, till I got close enough to see that the eyes were knots, washed white with rain, and the legs were broken limbs, and the ears and teeth only such because of the point from which they were seen.

As the day advanced the heat increased, and it was not until the afternoon that we reached the much-dreaded end of the journey. Here I found myself in the midst of a group of children of all sizes and of many colors—black, brown, copper-colored, and nearly white. I had not before seen so many children. As a newcomer I was an object of special interest. After laughing and yelling around me and playing all sorts of wild tricks, they asked me to go out and play with them. This I refused to do. Grandmamma looked sad, and I could not help feeling that our being there boded no good for me. She was soon to lose another object of affection, as she had lost many before. Affectionately patting me on the head, she told me to be a good boy and

READINGS—*continued*

go out to play with the children. They are "kin to you," she said, "go and play with them." She pointed out to me my brother Perry, and my sisters, Sarah and Eliza. I had never seen them before, and though I had sometimes heard of them and felt a curious interest in them, I really did not understand what they were to me or I to them. Brothers and sisters we were by blood, but slavery had made us strangers. They were already initiated into the mysteries of old master's domicile, and they seemed to look upon me with a certain degree of compassion. I really wanted to play with them, but they were strangers to me, and I was full of fear that my grandmother might leave for home without taking me with her. Entreated to do so, however, and that, too, by my dear grandmother, I went to the back part of the house to play with them and the other children. Play, however, I did not, but stood with my back against the wall witnessing the playing of the others. At last, while standing there, one of the children, who had been in the kitchen, ran up to me in a sort of roguish glee, exclaiming, "Fed, Fed, grandmamma gone!" I could not believe it. Yet, fearing the worst, I ran into the kitchen to see for myself, and lo! she was indeed gone, and was now far away, and "clean" out of sight. I need not tell all that happened now. Almost heartbroken at the discovery, I fell upon the ground and wept a boy's bitter tears, refusing to be comforted. My brother gave me peaches and pears to quiet me, but I promptly threw them on the ground. I had never been deceived before and something of resentment mingled with my grief at parting with my grandmother.

It was now late in the afternoon. The day had been an exciting and wearisome one, and I know not where, but I suppose I sobbed myself to sleep, and its balm was never more welcome to any wounded soul than to mine. The reader may be surprised that I relate so minutely an incident apparently so trivial, and which must have occurred when I was less than seven years old, but, as I wish to give a faithful history of my experience in slavery, I cannot withhold a circumstance which at the time affected me so deeply, and which I still remember so vividly. Besides, this was my first introduction to the realities of the slave system.

A Jewish Immigrant Discovers America

ABRAHAM CAHAN, EXCERPT FROM *THE RISE OF DAVID LEVINSKY*

The Rise of David Levinsky *was the first important Jewish novel written in America. It describes the early Russian childhood of David Levinsky, his arrival in America near the turn of the century, and his rise to wealth, promi-*

nence—and loneliness. A Talmudic scholar tells David, a newly arrived "green one," that "America is a topsy-turvy country." What does the scholar mean? What adjustment did the scholar have to make?

. . . When it grew dark and I was much in need of rest I had a street peddler direct me to a synagogue. I expected to spend the night there. What could have been more natural?

At the house of God I found a handful of men in prayer. It was a large, spacious room and the smallness of their number gave it an air of desolation. I joined in the devotions with great fervor. My soul was sobbing to Heaven to take care of me in the strange country.

The service over, several of the worshipers took up some Talmud folio or other holy book and proceeded to read them aloud in the familiar singsong. The strange surroundings suddenly began to look like home to me.

One of the readers, an elderly man with a pinched face and forked little beard, paused to look me over.

"A green one?" he asked, genially.

He told me that the synagogue was crowded on Saturdays, while on week-days people in America had no time to say their prayers at home, much less to visit a house of worship.

When he heard that I intended to stay at the synagogue overnight he smiled ruefully.

"One does not sleep in an American synagogue," he said. "It is not Russia." Then, scanning me once more, he added, with an air of compassionate perplexity: "Where will you sleep, poor child? I wish I could take you to my house, but—well, America is not Russia. There is no pity here, no hospitality. My wife would raise a rumpus if I brought you along. I should never hear the last of it."

With a deep sigh and nodding his head plaintively he returned to his book, swaying back and forth. But he was apparently more interested in the subject he had broached. "When we were at home," he resumed, "she, too, was a different woman. She did not make life a burden to me as she does here. Have you no money at all?"

I showed him the quarter I had received from the cloak contractor.

"Poor fellow! Is that all you have? There are places where you can get a night's lodging for fifteen cents, but what are you going to do afterward? I am simply ashamed of myself."

' "Hospitality,' " he quoted from the Talmud, " 'is one of the things which the giver enjoys in this world and the fruit of which he relishes in the world to come.' To think that I

READINGS—*continued*

cannot offer a Talmudic scholar a night's rest! Alas! America has turned me into a mound of ashes."

"You were well off in Russia, weren't you?" I inquired, in astonishment. For, indeed, I had never heard of any but poor people emigrating to America.

"I used to spend my time reading Talmud at the synagogue," was his reply.

Many of his answers seemed to fit, not the question asked, but one which was expected to follow it. You might have thought him anxious to forestall your next query in order to save time and words, had it not been so difficult for him to keep his mouth shut.

"She," he said, referring to his wife, "had a nice little business. She sold feed for horses and she rejoiced in the thought that she was married to a man of learning. True, she has a tongue. That she always had, but over there it was not so bad. She has become a different woman here. Alas! America is a topsy-turvy country."

He went on to show how the New World turned things upside down, transforming an immigrant shoemaker into a man of substance, while a former man of leisure was forced to work in a factory here. In like manner, his wife had changed for the worse, for, lo and behold! instead of supporting him while he read Talmud, as she used to do at home, she persisted in sending him out to peddle. "America is not Russia," she said. "A man must make a living here." But, alas! it was too late to begin now! He had spent the better part of his life at his holy books and was fit for nothing else now. His wife, however, would take no excuse. He must peddle or be nagged to death. And if he ventured to slip into some synagogue for an afternoon and read a page or two he would be in danger of being caught red-handed, so to say, for, indeed, she often shadowed him to make sure that he did not play truant. Alas! America was not Russia. . . .

PART TWO

Getting Together

CHAPTER 4

Sex and Age Roles Today

PREVIEW

To gain a sense of what you already know about the material covered in this chapter, answer "true" or "false" to the statements below. You will find the answers as you read the chapter.

1. Sex roles generally reflect the instinctive nature of males and females. True or false?
2. Sex role learning takes place during adulthood as well as during childhood. True or false?
3. Psychologists believe that the blurring of roles between males and females represents a decline in emotional health. True or false?
4. When men and women describe their "ideal man," they reveal substantially different ideals. True or false?
5. It is often possible to tell the sex of an infant based on its level of activity. True or false?
6. Peers are an important influence in the development of sex roles from birth onward. True or false?
7. People who are heavy television viewers tend to hold more liberal views about sex roles since they have a wider exposure to role models. True or false?
8. Traditional feminine sex roles discourage self-confidence in women. True or false?
9. Once an individual makes the decision to alter his or her sex role behavior, the change is relatively easy. True or false?
10. A double-standard in aging exists for men and women. As men age, they gain status as partners, as women age, they lose status as partners. True or false?

Outline

Not too long ago a national survey asked male and female Americans who their favorite heroes or heroines were (McBee, 1985). The top figure was Clint Eastwood, chosen by 30 percent of the participants; second was Eddie Murphy, by 24 percent; and third was Ronald Reagan, by 15 percent. When one young man was asked why he chose Eastwood, he explained, "I've always liked that tough-guy image." In recent years the tough guy, the macho male, has made a comeback in the American pantheon of heroes; the sensitive, liberated male, the hero of *Ms.* magazine, has taken a beating, to use "tough-guy" prose. He has become a "wimp" in media culture. On the surface, we seem to be returning to a time when men were men and women were cooking.

But if we look separately at those heroes chosen by men and those chosen by women, the picture changes. Men and women chose different heroes. Clint Eastwood was the top choice of 40 percent of the men, but of only 18 percent of the women. The number one choice of women was Jane Fonda, picked by 25 percent of them; she was not among the top ten choices of men. Eddie Murphy was the number two choice of men; Sally Field was the second choice for women. Ronald Reagan was the third choice of men but the ninth choice of women. (Eastwood was, however, the third choice for women. Sociologist William Simon [in McBee, 1985] reflected that Eastwood "represents the unambiguous masculine hero. He's the counterpart to true femininity for women still trapped in romance, who still read Gothic novels.") Among males, not a single woman was named as a hero.

The survey suggests that in terms of self-image, women are changing more than men. The female heroes women chose do not reflect the traditional passive, emotional, often helpless housewife-mother image of women. Instead, their heroes are assertive, achievement-oriented, and independent. Their traits and behaviors appear closer to those traditionally ascribed to males. Yet few would call Jane Fonda or Sally Field unfeminine or masculine. What the new female heroes represent is the androgynous person who embodies both masculine and feminine traits.

In another study, when men and women were asked to actually describe their ideals of both sexes, the descriptions did not follow sex-role stereotypes (Tavris and Wade,

1978) but rather reflected many androgynous characteristics. The respondents described their ideal man and woman as below.

Ideal Woman

As men describe her

1. Able to love
2. Warm
3. Stands up for beliefs
4. Gentle
5. Self-confident

As women describe her

1. Able to love
2. Stands up for beliefs
3. Warm
4. Self-confident
5. Gentle

Ideal Man

As men describe him

1. Able to love
2. Stands up for beliefs
3. Self-confident
4. Fights to protect family
5. Intelligent

As women describe him

1. Able to love
2. Stands up for beliefs
3. Warm
4. Fights to protect family
5. Gentle

Until recently, most Americans tended to look at men and women as polarized opposites, sharing few traits, behaviors, and attitudes. A man was considered masculine if he was achievement oriented, aggressive, instrumental, rational and so on; a woman was considered "feminine" if she was nurturing, subordinate, passive, emotional, and the like. Males traditionally suppressed "feminine" traits in themselves and females, "masculine" traits. What is apparently happening today, especially among women, is that sex roles are becoming more androgynous, incorporating both masculine and feminine traits. Growing evidence suggests that androgynous sex roles help us have more flexible and fulfilling relationships and lives.

Our sex roles have a tremendous impact on our lives. They influence our self-image, our dating and marital relationships, our achievement in school and careers, and many other aspects of our lives. In this chapter we look at sex roles: how they are formed and how they affect us.

☐ GENDER AND SEX ROLES

Each of us is born with an unorganized array of sensations, impulses, and possibilities. But at birth we are identified as either male or female. This identity, based on genitalia, is called *gender identity*, and we learn it at a very young age. It is perhaps the deepest concept we hold of ourselves. The psychology of insults suggests this depth, for few things offend a person so much as to be tauntingly characterized as a member of the "opposite" sex. Gender identity determines many of the directions our lives will take, for example, whether we will fulfill the role of husband or wife, father or mother. When the scripts are handed out in life, the one you receive depends on your gender identity.

Men and women move in different worlds. To understand the significance of sex roles, ask yourself these questions: Would you be the same "person" if you were the other sex? Would you be doing what you are doing this very instant if you were a

Throughout history the more complex activities have been defined and redefined, now as male, now as female—sometimes as drawing equally on the gifts of both sexes. When an activity to which each sex could have contributed is limited to one sex, a rich, differentiated quality is lost from the activity itself.

MARGARET MEAD

woman instead of a man? A man instead of a woman? Would your plans be different? Your activities, feelings, goals? Your clothes and mannerisms? Would you be a better student? A better athlete? All these questions relate to sex roles; significantly, however, they do not relate to gender identity. Biology creates males and females, but culture creates men and women.

Each culture determines the content of sex roles in its own way. Among the Arapesh of New Guinea (Mead, 1931), both sexes possessed what we consider feminine traits. Men and women alike tended to be passive, cooperative, peaceful, and nurturing. The father was said to "bear a child" as well as the mother; only the father's continual care could make a child grow healthily, both in the womb and in childhood. Eighty miles away, the Mundugumor lived in remarkable contrast to the peaceful Arapesh. "Both men and women," Margaret Mead (1948) observed, "are expected to be violent, competitive, aggressively sexed, jealous, and ready to see and avenge insult, delighting in display, in action, in fighting." She concluded: "Many, if not all of the personality traits which we have called masculine or feminine are as lightly linked to sex as are the clothing, the manners, and the form of head-dress that a society at a given period assigns to either sex. . . . The evidence is overwhelmingly in favor of social conditioning."

☐ SOCIALIZATION THEORIES

Although there are a number of ways of examining how we acquire our sex roles, two of the most prominent are social learning theory and cognitive-developmental theory.

Social Learning

Social learning theory is derived from behaviorist psychology. In explaining our actions, behaviorists emphasize observable events and their consequences rather than our internal feelings and drives. We learn attitudes and behaviors as a result of social interactions with others (hence the term *social* learning).

The cornerstone of social learning theory is the belief that consequences control behavior. Acts that are regularly followed by a reward, or *positive* reinforcement, are likely to occur again; acts that are regularly followed by a punishment are less likely to reoccur. Girls are rewarded for playing with dolls ("What a nice mommy!"), but boys are not ("What a sissy!").

What are little girls made of?
Sugar and spice
And everything nice.
That's what little girls are
    made of.

What are little boys made of?
Snips and snails
    and puppy dogs' tails.
That's what little boys are
    made of.

NURSERY RHYME

Most reinforcement, however, does not take place on the spot. It includes our ability to use language, anticipate consequences, and make observations. By using language, we can tell our daughter that we like it when she does well in school and that we don't like it when she hits someone. A person's ability to anticipate consequences affects behavior. A boy doesn't need to wear lace stockings in public to know that such dressing will lead to negative consequences. Finally, children observe what happens to others. A girl learns that she "shouldn't" play video games from hearing her father tell her sister that girls can't play video games well.

Reinforcement alone, however, cannot account for how we learn our appropriate sex roles. Most of us are not even aware of the many subtle behaviors that make up our sex roles: the ways in which men and women use different mannerisms and

Table 4–1 **Male and Female Stereotypes**

Male Role Tendency	*Female Role Tendency*
Instrumental leadership; task and power orientation	Expressive leadership; nurturance and support
Analytic reasoning; intellectualizing	Emotional reasoning; intuition
Generalizing	Personalizing
Identity based on achievement; how others see self less important	Identity dependent on feelings of others toward self; status traditionally based on relationships
Attention to issues of large systems; in a group, remarks impersonal and indirect	Attention to small number of others; in a group, remarks addressed personally to another
Anger and blame externalized; vengeance sought	Blame internalized; difficulty expressing anger
Physical distance; hostility-violence in crowded conditions	Greater comfort with being touched; cooperation under conditions of crowding
Fear of failure in the organizational world; get ahead at all costs	Ambivalence about success in the organizational world
Aggression; competition	Cooperation; support
Exhibit strength; hide weakness	Exhibit weakness; hide or repress strength

Source: Rosabeth Kanter, "Women in Organizations: Sex Roles, Group Dynamics, and Change Strategies," in A. Sargent, *Beyond Sex Roles* (St. Paul, Minn.: West), 1977, p. 382.

gestures, speak differently, use different body language, and so on. We don't "teach" these behaviors by reinforcement. Instead, we learn them by imitation. Learning through imitation is called *modeling*. Children tend to model friendly, warm, and nurturing adults; they also tend to imitate adults who are powerful in their eyes, that is, adults who control access to food, toys or privileges. Initially, the most powerful models children have are their parents; as they grow older and their social world expands, so do the number of people who may act as their role models: siblings, friends, teachers, media figures. Children sift through the various demands and expectations associated with the different models to create their own unique self.

Cognitive-Developmental Theory

In contrast to social learning theory, cognitive-developmental theory focuses on the child's active interpretation of the messages he or she receives from the environment. Whereas social learning assumes that children and adults learn in fundamentally the same way, cognitive-developmental theory stresses that we learn differently depending on our age. Swiss psychologist Jean Piaget showed that children's ability to reason and understand changes as they grow older (Santrock, 1984). Lawrence Kohlberg (1969) took Piaget's findings and applied them to how children assimilate sex role information at different ages. At age two, children can correctly identify themselves and others as boys or girls, but they tend to base this identification on superficial features such as hair and clothing. Girls have long hair and wear dresses; boys have short hair and never wear dresses. Some children even believe they can change their gender by changing their clothes or hair length. They don't identify gender in terms of genitalia as older children and adults do. No amount of reinforcement will alter their view because their ideas are limited by their developmental stage.

When children are six or seven, they begin to understand that gender is permanent; it is not something you can change as you can your clothes. They acquire this understanding because they are now capable of grasping the idea that basic characteristics do not change. A woman can be a woman even if she has short hair and wears pants. Oddly enough, although children can understand the permanence of gender, they tend to insist on rigid adherence to sex role stereotypes. Even though boys can play with dolls, children believe they shouldn't because dolls are for girls (unless, of course, dolls are redefined as excessively masculine "action figures" with guns and knotted biceps, such as G.I. Joe and He-man). Researchers speculate that children exaggerate sex roles to make the roles "cognitively clear."

According to social learning theory, boys and girls learn appropriate sex role behavior through reinforcement and modeling. But according to cognitive-developmental theory, once children learn that gender is permanent, they independently strive to act like a "proper" girl or boy. They do this on their own because of an internal need for congruence, or agreement between what they know and how they act. Also, children find performing the appropriate sex role activities rewarding in themselves. Models and reinforcement help show them how well they are doing, but the primary motivation is internal.

☐ LEARNING SEX ROLES

Although most research focuses on sex role learning during childhood and adolescence, such learning takes place throughout our lives, since what our culture prescribes as appropriate behavior for males and females changes depending on our age.

Sex Role Learning in Childhood

Infancy. It is difficult to analyze the relationship between biology and personality, for learning begins at birth. Evidence shows, for example, that infant females are more sensitive than infant males to pain and to sudden changes of environment. Such responses may be encouraged by learning that begins immediately after birth.

In our culture infant girls are usually held more gently and treated more tenderly than boys, who are ordinarily subjected to rougher forms of play. The first day after birth, parents rate their daughters as soft, fine featured, and small, and their sons as hard, large featured, big, and attentive. Fathers tend to stereotype their sons more extremely than mothers do (Rubin et al., 1974). Although it is impossible for strangers to know the sex of a diapered baby, once they learn the baby's sex, they respond accordingly. In one experiment, three groups played with Baby X (Condry and Condry, 1976). The first group was told the baby was a girl, the second group that the baby was a boy, and the third group was not told what sex the baby was. The group that did not know what sex Baby X was felt extremely uncomfortable, but they then made a decision based on whether the baby was "strong" or "soft." When the baby was labeled a boy, its fussing behavior was called "angry"; if the baby was labeled a girl, the same behavior was called "frustrated." The study was replicated with sixty college students playing with a baby—with the same general results (Sidorowicz and Lunney, 1980).

Parents as Socializing Agents.   During infancy and early childhood, a child's most important source of learning is his or her parents, especially the primary caretaker, whether the mother, father, or someone else. Most parents are not aware that their words and actions contribute to their children's socialization (Culp et al., 1983). Although parents may recognize that they respond differently to sons than to daughters, they usually have a ready explanation—the "natural" differences in the temperament and behavior of girls and boys. Parents may also believe they adjust their responses to each particular child's personality. In an everyday living situation that involves changing diapers, feeding babies, stopping fights, and providing entertainment, it is difficult for harassed parents to recognize that their own actions may be largely responsible for the differences they attribute to nature.

Children are socialized in sex roles through four very subtle processes: manipulation, channeling, verbal appellation, and activity exposure (Oakley, 1972). Parents *manipulate* their children from infancy onward. They treat a daughter gently, tell her she is pretty, and advise her that nice girls do not fight. They treat a son roughly, tell him he is strong, and advise him that big boys do not cry. Eventually, children incorporate their parents' views in such matters as integral parts of their personalities. Children are *channeled* by directing their attention to specific objects. Toys, for example, are sex differentiated. Dolls are considered appropriate for girls, cars for boys. *Verbal appellation* refers to the use of different words to describe the same behavior. A boy who pushes others may be described as "active," whereas a girl who does the same is usually called "aggressive." The *activity exposure* of boys and girls differs markedly. Although both are usually exposed to feminine activities early in life, boys are discouraged from imitating their mothers, whereas girls are encouraged

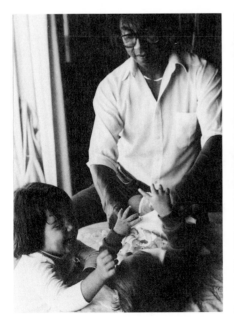

When a child observes a parent's nurturing behavior, he or she is in turn encouraged to be nurturing. If the parent and child are the same sex, the parent serves as a sex-role model for the child.

to be "mother's little helpers." In some homes even the chores children do are sex categorized. Girls may wash dishes, make beds, and set the table; boys are assigned to carry out trash, rake the yard, and sweep the walk. The boy's domestic chores take him outside the house, the girl's keep her in it—another rehearsal for traditional adult life.

Table 4–2   Stereotypic Sex Role Differences Compared to Research Findings

Stereotype	*Findings*
Perceptual Differences	
Men have: better daylight vision	Mild but in direction of stereotype.
faster reaction times	"
better depth perception	"
better spatial skills	"
are: less sensitive to extreme heat	"
more sensitive to extreme cold	"
Women have: better night vision	"
better hearing, especially in higher ranges	"
better manual dexterity and fine coordination	
are: more sensitive to touch in all parts of their body	"
less tolerant of loud sounds	"
Aggression	
Males are more aggressive.	Strong consistent differences in physical
Females are less aggressive.	aggression. Inconsistent finding with indirect aggression.
Dependency	
Females are more submissive and dependent.	Weak differences that are more consistent for
Males are more assertive and independent.	adults than for children.
Emotionality	
Females are more emotional and excitable.	Moderate differences on some measures. Overall,
Males are more controlled and less expressive.	findings inconclusive.
Verbal Skills	
Females excel in all verbal areas including reading.	Moderate differences, especially for children.
Males are less verbal and have more problems learning to read.	Moderate differences, especially for children.
Math Skills	
Males are better in mathematical skills.	Moderate differences on problem-solving tests,
Females are less interested and do less well in mathematics.	especially after adolescence.

Source: From Frank Cox, *Human Intimacy* (St. Paul, Minn.: West), 1984. Constructed from four main sources: Eleanor E. Maccoby and Carol N. Jacklin, *The Psychology of Sex Differences* (Palo Alto, Calif.: Stanford University Press), 1974; Daniel Goleman, "Special Abilities of the Sexes: Do They Begin in the Brain?" *Psychology Today*, Nov., 1978; Irene H. Frieze et al., *Women and Sex Roles* (New York: W. W. Norton), 1978; and Diane McGuiness and Karl Pribram, "The Origins of Sensory Bias in the Development of Gender Differences in Perception and Cognition," in Morton Bortner (ed.), *Cognitive Growth and Development*, essays in honor of Herbert G. Birch (New York: Brunner/Mazel), 1979.

As children get older, their social world expands and so do their sources of learning. Around the time children enter day care or kindergarten, teachers, peers, and the media (especially television) become important influences.

Teachers as Socializing Agents.   Teachers encourage different activities and abilities in boys and girls. They give children messages as to the appropriate activities for boys and for girls, such as contact sports for boys and gymnastics for girls. Academically, teachers tend to encourage boys more than girls in math and science and girls more than boys in language skills.

Although schools tend (often unintentionally) to reinforce traditional sex roles, they can also change them. As Tavris and Wade (1984) point out:

Nothing about children's classroom behavior is impervious to change. Using praise and attention as rewards, preschool teachers can get girls to be more independent and both sexes to play more with each other and select both boys' and girls' toys. The effects are surprisingly rapid; simply by moving in a particular area and giving attention to a particular type of play, a teacher, within minutes, can eliminate sex differences in play patterns that were "obvious" all semester. When the teacher withdraws attention or praise, children tend to revert rapidly to their previous sex-typed behavior. Still, the fact that such behavior can be eliminated quickly shows the enormous impact of the environment—including the teacher—on children's day-to-day conformity to sex roles.

Peers as Socializing Agents.   Peers—the child's age-mates—become especially important when children enter school. Their friends and playmates are important from grade school on throughout life. Through granting or withholding approval, they influence what games children play, what they wear, what music they listen to, what television programs they watch, what cereal they eat. Peer influence is so pervasive that it is hardly an exaggeration to say that in some cases children's peers tell them what to think, feel, and do. Although peer influence is perhaps strongest during adolescence, it is during these same years that a person needs to strengthen his or her own sense of individual identity. During adolescence parental and peer influences are in strong opposition to each other; and adolescents usually turn to their peers rather than their parents for guidance.

The Media as Socializing Agents.   The media are a powerful source of sex role learning from early childhood on. As we have seen, the top contemporary American heroes are media figures. They give us ever-present images of what it means to be a man or woman in America. But these images have little to do with the flesh-and-blood men and women that we ourselves are.

By the time a person is eighteen years old, he or she has spent more time watching television—more than sixteen thousand hours—than being in school. Children who are heavy television viewers (twenty-five hours or more a week) tend to have more stereotyped views of men and women than do light viewers (ten or less hours a week) (McGhee and Frueh, 1980). Similarly, adults who are heavy television viewers have more stereotypical sex role images than light viewers (Ross et al., 1982). Both groups see men as tough and competitive and women as gentle and noncompetitive. Men are problem solvers, creative, intelligent, authorities who give orders, people who save

If I had knowledge only of the anatomy and cultural capacities of men and women, I would predict that women rather than men would be more likely to gain control over the technology of defense and aggression, and that if one sex were going to subordinate the other, it would be female over male. While I would be impressed with the physical dimorphism—the greater height, weight, and strength of the males—I would be even more impressed by something which the females have and which the males cannot get—namely, control over the birth, care and feeding of babies. Women, in other words, control the nursery, and because they control the nursery, they can potentially modify any lifestyle that threatens them.

MARVIN HARRIS, COWS, PIGS, WARS, AND WITCHES

The media tend to be somewhat Neanderthal in its portrayal of male/female relations. The "Me-Tarzan-you-Jane" message from the media can be counterbalanced by the everyday interactions of real life.

others and are rewarded for their actions. Women, by contrast, are passive, compliant, and emotional; instead of giving orders, they obey them; instead of saving others, they themselves are saved.

Sex Role Learning in Adulthood

In adulthood, college, marriage, and the workplace provide new or different sources of sex role learning.

College.   The college and university environment, emphasizing independent behavior, contrasts markedly with the high school setting which emphasizes social conformity through dress codes and chaperoned dances and intellectual conformity through noncontroversial and watered-down subject matter.

Since a basic function of colleges and universities is the teaching of critical thought, conformity and prejudice are questioned, in some instances for the first time in a student's life. In the college setting many young adults learn to think critically, to exchange ideas, to discover the basis for their actions. In particular, in the college environment many young adults first encounter alternatives to traditional sex roles, either in their personal relationships or in their courses.

In Komarovsky's (1985) study of college women, she found that when students entered college as many as two-thirds suffered culture shock. Sex roles tended to become more liberal, and strongly traditional first-year women found themselves on the defensive. Male-female relationships were often transformed. A representative example was one young woman who, in high school, had believed that popularity with boys was the most important goal. Her self-esteem was linked to being sexually attractive. In college, however, she found that political and intellectual discussion was more satisfying than "partying." More important, she found that male approval was not her classmates' main goal in life. Her classmates felt free to disagree with men and did not change their manner whenever a man appeared on the scene.

Marriage.   Marriage is an important source of sex role learning. For many individuals, no one is more important than their partner for shaping sex role behaviors through interaction. Our partner has expectations of how we should act as a male or female and these expectations are important in shaping behavior.

If you would marry suitably, marry your equal.

OVID (43 B.C.–18 A.D.)

The role of provider is probably the primary traditional marital role for men, reinforcing the male-as-worker role. A man may evaluate himself both as a male and as a husband/father through his work identity and earning power. Even if a man's partner works, he still tends to identify himself as the provider (Weiss, 1985). Another man may come into marriage with the belief that he is the unchallenged head of the household, but interactions with his partner may lead him to see his role as an equal partner sharing power in the marriage.

For women, entrance into marriage gives two key adult roles: woman as wife and woman as mother. Although women today have greater latitude as wives—it is acceptable to work outside the home—they are still under considerable pressure to become mothers. Once a woman becomes a mother, she is likely to leave the work force until her youngest child enters kindergarten. Even young girls recognize this pressure and accept the notion of working until the arrival of the first child and then combining work and motherhood as the children get older (Archer, 1985). Once children are born, roles tend to become more traditional, even in nontraditional marriages. The wife remains at home, at least for a time, and the husband works. (For a college woman's personal views on choosing motherhood, see the reading "A Woman's Choice: Becoming a Parent" by Lisa Brown.)

The Workplace.   Workplaces have their own cultures that influence the way workers and managers feel about themselves as men and women.

It is fairly well established that men and women are psychologically affected by their occupations (Tavris and Wade, 1984). Work that encourages self-direction, for example, makes people more active, flexible, open, and democratic; restrictive jobs tend to lower self-esteem and make people more rigid and less tolerant. If we realize that female occupations are usually low status with little room for self-direction, then we can understand why women are not as achievement oriented as males. Because men and women have different opportunities for promotion, they have different attitudes toward achievement. Women typically downplay any desire for promotion, suggesting that promotions would interfere with their family responsibilities. But this may be related to a need to protect themselves from frustration, since most women are in dead-end jobs in which promotion to management positions are unlikely. One researcher found that when men's opportunities for advancement are blocked, they act in a stereotypical female manner: they express little interest in their jobs, emphasize their families over their work, and are indifferent to advancement (Kanter, 1976).

Household work affects women psychologically in many of the same ways that paid work does in female-dominated occupations (such as clerical and service occupations) (Schooler, 1984). Women in both situations feel greater levels of frustration owing to the repetitive nature of the work, time pressures, and being held responsible for things outside their control. Such circumstances do not encourage self-esteem, creativity, or a desire to achieve.

☐ TRADITIONAL SEX ROLES

Male in America

In every real man a child is hidden that wants to play.

FRIEDRICH NIETZSCHE (1844–1900)

Much is expected from boys simply because they are boys. (See Tables 4–1 and 4–2 for listing of sex role stereotypes.) We assume that boys will become men of destiny, while girls will become mothers. Pride in being male is instilled in boys to give them courage for the difficulties ahead. Thus *man's* history as recorded by *men* reaches heroic proportions. Men have dominated politics, the arts, religion, philosophy, industry, and commerce for thousands of years. Men make the laws, fight the wars, and write the histories that praise men for the laws and the wars they make and fight.

Rabbi Zusya said that on the Day of Judgment, God would ask him, not why he had not been Moses, but why he had not been Zusya.

WALTER KAUFMANN

The Male Image. What is it to be a "real" man in America? Bruce Feirstein parodied him in *Real Men Don't Eat Quiche* (1982):

QUESTION: How many Real Men does it take to change a light bulb?
ANSWER: None. Real Men aren't afraid of the dark.

QUESTION: Why did the Real Man cross the road?
ANSWER: It's none of your damn business.

In the last ten years, there has been growing interest in exaggerated masculinity, of which male body building is one aspect. In the media, "real men" such as Conan and Rambo are distinguished by their pectorals rather than their personalities.

This humor contains something both familiar and chilling. Feirstein discovered to his amazement that people were taking his book seriously. While appearing on a radio phone-in show, he received calls "like [from] the guy in Dallas who wanted to know what kind of gun a Real Man carries" (Mehren, 1982). Being a male in America carries a certain uneasiness. Men often feel they need advice about how to act out their male roles; they are unsure of what it means to be masculine.

No single image of the "real man" exists in our society. Instead, we have a number of images that are distinctly masculine: the football player, the jet-set playboy, the blue-collar brawler, the big-shot businessman, the Don Juan, the strong, simple workingman, the great man (David and Brannon, 1976). Stereotypes, however, have a significant impact on how men feel about themselves. David and Brannon described the stereotypes below.

- No Sissy Stuff: the stigma of all stereotyped feminine characteristics and qualities, including openness and vulnerability
- The Big Wheel: success, status, and the need to be looked up to
- The Sturdy Oak: a manly air of toughness, confidence, and self-reliance
- Give 'Em Hell!: the aura of aggression, violence, and daring.

Men and Work. A central part of the male identity is work. Ask any man about himself, and within a few moments he will be talking about what he does as a automobile worker, businessman, miner, engineer, writer, lawyer, sales clerk, and so on. In general conversation, if he does not talk about sports or politics, he will more likely talk about work than about his family. (See the reading by Jack Balswick and Charles Peek, "The Inexpressive Male.")

The male's work identity affects his family role as a husband or father. As we have noted, most men see their primary family function as provider, which takes precedence over all other family functions such as nurturing and caring for children, housework, preparing meals, being intimate, and so on. Because of this focus, men are often confused by their spouses' expectations of intimacy; they feel they are good husbands simply because they are good providers (Rubin, 1983).

Female in America

To be a "real" woman in America is to be young, beautiful, thin, compliant, and adoring. When she leaves adolescence the "real" woman gets married and has children, finding her total fulfillment in being a wife and mother. When she gets older she must deny the effects of aging (with the help of the cosmetic industry and the plastic surgeon).

The Female Image. The steps toward becoming a real woman are described by Helen Andelin, an advocate of traditional sex roles, in *Fascinating Womanhood* (1974):

Attitude: In acquiring femininity, you must first dispense with any air of strength and ability, of competence and fearlessness, and acquire instead an attitude of frail dependency. . . .

Femininity expresses the idea that there are things worth living for. Masculinity expresses the idea that there are things worth dying for.

JOHN WHEELER, *TOUCHED WITH FIRE*

The tendency to identify manhood with a capacity for physical violence has a long history in America.

MARSHALL FISHWICK

Why is it men are permitted to be obsessed about their work, but women are only permitted to be obsessed about men?

BARBRA STREISAND

Man's love is of man's life a part; it is woman's whole existence.

LORD BYRON (1788–1824)

When women are clearly subordinate, when they don't seek
to change their social status,
men seem free to delight in
them as physical beings. At
such a time, voluptuous
women may be welcome. But
in an age when women assert
their claim to power and autonomy, men have a different
response. The culture calls for
fashions that reflect a distinct
male fear of a mature woman's
power, particularly as it expresses itself through a woman's large body. . . . A woman
who wishes to conform to her
culture's ideal, in this age of
female assertion, will not be
large, mature, voluptuous,
strong or powerful. She . . . is
to make herself look like an
adolescent girl if she wishes to
appease her culture's anxiety
about female power.

KIM CHERNIN

The great question . . . which
I have not been able to answer,
despite my thirty years of research into the feminine soul,
is "What does a woman
want?"

SIGMUND FREUD

It is amazing how complete is
the delusion that beauty is
goodness.

LEO TOLSTOY

Stop doing the masculine work: Next, you will have to stop doing the man's work—stop lifting heavy boxes, moving furniture, mowing the lawn, painting, fixing motors, cleaning cars, changing tires, carpentry, or anything which is masculine responsibility. . . .

If stuck with a masculine job, do it in a feminine manner: . . . It is not up to you to perform masculine tasks with the skill that men do. . . . If you can do a job as well as a man can, he will never come to your rescue. . . .

Be submissive: . . . To be feminine, a woman must be yielding to her husband's rule, opinions, discretion, or judgment of another, or others. . . .

Don't subdue fearfulness: Feminine women tend to have a natural fear of dangers. They are afraid of snakes . . . bugs, spiders, mice, the dark, and strange noises, much to the amusement of men. . . .

Don't try to excel him: . . . Don't compete with men in anything which requires masculine ability. . . . Don't compete with them for scholastic honors in men's subjects. It may be all right to win over a man in English or social studies, but you are in trouble if you compete with a man in math, chemistry, public speaking, etc. . . .

Need his care and protection: Let him open doors for you, help you on with your coat, pull up your chair. . . . If he does not offer his help . . . then work on the other parts of femininity until he does. . . .

Live your feminine role: Perhaps in no way can a woman develop her femininity more than by living her feminine role as the wife, mother, and homemaker. . . .

Probably, there are no more "real" women in America than "real" men; few of either exist in reality. But the idea of the "real" woman places a burden on *real* women, who may feel inadequate because they don't fit the stereotypical image.

Women and Work. While the traditional roles for women have typically been those of wife and mother, in recent years an additional role has been added: woman as worker. The role of wage earner may appear to conflict with more traditional female roles, but often it does not. Indeed, the general expectation is that most women will be gainfully employed at various times in their lives. Work has become integrated into traditional female sex roles for the following reasons. First, work generally is not expected to take precedence over the functioning of women in their roles as wives and mothers. Women tend to work before they are married; when they marry, they generally continue working; but even if they are working full time, society continues to expect women to remain responsible for housework and child care. When a woman's first child arrives, the role of mother is expected to take priority over the role of worker. This expectation continues until the youngest child reaches at least school age. Second, women's work is generally in lower-status occupations than that of males—mainly in clerical or service fields where they do not directly compete with men for jobs or wages. Third, and perhaps most significant, industry needs a readily available pool of inexpensive labor, and families increasingly need to have two wage earners to make ends meet.

☐ LIMITATIONS OF TRADITIONAL SEX ROLES

Men's Limitations

Men are required to work and to support their families. The male as provider is probably a man's central role in marriage, accepted by himself and expected by his wife and children. In fulfilling his role, he does not have the freedom to *choose* to work as women have. Work and family life are often in conflict for men. When the man's role as worker and father come into conflict, usually it is the father role that suffers (Weiss, 1985). If a factory worker needs to spend time with his children to lighten his wife's burdens, his job does not allow flexibility. Because he must provide income for his family, he will not be able to be more involved in his parenting. In a familiar scene, a little boy comes into the father's study to play and the father says, "Not now. I'm busy working. I'll play with you later." When the boy returns, the "not-now-I'm-busy" is repeated. The scene occurs throughout the boy's growing up until one day, as his son leaves home, the father realizes that he never got to know him.

Emotionally, men have greater difficulty expressing their feelings than women do. Men cry less and show love, happiness, and sadness less (Balswick, 1980; Lombardo et al., 1983). When men do express their feelings, they do it more forcefully, domineeringly, and boastfully; women, in contrast, tend to express their feelings more gently and quietly (Kramarae, 1981).

When a woman asks a man how he feels, a common response is "I don't know" or "Nothing." These men have lost touch with their inner lives because they have repressed feelings that they have learned are inappropriate. Male inexpressiveness often makes men strangers to both themselves and their partners.

Men are taught to be instrumental, to be the ones who act, but the male sense of power and command does not facilitate personal relationships. Men who are unable to achieve power in their work relationships may seek power and status at home, displacing their frustration and anger into their personal relationships. But under such circumstances—without mutual respect and equality—genuine intimacy is difficult to achieve. One cannot control another person and at the same time be intimate with that person. Middle-class men often talk about egalitarian marriages but allow their partners relatively less power in the marital relationship. A tension exists between ideology and reality.

Although men generally hold greater power in personal relationships, they often may not realize it. Simone de Beauvoir (1952) wrote that many men believe themselves oppressed by women—as witnessed by the popular image of the henpecked husband. This feeling may derive directly from the denial of full equality to women. If, for example, the husband must earn the money, then the wife must demand the paycheck. If wives are kept out of the professions, then they may demand that their husbands be successful. The husband must give his wife more to compensate for her inequality, lack of economic control, and frustration. In denying equality to women, men become oppressed themselves because dependent women may make oppressive demands on their men. De Beauvoir explored this paradox in which men see themselves as victims and their wives as parasites. She wrote:

If he seems to be the victim, it is because his burdens are most evident; woman is supported by him like a parasite; but a parasite is not a conquering master. . . . If it is asserted that men

The wimp is the man who has a social conscience, who can understand the oppression of women, who is warm and caring, who fixes the family's meals after a rough day at the office. Women don't view such men as wimps; only other men see them that way.

LUCIA GILBERT

All males, without exception, whatever their age, suffer from penis rivalry . . . this trait has now become a threat to the future existence of the human race. . . . Today our phallic toys have become too dangerous to be tolerated. I see little hope for a peaceful world until men are excluded from the realm of foreign policy altogether and all decisions concerning international relations are reserved for women, preferably married ones.

W. H. AUDEN

oppress women, the husband is indignant; he *feels* that *he* is the one oppressed—and he is; but the fact is that it is the masculine code, it is the society developed by the males in their interest that has established woman's torment for both sexes.

Women's Limitations

There is considerable evidence that the traditional female sex role does not facilitate self-confidence or mental health. Both men and women tend to see women as less competent than men. One study found that women generally predicted they would not do as well on a test as the men taking the same test (Erkut, 1983). Another study of 1,850 men and women found that women had significantly lower self-esteem (Hoelter, 1983). (See the reading by Susan Brownmiller, "Femininity in the 1980's.")

Because of difference in sex roles, Bernard (1972) has suggested that each sex experiences marriage differently. There is, she argued, a "his" and "her" marriage. Men appear to be more satisfied in marriage than women (Rettig and Bubolz, 1983). More wives than husbands report frustration, dissatisfaction, marital problems, and desire for divorce. More wives than husbands experience anxiety or feel they are on the edge of a nervous breakdown; more wives blame themselves for their poor adjustment than do husbands (Mugford and Lally, 1981; Rubenstein, 1982). Unmarried women, Bernard suggested, tend to be happier and better adjusted than married women. (For a critique of "his" and "her" marriages, see Schvum, 1985.)

Finally, femininity is intimately tied to youth and beauty. As women get older, they tend to be regarded as more masculine. A young woman, for example, is "beautiful" but an older woman is "handsome." As Susan Brownmiller (1984) pointed out in her book *Femininity*,

Femininity is not something that improves with age, for girlishness, with its innocent modesty, its unthreatening impudence, and its promise of ripe sexuality in the rosy future, typifies the feminine principle at its best. Women who rely on a feminine strategy as their chief means of survival can do little to stop the roaring tide of maturity as they watch their advantage slip by.

Culture treats aging in men and women differently: as men age, they become distinguished; as women age, they get older. Men have an advantage in aging, while women are penalized for it. (See Feature, "The Double Standard of Aging," pp. 108–109.)

Resistance to Change

Discussions about the limitations of traditional sex roles often focus on the oppression of females by males. Although males generally hold more political and economic power than women, the question of who oppresses whom is not a simple one to answer. Perhaps it is not even the best question to ask. Collier and Williams (1981) observed:

Both [men and women] are equally constrained in the choices of behavior open to them. The male is imprisoned by his own and society's expectations of him as is the female by her own and society's expectations of her.

Women have served all these centuries, as looking glasses possessing the magic and delicious power of reflecting the figure of man at twice its natural size.

VIRGINIA WOOLF, A ROOM OF ONE'S OWN

If you are a married woman, very frequently you're asked who is going to take care of your children, how does your husband feel about your running [for political office]. That's a question a married man's never asked. . . . If [women are] single, the question is, "Why aren't you married?" Again, this is not asked of a single man.

GERALDINE FERRARO

When man lives he is soft and tender; when he is dead he is hard and tough. All living plants and animals are tender and fragile; when dead they become withered and dry. Thus it is said: The hard and tough are parts of death; the soft and tender are parts of life. This is the reason why soldiers when they are too tough cannot carry the day; when the tree is too tough it will break. The position of the strong and great is low, but the position of the weak and tender is high.

LAO-TSE (7th CENTURY B.C.)

Males interacting with other males reinforce "male" behavior patterns. Female interactions follow a parallel pattern. Similarly, females support idealized norms for males equally as much as males do for females. Thus males and females unconsciously and *bilaterally* function as agents of oppression . . . as they interact from day to day and moment to moment.

Despite the limitations traditional sex roles place on us, changing them is not easy. Sex roles are closely linked to self-evaluation. Our sense of adequacy depends on sex role performance as defined by parents and peers in childhood: "You're a good boy/ girl." Because sex roles often seem to be an intrinsic part of our personality and temperament, we may defend these roles as being natural even if the roles are destructive to a relationship or to ourselves. To threaten an individual's sex role is to threaten his or her sexual identity, since people do not generally make the distinction between sex role and gender identity. Such threats are an important psychological mechanism keeping people in traditional but dysfunctional sex roles.

Lillian Rubin (1983), a prominent psychologist, described her own difficulty in changing roles when her husband changed careers to become a writer and she assumed the primary provider role in the family. At first her husband was relieved to be freed from the financial responsibilities he had assumed for so many years. Then he fell into a six-month depression. Although Rubin was already a successful therapist, writer, and researcher, something in her life "had been altered profoundly." She grew angry. Her work was no longer voluntary. It was necessary to support the family, and she began to hate it. Rubin was stunned by her reaction. She and her husband had planned and agreed on the change; both felt he should be free to pursue his own interests. She wrote:

But speaking the words and living the results are two different things. Suddenly we found ourselves face to face with our inner sense of the way things *ought* to be. Suddenly, we had to confront the realization that we were still dominated by the stereotypic images of male and female roles—images we would have sworn we had, by then, routed from our consciousness.

He struggled with his sense of failure, with the fear that somehow his very manhood had been damaged. I—the liberated, professional woman—was outraged and enraged that he wasn't taking care of me any longer. I felt as if he had violated some basic contract with which we had lived, as if he had failed in his most fundamental task in life—to keep me safe and cared for, to protect and support me.

People can accept minor changes, Rubin found, but deep ones are more difficult.

Smaller changes may be tolerated quite easily. But one that puts a woman in a position of economic superiority and a man in the dependent female role is quite another matter. Most men still can't cope with not being able to support the family, and most women still have difficulty in accepting the need to support themselves.

Instead of seeking to blame one sex for the victimization of the other, we should try to understand the constraints placed on both sexes by rigid sex role stereotyping. What are the costs for males and females? Do traditional sex roles help us become more human or less human? Do they help us to love? To rear children well? To realize our potential?

We unwittingly set the stage for feelings of inadequacy and inferiority. The more rigidly we define ourselves the less likely we are able to cope with the infinite variety of life.

ERNEST ROSSI, *DREAMS AND THE GROWTH OF PERSONALITY*

Treat people as if they were what they ought to be and you help them become what they are capable of being.

JOHANN GOETHE (1749–1832)

The perpetual obstacle to human advancement is custom.

JOHN STUART MILL

Everybody wants to be somebody; nobody wants to grow.

JOHANN GOETHE

Young girls often dress up and play fantasy games that exaggerate their adult roles as women. They may also engage in activities that are traditionally reserved for boys in our culture. In middle childhood, girls are given greater leeway than boys in engaging in cross-sex activities. Such girls are accepted as "tomboys," while boys playing house, for example, are ridiculed as "sissies." But when girls reach adolescence, they experience greater pressure to conform to traditional female stereotypes.

☐ CHANGING CONCEPTS OF SEX ROLES

Bipolar Sex Roles

We forfeit three-fourths of ourselves to be like other people.

ARTHUR SCHOPENHAUER
(1788–1860)

The traditional view of masculinity and femininity is bipolar: masculinity and femininity are opposites, or mirror images, of each other. Our popular terminology reflects this. When people speak of members of the other sex, they speak of the "opposite" sex, suggesting that each sex has little in common with the other. Our sex role stereotypes fit this bipolar pattern, as we have seen: men, aggressive; women, passive; men instrumental; women, expressive; and so on. According to this view of sex roles, a *real* man possesses exclusively masculine traits and behaviors and a *real* woman possesses exclusively feminine traits and behaviors. Because the sexes have little in common, a "war of the sexes" is the norm.

But this older conception does not account for many people having traits ascribed to both sexes and still feeling profoundly masculine or feminine (Heilbrun, 1981). When people believe individuals should not have attributes of the other sex, males suppress their expressive traits and females suppress their instrumental traits. As a result, the range of human behaviors is limited by a person's sex role. Sandra Bem (1975) has argued that "our current system of sex role differentiation has long since outlived its usefulness, and . . . now serves only to prevent both men and women from developing as full and complete human beings."

Are men and women as different as traditional sex role stereotypes portray us? Certainly, we are different biologically and anatomically. Men impregnate and women gestate; men have penises and women have vulvas. But if we reflect on our own lives, whether we are male or female, we will see that men and women have much in common. If we are men, we seek intimacy as well as achievement, and if we are women we seek achievement as well as intimacy. We contain both "masculine" and "feminine" elements.

Today our ideas of what it means to be male and female are changing. For many, the old sex roles seem archaic, limiting, inappropriate, even dehumanizing. Confusion abounds. What is the new vision of being male and female in America?

Androgynous Sex Roles

Recent research on sex roles has rejected the traditional masculine-feminine dichotomy, looking instead at sex roles in terms of *androgyny* and *gender schema*. *Androgyny* is derived from the Greek *andros*, meaning "man," and *gyne*, meaning "woman." An *androgynous* person combines both masculine and feminine traits. An androgynous life style allows men and women to choose from the full range of emotions and behaviors, according to their temperaments and common humanity rather than their sex. Males may be expressive. They are permitted to cry and display tenderness; they can touch, feel, and nurture without being called "effeminate." Women can express the instrumental aspects of their personalities without fear of disapproval. They can be aggressive or career oriented; they can seek leadership, be mechanical or physical. Both sexes are permitted to express the traits that have previously been reserved only for the other sex. Both may express their maleness and their femaleness (see Zolla, 1981, for a discussion of androgyny in art and myth).

In Oriental philosophy the yin and yang represent the male and female principles which come together to form the whole. Both men and women partake of the opposite principle.

There is considerable evidence that androgynous individuals and couples have greater ability to form and sustain intimate relationships and adopt a wider range of behaviors and values. Androgynous college students and older individuals tend to have greater confidence in social situations than sex-typed individuals (Puglisi and Jackson, 1981; Spence et al., 1975). Also, androgynous couples may have greater satisfaction in their relationships than sex-typed couples. One study found that androgynous couples felt more commitment and satisfaction in their relationships than sex-typical couples (Stephen and Harrison, 1985). Even those couples in which only one partner was androgynous expressed greater satisfaction. Transcending traditional male and female behaviors and values, the androgynous couples were more flexible in their responses to each other and to the environment. As Sandra Bem (1974) observed in her pioneering study on androgyny, "In a society where rigid sex role differentiation has already outlived its utility, perhaps the androgynous person will come to define a more human standard of psychological health."

All are but parts of one stupendous whole
Whose body nature is, and God the soul.

ALEXANDER POPE (1688–1744)

Gender Schema

Although gender is not inherent in inanimate objects or in behavior, we treat both objects and behavior as if they were masculine or feminine or in some way related to gender. These gender divisions form a complex structure of associations that affect our perceptions of reality. Bem (1983) referred to this cognitive organization of the world by gender as *gender schema*. As we are socialized, we learn more than what constitutes appropriate behavior for males and females, Bem pointed out. Not only do we perceive males and females according to gender, but we also categorize much

All the world's a stage
And all the men and women
   merely players:
They have their exits and their
   entrances;
And one man in his time plays
   many parts,
His acts being seven ages. At
   first the infant,
Mewling and puking in the
   nurse's arms.
Then the whining school-boy,
   with his satchel
And shining morning face,
   creeping like snail
Unwillingly to school. And
   then the lover,
Sighing like furnace, with a
   woeful ballad
Made to his mistress's eyebrow.
   Then a soldier,
Full of strange oaths, and
   bearded like the pard,
Jealous in honor, sudden and
   quick in quarrel,
Seeking the bubble reputation,
Even in the cannon's mouth.
   And then the justice,
In fair round belly with good
   capon lined,
with eyes severe and beard of
   formal cut,
Full of wise saws and modern
   instances;
And so he plays his part. The
   sixth age shifts
Into the lean and slippered
   pantaloon,
With spectacles on nose and
   pouch on side,
His youthful hose, well saved,
   a world too wide
For his shrunk shank; and his
   big manly voice,
Turning again toward childish
   treble, pipes
And whistles in his sound.
   Last scene of all,
That ends this strange eventful
   history,
Is second childishness and
   mere oblivion,
Sans teeth, sans eyes, sans
   taste, sans every thing.

WILLIAM SHAKESPEARE, AS
   YOU LIKE IT

of the world by gender—jobs, toys, clothes, mannerisms, and so on. Mining is man's work, housework is woman's work; dolls are girls' toys, trucks are boys' toys; dresses are women's clothes, neckties are men's clothes; women walk with hips swaying, men stride forcefully; pink is feminine, blue masculine. Many languages even divide inanimate things into masculine and feminine. We think of America as a feminine entity. Regardless of their sex, we tend to think of cats as feminine and dogs as masculine. Both Freudian and Jungian psychology interpret symbols as masculine or feminine: spears and locomotives are masculine, for example, while oceans and houses are feminine.

Androgyny, like other personality theories, assumes that masculinity and femininity are basic aspects of an individual's personality. When we are active, we are expressing the masculine side of ourselves; when we are sensitive, we are expressing the feminine side of our personality. Living up to an androgynous sex role may be just as stultifying to an individual as trying to be traditionally masculine or feminine. In advocating the expression of both masculine and feminine traits, perhaps we are imposing a new form of sex-role rigidity on ourselves. Bem, who was one of the leading proponents of androgyny, has become increasingly critical of the idea. She believes now that androgyny replaces "a prescription to be masculine or feminine with the doubly incarcerating prescription to be masculine and feminine. The individual now has not one but two potential sources of inadequacy to contend with (Bem, 1983).

Perhaps the solution is to do away with the concept of masculine and feminine altogether. Gender schema, Bem argues, is not inevitable. In many cultures the masculine-feminine division is not as significant as it is in American culture. Instrumental and expressive traits should not be regarded as male or female traits but as human traits. Distinctions between the sexes should be based on anatomical and reproductive aspects of the person, not on personality characteristics.

☐ AGE ROLES

Few people realize how much age structures society. In all societies age is one of the key ways in which people are grouped. Individuals tend to associate with other people of the same age: we generally date and marry those in the same age group; we belong to clubs and other groups with others who are the same general age; and we go to school with people the same age. In many African and native American cultures, age groups are formalized in an age-graded system in which participation in particular societal activities—such as hunting, warfare, or religious ceremonies—is determined on the basis of age. In our culture "grade school," is an example of an age-grade activity.

Age and Expectations

Like sex roles, age roles have their basis in biology. Aging is a biological process, but we give it social meaning. As with sex roles, what is appropriate for certain ages in our culture is inappropriate in other cultures. An American fifteen-year-old is defined as an adolescent: he or she is probably unmarried, living at home under parental authority, and given little responsibility. But a fifteen-year-old in certain African tribes may already be a mother or a father, living separately from his or her own parents,

UNDERSTANDING YOURSELF

Learning Your Sex Role

Think about your sex roles. Would you describe yourself as masculine, feminine, or androgynous? Why? Do you have traits associated with the other sex? What are they? How do you feel about them? Do you consider them beneficial or not? How do other people respond to them?

How did your parents influence the development of your sex role? In what ways did you model yourself after your same-sex parent? In what ways are your conceptions of the appropriate sex role similar or different?

During high school, what influence did your peers have on your sex role development? How

important were your boyfriends/girlfriends in developing your sense of yourself as a female or male? What traits did they encourage or discourage? How is college different? Do you find your ideas about sex roles changing? In what ways?

Who are the people that most influence you today? Are they friends, teachers, parents, or media figures? What are the traits you admire in them? Are these traits similar to those you would like to have in a boyfriend/girlfriend or partner? In yourself?

with the rights and obligations of adulthood. The African adolescent is treated as an adult; the American teenager is still treated as a child (although the American teenager may already be chafing at the restraints imposed by parents).

Age and sex roles are closely related in our society. Age provides a rough timetable for our assuming the different aspects of our male and female sex roles. By age five, as we have seen, boys are expected to start acting in distinctly masculine ways; girls, however, have a grace period that may reach to puberty. But by the time they leave high school, both girls and boys are expected to act completely feminine or masculine. Family roles are also graded by age as well as by sex: a woman is generally expected to be married and a mother by age twenty-five; a man has more leeway in getting married and becoming a father, although he is expected to begin a career in his early twenties: "You can't play around forever, son. You've got to get a job," a father says to his twenty-two-year-old son. A woman's "career" is more often seen in terms of marriage.

Males are not only expected to act masculine; they are also expected to "act their age." Being masculine is different at age twenty than it is at age forty. A twenty-year-old man can be unruly, wild, spontaneous, and unmarried. But at forty he should be married, a father, dignified, settled down in his life and career. The expectations for a twenty-year-old woman differ from those for a woman who is forty. A twenty-year-old woman can be single, live experimentally, travel abroad, study. But at forty she had better be married and preferably a mother, for an unmarried woman of that age is looked on with suspicion. People who do not fulfill the age expectations of their sex role are called "immature" or "irresponsible"; children who act older than their age are called "precocious"; an older person who acts younger than his or her age role is "recapturing youth" or else "regressing to childhood." The most familiar reminders to people to fulfill their age roles are "grow up," "act your age,"

One's only real life is the life one never leads.

OSCAR WILDE (1854–1900)

FEATURE

The Double Standard of Aging

Due to the double standard of aging (as with the double standard of sex), women are shortchanged. Society is more tolerant of men who deviate from its standards than of women who do so. Masculinity is associated with independence, assertiveness, self-control, physical ability; with the exception of physical ability, none of these traits necessarily decrease with age. For the most part they intensify as one gains more experience in the world. But femininity is closely associated with attractiveness. Susan Sontag (1972) writes:

Being physically attractive counts much more in a woman's life than in a man's life, but beauty, identified as it is for women, with youthfulness, does not stand up well to age . . . "Femininity" is identified with incompetence, helplessness, passivity, non-competitiveness, being nice. Age does not improve these qualities.

From the beginning of dating in adolescence, girls tend to go out with boys their same age or older. When young women enter college, they generally go out with older men; for example, 18-year-old women often date 21-year-old men. In college, this situation leaves first-year men and senior women with much smaller groups from which to acquire dating partners. When Americans marry, a man is likely to marry a woman his same age or younger (in 85 percent of marriages this is the case; in 75 percent of marriages, the wife is less than five years younger than the husband). Less than 3 percent of the marriages in America include women who are five or more years older than the husband (Udry, 1974).

The explanation for women marrying older men is related to sex roles. Traditionally a woman's social status has depended on her husband's; he works and achieves status that reflects on her. Many women have therefore preferred to marry older men, who have probably worked longer and acquired greater status than younger men. Men have traditionally favored younger women because physical attractiveness is an important aspect of male mate selection processes and our society links the attractiveness of women to their youth.

"act maturely." These reminders are similar to "be a man" or "act like a lady," which many people have heard throughout their lives. Whereas acting masculine or feminine relates to a person's self-identity, acting your age relates to the fulfillment of societal obligations such as being married or having a job.

Age and Self-Evaluation

Life is a country that the old have seen, and lived in. Those who have to travel through it can only learn from them.

JOSEPH JOUBERT (1754–1824)

Age is one of the measures we use to evaluate ourselves by comparing our present life against earlier expectations. Neugarten (1972) observed:

It has become increasingly evident that each person interprets his present situation in terms of what his expectations have been. Man is a thinking and planning animal, he looks around, compares himself with others, anticipates, then compares reality with his anticipations. . . . The statement "I am 50 years old" has little significance; but, "I am 50 years old and farther ahead than I expected to be," or "farther behind than other men in the same line of work" [do have significance]. In such everyday phrases, the individual gives content and meaning to the passage of time.

FEATURE–*continued*

This arrangement places women at a disadvantage in several respects. First of all, if a woman marries a man older than herself, she is more likely to become a widow with many years left in her own life. In itself, the loneliness of widowhood can be a burden; but above and beyond that, it is more difficult for a widow than a widower to find a new partner. Her pool of eligible partners is limited to those of her own age or older. If she were a man, however, she could choose not only from those of her own age group but also from those who are younger. As women get older, they become less eligible for marriage because they are considered to have lost their attractiveness and because they have fewer potential partners. Women may also be at a disadvantage erotically. From the age of 18 on, men experience a declining interest in sexual contact. There is no such drastic decline for women; their sexual interest appears to increase in their mid-thirties (Kinsey, 1953). Thus, women are much more likely to find themselves sexually unsatisfied from middle age on. They often have stronger sexual desire than their mates, which may partly account for the increase in extramarital affairs among women as they reach their thirties and forties.

Self-evaluation against age appears to be crucial on certain birthdays that people often anticipate with anxiety: the twenty-first, thirtieth, thirty-fifth, fortieth, fiftieth, sixtieth, and sixty-fifth. Each birthday has its particular significance. The twenty-first signifies entering adulthood, whereas the thirtieth represents leaving youth behind. By the thirty-fifth birthday many people feel that half their lives have been lived, and the fortieth is the beginning of middle age. The fiftieth marks half a century, the sixtieth the beginning of old age, and the sixty-fifty the beginning of retirement, when a person is no longer deemed useful by society. Gail Sheehy (1975) refers to these ages as marking "predictable crises of adult life." They are times for role change, adaptation, reflection, and a growing awareness of the aging process itself. What has been accomplished so far in one's life? Has life been full or empty? The milestones of the aging process remind us that life is finite—that we must become now what we are capable of becoming. Think about your age and age roles. What is expected of you at this point in your life? What is expected five years from now? Ten years?

> When your friends begin to flatter you on how young you look, it's a sure sign you're getting old.
>
> MARK TWAIN

> Growing old isn't so bad when you consider the alternative.
>
> MAURICE CHEVALIER

☐ SUMMARY

- Sex roles are changing, especially for women. The ideal man and woman described by both sexes are remarkably similar.

- *Gender identity* is based on genitalia. *Sex roles* are the roles that tell us how we are to act as men and women. Sex roles are culturally relative, whereas gender identity is not.

- The two most important socialization theories are *social learning* and *cognitive-developmental theories*. Social learning emphasizes the learning of behavior from others through positive and negative reinforcement and modeling. Reinforcement takes place through the use of symbols, anticipation of consequences, and observation. Modeling is the imitation of the behavior of powerful figures.

Cognitive-developmental theory asserts that once children learn that gender is permanent, they independently strive to act like a "proper" boy or girl because of an internal need for congruence.

- Children learn their sex roles through *manipulation, channeling, verbal appellation,* and *activity exposure.* Parents, teachers, peers, and the media are important agents of socialization during childhood and adolescence.

- During adulthood, parental influence declines. For students, colleges and universities are important sources for sex role learning, especially for nontraditional roles. The workplace and marriage also influence the development of adult sex roles.

- Traditional male sex roles have certain core requirements, which can be labeled "no sissy stuff," "the big wheel," "the sturdy oak," and "give 'em hell!" Male models for relationships tend to be based on power; males tend to be less expressive of feelings than females.

- Traditional female roles emphasize passivity, compliance, physical attractiveness, and being a wife and mother. Work outside the home is acceptable as long as it does not interfere with other traditional role components.

- Changing sex role behavior is often difficult because each sex reinforces the traditional roles of its own and the other sex, because we evaluate ourselves in terms of fulfilling sex role concepts, and because we have internalized sex roles.

- *Androgyny* combines traditional male and female characteristics into a more flexible pattern of behavior, rather than seeing them as opposites. Evidence suggests that androgyny contributes to psychological and emotional health. Some researchers, however, believe that *gender schema,* which divides objects, activities, and behaviors into masculine and feminine categories, may impose a double burden of expectation on people. An alternative is to discard the idea of instrumental and expressive traits as masculine and feminine and think of them as human traits.

- Aging is a biological process that is given social meaning. Age roles are often closely aligned with sex roles. Society has definite expectations of people depending on their age as well as their sex. We use age as a measure of self-evaluation.

- Each age is marked by "predictable crises"—times of role change, adaptation, and reflection.

READINGS

The Inexpressive Male

JACK BALSWICK AND CHARLES PEEK, *THE FAMILY COORDINATOR*

*In this excerpt, the authors argue that men do not express
emotions to women. What evidence do they offer for this
view? Is their generalization valid? Why? Are Rambo,
Dirty Harry, and Rocky extensions of the "cowboy type" or
are they fundamentally different? The authors also suggest
that male inexpressiveness may be modified in marriage.
What function does this modification serve for marital stability? What are the benefits and costs of this modification?*

The Inexpresive Male as a Single Man

At least two basic types of inexpressive male seem to result
from this socialization process: the cowboy and the playboy.
Manville has referred to the *cowboy type* in terms of
a "John Wayne Neurosis" which stresses the strong, silent
and two-fisted male as the 100 percent American he-man.
For present purposes, it is especially in his relationship
with women that the John Wayne neurosis is particularly
significant in representing many American males. As portrayed by Wayne in any one of his many type-cast roles, the
mark of a real man is that he does not show any tenderness
or affection toward girls because his culturally-acquired
male image dictates that such a show of emotions would be
distinctly unmanly. If he does have anything to do with
girls, it is on a "man to man" basis: the girl is treated
roughly (but not sadistically), with little hint of gentleness
or affection. As Manville puts it:

> "The on-screen John Wayne doesn't feel comfortable
> around women. He does like them sometimes—God
> knows he's not *queer*. But at the right time, and in the
> right place—which he chooses. And always with his car/
> horse parked directly outside, in/on which he will ride
> away to his more important business back in Marlboro
> country."

Alfred Auerback, a psychiatrist, has commented more directly on the cowboy type. He describes the American male's inexpressiveness with women as part of the
"cowboy syndrome." He quite rightly states that "the cowboy in moving pictures has conveyed the image of the rug-
ged 'he-man,' strong, resilient, resourceful, capable of
coping with overwhelming odds. His attitude toward
women is courteous but reserved." As the cowboy equally
loved his girlfriend and his horse, so the present day American male loves his car or motorcycle and his girlfriend.
Basic to both these descriptions is the notion that the cowboy does have feelings toward women but does not express
them, since ironically such expression would conflict with

his image of what a male is.

The *playboy type* has recently been epitomized in *Playboy* magazine and by James Bond. As with the cowboy
type, he is resourceful and shrewd, and interacts with his
girlfriend with a certain detachment which is expressed as
"playing it cool." While Bond's relationship with women is
more in terms of a Don Juan, he still treats women with an
air of emotional detachment and independence similar to
that of the cowboy. The playboy departs from the cowboy,
however, in that he is also "non-feeling." Bond and the
playboy he caricatures are in a sense "dead" inside. They
have no emotional feelings toward women, while Wayne,
although unwilling and perhaps unable to express them
does have such feelings. Bond rejects women as women,
treating them as consumer commodities; Wayne puts
women on a pedestal. The playboy's relationship with
women presents the culmination of Fromm's description of
a marketing-oriented personality in which a person comes
to see both himself and others as persons to be manipulated and exploited. Sexuality is reduced to a packageable
consumption item which the playboy can handle because it
demands no responsibility. The woman in the process, becomes reduced to a playboy accessory. A successful "love
affair" is one in which the bed was shared, but the playboy
emerges having avoided personal involvement or a shared
relationship with the woman.

The playboy, then, in part is the old cowboy in modern
dress. Instead of the crude mannerisms of John Wayne, the
playboy is a skilled manipulator of women knowing when
to turn the lights down, what music to play on the stereo,
which drinks to serve, and what topics of conversation to
pursue. The playboy, however, is not a perfect likeness; for
unlike the cowboy, he does not seem to care for the women
from whom he withholds his emotions. Thus, the inexpressive male as a single man comes in two types: the inexpressive feeling man (the cowboy) and the inexpressive non-
feeling man (the playboy).

The Inexpressive Male as a Married Man

When the inexpressive male marries, his inexpressiveness
can become highly dysfunctional to his marital relationship *if* he continues to apply it across-the-board to all
women, his wife included. The modern American family
places a greater demand upon the marriage relationship
than did the family of the past. In the typical marriage of
100 or even 50 years ago, the roles of both the husband
and the wife were clearly defined as demanding, task-ori-
ented functions. If the husband successfully performed the

role of provider and protector of his wife and family and if the wife performed the role of homemaker and mother to her children, chances were the marriage was defined as successful, both from a personal and a societal point of view. The traditional task functions which in the past were performed by the husband and wife are today often taken care of by individuals and organizations outside the home. Concomitant with the decline of the task functions in marriage has been the increase in the importance of the companionship and affectionate function in marriage. As Blood and Wolfe concluded in their study of the modern American marriage, "companionship has emerged as the most valued aspect of marriage today."

As American society has become increasingly mechanized and depersonalized, the family remains as one of the few social groups where what sociologists call the primary relationship has still managed to survive. As such, a greater and greater demand has been placed upon the modern family and especially the modern marriage to provide for affection and companionship. Indeed, it is highly plausible to explain the increased rate of divorce during the last 70 years, not in terms of a breakdown in marriage relationships, but instead, as resulting from the increased load which marriage has been asked to carry. When the husband and wife no longer find affection and companionship from their marriage relationship, they most likely question the wisdom of attempting to continue in their conjugal relationship. When affection is gone, the main reason for the marriage relationship disappears.

Thus, within the newly defined affectively-oriented marriage relationship male inexpressiveness toward *all* women, wife included, would be dysfunctional. But what may happen for many males is that through progressively more serious involvement with women (such as going steady, being pinned, engagement, and the honeymoon period of marriage), they begin to make some exceptions. That is, they may learn to be *situationally rather than totally inexpressive*, inexpressive toward women in most situations but not in all. As the child who learns a rule and then, through further experience, begins to understand the exceptions to it, many American males may pick up the principle of inexpressiveness toward women, discovering its exceptions as they become more and more experienced in the full range of man-woman relationships. Consequently, they may become more expressive toward their wives while remaining essentially inexpressive toward other women; they learn that the conjugal relationship is one situation that is an exception to the cultural requirement of male inexpressiveness. Thus, what was once a double *sexual* standard,

where men had one standard of sexual conduct toward their fiancee or wife and another toward other women, may now be primarily a double *emotional* standard, where men learn to be expressive toward their fiancee or wife but remain inexpressive toward women in general.

To the extent that such situational inexpressiveness exists among males, it should be functional to the maintenance of the marriage relationship. Continued inexpressiveness by married males toward women other than their wives would seem to prohibit their forming meaningful relationships with these women. Such a situation would seem to be advantageous to preserving their relationships, since "promiscuous" expressiveness toward other women could easily threaten the stability of these companionship-oriented marital relationships.

In short, the authors' suggestion is that situational inexpressiveness in which male expressiveness is essentially limited to the marital relationship, may be one of the basic timbers shoring up many American marriages, especially if indications of increasing extramarital sexual relations are correct. In a sense, then, the consequences of situational inexpressiveness for marital relationships do not seem very different from those of prostitution down through the centuries, where prostitution provided for extramarital sex under circumstances which discouraged personal affection toward the female partner strong enough to undermine the marital relationship. In the case of the situationally inexpressive husband, his inexpressiveness in relations with women other than his wife may serve as a line of defense against the possible negative consequences of such involvement toward marital stability. By acting as the cowboy or playboy, therefore, the married male may effectively rob extramarital relationships of their expressiveness and thus preserve his marital relationship.

The inexpressiveness which the American male early acquires may be bothersome in that he has to partially unlearn it in order to effectively relate to his wife. However, if he is successful in partially unlearning it (or learning a few exceptions to it), then it can be highly functional to maintaining the conjugal relationship.

But what if the husband does not partially unlearn his inexpressiveness? Within the newly defined expressive function of the marriage relationship, he is likely to be found inadequate. The possibility of an affectionate and companionship conjugal relationship carries with it the assumption that both the husband and wife are bringing into marriage the expressive capabilities to make such a relationship work. This being the case, American society is ironically short changing males in terms of their ability to fulfill this

READINGS–*continued*

role expectation. Thus, society inconsistently teaches the male that to be masculine is to be inexpressive, while at the same time, expectations in the marital role are defined in terms of sharing affection and companionship which involves the ability to communicate and express feelings. What exists apparently, is another example of discontinuity in cultural conditioning. . . .

Femininity in the 1980's
SUSAN BROWNMILLER, EXCERPT FROM *FEMININITY*

What does it mean to be feminine, according to the author? Do you agree or disagree with her assessment? Why? The author suggests that femininity serves men. How? Does masculinity serve women? What does it mean to be unfeminine? What does being feminine and masculine mean to you?

Femininity, in essence, is a romantic sentiment, a nostalgic tradition of imposed limitations. Even as it hurries forward in the 1980s, putting on lipstick and high heels to appear well dressed, it trips on the ruffled petticoats and hoopskirts of an era gone by. Invariably and necessarily, femininity is something that women had more of in the past, not only in the historic past of prior generations, but in each woman's personal past as well—in the virginal innocence that is replaced by knowledge, in the dewy cheek that is coarsened by age, in the "inherent nature" that a woman seems to misplace so forgetfully whenever she steps out of bounds. Why should this be so? The XX chromosomal message has not been scrambled, the estrogen-dominated hormonal balance is generally as biology intended, the reproductive organs, whatever use one has made of them, are usually in place, the breasts of whatever size are most often where they should be. But clearly, biological femaleness is not enough.

Femininity always demands more. It must constantly reassure its audience by a willing demonstration of difference, even when one does not exist in nature, or it must seize and embrace a natural variation and compose a rhapsodic symphony upon the notes. Suppose one doesn't care to, has other things on her mind, is clumsy or tone-deaf despite the best instruction and training? To fail at the feminine difference is to appear not to care about men, and to risk the loss of their attention and approval. To be insufficiently feminine is viewed as a failure in core sexual identity, or as a failure to care sufficiently about oneself, for a

woman found wanting will be appraised (and will appraise herself) as mannish or neutered or simply unattractive, as men have defined these terms.

We are talking, admittedly, about an exquisite esthetic. Enormous pleasure can be extracted from feminine pursuits as a creative outlet or purely as relaxation; indeed, indulgence for the sake of fun, or art, or attention, is among femininity's great joys. But the chief attraction (and the central paradox, as well) is the competitive edge that femininity seems to promise in the unending struggle to survive, and perhaps to triumph. The world smiles favorably on the feminine woman: it extends little courtesies and minor privilege. Yet the nature of this competitive edge is ironic, at best, for one works at femininity by accepting restrictions, by limiting one's sights, by choosing an indirect route, by scattering concentration and not giving one's all as a man would to his own, certifiably masculine, interests. It does not require a great leap of imagination for a woman to understand the feminine principle as a grand collection of compromises, large and small, that she simply must make in order to render herself a successful woman. If she has difficulty in satisfying femininity's demands, if its illusions go against her grain, or if she is criticized for her shortcomings and imperfections, the more she will see femininity as a desperate strategy of appeasement, a strategy she may not have the wish or the courage to abandon, for failure looms in either direction.

It is fashionable in some quarters to describe the feminine and masculine principles as polar ends of the human continuum, and to sagely profess that both polarities exist in all people. Sun and moon, yin and yang, soft and hard, active and passive, etcetera, may indeed be opposites, but a linear continuum does not illuminate the problem. (Femininity, in all its contrivances, is a very active endeavor.) What, then, is the basic distinction? The masculine principle is better understood as a driving ethos of superiority designed to inspire straightforward, confident success, while the feminine principle is composed of vulnerability, the need for protection, the formalities of compliance and the avoidance of conflict—in short, an appeal of dependence and good will that gives the masculine principle its romantic validity and its admiring applause.

Femininity pleases men because it makes them appear more masculine by contrast; and, in truth, conferring an extra portion of unearned gender distinction on men, an unchallenged space in which to breathe freely and feel stronger, wiser, more competent, is femininity's special gift. One could say that masculinity is often an effort to please women, but masculinity is known to please by displays of

READINGS–*continued*

mastery and competence while femininity pleases by suggesting that these concerns, except in small matters, are beyond its intent. Whimsy, unpredictability and patterns of thinking and behavior that are dominated by emotion, such as tearful expressions of sentiment and fear, are thought to be feminine precisely because they lie outside the established route to success.

If in the beginnings of history the feminine woman was defined by her physical dependency, her inability for reasons of reproductive biology to triumph over the forces of nature that were the tests of masculine strength and power, today she reflects both an economic and emotional dependency that is still considered "natural," romantic and attractive. After an unsettling fifteen years in which many basic assumptions about the sexes were challenged, the economic disparity did not disappear. Large numbers of women—those with small children, those left high and dry after a mid-life divorce—need financial support. But even those who earn their own living share a universal need for connectedness (call it love, if you wish). As unprecedented numbers of men abandon their sexual interest in women, others, sensing opportunity, choose to demonstrate their interest through variety and a change in partners. A sociological fact of the 1980s is that female competition for two scarce resources—men and jobs—is especially fierce.

So it is not surprising that we are currently witnessing a renewed interest in femininity and an unabashed indulgence in feminine pursuits. Femininity serves to reassure men that women need them and care about them enormously. By incorporating the decorative and the frivolous into its definition of style, femininity functions as an effective antidote to the unrelieved seriousness, the pressure of making one's way in a harsh, difficult world. In its mandate to avoid direct confrontation and to smooth over the fissures of conflict, femininity operates as a value system of niceness, a code of thoughtfulness and sensitivity that in modern society is sadly in short supply.

A Woman's Choice: Becoming a Parent
LISA BROWN, *NEWSWEEK ON CAMPUS*

Prior to the women's movement, women had little choice or encouragement except for becoming mothers. According to the author of this essay, the situation has changed dramatically. Today, especially among many college women, motherhood has become a second-class profession; instead of

becoming mothers, women are expected to become professionals. It is the women who want to have children rather than careers who are now on the defensive. Do you agree with Lisa Brown's analysis? Do you think motherhood has been devalued? What caused the author to reevaluate her goals? Why? If you were given the choice between parenthood or a career, which would you choose? What personal and social factors influence your choice?

For years the theory of higher education operated something like this: men went to college to get rich, and women went to college to marry rich men. It was a wonderful little setup, almost mathematical in its precision. To disturb it would have been to rock an American institution.

During the '60s, though, this theory lost much of its luster. As the nation began to recognize the idiocy of relegating women to a secondary role, women soon joined men in what once were male-only pursuits. This rebellious decade pushed women toward independence, showed them their potential and compelled them to take charge of their lives. Many women took the opportunity and ran with it. Since then feminine autonomy has been the rule, not the exception, at least among college women.

That's the good news. The bad news is that the invisible push has turned into a shove. Some women are downright obsessive about success, to the point of becoming insular monuments to selfishness and fierce bravado, the condescending sort that hawks: "I don't need *anybody*. So there." These women dismiss children and marriage as unbearably outdated and potentially harmful to their up-and-coming careers. This notion of independence smacks of egocentrism. What do these women fear? Why can't they slow down long enough to remember that relationships and a family life are not inherently awful things?

Granted that for centuries women were on the receiving end of some shabby treatment. Now, in an attempt to liberate college women from the constraints that forced them almost exclusively into teaching or nursing as a career outside the home—always subject to the primary career of motherhood—some women have gone too far. Any notion of motherhood seems to be regarded as an unpleasant reminder of the past, when homemakers were imprisoned by husbands, tots and household chores. In short, many women consider motherhood a time-consuming obstacle to the great joy of working outside the home.

The rise of feminism isn't the only answer. Growing up has something to do with it, too. Most people find themselves in a bind as they hit their late 20s: they consider the ideals they grew up with and find that these don't necessar-

READINGS–*continued*

ily mix with the ones they've acquired. The easiest thing to do, it sometimes seems, is to throw out the precepts their parents taught. Growing up, my friends and I were enchanted by the idea of starting new traditions. We didn't want self-worth to be contingent upon whether there was a man or child around the house to make us feel wanted.

I began to reconsider my values after my sister and a friend had babies. I was entertained by their pregnancies and fascinated by the births: I was also thankful that I wasn't the one who had to change the diapers every day. I was a doting aunt only when I wanted to be. As my sister's and friend's lives changed, though, my attitude changed. I saw their days flip-flop between frustration and joy. Though these two women lost the freedom to run off to the beach or to a bar, they gained something else—an abstract happiness that reveals itself when they talk about Jessica's or Amanda's latest escapade or vocabulary addition. Still in their 20s, they shuffle work and motherhood with the skill of poker players. I admire them, and I marvel at their kids. Spending time with the Jessicas and Amandas of the world teaches us patience and sensitivity and gives us a clue into our own pasts. Children are also reminders that there is a future and that we must work to ensure its quality.

Now I feel challenged by the idea of becoming a parent. I want to decorate a nursery and design Halloween costumes; I want to answer my children's questions and help them learn to read. I want to be unselfish. But I've spent most of my life working in the opposite direction: toward independence, no emotional or financial strings attached. When I told a friend—one who likes kids but never, ever wants them—that I'd decided to accommodate motherhood, she accused me of undermining my career, my future, my life. "If that's all you want, then why are you even in college?" she asked.

The answer is simple: I want to be a smart mommy. I have solid career plans and look forward to working. I make a distinction between wanting kids and wanting nothing but kids. And I've accepted that I'll have to give up a few years of full-time work to allow time for being pregnant and buying Pampers. As for undermining my life, I'm proud of my decision because I think it's evidence that the women's movement is working. While liberating women from the traditional childbearing role, the movement has given respectability to motherhood by recognizing that it's not a brainless task like dishwashing. At the same time, women who choose not to have children are not treated as oddities. That certainly wasn't the case even 15 years ago. While the graying, middle-aged bachelor was respected, the female equivalent—tagged a spinster—was automatically suspect.

Today, women have choices: about careers, their bodies, children. I am grateful that women are no longer forced into motherhood as a function of their biology; it's senseless to assume that having a uterus qualifies anyone to be a good parent. By the same token, it is ridiculous for women to abandon all maternal desire because it might jeopardize personal success. Some women make the decision to go childless without ever analyzing their true needs or desires. They forget that motherhood can add to personal fulfillment.

I wish those fiercely independent women wouldn't look down upon those of us who, for whatever reason, choose to forgo much of the excitement that runs in tandem with being single, liberated and educated. Excitement also fills a family life; it just comes in different ways.

I'm not in college because I'll learn how to make tastier pot roast. I'm a student because I want to make sense of the world and of myself. By doing so, I think I'll be better prepared to be a mother to the new lives that I might bring into the world. I'll also be a better me. It's a package deal I don't want to turn down.

Ain't I a Woman?
SOJOURNER TRUTH

Sojourner Truth was born a slave in New York. She was a leader in the antislavery movement and also a champion for women's rights. The two selections that follow suggest that not all women accepted the stereotype of being passive and dependent. Sojourner Truth was attending a women's rights convention in 1851 when a man ridiculed women as being weak and helpless. She stood up and eloquently gave the famous speech from which this selection is taken.

The man over there says women need to be helped into carriages and lifted over ditches, and to have the best place everywhere. Nobody ever helps me into carriages and over puddles, or gives me the best place—and ain't I a woman?

Look at my arm! I have ploughed and planted and gathered into barns, and no man could head me—and ain't I a woman? I could work as much and eat as much as a man . . . and bear the lash as well! And ain't I a woman? I have born thirteen children, and seen most of 'em sold into slavery, and when I cried out with my mother's grief, none but Jesus heard me—and ain't I a woman?

READINGS–*continued*

In this second selection, from a speech given in 1867, Sojourner Truth points to a basic issue that is still with us today: the inequality of wages between men and woman.

I am above eighty years old; it is about time for me to be going. I have been forty years a slave and forty years free, and would be here forty years more to have equal rights for all. I suppose I am kept here because something remains for me to do; I suppose I am yet to help to break the chain. I have done a great deal of work; as much as a man, but did not get so much pay. I used to work in the field and bind grain, keeping up with the cradler; but men doing no more, got twice as much pay. . . . We do as much, we eat as much, we want as much. I suppose I am about the only colored woman that goes about to speak for the rights of the colored women. I want to keep the thing stirring, now that the ice is cracked. What we want is a little money. You men know that you get as much again as women, when you write, or for what you do. When we get our rights, we shall not have to come to you for money, for then we shall have money enough in our pockets; and maybe you will ask us for money. But help us now until we get it. It is a good consolation to know that when we have got this battle once

fought we shall not be coming to you any more. . . .

. . . I have lived on through all that has taken place these forty years in the anti-slavery cause. . . . We are now trying for liberty that requires no blood—that women shall have their rights—not rights from you. Give them what belongs to them; they ask it kindly too. I ask it kindly. Now, I want it done very quick. It can be done in a few years. How good it would be. I would like to go up to the polls myself. I own a little house in Battle Creek, Michigan. Well, every year I got a tax to pay. Taxes, you see, be taxes. Well, a road tax sounds large. . . . There was women there that had a house as well as I. They taxed them to build a road, and they went on the road and worked. It took 'em a good while to get a stump up. Now, that shows that women can work. If they can dig up stumps they can vote. It is easier to vote than dig stumps. It doesn't seem hard work to vote, though I have seen some men that had a hard time of it. . . . I don't want to take up your time, but I calculate to live. Now, if you want me to get out of the world, you had better get the women votin' soon. I shan't go till I can do that.

CHAPTER 5

Love

PREVIEW

To gain a sense of what you already know about the material covered in this chapter, answer "true" or "false" to the statements below. You will find the answers as you read the chapter.

1. Friendship and romantic love have little in common. True or false?
2. Everyone has a need for intimacy. True or false?
3. Love is able to fulfill all of a person's needs if he or she finds the right person. True or false?
4. Romantic love lasts "forever" if people are truly in love. True or false?
5. Love is instinctive. True or false?
6. Jealousy is a universal feeling. True or false?
7. Love is the development of mutual dependency. True or false?
8. Love is treating another as an end in himself or herself rather than as an object. True or false?
9. You always hurt the one you love. True or false?
10. Opposites attract. True or false?

Outline

Love is essential to our lives. Love binds us together as men and women, parents and children, friends and neighbors. It creates bonds that endure the greatest hardships, suffer the severest cruelty, overcome any distance. Ask us what love is, and we usually can't define it, although we often say we know it when we feel it. Often even this is not true, for we may torment ourselves with the question, "Am I *really* in love?" Many of us have gone through frustrating scenes such as the one below (Greenberg and Jacobs, 1966):

YOU: "Do you love me?"
MATE: "Yes, of course I love you."
YOU: "Do you *really* love me?"
MATE: "Yes, I really love you."
YOU: "You are *sure* you love me—you are absolutely sure?"
MATE: "Yes, I'm absolutely sure."
YOU: "Do you know the meaning of love?"
MATE: "I don't know."
YOU: "Then how can you be sure you love me?"
MATE: "I don't know. Perhaps I can't."
YOU: "You can't, eh? I see. Well, since you can't even be sure you love me, I can't really see much point in our remaining together. Can you?"
MATE: "I don't know. Perhaps not."
YOU: "You've been leading up to this for a pretty long time, haven't you?"

We are shaped and fashioned by what we love.

JOHANN GOETHE

Love is both a feeling and an activity. A person feels love for someone and acts in a loving manner. But we can also be angry with the person we love, frustrated, bored, or indifferent. This is the paradox of love: It encompasses opposites. Love includes affection and anger, excitement and boredom, stability and change, bonds and freedom. Its paradoxical quality makes us ask whether we *really* love someone when we are not feeling "perfectly" in love or when our relationship is not going smoothly. But love does not give us perfection; it gives us meaning.

In this chapter, we look at the development of intimacy using the "wheel theory" of love, the difference between love and friendship, and relationship between love and identity. Then we examine various approaches to the study of love. One approach is to study the styles in which people love. Another is to look at romantic love as the combination of a physiological response (say, a beating heart) with a label attached to the response (love). Still another way of looking at love is to compare romantic love with companionate love. We also look at some reasons for the many obstacles to lasting love that appear to exist in our society. These include using people as objects, the hidden taboo on love, and traditional sex roles. Finally, we examine jealousy.

☐ THE DEVELOPMENT OF INTIMACY

Everyone wants to fall in love, and doing it seems easy enough if the right chemistry exists. But what is it that creates the right chemistry? Falling in love, even though it may seem mysterious and instantaneous, is not as simple as it sounds. The development of love is actually a process.

The Wheel Theory

Sociologist Ira Reiss (1980) has suggested a "wheel theory" of love in which love develops through four processes: (1) rapport, (2) self-revelation, (3) mutual dependency, and (4) intimacy need fulfillment.

Rapport.   When two people meet, they quickly sense if rapport exists between them. This rapport is a sense of ease, the feeling each understands the other in some special way. This sense of rapport is dependent on our social environment in two ways. First, feeling rapport tends to depend on sharing the same social and cultural background, that is, factors of homogamy (see Chapter 6). If one person has a grade-school education and the other a college education, it is not likely they will share many of the same values; if one person is upper class and the other person is working class, their life experiences are probably quite different. Second, we tend to feel rapport with others who also share our role conceptions. Two people who believe in egalitarian sex roles, for example, are more likely to feel rapport than are a radical feminist and male chauvinist.

Self-Revelation.   If you feel rapport with someone, you are more likely to feel relaxed and confident. As a result, self-revelation, the disclosure of intimate feelings, is more likely to occur. But self-revelation also depends on what is considered proper by your socialization group. For example, upper-class people have a tendency to be more reserved about themselves, while middle-class people feel more comfortable in revealing intimate aspects of their lives and feelings.

Mutual Dependency.   After two people feel rapport and begin revealing themselves to each other, they may become mutually dependent. Each needs the other to share pleasures, fears, and jokes, as well as sexual intimacies; each becomes the other's confidant. Each person develops ways of acting and being that cannot be fulfilled alone. Going for a walk is no longer something you do alone; you do it with your partner. Sleeping no longer takes place in a single bed but in a double one with your partner. You are a couple.

Here too in the development of mutual dependency, social and cultural background

Love cannot save life from death, but it can fulfill life's purpose.

ARNOLD TOYNBEE

Love is patient and kind; love is not jealous or boastful; it is not arrogant or rude. Love does not insist on its own way; it is not irritable or resentful; it does not rejoice at wrong, but rejoices in the right. Love bears all things, believes all things, hopes all things, endures all things.

I CORINTHIANS 13:4–7

Absence extinguishes small passions and increases great ones, as the wind will blow out a candle, and blow in a fire.

FRANÇOIS de La ROCHEFOUCAULD (1613–1680)

are important. The forms of dependent behavior that develop are influenced by your conception of the role of courtship. Interdependency may develop through dating, getting together, or living together. Premarital intercourse may or may not be acceptable.

Need for Intimacy.   People, according to Reiss (1980), have a basic intimacy need, "the need for someone to love, the need for someone to confide in, and the need for sympathetic understanding." These needs are important for fulfilling our roles as a partner or parent. Reiss describes the relationship among the four processes, which culminate in intimacy, as follows:

By virtue of rapport, one reveals oneself and becomes dependent, and in the process of carrying out the relationship one fulfills certain basic intimacy needs. To the extent that these needs are fulfilled, one finds a love relationship developing. In fact, the initial rapport that a person feels on first meeting someone can be presumed to be a dim awareness of the potential intimacy need fulfillment of this other person for one's own needs. If one needs sympathy and support and senses these qualities in a date, rapport will be felt more easily; one will reveal more and become more dependent, and if the hunch was right and the person is sympathetic, one's intimacy needs will be fulfilled.

Intimacy is one of the basic needs of human beings. It develops through rapport and self-revelation.

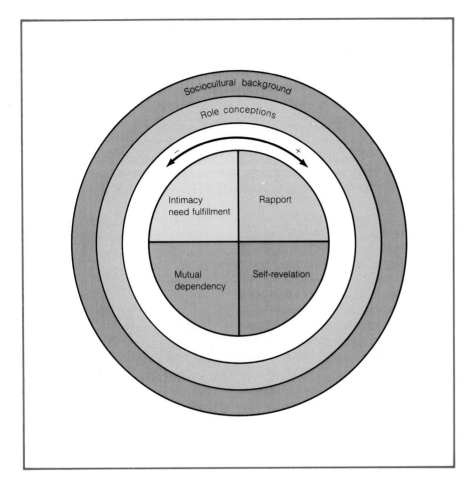

Figure 5–1

Graphic Presentation of the Wheel Theory of Love. (Revised, 1980.)

Reiss' Wheel Theory of Love. In the wheel theory of love, the development of intimacy takes place among those who share the same sociocultural background and role conceptions. Intimacy develops from a feeling of rapport, which leads to self-revelation; self-revelation leads to mutual dependency, which in turn may lead to intimacy need fulfillment.

How the Wheel Theory Works

Reiss calls the four processes—rapport, self-revelation, mutual dependency, and intimacy need fulfillment—the wheel theory to emphasize their interdependence: A reduction in any one affects the development or maintenance of a love relationship (see Figure 5–1). If a couple habitually argues, for example, the arguments will affect their mutual dependency and their intimacy need; this in turn will weaken the rapport.

The processes flow into one another in one direction to develop and maintain love; they flow in the opposite direction to weaken it. The "+" and "−" in the figure indicate the directions the processes can go to increase or decrease love. The outer ring on the diagram, "sociocultural background," produces the next ring, "role conceptions." All four processes are influenced by role conceptions, which define what a person should expect and do in a love relationship.

As you examine the diagram, ask yourself whether your love relationships follow the same course Reiss suggests. What creates rapport for you? What factors increase or decrease self-revelation? When self-revelation increases, does mutual dependency

The meeting of two personalities is like the contact of two chemical substances; if there is any reaction, both are transformed.

CARL JUNG

Upon my bed by night
I sought him whom my soul
    loves;
I sought him, but found him
    not;
I called him, but he gave no
    answer.
"I will rise now and go about
    the city,
    in the street and in the
    squares;
I will seek him whom my soul
    loves."
The watchmen found me
    as they went about in the
    city.
"Have you seen him whom my
    soul loves?"
Scarcely had I passed them,
When I found him whom my
    soul loves.
I held him, and would not let
    him go
    until I had brought him
    into my mother's house,
    and into the chamber of her
    that conceived me.
I adjure you, O daughters of
    Jerusalem,
    by the gazelles or the hinds
    of the field,
That you stir not up nor
    awaken love until it please.

SONG OF SOLOMON

also increase? If mutual dependency decreases, do self-revelation and rapport decrease? What impact have social background and role conceptions had on the development of your relationships?

☐ FRIENDS AND LOVERS

Love differs from admiration, wrote Woody Allen, because when you admire someone, you admire her from a distance. When you love someone, you want to be in the same room as she is, hiding behind the curtains! Friendship differs from love, we might add, because you can be in the same room as your friend *without* hiding behind the curtains. There seems to be something less complicated about friendship than love. What is it?

Reiss suggests that the wheel theory applies not only to the development of love relationships but also to other primary relationships like friendship. Recent studies comparing friendship and love found that friends and lovers also share certain characteristics (Davis, 1985):

- *Enjoyment* of each other's company
- *Acceptance* of each other
- *Trust* that each will act in light of the other's interests
- *Mutual respect* for each other
- *Mutual assistance*, especially in times of need or personal crisis
- *Confiding* experiences and feelings
- *Understanding* each other's feelings
- *Spontaneity* in being oneself

Because love and friendship have many similarities, friendships often grow into romantic relationships. Look at this photograph for clues. Would you guess that the man and woman walking together are friends or in love with each other? Why?

What seems to distinguish friendship from love, according to Davis, are two clusters of feelings: the passion cluster and the caring cluster. The passion cluster includes three characteristics: fascination, exclusiveness, and sexual desire. The caring cluster consists of giving the utmost and being a champion or advocate of the other.

In Davis's study, although the passion cluster clearly distinguished best friends from lovers and spouses, the caring cluster did not. Lovers or spouses gave more of their utmost to their partners than did friends, but there was not much difference between the two groups when it came to being a champion or advocate of the other. Perhaps not surprisingly in an age when marital instability is commonplace, friendships were seen as more stable than love or marriage relationships.

Due to the similarities between romantic relationships and friendship, it is not surprising that friendships are often transformed into love relationships. In the typologies of love developed by John Lee (1973), discussed later in this chapter, those most likely to transform friendship into love are those who seek companionable love.

☐ LOVE AND IDENTITY

The problem of identity may be the central problem of love. Erikson (1963) suggested that people are able to love and achieve intimacy only after they have established a firm identity. *Identity* means sense of self, the "I." This "I" establishes a person's feeling of place in the universe. When a person says "I love you," she or he must intuitively know what that "I" is. If a person is in a constant state of change, the "I" too may change. "I" may be different next week or next month. Among people whose identities are still unformed "I love you" may actually mean "I need you" or "The person I am today loves you." As their "I" changes, so will their needs. The love that they felt—based on their needs—may disappear.

It is, in the final analysis, love which transforms even ugly things into something beautiful. It is ourselves alone who can turn the primordial, uncouth and most ordinary contents of our unconscious—turnips, mice, toads—into the most refined products of our minds.

BRUNO BETTELHEIM, *THE USES OF ENCHANTMENT*

Being-Love and Deficiency-Love

Psychologist Abraham Maslow (1968) suggested that love may be divided into two kinds: deficiency-love and being-love. Deficiency-love is basically selfish, based on needs that the other person can fulfill. Being-love, however, is love for the very being of the other person—it is giving and unselfish. Deficiency-love is characteristic of people who lack important elements in their identity. Erik Fromm (1956) wrote of this type of love:

If a person has not reached the level where he has a sense of identity, of I-ness, rooted in the productive unfolding of his own powers, he tends to "idolize" the loved person. He is alienated from his own powers and projects them onto the loved person. . . . In this process he deprives himself of all sense of strength, loses himself in the loved one rather than finding himself. Since no person can, in the long run, live up to the expectations of his (or her) worshipper, disappointment is bound to occur, and as a remedy a new idol is sought for. . . . This idolatrous love is often described as the true, great love; but while it is meant to portray the intensity and depth of love, it only demonstrates the hunger and despair of the idolator.

Love gives itself; it is not bought.

HENRY LONGFELLOW (1807–1882)

It may be possible to tell infatuation from romantic love only in retrospect. If a relationship flowers, one continues to believes that he is experiencing true love; if a relationship dies, one concludes that he was merely infatuated.

ELLEN BERSCHEID and ELAINE WALSTER

In deficiency-love, the other person is frequently regarded as an object. Men love women who gratify them sexually, glory in *their* achievements, are subordinate and dependent, turn to them for advice and guidance, take care of their needs. Women love men who provide for them, satisfy them sexually, are successful, make all the important decisions, are smart, make life fun. Each is dependent on the other. Neither loves the other for his or her unique qualities but for the needs that are served. The man may say, "Yeah, Mabel, she's a good little wife," and the woman may say, "Charlie? Oh, yes, he's a wonderful provider for the family." Charlie doesn't say: "Mabel's fantastic," nor does Mabel say "Charlie's a wonderful person." They do not relate to each other as people but as roles, objects, and functions. Such love does not help people develop strong, independent identities.

In contrast to deficiency-love, being-love is rich, giving, and nonpossessive. Maslow (1968) wrote of being-love: "It gives him a self-image, it gives him self-acceptance, a feeling of love-worthiness, all of which permit him to grow. It is a real question whether the full development of the human being is possible without it."

> If you start with the belief that love is the pleasure of a moment, is it really surprising that it yields only a momentary pleasure?
>
> WALTER LIPPMANN, A PREFACE TO MORALS

Being-love is given without any desire for return, although this kind of love usually is reciprocal. No need motivation exists. A person does not love another to feel good or to gain status among friends. Being-love is disinterestd, free in the ultimate sense, given voluntarily with no strings attached. Since this love is not possessive, it nurtures growth and maturity; it is trusting and confident. The depth of understanding between the partners in being-love makes possible what Maslow described as "a mystic experience." It is not blind, but knowing. This love exists in the everyday world. It encompasses the whole spectrum of human emotions—anger, boredom, fear, compassion, sympathy—without being endangered. Being-love requires openness, knowledge, and the discovery of a sense of wonder in everyday life together.

The person with a strong identity values love but sees it as only one aspect of his or her identity. Traditional views of love see the couple relationship as satisfying all intimacy needs; Maslow's humanistic view sees the love relationship as satisfying only some intimacy needs. Other intimate relationships are also necessary, close friendships with members of both sexes among them.

Complementary Needs

The ancient Greek philosopher Plato related a myth about the origin of love. In the beginning, human beings were globular in shape, like wheels. But the gods became angry with humans' constant bickering and boastfulness, and as punishment Zeus cut each person in half; people no longer rolled but walked. Plato (1961 edition) wrote:

Now when the work of bisection was complete, it left each half with a desperate yearning for the other, and they ran together and flung their arms around each other's necks, and asked for nothing better than to be rolled into one.

When . . . [a lover] is fortunate enough to meet his other half, they are both so intoxicated with affection, with friendship, and with love, that they cannot bear to let each other out of sight for a single instant. It is such reunions as these that impel men to spend their lives together, although they may be hard put to it to say what they really want of one another, and indeed, the purely sexual pleasures of their friendship could hardly account for the huge delight they take in each other's company . . . .

And so all this to-do is a relic of that original state of ours, when we were whole, and now, when we are longing for and following after that primeval wholeness, we say we are in love.

> The head is always the dupe of the heart.
>
> FRANÇOIS De La ROCHEFOUCAULD

Plato's myth presents an alternative to Maslow's view that need is a deficiency. Plato suggests that no one is complete in himself or herself—someone else exists who can bring completeness by complementing our "incomplete" self.

Do we choose someone to love who is the same or who is different from us? Most research suggests that we love people who are similar to us in social class, values, religious background, and so on. But do we also choose people who resemble us psychologically—or do opposites attract?

Robert Winch's (1958) classic study of love relationships suggested that we love people who gratify our needs. These needs include achievement, autonomy, dominance, deference, nurturance, and recognition. The study, however, was limited (it involved only twenty-five married couples) and the results inconclusive. The hypothesis that received strongest support was that couples were complementary in two key dimensions: nurturant-receptive and dominant-submissive. Generally, it seemed, nurturing people married receptive people and dominant people married submissive ones.

It lies not in our power to love or hate,
For will in us is over-ruled by fate.

CHRISTOPHER MARLOWE,
HERO AND LEANDER

A problem with the complementary need idea is that it tends to divide people into submissive and dominant types and nurturing and receptive types. This division simplifies and polarizes human traits and seems to reflect traditional sex role stereotypes. It is quite possible for people to have needs to both nurture and receive nurturing, and to be both dominant and submissive. They can take turns nurturing and receiving nurturance, for example. They can dominate in some areas and be submissive in others.

☐ HOW DO I LOVE THEE? APPROACHES TO THE STUDY OF LOVE

"How do I love thee?" asked Elizabeth Barrett Browning in one of her poems. She went on to answer her own question:

I love thee to the depth and breadth and height
My soul can reach, when feeling out of sight
For the ends of Being and ideal Grace.
I love thee to the level of every day's
Most quiet need, by sun and candle-light.
I love thee freely, as men strive for right.
I love thee purely, as they turn from praise.
I love thee with the passion put to use
In my old griefs, and with my childhood's faith.

The heart has its reasons which reason does not understand.

BLAISE PASCAL (1623–1662)

We can look at love in many ways besides through the eyes of lovers, though other ways may not be as entertaining. Whereas love was once the province of lovers, madmen, poets, and philosophers, now social scientists have begun to appear on the scene. (See the readings by Daniel Goleman, "Psychologists Study Love" and John Scanzoni, "Love as an Exchange.") They have bravely disregarded William Blake's warning:

He who binds to himself a Joy
Doth the winged life destroy;
But he who kisses the Joy as it flies
Lives in eternity's sunrise.

Lovers and madmen have such seething brains,
Such shaping fantasies, that apprehend
More than cool reason ever comprehends.
The lunatic, the lover and the poet
Are of imagination all compact. . . .

WILLIAM SHAKESPEARE, A
MIDSUMMER NIGHT'S DREAM

Styles of Love

Sociologist John Lee has counted the ways differently than Elizabeth Barrett Browning. "I love thee erotically, obsessively, playfully, companionately, altruistically, pragmatically," he might say. Not only is there love but also there are styles of loving. Lee (1973) described six basic styles of love:

- Eros: love of beauty
- Mania: obsessive love
- Ludis: playful love
- Storge: companionate love
- Agape: altruistic love
- Pragma: practical love

In addition to these pure forms there are mixtures of the basic types: Storgic-Eros, Ludic-Eros, and Storgic-Ludis. The six basic types can be described as follows:

Eros.   Erotic lovers delight in the tactile, in the immediate; they are attracted to beauty (though beauty may be in the eye of the beholder). They love the lines of the body, its feel and touch. They are fascinated by every detail of their beloved. Their love burns brightly but soon flickers and dies.

Mania.   The word *mania* comes from the Greek word for madness. The Russian poet Lermontov aptly described a manic lover:

He in his madness prays for storms,
And dreams that storms will bring him peace.

For manic lovers, nights are marked by sleeplessness and days by pain and anxiety. The slightest sign of affection brings ecstasy for a short while, only to disappear into nothingness. Satisfactions last but a moment before they need to be renewed. Manic love is roller-coaster love. The French ballad "Plaisir d'Amour" is the manic lover's anthem.

The pleasures of love are but a moment long
But the pain of love endures the whole life through.

Ludis.   For ludic lovers, love is a game, something to play at rather than to become deeply involved in. Love is ultimately ludicrous. Love is for fun; encounters are casual, carefree, and often careless. "Nothing serious" is the motto of ludic lovers.

   The patron saint of ludic lovers is the poet Sir John Suckling (1609–1642), a favorite of the English court (and the inventor of cribbage), who, when banished, committed suicide. His poem "The Constant Lover" sums up the philosophy of the ludic lover.

Out upon it, I have loved
Three whole days together!
And am like to love three more,
If it prove fair weather.

Although youth believes love is its special province, it is as much the domain of the old.

Storge. Storge (pronounced *stor*-gay) is the love between companions. It is, wrote Lee, "love without fever, tumult, or folly, a peaceful and enchanting affection." It begins usually as friendship and then gradually deepens into love. If the love ends, it is also gradual and the couple often become friends once again. Of such love Theophile Gautier wrote: "To love is to admire with the heart; to admire is to love with the mind."

Agape. Agape (pronounced ah-*gah*-pay) is the traditional Christian love that is chaste, patient, and undemanding; it does not expect to be reciprocated. It is the love of saints and martyrs. As we might expect, Lee did not find any in his survey of lovers. Agape is more abstract and ideal than concrete and real. It is easier to love all of humankind in such a way than an individual.

Pragma. Pragmatic lovers are, first and foremost, logical in their approach to looking for someone who meets their needs. They are the only ones (in addition to students and researchers) who consciously consider endogamy and exogamy, homogamy and heterogamy, in choosing a mate. They look for mates who have the background, education, personality, religion, and interests that are compatible with their own. If they meet a person who meets their criteria, then erotic or manic feelings may develop. But as Samuel Butler warned "Logic is like the sword— those who appeal to it shall perish by it."

Love and you shall be loved. All love is mathematically just, as much as two sides of an algebraic equation.

RALPH WALDO EMERSON (1803–1882)

Lee believes that to have a mutually satisfying love affair, a person has to find a partner who shares the same style and definition of love. The more different two people are in their styles of loving, the less chance they will share in understanding each other's love.

Lee developed a test to help people recognize their own styles of loving (see Table 5–1 on page 129). You may wish to take the test and give it to your partner as well to see how closely your styles of loving match.

Romantic Love and Adrenalin

Love brings great pleasure. Christina Rossetti wrote:

My heart is like a singing bird
Whose nest is in a watered shoot;
My heart is like an apple-tree
Whose boughs are bent with thick-set fruit;
My heart is like a rainbow shell
That paddles in a halcyon sea;
My heart is gladder than all these
Because my love is come to me.

But love can also be torture, as the Roman poet Catallus complained in the first century B.C.:

I hate and I love.
You ask how that can be.
Yet I do not know.
But I feel it and I am tormented.

The contradictory nature of romantic love has confused lovers—and those who theorize about love—for centuries. Is passionate love pleasure or pain—or is it both?

The scientific explanation of romantic love was given a boost by Stanley Schachter's two-component theory of human emotions. According to his theory, for a person to experience an emotion, two factors must be present: (1) physiological arousal and (2) an appropriate emotional explanation of the arousal. By recognizing that love is accompanied by physiological arousal, psychologists are able to explain why both intensely positive and intensely negative experiences can lead to love. Stimuli that generate attraction, sexual arousal, jealousy, loneliness, rejection, relief, confusion, and gratitude, for example, can all produce intense physiological arousal. "Thus, these positive *and* negative experiences may all have the potential for deepening an individual's passion for another" (Berscheid and Walster, 1974).

The way people label their physiological responses is important in determining the way they feel. In a situation where those feelings may reasonably be labeled "love," the person may indeed experience love. We learn to label our physiological responses as we grow up. The adolescent girl may ask, "When I see Willie come into English class, my heart leaps. Does that mean I am in love?" Her response is crucial. If the answer is yes, she is going to identify the feeling with love. If a boy gets nervous every time he talks to a particular girl, he may label the nervousness "love" and fall in love; if he labels the nervousness "fear," he will not fall in love with the girl and may even avoid her. A number of unpleasant situations may generate physiological arousal, including fear, rejection, frustration, and challenge. Similarly, pleasant experiences may facilitate passion: attraction, sexual arousal, satisfaction of needs, excitement.

My love is like to ice, and I to fire:
How comes it then that this her cold so great
Is not dissolved through my so hot desire,
But harder grows the more I her entreat?
Or how comes it that my exceeding heat
Is not allayed by her heart-frozen cold,
But that I burn much more in boiling sweat,
And feel my flames augmented manifold?
What more miraculous thing may be told,
That fire, which all things melts, should harden ice,
And ice, which is congeal'd with senseless cold,
Should kindle fire by wonderful device?
 Such is the power of love in gentle mind,
 That it can alter all the course of kind.

EDMUND SPENSER (16th CENTURY)

I am not one of those who do not believe in love at first sight, but I believe in taking a second look.

HENRY VINCENT (1813–1878)

Table 5–1 Graph Your Own Style of Loving

Consider each characteristic as it applies to a current relationship that you define as love, or to a previous one if that is more applicable. For each, note whether the trait is *almost always* true (AA), *usually* true (U), *rarely* true (R), or *almost never* true (AN).

	Eros	Ludus	Storge	Mania	Ludic Eros	Storgic Eros	Storgic Ludus	Pragma
1. You consider your childhood less happy than the average of peers.	R		AN	U				
2. You were discontent with life (work, etc.) at time your encounter began.	R		AN	U	R			
3. You have never been in love before this relationship.				U	R	AN	R	
4. You want to be in love or have love as security.	R	AN		AA		AN	AN	U
5. You have a clearly defined ideal image of your desired partner.	AA	AN	AN	AN	U	AN	R	AA
6. You felt a strong gut attraction to your beloved on the first encounter.	AA	R	AN	R		AN		
7. You are preoccupied with thoughts about the beloved.	AA	AN	AN	AA		R		
8. You believe your partner's interest is at least as great as yours.		U	R	AN			R	U
9. You are eager to see your beloved almost every day; this was true from the beginning.	AA	AN	R	AA		R	AN	R
10. You soon believed this could become a permanent relationship.	AA	AN	R	AN	R	AA	AN	U
11. You see "warning signs" of trouble but ignore them.	R	R		AA		AN	R	R
12. You deliberately restrain frequency of contact with partner.	AN	AA	R	R	R	R	U	
13. You restrict discussion of your feelings with beloved.	R	AA	U	U	R		U	U
14. You restrict display of your feelings with beloved.	R	AA	R	U	R		U	U
15. You discuss future plans with beloved.	AA	R	R				AN	AA
16. You discuss wide range of topics, experiences with partner	AA	R				U	R	AA
17. You try to control relationship, but feel you've lost control	AN	AN	AN	AA	AN	AN		
18. You lose ability to be first to terminate relationship.	AN	AN		AA	R	U	R	R

	Eros	Ludus	Storge	Mania	Ludic Eros	Storgic Eros	Storgic Ludus	Pragma
19. You try to force beloved to show more feeling, commitment.	AN	AN		AA			AN	R
20. You analyze the relationship, weigh it in your mind.			AN	U		R	R	AA
21. You believe in the sincerity of your partner.	AA			U	R	U		AA
22. You blame partner for difficulties of your relationship.	R	U	R	U	R	AN		
23. You are jealous and possessive but not to the point of angry conflict.	U	AN	R			R	AN	
24. You are jealous to the point of conflict, scenes, threats, etc.	AN	AN	AN	AA	R	AN	AN	AN
25. Tactile, sensual contact is very important to you.	AA		AN		U	AN		R
26. Sexual intimacy was achieved early, rapidly in the relationship.	AA		AN	AN	U	R	U	
27. You take the quality of sexual rapport as a test of love	AA	U	AN		U	AN	U	R
28. You are willing to work out sex problems, improve technique.	U	R		R	U		R	U
29. You have a continued high rate of sex, tactile contact throughout the relationship.	U		R	R	U	R		R
30. You declare your love first, well ahead of partner.		AN	R	AA		AA		
31. You consider love life your most important activity, even essential.	AA	AN	R	AA		AA	R	R
32. You are prepared to "give all" for love once under way.	U	AN	U	AA	R	AA	R	R
33. You are willing to suffer abuse, even ridicule from partner.		AN	R	AA			R	AN
34. Your relationship is marked by frequent differences of opinion, anxiety.	R	AA	R	AA	R	R		R
35. The relationship ends with lasting bitterness, trauma for you.	AN	R	R	AA	R	AN	R	R

To diagnose your style of love, look for patterns across characteristics. If you consider your childhood less happy than that of your friends, were discontent with life when you fell in love, and very much want to be in love, you have "symptoms" that are rarely typical of eros and almost never true of storge, but which do suggest mania. Where a trait did not especially apply to a type of love, the space in that column is blank. Storge, for instance, is not the *presence* of many symptoms of love, but precisely their absence; it is cool, abiding affection rather than *Sturm und Drang*.

From J. A. Lee, "The Styles of Love, *Psychology Today*, 1974. Reprinted by permission.

There are few of us who have not fallen in love or had infatuations as a result of these strange, mysterious, and wonderful physiological arousal mechanisms.

We can turn to Shakespeare (as social psychologist), for an illustration of the two-component theory. In *A Midsummer Night's Dream*, Titania, Queen of the Fairies, is given a love potion that will make her fall in love with the first being she sees when she awakens from her sleep. The love potion is a stimulant that, like certain drugs, induces intense physiological responses. This stimulation is the basis for all love potions and spells, real or imagined. In this aroused state, Titania awakens and her eyes fall on Bottom, who has just been transformed into a donkey.

TITANIA: What angel wakes me from my flowery bed. . . .
          Thy fair virtue's force perforce doth move
             On the first view, to say, to swear, I love thee.
BOTTOM: Methinks, mistress, you should have little reason for that: and yet, to say the truth,
          reason and love keep little company together now-a-days. . . .

Of course, Bottom is neither wise nor beautiful; he is a donkey. But love aroused keeps no company with reason—although in a comedy about love, it is reasonable that Titania believes she is in love with a donkey. (We all may make that mistake sometime in our lives!) When the spell induced by the potion is broken (that is, when the physiological stimuli stop), Titania comes to see Bottom as the donkey he truly is.

So it is with all romantic love, according to Schachter's theory. It cannot endure. J. K. Folsom (quoted in Walster and Walster, 1978) wrote:

Love grows less exciting with time for the same biological reasons that the second run on a fast toboggan slide is less exciting than the first. The diminished excitement, however, may increase the real pleasure. Extreme excitement is practically the same as fear, and is unpleasant. After the excitement has diminished below a certain point, however, pleasure will again diminish, unless new kinds of pleasure have meanwhile arisen.

Ultimately, romantic love may be transformed or replaced by companionate love. Otherwise the relationship breaks up and each person searches for another who will once again ignite his or her passion.

Romantic Love versus Companionate Love

It may seem that the worst fate to befall romantic love is not its end but its transformation into mere companionship. *Companionate love*—the very term seems so comfortable, so lackluster, so dull. But romantic love alone is not enduring; it must be augmented or replaced (in part at least) by a different bond for a lasting relationship.

We have contradictory needs, wrote Walster and Walster (1978):

What we really want is the impossible—a perfect mixture of security and danger. We want someone who understands and cares for us, someone who will be around through thick and thin, until we are old. At the same time, we long for sexual excitement, novelty, and danger. The individual who offers just the right combination of both ultimately wins our love. The problem, of course, is that, in time, we get more and more security—and less and less excitement—than we bargained for.

Sidebar quotes:

I will reveal to you a love potion, without medicine, without herbs, without any witch's magic. If you want to be loved, then you must love.

HECATON OF RHODES

Love reckons hours for months, and days for years; and every little absence is an age.

JOHN DRYDEN (1631–1700)

Love is a flickering flame between two darknesses. . . . Whence does it come? . . . From sparks incredibly small. . . . How does it end? . . . In nothingness equally incredible . . . the more raging the flame, the sooner it is burnt out.

HEINRICH HEINE (1797–1856)

Love is such a tissue of paradoxes, and exists in such an endless variety of forms and shades that you may say almost anything about it that you please, and it is likely to be correct.

HENRY FINK, *ROMANTIC LOVE AND PERSONAL BEAUTY* (1902)

Companionate love is not the love of adventure or the thrill of anguish or rapture but the love of friendship and security. It is the love people seek after the excitement dies down; it makes it possible for them to widen the scope of their creative energies. In Tolstoy's *Family Happiness*, Sergei says to his wife, who mourns the loss of their romance:

In that summer when I first knew you, I used to lie awake all night, thinking about you, and I made that love myself, and it grew and grew in my heart. So again, in Petersburg and abroad, in the course of horrible sleepless nights, I strove to shatter that love, which had come to torture me. I did not destroy it, but I destroyed that part of it which gave me pain. Then I grew calm; and I feel love still, but it is a different kind of love.

In this love each knows he or she can count on the other. The excitement comes from the achievement of other goals as well as from the relationship; from being a creative person, from work, from childrearing, from friendships.

Walster and Walster (1978) wrote:

A husband and wife often enjoy being able to count on the fact that, while their friends must contend with one emotional upheaval after another, their lives drift on in a serene, unruffled flow. They enjoy the fact that they can share day-to-day pleasures and that, in old age, they'll be together to reminisce and savor their lives. This portrait is very alluring.

Companionate love, however, may slip into lacklustre love if the partners substitute routine for intimacy, if they take their love for granted. Maintaining romance within the context of companionate love becomes the challenge of an enduring relationship.

Individuals do not always feel passionate about the person who provides the most rewards with the greatest consistency. Passion sometimes develops under conditions that would be more likely to provoke aggression and hatred than love.

ELAINE WALSTER

François Gerard (1770–1837). "Cupid and Psyche." Romantic love is a fusion of psyche (mind) and eros (desire), as portrayed in this painting from Greek mythology.

□ OBSTACLES TO LOVE

Although love is one of the most important elements of our humanity, it may come and go. Perhaps the most profound question about love is not what it is but, as Tom Robbins (1980) noted, how to make it last.

Albert Camus wrote that the only serious question is whether to kill yourself or not. Tom Robbins wrote that the only serious question is whether time has a beginning or end. Camus clearly got up on the wrong side of the bed, and Robbins must have forgotten to set his alarm. There is only one serious question. And that is, Who knows how to make love stay?

Loving is learned behavior. Our ability to love develops from infancy on. If we were loved as infants and children, our potential to love as adults is heightened. Much of our ability to love is a result of our personal history. But much of it is cultural as well. Our parents lived in a particular time and place; their beliefs and attitudes about themselves and us were formed in large part by culture. As our parents related to us and to each other, so we tend to relate to our partners and children. But by becoming aware of the factors that influenced our development, we are in a better position to choose how we will love.

People as Objects

To be faithful to one is to be cruel to all others.

WOLFGANG AMADEUS
MOZART, *DON GIOVANNI*

The philosopher Martin Buber described two fundamental ways of relating to people: "I-Thou" and "I-It." In an I-Thou relationship, each person is treated as a "Thou," that is, as a person whose life is valued as an end in itself. In an I-It relationship, each person is treated as an "It"; the person has worth only as someone who can be used. When a person is treated as a "Thou," his or her humanity and uniqueness are paramount. But our culture encourages people to treat one another as objects. Each person tends to look on the other as an "It" rather than as a "Thou."

Such thinking led Fromm (1956) to write: "If we speak about love in contemporary Western culture, we mean to ask whether the social structure of Western Civilization and the spirit resulting from it are conducive to love." For Fromm the answer was no. He pointed out that capitalism—the basic economic structure of our culture—places profits above people. In the name of profits, people are reduced to mere objects. The result is alienation. "Modern man," wrote Fromm, "is alienated from himself, from his fellow men, and from nature. He has been transformed into a commodity. . . . Human relations are essentially those of alienated automatons." As a result, people are unable to love. "Automatons cannot love; they can exchange their 'personality packages' and hope for a fair bargain."

Culture affects our capacity to love. What ultimately lies at the roots of the dehumanization of humans may be mass society, whether capitalistic or socialistic. Mass societies depend on bureaucracies that turn people into numbers and categories. Identity becomes synthetic: plastic driver's licenses, social security cards, credit cards, student IDs. People are treated as consumers, employees, employers, students, administrators. Function replaces personhood. As a result, people who live in mass societies tend to become isolated; they find it difficult to make significant connections with one another. Their relationships are based on roles rather than personal characteristics. This general cultural atmosphere pervades all relations, including those of love.

The Hidden Taboo on Love

Another obstacle to love in our society is what psychologist J. K. Adams (1972) called "the hidden taboo on love." According to Adams, mass society cannot tolerate authentic love. Authentic love would undermine the impersonal relations that mass society requires to operate. Love would transform strangers into neighbors, enemies into friends; it would destroy sexism, racism, and nationalism. The radical potential for the Christian doctrine "Love thy neighbor" has not been realized in American mass society.

Adams named three necessary conditions for love, all of which contemporary society works against. First of all, we must be able to experience our basic feelings and impulses. If thwarted, our natural feelings will gradually disappear or else turn into qualitatively different kinds of feelings. We will be emotionally dead or overcontrolled. Thus anger (a hot emotion) will become hatred (a cold emotion). A warm love will become a cool love. Our culture discourages the expression of physical affection, although in recent years it has encouraged sexual expression. But sex and affection are not the same. One does not require the other. Affection and love may be more crucial than sex, but we are often willing to be satisfied with sex, mistaking it for love.

It is easier to stay out than get out.

MARK TWAIN

A second condition necessary for love is self-knowledge. As long as we disregard our feelings and emotions, we are prevented from truly knowing ourselves. We are strangers even to ourselves. As we have seen, self-knowledge is the basis of the "I" in "I love you"; it gives the statement its meaning.

A third condition of loving is respect for others. If we do not express our feelings, we cannot know ourselves. If we do not know ourselves, we cannot know others. If we do not know others, we cannot respect them. But our culture encourages us to treat people as objects; to know someone takes effort and insight, especially when culture works against this kind of knowledge.

Traditional Sex Roles

Yet another obstacle to love in our culture is traditional sex roles. Men are supposed to be strong, silent, controlling, reasonable, tough, successful, manipulative, unemotional; their very essence is supposed to be their independence, their ability to act alone. Women, in contrast, are supposed to be weak, talkative, compliant, emotional, soft, and dependent. They take their strength from others, especially men. Human beings, however, cannot be polarized in this manner. Most people are tough and soft, independent and dependent, emotional and rational.

No disguise can long conceal love where it exists, or long feign it where it is lacking.

FRANÇOIS De La ROCHEFOUCAULD

Traditional sex roles make it difficult for men to express their tender, intimate feelings; to touch and be touched; to be soft and vulnerable. They make it difficult for women to be assertive and independent, to express strength as well as weakness (Baruch et al., 1983). The result may be disastrous for love. Each person tends to look to the other sex for the sex role traits he or she lacks. Men cannot accept tenderness in themselves, thus they find it in women; women cannot accept strength in themselves, thus they find it in men. The ideal man and the ideal woman therefore have the characteristics that each sex dissociates from itself. As a result, we love a member of the other sex for precisely those traits we believe ourselves to lack. Such alienation is the basis for deficiency-love. Sooner or later, a woman may discover that her partner is not as strong as she has believed, and she may leave him as a result;

There is no love apart from the deeds of love; no potentiality of love than that which is manifested in loving. . . .

JEAN-PAUL SARTRE, *EXISTENTIALISM AS HUMANISM*

or a man may learn that his partner is not tender at all—he simply wanted to believe she was. Each sought to have his or her needs and deficiencies filled by the other. In reality, only they could have done that for themselves. When each only *needs* the other, love may vanish and each must begin again that lonely search for someone else to love.

☐ JEALOUSY

In Shakespeare's *Othello*, Othello murders his wife in a fit of jealous rage. Desdemona, however, was innocent of Othello's suspicions. When he learns the truth, Othello cries out, "He loved not wisely but too well." But does love necessarily inspire jealousy? Did Othello love "too well" or not well enough?

Social Components of Jealousy

Jealousy is not a universal feeling. Among most groups in our culture, if a man discovers that his wife is having an affair with his guest, he is likely to feel anger, resentment, betrayal, and jealousy; his friends and associates will feel pity or contempt for him. He is a cuckold. But in a culture where wife lending is practiced, as among the Eskimo, if a man does not share his wife with his guest he is considered inhospitable or stingy. Psychologist Ralph Hupka (in Adams, 1980), surveying world cultures, found great differences in the way cultures handled jealousy. Societies could be divided into low-jealousy cultures, such as the Todas of India, and high-jealousy cultures, such as the Texas Apaches. Little jealousy existed among the Todas, whose culture was characterized by a sharing attitude toward people and things, nonrestrictive attitudes toward sexual pleasure, and the separation of social recognition from marriage and progeny. In contrast, the highly jealous Apaches valued virginity, legitimized children through marriage, and believed that sexual pleasure needed to be earned by long periods of deprivation. Hupka concluded that jealousy is the result of socialization—learning what is valued and what is to be protected.

Our society has traditionally been a high-jealousy culture. In one study of 103 men and women (Pines and Aronson, 1983), half of the people in the study described themselves as a "jealous person." In some states laws have sanctioned murder as justifiable homicide if it is committed by a husband in a fit of jealous rage. A boot-hill epitaph at Dodge City reads:

Here lies the body of Mannie,
They put him here to stay;
He lived the life of Riley,
While Riley was away.

We curtail the sexuality of our children and adolescents, prize virginity, legitimize children only through marriage, and are highly possessive and competitive. Social changes of the last few decades, however, have undermined much of the traditional morality. Jessie Bernard (1972) has observed that "marital jealousy is declining as our conception of the nature of the marital bond itself is changing. . . . If monogamic marriage is changing, there may be less and less need for jealousy to buttress it, and less socialization of human beings to experience jealousy." With new feelings about sexuality and marriage, jealousy receives less approval and understanding. Jealousy itself has become a "problem," not the behavior that inspires it.

The Experience of Jealousy

Many people probably feel that jealousy is a "bad" feeling, that they should not have it, that it is irrational. But feelings are neither good nor bad; they are simply feelings. Jealousy, however, is an uncomfortable feeling, bringing rage or anger, fear, insecurity, distrust, and pain. Most of us would like to get rid of jealousy when we feel its nagging presence. Nevertheless, jealousy can have value. Psychologist Barbara Harris (1976) pointed out:

Feelings are signals, symptoms of complex reactions. Just as pain alerts us to a physical problem and spurs us to do something about it, so jealousy may be a way of calling our attention to an emotional problem we may not be aware of, or not want to face. What matters is not that we are jealous but whether we can find out *why*—and then how we deal with jealousy, what we learn about ourselves as a result, what we do about the situation.

Jealousy involves the fear of losing someone we love. Both men and women fear their partners' attraction to someone else because of dissatisfactions and the desire for sexual variety; women especially tend to fear losing their partner to a good-looking rival (White, 1981). Jealous fears may or may not be reasonable. For example, a person might be jealous because in fact his or her partner is in love with someone else and is about to leave. Jealousy in this instance is not blind but probably a realistic response to pain. But it is also common for people to provoke a jealous response in their partner as a means of exerting control (White, 1980a). Sometimes a jealous response is unrealistic. Your partner may have lunch with a friend of the other sex; you are jealous, fearing your partner may be falling in love with someone else. Although the relationship is strictly one of friendship, you feel threatened. This kind of unfounded jealousy is worth examining. Do you really trust your partner? Do you believe what your partner tells you? Are you projecting your own feelings onto your partner? Are you feeling insecure and blaming him or her?

All of us experience some kind of dependence on the person we love. As our lives become more and more intertwined, we become less and less independent. For some, this loss of independence increases the fear of losing the partner. Others fear the dependence of love itself. One of Lawrence Durrell's characters says in the novel *Justine* (1957): "But what made me afraid was that after quite a short time I found to my horror that I could not live without her. . . . I had fallen *in love*. The very thought filled me with an inexplicable despair and disgust." This despair and disgust is what Klein and Riviere (1953) call "the anxiety of dependency." But it takes more than simple dependency to make a person jealous. To be jealous we also need to feel insecure—either about ourselves or about our relationships (Berscheid and Frei, 1977).

Managing Jealousy

Jealous feelings become a problem when they interfere with a relationship. (See the reading "Types of Jealousy" by Gordon Clanton and Lynn Smith. Dealing with

A man was jealous of his wife, who, despite his jealousies, was always faithful. She gave him no reason to be jealous, but it did not matter; he tortured her with his constant tirades. Finally one evening she left and was never seen again. But outside the camp, her sons discovered a great rock which resembled her mother. Their father's jealousy, they said, had turned their mother to stone.

PLAINS INDIAN TALE

There is more self-love than love in jealousy.

FRANÇOIS de La ROCHEFOUCAULD

Jealousy is not a barometer by which the depth of love can be read. It merely records the degree of the lover's insecurity. . . . It is a negative miserable state of feeling having its origin in the sense of insecurity and inferiority.

MARGARET MEAD

feelings of jealousy may often be very difficult, for they touch deep recesses in ourselves. To work out jealous feelings, individuals need to feel that the relationship is worth the effort, that no other crises are occurring at the same time, and, most important, that their partner is supportive and nurturing. They need to understand their own jealousy as well as to learn to behave in ways that cause little jealousy in others. Clanton and Smith (1977) wrote:

Jealousy cannot be treated in isolation. *Your* jealousy is not *your* problem alone. It is also a problem for your partner and for the person whose interest in your partner sparks your jealousy. Similarly, when your partner feels jealous, you ought not to dismiss the matter by pointing a finger and saying "That's your problem." Typically, three or more persons are involved in the production of jealous feelings and behaviors. Ideally, all three should take a part of the responsibility for minimizing the negative consequences.

The jealous person must deal with his or her own jealousy on the personal level. The jealous person creates the feelings, interpretations, and perceptions that lead to jealousy. He or she must determine whether the jealous feelings are reasonable or irrational, arising from an actually threatening situation or from fears and insecurities. The partner of the jealous person must be honest. If the jealousy is irrational, the partner must reassure the jealous person that the relationship is secure, that the connecting bonds are not threatened. Since jealousy often reflects insecurity or lack of self-esteem, the partner must be reassuring and loving. Jealous persons may need considerable reassurance, often more than seems reasonable. But jealousy may not be irrational. In this case an important means of reassurance is for the partner to modify the relationship with the "third party" who initially caused the jealousy to flare up. This means recognizing that the jealousy was at least partly triggered by the situation. Modifying the third-party relationship, if only for a time, reduces the jealous response and, more important, symbolizes the partner's commitment to the primary relationship. These are only suggestions; each person must deal with jealousy using his or her own understanding and insights. As with most of life's puzzling problems, jealousy has no simple answers.

☐ SUMMARY

- Love signifies different things to different people. It is contradictory because it is both a feeling and an activity.

- The *wheel theory* of love developed by Ira Reiss states that love involves four processes: (1) *rapport*, (2) *self-revelation*, (3) *mutual dependency*, and (4) *intimacy need fulfillment*.

- Friendship and love have much in common: enjoyment, acceptance, trust, mutual respect, confiding, understanding, and spontaneity. Love differs from friendship in that love is characterized by passion, whereas friendship is not; both love and friendship display caring.

- The central requirement of love is identity. Without it, love may be based on dependency needs and be forever changing. *Deficiency-love* is basically selfish, based on needs the other person can fulfill; *being-love* is love for the other person as he or she is.

- The Greek philosopher Plato first posited the idea of *complementary* love in which each person searches for his or her "other half" to be complete. More recently, Robert Winch suggested that we love those who complement our needs, especially in terms of dominance/submission and nurturance/receptivity.

- According to John Lee, there are six basic styles of love: *eros*, *mania*, *ludis*, *storge*, *agape*, and *pragma*.

- The *two-component theory* of love suggests that physiological arousal and an appropriate emotional explanation of the arousal must be present for love to occur.

- *Romantic love* generally does not last and may be replaced by *companionate love*. Romantic love brings excitement but not stability. Companionate love gives stability but may not provide excitement.

- Many obstacles to love exist. They include (1) the tendency to treat people as objects, (2) a hidden taboo on love that our culture encourages through preventing us from experiencing our true feelings, knowing ourselves, and respecting others, and (3) traditional sex roles.

- Jealousy involves fear of losing the person we love. The fear may or may not be reasonable. Irrational jealousy is produced by insecurity as well as dependency. To work out jealous feelings, a person needs to feel that the relationship is worth saving, to have no other major crises occurring at the same time, and to have a supportive and nurturing partner.

READINGS

Psychologists Examine Love
DANIEL GOLEMAN, THE NEW YORK TIMES

Over the last decade or so, psychologists and sociologists have begun to investigate the nature of love. In this excerpt, three different psychologists examine love. What are their conclusions? How do they compare with each other? Which (if any) of these studies comes closest to your own understanding of love? Why?

Freud counted the ability to love, along with the capacity for work, as a hallmark of full maturity. Yet psychology's study of emotions has been oddly deficient in examining the nature of love. While such feelings as aggression and depression have been the objects of intense research, love has not.

That deficiency has begun to be remedied, with new research, public discussion and professional reports. Some of the new observations from psychological research and from the clinic, while perhaps less profound than the insights of poets, are nevertheless surprising and meaningful.

For example, the best predictor of how satisfied and

happy a couple are in a relationship, according to one recent study, is not how much or how little the partners love each other, but rather how equal their love is.

Also, it may come as a surprise to many men—but not to women—that women, on average, report loving their best friends as much as they do their lovers. And they report liking, as opposed to loving, their best friends a bit more than they do their lovers.

These are among the results reported by Robert Sternberg, a psychologist at Yale University, who is one of those doing major research on the nature of love. His work builds on that of several other researchers who, over the last decade, have devised psychological scales for measuring love. Dr. Sternberg has undertaken a comprehensive study that uses all the major measures in order to assess love's essential nature.

When it comes to the success of a romantic love relationship, men and women for the most part name the same factors as important, according to a report Dr. Sternberg published in the Journal of Personality and Social Psychology. The single most important element was found to be

READINGS—*continued*

sharing ideas and interests with one's lover. Also high on the list was the sense of growing personally through the relationship, as was taking pleasure in doing things for the other person.

Not of particular importance in the success of a romantic relationship, though, were such things as feeling that one's lover has great sex appeal or is seductive, feeling the lover to be particularly unique or feeling that other people would be impressed by one's lover.

While the sexes largely agree on what is important for success in romantic love, there were a few differences. One of the more striking, Dr. Sternberg finds, is that women, but not men, feel it is their own unselfishness that is crucial in the success of a relationship.

"Women, traditionally, have been more the maintainers of relationships than have men," Dr. Sternberg commented. "Even though sex roles are changing, this still seems to be true."

While romantic love has its special qualities, Dr. Sternberg finds that the different loving relationships in a person's life have much in common.

"There is a basic core of what love is that is the same in any loving relationship, whether with a lover or with one's child," according to Dr. Sternberg. That core includes such elements as being able to count on the loved one in times of need; having a mutual understanding and sharing oneself and one's things with the loved one; giving and getting emotional support; promoting the welfare of the person, and valuing and being happy when with the person.

"These are the things that really seem to matter when it comes to love," Dr. Sternberg said in an interview. "These qualities of loving are quite general. They can apply equally to a lover or to your child."

"But there are some additional components that differ in each kind of relationship that give love its different qualities," he added. "For example, with your parents there's a sense of gratitude and devotion for all they've done for you, while with your children, there's a strong element of identification—you see yourself in them."

Love in Equal Degrees

In a romantic relationship, Dr. Sternberg's research has shown, the single most important variable in how satisfied partners are with the match is whether they love each other in roughly equal degrees, not the absolute amount of love they feel. Here, he says, the least happy situation is when one loves one's partner much more, or much less, than the partner is perceived to love one in return.

An entirely different sort of insight into the nature of passionate love was offered at a conference sponsored by the Columbia University Center for Psychoanalytic Training and Research last week in New York.

Among the observations offered there was that passion—an intimate sexual abandon—amid the conventional responsibilities of matrimony can provide "an internal wildness that preserves marriage," in the words of Dr. Otto Kernberg, an eminent psychoanalyst.

On the other hand, sexual inhibition resulting from guilt is "a major source of boredom in otherwise happy couples," Dr. Kernberg said at the conference.

That inhibition "limits a couple to conventional standards which stifle passion." Pornography, or the active fantasy life it can stimulate, can be one antidote to such stifled passions, said Dr. Kernberg.

"A rebellious sex life within the bounds of a couple," he said, can be the cement of marriage.

Overcoming guilt and inhibition, and the subsequent sexual freedom, according to Dr. Kernberg, can be salutary, provided "the increased sexual temptations that go with increased sexual freedom are redirected into the couple's sexual life." If so, their sex life can be a major source of stability even in the face of conflicts in other areas.

Love, of course, has its pathologies. Dr. Kernberg, writing in *The Journal of the American Psychoanalytic Association*, describes a continuum in people's ability to fall and remain in love that ranges from severe problems to normality.

The most severe pathology of love, in Dr. Kernberg's view, is seen in the narcissist whose life is utterly devoid of love: he is socially isolated and expresses his sexual urges only in perverse masturbatory fantasies. A slightly better picture is seen in the narcissist who is sexually promiscuous, but feels no love for his partners—at least he has such relationships. And one step ahead is the person who can fall in love, but does so in a chaotic fashion, in a series of immature, promiscuous relationships. Somewhat better adjusted are those who can experience romantic tenderness but suffer sexual inhibitions.

Mature romantic love, in Dr. Kernberg's view, is a complex emotion that combines such elements as sexual excitement, an ecstatic mood, tenderness, commitment and, most particularly, an overriding passion that sets it apart from all other love relationships in one's life.

A major source of the excitement in romantic passion is the sense of mystery about one's lover. The roots of that mystery, Dr. Kernberg has written, can be seen in children's "intuition of an exciting, gratifying and forbidden relationship that links the parents and excludes the child, and their longing for and excitement about forbidden knowledge—particularly sexual knowledge."

"The experience of orgasm," Dr. Kernberg writes, "does not by itself represent sexual passion."

What is missing in orgasm alone is the psychological baggage of love, which brings to the union a set of inner meanings that resonate with the lovers' deepest identifications, conflicts and fantasies.

"Sexual passion," writes Dr. Kernberg, "reactivates the entire sequence of emotional states that assure the individual of his own, his parents', the entire world of objects' 'goodness' and the hope of fulfillment of love in the face of frustration, hostility and normal ambivalence."

Passion in sexual love, in his view, is the result of a unique facet of mature loving relationships: the crossing of psychological boundaries between oneself and one's lover. The sense of becoming one with the loved person, while simultaneously retaining one's sense of oneself, generates a feeling of transcendence.

This same sense of transcendence, in becoming one with the lover, can, paradoxically, add to love a poignant feeling of loneliness and longing at the frailty of such relationships, in Dr. Kernberg's view.

Emotional maturity is no guarantee of a couple's stability, Dr. Kernberg cautions. The complication is that as people change, the psychological grounds for the relationship are continually renegotiated, sometimes successfully, sometimes not.

If emotional maturity is no guarantee that a relationship will work out, what does matter?

"Marriages can rise or fall on how couples handle negative feelings," in the view of John Gottman, a psychologist at the University of Illinois, who has been studying marital satisfaction.

At the annual meeting of the American Psychological Association last summer, Dr. Gottman reported that in loving couples, the husband and wife each play a crucial, but distinctly different, role in managing negative emotions. The key interaction revolves around handling feelings such as anger.

In unhappy marriages, perhaps understandably, there is more open expression of negative feelings such as anger, fear, disgust and sadness, Dr. Gottman reported. Moreover, these feelings, once expressed, are reciprocated more often. Loving marriages, though, have a very different pattern when it comes to managing emotions.

"Happy couples are characterized by the ability to de-escalate conflicts," Dr. Gottman said in an interview.

"When tensions are low, it typically is the husband who plays the role of managing negative feelings. The wife will say something negative, and he'll respond in a positive way, keeping things from escalating. These husbands have a marvelously gentle way of deflecting their wives' negative feelings."

"But when things flare up, it's the wife who takes the crucial role in managing things," Dr. Gottman added. "Husbands don't seem as flexible as wives when feelings are intense; for example, men in both happy and unhappy marriages tend to respond to anger with anger. In happy marriages, though, the wives are able to switch to a de-escalating response during intense conflicts. Men are poorer at making up when things have gotten to this point."

"In unhappy marriages, there is an interlocking of negativity, which neither husband nor wife seem able to de-escalate," he said. "The couple get caught in a pervasive negative arousal pattern, which interferes with their ability to think of a new response. They get locked into a negative cycle where they fall back on an overlearned, automatic and negative response, which locks them into a destructive cycle."

There is a certain symmetry in the complaints made by husbands and wives in unhappy marriages, Dr. Gottman reported. Wives, he finds, complain that their husbands are too withdrawn; husbands complain that their wives complain too much, which may make the husbands withdraw more.

The most loving couples in Dr. Gottman's study discussed their conflicts and disagreements during moments of calm, not during arguments.

In a review of other research on marital interactions, Dr. Gottman reported that, in general, wives more readily become confrontational, while husbands tend to be conciliatory. This pattern becomes stronger, he finds, when the wife is pregnant.

One reason women more readily confront their spouses than do men, Dr. Gottman asserts, has to do with the different health consequences of negative emotions for each sex. He reported data showing that marital arguments are more damaging to the husband's health than to the wife's.

"Since marital arguments are more punishing for men than for women, men are more conciliatory," Dr. Gottman said. "They have more to gain from trying to head off arguments than do their wives."

Another perspective on love and the relationship between the sexes is offered by Carol Gilligan, a psychologist at Harvard University. In her view psychology, particularly psycho-

READINGS–*continued*

analysis, has been lacking an accurate understanding of how women love.

"Women's experience of love is better captured by the myth of Eros and Psyche than the story of Oedipus," Dr. Gilligan said. "The tale of Eros and Psyche is a story of passionate attachment which ends not in death, but with the birth of a child called "Pleasure.""

Love as an Exchange
JOHN SCANZONI, EXCERPT FROM *SEXUAL BARGAINING*

Sociologist John Scanzoni views love as an exchange. Does this view adequately explain romantic love and companionate love? When we view love as an exchange, what are the elements that lead to falling in love?

[Sociologist Peter] Blau suggests that "love is the polar case of intrinsic attraction." By "intrinsic attraction" he means a relationship that is considered an "end in itself," as contrasted with an *extrinsic* (or secondary) relationship in which the relationship is considered merely a means to ends beyond the relationship itself. For example, in a secondary relationship, a salesman takes a client golfing, but the "golfing relationship" serves *chiefly* as a means to sell a service or product. In an intrinsic relationship, it is sufficient for friends or lovers to be together, and simply to enjoy the other person for his own sake.

> Love appears to make human beings unselfish, since they themselves enjoy giving pleasure to those they love, but this selfless devotion generally rests on an interest in maintaining the other's love.

Love is generally conceived of in altruistic terms, but "even a mother's devotion to her children is rarely entirely devoid of the desire to maintain their attachment to her. *Exchange processes occur in love relations as well as in [extrinsic] social associations*" (italics supplied). . . . Male-female reward-seeking from each other begins prior to marriage at the very outset of their love relationship. The prospect of certain rewards from the other is what forms the basis of their relationship in the first place, but in order to receive those rewards each must in turn provide the kinds of rewards expected by the other. To be sure, rewards are furnished "to express and confirm his own commitment and to promote the other's growing commitment to the association." This ongoing process is labeled "social ex-

change" and is the basis for the formation and *maintenance* of *any* social relationship including love and marriage:

> A man falls in love if the attractiveness of a woman has become unique in his eyes. . . . His attraction to her makes him dependent on her for important rewards and anxious to impress and please her to arouse a reciprocal affection that would assure him these rewards. . . . Human beings evidently derive pleasure from doing things for those they love. . . . The repeated experience of being rewarded by the increased attachment of a loved one after having done a variety of things to please him may have the effect that giving pleasure to loved ones becomes intrinsically gratifying.

If a love relationship is "to develop into a lasting mutual attachment," then the "lovers' affection for and commitment to one another [must] expand at roughly the same pace." That is, if one lover makes significantly greater inputs than the other into the relationship, this "invites exploitation or provokes feelings of entrapment, both of which obliterate love. . . . The weak interest of the less committed or the frustrations of the more committed probably will sooner or later prompt one or the other to terminate it." Hence, if both parties define their inputs and rewards as "just," "beneficial," or "satisfactory," then the love relationship is quite likely to be maintained and to evolve into marriage. If one party does not feel that the cost-reward ratio is satisfactory to him, he (she) may cut back his inputs, thereby reducing the satisfactions of the other, and thus increasing the likelihood that the relationship will be terminated.

It is a general sociological principle that associations are formed and maintained on the basis of reciprocity—exchanged rewards and benefits. A love relationship is no exception. To be sure, since it is primarily an *intrinsic* relationship, persons are not overtly being "used" as means to extrinsic ends. But to conceive of love and marriage as purely altruistic is to miss the point that rarely, if ever, can human love be sustained unless it is requited. And although later we shall say more about common values and shared interests of a married couple, to posit value consensus or common interests as the prime basis for love and marriage exhibits only a tiny fraction of the iceberg, and totally misses the dynamics of marriage formation and subsequent interaction.

Jessie Bernard has tried to apply some of the ideas of game theory to marriage, and obviously one of the central notions of game theory is the seeking of individual rewards and interests. As long as players find the game rewarding, they will continue in it, and drop out when it ceases to

---

READINGS–*continued*

---

reward them. The individual reward-seeking is in no way inimical to the relationship. Indeed the more each feels rewarded the more solid it becomes.

Thus, there is no foundation for the assumption that individual interests and group interests are necessarily mutually exclusive or contradictory. Moreover, it is naïve to think that love and marriage relationships could be maintained unless individual gratifications were satisfied.

Types of Jealousy
GORDON CLANTON AND LYNN SMITH, EXCERPT FROM *JEALOUSY*

The authors suggest that there are several types of jealousy. What are they? Can you think of other types of jealousy? Is envy, for example, a type of jealousy? What types of jealousy have you experienced? Do you experience these types of jealousy differently? If so, how?

The deeper understanding and the management of jealousy require an appreciation of the specific types of jealousy and of the contextual factors which amplify or mute the jealous flash. The "sorting" of jealous feelings might well begin with this question: *Does a particular experience of jealousy come from feeling excluded or from a fear of loss?* The distinction is important; it is the difference between a small problem and a large one, between the benign and the malignant.

Feeling Excluded

Probably *most* jealous flashes come from feeling *left out* of an activity involving your partner and another (or others). When your partner "attends" (in whatever way) to another, his/her attention is elsewhere. When you notice that, before you process the implications or possible consequences, your first reaction is to note that they are "in," and you are "out." They are not noticing you—or, at least, not giving you as much attention as they are giving each other. You feel excluded, ignored, unappreciated. Perhaps you wish *you* could do what they are doing (whatever it is), but for reasons you don't quite understand, you can't.

This kind of experience is commonplace in our society, and dealing with it gracefully is part of the etiquette of our time—especially as women become more involved in occupational and social activities outside the home. The boss wants to dance with your wife. A woman takes more initiative in conversation with your husband than you would with a man you had just met. Your partner and a friend

both discover that they *adore* Bergman's films (which you never particularly enjoyed). And so on. Such experiences trigger the jealous flash, but typically, they do not fan it into a flame. The jealous feelings usually fade when the precipitating event is over—although one might still need to say, on the way home, "I cannot *imagine* what you and Pat could have found interesting enough to discuss for an hour."

If you find yourself troubled or upset by the "sharing" of your partner that is considered appropriate in your circle of friends, perhaps your "feeling excluded" is a symptom of an underlying fear of loss, the more serious "strain" of jealousy. If you literally cannot stand to let your partner out of your sight—and this is a condition observed among *both* the very conventional *and* some swingers—your jealousy is probably rooted in a persistent *fear* rather than in a temporary irritation.

Definitions of appropriate limits vary from one peer group to another, from one subculture to another. Behavior that is considered "friendly" in one circle may be viewed as "seductive" and "immoral" in another. What seems "proper" to my Uncle Calvin may seem "stuffy" or "cold" to Bob and Carol and Ted and Alice. We choose our values when we choose our neighbors, our workmates, our playmates, our helpmates.*

Fear of Loss

If your jealous flash signals *more* than irritation at being temporarily excluded, it probably reflects a *fear of loss*. This is more serious, but it need not be fatal to your self-esteem or to your relationship with your partner. To treat it you must diagnose it more precisely. *Exactly what is it you are afraid you might lose?* There are several possibilities, some more serious than others.

Perhaps it is *loss of "face"* that frightens you. If your wife is vivacious in company, perhaps the guys you drink with will think you "can't keep her in line." If your husband is appreciative of attractive women, perhaps your friends will suspect that he's dissatisfied with you. If your mate is too friendly with a person of the opposite sex, perhaps others

---

*Popular awareness of this variation is reflected in the bit of folk sociology which says that when two couples ride in one car, the seating arrangement will vary as follows: Working-class persons sit one couple in the front seat, the other in back. Middle-class couples regroup so that the men sit in front, the women in the back. The rich swap mates for the drive; each man sits next to the other's wife.

READINGS–*continued*

will assume that they are sexually involved. If you don't *like* the third party, if she seems "unworthy" of your mate's attention, the fear of loss of reputation can be especially powerful.

The fear of loss of face may be a minor problem or a major one, temporary or recurrent. It affects the way you feel about yourself and the way you present yourself to others. And these, in turn, influence your susceptibility to jealousy in the future.

But perhaps you fear *more* than loss of face; perhaps you fear that you are losing *control*—control of your spouse, control of the relationship, control of the future, control of your *self*. You cannot predict your partner's behavior. You are reluctant to voice complaints because you don't know how she will react. You are unsure of the motives of the third party. Your anxiety breeds tension which corrodes your relationship.

The fear of loss of control is rooted in insecurity and is a specific form of a neurosis that is quite general in our time. As we lose control of other sectors of our lives—or discover that we never really *had* control—we wish all the more to

be secure in our intimate relationships and family life. If things are chaotic at work, if the crime rate is going up, if political life is a tragi-comedy with a cast of criminals and incompetents, it becomes all the more important to keep things together at home.

The most serious jealousy is the jealousy which is *fear of loss of the partner*—and of all the love and affection, support and services s/he provides. This can be a terrifying feeling. To *lose* your partner may be to lose your history, your identity, your means of support, your housekeeper, your home, your children (or someone to help you rear them), perhaps even your reason for living. Not surprisingly, you become anxious and defensive. You assume— although this is questionable—that if you lose him/her it will be to another woman/man, so you view others with suspicion and fear. Such behaviors make you less attractive to your mate, and, perhaps, less entitled to consideration from the point of view of the third party. Thus jealousy begets aloofness and scorn, which deepen the fear that is at the root of the jealousy.

CHAPTER 6

Pairing and Singlehood

PREVIEW

To gain a sense of what you already know about the material covered in this chapter, answer "true" or "false" to the statements below. You will find the answers as you read the chapter.

1. Looking for a mate can be compared to shopping in a market. True or false?
2. Looks tend to be important when we first meet someone. True or false?
3. Interfaith marriages represent about ten percent of all marriages. True or false?
4. If a woman asks a man out on a first date, it is a sign that she is sexually attracted to him. True or false?
5. Because of the rise of egalitarian sex roles, both men and women commonly feel sexually pressured on dates. True or false?
6. An important problem men cite in dating is shyness. True or false?
7. Cohabitation before marriage substantially increases the likelihood of marital satisfaction. True or false?
8. Most dating couples feel they have equal power. True or false?
9. Men are less likely to fall in love first and consequently are more likely to end a relationship. True or false?
10. Pooling money, whether in cohabiting relationships or marriage, seems to indicate commitment to the relationship. True or false?

Outline

Although theoretically we have free choice in selecting our partners, in reality our choices are somewhat limited. These limits are universal enough in our culture to be virtually rules. If we know what the rules are, we can make deductions about whom we will be likely to choose as dates or partners.

There is a game you can play if you understand some of the principles of mate selection in our culture. Without ever having met a friend's new boyfriend or girlfriend, you can deduce many things about him or her, using basically the same method of deductive reasoning that Sherlock Holmes used to astound Dr. Watson. For example, if a female friend at college has a new boyfriend, it is safe to guess that he is about the same age or a little older, taller, and a college student; he is probably about as physically attractive as your friend (if not, they will probably break up within six months); his parents probably are of the same race and social class as hers; and most likely he is approximately as intelligent as your friend. If a male friend has a new girlfriend, many of the same things apply, except that she is probably the same age or younger and shorter than he is. After you have described your friend's new romantic interest, don't be surprised if he or she exclaims, "Good grief, Holmes, how did you know that?" Of course, not every characteristic may apply, but you will probably be correct in most instances. These guesses can apply as well for those whom you choose to date or mate. But these "guesses" are not so much guesses as deductions based on the principle of homogamy discussed in this chapter.

In this chapter we not only look at the general rules by which we choose partners but we also examine dating, premarital sexuality, the singles world, living together, and gay relationships. Over the last decade or two, most of these aspects of pairing have significantly changed, radically affecting marriage. Of course, unmarried people did have sexual intercourse and live together before the 1980s, but such behavior was disapproved of by society as a whole. Today, however, large portions of American society accept and approve of both premarital sex and cohabitation. Marriage has lost its exclusiveness as the only legitimate institution in which people can have sex and share their everyday lives. As a result, it has lost some of its power as an institution.

☐ THE MARRIAGE MARKET

How do we choose the people we date, live with, or marry? At first glance, it seems that we choose them on the basis of love, but other factors also influence our choice. These factors have to do with bargaining and exchange (as discussed in Chapter 2). We select the persons we date, fall in love with, live with, or marry in what might be called a marriage marketplace.

In the marriage marketplace, as in the commercial marketplace, people trade or exchange goods. Unlike a real marketplace, however, the marriage marketplace is not a place but a process. In the marriage marketplace, the goods that are exchanged are not tomatoes, waffle irons, or bales of cotton; *we* are the goods. When we come into this marketplace, each of us has certain resources, such as our social class, status, looks, and personality, that make up our marketability. We use these resources to bargain with. We size ourselves up and rank ourselves as a good deal, an average package, or something to be remaindered; we do the same with potential dates or mates.

The idea of exchange as a basis for choosing marital partners may not be romantic, but it is deeply rooted in marriage customs. In some cultures, for example, arranged marriages take place after extended bargaining between families. The woman is expected to bring a dowry in the form of property (such as pigs, goats, clothing, utensils, land) or money; or a woman's family may demand a bride-price if the culture places a premium on women's productivity. Traces of the exchange basis of marriage in our culture still exist in the traditional marriage ceremony in which the bride's father pays the wedding costs and "gives away" his daughter.

We tend to overlook the bargaining aspect of relationships because it doesn't seem very romantic. We bargain, nevertheless, but usually not openly or consciously. We exchange our social and personality characteristics. To get a sense of the complexity of bargaining in our culture, let's examine the role of physical attractiveness.

> A proposal of marriage in our society tends to be a way in which a man sums up his social attributes and suggests to a woman that hers are not so much better as to preclude a merger or partnership in these matters.
>
> ERVING GOFFMAN

Physical Attractiveness

Physical attractiveness, a prime resource in the dating and marriage marketplace, is particularly significant during the initial meeting and early stages of a relationship. If you don't know anything about a person, you tend to judge him or her on appearance.

Most people would deny that they are attracted to others just because of their looks. But we do so unconsciously by *infering* qualities based on looks. This inference is based on a "halo" effect: good-looking people are assumed to possess more desirable social characteristics than plain-looking people. In one well-known experiment (Dion et al., 1972), students were shown pictures of attractive people and asked to describe

> Taught from infancy that beauty is woman's sceptre, the mind shapes itself to the body, and roaming round its gilt cage, only seeks to adorn its prison.
>
> MARY WOLLSTONECRAFT (1797–1851), *A VINDICATION OF THE RIGHTS OF WOMEN*

Figure 6–1

Satisfaction with parts of the body differs according to sex. Our perception of ourselves as attractive or unattractive affects our social and sexual interactions. Figures indicate the percentages of respondents of each sex who expressed satisfaction. How do male and female responses differ? How do you account for the difference? (From *Sexual Choices: An Introduction to Human Sexuality* by G. D. Nass, R. W. Libby, and M. P. Fisher. Copyright © 1981 by Wadsworth, Inc. Reprinted by permission of Wadsworth Health Sciences Division, Monterey, California.)

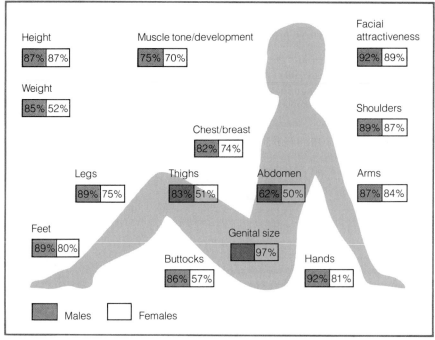

Note: Based on survey of 2000 *Psychology Today* readers approximating the national age and sex distributions.

The beautiful bird gets caged.

CHINESE PROVERB

what they thought these people were like. Attractive men and women were assumed to be more sensitive, kind, warm, sexually responsive, strong, poised, and outgoing than their peers; they were assumed to be more exciting and to have better characters than "ordinary" people. (See the reading by Ellen Berscheid, "Beautiful People: An Unfair Advantage," at the end of this chapter.)

In casual relationships the physical attractiveness of a dating partner is especially important for males, whereas personal qualities are more important for females. For more meaningful long-term relationships, however, both males and females rated personal qualities as more important than physical ones (Nevid, 1984).

But people don't necessarily gravitate to the most attractive person in the room; they tend to gravitate to those who are about as attractive as themselves. Sizing up someone at a party or dance, a man may say, "I'd never have a chance with her; she's too good looking for me." Even if people are allowed to specify the qualities they want in a date, they are hesitant to select anyone notably different from themselves in social desirability.

I'm tired about all this nonsense about beauty being only skin-deep. That's deep enough. What do you want— an adorable pancreas?

JEAN KERR

Trade-Offs

We tend to choose people who are our equals in terms of looks, intelligence, education, and so on (Walster and Walster, 1978). Matching, however, does not occur with each and every trait. If two people are different in looks or intelligence, for example, usually the individuals make a trade-off in which a lower-ranked trait is exchanged for a higher-ranked trait. For example, a woman who values status may accept a lower level of physical attractiveness in the man if he is wealthy or powerful. This trade-off phenomenon was demonstrated a few years ago when Henry Kissinger, a man not noted for his physical attributes, was at the height of his political power. During this time he was frequently seen in the company of beautiful women. When asked his secret, he remarked, "Power is the most important aphrodisiac known to man." Kissinger's female companions traded physical attractiveness for his aura of power.

We may daydream of movie-star lovers, but in real life we are more practical. Walster and Walster (1978) wrote:

Although we prefer partners who are more desirable than ourselves, our actual choices are influenced by matching considerations. We all tend to end up with partners of approximately our own social value. Thus, our selection of a mate appears to be a delicate compromise between our desire to capture an ideal partner and our realization that we must eventually settle for what we deserve.

> Style is the physiognomy of the mind, and a safer index to character than the face.
>
> ARTHUR SCHOPENHAUER (1788–1860)

The Marital Exchange

The Traditional Marital Exchange. The traditional basic marital exchange is related to sex roles. Traditionally, men have used their status, economic power, and role as protecter in a trade-off for women's physical attractiveness, nurturing, child-bearing, and housekeeping abilities; women in return have gained status and economic security. This exchange is embedded in the traditional conception of the "good" wife and the "good" husband.

Changing Terms of the Marital Exchange. As women enter careers and become more economically independent, the terms of bargaining change. When women achieve their own occupational status and economic independence, what is it they ask from men in the marital exchange? Safilios-Rothschild (1976) suggests many women expect men to bring more expressive, affective, and companionable resources into marriage. Independent women do not have to settle for a man who brings little more to the relationship than a paycheck; they want a man who is a companion, not simply a provider.

> The man who marries for money earns it.
>
> YIDDISH PROVERB

But even today a woman's bargaining position is not as strong as a man's in the marital exchange. Although women work, they make about 61 cents for every dollar that men make; they are still significantly underrepresented in the professions. Furthermore, many of the things that women traditionally used to bargain with in the marital exchange—children, housekeeping services, sexuality—are today devalued or available elsewhere. As we will see later (Chapter 12), children are not as highly valued as they once were. A man does not have to rely on a woman to cook for him (McDonald's and Lean Cuisine are available), sex is easily accessible in the singles world, and someone can be hired to do the laundry and clean the toilet.

Women are at a further disadvantage because of the double standard of aging. Physical attractiveness is a key bargaining element in the marital marketplace, but the older a woman gets, the less attractive she is considered. For women, youth and beauty are linked in most cultures. As women get older, their field of eligible partners declines because men tend to choose younger women for mates.

> Whom shall I marry? That question seems obviously about my choice. . . . The more researchers probe that question, however, the more they find a secret question, more destructive, more insistent, that is asked as well: Am I the kind of person worth loving? . . . The individual is faced with a terrible thought: if he or she is not chosen, then he or she may not be worth choosing.
>
> RICHARD SENNETT and JONATHON COBB, *THE HIDDEN INJURIES OF CLASS*

Cathy by Cathy Guisewite. Copyright © 1984, Universal Press Syndicate. Reprinted with permission. All rights reserved.

☐ THE FIELD OF ELIGIBLES

The men and women we date, live with, or marry usually come from the *field of eligibles*, that is, people whom our culture approves as potential partners. The field of eligibles is defined by two principles: (1) *endogamy*, marriage within a particular group and (2) *exogamy*, marriage outside the group.

People usually marry others from a large group such as nationality, race, or social class with which they identify because they share common assumptions, experiences, and understandings. Endogamy strengthens group structure. If people already have ties as friends, neighbors, work associates, or church members, a marriage between such acquaintances solidifies group ties. To take an extreme example, it is easier for two Americans to understand each other than it is for an American and a Fula tribesperson from Africa. Americans are monogamous and urban, whereas Fulanis are polygamous and wandering herders. But another, darker, force may lie beneath endogamy: fear and distrust of outsiders, those who are different from ourselves. Both the need for commonality and the distrust of outsiders work toward people marrying like individuals.

Yet the principle of exogamy requires us to marry outside of certain types of groups, specifically, members of our own family (however defined) and members of the same sex. Exogamy is enforced by taboos that are deeply embedded within our psychological makeup. The violation of these taboos may cause a deep sense of guilt. A marriage between a man and his mother, sister, daughter, aunt, niece, grandmother, or granddaughter is considered incestuous. Women are forbidden to marry their corresponding male relative. Beyond these blood relations, however, the definition of incestuous relations change. One society defines marriages between cousins as incestuous, while another encourages such marriages. Some states prohibit marriage between half-brothers and half-sisters as well as cousins. Others do not. During colonial times, marriage between second cousins was prohibited as incestuous. Although homosexuality has been decriminalized in a number of states, homosexuals are not legally permitted to marry. Homosexuals may have marriage ceremonies performed in some churches, but these marriages are not recognized by law.

Endogamy and exogamy interact to limit the field of eligibles. Although still quite large, the field of eligibles is further limited by society's encouragement of heterogamy and homogamy. Within the field of eligibles, *heterogamy* refers to the tendency to choose a mate whose personal or group characteristics differ from our own, whereas *homogamy* refers to the tendency to choose a mate whose personal or group characteristics are similar to ours. As a result of these limitations on whom we choose for our partners, mate choices in America follow certain patterns. (See the reading "Computer Dating Questionnaire" for an example of how the principles of homogamy are applied to matchmaking situations.) (For the pros and cons of marrying those with similar backgrounds, see Eshleman, 1985, and Dunham and Kidwell, 1985.)

- *Race.* Most marriages are between members of the same race; about 1.3 percent of all marriages are interracial. Between 1977 and 1981 the number of interracial marriages doubled, from 310,000 to 639,000. Only 21 percent of interracial marriages were between blacks and whites (0.3 percent of all marriages). In four-fifths of black-white marriages, black men are married to white women. Most interracial marriages are between whites or blacks and Orientals, Native Americans, or others (U.S. Bureau of the Census, 1982). It is not clear whether interracial marriages are equally or less stable than nonmixed marriages, since the few published studies are contradictory (Heer, 1974; Monahan, 1970).
- *Religion.* Until the late 1960s, religion was a significant factor affecting marital choice. Today, however, approximately 15 to 20 percent of all marriages are interfaith (Glenn, 1982). A report by the Notre Dame Study of Catholic Parish Life stated that a higher proportion of Catholics are involved in interreligious marriages: 21 percent of the Catholics compared to 11 percent of the Protestants ("Growing Numbers . . ., 1985"). Today almost one in four Jews chooses a non-Jewish partner, up from 6 percent in the early 1960s (Gruson, 1985).

  Religious groups tend to discourage interfaith marriages, believing they may weaken individual commitment and lead to children being reared in a different faith. "I regard interfaith marriage as the most serious problem facing American Jews today," said Rabbi Sol Roth, former president of the Rabbinical Council of America (Gruson, 1985). Only a few studies have been done on the impact of interfaith marriage on marital stability. These show that although divorce rates vary according to religions and denominations, in general interfaith marriages tend to have about a 10 percent higher divorce rate than marriages within the same faith (Bumpass and Sweet, 1972; also see Glenn, 1982, on marital happiness).
- *Socioeconomic Class.* Most people marry within their own socioeconomic class because of shared values, tastes, goals, occupations, and expectations. People tend to marry those who have the same educational background as themselves, reflecting the fact that educational attainment is related to class. Even if a person marries someone from a different race, religion, age group, or ethnic group, the couple will probably be from the same socioeconomic class. Women marry below their class in some instances, possibly as a result of their slightly lower status.
- *Age.* People tend to marry others within their same age group, although the man is usually slightly older than the woman. Age is important because we view ourselves as members of a generation, and each generation's experience of life leads to different values and expectations. Furthermore, different developmental and life tasks confront us at different ages. A twenty-year-old woman wants something different out of marriage and life than a sixty-year-old man does. By marrying people of similar ages, we ensure congruence of developmental tasks. (See Nera et al., 1985 and Atkinson and Glass, 1985 for discussion of age in marriage.)

These factors in the choice of partner interact with one another. Race and socioeconomic class, for example, are often closely related because of discrimination.

Fashionable ladies fall in love with acrobats and have to marry colonels. Shop assistants fall in love with countesses and are obliged to marry shop girls.

GEORGE BERNARD SHAW

Blacks and Mexican-Americans tend to be working class and not as well educated as whites. Whites generally tend to be better off economically and are usually better educated. Thus a marriage that is endogamous in terms of race is also likely to be endogamous in terms of education and social class.

Marriages that are homogamous tend to be more stable than heterogamous ones (Burr, 1973; but see Dean and Gurak, 1978; Udry, 1974). Three possible explanations have been given for this. First, heterogamous couples may have significantly different values, attitudes, and behaviors that may create a lack of understanding and conflict. Second, such marriages may lack approval from parents, relatives, and friends. Couples are then cut off from important sources of support during crises. Third, heterogamous couples are probably less conventional and therefore less likely to continue an unhappy marriage merely for the sake of appearances (Udry, 1974).

☐ THE NARROWING OF THE FIELD

Each individual theoretically has the freedom to choose any partner he or she wants. Yet most people freely choose partners of the same class, religious, racial, and educational background. Somehow (without anyone being forced) each person generally chooses someone who meets both family and societal requirements. How does that happen? What invisible hand brings about this harmony of individual and societal interests?

Traditionally, adolescents and college students develop their friends and peer groups in the environment of school. They spend considerable time together in school and go out together after school. Because schools usually reflect socioeconomic and racial patterns (through who goes to the school and who associates with whom), these peer groups tend to be homogeneous. Friends generally come from the same social background; indeed, they probably became friends in the first place because they shared values, aspirations, and goals reflecting their social and economic class.

Endogamy helps explain why people tend to marry those who live near them. "Cupid may have wings, but apparently they are not adapted for long flights," wrote James Bossard (1932), who first studied the idea of propinquity in mate selection. *Propinquity* refers to proximity or nearness in place. In his pioneer study, Bossard discovered that one-half of the couples issued marriage licenses in Philadelphia lived within twenty blocks of each other. One-sixth lived within a block, and one-third lived within five blocks. Residential propinquity reflects social class, race, and nationality; to a more limited extent it reflects religion. Suburbs may be primarily working class or middle class. If they are middle class, they are more likely white. These factors tend to reinforce one another. Propinquity, whether in neighborhood, school, places of entertainment, or work, leads to interaction, and the probability of marriage varies according to the likelihood of interacting. There are few mail-order brides now (but see the ads on page 163).

☐ DATING RELATIONSHIPS

Dating, going out, getting together—all such terms describe important rituals for pairing and in many cases for finding a marriage partner. In contemporary America most individuals find partners by dating. They narrow the field through a process of getting to know the other person. Those who do not fit the general characteristics required by endogamy tend to be weeded out through peer pressure or parental veto.

Functions of Dating

Although children may have friends of both sexes before puberty, once they enter adolescence friendships with the other sex often take on new meanings. In addition to its romantic or sexual aspects, dating is a significant means of developing intimate friendships with members of the other sex. It permits us to try out numerous relationships, learning about ourselves and others in the process. Sometimes this process of maturing is quite happy, other times painful, often both—but it is an important part of our growth.

There is considerable emphasis on acting out male and female sex roles; we learn to adjust these roles to our own personalities as we learn more about ourselves. Yet we experience considerable peer pressure—especially in adolescence—not to deviate from the traditional stereotypic sex roles. Boys with a gentle manner are often penalized by their peers for not being masculine; girls with an assertive temperament are considered unattractive because they do not meet the stereotype of femininity. So dating enables us to learn about ourselves, but (at the initial stages especially) it also includes considerable pressure for conformity.

The functions of dating vary with the age of the people and their motivations. These functions change over time. Initially, dating is for fun, to do something with someone—go to the beach, have coffee, see a movie, hang out. Through dating we learn how to relate to someone of the other sex. However, as people get older (late high school for some, college for others) dating begins to get more involved—choosing a marriage partner may be at stake. Is your date a potential mate? If so, will that person make a good mate? Will he or she be loyal, dependable, like children, work? Often such questions are never articulated; if they are, they are not always answered. The rush of romantic feelings sometimes makes such considerations seem irrelevant. But even if these kinds of issues are discussed, people never really know how one another will act in a marital or long-term relationship. Such a relationship takes trust, faith, and commitment, elements that are not always important or visible in dating relationships. (See Grover et al., 1985 for discussion of mate selection process and marital happiness.)

> Dreams are the touchstones of our character.
>
> HENRY DAVID THOREAU

Forms of Dating

Traditional Dating   The traditional dating pattern is formal. Each person has his or her role to play. The male initiates the date; the female waits to be called. The male is anxious lest he be turned down; he may feel his stomach churn while trying to appear calm and nonchalant as he calls up a female for a date or "accidentally" runs into her (after weeks of planning). The female's problems are complementary. She must wait to be called. Because she must appear demure, she can only express her interest indirectly by glances, tone of voice, body language, or playing helpless (Larkin, 1979). She may be so indirect that the male doesn't catch on. Also, she might not even be called by the person with whom she wants to go out—someone else may call instead. It is as difficult for some women to turn a man down as it is for some men to ask a woman out. "I don't want to hurt his feelings" is a common problem expressed by women who find themselves going out on a date with someone they don't particularly like.

On a formal date, both males and females play traditional sex roles: the male decides where to go, pays for the date, opens doors, is chivalrous. The dating couple often attend a movie, dance, concert, or sports event. Each dresses up. The symbolism

> Matrimony is a process by which a grocer acquired an account the florist had.
>
> FRANCIS RODMAN

of the male paying is especially important, for it signifies the female's economic dependence on the male, a precursor to traditional marriage. If the male pays, he often expects that he will get something in return, usually something sexual. The woman knows it. Depending on her age, she may feel obligated to kiss her date good night, "make out," or have sexual intercourse with him.

The female on a formal date is passive, expects to have her way paid, and tries to please the male without truly giving in. In accordance with the traditional female stereotype, she is expected to display less sexual interest than the man and to curtail the sexual advances of her date (Allgeier, 1982). The relationship is an exchange of favors. This type of dating is ultimately oriented toward mate selection. The sequence of steps is usually (1) dating, (2) engagement, and (3) marriage.

Getting Together. Over the last decade an alternative to the traditional dating pattern has emerged. It is often referred to as "getting together." Egalitarian sex roles probably more than any other factor are responsible for this emerging pattern. Getting together is based on mutuality and sharing. Equality is an important value, and to symbolize equality, each person pays his or her own way. Since each pays, the feelings of obligation that accompany one person spending money are absent. A man does not expect the woman to kiss him or go to bed with him in exchange for his showing her a good time. The woman does not feel that she owes the man anything. They go out together as equals.

Traditional sex roles are deemphasized in the getting-together pattern of dating. The woman may call up the man rather than wait for his call. Because there is less emphasis on traditional sex roles, masks that hide the real person are discouraged. Honesty and intimacy are highly valued and self-disclosure is considered an important quality (Rubin et al., 1980). Instead of being centered around an event, getting together emphasizes spontaneity. Males and females do not necessarily get together as couples, but often meet in groups. They get together informally for a pizza or hamburgers, for a picnic, or to study for a class. A man and a woman may begin to spend more time together as a result of these gatherings, but often it is within a group context. Neither has the responsibility for asking the other out. Much of the anxiety of formal dating is avoided.

Sexuality is moved from the realm of an exchange of favors to mutual involvement and satisfaction. Ideally, sexual involvement reflects true feelings and desires rather than the need to prove oneself or pay a debt. Friendship, respect, and common interests serve as the basis for decisions about whether to become sexually involved (Libby, 1976).

When people get together in this fashion, the pattern of mate selection may include the following sequence of steps: (1) getting together formally, (2) living together, and/or (3) marriage. When compared to dating, however, getting together is not as oriented toward eventual mate selection.

Problems in Dating

Dating, as we all know, whether as a source of recreation or a means of selecting a partner, can entail problems and create stress.

Dating rituals are in flux (Komarovsky, 1985). Although nontraditional women believe that the male prerogative of initiating the first date is a patriarchal holdover,

UNDERSTANDING YOURSELF

Getting Together and Dating

Make a list of your various attributes, such as intelligence, physical attractiveness, social class, and personality. Make a similar list for the person you are dating, going with, married to, or would like to meet. How do you compare? Are you about evenly matched in the various areas? If not, are there trade-offs? What are they? Have your dating or romantic experiences usually been with people with attributes equal to yours?

Think about your dating experiences. Do you date or "get together"? What is the difference in your own experience between the two? What different expectations have you found between the two forms of going out? How do sex roles

affect your interactions? What problems do you commonly experience on dates? How do you think they compare with the problems experienced by members of the other sex?

What does it mean to "be seeing" someone? What are the rules? Does going out a couple of times constitute "going together"? What makes two people who go out a "couple"? Often two people will be going together without an explicit commitment to seeing only each other; instead, they will have an "understanding" (that is sometimes understood by only one half of the couple). Why are commitments in dating relationships often unclear?

few dare violate this norm. After one or two dates and in established relationships, both men and women appear equally free to initiate dates (modified by power issues or personal involvement). Komarovsky wrote:

The strongest sanction against violating the male prerogative of the first move was the male interpretation of such initiative as a sexual come-on. Men described such aggressive women as "sluts." Indignant as the women were to this inference, they hesitated to expose themselves to the risks, unless they were among the very few who did so with full knowledge of the implications.

Komarovsky recounted the experiences of one first-year college woman who was eager to share some of the new ideas she encountered in her classes:

There was this one guy in my philosophy class who was really bright. He used to make brilliant comments in class and I wanted to get to know him, so I could talk to him about philosophy. So I approached him and asked him whether he would like to go out for a cup of coffee. My intention was to talk about the lecture, but when we sat down, all he wanted to talk about was how I felt about sex, and when we could go out on a date. I kept telling him that sex wasn't the reason I asked him out. I was trying to be honest and straight-forward with him, but he wouldn't believe it. He thought that the reason I asked him out for a cup of coffee was a sexual come-on. I never asked another guy out on a date.

Another problem is who pays. Some women in Komarovsky's study were fearful that male acquaintances would be put off if they offered to pay their share. Other women—whether traditional or egalitarian—who offered to pay found themselves

All tragedies are finished by a death.
All comedies are ended by a marriage.

LORD BYRON (1788–1824)

mocked by their dates. Some men who allowed their dates to pay still insisted on choosing where they went, whether the women wanted to go there or not. Still others allowed their dates to pay, but not publicly; instead, for example, the women secretly slipped money under the dinner table.

Divergent sex role conceptions also complicate dating in the initial stages (and sometimes beyond). Often when two people lack complementary sex role conceptions, the woman is the more egalitarian and the man the more traditional. The man may want the woman to be subordinate to his desires and wishes. She, however, may ask for an equal share in the decision making. In such cases, the relationship is not likely to become mutually satisfying.

Problems Among Women. According to a random study by Knox and Wilson of 227 college women and 107 men (cited in Knox, 1985), nearly 25 percent of the women said they received unwanted pressure to engage in sex, usually before the establishment of an emotional bond between the couple. Komarovsky (1985) cited male sexual pressure as a major barrier between men and women. Women who wanted to see the man again were placed in a dilemma: how to encourage the man to ask them out again without engaging in more sexual activity than they wanted. Men whose sexual advances were rejected by their dates often salved their hurt egos by accusing the women of having sexual hang-ups or being lesbians. Women rated places to go (23 percent) and communication (22 percent) almost as high on their list of dating problems as sexual pressure (Knox, 1985).

Problems Among Men. For men, the number one problem—cited by 35 percent— was communicating with their dates (Knox, 1985). They often felt they didn't know what to say, or they felt anxious about the conversation dragging. Communication may be a particularly critical problem for men, since traditional sex roles do not encourage the development of intimacy and communication skills among males. A second problem, shared by almost identical numbers of men and women, was where to go. A third problem, named by 20 percent of the men but not mentioned by women, was shyness. Although men can take the initiative to ask for a date, they also face the possibility of rejection. For shy men, the fear of rejection is especially acute. A final problem, again one not shared by women, was money, cited by 17 percent of the men. Men apparently accept the idea that they are the ones responsible for paying for a date.

The problems of shyness and money are related to traditional conceptions of dating in which the male initiates the first date and pays the woman's expenses. It seems that a common ground exists here for change, since women find themselves limited by not being able to initiate the first date and would often be happy to share expenses.

Power in Dating Relationships

Power doesn't seem to be a concern for most people in dating relationships. In fact, one study of dating couples found that both men and women felt they had about equal power in their relationship (Sprecher, 1985).

Most dating couples may not think about power too much, but that doesn't mean power is nonexistent in dating relationships. When a disagreement occurs, who generally wins? When one person wants to go to the movies and another wants to go to the beach, where does the couple go? If one person wants to marry and the other doesn't, what happens?

If power does become an issue or source of conflict in dating relationships, it may not become as intense an issue as in a marriage because a person can end a dating relationship more easily than a marriage. Intense power conflicts can be avoided by dissolving the relationship.

One of the primary resources for determining power in marriage is economic: the person with the most economic resources usually has the most power. Generally, this means men because they are more likely to be employed and to earn more money than women. In dating relationships, however, economic resources do not appear to be as important a power resource for men as is their ability to date other women (Sprecher, 1985). The easier men thought it would be to go out with other women, the more power they had in a dating relationship.

Controlling sex and the reciprocation of love is an important resource for women (Safilios-Rothschild, 1976, 1977). This seems to be true both in marriage and in dating relationships. As long as her partner is in love with her, the woman is able to use that love as a resource. One researcher (Sprecher, 1985) wrote:

Women probably have traditionally had to become skilled at controlling their emotions in heterosexual relationships in order to acquire any bargaining power. Indeed, evidence has been found that men are more romantic than women. . . . It has also been found that men are the first to fall in love . . . and the last to fall out of love. . . . The evidence suggests that men may value and need the love from a woman more than women value and need the love from men. Often unable to have access to other desirable resources (money, status), women have had to use the control of love as a means to gain some power in a relationship.

The more men and women contributed to the affective side of the relationship relative to their partners, the less power they felt they had. This was more true for women than for men. For women, in fact, the less they loved their partner, the more power they felt they had.

"Just Friends"

Relations between men and women who are "just friends" generally differ from those in which they are dating or are romantically involved (Komarovsky, 1985). Among those who are "just friends," women are more likely to share expenses, take the initiative in calling male friends, and self-disclose than they are in dating relationships. Since sex is not perceived as part of a friendship, many of the conflicts about sex are absent. Friendship offers many of the same qualities—such as acceptance, spontaneity, understanding—as does a romantic relationship (Davis, 1985).

Same-sex friendships tend to predominate, but male/female friendships are fairly common. In Davis's (1985) study of 250 students and members of the community, 56 percent of the men and 44 percent of the women had close friends of the other sex. But close male/female friendships differed from same-sex friendships. Same-sex friends tend to self-disclose more, offer practical help, have a greater sense of stability in the relationship, and show a greater willingness to give their utmost.

It is not uncommon for male/female friends to eventually become romantically involved. The development of both friendship and romantic relationships follow Reiss's

That person is able to dictate the conditions of association whose interest in the continuation of the affair is least.

WILLARD WALLER and REUBEN HILL

wheel theory (see Chapter 5): from rapport to self-revelation, to mutual dependency and intimacy need fulfillment. As friends make the transition to romantic partners, they may perceive a danger: friends tend to stay friends, but lovers may part. Because they value the stability, friends who fall in love with each other may hesitate to change their relationship. Others, however, feel that their friendship gives them a strong basis for love.

☐ BREAKING UP

Calculating the number of couples who break up is difficult because it is hard to say how many couples are going together. Sometimes when two people have gone out a couple of times, one (usually the woman) never hears from the other again; often no explanation is given. Sometimes two people just seem to drift apart; the time between their dates grows longer and longer until neither expects to see the other again. Feelings may be hurt, but neither person has the sense of breaking up; the experience is more of a disappointment than anything else.

"Most passionate affairs end simply," Walster and Walster (1978) note. "The lovers find someone they love more." Their love cools; it changes to indifference or hostility. This may be a simple ending, but it is also a painful ending because few relationships end by mutual consent (Hill et al., 1976). In Hill and his colleagues' two-year study of 231 college couples, the average couple had been going out for eight months; three-fourths were dating each other exclusively. Apparently, the men fell in love more rapidly and the women fell out of love more quickly. At the end of the study, only 128 couples were still together. Fifty-one percent of the breakups were initiated by the woman, men initiated 42 percent, and 7 percent were mutual. (If the man initiated the breakup, the chance was greater that the couple remained friends.)

Why were women less likely to fall in love as fast as men and more likely to end a relationship? Doesn't this contradict our image of women as more love and relationship centered than men? Yes and no. Since a woman depends far more on her husband than he does on her for income and status, she has to be more practical in choosing a relationship; he, by contrast, can afford to be romantic since he does not have as much at stake. Women also tend to be more sensitive to the quality of a relationship than men; as a result, they may expect more out of a relationship than their partners do. Women's greater practicality may also account for their ability to deal better with the end of a relationship than men do. In a study of 231 couples, among those who split up, women tended to be less depressed, lonely, and unhappy than men (Rubin et al., 1981).

☐ SINGLES

Culture and the Individual Versus Marriage

Despite the significance of intimate relationships for our development as human beings, our culture is ambivalent about marriage. Throughout most of its history, Christianity has celebrated religious devotion and celibacy over marriage. St. Paul (1 Cor. 7:7–9) declared it was best to remain chaste as he himself had done. "But if they cannot," he continued, "let them marry: For it is better to marry than to burn."

To forget someone means to think of him.

JEAN De La BRUYERE

There are two tragedies in life. One is to lose your heart's desire. The other is to gain it.

GEORGE BERNARD SHAW

The land of marriage has this peculiarity, that strangers are desirous of inhabiting it, whilst its natural inhabitants would willingly be banished from thence.

MICHEL De MONTAIGNE

FEATURE

Some Hints on Breaking Up

Breaking up is rarely easy, whether you are initiating the break up or "receiving" it. But thinking about the following may help.

If You Initiate the Break Up:

- *Be sure that you want to break up.* If the relationship is unsatisfactory, it may be because conflicts or problems have been avoided or been confronted in the wrong way. Instead of being a reason to break up, conflicts or problems may be a rich source of personal and couple development if they are worked out. Sometimes people erroneously use the threat of breaking up as a way of saying, "I want the relationship to change."
- *Acknowledge the fact that your partner will be hurt.* There is nothing you can do to erase the pain your partner will feel; it is only natural. Not breaking up because you don't want to hurt your partner may actually be an excuse for not wanting to be honest with him or her, or yourself.
- *Once you end the relationship, do not continue seeing your partner as "friends" until considerable time has passed.* Being friends may be a subterfuge for continuing the relationship on terms wholly advantageous to yourself. It will only be painful for your ex-partner, since he or she may be more involved in the relationship than you. It may be best to wait to become

friends until your partner is involved with someone else (and by then he or she may not care).
- *Don't change your mind.* Ambivalence after ending a relationship is not a sign that you made a wrong decision; neither is loneliness. Both indicate that the relationship was valuable for you.

If Your Partner Breaks Up with You:

- *The pain and loneliness you feel are natural.* Despite their intensity, they will eventually pass. They are part of the grieving process that attends the loss of an important relationship—but they are not necessarily signs of love.
- *You are a worthwhile person, whether you are with a partner or not.* Spend time with your friends; share your feelings with them—they care. Do things that you like; be kind to yourself.
- *Don't try to see your former partner.* If you broke up once, the chances are that you will break up again. If you try to continue seeing your former partner as a friend, it will prolong your distress. Instead, go cold turkey, as painful as it may be.
- *Repeat these clichés:* No one ever died of love. (Except me.) There are other fish in the ocean. (Who wants a fish?) In other words, keep a sense of humor; it may help ease the pain.

In contemporary culture we find two contradictory myths about marriage, which many people hold simultaneously. Richard Udry (1974) observed:

The first myth—"and they lived happily ever after"—portrays marriage as a continuous courtship. The second myth is the picture of the domestic grind: the husband sits behind the paper, the wife moves about in the morning disarray: the husband leaves for work, the wife spends the day among dishes, diapers, and dirty little children. Although, as with most myths, no one *really* believes either one of them, they continue to affect the behavior of most people.

A continuing tension exists between the alternatives of singlehood and marriage (Stein, 1976). The singles subculture is glorified in the mass media; the marriages

Table 6–1

A stage of tension exists between being single and being married. Those who are single are pulled (attracted) toward marriage by their desires for intimacy, love, children, and sexual availability; they are pushed (pressured) toward marriage by parents, loneliness, and fears of independence. Those who are married are pulled toward singlehood by the possibility of creating a new self, having new experiences, and achieving greater independence; they are pushed toward singlehood by restrictive roles, boredom, and unhappiness. Which of the pushes and pulls are true for you? Why?

Table 6–1   **Pushes and Pulls Toward Marriage and Singlehood**

Toward Marriage	
Pushes	*Pulls*
Economic security	Influence of parents
Influence from mass media	Desire for family
Pressure from parents	Example of peers
Need to leave home	Romanticization of marriage
Interpersonal and personal reasons	Love
Fear of independence	Physical attraction
Loneliness	Emotional attachment
Alternatives did not seem feasible	Security, Social Status, Prestige
Cultural expectations, Socialization	
Regular sex	
Guilt over singlehood	

Toward Singlehood	
Pushes	*Pulls*
Restrictions	Career opportunities
Suffocating one-to-one relationships, feeling trapped	Variety of experiences
Obstacles to self-development	Self-sufficiency
Boredom and unhappiness and anger	Sexual availability
Role playing and conformity to expectations	Exciting life style
Poor communication with mate	Freedom to change and experiment
Sexual frustration	Mobility
Lack of friends, isolation, loneliness	Sustaining friendships
Limitations on mobility and available experience	Supportive groups
Influence of and participation in Women's Movement	Men's and women's groups
	Group living arrangements
	Specialized groups

Source: Peter J. Stein. "Singlehood: An Alternative to Marriage." *The Family Coordinator* 24:4 (1975).

portrayed on television are situation comedies or soap operas abounding in extramarital affairs. *Playboy* extolls bachelorhood; *Cosmopolitan*, the single woman. But single persons are rarely fully satisfied with being single and may yearn for marriage. They are pulled toward the idea of marriage by their desires for intimacy, love, children, and sexual availability. They are also pushed toward marriage by parental pressure, loneliness, and fears of independence. Married persons, at the same time, are pushed toward singlehood by the limitations they feel in married life. They are attracted to singlehood by the possibility of creating a new self, having new experiences, and achieving independence. (See Table 6–1.) (For the pros and cons of singlehood, see Stein and Fingruid, 1985, and Schumm, 1985.)

Until recently, being single was viewed as abnormal or immoral in our society. Others saw single women as "old maids" and "spinsters" who were unable to find a man, and men as immature bachelors seeking fun rather than commitment (Yankelovich, 1981). But with the recent rise in the age of first marriage (in 1984 the median age for men was 24; for women, it was 22) and the rise in divorce, a significant percentage of American men and women are single at any one time. In 1984, 38 percent of the men and 26 percent of the women over age 25 had never married

(U.S. Census, 1984b). In 1970 there were 10.9 million singles; in 1982, 19.4 million, a 78 percent increase; singles represent around 40 percent of the adult population (Sanoff, 1983). The number of adults living alone increased 173 percent between 1960 and 1983 (Glick, 1984a). By 1983, 23 percent of households contained only one person (Alwin et al., 1985). If current trends continue, 10 percent of the men and 12 percent of the women will *never* marry. Of divorced men and women currently less than forty years old, 25 to 30 percent will not remarry (Glick, 1984b).

As with much behavior that is "abnormal" or "immoral," society will transform it into "normal" and "moral" behavior if enough people engage in it. This seems to be what is happening with singlehood. By the end of the 1970s, one public opinion poll found that 75 percent of the public considered being single "normal" (Yankelovich, 1981). Today, according to one study, singles consider themselves normal, have an explicit identity of themselves as single, and take themselves for granted (Cargan and Melko, 1982). In other words, they don't see anything unusual about themselves. (See the reading by Peter Stein, "Singlehood: An Alternative to Marriage.")

Some difference in attitudes and values appears to exist between singles and married people. Married people tend to embrace family values such as togetherness, stability, and loyalty more than single people do. Two researchers (Cargan and Melko, 1982) found that married people tended to see marriage, children, and love as more important than singles did, whereas singles saw friends and personal growth as more important. Since singlehood, however, tends to be transitional for most people, it is unlikely that singles will continue these attitudinal differences once they marry. Singles may possess these attitudes because they are single, not because they are inherently different from married people.

Not everyone who has not married is regarded by sociologists as single. Most college students are less than twenty-five years old, have not been married, are expecting to get married, and are looking for marital partners; they aren't "true" singles. Singles are generally at least twenty-five years old. Singles either have never been married or are divorced and usually do not have primary responsibility for children; they are generally working rather than attending school (Cargan and Melko, 1982).

> The hot narrow intimacy between man and wife was abhorrent. The way they shut themselves into their own exclusive alliance with each other, even in love, disgusted him. It was a whole community of mistrustful couples insulated in private houses or private rooms, always in couples, and no further life, no further immediate, no disinterested relationship admitted: a kaleidescope of couples, disjoined, separatist, meaningless entities of married couples.
>
> D. H. LAWRENCE, *WOMEN IN LOVE*

Marriage: Squeeze and Gradient

The Marriage Squeeze. One of the facts of life is that more women than men are eligible for marriage. After World War II through the early 1960s, there was a significant increase in the birthrate, resulting in the "baby boom." Since women tend to marry men several years older than themselves, "baby-boom" women reached the average age for marriage two years earlier than men born the same year. The result was a "marriage squeeze" in which there were greater numbers of women than men looking for marriage partners.

The marriage squeeze will partly reverse in the 1980s as the smaller number of women born after the baby boom will have more older men to choose from. In fact, that time has already arrived for women in the twenty- to twenty-four-year age bracket. A study based on 1980 population statistics found that white women in this age group are favored with 124 "suitable" men for every 100 "suitable" women (Goldman, 1984). Among blacks, there are 100 "suitable" men for every 93 "suitable" women. Suitability was defined by educational level and age preference. After age twenty-four, however, the marriage squeeze is in force again. White women in the twenty-five- to twenty-nine-year age bracket find 77 suitable men for every 100 suitable women; among blacks, the suitability ratio is about the same. As these women age, the marriage squeeze becomes even tighter.

The Marriage Gradient. "All the good ones are taken" is a common complaint among women in their mid-twenties and beyond. According to sociologist Jesse Bernard, they might be right. Bernard (1972) wrote:

> In our society, the husband is assigned a superior status. It helps if he actually *is* somewhat superior in ways—in height, for example, or age or education or occupation—for such superiority, however slight, makes it easier for both partners to conform to the structural imperatives. The girl wants to be able to "look up" to her husband, and he, of course, wants her to. The result is a situation known sociologically as the marriage gradient.

Men and women, as we have seen, tend to marry those with the same class and cultural background. But within this general homogamy, men tend to marry women slightly below them in age, education, occupation, and so on. This tendency creates the marriage gradient.

The result is that there is no one for the men at the bottom to marry, no one to look up to them. Conversely, there is no one for the women at the top to look up to; there are no men who are superior to them. . . . [The] never-married men . . . tend to be "bottom-of-the-barrel" and the women . . . "cream-of-the-crop."

Among college-educated men and women, the "cream-of-the-crop" by educational status, 93 percent of the men married but only 83 percent of the women married. By educational status, college-educated men represented the highest proportion of males who married, while college-educated women represented the lowest proportion of females who married (Glick, 1984b).

Bernard cautions us that when she speaks of "bottom-of-the-barrel" she is referring only to qualities specifically related to marriage, such as the desire to make a commitment, and not necessarily to attractiveness, occupational success, companionship, or charm. A man with these qualities may have everything but "marital aptitude."

Singles: Myths and Realities

Cargan and Melko (1982), in a study of 400 households in Dayton, Ohio, examined various myths and realities about singlehood. They concluded the following.

Myths.
- *Singles are dependent on their parents.* Few differences exist between singles and marrieds in their perceptions of their parents and relatives. They do not differ in perceptions of parental warmth or openness and differ only slightly in the amount and nature of parental conflicts.
- *Singles are self-centered.* Singles value friends more than do married people. Singles are more involved in community service projects.

Miss, n. A title with which we brand unmarried women to indicate that they are in the market. Miss, Missis (Mrs.) and Mister (Mr.) are the three most distinctly disagreeable words in the language, in sound and sense. Two are corruptions of Mistress, the other of Master. In the general abolition of social titles in this our country they miraculously escaped to plague us. If we must have them, let us be consistent and give one to the unmarried man. I venture to suggest Mush, abbreviated to Mh.

AMBROSE BIERCE (1842–1914?)

- *Singles have more money.* Fewer than half the singles they interviewed made more than $10,000 a year. Married couples were better off economically than singles, in part, because both partners worked.
- *Singles are happier.* Singles tend to believe they are happier than marrieds, while marrieds believe they are happier than singles. Single men, however, exhibited more signs of stress than did single women. A national survey conducted by Robert Weiss (1981) found that 23 percent of the single men and 27 percent of the single women felt lonely; by contrast, only 6 percent of the married women and 10 percent of the married men reported feeling lonely.
- *Singles view singlehood as a lifetime alternative.* The majority of singles expected to be married within five years. They did not view singlehood as an alternative to marriage but as a transitional time in their lives.

Realities.
- *Singles don't easily fit into married society.* Singles tend to socialize with other singles. Married people feel if they invite singles to their home, they must match them up with an appropriate single member of the other sex. Married people tend to think in terms of couples.
- *Singles have more time.* Singles are more likely to go out twice a week and much more likely to go out three times a week compared with their married peers. Singles have more choices and more opportunities for leisure-time activities.
- *Singles have more fun.* Although singles tend to be less happy than marrieds, they have more "fun." Singles go out more often, engage more in sports and physical activities, and have more sexual partners than marrieds. Apparently fun and happiness are not equated.
- *Singles are lonely.* Singles tend to be more lonely than married people; the feeling of loneliness is more pervasive for the divorced than the never-married singles.

> If you are lonely when you are alone, you are in bad company.
>
> JEAN-PAUL SARTRE

Singles Dating

Although dating in the singles world is somewhat different from dating in high school and college, there are similarities. Singles, like their counterparts in school, emphasize recreation and entertainment, sociability, and physical attractiveness. But unlike individuals in school, singles have considerably more casual sexual involvements. There are few virgins in the singles world. The casualness of sex may be a source of problems. Men often desire more casual sex and fewer commitments than women; women often want greater intimacy, commitment, and emotional involvement than men.

The singles world is big business, with the singles industry of bars, resorts, clubs, and housing bringing in billions a year. The singles bar has become the symbol of the singles scene, although most singles reject such bars as "meat markets" even though they may occasionally go to one. The problem of meeting other single people is very often the central problem of the singles world. In college, students meet each other in classes or dormitories, at school events, or through friends. There are many meeting places and large numbers of eligibles. Singles have less opportunity to meet available people. For one thing, there are fewer eligible persons. For another, singles do not have access to an informal network that facilitates meeting other singles such as school provides.

> It is always incomprehensible to a man that a woman should ever refuse an offer of marriage.
>
> JANE AUSTEN (1775–1817)

The singles industry is a thriving business with its bars, resorts, and clubs. The symbol of the singles world is the singles bar. Most singles, however, meet others through friends, work, or parties.

One single person (in Bradley et al., 1977) observed:

It seems very strange that there should be so many individuals who want to be married or have a love relationship and yet it is so hard for one individual to find another. There ought to be the old-fashioned big affairs where you had these hoards of men and these hoards of women playing some game like "Find the Shoe," where all the women's shoes are thrown in the middle of the floor and you date the person whose shoe you get.

As a result of this lack of structure, most singles have to rely on meeting someone through friends; the blind date and arranged dinner party are major devices for meeting others in the singles world. Another person (in Bradley et al., 1977) said:

COUNTRY-LOVING woman, 32, seeks caring relationships with nurturing men. Am pretty, sensual, creative, funny, independent and romantic. I value honesty, kindness, and physical and emotional intimacy. Enjoy photography, cooking, dancing, camping, homey coziness, travel. Love nature, animals, music, movies, children. Seeking mature, self-sufficient men who share above values and interests. Am content to enjoy several relationships but a special someone who shares my dreams of family life in the country could change all that! Photo appreciated.

I AM a sometimes spiritual, occasionally intellectual, invariably sensual, incurably romantic writer/photographer in my 30's (young at heart & looks).

Are you the attractive, intelligent lady of 22–40 who is missing from my otherwise very happy life and who, like me, wants to settle down and is more turned-on by old-fashioned loving relationships than current alternatives?

WARM, NURTURING, fun-loving but responsible, male writer, parttime college teacher, age 40, wants to meet warm, attractive, intelligent woman in her twenties or thirties with a sense of humor. Likes Woody Allen movies, 19th-century novels, Latin American travel, kids, cooking Mexican and Szechwan foods.

RUBENESQUE W/F, well-laughtered, 28 yrs young, with pretty face, looking for an unattached male who is intelligent, sensitive, independent, and not obsessed with finding Miss Perfect, but who wants to meet a compassionate, loving woman whose interests include cuddling, fishing, or spontaneous suggestions.

WALKS IN the country, evenings by warm fires, good music and films, dinners in quiet surroundings, are more enjoyable with a companion. Tall, slender, active white female, 68, would like to meet a compatible gentleman.

1963 W/M. Good condition. Not perfect but mechanically sound. Definitely one-of-a-kind model. Tall, muscular, very sporty, fun for around town and a blast on the open road. Performs great if taken care of, but should not be babied. Good choice for fun-loving, enthusiastic young lady. Best offer takes.

I will never say no when a friend says, "Hey, I'd like you to meet someone." I want to be totally open and available for any type of new meeting and encounter. Even if I'm tired, not feeling too well, doubtful, dubious, whatever, I'll usually make the effort to meet someone and consider the possibility, "This could be someone important. This could be someone wonderful."

Classified ads for relationships have become increasingly popular as a means for people to meet each other. Why? How are the principles of endogamy and exogamy at work in these ads? What do these ads tell us about the qualities people seek in potential partners? Which ads did you find interesting? Why? If you were to write an ad, what would it say? (For the pros and cons of non-traditional ways of meeting dating partners, see Becker, 1985, and Smart, 1985.)

Relationships

When people form relationships within the singles world, both the man and woman tend to remain highly independent (Gagnon and Greenblat, 1978). Singles work, and as a result, the man and woman tend to be economically independent of each other. They may also be more emotionally independent, since much of their energy may already be heavily invested in their work or careers. The relationship that forms consequently tends to emphasize autonomy and egalitarian roles. The fact that single women work is especially significant. In the past women were expected to marry on leaving school, or if they worked, their work was expected to be only temporary until they had children. Single women tend to be more involved with their work, either from choice or necessity, but the result is the same: they are accustomed to living on their own without being supported by a man.

Living in the singles world, like living together, tends to be transitory for most people. Most singles eventually seek a permanent relationship. Among divorced people, for example, half remarry within a year of their divorce. Among unmarried men in the twenty-five to twenty-nine age group, almost 45 percent marry by the time they reach thirty; among unmarried women, over half marry by age thirty.

☐ LIVING TOGETHER

The Rise of Cohabitation

In 1984 more than two million couples were living together in the United States (U.S. Bureau of the Census, 1984). In contrast, only 523,000 couples were cohabiting in 1970. Despite the striking increase, unmarried couples living together account for only 4 percent of the 52.9 million married and unmarried couples in the United States. (For census purposes, those who cohabit are called POSSLQs [pronounced possel-kews]—persons of the opposite sex sharing living quarters.)

Today 82 percent of cohabiting couples are less than forty-five years old; before 1970 the majority of cohabiting couples were more than forty-five years old. About 31 percent of the households of cohabiting couples include children under fifteen years of age. About 48 percent of the cohabiting individuals have never been married; another 36 percent were divorced (U.S. Bureau of the Census, 1984). (See Table 6–2 on page 166.)

Concerning cohabitation, Glick and Spanier (1980) noted: "Rarely does social change occur with such rapidity. Indeed, there have been few developments relating to marriage and family life which have been as dramatic as the rapid rise in unmarried cohabitation." Cohabitation is increasingly accepted at almost every level of society. Today the only difference between those who cohabit and those who do not lies not in social adjustment, family background, or social class, but in degree of religiousness. Those who have a high degree of religiosity and regular church attendance tend not to live together before marriage. For the religious, living together is still often considered "living in sin" (Newcomb, 1979).

Living together has become more widespread and accepted in recent years for several reasons. (For the pros and cons, see Gaylin, 1985, and Atwater, 1985.)

Property-Sharing Rights for Unmarried Couples

The fact that a man and woman live together without marriage, and engage in a sexual relationship, does not in itself invalidate agreements between them relating to their earnings, property, or expenses. Agreements between nonmarital partners fail to the extent that they rest upon consideration of meritricious sexual services.

CALIFORNIA SUPREME COURT, *MARVIN v. MARVIN*, 1976

- *The general climate regarding sexuality is more liberal than it was a generation ago.* Sexuality is more widely recognized as an important part of a person's life, whether or not he or she is married. The moral criterion for judging sexual intercourse has shifted; love rather than marriage is now widely regarded as making a sexual act moral.
- *The meaning of marriage is changing.* Because of the dramatic increase in divorce over the last two decades, marriage is no longer regarded as necessarily a permanent commitment. Permanence is increasingly being replaced by serial monogamy—a succession of marriages. Since the average marriage now lasts only seven years, the difference between marriage and living together is losing its sharpness.
- *Men and women are delaying marriage longer.* In the meantime, they want to have the emotional and physical closeness of marriage without the binding legal commitments.
- *Women are delaying having their first child.* As long as children are not desired, living together offers advantages for many couples. But when the couple want children, they usually will marry so the child will be "legitimate."

Despite some people's fears, cohabitation does not seem to threaten marriage. Most people who live together plan eventually to marry, although not necessarily each other. In one study about half the subjects who were living together stated they were planning to marry, although not in the near future (Danziger and Greenwald, 1973). The most significant social impact of cohabitation is that it delays the age of marriage for those who live together. As a consequence, cohabitation may actually encourage more stable marriages, since the older a person is at the time of marriage, the less likely he or she is to divorce. Furthermore, a later marriage is likely to produce fewer children, since an older woman has fewer reproductive years. Those who cohabit before marriage tend to want few or no children (Newcomb, 1979).

Types of Cohabitation

There is no single type of cohabitation just as there is no single type of person who cohabits. At least five different types of cohabitating relationships can be described, according to Eleanor Macklin (1978):

- *Temporary casual convenience.* Two people share the same living quarters because it is expedient and convenient to do so.
- *Affectionate dating or going together.* Two people live together because they enjoy being with each other; they will continue living together as long as it is mutually pleasurable.
- *Trial marriage.* This includes "engaged to be engaged" as well as couples who are trying to discover if they want to marry each other.
- *Temporary alternative to marriage.* Two people are committed to each other but are waiting for a better time to marry.
- *Permanent alternative to marriage.* Two people live together essentially as husband and wife but reject the idea of marriage.

Most college students who live together identify their cohabiting relationship as strong, affectionate, and monogamous. They share a deep attachment to each other but have not reached the point of making a long-term commitment. It is not known what proportion of older cohabiting couples fall into the various types (Macklin, 1978).

Living Together and Marriage Compared

Several features distinguish living together from marriage.

Transitory Nature of Living Together. Living together tends to be more transitory than marriage. A study based on national census figures indicates that 63 percent of such couples maintain a living-together relationship less than two years (Glick and Spanier, 1980). Either the couple split up or they get married. Those who marry after they have lived together usually do so because they want to formalize their commitment or to have children or because of pressures from parents or employers. Although cohabitation usually does not last as long as marriage, such relationships are often extremely satisfactory. They often end not because the relationship itself is bad but because marriage satisfies new or different needs.

Different Commitments. When a couple live together, their primary commitment is to each other. As long as they feel they love each other, they will stay together. In marriage the couple make a commitment not only to each other but to their marriage as well. Marriage often seems to become a third party that enters the relationship between a man and woman. Each will do many things to save a marriage; they may give up dreams, work, ambitions, and extramarital relationships to make a marriage work. A man and a woman who are living together may not work as hard to save their relationship. Although society encourages married couples to make sacrifices to

Table 6–2 **Cohabitation**

Characteristic	1984		1980		1970	
	Number (in 1000's)	Percent	Number (in 1000's)	Percent	Number (in 1000's)	Percent
Unmarried-couple households	1,988	100.0	1,589	100.0	523	100.0
Presence of children:						
No children under 15 years*	1,373	69.1	1,159	72.9	327	62.5
Some children under 15 years*	614	30.9	431	27.1	196	37.5
Sex of householder:						
Male	1,218	61.3	981	61.7	266	50.9
Female	770	38.7	608	38.3	257	49.1
Age of householder:						
Under 25 years	432	21.7	411	25.9	55	10.5
25 to 44 years	1,208	60.8	837	52.7	103	19.7
45 to 64 years	234	11.8	221	13.9	187	35.8
65 years and over	114	5.7	119	7.5	178	34.0
Marital status of householder:						
Never married	958	48.2	778	49.0	(NA)	(NA)
Married, spouse absent	160	8.0	144	9.1	(NA)	(NA)
Separated	138	6.9	121	7.6	(NA)	(NA)
Widowed	150	7.5	142	8.9	(NA)	(NA)
Divorced	719	36.2	525	33.0	(NA)	(NA)

*For 1970, children in unmarried couple households are under 14 years old.

Source: U.S. Bureau of the Census. Current Population Reports. Series P-20. No. 391, 1984.

save their marriage, unmarried couples rarely receive the same support. Parents may even urge their "living together" children to split up rather than give up plans for work, school, or career. If the couple is beginning to encounter sexual difficulties, it is more likely that they will split up if they are cohabiting than if they are married. It may be easier to abandon a problematic relationship than to change it.

Finances.   A striking difference between cohabiting and married couples is in the pooling of money as a symbol of commitment (Blumstein and Schwartz, 1983). People generally assume that in marriage the couple will pool their money. This arrangement suggests a basic trust or commitment to the relationship; the individual is willing to sacrifice his or her particular interests to the interests of the relationship. Among most cohabitating couples, money is not pooled. In fact, one of the reasons couples cohabit rather than marry is to maintain a sense of financial independence. One man said, "A strong factor in the success of our relationship is the fact that we're economically independent of each other. We make no decisions that involve joint finances and that simplifies life a great deal" (Blumstein and Schwartz, 1983).

Only if the couple expects to be living together for a long period of time or to marry do they pool their income. As Blumstein and Schwartz point out:

Since the majority of cohabitors do not favor pooling, these facts say important things about pooling and commitment. When couples begin to pool their finances, it usually means they see a future for themselves. The more the couple pools, the greater the incentive to organize future financial dealings in the same way. As a "corporate" sense of the couple emerges, it becomes more difficult for the partners to think of themselves as unattached individuals.

Work.   Traditional marital roles call for the husband to work; it is left to the discretion of the couple whether the woman works. The husband is basically responsible for supporting his wife and family. In cohabitating relationships, the man is not expected to support his partner (Blumstein and Schwartz, 1983). If the woman is not in school, she is expected to work. If she is in school, she is nevertheless expected to support herself. Married couples may fight about the wife going to work; no such fights occur among cohabiting couples.

Societal Support.   Compared to marriage, cohabitation receives relatively little social support (except from peers). It may be considered an inferior or immoral relationship—inferior to marriage because it does not symbolize lifetime commitment and immoral because it involves sexual activity without the sanction of marriage.

This lack of social reinforcement is an important factor in the greater instability of living-together relationships. Parents usually do not support cohabitation with the same enthusiasm as they would marriage. (If they do not like their son's or daughter's partner, however, they may console themselves that "at least they are not married.") Young adults often must hide the fact that they are living together for fear of parental rejection, anger, or reprisals.

Unmarried couples often find the greatest amount of social support from their friends, especially other couples who are living together. They are able to share similar problems with fellow cohabitants, such as whether to tell parents, how to handle visiting home together, difficulties in obtaining housing and so forth. Since unmarried couples tend to have similar values, commitments, and uncertainties, they are able to give each other support in the larger noncohabiting world.

Impact of Cohabitation on Marital Success

Although couples who are living together often argue that cohabitation helps prepare them for marriage, cohabiting couples are statistically as likely to divorce as those who do not live together prior to marriage. In 1972 Newcomb and Bentler (1980) interviewed 159 couples applying for marriage licenses. About half were living together at the time; the other half had not lived together. Four years later the researchers were able to interview 77 of these couples. Thirty-one percent had divorced. Those who had lived together were no less likely to have divorced than those who had not lived together. Among those still married, each group expressed about the same degree of marital satisfaction. Those who had lived together before argued less but had more problems with alcohol, drugs, and extramarital affairs. The differences probably have less to do with the impact of premarital cohabitation than with different personality characteristics. People who live together before marriage tend to be more liberal, more sexually experienced, and more independent than people who do not live together before marriage. Other studies have found that those who had cohabited before marriage were no more or less satisfied with their marriages than the other couples (Jacques and Chason, 1979; Watson, 1983).

A recent study noted slightly less marital satisfaction among married couples who had cohabited than among married couples who had not (DeMaris and Leslie, 1984). The researchers suggest that either cohabitating couples expect more out of marriage and are disappointed or else they are less likely to adapt well to traditional marital roles. They concluded:

The evidence accumulated to date would indicate that, while living together before marriage is increasingly becoming a common phase of courtship, cohabitation has no particular advantage over more traditional practices in assuring couple compatibility in marriage.

Cohabitation Among Young Adults

Before people live together they generally have dated each other for some time, have had reasonably good sex and have established a caring relationship. People who live together have almost invariably experienced premarital sex, whereas those who marry have not necessarily had premarital intercourse with each other. Two people who decide to live together go through steps similar to those of people who decide to marry. Studies indicate that men and women who live together have known each other for an average of eight months to two years (Danzinger and Greenwald, 1973; Macklin, 1972). Compared with dating relationships, living together offers more intimacy, emotional security, the chance to be with each other in everyday situations, and the opportunity to have sexual relations in a more personal setting. Companion-ship is especially important.

These advantages are similar to those of marriage over dating relationships. Yet people who live together feel that they do not want to make the permanent or long-term commitment of marriage. Perhaps they want more experience or they feel a need to test a relationship or to be free from more lasting commitments while they are still developing and discovering themselves. In his novel *Women in Love*, D. H. Lawrence implicitly argued for men and women living together outside of marriage. Two sisters, Gudrun and Ursula, are discussing marriage:

"You don't think one needs the *experience* of having been married?" [Gudrun] asked.
"Do you think it need *be* an experience?" replied Ursula.
"Bound to be in some way or other," said Gudrun, cooly. "Possibly undesirable, but bound to be an experience of some sort."
"Not really," said Ursula. "More likely to be the end of experience."

Cohabitation Among the Middle Aged and the Elderly

About 18 percent of unmarried households have a partner older than forty-five years. Generally, these unmarried couples are divorced or single people who have decided not to have children. Among the divorced, many are not willing to marry again (at least for awhile) because of their unhappy experiences during marriage.

About 31 percent of cohabiting divorced men and women have children from an earlier marriage living with them. Many children form powerful bonds with the nonparent, but if the couple splits up, the law does not protect the relationship between the child and nonparent (Newcomb, 1979). Unless the couples plan to marry, they usually choose not to have children of their own.

More than 114,000 couples over age sixty-five live together. Often they simply cannot afford marriage. Almost half the income of the elderly comes from pensions, and for many elderly people pensions and Social Security are the only income. If a widow remarries she often loses half or all of her pension, but if she lives with but does not marry a man, the two can pool their incomes without any cut. (The pooled income will be higher than that permitted a couple receiving Social Security.)

Companionship is often the core of such relationships, but they may have a sexual dimension as well. Relationships between elderly people often include affection, touching, kissing, and making love. Younger people may find it difficult to accept the extent of these sexual activities. Generally speaking, those who disapprove of elderly persons living together also disapprove of young adults living together. It is interesting to note that elderly people living together receive more support from middle-aged and older persons than from the young (Klemmack and Roth, 1980).

☐ GAY AND LESBIAN COUPLES

In contrast to studies of heterosexual relations, relatively little research has been done on gay couples—and most of that has been done on gay males. Generally, gay couples have been viewed as less committed than heterosexual couples because (1) gays cannot legally marry and (2) gays do not appear to emphasize sexual exclusiveness. One researcher has suggested, however, that gay couples may be no less committed than heterosexual ones—only differently committed (Lewis, 1981). Exclusive sexual relationships may not be as essential to gay love relationships as they are to heterosexual ones. One study found no association between sexual exclusiveness and relationship satisfaction among lesbians; some evidence indicated that sexually exclusive male

Although our culture celebrates love, it is generally hostile to the expression of love or intimacy between members of the same sex. As a result, gay men and women find little support for their relationships except within the gay subculture.

couples were happier, but the evidence was not conclusive and has been contradicted by other studies (Peplau, 1981).

Striking similarities exist between gay and heterosexual couples, according to Letitia Peplau (1981). Regardless of their sexual preferences, most people want a close, loving relationship with another person. For both gays and heterosexuals, intimate relationships provide love, satisfaction, and security. But there is one important difference. Heterosexual couples tend to adopt a traditional marriage model for their relationships, whereas gay couples tend to reject husband/wife roles. Freedom from such roles is often regarded as one of the major advantages of the gay life style. A gay male said, "Whenever I am asked who is the husband and who is the wife, I say, 'We're just a couple of happily married husbands' " (Saghir and Robins, 1973). Instead of adopting a marriage model, gay couples tend to have a "best-friend" mode. Peplau observed:

A friendship model promotes equality in love relationships. As children, we learn that the husband should be the "boss" at home, but that friends "share and share alike." Same-sex friends often have similar interests, skills, and resources—in part because they are exposed to the same gender-role socialization in growing up. It is easier to share responsibilities in a relationship when both partners are equally skilled—or inept—at cooking, making money, disclosing feelings, or whatever.

With this model, tasks and chores are often shared, alternated, or done by the person who has more time. Usually, both members of the couple support themselves; rarely does one financially support the other (Peplau and Gordon, 1982).

Two important factors contribute to egalitarianism in gay relationships (Harry, 1983). First, most gay couples are dual-worker couples; neither partner supports the other economically. Few gay relationships are divided into the traditional heterosexual provider/homemaker roles. Second, since gay couples are the same sex, the economic consequences of sex discrimination are absent. One does not have greater power based on income.

The relationships of many gay men, like those of heterosexual men, are often relatively short. In our culture it is common for men to first respond to a partner sexually and then emotionally. Most of the men in the study by Bell and Weinberg (1978), however, had at least one exclusive relationship with a male partner.

Lesbian women, like heterosexual women, appear to be more interested in emotional relationships. Most lesbians meet their partners through friends or social gatherings, and in contrast to gay men, have had fewer than ten sex partners during their adulthood. Their partners tend to be women they have known for a while and with whom they have had nonsexual intimacy (Bell and Weinberg, 1978).

Lesbians usually form more lasting relationships than do gay men, reflecting female socialization patterns; they are usually more committed to finding an enduring relationship based on love. Lesbian women have internalized equally as much as heterosexual women the norms of combining love and sexuality. Being a woman influences a lesbian's sexual behavior more than being homosexual. Both heterosexual and gay women tend to integrate sex, intimacy, and love more than men.

The gay world, however, is not always supportive of couple relationships. Blumstein and Schwartz (1983) comment:

The problem with gay male culture is that much of it is organized around singlehood or maintaining one's sexual marketability. Meeting places like bars and baths promote casual sex rather than couple activities. The problem with the lesbian world is quite different. Women

It is to be like a god, to sit
   before you and listen closely
To the sweet sounds and winning laughter
Which make my heart beat
   fast.
When I look on you, Brocheo,
   my speech
   stops short or fails me.
I am tongue-tied.

SAPPHO, (6th CENTURY B.C.)

are often tight-knit friendship groups where friends and acquaintances spend so much intimate time together that, it seems to us, opportunities arise for respect and companionship to turn into love and a meaningful affair. Thus, gay men imperil their relationships because of the availability of a singles market that draws men out of their relationships; lesbians are in jeopardy because of opportunities to fall in love. . . . If couplehood were an institution, participation in the gay world would not be detrimental; it would be supportive.

Gays and lesbians often achieve satisfying relationships only with difficulty because they lack the supports given to heterosexual people. They neither have the social nor legal sanction of our society. They generally lack, in addition, the bonding roles of mother or father provided by rearing children. As gays age, they develop friendship networks to replace missing or weak family ties (Rimmel, 1980).

□ SUMMARY

- The marriage marketplace refers to the selection activities of men and women when sizing someone up as a potential date or mate. In this marketplace, each person has resources, such as social class, status, age, and physical attractiveness. People tend to choose partners whose overall rating is about the same as their own.

- The marital exchange is based on sex roles. Men traditionally offer status, economic resources, and protection; women offer nurturing, childbearing, homemaking skills, and physical attractiveness. Recent changes in women's economic status give women more bargaining power; the decline in value of housekeeping and children and the increase of female sexual availability give men more bargaining power.

- The *field of eligibles* consists of those whom our culture approves of as potential partners. It is limited by the principles of *endogamy*, marriage within a particular group, and *exogamy*, marriage outside the group.

- The field of eligibles is further limited by *homogamy*, the tendency to choose a mate whose individual or group characteristics are similar to ours, and by *heterogamy*, the tendency to choose a mate whose individual or group characteristics are different from ours. Homogamy is especially powerful in our culture, particularly the factors of race, religion, socioeconomic class, and age.

- Functions of dating include cross-sex socialization, recreation, companionship, and mate selection. Traditional dating emphasizes formality, traditional sex roles, male aggressiveness, and female passivity. More recently, the idea of "getting together" has developed. Getting together emphasizes mutuality, spontaneity, and egalitarian sex roles. It is less oriented toward mate selection than is traditional dating.

- Friendship offers some of the same benefits as romantic or dating relationships. In contrast to dating relationships, sex is usually not an issue in friendships. Friendships may sometimes develop into romantic relationships.

- Problems in dating include who initiates the first date, who pays, and complementary roles. For women, problems include sexual pressure from men, communication, and where to go. For men, problems include communication, where to go, shyness, and money.

- Premarital sexuality is becoming widely accepted, especially among students who consider themselves in love. Virginity is also acceptable if it is tied to deeply held religious beliefs.

- Most breakups are initiated by the woman; few are mutual.

- Our culture feels ambivalent about marriage; continual tension exists between the alternatives of singlehood and marriage. The singles world consists of men and women over twenty-five who have never married or are divorced, who are working, and who do not have primary childrearing responsibilities. The singles world is a life style in which relationships tend to be casual; meeting other unattached persons is a major difficulty for singles.

- Singlehood is affected by the *marriage squeeze* and the *marriage gradient*. The marriage squeeze refers to the unequal ratio of men to women. In the 1980s, there are more suitable men than women in the twenty- to twenty-four-year age group; after age twenty-five, there are considerably more women than men. The marriage gradient refers to the relative inability of "cream-of-the-crop" women and "bottom-of-the-barrel" men to find suitable marriage partners.

- Cohabitation has become an acceptable alternative to marriage at virtually every level in society. At least five types have been noted: (1) temporary casual convenience, (2) affectionate dating or going together, (3) trial marriage, (4) temporary alternative to marriage, (5) permanent alternative to marriage. Compared with marriage, cohabitation is more transitory, has different commitments, and lacks extensive social support. It does not seem to have much impact on eventual marital success. Cohabitation has become increasingly popular because of a more liberal sexual climate, the changed meaning of marriage, delayed marriage, and delayed childbearing.

- Gay couples tend to adopt a best-friend model of relationships that implies equality in contrast to the traditional heterosexual model in which the male is dominant. Lesbians generally form more lasting relationships than gay men. The gay subculture emphasizes singleness and provides little support for couples.

READINGS

Computer Dating Questionnaire

COMPATIBILITY PLUS

This computer dating service relies on self reporting. Fill out this questionnaire. What items do you believe should be included? Deleted? After you have filled it out, examine it to see if your ideal match is similar or dissimilar to yourself. Do you see factors of homogamy at work in your choices?

QUESTIONNAIRE INSTRUCTIONS

Each question has two headings: "YOURSELF" and "IDEAL MATCH."

- For "YOURSELF" mark the box on the left that best describes you.
- Then, mark all the boxes on the right that best describe your "IDEAL MATCH."
- Please answer all the questions. If none of the choices is the exact answer you wish to give, then mark the answer that comes closest.

YOURSELF   IDEAL MATCH

1. Age _____ yrs.

2. **Minimum age acceptable**   _____ yrs.
   Maximum age acceptable   _____ yrs.

3. **Height:** ___ ft. ___ in.

4. **Minimum height acceptable**   ___ ft. ___ in.
   Maximum height acceptable   ___ ft. ___ in.

5. **Sex**
   ☐ 1) Male.................................☐
   ☐ 2) Female...............................☐

6. **Race**
   ☐ 1) White................................☐
   ☐ 2) Hispanic.............................☐
   ☐ 3) Oriental.............................☐
   ☐ 4) Black................................☐
   ☐ 5) Other _____☐
              (write in)

7. **Body Build**
   ☐ 1) Heavy................................☐
   ☐ 2) Moderately heavy.....................☐
   ☐ 3) Average ....☐
   ☐ 4) Moderately thin......................☐
   ☐ 5) Thin.................................☐

8. **Religion**
   ☐ 1) Catholic.............................☐
   ☐ 2) Protestant ....☐

   ☐ 3) Jewish...............................☐
   ☐ 4) Eastern Mysticism....................☐
   ☐ 5) Atheist or Agnostic ....☐
   ☐ 6) Other _____☐
              (write in)

9. **Economic Bracket**
   ☐ 1) Low income...........................☐
   ☐ 2) Average income ....☐
   ☐ 3) Above average........................☐
   ☐ 4) Much above average ....☐

10. **Furthest Education**
   ☐ 1) Grade School.........................☐
   ☐ 2) High School..........................☐
   ☐ 3) Some College.........................☐
   ☐ 4) Graduated College ....☐
   ☐ 5) Post-graduate study..................☐

11. **Diet**
   ☐ 1) No restrictions ....☐
   ☐ 2) No red meat ....☐
   ☐ 3) Kosher ....☐
   ☐ 4) Macrobiotic..........................☐
   ☐ 5) Vegetarian...........................☐

12. **Tobacco use**
   ☐ 1) Non-smoker (only)....................☐
   ☐ 2) Light smoker.........................☐
   ☐ 3) Regular smoker ....☐

13. **Children Living With You**
   ☐ 1) None ....☐
   ☐ 2) One ....☐
   ☐ 3) Two..................................☐
   ☐ 4) Three or more ....☐

14. **Political Outlook**
   ☐ 1) Liberal..............................☐
   ☐ 2) Moderate ....☐
   ☐ 3) Conservative.........................☐
   ☐ 4) Progressive–Radical ....☐
   ☐ 5) Other _____☐
              (write in)

15. **Affection**
   ☐ 1) Very affectionate ....☐
   ☐ 2) Moderately affectionate ....☐
   ☐ 3) Mildly affectionate ....☐
   ☐ 4) Non-demonstrative ....☐

16. **Sense of Humor**
   ☐ 1) Very funny or witty..................☐
   ☐ 2) Average ....☐
   ☐ 3) Mild.................................☐

READINGS–*continued*

17. **Assertiveness**
    - ☐ 1) Very assertive .... ☐
    - ☐ 2) Moderately assertive .... ☐
    - ☐ 3) Mildly assertive .... ☐
    - ☐ 4) Non-assertive .... ☐

18. **General Disposition**
    - ☐ 1) Easy going–flexible .... ☐
    - ☐ 2) Moderate .... ☐
    - ☐ 3) Firm .... ☐

19. **Favorite Parties**
    - ☐ 1) Loud and lively .... ☐
    - ☐ 2) Quiet and formal .... ☐
    - ☐ 3) Small and intimate .... ☐
    - ☐ 4) None–prefer one to one .... ☐

20. **Dancing**
    - ☐ 1) Love it .... ☐
    - ☐ 2) Like it .... ☐
    - ☐ 3) Mild interest .... ☐
    - ☐ 4) Dislike it .... ☐

21. **Sexual Activity**
    - ☐ 1) Very important .... ☐
    - ☐ 2) Moderately important .... ☐
    - ☐ 3) Not essential .... ☐

22. **Relationship Desired**
    - ☐ 1) Committed one to one .... ☐
    - ☐ 2) Friends and lovers .... ☐
    - ☐ 3) Nonsexual friendship .... ☐
    - ☐ 4) Just sexual .... ☐

23. **Favorite Activities and Interests**
    (Check all you enjoy)

☐ swimming	☐ dancing	☐ yoga
☐ surfing	☐ walking	☐ meditation
☐ sailing	☐ partying	☐ astrology
☐ bicycling	☐ playing music	☐ photography
☐ jogging	☐ listening to music	☐ art
☐ hiking	☐ concerts	☐ cooking
☐ skiing	☐ plays	☐ politics
☐ tennis	☐ movies	☐ shopping
☐ racquetball	☐ beach	☐ reading
☐ volleyball	☐ travelling	☐ bars
☐ aerobics	☐ golf	☐ television

24. **Personality Traits**
    (Check all that describe you)

☐ sexy	☐ intelligent	☐ emotional
☐ spontaneous	☐ considerate	☐ possessive
☐ romantic	☐ imaginative	☐ frugal
☐ playful	☐ conventional	☐ polite

☐ positive	☐ patient	☐ decisive
☐ energetic	☐ talkative	☐ reserved
☐ inquisitive	☐ generous	☐ moody
☐ sociable	☐ sincere	☐ serious
☐ athletic	☐ tolerant	☐ anxious
☐ relaxed	☐ loyal	☐ lazy
☐ open	☐ witty	☐ demanding

25. **Additional Remarks:**

_____

_____

_____

Beautiful People: An Unfair Advantage in Life
ELLEN BERSCHEID, *U.S. NEWS & WORLD REPORT*

Do physically attractive people have an unfair advantage? Does a person's sex have a bearing on the significance of attractiveness? How important is attractiveness beyond first impressions in a relationship? Do those of us who are not especially attractive have more difficulty in succeeding in life than our attractive counterparts? If so, in what ways?

Q *Professor Berscheid, do beautiful or handsome people get preferential treatment because of their good looks?*

A Yes. Society assumes that an attractive person is warm and responsive and sincere and has more potential for social, marital and occupational success. Attractive individuals are generally believed to be more sensitive, more kind, interesting, strong, poised, modest, sociable, outgoing and exciting.

This stereotype of physically attractive people helps explain why they get preferential treatment in a wide range of situations. Beauty affects job opportunities, for example. Even when appearance has no conceivable relationship to a person's functioning in a job, the hiring decisions of experienced personnel consultants are significantly influenced by the applicant's physical appearance.

We have been conditioned to expect good behavior and performance from attractive persons. And we may think we get it. Our expectations about attractive people sometimes come true because our favorable treatment subsequently elicits from them the desirable qualities we predicted they would have. We also tend to ignore those traits that don't fit the stereotype.

Q *Is this a growing problem in our society?*

A I think it is. The importance of first impressions and one-time interactions between people is increasing because of urbanization, greater geographic mobility, frequent job

READINGS—*continued*

changes and a rising divorce rate.

Since we more frequently interact with strangers, we more often judge others—and are judged ourselves—on the basis of first impressions that never get a chance to be corrected. Once these impressions are made, they are very difficult to overcome. Even if interaction continues, initial impressions set the course for what happens later.

So first impressions probably have become more important as our society has become increasingly fragmented. Since the turn of the century, the divorce rate has gone up over 700 percent. A child can't count on having the same set of parents for any length of time. We can't be certain of having the same marriage partner. People are thrown out on the dating-and-mating market at all ages—30, 40, 50 and 60.

We can't depend on having the same neighbors for any length of time, the same school friends, the same workmates or the same employer. As one result, people are more frequently assessed by others simply on the basis of their appearance because that's often the only information we have when we meet each other for the first time.

Q *Are you saying that the old axiom that "beauty is only skin-deep" is not true?*

A Based on many studies, we have to conclude that beauty is much more than skin-deep. Most of us, psychologists included, don't like to think that appearance makes an important difference in our lives. It is not a fact that makes us very comfortable.

When you start talking about personal characteristics that are genetically influenced—such as physical appearance, intelligence, race, sex and height—you immediately raise the specter of genetic determinism, which is anathema to our democratic tradition of equality. We Americans are very fond of the myth that everyone is born with equal assets and equal opportunities for survival and for living a happy and comfortable life. That simply isn't true, of course.

Q *Why is there such an obsession with beauty in the U.S.?*

A It always has been of some importance at all historical times, as Charles Darwin was the first to document in his studies of mate selection. In addition to social fragmentation, the current preoccupation with beauty may be due to the larger role the media play in our lives. Hollywood has always worshiped beauty, but now television holds before us 24 hours a day, every day, an extraordinarily high standard of physical attractiveness—one that may be too high, incidentally, for most people to achieve.

Advertising exhorts us to buy cosmetics and other devices to enhance our appearance. And we do, to the tune of billions of dollars. News announcers and game-show hosts who appear on our TV screens seem to be chosen in large part on the basis of their physical appearance. Even when they pan the football crowd or the studio audience, the camera stops and focuses on an attractive person.

Media consultants and political advisers know that physically attractive men and women capture more attention. And once they've got our attention, what they say is given more credibility and respect and tends to be remembered longer.

Television producers apparently know that viewers are likely to make a quick decision on announcers or performers based on that first impression and can switch the channel if they aren't immediately attracted by them.

Q *Does that mean that less attractive persons will find it hard to enter jobs in the public eye?*

A We all can hope not, since this will eliminate many talented people society can't afford to lose. But there's no question they are up against a social force that favors others, some of whom can't contribute as much. The wonderful thing about Walter Cronkite, for example, is that he looked like an ordinary human being. He and Harry Reasoner and other senior journalists may be "the last of the Mohicans," however. Not many of the new TV announcers look like anyone we might meet on the street.

The same is true for politicians. Politicians can be more sure that they will be seen than heard. No one has yet calculated precisely how many votes a bald head or a homely face will cost a candidate, but I think it is a question whether anyone like Abraham Lincoln could get elected in the television age. I doubt it.

Q *How early in life does favorable treatment of attractive people begin?*

A Virtually from the time the child draws a breath, studies are revealing. From infancy on, the treatment by mothers, fathers, nurses and teachers differs according to the level of attractiveness. Newborn infants that are independently judged to be attractive tend to be held, cuddled and kissed more than less attractive babies.

To take another example, the misbehavior of the unattractive child is regarded as evidence of a chronic antisocial nature, while a transgression on the part of an attractive child is thought to be a momentary aberration.

Teachers are prone to give attractive children more information, better evaluations, more opportunity to perform and more instruction. They think that such children are smarter and that their parents care more about their educational accomplishments.

READINGS–*continued*

Q *Besides their looks, how are attractive children different from the less attractive?*

A We don't yet know, because only recently did we begin to look for differences in how they're treated. We originally thought—hoped, to be more accurate—that children were immune from the effects we observed with adolescents and adults.

But more and more, psychologists suspect that unattractive and attractive children live in different worlds. They absorb from an early age the stereotype of who is pretty and who is homely. We did a study with nursery-school children who were rated by adults in terms of their attractiveness. We then asked the children to tell us which, if any, of their classmates they found "scary." They picked out classmates the adults had judged unattractive.

Q *Should persons, especially children, be made to understand that they may be unpopular partly because of their unattractiveness?*

A I think so. Knowledge is better than ignorance. People, children included, who understand what affects other people's treatment of them have a chance to do something about it—fight it, rise above it, go around it or otherwise deal with it. People who are ignorant don't have that chance, and they may never know what hit them.

When people deny the importance of physical attractiveness to children, the result can be bewilderment. Also, unattractive children who are treated poorly because of it may wrongly conclude there is some flaw in their character or personality, which just adds to their burden.

Q *Are people fooling themselves when they say they value social skills, intelligence, personality and good character in others more than physical appearance?*

A There is seemingly a paradox in what people say they regard as important in their feelings toward others and what actually influences them. I don't think people deliberately and consistently lie on this subject. We know that people often can't identify the forces that influence their behavior, including their feelings toward others.

Much of the unawareness in this case probably lies in the incredible speed with which the human mind processes a bit of information. For example, a person's physical-attractiveness level can be discerned from a photo tachistoscopically flashed on a screen for a bare fraction of a second. Almost instantaneously, we conjure up a mental image of that person's character.

With lightning speed, the human mind processes that information about the person's physical appearance against all the information held in memory about what physically attractive and unattractive people are like. So when we see

a beautiful woman or a handsome man, in the time it takes us to blink an eye we see standing before us a good and kind and sincere person. The fact that the individual is also physically attractive may seem incidental or just an irrelevant added bonus.

The mind works so fast that we're often not aware of where that inference of goodness and kindness came from or what information our mind used to reach that conclusion. And so we say we're responding to their character, not their appearance. We're not consciously lying. For those of us who have absorbed the stereotype about attractiveness, the effect may be virtually automatic and very compelling.

Q *As women become more of a force in the workplace, will appearance become more of a factor in their livelihood?*

A Less of a factor. For many years in this society, a woman's livelihood depended almost entirely on whom she married. Her economic security, her social status and the kind of life she and her children led depended very much on that marriage. And as long as men were choosing mates on appearance, then a woman's attractiveness played an especially heavy role in her destiny. Now more women feel that their brains count, too, and that their chances for a satisfying life depend more than before on factors other than physical attractiveness.

Q *What does all this emphasis on surface beauty say about our values?*

A The evidence is that we Americans delude ourselves by thinking that physical appearance isn't important in our lives. We cling to the idea that each of us at birth is dealt an equally good hand of cards to play—that appearance, intelligence, physical and mental health, and other genetically influenced factors don't make much difference in life. But they do.

Our Declaration of Independence says that each individual is created of equal value and worth as a human being. I didn't read anything that says we are all born with equal assets and opportunities. That certainly is not true of our physical features.

And I never read anything in there that said the child who is born with a deformity, the child who is born with a heart condition or who is born into poverty or has abusive parents has an equal chance with the child who does not have those handicaps.

The idea that pervades our society, as study after study has documented, is that we live in a just world where people get exactly what they deserve. The dark underside of that idea is our belief that if what they've gotten is misery, then they must have done something to deserve it since they started out equal. That is a cruel idea. But it is also a

READINGS–*continued*

convenient one for those of us who were gifted with a better-than-equal chance: What it does is absolve us from responsibility for someone else's misfortune.

Singlehood As an Alternative to Marriage
PETER J. STEIN, *THE FAMILY COORDINATOR*

What are the pushes toward marriage, according to the author? Why does the larger society oppose singlehood? Why do single men and women feel uncertainty about their social identity? How are singles devalued? Exploited? What kind of social context would need to be created to make singlehood an attractive alternative to marriage? Should such a social context be developed? Why?

The dominant value system in American society upholds the importance of marriage in such a way that singlehood is devalued and derogated by an array of social sanctions. Adams (1971) speaks of "the severe psychological and social devaluation that has settled like an accretion around the concept of singleness . . . this attitude is a societal product capable of being changed once its destructive potential is understood." This social bias results in overt and subtle pressures to conform to the marital norm, in discrimination by certain institutions, and in commercial exploitation. The social context is weighted against singlehood despite the growing numbers of singles and their emergent ideology. That the case for singlehood has not been presented to society is underscored by the stereotyping of singles, when, in fact, "the diversity of single life . . . contradicts both the old fashioned image of unmarried people as lonely losers and the current media picture of 'swingles' who cavort through an endless round of bars, parties and no strings attached sexual adventures" (Jacoby, 1974).

The prevailing attitudes which maintain that the most desirable and acceptable adult life condition lies within marriage generate pushes in the socialization process. For many, the pushes have been so well internalized that they appear as pulls in the outlook and behavior of young men and women. Marriage seems to them not only a desirable state, but also the only natural one. All of our interviewees, indeed most Americans, have been socialized according to the values of previous generations, wherein one's social status, sex-role, and self-image are embedded in marital status. Among the respondents, five have been married once, one twice, seven have lived in an exclusive relationship, and five have done both. Thus for eighteen of the 20 we spoke to, the pushes and pulls toward marriage or marriage-like living arrangements were strong enough to have convinced them at an earlier time in their lives that this was desirable. It was only after the marital situation was in effect that its underlying assumptions were questioned and largely rejected. Because of the social context, however, single persons continue to experience the contradictions stemming from a clash between the older values stressing marriage and parenthood, and the newer values stressing the choice to marry or remain single, the modification of traditional sex-roles, equalitarianism, individual freedom, and self-actualization.

This often creates for singles an uncertainty about their own social identity. This is heightened by a continuing push towards marriage in the form of pressure from parents, relatives, colleagues, and married friends. Such pressures were felt by many of our respondents. Jim, a writer, said that he felt

a non-specific pressure, a sort of wonderment that at 35 I can be alone. I sometimes feel pressure from my own confusion of how come I don't conform to the patterns of people who are in the same situation as I am in terms of career and age.

Brenda, who at 28 has never been married, sometimes feels that she should be. She feels her parents pressuring her to marry, and, although she does not plan to marry in the near future, she is concerned about what others think of her:

When I tell people I'm 28 and not married, they look at me like there's something wrong with me—they think I'm a lesbian. Some just feel sorry for me. What a drag.

A more subtle form of social pressure is illustrated by Phil, an assistant professor at a major university:

It was hard being the only single person in the department. I would be invited to social gatherings and would get pretty nervous about who my date should be. The men would get into shop talk and the women, in some other part of the house, would talk about their families, the school system, and summer vacations. My date and I would usually feel uneasy, not quite fitting in and yet feeling a bit guilty about not fitting in.

Lucile Duberman states that "unattached people, especially women, are considered a threat to married people." Most of our respondents corroborated this by indicating flatly that they "were not friendly with" or "avoided" married couples. Joan, one of the few who elaborated, speaking of her relationship with married couples whom she knows, said:

READINGS–*continued*

They're looking for a nice doctor for me to marry. I also found that when I'm friends with married people, I have to be very careful in how I act around husbands. Either one or both might think I'm coming on to the husband, when I'm really not.

A further example of the confusion and emotional frustration generated by singles' lower status may be seen in Ellen's statement:

> What does it mean for me to be single? There is a whole part of me that sees as freedom the possibilities of meeting different people and having different kinds of relationships, which is the exciting part. And then, there is the part of me that looks at where I'm not doing what I'm supposed to be doing, where I'll ultimately end up lonely, where something is the matter with me because I'm not in love with somebody, whatever that means.

Respondents in this study testified to the strength of the pushes brought to bear in a marriage-oriented society. For some this amounts to an assault on their identity. "Not being married seemed abnormal," commented Mike, a 45-year-old lawyer. While they may find some recourse in associating with others who share their life style, they must contend with misunderstanding and condemnation from the society at large. Natalie, who, as a programmer, works in a predominantly male occupation, reported a "depressing" conversation she'd had with several of her male colleagues, all of whom are married:

> My boss couldn't or didn't want to, understand why I was not married. He imagines all sorts of orgies going on. Two of the younger guys said they felt sorry for me, that I was missing out on a lot of fun. When I told them I was happy and that I neither wanted to marry nor be a mother, they looked upset . . . they couldn't understand my position and I think they didn't believe me. I was pretty upset by it.

As Natalie reflected further, she began to feel that her own certainty about remaining single had threatened her colleagues. Instead of dealing with and accepting her values, they challenged her perception of her needs and tried to convince her that she was wrong.

Lack of tolerance and perpetuation of stereotypes extends from attempts to dissuade singles to outright discrimination, as seen, for instance, in the job market. In a survey of fifty major corporations, it was found that 80 percent of the responding companies asserted that marriage was not essential to upward mobility; however, a majority indicated that only 2 percent of their executives, including junior management, were single. Over 60 percent reported that

single executives tend to make snap judgments, and 25 percent believed singles to be "less stable" than married people.

Without cultural support structures for remaining single, those who are not married are highly susceptible to commercial exploitation and mass misrepresentation. Singles are subjected to commercialized approaches and appeals that play up the ways and means of finding a mate. Whether the item being sold is an alluring cologne or a "singles weekend," the approach is essentially the same. Entrepreneurs have become skilled in exploiting the needs of single people for self-worth and meaningful relationships through the merchandising of images of glamour and adventure.

Singles bars serve as a prominent example. In an interesting ethnographic study, Allon and Fischel examine the social motivations of patrons. They report that men and women frequent singles bars in search of companionship, affection, excitement, and social acceptance. Using Seeman's discussion of alienation, they identify the singles' attempted moves from various degrees of powerlessness, isolation, normlessness, and self-estrangement in the direction of intimacy, social integration, opportunity for nurturant behavior, and reassurance of worth. Though some are successful in their search and make contact with others who can meet some of their needs, for most the singles bar scene is a disappointment. The amount of role-playing required severely limits the quality of interaction.

A number of respondents in our sample had experienced the exploitation of the "singles scene."

One of the men, who used to frequent various singles clubs on the east side of Manhattan, talked about his degrading and depressing experiences:

> I went into one place and I was ready to check the women over, but when they started checking me back, I panicked. Those questions about what I did, which meant like how much money I make and what I would be worth ten years from now, really threw me. I felt like I should carry a vita around and just hand it over.

Paul, corroborating the finding of Allon and Fischel, related one episode with a real sense of sadness:

> She was standing next to me . . . and I asked her if she'd ever been to this place before. Of course, we'd both been here before. We had a drink, exchanged lots of small talk . . ., and eventually split to her place. She kept saying that she didn't like New York and the scene, and I kept thinking about her large breasts and how much longer it would be before we got into bed . . . The next morning I lied about having an early appointment somewhere . . .

READINGS—*continued*

When I got home, my stomach started hurting and I had a bad headache. It's not what I wanted.

As Allon and Fischel report, "the goal of all these establishments is not to provide an adequate alternative to marriage, but to provide places where . . . singles can meet, have fun, and contemplate marriage." Certainly, the social settings provided by singles bars are not conducive to the development of meaningful relationships between men and women. They epitomize the commercial exploitation to which singles are subject in their search for "eligible" single members of the opposite sex. In the absence of places designed to meet the human needs of single people, in the absence of an ideology that makes singlehood a viable alternative, and in the absence of control by singles over their own lives and environments, the conditions of exploitation thus continue to flourish.

The consequence of exploitation, discrimination, and the misrepresented stereotypical image of singles is to be seen in a recent study of single men. Statistics indicate that single men, as opposed to married counterparts, are more prone to mental and physical problems, suicide, crime, and lower income status. In some cases the existence of such problems undoubtedly predates and accounts for the individuals' failure to marry. The probability, however, given the disproportion in statistics, is that the experience of the two groups are sharply differentiated: it is harder to be single in American society. Although Gilder uses this data to support the necessity of traditional marriage, it is here suggested that these statistics result not from failure to marry, in itself, but rather may represent in part the high cost of rigid social attitudes in a society that regards singles as deviants and as categorically unstable and incomplete.

PART THREE

Sexuality

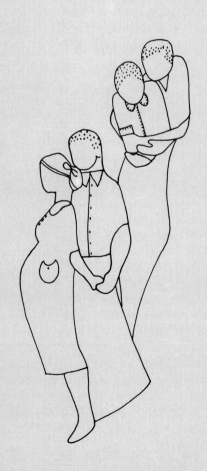

CHAPTER 7

Sexual Learning and Behavior

PREVIEW

To gain a sense of what you already know about the material covered in this chapter, answer "true" or "false" to the statements below. You will find the answers as you read the chapter.

1. Unlike most behavior, sexual behavior is instinctive. True or false?
2. Not all cultures view a woman's breasts as erotic. True or false?
3. During sexual intercourse, many physiological responses occur unnoticed. True or false?
4. Males more than females tend to view romantic activities as sexual signals. True or false?
5. Adolescents' perceptions of their friends' sexual activities are more important as models than their friends' actual behavior. True or false?
6. Men traditionally equate sex with intercourse. True or false?
7. Women have greater potential for multiple orgasms than men. True or false?
8. Sexual attitudes accurately reflect sexual behavior. True or false?
9. Although masturbation is common before marriage, after marriage few people masturbate because of the availability of a partner. True or false?
10. About 10 percent of the population engage in homosexual behaviors. True or false?

Outline

Although we are born with the potential to be sexual, we actually learn how to behave sexually. In this chapter, we examine how we learn to be sexual and how what we learn as males and females differs; we also examine male and female sexual structure, the sexual response cycle, and different types of sexual behavior.

☐ LEARNING TO BE SEXUAL

Imagine yourself sitting on the beach, reading; you see a man or woman walk by and feel a flash of sexual attraction to him or her. What is it that attracts you? Often we ascribe our attraction to the other person, saying that he or she has sex appeal. Actually, this sex appeal resides more in us than in the person to whom we are attracted. Our culture defines what is "sexy." Through learning we incorporate our culture's ideas of what traits, looks, body features, and so on are sexually appealing.

Beneath the apparent instinctiveness of sexuality lies a profound learning beginning with childhood. We learn to whom to be attracted, when to be attracted, what to do sexually, and how to feel about what we do. All of these are defined by culture and learned by each individual. (For a comprehensive discussion of human sexuality from a social learning perspective, see Gagnon, 1977; see Cook, 1981, for a collection of essays on sexual attraction from various perspectives. For an overview of human sexuality, see Strong and Reynolds, 1982; for new approaches to female sexuality, see Vance, 1984; for a discussion of the "feminist sexuality debates," see Freedman and Thorne, 1984; for bibliography on sexuality, see Mason, 1983.)

Cultures vary in what they consider sexually attractive and arousing (Dion, 1981; see Rosenblatt and Anderson, 1981). The aspects of beauty that appear universal are health and youth—both of which are linked to sexuality. The only cultural constants of male sexual attractiveness are his skills, prowess, strength, and health, not his appearance per se. In contrast to males, female sexual attractiveness tends to be perceived more in terms of physical appearance. Her attractiveness is based on what is appealing to males. The specifics of attractiveness vary from culture to culture. Many cultures view a woman's breasts as nonsexual; in our culture breasts are considered erotic. In Victorian America, a woman's ankles were seen as erotic; today no one pays attention to ankles. Obesity in men was valued in Polynesia; in the United States fitness and a trim body are the order of the day.

Adam was but human—this explains it all. He did not want the apple for the apple's sake, he wanted it only because it was forbidden.

MARK TWAIN

Sexuality is a good gift from God and is a fundamental means of realizing life-in-community. This gift includes all that it means to be male and female and is not limited to coital behavior. All expressions of human sexuality affect the emergence of genuine personhood and should reflect a concern for personal integrity, relational fidelity and the equality of men and women.

UNITED METHODIST CHURCH

The Role of Culture

Our sexual behaviors are the result of a complicated series of sexual decisions. These decisions, however, rarely reach our awareness because over time they have become automatic. Our decisions have become automatic for two reasons: (1) We have repeated the decision many times before. (2) We have been given a ready-made cultural script that encourages us to act in certain ways. As John Gagnon (1977) wrote:

There is nothing in any particular event in itself which produces sexual arousal—the classification of a stimulus as sexual and a response as sexual is the outcome of a history of decisions made by an individual in a particular society and culture. It is usually difficult for us to recall our first making the decisions to label and connect stimulus and response, partly because we often merely accept the models provided us.

Think again about reading on the beach and seeing the attractive, tanned man or woman walking along the water's edge. This time, the person smiles at you in passing. You might smile back briefly, then resume your reading. Or you might encode or define the event as sexual, the smile as a flirtation or a sexual invitation. If you encode the event as sexual, what will you do? A typical response in our culture is to begin a sexual fantasy of meeting the person later on the beach, walking in the moonlight, and spending the rest of the evening kissing or making love next to a brightly burning fire. Once you decide to define the event as sexual, the fantasy begins to unfold without much more ado. What you are not aware of is that you have learned to define certain kinds of smiles as flirtatious or erotic and people dressed in bathing suits as erotic objects. Being at the beach is a legitimate place for erotic fantasies, it is culturally appropriate to have fantasies about strangers (but not to engage in real-life sexual behaviors with them), and typical erotic fantasies in our culture include romance, kissing, or making love, for which you provide the details.

When we are engaged in sexual activities, we experience love, guilt, tenderness, anxiety, hostility, security, and so on. We may believe that the feelings come from the physical acts, but they are feelings we learned to associate with the acts. This learning can be explained by Stanley Schacter's two-component theory of emotion. As you recall from Chapter 5, he argued that two factors must coexist for a person to experience an emotion: (1) The person must be physiologically aroused. (2) It must be appropriate for the person to interpret the physiological arousal in emotional terms. Needless to say, sexual arousal and behaviors are strong physiological events; even the frustration caused by sexual inhibitions facilitates physiological responses. We have learned to associate these arousals with various emotions. Most of us learned in childhood and adolescence, for example, to associate masturbation with guilt. Our culture teaches us—especially females—to associate sexual intercourse with love. But love is no more a part of the physiological responses that make up sex than is guilt. We may even link hatred, jealousy, and pain to sexual arousal (Barclay, 1969; Dutton and Aron, 1974).

The link between emotions and sexual activity can be confusing. When two people make love, they may associate quite different emotions with the act: one person may feel a great sense of intimacy whereas the other person may feel alienation. We may mislabel our feelings about someone because of our arousal. People often ask themselves if it is sexual attraction or love that they feel: "Am I in love or in lust?"

Sin is geographical.

BERTRAND RUSSELL

Morality is the custom of one's country and the current feeling of one's peers. Cannibalism is moral in a cannibal country.

SAMUEL BUTLER (1612–1680)

Sin is whatever obscures the soul.

ANDRÉ GIDE

Sentiments are for the most part traditional; we feel them because they were felt by those who preceded us.

WILLIAM HAZLITT (1778–1830)

Sexual Scripts

Our sex roles are critical in learning sexuality. Sex roles tell us what behavior (including sexual) is appropriate for each gender. Our sexual impulses are organized and directed through our sexual scripts, which we learn and act out. A script is like a road map or blueprint that gives general directions; it is more like a sketch than a detailed picture of how our culture expects us to act. But even though a script is generalized, it is often more important in guiding our actions than our experiences themselves. Over time, we may modify, alter, or change our scripts, but we will not do away with them.

Sexual scripts define sexual sensations, events, objects, situations, and people. The scripts that permit sexual activity have two major components. The *intrapersonal* component, which includes internal psychological states that lead to sexual arousal. The *interpersonal* component, which is made up of the externally shared conventions and signals that enable two people to engage in sexual activity.

Intrapersonal Script.   On the intrapersonal level, sexual scripts enable individuals to give meaning to their physiological responses—to identify sensations as sexual or nonsexual. The internal scripts also determine which physiological events will be brought into a person's conscious mind. During sexual arousal a large number of physiological events are occurring simultaneously, but we are aware of only a few, such as increasing heartbeat and the tensing or contracting of muscles. Others—such as the increasing alkalinity of the vagina, and the emission of fluid from the Cowper's gland—do not filter through to our consciousness.

Interpersonal Script.   The interpersonal script is the area of shared conventions that makes sexual behavior possible. People follow a sequence of steps to define a situation as sexual and to act on that definition. Inviting a person to study with you at the library defines the situation as nonsexual; inviting a person to study with you in your apartment when your roommate is gone may define the situation as potentially sexual. More clues are needed to clear up ambiguity. Signs or gestures—verbal or nonverbal—also define encounters as sexual or nonsexual. People try to make their sexual motives clear (or unclear) by the way they look at each other, by the tone of their voices, by the movement of their bodies, and by other culturally shared phenomena: proximity, touching, glances, words. Moving from the living room to the bedroom to study further defines the situation as erotic. Once the situation is defined as erotic, the individuals must then decide on what sexual behaviors are going to take place: kissing, petting, oral sex, sexual intercourse, and so on. This decision is contingent on many factors: how much do I like or love this person? what are my moral values? is contraception available (or should I worry in the passion of the moment)? what if my roommate comes home? if I say no, what will be the consequences for our relationship? and so on.

If the couple decide to have intercourse, they will probably follow the general cultural script for sexual intercourse. Most people know the script, but it may not fit the particular situation or individuals. Although the script calls for the male to caress his partner's breasts, she may be self-conscious about their size and not respond to his touch. She may like having the light on, he may not. The man may prefer the woman-on-top position, although she expects him to be on top. Partners may be

Sex contains all, bodies, souls,
Meanings, proofs, purities, delicacies, results, promulgations,
Songs, commands, health, pride, the maternal mystery, the seminal milk
All hopes, benefactions, bestowals, all the passions, loves, beauties, delights of the earth,
These are contain'd in sex as parts of itself and justifications of itself.

WALT WHITMAN (1819–1892),
A WOMAN WAITS FOR ME

Because sexual desire is in the minds of most people coupled with the idea of love, they are easily misled to conclude that they love each other when they want each other physically.
. . . Sexual attraction creates, for the moment, the illusion of union, yet without love this "union" leaves strangers as far apart as they were before.

ERICH FROMM, *THE ART OF LOVING*

concerned about the way their genitals appear, whether the penis is too small, whether the vagina has an unpleasant odor. The man may worry about becoming erect; the woman about being orgasmic. The couple must discover how to interact compatibly with their bodies, how to move arms and legs and pelvises; how to move the genitals to give pleasure to both oneself and the partner. When it is over, the individuals must return to their nonsexual world—yet coitus has given new meaning to even this type of interaction. What do you say to each other now? To others? Only after partners have had experience with each other will the integration of sexual and nonsexual roles become easier.

As a couple spend more time together, they are able to integrate sexual intimacy with emotional intimacy, trust, and comfort. This allows many couples to experience greater satisfaction and fulfillment in their sexual experiences. Levine and Barbach (1985), in a study of 120 men, observed:

Part of the reason sex was better in an emotionally involved relationship was that the caring and comfort facilitated a level of communication that enhanced the physical experience. With time came a sense of safety and security that enabled the partners to risk communicating specific sexual information that was often necessary in order for the sex to be especially fulfilling.

Script Ambiguities.   One of the major problems men and women have is how to interpret signals—gestures, mannerisms, and so on—as sexual or nonsexual. Was the smile given to us by the man or woman on the beach actually flirtatious or was it merely friendly? Men are more likely to interpret the smile as flirtatious, while women are more likely to interpret it as friendly. Men and women tend to see the world of male-female relationships differently; men tend to sexualize relationships more than females. For example, if a woman initiates the first date, men are likely to view that as a sign that the woman is interested in sex (Komarovsky, 1985).

> For human beings, the more powerful need is not for sex per se, but for relationship, intimacy and affirmation.
>
> ROLLO MAY

In Los Angeles, researchers (cited in Tavris and Wade, 1984) asked more than four hundred adolescents about their expectations of sex and dating. Males and females differed considerably in their interpretation of sexual signals.

- Boys were more likely to interpret tight or revealing clothing as a sign that a person is sexually available. A woman may wear tight jeans because they are in style, but men are likely to conclude that she is trying to be seductive.
- Girls are less likely than boys to believe that a girl who accepts a date with a known Don Juan is implicitly agreeing to have sex with him.
- Boys are more likely than girls to believe that particular locations or activities are signals for sex. If a girl goes to a boy's house for a drink, he may assume that she is consenting to sex; she, however, may only be thirsty.
- Girls tend to view various verbal, physical, and romantic activities as signs of affection; boys, in contrast, view them as sexual signals. Such activities as talking about sex, playing with each other's hair, tickling, or telling a date that he or she is good looking or sexy consistently have different meanings for boys and girls.

Such differences lead to continuing misunderstandings over sex. Each sex misreads the signals of the other. Because much of our sexual and nonsexual interactions are nonverbal, they are ambiguous. We need verbal communication to reinforce or make clear our real intentions (see Chapter 14).

Sources of Learning

The cultural scripts we are given for sexual behavior tend to be traditional. These scripts are most powerful during adolescence, when we are first learning to be sexual. Gradually, as we gain experience, we modify and change these sexual scripts. Initially we learn our sexual scripts primarily from our parents, peers, and the media. As we get older, interactions with our partners become increasingly important.

Parents.   Parents, despite their best efforts, are usually not much help for adolescents trying to understand their emerging sexuality. Parents reveal little of their own sexual feelings while expecting to be privy to their child's sexual world. Such parents are in a dilemma: on the one hand, they are supposed to play a positive role in the development of their children's sexuality; on the other hand, almost no form of sexual behavior is approved by society before marriage. As a result, parents tend to limit their sexual teachings to prohibitions reflecting societal values. In fact, much of their efforts are directed toward limiting sexual behaviors rather than guiding them. One mother who found erotica in her son's room wrote to "Dear Abby," describing how she handled such problems:

When I find a girlie magazine in the room of any of our three teenage sons, I remove it and replace it with a 3 × 5 index card with a Bible verse covering that very subject. I've never had a complaint from any of them, as they know from the verses that they are to "abstain from fleshy lusts."

Needless to say, such acts, however well-intentioned, only make it more difficult for adolescents to turn to their parents.

Think about what you learned sexually from your parents. What did they teach you about sex? About morality? Guilt? How did they teach you about sex? What kind of models of sexuality did they present you? Do you view their contributions positively or negatively? What would you have done differently? How will (do) you teach your children about sex?

Peers.   Peers, especially from ages twelve to sixteen, are a powerful source of sexual learning (Gebhard, 1977). (See the reading, "The Slumber Party," by Wendy Hiller.) Unfortunately, the learning situation is something like the blind leading the blind. Because they lack experience and rely on the media for information, adolescent peers tend to reinforce sexual stereotypes. Adolescent males in particular camouflage their sexual ignorance, which leads to greater misinformation. Bill Cosby (1969) recalled early adolescence with its pressures to have sexual intercourse and his own ignorance. "But how do you find out how to do it without blowin' the fact that you don't know how to do it?" On his way to his first sexual encounter, he realized that he didn't have the faintest idea of what to do:

So now I'm walkin', and I'm trying to figure out what to do. And when I get there, the most embarrassing thing is gonna be when I have to take my pants down. See, right away, then, I'm buck naked . . . buck naked in front of this girl. Now, what happens then? Do . . . do you just . . . I don't even know what to do . . . I'm gonna just stand there and she's gonna say, "You don't know how to do it." And I'm gonna say, "Yes I do, but I *forgot.*" I never thought of her showing me, because I'm a man and I don't want her to show me. I don't want *nobody* to show me, but I wish somebody would kinda slip me a note. . . .

An adolescent's perception of peer's sexual behavior may be the most influential factor influencing his or her sexual behavior. But such perceptions are often unreliable indicators of actual behavior since boys tend to exaggerate their sexual experience and girls tend to understate it.

An adolescent's perception of peers' sexual behavior may be the single most important factor influencing his or her own sexual behavior. But such perceptions are often unreliable indicators of actual behavior. In keeping with traditional sex roles, boys tend to exaggerate their sexual experience and girls tend to understate it. Boys are expected to use whatever strategies they can to initiate sex, whereas girls are expected to use various strategies to avoid having sex (McCormick et al., 1984).

Think about your own childhood and adolescence. What did you learn from your peers about the sexual motivations and desires of males and females? About sexual intercourse? Masturbation? Pregnancy? What influence did your peers have on your sexual attitudes and behaviors? Did you ever pretend you had more (or less) sexual experience than you actually did? Why?

The Media.   Sex is a private act. We have little information about sexual interaction before we ourselves have had extensive experience. The media's portrayal of sex is often the only model we have for such behavior. Whether through television, movies, novels, magazines, song lyrics, or pornographic or erotic materials—the media fur-

FEATURE

Puberty

Puberty marks the beginning of our development as active sexual beings. It is the time when a child's body is transformed into an adult's body, with secondary sex characteristics—such as the development of breasts and hips in girls and musculature and deeper voice in boys—and the ability to reproduce. Young adolescents center much of their attention on the physical changes taking place in their bodies; they are fascinated by the "body mysterious" (Rierdon and Leoff, 1980). This physical development may cause worry and anxiety for adolescents if they seem to lag behind their peers.

For girls, menarche (men'-arky)—first menstruation (usually around age twelve to fourteen)—marks the beginning of fertility. Menarche is an event that in many cultures (but not our own) is celebrated as a girl's arrival into womanhood. It is the event that transforms a girl into a woman and underscores the importance that society places on

women's reproductive capacity. Menarche, however, is not associated with a girl's erotic transformation.

The development of breasts rather than menarche is the critical bodily event associated with erotic sexuality. Breasts are symbolic of female sexual attractiveness in our culture. Nora Ephron (1973) recalled the agony of being the "flattest" girl in eighth grade:

"Don't worry about it," said my friend Libby. . . . "When you get married your husband will touch your breasts and rub them and kiss them and they'll grow."

That was the killer. Necking I could deal with. Intercourse I could deal with. But it had never crossed my mind that a man was going to touch my breasts. . . . I became dizzy. . . . I knew no one would ever want to marry me. I had no breasts. I would never have breasts.

Here are some things I did to help: Bought a Mark Eden Bust Developer, Slept on my back for four years,

nish us with some of our most important models. One television critic (Mander, 1978) described his first kiss as a media kiss:

I was fourteen years old when I tried kissing for the first time. I imitated Humphrey Bogart's kiss, but I didn't feel it. Only later did I realize that perhaps Bogart didn't feel it either; he was merely kissing the way the director said he should. So there I was imitating a kiss that was never real in the first place, worrying that there might be something wrong with me for lacking the appropriate feelings and failing to obtain the appropriate response.

The media seduce us into imitating their images, but when we do, we become alienated from our true selves. Our kisses are media kisses, not our own; our sexual interactions are media interactions, not ours.

To get a sense of the significance of the media in portraying sexual interactions, think about your favorite television shows, movies, books, or magazines. Which characters do you identify with or find yourself attracted to? How do they depict sexuality? What motivates people to engage in sexual behavior in the media world? What is the relationship between sex and love? Sex and violence? Is the sex the media portray mostly premarital, marital, or extramarital? What are the differences in

Many people conceptualize their dissatisfaction with life in terms of sexual problems, but their real difficulty lies in misunderstanding the role of sex in life. As a rule, they feel that the meaning of sex in life is fixed, when in fact it is constantly developing and changing—it is free. That simple insight, when integrated fully into the lifestyle of an individual, can liberate him from the chains of his pain.

PETER KOESTENBAUM, *EXISTENTIAL SEXUALITY*

FEATURE–*continued*

Splashed cold water on them every night. . . . Ultimately, I resigned myself to a bad toss and began to wear padded bras.

Because breasts are a sexual symbol, women often feel anxiety about their breast size. The male preoccupation with breasts leaves many women feeling objectified as bodies.

For males, the comparable biological event to menarche is first ejaculation, which occurs usually around age thirteen to fourteen. (Although males may have orgasms from birth, it is not until the prostate gland—which produces the seminal fluid—becomes enlarged that a boy can ejaculate.) Although females tend to identify menarche with reproduction, males do not make a similar connection with first ejaculation. Kinsey (1948) reported that first ejaculation is seen as the turning point in adolescent male sexuality. Few men, regardless of their age, forget it (Sarrel and Sarrel, 1984). Males experiences are often mixtures of fear and delight. If they first ejaculate during masturbation, they may be frightened by the glutinous, milky ejaculate, fearing they have somehow grievously damaged themselves yet at the same time experiencing pleasure. It almost always leads to a fairly regular pattern of masturbation and/or nocturnal emissions ("wet dreams") within a few months. There is no comparable pattern among females with menarche.

First ejaculation is a sexual event, not a reproductive one. The association of ejaculation with erotic pleasure rather than reproduction is significant because men tend to dissociate sex and reproduction. Fertility is viewed as a female attribute rather than an attribute of both sexes. One important consequence of this belief is that women are given primary responsibility for birth control.

---

portrayal among these three forms? Who initiates sex? How? Do people use contraception in their sexual interactions? Have you ever consciously imitated media images or characters?

Partners. Parents, peers, and the media become less important in our sexual learning as we get older, to be replaced by our sexual partners. The experience of interpersonal sexuality is ultimately the most important source of modifying traditional male sexual scripts. Describing the sources of men's sexual learning, Levine and Barbach (1985) note:

Before their first sexual encounter, men could only rely on secondary sources for information about sex. But once they lost their virginity, women became their primary source of information. It was their continued sexual experience that ultimately expanded and enriched men's sexual repertoire. Their skill at the game of love evolved over time, through trial and error. Each experience left them with a clearer sense of themselves as sexual men. But until they acquired this self-confidence, many men were reluctant to drop their he-man façades and reveal to their partners that they were less than skilled lovers.

In relationships, men and women learn that the sexual scripts and models they learned from parents, peers, and the media do not necessarily work in the real world. They adjust their attitudes and behaviors in everyday interactions. If they are married, the sexual expectations and interactions become important factors in their sexuality (see Chapter 8).

☐ TRADITIONAL SEXUAL SCRIPTS

Traditional sexual scripts are most powerful when we are young and inexperienced. These scripts vary according to our gender. Males scripts tend to exaggerate sexuality, whereas female scripts tend to devalue it.

Male Sexual Scripts

In our society, intimacy is more frightening than sex. This is somewhat more of a problem for men, but it is also true for women.

HELEN SINGER KAPLAN

Sexual scripts given out to men and women in our culture have a number of components. Bernie Zilbergeld (1978) called the male sexual script the fantasy model of sex. The star of the male fantasy model is the penis, a "magical instrument of infinite powers." (In fact, the word *phallus* [penis] is from the Greek word meaning "shining one"). In the fantasy model, the penis is always ready for sex; the bigger the penis, the better. Satirizing male anxieties about penis size, Woody Allen once quipped that he was the only man who ever experienced penis envy; in fact, many men often feel their penises are not large enough. In the fantasy model, the penis is what every woman craves. Even if they deny it, they want the penis; the more often, the better. This belief leads some men to ignore women's expressed feelings about sex. When women say no, the model asserts, they really mean yes; they just need a little coaching, maybe even a little force.

Zilbergeld suggests that men hold a number of myths about sexuality, which include the following:

The war between the sexes is the only one in which both sides regularly sleep with the enemy.

QUINTIN CRISP

- *Men should not have (or at least should not express) certain feelings.* Men should not express doubts; they should be assertive, confident, and aggressive. Tenderness and compassion are not masculine feelings.
- *Performance is the thing that counts.* Sex is something to be achieved; to be a winner at. Feelings only get in the way of the job to be done. Sex is not for intimacy but for orgasm.
- *The man is in charge.* As in other things, the man is the leader, the person who knows what is best. The man initiates sex and gives the woman her orgasm. A real man doesn't need a woman to tell him what women like: he already knows.
- *A man always wants sex and is ready for it.* It doesn't matter what is going on, man wants sex; he is always able to become erect. He is a machine.
- *All physical contact leads to sex.* Since men are basically sexual machines, any physical contact is a sign for sex. Touching is seen as the first step toward sexual intercourse; it is not an end in itself. There is no physical pleasure except sexual pleasure.
- *Sex equals intercourse.* All erotic contact leads to sexual intercourse. Foreplay is just that: warming up, getting your partner excited for penetration. Kissing, hugging, erotic touching, oral sex are only preliminaries to intercourse.

- *Sexual intercourse leads to orgasm.* The orgasm is the proof of the pudding. The more orgasms, the better the sex. If a woman does not have an orgasm, she is not sexual. The male feels that he is a failure because he was not good enough to give her an orgasm. If she requires clitoral stimulation to have an orgasm, she has a problem.

Common to all these myths is a separation of sex from love (or any feelings). Sex is a performance.

Female Sexual Scripts

Whereas the traditional male sexual script focuses on sex over feelings, the traditional female sexual script focuses on feelings over sex, on love over passion. The traditional female sexual scripts cited by Barbach (1982) include the following:

- *Sex is good and bad.* Women are taught that sex is both good and bad. What makes sex good?—sex in marriage or a committed relationship. What makes sex bad?—sex in a casual or uncommitted relationship. Sex is good, so good in fact that you need to save it for your husband (or for someone you are deeply in love with). Sex is bad; if it is not sanctioned by love or marriage, you'll get a bad reputation.
- *Don't touch me "down there."* Girls are taught not to look at their genitals, not to touch them, especially not to explore them. (The Latin *pudendum*, meaning vulva, translates as "thing of shame"; contrast this to the Greek *phallus*). As a result, women know very little about their genitals. They are often concerned about their vaginal odors, making them uncomfortable about cunnilingus.
- *Sex is for men.* Men want sex, women do not. Women are sexually passive, waiting to be aroused. Sex is not a pleasurable activity; it is something performed by women *for* men. A popular nineteenth-century cartoon depicted a woman who has just taken choloroform lying on her marriage bed; next to her is a note to her husband reading "Do with me what you like." As a result of this script, women do not feel comfortable about asserting their sexual needs and desires.
- *Men should know what women want.* This script tells women that men know what they want—even if women don't tell them. Women are supposed to remain pure and sexually innocent. It is up to the man to arouse the woman, even if he doesn't know what a particular woman finds arousing. To keep her image of sexual innocence, she does not tell him what she wants.
- *Women shouldn't talk about sex.* Many women cannot easily talk about sex. Our language does not have many good words to describe sex. We only have scientific words ("sexual intercourse"), obscene words ("fuck"), and euphemisms ("make love"); the first seems cold, the second dirty, and the third coy. Not only the lack of words but also the admission of sexual feelings and the lack of sexual assertiveness inhibit communication. Women sometimes feel they don't know their partners well enough to communicate their needs. Ironically, they know their partners well enough to have sex, but not well enough to talk about it.
- *Women should look like Playmates.* The media present ideally attractive women as "playmates," beautiful models with slender hips, large breasts, no fat; they are always young, never with a pimple, wrinkle, or gray hair in sight. Ordinary women worry that they are too fat, too plain, too old. As a result of these cultural images,

Sex, depersonalized, allows us to avoid the challenge of using our whole self, our total energies and feelings, to present and communicate ourselves to another. Sex is the victim of the fear of love.

ROSEMARY REUTHER

"Do I choose to cope with the sexual aspect of my life or do I choose not to cope with this aspect?" Think about it for a while. Remember that you have already made some choice and that you are now living that choice. But you may have also chosen to forget the choice which you have in fact made, and which you are now living. Think again. Have you chosen to cope? Or have you chosen to give up? Do you like the choice you are living?

PETER KOESTENBAUM, *EXISTENTIAL SEXUALITY*

UNDERSTANDING YOURSELF

Your Sexual Scripts

Our sexual scripts tell us the whos, whats, whens, wheres and whys of sexuality (Gagnon, 1977). They tell us who to be sexual with, what to do sexually, when to be sexual, where to engage in sexual activities, and why. These scripts change over time, depending on a person's age, sexual experience, and interactions with intimate partners and others. Let's examine these in relation to yourself.

Who   The factors of homogamy and heterogamy are almost as strong in selecting sexual partners as they are in choosing marital partners, in part because marital and sexual partners are often one and the same. Society tells us to have sex with people who are not closely related to us, around our same age, and members of the other sex (heterosexual). Less acceptable is having sex with oneself, that is, masturbation, and sex with members of the same sex (homosexuality).

Examine the whos in your sexual script. With whom do you engage in sexual behaviors? How do your choices reflect homogamy and hetero-

gamy? What social factors influence your choice? Do your autoerotic behaviors change if you are in a relationship? How? Why?

What   Society classifies sexual acts as good and bad, moral and immoral, appropriate and inappropriate. What sexual acts are part of your sexual script? How are they regarded by society? How important is the level of commitment in a relationship in determining your sexual behaviors? What level of commitment do you need for kissing? Petting? Sexual intercourse? What occurs when you and your partner have different sexual scripts for engaging in various sexual behaviors?

When   When refers to timing. You make love when your parents are out of the house or, if a parent yourself, when your children are asleep. Usually, this type of when is related to privacy. But whens are also related to age. At what age is it appropriate for a person to engage in sexual activities? When does a person's sexuality end?

many women are self-conscious about their physical appearance. They often feel awkward without their clothes on to hide their imagined flaws.

- *Women are nurturers.* Women give, men receive. Women give themselves, their bodies, their pleasures to men. Everyone else's needs come first: his desire over hers, his orgasm over hers. If a woman always puts her partner's enjoyment first, she may be depriving herself of her own enjoyment. As Barbach (1982) points out, "If our attention is so totally riveted on another person, or on external events rather than on ourselves, it is impossible to experience the full pleasure and sensation of the sexual event."
- *There is only one right way to have an orgasm.* Women often "learn" there is only one "right" way to have an orgasm: during sexual intercourse as a result of penile stimulation. But there are many ways to have orgasm: through oral sex, manual stimulation before, during, or after intercourse, masturbation, and so on. For women who rarely or never have orgasm during heterosexual intercourse to believe

UNDERSTANDING YOURSELF–*continued*

When are the times you engage in sexual activities? Are the times related to privacy? When did you experience your first erotic kiss? At what age did you experience your first intercourse? If you have not experienced sexual intercourse, at what age do you think it would be appropriate? How was (or will) the timing for first intercourse be determined? What influences (friends, parents, religion) are brought to bear on the age timing of sexual activities?

Where   Where does society approve of sexual activities occurring? In our society it is usually the bedroom—where a closed door signifies privacy. For adolescents it may also be an automobile. Fields, beaches, motels, and drive-in theaters may be identified as locations for sex. Churches, classrooms, and front yards usually are not.

For yourself, where are acceptable places to be sexual? What makes them acceptable for you? Have you ever had conflicts with partners about the wheres of sex? Why?

Why   The whys are the explanations we give ourselves and others about our sexual activities. There are many reasons for having sex: procreation, love, passion, revenge, intimacy, exploitation, fun, pleasure, relaxation, boredom, achievement, relief from loneliness, exertion of power, and on and on. Some of these explanations are approved, others are not; some we conceal, others we do not.

What are your reasons for sexual activities? Do you have different reasons for different activities, such as masturbation, oral sex, or sexual intercourse? Do the reasons change with different partners? With the same partner? Which reasons are societally approved, and which are disapproved? What reasons do you make known, and which do you conceal? Why?

Which of these reasons have you used: "I did it for love." "I was carried away with passion." "I needed to feel close." "I was horny." "I did it for my partner." "I did it because it felt good."

---

this is the only legitimate way to orgasm deprives them of expressing themselves sexually in other ways.

☐ SEXUAL BEHAVIOR

Sexual behavior is a complex activity. It is more than the simple release of tension through orgasm. Orgasm does not even have to be the goal of erotic activity. We may engage in erotic activity for its own sake, for the sheer pleasure of touch and arousal. But whether or not our erotic activities include orgasm, they involve deep feelings about ourselves and others, ranging from ecstatic delight and pleasure to guilt and shame, from love to contempt, from self-respect to self-degradation. Although our culture gives us certain meanings to associate with sex (for example, masturbation is bad, oral-genital sex is dirty, sex within marriage is good), we ourselves are ultimately responsible for how we feel about our sexual behavior. Because we learn to be sexual,

What is it men in women do require?
The lineaments of Gratified Desire.
What is it women do in men require?
The lineaments of Gratified Desire.

WILLIAM BLAKE (1757–1827)

we can also unlearn those aspects of our sexuality—feelings, attitudes, or behaviors—that do not contribute to our functioning as healthy, happy human beings.

Sexual Attitudes and Behavior

The only way to get rid of temptation is to yield to it.

OSCAR WILDE

Abstinence sows sand all over
The ruddy limbs and flaming hair.

WILLIAM BLAKE

Social psychologists have been studying the link between attitudes and behavior for at least half a century. From their work, we know several things. First, attitudes and behavior do not fully correspond. Second, the causal relationship between attitudes and behavior is not clear. Do attitudes cause behavior or does behavior create our attitudes? (For a theoretical model of the development of sexual attitudes, see Byrne, 1971, 1977; Clore and Byrne, 1974.)

Think about the relationship between sexual attitudes and behavior. What is the relationship between your sexual attitudes and behavior? Are your sexual attitudes and behavior basically the same? In which areas do you find the greatest discrepancy between your attitudes and behavior? How do you handle the discrepancy? In your various relationships (past and present), do you tend to share the same sexual attitudes as your partner? If not, how does that affect your relationship?

Autoeroticism

Two monks, Tanzan and Ek-ido, were travelling down the road in a heavy rain. As they turned a bend, they came upon a beautiful young woman in a silk kimono. She was unable to pass because the rain had turned the road to mud.

Tanzan said to her, "Come on," and lifted her in his arms and carried her across the mud. Then he put her down and the monks continued their journey.

The two monks did not speak again until they reached a temple in which to spend the night. Finally, Ekido could no longer hold back his thoughts and he reprimanded Tanzan. "It is not proper for monks to go near women," he said. "Especially young and beautiful ones. It is unwise. Why did you do it?"

"I left the woman behind," replied Tanzan. "Are you still carrying her?"

ZEN TALE

The term *autoeroticism* was invented by Havelock Ellis (1936) to describe sexual activities that involve only the self. Autoeroticism is an intrapersonal activity rather than an interpersonal one. It may be the most diverse form of sexuality a person experiences, for it includes masturbation, sexual fantasies, and erotic dreams. Ironically, it is also the form of sexual behavior about which people experience the greatest anxiety and guilt.

Sexual Fantasies. "A fantasy is a map of desire, mastery, escape, and obscuration," wrote Nancy Friday (1980), "the navigational path we invent to steer ourselves between the reefs and shoals of anxiety, guilt, and inhibition." Erotic fantasy is probably the most universal of all sexual behaviors. Nearly everyone has experienced such fantasies, but because they touch on feelings or desires considered personally or socially unacceptable, they are not widely discussed. They may interfere with an individual's self-image, causing a loss of self-esteem as well as confusion. No necessary relationship exists between a person's sexual fantasies and what he or she does in real life.

Sexual fantasies serve a number of important functions in maintaining our psychological equilibrium. First of all, fantasies help direct and define our erotic goals. They take our generalized sexual drives and give them concrete images and specific content. These goals are generally conservative insofar as they usually do not greatly exceed idealized models of the type of person we are attracted to; we fantasize about certain types of men or women and reinforce our attraction through fantasy involvement. Second, sexual fantasies also allow us to plan or anticipate situations that may arise. Fantasies are a form of rehearsal in which we mentally practice how to act. Third, erotic fantasies provide an escape from a dull or oppressive environment. Fourth, even if our sexual lives are satisfactory, we may indulge in sexual fantasies to bring novelty and excitement into our relationship. Many people fantasize things they

"A fantasy is a map of desire, mastery, escape, and obscuration," wrote Nancy Friday, "the navigational path we invent to steer ourselves between the reefs and shoals of anxiety, guilt, and inhibition." Erotic fantasies are often expressive, reflecting unconscious feelings in the same manner as dreams.

would not actually do in real life; fantasy offers a safe outlet for sexual curiosity. Fifth, sexual fantasies also have an expressive aspect in somewhat the same manner as dreams do. Our sexual fantasies may offer a clue to our current interests, pleasures, anxieties, fears, or problems. Since fantasies select only a few details from the stream of reality, what we select is often significant, expressing feelings that often lie beneath the surface of our consciousness.

Masturbation. Individuals masturbate by stroking, rubbing, caressing, or otherwise stimulating their genitals to give themselves sexual pleasure. They may masturbate during particular periods of their lives or throughout their entire lives. Kinsey (1953) reported that 92 percent of the men and 58 percent of the women he interviewed said they had masturbated. Today both the incidence and frequency of masturbation appear to have increased slightly. One study indicated that two-thirds of the men and women interviewed believed that masturbation was not wrong (Hunt, 1974). Significantly fewer, however, believed it was a positive good. Many people continue to have feelings of shame or fear about masturbation, as did Philip Roth's (1968) hero in *Portnoy's Complaint*:

It was at the end of my freshman year of high school—and freshman year of masturbating— that I discovered on the underside of my penis, just where the shaft meets the head, a little

Masturbation is an intrinsically and seriously disordered act.

VATICAN DECLARATION CONCERNING SEXUAL QUESTIONS, 1976

Don't knock masturbation. It's having sex with someone I deeply love.

WOODY ALLEN

discolored dot that has since been diagnosed as a freckle. Cancer. I had given myself *cancer.* All that pulling and tugging at my own flesh, all that friction, had given me an incurable disease. And not yet fourteen! In bed at night the tears rolled from my eyes. "No!" I sobbed. "I don't want to die. Please—no!" But then, because I would be very shortly a corpse anyway, I went ahead as usual and jerked off.

Masturbation is one way in which people learn about their bodies. Through masturbation, boys and girls and men and women learn what pleases them sexually, how their bodies respond, and what their natural sexual rhythms are. Pioneer sex therapists William Masters and Virginia Johnson (1970) instructed their clients to masturbate as a means of overcoming specific sexual problems and discovering their sexual potential.

Although the frequency of masturbation often decreases significantly when a sexual partner is available, it is not necessarily a substitute for intercourse. Studies of married men and women suggest that both continue to masturbate (Petersen et al., 1983; Tavris and Sadd, 1977). The majority of wives who masturbate do so when their husbands are away. The more often a woman masturbates, the less likely it is that she regards her marital sex life as good (Tavris and Sadd, 1977). In one study, 70 percent of the women did not tell their husbands about masturbating (Grosskopf, 1983).

Husbands tend to masturbate more frequently than their wives; 43 percent of the husbands versus 22 percent of the wives in a *Playboy* study masturbated more than once a week (Petersen et al., 1983). Husbands' motives, however, were different from wives'. Husbands tended to masturbate as a supplement to intercourse rather than as substitute for it.

We don't know the impact of masturbation on marriage although guilt about masturbation may be a negative factor (Hessellund, 1976). The fact that most husbands and wives do not tell each other suggests that for whatever reason—guilt, embarrassment, or shame—they are not communicating about significant aspects of their sexuality. Whenever important information is withheld, the area of openness shrinks.

Erotic Dreams. Almost all of the men and two-thirds of the women in Kinsey's (1953) study reported having had overtly sexual dreams. From 8 to 10 percent of the women experienced homosexual dreams. Like fantasies, dreams do not usually go far beyond an individual's experience. But while fantasies tend to be logical and related to ordinary reality, the images of dreams are frequently very intense. Individuals may awaken in the night to find their bodies moving as if they were making love. They may also experience nocturnal orgasms.

Interpersonal Sexuality

Interpersonal sexuality is more complex than autoerotic sexuality because it involves two people with different scripts, moods, desires, cycles, and feelings who have to synchronize their sexuality with each other.

Pleasuring. Making love includes giving and receiving pleasure, yet many people—although they strive for orgasms and make love frequently—do not know how to experience erotic pleasure. Instead of having an erotic orientation, which includes the pleasure of touch, smell, sound, taste, and sight, they have a goal orientation: orgasm.

In the course of their sexual research, Masters and Johnson developed the idea of *pleasuring*, a way that couples get to know each other physically through touching. Pleasuring begins with nongenital touching and caressing. Neither partner tries to stimulate the other sexually—they simply explore each other. They discover how their bodies respond to touching. Masters and Johnson (1970) wrote:

The partner who is pleasuring is committed first to do just that: give pleasure. At a second level in the experience, the giver is to explore his or her own component of personal pleasure in doing the touching—to experience and appreciate the sensuous dimensions of hard and soft, smooth and rough, warm and cool, qualities of texture and, finally, this somewhat indescribable aura of physical receptivity expressed by the partner being pleasured. After a reasonable length of time . . . the partners are to exchange roles of pleasuring (giving) and being pleasured (getting) and then repeat the procedure.

No one can assume they know what any particular individual likes, for considerable variation exists among people. But pleasuring opens the door to erotic communication; couples discover that the entire body, rather than just the genitals, is erogenous. Pleasuring does not need to lead to sexual intercourse; it may be its own end whenever a couple chooses. As Shere Hite (1976) observed:

> In the beginner's mind there are many possibilities, in the expert's mind there are few.
>
> SHUNRYO SUZUKI, *ZEN MIND, BEGINNER'S MIND*

There is no reason why physical intimacy with men should always consist of "foreplay" followed by intercourse and male orgasm; and there is no reason why intercourse must always be part of heterosexual sex. Sex is intimate physical contact for pleasure, to share pleasure with another person (or just alone). You can have sex to orgasm, or not to orgasm, genital sex, or just physical intimacy—whatever seems right to you. There is never any reason to think the "goal" must be intercourse and to try to make what you feel fit into that context.

Oral-Genital Sex.   In recent years oral-genital sex has become accepted as a form of sexuality (Herold and Way, 1983). The word *cunnilingus* is derived from the Latin *cunnus*, which means "vulva," and *lingere*, meaning "to lick," and it refers to the erotic stimulation of a woman's vulva by her partner's mouth and tongue. *Fellatio*, derived from the the Latin *fellare*, meaning "to suck," refers to the oral stimulation of a man's penis by his partner's sucking and licking. Cunnilingus and fellatio may be performed singly or mutually. Between 60 and 95 percent of the men and women in various studies report they have engaged in oral sex (DeLamater and Mac-Corquodale, 1979; Petersen et al., 1983). Some women feel that fellatio is more intimate than sexual intercourse, whereas others feel it is less intimate. The overwhelming majority of men enjoy giving oral sex to their partners (Petersen et al., 1983).

> The only unnatural sex act is one that can't be performed.
>
> ALFRED KINSEY

Sexual Intercourse.   Sexual intercourse is a complex interaction. As with many other types of activities, the anticipation of reward triggers a pattern of behavior. The reward may not necessarily be orgasm, however, because the meanings of sexual intercourse vary considerably at different times for different people. People have many motivations for sexual intercourse; the release of sexual tension is only one. These motivations include showing love, having children, giving and receiving pleasure, gaining power, ending an argument, demonstrating commitment, seeking revenge,

> Spiritual and carnal love are inseparable.
>
> JOHN DONNE

(*Text continues on page 206.*)

FEATURE

Sexual Structure

THE MALE REPRODUCTIVE SYSTEM

The Penis

Both urine and semen pass through the penis. Ordinarily, it hangs limp and may be used for the elimination of urine, since it is connected to the bladder by the urinary duct. The penis is usually between two-and-one-half to four inches in length. When a man is sexually aroused it grows to about five to ten inches in length, is hard, and stands erect (hence the term *erection*). When the penis becomes erect, muscle contractions temporarily close off the urinary duct, allowing the ejaculation of semen.

The penis consists of three main parts: the root, the shaft, and the glans penis. The *root* connects the penis to the pelvis. The *shaft*, which is the spongy body of the penis, hangs free. At the end of the shaft is the *glans penis*, the rounded tip of the penis. The opening at the tip of the glans is called the *urethral meatus*. The glans penis is especially important in sexual arousal because it contains a high concentration of nerve endings, making it erotically sensitive.

When the penis is flaccid, blood circulates freely through its veins and arteries. But as it becomes erect, the circulation of blood changes dramatically. The arteries expand and increase the flow of blood into the penis. The spongelike tissue of the shaft becomes engorged and expands, compressing the veins within the penis so that the additional blood cannot leave it easily. As a result, the penis becomes larger, harder, and more erect.

The Testes

Hanging beneath the male's penis is his *scrotum*, a pouch of skin holding his two *testes* (singular *testis*; also called *testicles*). The testes are the male reproductive glands (also called *gonads*), which produce both sperm and the male hormone *testosterone*. The testes produce sperm through a process called *spermatogenesis*. Each testicle produces between one hundred million and five hundred million sperm daily. Once the sperm are produced, they move into the *epididymis*, where they are stored prior to ejaculation.

The Path of the Sperm

The epididymis merges into the tubular *vas deferens* (plural *vasa deferentia*). The vas deferens can be felt easily within the scrotal sac. Extending into the pelvic cavity, each vas deferens widens into a flasklike area called the *ampulla* (plural *ampullae*). Within the ampullae, the sperm mix with an activating fluid from the *seminal vesicles*. The ampullae connect to the *prostate gland* through the *ejaculatory ducts*. Secretions from the prostate account for most of the milky, gelatinous liquid that makes up the *semen* in which the sperm are suspended. Inside the prostate, the ejaculatory ducts join to the urinary duct from the bladder to form the urethra, which extends to the tip of the penis. The two *Cowper's glands*, located below the prostate, secrete a clear sticky fluid into the urethra that appears as small droplets on the meatus during sexual excitement.

If the erect penis is stimulated sufficiently through friction, an ejaculation usually occurs. *Ejaculation* is the forceful expulsion of semen. The process involves rhythmic contractions of the vasa deferentia, seminal vesicles, prostate, and penis. The first few contractions occur at about one-second intervals and usually include the expulsion of semen. Within three or four seconds, however, the contractions taper off. Altogether, the expulsion of semen may last from three to fifteen seconds. The pleasurable sensations that accompany the contractions and expulsion are called *orgasm*. It is

FEATURE–*continued*

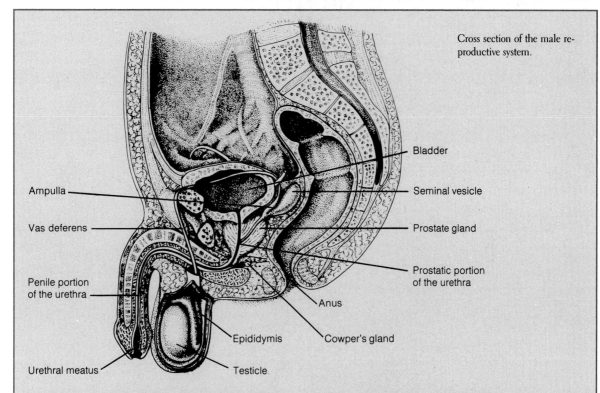

Cross section of the male reproductive system.

Ampulla

Vas deferens

Penile portion of the urethra

Urethral meatus

Epididymis

Testicle

Bladder

Seminal vesicle

Prostate gland

Prostatic portion of the urethra

Anus

Cowper's gland

also possible to have an orgasm without the expulsion of semen.

THE FEMALE REPRODUCTIVE SYSTEM

External Genitals

The female's external genitals are known collectively as the *vulva*, which includes the mons veneris, labia, clitoris, urethra, and introitus. The *mons veneris* (literally "mountain of Venus") is a protuberance formed by the pelvic bones and covered by fatty tissue. During puberty, it begins to be covered with pubic hair. The *labia* are the vaginal lips surrounding the entrance to the vagina. The *labia majora* ("major lips") are two large folds of spongy flesh extending back from the mons veneris along the midline between the legs. The outer edges of the labia majora are often darkly

pigmented and are covered with pubic hair. Usually the labia majora are close together, giving them a closed appearance. The *labia minora* ("minor lips") lie within the fold of the labia majora. The upper portion folds over the clitoris and is called the *clitoral hood*. During sexual excitement the labia minora become engorged with blood and double or triple in size. The labia minora contain numerous nerve endings that become increasingly sensitive during sexual excitement.

The *clitoris* is the center of erotic arousal in the female. It contains a high concentration of nerve endings and is highly sensitive to erotic stimulation. The clitoris becomes engorged with blood during sexual arousal and may increase greatly in size. Its tip, the *glans clitoridis*, is especially responsive to touch.

Between the folds of the labia minora are the urethral opening and the *introitus*, the vaginal

FEATURE–*continued*

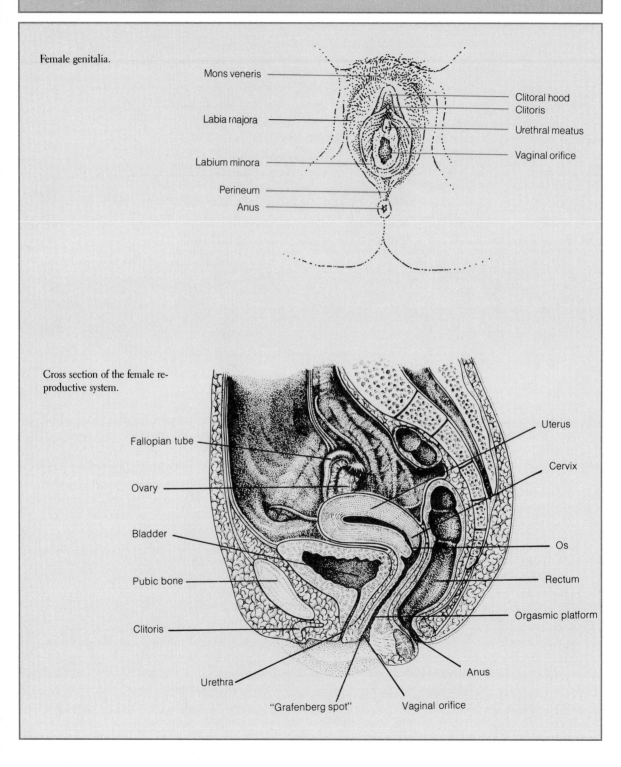

Female genitalia.

Mons veneris
Clitoral hood
Clitoris
Labia majora
Urethral meatus
Labium minora
Vaginal orifice
Perineum
Anus

Cross section of the female reproductive system.

Fallopian tube
Uterus
Ovary
Cervix
Bladder
Os
Pubic bone
Rectum
Clitoris
Orgasmic platform
Urethra
Anus
"Grafenberg spot"
Vaginal orifice

FEATURE–*continued*

opening. There is increasing evidence that some women emit or ejaculate fluids from their urethras during sexual excitement (Addigego et al., 1981; Ladas et al., 1982; Masters, Perry and Whipple, 1981; see Strong and Reynolds, 1982). The introitus is the opening to the vagina; it is often covered by a thin membrane called the *hymen*, which may be broken accidentally, or intentionally, before or during first intercourse.

Internal Genitals

The *vagina* is an elastic canal extending from the vulva to the cervix. It envelops the penis during sexual intercourse and is the passage through which a baby is normally delivered. The vagina's first reaction to sexual arousal is "sweating," that is, the production of lubrication through the vaginal walls.

A few centimeters from the vaginal entrance, on the vagina's anterior wall, there is, according to some researchers, an erotically sensitive spot that they have dubbed the "Grafenberg spot" or "G-spot" (Ladas et al., 1982; Whipple and Perry, 1981). It is a slight bump that may grow to twice its usual size as a result of stimulation; when it is stimulated it causes sensations similar to those of urination. The spot is associated with female ejaculation.

A female has two *ovaries*, reproductive glands (gonads) that produce *ova* (eggs) and the female hormones *estrogen* and *progesterone*. At the time a female is born, she already has all the ova she will ever have, more than forty thousand of them. About four hundred will mature during her lifetime and be released during ovulation; ovulation begins in puberty and ends at menopause.

The two *fallopian tubes* extend from the uterus up to, but not touching, the ovaries. When an egg is released from an ovary during ovulation, it drifts into a fallopian tube. If it is fertilized by sperm, this usually takes place within the fallopian tube.

The fertilized egg will move into the uterus. If the egg is not fertilized, it is discharged in the menstual flow approximately fourteen days after ovulation.

The *uterus* is a hollow, muscular organ within the pelvic cavity. The pear-shaped uterus is normally about three inches long, three inches wide at the top, and an inch at the bottom. The narrow, lower part of the uterus projects into the vagina and is called the *cervix*. If an egg is fertilized, it will attach itself to the inner lining of the uterus, the *endometrium*. Inside the uterus it will develop into an embryo and then into a fetus. If an egg is not fertilized, the endometrial tissue that developed in anticipation of fertilization will be shed. During menstruation, both the unfertilized egg and inner lining of the uterus will be discharged in the menstrual flow.

THE SEXUAL RESPONSE CYCLE

When a person is sexually aroused, he or she experiences a number of bodily responses. Most of us are conscious of some of these responses: a rapidly beating heart, an erection or lubrication, orgasm. But many other responses may take place below our threshold of awareness, such as curling of the toes, the ascent of the testes, the withdrawal of the clitoris beneath its hood, and a flush across the body.

Our various responses can be described in terms of the sexual response cycle. The sexual response cycle, according to Masters and Johnson (1966; see Strong and Reynolds, 1982), has four phases: excitement, plateau, orgasm, and resolution. The changes that take place in the cycle depend on two processes: vasocongestion and myotonia. *Vasocongestion* occurs when body tissues become engorged with blood. For example, blood fills the genital regions of both males and females, causing the penis and clitoris to enlarge. *Myotonia* refers

FEATURE–*continued*

MALE SEXUAL RESPONSE CYCLE

(a) EXCITEMENT PHASE

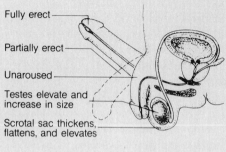

Fully erect

Partially erect

Unaroused

Testes elevate and
increase in size

Scrotal sac thickens,
flattens, and elevates

(b) PLATEAU PHASE

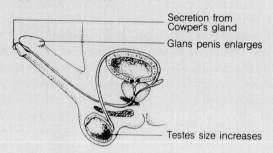

Secretion from
Cowper's gland

Glans penis enlarges

Testes size increases

(c) ORGASMIC PHASE

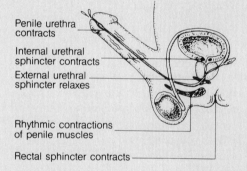

Penile urethra
contracts

Internal urethral
sphincter contracts

External urethral
sphincter relaxes

Rhythmic contractions
of penile muscles

Rectal sphincter contracts

(d) RESOLUTION PHASE

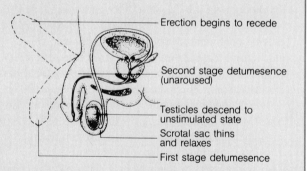

Erection begins to recede

Second stage detumesence
(unaroused)

Testicles descend to
unstimulated state

Scrotal sac thins
and relaxes

First stage detumesence

to increased muscle tension as orgasm approaches. Upon orgasm, the body undergoes involuntary muscle contractions and then relaxes.

Excitement Phase

In females, the vagina becomes lubricated and the clitoris enlarges during this phase. The vaginal barrel expands and the cervix and uterus elevate, a process called "tenting." The labia majora flatten and rise; the labia minora begin to protrude. The breasts may increase in size and the nipples may become erect.

In males, the penis becomes erect as a result of vasocongestion, and the testes begin to rise.

Plateau Phase

This phase is characterized by a marked increase in sexual tension above unaroused levels. In females, vasocongestion causes the outer third of the vagina to swell, narrowing the vaginal opening. This swelling forms the *orgasmic platform*. The entire clitoris retracts but remains sensitive to touch. Between 50 and 75 percent of women develop a "sex flush" resembling a rash on their chests.

(*Feature continues on page 206.*)

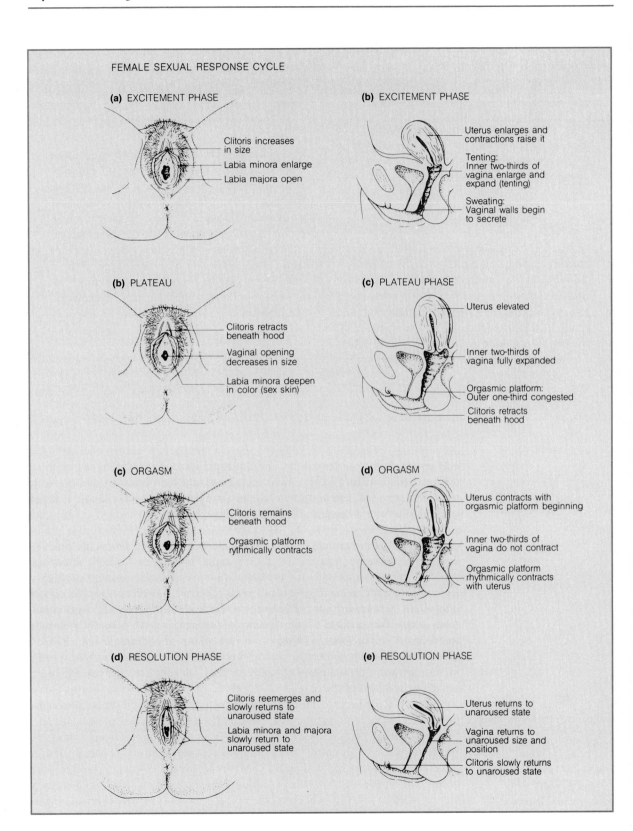

FEMALE SEXUAL RESPONSE CYCLE

(a) EXCITEMENT PHASE

Clitoris increases in size
Labia minora enlarge
Labia majora open

(b) EXCITEMENT PHASE

Uterus enlarges and contractions raise it

Tenting:
Inner two-thirds of vagina enlarge and expand (tenting)

Sweating:
Vaginal walls begin to secrete

(b) PLATEAU

Clitoris retracts beneath hood

Vaginal opening decreases in size

Labia minora deepen in color (sex skin)

(c) PLATEAU PHASE

Uterus elevated

Inner two-thirds of vagina fully expanded

Orgasmic platform: Outer one-third congested

Clitoris retracts beneath hood

(c) ORGASM

Clitoris remains beneath hood

Orgasmic platform rythmically contracts

(d) ORGASM

Uterus contracts with orgasmic platform beginning

Inner two-thirds of vagina do not contract

Orgasmic platform rhythmically contracts with uterus

(d) RESOLUTION PHASE

Clitoris reemerges and slowly returns to unaroused state

Labia minora and majora slowly return to unaroused state

(e) RESOLUTION PHASE

Uterus returns to unaroused state

Vagina returns to unaroused size and position

Clitoris slowly returns to unaroused state

FEATURE–*continued*

In males, the erection becomes firmer and the glans penis gets larger. The testes may enlarge up to 150 percent of their unaroused size. A sex flush develops in about 25 percent of men.

Orgasmic Phase

In females, this phase is characterized by simultaneous rhythmic contractions of the uterus, orgasmic platform, and rectal sphincter. In males, muscle contractions occur in the vasa deferentia, seminal vesicles, prostate, and urethral bulb and result in the ejaculation of semen. Ejaculation usually accompanies male orgasm, but ejaculation and orgasm are separate processes.

Resolution Phase

One of the most striking differences between male and female sexual responses occurs in the resolution phase. Females have the capacity to have multiple orgasms, that is, to have a series of orgasms without dropping below the plateau phase of arousal. Males, however, do not have this capacity. Following orgasm, their arousal level returns to prearousal or excitement levels. This is called the *refractory period*; during this time, additional ejaculations are impossible. Females do not have any comparable period.

---

proving masculinity or femininity, and degrading someone (including yourself). As one man said (in Hite, 1981): "Even more important than orgasm is being able to wrap your arms and legs and whatever else around another human being. It makes you feel less alone, more alive. There's nothing like it."

Orgasm. Orgasm has many functions. For males, it serves a reproductive function through the ejaculation of semen. It is a source of pleasure for both males and females. Orgasm—especially the male orgasm—is used in our culture as a signal for terminating sexual intercourse or other sexual behaviors. For many people, orgasm symbolizes their masculinity or femininity. Because of this powerful association, many people fake orgasms to hide feelings of inadequacy or to make their partners feel they are "good" lovers. But orgasm is also a form of communication. Partners may argue about whose orgasm is more important. "You always think of yourself first" is a common accusation of unhappy partners, who often transfer basic problems to the sexual relationship.

Males and females vary considerably in frequency of orgasm. In sexual intercourse women tend to be less orgasmic than men. Is this a matter of biology or technique? Sociobiologists argue that since female orgasm is not necessary for reproduction, the female orgasm was "invented" by culture; indeed, many cultures apparently do not recognize female orgasm (Symons, 1979). Unlike the male orgasm, these theorists believe, the female orgasm is learned. Most sex researchers, however, do not accept this approach to sexuality. They attribute women's tendency to have fewer orgasms in sexual intercourse to cultural roadblocks to female sexuality. (See the reading "Was

To be a really good lover, then, one must be strong and yet tender.

How strong?

I suppose being able to lift fifty pounds should do it.

WOODY ALLEN, *WITHOUT FEATHERS*

It Good For You?" by Sara Jennifer Malcolm.) Women are restricted from gaining sexual experience; they are taught to be sexually passive, to focus on male satisfaction in sexual intercourse rather than their own, and are discouraged from expressing their sexual needs to their partners.

Part of the problematic nature of female orgasm may lie in the role of the clitoris. Masters and Johnson established clinically that clitoral stimulation was the source of the female orgasm. They believed that the clitoris received sufficient stimulation through male thrusting, but Shere Hite's study (1976) on female sexuality suggested otherwise. As Hite pointed out, a precondition for participating in the Masters and Johnson study was that the women were orgasmic in heterosexual intercourse. This left out many women—perhaps the majority—who were not orgasmic in intercourse. Hite, in fact, found that only 30 percent of her 3,000 respondents experienced orgasm regularly through sexual intercourse "without more direct manual clitoral stimulation being provided at the time of orgasm." Hite concludes that many women need manual stimulation during intercourse to be orgasmic. They also need to be more assertive. She writes, "orgasm is more likely to come when the woman takes over responsibility for and control of her own stimulation." There is no reason, Hite points out, that a woman cannot be manually stimulated by herself or partner to orgasm before or after intercourse if she is not orgasmic in intercourse. But to do so, a woman needs to assert her own sexual needs and move away from the idea that sex is centered around male orgasm. The sexual script needs to be redefined to include orgasm as an experience for both men and women.

☐ SUMMARY

- Our sexuality depends more on learning than on biological drives. Sexual impulses are organized by our *sexual scripts*. Sexual scripts have two major components: the *intrapersonal* component is concerned with the internal and physiological states that lead to sexual arousal and orgasm; the *interpersonal* component is made up of the externally shared conventions and signals that enable two persons to engage in sexual activity. Sexual scripts are often ambiguous; males more than females tend to interpret signals as sexual.

- Sexual scripts are learned primarily through parents, peers, and the media. As a person becomes sexually experienced, his or her partners become extremely important as a source of learning.

- Male sexual scripts include denial or nonexpression of feelings, emphasis on performance and being in charge, belief that men always want sex and that all physical contact leads to sex, and assumptions that sex equals intercourse and that sexual intercourse always leads to orgasm.

- Female sexual scripts suggest that sex is both good and bad (depending on the context), genitals should not be touched, sex is for men, men should know what women want, women shouldn't talk about sex, women should look like Playmates, women are nurturers, and there is only one right way to experience an orgasm.

- A significant correlation exists between sexual attitudes and behavior.

- Autoerotic behavior is sexual activity that involves only the self. It includes sexual fantasies, erotic dreams, and masturbation.

- Sexual fantasies are probably the most universal of all sexual behaviors: they are normal aspects of our sexuality. Erotic fantasies serve several functions: (1) They take our generalized sexual drives and help define and direct them. (2) They allow us to plan or anticipate erotic situations. (3) They give pleasurable escape from routine. (4) They provide clues about the unconscious.

- People masturbate by stroking, rubbing, caressing, or otherwise stimulating their genitals or other erogenous parts of their bodies. Most men and the majority of women have masturbated. Masturbation is an important way to learn about our sexuality. People continue to masturbate during marriage, although married men tend to masturbate to supplement their sexual activities whereas women tend to masturbate as a substitute for such activities.

- Erotic dreams are widely experienced. People may have orgasms during their dreams.

- Pleasuring is a means by which couples get to know each other erotically through touching and caressing; it is erotic exploration.

- Oral-genital sex involves cunnilingus, fellatio, and mutual oral stimulation. Oral sex has become widely accepted.

- Sexual intercourse is a complex interaction. It is a form of communication that may express a host of feelings, including love, hate, need, and contempt.

- Orgasm has many functions. For males, it serves a reproductive function; for both males and females it is a source of pleasure and a proof of masculinity or femininity. The male orgasm often signals the termination of sexual intercourse or other sexual behaviors.

READINGS

The Slumber Party

MARILYN HILLER, FROM *SATURDAY NIGHT LIVE*

In this classic skit from the television series Saturday Night Live, *Gilda Radner, Laraine Newman, Jane Curtin, and Madeline Kahn portray 12-year-olds discussing sex. Although it is comedy, it strikes us as true. Why? At age twelve, what were your beliefs concerning sex? How did you learn about sex? What did your parents tell you?*

(A darkened living room, with single lantern-type of light used for camping. Girls huddled around Madeline on the floor with pillows, blankets, etc. Assorted old pizza boxes, coke bottles, strewn around them.)

MADELINE: (enormously confidential) . . . so then, the man gets bare naked in bed with you and you both go to sleep which is why they call it sleeping together. Then you both wake up and the man says, "Why don't you slip into something more comfortable"—no, wait, maybe that comes before—it's not important—and then the man says . . .

(light goes on at top of staircase)

MOTHER'S VOICE: Gilda, it's five a.m. When does the noise stop?

GILDA: We're just going to sleep, Mother.

MOTHER'S VOICE: What are you talking about at this hour?

GILDA: School!

MOTHER'S VOICE: Well save it for the morning.
(Door slams. Lights out)

READINGS—*continued*

JANE: (to Madeline, as if nothing has happened) And then the man . . .

MADELINE: Anyway . . . (Brings girls closer, whispers something inaudible. We finally hear:) . . . then the man (whispers) in you and then you scream and then he screams and then it's over.
(Moment of silence. The girls sit there shocked and horrified)

LARAINE: (making throwing-up sounds, pulling blanket up over her head) That's disgusting!

GILDA: You lie, Madeline.

MADELINE: Cross my heart and hope to die. My brother told me in my driveway.

GILDA: Your brother lies, Madeline.

MADELINE: No, sir.

JANE: Come on. Isn't he the one who said if you chew your nails and swallow them a hand will grow in your stomach.

MADELINE: Well, it's also true because I read it in this book.

JANE: What'd it say?

MADELINE: It said, "The first step in human reproduction is . . . the man
(whispers)

LARAINE: (hysterical, coming out from under covers) It's disgusting!
(Laraine, Gilda and Jane all do fake throwing up)

MADELINE: It's true.

JANE: Well, I just know it can't be true because nothing that sickening is true.

MADELINE: Boogers are true.
(the girls consider this for a moment)

GILDA: Well, I mainly don't believe it because I heard from my sister about this girl who this guy jumped out from the bushes and forced to have a baby.

MADELINE: (smugly) How?

GILDA: I don't know. I think he just said, "Have a baby right now."

MADELINE: Oh, sure, Gilda. And you think that would work if I tried it on you?

GILDA: (scared) Hey, don't. O.K.?

MADELINE: Well, don't worry. It wouldn't because that's not how it's done. How it's done is . . . the man . . .

LARAINE: Don't say it again, O.K.? I just ate half a pizza, O.K.?

GILDA: (thoughtfully) So that's why people were born naked.

JANE: Yeah.

LARAINE: But how could you face the man after? Wouldn't you be so *embarrassed*?

JANE: I'd have to kill myself after. I mean, I get embarrassed when I think how people standing next to me can see inside my ear.

MADELINE: Well, that's why you should only do it after you're married. Because then you won't be so embarrassed in front of your husband after because you're in the same *family*.

LARAINE: Oh, well, I really want to get married now. *Not!*

MADELINE: But the worst thing is—our *parents* do it, you know?

GILDA: Come on!

MADELINE: Gilda, think: none of us would be here unless our parents did it *at least once*.
(Moment of silence. They all consider the horror of this)

JANE: (horrorized) My parents did it at least twice. I have a sister.

GILDA: (greater horror) And my parents did it at least three times. I have a sister *and* a brother.
(they all turn to give her a "you're dirt" look)

GILDA: But, like, I know they didn't do it because they *wanted* to. They did it because they *had* to. To have children.

MADELINE: (accusing) They could have adopted children.

GILDA: Yeah, but adopted children are a pain. You have to teach them how to look like you.

LARAINE: Well, my father would never do anything like that to my mother. He's too polite.

MADELINE: My father's polite and we have six kids.

READINGS—*continued*

LARAINE: He's obviously not as polite as you think. (they glare at each other)

JANE: I wonder whose idea this was.

MADELINE: (off hand) God's.

JANE: Oh, come on. God doesn't go around thinking up sickening things like this for people to do.

GILDA: Maybe God just wants you to do it so you'll appreciate how good the *rest* of your life is.

JANE: Maybe.

LARAINE: (to Madeline) How long does it take?

MADELINE: Stupid! That depends on how big the girl's stomach is and how fast she can digest.

GILDA: Oh.

JANE: Can you talk during it?

MADELINE: You have to hold your breath or else it doesn't work.
(various vomit sounding shrieks, screams, etc.)

JANE: Well, I'm just telling my husband I'm not going to do it. (to heaven) Tough beansies.

MADELINE: What if he says he'll get divorced from you if you didn't do it?
(the girls consider this)

JANE: I would never marry someone like that.

MADELINE: What if you did by accident? What if . . . (making up story) . . . you met him in a war and married him real fast because you felt sorry for him since he's probably get killed only he didn't and then you were stuck with him?

GILDA: (moved by emergency) Look—let's make this pact right now that after we get married, if our husbands make us do it, we'll call each other on the phone every day and talk a lot to help keep our minds off it, like our mothers do.

JANE: Right.

MADELINE: Right.

LARAINE: Right, because it's *disgusting*.
(makes some throw-up sound. Ducks under covers)
(Laraine turns out flashlight)

JANE: Well, don't worry, we'll never have to keep this pact because I'll never do it.

GILDA: Me, neither.

MADELINE: Me, neither.
(there is a beat)

LARAINE: (quietly) I might.
(fade out)

___

Was It Good for You?
SARA JENNIFER MALCOLM, MS.

In this article from Ms. *magazine, a college sophomore reflects on female orgasm. While Masters and Johnson (1966) argued that females are "normally" orgasic in intercourse, Shere Hite (1976) contended that most women need direct manual stimulation of the clitoris to be orgasmic, either before, during, or after intercourse. What view does the author take? How does she support her view? What is her evidence? What forms of pressure do women feel regarding the need to be orgasmic?*

Over lunch with my mother, I finally mustered up the courage to talk about my problem. For more than six months, I'd been having a wonderful relationship—my first "real" sexual experience—and now my boyfriend and I were at an impasse. I knew my body was capable of orgasms during masturbation and foreplay, but I had never been able to reach a climax *during* sexual intercourse. I was frustrated and worried. What were we doing wrong?

Mom put down her coffee. "Where did you get the idea that women always have orgasms during intercourse?" She explained that few of us are biologically constructed to allow for such an orgasm. Many women, herself included, grew up believing that orgasm inevitably results from male penetration, while in reality the majority of women can only experience clitoral orgasm, that is, orgasm as a result of direct or indirect clitoral stimulation. I was dumbfounded. She smiled, adding, "We're having the same discussion I went through with my friends fifteen years ago."

I told her that my friend Lisa insisted she's had orgasms during intercourse. "Well, Lisa might be one of the rare ones." Mom responded. "Or she might be lying, as so many women do for the same reason you feared admitting it. Each woman thinks it's her own private, secret failure."

It turned out Lisa *had* been lying. Not only to me but to her sexual partners as well. When I told her my newly acquired information, she too admitted to years of faking orgasm and hiding her feelings of inadequacy. A few days after our conversation, Lisa worked up the nerve to raise the subject with her mother who admitted she had never had one orgasm during sexual intercourse. It was the first time they had had such an honest discussion about sex. I've never seen a friend so relieved. "I feel as though a weight has been lifted," Lisa said.

She wasn't the only one. The first time my friend Emily had sex, she wanted to say to the guy, "Is that what everyone's been making such a fuss about?" My friend Janet told me that in her 10 brief sexual relationships, she had only had three orgasms in total—not one of them coming as a result of intercourse. Again I heard the syndrome of self-criticism and embarrassment. She felt it was *her* fault—*she* wasn't able to relax, she was afraid of "letting go." It was an empty feeling and one she avoided confronting.

Another close friend, Rebecca, said, "I know a lot of my friends have faked it and they say the guy can't tell the difference." Women can't blame men for not knowing the truth about female sexuality if we are not even honest with ourselves. One woman's lie hurts all of us and silence leads to confusion and stifled desire.

The media is perhaps the largest source of misinformation. According to most films, women reach a climax almost every time a man gets on top of them. The sight of women writhing in bliss and coming to screaming sweaty orgasms on the screen sets up a standard that we aspire to. It makes us all think: What do these women know that we don't?

Jacqueline Bisset whimpers with ecstasy in both an airplane lavatory ("Rich and Famous") and a glass elevator ("Class"). I remember reading in one of those teen magazines that in "Endless Love" Brooke Shields had to facially express an orgasm during intercourse with her boyfriend in front of the fire. After many unconvincing takes, the director finally resorted to pinching her toe until her exclamation of pain constituted an authentic picture.

Because our society puts so much emphasis on intercourse, I anticipated not just the emotional climax but the ultimate physical peak as well. It didn't happen. As long as most young women approach sex with grand expectations for orgasm during intercourse, we're heading for inevitable disappointment.

What's worse, the stakes keep getting higher. The *latest* goal is the *simultaneous* orgasm. Each time we jump a hurdle, yet another is placed in our path to sexual fulfillment. Each one of these standards has a built-in feature. For myself, I was wrestling with trying to please my boyfriend while also trying to articulate how he should go

about pleasing me, while *also* trying to relax into being pleased. Once I became more at ease about all this—once I knew I was normal—the pressure was off. I enjoyed intercourse for what it gave me emotionally *and* physically, with no further unrealistic expectations. I realized that if I want sexual satisfaction, it's my responsibility to communicate what is and is not pleasurable.

Judging from my own and other young women's experiences, many men are under the impression that intercourse is as "good" for us as it is for them. I can't speak for them, but it does seem that men progress more directly toward a sexual peak while we, or at least I, tend to zigzag toward it.

For me, intercourse may not lead to ultimate sexual fulfillment, but I am now able to appreciate it for its own sensations and the power of its intimacy. I can accept that there are women who do experience vaginal orgasm without any clitoral stimulation, and others—such as my sister—who have experimented with different positions for more direct clitoral pressure during intercourse.

There seems to be a general consensus among women my age that finding the words (and the courage) to convey which sexual activities make us feel good is a task we're often tempted to avoid. We fear our being too aggressive and demanding will risk losing the romance and spontaneity. The deification of intercourse belittles the other aspects of lovemaking that are equally valid and often even more enjoyable. As Lonnie Barbach writes in *For Yourself: The Fulfillment of Female Sexuality* (Doubleday): "To make intercourse the goal of sex does a grave disservice to many enjoyable ways of touching."

It is ironic and distressing that something so universal as sex is a conversational taboo. Not only are we uncommunicative about it with our closest friends, but many of us don't talk openly with our partners. My friends and I have found that, in the long run, it is worth the struggle and the awkwardness. Once you have worked out with your partner what each of you specifically can do to make the other feel best, you'll find real sexual pleasure.

CHAPTER 8

Sexuality and Relationships

PREVIEW

To gain a sense of what you already know about the material covered in his chapter, answer "true" or "false" to the following statements. You will find the answers as you read the chapter.

1. While there is general toleration among college students of different sexual standards of morality, women who "sleep around" experience disapproval. True or false?
2. Both men and women report feelings of obligation or pressure to engage in sexual intercourse. True or false?
3. The decline in the frequency of intercourse generally indicates problems in the marital relationship. True or false?
4. It is common for couples to experience transitory sexual problems in their marriages. True or false?
5. Poor sexual technique is usually the basic problem in sexual difficulties. True or false?
6. Anger often leads to sexual problems in a relationship. True or false?
7. A sexually active, fertile woman has about a 50-percent chance of pregnancy within a year if she does not use contraception. True or false?
8. Men are more frequently fertile than women. True or false?
9. Extramarital affairs tend to be more sexual than emotional. True or false?
10. Fear of being nonorgasmic is a major concern of men. True or false?

Outline

The degree and kind of a person's sexuality reach up into the ultimate pinnacle of his spirit.

FRIEDRICH NIETZSCHE

We are sexual from birth to death. Our initial experiences are exploratory and tentative, especially in adolescence and early adulthood. For some, our first experience of intercourse is premarital; for others these experiences take place within marriage. Whatever their context, they are profound experiences, marking an important cultural transition from virgin to non-virgin status. In this chapter we will explore some of the meanings of our sexual experiences in premarital, marital, and extramarital contexts. Then we will examine sexuality and aging, common sexual problems in relationships, and homosexuality.

☐ PREMARITAL SEXUALITY

Over the last several decades, there has been a remarkable increase in the acceptance of premarital sexual intercourse. The advent of effective birth control devices and changing sex roles that permit females to be sexual have played a major part in this change. This widespread shift in acceptance of premarital intercourse has transformed both dating and marriage. Sexual intercourse has become an acceptable part of the dating process for many couples, whereas only petting was acceptable before. Furthermore, marriage has lost some of its power as the only legitimate setting for sexual intercourse (Furstenberg, 1980). Now sexual intercourse may occur before marriage with some of the same social legitimacy (at least among peers) that it has within marriage. One important result is that many people no longer feel that they need to get married to have their sexual needs fulfilled.

There appears to be a general expectation among students that they will engage in sexual intercourse sometime during their college career (Komarovsky, 1985) and that sexual involvement will occur within a loving relationship. The exceptions are those who, because of their religious beliefs, are committed to virginity until marriage.

Whatever people's beliefs about sexuality, most of them seem to accept divergent moral standards. When Komarovsky asked students, "Who, in your opinion is more on the defensive in this college—a virgin or a sexually experienced student?" the common response was the former.

While toleration was the ideal, there were limits. If a woman had sexual intercourse, it was to take place in the context of a committed relationship. Women who "slept around" were morally censured. Reflecting the continuing double standard, men are not usually condemned as harshly as women for sleeping around.

Virginity was acceptable if it reflected deeply-held religious beliefs. If a person was a virgin for moral rather than religious reasons, it was assumed he or she had psychological problems. Men and women who remained virgins generally developed groups of friends who shared their same religious values. In a generally permissive atmosphere, these groups provided support and validation for those who chose to remain virgins. (For the pros and cons of premarital sex see Broderick, 1985, and Rubin, 1985.)

What factors lead men and women to have premarital sexual intercourse? One study indicated that among men and women who had made the decision to have intercourse, the most important factors were their love (or liking) for each other, physical arousal and willingness of both partners, and preplanning and arousal prior to the encounter (Christopher and Cate, 1985). Among nonvirgins, as with virgins, love or liking between the partners was extremely important (Christopher and Cate, 1984). But feelings of obligation or pressure were about as important as actual physical arousal. Women reported affection as being slightly more important than did males. An interesting finding is that men perceived slightly more pressure or obligation to engage in intercourse than women.

Once people decide to have intercourse, how do they encourage their more reluctant partners to become more involved sexually? In one study about a third of the women and a quarter of the men were direct: they simply asked if their partners wanted to make love (Knox and Wilson, 1981). The others used indirect methods, such as setting the mood with music or candlelight, verbally expressing love, moving closer, or hinting. Women were more likely to move closer or hint.

As you consider these aspects of sexual decision-making, consider your own sexual decision-making. How important is loving or liking in the decision to have intercourse? Physical arousal? Pressure or obligation? Preplanning? If you are sexually interested in a person, do you make your interest known directly or indirectly? How? (See Jacoby and Williams, 1985, for effects of premarital sexual standards on dating and marital desirability.)

☐ MARITAL SEXUALITY

When people marry, they may discover that their sexual lives are very different than they were before marriage. Sex is now morally and socially sanctioned. It is in marriage that the great majority of heterosexual interactions take place. Yet if we were to judge by the media, little sex occurs within marriage. On television five times as much sex takes place between unmarried partners as between married ones. Men have sex more often with prostitutes than with their wives. Erotic activity is often linked with violence (Roberts, 1982). Sexual research is not much different from the media. There are literally hundreds of studies on premarital sexuality, extramarital sexuality, homosexuality, and sexual variations. Almost no studies exist on marital sexuality (Williams, 1980).

> It is better to marry than to burn.
>
> I CORINTHIANS 7:9

Frequency of Sex

Marital sex tends to diminish in frequency the longer a couple is married. For newly married couples, the average rate of marital intercourse is about three times a week. As they get older, the frequency drops. In early middle age, a married couple makes love an average of one and a half to two times a week. After age fifty, the rate is about

> Marriage has many pains but celibacy has no pleasures.
>
> SAMUEL JOHNSON (1709–1784)

UNDERSTANDING YOURSELF

Your Moral Standards and Premarital Intercourse

As we move from adolescence to adulthood, we reevaluate our moral standards, moving from moral decision making based on authority to standards based on our own personal principles of right and wrong (Kohlberg, 1969). We become responsible for developing our own moral code, which includes sexual issues. Then we undertake the difficult tasks of linking our behavior to our morality (see Kupersmid and Wonderly, 1980).

Sociologist Ira Reiss (1967) has described four moral standards of premarital sexuality. The first is the abstinence standard, which was the official sexual ideology in American culture until the 1950s and early 1960s. This belief holds that it is wrong for either men or women to engage in sexual intercourse before marriage regardless of the circumstances or their feelings for each other. The double standard, which was widely practiced but rarely approved publicly, permits men to engage in premarital intercourse. Women, however, are considered immoral if they have premarital intercourse. Permissiveness with affection represents a third standard. It describes sex between men and women who have an affectionate,

stable, and loving relationship. In contrast to twenty years ago, this standard is widely held today. Permissiveness without affection is the fourth standard. It holds that people may have sexual relationships with each other even if there is no affection or commitment.

Which of these moral standards most closely fits your standards for premarital sexual intercourse? Why do you hold these standards? Are these the same standards you held one year ago? Five years ago? If they have changed, how do you account for the change? What is the relationship between your moral standards and your sexual behaviors? Is your actual sexual behavior consistent with your moral standards? If your behavior is different from your moral standards, how do you account for the difference? How do you feel about the difference between the two? Are your moral standards the same as those of your current or most recent boyfriend, girlfriend, or partner? Have you been in relationships in which you and your partner had different standards? How were the differences resolved? Are your standards similar to those of your friends?

once a week or less. Sex also becomes more routine in marriage; the average time it takes married people to have sexual intercourse is ten to twenty minutes. For a couple in their early twenties, this means they spend about fifty hours a year having sexual intercourse. In contrast, the average couple will spend one thousand hours a year watching television.

Sex is only one bond among many in marriage. It is a more important bond in cohabitation than in marriage because cohabitors don't have the security and future-orientation of marriage to cement their relationship. Most married couples don't seem to feel that declining frequency is a major problem, especially if they rate their overall relationship as good. Blumstein and Schwartz (1983) found that most people attributed the decline to lack of time or physical energy or to "being accustomed" to each other. Also, other activities and interests engage them besides sex. But if the frequency of sex is low in cohabiting relationships, discord is likely.

New Meanings to Sex

Sexuality within marriage is significantly different from premarital or postmarital sex in at least three ways. First, sex in marriage is expected to be monogamous. Second, procreation is a legitimate goal. Third, it takes place in the everyday world. These differences present each person with important tasks.

Monogamy. The most significant factor shaping marital sexuality is the expectation of monogamy. Before or after marriage a person might have various sexual partners, but within marriage all sexual interactions are expected to take place between the spouses. This expectation of monogamy lasts a lifetime; a person marrying at twenty commits himself or herself to forty to sixty years of sex with the same person. Within a monogamous relationship, each partner must decide how to handle fantasies, desires, and opportunities for extramarital sexuality. Do you tell your spouse that you have fantasies about other people? That you masturbate? Do you flirt with others? Do you have an extramarital relationship? If you do, do you tell your spouse? How do you handle sexual conflicts or difficulties with your partner? How do you deal with sexual boredom or monotony? (For the pros and cons of monogamy, see Mace and Mace, 1985, and Whitehurst, 1985.)

Socially Sanctioned Reproduction. Sex also takes on a procreative meaning within marriage. Until recently, procreative sex within marriage was the only acceptable form of sex in Western culture. Now sex and reproduction can be separated by means of birth control (for a critique of this separation, see Germaine Greer's provocative *Sex and Destiny*). Although it is obviously possible to get pregnant before marriage, marriage is the only socially sanctioned setting in which to have children in our society. When a couple marry, they are confronted with the task of deciding whether to have children. It is one of the most crucial decisions they will make. Having children alters a person's life even more than marriage: marriages can be dissolved, but you never stop being a parent.

If the couple decides to have a child, the nature of their lovemaking may change from simply an erotic activity to an intentionally reproductive act as well. Many parents who planned their children speak of the difference between sex-as-pleasure and sex-as-reproduction. One woman recalled (in Strong and Reynolds, 1982):

> We wanted to have a child for a long time and when I quit taking birth control pills, we started making love to have a child. Each time we did it, we knew that we might be conceiving. That made it really different from before when it just felt good or was fun. I can't explain why, just that it was really different knowing that we might be creating something.

Changed Sexual Context. The sexual context changes with marriage. Because married life takes place in a day-to-day living situation, sex must also be expressed in the day-to-day world. Before marriage it may have taken place only in romantic or seductive settings, at home when parents were away, or in the back seat of a car. These situations make sexual encounters highly charged with emotions ranging from intense love to anxiety and fear.

After marriage, sex must be arranged around working hours and at times when the children are at school or asleep. Sometimes one or the other partner may be tired, frustrated, or angry. The emotions associated with premarital sex may disappear. Some of the passion of romantic love eventually disappears as well, to be replaced with a love based on caring and commitment.

A Frontier Guard

The bamboo leaves rustle
On this cold, frost night.
I am wearing seven layers of
   clothing
But they are not as warm, not
   as warm
As the body of my wife.

ANONYMOUS, 8TH-CENTURY JAPANESE

The vow of fidelity is an absurd commitment, but it is the heart of marriage.

ROBERT CAPON

Table 8–1 **Contraceptive Check List***

Type	Estimated Effectiveness	Risks	Non-Contraceptive Benefits	Convenience	Availability
Condom	64–97%	Rarely, irritation and allergic reactions	Good protection against sexually transmitted diseases, possibly including herpes and AIDS	Applied immediately before intercourse	OTC (over the counter)
Vaginal Spermicides (used alone)	70–80%	Rarely, irritation and allergic reactions	May give some protection against some sexually transmitted diseases.	Applied no more than one hour before intercourse; can be "messy"	OTC
Sponge	80–87%	Rarely, irritation and allergic reactions; difficulty in removal; very rarely, toxic shock syndrome	May give some protection against some sexually transmitted diseases	Can be inserted hours before intercourse, left in place up to 24 hours; disposable	OTC
Diaphragm with Spermicide	80–98%	Rarely, irritation and allergic reactions, bladder infection, constipation; very rarely, toxic shock syndrome	May give some protection against some sexually transmitted diseases	Inserted before intercourse, can be left in place 24 hours but additional spermicide must be inserted if intercourse is repeated	Rx (prescription required)
IUD	95–96%	Cramps, bleeding, pelvic inflammatory disease; rarely, perforation of the uterus	None	After insertion, stays in place until physician removes it	Rx
Birth Control Pills	97% (mini) 99% (comb.)	Not for smokers; blood clots, gall bladder disease, noncancerous liver tumors, water retention, hypertension, mood changes, dizziness and nausea	Less menstrual bleeding and cramping, lower risk of fibrocystic breast disease, ovarian cysts and pelvic inflammatory disease; may protect against cancer of the ovaries and of the lining of the uterus	Pill must be taken on daily schedule, regardless of the frequency of intercourse	Rx
Natural Family Planning or Rhythm	Very variable, perhaps 53–86%	None	None	Requires frequent monitoring of body functions and periods of abstinence	Instructions from physician or clinic
Vasectomy (Male Sterilization)	Over 99%	Pain; infection rarely; possible psychological problems	None	No care after surgery	Minor surgery
Tubal Ligation (Female Sterilization)	Over 99%	Surgical complications; some pain or discomfort; possibly higher risk of hysterectomy later in life	None	No care after surgery	Surgery

*Efficacy rates given in this chart are estimates based on a number of different studies. Methods which are more dependent on conscientious use and therefore are more subject to human error have wider ranges of efficacy than the others. Because the contraceptive sponge has only been on the market a short time, effectiveness estimates for it are not based on as many studies as those for the other forms of contraception.
Source: *FDA Consumer*, May, 1985.

A primary task in marriage is to make sex meaningful in the everyday world. Sex in marriage is a powerful bond. Although we may tend to believe that good sex depends on good techniques, it really depends more on the quality of the marriage. One woman remarked to her husband, "What really turns me on is to see you doing housework." The husband, perplexed, asked why, because housework did not make him feel particularly sexy. "Because when I see you vacuuming, it gives me a warm feeling of love for you, which makes me want to make love with you." If the marriage is happy, then the couple is more likely to have good sex; if it is unhappy, then the unhappiness is likely to be reflected in the sexual relationship.

Sex therapists are turning increasingly to examining the marital dynamics rather than the individual as the source of sexual problems (Kaplan, 1979). As Blumstein and Schwartz (1983) point out, "An unhappy sex life does not necessarily mean that a couple is sexually incompatible. Their sexual relationship may be undermined by other problems." It does not matter what the conflict is about—housework, children, money—it is likely to be carried over into the bedroom.

□ EXTRAMARITAL SEXUALITY

Extramarital involvements assume many forms (see Thompson, 1983 for a review of the research literature). They may be (1) sexual but not emotional, (2) sexual and emotional, or (3) emotional but not sexual (Thompson, 1984). Very little research has been done on extramarital relationships in which both people are emotionally but not sexually involved. Thompson's study, however, found that of 378 married and cohabiting individuals, the three types of extrarelational involvement were about

FEATURE

Using Contraception

A woman has about a 2–4 percent chance of becoming pregnant during intercourse without contraception. If intercourse occurs the day before ovulation, the chance of conception is 30 percent; if it occurs on the day of ovulation, there is a 50 percent chance of pregnancy. Over the period of a year, a couple that does not use contraception has a 90 percent chance of pregnancy.

Because the possibility of pregnancy is so high for a sexually active couple, it seems reasonable that sexually active men and women would use contraception to avoid unintended pregnancy (for a review of the contraceptive practices of American women between 1973 and 1982, see Zelnick and Shaw, 1983). Unfortunately, this is not the case. One major study found that during their first intercourse, fewer than half of the couples used contraception (Zelnick and Shaw, 1984). Of those who planned first intercourse (17 percent of the women and 25 percent of the men) almost three-quarters of the women used contraception. Another study of eighty-three adolescent couples found that the majority had discussed birth control, but rarely before their first intercourse (Polit-O'Hara and Kahn, 1985). As men and women age, they become more consistent contraceptive users. One

national study found that only about 7 percent of the sexually active women did not use contraception during intercourse (Bachrach, 1984). Twice as many single women (whether never-married, separated, or divorced) as married women did not use contraception.

The key to contraceptive effectiveness is diligent and consistent use of contraception. A diaphragm in the bathroom, a condom in the wallet, or pills in the dispenser are useless. Intentions may be good, but good intentions are not good contraceptives. (See Table 8–1 on page 218 for a contraceptive checklist.)

Most people know they are taking a chance when they don't use contraception. The more frequently a person takes chances with unprotected intercourse, however, the more likely he or she is to take chances again (Luker, 1975). A subtle psychology develops: somehow, apparently by will power, good vibes, or the gods' kindly intervention, the woman will not get pregnant. Eventually, the woman or couple will feel almost magically invulnerable to pregnancy. Each time they are lucky, their risk taking is reinforced.

The consequences of an unintended pregnancy—economic hardships, adoption, or abor-

O, what a tangled web we weave
When first we practise to deceive.

SIR WALTER SCOTT

Open Adultery: The smart new term not only dispenses with the sinful connotations of the traditional one but one that puts monogamists on the defensive.

HUGH RAWSON

equally represented. Twenty-one percent had been in relationships that were primarily sexual, 19 percent in relationships that were sexual and emotional, and 18 percent in relationships that were emotional but not sexual. All told, 43 percent had been in some form of extramarital relationship.

People who engage in extramarital affairs have a number of different motivations, and these affairs satisfy a number of different needs. John Gagnon (1977) described the attraction extramarital affairs have for the people involved:

Most people find their extramarital relationships highly exciting, especially in the early stages. This is a result of psychological compression: the couple gets together; they are both very aroused (desire, guilt, expectation); they have only three hours to be together. . . . Another source of attraction is that the other person is always seen when he or she looks good and is on best behavior, never when feeling tired or grubby, or when taking care of children, or when cooking dinner. . . . Each time, all the minutes that the couple has together are special because they have been stolen from all these other relationships. The resulting combination

FEATURE—*continued*

tion—may be overwhelming. So why do people take chances in the first place? Part of the reason is faulty knowledge. People often underestimate how easy it is to get pregnant. Also, people may not know how to use a contraceptive method correctly, especially if they use the rhythm method (which is none too reliable to begin with). Finally, Kristin Luker (1975) suggests that we can look at contraceptive use through a cost/benefit analysis. She observed, "The decision to take a contraceptive risk is typically based on the *immediate* costs of contraception and the *anticipated* benefits of pregnancy." But the anticipated benefits usually prove illusory. "The potential benefits of pregnancy seldom become real; they vanish with the verdict of a positive pregnancy test or [are] later outweighed by the actual costs of the pregnancy." Let us examine some of the costs and anticipated benefits.

ACKNOWLEDGING SEXUALITY

On the surface, it may seem fairly simple to acknowledge that we are sexual beings, especially if we have conscious sexual desires and engage in sexual intercourse. Yet acknowledging our sexuality is not necessarily easy, for sexuality may be surrounded by feelings of guilt, conflict, and shame. The younger or less experienced we are, the more difficult it is to acknowledge our sexuality.

PLANNING CONTRACEPTION

Planning contraception requires us to admit not only that we are sexual but also that we plan to be sexually active. Without such planning men and women can pretend that their sexual intercourse "just happens" in a moment of passion, when they have been drinking, or when the moon is full—even though it happens frequently.

Developments in recent years have shifted contraceptive responsibility from the man to the woman, requiring women to more consciously define themselves as sexual. To do so, they have had to abandon traditional, passive sexual roles. Many women are reluctant to plan contraceptive use because they fear they will be regarded as sexually aggressive or promiscuous.

Since it is women who get pregnant, men tend to be unaware of their responsibility or to downplay their role in conception and pregnancy. Males, especially adolescent males, lack the awareness that supports contraceptive planning (Freeman,

(*continued on next page*)

of guilt and excitement has a heightening effect, which tends to explain why people may claim that extramarital sex and orgasms are more intense.

The majority of extramarital sexual involvements are sporadic. Most people in extramarital relationships probably do not have extramarital sexual intercourse more than five times a year (Gagnon, 1977). It is not clear how many people become involved in extramarital sex. Numerous studies suggest that about fifty percent of men have extramarital affairs (Hassett, 1981; Petersen, et al., 1983). The *Redbook* study found that among women aged twenty to twenty-five, 25 percent had had extramarital sex; among women in the thirty-five-to-thirty-nine bracket, 38 percent had extramarital sex (Tavris and Sadd, 1977). More recently, the *Cosmopolitan* survey (Wolfe, 1982) found among female respondents eighteen- to thirty-four-years old, 50 percent had had at least one affair, and for women thirty-five years or older, 69 percent had had affairs. But how many of these women had meaningful involvements as

The knew each other too well to feel those mutual revelations of possession that multiply its joys a hundredfold. She was as sated with him as he was tired of her. Emma was finding in adultery all the banalities of marriage.

GUSTAVE FLAUBERT (1821–1880), *MADAME BOVARY*

FEATURE–*continued*

1980). Yet males are more fertile than females. The average male is fertile twenty-four hours a day for fifty or more years. Females, in contrast, are fertile only a few days of the month for thirty-five or so years.

CONTINUING CONTRACEPTION

Many people, especially women using pills or IUDs, practice contraception consistently and effectively within a steady relationship, but give up their contraceptive practices if the relationship breaks up. They define themselves as sexual only within the context of a relationship. When men or women begin a new relationship they may not use contraception because the relationship has not yet become long term; they do not expect to have sexual intercourse or to have it often. They are willing to take chances.

LACK OF SPONTANEITY

Using contraceptive devices such as condoms or a diaphragm may destroy the feeling of spontaneity in sex. For those who justify their sexual behavior by romantic impulsiveness, using these devices seems cold and mechanical. Others do not use them because it would mean untangling bodies and limbs, interrupting the passion of the moment.

OBTAINING CONTRACEPTION

Difficulty in obtaining contraception may be a deterrent to using it. It is often embarrassing for sexually inexperienced persons to buy contraceptives. Buying condoms, foam, or sponges at the local drugstore is a public announcement that a person is sexual. Who knows if your mother, teacher, or minister might be down the aisle buying toothpaste (or contraceptives, for that matter) and might see you?

ANTICIPATED BENEFITS OF PREGNANCY

Many men and women fantasize that even an "accidental" pregancy might be beneficial. These anticipated benefits include (1) proving womanhood or manhood, (2) proving fertility, (3) defining a commitment, and (4) defining or redefining the relationship to a person's parents. For yourself, how do the benefits of pregnancy weigh against the costs? Do you take chances?

opposed to one-time-only experiments is not known.

Men are more likely to have extramarital sex when they are younger; women when they are older. Women in their late thirties tend to be more interested in sex than they were when younger. This difference in the male-female sexual life cycle may account for women's increasing involvement in extramarital sex as they get older. The *Playboy* survey, however, found that among young marrieds significantly more women than men had affairs (Peterson et al., 1983).

Most extramarital sex is not a love affair, but is generally self-contained and more sexual than emotional (Gagnon, 1977). Affairs that are both emotional and sexual appear to detract most from the marital relationship, whereas affairs that are only sexual or only emotional seem to detract least (Thompson, 1984). More women than

The bonds of matrimony are so heavy that it takes two to bear them, sometimes three.

ALEXANDRE DUMAS, *FILS*

men have emotional affairs; almost twice as many men as women have affairs that are only sexual. About equal percentages of men and women are involved in affairs that are both sexual and emotional.

Studies have found little significant correlation between social background characteristics and extramarital sexuality (Thompson, 1983). A recent study (Weiss and Jurich, 1985) did find that the size of a community was directly related to extramarital attitudes; the smaller the community, the greater the disapproval. Personal characteristics and the quality of the marriage appear to be more important, and of the two, personal characteristics—alienation, need for intimacy, emotional independence, and egalitarian sex roles—were stronger correlates of extramarital sex than the quality of the marriage (Thompson, 1984). Generally, the lower the marital satisfaction and the frequency and quality of marital intercourse, the greater the likelihood of extramarital sexual relationships. Most people become involved in extramarital sex because they feel that something is missing in their marriage. Whatever the state of their marital relationship, they have judged their marriage defective, although not defective enough to consider divorce. Extramarital relationships are a compensation or substitute for these deficiencies (Cuber, 1969). They help maintain the status quo by giving emotional satisfaction to the unhappy partner.

Research by Ira Reiss and his colleagues (1980) suggested that extramarital affairs appear to be related to two variables: unhappiness of the marriage and/or premarital sexual permissiveness. Generally speaking, in happy marriages a partner is less likely to seek outside sexual relationships. If a person had premarital sex, he or she is more likely to have extramarital sex. Persons who break the social prohibition against premarital sex are less likely to be restrained by prohibitions against extramarital sex. Once the first prohibition is broken, the second holds less power.

Most married people feel that the spouse who is unfaithful has broken a basic trust. Sexual accessibility implies emotional accessibility. When a person learns that his or her spouse is having an affair, the emotional commitment of that spouse is brought into question. How can you prove that you still have a commitment? You cannot; commitment is assumed—it can never be proven. Furthermore, an affair implies indifference to the feelings of the marriage partner. Finally, it may imply to the partner (rightly or wrongly) that he or she is sexually inadequate or uninteresting.

There is an interesting fact regarding the relationship between extramarital affairs and the breakup of a marriage. Most men and women whose marriages break up after their involvement in an extramarital affair feel that the affair was an effect rather than a cause of marital problems. But if their spouse was involved in such an affair, they identify the spouse's infidelity as a cause of marital problems (Spanier and Margolis, 1983).

□ SEXUALITY AND AGING

Our bodies and our sexuality develop and change from birth through old age. Puberty, as we have seen, is the time during which a person develops secondary sex characteristics and becomes fertile. These changes are essential for the expression of adult sexuality, which is characterized by autoerotic and interpersonal sexual behaviors. It is not until middle age that additional significant bodily changes affecting sexuality occur.

Oh, I don't know that I love him [explains George's wife to her new lover]. He's my husband, you know. But I get anxious about George's health, and if I thought it would nourish him, I would fry you with onions for his breakfast and think nothing of it. George and I are good friends. George belongs to me. Other men may come and go, but George goes on forever.

GEORGE BERNARD SHAW

Gerald: You have never been married, Lord Illingworth, have you?
Illingworth: Men marry because they are tired; women because they are curious. Both are disappointed.
Gerald: But don't you think one can be happy when one is married?
Illingworth: Perfectly happy. But the happiness of a married man, my dear Gerald, depends on the people he has not married.
Gerald: But if one is in love?
Illingworth: One should always be in love. That is the reason one should never marry.
Gerald: Love is a very wonderful thing, isn't it?
Illingworth: When one is in love one begins by deceiving oneself. And one ends by deceiving others. . . .

OSCAR WILDE, A WOMAN OF NO IMPORTANCE

Rufus T. Firefly: What about
your husband?
Mrs. Teasdale: He's dead.
Rufus: He's just using that as
an excuse.
Teasdale: I was with him to
the end.
Rufus: No wonder he passed
away.
Teasdale: I held him in my
arms and kissed him.
Rufus: So—it was murder?

MARX BROTHERS, *DUCK SOUP*

Sexuality and Middle Age

Notable differences exist in male and female sexual expression (Kaplan, 1974). Among American women, sexual responsiveness continues to grow from adolescence until it reaches its peak in the late thirties or early forties; it is usually maintained at more or less the same level into the sixties and beyond. A male's orgasmic responsiveness (whether through masturbation or sexual intercourse) reaches its peak around eighteen years of age (Kaplan, 1974; Kinsey, 1948; but see Robinson, 1976). A gradual but not serious decline for males begins in their twenties. Changes in the male sexual response become apparent only when men are in their forties and fifties. As a man ages, achieving erection requires more stimulation and time and the erection may not be as firm. The refractory period following orgasm may lengthen from a few minutes to several days.

Around age fifty the average American woman begins menopause, which is marked by the cessation of the menstrual cycle. Menopause is not a sudden event. Usually, for several years preceding menopause the menstrual cycle becomes increasingly irregular. Menopause ends fertility but not an interest in sexual activities. There is no male equivalent to menopause. Male fertility slowly declines, but men in their eighties are often fertile.

Sexuality and the Aged

As you age, the desire remains
but it's not as strong, but neither is the emotion that goes
with it. So you're free to do
more useful things.

CARY GRANT

The sexuality of the aged tends to be invisible. Several reasons account for this in our culture (Barrow and Smith, 1979). First of all, we associate sexuality with the young, assuming that sexual attraction exists only between those with youthful bodies. Interest in sex is considered normal and virile in twenty-five-year-old men, but in seventy-five-year-old men it is considered lechery (Corby and Zarit, 1983). Second, we associate the idea of romance and love with the young; many of us find it difficult to believe that the aged can fall in love or love intensely. Yet a fifty-seven-year-old woman said of a seventy-two-year-old man she had recently met: "It was as if I were 17 and had never been on a date. I had never turned anybody on in my life, so far as I knew. Now, all of a sudden, it was Christmas. Believe it or not, we fell in love" (Barrow and Smith, 1979). Third, we continue to associate sex with procreation, measuring a woman's femininity by her childbearing and mother role and a man's masculinity by the children he sires. Finally, the aged do not have as strong sexual desires as the young and they are not expressed as openly.

Sexuality is one of the least understood aspects of life in old age (see Weg, 1983a, for a collection of essays on the sexuality of the aged). Many older people continue to adhere to the standards of activity or physical attraction they held when they were young. Sexual behavior is defined by researchers and the general population alike as masturbation, sexual intercourse, or orgasm. These definitions have "overshadowed the emotional, sensual, and relationship qualities that give meaning, beyond release, to sexual expression. . . . What has been ignored are the walking hand-in-hand or arm-in-arm; the caring for one another; the touching and holding, with or without intercourse" (Weg, 1983b).

Aged men and women face different problems sexually (Robinson, 1983). Physiologically, men are less responsive. The decreasing frequency of intercourse and the increasing time required to attain an erection produce anxieties in many older men about becoming impotent—anxieties that may very well lead to impotence. When the natural slowing down of sexual responses is interpreted as the beginning of impotence, this self-diagnosis triggers a vicious spiral of fears and even greater difficulty in having or maintaining an erection. But, as Masters and Johnson (1966) have pointed out, "Inevitably all physical responses are slowed down. . . . A man can't run around the block as fast as he could 20 or 30 years previously. Yet the simple fact that sexual functioning is but one more element in his total physiologic functioning has never occurred to him."

Women, who are sexually capable throughout their lives, have different concerns. They face greater social constraints than men (Robinson, 1983). Women are confronted with an unfavorable sex ratio (sixty-nine males for every one hundred females over sixty-five years), a greater likelihood of widowhood, norms against marrying younger men, less probability of remarriage, the double standard of aging, and inhibiting sex roles. "Biologically, men are at the greater disadvantage," wrote Simone de Beauvoir (1972) about the double standard of aging. "Socially, it is the women who are worse off, because of their condition as erotic objects."

To a large extent, women are viewed by potential partners in terms of their attractiveness. Yet in our culture, beauty is equated with youth. Thus, as women grow older, they lose one of the major aspects of their femininity. Although they have more sexual desire than they had in youth, older women usually have increasing doubts of their sexual appeal. The double standard of aging places women in a difficult position. They outnumber men of their own age—and many of these men seek younger women, a situation that is considered acceptable socially, although the union of an older woman with a young man is not.

The greatest determinant of an older individual's sexual activity is the availability of a partner. Those who do not have partners may turn to masturbation as an alternative. In one study of older people, only 7 percent of those who were single, divorced, or widowed were sexually active, in contrast to 54 percent of those living with a partner (Verwoerdt et al., 1969). Frequency of sexual intercourse for the latter group—average age seventy years—ranged from three times a week to once every two months. Those who described their sexual feelings as having been weak or moderate in their youth stated they were without sexual feelings.

After age seventy-five a significant decrease in sexual activity takes place. This seems to be related to health problems, such as heart disease, arthritis, and diabetes. But often these people indicate that they continue to feel sexual desires; they simply lack the ability to express them because of their health (Verwoerdt et al., 1969). Social attitudes toward the aged also discourage the expression of sexual desires. Such desires may be labeled abnormal, dirty, or inappropriate. The old, fearing ridicule and disapproval, may incorporate these attitudes into their own perception of themselves.

☐ SEXUAL PROBLEMS IN RELATIONSHIPS

At various times, couples may experience difficulties in their sexual relationships. Often these are transitory, lasting anywhere from a few days to a few weeks or months, and may occur because of fatigue, stress, or situational problems. If such problems persist, however, they may result in sexual dysfunctions, that is, inability to give and receive sexual satisfaction. Dysfunctions are extremely common in marriage, both for short and long periods of time (Masters and Johnson, 1970).

The most common dysfunctions among men include *erectile dysfunction*, the

So, lively brisk old man
Do not let sadness come over
  you;
For all your white hairs
You can still be a lover.

JOHANN GOETHE

So we'll go no more a-roving
  So late into the night,
Though the heart be still as
  loving
  And the moon be still as
  bright.
For the sword outwears its
  sheath,
  And the soul wears out the
  breast,
And the heart must pause to
  breathe,
  And love itself have rest.
Though the night was made
  for loving,
  And the day returns too
  soon,
Yet we'll go no more a-roving
  By the light of the moon.

LORD BYRON

I believe in the flesh and the
  appetites,
Seeing, hearing and feeling are
  miracles, and each part and
  tag of me is a miracle.

WALT WHITMAN

Playfulness is an important aspect of sexuality, banishing boredom and routine, making each encounter fresh and new.

Some obstacle is necessary to swell the tide of libido to its height; and at all periods of history whenever natural barriers in the way of satisfaction have not sufficed, mankind has erected conventional ones in order to enjoy love.

SIGMUND FREUD

inability to achieve or maintain an erection; *premature ejaculation*, the inability to delay ejaculation after penetration; and *delayed orgasm*, difficulty in ejaculating. Among women the most common dysfunctions are *orgasmic dysfunction*, the inability to attain orgasm; *arousal difficulties*, the inability to become erotically aroused; and *dyspareunia*, painful intercourse. Both sexes may suffer from *inhibited sexual desire*, the lack of sexual desire, a common but only recently recognized problem.

Research and treatment of sexual dysfunctions have been directed toward resolving problems of impotence, premature ejaculation, and lack of orgasm. In these areas successful treatment may reach 70 to 80 percent. Now therapists are finding a widespread incidence of inhibited sexual desire (ISD). ISD responds to treatment in only about 10 percent of the cases. Inhibited sexual desire is related to other sexual dysfunctions insofar as it is rooted in anxiety. Usually, however, it stems from deeper, more intense sexual anxiety, greater hostility toward the partner, and more pervasive defenses than those found among people with erectile and orgasmic difficulties (Kaplan, 1979). Sometimes it is a means of coping with other sexual dysfunctions that precede it. Kolodny and his colleagues (1979) observed: "By developing a low interest in sexual activity, the person avoids the unpleasant consequences of sexual failure such as embarrassment, loss of self-esteem, and frustration."

Although some sexual dysfunctions are physical in origin, most are psychological (Kaplan, 1979). Some dysfunctions have immediate causes, others originate in conflict within the self, and still others in a particular sexual relationship. Still, the possibility of a physical basis for a sexual dysfunction should be the first to be explored, especially if the male has prostate problems (Roen, 1983) or if there is chronic pain (Maruta and McHardy, 1983).

Individual Causes of Dysfunctions

Dysfunctions tend to be rooted in marital interactions, but the causes may also be individual. Sometimes it is simple sexual ignorance that prevents couples from being fully sexual with each other. "Many couples do not know very much about sexuality and are too guilty and frightened to explore and experiment" (Kaplan, 1978).

Performance Anxieties.   The fear of failure is probably the most important immediate cause of erectile dysfunctions and, to a lesser extent, of orgasmic dysfunctions in women (Kaplan, 1978). If a man does not become erect, anxiety is a fairly common response. Some men experience their first erectile failure when a partner initiates or demands sexual intercourse. Women are permitted to say no, but many men have not learned that they too may say no to sex. Women suffer similar anxieties, but theirs tend to center around their orgasmic abilities rather than the ability to make love. If they are unable to experience orgasm, a cycle of fear may arise, preventing future orgasms. Often a man will insist that his partner have an orgasm; but the orgasm is not so much for her as it is for reassurance and proof of his sexual ability. Such demands often lead a woman to fake an orgasm. A related source of anxiety is an excessive need to please one's partner (Kaplan, 1978).

Conflicts Within the Self.   People often feel guilty about their sexual feelings. But guilt and emotional conflict do not usually eliminate a person's sexual drive; rather, they inhibit the drive and alienate a person from his or her sexuality. A person comes to see sexuality as something bad or "dirty," not something to be happily affirmed. Sexual expression is forced, Helen Kaplan (1978) wrote, "to assume an infinite variety of distorted, inhibited, diverted, sublimated, alienated and variable forms to accommodate the conflict." Sometimes the conflicts result in less than satisfying sexual interaction, a lowering of pleasure, a fear of sexuality. These psychic conflicts are deeply rooted; often they are unconscious.

Relationship Causes of Dysfunctions

Rage, anger, disappointment, and hostility sometimes become a permanent part of marital interaction. Such factors ultimately affect the sexual relationship, for sex is like a barometer for the whole relationship. Kaplan (1978) suggested that marital discord has its sources in six areas: (1) transferences, (2) lack of trust, (3) power struggles, (4) contractual disappointments, (5) sexual sabotage, and (6) lack of communication.

Transference.   Transference refers to the redirection of feelings we have about someone else (usually parents or other significant persons) toward our partners. For example, if we had an unhappy love affair in the past, we may transfer some of our feelings about our previous partner to our present one. If we feel we were deprived of our mother's attention, we may feel our partner is similarly depriving us.

> We have reduced physical impotence to a disunion between the tender and sensual currents of erotic feeling. . . . I shall put forward the proposition that physical impotence is far more widespread than is generally supposed, and that some degree of this condition does in fact characterize the erotic life of civilized peoples . . . it would comprise, to begin with, all those men who are described as psychoanesthetic, i.e., who never fail in the act but who perform it without special pleasure—a state of things which is commoner than one might think.
>
> SIGMUND FREUD

Lack of Trust. Love, intimacy, and sexuality require trust. Without trust in the other, we are unwilling to expose ourselves, our feelings, or our sexuality. With trust we become transparent; it is no slight coincidence that we speak of standing naked before the other both metaphorically and physically. We are at our most vulnerable when we are sexually intimate; we must trust that we have nothing to fear if we give ourselves sexually.

Being forced is poison for the soul.

LUDWIG BORNE (1786–1837)

Power Struggles. Power struggles take place when domination is a central theme in a relationship. Sexuality becomes a tool in struggles for control in intimate relationships. A man may force his wife to submit to him sexually or engage in sexual activities she does not like. She may humiliate him by forcing him to perform, by withholding sex, or by being nonresponsive or nonorgasmic. The results of such unconscious power struggles may be lessened desire, poor sexual interaction, impotence, or orgasmic dysfunction. Sexual responsiveness to the partner becomes tantamount to submission; sexual pleasure is forgotten.

Contractual Disappointments. Contractual disappointments stem from the unwritten marriage contracts between couples. These unwritten contracts are the assumptions and expectations—usually unconscious—about how each should act in the marriage. A man, for example, may assume he and his wife will have children when they marry; she does not want them. Because they never discuss the issue it does not become a source of discord until after marriage.

Figure 8–1

What Prevents People from Expressing Their Sexuality. A 1983 survey of 12,000 readers of *Psychology Today* found substantial differences between males and females regarding sexual inhibitions. Do you think that the increasing incidence of Acquired Immune Deficiency Syndrome (AIDS) is increasing the fear of disease? Why? Source: Carin Rubenstein, "The Modern Art of Courtly Love," *Psychology Today*, 1983.

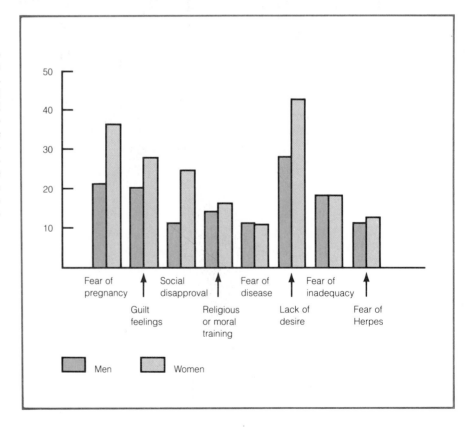

Sexual Sabotage.   A couple may engage in sexual sabotage with each other by, for example, asking for sex at the wrong time, putting pressure on each other, or frustrating or criticizing each other's sexual desires and fantasies. People most often do this unconsciously; to engage in sexual sabotage consciously would appear to be vicious. This lack of awareness may partly absolve a person, but makes solving the problem more difficult.

Communication Problems.   Finally, lack of communication is one of the most important factors underlying sexual dysfunctions. A person cannot be a sexual mind reader; each partner must know how the other feels about sex and about ways of being sexual. If neither knows how the other feels—especially if one or both partners fake responses—a great amount of harmful misinformation may be conveyed. (See Chapter 14 for a comprehensive discussion of communication.)

☐ HOMOSEXUALITY

Sexual behavior may be heterosexual, homosexual, or bisexual, depending on a person's sexual object. Heterosexual behavior occurs between males and females, homosexual behavior between members of the same sex. Bisexuals are men or women who engage in sex with both sexes. Although homosexuals of both sexes may be known as "gays," to distinguish the sexes males often identify themselves as gays and females identify themselves as lesbians.

Homosexuality has been variously called a sin, sickness, perversion, or deviation. These labels, however, do not broaden our understanding of homosexuality but narrow it by focusing on moralistic and causal issues that can never be scientifically resolved. A more useful approach is to look at homosexuality as a sexual variation or difference and to try to understand the world in which gay men and women live.

Homophobia

One of the most powerful forces affecting gays and lesbians is homophobia, literally fear of homosexuals. Although homosexuality is condemned in both Jewish and Christian scripture—"Thou shalt not lie with mankind, as with womankind (Leviticus 18:22)—there was little persecution of homosexuals until the Middle Ages (Boswell, 1980) when they were burned, hanged, beaten, and mutilated. Until the nineteenth century in America, homosexuality was punishable by death (Marmor, 1980).

Homophobia, fear and hatred of homosexuals, is derived from several sources (Marmor, 1980): (1) a deeply rooted insecurity about one's own sexuality and gender identity, (2) a strong fundamentalist religious orientation, and (3) ignorance about homosexuality. In addition, homophobic individuals are less likely to have had personal contact with gays or lesbians and more likely to be older and less well educated, to express traditional, restrictive attitudes toward sex, and to manifest more guilt about sex (Herek, 1984). Many of them view AIDS as a punishment sent for homosexuality. In a controversial essay on "heterosexism," feminist Adrienne Rich (1983) suggests that homophobia serves males by preventing women from naturally forming strong bonds (and possibly sexual relationships) with other women.

Zeus was the father of the gods, and Hera, his wife (and sister) was the mother of the gods. But the two lived in constant battle with each other. Zeus was perpetually unfaithful, taking many forms to go upon the earth and seduce young women. Hera was as jealous as Zeus was unfaithful. Once she plotted to drug him; other gods crept up to him to tie him down. But Zeus awoke and they fled, confessing that Hera had set them against him. In his anger, Zeus tied Hera by her heels and let her dangle from the clouds amidst tears that fell like rain. Then they promised to love each other, Zeus by being faithful and Hera by being trusting. The agreement was soon broken and once again earthquakes shook all of Greece from their unending arguments.

ANCIENT GREEK MYTH

Homosexuality: Behavior or Identity?

A far-reaching debate is currently going on about the nature of homosexuality: Is homosexuality fundamentally an identity or is it an erotic relationship between individuals of the same sex—a set of behaviors (De Cecco and Shively, 1983/1984)? (See three special issues of the *Journal of Homosexuality*: 9:2/3 [Winter 1983/Spring 1984]; 10:1/2 [Fall, 1984]; and 10:3/4 [Winter 1984]). The idea that homosexuality is an identity has only existed for a little more than a decade but it has become a key concept (Cass, 1983/1984). The classification of individuals according to their sexual orientation, that is, heterosexual, homosexual, or bisexual, has been done for little more than a hundred years; Sigmund Freud popularized this classification around the turn of the century (De Cecco and Shively, 1983/1984). If it is an identity, then a person who engages in sexual relations with members of the same sex *is* homosexual. Homosexuality is part of the person's core identity; it is not likely to change. The older view that homosexuality is certain sexual behaviors conducted between members of the same sex, implies that a person is not inherently homosexual, but only behaviorally so. The belief that homosexuality describes behaviors rather than identities was given credence by Alfred Kinsey in his studies of sexual behavior (1948, 1953; see Robinson, 1976, for a critique).

With no warning,
Like a whirlwind swoops on an
   oak,
Love shakes my heart.

SAPPHO

Homosexuality as Behavior and Relationship.   Only a small number of people are exclusively homosexual in their relationships. Kinsey estimated that among those between the ages of twenty and thirty-five, only 1 to 3 percent of women and 2 to 16 percent of men have been exclusively homosexual at any one period. Based on numerous other studies, one researcher estimated that the incidence of more or less exclusive homosexuality in Western culture ranges from 5 to 10 percent for men and 3 to 5 percent for women. If persons involved in bisexual activities were included, the figures would double (Marmor, 1980).

In a study by Bell and Weinberg (1978), three-quarters of the gay males considered themselves exclusively homosexual in behavior, although only 42 percent felt themselves exclusively homosexual in feelings. In contrast, lesbians were more heterosexual in feelings and behavior; this may reflect a history of sexual accommodation to males or conformity to societal expectations. The lives of a considerable number of people include both homosexual and heterosexual responses or experiences. Yet behavior is often categorized as normal or abnormal, heterosexual or homosexual, without recognizing gradations. A person with only one homosexual experience may be placed in the "homosexual" category and lose his or her job—or, if a male, may even be jailed.

Kinsey's research led him to believe that heterosexuality and homosexuality do not describe people's identities but their sexual responses. He placed responses on a continuum rather than identifying people as homosexual or heterosexual (see Table 8–2). The zero category indicated no homosexual responses; one indicated almost exclusive heterosexuality with some homosexual interest; two, basic heterosexuality, but with active interest in homosexual activity; three, equal heterosexual and homosexual interest; four, greater interest in homosexuality, with active interest in heterosexuality; five, predominant homosexuality, with some heterosexual interest; six, exclusive homosexuality.

Many people who identify themselves as heterosexual—as many as 37 percent of the males and 13 percent of the females in Kinsey's (1948, 1953) studies—have had

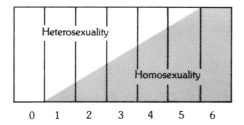

Figure 8–2

Alfred Kinsey's Heterosexual–
Homosexual Continuum.

overt homosexual experiences. Are these people bisexual, homosexual, or heterosexual? The fact that their choice of sexual partners contradicts their sexual identity as heterosexual points out the limitation of the concept of sexual identity. Our sexual identity is not only an objective definition but also a subjective one. Some researchers would argue that such difficulties make the concepts of heterosexual, homosexual, and bisexual identities meaningless (see De Cecco and Shivley, 1983/1984).

Why do most people who have experiences with both sexes tend to identify themselves as heterosexual rather than bisexual or homosexual? Part of the explanation lies in people's reluctance to assign themselves deviant labels. More important, however, may be the context in which these homosexual experiences took place. Most homosexual experiences occur either in adolescence or in sexually segregated situations. The great majority of heterosexuals with homosexual experiences had them in adolescence (Kinsey, 1948, 1953). Such experiences are a form of sexual experimentation and do not represent a commitment to homosexuality; they generally end by middle adolescence (Hass, 1979). Situational homosexuality takes place when the sexes are isolated from each other—most frequently in prisons, the military, and sexually segregated schools and colleges.

Homosexuality as Identity.   Since the 1970s, the concept of homosexual identity has been one of the dominant themes in homosexual research. Those who use the identity concept believe that a person's sexuality as heterosexual or homosexual is established by age four or five (Marmor, 1980). But identifying oneself as gay takes considerable time and includes several phases, usually beginning in late childhood or early adolescence. Homosexual feelings almost always precede homosexual activity by several years (Bell et al., 1981). Various studies have indicated that the average male homosexual does not identify himself as gay until ages nineteen or twenty-one (Troiden and Goode, 1980). The more heterosexual experiences during high school a boy has beyond kissing, the longer it takes him to recognize that he is fundamentally homosexual. The significant factor is that he is less likely to enjoy his youthful heterosexual encounters (Bell et al., 1981).

The first phase in acquiring a gay identity is marked by fear and suspicion that somehow one's desires are different. At first, the person finds it difficult to label these emotional and physical desires for the same sex. When an older child or young adolescent first experiences these desires, his or her initial reactions are often fear, confusion, or denial. Worse, adolescents fear their family's discovery of their homosexual feelings. "Nowhere has the hostility to homosexuality been more frightening to large numbers of gay men and lesbians than in their own families forcing them to feel like minority group members in their own homes" (Voeller, 1980). In the second phase, the person actually labels these feelings of attraction, love, and desire as homosexual. If the feelings recur often enough, a person is eventually forced to acknowledge that they are homosexual feelings. The third phase includes the person's self-definition as gay. This may take considerable struggle, for it entails accepting a label that society generally calls deviant. Questions then arise about whether to tell parents or friends—whether to hide one's identity (go into the closet) or make the identity known (come out of the closet).

Some gays may go through two additional phases. One phase is to enter the gay subculture. A gay person may begin acquiring exclusively gay friends, going to gay bars, baths, and clubs, or engaging in cruising or anonymous sexual encounters. The final phase begins with a person's first homosexual love affair. This marks the commitment to unifying sexuality and affection. Sex and love are no longer separated. Most gays have had such love affairs, despite the stereotypes of anonymous gay sex. Bell and Weinberg (1978) found that virtually every gay and lesbian they interviewed had experienced at least one long-term relationship.

Coming Out.   Publicly avowing one's homosexuality is a major decision, since it may jeopardize many relationships. Yet Weinberg and Williams (1974) concluded that once homosexuality is revealed, apprehension gives way to relief. Coming out of the closet is an important means of self-validation. By publicly acknowledging homosexuality, a person begins to reject the stigma and condemnation associated with it (Friend, 1980). Generally, this occurs in stages, first involving family members, especially the mother, then siblings, and last the father. Coming out to the family is often regarded as a crisis, but generally the family accepts the situation and gradually adjusts. After the family, friends may be told, and in fewer cases employers and coworkers. The higher a person's status, however, the less likely a person is to come out of the closet. The majority of homosexuals, both male and female, remain covert (Bell and Weinberg, 1978).

AIDS.   Acquired Immune Deficiency Syndrome (AIDS) has taken the lives of over 8000 Americans, the majority of whom were homosexuals. But AIDS is not a homosexual disease; it is a blood contamination disease (see Resource Center). In the United States it has been found primarily among homosexuals, who are particularly vulnerable to it for two reasons. First, the rectal walls are easily ruptured during anal intercourse, thereby allowing semen containing the AIDS virus to enter the bloodstream. Second, homosexuals tend to have a larger number of sex partners than heterosexuals, giving them more opportunities for exposure to the virus. Incidental reports suggest that gay men are beginning to change their sexual behaviors by using condoms and avoiding casual sexual encounters. As Arthur Kretchmer (1986) wrote: ". . . we require the courage to look at the victims and understand that they are victims. They have not committed sin, they have committed sex; and sex served as the pathway to a tragedy."

☐ SUMMARY

- Premarital sexual intercourse is widely accepted. On campuses there is widespread acceptance of divergent sexual standards. The sexual double standard continues, however; women are condemned if they engage in sexual intercourse outside of a committed relationship, while men are not.

- In sexual decision making, loving or liking is often the most important factor determining first intercourse or intercourse with a new partner.

- Marital sexuality is generally expected to be monogamous, takes place in a day-to-day context, and has reproduction as a socially sanctioned goal. Sex is only one bond among many in marriage. Marital sex tends to decline in frequency over time but this does not generally signify marital deterioration.

- Extramarital sexual involvements assume three basic forms: primarily sexual, primarily emotional, and emotional and sexual. Women are increasingly engaging in extramarital affairs; male involvement has remained relatively high. Most people have extramarital affairs because they feel something is lacking in their marriage. The two most important factors predicting extramarital involvement are whether the marriage is happy and whether the individual was permissive about premarital sex.

- Women reach their sexual peak in their late thirties and early forties and usually maintain the same level through their sixties. Men reach their sexual peak, measured by orgasmic frequency, at age eighteen; their sexual responsiveness gradually declines, although it is usually not noticeable until they reach their forties or fifties. Around age fifty, women enter menopause and their menstrual cycle ends marking the end of fertility; men are often fertile in their eighties.

- The sexuality of the aged tends to be invisible because we associate sexuality with youth and because the old themselves do not have as strong sexual desires as they did when younger. Men fear impotence, while women may dread the loss of their physical attractiveness. The main determinants of sexual activity in old age are the availability of a partner and health.

- Sexual dysfunctions are problems in giving and receiving erotic satisfaction. The most common male problems are *erectile dysfunction, premature ejaculation,* and *delayed orgasm.* The most common female problems are *orgasmic dysfunction, arousal difficulties,* and *dyspareunia* (painful intercourse). A recently recognized sexual dysfunction is *inhibited sexual desire* (ISD).

- Most sexual dysfunctions are psychological in origin, but physical or hormonal causes should not be discounted. There are a number of causes of sexual dysfunctions, including sexual ignorance, performance anxieties, excessive need to please, conflicts within the self, and marital discord.

- Only a small number of people are predominantly homosexual. Large numbers of people have had both heterosexual and homosexual experiences; of these, some consider themselves homosexuals, others believe that they are bisexual, but the great majority consider themselves heterosexual. Kinsey argued that heterosexuality and homosexuality are behaviors, which exist on a continuum.

- Identifying oneself as gay or lesbian occurs over considerable time, usually beginning in late childhood or adolescence. The earliest phase begins with fear or suspicion that one's sexual desires are different or strange. In the second phase the person labels these feelings as homosexual. The last phase consists of defining oneself as gay or lesbian. Two additional phases are entering the gay subculture and having a long-term homosexual affair. AIDS is not a homosexual disease but a blood contamination disease.

READINGS

Initiating and Refusing Sex

PHILIP BLUMSTEIN AND PEPPER SCHWARTZ, EXCERPT FROM
AMERICAN COUPLES

According to the authors, why do men initiate sex in relationships? What prevents women from initiating sex? Is the man's "right" to initiate sex and the woman's "right" to refuse necessarily a reflection of power in the relationships, as the authors suggest? Why? How do you think men feel about being responsible for initiating sex? How do women feel about refusing sex? How do partners indicate that they are interested or not interested in sex at a particular time?

Among heterosexual couples, men have traditionally been the sexual aggressors and women have traditionally waited for men to approach them. A woman might then be free to refuse, but a man was expected to be ever-ready. Nowadays, men and women are moving away from such narrow definitions of what "men must always do" and "women must never do." We might expect to have reached a time when the majority of our couples feel they can share the roles of initiator or refuser fairly evenly. Our evidence, however, strongly suggests that the old traditions are still alive.

When initiating sex, a partner is making something between a request and a demand: He or she may be invoking a right or seeking a special privilege. When refusing sex, a partner may be exercising an established prerogative or declining a sacred duty. The acts of initiating and refusing sex take on different meanings for different couples. These acts can tell us the degree of power or dependency each partner has, and the many ways in which partners use sex to control each other. By viewing requests and rejections in the bedroom, we get a unique perspective on the most basic aspects of a couple's life together. . . .

The evidence clearly points to initiation as a largely male responsibility among heterosexual couples. This is especially true for married couples, but it shows up strongly among the cohabitors as well. The man is the initiator in more than twice as many couples as the woman.

We might expect same-sex couples to display more equality, since they do not have one man and one woman to play traditional roles in the bedroom. Yet fewer than 40 percent of same-sex couples tell us they initiate equally.

Often, married women do not feel that initiating sex is their right. Cohabiting women, frequently the first to experiment with changing female roles, *do* initiate sex with their partners more than married women do. Seeking equality with men on all issues, they want an equal say in establishing how often the couple has sex. . . .

Some wives feel that husbands who insist on controlling the relationship do so out of insecurity. These men do not allow their spouses to take over the smallest area of male territory. Folk wisdom tells these wives to tread lightly on their husband's egos. In our interviews, we heard from wives that when their husbands were having trouble at work or in some other area of their lives, the wives were more timid about making sexual advances. We think husbands become more proprietary about male prerogatives when other sources of prestige and power are disturbed.

This is an understandable pattern; men have traditionally had the right of sexual access to their wives. This right was even written into religious and civil law, and women were expected to be sexually available as part of their duty. But if men had the right to ask for—and expect—sex, they also had the *duty* to initiate it. To this day, men take this prescription very seriously. They often become angry when they ask for sex and their partners refuse. And they also feel guilty when they do not fulfill their duty to initiate sex.

From the interviews, we see that wives know implicitly when circumstances have made their husbands less secure; in turn they know they must be careful to reinforce their husbands' need to be in control. They frequently remark upon the delicacy of the issue of who starts sex. The inhibitions these women face are complex. They do not want to usurp what they know are historic male prerogatives and they fear bruising the male ego. Rita gave us a sense of the dilemma she faces. She is thirty-three, a caterer, and has been married to Angelo, thirty-eight, an out-of-work manager, for only a year. Although their relationship has a great degree of conflict, they express a strong commitment to each other. A major source of trouble is sex. They are both "very physical people," but Rita still feels she has to handle sexual matters very gingerly.

Sex went from all the time to once a week or twice a week after three or four months. I became a given in his life and so he is no longer overwhelmed, and therefore his problems with business and with the apartment overwhelm him more. Whereas I think I have a greater capacity to separate things and say, "That's all back there."

He tries to be very affectionate with me. The difficulty is that when he gets out of bed to watch a late movie, I feel totally abandoned. He doesn't feel this way. I suppose if I was the one to get out of bed for a late movie I wouldn't feel that way either. But it never is me. I wouldn't leave a bed to watch a late movie.

I really don't know how to deal with it. At first, I felt honesty was everything. But now, I don't know. . . . There is this friend of mine and there is one thing she said: "Don't ever tell a man you are sexually displeased.

READINGS–*continued*

Manipulate it the next time it comes up or say, sweetly, what you want." But I don't have that sweetness capacity. But she says that men's egos are frail. They can't deal with [honesty]. And I don't know if she's right or wrong.

Because of her concern for Angelo's feelings, Rita neither discusses sex nor feels she can initiate it. The matter is talked about in coded ways. This is frequently the way couples discuss the "undiscussable." But when it does come up, we see that both partners measure themselves against the traditions of male and female conduct. The following dialogue—their response to our asking what gives the most satisfaction in the relationship—is a prime example:

ANGELO: If I was going to answer for you, what would I say?

RITA: Yes.

ANGELO: Sex, for you. Not for me. It would be the time we spend together.

RITA: I'm just an animal.

ANGELO: That's it.

RITA: Thank you.

ANGELO: You're after my body. The first minute I walk through the door.

RITA: That's true, but it doesn't mean it's the *most* rewarding thing in the relationship.

ANGELO: [He snickers, as if to say, "Oh, yeah?"]

Comments like these in their interview with us were the closest this couple could come to an open discussion of their sexual needs and Rita's role as sexual aggressor. It is clear that Angelo's words serve as both reproach and warning: They remind Rita what is—and what is not—"appropriate" behavior for a wife in the bedroom. . . .

As sexually egalitarian as the cohabiting woman can be, she, too, is careful about making requests for sex. Franklin and Cassie have been living together for a little more than a year. Both are nineteen, and Franklin works part time in a cannery. He has strong feelings about sex:

I have this design in my head for what is going to happen and I don't want it messed up. . . . We were in bed and she was saying, "Do this lighter," or "Do this softer," and I just told her that I was making love to her and she was going to have to let me do it my own way. . . . You don't want to feel bossed around. . . . You don't want to be feeling like a machine.

Even if a male cohabitor encourages his partner to be sexually aggressive, she may still have to be cautious. Ron is thirty-seven, a production manager in graphic arts, and Trish is twenty-eight, a lawyer. They have lived together for

two years in an uncertain relationship. Ron feels that Trish hesitates to initiate sex because she is insecure.

I initiate most of the time, the reason being she has a real hang-up about being rejected sexually. If she catches me in a mood when I'm not interested, she's terribly hurt, and so as a result, she doesn't start anything.

Trish has another explanation:

It is sort of an issue in that I don't initiate sex. I would always wait for him. And finally he said, "Look, I'm not going to initiate sex all the time," and I would give him the argument: "Oh, men say they want women to initiate sex, but really when it happens they're, like, 'I have a headache tonight, honey.'" So in my mind there was a reason not to initiate it because it threatened him. Even now I'm perfectly willing to say, in a joking sort of way: "Do you want to fool around tonight?" Almost like we make fun of it. And that's to ease my feeling about the fact that if I were really making a serious sexual advance, I think it would bother him.

Another couple who live together, Bill and Christina, aged twenty-eight and twenty-two, do not share equally in the task of starting sex—but for a very different reason. Their problems do not arise out of fear of rejection, but have a lot to do with something we hear about more often from young cohabiting women than from young wives: too little sex and what to do about it. When the man always takes the lead, his sexual appetite is the only one that has to be directly satisfied (although he may feel it his duty to suggest sex because of what he perceives to be his partner's need). Part of the male role means living up to the image of a man with a substantial sexual appetite, certainly greater than his female partner's. This image is unlikely to be challenged when he is the sole initiator, even though his partner's fulfillment may not be achieved. As the woman initiates more, the issue of her having the bigger appetite emerges and with it a challenge to the man's sense of worth. . . .

Saying no to men when they ask for sex is one of the rights of women, partly because of the image society has ascribed to them of being the "less sexual sex." When a woman refuses sex, a man can interpret it as a sign of her smaller appetite, not a rejection of him. When a woman takes the initiative, she wants her partner to be glad she asked and have him eager to oblige. If he refuses, she is likely to think he is uninterested in *her* rather than uninterested in having sex. A woman who has been living with a man for ten years told us:

He has a wall that he puts up that I feel like I can't

READINGS–*continued*

penetrate. Sexually I can't even attempt to because I feel so vulnerable about it. So if he backs off in a little bit of a way, it affects our relationship. I feel rejected very easily and that doesn't help.

It is clear that both married and cohabiting couples share many of the same strains over who initiates sex. Problems arise because these couples feel restricted in what they are allowed to do by virtue of their being men and women.

Women and the Abortion Controversy
KRISTIN LUKER, *FAMILY PLANNING PERSPECTIVES*

In this excerpt, Kristin Luker argues that female prochoice and prolife activists hold different world views regarding sex roles and sex. What are these separate world views? With which do you most agree? Is there a relationship between your world view and your views concerning abortion? (For the pros and cons of abortion, see Marshner, 1985, Balis, 1985, and Caldwell and Solomon, 1985.)

Women (and to a lesser extent male) activists are separated by far more than their values on abortion. Beliefs about abortion, as many of them noted, are simply the "tip of the iceberg." The two sides have very little in common in the way they look at the world, and this is particularly true with regard to the critical issues of gender, sex and parenthood. The views on abortion of each side are intimately tied to, and deeply reinforced by, their views on these other areas of life. Even if the abortion issue had not mobilized them on opposite sides of the barricades, they would have been opponents on a wide variety of issues.

With respect to gender, for example, prolife activists believe that men and women are intrinsically different, and that this is both a cause and a product of the fact that they have different "natural" roles in life. Here are some representative comments from the interviews:

The women's lib thing comes in, too. They've got a lot of good ideas, but their whole thing ran off so far from it. How can they not see that men and women are different? Men and women were created differently, and were meant to complement each other, and when you get away from our proper roles as such, you start obscuring them. That's another part of the confusion going on now; people don't know where they stand, they don't know how to act, they don't know where they're coming from, so your psychiatrists' couches are filled with lost souls, with people who have gradually been led into confusion and don't even know it.

Men, the prolife activists believe, are best suited to the public world of work, and women to the private world of rearing children, managing homes and caring for husbands. Most prolife activists believe that the raising of children is the most fulfilling work women can have. They subscribe quite strongly to the traditional belief that women should be wives and mothers *first*. Mothering, in their view, is so demanding that it is a full-time job, and any woman who cannot commit herself fully to it should avoid it entirely. Moreover, they believe that the kinds of emotional sets called for in the larger world are at odds with those needed at home:

When you start competing in the marketplace for what you can do and how you can get one-up or whatever, then I think we get into problems. It's harder to come down off that plane [of activity] and come home to a life where everything is quite mundane, and the children are way beneath you. It's hard to change from such a height to such a depth in a short time, and it becomes more and more difficult, I would think, as time goes on, to relate to both planes.

Prolife activists see the world divided into two spheres—public and private life—and each sex has an appropriate, natural and satisfying place in his or her own sphere. In this view, everyone loses when traditional roles are lost. Men lose the nurturing that women offer, the nurturing that gently encourages them to give up their potentially destructive and aggressive urges. Women lose the protection and cherishing that men offer. And children lose full-time loving by at least one parent, as well as clear models for their own futures.

Prochoice activists reject this notion of separate spheres. They believe that men and women are fundamentally equal, by which they mean substantially similar, at least as regards rights and responsibilities. As a result, they see women's reproductive and family roles not as a natural niche, but as a potential barrier to full equality. So long as society is organized to maintain motherhood as an involuntary activity, they argue, "women's sphere" connotes a potentially low-status, unrewarded role to which women can be relegated at any time.

I just feel that one of the main reasons women have been in a secondary position culturally is because of the natural way things happen. Women would bear children because they had no way to prevent it, except by having no sexual involvement. And that was not practical down through the years; so without knowing what to do to prevent it, women would continually have children. And then if they were the ones bearing the child, nursing the child, it just made sense for them to be the ones to rear

READINGS–*continued*

the child. I think that was the natural order. When we advanced and found that we could control our reproduction, we could choose the size of our families, or whether we wanted families. But that changed the whole role of women in society. . . . It allowed us to be more than just the bearers of children, the homemakers. That's not to say that we shouldn't continue in that role. It's a good role, but it's not the only role for women.

These different views about the intrinsic nature of men and women in turn help to shape how the two sides view sexuality. For the prolife people we talked to, the primary purpose of sexuality is procreation:

You're not just given arms and legs for no purpose. There must be some cause for sex, and you begin to think, well, it must be for procreation ultimately, and certainly procreation in addition to fostering a loving relationship with your spouse.

It is not surprising, given this commitment to the procreative dimension of sexuality, that the prolife activists in this study are opposed to most contraceptives. Although they are careful to point out that the prolife movement is officially neutral on the topic, most of the activists are confident that any law outlawing abortion would also outlaw the pill and the IUD, a result that they favor.

I think it's quite clear that the IUD is an abortifacient 100 percent of the time and the pill is sometimes an abortifacient—it's hard to know just when, so I think we need to treat it as an abortifacient.

Moreover, a substantial number of prolife activists use periodic abstinence, or natural family planning, as their only form of fertility control, rejecting other methods of contraception on moral and social grounds.

Well, you know the natural family planning books make a big thing out of how affection should be shown during the period of abstaining, and how this can bring you closer together than you might otherwise be. It would be easy to fall into a mechanical view of the spouse if you were to use a mechanical means of contraception. You have a better buttress if you use a natural means.

Because prolife activists regard the procreative dimension of sex as the most valuable, when they do use natural family planning, they use it to time the arrival of children, rather than to foreclose entirely the possibility of having them. For them, the fact that the method may not be highly effective in preventing pregnancy is a plus, not a minus:

The frame of mind in which you know there might be a conception in the midst of the sex act is quite different

from that in which you know that there could not be a conception. . . . I don't think that people who are constantly using physical, chemical means of contraception ever really experience the sex act in all of its beauty.

Thus, the one thing family planners commonly assume that everyone wants from a contraceptive—that it be 100 percent effective and reliable—is precisely what prolife people do *not* want from their chosen method of fertility control. And, as is so often the case, the attitudes that prolife activists hold toward contraception are intimately tied to the realities of their lives. Since prolife men and women believe in, and live in, a world of separate spheres where each sex has its appropriate task, for them to accept contraception (and by extension, abortion) would devalue the one secure resource prolife women have—the private world of home and hearth. This would be disastrous not only in terms of status but also in terms of meaning. For prolife men and women to accept highly effective contraception, which symbolically and actually subordinates the role of children in the family to other needs and goals, would be to take away the meaning from at least one partner's life. Contraception, therefore, which sidelines the reproductive capacities of men and women, is both useless and threatening to prolife people. Moreover, if positive values about fertility and family are not essential to a marriage, they ask, what support does a traditional marriage have in times of stress?

These views about gender roles and the purpose of sexuality come together to shape attitudes toward premarital sex, particularly among teenagers.* People who feel that sex should be procreative find premarital sexuality disturbing. Since, for them, the purpose of sex is procreation (or at the least requires a willingness to be "open to a new life"), people who are sexually active before marriage are by definition not actively seeking procreation: and in the case of teenagers, they are seldom financially and emotionally prepared to become parents. So for prolife people, premarital sex is both morally and socially wrong. Although prolife people agree that teenage pregnancy poses a very real problem in the United States today, they feel that the availability of contraception is what encourages teenagers to have sex in the first place, so that sex education and contraception only add fuel to the fire:

---

*People interviewed in this study tended to use the terms teenage sex and premarital sex interchangeably. But teenage premarital sex represents the worst of both worlds for most prolife people. In their view, teenagers should not be having sex because they are not married and are too young even to contemplate marriage seriously.

READINGS–*continued*

Planned Parenthood . . . it seems so logical—we've got all of these problems here, and if we just do sex education and contraceptives and everything, we'll solve all of them. It's kind of like two people coming to a fire. One says, "Let's put this fire out by throwing water on it." The other says, "Oh, no, we always did it that way. I've got something better, it's called gasoline, and it's *cooler* than water." Well, there's a term that's being overlooked, and that term is responsibility—caring, real honest-to-God caring for other people.

On all of these dimensions, prochoice attitudes are very different. For example, prochoice people in this study focus on the emotional aspects of sexuality—what our 19th century ancestors called amative sex—rather than on the procreative aspects. Prochoice people, therefore, value sex as an end in itself rather than as a means to procreation. For much of a lifetime, they argue, the main purpose of sex is not to produce children but to afford pleasure, human contact and, perhaps most important, intimacy. In their view, too exclusive a focus on the procreative function of sexuality leads to social control of sexuality, and, in turn, what they call sex-negative values. When prochoice people speak of sex-negative values, they mean values that prevent people from talking openly about sex, and thinking of sex as something to be enjoyed for its own sake, but that lead them to treat budding childhood sexuality—masturbation and adolescent flirtation—harshly.

Such harsh and negative treatment of sex makes sense, of course, if a community believes strongly that it is the only way to control the production of children and, in particular, the production of children born out of wedlock. But prochoice activists, in part because of their faith in the ability of humans to use reason to change the environment, believe that there are better ways to control the consequences of sexuality than to repress it and, in turn, to keep close control over women. As a result, prochoice people see contraception as a social good. In their view, the point of sexuality is intimacy; but since such closeness requires trust, familiarity and security, the establishment of intimacy takes practice. As a result, contraception, which allows people to focus on the *emotional* aspects of sex without worrying about its procreative aspects, is a social good.

For virtually all of the prochoice people in this study, contraception is not a moral issue. While they do have some pragmatic concerns about contraceptive methods—how unpleasant or how unsafe some are—contraceptive use in itself has no moral connotations. A good contraceptive method, from the prochoice point of view, is one which is safe, undistracting and pleasant to use—in short, one

which enhances the intimacy available during sex, rather than one which detracts from it.

What is perhaps surprising to those unfamiliar with the issue is that prochoice people do have one moral concern about an aspect of birth control. With very few exceptions, the prochoice people interviewed do not accept abortion as a routine method of fertility control:

> I take the idea of ending the life of the fetus very, very gravely. . . . That doesn't in any way diminish my conviction that a woman has the right to do it, but I become distressed when people regard pregnancy lightly and ignore the spiritual significance of a pregnancy.

A great many prochoice people in this study, particularly those active in helping women obtain abortions, find multiple abortions morally troubling. Some of them even volunteer the information that they feel like personal failures when a woman comes back to them for a repeat abortion. At first glance, this reaction would appear to be illogical. If the first abortion is a morally acceptable act, why isn't the second or the fifth abortion equally moral?

Prochoice opposition to abortion as a routine method of birth control is based on complex and subtle moral reasoning. For most prochoice people, personhood does not exist at conception, but it does develop at some later time. The prochoice view of personhood is therefore a *gradualist* one. A fetus may not be fully a person until it is viable, but it does have potential rights at all times, and these rights increase in moral weight as the pregnancy continues. Prochoice people tend to argue that the potential rights of the embryo or fetus at times must be sacrified to the actual rights of the woman involved. But a woman who carelessly or capriciously conceives when she has the alternative of preventing pregnancy by the use of birth control is seen by prochoice activists as unjustifiably usurping the potential rights of the embryo by trivializing them.

Thus, for prochoice people, opposition to abortion as a routine form of fertility control stems from both the gradualist and contextual moral reasoning outlined above. A first abortion represents presumably the lesser of two evils, because the abortion of an embryo or fetus is seen as less morally wrong than to bring a child into the world whom the woman cannot properly raise. Since most women are offered a contraceptive method after an abortion, every abortion after the first represents a case where a woman had the option of avoiding pregnancy and did not do so; in most cases, prochoice people tend to find that kind of carelessness morally wrong.

CHAPTER 9

Pregnancy
and
Childbirth

PREVIEW

To gain a sense of what you already know about the material covered in this chapter, answer "true" or "false" to the statements below. You will find the answers as you read the chapter.

1. One out of every six American couples is infertile. True or false?
2. Fertility problems are often emotional in origin. True or false?
3. Untreated venereal disease is a primary cause of infertility in women. True or false?
4. Using newly discovered techniques, it is possible to select the sex of your child with a high degree of accuracy. True or false?
5. A moderate amount of alcohol consumption does not affect the fetus. True or false?
6. A woman with genital herpes must deliver her baby by cesarean section. True or false?
7. The United States has a high rate of infant mortality compared with other industrialized nations. True or false?
8. One out of every five births is by cesarean section. True or false?
9. Medically supervised home births have been found to be safer than hospital births. True or false?
10. Bottle feeding with an appropriate formula is superior to breastfeeding. True or false?

Outline

Pregnancy and childbirth are among the most important experiences in human life. In the long run they ensure the continuation of human life; more immediately, they transform women and men into mothers and fathers and create families—the basic unit of society. Some of society's most fundamental roles and institutions are formed by or reflected in the experience of childbirth. In this chapter we view pregnancy and childbirth not only as biological processes but as social processes as well. Childbirth is a biological fact, but where and how childbirth takes place are determined by society. We look at childbirth both in the hospital and at home and examine traditional and alternative birth practices. First, we look at the problem of infertility and its treatment and at adoption as an alternative to childlessness.

☐ INFERTILITY

Infertility is generally defined as the inability to conceive a child after trying for a year or more. Until recently, the problem of infertility attracted little public attention. In the last few years, however, a large number of couples who have deferred pregnancy because of career plans or later marriages have discovered they are infertile; they are unable to conceive or the woman is unable to carry a pregnancy to live birth (see Clark et al., 1982; Wallis, 1984). Such couples have not previously tested their fertility. As more of them try to have children, statistics are indicating that infertility is reaching "epidemic" proportions. Its incidence has tripled in the past twenty years. Approximately one in six American married couples are involuntarily childless; another 10 percent have fewer children than they want. This amounts to about ten million Americans (Menning, 1977). Every year more than a million American couples seek help for infertility.

Emotional Responses to Infertility

Many people look forward to becoming parents when they marry; they may have chosen each other partly on the basis of their qualities as potential parents. To some couples, having a child together is a symbol of the completeness of their relationship. By the time an infertile couple seek medical advice, they may have already experienced a crisis in confronting the possibility of not being able to become parents. After seeking help, childless couples typically go through three phases, according to Miriam Mazor (1979):

The first phase revolves around the injury to the self implicit in the situation. Patients are preoccupied with the infertility study and with formulating theories about why it is happening to them, what they have done wrong, why they are so defective and bad that they are denied something the rest of the world takes for granted. The second phase occurs when treatment is unsuccessful; it involves mourning the loss of the children the partner will never bear and an intense examination of what parenthood means to them as individuals, as a couple, and as members of families and of society. Finally, in the third phase, they must come to terms with the outcome of the study: they must make some kind of decision about their future, whether to pursue plans for adoption or for donor insemination or to adjust to childlessness and go on with life.

If the male is the infertile partner, treatment may not be successful. If the woman is infertile, there may be a better chance of restoring fertility, depending on the cause. Alternatives include artificial insemination if the man is infertile and in vitro fertilization if the woman is infertile because of blocked fallopian tubes (Figure 9–1). Advances in reproductive technology have given hope to couples who can afford such services; they have also raised new ethical questions.

> Ancient man knew nothing of the sperm and the ovum. This knowledge belongs to the era of the microscope. For him the seminal fluid was the substance that grew into the child—drawing sustenance from the womb of the pregnant woman, absorbing the blood that issued periodically from the womb when there was no child there. The woman's body nurtured the seed, as the soil nurtured the grain of rice. But the seed was the man's seed and the child was the man's child. It was his ongoing spirit, his continuing life.
>
> DAVID MACE and VERA MACE, *MARRIAGE: EAST AND WEST*

Female Infertility

The leading cause of female infertility is blocked fallopian tubes. This may be the result of a number of factors, including pelvic inflammatory disease (PID), septic abortions, and abdominal surgery. About 40 percent of infertile women have such physical problems. The second leading cause of infertility in women is endometriosis; it is sometimes called the "career woman's disease" because it is most prevalent in women aged thirty and over, many of whom have postponed childbirth. In this disease uterine tissue grows outside the uterus, often appearing on the ovaries, fallopian tubes (where it may also block the tubes), and in the abdominal cavity. In its most severe form it may cause painful menstruation and intercourse, but most women with endometriosis are unaware they have it. Why endometriosis causes infertility (except when it blocks the fallopian tubes) is not known (Kolata, 1979). In addition to physical causes, there may be hormonal reasons that a woman is unable to conceive. As many as 20 percent of women with infertility problems have hormonal abnormalities (Kolata, 1979). Finally immunological causes may be present, the most important of which is the production of sperm antibodies by the woman. For some unknown reason, the woman is allergic to her partner's sperm, and her immunological system produces antibodies to destroy them.

Infertility appears to be an increasing problem for women. Toxic chemicals threaten a woman's reproductive capacity. Smoking has been shown to reduce fertility in women (Baird and Wilcox, 1985). Increasing evidence indicates that the daughters of DES mothers (women who were prescribed diethylstilbestrol to increase their fertility) have a significantly higher infertility rate, although studies remain somewhat contradictory. As the current epidemics of chlamydia and gonorrhea continue, more and more women risk contracting pelvic inflammatory disease as a consequence (Strong and Reynolds, 1982). (See Resource Center for more information on sexually transmitted diseases and their treatment.) IUDs have also been implicated in the development of PID. PID may leave a woman's fallopian tubes scarred, preventing the ova from reaching the uterus. Abortions also put women at higher risk of sterility if more than one has been performed. One abortion does not affect a woman's reproductive capabilities, but her chances of conceiving diminish proportionally to the number of abortions she has had after her first one.

Male Infertility

The primary causes of male infertility are low sperm count, lack of sperm motility (ability to move spontaneously), or blocked passageways (Lock and Dworkin, 1981). As with women, environmental factors may contribute to infertility. Increasing evidence suggests that toxic chemicals are responsible for decreased sperm counts in men and that smoking may produce reduced sperm counts or abnormal sperm (Evans, 1981). Large doses of marijuana have a similar effect, which is reversed when marijuana smoking is stopped (Castleman, 1981). Sons of DES mothers may have increased sperm abnormalities and fertility problems. Too much hot tubbing may temporarily reduce the sperm count in men; couples trying to conceive may want to stay out of their hot tubs for a while (Paulson, 1980). A fairly common problem among men is the presence of a varicose vein above the testicle, called a *varicocele*, which apparently damages the testicle. It may be surgically removed, but unless the man has a fairly good sperm count to begin with, his fertility may not improve.

Treatment of Infertility

Almost without exception, fertility problems are physical, not emotional (despite myths to the contrary that often prevent infertile couples from seeking medical treatment). The two most popular myths are that anxiety over becoming pregnant leads to infertility and that if an infertile couple adopts a child, the couple will be able to conceive a child on their own (Kolata, 1979). Neither has any basis in medical fact.

What did you look like before you were conceived?

ZEN KOAN (RIDDLE)

Adequate treatment for infertility requires that both the man and woman be examined medically to determine whether the problem is related to one individual or to both. The woman is judged infertile in about half the cases. Studies have shown that the man is the primary cause of infertility in 30 to 40 percent of infertile couples and a contributing cause in 10 to 20 percent (Brody, 1985; Culverwell, 1984). The success rate for solving fertility problems has risen from 50 percent in the 1960s to 70 percent today. Many kinds of diagnostic tests are available from gynecologists, urologists, or endocrinologists. (The Resource Center section of this book has information on predicting ovulation; it also has the names and addresses of organizations that will give you further information on infertility.)

All-Round "Typical Boy"

Sturdy, durable child comes in choice of colors, including blue-eyed blond (shown here) and various ethnic models (please specify when ordering). Nicely behaved with just that right touch of boyish mischief. Will do well in all sports. Stands up well under frequent washing. Clothing, baseball bat not included. Available in Normal, Very Normal and Supernormal sizes.
4891W All-Round "Typical Boy," $5,200 per year.

Academic Achiever

Meets highest standards for professional advancement. Developed to be a high-performance, hard-charging model that tests well (over 95th percentile). Available in choice of sex, as well as many colors and sizes.
8194E Academic Achiever, $7,200 per year (price does not include school or college tuition).

Our Latest Model Girl

Certified free of math anxiety, this model possesses traditional virtues but is adaptable to changing roles. Equally at home on soccer field and in schoolroom. Mary Lou Retton Gymnast model also available. Wide choice of colors, sizes.
94188 Our Latest Model Girl, $5,200 per year.

L.L.Gene's Own Super-tall

Our original model, the most copied genetic variation in the world, has been in our line since 1985. You'll find it on basketball courts everywhere. Available in many colors, including Larry Bird Blond (shown here), and in our exclusive Growthspurt© model.
4189T L.L.Gene's Own Super-tall, $8,200 per year.

The "L. L. Gene" catalogue presents a humorous view of reproductive technology.

Artificial Insemination

When childlessness is the result of male infertility or a genetically transmitted disease carried by the male, some couples may try *artificial insemination*. Single women who want children but who have not found an appropriate partner or who wish to avoid emotional entanglements have also made use of this technique, as have lesbian couples. During ovulation, semen is deposited by syringe near the cervical opening. The semen may come from the partner; if he has a low sperm count, several collections of semen may be taken and frozen, then collectively deposited in the woman's vagina, improving the odds of conception. If he had a vasectomy earlier, he may have had the semen frozen and stored in a sperm bank. If the husband is sterile or has a genetically transferable disorder, artificial insemination by donor (AID) may be used. Anonymous donors—often medical students—are paid nominal amounts for their deposits of semen, which may be used at once or frozen. Artificial insemination tends to produce males rather than females; in the general population, about 51 percent children born are male, but this figure reaches almost 60 percent when conception is achieved artificially. Artificial insemination has a success rate of about 60 percent for infertile couples.

FEATURE

The Ethics of Reproductive Technology

The last twenty years have witnessed an explosion of scientific and technological developments in the area of reproduction. In the wake of this explosion, we are left with legal, moral, and ethical questions unlike any that humanity has had to face before; many of these questions have no apparent answer but only beget more questions.

The infertility "epidemic" that appears to have struck the United States has created opportunities for scientific research and economic opportunism. The paramount value that many of us place on fertility—equating it with maturity, creativity, productivity, accomplishment, and the essence of our maleness or femaleness—has fueled the engine of reproductive technology. The techniques and technologies developed to achieve conception include artificial insemination (AI) and the establishment of sperm banks, in vitro fertilization (IVF) (including embryo freezing), and surrogate motherhood (the hiring of a woman to "carry" a couple's child, usually involving AI by the father), and will

likely soon include human embryo transplants.

Sex preselection techniques are also a subject of much interest, although consistently reliable methods for assuring you the gender of your choice do not yet exist. (Research indicates that the odds in favor of a particular sex may be slightly swayed one way or the other.)

In addition to the desire to bear children, the desire to bear *healthy* (perfect?) children has encouraged diagnostic technologies such as ultrasonagraphy, which takes pictures of the fetus by bouncing sound waves off it, amniocentesis, and a variety of other methods that involve sampling bits of fetal and maternal tissues and fluids. If a fetus is determined to be defective, it may be carried to term, aborted, or in rare but increasing instances, surgically treated while still in the womb. The implementation of gene therapy, in which defective enzymes in the genes of embryos are replaced by normal ones, is considered an exciting frontier of reproductive medicine (Lyon, 1985).

Most doctors inseminate women twice during their cycles; on the average, women who become pregnant have received inseminations over a period of 3.7 months (Curie-Cohen, 1979). The process of artificially collecting, storing, and depositing sufficient viable sperm into a woman's uterus is difficult. Furthermore, when frozen sperm is used, only about 15 percent of the sperm survive freezing sufficiently to initiate conception. As a result, sperm freezing preceding vasectomy is not a dependable method for ensuring parenthood at a later date. There is also growing criticism that donors are not adequately screened for possible genetic defects and that current AID practices are designed to protect the practitioners and donors rather than the recipients and their children (Annas, 1981). In the United States, probably more than 20,000 babies a year are conceived by donor insemination (Fromer, 1983).

Adoption

Adoption is a traditionally acceptable alternative to pregnancy for infertile couples. In recent years many Americans—married and single, childless or with children— have been choosing to adopt for other reasons as well. (See the reading, "Infertility

The desire to have healthy, happy, beautiful children is understandable, basic, and human. But the questions of the lengths to which we are willing to go, the risks we are willing to take, and the costs we are prepared to bear to achieve this end need to be carefully examined. Some of the crucial ethical questions raised are the following:

- How invasive is the technique in question? What is the probability of injury to the mother and to the fetus?
- What are the legal rights and responsibilities of *all* the parties involved (parents, donors, surrogates, child, practitioner, storage facility)? What are the embryo's legal rights?
- Who is profiting by the technology (scientists, physicians, business people, donors, parents)? Who is taking the greatest risks? How great are the costs and who is paying them?
- What are the long-range goals of reproductive technology? Are we trying to develop the perfect human being? Are we "playing God"? How might this knowledge be abused?

- When does human life begin and when, if ever, does a human being have the right to take that life? For example, is it acceptable to have an abortion if your fetus is discovered to be of the "wrong" sex? (In China female fetuses are often aborted; "gender abortions" are also performed in this country.) What if the fetus has a severe deformity or major brain damage? What if the fetus has a minor disability (such as a deformed limb)? What if the pregnancy is accidental and unwanted? What if the pregnancy is the result of rape or incest?
- What is the relation between fertility and fulfillment? Are our own values congruent with reality, given the world's population problems? Are there (or can there be) viable alternatives to conceiving or bearing a child (adoption, foster parenting, extended or communal families, working with children, other creative work)?

For further discussion of these issues, see Corea, 1985; Fromer, 1983; Lyon, 1985.

and Adoption," by Abby Sylviachild). They may have concerns about overpopulation and the number of homeless children in the world. They may wish to provide families for older or disabled children. Although tens of thousands of parents and potential parents are currently waiting to adopt, there is a shortage of available healthy babies in this country. In 1970 the number of adoptions per year peaked at 175,000; today the number has declined to about 100,000 owing to more effective birth control and an increase in the number of single mothers who choose to keep their children. The wait for a healthy infant or toddler averages one to five years (Kennedy, 1984).

Foreign adoptions are increasingly favored because the process takes relatively less time, although it may involve considerably greater expense than domestic adoptions arranged through public agencies. As of 1982, South Korea and India (major sources of children) have severely limited the number of available children, causing greater numbers of adoptive families to look to Latin America, where the waiting period is one to two years (Colamosca, 1983; Kennedy, 1984). Because of the delays and frustrations of standard adoptions, many couples obtain children through the illegal "baby black market" where, although the paperwork and red tape are minimal, a healthy, white infant may cost as much as $50,000 (Kennedy, 1984).

Figure 9–1

New Ways to Make Babies

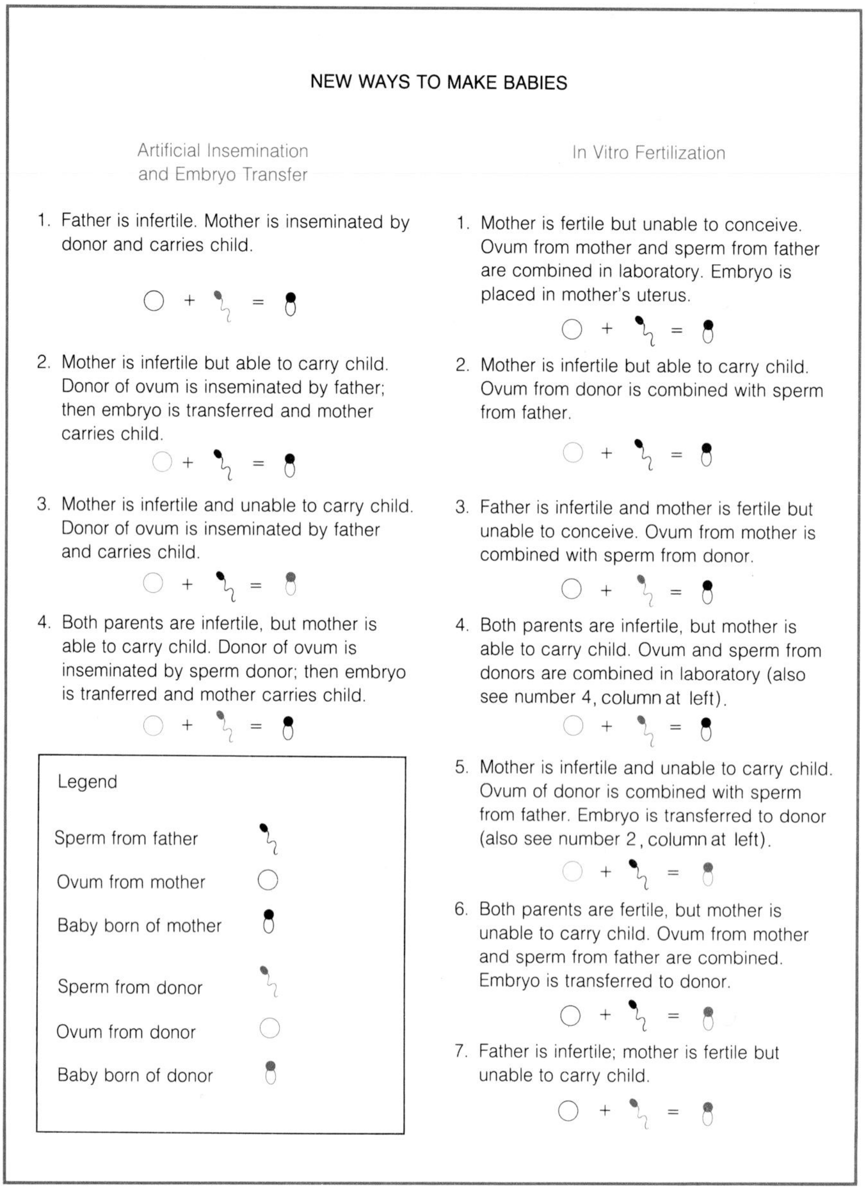

NEW WAYS TO MAKE BABIES

Artificial Insemination and Embryo Transfer | In Vitro Fertilization

1. Father is infertile. Mother is inseminated by donor and carries child.

2. Mother is infertile but able to carry child. Donor of ovum is inseminated by father; then embryo is transferred and mother carries child.

3. Mother is infertile and unable to carry child. Donor of ovum is inseminated by father and carries child.

4. Both parents are infertile, but mother is able to carry child. Donor of ovum is inseminated by sperm donor; then embryo is tranferred and mother carries child.

Legend

Sperm from father

Ovum from mother

Baby born of mother

Sperm from donor

Ovum from donor

Baby born of donor

1. Mother is fertile but unable to conceive. Ovum from mother and sperm from father are combined in laboratory. Embryo is placed in mother's uterus.

2. Mother is infertile but able to carry child. Ovum from donor is combined with sperm from father.

3. Father is infertile and mother is fertile but unable to conceive. Ovum from mother is combined with sperm from donor.

4. Both parents are infertile, but mother is able to carry child. Ovum and sperm from donors are combined in laboratory (also see number 4, column at left).

5. Mother is infertile and unable to carry child. Ovum of donor is combined with sperm from father. Embryo is transferred to donor (also see number 2, column at left).

6. Both parents are fertile, but mother is unable to carry child. Ovum from mother and sperm from father are combined. Embryo is transferred to donor.

7. Father is infertile; mother is fertile but unable to carry child.

The principal issues of concern in adoption include the rights of the biological mother (or parents), the expectations of the adoptive parents, the question of whether to tell the child of the adoption, and the right of the child to know the identity of the biological parents (Lifton, 1975, 1979). Several states have now enacted laws allowing adult adoptees to get copies of their original birth certificates. Others have set up voluntary registries to assist adoptees and biological parents who wish to meet each other.

Despite the unique problems and stresses of acquiring and raising an adopted child, Laurie M. Flynn, director of the North American Council on Adoptable Children, has stated, "Adoptive parents are finding that parenthood is so much more

Adoption provides unique challenges and rewards to parents who reach out to share their lives with children in need. Foreign adoptions are increasingly favored in the United States today. This family has adopted children from the United States, Korea, and Columbia.

than giving birth. It is the joy that comes from sharing their lives with a needy child" (Kennedy, 1982; also see Riben, 1983). (See Resource Center for agencies to contact about adoptions.)

☐ PREGNANCY TESTS

Chemical tests designed to detect the presence of *human chorionic gonadotropin* (HCG), a hormone secreted by the placenta, usually determine pregnancy approximately two weeks following a missed (or spotty) menstrual period. In the *agglutination test* a drop of the woman's urine causes a test solution to coagulate if she is not pregnant; if she is pregnant the solution will become smooth and milky in consistency. Home pregnancy tests to detect HCG may be purchased in most drugstores. The directions must be followed closely. Although such tests predict pregnancy with better than 95 percent accuracy, no absolute certainty exists until fetal heartbeats and movements can be detected.

The first reliable physical sign of pregnancy can be distinguished about four weeks after a woman misses her period. By this time, changes in the woman's cervix and pelvis become apparent during a pelvic examination. *Hegar's sign*—a softening of the uterus just above the cervix, which can be felt through the vagina—is particularly useful to the examiner. A slight purple hue colors the minor vaginal lips; the cervix also takes on a purple color rather than its usual pink.

Predicting the Date of Birth

Everyone wants to know when his or her baby's going to be born. It is fairly simple to figure out the date: add seven days to the first day of the last menstrual period. Then subtract three months and add one year. For example, if a woman's last menstrual period began on July 17, 1986, add seven days (July 24). Next subtract three months (April 24). Then add one year. This gives the expected date of birth as April 24, 1987. Few births actually occur on the date predicted, but 60 percent of babies are born within five days of the predicted time.

FEATURE

Pregnancy After Age Thirty-five

As more women defer childbirth because of their careers or economic necessity, understanding what chances a woman takes in having a late pregnancy is increasingly important. The three most common difficulties are declining fertility, increased chance of birth defects, and increased incidence of miscarriage.

Around age thirty-five fertility begins to drop dramatically. Long before menopause, women begin to ovulate less frequently, although they continue to menstruate each month. These menstrual periods are longer and spottier. By the time a woman reaches forty, a quarter of her menstrual cycles are anovulatory, that is, do not produce an ovum (egg cell). By age forty-six, she may ovulate only seven times a year. Furthermore, the woman may be developing infertility problems, such as endometriosis, without being aware of them if she has not tried to become pregnant.

A woman over thirty-five years of age is more likely to give birth to children with congenital defects (birth defects). A woman's ova, all of which are in place at birth, are subject to stress from medication, pollutants, infections, and radiation. As the eggs mature, they are more likely to develop chromosomal abnormalities, such as having one chromosome too many, which causes Down's syndrome, characterized by mental retardation as well as a characteristic physical appearance. (Men over fifty-five years also contribute to Down's syndrome in about a quarter of all cases.) There is one chance in five hundred that a woman at age twenty will have a child with a chromosomal defect. By age thirty-five, the chances reach 1 percent, but by age forty-five, the chances increase to 10 percent. Down's syndrome accounts for about a third of chromosomal defects.

Miscarriages also increase as women grow older,

☐ PSYCHOLOGICAL EFFECTS OF PREGNANCY

Since mother is not all there is to any woman, once she becomes a mother, how does a woman weave the mother into her adult self?

ANDREA EAGAN

A woman's feelings during pregnancy will vary dramatically according to who she is, how she feels about pregnancy and motherhood, whether the pregnancy was planned, whether she has a secure home situation, and many other factors. (See the reading, "A Native American Birth Story," by Marcie Rendon.) A woman's first pregnancy is especially important because, in our culture, it symbolizes her transition to maturity (Zajicek, 1981). Her feelings may be ambivalent; they will probably change over the course of the pregnancy. Sheila Kitzinger (1974) wrote about first pregnancy:

We all know that an expectant mother is emotionally vulnerable and tends to get weepy and fly off the handle about little things, and society as a whole tolerates this with a certain degree of amusement. It is usually accounted for physiologically and put down to hormone and other changes in her body. But this is by no means the whole of the story. There are enormous emotional adjustments to be made too, so that she can grow up enough to be not just a bride but a mother and to be able to be not only a wife to her husband but a mother to her children, and to tie these relationships together in such a way that they do not conflict.

The pregnant woman increasingly turns to her partner for emotional support. She may look at and experience her relationship with him more deeply and intensely.

FEATURE–*continued*

but this may not necessarily be a disadvantage; spontaneous abortions tend to occur when the fetus is defective. For example, there is a 24 percent chance of miscarriage in the last half of pregnancy if the fetus suffers from Down's syndrome; this figure is six times the rate of miscarriage for an apparently healthy fetus at this stage of pregnancy (Hook, 1978).

Recent developments in fetal screening make early diagnosis of birth defects possible in many cases. Ultrasound, amniocentesis, and alpha-fetoprotein (AFP) screening are the most common procedures. Fetal abnormalities, including neural tube disorders (such as spina bifida), Down's syndrome, Tay-Sachs disease, and other metabolic disorders can be detected with these tests. Ultrasound and AFP screening (one or a series of blood tests) are relatively simple procedures. Amniocentesis is more complex and expensive and carries a slight risk (less than 1 percent chance of miscarriage or infection) (Boston Women's Health Collective, 1984). For approximately 95 percent of women who undergo prenatal testing, the results are negative. But the results of amniocentesis and AFP screening can't be determined until approximately twenty weeks of pregnancy; consequently, if the pregnancy is terminated through abortion at this stage, the process is likely to be physically and emotionally difficult. A promising alternative to amniocentesis, recently introduced in the United States, is chorionic villus biopsy. This procedure involves removal (through the cervix) of tiny pieces of the membrane that encases the embryo; it can be performed between eight and twelve weeks of pregnancy. So far, chorionic villus biopsy is not widely available and its relative safety has not yet been determined. Before undergoing any type of prenatal testing, it is crucial for a pregnant woman to get complete and accurate information so that she may make informed decisions about which tests, if any, are appropriate to her particular situation.

Does she love him? Does he love her? Is he a source of emotional support for her? Will they assist each other in rearing the child? Will the child enhance or detract from their relationship? Will he accept his responsibilities as a father? Can they relate to each other as parents as well as partners? This is a period in which both partners must develop confidence in each other. If her partner is not supportive or if she does not have one, it is important that she find other sources of support—family, friends, women's groups—and that she not be reluctant to ask for help.

At the same time, a pregnant woman may change her relationship with her mother. In a certain sense, becoming a mother makes her the equal of her own mother. She can now lay claim to being treated as an adult. Women who have depended on their mothers tend to become more independent and assertive as their pregnancy progresses. Women who have been distant, hostile, or alienated from their own mothers begin to identify with their mothers' experience of pregnancy. This process of identification resolves many of the leftover conflicts of growing up (Bibring, 1975).

The first trimester (three months) of pregnancy may be difficult physically for the expectant mother. She may experience nausea, fatigue, and painful swelling of the breasts. She may also have fears of miscarriage or of producing a malformed child, although these fears are usually transitory. Her sexuality may undergo changes, resulting in unfamiliar needs (for more, less, or differently expressed sexual love), which may in turn cause worry, anxiety, or guilt (Strong and Reynolds, 1982; White,

If your parents didn't have any children, there's a good chance that you won't have any.

CLARENCE DAY

1982). Education about the birth process and her own body's functioning and support from partner, friends, relatives, and health-care professionals are the best antidotes to fear.

During the second trimester, most of the nausea and fatigue disappear, and a pregnant woman can feel the fetus move within her. Worries about miscarriage begin to disappear too, for the most dangerous part of fetal development has passed. The pregnant woman may now be concerned about whether her own body is growing properly: Is she gaining too much weight? Will she be able to nurse? She may wonder whether the baby's kicking is normal.

The third trimester is the time of the greatest hardships in daily living. Water retention (*edema*) is a common, painful problem during late pregnancy. Edema may cause swelling in the face, hands, ankles, and feet, but it can often be controlled by cutting down on salts and carbohydrates in the diet. If dietary changes do not help this condition, a pregnant woman should consult her physician. Her physical abilities are limited by her size and ungainliness. She may be forced to stop working (many public schools, for example, do not allow women to teach after their sixth month). A family depending on the pregnant woman's income may suffer a severe financial crunch.

The woman and her partner may become increasingly concerned about childbirth—whether the labor will be easy or hard, whether the doctor or midwife will be able to deliver the baby without complications. Many women experience periods of depression in the month preceding their delivery. They are uncomfortable and im-

During pregnancy, both partners need to develop confidence with one another. A woman without a supportive partner should seek out other sources of support—family, friends, or women's groups.

patient. They may feel physically awkward and sexually unattractive; they may feel an exhilarating sense of excitement and anticipation marked by energetic bursts of industriousness. They often feel that the fetus is a "member of the family" (Stanton, 1985).

The principal developmental tasks for the expectant mother may be summarized as follows (Valentine, 1982; also see Wolkind and Zajicek, 1981):

1. Development of an emotional attachment to the fetus
2. Differentiation of the self from the fetus
3. Acceptance and resolution of the relationship with her own mother
4. Resolution of dependency issues (generally involving parents or husband/partner).

And for the expectant father (see the reading, "When My Son Was Born," by James Webb):

1. Acceptance of the pregnancy and attachment to the fetus
2. Evaluation of practical issues such as financial responsibilities
3. Resolution of dependency issues (involving wife/partner)
4. Acceptance and resolution of the relationship with his own father.

☐ COMPLICATIONS OF PREGNANCY

Usually, pregnancy proceeds without major complications. Good nutrition is probably one of the most important factors in having a complication-free pregnancy. However, some women experience minor to serious complications, which we discuss here.

The Placenta and Harmful Substances

Substances other than nutrients may reach the developing embryo or fetus through the placenta. Whatever a woman eats or drinks is eventually received by the embryo or fetus in some proportion. Studies have linked chronic ingestion of alcohol during pregnancy to fetal alcohol syndrome (FAS), which includes congenital heart defects, defective joints, and mental retardation. About one of every 750 babies has FAS. Even moderate alcohol consumption has been shown to have a detrimental effect on birth weight ("How Much . . ." 1985). Mothers who regularly use opiates—heroin, morphine, codeine, and opium—are likely to have infants who are addicted at birth. Cigarettes also affect the unborn child. Babies born to women who smoke during pregnancy are an average of one-fourth to one-half pound lighter at birth than babies born to nonsmokers. Tetracycline must be avoided by pregnant women, who are highly susceptible to liver damage caused by this antibiotic. Furthermore, tetracycline passes through the placenta to the fetus, damaging its teeth and bones.

Although few extensive studies have been done on the subject, environmental pollution may also affect the health of the fetus. One of the most startling cases of environmental pollution occurred in Minamata, Japan, where scores of infants were born deformed as a result of their mothers' eating fish caught in mercury-contaminated water. (Dangerously high levels of mercury contamination have also been reported in water supplies in various areas of the United States.) Alcohol, tobacco, marijuana, sleeping pills, aspirin, and other drugs, as well as large quantities of caffeine-bearing food and drink (coffee, tea, colas, chocolate), should be avoided or used only with medical supervision.

Union between man and woman is a creative act and has something divine about it. . . . The object of love is a creative union with beauty on both the spiritual and physical levels.

PLATO, *THE SYMPOSIUM*

Yes—the history of man for the nine months preceding his birth would, probably, be far more interesting, and contain events of greater moment, than all the three score and ten that follow.

SAMUEL COLERIDGE

Infectious Diseases

Infectious diseases can also damage the fetus. If a woman contracts German measles (rubella) during her first three months of pregnancy, her child may be born deformed or retarded. Immunization against rubella is available, but it must be received before the woman is pregnant; otherwise the injection is as harmful to the fetus as the disease itself. Venereal disease may also damage the fetus. A woman with gonorrhea may have a child who becomes blind after passing through the infected vagina. A woman with syphilis may have a spontaneous abortion, her baby may be born dead, or it may be deformed, blind, or deaf, and may have syphilis itself. A woman with AIDS may pass the disease to the fetus.

The increasingly widespread incidence of herpes simplex II may present some hazards for the pregnant woman and her infant. These hazards, however, can be greatly minimized if certain precautions are taken. The virus may be passed to the fetus through the placenta of the pregnant woman, but only during the initial outbreak; recurrences of genital herpes are not infectious to the fetus. An outbreak of genital herpes in the mother at the time of delivery is more dangerous, especially if it is the initial outbreak. When the infant passes through the birth canal, it has a 40 to 50 percent chance of contracting the herpes virus. About half the infants infected with herpes simplex II die and many of the survivors suffer tragic brain damage or blindness. Dr. Anne Yeager (1979), head of the Stanford Perinatal Herpes Simplex Program, wrote about herpes and childbirth: "If an active, visible lesion is present at the time of delivery, a C-section should be done. If no lesion is present and the cultures are negative, a vaginal delivery can be permitted." Dr. Margaret Lynn Yonekura (quoted in "Neonatal Herpes . . ." 1984) of the University of Southern California's School of Medicine has said that many women's "fears of infecting the newborn child [with genital herpes] . . . are exaggerated. . . . Though genital herpes can be devastating to newborns, the chance of infection during birth is minimal if proper procedures are followed."

Once the baby is born, a mother who is experiencing a herpes outbreak should always wash her hands carefully and not permit contact between her hands, contaminated objects, and the baby's mucous membranes (inside of eyes, mouth, nose, penis, vagina, and rectum). If the father is infected, he should do likewise until the lesions have subsided. (See Resource Center for additional information on herpes simplex II and other sexually transmitted diseases.)

Other Complications

In *ectopic pregnancy*, which occurs in about 2 percent of all pregnancies, the fertilized egg implants itself in the fallopian tubes. Generally this occurs because the tube is obstructed, often as a result of pelvic inflammatory disease. The pregnancy will never come to term. The embryo may spontaneously abort or the embryo and placenta will continue to expand until they rupture the fallopian tube. Salpingectomy (removal of the tube) and abortion of the fetus may be necessary to save the life of the mother.

Spontaneous abortion (miscarriage) is a powerful natural selective force toward bringing healthy babies into the world. Between 10 and 25 percent of all pregnancies end in spontaneous abortion; studies indicate that at least half of all miscarriages are due to defects in the fetus. Furthermore, as many as one-third of all fertilized eggs abort before the next menstrual period is late (James, 1970). The first sign that a pregnant woman may miscarry is vaginal bleeding ("spotting"). If a woman's symptoms of pregnancy disappear and she develops pelvic cramps, she may be miscarrying. During a miscarriage, the fetus is usually expelled by uterine contractions. Most miscarriages occur between the sixth and eighth weeks of pregnancy (Welch and Herrman, 1980). Evidence is increasing that certain occupations involving exposure to chemicals increase the likelihood of spontaneous abortions (Hemminki et al., 1983; Strong and Reynolds, 1982).

Toxemia is characterized by high blood pressure and edema (fluid retention and swelling). It is not clear what causes toxemia, but it seems to be related to poor nutrition. Toxemia does not usually appear until the twentieth to twenty-fourth week of pregnancy. Immediate medical attention is imperative. A woman with toxemia in its most severe form, experiences convulsions, falls into a coma, and may die.

Prematurity or *low birth weight (LBW)* is a major complication in the third trimester of pregnancy, affecting about 7 percent of newborns (230,000 babies yearly) in the United States. The most fundamental problem of prematurity is that many of the infant's vital organs are insufficiently developed. An LBW baby usually weighs less than 5.5 pounds at birth. Most premature infants will grow normally, but many will experience disabilities. LBW infants are subject to various respiratory problems as well as infections. Feeding too is a problem because the infants may be too small to suck a breast or bottle and their swallowing mechanisms may be too underdeveloped to permit them to drink (Trotter, 1980). As premature infants get older, problems such as low intelligence, learning difficulties, poor hearing and vision, and physical awkwardness may become apparent. Although existing problems can be detected, a major task for developmental psychology is to devise a method to identify which premature infants may need special treatment (Trotter, 1980). Premature delivery is one of the greatest problems confronting obstetrics today. About half the cases are related to teenage pregnancy, smoking, poor nutrition, and poor health in the mother; the causes of the other half are unknown. Prenatal care is extremely important as a means of preventing prematurity; for this reason, the federal government's reduction or elimination of supplemental assistance for pregnant women on welfare has created alarm among a number of health professionals.

Infant Mortality

The U.S. infant mortality rate has halted its decreasing trend and seems to be stabilized at approximately 11 deaths per 1,000 births. Approximately 40,000 American babies less than one year old die each year; the infant mortality rate for blacks is almost twice that for whites. Governor Thomas H. Kean of New Jersey, chairman of the National Governors Association Committee on Human Resources, stated that infant deaths are the result of "social factors—poverty, age, race, nutrition, and substance abuse." He recommended increasing Medicaid eligibility and benefits (Pear, 1985). In some areas with high unemployment, such as Detroit and Baltimore, the infant mortality rate approaches that of underdeveloped countries (Warshaw, 1984). Since 1981 the federal government has cut pregnancy and infant care programs by 25 percent; WIC (Women, Infants, and Children) programs have been cut by one-third (Robbins, 1983). On the state level also, the current trend is to cut back on medical and health care for low-income people.

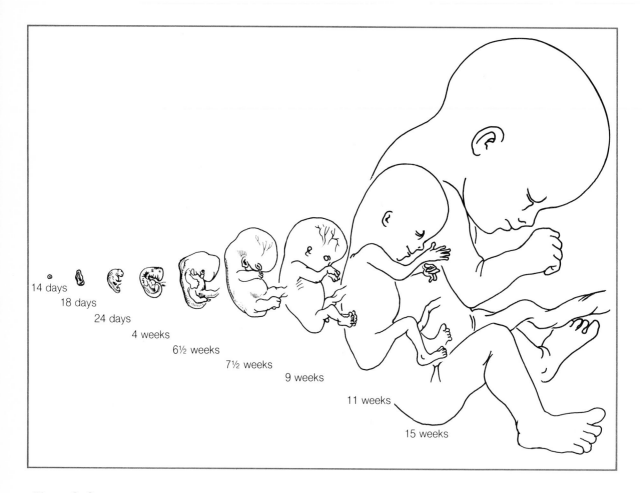

14 days
18 days
24 days
4 weeks
6½ weeks
7½ weeks
9 weeks
11 weeks
15 weeks

Figure 9–2

Embryo and Fetus Growth. Figure represents the actual sizes of the developing embryo/fetus. At four weeks, the fetus' heart is pumping blood and its digestive system is beginning to form. At eight weeks, face and features begin to form, limbs begin to show distinct divisions, bones and internal organs begin to develop. At twelve weeks, arms, hands, fingers, legs, feet and toes are fully formed and eyes are almost fully developed. At fifteen weeks, the fetus has a strong heart beat, fair digestion and active muscles. Most bones are developed; eyebrows appear. Its skin is covered with fine downy hair.

□ BIRTH

Normal Labor and Delivery

Throughout a woman's pregnancy she occasionally feels contractions of her uterus that are strong but usually not painful. These are called *Braxton Hicks* contractions, and they exercise the uterus, preparing it for labor. During labor these contractions also begin the *effacement* (thinning) and *dilation* (opening up) of the cervix. It is difficult to say exactly when labor begins, which helps explain the great differences reported in lengths of labor for different women. When the uterine contractions become regular, true labor begins. During these contractions the lengthwise muscles of the uterus involuntarily pull open the circular muscles around the cervix. This process generally takes from two to thirty-six hours. Its duration depends on the size of the baby, the baby's position in the uterus, the size of the mother's pelvis, and the condition of the uterus. Sometimes labor takes even longer, but it tends to shorten after the first birth experience.

Labor can be divided into three stages (see Figure 9–4). The first stage is usually the longest, lasting from four to sixteen hours. An early sign of first-stage labor is the expulsion of a plug of slightly bloody mucus that has blocked the opening of the cervix during pregnancy. At the same time or later on there is a second fluid discharge

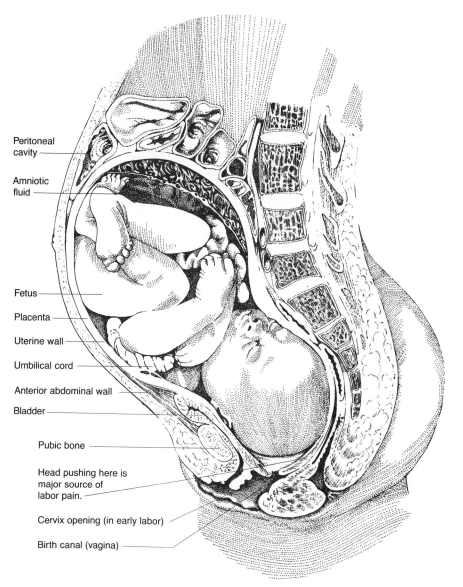

Peritoneal cavity

Amniotic fluid

Fetus

Placenta

Uterine wall

Umbilical cord

Anterior abdominal wall

Bladder

Pubic bone

Head pushing here is major source of labor pain.

Cervix opening (in early labor)

Birth canal (vagina)

Figure 9–3

The Fetus (Full Term). At five months, the fetus is 10–12 inches long and weighs ½ to one pound. The internal organs are well developed although the lungs cannot function well outside of the uterus. At six months, the fetus is 11–14 inches long and weighs over a pound; the eyelids separate and eyelashes are formed. At seven months the fetus is about 13–17 inches long and weighs about 3 pounds; its skin is red and wrinkled. During its eighth and ninth months, the fetus matures rapidly, "growing into" its wrinkled skin. Average length at birth is 20 inches, average weight 7 pounds.

from the vagina. This discharge is the amniotic fluid, which comes from the ruptured amniotic membrane. (Because the baby is subject to infection after the protective membrane breaks, the woman should receive medical attention soon thereafter, if she has not already.) The contractions at the end of the first stage now come more quickly and are much more intense. Many women report this is the most difficult part of their labor. A major factor in a woman's experience during first-stage labor is her attitude toward pain (discussed in the natural childbirth section of this chapter).

During the last part of first-stage labor—called *transition*—the baby's head enters the birth canal. This marks the shift from dilation of the cervical opening to expulsion of the infant. The cervix is now almost fully open, but the baby is not yet completely in position to be pushed out. Some women may feel despair, isolation, and anger at

It is not to diffuse you that you were born of your mother and father—it is to identify you,
It is not that you should be undecided, but that you should be decided.
Something long preparing and formless is arrived and formed in you,
You are thenceforth secure, whatever comes or goes.

WALT WHITMAN

Figure 9–4

Stages of Labor. A. Several weeks or days before birth, the fetus descends lower into the pelvis, a process called "lightening." B. The first stage of labor opens the cervix so that the baby may enter the birth canal. The last (and most intense) part of first stage labor is transition. C. During second stage labor, the baby is pushed through the birth canal. D. Second stage labor ends with the baby's actual birth. Generally, the baby's head rotates to the side just prior to birth. In third stage labor, the placenta is expelled.

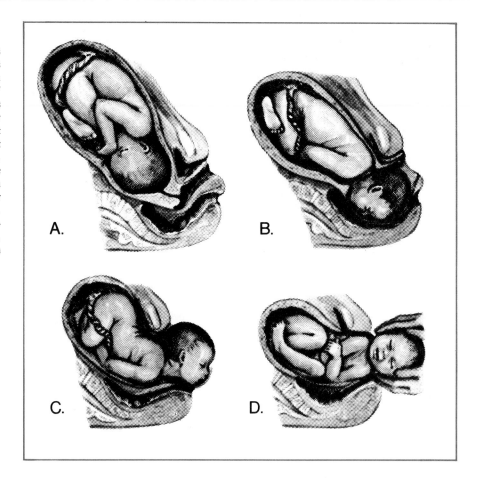

A.   B.

C.   D.

Odds of Multiple Births

Twins: one out of every 90 births.

Triplets: one out of every 9000 births.

Quadruplets: one out of every 500,000 births.

this point (Colman and Colman, 1972). Many lose faith in those assisting in the birth. A woman may find that management of the contractions seems beyond her control; she may be afraid that something is wrong. At this time she needs the full support and understanding of her helpers. Transition is usually, though not always, brief (half an hour to one hour).

Second-stage labor begins when the baby's head moves into the birth canal and ends when the baby is born. During this time many women experience a great force in their bodies. Some women find this the most difficult part of labor. Others find that the contractions and bearing down bring a sense of euphoria. The baby is usually born gradually. With each of the final few contractions, a new part of the infant emerges. The baby may even cry before he or she is completely born, especially if the mother did not have medication. The baby will still be attached to the umbilical cord connected to the mother, which is not cut until it stops pulsating. The baby will appear wet, often covered by a milky substance called *vernix*. The baby's head may look oddly shaped at first, due to molding during birth. This queer shape is temporary, and the baby's head will soon achieve a normal appearance, although both parents may feel some anxiety in the meantime.

After the baby has been delivered, the uterus will continue to contract, expelling the *placenta* (afterbirth), and completing the third stage of labor. The doctor or midwife will examine the placenta to make sure it is whole. If the practitioner has any doubt that the entire placenta has been expelled, he or she may examine the uterus to make sure no parts of the placenta remain to cause adhesions or hemorrhage.

Following labor, the mother will probably feel intense contractions as the uterus begins to return to its normal size and shape. This process takes about six weeks. She will also have a bloody discharge, called *lochia*, which continues for several weeks.

Cesarean Section

Cesarean section (C-section) is the removal of the fetus by an incision in the mother's abdominal and uterine walls. The term *cesarean birth* originated, by tradition, when Julius Caesar was cut out from his mother's womb immediately after her death. The first reported cesarean section performed on a living women occurred in the seventeenth century when a butcher cut open his wife's uterus to save her and their child. In 1970, 5.5 percent of births to American women were done by cesarean section. Today cesarean births account for 20 percent of all births; more than a half-million women have C-sections each year. This represents almost a 400 percent increase in the last fifteen years. Although infants born by C-section have a decreased mortality rate, that for mothers is significantly higher.

The National Institutes of Health issued guidelines in 1980 to reduce the alarming increase in C-sections. These recommendations can be summarized as follows:

- Because a woman has had a previous cesarean delivery does not mean that subsequent deliveries must be C-sections; whenever possible, women should be given the option of vaginal birth.
- Abnormal labor does not mean that a C-section is necessary. Sleep or medication may resolve the problems. Only after other measures have been tried should a physician perform a cesarean, unless the infant is clearly in danger.
- Breech babies (those who come out of the womb buttocks or feet first) do not necessarily require C-sections. In 1970, only 11.6 percent of breech presentations were delivered through surgical procedures; by 1978, 60 percent of breech babies were delivered by C-section. A physician's experience using his or her hand or forceps to turn the baby for a normal vaginal delivery is crucial.

If a woman does not want a C-section unless it is absolutely necessary, she should learn about her attending physician's attitude and record on cesareans. Otherwise, the chances are one out of five that she will have a cesarean delivery.

Natural Childbirth

Natural childbirth was popularized by Grantly Dick-Read (1972) in the first edition of his book *Childbirth Without Fear* in the 1930s. He observed that fear causes muscles to tense, which in turn increases pain and stress in childbirth. By teaching both partners about childbirth and giving them physical exercises to ease muscle tension, he became a pioneer in returning childbirth to women. Using his methods, many women reject anesthetics during labor and delivery and are consequently able to take an active role in their delivery as well as be more aware of the process.

FEATURE

Couvade

Pregnancy and childbirth are two of the most profound experiences known to *man*. Throughout the world males envy and imitate both. In our own culture some men have sympathetic pregnancies in which they develop physical characteristics similar to their pregnant partners. If she has morning sickness, so does he; if her belly swells, so does his. Someone wrote, "Man is a rational animal, but only women can have babies." And so men often use images of pregnancy to describe their creative work. A man "conceives" an idea. He "gives birth" to a new theory. He is in a "fertile" period of artistic development. His book is "pregnant" with ideas. Less fortunate men find their careers "aborted," while others have "stillborn" ideas. It has even been suggested that men often discriminate against women in the arts and sciences precisely because these are areas of highly creative work; men who feel jealous of women's biological creativity thus keep these domains for themselves.

Other cultures have the ritual of *couvade*. The word comes from the French *couver*, which means to hatch or brood. Couvade involves a number of different activities in different cultures. In many, the father must follow certain rest patterns, work restrictions, and dietary practices. Among the Hopi, for example, a man must avoid hurting animals. If he does not, his child is likely to be born deformed. The Ifage males in the Philippines are prohibited from cutting or killing anything during their partner's pregnancy.

Most startling to the Westerner are the male imitations of childbirth. Among the Chaorti in

In the 1950s Fernand Lamaze (1956; rev. ed. 1970) developed a method of natural childbirth based on knowledge of conditioned reflexes. Lamaze developed a method for women to separate mentally the physical stimulus of uterine contractions from the conditioned response of pain. Using various physical positions and breathing techniques during labor, a woman may free herself of much of the pain and anxiety associated with uterine contractions. Other benefits may occur as well. One hospital study observed, "In virtually every category of obstetric performance the data suggest that the Lamaze method is beneficial" (Hughey et al., 1978); the study found one-fourth the number of cesareans, one-fifth the amount of fetal distress, and one-fourth the usual perinatal mortality. These results probably reflect the Lamaze-trained couple's more active participation in pregnancy decisions and their rejection of drugs during labor and delivery.

More recently, Frederick Leboyer has popularized a method of natural childbirth, described in his book *Birth Without Violence* (1975), that emphasizes welcoming the infant into the world with warmth. The traditional slap is done away with as a vestige of barbarism. Instead, the lights are lowered and the baby is placed on the mother's abdomen with its umbilical cord still attached. The baby continues to receive oxygen through the umbilical cord until it begins to breathe on its own. The newborn is then gently placed in a bath of warm water and lovingly caressed (also see Odent, 1984).

One review of clinical studies on prepared childbirth found that such techniques were effective in reducing subjective pain perception and in increasing pain endurance

South America, the man takes to his hammock for several days during and after the delivery. In many tribes a man imitates his wife in childbirth, wrapping his arms around his belly and mimicking labor contractions. After birth he will pretend he is entering a postpartum period. The couvade is a dramatic symbol of the male's paternity and his "magical" relation to the child (LaBarre, 1968). By pretending he is pregnant, he distracts evil spirits from harming his baby. Describing the magical impact of the couvade, Arthur and Libby Coleman (1971) wrote:

The couvade phenomena have the important side effects of helping a husband play an important part in pregnancy in childbirth. . . . They help a man cope with the envy and competitiveness which he may feel at his wife's ability to perform such a fundamental and creative act. Lastly, in his activities to deceive the evil spirits, a man may also find a reasonable outlet for his own desire to take on something of the female role in his life.

Some American males may experience what medical researchers called the "couvade syndrome." A study of the partners of 267 postpartum women found that 22.5 percent of the males experienced nausea, vomiting, anorexia, abdominal pain and bloating, and other symptoms of pregnancy that could not be objectively explained (Lipkin and Lamb, 1982). These men had four times more symptoms than before their partners' pregnancies. Other studies suggest that between 11 percent to 65 percent of males with pregnant partners experience sympathetic pregnancies (see Trethowan, 1968, 1972; White and Bulloch, 1980).

(Conway, 1980). Prepared mothers successfully handled childbirth pain, cooperated with the physician, used fewer drugs and anesthetics, expressed greater satisfaction with their childbirth experiences, and experienced less postpartum depression than women undergoing routine hospital births. But as Conway noted, "The question of whether these techniques, particularly attention focusing and feedback relaxation, actually alter or decrease the subjective pain experience remains unanswered and debated."

Choosing the Birthplace

Hospital Birth. The impersonal, routine quality of hospital birth is increasingly being questioned. Hospital conditions have generally been designed not for the woman who is giving birth but "primarily to facilitate the ministrations of the obstetrician" (Mead, 1968). One woman described the experience of her first birth (Boston Women's Health Collective, 1978):

Man is a rational animal, but only women can have babies.

ANONYMOUS

I remember feeling very strange, to have experienced the most remarkable of all things, the birth of my first child, and then to be left all alone. First they took the baby into the nursery. Then I was wheeled into my room, where my husband was able to stay and chat for a while. . . . I was tired, but too excited to sleep. So there I was, alone, remembering the experience full of wonder and amazement that we had all shared. But for the next few hours, we were not sharing. The hospital had separated us.

Some hospitals are responding to the need for a family-centered childbirth. The father does not always need to handcuff himself to the delivery table (as one man did) to be present during the birth. Indeed, fathers may often participate today. Nor do the woman and the infant always need to be separated immediately after birth. Hospitals may permit rooming-in (the baby stays with the mother rather than in the nursery) or a modified form of rooming-in. This arrangement is expensive and consequently is not available to most families. Women who would prefer some form of rooming-in should check with the hospital to see if it is allowed. A woman should also check to find out when the father and the other family members and friends are allowed to visit. Some hospitals restrict visits to regular visiting hours, even if the mother and the child are in the same room.

But the norm is still the impersonal birth. During one of the most profound experiences of her life, a woman has her baby among strangers to whom birth is merely routine. Moreover, the baby is delivered on a table, against the force of gravity. In most cultures, a woman gives birth while sitting in a birthing chair, kneeling, or squatting. Until the present century, most American women used birthing chairs; the delivery table was instituted for the convenience of the physician (Wirtz and Wirtz, 1978). Recently, however, a motorized birthing chair has been developed that can be raised, lowered, or tilted according to the physician's and the woman's needs. It is now used in more than two hundred hospitals throughout the United States and abroad.

Following birth (which often takes place while the mother is heavily medicated), the baby is generally taken off to a nursery. Its lips are ready for sucking, seeking the breast that is not there. Its crying brings no relief. Often, if it is a male, the foreskin of his penis is cut off; medical reasons may be given for circumcision, but it is (as is acknowledged in some other cultures) basically a pain-inducing ("welcome to the 'real' world") ritual or a matter of fashion. The infant is diapered and clothed, his or her first lesson, observes Margaret Mead (1948), "in expecting cloth to intervene between one body and the next." During the next two or three days, the infant is brought to the mother at scheduled intervals for feeding and visiting. In the last few years some hospitals have tried to comply with mothers' wishes for "demand" feeding (when the baby feels hungry as opposed to when the hospital wants to feed it), but because most hospital maternity wards are busy places, they often find it difficult to meet the individual needs of many infants and mothers. If the mother is breastfeeding, a rigid schedule can make the establishment of a feeding routine between her and her child almost impossible.

Childbirth does not have to be this way. More Americans are making alternative choices of natural childbirth, rooming-in, birthing centers, home births, and mid- wives. The chief of obstetrics at a major hospital observed: "It's a major upheaval in medicine, and the conflict has tended to polarize the consumer and the care giver. The basic problem is that we have changed obstetrics with the latest medical advances and not incorporated essentially humanistic considerations" (see Pallow-Fleury, 1983, for questions to ask about a hospital's birth policies).

Birthing Rooms and Centers. Birth (or maternity) centers, institutions of long standing in England and other European countries (see Odent, 1984), now are being developed in the United States; in 1984 there were more than 120, with at least 300 more planned (Carey, 1984). Although they vary in size, organization, and orienta- tion, birth centers share the view that childbirth is a normal, healthy process that can be conducted by skilled practitioners (midwives or physicians) in a homelike setting. The mother or couple has considerable autonomy in deciding the conditions of birth—lighting, sounds, visitors, delivery position, and so on. Some of these centers can provide some kinds of emergency care; all have procedures for transfers to hospitals if necessary.

Some hospitals now have their own birthing centers (or rooms) that provide for labor and birth in a comfortable setting and allow the mother or couple considerable autonomy. Hospital practices vary widely, however; prospective parents should carefully determine their needs and thoroughly investigate their options.

Home Birth.   Home births have increased in the last few years, although they still constitute a small fraction of total births, amounting to not quite 2 percent according to available data. Home births tend to be safer than hospital births if they are supervised by midwives or physicians. Without medical supervision, however, they have a significantly higher infant mortality rate (JAMA, 1980). Supervised home births are safer than hospital births as a result of careful medical screening and planning that eliminate all but the lowest-risk pregnancies. A couple can create their own birth environment at home, and home births cost considerably less, usually at least one-third less, than hospital delivery. With medical supervision, a couple has little to worry about. But if a woman is at risk, she is wiser to give birth in a hospital where medical equipment is readily available.

Midwifery

The United States has an increasing number of certified nurse-midwives who are trained not only as registered nurses but in obstetrical techniques as well. They are well qualified for routine deliveries and minor medical emergencies. They also often operate as part of a total medical team that includes a backup physician, if needed. Their fees are generally considerably less than a doctor's. Nurse-midwives usually participate in both hospital and home births, although this may vary according to hospital policy and the midwives' preference.

Lay midwifery, in which the midwives are not formally trained by the medical establishment but by other experienced midwives, has also increased in popularity in the past decade. Many satisfactory births with lay midwives in attendance have been reported, but extensive, reliable information is not available, owing to the "underground" nature of lay midwifery, which is often practiced outside of (and without the support of) the regular practice of medicine.

Women who choose midwives for home or hospital births do so for several reasons. Some prefer the empathy offered by other women (although some midwives are male), some cannot afford hospital births, others are reluctant to undergo the routine drug and surgical techniques done by obstetricians, and still others prefer the warm environment of their home and family. Physicians in the hospital setting, using forceps, drugs, scalpels, and electronic monitoring, tend to intervene medically more than home practitioners. One study found more complications and injuries in hospital births, a greater number of damaged babies, and more torn or hemorrhaging mothers (Mehl, 1977).

If a woman decides she wants to give birth with the aid of a midwife, she should have thorough medical screening to make sure she or her infant will not be at risk

How have women given birth, who has helped them, and how, and why? These are not simply questions in the history of midwifery and obstetrics: they are political questions. The woman awaiting her period, or the onset of labor, the woman lying on a table undergoing abortion or pushing her baby out, the woman inserting a diaphragm or swallowing her daily pill, is doing these under the influence of centuries of imprinting. Her choices—when she has any—are made, or outlawed within the context of laws and professional codes, religious sanctions and ethnic traditions, from whose creation women have been historically excluded.

ADRIENNE RICH, OF WOMAN BORN

FEATURE

Childbirth in Historical Perspective

Until the nineteenth century, American childbirth was a female-centered event, taking place at home, under supervision of a skilled female midwife. The pregnant woman was surrounded by friends and relatives who shared their knowledge and experiences; the younger women in attendance learned first hand what to expect when they themselves gave birth. After giving birth, the new mother began "lying-in," a period of several days to several weeks during which friends, neighbors, and relatives cooked, took care of the other children, and tended to her wifely duties. At the end of this period, the new mother gave a "groaning party" for the women who had helped her—a feast and celebration marking the end of her lying-in. The groaning referred to both the groaning of labor and the groaning of the guests who ritualistically overate (Wirtz and Wirtz, 1978). Little remains today of the lying-in tradition except for mothers or mothers-in-law occasionally coming to help in the days immediately before and after delivery.

Childbirth, however, was not viewed as an especially joyful occasion, as it is today. Rather, it was seen as a time that revealed the power of God and nature over women. Through the pain of childbirth women were reminded of God's curse on Eve for tempting Adam and eating the forbidden fruit: "In sorrow thou shalt bring forth children" (Genesis 3:16). Because women frequently died in childbirth, it was a time of foreboding. Anne Bradstreet (1612–1672) wrote "Before the Birth of One of Her Children" for her husband:

How soon, my Dear, death may my steps attend,
How soon't may be thy lot to lose thy friend,
We both are ignorant, yet love bids me
These farewell lines to recommend to thee,
That when that knot's untied that made us one,
I may seem thine, who in effect am none.

Until the nineteenth century, most midwives had been women. Then an important device, invented in the early seventeenth century, ultimately helped replace the female midwife with the male obstetrician. This was the forceps, a device like two enlarged spoons with handles that could be inserted in the birth canal to draw out the fetus in a difficult delivery. Until its invention by Peter Chamberlen, fetuses that could not travel through the birth canal were killed and then dismembered with sharp hooks. Chamberlen, however, did not reveal his secret instrument to anyone; instead, the forceps were kept a family secret for over a century. Chamberlen (quoted in Rich, 1976) wrote:

My Father, Brothers, and myself . . . have, by God's

during delivery. When she finds a midwife, she should learn about the midwife's training and experience; what type of backup services the midwife has in the event of complications or emergencies; and how the midwife will handle a transfer to a hospital if it becomes necessary (Levinson, 1980).

☐ BREASTFEEDING

About three days after childbirth, *lactation*—the production of milk—begins. Before lactation, as early as the second trimester, a yellowish liquid called *colostrum* may appear at the nipples. It is what nourishes the newborn infant before the mother's milk comes in. Colostrum is high in protein and contains antibodies that help protect a baby from infectious diseases. Hormonal changes during labor begin the changeover

FEATURE–*continued*

blessing and our Industry, attained to, and long practiced a way to deliver women in this case, without any prejudice to them or their infants; tho all others . . . do and must endanger, if not destroy, one or both with hooks.

When he and his brothers arrived at a difficult birth, they took from their carriage a massive dark chest whose contents they revealed to no one. Upon entering the birthing room, they blindfolded the women they delivered to prevent their secret from being discovered.

Eventually, the forceps became well known. Male midwives used them, but female midwives did not. This may have been because of a tradition that associated males with instrumental interference, because surgeon guilds refused to permit midwives to use them, or because forceps were associated with the deadly hooks that destroyed fetuses. Surgeons began using forceps not only for difficult deliveries but also to speed up labor. When the earliest medical schools were established in the United States they included midwifery as the first medical specialty. In the nineteenth century, medicine was neither an affluent nor a highly respected profession. To increase both status and income, physicians attempted to become more scientific. In doing so, they rejected the female midwives as relying more on nature than on "scientific" training and medical techniques. A medical school education, however, did not necessarily give physicians much expertise. One obstetrician recalled his first delivery in 1850 (quoted in Wirtz and Wirtz, 1978):

I was left alone with a poor Irish woman and one crony, to deliver her child . . . and I thought it necessary to call before me every circumstance I had learned from books—I must examine and I did—But whether it was head or breech, hand or foot, man or monkey that was defended from my uninstructed finger by the distended membranes, I was uncomfortably ignorant, with all my learning, as the fetus itself that was making all this fuss.

Midwifery, nonetheless, was attacked, and the male midwives eventually became known as obstetricians. By the middle of the nineteenth century, most middle-class women gave birth at home with the assistance of a male obstetrician. Childbirth as a female ritual was giving way. Soon it was to be transferred from the home to the hospital.

In 1847, to the horror of his colleagues, a physician administered chloroform to a woman in labor to ease her birthing pains. Physicians had feared that anesthesia would cause the labor contractions to stop. The labor, however, went normally despite the fact that the woman was unconscious. Women now had the possibility of giving birth without pain. Before, women had

(Continued on next page.)

from colostrum to milk, but unless a mother nurses her child, her breasts will soon stop producing milk. If she chooses not to breastfeed, she is usually given an injection of estrogen soon after delivery to stop lactation. It is not certain, however, whether estrogen is actually effective; furthermore, it may cause an increased risk of blood clotting.

Almost 58 percent of American women breastfeed their children today (Wootan, 1985). In 1973 only about 25 percent of mothers in this country breastfed. A mother's milk—if she is healthy and has a good diet—offers the best nutrition for the baby. In addition, her milk contains antibodies that will protect her child from infectious diseases. Finally, a breastfed baby is less likely to become constipated, contract skin diseases, or develop respiratory infections. Low birth-weight babies, similarly, do best with mother's milk rather than formula or mature milk from a donor, since "nature

FEATURE—*continued*

accepted birthing pains as part of the natural order. As noted, in the Christian tradition the travail of labor was looked on as Eve's (and women's) punishment for leading Adam astray. When women began to ask for anesthetics during childbirth to relieve their pain, there was an outcry from the religious community: painless childbirth was blasphemy against God. But after England's Queen Victoria gave birth under anesthesia, the religious opposition discreetly disappeared. The Bible was reinterpreted to make the use of anesthesia acceptable during labor. The acceptance of painless labor was crucial in moving childbirth from the home to the hospital. With the introduction of anesthesia, the nineteenth century witnessed a new attitude toward pain, especially pain affecting women. "Victorian culture encouraged women to

be more sensitive to pain than men and to express openly their aches and illnesses," wrote Wirtz and Wirtz (1978). Pain became subjectively perceived as more painful than before and women as no longer capable of enduring it.

Hospitals expanded their facilities to meet women's new needs for anesthesia. In doing so, however, birth changed from a female-centered natural process taking place in the home to a process dominated by male experts, requiring medical skill, and taking place in a hospital. This transformation was completed in less than a hundred years. In 1900 only 5 percent of all births took place in hospitals; by 1981 more than 95% of all births occurred in hospitals. A hundred years ago, hospital births were suspect; today it is home birth that is suspect.

---

adapts mother's milk to meet infant's needs" (JAMA, 1980; Johnson and Goldfinger, 1981). A benefit to the mother is that hormonal changes, stimulated by breastfeeding, cause the uterus to contract and help ensure its return to a normal state. The American Academy of Pediatricians endorses total breastfeeding for a baby's first six months.

Breastfeeding has psychological as well as physical benefits. Nursing provides a sense of emotional well-being for both mother and child through close physical contact. A woman may feel that breastfeeding affirms her body, giving her assurance that she is plentiful, capable of nourishing, able to sustain the life of another through her milk (see Lainson, 1983; Stone, 1983). Some men feel jealous of the baby's intimate relationship with their partners. Others feel incompetent because they cannot contribute to nourishing their child (Waletzky, 1979).

Many American women choose not to breastfeed. Their reasons include the inconvenience of not being able to leave the baby for more than a few hours at a time, tenderness of nipples (which generally passes within several days to two weeks), and inhibitions about nursing a baby, especially in public. If a woman works, bottle feeding may be her only practical alternative, as American companies rarely provide leaves, part-time employment, or nursing breaks for their female employees. Some women may have a physical condition that precludes breastfeeding.

American mothers may also worry about whether they will be able to breastfeed "properly." As Niles Newton (1955) wrote:

Unsuccessful breast-feeding is a type of breast-feeding that is typical of the modern American urban mother. This type of breast-feeding is a difficult and tenuous process. There is constant worry about whether there is enough milk for the baby . . . The pain, the work, and the worry

Breastfeeding provides extensive physical and psychological benefits for both mother and child. The American Academy of Pediatricians endorses total breastfeeding for an infant's first six months.

All is beautiful
All is beautiful
All is beautiful
All is beautiful, yes!

Now Mother Earth
and Father Sky
Join one another and meet
forever helpmates
   All is beautiful
   All is beautiful
   All is beautiful, yes!

Now the night of darkness
And the dawn of light
Join one another and meet
forever helpmates
   All is beautiful
   All is beautiful
   All is beautiful, yes!

Now the white corn
And the yellow corn
Join one another and meet
forever helpmates
   All is beautiful
   All is beautiful
   All is beautiful, yes!

Life that never ends
Happiness of all things
Join one another and meet
Forever helpmates
   All is beautiful
   All is beautiful
   All is beautiful, yes!

NAVAJO NIGHT CHANT

of unsuccessful breast-feeding make early weaning part of the unsuccessful breast-feeding pattern. . . . Successful breast-feeding is the type of feeding that is practiced by the vast majority of mothers all over the world. It is a simple, easy process. When the baby is hungry, it is simply given a breast to suck. There is an abundance of milk, and the milk supply naturally adjusts itself to the child's growth and intake of other foods.

La Leche League, which has many nationwide chapters, is an excellent source of assistance and support to mothers in establishing breastfeeding (see Resource Center).

Bottlefeeding an infant does make it possible for the father and other caregivers to share intimately in the nurturing process. Some mothers (and fathers) have discovered that maximum contact and closeness can be enjoyed when the infant is held against their naked breast while nursing from a bottle.

☐ MAKING ADJUSTMENTS

The time immediately following birth is a critical period of family adjustment (Grossman et al., 1980). No amount of reading, classes, and expert advice can prepare expectant parents for the real thing (see Feldman and Nash, 1984). The month or so following childbirth is called the *postpartum period*. This time is one of physical stabilization and emotional adjustment. It also may be a time of significant emotional upheaval. Even women who had easy and uneventful births may experience a period of "postpartum blues" characterized by alternating periods of crying, unpredictable mood changes, fatigue, irritability, and occasionally mild confusion or

UNDERSTANDING YOURSELF

Exploring Your Reproductive Values

Is the ability to create a child important to your own sense of self-fullment? Do you definitely know that you are fertile? If you discovered that you were infertile, what do you think your responses would be? How would infertility change your plans about the future?

What concerns do (or will) you (and your partner) have about the prenatal health of a child you have conceived? (Think in terms of your own health, medical history, genetic background, drinking and smoking habits, exposure to disease, chemicals, radiation, and so on.) If you have legitimate concerns: where can

you get more information? In what practical ways can you deal with your concerns?

In having a baby, what factors are (or will be) important to you in choosing a birth method, setting, practitioner, and so on?

If you are a male: how have you chosen (or will you choose) to be involved in the birth of your child? What kinds of obstacles, if any, might you expect to your participation? If you are a female: what extent of participation in childbirth do (or will) you expect from your partner?

In traditional sexual thought sex was justified primarily, sometimes exclusively because it was necessary to the propagation of the species. Since one of the premises of the modern tradition in sexual thought has been that sex is a valuable end in itself, modern theorists, by way of reaction, have generally inclined to belittle the reproductive perspective on sexuality.

PAUL ROBINSON, *THE MODERNIZATION OF SEX*

lapses of memory (Young and Ehrhardt, 1980). A woman has irregular sleep patterns because of the needs of her newborn, the discomfort of childbirth, or the strangeness of the hospital environment. Some mothers may feel lonely, isolated from their familiar world. Many women blame themselves for their fluctuating moods. They may feel that they have lost control over their lives because of the dependency of their newborns. One woman commented (Boston Women's Health Collective, 1978):

We often feel guilty, because we think our own inadequacies are the cause of our unhappiness. We rarely question whether the roles we have are realizable. Because of social pressures surrounding motherhood, and the mystique of the maternal instinct . . . many women are unable to pinpoint their feelings of confusion and inadequacy or are unable to feel that it is legitimate to verbalize their hestiation and problems.

Biological, psychological, and social factors are all involved in postpartum depression. Biologically, during the first several days following delivery, there is an abrupt fall in certain hormonal levels. The physiological stress accompanying labor, dehydration, blood loss, and other physical factors contribute to lowering the woman's stamina. Psychologically, conflicts about her ability to mother, ambiguous feelings toward or rejection of her own mother, and communication problems with the infant or partner may contribute to the new mother's feelings of depression and helplessness. Finally, the social setting into which the child is born is significant, especially if the infant represents a financial or emotional burden for the family (Young and Ehrhardt, 1980).

Although the postpartum blues are felt by many women, they usually don't last more than a couple of weeks. Interestingly, men seem to get a form of postpartum blues as well. Dr. Martha Zaslow and her colleagues (1981) of the National Institute of Child Health observed: "It looks increasingly as if a number of the things we assumed about mothers and motherhood are really typical of parenthood." When infants arrive, many fathers do not feel prepared for their new parenting and financial responsibilities. Some men are overwhelmed by the changes that take place in their marital relationship. Fatherhood is a major transition for them, but their feelings are overlooked, since most people turn their attention to the new mother.

Perhaps the new father will be allowed (or expected) to have equal status with the mother as a nurturing parent and to take on an equal share of household and childrearing duties. Then not only will the mother be able to experience some relief from the physical drain of motherhood but the father also may experience his family from within rather than as a burdened provider watching from the outside. Studies indicate that "parental similarities far outweigh differences, suggesting that beyond the biological advantage accorded the mother by virtue of her physiology, both parents are equally capable of caring for their young" (Belsky et al., 1983). Both traditional sex roles and our traditional work structure, which does not permit men the opportunity to be at home or to work part time, stand in the way of fathers participating equally (or replacing mothers) as the primary nurturers. In contrast to the United States, Sweden guarantees by law the right of the father to take a leave of absence from his job to care for his newborn. Nature does not prevent men from nurturing; societal expectations and the social structure do. (For a discussion of the transition to parenthood for men and women, see Feldman and Nash, 1984.)

☐ SUMMARY

- The primary causes of male infertility are low sperm count, blocked passageways, and lack of sperm motility. The primary causes of female infertility are blocked fallopian tubes, endometriosis, and hormonal abnormalities.

- *Artificial insemination* involves depositing sperm artificially (by syringe) in a woman's vagina. It is successful about 60 percent of the time.

- Adoption is an alternative to pregnancy that is considered by both infertile and fertile couples and by singles. It is a tedious and often expensive process with unique problems and rewards. Approximately 100,000 children are adopted yearly in the United States, mostly by relatives.

- The first reliable test of pregnancy can be made two to four weeks after a woman misses her menstrual period. A chemical test called the *agglutination test* will determine the presence of human chorionic gonadotropin (HCG) in the urine. *Hegar's sign*, a softening of the uterus, can be detected by a trained examiner. The only absolute indication of pregnancy is the detection of fetal heartbeats and movements.

- A woman's feelings will vary greatly during pregnancy owing to a number of factors. It is important for her to be able to share her fears and to have support from her mate, friends, relatives, and health-care workers.

- Harmful substances may be passed to the embryo or fetus through the placenta, including opiates, tobacco, alcohol, marijuana, barbiturates, and caffeine. Infectious diseases, especially rubella, may damage the fetus. Sexually transmitted diseases may be passed to the infant through the placenta or through the birth canal during childbirth.

- *Ectopic pregnancies, spontaneous abortion, toxemia,* and *prematurity* are the most significant complications of pregnancy. Toxemia is characterized by high blood pressure and *edema* (swelling caused by water retention). Premature or low birth weight (LBW) babies usually weigh less than 5.5 pounds at birth; often their vital organs are not sufficiently developed.

- A woman feels *Braxton Hicks* contractions, which exercise the uterus in preparation for labor, throughout pregnancy. The Braxton Hicks contractions also begin the *effacement* (thinning) and *dilation* (opening up) of the cervix to permit delivery. Both continue throughout the second stage of labor.

- Labor can be divided into three stages. The woman enters first-stage labor when her uterine contractions become regular. When the cervix has dilated approximately 10 centimeters, the baby's head enters the birth canal; this is called *transition.* In second-stage labor the baby emerges from the birth canal. In third-stage labor the *placenta* (afterbirth) is expelled.

- *Cesarean section* is the removal of the fetus by an incision through the abdomen into the woman's uterus. A dramatic increase in C-sections in recent years has led to criticism that the procedure is used more often than necessary.

- Natural childbirth encompasses a variety of methods that basically stress the importance of relaxation and emotional support of the mother during childbirth.

- Hospital birth practices, which are designed for the convenience of the hospital rather than that of the mother, father, and child, have come under increasing criticism. Professionally staffed birthing centers and special birthing rooms in hospitals are providing attractive alternatives to mechanized hospital birth settings.

- The incidence of home births is increasing. If home births are supervised by trained midwives or physicians they tend to be safer than hospital births. One reason for this is that all but the lowest-risk pregnancies are excluded.

- Nurse- and lay-midwives are trained in obstetric techniques. Many women are now choosing midwives to deliver their babies because they want home births, cannot afford physicians, or prefer the attendance of a woman (most physicians are male, most midwives female).

- Almost 58 percent of American women breastfeed their children today. Mother's milk tends to be more nutritious than formula or cow's milk and provides immunities to many diseases; nursing offers emotional rewards to mother and infant.

- A critical adjustment period follows the birth of a child. The mother may experience feelings of depression (sometimes called "postpartum blues") that are a result of biological, psychological, and social factors. Participation of the father in nurturing the infant and performing household duties may help alleviate both the mother's and father's feelings of confusion and inadequacy.

READINGS

A Native American Birth Story

MARCIE RENDON, FROM *BIRTH STORIES* (EDITED BY JANET ISAACS ASHFORD)

Marcie Rendon, a Native American midwife, recalls the births of each of her three daughters. How does each birth situation reflect the prevailing attitudes of its time and place? Rendon asks if a Native American birth story is "any different than any woman's birth story." What do you think? What is the story of your birth?

A Native American birth story. Is it any different than any woman's birth story? Any mother, the world over, could come upon a woman in labor anyplace and recognize what was happening. And feel at one with, be supportive of, the woman in labor.

Ever since I can remember, I knew I wanted to have my babies at home. There was never a question in my mind whether I would have children or not. I just knew I would and that I wanted them born at home. I figured, women have given birth since time began, our bodies know what to do and how to do it.

There isn't a birth story. There are birth stories. Mine began with my asking, "Grandpa, tell me again, how were you born?"

"In the snow, girl, just dropped in the snow. My ma didn't know nothin. Raised in mission schools. Didn't know nothin. Just dropped in the snow. Till my grandma heard her cryin and came out and found us. Thought she had to go to the bathroom; went out and dropped me right in the snow. Raised in mission schools. Didn't know nothin.

"Now your ma, she was born the old way. In the fall, during wild rice season. Right there in ricing camp. Your grandma and me were ricing when your ma started to be born. Three old ladies helped her. They stuck sticks in the ground like crutches. Your grandma squatted, hanging on them under her arms. They had medicines for her. Right there. Knew what to do to help your ma be born. Yep, right there in ricing camp, your ma was born. The old way, no trouble. Me, I was dropped in the snow. Thought she had to go to the bathroom. Didn't know nothing. Raised in mission schools."

My birth. Born to an alcoholic mother. Suffering withdrawal along with her during the hospital stay. Nursing, etched in my being as a wordless memory. Remembering her story, laughing. "When I was nursing I had so much milk. My breasts were so big I'd take bets in the bar. I'd take bets that I could set a glass of beer on my tits and drink the foam off. Got a lot of free drinks that way."

Laughter. Laughter that filled the whole room. Caught everyone up in it. My mother, dead in my eighteenth year, from alcohol.

Birth stories. My daughters, children of my grandfathers' and grandmothers' dreams. You were a reality long before my passion and your father's seeds conceived you on those winter and spring nights. Visions preceded flesh from my womb. And my generations shall be as one. Spirits healing my mother's madness, my father's sadness. As the daughters of my grandfathers' and grandmothers' dreams touch hands with wind and water, light and love.

"Tell me Mom, how was I born?" asks my seven-year-old.

Conception. Christmas Eve. Warm glow as the spark of your being ignites. I remember standing at the window that night watching the lights glitter on the snow, knowing that night that you were started in me.

"Your daddy told me I was crazy because I wanted to have you at home. I asked all over, trying to find a midwife. Everyone told me there weren't any, that midwives were a hundred years ago. So I decided I'd have you at home alone. I kept saying, 'Women have given birth since time began; my body knows what to do.' And your daddy just kept telling me I was crazy. As it was, I didn't get any support to have you at home and we ended up in the hospital. They strapped me down and I had to physically fight the nurses, doctor and anesthesiologist not to be gassed or drugged. Your daddy just kept telling me to be good and cooperate. I had back labor and I just kept seeing the fear in his eyes and wishing it would go away. I just wanted to have you my way, with no interference. And you ended up being born by forceps because I wouldn't cooperate. All my energy went into fighting the nurses and doctors until my body just gave up and they pulled you out. But you were a beautiful little girl. When I first got to hold you and nurse you, you just smiled right at me. They didn't want me to nurse you. They kept giving me sugar water to give to you. They told me you'd dehydrate and have brain damage if I didn't give it to you. So I'd drink it myself or pour it down the toilet to keep them off my back. When we went home I was black and blue from where the straps had been, from fighting them so hard to have you the way I'd wanted to have you." My first daughter. Rachel Rainbeaux. My "One of Many Dreams." Rainbeaux. The one who fights for life with every ounce of muscle and energy in her little body.

"And me, Mommy, how was I born?" asks my five-year-old.

"You, my girl, were born in a midwife unit. Again, I wanted to have you at home, but couldn't find a midwife to come. So the midwife unit was a compromise to your dad, who was still too scared to do it alone at home.

"You were conceived in Denver. I remember standing outside after work, waiting for your daddy to pick me up. It was April and it started to rain snow. Huge, soaking wet snowflakes. At the same time I could feel my body ovulating. That night we made love and right afterwards my whole body started to shake. I told your daddy, 'I'm pregnant. You have to get me something to eat.' He thought I was being really silly. I said, 'No, for real, get me something to eat.' So he brought me a big bowl of cornflakes. That's the night you were started.

"You were born in a hospital midwife unit. The whole birth was beautiful. Calm. Peaceful. Except I had back labor again, even though I'd made one of the nurse-midwives promise I wouldn't have back labor twice in a row. Only during transition did I lose it; the back labor got so bad I said, 'That's it. I quit. Give me a cigarette. I'm done.' Everyone just laughed at me and ten minutes later you were born. Another beautiful girl who smiled right at me. I got to hold you right away. Hold you. Love you. Nurse you."

"And my foot, Mom. Tell me about my foot."

"You were born with a crooked foot. So they put a tiny little cast on it the day after you were born and then you had surgery on it when you were four months old."

Simone. My Starfire, with the warmth of a soft summer night, the flicker of eternity in her eyes. Rainy Day Woman—life giver—love flows out of your being and waters the souls of those you touch.

The next four years. Mothering. A divorce. Single parenting. Welfare. Apprenticing. Midwifing. Mothering.

"And the baby, Mom," the seven and five-year-old say. "Where was she born? You finally got to have one of us at home, didn't you?"

My baby, four months old and growing. My home birth. What will I tell her when she's old enough to ask?

"You, my baby girl, were born at home. On the living room floor. Twenty-four hours of the hardest work I ever hope to do. Twenty-four hours of excruciating back labor. You were conceived November 2, 1982. It was right after the full moon, but it was a really cold, dark, hard night. Your dad and I had been seeing each other off and on. That just happened to be one of the 'on' nights. But the thing I remember most was that for about a month before that, every night when I'd go to bed, I'd hear three knocks on the window. I'd say, 'Bendigan, come in,' like I was taught to say when spirits are heard. Well, November 2nd was the last night I heard the three knocks. Again I knew I

was pregnant right away. It was so free this time, because I knew I could do whatever I wanted with the pregnancy and birth. I could have women around me to be supportive of me. I spotted a little blood in the third month, so in the seventh month we went up north to be doctored by a medicine man for a low placenta. The very first time he saw me, he said, 'Another girl, huh? Well, we'll keep prayin for a boy.' He also told me my delivery would be dangerous, to not have anyone around who would be afraid. Well babe, you were born in the heat of the hottest summer I remember. We spent all our money all summer going where it was cool—swimming, air-conditioned shopping malls, swimming, to friends' houses that had air-conditioning, and swimming again. Your birth. Like I said, long and hard. Twenty-four hours of excruciating back labor. I walked and squatted the whole time. Trying to dance you down into a more straight up and down position. We had a grandmother, a midwife and an apprentice here to help us. Three of the most beautiful women I've ever seen. At one point I got a contraction band around my uterus, looked like a rubber band being tightened around my belly. I got scared for you. I said, "I want to go in." I started praying the Serenity Prayer—God grant me the serenity to accept the things I cannot change (the band, the back labor, the pain), and the courage to change the things I can (my position). I walked from the dining room to the living room and squatted down by a chair. The band disappeared and I started pushing. Hard work. Three hours of pushing during which time I visualized the Viet Nam war. Telling myself, if my brother could live through that, I could live through pushing one baby out. Just before you were born I told them I was bleeding. They said no, there wasn't any blood. You head was born, your shoulders stuck. As soon as you were completely born the blood gushed out. Your cord was too short to nurse you or even pick you up enough to tell if you were a girl or boy. But you were lying on my belly. The first thing you did was lift your head up, look at me and smile. Another beautiful girl. They had to call another midwife to help stop the bleeding and fix the tear. And you baby, you never missed a beat. Like a turtle, your little heart never even flickered a sign of distress. Born at home. I held you, nursed you, loved you. Another beautiful, beautiful girl."

Awanewquay. Quiet, calm, peaceful little woman. Awan. Fog Woman. Three knocks announcing your intention. Birth and death inseparable. Birth—the coming of the spirit to this world. Death—the going of the spirit to that world. Fog Woman. The cloud of mystery. With your two sisters I felt strong, powerful. After they were born I felt, if I can do that, I can move mountains. Well, honey, with you I moved the mountain. With all humbleness, I moved the mountain.

A Native American birth story. It is the story of the generations. I gave birth because I was born a woman. The seeds of the future generations were carried in my womb. I remember conception because the female side of life is always fertile first. I gave birth three times as naturally as possible, given the situation, because as a woman my body and heart knew what to do. I nursed because my breasts filled with milk. I remember their names because that is how they will be recognized by their grandfathers and grandmothers who have gone on before. I am a mother because I was given three daughters to love. I am a midwife because women will continue to give birth. That is my story. Megwitch. I am Marcie Rendon, Awanewquay, of the Eagle Clan, Ojibwe.

Infertility and Adoption

ABBY JOAN SYLVIACHILD, FROM *BIRTH STORIES* (EDITED BY JANET ISAACS ASHFORD)

"Our bodies betray us," writes Abby Joan Sylviachild. What does she mean? What are the stages of the emotional process experienced by infertile couples, according to Sylviachild? In terms of the effect on the functioning of the household, how does the arrival of an adopted infant differ from that of an infant who is born into the family? How is it similar?

We have always been planners. We planned our educations, our travels abroad, our garden rows, and our childbearing. We planned to get pregnant when things were just right. We thought that having a child would be another accomplishment we could complete by choice, like the new house or job or degree. But the supposedly simple act of getting pregnant can sometimes turn out to be much harder than we think. Months and menstrual periods go by without any sign that our bodies are aware of our longings, dreams and hopes. Our bodies betray us by being beyond our control. Like so many infertile couples, our feelings began with surprise and shock, then led to disappointment, denial of the reality, anger, isolation, depression, guilt, appeasement, then finally grief and mourning for the biological child never-to-be. Finally we came to some resolution as we planned, again, to reach our goal of parenthood another way. . . .

One out of every six couples of reproductive age is infertile and at last there is an organization for us, RESOLVE,

Inc., a national, nonprofit, grass-roots organization giving information, support, referrals, and counseling to people with infertility. In the forty-five local chapters around the country, people like me can find others to talk to about the effects of infertility on their personal lives, and we can compare notes on diagnostic tests, treatments, and doctors. Through RESOLVE I found out that I was not "crazy" for crying every time I got my period and that I was not "unbalanced" to have feelings of jealousy and anger toward every pregnant woman I saw, whether among my family, friends, or strangers on the street. Through RESOLVE I learned that what seems an obsession to others—perhaps even to our husbands—is just the way this life crisis behaves: infertility takes over our lives entirely until we resolve it. I found out that not being able to look at or be in the same room with anybody else's baby or small child is also "normal" for infertiles. And I discovered that while fifty percent of us will be helped to achieve a successful pregnancy and give birth to a baby, many of the rest of us will be able to build our families through adoption. Through RESOLVE I learned what my options were.

Infertility can become the center of a couple's life. It is only when the difficulty of the treatments and the small percentages of success seem not worth the trouble, and when we realize that we want to have a child with or without a pregnancy, that the option of adoption becomes the next and very positive step. Many couples refuse to consider adoption when they are in the thick of their infertility workup. They think that even considering adoption means that they are giving up on their infertility. But it is possible and even common for couples to look into adoption and continue their medical treatments at the same time. . . .

After three years we were reaching the limit of our ability to be infertile and childless (we thought). There is a six to twelve month optimum time in which to get pregnant after conservative surgery for endometriosis. At about that time we became very serious about adopting a child. We investigated every available piece of information and learned about the various routes of adoption open to us. In the U.S.A. we could choose between public or private agencies or independent, also called private, adoption. We could also adopt abroad through an international adoption agency, perhaps in Mexico, Central or South America, or in Asian countries like Korea or India. By then we were in a hurry, so we tried everything. We started a home study locally for a Korean child, put our names on every agency list in the state, and went to every adoption information meeting and agency orientation that we could. We also started "putting out the word" that we were hoping to adopt

READINGS—*continued*

a baby. We began to tell everyone we knew, and had our families and friends do the same, and we followed up all the leads we heard about, no matter how strange. Within two months we heard that someone knew someone who knew someone who knew a pregnant woman who was considering adoption for the baby. From that phone call on we were so exhilarated at our chance to be parents, and so frightened that it might not work out, that we could hardly concentrate.

The elevator ride up to the nursery floor of a small community hospital was the most intensely exciting moment of my life. I was about to meet my newborn daughter. After three and a half years of doctors, tests, temperature charts, drugs, surgeries, X-rays, a miscarriage, and the depression, sadness, and loneliness of being among dear friends with children, I was at last becoming a parent. . . .

An 8:30 A.M. telephone call saying, "It's a girl, very big, very healthy," was our first information about our daughter. It came when she was about fifteen hours old. A day later we told her four grandparents that, if all went well, we'd have our baby girl in two more days. We chose my grandmother's name for her but didn't dare to buy a single baby item until the papers were signed. It would have been too cruel to look at tiny new baby things in our home if the adoption hadn't taken place.

The morning of that exciting day, we were up and dressed early to go to the county court house. There we were interviewed about our ages, address, marriage, and state residency. The birthparents had had a parallel experience before us. We had a quick hearing in front of a judge who asked us if we were aware that adoption meant our taking on the "care, custody, and control" of this baby for the rest of our lives. Of course we were aware! That was the whole object of becoming parents by adoption: to be our child's parents. At the time I couldn't believe the judge really asked us that, though I didn't make a peep in the courtroom.

From court we went to the hospital, an easy and familiar drive that seemed to take forever. We stopped only to call our parents. Mine were waiting back East for our call so that they could jump on the first airplane to be with us at this exciting time.

I will never forget riding up that hospital elevator, with our attorney who had to check the baby out of the hospital. Seeing our baby daughter for the first time, in a tiny examining room on the maternity floor, was dreamlike. Here was this *beautiful* baby who was going to be *mine/ours*. I watched the nurse dressing her. I was entranced, though holding back. I don't know why I didn't just pick her up

and hug her, but I guess I still felt that maybe it was not going to happen, that something else would happen to keep me from being a "Mommy."

Finally all the paperwork of hospital checking-out was completed and a volunteer brought a wheelchair for me, just the way they do for every other new mom, even though I had walked in there by myself just twenty minutes before. A nurse held my daughter all the way down the elevator and out the front door to the car. Then, at last, she put the baby in my arms in the car and wished us good luck.

We had only one hospital pack of formula, so we stopped at our corner drugstore for our first baby shopping: formula, bottles, nipples, cotton and alcohol for her navel, a box of diapers until diaper service started, and a baby thermometer. We took several instant print photos and mailed them right away to her other grandparents, who would come to visit the very next weekend.

At home we just sat and looked at her sleeping. We couldn't take our eyes off her. We watched her breathing, her face movements, the flexing of her fingers and toes. We were fascinated, falling in love, amazed, and in awe of such a miracle. We also didn't know what to do until she woke up and needed to be fed or changed. We phoned a few more family members and a friend who started calling our other friends to spread the good news. . . .

The baby was asleep on our bed when her grandparents saw her for the first time. They beamed; they exclaimed; they cooed about her beauty, her size, her loveliness, her skin, her hands. We all felt so filled with incredibly good feelings. After she woke up, we all worked on changing and feeding her, with much discussion of the right temperature for the bottle, whether the water to dilute the formula had to be boiled (yes, until she was four weeks old said the pediatrician later), and how often to burp her. She helpfully fell asleep after two and a half ounces, so we all could relax again and watch her sleep. This was a most fascinating activity and one which, before the day I became a mother, I had never even known about. . . .

By supper, we were exhausted. We were all floating on clouds of happiness and incredibly high on this one little baby. We fed and changed her a few more times before we all went to sleep. The first time she woke us at 1:00 A.M., I really didn't know where I was (in the living room on the sleepersofa) or what was happening. Her cries seemed so loud in the otherwise silent house. She seemed so intensely hungry. We tried to get the bottle warmed up as quickly as we could, but she woke her grandparents anyway. My mom took over this feeding and I gratefully snuggled back under the covers for another three hours of sleep. By 4:30 A.M.

READINGS—*continued*

my arms and legs felt leaden when I tried to move out of bed for her feeding. I wondered how anyone could continue to function after a night of being awake for forty-five minutes every three hours.

In the morning, the most ordinary things seemed changed. Everything was revolving around the baby. My thoughts were: is she up? is she wet? is the formula warm? do we have more pins for the diapers? can the basinette go out on the patio? do we need mosquito netting? How busy we were—all four grown people not finishing our breakfasts without running to look at her, do some laundry of hers, wash and boil her bottles and nipples, call some more friends and family, get referrals for a pediatrician in town for her first visit. And in between, we all smiled at each other as we bent over the basinette to look at her and listen to her breathe, watching her turn her head from side to side, yawn, or sneeze.

That day progressed like a carnival, with telephone calls ringing in with congratulations and friends stopping by to welcome our daughter. They brought with them treasured collections of their own children's outgrown baby equipment and clothes to share. A car seat, stroller, car bed, swingomatics, playpen, high chair, infant seats, baby bath, and changing table arrived until the patio looked like a baby-land garage sale, with all the stuff being scrubbed clean and drying in the sun. My friends had saved their kids' stuff for my child-to-be, whenever she would arrive. Before, when I was suffering with my infertility and childlessness, they had agreed among themselves not to talk about their children when I was around. I did not know about their consideration until much later. I felt so much more connected to all of them now that we were sharing this mothering experience and now that they could talk "mother talk" freely with me.

Adoption is another way of building families; for after our child is with us, the same issues of sleeping through the night, parent exhaustion, learning to parent, coping with the first fever, bad diaper rash, ear infections, enjoying, worrying, teaching and learning with our child, and all the other wonderful and frustrating parts of being a family occur whether we have adopted or given birth to our child.

When My Son Was Born
JAMES WEBB

U.S. Assistant Secretary of Defense James Webb recounts how witnessing his son's birth profoundly affected his life. As

you read, consider the effect that sex role formation has on our perceptions of the birth process. Do you agree with Webb that "men are essentially interlopers in the life process"? Do you agree with him that it is a father's duty "to challenge and toughen" his sons? Does a father's duty to his daughter differ from his duty to his son? What is the nature of the paradox experienced by Webb? Do you think that all fathers (or parents) must necessarily experience the same paradox? Why or why not?

I was raised from my mother's milk to be a man.

I was taught to do physical labor, to be embarrassed if my palms did not display the calluses of a "working man's hands." I received my first rifle, a gift from my father, on my ninth birthday; I was already an excellent shot. I boxed "under the lights" for eight years—Junior Gloves, Golden Gloves, military boxing. I served in the Marine Corps infantry and was wounded in Vietnam. I grew to manhood believing that nothing was out of my reach if I was willing to sacrifice for it—if I would, on the one hand, perform and, on the other, take the punishment that so often comes with success.

There was no pain that I could not endure. I have been laughed at, called a dirtball, an arrogant redneck. I've been hit in the face, booted in the belly, shot at, blown into the air by enemy grenades, cut on by face-masked doctors. I have endured good relationships that went bad and bad ones that stayed bad, and I finally found one that will always stay good. But not a bit of all this ever got me to the point that I felt my guts had been ripped apart. That was merely life.

My life, that is. Somehow, that made chaos acceptable. Real pain, for me, is to watch one of my children cry.

I have not always been such an easy touch. I began fatherhood with the same intensity that I put into all the other things. My oldest daughter worked very hard to tame me and had some success, teaching me from her crib that one cannot order a newborn babe to cease its crying, that no amount of forceful logic can keep a diaper dry.

But the capstone came when my son was born: The doctors let me inside the delivery room and, in so doing, opened up a world for the most part kept from men. They gave me a glimmer of those first moments of life, made me comprehend the fragility of creation. They helped me see my children, however awkwardly, as their mother does every day.

This is not a testimonial for the Lamaze technique or for the recent trend that allows father inside the delivery room. The availability of either or both, while nice, does not translate into automatic understanding. Men are essentially interlopers in the life process. They are indispensable to creation, but only as something of a catalyst. After that, they are totally dispensable. Their primary function is to drive a car, hold somebody's hand and say nice words. For the most part, they must step back and watch. Even the most well-intentioned male would never presume to be more.

March 9, 1982. For the first time, I witnessed actual birth. JoAnn had a difficult labor. After 36 hours, the doctor decided to perform a cesarean section, since JoAnn was not dilating. The baby had been ramming itself against the undilated cervix as JoAnn's body trembled and undulated, until I became worried for them both.

I was allowed free movement in the delivery room. I was close enough, when the doctors made the incision on her belly, to be splattered with her blood. They pushed and pulled inside her, talking clinically to each other, worrying about the positioning of the baby's head, which was tightly against the cervix, at the beginning of the vaginal canal. I was afraid he was damaged, or even stillborn, since her water had broken hours before.

Suddenly, one doctor reached inside and pulled out a bluish form that reminded me in that instant of a fish, all slick with a coating of placenta, the umbilical cord still joining him with his mother in this last moment of shared existence. I was stunned at his appearance—his size, his color, his immediate reaching and twisting as the doctor held him on display (indeed, like a fish) by one leg. But with that twisting, and the brief wailing sound he made, the fish became a boy.

The nurses wiped him down on a nearby table, dropped liquid into his eyes and gave him a shot. Then they wrapped him, put a stocking cap on his head and handed him to me. After showing him briefly to JoAnn, I was permitted to carry him to the recovery room.

And in the hallway, as we checked each other out, he robbed me of the certainty of my youth. Or maybe I gave it away without a fight.

He was *aware.* That was my first and deepest revelation—birth was not a clear demarcation in the life cycle. He had been alive, and now he was born. There was in his face not a slow awakening that would indicate the turning on of a brain but a conscious comparing, an active mind absorbing a new environment. He did not cry. He lay still in my arms, his clouded little eyes sweeping back and forth, evaluating, and I thought of Dorothy when she landed in Oz: "Toto—I have the feeling we're not in Kansas anymore."

He became so precious to me in those few moments that I did not want to let him out of my arms. I was awash with a mix of emotions and memories, each one indefinable yet all going off in my mind at once, like a sky full of brightly shining stars. I remembered the admonitions of my parents, their attempts to keep me from boxing and their quiet wishes that I not go into the infantry. I recalled my own feelings of immortality at the time, my belief that they were worried that I would not perform well rather than that I might be hurt.

I knew then, as I watched blue eyes that could have been my own seeking to follow different sounds in the sanctity of my cradling arms, that he would in his own way do to me what I had done to them. I knew also that, although the hurt might kill me, I would want him to. Although there could be no greater pain in my life than to see one of my children hurt or lost, it would be my duty to challenge and toughen him, to teach him all the intangibles without which there cannot be strength and honor and achievement. So I danced on the razor's edge of a paradox: I felt at once so joyous, so filled with a love that knew no bounds, yet so afraid that the fruits of my own way of living might someday take my boy away.

In short, for the first time, I looked at life as women always have.

Isn't this what women do? Do they not comprehend better than we men the fragility of life, having nurtured it from nothing? And from the first moment they lose the child from the womb, do they not confront a powerlessness that men rarely even consider? I see all my children differently after that moment with my newborn son. I marvel at their growth, I hope for their future, but deep inside I harbor an agony, knowing how easily fate might bear them away from me. I love them with the knowledge that they are every day moving away, in directions that can perhaps be encouraged but never controlled.

Nothing in my male environment prepared me for this paradox. Instead, it responded to power. The duty of the honorable man was to confront issues with dignity. I learned to be tough. I learned to fight back. I even learned humility. I did not learn that pain administered to someone else might crush me.

A man's relationship with his children begins at a conscious level and grows out of negotiation, however unarticulated. The kids are born, Dad and kids check each other out and become mutually satisfied and then, as the psychologists like to say, they "bond."

This process is deeper for mothers, more fundamental,

READINGS—*continued*

unavoidably biological. I see this in my wife. No matter how much I love my children, no matter how deeply they love me, we began at a different starting point. We developed our love as separately existing individuals. I learned something when that glistening creature was pulled out of my wife's insides and became a boy, but I still doubt that I comprehend the knowledge of human frailty that comes from months of carrying someone in your womb, sharing your blood and body.

My wife is pregnant again. She becomes radiant when with child, at times imperious, at times forgiving but always just a little removed from the rest of us. She smiles and growls just as before, she gives her time and energy to us as she always has, she does not alter her routine. But she is, indeed, in a place that none of us can share. Conception hits her like a hangover as her system adjusts to the presence of another living thing. The baby takes from her, leaving her at first draggy and sleepy. It grows. Her system rights itself. She takes command of her body again, but always with the knowledge that just below her heart she is carrying a part of our future.

At night, I watch her curl on her side and talk to this thing that will soon be her baby. Its elbows and knees make dimples on her belly, and she alternately comforts it and teases it. She knows when it is "awake," and she knows when it "takes a nap." It is alive. And I know nothing of it, except what I learn from her.

PART FOUR

Marriages and Families

CHAPTER 10

Marriage as Process

PREVIEW

To gain a sense of what you already know about the material covered in this chapter, answer "true" or "false" to the following statements. You will find the answers as you read the chapter.

1. How well a couple gets along during their engagement usually indicates how well they will get along after marriage. True or false?
2. Marriage more than parenthood radically affects a woman's life. True or false?
3. The advent of children generally increases a couple's marital satisfaction. True or false?
4. The law usually assumes that the husband is the head of the household. True or false?
5. Although it is generally acceptable for married women to work before they have children, after they become mothers they are likely to experience social pressure to remain at home caring for their young children. True or false?
6. The number of adult children (twenty-one or older) living at home has been increasing in recent years. True or false?
7. The empty nest syndrome, characterized by a mother's depression after the last child leaves home, is a major problem for American families. True or false?
8. Enduring marriages usually have a high level of marital satisfaction. True or false?
9. Most elderly men and women see their children about six times a year. True or false?
10. Despite the image of the isolated American family, considerable interaction takes place between extended family members. True or false?

Outline

Marriage is a process in which people interact with each other, create families, and give each other companionship and love. Marriage is not static—it is always changing to meet new situations, new emotions, new commitments and responsibilities. The marriage process formally begins with engagement; it ends with divorce or with the death of a partner. We may begin marriage thinking we know how to act within it, but we find that the reality of marriage requires us to be more flexible than we had anticipated in order to meet our own needs and the needs of our partners and the marriage. We may have periods of great happiness and great sorrow within marriage. We may find boredom, intensity, frustration, and fulfillment. Some of these may occur because of our marriage; others may occur in spite of it. But as we shall see, marriage encompasses many possibilities.

In this chapter we look at engagement, the wedding ceremony, and the process of entering marital roles. We explore these new roles and how partners go about making adjustments to them. Then we look at the family life cycle to see how families change over time. We examine young, middle aged, and aging families and the theme of marital satisfaction. Next we explore the issue of whether happiness is a necessary quality for enduring marriages by looking at the types of marriages that do endure. Finally, we look at the social context in which our marriages exist and examine the roles that kin and friends play in sustaining marriages.

☐ ENGAGEMENT

Before marriage, prospective partners tend to draw apart from their friends and families, spending more and more time with each other. The relationship becomes so significant that the couple could stand against their friends and family if such a necessity arose. Sociologist Philip Slater (1963) calls this process of isolation *dyadic withdrawal*.

Engagement is the culmination of the formal dating process. Couples who start out in the less traditional "getting together" pattern are less likely to become formally engaged. Instead, they announce that they "plan to get married." Because it lacks the formality of engagement, planning to get married is also less socially binding, although not necessarily less personally binding.

To speak frankly, I am not in favour of long engagements. They give people the opportunity of finding out each other's character before marriage, which I think is never advisable.

OSCAR WILDE, *THE IMPOR-TANCE OF BEING EARNEST*

Functions of Engagement

Engagement performs several functions. First, it prepares couples for marriage by requiring them to think about the realities of everyday married life—money, friendships, religion, in-laws. Second, engagement is the beginning of kinship. Parents, family, and friends become more involved with the couple. The future marriage partner begins to be treated as a member of the family. Third, engagement allows the prospective partners to strengthen themselves as a couple. The engaged pair begin to experience themselves as a social unit. Some couples who have refrained from premarital intercourse may feel that intercourse is now legitimate. Engagement is *almost* like marriage.

When couples announce their engagement, their lives cease being altogether a private matter. They have made a public announcement and thus begin to move into a public sphere. They leave the youth or singles' culture and prepare for the world of the married, which is a remarkably different world. Relationships with parents are reestablished as plans for the wedding are made. Whom to invite, where the wedding and reception are to be held, decisions about the trousseau and the honeymoon—all may require considerable planning with both the bride's and groom's parents, especially the bride's.

Marriage often unites for life two people who scarcely know each other.

HONORÉ DE BALZAC (1799–1850)

Wedding Preparations

In recent years weddings have changed significantly, reflecting changes in who is getting married (Leo, 1982). Today the average bride is in her mid-twenties rather than in her late teens or early twenties. She is more independent and mature. She may be getting married for the second time; she does not approach the wedding as a blushing bride. As a result, the bride-to-be has much more control than previously in planning the wedding. According to Jacqueline Leo, an editor of *Modern Bride* (quoted in Stanyon, 1982), the contemporary bride is very different from her mother:

She's away from home, usually earning her own living. Sometimes she's living with her husband-to-be, sometimes not. Whatever, she is old enough to feel sure he is the one she wants to marry. She has rationally put off marriage until she feels that certainty. The modern bride wants to plan the wedding on her turf, not her parents'. The guests are more apt to be mainly her colleagues, and his, than her dad's golf partners or equivalent associates of her mother.

Since 40 percent of marriages today involve remarriage for at least one partner, children are also often included in the wedding preparations. Some suggest that when such a couple decides to marry, the children should be the first ones told; one child suggested that when parents announce wedding plans to their children they should make it a celebration with an "ice cream sundae to make it official" (Stephen, 1982).

Most couples experience anxiety and stress during their engagement. Some will break the engagement, but most will marry. Of those who do marry, their period of engagement is the best indicator of how successful their marriage will be. Ernest Burgess and Paul Wallin (1953), whose famous study of engagement is still the most authoritative, found that couples who got along well during engagement generally got along well in marriage. Almost half of those in this study found themselves uncertain or anxious during engagement about whether they were marrying the right person. Both the amount of time engaged couples spent together and the length of their engagement were positively related to their marital success.

☐ THE WEDDING

Historical Background

Weddings are ancient rituals that symbolize a couple's commitment to each other. The word *wedding* is derived from the Anglo-Saxon *wed*, meaning "pledge" (Chesser, 1980). The rituals, however, have changed over time. Today it is common for people to devise their own wedding ceremonies, for which they write their own pledges, choose their own settings, and set their own atmosphere. Although wedding ceremonies vary greatly, some aspects remain timeless. The exchanging of rings dates back to ancient Egypt and symbolizes trust, unity, and timelessness, since a ring has no beginning and no end. It is a powerful symbol. (When people meet for the first time, one of their first acts is to glance at each other's fingers to see if the other is wearing a wedding ring.) To return a ring or take it off in anger is a symbolic act. Not to wear a wedding ring is a symbolic statement about a marriage. Carrying the bride over the threshold was practiced in ancient Greece and Rome. It was a symbolic abduction growing out of the belief that a daughter would not willingly leave her father's house. The eating of cake is similarly ancient, representing the offerings made to household gods. The cake made the union sacred (Coulanges, 1960).

The custom of church weddings, however, is more recent (see Chapter 3). It dates back to the Middle Ages when the church was expanding its powers. Before that time, marriage was a family affair in which the father "gave" his daughter away in marriage. The church usurped the family's power and declared marriage a sacrament. As a divine institution, marriage could not be dissolved.

Contemporary American Weddings

Most American weddings are traditional, religious, and formal. First weddings especially are formal, the brides wearing floor-length gowns, mostly white or ivory. But because so many weddings are remarriages, a new etiquette is developing (Leo, 1982). Most second weddings tend to be intimate rather than grand affairs; the woman wears a dress reflecting her own personal style; her father does not give her away again; and she hosts the reception in her own manner. If the bride or groom has children, they are usually given a special place in the ceremony.

Whether a first or second marriage, the central fact about a wedding is that it symbolizes a major transition in life. Most significantly, the man and woman take

Weddings are ceremonies that publicly mark the transition from singlehood to marriage. They symbolize the entrance into society's major adult roles: husband, wife, and (potentially) socially-approved parenthood.

on marital roles. For young persons entering marriage for the first time, marriage signifies a major step in adulthood. Some of the apprehension about marriage felt by engaged couples is probably related to their entering these significant new roles. They take on new responsibilities. Many will have a child within the first year of marriage. So the wedding must be considered a major rite of passage. When a man and woman enter the place where they are going to be married, they are single, their primary responsibilities are to themselves, and their parents may have greater claims on them than they do on each other. But with the exchange of a few words, they are transformed. When they leave the wedding scene, they leave behind the life of being single. They are now responsible to another person as fully as they are to themselves and more than they are to their parents. (See the reading "A Gay Wedding" by Philip Zwerling.)

. . . until two people, who are married, look into each other's eyes and make a solemn commitment to each other—that they will stop at nothing, that they will face any cost, any pain, any struggle, go out of their way so that they may learn and seek in order that they may make their marriage a continuously growing experience—until two people have done that they are not in my judgment married.

DAVID MACE and VERA MACE

☐ THE FAMILY LIFE CYCLE

Just as individuals have life cycles with specific stages, so do marriages and families. Within these stages each marriage and family has its own unique history (Aldous, 1978). The family life cycle approach uses a developmental framework to explain people's behavior in families. According to the developmental framework, families change over time in terms of both the people who are members of the family and the roles they play. At various stages in the family life cycle, the family has different developmental tasks to perform. The behavior of family members can be explained in terms of the family's developmental stage. The key factor in such developmental studies is the presence of children. The family organizes itself around its childrearing responsibilities. (For a developmental approach centering on age, see Neugarten, 1979, and Neugarten et al., 1973.) A woman's role as wife is different when she is childless than when she has children. A man's role as a father is different when he is the father of a one-year-old than when he is the father of a fifteen-year-old.

There are a number of ways of looking at the stages of the family life cycle (Norton, 1983). Most of them, however, assume that the family is the contemporary intact nuclear family; marriages without children, single-parent and blended-families generally are not incorporated into the developmental framework (McGoldrick and Carter, 1982; for a chart describing the developmental tasks of the blended-family, see Chapter 17). Single adults have a unique "family" life cycle (Stein, 1978).

The family life cycle approach gives us important insights into the complexities of family life. Not only is the family performing various tasks during its life cycle but each family member is also undergoing developmental tasks in his or her life cycle (see Chapter 1 for Erikson's description of the individual life cycle). The task for families with adolescents is to give their children greater autonomy and independence. While the family is coping with this new developmental task, an adolescent daughter has her own individual task of trying to develop a satisfactory identity. Meanwhile, her older brother is struggling with intimacy issues, her younger sister is developing industry, her parents are dealing with issues of generativity, and her grandparents are confronting the issue of integrity.

One of the most widely used approaches divides the family life cycle into eight stages (Duvall, 1975; but also see McGoldrick and Carter, 1982, who include singlehood as part of the family life cycle). As you examine the different stages, find which stage your family of origin is in. What are the tasks it confronts? In what individual developmental tasks are the different members of your family engaged?

- *Stage I: Beginning Families.* During this stage the married couple has no children. In the past this stage was relatively short, since children soon followed marriage. Today, however, it may last until a couple is in their late twenties or early thirties. On the average, it seems to last about two to three years. In the 1980s the average age for women at the birth of their first child is twenty-five years. Most studies on marital satisfaction agree that couples experience their greatest satisfaction in this stage (Glenn and McLanahan, 1982).
- *Stage II: Childbearing Families.* Because families tend to space their children about thirty months apart, the family is still considered to be forming. By this time the oldest child is about thirty months old. The average family has 2.3 children. Since the woman is deeply enmeshed in childbearing and childrearing, this is the

time when she is least likely to work. Increasing parental responsibilities also mean less time together for the couple. Marital satisfaction begins to lessen and continues to decline through the end of the preschool or school-age family. This stage lasts around two and a half years. Most studies (Rollins and Cannon, 1974; Spanier et al., 1975) suggest that marital satisfaction does not increase again until the children begin to leave home.

- *Stage III: Families with Preschool Children.* This family's oldest child is age thirty months to six years. The mother is still deeply involved in childrearing. This stage lasts about three and a half years.
- *Stage IV: Families with Schoolchildren.* This family's oldest child is between six and thirteen years of age. With the children in school and more free time, the mother has more options available to her. This is when most women reenter the job market. This stage lasts about seven years.
- *Stage V: Families with Teenagers.* In a family with adolescents the oldest child is between thirteen and twenty years old. This stage may last seven years.
- *Stage VI: Families as Launching Centers.* By this time the first child has been launched into the adult world. This stage lasts until the last child leaves home, a period of about eight years. Virtually all studies show that marital satisfaction begins to rise for most couples during this stage.
- *Stage VII: Families in the Middle Years.* This stage lasts from the time the last child has left home to retirement. The "empty nest phase," that is, the time from the departure of the last child to old age, is a distinct new phase in the family life cycle (Borland, 1982). Until this century most parents continued to have children until middle age, and the childrearing and launching periods were extended into old age. The empty nest period has increased from two to thirteen years in this century; it is one of the most dramatic changes that has occurred in the family life cycle pattern (Glick, 1977a).
- *Stage VIII: Aging Families.* The working members of the aging family have retired. Usually, the husband retires before the wife since he tends to be older; if she works, he may be left at home alone until she also retires (Keith et al., 1981). Chronic illnesses begin to settle in and take their toll. Eventually, one of the spouses dies, usually the husband. Women have an average life expectancy of seventy-nine years, whereas men's life expectancy averages about seventy-two years; 69.7 percent of American women over the age of seventy-five are widows. Few remarry at that age. They live out their remaining years as widows, what one researcher calls a "roleless role" (Hiltz, 1978).

For everything there is a season, and a time to every purpose under heaven:
a time to be born and a time to die;
a time to plant, and a time to pluck up what is planted;
a time to kill, and a time to heal;
a time to break down, and a time to build up;
a time to weep, and a time to laugh;
a time to mourn, and a time to dance;
a time to cast away stones and a time to gather stones together;
a time to embrace, and a time to refrain from embracing;
a time to seek, and a time to lose;
a time to keep, and a time to cast away;
a time to rend, and atime to sew;
a time to keep silence, and a time to speak;
a time to love, and a time to hate;
a time for war, and a time for peace.

ECCLESIASTES

☐ BEGINNING MARRIAGES AND FAMILIES

The first stage of the family life cycle begins with the wedding. But a wedding is not a marriage. It is only the ceremony that represents the beginning of marriage. The first year that follows marks the real beginning of the marriage, and it is an especially crucial year. Mace and Mace (1980) observed: "Following the wedding, marriages begin to take shape in that first year, and sometimes it is a good pattern, in which case the marriage will keep on growing, and sometimes it is a bad pattern, in which case the marriage will probably go on deteriorating." Whatever direction the marriage may take, it now begins in earnest.

It is an easier thing to be a lover than a husband, for the same reason that it is more difficult to be witty everyday than now and then.

HONORÉ DE BALZAC

. . . in all countries there are many women who manage to dominate the man, but it seems likely that in most countries, when the husband tries to dominate he can still do this. Even when the husband performs the household chores, his participation means that he gains power—the household becoming a further domain for the exercise of prerogatives for making decisions.

WILLIAM GOODE

Marriage is that relation between men and women in which the independence is equal, the dependence mutual, and the obligation reciprocal.

L. ANSPACHER

Role Expectations

The expectations that two people have about their own and each other's marital roles are based in law and their own experience.

Legal Assumptions.   As they begin marriage, two people discover that they each have very powerful expectations of how they are supposed to act. The role responsibilities of husbands and wives are even included in the legal code (Weitzman, 1981). The four main legal assumptions about the responsibilities of husbands and wives are as follows (Weitzman, 1978):

- The husband is the head of the household.
- The husband is responsible for supporting the family.
- The wife is responsible for domestic work.
- The wife is responsible for childrearing.

Even if the couple have drawn up their own marriage contract, if any part of it contradicts the legal assumptions, the contract may be invalid in a court of law. The state is a profound force shaping the ways in which we choose to live (Weitzman, 1981).

Contemporary Marital Roles.   Although the law requires husbands and wives to be responsible for certain aspects of the family, the rigidity of these distinctions has been breaking down for some time. The law does not necessarily reflect marital reality. For example, the husband may be head of the household legally, but power tends to be shared. With the rise of dual-worker families, both men and women contribute to the financial support of the family. Although responsibility for domestic work still tends to reside with women, men are beginning to assist in housework. The mother is still generally responsible for childrearing, but fathers are beginning to participate more.

According to one researcher (Nye, 1976), there are at least eight roles within the contemporary American family (see below). As you examine these stages, how do you think the responsibilities should be divided between men and women? How are they divided in your family of origin? If you are cohabiting or married, how are these responsibilities divided in your relationship? Compare your responses to your partners; you might be surprised.

- *The housekeeper role*: responsibility for cleaning the house, washing clothes and dishes, shopping and preparing meals, and maintaining household accounts.
- *The provider role*: responsibility for earning money to support the family.
- *The child-care role*: the physical care of the children—feeding, dressing, washing, and protecting them.
- *The child socialization role*: teaching children values, attitudes, skills, and approved behaviors.
- *The sexual role*: responding to the partner's sexual needs.
- *The kinship role*: maintaining contact with relatives and assisting them in times of need.
- *The recreational role*: organizing family recreation.
- *The therapeutic role*: listening to, understanding, sympathizing with, helping, and caring for other members of the family.

Although law and tradition have assigned these responsibilities along sex lines, they do not always fit the temperament and abilities of a particular husband and wife.

Identity Bargaining

At the outset of a marriage, each partner must take the roles and stereotypes he or she has learned and adjust them to the reality of the marriage. The most significant person for teaching proper roles is the partner. As Mirra Komarovsky (1967) points out, "No one has a more vital stake in getting his partner to fulfill his obligations than his spouse. Hardly any aspect of marriage is exempt from mutual instruction and pressures to change."

People carry around idealized pictures of marriage long before they meet their marriage partner. They have to adjust these preconceptions to the reality of their partner's personality and the circumstances of their marriage. This process of adjustment is called *identity bargaining* (Blumstein, 1975). It is a three-step process.

First, a person has to identify with the role he or she is peforming. A man must feel as if he is a husband and a woman must feel as if she is a wife. The wedding ceremony acts as a catalyst for role change from the single state to the married state.

Second, a person must be treated by the other as if he or she fulfills the role. The husband must treat his wife as a wife; his wife must treat him as a husband. The problem is that a couple rarely agrees on what actually constitutes the roles of husband and wife. This is especially true now as the traditional content of marital roles is changing.

Third, the two people must negotiate changes in each other's roles. A woman may have learned that she is supposed to defer to her husband, but if he makes an unfair demand, how can she? A man may believe his wife is supposed to be sexually passive, but if she is not, should he lose respect for her or should he accept her as an active sexual being? A woman discovers she does not like housework, but she is expected to do it as part of her marital role. Does she then do housework or does she ask her husband to share responsibility with her? A man knows he is supposed to be strong, but sometimes feels small and weak—does he reveal this to his wife? Eventually, these adjustments must be made, but at first there may be confusion; both partners may feel inadequate because they are not fulfilling their role expectations.

> Married in haste, we repent at leisure.
>
> WILLIAM CONGREVE (1670–1729)

Male Adjustments. Although both husband and wife must make adjustments to each other, the life of the man usually changes less drastically with marriage than the life of the woman. The man has been trained since early boyhood to go out into the world, to be active; his role as husband continues that direction as he helps support his wife and family through his work or career (Weiss, 1985).

> The whole world is a comedy to those that think, a tragedy to those who feel.
>
> HORACE WALPOLE (1717–1797)

Female Adjustments. In contrast to men, a woman's role in marriage is discontinuous with her earlier life. True, she has been socialized to be a wife and mother; her girlhood and adolescence have been a training ground for her marital role. But marriage takes her outside the social context in which she used to live; her world changes dramatically. She is expected to remain at home. Even if she works, she is under subtle pressure to have a baby and return to the home to fulfill her duties as a housewife and mother. Since nearly one-fifth of all marriages take place when the woman is already pregnant, she is soon at home as both a wife and a mother.

Table 10–1 **Changing Marital Roles**

Domain	Norms	Change Occurred[1]	Implementation By Majority[1]
1. Division of Labor			
Economic	acceptance of wives' and mothers' labor force participation	yes	yes
	acceptance of shared responsibility for provider role	low	no
Housework	acceptance of mutual and flexible participation in housework	yes	yes
	acceptance of shared responsibility for housework	low	no
Childcare	acceptance of mutual and flexible participation in childcare	yes	yes
	acceptance of shared responsibility for children	low	no
Total work	acceptance of equality in spouses' work load	yes	yes
2. Authority	acceptance of shared participation in all family decisions	yes	yes
	acceptance of shared authority	low	no
	acceptance of use of similar power tactics	?[3]	?
	rejection of use of physical force[2]	?	(yes)
3. Sexual relations	acceptance of same sexual standards for both sexes	yes	partially
	acceptance of right to equal sexual gratification	yes	yes
	acceptance of shared participation in sexual decisions	yes	no

Domain	Behaviors	Change Occurred[1]	Implementation By Majority[1]
1. Division of Labor			
Economic	wives' and mothers' labor force participation	yes	yes
	equal contribution of spouses to family income	some	no
Housework	mutual and flexible participation in housework	low	no
	equal time spent with housework	low	no
Childcare	mutual and flexible participation in childcare	some	no
	equal time spent with childcare	low	no
Total work	equal workload of spouses	low	no
2. Authority	shared participation in all family decisions	low	no
	not applicable		
	use of similar power tactics by both partners	?	no
	use of physical force	?	(yes)
3. Sexual relations	equal participation in sexual activities	yes	partially
	equal sexual gratification	yes	partially
	shared participation in sexual decisions	some	no

[1]Change refers to evidence regarding increased acceptance/enactment of norms/behaviors characteristic of the sex-role transcendent model, implementation refers to the acceptance/enactment of such norms/behaviors by the majority (over 50%).

[2]Application of the majority rule is probably inappropriate here, but the majority of respondents reject use of physical force in marital relations.

[3]? indicates lack of clear empirical evidence.

Establishing Boundaries

When people marry they often have strong ties to their parents. Until the wedding their family of origin has greater claim to their loyalties than their spouse-to-be. Once the ceremony is completed, however, the newlyweds must establish their own family independently of their families of origin. The couple must negotiate a different relationship with their parents, siblings, and in-laws. Loyalties must shift from their families of origin to their newly-formed family. The families of origin must accept and support these breaks (Minuchin, 1974). Indeed, opening themselves to outsiders who have become official members through marriage places no small stress on families (McGoldrick and Carter, 1982).

The new family must establish its own boundaries. The couple must decide how much interaction with their families is desirable and how much influence their families of origin may have. There are often important ties to the parents that may prevent new families from achieving their needed independence. First is the tie of habit. Parents are used to being superordinate; children are used to being subordinate. The tie between mothers and daughters is especially strong; daughters often experience greater difficulty separating themselves from their mothers than do sons. These difficulties may show up in a woman feeling conflicting loyalties toward her mother and husband (see Cohler and Geyer, 1982). Much in-law conflict occurs when a spouse feels an in-law is exerting too much influence on his or her partner: a mother-in-law insisting that her son visit each Sunday and the son accepting despite the protests of his wife; a father-in-law warning his son-in-law to establish himself in a career or risk losing his wife. If conflict occurs, husbands and wives need to put the needs of their spouses ahead of their parents.

Another tie to the family of origin may be money. Newly married couples often have little money or credit with which to begin their families. They may turn to parents to borrow money, cosign loans, or obtain credit. But financial dependence keeps the new family tied to the family of origin. The parents may try to exert undue influence on their children because it is their money, not their children's money, that is being spent. They may try to influence their children's purchases; they may refuse to loan money to buy something of which they disapprove.

The critical task is to form a family that is interdependent rather than totally independent or dependent. It is a delicate balancing act as parents and their adult children begin to make adjustments to the new marriage. We need to maintain bonds with our families of origin and to participate in the extended family network, but we cannot let those bonds turn into chains. (See the reading "Marital Tasks: Breaking Parental Ties" by Jean Marzollo.)

> When a young man marries, he divorces his mother.
>
> YIDDISH PROVERB

> Some young men and women use marriage as a means of breaking away from over-possessive parents. But marriage which is considered by the participants as part of the strategy of emancipation from parents will bring with it tremendous psychological hazards. Despite their ostensible defiance, children who seek so drastic a means of establishing their independence have by no means done so effectively. The complexities and subtleties of this parent-child battle reflect themselves in the marriage itself. In-law problems may thus be one phase of parent-child relational problems.
>
> JESSIE BERNARD, *REMARRIAGE*

☐ YOUTHFUL MARRIAGES

Youthful marriages represent stages II-IV in the family life cycle: childbearing families (stage II), families with small children (stage III), and families with school-age children (stage IV).

Impact of Children

Husband and wife both usually work until their first child is born; then the woman generally quits working to attend to childrearing duties. The husband continues his

FEATURE

Concepts of Marriage

Through our lifetime we tend to hold different views of marriage that evolve throughout our lives. Tamashiro (1978) describes individuals' conceptions of marriage as consecutive stages: magical, idealized convention, individualistic, and affirmational.

In the first stage, the *magical stage*, people see marriage as a fairy tale that ends in "and they lived happily every after." Simplistic beliefs such as money brings happiness, good sex makes a good marriage, and children guarantee marital and personal fulfillment are part of the magical stage.

The second stage, *idealized convention*, views marriage according to strict conventional rules. People accept the rules without criticism; they believe that following the rules will bring happiness. Thus a husband does not do housework, a wife does not work outside the home. The couple judge their relationship by external factors like personal appearance, friendliness, health, reputation, and status. "Getting along together" is seen as the basis of the relationship.

The third stage, the *individualistic stage*, is marked by the individual's growing awareness of inner feelings and emotions. The individual discovers that conventionality does not lead to an emotionally fulfilling marriage. During this stage, conventional standards are replaced by the individual's personal preferences and desires. People assess their marriage in terms of their sense of well-being, personal development, and sense of self. They view the marriage as worthwhile only if it furthers personal goals and allows them the maximum amount of freedom. Self-enhancement is the major concern in this stage.

The final stage is the *affirmational stage* in which individuals acknowledge their inner dilemmas and face their vulnerability. They conceptualize marriage as multifaceted; they express a deepened concern for themselves and their partners. They tend to be more open and positive in their concept of marriage.

At which stage is your concept of marriage? What brought you to this stage? Did you go through earlier stages consecutively as Tamashiro suggests is necessary?

job or career. Although the first child makes him a father, fatherhood does not radically alter his relationship with his work. The wife's life, however, changes dramatically with motherhood. Her contacts during most of the day are with her children and with other mothers. This relative isolation requires her to make a considerable psychological adaptation. She may experience a severe identity crisis. Because she is fulfilling her traditional roles as wife and mother, her partner may not understand why she is unhappy. She may not fully understand the reasons herself. The husband and wife may grow increasingly apart during this period: throughout the day they move in different worlds, and at night they cannot relate easily to each other because they do not understand each other's experiences.

Typical struggles in families with young children concern child-care responsibilities and parental roles. Sometimes parents do not accept themselves as authority figures and find it difficult to exert control over their children. If they are unable to assume adequate parent roles, they may placate or spoil their children or be overly critical of them (McGoldrick and Carter, 1982).

Although parenthood takes away from a couple's time, it is also a source of great pleasure for most parents. Their need to establish generativity is met through rearing their children.

Individual Changes

When people enter their thirties, the marital situation begins to change somewhat. The children have usually started school and the wife now begins to have some time free from childrearing duties. What does she do? Does she return to school to finish her degree or go back to the world of work? Will her husband support her decision to leave the home or does he want more children? In her late thirties she may enter a midlife crisis. The majority of women return to the workplace by the time their children reach adolescence. By working, women generally increase their marital power.

Husbands, too, may enter a midlife crisis. Blue-collar men often find that their jobs have already peaked; they can no longer look forward to promotions. They may feel stalled and become depressed as they look into the future, which they see as nothing more than the past repeated for thirty more years. Their families may offer emotional satisfaction and fulfillment, however, as compensation..

Middle-class men also may undergo a crisis in their thirties. They may have found success, but not the success they dreamed of when they were younger. They will not be vice-president of the company; they will not be elected president; they will not be the greatest athlete—or lover—in the world. They then may experience whatever success they have achieved as failure, for they have not attained the unattainable. Alternatively, they may find that the cost of their success is not worth it: they may have lost touch with their partners; they may not have had time to be a good father

I am referred to in that splendid language [Urdu] as "Fella belong Mrs. Queen."

PRINCE PHILIP, DUKE OF EDINBURGH

to their children. At this time, they may renew their involvement with their families.

Corporate families in this period are faced with both acute and chronic stress. Employment insecurity and career mobility, job content and satisfaction, heavy work loads, geographic mobility, and the expectation that the executive be married to the corporation as well as to his or her partner all drain the family (Voydanof, 1980). Spouses may develop separate lives and fail to establish community ties; their children may be unable to form lasting friendships because of constantly moving.

☐ MIDDLE-AGED MARRIAGES

Marriage must continually vanquish the monster that devours everything, the monster of habit.

HONORÉ DE BALZAC

Middle-aged marriages generally represent stages V–VII in the family life cycle: families with teenagers (stage V), families as launching centers (stage VI), and families in the middle years (stage VII). Couples in these stages are usually in their mid-thirties, forties and fifties.

Families with Adolescents

Increased family conflict usually occurs as adolescents begin to assert their autonomy and independence. Some parents cannot face seeing their children grow up. As McGoldrick and Carter (1982) pointed out:

Families with adolescents must establish qualitatively different boundaries than families with younger children. . . . Parents can no longer maintain complete authority. Adolescents can and do open the family to a whole array of new values as they bring friends and new ideas into the family arena. Families that become derailed at this stage are frequently stuck in an earlier view of their children. They may try to control every aspect of their lives at a time when, developmentally, this is impossible to do successfully. Either the adolescent withdraws from the appropriate involvements for this developmental stage or the parents become increasingly frustrated with what they perceive as their own impotence.

When Children Leave Home

Some couples may happily or even gratefully see their children leave home, some experience difficulties with this exodus, and some continue to accommodate their adult children under the parental roof.

The Empty Nest.   As their children leave home, parents are faced with the "empty nest." For some parents, the empty nest is seen as the end of the family: children have been the focal point of much family happiness and pain—and now they are gone. Research has been inconsistent as to whether departure of the last child from home (the end of childrearing responsibilities) necessarily leads to the *empty nest syndrome,* characterized by depression and identity crisis. Some studies suggest that individuals find their lives more satisfying during this stage (Petranek, 1970). If the syndrome does occur, it generally seems to be restricted to white, middle-class women who have led traditional lives centered around their roles as mothers (Bart, 1972;

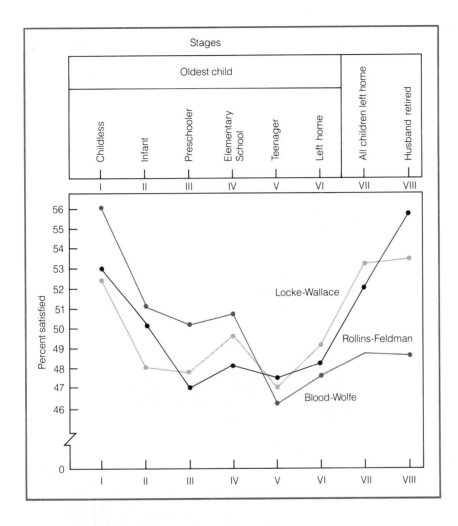

Stages

Figure 10–1

This figure shows the average standard scores on marital satisfaction over eight stages of the family life cycle, as indicated by three separate studies. Note that all three record a sharp decline in marital satisfaction around the time of the birth of children and a sharp increase in marital satisfaction when children leave home. (From Boyd C. Rollins and Kenneth L. Cannon, "Marital Satisfaction over the Family Life Cycle," *Journal of Marriage and the Family*, May 1974.) Also see Table 16–1 (p. 295) for the relationship between the stages of the family life cycle and stress.

Lurie, 1974; Williams, 1977). It does not seem to occur in Mexican-American and black families (Borland, 1982).

The couple must now recreate their family minus their children. The husband and wife must rediscover themselves as man and woman and no longer relate to each other primarily as parents—the mainstay of their relationship for perhaps twenty years. Some couples may divorce at this point if the children were the only reason the pair remained together.

Continuing Parental Control. Even after a child has left home, parents may be reluctant to abandon their roles as parents. This is especially true if their children are financially dependent on them, as when they are in college. If the parents control the purse, they may feel they have a right to impose their standards and judgments on their children: to decide whether the son or daughter can live with someone, go to Europe, stay at home over the summer, and so on. Only when their children have lived away from home for some time or marry do parents begin to fully relinquish their parental role.

Adult Children at Home

Just how empty homes actually are after children reach eighteen years of age is open to question. Children do not necessarily leave home after they turn eighteen. In fact, most single children do not leave home until they are more than twenty-four years old. They may live at home while attending college or working. Most children move away from home when they get married. The statistics are quite startling: In 1983, 7.4 percent of families had one child between eighteen and twenty-four years living at home and 4.2 percent had two children living at home. Almost 4 percent of the families had one child over age twenty-five living at home; about 1 percent had two children over twenty-five living at home (Clemens and Axelson, 1985). In 1980, 69 percent of single men between the ages of twenty and twenty-four and 42 percent of those between the ages of twenty-five and twenty-nine still lived at home. Among women, 64 percent and 32 percent of these age groups, respectively, lived at home (U.S. Bureau of the Census, 1981). Although stereotypes suggest that men are more independent than women, when it comes to leaving home men apparently exhibit more dependent behavior.

In one study the most frequently reported reasons adult children live at home, apart from educational ones, were financial problems, saving money, unemployment, waiting to begin a new job, and inability "to get on his or her feet" (Clemens and Axelson, 1985). (Some of these reasons overlap.) About 80 percent of the parents with children twenty-two years and over had not expected the child to be living at home. Most wanted their children to be "up, gone, and on their own." For parents, the most frequently mentioned problems were the hours of their children's coming and going and their failure to clean and maintain the house. Almost half reported serious conflicts with their children.

Reevaluation

Middle-aged persons find that they must reevaluate relations with their children who are becoming or have become independent adults and with their own parents who are becoming more dependent as they age (see Thompson et al., 1985, and Thompson et al., 1985b).

Seldom, or perhaps never, does a marriage develop into an individual relationship smoothly and without crises; there is no coming to consciousness without pain.

CARL JUNG

Examining Goals.   Couples in middle age tend to reexamine or finish examining their aims and goals. On the average, husbands and wives have eleven more years of marriage without children than they used to, and during this time their partnership may become more harmonious or more strained. The man may decide to stay at home more, not to work as hard as before. The woman may be tired of being at home and decide to work—or she may remain at home, enjoying her new child-free leisure. Because the wife often returns to work and childrearing expenses have stopped, this period may represent the financial peak for a couple (Glick, 1977). In fact, 31 percent of all Americans between forty-five and sixty-four years earn more than $35,000 a year; they have in their hands more than one-third of all discretionary income (Doan and Thornton, 1983).

As people enter their fifties, they probably have advanced as far as they will ever advance in their work: they have accepted their own limits. But they also have an increased sense of their own mortality. Not only do they feel their bodies aging, but also around them people their own age are beginning to die. Some continue to live

Table 10–1 **Individual and Marital Stages of Development**

Item	Stage 1 (18–21 years)	Stage 2 (22–28 years)	Stage 3 (29–31 years)	Stage 4 (32–39 years)	Stage 5 (40–42 years)	Stage 6 (43–59 years)	Stage 7 (60 years and over)
Individual stage	Pulling up roots	Provisional adulthood	Transition at age 30	Settling down	Mid-life transition	Middle adulthood	Older age
Individual task	Developing autonomy	Developing intimacy and occupational identification; "getting into the adult world"	Deciding about commitment to work and marriage	Deepening commitments; pursuing more long-range goals	Searching for "fit" between aspirations and environment	Restabilizing and reordering priorities	Dealing effectively with aging, illness, and death while retaining zest for life
Marital task	Shift from family of origin to new commitment	Provisional marital commitment	Commitment crisis; restlessness	Productivity: children, work, friends, and marriage	Summing up: success and failure are evaluated and future goals sought	Resolving conflicts and stabilizing the marriage for the long haul	Supporting and enhancing each other's struggle for productivity and fulfillment in face of the threats of aging
Marital conflict	Original family ties conflict with adaptation	Uncertainty about choice of marital partner; stress over parenthood	Doubts about choice come into sharp conflict; rates of growth may diverge if spouse has not successfully negotiated stage 2 because of parental obligations	Husband and wife have different and conflicting ways of achieving productivity	Husband and wife perceive "success" differently; conflict between individual success and remaining in the marriage	Conflicting rates and directions of emotional growth; concerns about losing youthfulness may lead to depression and/ or acting out	Conflicts are generated by rekindled fears of desertion, loneliness, and sexual failure
Intimacy	Fragile intimacy	Deepening but ambivalent intimacy	Increasing distance while partners make up their minds about each other	Marked increase in intimacy in "good" marriages; gradual distancing in "bad" marriages	Tenuous intimacy as fantasies about others increase	Intimacy is threatened by aging and by boredom vis-à-vis a secure and stable relationship; departure of children may increase or decrease intimacy	Struggle to maintain intimacy in the face of eventual separation; in most marriages this dimension achieves a stable plateau
Power	Testing of power	Establishment of patterns of conflict resolution	Sharp vying for power and dominance	Establishment of definite patterns of decision making and dominance	Power in outside world is tested vis-à-vis power in the marriage	Conflicts often increase when children leave, and security appears threatened	Survival fears stir up needs for control and dominance
Marital boundaries	Conflicts over in-laws	Friends and potential lovers; work versus family	Temporary disruptions including extramarital sex or reactive "fortress building"	Nuclear family closes boundaries	Disruption due to reevaluation; drive versus restabilization	Boundaries are usually fixed except in crises such as illness, death, job change, and sudden shift in role relationships	Loss of family and friends leads to closing in of boundaries; physical environment is crucial in maintaining ties with the outside world

From Levinson et al., 1974. Reprinted with permission from Berman, E. & Lief, H. Marital therapy from a psychiatric perspective: An overview. *American Journal of Psychiatry*, 132(6): 586, June 1975.

FEATURE

Examining Marital Satisfaction

CHILDREN AND THE LIFE CYCLE

Since marriage and the family have moved to the very center of people's lives as a source of personal satisfaction, we now evaluate marriage and family according to how well they fulfull emotional needs. Paradoxically, however, marriages seem to give the most satisfaction when no children are present; nevertheless, people continue to have children. Children and marital satisfaction seem opposed to each other. Virtually all studies come to that same dismal conclusion. Studies indicate a U-shaped curve of marital satisfaction (see Figure 10–1). Satisfaction is highest at the first stage of the family life cycle before children. The arrival of the first child marks a steady decline; satisfaction does not begin to increase until the children start to leave home.

We have to be careful however, when we interpret the relationship between marital satisfaction and children.

1. When you examine the U-shaped curve in Figure 10–1, notice that the steepness of the curve *visually* distorts the amount of change. Most of the variation covers the range from 46 to 56, a fairly small range of the response.

2. Changes in marital satisfaction may not be due to changes in the family life cycle as much as to other factors, such as increasing work commitments and role strain, conflicting family, work, kinship, and community roles. Children come at a time when work commitments are heaviest for both men and women. The workplace makes few if any adjustments to family needs. Rollins and Cannon (1974) suggest that less than 10 percent of the decline in marital satisfaction can be attributed to changes in the family life cycle per se.

3. The methodology itself might be flawed. Most studies relating changes in marital satisfaction

---

as if they were ageless—running, working hard, keeping up or even increasing the pace of their activities. Others become more reflective, retreating from the world. Some may turn outward, renewing their contacts with friends, relatives, and especially their children.

The Filial Crisis. During this time, parents must accept the marriages of their children and new members entering their family as in-laws. They must accept themselves as grandparents. At the same time, they must deal with a different kind of relationship with their own parents who may become dependent on them. Eighteen percent of the elderly live with an adult child. At least five million men and women are caring for an aged parent on any single day. Such care often is the source of profound stress (Gelman et al., 1985):

. . . there is a welter of conflicts, anxiety about their parents' needs colliding with the needs of their own families, the guilty longing for freedom rubbing up against the guilty conviction that they are not doing enough. For some, the ironic role reversal in becoming a parent to the parents is unsettling at a deep psychic level. The sudden or growing helplessness of people who were the authority figures in a child's life can be overwhelming.

> Anyone who fails to go along with life remains suspended stiff, and rigid in mid-air. That is why so many people get wooden in their old age; they look back and cling to the past with a secret fear of death in their hearts. From the middle of life onward, only he remains virtually alive who is ready to die with life, for in the secret hour of life's midday the parabola is reversed, death is born. We grant goal and purpose to the ascent of life, why not to the descent?
>
> CARL JUNG

FEATURE–*continued*

to the family life cycle are cross-sectional studies; that is, a number of families at different stages in their life cycle are asked to rate their satisfaction. If the studies are done longitudinally (studying the same families over their entire life cycle), would the same changes be found? In the cross-sectional studies, for example, marital satisfaction might have risen during the later stages because the unhappy couples had divorced and thus were not included. A recent study controlled number of children, their age, and sex and found that marital satisfaction declined for mothers of two children and for mothers with male children (Abbott and Brody, 1985). There were no significant differences between the marital satisfaction of women with female children and wives without children.

Although many societal factors make childrearing a difficult and sometimes painful experience for many families, it is also important to note that children create parental roles and the family in its most traditional sense. The marital relationship may be less than fulfilling, but many couples may make a trade-off for fulfillment in their parental roles. In times of marital crisis parental roles may be the glue that holds the relationship together until the crisis passes. Many couples will endure intense situational conflict, not for the sake of the marriage, but for the sake of the children. If the crisis can be resolved, the marriage may be even more solid than before.

In looking at marital satisfaction in terms of children, we need to balance it against family satisfaction. In Leo Tolstoy's poignant novella *Family Happiness*, Marya struggles over her changing feelings toward her husband after their marriage. "To love him," she muses, "was not enough for me after the happiness I had felt in falling in love." She wants her marital relationship to have the same romance that it had when they courted and were first married. At last, she and her husband talk about the changes in their relationship. The

(*Continued on page 298.*)

This role reversal of aging parents and their children is called the *filial crisis* (Santrock, 1983). Women, in particular, feel the stress since they tend to be the ones responsible for intergenerational care. Not only are they frequently mothers but they are also workers; an infirm parent can sometimes be an overwhelming burden to an already overburdened woman. The filial crisis calls for viewing parents in a new perspective, appreciating their strengths and weaknesses, and accepting their increasing dependence.

☐ AGING MARRIAGES

Aging marriages represent the last stage (stage VIII) in the family life cycle. During this period, the aging family faces two important tasks: adjustment to retirement and the loss of the spouse. Individuals must deal with their own biological aging and ultimate deaths.

Stages of Aging

We can look at stages of aging chronologically and by tasks confronting people at different stages.

Better a Socrates dissatisfied than a pig satisfied.

JOHN STUART MILL

The pursuit of happiness is a most ridiculous phrase: if you pursue happiness you'll never find it.

C. P. SNOW

Love seems the swiftest, but it is the slowest of all growths. No man or woman really knows what perfect love is until they have been married a quarter of a century.

MARK TWAIN

FEATURE–*continued*

novella concludes in a poignant but bittersweet manner: "With that day ended my love-story with my husband, the old feeling became a precious memory never to return; but the new feeling of love for my children and the father of my children laid the foundation of another life, happy in quite a different way, which I am still living up to the present moment."

SOCIAL AND PERSONAL FACTORS

Although the most consistent finding about marital satisfaction concerns children, other social factors are also important. First, income level is a significant factor. Blue-collar workers have less marital satisfaction than white-collar, managerial, and professional workers for the simple reason that they make less money (Feldman and Feldman,

1975). High unemployment and the increasing shift of the tax burden to individuals also directly affect marital satisfaction. Much marital conflict is about money. People do not live on love alone—they live on love *and* money.

Race is also associated with marital satisfaction. Blacks tend to be less satisfied in their marriages than whites; younger black women tend to be more dissatisfied with their marriages than their white peers (Renne, 1970).

As we might guess, love, esteem, and affection for each other are also related to marital satisfaction (Hicks and Platt, 1970). A high self-concept—how a person perceives himself or herself and how the spouse perceives the person—contribute to marital satisfaction. Happily married couples talk to each other more, are more sensitive to each other's needs, and give each other positive reinforcement in nonverbal ways (Narvan, 1967).

The greatest happiness you can have is knowing that you do not necessarily require happiness.

WILLIAM SAROYAN

Six Rules for Staying Young

1. Avoid fried meats which angry up the blood.
2. If your stomach disputes you, lie down and pacify it with cool thoughts.
3. Keep the juices flowing by jangling around gently as you move.
4. Go very lightly on the vices, such as carrying on in society. The social ramble ain't restful.
5. Avoid running at all times.
6. Don't look back. Something might be gaining on you.

SATCHEL PAIGE

The Young-Old, Old-Old, and Oldest-Old. The aged are not a monolithic group of feeble men and women living in convalescent hospitals. The aged can be divided into three groups based on longevity: the *young-old* (ages fifty-five to seventy-four), the *old-old* (ages seventy-five to eighty-four), and the *oldest-old* (eighty-five years and older). These age divisions reflect health, activity, and economic status.

The young-old are relatively healthy and active, economically comfortable, better educated than earlier generations, seeking meaningful self-fulfillment, and involved in community service. Their lives change as they move into the old-old group, those over age seventy-five years. But it is not age alone that makes the old-old old; rather it is their failing health and psychological dependency. About 5 percent live with their children, 40 percent are married, and 7 percent live in institutions (Gelman et al., 1985).

Those over eighty-five years—the oldest-old—represent 1.1 percent of the population. Because of increasing longevity, however, today's baby boomers will be tomorrow's oldest-old; they are expected to represent 5 percent of the population in 2050 (Collins, 1985). It is with the oldest-old that the most severe problems occur. In 1983, 11 percent of the oldest-old lived with their children; only a fifth of the oldest-old were married. In 1980, 23 percent lived in institutions.

Tasks of Aging. Robert Peck (1956) described three stages of aging according to tasks people must confront. The first stage is *ego differentiation versus work-role*

Relatively few widows over age 55 remarry. This widow, who never remarried, makes a birthday wish during the first year of her widowhood. (She is the young girl in the 1901 portrait on page 72.)

preoccupation. This is the stage in which men and women reevaluate whether their work lives brought them personal meaning. They appreciate the limitations of time and turn to activities that are personally rewarding rather than conforming to the standards of their families, friends, or society.

The second stage is *body transcendence versus body preoccupation.* In this stage older people must transcend concerns about their aging bodies. They must accept declining health, impaired hearing, poor eyesight as aspects of aging and their own mortality. Rather than reject or deny the natural aging process, individuals need to adjust their activities to it.

The third stage is *ego transcendence versus ego preoccupation.* This is the stage in which the aging person realizes and accepts that death may come at any moment regardless of all efforts against it. This stage calls for awareness of the meaning and continuity of life, the knowledge that even though the individual dies, life itself continues.

Tho' much is taken, much
   abides; and tho'
We are not now that strength
   which in old days
Moved earth and heaven; that
   which we are, we are—
One equal temper of heroic
   hearts,
Made weak by time and fate,
   but strong in will
To strive, to seek, to find, and
   not to yield.

ALFRED, LORD TENNYSON

Retirement

Retirement, like other life changes, has the potential for satisfactions and problems.

Retired Men. When men reach their sixties, they usually retire, losing a major activity through which they defined themselves. Many men look upon retirement with dread. They no longer have the satisfaction of being respected for their work. In large part, men fulfill their family roles as good husbands and fathers through being

Many a man that cudden't direct ye to th' drug store on th' corner whin he was thirty will get a respectful hearin' whin age has further impaired his mind.

FINLEY PETER DUNNE, OLD AGE

good providers, that is, through their work roles. Now they are at home, and their wives must adjust to having someone around the house all day long. The men must adjust too. Women traditionally have kept themselves busy with housework, but retired men usually resist housework as they did when they were working. They have to find something to do. Some men turn to hobbies; others do little more than watch television. (See the reading "A Retired Husband Underfoot" by Hannah Sampson.)

Retired Women. If the woman worked outside the home, she may experience many of the same problems a retired man does but they tend to be less severe (Lowenthal et al., 1975). A retiring woman may not find herself facing the same identity issues as a man since women often have had (or continue to have) important family roles as wife, mother, and homemaker. She can return to homemaking in retirement and feel a sense of role fulfillment. If she identified herself through her career, she may feel a sense of loss (Johnson and Price-Bonham, 1980).

If a woman has been a full-time homemaker, she probably experiences no abrupt role change in her sixties. There is no retirement for homemakers, however ironic that may be. Because "a woman's work is never done," homemakers may have a bitter last laugh, for they can perform their traditional role without any interruption throughout their entire lives if they so choose.

We don't know life: how can we know death?

CONFUCIUS (541–479 B.C.)

Husband-Wife Interaction. The retired family experiences the highest degree of marital satisfaction since the first family stage, when they had no children (Spanier et al., 1975). A study by Hill and Dorfman (1982) found that wives generally felt positive about their husband's retirement. The most consistent factor associated with several measures of satisfaction among wives was the participation of their husbands in household tasks. Eighty-one percent of the wives felt that retirement gave the couple time to do what they wanted; 67 percent said that they gained increased companionship. Negative aspects of retirement were also apparent: 36 percent mentioned financial problems and 31 percent noted that their husbands did not have enough to do. When asked what advice to give other women whose husbands were about to retire, the respondents made these suggestions:

- Wives should try to keep their husbands busy.
- Wives should try to continue the activities in which they were involved before their husband's retirement.
- The couple should do more things together.
- Wives should try to maintain some privacy.

As married people faced retirement, according to one study (Lowenthal et al., 1975), the couple experienced renewed interest in each other. The majority felt that their marriages had improved since their children had gone.

Grandparenting

Grandparenting is expanding tremendously these days, creating new roles that relatively few Americans played a few generations back. Three-quarters of older Americans are grandparents and 40 percent of them are also great-grandparents! Although roles for grandparents are defined, if somewhat vaguely, the phenomenon of great-grandparenting is too new to have developed roles.

Simone de Beauvoir (1972) wrote, "The warmest and happiest feelings that old people experience are those which have to do with their grandchildren." At the same time, people may find themselves shocked when they first become grandparents: it confirms that they are no longer young. Becoming a grandparent may also intensify rivalry between the grandmother and her daughter or daughter-in-law. Since women prize themselves as mothers, Beauvoir observed, it is in the mother role that rivalry between an older woman and her daughter or daughter-in-law may begin or resume. The middle generation is usually responsible for determining how much interaction takes place between grandparents and grandchildren (Robertson, 1975). If rivalry rather than cooperation ensues, the middle generation may restrict grandparent-grandchildren interaction. But most families gain from such interactions (Barranti, 1985).

Widowhood

Marriages are finite; they do not last forever. Eventually, every marriage is broken by divorce or death. Somehow we are willing to recognize divorce but usually avoid recognizing death as an end to marriage. We can think of divorce as a result of irreconcilable differences, but what is death a result of? Death is unthinkable. Yet most marriages end with death, not divorce: "until death do us part" is a fact for most married people.

Only about half of the men and women over sixty-five years are married; most of the others are widowed. In 1983, there were 10,896,000 widows; of these, 7.6 million were over sixty-five years. By contrast, only 1,940,000 American men were widowers; 1.4 million were over sixty-five years (Department of Commerce, 1985). One researcher estimated that fewer than 5 percent of women widowed after age fifty-five will remarry (Hiltz, 1978). If a woman is widowed at fifty-five and dies at seventy-five, she may have spent as much time as a widow as she spent raising children.

People who are widowed may be thrown into trauma and despair. Even if they did not love their spouses, they go through a difficult period of making a new life without them. When one woman, Lynn Caine (1974), lost her husband, her first response was numbness and disbelief, which was a period of grace before the overwhelming sense of loss.

When that protective fog of numbness had finally dissipated, life became truly terrifying. I was full of grief, choked with unshed tears, overwhelmed by the responsibility of bringing up two children alone, panicked about my financial situation, almost immobilized by the stomach-wrenching, head-splitting pain of realizing that I was alone.

She then went through a period of madness that many people experience after their spouse's death. Some grieve for long periods; others "see" their dead partner. Lynn Caine did not know what she should do. She called an ex-lover from eighteen years before, hoping in some way that he would save her: "When he answered I said, 'You told me I could always call you if I were in trouble.' I started crying. 'I'm in very bad trouble,' I sobbed. 'Martin is dead and I have two children.' He didn't know who I was!"

Recovering from the loss of a spouse is often difficult and prolonged (Kubler-Ross, 1982). Suicide rates among widowed people are significantly higher than for married people within the same age group (Gubrium, 1974). The woman may experience

Objects were memory inert. Desk, the bed, et cetera. Objects would survive the one who died first and remind the other of how easily halved a life can become. Death, perhaps, was not the point so much as separation. Chairs, tables, dressers, envelopes. Everything was a common experience, binding them despite their indirections, the slanted apparatus of their agreeing. That they did agree was not in doubt. Faithlessness and desire. It wasn't necessary to tell them apart. His body, hers. Sex, love, monotony, contempt. The spell that had to be entered was out there among the unmemorized aces and uniform cubes of being. This, their sweet and mercenary space, was self-enchantment, the near common dream they'd countenanced for years. Only absences were fully shared.

DON DELILLO, *PLAYERS*

When a man could endure no longer, death came and set him free.

MARK TWAIN

FEATURE

Five Stages of Dying

What happens when a person is dying? According to Elisabeth Kubler-Ross (1969), most people go through five stages: (1) denial and isolation, (2) anger, (3) bargaining, (4) depression, and (5) acceptance. (For a powerful expression of the experience of dying, see Leo Tolstoy's story *The Death of Ivan Ilych*.)

Denial and Isolation. When dying people are first told they are dying, their response is usually, "Not me; it can't be true." This denial is an important response because it gives the person time to gather his or her thoughts, to make some kind of adjustment to the fact. Then the person begins to accept the idea, but feels isolated: it is his own or her own death and no one else can understand its uniqueness and ultimate personal meaning.

Anger. When their approaching death can no longer be denied, dying people get angry. They shake their fist at fate or at God and ask, "Why me? Why not someone else?" This stage is often very difficult for the dying person's family, since the rage is generalized or displaced. The dying person revives old feelings, including past injustices and resentments.

Bargaining Bargaining is really an attempt to postpone or delay death. But death makes no bargains. Promising to turn over a new leaf or begging for more time means nothing. People usually try to make these kinds of bargains with God. Sometimes a spiritual crisis occurs: nonbelievers may suddenly believe or believers may lose their faith when it becomes obvious that God will not spare them.

Depression. In the fourth stage dying people go into a deep depression. They can do nothing to postpone death. Their condition worsens, they feel themselves weakening. The financial expenses of medical treatment become more pressing, often forcing dying people to use up their savings or sell their homes. But the depression often changes its quality, moving from a reaction to impending death to a depression preparing the person for death.

Those who are close to dying people often find this depression unbearable and try to cheer the

considerable disorientation and confusion from the loss of her role as wife and companion (Lopata, 1973). Having made much of her life, not as an individual, but as part of a couple—having mutual friends, common interests, shared goals—the widow suddenly finds herself alone. Whatever the nature of her marriage, she experiences grief, anger, distress, and loneliness.

Widowed persons go through a three-stage healing process of grief (Baldwell, 1981). First, they experience shock and bewilderment, a stage lasting anywhere from one day to several months that is characterized by numbness and purposeless activity. In the second stage the person has a sharp, cutting sense of loss, sometimes feelings of guilt. This period generally lasts from one to twelve months. Finally, in the third stage the widowed person tries out new roles; it is a time often marked by despair and a feeling of helplessness as new roles are tried and discarded. The wounds are beginning to heal, however, and the widowed person begins to make his or her way back into society. If the person is male, the chances are that he will remarry; if female, she is less likely to remarry because the pool of eligibles is significantly

FEATURE–*continued*

dying. When depression is a response to the impending loss of everyone a person loves, it is a form of grief that prepares the dying for the acceptance of death. Although the people around the dying will try to avoid talking about death, it is the most important thing for the dying person to understand. Talking about it helps clarify a person's feelings. Once feelings are clarified, however, there is little more to be said. The dying tend to be silent in their depression. Kubler-Ross (1969) wrote, "The patient is in the process of losing everything and everybody he loves. If he is allowed to express his sorrow he will find a final acceptance much easier, and he will be grateful to those who can sit with him during this stage of depression without constantly telling him not to be sad."

Acceptance. The final stage—which is neither happy nor sad—is acceptance. Feelings are almost absent. If the dying person has been able to express his or her resentment, anger, and questioning, then it is likely this last stage will be a peaceful one, a period of rest, contemplation, and acceptance. This stage is probably the hardest for the family of the dying person, for now they must begin their own period of grief.

When a family member is dying, the family itself goes through many of the same stages as the dying person—at first, disbelief, then anger when reality is faced. Next comes the bargaining with fate or God, then depression, and finally acceptance. The way the family handles this period depends in large part on how the dying person handles it. Kubler-Ross (1969) wrote, "If they are able to share their common concerns, they can take care of important matters early and under less pressure of time and emotions. If each one tries to keep a secret from the other, they will keep an artificial barrier between them which will make it difficult for any preparatory grief for the patient or his family."

There are, however, different kinds of death. If the death is sudden, as in an accident, then the stages for the family are compressed. If the person is dying from cancer, then the family usually has more time (but they also must endure the physical wasting away). With people suffering from heart disease, death can come suddenly: family members of heart disease patients are often afraid of discussing death because they fear they might cause the fatal heart attack. (See the reading "A Mother's Death" by Bob Greene.)

smaller. Not only are there fewer males available but also those who are available most frequently choose younger women. The double standard of aging takes its toll.

Many widows live below the poverty line. Widows receive about 75 percent as much annual income as widowers (Lopata, 1978). They and their families are usually left with almost nothing with which to begin over again. They may be forced to seek employment after years of being homemakers, but they are at a disadvantage because they lack skills or their old skills have become dated. Similarly, laws place widows at a severe disadvantage in most states. Since women are regarded as economic dependents, having no income, they must pay a heavy inheritance tax on their community property when their husbands die. A husband, by contrast, does not pay an inheritance tax if his homemaking wife dies first, since she is assumed to have nothing for him to inherit.

Eventually widows adjust to the loss. Most do not plan to remarry. Some like their new freedom. Others feel they are too old to remarry; still others cannot imagine living with someone other than their former husband. (Those who had good marriages

Chasuble: Dear Mr. Worthing, I trust this garb of woe does not betoken some terrible calamity?
Jack: My brother.
Miss Prism: More shameful debt and extravagance?
Chasuble: Still leading his life of pleasure?
Jack (shaking his head): Dead!
Chasuble: Your brother Ernest dead?
Jack: Quite dead.
Miss Prism: What a lesson for him! I trust he will profit by it.

OSCAR WILDE, *THE IMPORTANCE OF BEING ERNEST*

think of remarrying more often than those who had poor marriages.) A large number of elderly men and women live together without remarrying. For many widows, widowhood lasts the rest of their lives.

☐ ENDURING MARRIAGES

The search for marital satisfaction and happiness is continual—for both married couples and researchers. The very nature of the search, however, may cause it to lead nowhere. Happiness (or at least a steady, uninterrupted stream of happiness) may not be the basis of a good relationship, for happiness does not work that way. Those who score high on happiness scales, wrote George Simpson, "may not be happy, but slap-happy." On study he cited asked the question: "Do you ever regret your marriage?" One subject replied "occasionally," three "rarely," and five "never." Simpson (1960) observed:

But a mature answer is: of course, but the very regret is the ambivalent aspect of my joy in it. All human satisfaction is tinged with dissatisfaction; by taking up one option, we surrender others. The human psyche is not structured in such a way that answers to such questions give any indication of fundamental personality traits or make possible understanding of an individual's capacity for being interrelated with another.

Another way of looking at marriage is not according to satisfaction but stability. What we find is what many of us already know: often little correlation exists between happy marriages and stable ones. Many unhappily married couples stay together; some happily married couples undergo a crisis and break up. John Cuber and Peggy Haroff (1965) studied more than four hundred married persons who had "normal" marriages. Subjects were upper middle class, ranging in age from thirty-five to fifty-five. Each person in the marriages under study considered himself or herself content, if not actually happy. Cuber and Haroff found several distinct types of marriages representing "different kinds of adjustment and different conceptions of marriage." These types of marriage were (1) conflict-habituated marriage, (2) devitalized marriage, (3) passive-congenial marriage, (4) vital marriage, and (5) total marriage.

Partners gave their own personal meaning to their marriage. In none of the types of marriage did there seem to be a cycle in which a marriage began blissfully and ended in disillusionment or disengagement. For example, many of the passive-congenial marriages (described briefly below), began that way and continued on the same level; neither partner experienced any particular disappointment with the habits of living they had fashioned. Some couples may move from one style of marriage to another, but it is infrequent. Cuber and Haroff emphasized that relationships tend to continue their style over long periods of time without changing.

The Cuber and Haroff study is a descriptive study of marriages that stands in remarkable contrast to studies that look at marital satisfaction. Beneath the studies of happiness and satisfaction lie certain value judgments about how marriages ought to be. They assume there are good marriages and bad marriages, but people with different values will judge marriages differently. Generally, these studies begin with the idea that marriage (*ought to* is the hidden term) provides companionship, shared activities, intimacy, and love. But Cuber and Haroff found that these characteristics are not necessary for partners to feel that their marriage is good. The five types of marriage are described below.

Conflict-Habituated Marriage

This form of marriage may be described as the "Who's-Afraid-of-Virginia-Woolf?" type of marriage. Conflict, not harmony, is its most distinguishing characteristic. In this type, couples fight and fight and fight; they need each other for sparring partners. They may bruise each other both physically and emotionally, but they do not believe such fighting is a reason for divorce. They sense they could probably not get along with anyone else any better; fighting is acceptable behavior for them.

Few people outside the family group may know about the fighting, which is usually discreet, rarely taking place in front of others. Although a couple may engage in recriminations about the past or bitter personal attacks, their conflict usually takes the form of small quarrels: "You didn't put the cap on the toothpaste"; "Look at the dishes! You call *that* clean!" A few days after a fight, the couple may not even be able to remember what they fought about, but they fight continually. The channeling of conflict and the repression of hostility become a dominant force in their lives. Conflict and hostilty make up a considerable portion of their interaction.

Devitalized Marriage

This type of marriage is most marked by the contrast between its earlier years and its present. At first, this kind of marriage was filled with vitality; the husband wife were deeply in love with each other, spent considerable time together, and had a good sex life. They enjoyed each other and were closely identified with each other. Now whatever time they spend together is "duty time," whether it is entertaining, spending time with their children, or meeting their community responsibilities. Yet they get along well enough with each other so that they do not contemplate divorce. Sometimes the wife may be unhappy if she does not have a career to compensate for the deficiencies of the relationship. Both partners sense a lack of alternatives or possibil-

> It is not lack of love but lack of friendship that makes unhappy marriages.
>
> FRIEDRICH NIETZSCHE

Drawing by D. Fradon; © 1969 The New Yorker Magazine, Inc.

ities; both are unwilling to take the chance of finding a better partner, believing they have too much to lose if they fail. Psychological comfort is a key value for them.

Passive-Congenial Marriage

This type of marriage varies little from the devitalized marriage except that the couple never had high emotions to begin with. Couples begin passive-congenial marriages with low expectations, which change little over the years. Partners do not gain their satisfaction from each other but from their outside relationships. The husband gains it from his work and from his male companions, with whom he goes fishing, bowling, or to sports events. The wife achieves satisfaction from her children, her friends, and her job or career, if she has one.

Considerable role segregation exists in these marriages. Each partner has his or her proper sphere of activities, duties, and responsibilities. Some people drift into passive-congenial relationships. Expected to marry, not wanting to be lonely, they choose a partner without feeling deep involvement. Others pick this relationship because it fits their career needs and gives them considerable independence. Devoting themselves to their careers rather than to each other, they are freed from having to adjust to their spouse's needs. Cuber and Haroff point out that "the passive-congenial marriage is thus a mood as well as a mode."

Vital Marriage

In this type of marriage the partners' lives are closely intertwined through matters that are important to both of them. Being together brings mutual excitement, satisfaction, and pleasure. One man said of his wife: "The things we do together aren't fun intrinsically—the ecstacy comes from being *together in the doing.*"

Outwardly, the lives of those engaged in vital marriages look like most other marriages. Partners in vital marriages belong to groups, entertain, and care for their children just like everybody else, but they privately experience a strong, positive psychological bonding. Conflict is not central to their relationship. When conflict does occur, it is about matters that are important to both, rather than trivial problems.

Both partners are willing to compromise and to sacrifice for the sake of each other and their relationship. This type of marriage and the total marriage described next conform more closely to the marriage ideals of our culture; however, only about one-fifth of the marriages in the study were vital or total.

Total Marriage

The total marriage is similar to the vital marriage, except that husband and wife participate in each other's lives more completely and on more levels. The husband and wife, for example, may work together on projects such as research or counseling or they may be craftspeople who share the labor of making and selling their own products. Total marriages have few areas of tension since difficulties are resolved as they arise, preventing a spillover into other areas or a slow simmering of hostility. "When faced with differences, they can and do dispose of the difficulties without losing their feeling of unity or their sense of the vitality and centrality of their relationship. This is the mainspring" (Cuber and Haroff, 1965).

Cuber and Haroff view the first three types of marriages—conflict habituated, devitalized, passive-congenial—as *utilitarian* marriages. They are based on convenience and lack of better alternatives. The last two—vital and total marriages—are viewed as *intrinsic* marriages; the marriage interactions are inherently rewarding. They estimate that about 80 percent of American marriages are utilitarian, 15 percent are vital, and 5 percent are total.

What these five types of marriages have in common is that they are all enduring. They do not represent degrees of marital happiness and satisfaction. A variety of approaches are used in looking at marriages and marital interaction. Some studies find considerable happiness or misery; others find marriages hopelessly inegalitarian. As we have noted, however, most of these studies rely on value judgments in measuring marital success. As R. G. Ryder (1967) pointed out:

There is no descriptively defined entity that can reasonably be called a successful marriage because there is no general agreement as to what marriages should be. Yet study after study has contrasted "good" marriages with "bad" marriages as if there were such an entity. A successful marriage is clearly one of which we approve. The concept is a value judgment dressed up to look like a matter of objective descriptive fact.

☐ THE SOCIAL CONTEXT

Despite the widespread belief in the isolation of the nuclear family, most marriages and families are not truly isolated. Most of us live in a rich social environment in which we may find help, sustenance, nurturing, and caring; we have kin, friends, and neighbors with whom we often interact regularly. They are there in both good times and bad times, and they are an important resource in times of stress and crisis (Troll, 1971).

Helping Kin

Few aspects of family life exist to which relatives (especially parents and siblings) do not make a contribution (Schneider, 1980). Parents will loan money to their children

UNDERSTANDING YOURSELF

What Makes Commitments Last?

Commitment is almost a cliché. We all say that we have a commitment to our relationship, our partner, our marriage. People make commitments with the best intentions of making them stick, but not all commitments endure. Making a commitment last is more than simply an act of will, a reflection of character and integrity. Interpersonal and social factors that enhance or detract from commitments are also at work..

Sociologist Ira Reiss (1980) suggests that dyadic commitments, that is, commitments between two people in a paired relation, are affected by three factors: (1) the balance of rewards to tensions in the relationship, (2) normative inputs, and (3) structural constraints. An interplay of these three elements maintains or erodes commitment. It is possible, for example, to have an unfavorable balance between rewards and tensions but strong normative inputs and structural restraints that will sustain a relationship.

The Balance Between Rewards and Tensions We can look at relationships according to a cost-benefit ratio. If the benefits outweigh the costs, then a greater likelihood exists that the commitment will endure. In your own relationship, do you and your partner generally agree about your sex roles and marital roles? What benefits do you derive from your relationship? Are your intimacy needs fulfilled? Do you visit friends together, go out together, entertain friends at home, express affection toward each other, do something that your partner particularly appreciates?

What tensions do you experience in your relationship? Do you fight about time spent with friends, where to go out, household expenses, being tired or away from home too much, disciplining children, not expressing love, in-laws, work, religion, personal habits? What are the costs of maintaining your relationship?

Normative Inputs Normative inputs are the values you hold about marriage and the family. How do you feel about the marriage commitment? Do you believe that marriages are for life and divorce is unacceptable? Under what circumstances, if any, would you consider divorce? Does the presence of children affect your marriage beliefs? If a couple has children, is divorce preferable to an unhappy marriage but an intact family? What are the values of your friends, family, and religion about marriage and divorce? Do their values reinforce or conflict with yours?

If you are dating or living with someone, what are the norms governing your particular

at no or low interest or give them practical gifts such as appliances and clothes (especially for grandchildren). Sometimes parents will pay the expenses of their children's coming home for a visit. They frequently loan their children money to make a down payment for a home. The obligations that these loans and gifts entail differ according to a person's age and marital status. If the children are young and single, parents may still expect to exercise considerable control over their children's behavior in return for their support. But if the children are older or—more important—married, there are fewer obligations.

UNDERSTANDING YOURSELF–*continued*

relationship? What kind of social support do you receive?

Structural Constraints: Parenthood, Occupation, and Relationships   The parent role is primary in families, but our role as parent often conflicts with the demands of our role as husband or wife. When the children need attention, how can we go out for a night alone with our partner? In general, as we have seen, marital satisfaction declines with the arrival of the first child and does not increase significantly until the children leave home. Will children add or detract from your marital commitment? What role do you think children will have in your marital happiness? Why? What strategies can you plan to minimize conflicts between your marital and parental roles? In your family of origin, did your parents' marriage improve or decline when the children left home? How have children affected the marriages of your relatives and friends?

Our occupational role is another type of structural constraint on marriage. Does economic security and success increase the likelihood of maintaining a commitment? Or do the sacrifices entailed in such security and success—long hours, time away from home, fatigue—weaken commitment by alienating the person from his or her partner? In the utilitarian marriages described by Cuber and Haroff (1965), economic success seemed to lead to low levels of intimacy but nevertheless enduring marriages. Other studies suggest a higher divorce rate among the poor (see Chapter 16). Where do you set your priorities—in work or marriage? How can you tell if your work is interfering with the quality of your marriage? What standard of living do you expect in your marriage? Will success hold your marriage together? Will you have to pay a price for such success?

When husband and wife share ties to kin and friends, the dyadic commitment probably increases since such ties lead to additional sources of satisfaction. Both kin and friends are a rich source of emotional support as well as physical and financial support in times of need. If the husband and wife are in conflict over kin and friendship relationships, the marital relationship may suffer. Think about the relationships you have with your partner's kin and friends. Do you like your partner's friends, parents, and siblings? How do your feelings for them affect your relationship? How does your partner feel about your friends and family? Do your partner's friends and family support the relationship?

Kin Exchange.   In primitive cultures where most work is done by the family, one of the primary reasons for marrying is to gain in-laws. When one family forms an alliance with another through marriage, cooperation replaces competition. Margaret Mead (1948) suggested that the basis of the incest taboo is the need for families in such societies to establish new ties. "If you married your sister, the Arapesh say, you would have no brother-in-law. With whom would you work? With whom would you hunt? Who would help you?" Within American culture, kinship ties are the basis for the exchange of many services, just as they are in primitive societies.

Among blue-collar families, relatives often exchange services that more wealthy families might purchase, such as help with moving, painting, house repairs, child care, and so on (Rubin, 1976). Middle-class families often pay to have their house repainted or their children cared for. By paying for such services, they isolate themselves from kin interaction, depriving themselves of significant personal relations. Assistance is generally given along traditional sex role lines. Since women are traditionally expected to keep house and rear children, assistance is given to the daughter by the mother in the form of helping around the house or caring for the children. Parents assist their son by giving or loaning him money. These forms of aid permit their children to fulfill their traditional marital roles of the woman as homemaker and the man as breadwinner. Parents less frequently offer to help their married daughters financially or help their married sons with housework if they become househusbands.

Kin Relations.   Although in theory most people believe both sets of parents should be treated equally in visits and gifts, this is not the case in practice. Married couples visit the relatives of the wife more often, especially her parents. We can see two reasons for this behavior: (1) Women are usually more attached to their parents than men are to theirs. (2) Women are generally responsible for planning social activities within the family. As married women grow older, their emotional ties with their mothers tend to grow stronger; by contrast, men's ties become weaker and weaker. This trend, however, reflects fundamental aspects of sex role socialization: Women are reared to live within the family and to bind the family together; men are reared to become independent and to be concerned with achievement rather than feelings (Rubin, 1976; Rosenthal, 1985).

This does not mean that men are not concerned for their parents' well-being or welfare but that they do not share important aspects of their lives with them. They do not confide feelings of frustration in their marriage, express warmth, or share fears. If they are close to a parent, it is usually to the mother, who encourages intimacy. Because fathers usually are not intimate with their sons as they are growing up, they are not intimate with them later. A study by Komarovsky (1967) found that 25 percent of sons were hostile to their fathers; only 9 percent expressed similar estrangement from their mothers.

Contacts with kin are an important element in the lives of the aged. Among older persons in a national study, 52 percent of elderly men and women not living with a child had seen their children within the previous twenty-four hours; 78 percent had seen their children within the previous week; and 40 percent had seen a sibling during the previous week (Shanas, 1977).

Friendship

Married couples find their friends among a number of groups, and these friends fill important needs.

Friendship Needs.   Whether we are married or single, we need friends with whom we can be intimate. Neither couples nor individuals can function well in isolation. Robert Weiss (1969) noted that people have needs that can be met only in relationships with other people. These needs can be summarized as follows:

Grownups were so immense, slow moving, carrying great burdens; they sank into chairs with a great sigh and remained there for long periods as we fetched a newspaper, got ice cream for them, rubbed their necks. "Rub my neck, wouldja," one would say and so we did as the poor thing groaned. They had so many aches and pains, we never expected them to play with us. Aunt Flo did, sometimes, take her ups and give the ball a whack, but she only visited the game, she didn't stay in it.

They kept to the porch in the summer when they weren't working, sunk into porch chairs. Their dogs barked. Their eyes burned. They had dust in their mouths, we got them Kool-Aid. "I don't know when I've felt so exhausted before," they said day after day, always beating their old records. Their weariness was honorable, even awesome. They had done everything they could do for us. We could ask no more.

GARRISON KEILLOR, *LAKE WOBEGON DAYS*

Regardless of our age, friends are important to our sense of well-being; they share our joys and sorrows.

1. *Nurturing others.* This need is filled through caring for a partner, children, or other intimates both physically and emotionally.
2. *Social integration.* We need to be actively involved in some form of community; if we are not, we feel isolated and bored. We meet this need through knowing others who share our interests.
3. *Assistance.* We need to know that if something happens to us, there are people we can depend on for help. Without such relationships, we feel anxious and vulnerable.
4. *Intimacy.* We need people who will listen to us and care about us; if such people are not available, we feel emotionally isolated and lonely.
5. *Reassurance.* We need people to respect our skills as persons, workers, parents, and partners. Without such reassurance, we lose our self-esteem.

Although many of these needs may be met within marriages and families, they do not necessarily have to be met there. It may be difficult to have all of them met within the marriage. Your partner may not share your interests and activities or respect your skills; he or she may not be able to assist you in certain situations or crises. We usually need further support. Even the best marriage cannot meet all our needs (Fischer, 1982, 1983). In beginning marriages, friends appear to be especially important in solidifying the relationship (Lingren et al., 1982).

Sources of Friendship.   Friends come from many sources. One important source is our families. Komarovsky (1967) found in her study that almost three-fourths of the intimate confidants of blue-collar wives were relatives by blood or marriage;

No man is an island, entire of itself; every man is a piece of the continent, a part of the main; if a clod be washed away by the sea, Europe is the less, as well as if a promontory were, as well as if a manor of thy friends or of thine own were. Any man's death diminishes me, because I am involved in mankind. And therefore never send to know for whom the bell tolls. It tolls for thee.

JOHN DONNE

mothers and sisters were especially important as confidants. Among the men studied, the only relatives they tended to be close to were brothers. Very rarely did fathers become confidants of their married children. A study by Rubin (1976) had similar findings.

Middle-class husbands and wives are less likely to have as many relatives who are also friends. Because they are more mobile geographically and socially, their ties to relatives are weaker (Leigh, 1982). They are not as likely to live near parents, brothers, or sisters; if they now have higher social status than formerly, they are not as likely to interact with relatives because they no longer share common tastes and goals.

Friends also come from childhood playmates, college friends, coworkers, and neighbors. Most friends among the middle class are from outside the family. But having friends who are not relatives can be a problem. When people marry, they often lose a number of friends, especially those of the other sex whose friendship may be threatening to the new husband or wife. New friends are made within the context of the marriage, and the requirements for such friends are often unspoken. The most important requirement is that each partner's friends be of the same sex (unless the friend is also a relative). The threat of jealousy is a powerful deterrent to finding new friends of the other sex. The result is that a person generally must be satisfied with having intimate friends of only the same sex.

Patterns of Friendship. Two common patterns of friendship are found within marriage. Among marriages in which there is a strict division of male and female worlds along traditional sex role lines, few couples are friends (Rubin, 1976). The wife's friends are women, the husband's friends are men; neither shares his or her friends with the other. The wife will shop or spend time with "the girls"; the husband will bowl or play poker with "the boys."

Middle-class marriages usually include more shared activities between partners; companionship and intimacy are the ideals of middle-class marriages. As a result, friends are often shared friends who are compatible with the ideals of companionate marriage. Helena Lopata (1975) wrote: "Strong sex-segregated friendships are not encouraged, however, in modern marriage because they are seen as threatening the marital unit's relation, competing for time, attention, and fulfillment of needs, and preventing its full development into self-sufficient and self-revealing intimacy."

☐ SUMMARY

- Engagement is the culmination of the formal dating pattern. It prepares the couple for marriage by involving them in discussions about the realities of everyday life; it involves family members with the couple; and it strengthens the couple as a social unit.

- A wedding is an ancient ritual that symbolizes a couple's commitment to each other. It marks a major transition in life as the man and woman take on marital roles.

- The family life cycle consists of eight stages: *beginning families, childbearing families, families with preschool children, families with schoolchildren, families as launching centers, families in the middle years,* and *aging families.*

- Marriage involves many powerful role expectations. These are supported by legal assumptions that the husband is head of the family and is expected to support it and that the wife is responsible for housework and childrearing.

- There are at least eight roles in marriage: the *housekeeper, provider, child-care, child socialization, sexual, kinship, recreational,* and *therapeutic* roles.

- Couples undergo *identity bargaining* in adjusting to marital roles. This is a three-step process: a person must identify with the role, the other person must relate to him or her in that role, and both people must negotiate changes in each other's roles.

- Women's roles tend to change more drastically with marriage than men's because women usually leave the workplace to become mothers and continue that role for at least several years.

- A critical task in early marriage is to establish boundaries separating the newly formed family from the couple's families of origin. Ties to the families of origin may include habits of subordination and economic dependency.

- In youthful marriages, the arrival of children usually leads to the mother quitting paid employment to begin childrearing. As parents reach their late thirties, they may experience a mid-life crisis. Women may question their roles as mother; men often feel disappointment with their work.

- In middle-aged marriages, families must deal with issues of independence of their adolescent children. Most women do not suffer from the *empty nest syndrome,* that is, depression over the end of their active mother role. In fact, for many families there is no empty nest because of the increasing presence of adult children in the home. As children leave home, parents reevaluate their relationship with each other and their life goals.

- Marital satisfaction usually declines with the arrival of children and does not rise again until they reach adolescence. Part of this decline, however, may be attributed to work and role strain. Most studies are cross-sectional rather than longitudinal, which may distort the results. Parental roles often compensate for decreased satisfaction in marital roles.

- The aging family must deal with issues of retirement and the death of a spouse. The aged are not a monolithic group; they can be divided into the young-old, old-old, and oldest-old. The aged have three psychological tasks: *ego differentiation versus work-role preoccupation, body transcendence versus body preoccupation,* and *ego transcendence versus ego preoccupation.*

- In retirement, men have to adjust to the loss of their roles as worker and provider. Retiring women may not find themselves facing the same identity issues as men since they often have had (or continue to have) important family roles as wife, mother, and homemaker. Marriages are generally at high levels of marital satisfaction during retirement.

- Grandparenting is an important role for the aged: it provides them with a sense of continuity. Conflicts may arise between the grandmother and her daughter or daughter-in-law over issues of mothering. The middle generation usually determines the amount of interaction of grandchildren and grandparents.

- Most marriages end in death rather than divorce. The loss of a spouse is emotionally traumatic. The survivor generally goes through a three-stage process: (1) shock and bewilderment, (2) a sharp sense of loss, and (3) gradual healing and resumption of normal activities.

- Enduring marriages can be divided into five basic types: *conflict habituated, devitalized, passive-congenial, vital,* and *total.* The fact that a marriage endures does not necessarily mean that it is a happy one, although couples in enduring marriages usually describe their marriages as satisfactory.

- Marriages and families exist in a rich social context. Kin, friends, and neighbors all contribute to our well-being. They provide assistance and emotional support that give our marriages added strength.

READINGS

Marital Tasks: Breaking Parental Ties
JEAN MARZOLLO

One of the most important tasks a newly-married couple (especially a young couple) must perform is to establish their own family separate from the family of their parents. Why is forming a separate family unit sometimes a problem? Do men and women experience this problem differently? Why? What can be done to overcome conflicting demands between the spouse and his or her parents.

Ellen holds the set of calligraphy pens tightly on her lap and eyes the sleet hitting the windshield. "Please slow down," she says tensely.

"I'm not speeding," Tom answers, equally on edge. They are driving home from Ellen's mother's house, where they have been to a disastrous birthday party for Ellen. Although they've been married only six months, they don't feel like newlyweds.

"I really do like the pens," says Ellen, who has recently taken up calligraphy.

"I felt so stupid when you were opening them," Tom replies. "Your mother and father gave you so many presents, and they know I can't afford to give you much. I told you I didn't want to go there. Why couldn't we have gone out to dinner alone?"

"You know how Mother is," Ellen says. "She lives for our visits. And she loves birthdays. It would have hurt her terribly if we hadn't shown up."

"Well, I hate having to play second fiddle. I mean—for Pete's sake, your mother gave you a carload of expensive things and I gave you three felt-tipped calligraphy pens."

"No one cared. Why did you have to ruin the whole party with your sulking?"

Ellen begins to cry. She feels sorry for herself, it's her birthday after all—and sorry for her mother, who only wanted the evening to be festive. Ellen has always been her mother's pride and joy, and she feels it would be selfish not to visit as often as possible. She wonders why Tom can't understand.

Julie often feels just as Ellen does.

Julie's father, retired and recently widowed, lives alone in a town in Florida. She lives an hour away with her husband Wayne and their 2-year-old son, Wayne Jr. Every day after Wayne leaves for work, Julie puts Wayne Jr. into his car seat and drives the 40 miles to her father's house. There, her father and the baby watch TV while Julie cleans the house, weeds the garden, shops at the local supermarket and cooks a hearty, nutritious lunch with enough leftovers for her dad's dinner.

Often, Julie returns home too exhausted to shop and cook again, so when her husband comes home, she frequently suggests going to McDonald's. Wayne doesn't mind a burger and fries once in a while, but he misses Julie's cooking. He's beginning to feel angry that Julie cooks every day for her father and rarely for him. Their dinner hour, once a special time, is now hurried and harried.

Wayne's afraid to tell Julie what's really on his mind because he knows how much Julie loves her father and he's ashamed of feeling jealous of a lonely old man. He's afraid, too, that if he complains, Julie will suggest that her father move in with them. Wayne wants to avoid that because whenever Julie's dad is around, Wayne feels left out.

For her part, Julie's not happy about devoting more time and energy to her father than to her husband, but she believes that her dad really needs her. She's sure that if she stopped seeing her father so often, there would be a hole in his life that no one else could fill.

Ellen and Julie are having trouble with their marriages because they are too close to their parents. To complicate matters, neither woman realizes that the parents are the problem—both believe that the fault lies with their husbands.

A great many young wives find themselves similarly torn between their husbands and their parents. Even though they're married, they haven't yet left the nest. According to Dr. Bruce M. Forester, assistant professor of psychiatry at Columbia University and a psychiatrist in private practice in New York City, "Overinvolvement with parents causes the most trouble in early marriage—more than sex or any other issue."

If you sense such a conflict in your marriage, keep these questions in mind:

● Who has the most control over your actions—you, your parents or your husband?
● Whom do you care most about pleasing—yourself, your parents or your husband?
● Who depends on you most—your parents or your husband?

If your most frequent answer is "my parents," you do indeed have a problem. Being so involved with Mom and Dad endangers your marriage because it creates an imbalance, your life is weighted too heavily in your parents' favor. The solution isn't to shift all the weight over to your husband; instead, you need to put yourself in charge. You are the core of your own life, and you're now establishing the most intimate bond you'll ever experience—the one with your mate. That bond requires most of your attention right now because you're laying the foundation for a lifetime partnership. To be successful, you must let go of your parents.

Dr. Sonya Rhodes, a New York City family therapist and co-author of *Surviving Family Life* . . ., has writen about stages in family development. She says you can be shackled to your parents by some very powerful bonds.

If you need your parents' money, for example, you may feel emotionally indebted to an excessive degree. Or if your parents are very attached to you and have centered their lives around you, you may feel extremely guilty about going your own way. You may fear that you will make your parents angry, sad—even sick—if you "abandon" them.

How to Loosen the Bonds

The first step, according to Forester, is to talk to your hus-

band. How is he feeling—left out? Jealous? Hurt? Talk about your own feelings, which might include guilt, fear and confusion.

Once you've established that you do have a problem, "The next step is to draw up a plan together," says Forester. "You must work out a strategy that will gradually loosen the parental tie, but in a very tactful way."

If you're lucky enough to be able to talk directly to your parents, do so. For example, Julie might say to her father, "I love you very much, but I feel that visiting you every day is hurting my marriage. You're in good health and sociable. Maybe it's time you went out and met more people. Seeing less of each other will be better for both of us. From now on, I'll just come once a week."

Forester suggests that if you don't feel you can be blunt without causing tremendous hurt, you can back off more subtly.

For example, says Forester, if Julie couldn't speak frankly to her father, she might try withdrawing gradually. "In the first week, Julie can say, 'Look, Dad, I won't be able to come this Thursday.' And she can continue to cancel once a week for a few weeks. Then she can start canceling twice a week, always giving advance notice. Finally she can say, 'You know, it'd be great if you started seeing friends more often. I care about you and I want you to have companionship.' This way, everyone knows what's going on but no one needs to feel hurt or rejected."

Remember too that although making the break is very tough for both you and your parents, this crisis can bring you and your husband closer. It can reinforce your mutual commitment and strengthen your confidence in your ability to weather future crises together. Breaking away from your parents is almost guaranteed to be very hard, but the eventual rewards for everyone involved are immeasurable.

It isn't only wives who have trouble breaking away from Mom and Dad. Husbands can be overinvolved with parents too.

Gwen and Mark, for example, have been married a year. They don't have children yet, but Gwen feels they're already a family of three: Gwen, Mark and Mark's mother. Mark's mother, a widow, is in the habit of dropping by a couple of times a week with homemade goodies. Naturally, she likes to chat awhile.

Mark doesn't mind his mother's frequent visits, but Gwen does. She has asked Mark to explain to his mother that the two of them, who both work, need more time alone. Lately, she hears herself nagging, and that frightens her. Mark feels torn between his mother and his wife. He wishes Gwen would understand his mother's good inten-

READINGS–*continued*

tions and be nicer to her.

If you, like Gwen, are married to a man who's tied to his parents, you will have to tread carefully.

- Approach him gently. Be honest with your husband about the problems, but talk to him in a way that shows how much you care. Dr. Bruce M. Forester recommends saying something like, "I know you love your parents very much, and I love them too, but I think we're spending too much time with them. I'd like to be alone with you more often. How can we work this out?"
- Avoid, at all costs, hurling accusations at your husband or his parents. "If you scold, you're acting like a mother," Dr. Forester says. "If his real mother is apt to yell at him too, he'll feel that everyone is treating him like a kid."
- If you resent visiting his parents often, Dr. Penelope Russianoff suggests your husband go alone occasionally. "You can say, 'I have a feeling your parents might enjoy being alone with you sometimes. Why don't I visit some friends while you go to your folks' this Sunday?' Afterward you can tell him what a great time you had," Russianoff adds. "He may feel more inclined to join you next time."
- You can't change his relationships with his parents overnight. It helps if you can see that his parents are probably well-meaning; they're not deliberately trying to interfere.

A Gay Wedding
REVEREND PHILIP ZWERLING

A minister performed a gay marriage for the first time, and these are his reflections on it. Why did he feel it was appropriate to marry the gay couple? Do you agree with him? Should legal marriage be extended to gays and lesbians? What impact would the ability to legally marry have on gay relationships? On society?

I've done nearly one hundred weddings now, and so I had become a bit blasé about the ceremony and the emotions that surround it. At least that was true until last month when two young men came to me to request a wedding. Gay marriages are not yet legally recognized in the state of California, but many clergy have performed weddings for gay people. This was only a first for me, and so I had to think about it a bit.

I had long ago ceased to judge the fitness of my prospec-

tive brides and grooms. Some of those couples I thought least sympatico are still together, where others who had seemed so well suited to each other have since moved to divorce.

And long ago I had stopped looking upon marriage as a permanent institution. People continue to change and grow after marriage, and I came to understand that even a marriage that ended in divorce need not have been a failure; that even in its limited span such a relationship could have been helpful and worthwhile to a couple who later ended their marriage.

And yet, I had never married two people of the same sex. I finally realized that their sexual orientation did not lessen their commitment to each other, or their love for each other. Certainly I cannot now predict the future of their relationship, but I do believe that they freely chose what both believed best for them.

Their ceremony was lovely; family and friends attended; vows and rings were exchanged; the newly-married couple looked exceedingly happy.

Gay people have the same desire for happiness in our society as heterosexuals. And one of those rights is the chance (with the same lack of guarantees of success or permanence we all struggle with) to create a marital relationship of depth and love.

A Retired Husband Underfoot
HANNAH SAMPSON

One of the issues of retirement involves the impact of having a formerly-working spouse around full-time. What readjustments take place according to this article? What other adjustments do you think the couple will face as the retirement progresses?

You talk about it and talk about it. Then it happens. We're retired. Yes, "we." After all, you can't go through that lifetime together, accepting invitations for "us," arguing over "our" children, agonizing about "our" car, "our" weedy lawn, "our" dog sanitation—*your* mother, I'll grant—and not wind up with "our" retirement.

So, of course, we did talk about the coming retirement. But what was the talk about, really? Money. Would there be enough? The rest was uncharted territory. Silently, I wondered and worried. Like everyone, I'd read the literature on the perils of retirement. Some cynic had written: *What is retirement? Twice as much husband and half as much pay.* Ha, ha. I had laughed along with the rest.

READINGS–*continued*

Would it be a laughing matter? Would he be all over the place, driving me bananas? Would familiarity breed, well, what familiarity is supposed to breed? Would he be bored? Some men, I'd read with a sinking heart, die soon after retirement.

What were we getting into?

Saturday and Sunday don't count, of course, but here's the scene that first Monday.

He comes into the kitchen rubbing his hands briskly, slickly decked out in his baby-blue Christmas cardigan carefully coordinated with his slate-colored pants. Shoes like twin mirrors. Like something out of a Brooks Brothers ad. I resemble nothing so much as the remains of a garage sale—fuzzy, familiar slippers and my ancient Indian-blanket bathrobe.

I'm inoculating myself with coffee, trying to get an eye open. He starts rummaging around in the refrigerator. What is he looking for? Kippers. Don't we have kippers? On Monday morning? Does he think that this is the Beverly Hills Hotel? Although I am less than half-awake, I don't want to spoil his first day of freedom, so I rustle up a pretty fair omelet and throw in yesterday's leftover hashbrowns.

Before he's finished this celebration of retirement, one of the usual steady stream of real-estate sales people is at the door. I take the emery board with her agency's advertising on one side and toss it into the flower bowl that's full of emery boards with advertising on them and, smiling enigmatically, I prepare to close the door.

Ah, but this morning I am not alone. He squeezes in front of me and starts a passionate flirtation with I'm Melodie-I'm-your-neighborhood-professional. Suddenly he's a master of innuendo.

"Neighborhood professional *what*?" And he waggles his eyebrows at her.

"Oh, you're terrible," simpers Miss Real Estate. . . . My, they have a good thing going—good enough to stir the retired blood? Do I know this man? Not on your life.

The days go by. He's increasingly unrecognizable. I am no longer confident—as, I confess shamefacedly, I once was—that I know what he'll do next. When my friend Fannie drops in for a cup of coffee and an exchange of gossip, he sweeps the newspapers from a chair and, as if he were D'Artagnan, bows and beckons her to take a seat. "Make believe I'm not here," he grins. Since his usual (past) greeting to her has been an absentminded "Hi," Fannie lies and says that she came only to borrow sugar, and takes off in confusion.

"So what's on the agenda for today?" inquires the bright-faced retiree. Ayee! Has this clown got to be entertained?

Now he's looking for Tensor lamp bulbs. He'll never find them; they're only as big as poppy seeds. Nevertheless, he's all over the cupboard. Now he's straightening the top shelves "as long as I'm here." I haven't been up there since I stopped wearing high heels.

Boredom? My husband's certainly not dying of boredom. Or of anything else. He's happy as a clam. "Here, let me do that," he keeps telling me. Freed at last from his lifetime of teaching, which had become less and less fulfilling, he's overoccupied with plans, deeds and *me*.

It's not long before he's back to wearing his chino work pants and his Montgomery Ward plaid shirts, although he can't seem to stop polishing his shoes. What's more, I'm now the owner of a couple of long housecoats—the kind that can cover a multitude of shabby-nightgown sins. And I'm now combing my hair before I come into the kitchen.

As if there were company in the house.

I find myself thinking about him at odd moments during the day. Who is he, really? I long to know. Is he truly as interested in all the daily trivia as he appears to be? All of the tiny inconsequentials that I'd made practically a religion of not bothering him with?

"Now that I see so much of you, I see you're not the person I thought you were," he says suddenly one morning.

There you are. He hates me. And it's not even me. I'm a stranger, even to myself.

"How different?" Heart sinking.

"Can't put my finger on it. Different, is all." Clears his throat. Smiles shyly. "As if we'd just met . . . and I want to make a good impression on you. . . ."

A Mother's Death
BOB GREENE

We often take our parents and other family members for granted until death intervenes and we witness our connectedness. And although life goes on, death does not end the relationship, for you may discover how the other person was "a part of you," as did the woman in this essay. As you read this essay, what feelings do you get about members of your family to whom you are close? Has there been a death in your family? What was your experience of the death? Other members' experience?

At 36, she is a high school teacher living in a big metropolitan area; she has never been married. She had driven to her small hometown to visit her parents; her mother, who had been suffering from cancer for three years, was not doing well.

It was a Friday night. Her mother was in bed; she was hooked up to an oxygen tank by a long cord. The daughter climbed onto the bed next to her mother, just as she had as a little girl. The two of them watched "Dallas" and "Falcon Crest." The daughter sensed her mother was thinking something but not saying it.

The mother looked over. She said the words:

"I just don't want to leave yet."

The two women both started to cry. They held each other, and the daughter could not tell who was rocking whom: the mother rocking the daughter, as in days long ago, or the daughter rocking the mother. They spoke of death; the daughter said she was afraid she would never get over missing this woman who had been there for her for a lifetime.

The mother said that in time, it happens; the hurt begins to let up. She said she had been 40 when her own mother died; all these years since, she had missed her. They kept rocking each other, the mother and the daughter, and they said all the words that needed to be said.

At the end of the weekend, the daughter drove back to the city where she now lives. Within days the news came from her hometown: The mother had taken a bad turn. She was in the hospital.

So the daughter made the drive again. A nurse stopped her in the hallway; the nurse warned that the mother looked much worse than she had even four days before. In the hospital room the daughter saw her mother propped up in bed, her eyes seeming to focus on someplace beyond the four walls.

The daughter's father and brother were there, too, as they had been all day. They said they were going to go away for a few hours; the daughter said she would stay with her mother. The mother drifted into a drugged sleep; once she woke up, apparently startled to find the daughter there. She asked: "How much longer will it be?" She didn't wait for an answer. Another time she opened her eyes and said she "was ready."

"Dallas" was on the television set. The daughter thought: Had it really been a week since they had sat together and watched the show? She stroked her mother's hand and talked softly to her; her mother said the daughter looked tired and should go home. The daughter said she would rather stay. A nurse came in and gave the mother a shot; it hurt, and she turned onto her side because her back was sore, and the daughter massaged her. Once the mother

opened her eyes and the daughter smiled and said the mother was missing "Dallas."

At 11 p.m. the daughter's brother came back. The mother was having trouble breathing; the daughter let the mother rest her head on her shoulder, and the daughter held her up like a baby. Several hours later—about 2:30 a.m.—the mother sat upright and let her legs dangle over the side of the bed. She wouldn't lie back down.

The nurse who was present asked the mother if she knew her daughter and son were there. She nodded yes. She was awake, but this was clearly the end.

The daughter thought: So this is what death is like.

The two children embraced their mother for 30 or 40 minutes. They could hear that she was having great difficulty breathing. No one really spoke; they just held on. Finally, with her tired back resting against her daughter's chest and her head leaning against her daughter's shoulder, she closed her eyes and died.

The daughter thought: This wasn't frightening and it wasn't awful and it wasn't terrible. A woman had died in the arms of her children, knowing that she was loved.

The daughter thought: I don't know how I will get over this. I have called this woman on the telephone every night of my life since I was in college. This woman has told me I am all right all of my life, even during times when I wasn't so sure myself. I always hoped if I ever got married, this woman would be there. But she never bothered me about it. She always said, "You're doing fine, your life is great."

It was 25 minutes before the daughter's father arrived back at the hospital. For that whole time, the daughter continued to hold her mother in her arms.

Now that it is over, the daughter lies in bed in her apartment, and she feels as if her mother is still alive. She feels as if her mother is watching her life. "It's like my mother is still in on it," the daughter will think. "It's as if she's in me. She's a part of me."

Of course there are days when the daughter will think of her mother constantly. She will be watching television and suddenly she will start crying. She will see mothers and daughters on the street and again the tears will come.

But there are also days—more and more of them recently—when she will realize she has not thought about her mother. This surprises her; she had assumed such a time would never come.

"It's the life-and-death of it," she says. "It's the life-and-death of it that spooks me. Life goes on. Oh my, my."

CHAPTER 11

Marriage, Work,
and Economics

PREVIEW

To gain a sense of what you already know about the material covered in this chapter, answer "true" or "false" to the following statements. You will find the answers as you read the chapter.

1. Satisfaction with the homemaker role tends to be related to class background rather than the homemaker's duties. True or false?
2. Blue-collar women, in contrast to middle-class women, tend to attach little status to the homemaker role. True or false?
3. About 50 percent of all mothers with young children are employed. True or false?
4. Women tend to interrupt their careers for family reasons about ten times as much as men. True or false?
5. Career women generally follow the same career patterns as men. True or false?
6. Women make about 90 cents for every dollar a man makes. True or false?
7. Of the six million employers in the United States, about 15,000 provide some kind of day care assistance for their employees. True or false?
8. The majority of female welfare recipients are on welfare as a result of a change in their marital status. True or false?
9. Children represent 20 percent of the poor in America. True or false?
10. The average food stamp recipient receives 48 cents per person per meal. True or false?

Outline

In this chapter we look first at how work—both paid work outside the home and unpaid work inside the home—contributes to and conflicts with family life today. As women work outside the home, child care becomes a central issue in their lives: Women, rather than men, tend to be responsible for caring for the children, even if both husband and wife work. The lack of adequate child care severely hampers women's employment and educational opportunities. Then we examine the impact of unemployment on families. Next we examine poverty. Finally, we look at how the family manages its finances through credit cards, indebtedness, and styles of financial planning.

☐ EMPLOYMENT AND THE FAMILY

Work and economics shape the quality of family life. They shape time, roles, incomes, spending, leisure, even individual identities. We can see the close relationship between work and identity in many surnames. For example, John Miller's ancestor in medieval England was John the Miller who ground the flour in Nottingham; Mary Cooper's ancestor was John the Cooper who made barrels in London. One of the first things we ask someone we meet is, "What do you do?" and the person replies that he or she is a student, teacher, truck driver, salesperson, cook, and so on. Within our families, the time we have for each other, for leisure, for our children, even for sex is the time that is not taken up by work. The main characteristic of work in relation to the family is its inflexibility. Work regulates the family (Lopata, 1978). Today, as in the past, a woman's work molds itself to her family, but a man's family molds itself to his work (Degler, 1980).

If you don't want to work you have to work to earn enough money so that you won't have to work.

OGDEN NASH

For many people, the external rewards of work—income, power, and status—are the most important motivations for work. The process of work itself is secondary. Most people work in jobs, wrote sociologist Bennet Berger (1960), "in which one neither rejoices nor suffers, but with which one puts up with more or less grace for the sake of other things that are supposed to be important—those other things being typically connected with one's private life."

Of all the private satisfactions that work offers, Americans find that providing for their family is often the most important. It is frequently the primary motivation for continuing work that otherwise would be intolerably deadening. Mary Howell (1975) noted:

We are carefully instructed from our early years that most people would not work at necessary jobs unless it is arranged that their very livelihood—that is, their ability to feed and clothe and shelter themselves and their families—is at stake. The dreariness and the impossibility of creative investment in most jobs for pay is thereby accepted, for we have been taught that we are basically lazy and that we will do only what needs to be done with that stick of financial fear at our backs.

The rhythms of contemporary family life depend on the type of work the breadwinner does. Blue-collar and low-level white-collar workers have little time flexibility in their jobs. These workers punch in during the early morning and punch out in the late afternoon. During the work week, they cannot easily take time off for such activities as driving a sick child to the doctor or watching their children play soccer. Time for their family is limited to evenings and weekends. The quality of that "family" time depends on how tired the working person is.

Professionals and men and women working at the managerial level have more flexible work hours they can take advantage of to meet family needs. But flexibility in itself may not be an advantage, for professionals and executives may take their work home with them. Blue-collar and many white-collar workers may find their work tedious, boring, and alienating, but they leave it behind when they punch out at the factory or the office.

Spouses of managers and professionals often complain that their partners are married to their jobs. Work and family compete for evenings and weekends. Robert Weiss (1985) noted in his study of successful professional men:

Because respondents saw their own working as a family responsibility, they could believe themselves to be demonstrating concern for their families when they worked hard. They could, at least to an extent, justify the time and energy they gave to their work, including absences from home during the family times of evenings and weekends.

Success in work—especially for men—undercuts the emotional cohesiveness of the family and generally leaves the members to fend for themselves. These effects may be less painful when the family itself identifies with success.

☐ HOUSEHOLD WORK

In the traditional division of labor in the family, the husband is expected to work outside the home for wages; the wife is expected to remain at home caring for children and maintaining the household. Although women with children have increasingly

One day Sisyphus, King of Corinth, saw a great eagle flying overhead, larger and more beautiful than any bird he had ever before seen. It was carrying a young girl off to a distant island. When Asopus the river god saw Sisyphus, he asked the king for help in finding his daughter who, he believed, had been carried off by Zeus. Sisyphus told the river god what he had seen. Zeus, angry at Sisyphus, condemned him to forever roll a great rock up a mountainside; when his labor was completed, the rock would roll down and Sisyphus would again push it up through eternity. Sisyphus' labor would never be completed; it would remain meaningless work forever.

GREEK MYTH

Work is the refuge of people who have nothing better to do.

OSCAR WILDE

Work expands so as to fill the time available for its completion.

NORTHCOTE PARKINSON

entered the work force, altering the traditional division of labor, women—whether or not they are employed outside the home—remain primarily responsible for household tasks.

Men's Household Work

Men's work generally takes place outside the home where they sustain their primary economic role as provider. The husband's role as provider is probably the male's most fundamental role in marriage (Rubin, 1983; Scanzoni, 1979). The basic equation for men in marriage is that if the male is a good provider, he is a good husband and a good father. This core concept seems to endure despite trends toward more egalitarian and androgynous marriage and personal roles.

> It is not enough to be busy
> . . . the question is: what are
> we busy about.
>
> HENRY DAVID THOREAU

The devastating inflation that began in the 1970s drove increasing numbers of married women into the workplace to maintain the family standard of living. Men seem to have accepted the necessity of their wives working, although they continue to believe it is "his responsibility, not his wife's, to produce income for the family" (Weiss, 1985).

Men are traditionally expected to contribute to household maintenance primarily in the form of repairs, light construction, mowing the lawn, and other activities that are consistent with instrumental male norms. But many professionals and executives do not find such work rewarding; the small sense of satisfaction they get is not nearly as great as the satisfaction they receive from their work outside the home (Weiss, 1985).

Men often contribute to housework and child care, although their contribution may not be significant in terms of the total amount of work to be done. Men tend to see their role in housekeeping or child care as "helping" their partner, not as assuming equal responsibility for such work.

Some redistribution of household tasks takes place when the wife is employed. A recent study of employed women, for example, found that only 39 percent had sole responsibility for child care (compared with 56 percent of nonemployed wives); 42 percent of employed wives were solely responsible for housework (compared with 57 percent of nonemployed wives); 34 percent of employed wives were solely responsible for washing the dishes (compared with 49 percent of nonemployed wives) (Maret and Finlay, 1984).

Women's Household Work

Household tasks are considered the woman's duty. Even the law assumes that the wife is responsible for domestic work and childrearing (Weitzman, 1981). No matter what kind of work the woman does outside the home or how nontraditional she and her husband may consider themselves, when it comes to housework there is seldom much equality. Men may help their partners with washing dishes, vacuuming, or doing the laundry, but few relationships can be found where such work is split on a fifty-fifty basis. The ultimate responsibility for housework and childcare remains with the women.

☐ THE HOMEMAKER ROLE

Women's work consists of two kinds: unpaid work at home as a homemaker and paid work outside the home, generally as an employee. When we think of work, we tend to think of paid labor. Because the work of homemakers is performed by women and is unpaid, it has been denigrated as "women's work"—inconsequential and unproductive. The work homemakers do is actually extremely productive and important, but it lacks status in a society where value is equated with economic achievement.

The housewife is a nineteenth-century invention (Degler, 1980). Industrialization removed many of women's productive tasks from the home and placed them in the factory. Even then, although women made fewer things at home, they nevertheless continued their service and childrearing roles: cooking, cleaning, sewing, raising children, and nurturing the family. With the rise of a money economy in which only paid work was recognized as real work, women's work in the home went unrecognized as necessary and significant labor (Andre, 1981; Bernard, 1982). Even when women work for wages, their contribution to family income is often underrated (Bird and Bird, 1985).

Characteristics of the Homemaker's Work

Sociologist Ann Oakley (1974) described four characteristics of a homemaker's work:

1. Exclusive allocation to women, rather than to adults of both sexes
2. Association with economic dependence, that is, with the dependent role of the woman in modern marriage
3. Status as nonwork—or its opposition to "real," economically productive, work
4. Primacy to women, that is, its priority over other roles

Despite its routine nature, housework has been glorified as emotionally fulfilling since the early part of the twentieth century. Ruth Cowan (1976) observed that before the First World War, housework was considered a chore, a series of menial, unpleasant tasks. But after the war it slowly began to be characterized as meaningful work:

Laundering was not just laundering, but an expression of love; the housewife who truly loved her family would protect them from the embarrassment of tattletale grey. Feeding the family was not just feeding the family, but a way to express the housewife's artistic inclinations and a way to encourage feelings of family loyalty and affection. Diapering a baby was not just diapering, but a time to build the baby's sense of security and love for the mother. Cleaning the bathroom sink was just not cleaning, but an exercise in protective maternal instincts, providing a way for the housewife to keep her family safe from disease.

Attitudes Toward Homemaking

A woman's feelings about being a homemaker depend on the answers to two questions: Does she receive status for her homemaker role—that is, is her work valued and recognized? Is the work itself rewarding?

Class Differences in the Status of Homemaking. Whether housewifery is valued depends in part on social class. Lillian Rubin's study of working-class families (1976) found that two-thirds of the homemakers and mothers were satisfied; they believed

Therefore I tell you, do not be anxious about your life, what you shall eat or what you shall drink, nor about your body, what you shall put on. Is not life more than food, and the body more than clothing? Look at the birds of the air; they neither sow nor reap nor gather into barns, and yet your Heavenly Father feeds them. Are you not of more value than they? And which of you by being anxious can add one cubit to his span of life? And why are you anxious about clothing? Consider the lilies of the field, how they grow; they neither toil nor spin; yet I tell you, even Solomon in all his glory was not arrayed like one of these.

MATTHEW 6:25–29

their roles were important and gratifying. They displayed little trace of the attitude "I'm just a housewife" which reflects low esteem for the role. The women were not necessarily content in their lives as homemakers, but the discontent was not due to their roles' lacking significance. Those who worked before becoming full-time home-makers gave no indication that the transition involved any loss of prestige.

Working-class women often do not judge their worth by achievement and success but rather by fulfilling their marital roles. The working-class wife respects herself, as do her husband, relatives, and friends, for her skills as cook, seamstress, housekeeper, and mother. These skills may give her more pleasure and satisfaction than they do her middle-class counterpart.

Middle-class, college-educated women have different values and aspirations. A middle-class woman's husband may work in the white-collar world of managers and executives in which competition is fierce, achievement prized, and material success admired. In contrast to her husband, she is "only a housewife." Yet in many cases, she herself was once an achiever in high school and college. Such women chafe, wrote Komarovsky (1967), "because of the low prestige society attaches to her role. She no longer receives recognition of her skills as a housekeeper. Whatever lip service is paid to the importance of the home, the housewife herself notes that social esteem and economic rewards go to women who achieve success in careers outside the home." In fact, nonemployed married women are perceived as having less favorable personality traits and professional competencies than employed married women (Etaugh and Petroski, 1985). Because of the middle-class prejudice against homemaking, middle-class homemakers tend to be more dissatisfied with their status.

Is the Work Rewarding?   What about the nature of homemaking? Do women find it fulfilling? Generally not. As Komarovsky (1967) wrote, "The esteem [homemakers] attach to their roles does not . . . ensure their contentment in it." Both working-class and middle-class women tend to feel tied down by their duties as wives and mothers.

Women's reactions to homemaking can be categorized as follows:

1. Homemaking tends to isolate a woman at home. She cleans alone, cooks alone, launders alone, cares for children alone. Loneliness is a common complaint (Oakley, 1974). One study found that twice as many homemakers who were socially isolated felt unhappy compared with those with daily contacts (Ferree, 1976).

2. Homemaking is unstructured, monotonous and repetitive. A homemaker never feels that her work is done. Housework is open-ended and unending. There is always more dust, more dishes, more dirty faces. In "The Housewife's Lament," a nineteenth-century folk song, the housewife complained:

> With grease and with grime from corner to center
> Forever at war and forever alert.
> No rest for a day lest the enemy enter,
> I spend my whole life in struggle with dirt.

The order of preference of household tasks are cooking, shopping, laundering, housecleaning, dishwashing, and ironing (Oakley, 1974).

3. The homemaker role is restricted. It is essentially the woman's only role. By contrast, a man's role is dual: employed worker and husband/father. If the man finds one role unsatisfactory, he may find satisfaction in the other. The woman's homemaker role as wife/mother is largely subsumed in the role. It is much more

Housework continues to be defined as a woman's responsibility. Because husbands rarely make a substantial contribution to household work, the total work week (including housework) of an employed woman with two children is estimated at seventy-one to eighty-three hours. As a result, today's woman may be working longer hours than her grandmother, who had no food processor or microwave.

difficult for her to separate the satisfaction she may get from being a mother from the dissatisfaction of household work.

4. Housework is autonomous. This is the most-liked aspect of the housewife role (Oakley, 1974; Rubin, 1976). Being her own boss allows a woman to direct a large part of her own life. In contrast to employment, this is a definite plus.

5. Homemakers work long days and nights. Most women know that the old ditty

> A man's work is from sun to sun,
> But woman's work is never done

reflects considerable truth. Women work in the home anywhere from fifty to one hundred or more hours a week. Their work weeks are considerably longer than their partners'.

Still, many women find satisfaction in the homemaker role—even in housework. One woman (quoted in Lopata, 1972), a mother of three children under four years, said: "You get satisfaction seeing anything you accomplish look nice. Each thing you do is an improvement." Young women may get increasing pleasure from their homemaker responsibilities as they experience a sense of mastery. If they have formed a network among other women—friends, neighbors, relatives—they may be able to share many of their responsibilities with others. The "coffee klatch"—when women get together to talk—is often mocked by men, but it is a significant networking device (Lopata, 1972). In it women discuss ideas and feelings and give each other support; they exchange information on child care, shopping, cleaning, and other homemaker responsibilities. They share joys as well as problems.

As we saw in Chapter 10, the contemporary American family performs at least eight functions. A homemaker must often fulfill not only a housekeeper role, but also child care, child socialization, sexual, kinship, recreational, and therapeutic roles. She may find her greatest rewards as companion and mother (Lopata, 1972; Rubin, 1976). One woman (quoted in Alter, 1979) said of her life as a homemaker:

I find the responsibilities that make up my life very rewarding. I get a lot of pleasure from running the house. . . . I'm very good at handling household routines. I can't say that the time both kids came down with the chicken pox, the washing machine overflowed and the housebroken dog regressed was my finest hour . . . Times like that don't do me in—they're all part of a day's work.

Most of my early evening hours are spent with the kids, helping with homework, playing a game. . . . After they're in bed, Larry and I usually spend a quiet hour or two just listening to a good record . . . and *talking*.

The Displaced Homemaker

In recent years increasingly large numbers of women are being forcibly displaced from their roles as wife and mother. Homemakers often find it necessary to enter or reenter the job market as a result of divorce or death, the disability of their spouses, or the termination of public assistance that permitted them to remain at home until their children turned eighteen. Such women are called *displaced homemakers*. There are approximately four million displaced homemakers in the United States (Marano et al., 1980). As a result of women living on the average eight to ten years longer than their husbands and a soaring divorce rate, the number of displaced homemakers is rapidly growing. The annual income for families headed by displaced homemakers rarely exceeds $5,000 (Marano, 1980).

Yvonne Braithwaite Burke (quoted in Strong et al., 1979) wrote of displaced homemakers:

The stoical scheme of supplying our wants by lopping off our desires is like cutting off our feet when we want shoes.

JONATHON SWIFT (1667–1745)

It is the payoff to a woman who has fulfilled society's traditional definition of a woman's role. She is encouraged to stay home and care for her family, but when she grows old, she is penalized for not having "worked." She must therefore settle for a job with low status, low responsibility, and low pay, if she is lucky enough to get a job at all. Prevailing cultural attitudes, sexism, and ageism all work against her.

The loss of job experience and skills severely handicaps women when they must return to work (Ferber and Birnbaum, 1980). While their spouses were upgrading their skills and careers, full-time homemakers devoted their energies to their homes and families. Their experiences at home do not translate easily into good jobs. Displaced homemakers must assess the skills they acquired during homemaking, their volunteer experiences, their education, and their past work experiences, and learn how to market them.

Many displaced homemakers devalue their past experiences and marketable skills. They must often deal not only with finding employment but also with their own feelings of anger, failure, and guilt. They are likely to feel powerless, tense, desperate, inadequate, and isolated. These feelings are exacerbated by having to deal with several crises at once (Marano, 1980). Displaced homemakers are only now being recognized as a group often in desperate need of emotional and financial support.

☐ WOMEN IN THE LABOR FORCE

Women have traditionally been members of the work force. When the first factories started up in the early nineteenth century, single women were their most important source of labor (Degler, 1980). Since the 1890s, more than 40 percent of all single women have worked.

Participation in the Labor Force

In 1984 women made up 44 percent of the work force; 54 percent of women were employed or seeking employment (Waldman, 1985). Nearly twenty-seven million married women are currently employed; more than half—14.5 million—are performing the roles of wife and mother as well as worker. In addition, ten million single mothers are employed; more than two-thirds have preschool or school-age children.

Between 1970 and 1983, the number of women in the labor force rose by seventeen million. More than 60 percent of this increase came from women in the twenty-four- to thirty-five-year age bracket. In the past these women stopped working when they married or had children. In 1970 only 24 percent of the women in this age group worked; by mid-1984, an astounding 69 percent worked (Waldman, 1985). Half of all mothers with young children are currently in the work force. These changes have more than economic significance. In fewer than fifteen years, the responsibility for childrearing shifted. Half of America's young children today are being reared in part by people other than their parents.

Women's participation in the labor force, according to one researcher, represents "a revolution in social values" (Waldman, 1985). Women's working outside the home has altered their relationship to the family. As workers, wives and mothers have challenged traditional family roles (see Kessler-Harris, 1982; Mattaei, 1982). To name just a few of the consequences:

- Families increasingly rely on the wife's earnings to maintain their standard of living.
- As women gain economic independence, they also gain power in the marital relationship.
- Household duties and responsibilities are being renegotiated so that the husband takes on more day-to-day tasks.
- Childrearing patterns are changing as the children of working parents spend more time in day care rather than with one (usually the mother) or both parents.
- Women's economic self-sufficiency means they are more likely to leave an unsatisfactory marriage.

Single women experience little resistance to their working because working does not violate the traditional norm that married women with children remain home. But when they become mothers, the pressure to quit working mounts (Klemsrud, 1983). A notable exception to this is the expectation that single mothers should work to avoid welfare. If they do not work, they are often stigmatized as "lazy," "no good," or "cheats"; sometimes they are accused of having children so they may go on welfare. The poor are blamed for their poverty.

Women's Employment Patterns

The majority of women are employed in low-paying, dead-end jobs in which women are overrepresented. College-educated women are similarly overrepresented in traditional female occupations, which offer less pay and status than traditional male occupations. In part, this is a result of the family orientation of women's sex roles. Many of women's choices about work and careers are based on their plans for a family and whether and when they will want to work (Burroughs et al., 1984). Low pay, low-status work offers women more flexibility for planning families than professional

As a result of the women's movement in the 1970's, many women are moving into occupations formerly defined as male.

and managerial work because traditional female jobs require less preparation and less commitment.

Work Interruptions.   Because of family responsibilities, women tend to interrupt their work lives significantly more than men. Work interruptions have an important impact on wages: the more or longer the interruptions, the lower the wages. A study by the Bureau of the Census ("Work Interruptions and Earnings," 1985) found that one-fourth of the men but three-fourths of the women had work interruptions lasting six months or longer. Sixty-seven percent of women's work interruptions were for family reasons; only 2 percent of men's work interruptions were for family reasons. Similar differences are found comparing women who have been married (with children) to women who have never been married (without children). Among women age twenty-one to twenty-nine years, 21 percent of the never-married have had a work interruption but 81 percent of the married have had work interruptions.

The employment of women has generally followed a pattern that reflects their home and child-care responsibilities. Women's employment rates follow an M-shaped curve. Women's entry into the job market rises from age sixteen to twenty-four; at age twenty-five, their participation drops as they begin engaging in homemaking and child-care activities. Then, after thirty-five, the rates go up again, falling toward zero as women near retirement.

This M-shaped pattern, however, may be changing, since half of the mothers with small children work. According to one study, the mothers in this age group place children and their welfare as their highest priority until the youngest child reaches age four; after age four, with children entering kindergarten, women begin entering the job market again (Krogh, 1985). Mothers with high achievement motivation were more likely to have a job than those with low achievement motivation. Among employed mothers, those with nontraditional sex role orientations were more likely to work more hours a week. (Also see Avioli, 1985, and Belsky et al., 1985.)

Researchers have found that a woman's decision to remain in the work force or to withdraw from it during her childbearing and early childrearing years is critical for her later work-force activities (Rexroat, 1985). If a woman chooses to work at home caring for her children, she is less likely to work outside the home later. If she does return to the work force, she will probably earn substantially less than women who remained in the work force (Rexroat, 1985; Velsor and O'Rand, 1984).

Careers. In contrast to a job, a career is more likely to require extensive training, continuity, and mobility. For career-oriented people, their work is often an end in itself; for job-holding people work is usually a means to an end, such as supporting oneself or a family. Working at McDonald's as a short-order cook is usually a job; working as a family therapist is usually a career. Men with careers generally follow a single pattern: they begin careers and continue them uninterrupted by family concerns until they retire. Career women, however, have four possible career patterns they may follow (Poloma et al., 1982): *regular, interrupted, second,* and *modified second.* In the regular career pattern, the woman is involved full time. Her work is similar to that of a man in a similar career except it is limited by compromises required by family life:

Lectures, evening work, travel, and annual meetings often could not be integrated into their hectic schedules. They found their professional involvement greatly curtailed when their children were younger, gradually increasing as they got older, and leading to greater involvement . . . only after the children had been launched.

An interrupted career begins and continues like a regular career, except that is is interrupted, usually by the birth of the first child. Some women then stop working altogether, whereas others with more flexible careers such as medicine, law, and college teaching, work part time. A second career is a career that begins around the time that the children are grown or a divorce occurs. Modified second careers begin when the woman believes her children no longer need her full-time care, usually when they are between the ages of three and seven years.

In these women's career patterns, it is not marriage but the birth of the first child that affects their career most significantly. Career women with children do not reach the peak of their career until at least after the first child has left home (Poloma et al., 1982).

Why Women Work

Most women work out of economic necessity. Nearly two-thirds of the women in the work force in 1984 were single (26 percent), divorced (11 percent), widowed (11 percent), separated (4 percent), or had husbands whose income was less than $15,000 (19 percent), according to the Women's Bureau (U.S. Department of Labor, 1984). But there are other reasons why women work. The routine nature of housework (and its low status) often sends some women looking for more interesting and fulfilling

Women constitute half the world's population, perform nearly two-thirds of its work hours, receive one-tenth of the world's income, and own less than one-hundredth of the world's property.

UNITED NATIONS REPORT, 1985

FEATURE

When Wives Earn More Than Their Husbands

In a large number of marriages the wife earns more than the husband. In 1981, for example, wives earned more than their husbands in 12 percent of all American marriages and 15.5 percent of all dual-career marriages. This amounts to 5.9 million American families. Four million of these families are dual-worker families, whereas in 1.9 million the woman is the only wage-earner. Thirty-six percent of the women in families where the wives earn more hold professional or managerial jobs; a large proportion of the couples—55 percent—do not have children at home. Their median income is $23,547, substantially less than that of families in which the husband earns more than his wife (Sanoff, 1984). Studies of the marital impact of this phenomenon are mixed; some suggest higher divorce rates, others find no correlation (Atkinson and Boles, 1984).

In some of these marriages, what have been called "Wife-As-Senior-Partner" or WASP marriages, marriage and family life are organized around the wife's job or career rather than the husband's (Atkinson and Boles, 1984). These marriages are characterized by the woman having a traditionally male job, flexibility in the husband's work, and the absence of children. A major problem with such marriages is their perception as deviant by friends, coworkers, and relatives. Atkinson and Boles (1984) reported these responses:

Husbands were perceived as losers, e.g., lazy, irresponsible, and unmasculine. One father said of his son, who was relocating for his wife's career: "If he were any kind of a man, he wouldn't be following her like that." Wives are seen as "unladylike," domineering, and manipulative. One comment addressed to the husband of an office manager was, "Does she manage you too?" A wife asked, "What kind of drugs do you give him anyhow?" A young woman said to an older colleague, "I'd rather die than end up like you."

Such marriages are under considerable stress. Wives reported the main disadvantages as having the major responsibility for financially supporting the family (62 percent); being tired (53 percent); feeling guilt over not being a "good wife" (41 percent); and lacking time with husband and children (54 percent). Men mentioned fewer problems. The three most-mentioned disadvantages were the wife's time away from home (46 percent); lack of household services provided by the wife (33 percent); and sacrifices in their own careers (23 percent). In many ways, these are the traditional complaints of husbands and wives, only reversed.

occupations. A thirty-one-year-old factory worker (quoted in Rubin, 1976), the mother of five children, told how she felt about working:

I really love going to work. I guess it's because it gets me away from home. It's not that I don't love my home; I do. But you get awfully tired of just keeping house. . . .

You know, when I was home, I was getting in real trouble. I had that old housewife's syndrome, where you either crawl in bed after the kids go to school or sit and watch TV by the hour. I was just dying of boredom.

Yet work must present a real alternative to women, whether in increased income, more opportunity for social contact, or greater sense of personal fulfillment. Married women have to balance gains against losses. Can a good job be found? How will her husband react? Will the children feel neglected? Is good day care available?

Men do not have to take such considerations into account. First of all, men have a much better chance of getting a good job. The average woman earns only about three-fifths of what a man earns. Second, both men and women expect the husband to work. The husband often suffers both in his own eyes and in those of his partner if he does not. Third, the man is not expected to rear the children, so concern for child-rearing rarely enters into his decision to work. His responsibility to the children is traditionally shown by being the family provider (that is, the "worker"). The questions a man must face concerning work are of an entirely different character than those faced by a woman.

Economic Discrimination

It is well known that women are discriminated against economically: they make less money than men for the same work and they have fewer career opportunities. But other forms of discrimination exist that are less apparent but no less real. Most important is the discrimination businesses practice by the way they organize work and the workplace. Businesses do not recognize that the family has radically altered in the last fifty years. Businesses are run as if every worker were male with a wife at home to attend to his and to his children's needs. But the reality is that women make up a significant part of the work force and they don't have wives at home. Allowances are not made in the American workplace for the special needs of working mothers: flexibility in work schedule, day-care, emergency time off to look after sick children, and so on. In Sweden, on the other hand, working parents are given up to sixty days paid leave to attend to sick children (Pogrebin, 1982b).

The effects of economic discrimination can be devastating for divorced women. Women make 61 cents for every dollar that men make. (In Sweden, they make 90 cents for every dollar made by men.) Single-parent families account for 22 percent of America's families with children; 89 percent are headed by women (Glick, 1984a). Thirty-six percent of female single-parent families live beneath the poverty level, compared with 13 percent for single-parent families headed by men (Weinberg, 1985). Women head 89 percent of all single-parent families and generally have to support these families. Because of the great difference in women's and men's wages, many women are condemned to poverty and are forced to accept welfare and its accompanying stigma.

> There is a simple way to define a woman's job. Whatever the duties are—and they vary from place to place and from time to time—a woman's job is anything that pays less than a man will accept for comparable work.
>
> CAROLINE BIRD

Comparable Worth

Title VII of the 1964 Civil Rights Act prohibited pay and employment discrimination. But the law did not end the pay discrepancy between men and women. Much of the earnings gap we have noted is the result of occupational differences and segregation, not unequal pay for the same job (Beller, 1984). Earnings are about 30–50 percent higher in traditional male occupations, such as truck driver or corporate executive, than in predominantly female or integrated occupations, such as secretary or school teacher (Beller, 1982). The more an occupation is dominated by women, the less it pays.

In the last few years, the idea of "comparable worth" has been proposed as a means of closing the gap between men's and women's wages. Many believe that jobs held mostly by women pay less than jobs held mostly by men because they are seen as "women's work" and are consequently devalued. Supporters of comparable worth argue that secretaries, nurses, and clerks should earn as much as truck drivers, mechanics, and construction workers according to measurements of the inherent worth of such jobs in terms of experience, knowledge and skills, mental demands, accountability, and working conditions. Using such criteria, Minnesota evaluated its state employees. It found that although registered nurses (mostly females) and vocational education instructors (mostly males) were ranked equally, the nurse was paid $1,732 a month, whereas the instructor was paid $2,260 a month (Beck, 1984). In a study in Washington state, the jobs held mostly by women paid about 20 percent less on the average, than comparable jobs held by men (Goodman, 1984). (For comparable worth and college professors, see Bergmann, 1985.)

Since 1984, Minnesota, South Dakota, New Mexico, and Iowa have appropriated millions of dollars to raise wages for female employees; many states have begun studies of comparable worth and the city of San Jose, California, and the county of Los Angeles have adopted comparable worth policies (Lawson, 1985).

Comparable worth is controversial. Opponents argue that occupational wage differentials are the result of social norms, market forces, and women's own choices of putting family ahead of work. They argue that "inherent worth" is a subjective judgment and that wages should be set by the marketplace. Furthermore, they say, the cost of raising women's wages is prohibitively high. It would cost the federal government more than $10 billion (about 3 percent of the proposed 1986 military budget) to effect comparable worth. Clarence Pendleton, the head of the U.S. Civil Rights Commission, calls the idea "the looniest thing since Looney Tunes"; the Civil Rights Commission voted to oppose it. President Ronald Reagan opposes the idea and threatens to veto any such measure. In 1985, a federal circuit court struck down a Washington state court decision favoring comparable worth, declaring that wage differentials between men and women were not the result of sex discrimination. By contrast, liberal Democrats, many unions, the National Organization of Women, and other women's groups support comparable worth.

☐ EMPLOYMENT AND CHILD CARE

Employment Opportunities and Child Care

For women, lack of child care or inadequate child care is one of the major barriers to equal employment opportunity (U.S. Commission on Civil Rights, 1981). Many women would like to work but they are unable to find adequate child care or cannot afford it. This is especially true for young, unmarried, black, and poor mothers.

Personal Consequences of Inadequate Child Care. Even if mothers are working, they may not have child care. In the United States at least two million "latchkey children" between the ages of seven and thirteen come home from school to an empty house. Some estimates run as high as fourteen million. Latchkey children are not only found in poor families. A recent paper presented results of a study of over 300 children in a well-to-do suburb near Dallas and found that 23 percent were latchkey children (Vandell and Corasaniti, 1985). Latchkey children are left alone without supervision. Sometimes they are frightened; other times they get into mischief; some

Inequality is as dear to the American heart as liberty itself.

WILLIAM DEAN HOWELLS

enjoy their independence. Their mothers often worry, feel guilty, or experience anxiety. "Sometimes I just have anxiety attacks when I am at work," one mother said. "I really am so far away. It happens usually around 3 o'clock. My heart like stops and I think, 'Oh, my God, in 30 minutes everybody's supposed to be home or check in. I hope everything's OK! . . ." (U.S. Commission on Civil Rights, 1981.)

Employment Consequences of Inadequate Child Care.   In one survey of working women, 29 percent of the clerical, service, factory, and plant workers cited child care as a major problem. Among professional, managerial, and technical workers, the figure rose to 36 percent (cited in U.S. Commission on Civil Rights, 1981). Unfortunately, of the six million employers in the United States, only 1,500 provide some kind of child-care assistance to their employees; often this is only in the form of referrals (Select Committee, 1985).

Finding adequate care can be a frustrating task. It may involve constant switching of arrangements depending on who or what is available and the age of the child or children (Floge, 1985). Women often use three or four different arrangements—child's father, relatives living in or outside the household, day care, or a combination of these—before a child reaches school age. Most women change their child-care arrangements several times before their children reach school age.

Childrearing responsibilities make it more difficult for women to compete with men for equal employment. One unemployed mother complained: "You got children to take care of. And a man does not have that hanging around his neck. You have to be superwoman in order to get the same job that the man would very easily fall into because he doesn't have to worry about the children going to the doctor; he doesn't have to worry about the children getting sick" (U.S. Commission on Civil Rights, 1981).

In a report issued by the U.S. House of Representative's Select Committee on Children, Youth, and Families (1985), the committee found that nearly 20 percent of the working parents said they would work more hours if adequate and affordable child care were available. More than 25 percent of nonworking parents said they would work if they could find such care. The committee also reported that in nearly 25 percent of all households with young children, one or more adults had to give up work, were unable to take a job, or had to discontinue education or training because of lack of child care.

The U.S. Commission on Civil Rights (1981) concluded that the lack of child care or inadequate child care

- Prevents women from taking paid jobs
- Keeps women in part-time jobs, most often with low pay and little career mobility
- Keeps women in jobs for which they are overqualified and prevents them from seeking or taking job promotions or the training necessary for advancement
- Conflicts sometimes with women's ability to perform their work
- Restricts women from participating in education programs

Lack of Government Support.   Currently, there may be a million day-care providers who take care of children in their homes. But their numbers are likely to decline in the 1980s as these day-care workers seek other employment because of low pay and cuts in federal funding. Yet an estimated one million more homes will be needed by 1990 (U.S. Commission on Civil Rights, 1981). The expansion of day-care facilities

Ah, the little troubles, Mr. Oliver, they ruin a woman's life. It's the devil, I do believe, as sends us the toothache and the east wind and tax on beer. As for your grand sorrows . . . it's almost a pleasure to grieve, all hung in weeds, like a weeping willow. But the price of eggs, Mr. Oliver, the price of eggs.

GEORGE SANTAYANA, *THE LAST PURITAN*

will have a direct relationship on women's ability to compete equally with men in the job market.

Because of a 21 percent cut in day-care funding for low- and moderate-income families by the Reagan administration in 1981, the use of the child-care tax credit has become the largest single source of funding for child care (Select Committee, 1985). The tax credit provides approximately $1.7 billion in relief for child-care expenses. Two-thirds of this credit, however, goes to families with above-median incomes; only 7 percent goes to families making less than $10,000. *None* goes to the millions of families who have insufficient income to take advantage of it.

Why has child care received so little government support in the face of such direct need? Part of the answer lies in the traditional belief that women should care for their young children rather than work or attend school. This belief translates itself into government policies designed to discourage women with children from seeking employment outside the home. Child care is actually a political issue. Letty Pogrebin (1982a) wrote:

The split between love and power—or between love and work—allows most men, whether legislators, economists, employment specialists, or fathers, to ignore the problem of caring for children. Children are lumped into the love sphere, the female sphere. Therefore, few men ever experience the direct *connection between the responsibilities of love and depletion of power* . . . Work-family conflicts—the tradeoffs of your money for your life, your job or your child— would not be forced upon women with such sanguine disregard if men experienced the same career stalls caused by the buck-stops-here responsibility for children. Children would be better off if the *care* aspect of life were not so relentlessly privatized and feminized. In sum, child care is an employment issue *and* a family issue, not "just" a woman's issue. Child care is an issue of power as well as love.

Women are forced to make a choice, Pogrebin argued, between working or caring for their children.

Child Care and Women's Educational Opportunities

There are well over eleven million women age twenty-five and up enrolled in colleges and universities; a substantial number of them have children at home. Child care is a major problem for these women as well as for younger ones with families. At the University of Michigan, one-fifth to one-fourth of the students surveyed would seek more employment or education if child-care services were available. At University of California campuses, 7,500 students (6.5 percent) have children; 19 percent of these student parents are single parents. Two-thirds of these student parents used some form of child care, but 64 percent still had additional child-care needs. One student testified before the Select Committee (1985) about her child-care difficulties:

For a year I had to drive 40 miles a day to take my infant son to a Title XX [child care for low- and moderate-income families] licensed child-care provider. Several times I was nearly forced to terminate my schooling because I had no infant care. I have often missed exams and have had to take incomplete grades because of a sick child.

For some, child care determines the pace of their academic career; for others, it determines whether additional education can be pursued. A study at Portland State

University in Oregon found that a third of the students having problems with child care would increase their course load by 3.6 credits if they could resolve their difficulties. At the University of California, more than a third of the student parents indicated that they could have completed their degree earlier if they had adequate child care (Select Committee, 1985).

Forty percent of colleges and universities—approximately 1,000—provide day-care facilities for students, and waiting lists are long. What is the situation at your college or university? How have child-care problems affected student parents in this course? What can be done about it?

☐ DUAL-WORKER MARRIAGES

Effects on Marriage

The fact that women work affects marriage and the family in various ways (Hefferan, 1982b). For example, working wives contribute to family income, but this economic contribution may also be a threat to those husbands whose self-image is based on being the household provider (Pearlin, 1975). Also, work gives women increased independence. One consequence is that such women are more likely to divorce (Ross and Sawhill, 1975). Divorce may be more likely among working women either because economically independent women do not have to tolerate unsatisfactory marriages or because independent-minded women do not conform to traditional sex roles, causing tension and conflict in the marriage. Both interpretations may be partly correct. Moore and Sawhill (1978) comment:

> The recent upsurge in divorce rates reflects both greater economic independence among women and the marital strains engendered by changing attitudes about the position of women. Once society has adjusted to more egalitarian norms, the divorce rate might decline somewhat, but if the economic achievements of women continue to undermine the utilitarian character of traditional marriages, a permanently higher rate of divorce is a likely outcome.

Another consequence of women working is a shift in the decision-making patterns in a marriage. Although decision-making power in a given family is not based solely on economic resources (personalities, for instance, also play a part), economics is a major factor. A number of studies suggest that employed wives exert greater power in the home than nonemployed wives (Bahr, 1974). Marital decision-making power is greater among women who are employed full-time than among those who are employed part time. Wives have the greatest power (which may or may not equal the husbands) when they are employed in prestigious work, are committed to it, and have greater income than their husbands.

Role Overload and Role Strain

Research indicates that work-related problems may be more severe for working parents than nonparents (Voydanoff and Kelly, 1984). Being a working parent means performing three roles simultaneously: worker, parent, and spouse (in most cases). Because the time, energy, and commitment needed to carry out these roles are interdependent, considerable *role strain* can result. Voydanoff and Kelly (1984) observed that two types

The employment of women affects the power structure of the family by equalizing the resources of husband and wife. A working wife's husband listens to her more, and she listens to herself more. She expresses herself and has more opinions. Instead of looking up into her husband's eyes and worshipping him, she levels with him, compromises on the issues at hand. Thus her power increases and, relatively speaking, the husband's falls.

ROBERT BLOOD

All happiness depends on a leisurely breakfast.

JOHN GARDNER

of role strain are likely to occur, *role overload* and *interference* (also see Kelley and Voydanoff, 1985):

Overload occurs when the total prescribed activities of one or more roles are greater than an individual can handle adequately or comfortably. Interference exists when responsibilities conflict—that is, the expectations are contradictory or an individual is required to do two things at the same time. Thus, time shortage is an important type of work/family role strain among employed parents.

Role overload is a common plight for women who try to combine work, marriage, and family roles (Frieze et al., 1978). Although a woman may work full time, she is also often expected to perform her full-time wife and mother duties. Women today may very well be working longer hours than their grandmothers (Vanek, 1974). The estimated total work week for an employed women with two children varies from seventy-one to eighty-three hours (Ferber and Birnbaum, 1980).

Conflict Between Work and Family Life

Excessive work time is the major cause of conflict between work and family for men. For married women, it is fatigue and irritability (see Tables 11–1 and 11–2). Joseph Pleck and his colleagues (1980) noted:

The greater family responsibilities for women may be the reason for higher reports that the physical and psychological consequences of work caused family problems. Fatigue and irritability brought home from work often makes performing family tasks more difficult. . . . Husbands generally spend longer hours on the job but perform fewer household tasks. Having the opportunity to rest after work may help make fatigue and irritability less of a problem for husbands.

Conflict often centers on the division of household and child-care responsibilities. Generally, husbands spend only a few hours a week doing housework, even if their wives work as long and hard as they do (Nichols and Metzer, 1982). Men tend to do domestic chores such as shopping, rather than mopping floors, cleaning toilets, ironing, or washing dirty diapers. One study found that husbands contributed about eleven hours a week to household work, whereas wives contributed fifty-one hours (Walker and Woods, 1976). If the homemaker was employed thirty hours or more a week, she spent about five hours a day on housework instead of the eight hours full-time homemakers spent. The husband's contribution remained basically unchanged regardless of his wife's employment status. Men, however, tend to perceive that they do more housework than they actually do (Condran and Bode, 1982). Reviewing the literature on household task performance, Scanzoni and Fox (1980) found little evidence of egalitarianism in marriages when it comes to housework. (This comes as no surprise to most working wives and mothers.) They came to five conclusions:

- Working wives continue to have primary responsibility for running the family.
- Whether wives are employed or not has little impact on their husband's sharing the housework.
- The woman's day is increased at the expense of her sleep and leisure.
- Working wives spend less time on housework.
- Older children in families where the mother works may do more housework chores.

If you make money your god, it will plague you like the devil.

HENRY FIELDING (1707–1754)

Table 11–1 **Percent of Family Members Reporting Work-Related Conflict**

Group	No Conflict	Little Conflict	Moderate Conflict	Severe Conflict
All family members*	24	41	24	10
Employed husbands with employed wives	27	42	21	11
No children	35	37	20	7
Preschool children	23	41	23	13
School-age children	20	47	21	12
Employed wives with employed husbands	23	39	28	10
No children	37	34	19	11
Preschool children	12	40	36	12
School-age children	16	44	31	9
Employed women in one-parent families	17	58	14	11
Preschool children	19	56	9	16
School-age children	16	60	18	7

*Total sample size is 1,064; percentages based on weighted sample.

Note: Figures may not add up due to rounding.

Source: Joseph H. Pleck, Graham L. Staines, and Linda Lang, "Conflicts between work and family life," *Monthly Labor Review* 103(3):29–32, U.S. Department of Labor, Bureau of Labor Statistics, 1980.

A more recent study showed that sex role orientation seems to affect the sharing by men in household tasks (Bird et al., 1984). Men who believed in egalitarian roles accepted more responsibility for child care, meal preparation, and cleaning. Husbands' sharing of household work was also related to their wives being employed, especially if their wives were career oriented. As wives' income rose, they reported more participation by their husbands in household tasks. Whereas for men, sex role orientation and their wives' employment is important for sharing household work, for women, increased income and job status motivate them to secure their husbands' sharing of tasks. Another study found that the more expressive and mastery oriented the wife, the more assistance she obtained from her husband (Nyquist et al., 1985). Men who were relatively expressive helped their wives more than men who were relatively aggressive, dominant, and emotionally "tough."

But regardless of sex roles, wives' income, and expressiveness, as one researcher reported, "No matter how much help the women received, the domestic realm was defined ultimately as her responsibility; it was not defined as a responsibility to be shared equally by both spouses" (Holmstrom, 1972). (See the reading "The Politics of Housework" by Pat Mainardi.)

Dual-Job Versus Dual-Career Marriages

More than half of all married women held jobs in 1984, but the great majority of women were employed in low-paying, low-status jobs: secretaries, clerks, nurses, social workers, and the like. The ravages of inflation pushed most of them into the job market. Employed mothers do not seek personal fulfillment in their work as much as they do additional income to help make ends meet. Their families are their top priorities. Yet they often enjoy employment as a means of getting out of the house and breaking the routine of housework (Rubin, 1976).

Career-oriented women, however, have different characteristics from job-holding

Table 11–2   **Percent of Family Members Reporting Common Types of Work–Family Conflicts**

Group	Excessive Work Time	Schedule Incompatibility	Fatigue and Irritability
All family members*	50	28	15
Employed husbands with employed wives	63	22	11
Employed wives with employed husbands	39	39	27
Employed women in one-parent families	10	50	15

*Total sample size is 372; percentages based on weighted sample of those experiencing moderate or severe conflict.
Note: Figures may not add up due to rounding.
Source: Joseph H. Pleck, Graham L. Staines, and Linda Lang, "Conflicts between work and family life," *Monthly Labor Review* 103(3):29–32, U.S. Department of Labor, Bureau of Labor Statistics, 1980.

women (Rice, 1979). They have a strong need for achievement and rely on an extrinsic reward system, such as promotion, recognition, status, or spousal approval. Unfortunately, career women may have conflicts in achieving both their professional and family goals (Kilpatrick, 1982). Often they have to compromise one goal to achieve the other, since the work world generally is not structured to meet the family responsibilities of its employees.

Problems in Dual-Career Marriages

Role Problems.   The impact of dual-career marriages affects women more than men. We have already seen the stressful nature of role overload. In addition, both career- and job-oriented women continue to feel some identity conflicts. They have usually been reared to expect both men and women to follow traditional roles. Dual-career families experience some strain as they attempt to make roles more androgynous to lighten the home burdens of women (Skinner, 1980).

Even though a dual-career couple may adjust roles to help each other, society still expects husband and wife to follow traditional sex roles (Heckman et al., 1977). A male vice president who wields a broom at home, scrubs toilets, and takes time off for a sick child may be the object of ridicule at corporate headquarters. (This is a problem even in liberal Sweden where the postmaster general, Ove Rainer, took a month's paternal leave to be with his newborn and became the center of controversy. Corporation leaders attacked him as "a traitor to his sex." When another government leader was asked if he had taken care of his children, he laughed and said, "How would it be if Swedish generals told the enemy in wartime that we had to stay home?" "I told him," said Rainer, "that no leader is indispensable. We are only indispensable to our children" [Pogrebin, 1982b].)

Occupational Problems.   Many career-oriented women experience difficulties with the occupational structure. To advance they must be willing to move and devote themselves to full-time, continuous careers (Holmstrom, 1972). A random study (Markham et al., 1983) of 879 federal government employees and supervisors found that women were much less willing to move than men. Those who identified themselves as unwilling to move "ran the risk of being labeled unsuitable for high-level positions." The demands for geographical mobility are particularly difficult. When

Money is a source of power that supports male dominance in the family. . . . Money belongs to him who earns it, not to her who spends it, since he who earns it may withhold it.

REUBEN HILL and HOWARD BECKER

a partner's career requires moving, the man's career requirements usually take precedence over the woman's, regardless of how egalitarian the marriage is.

Marital Satisfaction. What about marital satisfaction in dual-career marriages? Does a woman's pursuit of a career affect her marriage? In general, dual-career and dual-job marriages require greater adjustments on the part of women. Role overload is a constant factor for women. Overinvolvement in work can lead to marital dissatisfactions. One study found that marital adjustment was highest when the husband's involvement in work was "medium" and the wife's involvement was "low" (Ridley, 1973). Presumably, low work involvement for women gave them more time for greater involvement in their family roles.

Some husbands may feel less satisfied with their marriages if their partners work because men lose some of their "active support system" and have to perform more housekeeping tasks (Burke and Weir, 1976). But one study found that dual-career husbands experienced less stress than their conventional counterparts because additional money and greater fulfillment for their wives outweighed the disadvantages (Booth, 1977; also see Gaesser and Whitburne, 1985; Benin and Nienstadt, 1985).

Coping with Dual-Worker Marriages

Dual-worker marriages are here to stay. They are particularly stressful today because society has not evolved ways to make them more manageable. The three greatest social needs in dual-worker marriages are redefining sex roles to eliminate role overload for women, providing adequate child-care facilities for working parents, and restructuring the workplace to recognize the special needs of parents and families (see Boken and Viveros-Long, 1981; Regan and Roland, 1985).

Meanwhile, women in dual-worker marriages use a variety of coping strategies. One study (Poloma, 1972) noted four techniques such women used to manage stress in their families (all of which required the woman rather than her husband to make sacrifices):

- They reduced conflicts over their roles as wives, mothers, and workers by defining their dual-worker arrangement as the best alternative for themselves and their families. One woman saw herself as a better wife and mother because she was employed; another emphasized her work as an economic necessity for the family.
- They established role priorities: Their first priority was to their marriages and families, and if their work roles conflicted with their family roles, their families came first.
- They compartmentalized their roles as much as possible—they tried not to bring their work home—which enabled them to devote their energy at home to their husbands and children.
- They compromised their career aspirations to avoid conflicts at home. They turned down promotions if the new job required a move. They minimized business travel to spend more time at home. They gave up the idea of becoming tops in their field if it meant sacrificing too much of their family lives.

Other strategies include reorganizing the family system and household expectations (McCubbin, 1979). Husbands may do more housework. Children may take on more household tasks than before (Coggle and Tasker, 1982). Household standards—such

Husband and wife are the same flesh but they have different purses.

YIDDISH PROVERB

UNDERSTANDING YOURSELF

The Division of Labor:
A Marriage Contract

How do you expect to divide household and employment responsibilities in marriage? More often than not, couples live together or marry without ever discussing basic issues about the division of labor in the home. Sometimes they feel that things will "just" work out. Other times they believe they have an understanding only to discover that they do not.

The following questions cover important areas of understanding for a "marriage contract." These issues should be worked out before marriage. Although marriage contracts dividing responsibilities are not legally binding, they make explicit the assumptions couples have about their relationships.

Answer these questions for yourself. If you are involved in a relationship, live with someone, or are married, answer them with your partner. Put your answers down in writing.

- *Which has the highest priority for you: marriage or work? What will you do if one comes in conflict with the other? How will you resolve the conflict? What will you do if your job requires you to work sixty hours a week? Would you consider that such hours conflict with your marriage goals and responsibilities? What would your partner think?*

 Do you believe that a man who works sixty

hours a week shows care for his family? Why? What about a woman who works sixty hours a week?

- *Whose career or work is considered the most important—yours or your partner's? Why?*

 What would happen if both you and your partner worked and you were offered the "perfect" job five hundred miles apart from each other? How would the issue be decided? What impact do you think this would have on your marriage?

- *How will household responsibilities be divided? Will the woman be entirely, primarily, equally, secondarily, or not responsible at all for housework? How will this be decided? Does it matter whether the woman is employed full-time as a clerk or lawyer in the amount of housework she should do?*

 Who will take out the trash? Vacuum the floors? Clean the toilet? How will these tasks be decided?

- *If you both work and then have a child, how will the birth of a child affect your employment? Will one person quit work to care for the child? Who will that be? Why? Who will be responsible for child care? If both of you work and the child is sick, who will remain home to care for the child? Why?*

---

as a meticulously clean house, complicated meal preparation, and washing dishes after every meal—may be changed. Careful allocation of time and flexibility assist in coping. Home economist Kathryn Walker (1982) suggested that the best way to organize is to ask fundamental life questions: "One begins any such process by asking: What do I want to get out of home life? Until we determine what is important and identify values and goals, we cannot really plan time." Dual-worker couples often hire outside help, especially for child care, usually a major expense for most couples. About 3 percent of the couples in Walker's study hired outside help for the various domestic chores (Walker, 1982).

One man eats very little and is always full. But another man constantly eats and is always hungry. Why is that?

ZEN RIDDLE

The goal for most dual-worker couples is to manage their relationships with each other and with work to achieve a reasonable balance of strains versus gains. When the gains outweigh the strains, they have succeeded. But achieving such success will continue to be a struggle until society and the workplace adapt to the needs of dual-worker marriages and families.

☐ UNEMPLOYMENT

Unemployment is a structural part of the American economy; it is there in good times and bad times. In the best of times there has been a 4 percent unemployment rate. Today, "full-employment" is defined as a 6-percent unemployment rate; in 1985 unemployment averaged about 7 percent. During the 1981–1982 recession, more than 10 percent of the work force was unemployed; the average worker was unemployed eighteen weeks or longer. People tend to overestimate the benefits the unemployed receive from social welfare programs (Liem and Rayman, 1982). In 1982, for example unemployment insurance covered only about 40 percent of the unemployed (Thurow, 1982)—only five million out of twelve million unemployed workers.

Impact on Families

The types of families hardest hit by unemployment are single-parent families headed by women, black families, and young families (see Table 11–3). Both black families and single-parent families headed by women tend to be unemployed longer than other types of families. Young families with preschool children often lack the seniority,

When, in a city of 100,000, only one man is unemployed, that is his personal trouble, and for its relief we properly look to the character of the man, his skills, and his immediate opportunities. But when in a nation of 50 million employees, 15 million men are unemployed, that is an issue, and we may not hope to find its solution within the range of opportunities open to any one individual. The very structure of opportunities has collapsed. Both the correct statement of the problem and the range of possible solutions require us to consider the economic and political institutions of the society, and not merely the personal situation and character of a scatter of individuals. . . .

C. WRIGHT MILLS, *THE SOCIOLOGICAL IMAGINATION* (1959)

Table 11–3   Labor Force Status of White, Black, and Hispanic Origin Women Maintaining Families, by Presence of Children and Marital Status, March 1983 (Numbers in thousands)

Race, Hispanic Origin, and Marital Status	Total			With Children Under Age 18			With No Children Under Age 18[1]		
	Population	Labor Force Participation Rate	Unemployment Rate	Population	Labor Force Participation Rate	Unemployment Rate	Population	Labor Force Participation Rate	Unemployment Rate
White women, total	6,783	60.5	10.9	3,959	70.3	13.4	2,824	46.8	5.6
Never married	842	53.6	12.4	442	47.5		399	60.4	3.7
Separated	1,117	62.1	16.9	918	62.0	16.3	200	62.5	19.2
Widowed	1,963	34.6	7.4	376	59.0	12.6	1,588	28.8	4.8
Divorced	2,861	79.7	9.9	2,224	80.0	11.5	637	78.3	4.0
Black women, total	2,808	57.1	21.7	1,923	60.3	25.7	885	50.2	11.3
Never married	940	57.0	28.2	785	54.0	30.4	155	72.3	19.6
Separated	657	62.1	22.8	504	62.7	25.3	153	60.1	14.1
Widowed	536	32.5	13.8	132	39.4	(2)	404	30.2	8.2
Divorced	675	71.9	16.5	502	72.9	20.2	173	68.2	4.2
Hispanic women, total	800	49.0	13.5	585	48.2	16.0	214	51.4	6.4
Never married	193	47.2	14.3	136	33.8	(2)	57	(2)	(2)
Separated	255	39.2	20.0	209	38.8	21.0	46	(2)	(2)
Widowed	123	35.0	(2)	51	(2)	(2)	72	(2)	(2)
Divorced	229	69.0	9.5	189	68.3	9.3	40	(2)	(2)

[1]*Children are defined as "own" children of the family. Included are never-married daughters, sons, stepchildren, and adopted children. Excluded are other related children such as grandchildren, nieces, nephews, cousins, and unrelated children.*

[2]*Rate not shown where base is less than 75,000*

experience, and skills to quickly regain employment. "Since the parents of preschoolers are also the ones most likely to lose their jobs," observed Moen (1983), "the largest toll in an economic downturn is paid by families in the early years of childbearing and childrearing."

A common public policy assumption is that unemployment is primarily an economic problem. But joblessness also seriously affects health and the family's well-being (Liem and Liem, 1982; Riegle, 1982). Two psychologists call for "radically reshaping our sense of unemployment as not simply a problem in economics but as a factor in human and social welfare" (Liem and Rayman, 1982). What is an economic downturn for economists, corporate executives, and Washington policy makers is often a social and personal disaster for families.

In times of economic hardship, strains increase and the rates of infant mortality, alcoholism, family abuse, homicide, admissions to psychiatric institutions and prisons, and suicide sharply increase (Brenner, 1973, 1976; Kasl, 1979; see Liem and Rayman, 1982 for a review of the literature on the health and social costs of unemployment.)

The families of the unemployed experience considerably more stress than employed families (see Gnezda, 1984, for a review of the effects of unemployment on family functioning). The most extensive work on the effects of unemployment has been done in the Boston area. Preliminary reports by Leim and colleagues (cited in Gnezda, 1984) indicate that in the first few months of unemployment, mood and behavior changes cause stress and strain in family relations. As families adapt to unemployment, family roles and routine change. The family spends more time together, but

> We spend more than $1 million a minute on the arms race in a world where 40,000 children in the developing countries die—not every year or every month but every day.
>
> JAVIER PEREZ DE CUELLAR, SECRETARY GENERAL, UNITED NATIONS, 1982

wives often complain of their husbands "getting in the way" and not contributing to household tasks. Wives may assume a greater role in family finances by seeking employment if they are not already employed. After the first few months of unemployment, wives begin to feel emotional strain, depression, anxiety, and sensitiveness in marital interactions. The children of the unemployed are more likely to avoid social interactions and tend to be more distrustful; they report more problems at home than children in employed families. Families seem to achieve stable patterns around new roles and responsibilities after six or seven months. If unemployment persists beyond a year, the family becomes highly vulnerable to marital separation and divorce; family violence may begin or increase at this time, according to Leim.

Unemployment does not necessarily lead to family disruption; some families experience increased cohesion (Gnezda, 1984). The family's response to a crisis is not unique; it reflects its established pattern of interactions (see Chapter 13). Strong families draw together; families with serious problems may draw apart.

Stages of Response

Powell and Driscoll (1973) studied a number of scientists and engineers who were suddenly unemployed and found they went through a series of predictable stages. The first was *relaxation and relief.* These unemployed professional men initially looked on the period of their job loss as a time to take it easy, catch up on their reading, be with the family, take a vacation. They felt they were simply between jobs and made no serious efforts to seek work.

The second stage was a period of *concerted effort.* After about three to four weeks, they began to get bored at home. Now they started seriously looking for work. The men were usually optimistic, taking rejection letters in stride. Relations with their families were generally good during this time, and their wives were supportive.

The third stage was one of *doubt and indecisiveness.* By this time the men had been out of work longer than ever before in their lives. They now began doubting their judgment and giving thought to other careers. Finding the old ways of searching for work unsuccessful, they became more sporadic at job hunting. They alternated between looking hard and not looking at all. They became more moody and frustrated, prone to sudden anger. Their family and marital relations began to deteriorate. Feeling unproductive, they believed themselves to be a burden on their respective families, who had to cope with mood swings and dwindling savings. After three to nine weeks in this stage, they gave up looking for a job. They felt over the hill, past their prime— that being over thirty-five was a handicap, which in our society it often is.

They now entered the fourth stage: *malaise and cynicism.* If they continued to seek work at all, they limited their job-search efforts only to ads asking for resumés, so they did not have to meet rejection face to face. They eventually ceased to care about anything—work or family—and felt totally helpless. Most gave up and no longer saw themselves as workers.

Coping with Unemployment

Louis Ferman of the University of Michigan's Institute of Labor and Industrial Relations suggests a number of coping mechanisms for unemployment (in Brody, 1983; also see Resource Center):

Richard Cory

Whenever Richard Cory went
      down town,
   We people on the pavement
      looked at him:
He was a gentleman from sole
      to crown,
   Clean favored, and imperi-
      ally slim.

And he was always quietly
      arrayed,
   And he was always human
      when he talked;
But still he fluttered pulses
      when he said,
   "Good-morning," and he
      glittered when he walked.

And he was rich—yes, richer
      than a king,
   And admirably schooled in
      every grace:
In fine, we thought that he
      was everything
   To make us wish that we
      were in his place.

So on we worked, and waited
      for the light,
   And went without the meat,
      and cursed the bread;
And Richard Cory, one calm
      summer night,
   Went home and put a bullet
      through his head.

EDWIN ARLINGTON ROBINSON

- *Planning ahead.* If job loss looks imminent, take stock of your resources. Find out what community services offer assistance or counseling, what medical clinics and lawyers offer sliding-scale or free services, where to obtain public food, child care, financial advice and so on.
- *Income gathering.* Look at the entire family as an income unit. Adolescent children can contribute to the family through delivery services, child care, house cleaning. Who can work at what? Brainstorm possibilities.
- *Financial planning.* List your assets and decide which are the most expendable; reexamine your expenditures to determine which are absolutely necessary.
- *Support groups.* Find others who are unemployed and form a support group to talk about your feelings; in this way, some of the emotional consequences of unemployment may be eased.

☐ POVERTY AND THE FAMILY

The law, in its majestic equality, forbids the rich as well as the poor to sleep under bridges, to beg in the streets, and to steal bread.

ANATOLE FRANCE (1844–1924)

In 1984, more than thirty-three million Americans—14.4 percent of the population—live in poverty (for a discussion of how the government defines "poverty," see Weinberg, 1985). Poverty has been increasing since 1981, primarily as a result of high sustained unemployment, the increase in single-parent families, and government cutbacks in aid to the poor (see "The Welfare State in America," special issue of *Annals of the American Academy,* 1985; Kelley, 1985).

Poverty can touch almost anyone from any class. About a quarter of the American population requires welfare assistance at one time or another in their lives, according to a study by the University of Michigan's Institute for Social Research (Duncan

Since 1981, because of federal and state welfare cuts, children have become especially vulnerable to poverty. Today they make up over 40 percent of the poor; they are the fastest growing segment of the homeless population.

In 1984, 300,000 to 3 million Americans were homeless, according to various estimates; poor families made up about 21 percent of the total. According to Harvard professor Ellen Bassuk, "The issue with homeless women and children is not merely the economics of poverty, but the breakdown of the family" (Karlen, 1986). The majority of homeless families are single-parent families headed by women. As many as 40 percent of the women in public shelters are battered wives; two-thirds have experienced major family shake-ups. Two-thirds of their children are under five years (Bassuk, 1984).

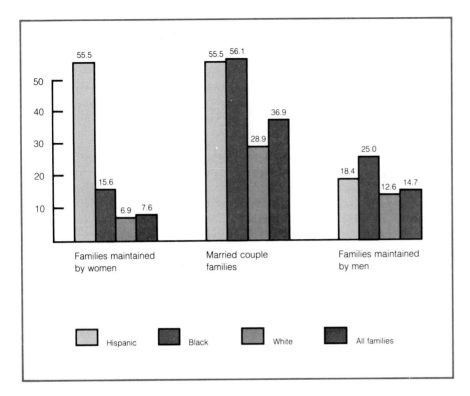

Figure 11–1

Families living in poverty, 1983.
(Source: U.S. Department of
Labor. Bureau of Labor Statistics,
1984. Bulletin 2209.)

et al., 1984). Because of changes in families due to divorce, unemployment, illness,
disability, or death, people on all rungs of the economic ladder may find themselves
requiring welfare assistance. According to the study, "Many families receiving welfare
were in the early stages of recovery from an economic crisis caused by the death,
departure, or disability of the family's major wage earner." Many who accepted
government assistance returned to self-sufficiency within a year or two. Only about
2 percent of the population depend heavily on welfare for more than seven out of ten
years. Most of the children in these families do not receive welfare after they leave
home.

Welfare Benefits

A 1983 study of recipients of Aid to Families with Dependent Children (AFDC)
found that one-third of the women left the program within a year, half the end of
two years, and two-thirds within four years. Most of the women went on AFDC as a
result of changes in their family situation: 45 percent after separation or divorce; 30
percent after becoming unmarried mothers. About a third left the program because
their income had increased, another third when they remarried or reconciled with
their mate, and 14 percent when their children left home or grew up.

Nineteen percent of all American households received benefits based on need in
1984. These programs include welfare, food stamps, subsidized housing, veterans'
pensions, free and reduced-price school lunches, and Medicaid (the health program

"We [a migrant family] travel
a lot, and sometimes I don't
know where we are. Then I see
the flag and I know it's still
America; and, like the teacher
says, we are free to say what we
want. But my parents say that
if only we could make more
money, we'd not be having
such a tough time, and we'd
know where our next meal is
coming from."

ROBERT COLES, "WHAT IT
MEANS TO LOVE AMERICA"

Figure 11–2

Percent distribution of aggregate income, 1983. (Source: U.S. Statistical Abstract, 1985.)

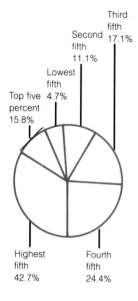

for the poor). Seventy percent of single-parent families headed by women received government assistance, most often Medicaid or school lunches. Nine percent of all households received Medicaid benefits; 8 percent received food stamps; 7 percent had children receiving free or low-priced school lunches; 5 percent received AFDC; and 4 percent lived in subsidized housing (Pear, 1985).

Effect of Federal Policies on the Poor

Between 1981 and 1984, as a result of government policy, 500,000 families with children had been removed from AFDC; many of these families were poor when their assistance was ended or were pushed into poverty as a result of the cuts (Greenstein, 1984). Since being dropped from the program, 30–60 percent of these families have had no health-care coverage for themselves or their children; more than half have run out of food at least once; and more than a quarter have had a utility shut off.

Not only are fewer families receiving benefits but also inflation has seriously eroded the value of these benefits. The value of combined welfare and food-stamp benefits for a family of four with no other income dropped 22 percent between 1972 and 1984. Such a family received $6,955 in benefits in 1984 compared with $8,894 (in 1984 dollars) in 1972. A working mother with income at half the poverty level who received welfare benefits had 28.5 percent less purchasing power in 1984 than in 1972. The average food stamp recipient received 48 cents per meal per person; the highest amount received is 70 cents (Press, 1985). The buying power of the working poor decreased because of higher Social Security and income taxes and reductions in welfare benefits ("Big Erosion . . . ," 1985).

Recent tax changes have hurt the poor especially. The poor paid twice as much in taxes in 1984 as they did in 1980. According to a 1984 report from the Congressional Budget Office, the net effect of tax cuts and spending reductions gave those earning $10,000 a year or less a net loss of $390; those earning $40,000 to $80,000 had a net gain of $2,900; those earning $80,000 or more had a net gain of $8,270 ("Soaking the Poor," 1984). In the same period, the share of federal revenue from corporate

Table 11–4 Money Income of Families—Income at Selected Positions Received by Each Fifth and Top 5 Percent of Families: 1983

			Race	
			Black and Other Non-white	
Item	*All Families*	*White*	*Non-white*	*Black*
Number (1,000)	61,997	53,934	1,298	6,675
Income at Selected Positions (dollars)				
Upper limit of each fifth:				
Lowest	11,629	12,878	6,206	5,915
Second	20,060	21,288	12,000	11,025
Third	29,204	30,255	20,120	18,300
Fourth	41,824	42,915	32,011	29,100
Top 5 percent	67,326	69,342	52,712	47,610

Source: Adapted from U.S. Bureau of the Census, *Current Population Reports*, series P–60, No. 145.

taxes decreased from 12.5 percent to 6.2 percent (Greenstein, 1984; Hershey, 1984). (See Table 11–4 on the distribution of income.)

The "feminization of poverty" is a painful fact. It has primarily resulted from high rates of divorce and increasing numbers of unmarried women with children (Hill, 1985). When women with children divorce, their income falls dramatically; 73 percent of the women experience a decline in their income after divorce (42 percent of the men's income increases) (Bohen, 1984). Women represent 61 percent of all persons age sixteen and over who were below the poverty level in 1983. Children represent 40 percent of the poor. If we are going to protect our families, we need to protect our poor. (See the reading "Being on Welfare" by Barbara McIntosh.)

☐ FINANCIAL PLANNING

"Money is a terrible master but an excellent servant," P. T. Barnum once said. He also said there's a sucker born every minute. Both are useful to keep in mind when we think about money.

Indebtedness

We are a nation of debtors. In 1984, Americans owed $460 billion in installment debts (from credit card purchases and automobile and other personal loans—but not home mortgages); this is an increase of about 20 percent over the previous year. About 600 million credit cards are in circulation representing debts totaling $75 billion (Proxmire, 1984). Seven out of ten consumers use credit cards; the average cardholder has 5.2 cards.

Why do people go into debt? First, many poor people must go into debt to live. The wolf is always at the door. They have no choice but to borrow to make ends meet. Second, money is many things besides the ability to buy. It symbolizes power, status, achievement, work, and love. "Money talks" is an old expression. ("Money doesn't talk/It swears," sang Bob Dylan in his younger days.) "For many people to admit they can't afford the things they want," explained a psychiatrist at Harvard Medical School, "means they are placing themselves in a position of weakness. They have to say no to themselves, and nobody likes to do that" (Friedrich, 1982). Third, with inflation, people tend to buy rather than to save, since savings are eaten up by inflation. If you wait to buy a new television set until next year, it may cost $50 more. If you don't have the money now, you use your credit card.

Credit Cards

Credit cards allow people to buy goods easily, but credit cards are not free. Credit card owners often pay annual fees for the use of their cards as well as high interest (ranging in 1986 around 19.8 percent for the major cards). But there is another cost as well: higher prices. The merchant must pay the credit card company for all sales made with the company's card. This cost averages 3 percent, but it is sometimes as high as 6 percent. As William Proxmire (1984) points out:

Who pays the cost of the merchant discount? All consumers do, including those who pay cash. The merchant discount may be hidden, but its cost must be recovered in the price of

---

Prosperity doth best discover vice; but adversity doth best discover virtue.

FRANCIS BACON (1561–1626)

Many workers, in the elation of the first days after their honey-moon, lock themselves into a lifetime of debt when they buy a house and furniture to add on the payments they are already making on their car. From then on, their freedom to travel, or to try a new job, or just engage in a range of activities outside work is taken from them by the structure of debt in which they are enmeshed.

A. LEVINSON, *THE WORKING-CLASS MAJORITY*

Money is a good thing to have. It frees you from doing things you dislike. Since I dislike doing nearly everything, money is handy.

GROUCHO MARX

What shall it profit a man, if he shall gain the whole world, and lose his own soul?

MARK 8:36

Financial Danger Signals

- Routine payment of only minimum amount due on monthly accounts.
- Use of savings or loans to keep up with monthly bills.
- Use of credit to pay for items usually paid for in cash, such as entertainment, clothes, and food.
- Dependence on additional income such as overtime or moonlighting to keep up with bills.

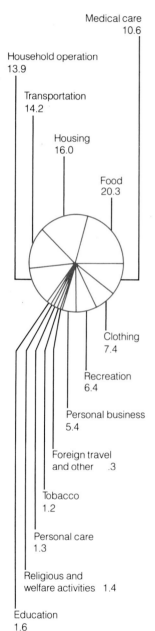

Figure 11–3

Where the dollar goes. (Source: Bureau of Economic Analysis, 1982.)

Medical care 10.6

Household operation 13.9

Transportation 14.2

Housing 16.0

Food 20.3

Clothing 7.4

Recreation 6.4

Personal business 5.4

Foreign travel and other .3

Tobacco 1.2

Personal care 1.3

Religious and welfare activities 1.4

Education 1.6

the goods sold. Thus, cash customers are paying for a service they don't receive. Since cash buyers tend to be those who don't qualify for credit cards, we have a case of the poor subsidizing the rich.

Styles of Planning

In the face of rising debts and economic uncertainties that have become part of the American economic way of life, financial planning is more important than ever. The first thing to do is to decide on a budget. Most people who are in financial trouble do not know how much they owe, much less the exorbitant interest they are probably paying. Most people have no idea how much they really spend. For example, take a moment and figure out what you spent last month. After you make a rough estimate, turn to the budget section of the Resource Center and, using the form provided, compute what you actually spent during that time. You may be surprised to find a considerable difference between your estimated and actual expenditure. People tend to figure in their major items but overlook smaller expenses, which add up. What items do you tend to overlook when figuring your expenses?

People have certain styles in financial planning (Hefferan, 1981). Your style of planning may be as important as your style of loving. It may have a lot to do with how well your love relationships work. *Morphostatic* planners are oriented toward the present, buying what they want now rather than waiting; their standards are inflexible—they want the best there is. They go by the rules and are conventional in their buying and planning. In contrast, *morphogenic* planners are flexible, want all family members to participate in the planning, and have foresight about the consequences of their current financial activities (Beard and Firebaugh, 1978).

When we are making financial plans, we must clarify our goals and values. Families that engage in financial planning tend to be motivated by very strong goals, especially home ownership, education of children, and adequate retirement (Hefferan, 1981). Strong goal commitments influence the way we spend our money. If a couple is committed to buying a house, both partners are more likely to be working and willing to reduce luxury items such as dinners out, movies, and other recreational items.

It is also important to begin making positive, long-term financial plans at the beginning stages of the family life cycle (Hefferan, 1981). Although money helps in long-term planning, low-income families in the early stages of their family life cycle—especially recent high school or college graduates—are able to make plans based on their expected income rather than their current income. In the early stages of the family life cycle, we usually spend our money on furniture, housing, automobiles, and recreation; later, when our children reach adolescence, we begin to spend heavily on their needs. These two times are the periods of greatest expenses for most families. Although our needs and circumstances may change, they usually only temporarily alter our established patterns of planning behavior. (For information on establishing credit, budgeting, and other aspects of financial planning, see the Resource Center.)

More than one hundred years ago, Charles Dickens in *David Copperfield* produced a sound formula for financial planning: "Annual income twenty pounds, annual expenditure nineteen nineteen, result, happiness. Annual income twenty pounds, annual expenditure twenty pounds ought and six, result misery." It is as worth remembering now as it was in the past.

☐ **SUMMARY**

- The structure of work regulates the family and determines its rhythms. Working-class men and women have little work flexibility and experience high unemployment rates, which adversely affect their marriages and families.

- White collar, managerial, and professional workers have higher incomes, greater work flexibility, and higher status, but their work requires greater personal and emotional commitment. Their work may compete with their families as a means of satisfaction.

- In the traditional division of labor in the family, the husband works outside the home for wages and the wife works inside the home without wages. Men's participation in household work is traditionally limited to repairs, construction, and yard work. Some redistribution of household work may take place if the wife is also employed. Women's responsibility for household work is part of the traditional marriage contract.

- Four characteristics of the homemaker role are (1) exclusive allocation to women, (2) association with economic dependence, (3) status as nonwork, and (4) priority over other roles.

- Status accorded to homemakers depends on class. Working-class families accord homemakers greater status than middle-class families.

- Five characteristics of housework are (1) It isolates the person at home. (2) It is unstructured, monotonous, and repetitive. (3) It is often a restricted, full-time role. (4) It is autonomous. (5) It is "never done."

- In recent years large numbers of middle-aged women have been forced to enter or reenter the job market as a result of divorce, death, or economic hardship. There are about four million of these *displaced homemakers.*

- Women workers make up 44 percent of the work force; 54 percent of adult women are employed or seeking employment. Nearly twenty-seven million women are currently employed, the majority in low-paying, dead-end jobs.

- Women's employment pattern follows an M-shaped curve, reflecting their home and child-care responsibilities. Women's labor force participation is interrupted for family reasons almost forty times as much as it is for men.

- Women tend to have four career patterns: regular, interrupted, second, and modified second; men only have one pattern, regular.

- Comparable worth supporters argue that traditional male and female occupations should receive comparable wages when it can be shown that the occupations have comparable intrinsic worth, measured in terms of education, skill levels, and the like. Opponents argue that the marketplace should set wages.

- The lack of adequate child care severely handicaps women's employment and educational opportunities. Since 1981 the federal government has severely cut day-care funding.

- In dual-worker marriages, women are more independent and have increased power in decision making. They are affected, however, by *role overload* and *role strain* because they must play the roles of wife, mother, and worker. Husbands generally do not significantly increase their share of household duties. The major conflict that married women experience in work and family life is irritability and fatigue as a result of role overload.

- Unemployment most frequently affects female single-parent families, black families, and young families. Unemployed families experience greater stress than employed families. Unemployment causes family roles to change; families spend more time together, but wives complain husbands don't participate in household tasks. After about six months, a stable family pattern is established. If unemployment continues beyond a year, the family is vulnerable to separation and divorce.

- Unemployed males may go through four stages in response to unemployment: (1) relaxation and relief, (2) concerted job search effort, (3) doubt and indecisiveness, and (4) malaise and cynicism.

- Families may cope with unemployment by (1) planning ahead, (2) income gathering, (3) financial planning, and (4) finding support groups.

- More than 15.3 percent of the population lives in poverty. The majority of poor people are women and children. Although most welfare recipients are on welfare less than two years, welfare is stigmatized. Welfare benefits have been woefully inadequate; since 1981 the poor have been increasingly penalized through taxes.

- We are a nation of debtors; the average person has at least five credit cards. People go into debt because (1) they can't afford to buy goods (including necessities), (2) money means power and status, and (3) in inflationary times, people buy rather than save.

READINGS

The Politics of Housework

PAT MAINARDI

Why is housework considered a "political" issue between men and women? What are the arguments in favor of men participating equally in housework? Against equal participation? What would you consider the basis for a fair distribution of housework? Would gender be a consideration in such a distribution? Why?

We both had careers, both had to work a couple of days a week to earn enough to live on, so why shouldn't we share the housework? So I suggested it to my mate and he agreed—most men are too hip to turn you down flat. You're right, he said. It's only fair.

Then an interesting thing happened. I can only explain it by stating that we women have been brainwashed more than even we can imagine. Probably too many years of seeing media-women cooing over their shiny waxed floors or breaking down over their dirty shirt collars. Men have no such conditioning. They recognize the essential fact of housework right from the very beginning. Which is that it stinks.

Here's my list of dirty chores: buying groceries, carting them home and putting them away; cooking meals and washing dishes and pots; doing the laundry; digging out the place when things get out of control; washing floors. The list could go on but the sheer necessities are bad enough. All of us have to do these jobs, or get someone else to do them for us. The longer my husband contemplated these chores, the more repulsed he became, and so proceeded the change from the normally sweet considerate Dr. Jekyll into the crafty Mr. Hyde who would stop at nothing to avoid the horrors of—housework.

So ensued a dialogue that's been going on for several years. Here are some of the high points:

"I don't mind sharing the housework, but I don't do it

very well. We should each do the things we're best at."

Meaning: Unfortunately I'm no good at things like washing dishes or cooking. What I do best is a little light carpentry, changing light bulbs, moving furniture. (How often do you move furniture?)

Also meaning: Historically the lower classes (blacks and women) have had hundreds of years doing menial jobs. It would be a waste of manpower to train someone else to do them now.

Also meaning:I don't like the dull stupid boring jobs, so you should do them.

"I don't mind sharing the work, but you'll have to show me how to do it."

Meaning: I ask a lot of questions and you'll have to show me everything, every time I do it because I don't remember so good. Also, don't try to sit down and read while I'm doing my jobs because I'm going to annoy hell out of you until it's easier to do them yourself.

"I've got nothing against sharing the housework, but you can't make me do it on your schedule."

Meaning: Passive resistance. I'll do it when I damn well please, if at all. If my job is doing dishes, it's easier to do them once a week. If taking out laundry, once a month. If washing the floors, once a year. If you don't like it, do it yourself oftener, and then I won't do it at all.

Being on Welfare
BARBARA McINTOSH

Women on welfare are often stigmatized as "welfare queens"; sometimes they are accused of having children in order to receive welfare benefits. Why do we "blame the victim" for being poor? What are the most frequent reasons that women go on welfare? What does government do to perpetuate welfare dependency? What could be done to assist women on welfare to become self-sufficient?

Despite their briefcase-toting image, women as a class are growing poorer. Currently, two-thirds of people officially classified as poverty-stricken are women.

Divorced and never-married women constitute the fastest growing segment of the female disadvantaged.

What sociologists see developing is a significant subculture of women . . . who are waging frustrated, often isolated, battles to care for their children under great economic and emotional strain. They exist on an erratic mix of miserable salaries, child-support payments and, sometimes, subsistence-level welfare benefits.

This increasing impoverishment is tidily referred to as the "feminization of poverty." It is related to a dramatic increase in the numbers of mothers who support families by themselves, due largely to high rates of divorce and unwed pregnancy.

Fifty percent of all poor families in this country are headed by women. By 1982 standards, the most recent available, that means a woman with three children is trying to live on $190 or less a week.

The most severely affected are women who have always borne the brunt of poverty—the elderly, black, Hispanic and disabled. And they are losing even more ground as a new category of poor, middle-class women slip downward.

Consider Elizabeth. At first glance, she looks like any other suburban housewife. She lives in an expensive house with her two young daughters on a cul-de-sac in Los Altos.

A college graduate, she worked for years as a school psychologist. She is articulate and witty. She has stylish blonde streaks in her pixie-cut hair. Three dainty gold necklaces adorn her neck.

One has to look very carefully to see hints of the truth. Elizabeth is a member of the new poor. Like many other middle-class women, her financial troubles began with a broken marriage.

The faint circles under her eyes suggest the many sleepless nights she has spent asking the darkness the same questions: "Where will I ever get the money? How will I ever survive this?"

On closer inspection, her ranch-style home shows signs of deterioration. The paint is peeling, the roof needs patching and the lawn is growing weedy. Once there were four cars in the driveway. Now there is only one—a 1977 model in shaky condition.

Although Elizabeth dabbled in modeling as a young woman, fashion isn't the reason she wears layered jogging clothes at home. She's trying to keep the cold out. Money is so tight she doesn't want to turn on the heat.

This 41-year-old woman is a disappointed investor in the American Dream. She married in a white gown at a big church, bore two children and, after a few years of hard work, moved into a dream house with her family.

Elizabeth and her husband separated last year—a few days before she lost her job in education because of budget cutbacks. Only dust stirs in the formal dining room now. The blender, microwave and other status symbols of modern homemaking sit on cabinets empty of food. The ceiling above the sunny breakfast nook is caving in because of rain leaks.

Elizabeth is currently involved in a messy divorce. She

READINGS—*continued*

receives $600 a month in temporary family support from her husband. . . . [She] must declare that support from her taxes as income. He gets to deduct it.

Her husband's lawyer is trying to get her child support payments reduced on the grounds that Elizabeth is employable. She is trying to keep the house so her children won't have to switch schools, but that payment alone is $1,035 a month and there is an outstanding $3,000 in back taxes on the property. She also faces $5,000 in legal fees.

Elizabeth recently rented out the downstairs family room to help defray costs. She has looked for a job in counseling, to no avail. "I've decided I can't be picky," she says. "I'm thinking about restaurant work, anything, to bring in some money."

Divorce doesn't automatically equal destitution, of course, but for many single mothers it does mean a significant financial decline. For example, a recent California study found that after divorce a woman's standard of living decreased by about 73 percent while a man's increased by 42 percent.

A major reason: Most often a man becomes single when he divorces; a woman becomes a single mother.

As a group, females divorce most often between the ages of 30 and 44, the primary child-rearing years for most Americans.

And, contrary to the "Kramer vs. Kramer" storyline, most men do not fight for legal custody of their children. While some fathers do conscientiously pay child support, many do not. Non-payment of child support is at its highest level ever.

In California, only about one-fourth of the children of divorce receive any financial support from their absent fathers. Of those men who do contribute, half pay less than 10 percent of their annual incomes.

Nationally, the average support payment in 1981 was about $176 per month for one child. For a full-time working mother, that amount does not even cover the cost of $2-an-hour day care. Children become more expensive to rear as they grow older, but most child-support allotments do not include automatic escalators to account for age or changes in the cost of living.

Minority families fare the worst in courts. While more than 70 percent of white children are awarded some level of support, only about 44 percent of Hispanic and 29 percent of black youngsters receive any court-ordered allotment.

Olive Luton doesn't own a house or car. Her child-support payment for her three sons is $400 a month. As a 40-year-old black woman, she faces the triple whammy of possible age, race and sex discrimination.

She was raised in Harlem, the daughter of a brick mason. "My family never encouraged me to get an education," she says. "I was just supposed to get married."

She obliged. She wed a military man and began a family. They lived at bases all over the world until their 12-year marriage ended in 1976, making Luton a displaced homemaker with no marketable job skills.

For a while, Luton and her children managed to live in San Jose on a small inheritance her mother left her. She decided to capitalize on her considerable talent as an amateur artist by enrolling in a graphic design program at San Jose State University with student financial aid.

Luton should do well in a job interview. She speaks concisely, dresses conservatively and is the winner of several scholastic awards. Yet, since her graduation in 1982, she has been unable to find a permanent position as a graphics designer.

She and her family live on public assistance, receiving $625 a month and $104 in food stamps. She relinquishes her monthly child-support payment to the government, as do all single parents on welfare.

Bitterly disappointed that her college degree hasn't helped her find graphics work, Luton has decided any job is better than no job. She recently completed a vocational-education course in computer operation, but so far hasn't found a full-time job in either printing or office work.

"You know, sometimes I think it's how old I am," she says. "The first thing I did after my divorce was color my hair so the gray wouldn't show. I'm having to compete with kids right out of school who are half my age."

Single mothers like Olive Luton share an impoverishment that is often different from that affecting men. Their financial distress is dictated much less by the rising and falling of the unemployment rate.

While the cure for most male poverty is a job, many women are employed full-time and still live below or just above the poverty line because of the type of work available to them and the high cost of day care and child-rearing.

These women find themselves in the position of supporting a family within an economic system based on the idea that Daddies bring home the bacon. That assumption, once largely true, no longer holds. Only 7 percent of American families fit into the traditional breadwinner Pop, homemaker Mom and dependent children mold anymore.

Yet, wage discrimination between men and women not only exists, it has worsened. In 1957, working women on the average earned 64 cents for every $1 that men received; by 1980, that figure had slipped to about 59 cents.

READINGS–*continued*

For women, education does not translate as easily into earning power as it does for males. Female college graduates earn, on the average, the same salary as a male with an eighth-grade education, and an estimated one-third of black women with college degrees live below the poverty line.

Sociologist Diana Pearce of Catholic University says while it's true individual females have made great strides in the last decade, the majority of women remain "as occupationally segregated as during the Victorian era." Most still work in the pink ghetto of women's work—retail sales, clerical, restaurant, domestic and light assembly—in positions that often have poor benefits and limited chances of advancement.

When Sonia Lewis' three-year marriage ended last year she considered suicide, but opted for welfare.

"It almost killed me," she says. But Lewis had Tracie, her 2-year-old daughter, to consider. She put off applying for welfare as long as she possibly could. After her separation, she and the child were evicted from a Sunnyvale apartment. They tried staying in a one-bedroom apartment with seven other people. When that became unbearable for all concerned, Lewis resorted to living in her car for two weeks. She used the money she had left to place Tracie in a 24-hour day-care facility.

"I'd go to see her and be afraid she wouldn't remember who I was," Lewis says. That's when she applied for aid.

"I felt like crying," she says. "I used to work for the school district in a migrant-education program. I filled out papers for Mexican families to receive welfare and here I was in the same boat. I was so ashamed."

At least one major study suggests most single mothers do try to avoid public assistance. According to research at Syracuse University, the majority of divorced or separated welfare recipients do not start receiving aid until about two years after their marriages end, an indication that they try to make it on their own first.

The average time an AFDC recipient receives benefits is about 22 months. But the unusual thing about single mothers is that they tend to fall in and out of poverty because their financial and home situations are so precarious. A sick child, an increase in day-care expense or a reduc-

tion in working hours can put them right back on the welfare rolls.

. . . "You know, sometimes I get the feeling the government doesn't want women to get any better off. Like, maybe there's a conspiracy or something against mothers like me," says Brandie McClatchy, a 29-year-old divorced mother of three boys, all under the age of 7.

The first thing one senses about McClatchy is an anger and desperation. Very recently, she and her sons stayed in area shelters because no landlord would allow them to move into a one-bedroom apartment. Yet, that was all McClatchy could afford on her $625 welfare allotment for a family of four.

Finally, her sister consented to move in with them and share the rent in a small, two-bedroom apartment near downtown San Jose. McClatchy, a recent Catholic convert, has filled it with pictures of Christ and the Virgin Mary.

McClatchy wants to expand her job skills—which have limited her to working at a doughnut shop, dry cleaners and as a waitress—in order to support her sons without aid.

So, she recently enrolled in a four-year accounting program at a San Jose college. The school solved one of her major problems by offering her free child care in a program available only to full-time students.

But McClatchy found her aspirations are against the law. As a welfare mother, she cannot carry a full college load without having her benefits cut or eliminated.

She is now required to sign up for the state work incentive program (WIN), which requires her to register for an intensive month-long work search and accept any job for which she is qualified. Usually single mothers with children under the age of 6 are not required to participate in the program, partly because of the high cost of day care.

But according to bureaucratic reasoning, if McClatchy goes to school full time—even though it is possible only because she gets free child care—then she is theoretically capable of working full time.

"That means I'd be stuck in another minimum-wage job going nowhere," McClatchy says. "I still couldn't afford day care. I still wouldn't have insurance. I don't want to stay on welfare, but if it means taking better care of my boys, I will."

CHAPTER 12

Parents and Children

PREVIEW

To gain a sense of what you already know about the material covered in this chapter, answer "true" or "false" to the following statements. You will find the answers as you read the chapter.

1. Egalitarian marriages usually remain so after the birth of the first child. True or false?
2. Specific strategies may be developed to cope with parental stress. True or false?
3. A maternal instinct has been proven to exist in humans. True or false?
4. Playing with dolls can help both girls and boys to become good parents. True or false?
5. The great majority of married men say they get more satisfaction from the husband-father role than from their work. True or false?
6. Most studies show that regular day care by nonfamily members is detrimental to intellectual development. True or false?
7. A link between television violence and aggressive behavior in children has not yet been proven scientifically. True or false?
8. Many parents follow the advice of "experts" even though it conflicts with their own opinions, ideas, or beliefs. True or false?
9. Among siblings, the order of birth and spacing between births influence the development of each child. True or false?
10. There is evidence that children are biologically equipped to discern the difference between right and wrong. True or false?

Outline

Many Americans feel deeply ambivalent about parenthood. More people in this country than ever before are asking if they even want to be parents. The increasing numbers of child-free marriages, single-child families, and deferred families all point to changed feelings about having children and parenting among large segments of the population. These changes have occurred mostly among the young and well-educated, who are often in the vanguard of change in society as a whole.

In this chapter we discuss the unique challenges that the transition to parenthood presents to both mothers and fathers. The roles of outside childcare and of television as child socializers are also examined. Next, we look at theories of child development, styles of childrearing, and the needs of children and parents. Finally, we explore some specific contemporary childrearing strategies.

☐ SHOULD WE OR SHOULDN'T WE? CHOOSING TO HAVE CHILDREN

Aunt Tillie: Do you like children?
Uncle Gus: I do if they're properly cooked.

W. C. FIELDS

Parenthood may now be considered a matter of choice owing to widespread acceptance of birth control. If men and women want to have children, they can decide when to have them. As a result, America's birthrate has fallen to an average of two children per marriage, the ideal number expressed by 56 percent of the people interviewed in a 1985 Gallup poll. A little more than twenty-five years ago, 37 percent of those interviewed wanted a large family of four or more children. Today only 11 percent want so large a family. Approximately 2 percent want no children at all.

In some areas "reproductive decision-making" workshops and classes are being offered to help women order their priorities about career, life style, and childrearing.

One study found that 42 percent of the women who attended such a workshop were able to make a clear reproductive choice at the program's conclusion (Daniluk and Herman, 1984). (See the reading "No Children Allowed" by Linda Lee.)

Child-Free Marriage

In recent articles and discussions of marriages in which there are no children, the term "childless" is often replaced by "child-free." This change in terminology reflects a shift of values in our culture. Couples who do not choose to have children need no longer be viewed as lacking something hitherto considered essential for personal fulfillment. Indeed, the use of the suffix "-free" suggests liberation from the bonds of a potentially oppressive condition (also see Callan, 1985). Women who choose to be child-free are generally well educated and career oriented. They feel that children will disrupt their marriages or other relationships, limit their careers, and restrict their life-style options. One woman expressed her feelings as follows (in Boston Women's Health Book Collective, 1978):

When I see someone who's dragging along a child who's crying and screaming and I'm on a date with a man who's saying "You're not a whole woman if you can't have my baby," then I say, "Why don't you go over there to that child and listen to the screaming for a few minutes?" The reality is that there's a lot of noise. There's a lot of mess. And it's not just for a few days. It's for years.

The National Alliance for Optional Parenthood and the National Organization for Non-Parents (NON) are groups that provide emotional support for the voluntarily childless. Even when familial and societal pressure to reproduce is lessened, the decision to remain without children is not always easily attained and sustained. But as a member of NON stated, "The fact is we're severely overpopulated. So there's really no reason to have a child unless you know you really enjoy the process of raising one" (Boston Women's Health Book Collective, 1978).

> In the time it takes to read this sentence, world population will have increased by three.

The partners in some child-free marriages have never felt they wanted to have children. But for most the decision seems to have been gradual. Veveers (1973) identified four stages of this decision process:

1. The couple decides to postpone children for a definite time period (until he gets his degree, until she gets her promotion, and so on).
2. When the time period expires, they decide to postpone children indefinitely (until they "feel" like it).
3. They increasingly appreciate the positive advantages of being child free (as opposed to the disadvantages of being childless).
4. The decision is made final—generally by the sterilization of one or both partners.

Couples usually have some idea that they will or will not have children before they marry. If the intent isn't clear from the start or if one partner's mind changes, the couple may have serious problems ahead. A New York banker, aged forty-four, whose wife had been continuing to postpone childbirth, complained in frustration, "What these intelligent women owe the world is not just what they do or who they are—they owe the world a legacy to pass on" (in Francke, 1980).

Studies of child-free marriage generally indicate a higher degree of marital adjustment or satisfaction than is found among couples with children. In one study

FEATURE

Ten Myths of Parenting

Parental needs and expectations have generated a number of myths about parenting (Okun and Rappaport, 1980). How do these myths affect parenting? Which, if any, do your parents believe? Which of them do you believe?

1. The birth of a child will save a disintegrating marriage.
2. The child is an extension of the parent and will think, feel, and behave as the parent did in childhood.
3. Children will care for aged parents.
4. Children will respect and obey parents.
5. A child will always love its parents and be a best friend to them.
6. A child will give parents a "second chance" to achieve what they should have achieved.
7. With the right techniques parents can mold their children into whatever they want.
8. It is the parents' fault if their child fails.
9. Mothers are instinctively better parents than fathers.
10. Parenting is instinctual and requires no training or instruction.

child-free women reported more frequent exchange of stimulating ideas with their husbands, more shared projects and outside interests, and greater agreement on household tasks and career decisions (Houseknecht, 1982). These findings are not particularly surprising if we consider the great amount of time and energy that childrearing entails. It has also been observed that divorce is more probable in child-free marriages, perhaps because, unlike some other unhappily married couples, they do not stay together "for the sake of the children" (Glenn and McLanahan, 1982). (See the reading "On Not Having Children" by John Hubner.)

Deferred Parenthood

A report from the National Center for Health Statistics in 1982 indicated that a "baby boomlet" was in progress in the early 1980s. This increase in births is credited to the fact that women in their thirties (themselves products of the post-World War II baby boom) have postponed childbirth. First births to women in their thirties increased from 54,000 in 1970 to 116,000 in 1979 and have continued to increase in the 1980s. A definite trend toward later marriage and childbearing has been apparent since 1965. Although most women still begin their families while in their twenties, demographers predict that the trend toward later parenthood will continue to grow, especially in middle- and upper-income groups (Price, 1982).

The average age at marriage has increased slowly and steadily since 1960. More career and life-style options are available to single women than in the past. Marriage and reproduction are no longer economic or social necessities. People may take longer to search out the "right" mate (even if it takes more than one marriage to do it), and they may wait for the "right" time to have children. Increasingly effective birth-control (including safe, legal abortion) has also been a significant factor in the planned deferral of parenthood.

Besides giving parents a chance to complete education, build careers, and firmly establish their own relationship, delaying parenthood can also be advantageous for other reasons. Maternity and medical expenses, food, furniture and equipment, clothes, toys, baby-sitters, lessons, summer camp are costly—it has been estimated that the cost of raising a typical American child from birth to age eighteen years is between $80,000 and $90,000 in noninflation dollars. Obviously, parents who have had a chance to establish themselves financially will be better able to bear the economic burdens of childrearing. Older parents may also be more emotionally mature and thus more capable of dealing with parenting stresses (although age isn't necessarily indicative of emotional maturity). In addition, as Jane Price (1982) wrote, "Combating the aging process is something of a national preoccupation. . . . In our society, the power of children to revitalize and refresh is part of the host of forces encouraging men and women to become parents much later than they did in the past."

☐ BECOMING A PARENT

A man and woman who become parents enter a new phase of their lives. More than marriage, parenthood signifies adulthood: the final, irreversible end of youthful roles. A person can become an ex-spouse, but never an ex-parent, for the tie of blood always exists. The irrevocable nature of parenthood may make the first-time parent doubtful and apprehensive, especially during the pregnancy. Yet people have few ways of preparing for parenting. Parenthood has to be learned experientially (although ideas can modify practices). A person may receive assistance from more experienced parents, but each new parent has to learn on his or her own.

"If I pay the basic price of $80,000 to raise a child for the next 18 years, plus all the extras that you've mentioned, is there any guarantee it will turn out all right?"

"There is no warranty with the price whatsoever. You pay your money and you take your chances. We no longer guarantee that when it gets to be 18, it will be able to read and write. Frankly, you'll be lucky if it volunteers to cut your lawn or do the dishes once a week. And if you think for 80 grand it's going to clean up it's own room, you're living in a dream world."

ART BUCHWALD, "BOTTOM LINE ON CHILD-REARING COSTS"

Parenthood is a role that is acquired literally overnight. One day you're not a parent . . . and the next day you are—irrevocably! The family today emphasizes the expressive (emotional) qualities of all its members, including the father, much more than in the past.

FEATURE

Am I Parent Material?

Here are some questions for you to consider before you deal with the important decision of whether or not to have a child.

If you decide to have a child, it'll be a decision that will affect you for the rest of your life. Think about it. . . . Taking responsibility for a new life is awesome.

These questions are designed to raise ideas that you may not have thought about. There are no "right" answers and no "grades"—your answers are "right" for you and may help you decide for yourself whether or not you want to be a parent. Because we all change, your answers to some of these questions may change two, five, even ten years from now.

You *do* have a choice. Check out what you know and give it some thought. Then do what seems right for you.

DOES HAVING AND RAISING A CHILD FIT THE LIFE-STYLE I WANT?

1. What do I want out of life for myself? What do I think is important?
2. Could I handle a child and a job at the same time? Would I have time and energy for both?
3. Would I be ready to give up the freedom to do what I want to do, when I want to do it?
4. Would I be willing to cut back my social life and spend more time at home? Would I miss my free time and privacy?

5. Can I afford to support a child? Do I know how much it takes to raise a child?
6. Do I want to raise a child in the neighborhood where I live now? Would I be willing and able to move?
7. How would a child [affect] *my* growth and development?
8. Would a child change my educational plans? Do I have the energy to go to school and raise a child at the same time?
9. Am I willing to give a great part of my life— AT LEAST 18 YEARS—to being responsible for a child? And spend a large portion of my life being concerned about my child's well being?

WHAT'S IN IT FOR ME?

1. Do I like doing things with children? Do I enjoy activities that children can do?
2. Would I want a child to be "like me"?
3. Would I try to pass on to my child my ideas and values? What if my child's ideas and values turn out to be different from mine?
4. Would I want my child to achieve things that I wish I had, but didn't?
5. Would I expect my child to keep me from being lonely in my old age? Do I do that for my parents? Do my parents do that for my grandparents?
6. Do I want a boy or a girl child? What if I don't get what I want?

Transition: Parental Stress

The abrupt transition from a nonparent to a parent role may create considerable stress. Parents take on parental roles literally overnight, and the job goes on without relief on a round-the-clock basis. Parents have to learn to interpret the needs of their dependent infant from the child's crying, sniffling, and gurgling. Sometimes these cues are ambiguous. Many parents wonder about their ability to meet all the responsibilities of childrearing. But despite parental fears and anxieties, children somehow manage to grow up (also see Kliman and Vukelich, 1985).

FEATURE–*continued*

7. Would having a child show others how mature I am?
8. Will I prove I am a man or a woman by having a child?
9. Do I expect my child to make my life happy?

RAISING A CHILD: WHAT'S THERE TO KNOW?

1. Do I like children? When I'm around children for a while, what do I think or feel about having one around all of the time?
2. Do I enjoy teaching others?
3. Is it easy for me to tell other people what I want, or need, or what I expect of them?
4. Do I want to give a child the love (s)he needs? Is loving easy for me?
5. Am I patient enough to deal with the noise and the confusion and the 24-hour-a-day responsibility? What kind of time and space do I need for myself?
6. What do I do when I get angry or upset? Would I take things out on a child if I lost my temper?
7. What does discipline mean to me? What does freedom, or setting limits, or giving space mean? What is being too strict, or not strict enough? Would I want a perfect child?
8. How do I get along with my parents? What will I do to avoid the mistakes my parents made?
9. How would I take care of my child's health and safety? How do I take care of my own?

10. What if I have a child and find out I made a wrong decision?

HAVE MY PARTNER AND I REALLY TALKED ABOUT BECOMING PARENTS?

1. Does my partner want to have a child? Have we talked about our reasons?
2. Could we give a child a good home? Is our relationship a happy and strong one?
3. Are we both ready to give our time and energy to raising a child?
4. Could we share our love with a child without jealousy?
5. What would happen if we separated after having a child, or if one of us should die?
6. Do my partner and I understand each other's feelings about religion, work, family, child raising, future goals? Do we feel pretty much the same way? Will children fit into these feelings, hopes and plans?
7. Suppose one of us wants a child and the other doesn't? Who decides?
8. Which of [these] questions in this pamphlet do we need to *really* discuss before making a decision?

National Alliance for Optional Parenthood

Although couples may have an egalitarian marriage before the birth of the first child, the marriage usually becomes more traditional once a child is born. The wife often will give up her job to rear the child. Because her husband is away at work during the day, the housework becomes her full responsibility. Her world narrows, focussing increasingly on the demands of motherhood. However, if the couple develops a close, mutual relationship before the first child arrives, they are likely "to establish some barriers between themselves and their children, a marital defense against the institution of parenthood" (Rossi, 1968).

Generally the stresses of the first year of childrearing do not seem to overwhelm

We learn from experience. A man never wakes up his second baby just to see it smile.

GRACE WILLIAMS

parents. The couple experience less stress if they have already developed a strong relationship, are open in their communication, have agreed on family planning, and originally had a strong desire for the child (Russell, 1974). If, however, the couple had their first child to save their marriage, then the diapers, sleepless nights, and curtailed social life are likely to precipitate the end of the marriage.

The stresses each parent experiences are different, and these differences closely reflect sex roles (Gilbert et al., 1982). If parental roles altered, so would the stresses. One study found that new mothers were worried about their personal appearance and were physically tired and worn out from constant child-care duties (Russell, 1974). During their child's first year, new mothers are more easily upset and emotional. They complain of lack of uninterrupted sleep. Fathers also complain of their babies interrupting their sleep. But fathers also complain of interference from their mothers-in-law, increased financial strains, the necessity of changing plans, and the extra work a baby causes. Mothers and fathers both report that their sexual relationship suffers following childbirth (Harriman, 1983).

Mothers generally have greater stress than fathers in adjusting to parenthood (Harriman, 1983). A study by Judith Myers-Walls (1984) found that mothers' adjustment to fulfilling multiple roles (work, social life, marriage, housework, and parenthood) was made easier if they used the following coping strategies: (1) holding a positive view of the situation, (2) developing a "salient" role (deciding which role should dominate when conflict arose), (3) compartmentalizing roles, and (4) compromising standards. (For a discussion of the transition to parenthood, see Belsky, 1985, Belsky et al., 1985a, Belsky et al., 1985b, Teachman and Polonko, 1985.)

People can debate endlessly whether to have children. But once a child is born, the question is moot. The decision has been made and a parent must live with that decision. The rewards of parenting are great, but so are the constraints. Being a parent gives a person rewards he or she cannot get anywhere else (Pohlman, 1969). The bond between parent and child is unbreakable; the relationship—which is a complex one involving many emotions—endures throughout a person's life and lasts in memory long after the death of the parent or child.

Cleaning and scrubbing can wait till tomorrow.
For babies grow up we've learned to our sorrow.
So quiet down cobwebs, dust go to sleep.
I'm rocking my baby and babies don't keep.

ANONYMOUS

Motherhood

Many women see their only destiny as motherhood. Given the choice (made possible through birth control) of becoming mothers or not, most women would probably choose to become mothers at some point in their lives (see Cook et al., 1982)—and they would make this choice for very positive reasons. But many women make no conscious choice; they become mothers without weighing their decision or considering its effect on their own lives and the lives of their children and mates. The consequences of a nonreflective decision may be great: bitterness, frustration, anger, or depression. But it is also possible that a woman's nonreflective decision will turn out to be "right" and that she will experience unique personal fulfillment as a result.

The decision to become a mother is momentous. In the novel *Fear of Flying* by Erica Jong (1975), the heroine thought over this problem of choice:

How did people decide to get pregnant, I wondered. It was such an awesome decision. To undertake responsibility for a new life when you had no way of knowing what it would be like. I assumed that women got pregnant without thinking about it, because if they ever once considered what it really meant, they would surely be overwhelmed with doubt.

Powerful social forces impel women toward motherhood. Some women become pregnant without much planning or forethought, while others carefully weigh the pros and cons. This baby's two mothers had many factors to consider prior to choosing to become parents; their desire for a child was strong enough to overcome a number of social and practical obstacles.

One woman wrote (in Bernard, 1972), "I was forty years old before it dawned on me that I really had a choice about becoming a mother. Not that I didn't know about contraception, but that it had never occurred to me that anything else was possible." She was indignant that she did not know she had a choice. She would have chosen motherhood anyway, she said, but there was something else that bothered her: she had not exercised autonomy. Another woman with a small child wrote (in Bernard, 1972):

I do not know if it was pure biological urge that made it imperative that I bear a child. I doubt it. The thrust of my child's conception was fueled by many vested interests. "They" wanted it, and "they" delight in it to this very moment. . . . In every childhood fantasy of the future, I pictured myself surrounded by my adoring children. Never did the possibility of choice enter my mind.

The closest researchers have come to finding a maternal instinct is in some studies of nurturing behavior in mammals, where the presence of an infant will stimulate such behavior in most mothers. But some animals may reject their offspring in the same manner as negligent parents. In the Central Park Zoo, for example, a gorilla gave birth to an infant the zookeepers called "Sunny Boy"; but instead of nurturing its tiny baby, the mother rejected it so soundly that a human had to take it home and raise it herself. The same year, however, in the Washington (D.C.) Zoo, another gorilla gave birth, danced around her cage in glee, burst into smiles to visitors, and swung around happily with her child.

Although researchers are unable to find any instinctual motives for having children among humans (which does not necessarily mean such motives do not exist), they recognize many social motives impelling women to become mothers. These are so powerful, so all-pervasive, that they seem to be instinctive. Jessie Bernard (1972) wrote: "An inbred desire is no less potent than an instinctive one. The pain and anguish resulting from deprivation of an acquired desire for children are as real as the pain and anguish resulting from an instinctive one." How do women acquire the desire to be mothers?

. . . we have attributed the influence to [the mother] as if she was a sorceress. She's a good witch if the child turns out fine and a bad witch if he doesn't.

JEROME KAGAN

Adult sex roles are defined in large part by their parenting components. When a woman becomes a mother, she may feel that her identity as an adult is confirmed. She is no longer a child, no longer a girl, but a woman. Having a child of her own proves her womanliness. From her earliest years, a woman is trained to assume the role of mother. She changes dolls' diapers and pretends to feed them, practicing infant care. She plays house while her brother builds forts. The stories a girl hears, the games she plays, the textbooks she reads, the religion she is taught, the television she watches—all socialize her for the mother role.

Fatherhood

When we speak of "mothering" a child, everyone knows what we mean: nurturing, caring for, feeding, diapering, soothing, loving. Mothers generally "mother" their children almost every day of the year for at least eighteen consecutive years. The meaning of "fathering" is quite different. "Fathering" a child need take no more than a few minutes if we understand the term in its traditional sense, that is, impregnating the child's mother. Nurturant behavior by a father toward his child has not typically been referred to as "fathering." ("Mothering" doesn't seem appropriate either in this context.) The verb "to parent" has been coined to fill the need for a word that adequately describes the child-tending behaviors of both mothers and fathers (see also Verzaro-Lawrence, 1981).

As we have seen, the father's traditional roles of provider and protector are instrumental; they satisfy the family's economic and physical needs. The mother's role in this traditional model is expressive, giving emotional and psychological support for her family. However, the lines between these roles are becoming increasingly blurred owing to economic pressures and new societal expectations. From a developmental viewpoint, the father's importance to the family derives not only from his role as a representative of society, connecting his family and his culture, but also from his role as a developer of self-control and autonomy in his children. A great deal of recent research has examined the role of the father in influencing his child's (usually his son's) sex role formation.

Research indicates that although mothers are inclined to view both sons and daughters as "simply children" and to apply similar standards to both sexes, fathers tend to be differently involved with their male and female children. This may place a daughter at a disadvantage, since she has less opportunity to develop instrumental attitudes and behaviors. It may also be disadvantageous to a male child as it can limit the development of his own expressive patterns and interests (Gilbert et al., 1982).

LeMasters (1974) concluded from his study that the American father role has three characteristics:

1. Parenting is a peripheral role for males; breadwinning is the principal one.
2. No attachment or "bonding" process is seen between fathers and children as between mothers and children. (Although the debate over the existence of a biological basis for such attachment goes on and on, the fact remains that men do not have the experience of childbirth and breastfeeding and have not generally been encouraged to spend time engaging in nurturant behavior.)
3. The "fathering" role is closely tied to the success of the marriage relationship. A good father is seen as necessarily being a good husband. If a divorce occurs the mother traditionally retains custody (the expressive role) and the father continues to provide support (the instrumental role).

Rebelsky and Hanks (1971) found that fathers interacted an average of 37.7 seconds per day with their infant children (between two weeks and three months of age). In other studies half the preschool children questioned said they preferred the television to daddy, and one child in ten said the person that the child feared the most was his or her father (none of them named mother as most feared) (Pogrebin, 1982a). Although fathers certainly participate more in pregnancy and birth processes today than in our society's past, evidence about whether this involvement predisposes the father to greater participation with his children later on is conflicting (Bigner, 1979).

It appears that the family today emphasizes the expressive qualities of all its members, including the father, much more than in the past (Bigner, 1979). The "emergent" perspective described by Fein (1980) views men as psychologically capable of participating in virtually all parenting behaviors (except gestation and lactation). It further believes that such participation is beneficial to the development and well-being of both children and adults. The implicit contradiction between the terms "real man" and "good father" needs to be resolved if boys are to develop into fathers who feel their "manhood enlarged and not depleted by active, caring fatherhood" (Pogrebin, 1982a). We see this contradiction epitomized by parents' fear of allowing boys to play with dolls. When a child plays with a doll, he or she is modeling the familiar parent-child relationship. By discouraging boys from "playing house" we create "an aversion to the very activities that make a man a good father" (Pogrebin, 1982a).

In support of this emergent view of fatherhood, Dr. Benjamin Spock (1968, 1976) has made a number of changes in his *Baby and Child Care* (otherwise known as the "Baby Bible"). On the subject of father participation in childrearing, the original version (1945) said, "A man can be a warm father and a real man at the same time. . . . Of course I don't mean that the father has to give just as many bottles or change just as many diapers as the mother. But it's fine for him to do these things occasionally. He might make the formula on Sunday." The revised edition (Spock and Rothenberg, 1985) advises *all* fathers to take on at least half of the child management duties and participate in the housework:

When a father does his share as a matter of course . . ., it does much more than simply lighten his wife's work load and give her companionship. . . . It shows that he believes this work is crucial for the welfare of the family, that it calls for judgement and skill, and that it's his responsibility as much as it is hers. . . . This is what sons and daughters need to see in action if they are to grow up without sexist attitudes.

A 1983 Gallup poll found that 25 percent of expectant fathers expected to be the

primary parent when their wives returned to work. Eighty percent said they changed diapers. In another poll, 90 percent of the men said that being a husband and father was the most satisfying role in their lives (Findley, 1984). Although mothers, especially those with jobs or schooling that takes them away from home, may welcome and indeed rely on fathers' participation in childrearing and household duties, institutions change slowly. Most employers don't provide much in the way of maternity leave, sick-child leave, and so on for mothers, let alone the equivalent for fathers. One exception is the Ford Foundation, which gives paternity leave for two months with full pay (Korpivaara, 1982).

In Sweden, where social policies tend to be more progressive than our own, mothers and fathers are allowed leave with 90 percent pay in the months following the birth of a child. They are similarly granted leave during the illness of a child if their presence is needed at home. During the first year of enactment, the paternity leave policy was taken advantage of by only 1 to 2 percent of fathers; currently, about 12 percent use it (Pogrebin, 1982b). Closer to home, the Fatherhood Project at the Bank Street College of Education in Manhattan has been formed to promote awareness of fathers' roles and to serve as a clearinghouse for information on fatherhood (see Klinman et al., 1984, for a guide to programs, services, and resources for fathers). The project director, James A. Levine (quoted in Korpivaara, 1982), stated, "As more mothers are working outside the home, the reexamination of women's roles leads to a reexamination of men's roles that will filter into the educational system, the legal system, and every area of society."

> Don't be the man you think you should be, be the father you wish you'd had.
>
> LETTY COTTIN POGREBIN

☐ OTHER SIGNIFICANT CHILD SOCIALIZERS

Child Care

Supplementary child care is a crucial issue for today's parents of young children. Dual-worker and single-parent families have doubled in the past decade; they are now the rule rather than the exception. Many parents must look outside their homes for assistance in childrearing. About two million children currently receive formal, licensed day care, and another five million attend nursery schools. Uncounted millions are cared for by relatives or baby-sitters, and perhaps five million children under the age of ten have no one at all to look after them (Watson, 1984). (See Chapter 11 for a discussion of the role of day care in maternal employment.) Day-care homes and centers, nursery schools, and preschools can relieve parents of some of their childrearing tasks and also furnish them with some valuable time of their own. Dr. Nathan Talbot (1976), professor of pediatrics at Harvard University, wrote:

> With three provisos, these out-of-home experiences can so enrich a father's or mother's personal life that s/he is better able to serve the needs of the children than s/he would be if s/he stayed home all the time. The first proviso is that the children are well cared for. . . . The second is that at least one parent continues to be readily available to the children for a minimum of one or two hours most days. The third is that a parent . . . remain the person responsible for the upbringing of the children. . . . Supplementary child care can solidify rather than disrupt the family and can improve rather than hurt the children's chances for happy and developmentally rich lives.

What of the children? What does group care have to offer them? Studies of infants and young children in group-care situations have shown that their development is stimulated or enhanced by enriched child-care environments (Bigner, 1979). Emotional security and patterns of attachment to parents do not seem to be significantly altered by group-care experiences. Other studies have indicated that the overall effect of day care on intellectual development is neither beneficial nor adverse. Furthermore, in the case of disadvantaged families, high-quality child care has great positive impact (Belsky et al., 1984). Among children who must care for themselves (latchkey children), some report being afraid of being home alone while others enjoy the independence. Mothers of these children report feelings of anxiety and guilt over leaving their children alone. Only a few studies have investigated this significant area (Vandell and Corasaniti, 1985).

Dr. Burton White, director of Boston's Center for Parent Education, sees the trend toward increasing use of day care as a "disaster": "Both parents don't *have* to work—they both *want* to work to maintain a house and lifestyle. They are putting their desires above the welfare of the baby" (cited in Watson, 1984). Yet as Jay Belsky and colleagues (1984) point out, "Since it is unlikely that mothers will return in large numbers to the role of full-time homemakers, and that day care will go away, . . . the critical issue [in day care] is the condition of care."

National concern has recently been focused on day-care practice by revelations of sexual abuse of children by their caregivers. Although these revelations have brought providers of child care under close public scrutiny and have alerted parents to potential dangers, they have also produced a backlash within the child-care profession. Some caregivers are now reluctant to have physical contact with the children; male child-care workers feel especially constrained and may be finding their jobs at risk (Chaze, 1984). Yet one survey revealed that out of 50,000 reported cases of child sexual abuse, only 18 percent involved someone other than a relative and only 1.5 percent involved day-care workers or baby-sitters. In 1985 the U.S. Department of Health and Human Services announced new day-care guidelines, calling for training of staff in prevention and detection of child abuse, thorough checks on prospective employees, and allowing parental visits at any time. But critics feel that the government should go farther in establishing standards for day care itself. Senator Paula Hawkins (quoted in Collins, 1985) stated, "They really have to consider the quality of the care, and not just the quality of the care-givers." Government funding and assistance for day-care programs remain small to nonexistent.

What can parents do to ensure quality care for their children? In addition to the obvious requirements of cleanliness, comfort, good food, a safe environment, and attentive, trained staff, parents should look for the following (from Watson, 1984b):

- A *stable staff.* Children are more secure when they know who is caring for them. Ideally, the staff should be trained in child development or psychology.
- *Small groups.* Infants especially need close attention and stimulation. Older preschoolers can function in groups of four to eight children per adult, depending on the children's ages.
- *Appropriate attention.* Children need attention appropriate to their developmental stage.
- *Appropriate activities.* Activities should be appropriate to the children's developmental stage, reflecting their needs to learn about themselves and their environment.
- *Parental involvement.* Parents should be welcomed and their involvement with the child-care program encouraged. (For more information, see Resource Center.)

As with a number of critical services in our society, those who most need supplementary child care are those who can least afford it. Child care done properly is a costly business (even though child-care work remains a relatively low-paying, low-status job). The United States is one of the few industrialized nationals that does not have a comprehensive national day-care policy. The Reagan administration has consistently cut federal contributions to day care and many state governments are following that example. Nathan Talbot (1976) observed that "we are shortchanging ourselves and the future of our nation by failing to invest in our children as our best and most critically important asset. . . . Child care is worthy of a position close to the top in our national hierarchy of priorities."

Television

The average American child between the ages of two and eleven watches television twenty-seven hours and twenty-one minutes a week, according to an A. C. Nielsen Company survey (Tooth, 1985); some studies have placed the average as high as fifty-four hours per week (Winn, 1978). By the time a child finishes high school, he or she will have spent at least eighteen thousand hours in front of the set as opposed to twelve thousand hours at school and studying. Thirty hours of television viewing includes about four hundred commercials and provides a "fast-moving melange of Batman, Bulletman, Spiderman, Jeannie, Barbie, Ring Dings, Milk Duds, Sugar Smacks, violent acts, Mork, Mindy, and money" (Moody, 1980). Thirty hours of watching television is thirty hours not spent interacting with family members, playing outside, playing creatively, reading, fantasizing, doing homework, exploring, or even napping. Besides limiting children's time for such pursuits, television has also been implicated in a number of individual, familial, and societal disorders (see also "Media and the Family," special issue of *Journal of Family Issues*, June 1983).

Researchers have documented a variety of physiological effects produced by television, including altered brain wave (trancelike) states and hyperactivity, impaired eye movements, and impaired hand and body use. Low levels of microwave radiation are emitted by color sets. Although the manufacturers assure us that we are in no danger, we are also cautioned not to sit too close "just in case." Television has also

. . . TV causes . . . serious and pervasive violence in normal . . .youngsters who watch TV attentively and regularly. What results from this psychic abuse is the impoverishment of personality and the trivialization of life.

HERB KOHL

Time spent watching television is time not spent playing creatively, playing outside, reading, fantasizing, exploring or interacting with others.

been observed to have deleterious effects on learning and perception, nutrition, life style, and family and social relationships (Moody, 1980).

Television is a strong authoritative force in young children's lives. One expert testified before Congress that "an advertisement to a child has the quality of an order, not a suggestion." The power of television can be illustrated by the following incident. Soupy Sales, a popular children's television personality, had an early morning children's show. One morning, looking out into the eyes of millions of children, he asked in a low, secretive voice: "Is Daddy asleep? He is? Good! Find his wallet and slip out some of those funny green pieces of paper with all those nice pictures of George Washington, Abraham Lincoln, and Alexander Hamilton, and send them along to your own pal, Soupy, care of WNEW, New York." The next day he began to receive the loot from throughout the country. Soupy had meant this order as a gag, but hundreds of children were unable to make the distinction. Soupy and his producer were temporarily suspended by the station (Helitzer and Heyl, 1970).

Anyone watching television, especially children's television, cannot help but be aware of the amount of junk food (breakfast cereals, candy, snacks) and toy advertising directed toward children. Much parent-child conflict revolves around eating habits. Although most parents want their children to eat nutritiously, television encourages poor eating habits. The director of the Society of Nutrition Education observed (in Federal Trade Commission Staff Report, 1978):

The nutritional message which is delivered to the child day after day in many TV ads promotes a completely unbalanced diet. When almost all the choices advertised on programs aimed at children are pre-sweetened cereals, candy and soft drinks with a message that these are the only foods needed for a good life, it is not difficult to realize the result would be a totally inadequate diet.

Responsible parents are put in the position of having to defend good nutrition against the incessant bombardment of commercials. Advertisers are aware of this situation;

nevertheless, they encourage children to confront their parents. The American Academy of Child Psychiatry is concerned about the impact of this mental exploitation of children. A former president of the academy noted (in Federal Trade Commission Staff Report, 1978):

Many of these advertisements are directed to the attention of children in order to bring pressure to bear upon the parents to purchase these products. . . . Furthermore, the advertisements encourage confrontation and alienation on the part of children toward their parents and undermine the parents' child rearing responsibilities.

Furthermore, although the advertising of products for adults has been traditionally directed at adults, William Melody (1977) observed a shift: advertisers are developing the idea that children may be the best target for the promotion of adult products. The reason is quite simple. When family members do not have a brand preference and the mother regards all brands as more or less equal, the children's preferences are likely to determine what specific brand is purchased. On the average, the mothers surveyed indicated that they spent $1.66 more each week on groceries because their children asked for specific products and brands. Although this figure may seem low, it comes to more than $85 per year. Over the portion of the family life cycle during which children are at home, the additional costs may run between $1,500 and $2,500 or more. In the national market, the results are astounding: " 'Childpower' adds at least $30 million weekly, or $1.5 billion annually, to grocery retail sales—just to make Junior happy" (Helitzer and Heyl, 1970).

Because of the constant pressure to buy and the necessity of regulating their children's viewing habits, some parents choose not to have a television. Once the television is gone, it is often not missed. It may be missed more by adults who use it for their own entertainment and as a baby-sitter for their children. Children are peer oriented and have their friends to play with. The use of television as a baby-sitter underlines a dilemma for many parents: they disapprove of what their children see, but they also want to have the time to themselves that may be obtained by letting their children watch television.

Children learn about the world from watching television. Although some valuable

We are drowning our youngsters in violence, cynicism and sadism piped into the living room and even the nursery. The grandchildren of kids who used to weep because the Little Match Girl froze to death now feel cheated if she isn't slugged, raped, and thrown into a Bessemer converter.

JENKIN LLOYD JONES

"Let's wait. Maybe he kills her or something."

Drawing by Weber; © 1966 The New Yorker Magazine, Inc.

FEATURE

Evaluating Children's TV Programs

In *Growing Up on Television*, Kate Moody (1980) suggests the following criteria for helping parents to evaluate what their children watch.

1. What kind of distinction is made between reality and make-believe? If there is a transition between the two, is it clearly signaled to children?
2. Is the program geared to the child's level of understanding?
3. How are problems solved? By using others? By hitting? Revenge? Money? Magic? Cooperation?
4. What role models are offered? Are sex stereotypes reinforced?
5. What is the pace of the program? Angle change? What special effects are used? What is the noise/confusion level?
6. How is humor used? Does a laugh track tell the child what is to be considered funny?
7. How is the world portrayed? As a dangerous and fearsome place?
8. What kind of commercials are associated with the program? Junk food? Fast cars? Personal hygiene products?
9. What is the child's response to the program? Is he or she aggressive, cooperative, excitable, calm? What kinds of play follow viewing?
10. Is the program good enough to be worth the parent's time?

---

and thought-provoking insights may be gained from it, much of television programming promotes or condones racist, sexist, ageist, and other negative stereotypes. It also promotes violence and fear (see Waters, 1982). Dr. George Gerbner (in Moody, 1980) stated: "There is a consistent relationship between fear and the amount of television watched. They [heavy watchers] do perceive the world as much more violent, and they are much more fearful." A report issued by the National Institute of Mental Health stated that "overwhelming" evidence indicates that "excessive" violence on television causes aggressive behavior in children ("A New Indictment . . .," 1982, Tooth, 1985). This conclusion was based on the results of approximately 2,500 separate studies conducted since the early 1970s. Besides encouraging aggressive behavior, television also has the effect of desensitizing viewers to observed violent acts. Children may learn to see violence as an acceptable means of problem solving and to show no moral outrage at acts of destructive aggression. As Peggy Charren, president of Action for Children's Television, commented, "Parents [should] understand that the box in the living room is not necessarily a friend of the family."

> Jesse James shot children, but only in fact, not in folklore.
>
> JOHN GREENWAY

☐ WHO IS THE CHILD? THEORIES OF SOCIALIZATION

Historical Background

Until the middle of the nineteenth century, Christians viewed the newborn child as a tiny demon filled with unruly desires (see Chapter 3). Orthodox Christianity taught that infants are "by nature sinners, and show us that . . . they go astray as soon as they be born, speaking lies." Because children were born in sin, their will had to be broken and destroyed—only submission to authority would save the child. The goal of childrearing was obedience, and punishment was its instrument. Love, although important, could not curtail the child's inherent evil. Preparing the child for the world meant following absolute rules. (See Boggs, 1983, for an analysis of contemporary fundamentalist Christian childrearing.)

In the nineteenth century a gentler view of the child took hold. The child was now an innocent whose impulses and desires were neither good nor evil but instead could be molded through love and kindness. This new form of childrearing was more appropriate in a swiftly developing nation that was leaving tradition behind. One historian (Wishy, 1968) wrote:

> Harsh and minute prescriptions gave way to general, more benign principles of behavior because Americans could not anticipate that a closely drawn code of behavior appropriate to a traditional society would serve the child well in a fast-changing world. The call for more affectionate and tender care also suggested a way of winning the life-long love of offspring who in America had no need to remain indefinitely at home under the rule of a patriarch whose favor determined their chance in life. Both the generality and mildness of the new rules of nurture thus reflected the instability and unpredictability of American life, a culture in which everything in life was a problem and a gamble. . . . Minute authoritarian codes were not so much right or wrong as they were useless.

Theories of Socialization

Twentieth-century attitudes toward the child have been influenced by several theories of socialization.

The Psychoanalytic Model.   The modern heir to the ancient doctrine of inherent evil is the "impulse-taming" Freudian school of thought. Although Sigmund Freud's contribution to the understanding of the human psyche is profound, his view of humankind is dark and forbidding. It holds that beneath the surface of each individual's consciousness is the repressed unconscious—a storm of contradictory impulses, controlled only by the individual's gradual internalization of societal restraints. These restraints are first imposed by both parents; then slowly the child identifies with the parent who is of the same sex. Wanting to be like that parent, the child takes on the adult's values. Not becoming like that parent is a failure to reach maturity: the rebel is described as "infantile." Such a doctrine is fundamentaly conservative and deems the world a place in which control must be paramount because change is threatening.

The scientific thought of Freud's time was greatly influenced by Charles Darwin's theories on evolution. As Jerome Kagan (1984) has pointed out, Freud viewed evolution as an apt metaphor for human behavior and constructed his theories in accordance with the scientific thought of his day. His psychoanalytic principles resembled those of zoology, physiology, and physics and brought humans and animals conceptually closer.

Stages of Development.   Beginning in the 1920s, the work of Jean Piaget continued to make use of the evolutionary model. Piaget observed that cognitive development occurs in discrete stages through which all infants and children pass. These stages can be seen as building blocks, each of which must be completed before the next

Table 12–1

STAGES OF DEVELOPMENT: FREUD, PIAGET AND ERIKSON COMPARED

	Freud		Piaget	Erikson
Infancy	Oral Anal		Sensorimotor	Trust vs. mistrust Autonomy vs. shame/doubt
Early childhood	Phallic		Preoperational	Initiative vs. guilt
Late-middle childhood	Latency		Concrete operational	Industry vs. inferiority
Adolescence	Genital		Formal Operational	Identity vs. role confusion
Early adulthood				Intimacy vs. isolation
Middle adulthood				Generativity vs. stagnation
Late adulthood				Ego integrity vs. despair

Table 12–1

Stages of Development: Freud, Piaget, and Erikson Compared

one can be put into place. In Piaget's view, children develop their cognitive abilities through interaction with the world and "successful accommodations to new challenges" (Kagan, 1984).

Social Molding. In the mid-1900s, as social and political liberalism began to flourish, it seemed reasonable to remove the origin of human frailty and suffering from the individual's biological makeup and place it in the social realm. Theories of *social molding* view social experiences as the principal source of human variation. To this way of thinking, human nature is formed by culture, society, and the family. True, the infant or young child embodies a host of impulses, but these are given shape and direction through interactions. Children are first socialized through parental direction of their behavior. Parents teach them what is good, what is bad, what to eat, what not to eat, what to keep, what to share, how to talk, what to feel, what to think.

Erik Erikson's work emphasizes parental and societal responsibilities in children's development. Each of Erikson's life-cycle stages (see Chapter 1) is centered around a specific emotional concern based on individual biological pressures and external sociocultural expectations and actions.

Relativity of Theories. Jerome Kagan (1984) has noted that theories of child development and childrearing reflect the scientific and moral climate of the times. This century has witnessed popular trends emphasizing, in chronological order, self-control, adjustment to social demands, and maternal attachment. Current scientific

Children begin by loving their parents; after a time, they judge them; rarely, if ever, do they forgive them.

OSCAR WILDE

The chief cause of human errors is to be found in the prejudices picked up in childhood.

RENÉ DESCARTES (1596–1650)

interest in child development stresses cognitive aspects: perception, memory, and categorical functioning. Kagan suggests that current interest in morality will lead to a new focus on the "behavioral previews of will, intention and choice because they are the essential elements of conscience." He expects childrearing practices to become "more restrictive rather than less, for . . . the popularity of restriction cycles about every one hundred years."

The Sense of Self.   The three models we have described leave out something very crucial about human personality. Each person knows that his or her basic motives are not simply the result of biological drives nor that everything he or she does is just the result of socialization. Something more human about human beings exists than these models admit. This is the "I" within each person; it may be what philosophers have called the soul or it may be something else, but it has an existence of its own that resists biological and environmental pressures. Erik Erikson (1968) wrote:

What the "I" reflects on when it sees or contemplates the body, the personality, and the roles to which it is attached for life—not knowing where it was before or will be after—are the various selves which make up our composite Self. One should really be decisive and say that the "I" is all-conscious, and that we are truly conscious only insofar as we can say "I" and mean it . . . to ignore the conscious "I" . . . means to delete the core of human self-awareness.

Developmental Interaction.   Parents do not simply give birth to children and then "bring them up." The growth and development of children takes place within a complex and changing family system. Children are not only socialized by their parents but they are also socializers in their own right. When an infant cries to be picked up and held, to have a diaper changed, or to be burped or smiles when being played with, fed, or cuddled, the parents are being socialized. The child is creating strong parental bonds. Crying and smiling are the two most important means of

Children are not only socialized by their parents; they are also socializers in their own right. Smiling is an important means by which children control their parents.

controlling his or her parents. Although the infant's actions are not at first consciously directed toward reinforcing parental behavior, they nevertheless have that effect. In this sense, children can be viewed as participants in creating their own environment and contributing to their further development.

In the *developmental interaction* model of family growth, social and psychological development are seen as lifelong processes, with each family member having a role in the development of every other.

Siblings influence one another according to their particular needs and personalities. Also, sibling influence (or the lack of it in the case of only children) is significant in subtle yet powerful ways as the result of birth order and spacing (the number of years between sibling births) (Belsky, 1984). A study at Colorado State University, for example, found that a firstborn's self-esteem suffers if a sibling is born two or more years later but is not affected if the sibling is born less than two years later (Goleman, 1985). Furthermore, if the firstborn child is already five or six years old, the birth of a second sibling does not have the same impact.

In terms of the eight developmental stages of a human life cycle described by Erikson, parents are generally at the seventh stages (generativity) during their children's growing years, and the children are probably anywhere from the first stage (trust) to the fifth (identity) or sixth (intimacy). The parents' need to establish their generativity is at least partly met by the child's need to be cared for and taught. And the parents' approach to childrearing will inevitably be modified by the child's inherent nature.

☐ STYLES OF CHILDREARING

A parent's approach to training, teaching, nurturing, and helping a child will vary according to cultural influences, the parent's personality, the parent's basic attitude toward children and childrearing, and the role model the parent presents to the child (Bigner, 1979). Role modeling is based on the parent's own experiences during childhood, and the influence of those experiences may not be consciously felt. The three basic styles of childrearing may be termed authoritarian, permissive, and authoritative (Baumrind, 1971, 1983).

Authoritarian Parents

Authoritarian parents typically require absolute obedience. The parents' maintaining control is of first importance. "Because I said so," is a typical response to a child's questioning of parental authority, and physical force may be used to assure obedience. Working-class families tend to be more authoritarian than middle-class families (Kohn, 1959). Diana Baumrind found that children of authoritarian parents tend to be less cheerful than other children and correspondingly more moody, passively hostile, and vulnerable to stress (Belsky, 1984). The effects of punishment have been described by Sears et al. (1976):

Because it's good for you. Reason given to make child eat food it does not want.

MISS MANNERS

Punitiveness, in contrast with rewardingness, was a quite ineffectual quality for a mother to inject into her child training. . . . The unhappy effects of punishment have run like a dismal thread throughout our findings. Mothers who punished toilet accidents severely ended up with bed-wetting children. Mothers who punished dependency to get rid of it had more dependent children than mothers who did not punish. Mothers who punished aggressive behavior severely had more aggressive children than mothers who punished lightly.

Permissive Parents

Permissive attitudes are more popular in middle-class families than in working-class families. The child's freedom of expression and autonomy are valued. Permissive parents rely on reasoning and explanations. Yet permissive parents may find themselves resorting to manipulation and justification. When Johnny says he wants to go to Disneyland for his family's summer vacation, his father may say, "Yes, that sounds really good. But you know, I think you might like going to the Maine coast even better. You can go swimming every day, and fishing and hiking. . . . You still want to go to Disneyland, huh? . . . Well, did you know that Disneyland is going to be closed during the time I have my vacation? Yeah, the Jungle Cruise boat sank and they have to shut the whole place down to fix it. So I think maybe we should plan to go to the coast, don't you? . . . Oh, good, I knew you'd like it."

Sometimes parents justify their needs in terms of the child's. "Let's send Deborah to summer school, it will give her a chance to be in a learning environment," says a mother. But her real meaning is that she needs some time to herself without the constant demands of childrearing. Unable to accept that need because it conflicts with her image of the caring mother, she rationalizes it as being the child's need.

Although the permissive family emphasizes the child's freedom, that freedom may be illusory. The child is free from external restraints but not from internal ones. The child is supposedly free because he or she conforms "willingly," but such freedom is not authentic. Kohn (1959) observed, "The child is to act appropriately, not because the parents tell him to, but because he wants to. Not conformity to authority, but inner control; not because you're told to, but because you take the other person into consideration—these are the middle-class ideas." This form of socialization creates a bind. For example, parents tell a son to brush his teeth regularly but also tell him it is his own responsibility to do it. The parents insist that he take the initiative in brushing his teeth, although it is not important to him. The message is this: "Do what we tell you to do because *you* want to do it." Two psychologists commented on internalized control as a means of socialization as follows (Sluzki and Eliseo, 1971):

> "If you do not obey, we shall be angry with you, but if you obey only because we are telling you, we shall also be angry, because you should be independent." (That is, *want* to do whatever one *should* do of one's own will.) This injunction creates an untenable situation, because it demands that an external source be confused with an internal one.

Authoritarian socialization based on obedience eliminates this problem: "Do what we want you to do because *we* want you to do it." The message is much clearer. As a result, some psychologists suggest that middle-class boys feel more guilt than their working-class counterparts (Green, 1946). Because the repressive, punitive behavior of their parents is very clear, the latter boys are able to reject their parents and establish their own autonomy. Because middle-class parents try to control their children with explanations, love, and rewards, their children feel guilty when they try to assert their independence. One of the most guilt-producing weapons parents use against their children in such situations is "After all we have done for you, you want to do *this* to us." The child, who just desires to become independent, may not want to do anything to hurt his or her parents. But the parents' response creates guilt, ambivalence, and conflict in the child. Baumrind (1973) found that although children of permissive parents are generally cheerful, they exhibit low levels of self-reliance and self-control.

It takes 18 years of constant work to get one into presentable shape so that a college will take him or her off your hands for the winter season, and it can easily take another 10 years of coaching and reviewing before someone will consent to take the child on permanently.

MISS MANNERS

Authoritative Parents

Parents with *authoritative* attitudes toward childrearing rely on positive reinforcement and infrequent use of punishment. They direct the child in a manner that shows awareness of his or her feelings and capabilities. Parents encourage the development of the child's autonomy within "reasonable limits" and foster an atmosphere of "give and take" in parent-child communications. Children raised by authoritative parents tend to approach novel or stressful situations with curiosity and show high levels of self-reliance, self-control, cheerfulness, and friendliness (Baumrind, 1973). The childrearing strategies discussed later in this chapter may be used by parents who take an authoritative approach to childrearing.

☐ HOW TO RAISE YOUR CHILD

The Rise of Experts

About 150 years ago, Americans began turning to books to learn how to act and live rather than turning to each other; they began to lose confidence in their own abilities to make appropriate judgments. The vacuum that formed when traditional ways broke down under the impact of industrialization was filled by the so-called expert. The old values and ways had been handed down from parent to child in an unending cycle. Men and women had learned how to be mothers and fathers from their own parents, but with increasing mobility the continuity of generations ceased. A woman's mother was often not physically present to help her with her first child. New mothers were not able to turn to their more experienced kin for help. Instead, they enlisted the aid of new authorities—the experts who through education and training supposedly knew what to do. If your baby was colicky, the experts advised a drop of laudanum in the baby's bottle. (The laudanum would put the baby to sleep, but it would also make him or her a heroin addict by the end of a year.) If your husband was impotent, you were advised to purchase a cannabis extract from your pharmacist and have your husband drink it; it would restore his desire—and the only side effect would be a feeling of euphoria.

Modern parents may still follow experts' advice even if it conflicts with their own beliefs. Yet if the expert's advice counters their own understanding, they should carefully examine that advice as well as their own beliefs. All parents should take an expert's advice with at least a grain of salt. It is the parents' responsibility to raise their children, not the expert's.

The perniciousness of so much of the advice from experts that pervades the media is that it undermines the confidence of parents in their own abilities and values, overemphasizes the significance of specific child-rearing techniques, and grossly misrepresents the contribution of the expert in psychiatry or education can make to the conduct of ordinary family life.

RITA KRAMER

Children's Developmental Needs

As we noted earlier, academic thinking about child development tends to reflect contemporary scientific and moral concerns. Although the relative effects of physiology and environment are much debated by today's experts, it is clear that both "nature" and "nurture" play significant roles in human development. Jerome Kagan (1984) has recently presented a strong case for the role of biology in early development. He holds that the growth of the central nervous system in infants and young children assures that such motor and cognitive abilities as walking, talking, using symbols, and becoming self-aware will occur "as long as children are growing in any reasonably

We can expect a conscience of every child. We don't have to build it in. All we have to do is arrange the environment so they don't lose it.

JEROME KAGAN

One of children's basic needs is to feel valued by parents and other special adults. (Parents need to feel valued too.)

Conscience is the inner voice which warns us that someone may be looking.

H. L. MENCKEN

varied environment where minimal nutritional needs are met and [they] can exercise emerging abilities." Furthermore, according to Kagan, children are biologically equipped for understanding the meaning of right and wrong by the age of two; but although biology may be responsible for the development of conscience, social factors encourage its decline.

In addition to physiological maturation, significant factors affecting early development are (1) the acquisition of knowledge, (2) the formation of attachments (especially maternal), and (3) individual temperamental differences (such as inhibited/restrained/watchful or uninhibited/energetic/spontaneous) (Kagan, 1984). Development in later childhood can also be profoundly affected by social forces.

Parents often want to know what they can do to raise healthy children. Are there specific parental behaviors or amounts of behaviors (say, twelve hugs a day?) that all children need to grow up healthy? Apart from saying that basic physical needs must be met (adequate food, shelter, clothing, and so on) along with some basic psychological ones, experts cannot give us detailed instructions. Jerome Kagan (1976) wrote:

Children do not require any specific actions from adults to develop optimally. There is no good evidence that children must have a certain amount or schedule of cuddling, kissing, spanking, holding, or deprivation of privileges in order to become gratified and productive adults. The child does have some psychologic needs, but there is no fixed list of parental behaviors that can be counted on to fill those requirements.

The psychological needs of children vary with age and the context of their growth. According to Kagan, in our society a child needs to:

1. Feel valued by parents and a few special adults (such as a teacher, aunt, or grandparent).
2. Develop autonomy in attitudes and behaviors.
3. Develop and perfect talents that are desirable in society.
4. Be successful in a sexual context; love and be loved.

FEATURE

Self-Esteem

High self-esteem, what Erik Erikson called "an optimal sense of identity," is essential for growth in relationships, creativity, and productivity in the world at large. Low self-esteem is a disability that afflicts children (and the adults they grow up to be) with feelings of powerlessness, poor ability to cope, low tolerance for differences and difficulties, inability to accept responsibility, and impaired emotional responsiveness. Self-esteem has been shown to be more significant than intelligence in predicting scholastic performance.

Clemes and Bean (1983) describe four conditions necessary for developing and maintaining high self-esteem. The first condition is a sense of *connectiveness*—of being an important part of a family, class, team, or other group and of being connected ("in touch") with our bodies. The second condition is a sense of *uniqueness*—a feeling that our specialness and differentness are supported and approved by others. Third is a sense of *power*—the belief that we have the capability to influence others, solve problems, complete tasks, make our own decisions, and satisfy our needs. Children develop a sense of power through sharing duties and responsibilities in the home and having clear limits and rules set for them. The fourth condition for the development of self-esteem is a sense of *models*. Human, philosophical, and operational (mental constructs and images derived from experience) models help us establish meaningful values and goals and clarify our own standards.

Parents can foster high self-esteem in their children by (1) having high self-esteem themselves, (2) accepting their children as they are, (3) enforcing clearly defined limits, and (4) respecting individuality within the limits that have been set. Furthermore, "acknowledging your own needs and accepting them," according to Clemes and Bean, "can help you have patience and compassion for [children's] efforts to realize high self-esteem."

Kagan also observed that because our values derive from our profit-oriented economic system, crowded urban conditions, and competitive institutions in general, they tend to emphasize self-interest, competitiveness, and narcissism. More humanistic values would foster intimacy, cooperation, and altruism.

Children have more strength, resiliency, and resourcefulness than people may ordinarily think. They can adapt to and overcome many difficult situations. Parents do not have to be overly concerned that their every action will overwhelmingly influence their child's life. A mother can lose her temper and scream at her child and the child will most likely survive. A father can turn his child away with a grunt because he is too tired to listen and the child will not necessarily grow up neurotic as a result.

Parents' Needs

Although some parents' needs are met by their children, they have other needs as well. Significant needs of parents during the years of childrearing are personal developmental needs (such as social contacts, privacy, and outside interests) and the need to maintain marital satisfaction. Yet so much is expected of parents that they

Warning! The Surgeon General has determined that trying to be a good parent can be hazardous to your health.

ART DWORKEN

often neglect these needs. Parents may feel a deep sense of guilt if their child is not happy or has some defect, an unpleasant personality, or even a runny nose. The burden is especially heavy for mothers because their success is often measured by how perfect their children are. But children have their own independent personalities, and many forces affect a child's development and behavior. Nevertheless, as Philip Slater (1971) wrote: "Deep in their hearts most middle-class Spock-taught mothers believed that if they did their job well enough, all their children would be creative, intelligent, kind, generous, happy, brave, spontaneous, and good—each, of course, in his or her own special way." (See the reading "Egalitarian Childrearing" by Letty Pogrebin.)

Accepting our limitations as parents (and as human beings) and accepting our lives as they are (even if they haven't turned out exactly as planned) can help us cope with the many stresses of childrearing in an already stressful world. Contemporary parents need to guard against the "burnout syndrome" of emotional and physical overload (Dworken, 1984). Parents' careers and children's school activities, organized sports, scouts, music, art, or dance lessons compete for the parents' energy and rob them of the unstructured (and energizing) time that should be spent with others, with their children, or simply alone. Learning to prioritize activities—deciding which are essential and which can be eliminated or postponed—is a valuable parenting skill.

The Meaning of Being Me

Who Am I? Who Am I?
Growing up isn't easy, no matter what you think.
No. No. It's hard. It's hard.
It's standing on the brink
  of a mountain that
  you're afraid of.
  Sometimes I ask you who I am, but you don't tell me.
  Sometimes I ask myself who I am. . . .
Still a kid?
Soon a grown-up person. (Will it be better then?
Can you tell me that . . . can I believe it?)
I hear a certain song and I get
  tears in my eyes. . . .
I see a person and I get so angry—and he never even said a word. . . .
It's hard, growing up . . . it's so hard. Why must it be so hard. . . .
The littlest rough spot and there I go—crying,
angry . . . up to my room to break down—to kick—to have bad dreams—
I hurt you, and you, and you, sometimes—but I hurt me more times.
I don't want to hurt you, and I don't want to hurt me—
But it hurts so much not to know
  how to answer,
Who am I?

Susan, age 11
From *The Myth of the Happy Child* by Carole Klein

FEATURE

The Family and the Disabled Child

The advent of disability in a family, whether through birth, illness, or accident, is a source of tremendous stress on the family unit, especially at first. Parents may be overwhelmed with feelings of guilt, uncertainties about their parenting abilities, and fears about the future. Mothers especially feel the effects of this stress since they are generally responsible for the child's day-to-day care. Siblings of disabled children also experience added stress (Harris, 1984). Studies indicate that the marital relationship may suffer in families with a disabled child, although it is only the already shaky marriages that are seriously threatened (Harris, 1984). Healthy marriages may actually be enhanced through the experience of rearing a "special" child (Belsky et al., 1984).

Schneider (1983) developed a model describing stages of grief that is applicable to all life circumstances involving significant loss. The six stages of this model are as follows:

1. Initial awareness, often accompanied by guilt and panic. If the loss event occurs at birth, the mother is especially tired and vulnerable at this stage.
2. Strategies to overcome loss, characterized by the ambiguity of holding on and letting go simultaneously.
3. Awareness of the extent and complications of loss. Much energy is consumed in dealing with

this phase, often resulting in poor physical health. The griever experiences resentment, cynicism, and anger.
4. Completions: healing, acceptance of loss, resolution. This may be a lengthy process.
5. Resolution and reformations, bringing an enhanced sense of personal power.
6. Transcending loss, being free of its power to bind and limit. New energy and growth are now possible.

Children are subject to numerous disabling afflictions and conditions—Down's syndrome, autism, cerebral palsy, cystic fibrosis, blindness, physical abnormalities, growth disorders, injuries, to name just a few. Some of these disabilities are physical, some developmental, some both. Despite the prevalence of such conditions, we tend to shy away from anyone who is not "normal." This type of denial not only deprives the disabled and their families of much needed support and acceptance but it also deprives the rest of society of valuable relationships and interactions. Families with disabled members need to fight social isolation by reaching out to their friends for assistance, forming networks with similar families, and learning to use existing community resources (see Resource Center at end of text).

☐ CHILDREARING STRATEGIES

One of the most challenging aspects of childrearing is how to change, stop, encourage, or otherwise influence children's behavior. We can request, reason, explain, command, cajole, compromise, yell and scream, or threaten with physical punishment or the suspension of privileges; or we can just get down on our knees and beg. Some of these approaches may be appropriate at certain times; others clearly are never appropriate. Some may prove effective some of the time, some may never work very

The chief tools of proper child rearing are example and nagging.

MISS MANNERS

well, and no technique will work every time. We describe a few contemporary strategies in parenting in the following sections.

Behavior Modification

The basic principles of *behavior modification* are *positive reinforcement*—the prompt rewarding of the desired behavior—and *negative reinforcement*—giving a person the opportunity to terminate a mildly aversive situation by improving his or her behavior (for example, a whining, demanding child is sent to his or her room and allowed to come out as soon as the unacceptable behavior stops). Parents may feel uncomfortable with this approach; reinforcement is a powerful tool that can be used by the strong to take advantage of the weak, as in the case of bribery or blackmail. However, many parents and teachers use some behavior modification principles in their dealings with children. They often find that once the child has changed a particular behavior successfully, the reinforcement is no longer necessary.

Democratic Child Training

In the *democratic child-training* strategy, described by Rudolph Dreikurs (1964), the family unit is viewed as the shaper of the child's behavior patterns. The child makes his or her decisions within the context of family discussions and mutually established rules. The proponents of democratic childrearing believe that the child will learn quickly by experiencing the *logical consequences* of his or her acts and will conform quickly to "expected standards that ensure the fair treatment of all family members" (Bigner, 1979). The concept of logical consequences may occasionally be difficult for a parent to apply, or application may be unwise if it appears that the consequences will be severe.

The Humanistic Approach

The *humanistic* approach to parent-child relations, formalized by Dr. Haim Ginott (1965), centers on effective communication. Parents should be empathetic counselors who respect their children's views and feelings. Some characteristics of the humanistic strategy are as follows: (1) Parents and children are both entitled to their feelings. (2) Feelings can be expressed without attacks on personalities. (3) Certain behaviors, such as the use of threats, bribes, and sarcasm, are self-defeating. (4) Physical punishment is damaging as well as only minimally effective. (5) Children are capable of learning, through reasonable limits, to accept responsibility and regulate their own behavior.

Parent Effectiveness

Psychologist Thomas Gordon (1978) has devised a parenting strategy called *Parent Effectiveness*, which emphasizes *active listening* and *no-lose problem solving*. By using active listening, verbally "feeding back" to the child his or her communications, the

UNDERSTANDING YOURSELF

Your Children: Planning and Rearing

Children are central to our feelings about family. Our culture expects a family to have children. Yet technically, a family can be a family if it consists of only a husband and wife, whether they have never had children or their children have left. Why do you think it is that children are so important to our sense of family in America?

If you don't have children: Do you want children? When? How many? What factors do you need to take into consideration when contemplating a family for yourself? Does your partner (if you have one) agree with you about having children? If you and your partner disagree about having children, how will that affect your relationship? If you discovered that you were infertile, how would that affect your feelings about family?

If you have children: Did you plan to have them? What considerations led you to have them? How do you feel about being a parent? What adjustments have you had to make as a

result? How did your relationship with your partner change? Do you want to have more children?

How should childrearing tasks be delegated between spouses (or partners)? Are there any particular tasks you feel either men or women should not do? How are tasks delegated in your household? Who should be responsible for children if they are ill? Who should be responsible for making baby-sitting or child-care arrangements?

In your family of origin, what childrearing attitudes (authoritarian, permissive, or authoritative) predominated? Do you think these attitudes influenced your own development? How has your attitude been influenced by your upbringing? What childrearing strategies might (or do) you find useful in raising your children?

parent helps the child solve his or her own problems. The task of the parent is to try to understand the child and help the child understand the nature of the problem by mirroring the child's feelings. In the no-lose method of problem solving, parent and child work together to identify the problem, generate and evaluate possible solutions, choose the best solution for both parties, and then evaluate how well it has worked. *"I" messages* are important in parent effectiveness because they impart facts without placing blame and are thus less likely to promote rebellion in children than are "you" messages. (*"I get grouchy when you wake me up early on Sunday"* versus *"You are a rude child to wake up your poor mother."*)

> Child rearing is the only task in the world where you goal is to make your own job obsolete.
>
> MISS MANNERS

Although none of these strategies will be successful all the time, it is important for families to keep seeking ways to improve their communication and satisfaction. It is also important for parents to develop and maintain confidence in their own parenting skills, common sense, and love for their children.

"Wrong Reasons"

60-Second Television Message*

ANNCR(VO): A lot of people have children for the wrong reasons.

GRANDMOTHER: You've been married a year now. When are we going to see some grandchildren?

YOUNG MAN: You want to have a baby, Evelyn? All right, we'll have a baby! Maybe that'll patch things up!

YOUNG WIFE: We only want two children. But if one of them isn't a boy— we'll keep trying.

WOMAN: Why knock myself out working when I can have a baby.

MAN: Heh-heh, hey Harry. What are you and Marge waiting for— huh?

YOUNG GIRL: Sure I want another baby. What else is a woman for?

ANNCR(VO): As we said, there are a lot of wrong reasons to have a child— but only one right reason: because you really want one. And that takes planning.

Planned Parenthood
Children by choice.
Not chance.

ANNCR(VO): For more information, write Planned Parenthood, Box 840, New York, 10019.

Printed by permission of Planned Parenthood Federation of America, Inc.

☐ SUMMARY

- Parenthood can now be considered a matter of choice owing to effective methods of birth control. Child-free marriage and deferred parenthood are alternatives that are growing in popularity.

- Parental roles are acquired virtually overnight and can create considerable stress. The parent-child relationship is lifelong.

- Many women find considerable satisfaction and fulfillment in motherhood. Although we have no concrete evidence of a biological maternal drive, it is clear that socialization for motherhood does exist.

- The role of the father in his children's development is currently being reexamined. The traditional instrumental roles are being supplemented, if not supplanted, by expressive ones.

- Supplementary child care outside the home is a necessity for many families. The development and maintenance of quality day-care programs should be a national priority.

- Television has recently been implicated in a number of individual, familial, and societal disorders. Commercials generally encourage poor nutritional habits and conflict between parent and child. Violence on television has been demonstrated to cause aggressive behavior in children.

- Models of child socialization include Freud's *psychoanalytic* model, Piaget's *stages of cognitive development*, and the *social molding* model used by Erikson. Each of us also has an "I"—sense of self—that resists biological and environmental pressures.

- In the *developmental interaction* model of the family, family members are viewed as interdependent in their growth, which continues throughout their lives. Birth order and space between births are significant.

- Basic attitudes toward childrearing can be classified as *authoritarian, permissive,* and *authoritative.*

- Expert advice is often relied upon by today's parents. It needs to be tempered by parents' confidence in their own parenting abilities and in their children's strength and resourcefulness.

- Biology, particularly central nervous system growth, strongly influences the child's development in the first few years of life. Other factors affecting early development are the acquisition of knowledge, the formation of attachments, and individual temperamental differences. Social forces are also significant for development in later childhood.

- Contemporary strategies for childrearing that parents find useful include behavior modification, democratic child-training, the humanistic approach, and Parent Effectiveness.

READINGS–*continued*

No Children Allowed!

LINDA LEE, REDBOOK

*What evidence does Linda Lee offer to support her conten-
tion that "America is anti-kid"? How does her assessment
coincide with your own experience or that of parents of your
acquaintance? Do you think there is a legitimate "other
side" to this issue? Why or why not?*

You know the old joke about the couple trying to rent a
house? "Steadily employed?" the owner asks them. "Yes,"
they reply. "Children?"—"Two of them, aged five and
nine." "Animals?"—"Now, wait a minute," the parents say.
"They may be rough, but they're not animals."

These days in many parts of the United States, if you
had answered yes to children, the owner would have turned
you down. There would have been no need to go on to the
question about animals. In fact, animals may get more respect than children: America has become anti-kid.

Vance Packard notes in *Our Endangered Children* (Little, Brown and Company, 1983) that in 1979 all four of
Atlanta's newest housing complexes barred children, 90
percent of Denver's complexes were "adults only" and virtually all of Houston's new developments either excluded
children outright or restricted them to certain buildings.
Marian Wright Edelman, president of the Children's Defense Fund, notes: "In 1980, 76 percent of the rental apartment units in the nation had policies to keep out or restrict
children."

So, what's wrong with that?

Nothing, if you really and truly don't want to live near
children—even your own. But what message are we getting
here? That children are unsavory characters? That older
people have a right to live apart from younger people, even
though we insisted on the integration of whites and blacks
in our country 20 years ago? That indeed, as Letty Cottin
Pogrebin says in *Family Politics* (McGraw-Hill, 1983), "An
entire class of human beings, children, are characterized in
advance as undesirable before any individual child has a
chance to be noisy or . . . obtrusive."

A case in point: Erica Pomerantz, nine months old, has
officials in Broward County, Florida, in an uproar. They
have promised to fight her all the way to the Supreme
Court. Her crime? She was born to parents who live in a
no-children-allowed community. Why, even now she's
being seen—in public—sitting in her stroller. Next she'll
be walking and talking. Who knows where things will go
from there?

In some cases the anti-child bias is less explicit—but just
as strong. A friend of mine nearly lost his chance to bid on
an expensive co-op apartment in New York City when the
co-op board learned that he had three children. Only after
he explained that one son was living apart and getting married, that another son was in law school and that the at-
home daughter did not play any percussion instruments,
would not roller-skate in the halls and never invited friends
over was he allowed to offer money for the apartment.
Didn't that make him mad? I asked him later. "Not at all,"
he said. "Most people in the building are older. They don't
want kids around, and frankly, neither do I. I don't want to
hear a baby crying all night. I don't want to trip over a
tricycle some kid leaves in the hall. I've done that already.
I've earned a little peace and quiet."

Apparently people on airplanes feel the same way. Have
you ever staggered onto a plane loaded with carry-on baby
and bags? Have you noticed how the eyes of the other pas-
sengers widen like those of frightened deer? They react as if
you were carrying a vial of deadly plutonium, when all
you've got is a sleeping baby. Suddenly everyone in your
section decides to change seats.

Feel lonely sitting there, just you and the baby? Need a
hand? I'll bet that nice stewardess will help.

Not a chance. The stewardess is probably directing her
attention to frequent flyers, the kind of people who are
good for business. Babies, stewardesses seem to feel, are
more trouble than they're worth—nonpaying, squalling
baggage.

I've raised a son in big-city America and I can tell you
from experience that people hate kids. My friends started in
on me when I was pregnant. "What do you want a kid for,"
they asked. "All that crying and fussing. Get a cat!" Is there
no place in our society for children? When I carried one-
year-old Evan into a restaurant, people looked at me as if I
had chosen to dine with a Saint Bernard. Bus drivers
snarled at me for trying to bring a baby and a stroller on
board. If we got on, no one offered us a seat. We couldn't
get up stairs or down escalators or through revolving doors
without exertion, contortion or both. Again, no one
helped.

Well-dressed people rushing to work in the morning
tripped over the two of us—the slow-moving mother with
the child learning to walk. They didn't apologize, either.
They glared. And more than once we've been rudely el-
bowed aside in the supermarket. Only recent immigrants to
America—the Koreans at the corner fruit stand, the Arabs
selling newspapers, the Viennese lady at the bakery—noticed my little boy and asked his name. To all other Americans he seemed at best nonexistent, at worst a menace.

Okay, so people in big cities don't have enough space.

READINGS—*continued*

They are in a hurry and under pressure. We don't give our old people enough respect (or money) and the old people take it out on the only creatures who are lower than they are on the social totem pole—kids. But how does that explain what happened recently when I took my son to see a Walt Disney movie, *Fantasia?* It was Saturday afternoon, prime kid-time. When my son started to ask me what was going on in the movie, with all the lava and the dinosaurs, we got a chorus of "sssssssshhhhhs." It turned out that the theater was filled with grownups—grownups without children—who were there to relive their own childhoods. They wanted no part of real, live, here-and-now children.

"Why is this child out with you all the time?" people ask. "Why isn't he in school? Why isn't he home, where he belongs?" But of course, he must be out to commute between home and school. Besides, my child belongs anywhere he wants to be: at a movie, at a restaurant, in a nice apartment building and, yes, even on an airplane. He is polite, bright and well-behaved. He is not a burden to anyone. Why, then, does our society treat him like an unwelcome guest?

On Not Having Kids
JOHN HUBNER

What does this article say about society's response to childlessness in its members? What are the author's reasons for not wanting children? Do you think they are valid? Should the decision to be child-free even need to be defended? Why? Compare Hubner's view of a pro-parenthood society to Lee's anti-child society. Can you reconcile both views? How?

Before we left Boston for San Jose last fall, we had dinner with two couples we've known for years. We used to spend hours with them, discussing the pros and cons of starting a family. Within a few months, both couples had children. We thought it was going to be a bittersweet goodbye dinner, but they ganged up on us about having children as soon as we got our coats off. They kept telling us we didn't know what we were missing. We suggested they were missing a lot, too. That, they didn't like. "Well, people are having children later these days," one proud mother said. "There's still time. It's a matter of maturity. When you're ready, you'll know it."

That, I didn't like. Why should maturity be equated with having children? Before I could react, they hit us rapid-fire with a series of questions that probed like a scal-

pel. One new father, a psychiatrist, wondered if we might be just a bit narcissistic. His wife, a clinical psychologist, asked if we were perennial adolescents, afraid of the responsibility that comes with parenthood. She suggested that our relationship was too fragile for the strains of raising kids. They were as obnoxious as est graduates. We had two choices: laugh it off or tell them off.

"You want the truth?" I said. "Our sex life is so kinky, we'll never reproduce."

Nobody laughed. It was as if I'd committed heresy, joking about the hallowed act of creation. After a pause, the conversation shifted to a safer topic: California.

Ann and I are not narcissistic. Our relationship has endured worse strains than the "terrible twos." It's not that we do not like children, either. We have loved several. We have friends here who have a wonderful 2-year-old daughter, so I catch glimpses of what I'm missing. The point is, I've chosen to miss it. We do not have children because we do not want any. If we did, we would have them.

I have no deep biological urge to reproduce myself. The world will get along fine without my kids, just as it will get along fine without me when I'm gone. I lack the drive to love, to nurture, and to shape another human being. Babies don't fascinate me. I'm like Queen Victoria: I like kids after they've left what she called the "frog stage."

I worry about money like most of us do, but if we had kids, I'd *really* worry about money. I don't want to spend money on Gerber's and Pampers and life insurance. I don't want to save for a college education. I'd rather save so I can go back to Morocco. I don't want to spend nights babysitting. I want to go to country bars. I don't want to spend Saturdays taking 5-year-olds to Great America. I want to go to Reno. If this sounds hedonistic, perhaps it is. But it is not self-destructive. Aristotle, a really nifty definition-maker, said that to be happy is to be always learning something. My job does that for me. I've chosen not to learn about the things a child could teach me.

I'm not convinced I would love my child simply because he or she was mine. Plenty of parents do not like their kids. You've seen them. We have a great friend who is a successful novelist. She has reached her 60s, has no children, and has no regrets. "It's a real longshot to produce a child that you would choose as a friend," she says. "Think about your family: Your child could turn out to be like any one of them. How many of them do you like enough to want to spend the next 18 years with?"

I suspect that in many cases, it is the parents' fault if they don't like their children. We had friends we stopped seeing because they have a kid who is a monster. The terror

READINGS–*continued*

I'll call Joey is out of control the second his feet hit the floor. He is the product of what I call child idolatry: the child as center of the universe. The little creep controls every situation. Joey's parents are little more than serfs, the loyal subjects of a 4-year-old despot. "No Joey, daddy can't read you a story now, daddy is busy talking . . . Joey, don't shout at daddy . . . Please don't shout, Joey . . . Joey, don't cry . . . Oh, all right Joey! Get the damn book."

I think that if I had a child, I would spend most of the day worrying about him. Jeffrey is the closest I've come to being a father; he and his mother moved in next door to us when he was 2. He was so beautiful, his hands and cute little legs emerging from his favorite Levi cutoffs so delicate, that I wanted to pick him up and hug him and never let go. Every time he laughed, 1,000 volts shot up my spine. I'd think, do that again Jeffrey and I'll give you my house. If your best friend is the person you most enjoy being with, then that's what Jeffrey was to me. I liked the things he said and the way he said them. I liked watching *Sesame Street* with him. I liked the way he conned me into stopping for ice cream cones.

When Jeffrey was 6, they discovered he had cancer. His doctors told me he had a 50-50 chance to live six months. They wouldn't even give odds on a year. I took long walks, hunting the catharsis, trying to cry. Once I screamed and kicked a tree, but it was self-conscious and didn't help. Jeffrey was going to die.

He went through radiation and chemotherapy. When he lost his hair, his mother bought him a Dodger hat. He went back to school and never took the hat off. Any kid who tried to take it off was in for a fight. I refused to let myself hope, even when the cancer mysteriously went into remission.

Jeffrey survived! It is the one miracle I've seen. The cancer gradually disappeared; the doctors can't explain it. Jeffrey is 13 now, and he's still my man. But I never, ever, want to go through anything like that again.

Sometimes I think about moving into middle age, and then old age, without children. It is frightening. Loneliness is the enemy. For three years, we lived in New Hampshire, surrounded by retired couples. They wouldn't have had much to do besides read the *Boston Herald American* and bowl candlepins if it weren't for their children. Their families were scattered all over the country, so they didn't see their children or grandchildren often, but their families gave them a lot to think about. A letter or phone call was a major event. Still, with children or without, life for the elderly in this country is pretty bleak. We isolate old people. Those I've known spend far too much time alone. I'm

hoping that if I make it to my 70s, there will be old-folks communes by then that will let me in.

As resolved as I am to not having children, I will always wonder what I have missed. The other day, I was walking around Vasona Park. I noticed a man who apparently had arrived late for a picnic. He was walking up a slight hill when his kids saw him. They jumped away from the picnic table and went running down the hill. The father scooped one up and swung him 'round and 'round while the other child danced about, waiting for an opening. Finally, the kid charged in and grabbed his father's leg. They wrestled for a while, and then walked hand-in-hand up to the picnic table.

As I watched, I wondered if the love that father has for his children is more profound than any love I've known. I'll always wonder about that.

Egalitarian Childrearing
LETTY COTTIN POGREBIN, EXCERPT FROM *GROWING UP FREE*

The author offers advice for both mothers and fathers on providing children with non-stereotypical sex role models. What kinds of ideas and attitudes does she advise mothers to let go of? How does she advise fathers to change in terms of attitudes and actions? What impact do you think her suggestions would have on parents and children?

Advice for Mothers   Feeding, cleaning and dressing a child are not acts of love. They're functions you perform lovingly. Not performing them constantly or exclusively does not constitute bad motherhood. No one should feel guilty about wanting to share the work of child care, because that's what it is: work—repetitive, tedious, often lonely and exhausting work. To romanticize it, as our culture has done, is to mislead women (and men) and make real-life parenthood ultimately disillusioning.

This second bit of advice for mothers is tougher than it sounds. Let go. Stop getting an easy high from being maven of the manse and honcho of the household.

Don't view a man's way of doing housework as a personal attack. His method is not a criticism of your methods; it is his method. And don't view his participation as a favor or a gift; it's a normal obligation: "We both eat, so we both shop, cook and do dishes. We both contribute to the mess, so we both clean it up. We both wear clothes, so we both do laundry."

Let go for your children's sake, too. When a man shares housework (not just "helps around the house"), it's easier to rear your son to be that kind of man, and your daughter to expect that kind of behavior.

If working outside the home is what you need to make you happy, or what the family needs to make ends meet, deal with it. Do not be deterred by a shrieking child barring the front door or wrapped around your legs. Children, like the rest of us, become addicted to the full-time service and attention of another person. This doesn't mean it's beneficial for them to have it, and it doesn't mean they won't get used to it if they don't.

A mother's self-esteem, energy level, and feelings of personal worth—whether they derive from an executive job, blue-collar work, or homemaking—determine not only the quality of her maternal behavior, but the messages she transmits to her children about female competence and dignity.

Advice for Fathers How can you reverse gears? How can you change your attitude and actions before it's too late? Accepting your wife as an equal, primary or sole wage-earner might be the first prerequisite.

The second prerequisite for change is to analyze the state of your finances. Naturally, if both you and your wife are working full-time and still can't stay out of debt, then there's little room to maneuver. But if you are working harder than you have to, making more than you really need just because of the onward-and-upward habit, or pursuing a Big Shot job just for the victory of winning it—or if your wife is not working because you need the "masculine" status of being sole support, or if she is holding back on her earning potential to protect your ego—then the two of you are cutting off your options and spiting your children.

If you can afford to make radical changes in your work schedule, here are some possibilities:

● Drawing the line: Make 6 p.m. the absolute cutoff between your paid job and your father-job; give up all over-

time work; stop bringing a briefcase home.
● Exploring flexible schedules: Could you live nearly as well on two part-time salaries as on one full salary?
● Reassessing what everything means to you: Maybe you are on someone else's treadmill; maybe you really want to be a poet or a potter. Think about going back to school, changing fields, taking a year or two off.

Whatever economic or scheduling adjustment you can afford should have one objective at heart: to balance love and work more sensibly so that your children can have a real father, and you can have the pleasure and humanity most men find out too late that they missed.

Adjustments of attitude and time make a man available for fatherhood. What makes him a father (and not a mother's helper) is involvement in the dailiness of children's lives at every level.

You will have to learn the physical duties—the feeding, holding, diapering, bathing, dressing, toilet-training—the way most mothers learn them: by doing them, reading about how to do them and talking to experienced parents who do them well.

Practice listening to your children without asking questions, and without giving advice (unless it is sought), and without jumping to conclusions before the child has been fully heard. Many fathers try to be instant problem-solvers, when all a child wants is a confidante or a word of fatherly support.

The man who knows the difference between quiet time and other times, between ten minutes rocking a child in his lap and ten minutes playing catch with her, between being there for a teenager with love problems or tossing him the keys to the car—the man who knows those differences, and can act upon them appropriately, knows emotionally how to father a child.

PART FIVE

Interiors

CHAPTER 13

Hidden Realities: What Goes On Inside Families

PREVIEW

To gain a sense of what you already know about the material covered in this chapter, answer "true" or "false" to the statements below. You will find the answers as you read the chapter.

1. The public and private behaviors of a family usually coincide. True or false?
2. A family's rules are often hidden from its members. True or false?
3. Our emotions are often a product of our family environment. True or false?
4. If a person is powerful enough, he or she can single-handedly control the family. True or false?
5. Families constantly seek to change their structures and patterns of interaction. True or false?
6. A person's response to a family member's action is modified by family rules. True or false?
7. Families that tend to be closed to outsiders are likely to have members with high self-esteem. True or false?
8. Family rules can be easily changed through discussion. True or false?
9. Healthy families resist change because change may destroy the family unit. True or false?
10. Families sometimes engage in conflicts about *whose* feelings will be validated as "real." True or false?

Outline

What is the price of
   experience?
Do men buy it for a song?
Or wisdom for a dance in the
   street?
No, it is bought with the price
Of all that a man hath.
Wisdom is sold in the desolate
   market where none come to
   buy.

WILLIAM BLAKE

Families are mysterious entities in many ways. Each of us knows very little about what goes on in families other than our own. People present public images of their family life that may be very different from the family's life outside public view. If we hide much of the family from the public, we also hide much of it from our family members. Marriages and families have their secret loves and hates, their peculiar relationships, their private ambitions and desperations about which some or all members are kept in the dark. These secrets are not necessarily sinister; they are merely secrets. For example, a married man flirts with someone at a party but does not tell his spouse, or a married woman enjoys erotic fantasies about a neighbor.

Other secrets are more important: a woman is angry at her husband's desire to spend vacation time with his male friends but does not show it. Some secrets may be of overwhelming emotional impact: a man hides from his wife the fact that he has been threatened with dismissal from his job because of his drinking problem. Laing (1972) observed: "There is concerted family *resistance* to discovering what is going on, and there are complicated strategems to keep everyone in the dark. . . . We would know more of what is going on if we were not forbidden to do so, and forbidden to realize that we are forbidden to do so."

☐ HIDING FROM OUTSIDERS

Front-Stage Behavior

The facts are always friendly.
Every bit of evidence one can
acquire, in any area, leads one
that much closer to what is
true.

CARL ROGERS, ON BECOMING
PARTNERS

We divide our lives into public and private arenas. We allow anyone to see certain of our activities, such as buying groceries, but keep others, such as bathing, private. Bathing is intimate, and we allow only those with whom we are intimate—if anyone— to see us nude. Sociologist Erving Goffman (1959) describes life as a drama in which we perform our roles on stage. There are two stages, however: front stage and backstage. Some performances are appropriate for what Goffman calls front-stage behavior, for which we have a nonintimate audience such as strangers, acquaintances, or work associates. Backstage behavior takes place among intimates. In our front-stage behavior, we keep people at a distance by being polite, following rules, exercising self-control, and acting according to our roles. In this manner, we keep people from seeing us too closely, knowing us too intimately. Behavior such as addressing each other as "Mr. Jones" instead of "Joe" or "Professor Smith" instead of "Sue" indicates that we are acting publicly on front stage. Body movement, interpersonal space, touching, and gestures help define which stage we are on: a handshake is usually front stage. Where we are—in a restaurant, classroom, or at home—helps define whether behavior can be formal or intimate. Clues that define situations and roles as formal or informal are often very subtle, but they establish certain rules that people do not violate. They create the front-stage framework within which we perform our roles.

A moderately honest man with a moderately faithful wife, moderate drinkers both, in a moderately healthy house: that is the true middle-class unit.

GEORGE BERNARD SHAW

Backstage Behavior

The backstage is quite different from the front. Goffman (1959) wrote:

Throughout Western society there tends to be one informal or backstage language of behavior and another language of behavior for occasions when a performance is being presented. The backstage language consists of reciprocal first-naming, cooperative decision making, profanity, openly sexual remarks, elaborate griping, smoking, rough informal dress, "sloppy" sitting and standing posture, use of dialect or sub-standard speech, mumbling and shouting, playful aggressivity and kidding, inconsiderateness for the other in minor but potentially symbolic acts, minor physical self-involvements such as humming, whistling, chewing, nibbling, belching, and flatulence.

In the backstage area, we take off our masks: when people are "up front" with others, they bring backstage attitudes to the front stage. Backstage is where people can feel at ease, be themselves, feel "at home" (since that is where backstage behavior usually occurs in the family). Backstage is the private arena where daily activities of married and family life take place. Here most intimate activities are performed, hidden from public view.

I hope you have not been leading a double life, pretending to be wicked and being really good all the time. That would be hypocrisy.

OSCAR WILDE

Homes have front stage and backstage spaces. The "front" room is front stage and public. It usually presents a conventional image of family life. Backstage areas, which usually include bedrooms, are private and informal; only family and close friends are allowed in backstage areas.

We rarely see more than the front-stage roles of a family: happy, loving husband and wife; adorable, polite children. People like to show only their "best" side, which is usually their public side. The distinction between front-stage and backstage behavior helps explain why, when couples split up or divorce, friends are frequently surprised. Bewilderment is a common response—"But I thought you were both happy." What the friends saw, however, was only the public side of the marriage; the private side (say, the endless fights, unsatisfactory sex, and money disagreements) remained hidden—rarely discussed except between husband and wife. This underside of family life is seldom seen by outsiders. It is often hidden from family members as well.

Backstage behavior includes such activities as dressing, undressing, sleeping, and putting on makeup. Arguments are private; sexual intercourse is private. The world sees neither the daily struggles and pain nor the quiet intimacies, the tenderness. Nor does it usually see the husband or wife at their everyday tasks—cleaning, scrubbing the floors, preparing meals. People try to hide their backstage behavior.

Front-stage and backstage spaces exist even within homes. The front yard is public, or front-stage; the backyard is less public and is backstage. The living room and dining room are front-stage; the bathroom and bedroom, backstage. These backstage areas are usually reserved for private activities such as sleeping, dressing, making love, relieving oneself, and cleaning. When a person is awake, clean, and dressed, then he or she will move into the living room (sometimes called the "front" room), where friends and strangers can be met (for the social history of the "family room," see Langdon, 1983).

People guard against others intruding into their private backstage areas, but it is almost impossible to keep backstage areas totally private. We often unexpectedly see others' backstage behavior—say, a couple kissing or arguing—and we pretend not to notice. Partners may agree not to discuss certain matters with outsiders. But, of course, sometimes the agreement breaks down. They agree not to fight in public, but an argument ensues anyway, perhaps at a dinner party. Each spouse is angry at the other not only because they fought but also because they fought in public. They both have to contend with the social embarrassment of having fought in public— for bringing backstage behavior up front.

While front-stage behavior is formal and role-oriented, backstage behavior is informal and considerably more fluid. It is in the backstage area that we see the informal family system at work.

Underneath the surface is a vast amount of conflict and violence—including bitter feelings, anger, hatred, much physical punishment of children, pokes and slaps of husbands and wives, and not altogether rare pitched battles between family members.

S. K. STEINMETZ AND M. A. STRAUS, *VIOLENCE IN THE FAMILY*

Nothing is so firmly believed as that which is least known.

FRANCIS JEFFREY (1773–1850)

☐ THE FAMILY AS A SYSTEM

Since the 1970s, the study of family relationships has been increasingly enriched by systems theory. Compared with other theories such as structural functionalism and symbolic interaction, systems theory is still in its infancy. Many of its basic concepts are still in dispute even among its adherents (Melito, 1985). In fact, some argue that there is no such thing as system theory; rather, systems analysis is a "loosely connected series of concepts" (Papp, 1983). (Systems approaches to the family are often technical; but for clear introductions, see Virginia Satir's *Peoplemaking* [1972], August Napier and Carl Whitaker's *The Family Crucible* [1978], Salvador Minuchin's *The Family Kaleidoscope* [1984]; also see Weber et al., [1985] and Merkel and Rudisill, [1985].)

In some ways, systems theory combines basic ideas from both structural functionalism and symbolic interaction (see Chapter 2). Like structural functionalism, systems theory views the family as a structure of related parts or subsystems. Each part carries out certain functions. These parts include the spousal subsystem, the parent-child subsystem, the parental subsystem (husband and wife relating to each other as parents), and the personal subsystem (the individual and his or her relationships). Salvador Minuchin (1974) describes that family structure as "the invisible set of functional demands that organizes the ways in which family members interact."

The subsystems interact with each other as well as with the world outside. One of the important tasks these subsystems have is to maintain their boundaries. For the family to function well, the subsystems must be kept separate (Minuchin, 1981). Husbands and wives, for example, should prevent their conflicts from spilling over into the parent-child subsystem. When husband and wife become estranged, one parent may encourage the children to disobey the other parent; a husband may take out his anger for his wife on his daughter (Minuchin, 1974). Sometimes a parent will turn to the child for the affection that he or she ordinarily receives from a spouse. When the boundaries of the separate subsystems blur, family dysfunctions may result.

As in symbolic interaction, interaction is significant in systems theory because a system is more than the sum of its parts. The family system is more than simply its members. It is also the *pattern* of interactions of family members: their communication, roles, beliefs, and rules. This emphasis on the pattern of interactions within the structure is a distinctive feature of the systems approach.

Transactional Patterns

Marriage is much more than two people acting out their prescribed marital roles. It is a relationship between a husband and wife *and* their pattern of interactions. The structure of marriage is determined by how the spouses act in relation to each other over time (Lederer and Jackson, 1968). Each partner influences the other and in turn is influenced by the partner. Each interaction is limited by the marital structure created by their patterns.

The interactions of spouses and family members help create a family system. Minuchin (1974) describes the family system as follows:

A family is a system that operates through transactional patterns. Repeated transactions establish patterns of how, when, and to whom to relate, and these patterns underpin the system. When a mother tells her child to drink his juice and he obeys, this interaction defines who she is in relation to him and who he is in relation to her, in that context, and at that time. Repeated operations in these terms constitute a transactional pattern.

Transactional patterns are the ways people habitually relate to each other. They regulate the behavior of family members. These patterns are maintained by a culture's rules governing family organization and by the family's own rules. The cultural rules establish the functions and organization of the family. Families, for example, are responsible for nurturing and socializing children; spouses are expected to provide intimacy for each other. Families are also constrained by the family's own unique expectations or rules. Rules are often covert and unarticulated, but family members *feel* their existence. A family rule such as "Never talk or think about your 'real' father" does not need to be expressed for a child to know it exists. It is said by the parent with a glance, gesture, or attitude. These rules may govern individuals' interactions in families: think how often you abide by your family's, parents' or partner's rules. Although rules are unwritten, they are often as powerful as the law itself.

We all think we can choose when a choice comes, but our choice is really made not at the moment, but by our life hitherto. You choose according to that which you have chosen a hundred times before. Your destiny is not that which you will do, but that which you have done. Your future is behind you, in your past.

E. F. BENSON

Because our emotions are experienced in a social context, systems researchers argue that they cannot be understood outside the family context. For example, among friends, you may be outgoing; at home, you may be withdrawn. Are you then an "outgoing" or a "withdrawn" person? The family is so powerful in affecting a person's emotional state that some researchers argue that you cannot label a person as either "outgoing" or "withdrawn." They suggest that when forming a hypothesis we should substitute the verb *to show* for *to be*. Instead of saying, "The daughter is withdrawn and the mother is scornful," it is more accurate to say "The daughter shows withdrawal behavior when in the presence of the mother who shows scornful behavior to her." This mode of speaking describes interconnected responses and relates them to their context. Exploring the interconnectedness further, we could say, "The daughter shows withdrawal behavior when in the presence of the mother who shows scornful behavior to her. Her mother shows scorn toward her after her husband shows disregard when he returns home from work following arguments with a coworker. The father sides with the daughter against the mother to show anger with his wife for not showing submissiveness. His wife shows scorn for her daughter who has replaced her in her husband's affections."

In systems analysis no single person has unilateral control over another. Rather, the control is exercised by interactions and feedback. No single event or behavior causes another. Each is linked in a circular manner to many other events and behaviors, which form a pattern over time. The mother's and daughter's responses are viewed as moves and countermoves in the family game that also includes the husband/father (Papp, 1983). If we want to change a behavior, we must change the system. In this case, if the family wants the daughter to be emotionally engaged with the family, changes must occur in interactions between the daughter, mother, father, and the father's interactions with his coworkers.

Characteristics of the Systems Approach

In looking at family systems, researchers and therapists make a number of assumptions about the nature of families and their interactions.

1. Interactions must be studied in the context of the family system. Each action affects every other person in the family. The family exerts a powerful influence on our behaviors and feelings just as we influence the behaviors and feelings of other family members.

2. The family has a structure that can only be seen in its interactions. Each family has certain preferred patterns of transactions that ordinarily work in response to day-to-day demands. For example, a family may decide that both husband and wife will work to earn its income. Under most circumstances, the husband and wife will make an arrangement that allows them both to work; they organize their lives around that commitment.

3. The family is a purposeful system; that is, it has a goal. In most instances, its goal is to maintain itself intact as a family. It seeks *homeostasis*, that is, stability.

4. Each family system is transformed over time. A well-functioning family system constantly changes and adapts in response to its members and the environment to maintain itself. The system changes through the family life cycle as partners age and as children are born, grow older, and leave home (see Table 13–1). A parent, for example, must adapt to an adolescent's increasing independence by relinquishing

Table 13–1   **The Stages of the Family Life Cycle: Stress Points**

Family Life Cycle Stage	Emotional Process of Transition: Key Principles	Second-Order Changes in Family Status Required to Proceed Developmentally
1. Between families: the unattached young adult	Accepting parent-offspring separation	a. Differentiation of self in relation to family of origin b. Development of intimate peer relationships c. Establishment of self in work
2. The joining of families through marriage: the newly married couple	Commitment to new system	a. Formation of marital system b. Realignment of relationships with extended families and friends to include spouse
3. The family with young children	Accepting new members into the system	a. Adjusting marital system to make space for child(ren) b. Taking on parenting roles c. Realignment of relationships with extended family to include parenting and grandparenting roles
4. The family with adolescents	Increasing flexibility of family boundaries to include children's independence	a. Shifting of parent/child relationships to permit adolescent to move in and out of system b. Refocus on mid-life marital and career issues c. Beginning shift toward concerns for older generation
5. Launching children and moving on	Accepting a multitude of exits from and entries into the family system	a. Renegotiation of marital system as a dyad b. Development of adult to adult relationships between grown children and their parents c. Realignment of relationships to include in-laws and grandchildren d. Dealing with disabilities and death of parents (grandparents)
6. The family in later life	Accepting the shifting of generational roles	a. Maintaining own and/or couple functioning and interests in face of physiological decline, exploration of new familial and social role options b. Support for a more central role for middle generation c. Making room in the system for the wisdom and experience of the elderly; supporting the older generation without overfunctioning for them d. Dealing with loss of spouse, siblings and other peers and preparation for own death. Life review and integration

Source: E. A. Carter and M. McGoldrick (eds.), *The Family Life Cycle: A Framework for Family Therapy* (New York: Gardner), 1980. Reprinted by permission.

some parental control. The parent must allow the parent-child relationship to change. If a child becomes disabled, the family changes to adapt to the disability; the mother or father may quit work to care for the child, family finances may become tight, parents have less free time. Similarly, if the primary wage earner loses his or her job, the family adapts to the loss in income; the children may seek work, recreation is cut, the family may be forced to move. The family system adapts to stresses in ways to maintain family continuity while making restructuring possible. The family needs to be able to mobilize alternative transactional patterns if internal or external conditions require restructuring (see Graham-Combrink, 1985 for a developmental systems model).

Virginia Satir (1972) compares the family system to a hanging mobile. In a mobile all the pieces, regardless of size and shape, can be grouped together and balanced by changing the relative distance between the parts. If you think of the family as a mobile, the family members, like parts of the mobile, require certain distances between each other to maintain the balance. Any change in the family mobile— such as a child leaving the family, family members forming new alliances, hostility distancing the mother from the father—affects the stability of the mobile. To form a

Families are somewhat like mobiles. A family tries to maintain its equilibrium by balancing its members in relation to each other much as a mobile balances its parts. If a family member changes his or her position in the family mobile, the family suffers disequilibrium. Such disequilibrium often manifests itself in emotional turmoil and stress. The family may try to restore the old equilibrium by forcing its "errant" member to return to his or her former position or it may adapt and create a new equilibrium with its members in changed relation to each other.

It happens often enough that the lie begun in self-defense slips into self-deception.

JEAN-PAUL SARTRE

new family balance, each member has to change his or her distance from other family members.

☐ THE FAMILY AS AN INFORMATION-PROCESSING UNIT

In family systems analysis, the family is seen as an information-processing unit. It takes input—information from the environment such as a person's mood, an accident, the birth of a child—and processes it according to family rules. The family's response is its output. For example, the family receives input from the husband/father in the form of his loving behaviors. This information is interpreted by individual family members and the family as a unit; each family member individually acts according to the interpretation both his or her interpretation and the family's interpretation.

Family Rules

Rules are patterned or characteristic responses. Family rules are generally unwritten; in fact, most of the time we probably don't even know we have them. They are formed from habit; like any habit, they are difficult to change.

All families have a hierarchy of rules. Individuals have their rules; so does each family member in his or her role as mother, father, son, daughter, and so on. Above individual and member rules are family rules. Family rules are the combined members' rules. They are arrived at either consensually or through power struggles—both of which may be unconscious. These family rules are "policies" that evolve over time, such as "No one will discuss Daddy's drinking." The rules may be overt (openly recognized) or they may be covert (hidden and unrecognized).

Superior to family rules in the hierarchy are what are called "meta-rules." Meta-rules are different from individual and family rules primarily because they are more abstract. If not discussing Daddy's drinking is a family rule, the meta-rule is "Don't discuss anything that will cause a problem." When we talk of conspiracies of silence, we are usually talking about meta-rules. Meta-rules are much more difficult to change.

Laing (1969) illustrates a typical family rule:

A family has a rule that little Johnny should not think filthy thoughts. Little Johnny is a good boy; he does not have to be told not to think dirty thoughts. He never has. They never have *taught* him not to think filthy thoughts. He never has. So, according to the family, and even little Johnny, there is no rule against filthy thoughts, because there is no need to have a rule against what never happens. Moreover, we do not talk in the family about a rule against filthy thoughts, because since there are no filthy thoughts, and no rule against them, there is no need to talk about this dreary, abstract, and even vaguely filthy subject. There is no rule against talking about a nonexistent rule about nonexistent filthy thoughts: and no rule against talking about nonexistent talk about a nonexistent rule about something that is nonexistent.

Feedback

The way each person responds influences every other person through feedback. Let us say the family rule is that no one confronts the father about his yelling at other family members. The wife responds by withdrawing affection, the son goes into his

They are playing a game. They are playing at not playing a game. If I show them I see they are, I shall break the rules and they will punish me. I must play their game, of not seeing I see the game.

R. D. LAING, *KNOTS*

"I can't tell you just now what the moral of that is, but I shall remember it in a bit."

"Perhaps it hasn't one," Alice ventured to remark.

"Tut, tut, child!" said the Duchess. "Everything's got a moral, if only you can find it."

LEWIS CARROLL, *ALICE IN WONDERLAND*

room and shuts the door, a daughter tries to placate her father. These responses become new input. The father feels that his daughter is supportive of him; he is angry at his wife for withdrawing. The mother is angry at her daughter for responding to her father's yelling and ignoring her. The son is an absent member of the family.

Feedback is the basic principle for processing information. Feedback permits the system to alter its activities, structure, and direction to further its own goals. Information is processed through a feedback loop. The input becomes the system's output; the output in turn becomes new input. There are two types of feedback: negative feedback and positive feedback. Negative feedback tells the system that everything is okay, that things are normal or returning to normal. In the example above, the feedback the father received was basically negative feedback because no one confronted him and said his behavior was unacceptable. The feedback did not tell him that he had to change.

Positive feedback tells the system that things are changing, that the system is deviating from its normal state. Positive feedback *amplifies* the original input. If the mother had responded to her husband's yelling behavior by telling him to stop, he would have received positive feedback. But because the family rule is to avoid confrontation, the father received no such positive feedback. Imagine, however, that the family rule was to meet outburst with outburst. If the family rule called for anger, then the output would be quarreling and discussion in the family. This angry output then would become new input into the family system. If the family rule allows the unbridled expression of anger, then the anger will be amplified until it goes out of control. This process causes polarization and escalation. It is known as the *positive feedback spiral*.

Family rules and meta-rules are also known as *rules of transformation* because they transform or interpret input as it becomes output. If the husband loses his job, a family rule might call for blaming. As a result of the family rule, the job loss might generate hostility, family disintegration, and a major crisis. A different family could have different rules dealing with similar input. If the husband loses his job, the family rule might call for unity. In this case, the output would be family solidarity, which might reduce the crisis (Broderick and Smith, 1979).

Changing Family Rules

To show how the family processes information, let's take an extended example used by Mary Hicks and her colleagues (Hicks et al., 1983). As you read this example, remember that we are discussing an *interactive* process. The family reacts to input, processes the input, and then sends it back to the environment as output, which becomes additional input. Here is an illustration concerning a woman working outside the home:

- *Environmental input*: Men and women are equal.
- *Wife's rule*: "I should be able to work outside the home and get help from my husband in household work."
- *Husband's rule*: "I should give my full energy to my career; my wife should support me in this."
- *Family rule*: "Husband should work and wife should be responsible for child care and housework."

"When I want to look at the world I see it the way you do. Then when I want to see it I look at it the way I know and I perceive it in a different way."

"Do things look consistently the same every time you see them?"

"Things don't change. You change your way of looking, that's all."

CARLOS CASTENADA, *A SEPARATE REALITY*

- *Meta-rule*: "Husband is primary and wife is subordinate."
- *System output*: "Husband is breadwinner; wife supports husband through child care, housekeeping, and additional income."

Look at these rules carefully. This family system is experiencing stress because the wife is out of step with the rest of the system. The wife is providing *positive feedback*. Through a process of negotiation between husband and wife, the rules in the hierarchy will change, although it will probably take considerable time and negotiation.

New rules evolve as society continues to change and move toward more egalitarian norms. "After many cycles and over an extended period of time," noted Hicks and her colleagues, "the combination of inputs, rule transformations, and outputs may result in a situation such as the one that exists in contemporary Western societies, in which an egalitarian norm is evolving, but with husbands' and families' rules still slow to change." If the family evolves these norms, the rules for the preceding example may be somewhat like the following:

- *Environmental input*: "Men and women are equal."
- *Wife's rule*: "I should be able to work and receive help from my husband."
- *Husband's rule*: "My wife should be able to work, but my career is primary."
- *Family rule*: "Wife can work; husband will share in household work and child care as long as it does not interfere with his career."
- *Meta-rule*: "Husband is senior partner; wife is junior partner."
- *Family system output*: "Wife will increase financial contribution and husband will increase child care and household work."

As Hicks and her coworkers point out, some changes have been made in all components, but the husband's, family's and meta-rules are still resistant to an egalitarian ethic. Since disparity still exists, stress will continue.

☐ OPEN, CLOSED, AND RANDOM FAMILIES

Family systems can be categorized as closed, open, and random systems (Kantor and Lehr, 1975).

Closed-Type Families

In closed-type systems, families emphasize obligations, conformity to tradition, and stability. Kantor and Lehr (1975) described the affective qualities of the closed-type system:

The closed-type family strives after an intimacy and nurturance which is stable. Affections are characterized by earnestness and sincerity rather than passion. . . . Loyalties based on blood ties are usually honored above those to friends. Affections are deeply rooted in each member's strong and enduring sense of belonging. Feelings of tenderness predominate. . . . Members' relations with one another are fastidious and sensible. The emotional, or affect, mandate is to *care deeply but be composed*. . . . Durability, fidelity, and sincerity are the closed system's ideals in the affect dimension.

Habit is the enemy of truth; lies deny truth but habit ignores it.

FLOYD ZIMMERMAN

Permanence? Stability! I can't believe it's gone. I can't believe that the long, tranquil life, which was just stepping a minuet, vanished in four crashing days at the end of nine years and six weeks. Upon my word, yes, our intimacy was like a minuet, simply because on every possible occasion and in every possible circumstance we knew where to go, where to sit, which table we unanimously should choose; and we could rise and go, all four together, without a signal from any one of us, always to the music of the Kur orchestra, always in the temperate sunshine, or, if it rained, in discreet shelters. No, indeed, it can't be gone. You can't kill a minuet de la cour.

No, by God, it is false! It wasn't a minuet that we stepped; it was a prison—a prison full of screaming hysterics, tied down so that they might not outsound the rolling of our carriage wheels as we went along the shaded avenues of the Taunus Wald.

FORD MADDOX FORD, *THE GOOD SOLDIER*

Family rules are covert, rigid, and out-of-date; family members are required to change their needs to conform to the family rules. Communication is indirect, unclear; members have a tendency to blame, placate, distract, or be excessively rational. Family members are restricted in their ability to comment about what is going on in their family. Such families often have low self-esteem (Satir, 1972).

Open-Type Families

Open-type families emphasize consent in opinions and feelings in running the family. They seek intimacy and nurturance but not at the expense of the individual's identity. Kantor and Lehr (1975) wrote:

Members are encouraged to reveal their honest feelings and thoughts to each other. Feelings of all kinds are permissible, as long as they are true ones. Members may communicate a greater intensity as well as a larger range of emotions than can those in a closed system. In addition, emotions may be more readly tapped. If a member is not showing his or her feelings, others are free to ask him to do so. . . . Its emotional mandate is to *share and not withhold* whatever is being felt. . . . In sum, responsiveness, authenticity, and the legitimacy of emotional latitude are the open system's major affect ideals.

Families in such a system have high self-esteem. Communication is clear, direct, specific, and honest. The family rules are overt, up-to-date, human; they change as the need arises. Family members are free to comment on anything going on in the family (Satir, 1972).

Random-Type Families

The random-type family emphasizes individual expression; its highest value is for each member to exercise his or her freedom unfettered by either tradition or consent. Free exploration by the individual is the basic purpose of the random-type family. Kantor and Lehr (1975) described the random-type family:

Emotions wander and are characterized by passion. They can be trenchant, profound, caustic, electric, tender, romantic, or hysterical. In short, members' emotions are unlimited. Random family affections are penetrating and penetrable, rapt and quick. Intense emotional moments, which spring unplanned from nowhere, are preferred to planned or habitual experiences. . . . The random affect mandate is to *raise experience to levels of originality and inspiration*.

A monk asked: "How does one get emancipated?" The master said: "Who has ever put you in bondage?"

D. T. SUZUKI

The random-type family is really a roller-coaster family. Its rules call for no rules, for doing what each member wants regardless of the consequences; "I do my thing and you do your thing" is its motto. Little family cohesion exists; self-esteem is basically low, despite appearances of megalomania. Communication is erratic, high decibel, hysterical.

As you look at these family types, how would you identify your family? (Remember, however, that families often combine aspects of these different models.) What are the consequences of being in such a family? If your family of origin is a certain type of family, will the family you create be similar? Why? Can a closed family be transformed into an open family?

UNDERSTANDING YOURSELF

Your Family Rules

Every family has rules governing its behavior. But, as we have seen, these rules are often difficult to pinpoint because they are unwritten, unspoken, and often unconscious. As Laing pointed out, the rules often forbid us to know that we have rules.

Look at the rule about freedom to comment in your family. Freedom to comment refers to the ability of family members to speak their minds freely on any subject (Satir, 1972).

- *What can you say about what you see happening in your family?*
- *To whom can you talk about what is happening?*
- *What do you do if you approve or disapprove of someone or something?*
- *How do you question something you don't understand? Or do you even question?*

After you look at your family's freedom-to-comment rule, think about who made it. How was it made? What was your role in making and maintaining it? What is its function in
your family? Does it bring you closer together or keep you apart? Who enforces the rule? How? What happens when the rule is broken? Who usually breaks the rule?

Now examine your family rules more closely. What are the various rules about the expression of your feelings? Write them down.

- *Environmental rule:*
- *Your rule:*
- *Your mother's rule:*
- *Your father's rule:*
- *Your brother's rule:*
- *Your sister's rule:*
- *Family rule:*
- *Meta-rule:*

What is the purpose of these rules? Who is the dominant rule maker? Have you tried to change the rules? What happened? Are you happy with the rules? How do these rules affect your other relationships with friends, partner, husband or wife?

☐ FAMILY RESISTANCE TO CHANGE

For families to function well, they must adapt to changing circumstances, whether those changes come from outside the family or from inside. But families have a tendency toward inertia (homeostasis). They resist change. This resistance to change is necessary for the family to maintain its unity; but excessive resistance to needed change can be dysfunctional. Several of the ways that families resist change are through scapegoating, pseudomutuality, and what Laing calls "the politics of experience."

Scapegoating

One of the ways that families try to avoid change is to assign blame. The family finds a scapegoat, and all the family problems are viewed as being caused by that person. Scapegoating creates the illusion that an individual rather than the family is responsible. As Napier and Whitaker (1978) pointed out:

Blaming is a very powerful process, the members not only hurling accusations at someone else, but defending themselves in turn. . . . Each feels herself powerless, victimized; she sees the "other" as the one in power, the one who controls her fate. . . . Each reveals an intense awareness of the other person, but a profound lack of awareness of herself. They are not aware of their own feelings, nor do they recognize their own potential for action and change. . . . It is always the other person they talk about, the other person who must change.

Pseudomutuality

One of the most fundamental human needs is to relate to people in intimate ways, expressing our feelings, sharing our laughter and interests as well as our burdens, revealing our hopes as well as our fears. We also need to develop a sense of our own unique identity. Although our identity is the very core of what we are, it is not fixed; we are different today than we were ten years ago.

Relatedness and identity are closely connected; much of our identity is formed through our relations with other people, especially family members. Yet relationships with others eventually may block or freeze vital aspects of our changing identities. A husband fears his wife's desires for independence; a mother fears her daughter growing up. Both try to prevent the other person from changing. People who find themselves constrained by this type of relationship sometimes have only two realistic choices: they must attempt to alter the character of the relationship; if that fails, they may have to end the relationship. Either solution may be very painful; avoiding pain is one reason we resist change. If people resist confronting the alternatives, they may invent a third: they pretend nothing is wrong. Pseudomutuality develops from the third alternative.

It is possible for a man to wholly disappear and be merged in his manners.

HENRY DAVID THOREAU

Mutual and Pseudomutual Responses. The two main types of responses to the problem of relatedness and identity are called mutuality and pseudomutuality. A *mutual* relationship is one in which each person recognizes that the other has interests, desires, and needs that may differ from his or her own. This recognition is more than simple tolerance. It is positively accepting the differences and appreciating what the other brings to the relationship. Neither person feels unloved or threatened by the identity of the other, and each views the other as a unique person rather than a stereotype. In such relationships a man accepts his wife's desire to return to school or begin a career when she finds that she is no longer satisfied with her role as a homemaker. He respects her desire for an identity independent of her family roles. Similarly, a woman accepts her children's growing independence; she does not try to prolong their babyhood but encourages their development as autonomous persons.

In *pseudomutual* relationships, however, people direct their energies toward fulfilling role expectations rather than developing their individual identities. The roles are usually static; changes are seen as threatening. Although people involved in pseudomutual relationships usually feel frustrated, unfulfilled, and unhappy, they may refuse to seek a real solution to their problems.

Characteristics of Pseudomutuality. Psychiatrist Lyman Wynne and his colleagues (1958) described four characteristics of pseudomutual relationships.

1. *Rigidity.* Despite changes in a family's physical and emotional circumstances, roles and role structures remain essentially unchanged. In one family the children

are all in high school; their mother has little to do during the day except watch television and clean house. She is depressed; her life has little meaning. When her children were smaller, she received great pleasure and fulfillment in caring for them; now they have no need for such nurturing. She does not know what to do with herself.

2. *Fear of Change.* She is thinking of returning to work, but a second characteristic of pseudomutuality interferes with this course: there is intense concern about anyone changing his or her roles. Her husband does not want her to return to work; his role is family breadwinner, for which he justifies working at a tedious, meaningless job. He is also afraid that she might leave him if she became financially independent or met someone else at work. She knows that her husband does not want her to return to work. She also feels that her children have grown emotionally apart from her as they have grown older; she wants to hold on to them because they are her only reason for continuing in her mother role. She cannot relate to them except as dependents.

3. *Insistence on Roles as Proper.* A consequence of rigidity and a fear of change is that family members insist their roles are both desired and proper. Because she knows her husband will violently oppose her going to work, she convinces herself that it is wrong to work outside the home. She insists that her children need her. She says she

People often mask their real selves, even in intimate situations.

The imaginations which people have one another are the solid facts of human life.

CHARLES COOLEY

loves being a mother and homemaker, and that *all* women should be mothers and homemakers. She mocks women who seek egalitarian relationships. Her husband agrees with her. "A woman's place is in the home," he says. Their children are largely indifferent to what she does. Her overprotectiveness and demands for affection made them distance themselves from her a long time ago. But they want her to stay at home so that they do not have to assume responsibilities such as cleaning, cooking, or doing the laundry.

4. *Absence of Spontaneity.* All these factors converge in a fourth characteristic of pseudomutuality: an absence of spontaneity, novelty, warmth, and affection in family interactions. The woman cannot discuss her depression with her husband because that would violate a basic family rule: "No one rocks the boat." So she represses her spontaneous feelings which could lead to her discovering that she wants to go to work. Her husband acts accordingly; he does not want to inquire too deeply into his wife's feelings because he too knows she is depressed and in need of change. The children feel the tension in the house; they stay away as much as possible. They are polite rather than warm. They return only to eat, sleep, or watch television—which is another escape from their family.

In such families people do not ask how others feel or what they desire. Feelings are unexpressed. Originally, psychiatrists believed that pseudomutuality was a characteristic only of severely disturbed families. But most families can be placed somewhere on a continuum between mutuality and pseudomutuality. The masks we wear are not necessarily dysfunctional; they may be necessary adaptations. By making use of masks, for example, children can sometimes lead relatively healthy lives in families that disregard their need to develop autonomy. Such masks also permit compromises and make it possible to avoid minor disagreements. Our roles can facilitate smooth interactions. It is only when our roles are rigid, blocking development and change, that they become destructive.

The Politics of Experience

A third way that families resist change is by playing the politics of experience.

The Definition of Reality. R. D. Laing (1967) developed the idea that struggles often take place within a family over what is defined as real. He called these struggles the *politics of experience.* These struggles take several forms that are often related. One is the struggle to define what is really going on in a family. A couple may constantly fight over money. The husband insists that his wife spends too much on clothes. He is angry at seeing her spend "his" money. The wife insists that she only buys what she needs and, furthermore, that he has no right to control her. He replies that he is not trying to control her, just trying to get her to spend less. What is going on? Are they really arguing about money?—or are they fighting about control and independence? The husband insists they are fighting about her spending habits; the wife maintains they are fighting about control.

Whose Reality Is Real? A second struggle in the politics of experience is over whose definition of experience is going to be validated as real and whose is going to be invalidated. Let us return to the warring couple. She calls him a "bully"; he calls her a "spendthrift." He does not feel he is a bully. He feels that he has always been

No man, for any considerable period, can wear one face to himself, and another to the multitude without finally getting bewildered as to which may be true.

NATHANIEL HAWTHORNE

I do not know what I do not know.

LUDWIG WITTGENSTEIN

There are often struggles within families about the definition of reality and whose definition of reality is going to be accepted.

considerate of her. She denies that she spends money carelessly. They continue arguing about money for almost three months. The husband carefully "explains" their finances to his wife and finally convinces her that he does not care about controlling her. He believes, he says, in egalitarian marriage. They stop fighting about money; she now believes that she is a spendthrift and that her husband was right. She has a clothes budget that they have both agreed on. She "realizes" the conflict was her fault. The resolution, however, is ultimately unsatisfactory: the conflict about money *was* really a conflict about control. Her husband has defined reality according to his terms and she has accepted it. Soon, however, they begin to fight about sex: he accuses her of being cold, she accuses him of being insensitive. Both are wrong. Again, the conflict is about control.

Other Methods of Obscuring Reality

The reality of a marriage or of a family is hidden from its members in other ways too (also see Pollner and Wikler, 1985; Reiss, 1985).

Imperviousness. Imperviousness is one way to ignore reality: people can ignore what is being said to them while pretending to listen. If a woman says she needs some time to herself each day, her husband may agree with her. But he may do nothing to change the situation; he could (but does not) take the children out for a walk or watch them while she goes out. In effect, he is ignoring her. But she will have a hard time making him (and maybe even herself) realize that she is being ignored.

Mystification.   Mystification is another way of disguising what is happening within a family. Experience is mystified when people do something in their own self-interest and then justify what they have done by maintaining that they did it for the good of another. For instance, a father sends his children outside to play when they want to be inside with him. "Go down to the park and play for a while. It will do you good to get outside more." But the father is actually acting for his own good. He is tired and wants to rest. He sometimes complains that he works so hard only because of his family's needs. In reality, he works hard because he likes his career. His children may grow up believing he placed their interests first despite the fact that his own interests always had the highest priority.

Punishment is usually justified as being for the benefit of the person who is being punished rather than the person who is doing the punishing. An angry mother may spank her daughter "for your own good" when in fact the daughter is being spanked because the mother is frustrated. Eventually, the child may believe that being spanked is necessary as she has done something wrong. When the daughter grows up, she may justify (mystify) spanking in the same terms.

Mislabeling.   Mislabeling inner states may also hide reality from family members. A parent may want a child to take a nap. The parent looks at the child and says "You're sleepy" and puts the child to bed. The child, however, is not sleepy. A man is angry but his partner says, "You're very tired, aren't you?" He may begin to believe that whenever he feels angry, he is not really angry but tired.

Double Binds.   Double binds are particularly confusing. The basic ingredient of a double bind is the repetition of a situation in which people are faced "with the dilemma either of being wrong or being right for the wrong reasons or in the wrong way" (Bateson, 1967). Regardless of how they respond, they are punished in some form. A classic double bind involves saying one thing while doing another. For example, a woman greets a man, putting her arm around him affectionately. When his body stiffens and she senses disapproval, she takes her arm away. "Don't you love me, dear?" he asks. She is confused, and he says, "Darling, don't be embarrassed about showing your feelings. People *ought* to show their feelings." He has given one message verbally while his body has given another message that contradicts the verbal one. Over time, the woman is presented with a dilemma: if she wants to keep her relationship with him, she must not show that she cares about him; but she fears he will leave her if she doesn't show affection.

The overall impact of scapegoating, pseudomutuality, the politics of experience, and other methods of obscuring reality is to hide the inner workings of the family from its members. Most of us practice these deceptions to varying degrees (Henry, 1971). Problems may arise when such deceptions are the major part of family interactions. Mostly, these masks and disguises do not destroy the family unit; they simply hide important aspects of family life from view. We are left wondering what *really* is going on in our family, which we thought we knew so well.

"Momma" by Mell Lazarus. Courtesy of Mell Lazarus and New America Syndicate.

☐ STRESS AND THE FAMILY SYSTEM

Life involves constant change to which both the individual and the family must adjust (Bell et al., 1980); change brings stress. It does not matter whether the change is for the better or for the worse; both produce stress.

A high degree of stress may ultimately cause illness. Constant stress is difficult to escape, for one stressful event helps create another. For example, if a man loses his job, he experiences the stress of unemployment. But that one event creates other stresses. He is unable to fulfill his family role as the breadwinner. His wife resents him for his inability to get another job. They quarrel and their relationship is increasingly tense. Both parents take out their frustrations on their children, who in turn become disobedient. The family now verges on disintegration. The wife threatens divorce, the man turns to alcohol, the children withdraw to escape the conflict within the family.

Both individuals and families want to maintain their equilibrium in the face of stress (Reiss, 1981). They want to keep their identity and family structure intact, and they try to do this in many different ways. How a person or family copes with stress determines whether or not it precipitates a crisis. Some stress situations can be easily alleviated, and we can return to our normal state; others are either so charged with meaning or so mishandled that we may enter a state of crisis. The way a family handles stress and crisis depends largely on how it interprets them through its rules.

> We are never deceived: we deceive ourselves.
>
> JOHANN GOETHE

Mishandling Stress

The three most common ways of mishandling stress are *avoidance*, *denial*, or *misidentification*. Psychologist Jerry Lewis (1979) recounts the following incident that shows how families deny the existence of a problem. Lewis was interviewing a family with a severely disturbed fifteen-year-old son who heard voices, thought his teachers were planning to kill him, and carried a loaded gun. Lewis suggested that the boy seemed to be very distressed and struggling with painful feelings. They responded:

MOTHER: Oh, he's . . . well, perhaps a little tense . . . but nothing serious.
FATHER: That's right, doctor, it may be that he isn't quite himself—but Owen will be fine, won't you Owen?
OWEN: They're after me . . . they say . . . (inaudible) . . . killing . . . going to get me.

> When a thing is funny, search it for a hidden truth.
>
> GEORGE BERNARD SHAW

FATHER: That's why we're here—we know that there really isn't anything wrong,
but the principal said Owen couldn't return to school without clearance,
and our family doctor insisted that we see you.

This family dealt with their son's clearly apparent and dangerous disturbance by
denying that it existed.

When people respond to stress with avoidance, denial, or misidentification, they
do not deal realistically with the problem. The son may actually kill someone; or the
family may stabilize around the son's disturbance and continue to function, but it
will function as a disturbed family, not as a healthy one. The stress will still exist
and the different family members—not only the son—may show psychological or
physical symptoms of stress such as fear, anxiety, loss of appetite, ulcers, depression,
insomnia, or lessened sexual drive and response.

Handling Stress

The answers to a number of questions help identify factors that determine how well
a family may handle stress (also see Walker, 1985).

Interpretation of Events.   First, will the family interpret a given event as trivial or
as a major catastrophe? In some families, the love of the parents for their child will
not be affected by the child's failing in high school. Stress is minimal. In others,
such a situation may cause the parents to withdraw their love. Stress is considerable,
and a crisis ensues. The tendency to identify stress as a crisis leads to crisis—a pattern
that will eventually exhaust the family psychologically. Ultimately, a family may be
destroyed by such catastrophic interpretations of events.

Resources.   Second, does the family have the available resources (both emotional
and financial) to deal with stress? Different families have different resources, and
what they have available may not be what they need for a particular crisis. If, say,
the working parent in the family loses his or her job, there may be sufficient savings
to meet house payments and regular living expenses without strain; or the spouse
may go to work if he or she is not already working. Such a family can endure this
kind of stress without severe disruption. But if one of the spouses in the same family,
rather than losing a job, has a prolonged affair, the marriage may flounder and end
in divorce because neither partner is able to deal with the resulting emotional stress.
The highest divorce rates are found among the poor, whose economic resources and
personal relationships are usually strained by living on the edge of crisis. "Lower-
class life is crisis-life, constantly trying to make do with string where rope is needed,"
wrote sociologist S. M. Miller (1970). "Anything can break the string. Individuals
do not develop an image of the world as predictable and as something with which
they are able to cope."

Interaction of Family Members.   Third, how do family members usually interact
with each other (see Kantor and Lehr, 1975)? If the family is tightly knit and orderly,
each person having a place and a specific role in relation to everyone else, then the
family is like a row of dominoes. If something happens to one person, everyone else
will immediately be affected. For instance, if two children have a quarrel, everyone

else in the family immediately steps in to end it. They cannot tolerate anything that disrupts the family unit. Each fight is a crisis to the family. But this response (if it constantly occurs) may alienate the two children who were fighting. They may feel that the others had no right to interfere.

The members of a family at the other extreme may be so distant from each other that they will not respond to problems requiring immediate attention. If one person is having a nervous breakdown, no one may do anything about it. If a child locks himself or herself in a room, does not come out to eat, and cries constantly, no one may respond. Such behavior simply does not touch any other member of the family. It is as if the dominoes were placed a foot apart instead of half an inch. If one falls, none of the others are affected because each is out of range of the other.

External versus Internal Stress.   Fourth, does the stress come from internal or external sources? External events can foster family unity if they are not so constant or overwhelming that they destroy the family. Natural disasters such as floods and hurricanes encourage family cooperation. Families tend to meet these kinds of events head on. Wars and persecution have similar effects. But stress that takes place within the family can break it apart. A parent losing his or her job, a child failing in school, or a parent or child developing an alcohol or drug problem can destroy the same family that heroically withstood a natural disaster or human persecution.

The addition of another family member—a disabled child or adult, an aged parent moving in—can create another kind of internal stress. Families with a developmentally disabled child, for example, experience more stress, have less marital satisfaction, feel less psychological well-being, and have less social support, according to a study of thirty-four developmentally disabled nine-year-olds (Friedrich and Friedrich, 1981). Still another cause of internal stress may be the departure of a family member, whether by death, divorce, prolonged illness, or a stint of military service. Such absence may break up the family structure of interaction and roles; other family members may have to take on new responsibilities; the support of the absent person is lost. The result may be disorientation and confusion (Nelson, 1982). But this kind of loss may also lead to family unification in the face of the crisis.

Internal stresses may be hard to recognize, especially if they are not physical. Most external stresses are visible. We can see a flood or fire or hurricane. But internal stresses are not visible in the same sense. We can see a couple fight and the fight will end; the family unit will still be physically intact. But the fight may leave an invisible emotional wound or scar, however small. Other stresses may aggravate this unseen wound until a family is in crisis without realizing it. The crisis may be unseen although everyone experiences the tension, distance, and anger in the household. But the cause cannot be identified in the same way it could if the house burned down. Family members who are not directly involved in the fighting do not recognize that they contribute to the stress. Children taking sides against one parent or withdrawing can increase the tension. Taking sides isolates the family members from each other, forcing them into antagonistic camps, and withdrawing increases alienation. Harvey Ruben (1976) wrote:

The resolution of a family's internal crisis can only begin to come about when the family accepts itself as the source of the stress and then subsequently proceeds to an accurate identification of each member's role in the crisis and how the crisis is affecting him as well as the whole family. Then the family will be in a position to begin to try to cope.

The human condition is such that pain and effort are not just symptoms which can be removed without changing life itself; they are rather the modes in which life itself, together with the necessity to which it is bound, makes itself felt. For mortals, the "easy life of the gods" would be a lifeless life.

HANNAH ARENDT

FEATURE

Stress and the Family: How Much Can Affect Your Health?

Change, both good and bad, can create stress and stress, if sufficiently severe, can lead to illness. Drs. Thomas Holmes and Minoru Masudu, psychiatrists at the University of Washington in Seattle, have developed the Social Readjustment Rating Scale. In their study, they gave a point value to stressful events. The psychiatrists discovered that in 79 percent of the persons studied, major illness followed the accumulation of stress-related changes totaling over 300 points in one year. Examine the scale that follows. Notice how most directly or indirectly relate to marriage and family. What stresses have you experienced in the past six months? What stresses do you expect to experience in the next six months?

Life Event	Past	Value	Future
Death of spouse	☐	100	☐
Divorce	☐	73	☐
Marital separation from mate	☐	65	☐
Detention in jail or other institution	☐	63	☐
Death of a close family member	☐	63	☐
Major personal injury or illness	☐	53	☐
Marriage	☐	50	☐
Being fired at work	☐	47	☐
Marital reconciliation with mate	☐	45	☐
Retirement from work	☐	45	☐
Major change in the health or behavior of a family member	☐	44	☐
Pregnancy	☐	40	☐
Sexual difficulties	☐	39	☐
Gaining a new family member (e.g., through birth, adoption, oldster moving in, etc.)	☐	39	☐
Major business readjustment (e.g., merger, reorganization, bankruptcy, etc.)	☐	39	☐
Major change in financial state (e.g., a lot worse off or a lot better off than usual)	☐	38	☐
Death of a close friend	☐	37	☐
Changing to a different line of work	☐	36	☐
Major change in the number of arguments with spouse (e.g., either a lot more or a lot less than usual regarding childrearing, personal habits, etc.)	☐	35	☐
Taking out a mortgage or loan for a major purchase (e.g., for a home, business, etc.)	☐	31	☐
Foreclosure on a mortgage or loan	☐	30	☐

☐ SUMMARY

• Family life may be described as the acting out of a drama in which we perform our roles on two kinds of stages: front stage and backstage. *Front-stage* behavior takes place publicly among nonintimates. *Backstage* behavior takes place privately among intimates.

• Systems theory approaches the family in terms of its structure and pattern of interactions. The transactional patterns are maintained by society's and the family's rules. Each family system has a hierarchy of rules, including individual, family, and meta-rules.

• Systems analysts believe that (1) interactions must be studied in the context of

FEATURE–*continued*

Major change in responsibilities at work (e.g., promotion, demotion, lateral transfer)	☐ 29 ☐	
Son or daughter leaving home (e.g., marriage, attending college, etc.)	☐ 29 ☐	
In-law troubles	☐ 29 ☐	
Outstanding personal achievement	☐ 28 ☐	
Wife beginning or ceasing work outside the home	☐ 26 ☐	
Beginning or ceasing formal schooling	☐ 26 ☐	
Major change in living conditions (e.g., building a new home, remodeling, deterioration of home or neighborhood)	☐ 25 ☐	
Revision of personal habits (dress, manners, association, etc.)	☐ 24 ☐	
Troubles with the boss	☐ 23 ☐	
Major change in working hours or conditions	☐ 20 ☐	
Change in residence	☐ 20 ☐	
Changing to a new school	☐ 20 ☐	
Major change in usual type and/or amount of recreation	☐ 19 ☐	
Major change in church activities (e.g., a lot more or a lot less than usual)	☐ 19 ☐	

Major change in social activities (e.g., clubs, dancing, movies, visiting, etc.)	☐ 18 ☐	
Taking out a mortgage or loan for a lesser purchase (e.g., for a car, TV, freezer, etc.)	☐ 17 ☐	
Major change in sleeping habits (a lot more or a lot less sleep, or change in part of day when asleep)	☐ 16 ☐	
Major change in number of family get-togethers (e.g., a lot more or a lot less than usual)	☐ 15 ☐	
Major change in eating habits (a lot more or a lot less food intake, or very different meal hours or surroundings)	☐ 15 ☐	
Vacation	☐ 13 ☐	
Christmas	☐ 12 ☐	
Minor violations of the law (e.g., traffic tickets, jaywalking, disturbing the peace, etc.)	☐ 11 ☐	

Source: Reprinted with permission from the *Journal of Psychosomatic Research*, Vol. 11, pp. 213–218, T. H. Holmes, M.D.; The Social Readjustment Rating Scale © 1967, Pergamon Press Ltd.

the family; (2) family structure can only be seen in its interactions; (3) the family is a purposeful system; (4) family systems are transformed over time.

- Systems theory views families as information-processing units. The family takes input and processes it according to family rules. The information becomes output, which becomes new input in a process called *feedback*. There are two kinds of feedback: *negative feedback* and *positive feedback*. Negative feedback tells the system that everything is normal; there is no need for change. Positive feedback tells the system that things are out of balance. Positive feedback tends to amplify the original input; the situation may escalate in a positive feedback spiral.

- Three types of families are *closed, open,* and *random.* Closed families emphasize obligations, conformity, and stability. Open families emphasize intimacy and nurturance; communication is clear and open. Random families emphasize self-expression, freedom, intense emotions, individualism; communication is erratic.

- Family resistance to change may take place through scapegoating, pseudo-mutuality, and the politics of experience, as well as other ways of obscuring reality.

- *Scapegoating* occurs when one person is blamed as the cause of all family problems.

- *Pseudomutuality* refers to the fulfillment of role expectations at the expense of the development of individual identity. Four characteristics of pseudomutual relationships are as follows: (1) Roles and role structure remain essentially unchanged over time despite changing circumstances. (2) The family has intense concern about anyone changing his or her role. (3) Family members insist that their roles are both desired and proper. (4) Family interactions are characterized by an absence of spontaneity, warmth, and affection.

- The *politics of experience* refers to struggles within the family over what is "real." These struggles take several forms: for example, the struggle to define what is really going on in a family and the struggle over whose definition is going to be accepted.

- Family reality is obscured in various ways, including (1) *imperviousness*, or ignoring what someone says while pretending to listen; (2) *mystification*, or obscuring the true reasons for behavior; (3) *mislabeling*, or assigning the wrong labels to inner stress; and (4) *double binds*, or the dilemma of either being wrong or being right for the wrong reasons or in the wrong way.

- Stress occurs as a result of change. Both families and individuals attempt to maintain equilibrium in the face of stress. Stress may be mishandled through *avoidance, denial,* or *misidentification.* How families handle stress depends on their interpretation of the event, resources, family interactional patterns, and whether the stress is external or internal.

READINGS

A Family In Crisis

AUGUSTUS NAPIER AND CARL WHITAKER, EXCERPT FROM
THE FAMILY CRUCIBLE

In this classic work describing a family in therapy, Napier and Whitaker utilize systems theory to explain what is going on in the Brice family. The family originally came into therapy because of conflict between Claudia, a sixteen-year-old daughter, and her mother, Carolyn. Using systems theory, however, the therapists unravel a much more complicated problem. In such families, triangulation, blaming, and identity diffusion are critical issues. What do these terms signify? Do you believe triangulation is often present in family conflicts? Why? Have you experienced triangulation, blaming, or identity diffusion in your family? How?

We didn't have to look far to find what Jay Haley has called the basic problem in emotional disturbance: the triangle. In almost every instance of "symptomatic" behavior, Haley finds this simple, sad, common story: two parents are emotionally estranged from each other, and in their terrible aloneness they overinvolve their children in their emotional distress. Then these children grow up disturbed and repeat the pattern in their own families.

There was no question that Carolyn and David's marriage was in trouble, though until we mentioned it, this trouble had been only a flitting shadow across their consciousness. But when we brought it up, they admitted it readily: their marriage had been cool and distant for years,

READINGS—*continued*

and it was getting cooler. There also seemed to be little question that Claudia's troubles were intimately related to the problems in the marriage, though the nature of the connection and what could be done about it remained in doubt for a while.

One way of looking at the triangle between the couple and Claudia was to see it in old-fashioned sexual terms. As in Freud's description of the Oedipus and Electra complexes, David, estranged from his wife, began to lean too heavily on his daughter for emotional closeness, and with time this relationship became tinged with an inappropriate sexuality. David didn't recognize it, but he was using Claudia as a wife substitute.

Carolyn didn't realize why she was so angry with Claudia, but it was partly because of the way David stroked Claudia's hair, the way he spoke to her first when he came home in the evening, the fondness in his voice when he talked to her, the amount of time he spent helping her with her homework. Carolyn was, in fact, furiously jealous of her own daughter.

As far as it goes, this analysis of the situation was correct. But there were some obvious problems in this view. One problem is the language of causality: "David became overinvolved with Claudia, and this was the cause of Carolyn's anger." David did something *to* Claudia. But to put it that way is to make David the real villain and the two women mere reactors. This is the old cause-and-effect language of physics, a language that is old-fashioned even in physics. And it is definitely inadequate in helping us analyze the beehive of complexity and complicity in the family.

Look at it this way: David and Carolyn evolved a mutually agreed-up distance in their marriage. For the moment never mind *why*—it just happened. David didn't do it; Carolyn didn't do it. They both did it—by gradual degrees, over a period of years, and unconsciously. But the psychological space between the couple didn't remain a vacuum. Into it moved their children, most prominently Claudia. Nor were the spouses merely cool and aloof from each other. As Claudia grew, she became a pawn in the unspoken but intense conflict between her parents. David could meet some of his needs for emotional closeness by snuggling up to his daughter, and Carolyn could express some of her anger at David indirectly—by yelling at Claudia instead of at David. The couple lived vicariously, indirectly, through their daughter. And this situation was obviously very confusing and painful for Claudia.

But Claudia was more than victim. On some level, she too agreed that she would participate in this folly, partly, one suspects, because she gained power by doing so. Claudia was "promoted" into semiadult status by her parents, and this induction into their marriage gave her a powerful leverage. If Mother said no to a request, Claudia could count on her father as a covert ally, and she would readily defy her mother and get away with it. At times Carolyn was imploring and inadequate in the face of her daughter's defiance, and this came about precisely because of the split between the couple, a split which Claudia knew about and used to her advantage.

So they all were guilty in the unconscious collusion that produced this absurd situation, even Claudia; yet at the same time no single person was guilty *by himself.* It took everyone performing a particular step to produce the whole dance. For a while the dance seemed mutually advantageous, but a point came when it lost its usefulness to the family and became the painful caricature of family life which we saw at the beginning of therapy.

But *why* this crazy war between Carolyn and Claudia that threatened to tear the family apart? Why couldn't Carolyn and David address their conflicts with each other directly? Why destroy Claudia's life by fighting through her? Because, we assume, the couple was simply too frightened of the implications of an open war between them. They loved each other enough, and were dependent enough on each other, for it to be too risky to acknowledge their hostility. Although they appeared distant from each other, beneath the surface they had formed a tight, frightened togetherness. The clear-cut, honest divergence of a good fight was hazardous to this togetherness. The tension had to emerge elsewhere: between Carolyn and Claudia.

An interesting hypothesis about the escalating war between Claudia and her mother is that it was really part of increased tensions within the marriage and that it *helped stabilize that tension.* For various reasons, there was a largely covert increase in the conflict between Carolyn and David, and the family agreed tacitly to help the two of them deal with it by the creation of a war between Carolyn and Claudia. What is more, the war between mother and daughter, however disruptive and tragic it seemed, actually did result in the parents moving closer together. They couldn't help it; they had to cooperate in order to cope with their daughter. Claudia even complained about the result she had helped expedite: "Dad, you're agreeing more with Mother these days."

. . . This is a terrible price to pay for marital stability: the expulsion of one of the children, with great pain, from the family.

An integral part of the family's agony is its fascination with finding someone to blame. Blaming is a very powerful process, the members not only hurling accusations at someone else, but defending themselves in turn. Carolyn is sure that if Claudia would only change, the family would relax. Claudia is certain that if only her mother would change, the family and she would relax. Each feels herself powerless, victimized; she sees the "other" as the one in power, the one who controls her fate.

As Carolyn and Claudia sit looking balefully at each other, each pressuring the other, they betray more than a misunderstanding about issues and ideas. Each reveals an intense awareness of the other person, but a profound lack of awareness of herself. They are not aware of their own feelings, nor do they recognize their own potential for action and change. In the beginning they can't even *talk* about themselves very well, much less consider the possibility that they themselves can be different. It is always the other person whom they talk about, the other person who must change.

Claudia and Carolyn really fail to see each other as separate human beings. They are abstractions to each other; powerful entities; threatening forces; wild images; symbolic strangers in a jungle of anxiety. For Claudia, her mother is Punitive Authority, or Betrayal, or Smothering Fog. To her mother, Claudia is Rebellion, or Ungrateful Scorn, or Intimidation. Who knows what they *really* see as they stare? Does Carolyn see her husband as she looks at her daughter? Does she see her own mother? Herself? A sibling? Enormous complexity is mixed into this fight, giving it a supercharged quality that almost completely obscures the real people. Carolyn certainly doesn't see very clearly the scared, lonely, confused daughter whom Carl and I see, nor does the daughter perceive the painful intimidation and shyness in the mother, or her loneliness. Caught in the storm of anger, each is Threat to the other, not a person.

We are talking about much more than a perceptual problem based on misunderstanding, however. The trouble is far more serious. Perception of Other is rooted in experience of Self, and the limitations the family members have in seeing one another as truly human are really limitations in self-experience. We can't teach people intellectually to see one another differently. First, they must experience *themselves* differently. And that is what this approach to family therapy is all about: experience.

There is an even more serious problem in families than a political war between various family antagonists. The assumption that this is only a sexual-political conflict may overestimate the maturity of the family members. Carl and I believe that in a family where there is a problem of any

seriousness, the family is likely to have a tense, difficult kind of relatedness in which no one member is free to be autonomous and independent. They may not be grown up enough for that, adult though some of them are. There is often a *family-wide symbiosis* which inhibits the individuality of every member. They are so dependent on one another, so afraid of losing one another's support, that in this fear they all agree intuitively not to "rock the boat." They fall into rigid patterns with one another, contriving intricate and tortuous routines that preserve their unity at the expense of their individuality. Carolyn might like to say something direct and challenging to David, but she is afraid to. He might like to go camping alone for a weekend, but he doesn't dare. The family's spontaneity, their creativity, their very liveliness are compromised again and again in the interest of pleasing one another and keeping the peace. None really dares be himself for fear of—what? They don't even know what they are afraid of.

Instead of a family of five separate persons, there is a conglomerate person, *the* family. And instead of the members controlling the family, they are rigidly controlled by their roles in the family system. The family rules them all with a steel hand. This symbiotic togetherness, which is probably basically a response to stress, produces a stress of its own because of the fact that *it threatens the individuality and autonomy of the family members.* Everyone is panicked by the fear of losing his or her individuality in the morass. One of the methods the family evolves to deal with this fear of loss of self is to create conflict. The battles indicate the family's need for separateness, and a war with somebody is one way of developing independence from him or her. The problem is that sometimes the war isn't enough or that it becomes far too destructive and costly.

By the time the family has entered treatment every one of its members is usually crying out about being intimidated by someone. It is clear that each means it. They really do *feel* intimidated. But the husband and wife or mother and daughter who point accusingly at each other, saying, in unison, "You are intimidating me," are not intimidated so much by each other as individuals as by their *mutual need for each other.* Their insecurities are profound enough that, in the interest of security, they subjugate themselves to the relationship and its demands. *It is the relationship, the system, the dance that intimidates them, enslaves them. It is the family itself from which they beg freedom.*

READINGS–*continued*

Family Roles

DAVID KANTOR AND WILLIAM LEHR, *INSIDE THE FAMILY*

In this important work describing systems theory, Kantor and Lehr suggest that there are four basic parts that family members play. What are they? In your family, identify the part each of your family members plays. Describe a situation in which your family members played these parts.

It is our belief that each individual seeks and negotiates for a place in the family system, in order that his personality may be affirmed by the family in ways that are compatible with his own needs and, optimally, with the goals of the family establishment. With this goal in mind, the individual family member consciously develops personal strategies in response to his family's strategies. These strategies are intended to provide him a place within the family in which he can use the space, time, and energy available to him in order to gain access to the targets of intimacy, nurturance, efficacy, and identity he is seeking. Every individual asks and tries to answer, at least for himself, a battery of fundamental questions about his family. Do I have a place here? What is my place? Is it a good place? Is support given or withheld? What are other members like? What is their style? What is my style? Am I alike or different from the rest of my family? If different, dare I show my difference? What alternatives to my family are there for me? Do I have a place somewhere else? One's answers to these questions are the bases for his psychopolitical maneuvers toward other family members. In effect, each individual must decide whether he wants to live in ways that are approved or disapproved by his family, because every family action triggers an individual reaction, and every individual action triggers a family reaction. The lives and processes of individual and family are inextricably bound. As a result, one can gain no real understanding of an individual action or a strategy unless one can also identify those family actions that have stimulated it and those that have occurred in response.

Family observers frequently make the mistake of thinking that family power or love or ideology can be located in one single person and that this one person can employ it for the benefit or detriment of the others. Such mistaken observations are founded on the premise that a certain member can become dominant over the others. All students of family have witnessed such dominance, but we would assert that its existence is due not only to the strategic moves of the "dominant" party, but also to the strategic moves of the family as a whole, including the moves of the "submissive" parties. Even the pathogenic mother, the focus of so much literature on disturbed families. does not wield her power in a vacuum, but with the compliance of a family system made up of members who allow and may even encourage her to exercise such authority. The reality of such individual-family phenomena suggests two rather basic interface questions. How do individual family members, occupying the same social space, work out in observable interactions their psychopolitics toward each other and toward the family as a whole? From the opposite perspective, how do members' separate individual behaviors and strategies reveal their private psychopolitical views, both of themselves and of the family? Our four-player model delineates a conceptual framework in which these and other interactional questions may be coherently addressed.

We contend that members of a family (indeed, members in any social system) have four basic parts to play: *mover, follower, opposer,* and *bystander.* Our premise is that any social action initiated by one member of a family stimulates a reaction from the other members. The initiator of such an action is the mover of the action. The responders are co-movers. They may exercise one of three logical options: following—agreeing with the action taken by the mover; opposing—challenging the action of the mover; or bystanding—witnessing the mover's action but acknowledging neither agreement nor disagreement with it. Any two or more people meeting for the first time have the same basic options at their disposal in the genesis of roles they evolve in relation to each other. Even when there are only two persons present, there are four parts ready to be played, and if the relationship is to continue, all four parts most certainly will be played. This potential for parts remains the same whether the social system consists of two, three, four, seven, nineteen, or two thousand members.

If there are only four parts to be played, how do we justify the claim that our interactional system of analysis applies to contexts in which there are more than four participants? The answer is that any one part can be played by any number of participating players. Consequently, within a sequence any number of people may be playing the various co-moving parts. For instance, there may be three followers, one opposer, and four bystanders of a mover's move. Is it then possible that we might categorize highly individual members into strategic parts that are too broadly defined? We will not do so if we are careful to differentiate among those playing the same part. For example, if there are three followers, each may emphasize something different from the others. Follower A may say to a mover, "Yes, I am with you, sink or swim, because I love you." Follower B may announce, "Regarding this value I believe the same as you." Follower C may suggest, "Anyone who doesn't restrict my freedom has my support." Thus, they each follow the mover's lead, but within different spheres—A in affect, B in meaning, C in power. Though each plays the same part, we can distinguish them from each other by understanding the direction and destination of their separate following strategies. More precisely, the separate players within each part are differentiated by discovering (1) in what order or sequence they act, (2) in what situations and contexts, (3) with what flexibility, (4) in what combinations, (5) according to which meanings and images, (6) with which particular system strategies (including both enabling and disabling strategies), (7) in which access spheres, and (8) toward what targets. Patterns of sequence develop in every family as individual family members tend to play a part or combination of parts more than others. Sometimes a person is associated with a particular part in all six access and target spheres. More often, however, a person characteristically plays one part in one sphere and a different part in another sphere. For instance, a family may be so organized that mother is a mover in its power sphere, in which she experiences father's opposition, whereas in the meaning sphere Father more often exercises the mover op-

tion while Mother stands by and their son plays the follower.

If we envision the spatial organization of the four-player model, the four basic strategic parts encompass all potential moves individuals may make in an interactional system. Together they enable us to perceive, understand, and conceptualize the various patterns of behavior in human systems. Spatially, the mover is often at the center of things. His act of moving defines the space in which an action takes place. The act of following is associated with a validation of the action initiated by the mover. Characteristically, a follower moves in support of the center of action, or else promotes the supportive moves of other members. The opposer either obstructs the action of the mover, or pulls away from it. Persons playing the bystander part tend to place themselves on the periphery of an action field. From that position the bystander has three options: to remain in position as bystander, to move into the action as an opposer or a follower, or to leave the field in order to act as a mover in a new action sequence, to which the other players may or may not respond. As long as the initial action continues and a player maintains his position as a mover, follower, or opposer, he cannot leave the field. Only the bystander can leave the field.

CHAPTER 14

Communication and Conflict Resolution

PREVIEW

To gain a sense about what you already know about the material in this chapter, answer "true" or "false" to the statements below. You will find the answers as you read the chapter.

1. Remaining silent is an effective form of noncommunication. True or false?
2. Always being pleasant and cheerful is the best way to avoid conflict and sustain intimacy. True or false?
3. Nonverbal communication is a significant form of communication in intimate relationships. True or false?
4. Most people feel satisfied about their communication in marriage. True or false?
5. Conflict and intimacy go hand in hand in intimate relationships. True or false?
6. Good communication is primarily the ability to offer constructive criticism and resolve problems effectively. True or false?
7. Coercion is the most frequently used power resource by husbands if disagreement arises between themselves and their wives. True or false?
8. The partner with the least interest in continuing a relationship generally has the most power in it. True or false?
9. If you and your partner disagree about something, you should give in to avoid conflict. True or false?
10. Anger may be an indication that something needs to be changed in a relationship. True or false?

Outline

One of the primary functions of marriage is to provide intimacy. Today, communication has become the very foundation of marriage because intimacy and communication are inextricably intertwined. Through communication we disclose who we are, and through this self-disclosure intimacy grows. Perhaps the most common complaint of married partners is "We don't communicate." But often what is really being said is not that a couple doesn't communicate but something even more basic—that the couple isn't intimate (see Stephen, 1985).

When we speak of communication, we mean more than just the ability to discuss problems and resolve conflicts. We mean communication for its own sake: the pleasure of being in each other's company, the excitement of conversation, the exchange of touches and smiles, the loving silences.

In this chapter we examine nonverbal communication, how to develop communication skills, how to self-disclose, how to give feedback and affirm your partner. We also discuss the relationship between conflict and intimacy, exploring the types of conflict and the role of power in marital relationships. We look at conflicts about children, sex, in-laws, and money. Finally, we explore some ways of resolving conflicts.

☐ NONVERBAL COMMUNICATION

There is no such thing as not communicating. People tend to think of communication as verbal communication. But even when you are not talking, you are communicating by your silence (an awkward silence, a pregnant silence, a tender silence); you are communicating by the way you position your body and tilt your head, through your facial expressions, your physical distance from another person, and so on. (Look around you: How are the people in your presence communicating nonverbally?)

Much of our communication of feeling is nonverbal. We radiate our moods: a happy mood invites companionship; a solemn mood pushes people away. Joy infects;

Married couples who love each other, tell each other a thousand things without talking.

CHINESE PROVERB

depression distances—all without a word being said. Nonverbal expressions of love are particularly effective: a touch, a loving glance, a small gift, a flower left on a pillow—all make up the poetry of love.

One of the problems, however, with nonverbal communication is the imprecision of its messages. Is a person frowning or squinting? Does the smile indicate friendliness or nervousness? A person may be in reflective silence, for example, but we may interpret the silence as disapproval or distance.

Functions of Nonverbal Communication

A recent study of nonverbal communication and marital interaction found that nonverbal communication has three important functions in marriage (Noller, 1984): (1) conveying interpersonal attitudes, (2) expressing emotion, and (3) handling the ongoing interaction.

Conveying Interpersonal Attitudes. Nonverbal messages are used to convey attitudes. Gregory Bateson described nonverbal communication as revealing "the nuances and intricacies of how two people are getting along" (quoted in Noller, 1984). Holding hands can suggest intimacy, sitting on opposite sides of the couch can suggest distance; not looking at each other in conversation can suggest a lack of intimacy or awkwardness.

Expressing Emotion. Our emotional states are expressed through our bodies. A depressed person walks slowly; a happy person walks with a spring. Smiles, frowns, furrowed brows, tight jaws, tapping fingers—all express emotion. Expressing emotion is important because it lets our partner know how we are feeling so that he or she can respond appropriately. It also allows our partner to share our feeling—to laugh or weep with us.

Handling the Ongoing Interaction. Our nonverbal communications help us handle the ongoing interaction by indicating interest and attention. An intent look indicates our interest in the conversation; a yawn indicates boredom. Our posture and eye contact are especially important. Are we leaning toward the person with interest or slumping back, thinking about something else? Do we look at the person who is talking or are we distracted, glancing at other people as they walk by, watching the clock?

Relationship Between Verbal and Nonverbal Communication

The messages we send and receive contain a verbal and a nonverbal component. The verbal part expresses the basic content of the message, while the nonverbal part expresses what is known as the "relationship" or "command" part of the message. The relationship part of the message tells the attitude of the speaker (friendly, neutral, hostile) and how the words are to be interpreted (as a joke, request, or command). The full content of any message has to be understood according to both the verbal and nonverbal parts.

For a message to be most effective, both the verbal and nonverbal components must be in agreement. If you are angry and say, "I am angry" and your facial

Do you hide a spear within a smile?

DOGEN, *A PRIMER OF SOTO ZEN*

No matter how grouchy you're feeling
You'll find the smile more or less healing:
It grows a wreath all around the front teeth,
Thus preserving the face from congealing.

ANTHONY EUWER

The Latin word for inner or innermost is intimus. If one knows, grasps, the inner reality of someone, he grasps the intimus, the inmost character of the person.

THOMAS ODEN, *GAME FREE*

It was fortunate that love did not need words, or else it would be full of misunderstandings and foolishness.

HERMAN HESSE, *NARCISSUS AND GOLDMUND*

FEATURE

Ten Rules for Avoiding Intimacy

If you want to avoid intimacy, here are ten rules that have proven effective in nationwide testing with men and women, husbands and wives, parents and children. Follow these guidelines and you'll never have an intimate relationship.

1. *Don't talk*. This is the basic rule for avoiding intimacy. If you follow this one rule, you will never have to worry about being intimate again. Sometimes, however, you may be forced to talk. If you have to talk, don't talk about anything meaningful. Talk about the weather, baseball, class, the stock market—anything but feelings.

2. *Never show your feelings*. Showing your feelings is almost as bad as talking because feelings are ways of communicating. If you cry or show anger, sadness, or joy, you are giving yourself away. You might as well talk, and if you talk you could become intimate. So the best thing to do is remain expressionless (which, we admit, is a form of communication, but at lease it is giving the message that you don't want to be intimate).

3. *Always be pleasant*. Always smile, always be friendly, especially if something's bothering you. You'll be surprised at how effective hid-

ing negative feelings from your partner is in preventing intimacy. It may even fool your partner into believing that everything's okay in your relationship. Then you don't have to change anything or be intimate.

4. *Always win*. Never compromise, never admit that your partner's point of view may be as good as yours. If you start compromising, that's an admission that you care about your partner's feelings, which is a dangerous step toward intimacy.

5. *Always keep busy*. If you keep busy at school or work, your work will take you away from your partner and you won't have to be intimate. Your partner may never figure out that you're using your work to avoid intimacy. Because our culture values hard work, he or she will feel unjustified in complaining. Incidentally, devoting yourself to your work will nevertheless give your partner the message that he or she is not as important as your work. You can make your partner feel unimportant in your life without even talking!

6. *Always be right*. There is nothing worse than being wrong because it is an indication that you are human. If you admit you're wrong,

---

Words are given to man to enable him to conceal his true feelings.

VOLTAIRE (1694–1778)

expression and voice both show anger, the message is clear. But if you say, "I am angry" in a neutral tone of voice and smile, your message is ambiguous. If you say, "I'm not angry" but clench your teeth and use an angry voice, your message is also unclear. The person you're addressing is left wondering: are you really angry? how angry are you?

Silence as a Nonverbal Message

Of all the nonverbal messages, perhaps the most potentially destructive is silence: the silence that distances the heart, the dark silence of separateness, the silence of fear and mistrust, the silence of hatred itself. One of the most common complaints that wives make about their husbands is that they don't talk. Husbands are called the

FEATURE–*continued*

then you might have to admit your partner's right and that will make him or her as good as you. If he or she is as good as you, then you might have to consider your partner and before you know it, you are intimate!

7. *Never argue.* If you argue, then you might discover that you and your partner are different. If you're different, you may have to talk about the differences so that you can make adjustments. And if you begin making adjustments, you may have to tell your partner who you *really* are, what you *really* feel. Naturally, these revelations may lead to intimacy.

8. *Make your partner guess what you want.* Never tell your partner what you want. That way, when your partner tries to guess and is wrong (as he or she often will be), you can tell your partner that he or she doesn't really understand or love you. If your partner did love you, then he or she would know what you want without asking. Not only will this prevent intimacy but it will drive your partner crazy as well.

9. *Always look out for number one.* Remember, you are number one. All relationships exist to fulfill *your* needs, no one else's. Whatever you feel like doing is okay. You're okay—your partner's not okay. If your partner can't satisfy

your needs, he or she is narcissistic; after all, you are the one making all the sacrifices in the relationship.

10. *Keep the television on.* Keep the television turned on at all times, during dinner, while you're reading, when you're in bed, while you're talking (especially if you're talking about something important). This rule may seem petty compared with the others, but it is good preventive action. Watching television keeps you and your partner from talking to each other. Best of all, it will keep you both from even noticing that you don't communicate. If you're cornered and have to talk, you can both be distracted by a commercial, a seduction scene, or the sound of gunfire. When you actually think about it, wouldn't you rather be watching "Miami Vice" than talking with your partner anyway?

We want to caution the reader that this list is not complete. Everyone knows additional ways for avoiding intimacy. These may be your own unique inventions or techniques you learned from your boyfriend or girlfriend, friends, or parents. To round out this compilation, list additional rules for avoiding intimacy on a separate sheet of paper.

"silent partner" in marriage. Helen Rowland (quoted in Pogrebin, 1983) remarked wryly, "Marriage is the only thing that affords a woman the pleasure of company and the perfect sensation of solitude at the same time" (see Newman, 1985).

Silence is also a prominent feature of communication of adolescents in their families. Dolores Curran (1983) wrote:

The most common reaction technique of youths in conflict with their families is silence. Often silence is the only reaction acceptable in the family. If youths can't expose what's bothering them for fear of ridicule or censure, or if they're not allowed to argue, then they will revert to silence. The sad irony discovered by so many family therapists is that parents who seek professional help when their teenager becomes silent have often denied him or her any other route but silence in communicating. And although they won't permit their children to become angry or to reveal doubts or to share depression, they do worry about the silence that results. Rarely do they see any relationship between the two.

If you don't say anything, you won't be called on to repeat it.

CALVIN COOLIDGE

The cruelest lies are often told in silence.

ROBERT LOUIS STEVENSON (1850–1890)

Healthy families recognize positive nonverbal communication as an important part of their lives. They display positive emotions nonverbally through touching, gifts, favors, smiles, cooperativeness. They don't depend merely on words to discover if something is bothering a member. They are quick to pick up on nonverbal clues.

☐ DEVELOPING COMMUNICATION SKILLS: FEELINGS AND SELF-AWARENESS

Why People Don't Communicate

We can learn to communicate, but it is not always easy. Male sex roles, for example, work against the idea of expressing feelings. The traditional male sex role calls for men to be strong and silent, to ride off into the sunset—alone. If men talk, they talk about things—cars, politics, sports, work, money—but not about feelings. Also, people may have personal reasons for not expressing their feelings. They may have strong feelings of inadequacy: "If you *really* knew what I was like, you wouldn't like me." They may feel ashamed or guilty of their feelings: "Sometimes I feel attracted to other people and it makes me feel guilty because I *should* only be attracted to you." They may feel vulnerable: "If I told you my *real* feelings, you might hurt me." They may be frightened of their feelings: "If I expressed my anger, it would destroy you." Finally, people may not communicate because they are fearful that their real feelings and desires will create conflict: "If I told you how I felt, you would get angry" (also see Cole and Cole, 1985).

Obstacles to Self-Awareness

Before we can communicate with others, we must first know how we ourselves feel. Yet we often place obstacles in our way. First, we suppress "unacceptable" feelings, especially feelings such as anger, hurt, and jealousy. After a while, we don't even consciously experience them. Second, we deny our feelings. If we are feeling hurt and our partner looks at our pained expression and asks us what we're feeling, we may reply, "Nothing." We may feel nothing because we have anesthetized our feelings. Third, we displace our feelings. Instead of recognizing that we are jealous, we may accuse our partner of being jealous; instead of feeling hurt, we may say our partner is hurt.

Becoming aware of ourselves requires us to become aware of our feelings. Perhaps the first step toward this self awareness is realizing that feelings are simply emotional states—they are neither good nor bad in themselves. As feelings, however, they need to be *felt*, whether they are warm or cold, pleasurable or painful. They do not necessarily need to be acted out or expressed. It is their acting out that holds the potential for ill.

. . . analysis is not the only way to resolve inner conflicts. Life itself still remains a very effective therapist.

KAREN HORNEY

Feelings as Guides for Actions

Feelings are valuable guides for actions. If we feel irritated at a partner, our irritation is a signal that something is wrong and we can work toward change. But if we suppress or deny our feeling—perhaps because we are fearful of conflict—we do not have the impetus for change. The cause remains and our irritation increases until it is blown out of proportion; a minor irritation or annoyance becomes a major source of anger. If we are bothered by our partner leaving dirty dishes scattered around the house, we can tell our partner how we feel and he or she has the option to change. But if we suppress or deny our irritation, the piles of dirty dishes may grow to towering heights, green mold may invade the house, and we may feel alienated from our partner without giving him or her the opportunity to change. Finally, when we become aware of our feeling, it may have grown to such intensity that we fly into a rage when we see one dirty plate, crash the dish to the floor, slam the door and walk out.

She generally gave herself very good advice (though she seldom followed it).

LEWIS CARROLL

☐ SELF-DISCLOSURE

Through communication we reveal ourselves to others. Revealing ourselves is called *self-disclosure*. We live much of our lives playing roles—as student, worker, husband, wife, son, or daughter. We live and act these roles conventionally. They do not necessarily reflect our deepest selves. If we pretend we are only these roles and ignore our deepest selves, then we have taken the path toward loneliness, isolation, and despair. We may reach a point at which we no longer know who we are. More than one hundred years ago Nathaniel Hawthorne cautioned, "No man, for any considerable period, can wear one face to himself, and another to the multitude, without finally getting bewildered as to which may be true." In the process of revealing ourselves to others, we discover who we ourselves are. In the process of sharing, others share themselves with us. Self-disclosure is reciprocal.

Whenever a feeling is voiced with truth and frankness . . . a mysterious and far-reaching influence is exerted. At first it acts on those who are inwardly receptive. But the circle grows larger and larger. . . . The effect is but the reflection of something that emanates from one's own heart.

I CHING

Keeping Closed

If I do not disclose myself, I receive no feedback from my partner. Our relationship remains closed. We are isolated, untouched by each other. If I do not disclose myself, neither will my partner. My silence obliges him or her to remain silent. If I do not disclose myself, I will remain ignorant of myself for my partner will not speak to me

"Why did I ever marry below my emotional level?"

truthfully. My partner will tell me only what he or she believes I want to hear. But my partner does not know truly what I want to hear, because I am afraid to reveal myself.

Men are less likely than women to disclose intimate things about themselves (Gilbert, 1976). (See the reading by Nancy Henley, "Male/Female Differences in Communication.") Having been taught to be strong, they are more reluctant to express feelings of weakness or tenderness (Cozby, 1973). Women find it easier to disclose their feelings, perhaps because from earliest childhood females are encouraged to express their feelings (see Notarius and Johnson, 1982). These differences can drive wedges between men and women. One sex does not understand the other. One man complained of his wife: "Yakketty-yakkers, that's what girls are. Well, I don't know; guys talk too. But, you know, there's a difference, isn't there? Guys talk about things and girls talk about feelings" (Rubin, 1976). The differences may plague a marriage until neither partner knows what the other wants; sometimes partners don't even know what they want for themselves. In one woman's words (quoted in Rubin, 1976):

I'm not sure what I want. I keep talking to him about communication, and he says, "Okay, so we're talking; now what do you want?" And I don't know what to say then, but I know it's not what I mean. I sometimes get worried because I think maybe I want too much. He's a good husband; he works hard; he takes care of me and the kids. He could go out and find another woman who would be very happy to have a man like that, and who wouldn't be all the time complaining at him because he doesn't feel things and get close.

What is missing is the intimacy that comes from self-disclosure. People live together, are married, but they feel lonely. There is no contact. And the loneliest loneliness is to be alone with someone to whom we want to feel close.

How Much Openness?

Can too much openness and honesty be injurious to a relationship? How much should intimates reveal to each other? Some studies suggest that less marital satisfac-

If you are afraid of loneliness, don't marry.

ANTON CHEKHOV

When in doubt, tell the truth.

MARK TWAIN

A half truth is a whole lie.

YIDDISH PROVERB

To say what we think to our superiors would be inexpedient; to say what we think to our equals would be ill-mannered; to say what we think to our inferiors is unkind. Good manners occupy the terrain between fear and pity.

QUENTIN CRISP

tion results if partners have too little or too much disclosure; a happy medium offers security, stability, and safety. One study on marital communication and satisfaction suggested that the question most likely to distinguish happy from unhappy marriages was "Does your spouse have a tendency to say things that would be better left unsaid" (Bienvenu, 1970)? Those who were unhappily married were considerably more likely to respond "yes" than those who were happily married.

Not everyone agrees with this too-little/too-much curvilinear model of communication. In an alternate, linear model of communication, the greater the self-disclosure, the greater the marital satisfaction, provided the couple is highly committed to the relationship and willing to take the risks of high levels of intimacy (Gilbert, 1976). Such a relationship offers greater flexibility, commitment, and intimacy, but also greater risk. Two researchers who tried to test the two approaches empirically found evidence to support only the linear model (Jorgensen and Gaudy, 1980). They cautioned, nevertheless, that couples unskilled or not used to high levels of self-disclosure might need to understand its significance before embarking on such a highly charged undertaking.

How far are couples committed to openness in dating relationships? One study of 231 college couples found that a fairly high proportion said they "fully" disclosed their thoughts to their dates in most areas (Rubin et al., 1980). Men as well as women appeared committed to an ethic of openness. However, the researchers found some limiting (and "traditional") aspects of this self-disclosure. Women revealed more than men in certain areas, including their fears. Although this study may indicate a substantial change, it may also simply reflect a shift in conventions rather than behaviors; it may be more acceptable to appear sensitive rather than silent.

☐ GIVING FEEDBACK

Self-disclosure is reciprocal. If we self-disclose, we expect our partner to self-disclose as well. As we self-disclose, we build trust; as we withhold self-disclosure, we erode trust. To withhold ourselves is to imply that we don't trust the other person, and if we don't trust the other person, the other person will not trust us.

A critical element in communication is feedback. If someone self-discloses to us, we need to respond to his or her self-disclosure. This response is called *feedback*. The purpose of feedback is to provide constructive information to increase another's self-awareness of the consequences of his or her behavior on you.

If your partner discloses to you his or her doubts about your relationship, you can respond in a number of ways. Among these are remaining silent, venting anger, expressing indifference, or giving helpful feedback. Of these responses, feedback is the most constructive and most likely to encourage change. (See the reading by Judith Viorst, "How to Fight Fair.")

You can remain silent; silence, however is generally a negative response, as powerful perhaps as saying outright that you do not want your partner to self-disclose this type of information. You can respond angrily, which may convey the message to your partner that self-disclosing will lead to arguments rather than understanding and possibly change. Third, you can remain indifferent, not responding to your partner's self-disclosure. Fourth, you can acknowledge your partner's feelings as valid (rather than "right" or "wrong") and disclose how you feel in response to his or her statement.

Consider what life would be like if everyone could lie perfectly or if no one could lie at all. . . . If we could never know how someone really felt, and if we knew that we couldn't know, life would be more tenuous. Certain in the knowledge that every show of emotion might be a mere display put on to please, manipulate, or mislead, individuals would be more adrift, attachments less firm. And if we could never lie, if a smile was reliable, never absent when pleasure was felt, and never present without pleasure, life would be rougher than it is, many relationships harder to maintain. Politeness, attempts to smooth matters over, to conceal feelings one wished one didn't feel—all that would be gone. There would be no way not to be known, no opportunity to sulk or lick one's wounds except alone.

PAUL ECKMAN, *TELLING LIES: CLUES TO DECEIT IN THE MARKETPLACE, POLITICS, AND MARRIAGE*

We longed to have no secret from each other. We yearned for the courage to surrender ourselves. But when it finally happened, we were no longer living together.

Our needs were impossible to satisfy.

That became our hell. Our drama.

There was a door in his study, which we covered with hearts and crosses and tears and black rings. Symbols of what we had been to each other that day.

Nothing existed outside ourselves. No joy or pain that had not been inflicted by the other.

Slowly this became the grounds for the breakup.

LIV ULLMAN, *CHANGING*

UNDERSTANDING YOURSELF

Styles of Miscommunication

Virginia Satir (1972) noted that people use four styles of miscommunication: placating, blaming, computing, and distracting. Read the following descriptions and try to identify which (if any) style you and your partner tend to use.

Placaters. Placaters are always agreeable. They are passive, speak in an ingratiating manner, and act helpless. If a partner wants to make love when they do not, they will not refuse because that might cause a scene. No one knows what a placater really wants or feels—and they themselves often do not know.

Blamers. Blamers act superior. Their bodies are tense, they are often angry, and they gesture by pointing. Inside, they feel weak and want to hide this from everyone (including themselves). If a blamer runs short of money, the partner is at fault; if a child is conceived by accident, the partner is responsible. The

blamer does not listen and always tries to escape responsibility.

Computers. Computers are very correct and reasonable. They show only printouts, not feelings (which they consider dangerous). "If one takes careful note of my increasing heartbeat," a computer may tonelessly say, "one must be forced to come to the conclusion that I'm angry." The partner computer does not change expression and replies, "That's interesting."

Distractors. Distractors act frenetic and seldom say anything relevant. They flit about in word and deed. Inside, they feel lonely and out of place. In difficult situations distractors light cigarettes and talk about school, politics, business, anything to avoid discussing relevant feelings. If a partner wants to discuss something serious, distractors change the subject.

It is a luxury to be understood.

RALPH WALDO EMERSON (1803–1892)

The only way to speak the truth is to speak lovingly.

HENRY THOREAU

Excuses are always mixed with lies.

ARABIC PROVERB

This acknowledgment and response is constructive feedback. It may or may not remove your partner's doubts, but it opens up the possibility for change, whereas silence and anger to not.

Some guidelines (developed by David Johnston for the Minnesota Peer Program) will help you engage in dialogue and feedback with your partner:

1. *Focus on "I" statements.* An "I" statement is a statement about *your* feelings: "I feel annoyed when you leave your dirty dishes on the living-room floor." "You" statements tell another person how *he* or *she* is, feels, or thinks: "You are such a slob. You're always leaving your dirty dishes on the living-room floor." "You" statements are often blaming or accusatory. Because "I" messages don't carry blame, the recipient is less likely to be defensive or resentful.

2. *Focus on behavior rather than on the person.* If you focus on a person's behavior rather than on the person, you are more likely to secure change. A person can change behaviors, but not himself or herself. If you want your partner to wash his or her dirty dishes, say, "I would like you to wash your dirty dishes; it bothers me when I see them gathering mold on the living-room floor." This statement focuses on behavior that can be changed. If you say, "You are such a slob, you never clean up after yourself," then you are attacking the person and he or she is likely

There can be no intimacy without conflict, but for conflict to enhance intimacy each partner must learn to give and receive feedback.

to respond defensively. "I am not a slob. Talk about slobs, how about when you left your clothes lying in the bathroom for a week?"

3. *Focus feedback on observations rather than on inferences or judgments.* Focus your feedback on what you actually observe rather than what you think the behavior means. "There is a towering pile of your dishes in the living room" is an observation. "You don't really care about how I feel because you are always leaving your dirty dishes around the house" is an inference that a partner's dirty dishes indicate a lack of regard. The inference moves the discussion from the dishes to the partner's caring. The question "What kind of person would leave dirty dishes for me to clean up?" implies a judgment: Only a morally depraved person would leave dirty dishes around.

4. *Focus feedback on observations based on a more-or-less continuum.* Behaviors fall on a continuum. Your partner doesn't *always* do a particular thing. When you say your partner does something sometimes or even most of the time, you are actually measuring behavior. If you say your partner always does something, you are distorting reality. For example, there were probably times (however rare) when your partner picked up the dirty dishes. "Last week I picked up your dirty dishes three times" is a measured statement. "I *always* pick up your dirty dishes" is an exaggeration that will probably provoke a hostile response.

5. *Focus feedback on sharing ideas or offering alternatives rather than giving advice.* No one likes being told what to do. Unsolicited advice often produces anger or resentment because advice implies that you know more about what a person needs to do than the other person does. Advice implies a lack of freedom or respect. By sharing ideas and offering alternatives, however, you give the other person the freedom to decide based on his or her own perceptions and goals. "You need to put away your dishes immediately after you are done with them" is advice. "Having to step around your dirty dishes bothers me. What are the alternatives other than

Wives and husbands are, indeed, incessantly complaining to each other; and there would be reason for imagining that almost every house was infested with perverseness or oppression beyond human sufferance, did we not know upon how small occasions some minds burst out into lamentations and reproaches, and how naturally every animal revenges his pain upon those who happen to be near, without any nice examination of its cause. We are always willing to fancy ourselves within a little of happiness and when, with repeated efforts we cannot reach it, persuade ourselves that it is intercepted by an ill-paired mate since, if we could find any other obstacle, it would be our own fault that it was not removed.

SAMUEL JOHNSON

A sound marriage is not based on complete frankness; it is based on sensible reticence.

MORRIS L. ERNST

my watching my step? Maybe you could put them away after you finish eating, clean them up before I get home, or eat in the kitchen? What do you think?" is offering alternatives.

6. *Focus feedback according to its value for the recipient.* If your partner says something that upsets you, your initial response may be to lash back. A cathartic response may make you feel better for the time being, but it may not be useful for your partner. For example, your partner admits lying to you. You can respond with rage and accusations or you can express your hurt and try to find out why he or she didn't tell you the truth.

7. *Focus feedback on the amount the recipient can process.* Don't overload your partner with your response. Your partner's disclosure may touch deep, pent-up feelings in you, but he or she may not be able to comprehend all that you say. If you respond to your partner's revelation of doubts with a listing of all the doubts you have ever experienced about yourself, your relationship, and relationships in general, you may overwhelm your partner.

8. *Focus feedback at appropriate time and place.* When you discuss anything of importance, choose an appropriate time and place so that nothing will distract you. Choose a time when you are not likely to be interrupted. Turn the television off and take the phone off the hook. Also choose a time that is relatively stress free. Talking about something of great personal importance just before an exam or a business meeting is likely to sabotage any attempt at communication. Finally, choose a place that will provide privacy; don't start an important conversation if you are worried about people overhearing or interrupting you. A dormitory lounge during the soaps, Grand Central Station, a kitchen filled with kids, or a car full of people are inappropriate places.

☐ MUTUAL AFFIRMATION

Good communication includes three elements: (1) mutual acceptance, (2) liking each other, and (3) expressing liking in both words and actions. Mutual acceptance means people accepting each other as they are, not as they would like each other to be. People are who they are and not likely to change in fundamental ways without a tremendous amount of effort, as well as a significant passage of time. The belief that an insensitive partner will somehow magically become sensitive after marriage, for example, is an invitation to disappointment and divorce.

If you accept people as they are, then you can like them for their qualities. Liking someone is somewhat different from being romantically in love. It is not rare for people to dislike those whom they romantically love.

Mutual affirmation means people telling their partners that they like them for who they are, that they appreciate the little things as well as the big things they do. Think about how often you say to your partner, your parents, or your children, "I like you" or "I love you," "I appreciate your doing the dishes," "I like the way you look," "I like your smile." Affirmations are often highest during dating or the early stages of marriage or living together. But as you get to know a person better, you may begin noting things that annoy you or are different from you. Acceptance turns into negation and criticism: "You're selfish," "Why don't you clean up after yourself," "Stop bugging me," "You talk too much."

To get a sense of how much you affirm or negate someone, keep track of your

Words must be supported by one's entire conduct. If words and conduct are not in accord and not consistent, they will have no effect.

I CHING

Pass no judgement, and you will not be judged; do not condemn, and you will not be condemned; acquit, and you will be acquitted; give and gifts will be given to you . . . for whatever measure you deal out to others will be dealt to you in return.

LUKE 6:37–38

Kindness in words creates confidence. Kindness in thinking creates profoundness. Kindness in giving creates love.

LAO-TZE

A little sincerity is a dangerous thing, and a great deal of it is absolutely fatal.

OSCAR WILDE

affirmations and negations. On a sheet of paper label one column affirmations and the other column negations. Each time you make an affirmation of that person, give yourself a plus; each time you make a negation, give yourself a minus. At the end of the day, compare the numbers of pluses and minuses.

If you have a lot of negatives in your interactions, don't feel too badly. Many of our negations are habitual. When we were children, our parents were always negating: "Don't leave the door open," "Don't leave your clothes piled in the bathroom," "Don't chew with your mouth open." How often did they affirm? Once you become aware that negations are often automatic, you can change them. Because negative communication is a learned behavior, you can unlearn it. One way is to consciously make the decision to affirm what you like; too often we take the good for granted and only feel compelled to point out the bad.

People like and love those with whom they feel comfortable, who give them support and reinforcement. They don't like or love those who make them feel uncomfortable, who chip away at their self-respect. If affirmation turns to negation, then a couple is in trouble. For once affirmation goes, so do liking and acceptance.

☐ CONFLICT AND INTIMACY

Conflict between people who love each other seems to be a mystery. We expect love to unify us; but sometimes it doesn't. The coexistence of conflict and love has puzzled human beings for centuries. An ancient Sanskrit poet asked

In the old days we both agreed
That I was you and you were me.
But now what has happened
That makes you, you
And me, me?

Two people do not become one when they love each other, although at first they may have this feeling. Their love may not be an illusion, but their sense of ultimate oneness is. In reality, they retain their individual identities, needs, wants, and pasts while loving each other—and the more intimate two people become, the more likely they may be to experience conflict. But it is not conflict itself that is dangerous to intimate relationships—it is the manner in which the conflict is handled.

A tension may exist between the individual's need for maintaining a sense of personal identity and the need of the couple for maintaining stability (Askham, 1976). For personal identity, men and women need relationships in which this identity can continue to develop. They need privacy; they need flexible roles; they need relationships that are flexible enough to incorporate individual change; they need friends with whom to discuss their most intimate thoughts.

While the fulfillment of such needs helps a person achieve a sense of personal identity, it may interfere with the stability needs of the relationship. To create stability within a relationship, the couple may have to avoid topics that threaten the relationship or that reveal deep differences. Individual change may be threatening. Intimate friends (especially of the other sex) may appear to compete with the relationship. These conflicting aspects of identity and stability needs can be resolved in several ways, according to Askham. A person may compromise both needs, gaining a limited satisfaction in both areas. A person may stress one need first and then the other. He

The union and interaction of individuals is based upon mutual glances. This is perhaps the purest and most direct reciprocity that exists anywhere. . . . So tenacious and subtle is this union that it can only be maintained by the shortest and straightest line between the eyes, and the smallest deviation from it, the slightest glance aside, completely destroys the unique character of this union. . . . The totality of social relations of human beings, their self-assertion and self-abnegation, their intimacies and estrangements, would be changed in unpredictable ways if there existed no glance of eye to eye. This mutual glance between persons, in distinction from the simple sight or observation of the other, signifies a wholly new and unique union between them.

GEORGE SIMMEL, *SOCIOLOGY*

All intimacies are based on differences.

HENRY JAMES (1843–1910)

Love can be angry . . . with a kind of anger in which there is no gall, like the dove's and not the raven's.

AUGUSTINE

There is perhaps no phenomenon which contains so much destructive feeling as *moral indignation*, which permits envy or hate to be acted out under the guise of virtue.

ERICH FROMM

or she may sacrifice one need to the other. Finally, a person can have one need met in a particular relationship and the other met in a second relationship. This often occurs in extramarital relationships when identity needs are met in the affair and stability needs in the marriage.

Conflict is natural in intimate relationships. That is the paradox of love: the more intimate a couple becomes, the more likely they are to have differences. If this is understood, then the meaning of conflict changes; conflict will not necessarily represent a crisis in the relationship. David and Vera Mace (1979), prominent marriage counselors, observed that on the day of marriage, people have three kinds of raw material with which to work:

First, there are the things you have in common, the things you both like. Second are the things in which you are different, but the differences are complementary. . . . Third, unfortunately, are the differences between us which are not at all complementary, and cause us to meet head-on with a big bang. In every relationship between two people, there is a great deal of those kinds of differences. So when we move closer together to each other, those differences become disagreements.

The presence of conflict within a marriage or family does not necessarily indicate that love is going or gone. It may mean just the opposite.

□ TYPES OF CONFLICT

Basic Versus Nonbasic Conflicts

If conflict unites marriages, what tears marriages apart? Paradoxically, it is also conflict. Two types of conflict affect the stability of a relationship: basic and nonbasic. Basic conflicts challenge the fundamental assumptions or rules of a relationship, whereas nonbasic conflicts do not.

Basic Conflicts. Basic conflicts revolve around carrying out marital roles and the functions of marriage and the family, such as providing companionship, work, childrearing, and so on (see Chapter 1). It is assumed, for example, that a husband and wife will have sexual relations with each other. But if one partner converts to a religious sect that forbids sexual interaction, a basic conflict is likely to occur because the other spouse considers sexual interaction part of the basic marital premise. No room for compromise exists in such a matter. If one partner cannot convince the other to change his or her ground, the conflict is likely to destroy the relationship. Similarly, despite recent changes in family roles, it is still expected that the man will work to provide for the family. If he decides to quit work altogether and not function as a provider in any way, he is challenging a basic assumption of marriage. His partner is likely to feel that his behavior is unfair. Conflict ensues. If he does not return to work, she is likely to leave him.

Nonbasic Conflicts. Nonbasic conflicts do not strike at the heart of a relationship. If the husband wants to change jobs and move to a different city, the wife may not want to move. This may be a major conflict, but it is not a basic one. The husband is not unilaterally rejecting his role as a provider. If a couple disagree about the frequency of sex, the conflict is serious but not basic because both agree on the desirability of sex in the relationship. In both these cases, resolution is possible.

Against all the evidence of his senses the man in love declares that he and his beloved are one, and is prepared to behave as if it were a fact.

SIGMUND FREUD

Some people are proud of their handful of justice and commit outrages against all things for its sake, till the world is drowned in their injustice.

FRIEDRICH NIETZSCHE

The return of understanding after estrangement: Everything must be treated with tenderness at the beginning so that the return may lead to understanding.

I CHING

Epitaph on His Wife

Here lies my wife; here let her lie!
Now she's at rest.
And so am I.

JOHN DRYDEN

Be to her virtues very kind,
Be to her faults a little blind.

MATTHEW PRIOR (1664–1721)

The types of conflicts are basic and nonbasic, personality and situational. Nonbasic and situational conflicts may be difficult but they can be resolved through negotiation and compromise. Basic conflicts, which involve fundamental marital roles and assumptions, and personality conflicts are more difficult if not impossible to resolve.

Situational Versus Personality Conflicts

Some conflicts occur because of a situation and others occur because of the personality of one (or both) of the partners.

Situational Conflicts. Situational conflicts occur when at least one partner needs to make changes in a relationship. Such conflicts are also known as *realistic* conflicts. They are based on specific demands like putting the cap on the toothpaste, dividing housework fifty-fifty, sharing child-care responsibilities, and so on. Conflict arises when one person tries to change the situation about the toothpaste cap, housework, or child care.

> "You're irresponsible, but for reasons for which you may not be entirely responsible."
>
> PETER DE VRIES, *MADDER MUSIC*

Personality Conflicts. Personality conflicts arise, not because of situations that need to be changed, but because of personality, such as needs to vent aggression or dominate. Such conflicts are essentially unrealistic. They are not directed toward making changes in the relationship but simply toward releasing pent-up tensions. Often this takes the form of violence: slapping, hitting, pushing, and shoving. Whereas situational conflicts can be resolved through compromise, bargaining, or mediation, personality conflicts often require a therapeutic approach. Other such personality conflicts pit a compulsive type individual against a free spirit or fastidious personality against a sloppy one.

> Keep thy eyes wide open before marriage, and half shut afterwards.
>
> BENJAMIN FRANKLIN, *POOR RICHARD'S ALMANAC*, 1738

Power Conflicts

The politics of family life—who has the power, who makes the decisions, who does what—can be every bit as complex and explosive as politics at the national level. Power is the ability or potential ability to influence another person or group (Scanzoni, 1979). Most of the time we are not aware of the power aspects of our relationships.

One reason for this is that we tend to believe that intimate relationships are based on love alone. Another reason is that the exercise of power is often subtle. When we think of power, we tend to think of coercion or force; as we shall see, marital power takes many forms. A final reason is that power is not constantly exercised. Power comes into play only when (1) an issue is important to both people and (2) people have conflicting goals.

Changing Sources of Marital Power. Traditionally, husbands have held ultimate authority over their wives. In Christianity, the subordination of wives to their husbands has its basis in the New Testament. Paul stated: "Wives submit yourselves unto your husbands, as unto the Lord. For the husband is the head of the wife, even as Christ is the head of the Church: and he is the savior of the body. Therefore, as the Church is subject unto Christ, so let the wives be to their own husbands in everything" (Colossians 3:18–19). Such teachings reflected the dominant themes of ancient Greece and Rome. Western society continued to support wifely subordination to husbands. The English common law stated: "The husband and wife are as one and that one is the husband." A woman assumed her husband's identity, taking his last name on marriage and taking up her husband's domicile.

The courts have institutionalized these power relationships. The law, for example, supports the traditional division of labor in most states. The husband is legally responsible for supporting the family and the wife is legally responsible for maintaining the house and rearing the children. She is legally required to follow her husband if he moves; if she does not, she is considered to have deserted him. But if she moves and her husband refuses to move with her, she is also considered to have deserted him (Weitzman, 1981).

However, absolute control of the family by the husband has substantially declined since the 1920s and an egalitarian standard for sharing power in families has taken much of its place (Sennett, 1980). The wife who works has especially gained more power in the family. She has greater influence in deciding family size and how money is to be spent (Safilios-Rothschild, 1969). Her status has risen to that of *junior partner*; few women achieve absolute equality with husbands in power, resources, and authority (Scanzoni, 1979). With the commitment to egalitarian relationships, however, men must exercise their power differently and more subtly. Since husbands continue to exercise dominant power while theoretically believing in egalitarian relationships, a tension exists between ideology and reality. Sociologist William Goode (1963) observed: "One partial resolution of the . . . tension is to be found in the frequent assertion from families of professional men that they should not make demands which would interfere with his work: he takes preference as a *professional*, not as a family head or as a male."

The formal and legal structure of marriage makes the male dominant, but the reality of marriage may be quite different. Sociologist Jessie Bernard (1972) made an important distinction between authority and power in marriage. Authority is based in law but power is based in personality. A strong, dominant woman is likely to exercise power over a weak, passive man simply by force of her personality and temperament. Bernard wrote: "Power, or the ability to coerce or to veto, is widely distributed in both sexes, among women as well as among men. And whatever the theoretical or conceptual picture may have been, the actual day-to-day relationships between husbands and wives have been determined by the men and women themselves. . . . Thus, keeping women in their place has been a universal problem, in spite of the fact that almost without exception institutional patterns give men positions of authority over them."

If we want to see how power really works in marriage, we must look beneath the stereotypes we hold of men and women. Women have considerable power in marriage, although they often feel they have less than they actually do. They fail to recognize their power because cultural norms theoretically put power in the hands of their husbands and they look at norms rather than their own behavior (Turk and Bell, 1976). A woman may decide to work, even against her husband's wishes, and she may determine how to discipline the children. Yet she may feel that her husband holds the power in the relationship because he is supposed to be dominant. Similarly, husbands often believe they have more power in a relationship than they actually do because they only see traditional norms and expectations (Cromwell and Olson, 1975).

Bases of Marital Power. Power is not a simple phenomenon. According to French and Raven (1959), there are six bases of marital power: (1) *coercive power*, based on the fear that the partner will punish the other; (2) *reward power*, based on the belief that the other person will do something in return for agreement; (3) *expert power*, based on the belief that the other has greater knowledge; (4) *legitimate power*, based on acceptance of roles giving the other person the right to demand compliance; (5) *referent power*, based on identifying with the partner and receiving satisfaction by acting similarly; and (6) *informational power*, based on the partner's persuasive explanation.

Raven and his colleagues (1975) studied 746 men and women in Los Angeles to see how common these various sources of power were. Coercion and reward were not particularly significant. Among wives, women described the source of their husbands' power as expert (37 percent), referent (36 percent), and legitimate (18 percent). Among husbands, men described the source of their partners' power as referent (48 percent), legitimate (22 percent), and expert (21 percent). Women tended to attribute the source of their husbands' power to expertness. By contrast, men tended to attribute referent power to their wives.

The basis of power varied according to the domain. Decisions to visit a friend or relative tended to be based on legitimate (43 percent) or referent (27 percent) power. Cleaning or repairing something in the house tended to be based on legitimate (35 percent) or expert (28 percent) power. Significantly, the basis of a spouse's power also varied according to marital satisfaction. Among highly satisfied couples, 49 percent attributed their spouses' power to referent power and 2 percent to coercion. Among those couples not satisfied at all, only 21 percent said their spouses' power was referent, whereas 42 percent believed their spouses' power lay in coercion (see also Bell et al., 1981).

Relative Love and Need Theory. Another way of looking at the sources of marital power is *relative love and need theory*, which explains power in terms of the individual's involvement and needs in the relationship. Each partner brings certain resources, feelings, and needs to a relationship. Each may be seen as exchanging love, companionship, money, help, and status with the other. What each gives and receives, however, may not be equal. One partner may be gaining more from the relationship

If I speak in the tongues of men and of angels, but have not love, I am as a noisy gong or a clanging cymbal.

I CORINTHIANS 13:1

It is almost as important to know what is not serious as to know what is.

JOHN KENNETH GALBRAITH

than the other. The person gaining the most from the relationship is the one who is
most dependent. Constantina Safilios-Rothschild (1970) observed: "The relative degree to which the one spouse loves and needs the other may be the most crucial
variable in explaining total power structure. The spouse who has relatively less feeling
for the other may be the one in the best position to control and manipulate all the
'resources' that he has in his command in order to effectively influence the outcome
of decisions." Love is a major power resource in a relationship. Those who love
equally are likely to share power equally (Safilios-Rothschild, 1976). Such couples
are likely to make decisions according to referent, expert, and legitimate power.

Principle of Least Interest.   Akin to relative love and need as a way of looking at
power is *the principle of least interest.* Sociologist Willard Waller (Waller and Hill,
1951) coined this term to describe the curious (and often unpleasant) situation in
which the partner with the least interest in continuing a relationship has the most
power in it. At its most extreme form, it is the stuff of melodrama: "I will do anything
you want, Charles," Laura said pleadingly, throwing herself at his feet. "Just don't
leave me." "Anything, Laura?" he replied with a leer. "Then give me the deed to
your mother's house." Quarreling couples may unconsciously use the principle of
least interest to their advantage. The less-involved partner may threaten to leave as
leverage in an argument: "All right, if you don't do it my way, I'm going." The threat
may be extremely powerful in coercing a dependent partner, while having little effect
if coming from the dependent partner because he or she has too much to lose to be
persuasive. The less-involved partner can easily call the bluff.

Power Versus Intimacy.   The problem with power imbalances or the blatant use
of power is their negative effect on intimacy. As Ronald Sampson (1966) observed in
his study of the psychology of power, "To the extent that power is the prevailing force
in a relationship—whether between husband and wife or parent and child, between
friends or between colleagues—to that extent love is diminished." If partners are not
equal, self-disclosure may be inhibited, especially if the powerful person believes his
or her power will be lessened by sharing feelings (Glazer-Malbin, 1975). Women
who feel vulnerable to their mates may withhold feelings or pretend to feel what they
do not (Halleck, 1969). Unequal power in marriage may encourage power politics.
Each may struggle with the other to keep or gain power (Cadden, 1973).

It is not easy to change unequal power relationships after they become embedded
in the overall structure of a relationship. Yet they can be changed. Talking, understanding, and negotiation are the best approaches. Still, in attempting changes, a
person may risk estrangement or the breakup of a relationship. He or she may weigh
the possible gains against the possible losses in deciding whether change is worth the
risk.

Genuine intimacy appears to require equality in power relationships. Decision
making in the happiest marriages seems to be based not on coercion or tit-for-tat but
on caring, mutuality, and respect for the other person.

☐ AREAS OF CONFLICT

Even if, as Tolstoy suggested, every unhappy family is unhappy in its own way, still
marital conflicts tend to center around certain issues, especially communication,

children, sex, money, how to spend leisure, in-laws, infidelity, housekeeping, and physical abuse. In this section, we focus on childrearing, sex, money, and relatives.

Fighting About Children

Conflict about children is experienced by as many as half the couples who come into counseling. Sometimes the conflict is about differences in childrearing beliefs between parents; other times the conflict is between parents and children. Conflicts with children become most intense during adolescence, when the children are seeking to establish independent identities. This is also the period during which marital satisfaction is at its lowest point. Fortunately for both parents and children, the children are eventually launched (sometimes pushed) from home; once children leave home, marital satisfaction generally reaches its highest point since the arrival of the first child. (Parent-child relations are discussed in detail in Chapter 12.)

Fighting About Sex

Fighting and sex can be intertwined in several different ways (Strong and Reynolds, 1982). A couple can have a specific disagreement about sex that leads to a fight. One person wants to have sexual intercourse and the other does not, so they fight. A couple can have an indirect sex fight. The woman does not have an orgasm, and after intercourse her partner rolls over and starts to snore. She lies in bed feeling angry and frustrated. In the morning she begins to fight with him because he never does his share of the housework. The housework issue obscures why she is really angry. Sex can also be used as a scapegoat for nonsexual problems. A man is angry that his wife calls him a lousy provider. He takes it out on her sexually by calling her a lousy lover. They fight about their lovemaking rather than the issue of his provider role. A couple can fight about the wrong sexual issue. A woman will berate her partner for being too quick in sex, but what she is really frustrated about is that he is not interested in oral sex with her. She, however, feels ambivalent about oral sex ("Maybe I smell bad"), so she cannot confront him with the real issue. Finally, a fight can be a cover-up. If a man feels sexually inadequate and does not want to have sex as often as his partner, he may pick a fight and make his partner so angry that the last thing she would want to do is to have sex with him.

It is hard to tell during a fight if there are deeper causes than the one a couple is fighting about. Are you and your partner fighting because you want sex now and your partner doesn't? Or are there deeper reasons involving power, control, fear, or inadequacy? If you repeatedly fight about sexual issues without getting anywhere, then the ostensible cause may not be the real one. If fighting does not clear the air and make intimacy possible again, you should look for other reasons for the fights. It may be useful to talk with your partner about why the fights do not seem to accomplish anything. Step back and look at the circumstances of the fights, what patterns occur, and how each of you feels before, during, and after a fight.

Money Conflicts

An old Yiddish proverb puts the problem of managing money quite well: "Husband and wife are of the same flesh but they have different purses." Money is a major

Marriage is one long conversation, chequered by disputes.

ROBERT LOUIS STEVENSON (1850–1894)

Silence is the one great art of conversation.

WILLIAM HAZLITT

For neither man nor angel can discern
Hypocrisy, the only evil that walks
Invisible . . .

JOHN MILTON

source of marital conflict. Intimates differ about spending money probably as much as or more than any other single issue. One nationwide study found that 54 percent of the families studied frequently argued about money (Yankelovich, Skelly, and White, 1975). Among those families with financial worries, 64 percent argued frequently about money. The most frequently argued-about money subjects included money in general, 59 percent; need for family to economize, 47 percent; wasting money, 42 percent; unpaid bills, 38 percent; keeping track of where money is spent, 33 percent; saving for the future, 25 percent; borrowing money, 17 percent.

Why People Fight About Money. Couples disagree or fight over money for a number of reasons. One of the most important reasons is power. Reuben Hill and Howard Becker observed: "Money is a source of power that supports male dominance in the family. . . . Money belongs to him who earns it, not to her who spends it, since he who earns it may withhold it." Earning wages has traditionally given men power in families. A woman's work in the home has not been rewarded by wages. As a result, women have been placed in the position of having to ask their husbands for money. In such an arrangement, if there are disagreements, the woman is at a disadvantage. If she is deferred to, the old cliché, "I make the money but she spends it," has a bitter ring to it. But as women increasingly participate in the work force, power relations within families are shifting. Studies indicate that women's influence in financial and other decisions increases if they are employed outside the home (McDonald, 1977).

Another major source of conflict is allocation of the family's income. Not only does this involve decisions about who makes the decision but it also includes setting priorities. Is it more important to pay a past due bill or to buy a new television set to replace the broken one? Is a dishwasher a necessity or a luxury? Should money be put aside for long-range goals or should immediate needs (perhaps those your partner calls "whims") be satisfied? Setting financial priorities plays on each person's values and temperament; it is affected by basic aspects of an individual's personality. A miser cannot be happily married to a spendthrift. Yet we know so little of our partner's attitudes toward money before marriage that a miser might very well marry a spend-thrift.

Dating relationships are a poor indicator of how a couple will deal with money matters in marriage. Dating has clearly defined rules about money: the man pays, both pay separately, or each pays alternately. In dating situations each partner is financially independent of the other. Money is not pooled as it usually is in marriage, and power issues do not necessarily enter spending decisions, since each has his or her own money. Differences can be smoothed out fairly easily. Both are financially independent before marriage but are financially interdependent after marriage. It is the working out of financial interdependence in marriage that is often so difficult.

Talking About Money. Talking about money matters is difficult. People are very secretive about money. It is considered poor taste to ask people how much money they make. Children often do not know how much money their family earns; sometimes spouses don't know either. One woman recently remarked that it is easier to talk about sexual issues that money matters: "Money is the last taboo," she said. But, as with sex, our society is obsessed with money.

We find it difficult to talk about money for several reasons. First of all, we don't

Money is often a difficult subject to discuss. One way to begin talking about money is for each partner to make a separate monthly budget and then compare the two.

want to appear unromantic or selfish. If a couple is about to marry, to discuss attitudes toward money may lead to disagreements, shattering the illusion of unity or selflessness. Second, sex roles make it difficult for women to express their feelings about money. Women are traditionally supposed to defer to men in financial matters. Third, since men tend to make more money than women, women feel their right to disagree about financial matters is limited. This is especially true if the woman is a homemaker and does not make a financial contribution. She herself tends to devalue her economic contribution through child care and housework.

> We are all inclined to judge ourselves by our ideals; others by their acts.
>
> HAROLD NICHOLSON

One way for you and your partner to begin talking about money is to each make out a budget for one month. Then sit down and compare notes. What are the areas of agreement and disagreement? What do these say about priorities and values? How can you resolve your differences? Another approach is to imagine that you have $25 left over at the end of the month to spend in whatever way you choose. How would you spend it? Would your partner agree to spending it in that manner if the money belonged to both of you? How would your partner spend it?

In-Law Conflicts

Many men dread their mother-in-law; myths have grown up around her; bad jokes and clichés abound. Throughout the world, the mother-in-law is someone to avoid. In northern Australia, a man who speaks to his mother-in-law can be put to death. In some parts of the South Pacific, both must take their own lives if they speak. In Yucatan, Mexico, the Mayan Indians believe that a man who meets his mother-in-law face to face will become sterile; whenever he ventures into her territory, he takes elaborate precautions. Mothers-in-law are believed by Navajo men to cause blindness;

> The greatest thing in family life is to take a hint when a hint is intended—and not to take a hint when a hint isn't intended.
>
> ROBERT FROST

hence Navajo mothers are forbidden even to attend their daughters' weddings (Schlien, 1962).

Ironically, with so much ado about mothers-in-law, it is usually wives, not husbands, who have the greatest mother-in-law difficulties. The bond between the mother and her children is frequently intense in American culture. Much of the mother's performance as a woman is judged according to whether she is a good mother. Rearing her children, she teaches her daughter to be a good wife, to look after the emotional and physical needs of her future husband. She likewise rears her son to be a good husband. But being a good husband is basically defined as being independent and (at the same time) dependent on a woman to take care of physical and emotional needs. When a daughter marries, the new son-in-law does not compete directly with the mother's role. But when a son marries, his wife takes care of him, replacing his mother as the person who does the cooking, mending, straightening up, listening, and caring. The mother judges and criticizes the way her daughter-in-law performs these functions. As Leslie (1976) points out:

> The wife is thrown into direct competition with the husband's mother and will be judged in terms of her ability to keep house, cook, and otherwise cater to her husband's needs; moreover, she competes with a woman with twenty or more years' experience on the job. The husband will be judged too—but not so much in terms of his performance as a husband. He will be judged in terms of his success in the occupational world.

In-law difficulties are closely associated with age. Young couples who are trying to separate from their families of origin have greater in-law difficulties than older couples. A study of wives showed that of those who married between the ages of seventeen and nineteen, only 45 percent reported an excellent adjustment with their in-laws (Landis and Landis, 1973). By contrast, 63 percent reported excellent in-law adjustment if they were twenty-four years or older when they married. Another study suggested that in-law difficulties decreased as the couple got older (Blood and Wolfe, 1960).

The roots of in-law difficulties lie in the need for young adults to be independent of their parents. This is difficult to achieve. If parents (especially the mother) encourage the married son or daughter to continue being dependent, the other spouse is liable to view the mother as interfering. Dependence after marriage is considered legitimate only between husband and wife. Dependence of married children on their parents is unacceptable and violates basic loyalty patterns. (See the reading by Jean Marzollo, "Marital Tasks: Breaking Away from Family Ties," in Chapter 10.)

☐ ANGER AND CONFLICT

Differences can lead to anger and anger transforms differences into fights, creating tension, division, distrust, and fear. Most people have learned to handle anger by either venting or suppressing it. David and Vera Mace (1980) suggest that most couples go through a love-anger cycle. When a couple come close to each other, they may experience conflict and they recoil in horror, angry at each other because just at the moment they were feeling close their intimacy was destroyed. Each backs off; gradually they move closer again until another fight erupts, driving them away from each other. After a while, each learns to make a compromise between closeness and distance to avoid conflict. They learn what they can reveal about themselves and what they cannot. Because closeness brings conflict, they stop being close and their relationship becomes empty and meaningless.

Another way of dealing with anger is by suppressing it. Suppressed anger is dangerous because it is always there, simmering beneath the surface. Ultimately, it leads to resentment, that brooding, low-level hostility that poisons both the individual and the relationship.

Anger can be dealt with in a third way: recognizing it as a symptom of something that needs to be changed. If we see anger as a symptom, then we realize what is important is not venting or suppressing the anger but finding its source and eliminating it. David and Vera Mace (1980) wrote:

> When your disagreements become conflict, the only thing to do is to take anger out of it, because when you are angry you cannot resolve a conflict. You cannot really hear the other person because you are just waiting to fire your shot. You cannot be understanding; you cannot be empathetic when you are angry. So you have to take the anger out, and then when you have taken the anger out, you are back again with a disagreement. The disagreement is still there, and it can cause another disagreement and more anger unless you clear it up. The way to take the anger out of disagreements is through negotiation.

☐ CONFLICT RESOLUTION

There are a number of ways to end conflicts. You can give in, but unless you feel that the conflict ended fairly, you are likely to feel resentful. You can try to impose your will through the use of power, force, or the threat of force. But using power to end conflict leaves your partner with the bitter taste of injustice. Finally, you can end the conflict through negotiation. In negotiations both partners sit down and work out their differences until they can come to a mutually acceptable agreement.

Conflicts can be solved through negotiation in three major ways: (1) agreement as a gift, (2) bargaining, and (3) coexistence.

Agreement as a Gift

If you and your partner disagree on an issue, you can freely agree with your partner as a gift. If you want to go to the Caribbean for a vacation and your partner wants to go backpacking in Alaska, you can freely agree to go to Alaska. An agreement as a gift is different from giving in. When you give in, you do something you don't want to do. But when you agree without coercion or threats, the agreement is a gift of love. As in all exchanges of gifts, there will be reciprocation. Your partner will be more likely to give you a gift of agreement. This gift of agreement is based on referent power, discussed earlier.

Bargaining

Bargaining means making compromises. But bargaining in relationships is different from bargaining in the marketplace or in politics. In relationships you don't want to get the best deal for yourself but the most equitable deal for both you and your partner. At all points during the bargaining process, you need to keep in mind what is best for the relationship as well as for yourself and trust your partner to do the same. In a

Anger causes a man to be far from the truth.

HASIDIC SAYING

Argument is the worst sort of conversation.

JONATHON SWIFT (1667–1745)

What manner of communications are these that you have one with another?

LUKE XXIV:17

Without forgiveness life is governed by . . . an endless cycle of resentment and retaliation.

ROBERTO ASSAGIOLI

In love it is enough to please each other by loveable qualities and attractions; but to be happy in marriage it is necessary to love each other's faults, or at least to adjust to them.

NICHOLAS CHAMFORT

marriage both partners need to win. The purpose of conflict in a marriage is to solidify the relationship, not make one partner the winner and the other the loser. To achieve your end by exercising coercive power or withholding love, affection, or sex is a destructive form of bargaining. If you get what you want, how will that affect your partner and the relationship? Will your partner feel you are being unfair and become resentful? A solution has to be fair to both or it won't enhance the relationship.

Coexistence

Sometimes differences can't be resolved but they can be lived with. If a relationship is sound, differences can be absorbed without undermining the basic ties. All too often we regard differences as threatening rather than as the unique expression of two personalities. If one person wants to go to the Caribbean for vacation and the other wants to go backpacking, each can take a separate vacation. Or, rather than being driven mad by the cap left off the toothpaste, you can probably learn to live with it.

Deep-seated preferences cannot be argued about—you cannot argue a man into liking a glass of beer.

OLIVER WENDELL HOLMES, JR.

☐ SUMMARY

- Communication includes both *verbal* and *nonverbal communication.*

- The functions of nonverbal communication are to convey interpersonal attitudes, express emotion, and handle the ongoing interaction. For communication to be unambiguous, verbal and nonverbal messages must agree. Silence can be a particularly destructive form of nonverbal communication.

- Barriers to communication are the male sex role (because it discourages the expression of emotion), personal reasons such as feelings of inadequacy, and the fear of conflict.

- To express yourself, you need to be aware of your own feelings. We prevent *self-awareness* through *suppression, denial,* and *displacement.* A first step toward self-awareness is realizing that our feelings are neither good nor bad but are simply emotional states.

- *Self-disclosure* is the revelation of yourself to another. Without self-disclosure, a relationship remains closed. Men are less likely to self-disclose than women.

- According to some researchers, both low and high self-disclosure are related to low marital satisfaction (curvilinear model). Other researchers maintain that high self-disclosure is related to high levels of marital satisfaction, although it entails greater risks (linear model).

- *Feedback* is constructive response to another's self-disclosure. Giving constructive feedback includes (1) focusing on "I" statements, (2) focusing on behavior rather than the person, (3) focusing feedback on observations rather than on inferences or judgments, (4) focusing feedback on the observed incidence of behavior, (5) focusing feedback on sharing ideas or offering alternatives rather than giving advice, (6) focusing feedback according to its value to the recipient, (7) focusing feedback on the amount the recipient can process, and (8) focusing feedback at an appropriate time and place.

- *Mutual affirmation* includes mutual acceptance, mutual liking, and expressing liking in words and actions.

- Conflict is natural in intimate relationships. People must balance personal identity needs against stability needs of the relationship.

- Types of conflict include *basic* versus *nonbasic* conflicts and *situational* versus *personality* conflicts. Basic conflicts may threaten the foundation of a marriage because they challenge fundamental roles; nonbasic conflicts do not threaten basic assumptions and may be negotiable. Situational conflicts are realistic conflicts based on specific issues; personality conflicts are unrealistic conflicts based on the need of the partner or partners to release pent-up feelings.

- Power is the ability or potential ability to influence another person. Traditionally, legal as well as de facto power rested in the hands of the husband, but recently wives have been gaining more actual power in relationships although the power distribution still remains unequal.

- The six bases of marital power are *coercive, reward, expert, legitimate, referent,* and *informational*. These bases of power shift in different domains. Other theories of power include *relative love and need* and the *principle of least interest*.

- Four major sources of conflict include children, sex, money, and in-laws. Conflicts about children can focus on differences in childrearing beliefs between partners or parent-child relations. The latter conflict is highest during adolescence. Conflicts about sex can be specifically sexual disagreements, indirect disagreements in which a partner feels frustrated or angry and takes it out in nonsexual ways, arguments that are ostensibly about sex but are really about nonsexual issues, or disagreements about the wrong sexual issue. Money conflicts occur because of power issues, disagreements over the allocation of resources, or differences in values. In-law conflicts tend to occur most frequently between wives and mothers-in-law in the earlier years of marriage.

- People usually handle anger in relationships by suppressing or venting it. Anger, however, makes negotiation difficult. When anger arises, it is useful to think of it as a signal that change is necessary.

- *Conflict resolution* may be achieved through negotiation in three ways: *agreement as a freely given gift, bargaining,* or *coexistence*.

READINGS

Male/Female Differences in Communication

NANCY HENLEY, EXCERPT FROM *BODY POLITICS*

According to this reading, what are the two widely-held myths regarding sex differences in language? What are some examples from your own experience that support these myths? That challenge them? In classroom discussion and personal conversations, which sex tends to dominate, control, and interrupt? Are there differences in self-disclosure between men and women? If so, what do you think is the cause of these differences—socialization? Power distribution? Heredity?

[There are] two particularly widespread myths about sex differences in language.

Myth I—Do Women Talk Too Much? The first myth is that women speak more and longer than men. This is simply not so. In study after study, men have been found to speak more often and at greater length than women, and to interrupt other speakers more than women do. This finding applies to all kinds of social situations—alone, in single-sex or mixed-sex pairs, and in groups; it has been found at all occupational levels; and it applies to "real-life" couples (e.g., husbands and wives) as well as to experimentally-created dyads and groups.

Sociologist Jessie Bernard has observed that on TV panel discussions males out-talked females by a considerable margin, and that as a general conversational pattern, women have a harder time getting the floor in groups and are more often interrupted than men. The obvious power advantages of monopolizing and controlling conversation can be seen, but there is the additional advantage that studies of leadership have consistently found that those who talk more are perceived as leaders. Thus sheer volume gives power to influence.

As Bernard indicates, women find it difficult to be able to say anything even if they wish to, because they are eminently interruptible. Add to this that they themselves are extremely unlikely to interrupt others (or if they do, are unlikely to be successful at it). Several studies have found that males interrupt more than females; the best research in this area is based on conversations of same-sex and mixed-sex pairs taped unobtrusively in natural settings. Here it was found that 96% of the interruptions, and 100% of the overlaps, in conversation were made by male speakers.

The authors of this last study give us an interesting example of the murder of attempts at assertiveness, in their analysis of silences. They found that overwhelmingly the greatest amount of conversational lapses was exhibited by

females in female–male conversations. Silences were both more frequent and of longer duration following three types of male response: interruption, overlap, and delayed minimal response (giving an *mm-hmm* type response after a long delay instead of within the speaker's utterance, the supportive way). In an example they present, the female speaker's silences seem to grow longer with succeeding delayed minimal responses. If this pattern is true, we can see another example of extinction, behavior being killed off this time by (it seems) negative reinforcement as well as an absence of positive response.

Myth 2—Beast and Bird; How Males and Females Sound. The second myth attributes the high pitch of women's speech to anatomical differences alone. While it is true that there are anatomical differences between females and males that produce slightly higher pitch in females, the anatomical difference is nowhere near so great as to produce the difference that is heard. Recent investigators have concluded that at least some of this difference is learned and constitutes a linguistic convention. *Males and females talk at greatly different pitches because that is the requirement of their social roles*, a requirement so strong that the differences in pitch exceed the expectation from the anatomical differences even in children, before the male voice change of puberty.

The prescription that male voices should be low and female voices high is so strong, also, that any deviation from this expectation produces a powerful effect on other people's impressions of one's personality. Males with high-pitched voices may be reacted to as female in phone conversations and treated accordingly, disregarded in group conversations, and ridiculed behind their backs. But female announcers and newscasters with lower pitch are preferred and hired over other females: since lower pitch is associated with males, who have more authority in our society, it carries more authority when used by females also.

The tendency to hesitate, to apologize, and to disparage one's own statements, all patterns associated with subordinates, are also associated with females. Terms of address, too, as well as reflecting status differences, may reflect sex status; several linguists and psychologists have observed that women are more frequently and readily addressed by their first names than are men, but there are no hard data to support this speculation (other than women's generally more subordinate occupational positions, which of themselves receive subordinate address).

Control of a conversation's direction reflects status and power. Partly because of male patterns of interruption and of female patterns of support and agreement, control of

READINGS–*continued*

conversational topics generally rests with the males, and women may find it difficult or impossible to initiate a topic when conversing with men. That control need not come solely from men's own initiation of topics, but may well flow from their failure to respond to many female-initiated topics. Phyllis Chesler has written,

> Even control of a simple—but serious—conversation is usually impossible for most wives when several men, including their husbands, are present. . . . Very rarely, if ever, do men listen silently to a group of women talking.

Self-Disclosure. Self-disclosure is another aspect of conversation that varies with gender. A number of research studies have found that women disclose more personal information to others than men do, just as subordinates in general are more self-revealing. Women who obtain authoritative positions presumably are less self-disclosing than the rest of us, and like powerful men, keep their cool in ruffling circumstances. Most women, however, have been socialized to display their emotions, their thoughts and ideas. Giving out this information about themselves, especially in the context of inequality, is giving others power over them. Self-disclosure (including emotional display) is not itself a weakness or negative behavior trait: like other gestures of intimacy, it has positive aspects, such as sharing of oneself and allowing others to open up, *when the self-disclosure is voluntary and reciprocal.*

Men's self-disclosure often seems very exclusive: many women will testify about a man, that they alone see his emotional and tender side. They feel privileged at being allowed this intimate peek, and seem to suggest the man's negative public self should be forgiven on the basis of this vulnerable alter-ego. This is a dangerous tradition, however: the more women make it possible for men to dichotomize themselves this way, the less will men free their emotionality, to be shown before others and accepted as an integral part of themselves; and the more entrenched will become the hard side they show to other males, and their deprecation of women, as weak and emotional.

Women function as this kind of emotional service station to men (and their families and to a lesser extent, other women) in other ways relevant in an analysis of power. In particular, they take part in cooling-out anger in men, assisting them to accept inferior status, injustice, and all the daily inequities they are subject to. In this capacity they function to perpetuate the hierarchical system between men as well as to preserve sex roles.

How to Fight Fair
JUDITH VIORST, *REDBOOK*

In this reading, Judith Viorst suggests fifteen ways to keep your fights fair. By fighting fairly, couples can use their inevitable conflicts to solidify rather than destroy their relationships. As you read her fighting rules, ask yourself which ones you tend to follow and which ones you tend to ignore. Do you use different rules when you fight with different people, such as friends, dates, partners, siblings, and parents? Why? What other rules can you add to her list?

I was not fighting fair when I accused Milton of refusing to buy a new car because he was saving the money for the teenaged nymph he was doubtless planning to marry the minute I died an untimely death after the engine of our miserable blue station wagon stalled (yet again) in the middle of a highly trafficked intersection.

Wally was not fighting fair when he blamed his tension and subsequent defeat in the Shadybrook Tennis Club tennis finals on Annabel's not wanting to make love that morning.

And Shari was not fighting fair when she told Mike, who had promised to show up at three and showed up at four, that he was unconsciously perceiving her as the feared and hated mother of his childhood and making her pay for his mother's rejection of him.

No fair!

Now you may want to raise the question of whether it's possible in a marriage to feel furious, hurt, humiliated and/or betrayed and still have sufficient self-restraint to hit above the belt, to fight fair. And you may want to ask another, far more fundamental question: Can two normal people be married and never fight?

I'll start with that second question, to which I have a simple answer: Certainly not.

For the first thing we need to concede is that marriage is a difficult living arrangement and that, as William Dean Howells once wrote, ". . . the silken texture of the marriage tie bears a daily strain of wrong and insult to which no other human relation can be subjected without lesion."

And the next thing we need to concede is that, much as we deeply love and respect our spouses, there will be times when we deeply hate and despise them.

And the third thing we need to concede is that, rational and civilized though we may be, not all our marital differences can be resolved by simply sitting down and *talking* about them. Sooner or later, some feelings we feel and points we need to make will have to be communicated more . . . vigorously.

READINGS–*continued*

That vigorous form of communication is what most people mean when they use the word "fight."

Actually, I have become considerably less of a marital fighter in recent years—I just don't enjoy a good fight the way I used to. And although I still firmly believe that it is sometimes absolutely essential to have a fight, I am now more inclined to ask myself before I launch an attack—or before I respond to one—"Is this fight necessary?"

By that I mean: Will this fight resolve a current problem or prevent a future problem or provide a badly needed emotional outlet? Or will we both just wind up feeling bruised? And sometimes—not always, but sometimes—having decided a fight can't do anything but hurt, I am able to persuade myself not to fight.

But what is a wife who decides not to fight to do with her feelings of anger? Linda offers one ingenious solution. When her husband Phil called from Albany and said that he was tied up and couldn't make the party that he'd practically sworn on his life he was going to make, Linda was apoplectic, but she also knew that she couldn't change his mind. "Hang on, Phil," she told him. "Let me take this in the kitchen." And she put down the phone and ran from the second floor, screaming at the top of her lungs all the way down the stairs: "Miserable, rotten, no-good son of a . . ." and a few other words I'd just as soon not mention. After that, she said, she was able to lift the receiver and ask, with relative calm, "So tell me, Phil, what time *should* I expect you?"

Now there is no point in not having a fight if what we have instead is a cold war (no talking except for basic queries like, "Would you consider it a vicious attack on your masculinity if I asked you to pass the butter?"), or if we translate our repressed rage into bleeding ulcers or headaches, or if we engage in some major marriage-threatening activity like taking a lover or hiring a divorce lawyer. But if we have to fight, and if we want to preserve—not massacre—our marriage, what are the limits we need to set to keep the fight we're fighting clean and constructive? Here, from some fighters I've talked with, are several suggestions.

1. *Avoid paranoid overstatements.* (See Milton and Judy's fight.)

2. *Accept responsibility for your own failures.* (See Wally and Annabel's fight.)

3. *Do not practice psychiatry without a license.* (See Shari and Mike's fight.)

4. *Don't wait too long.* We need to consider the story of the genie in the bottle who, during his first thousand years of incarceration, thinks, "Whoever lets me out will get three wishes," and who, during his second thousand years

of incarceration, thinks, "Whoever lets me out I'm gonna kill." Many of us, like that genie, seem to get meaner and more dangerous the longer our grievances are bottled up.

5. *Know what you want.* My friend Nina says that her idea of a clean fight is the delivery of the following crystal-clear message: "I'm upset; here's why I am; here's what I want"—though it may take some time to figure out what she wants. Recently, for instance, while fighting with her husband yet again about working late at the office night after night, it suddenly struck her that she didn't actually want him to say to hell with the work and miss his deadline, that all she really wanted was for him to say, "I miss you. I miss the baby. I feel terrible about not being home. And you're such a fabulous person for being able to handle everything while I'm gone."

She got it.

6. *Figure out what you're really, really fighting about.* There are many battles about, say, his forgetting to make hotel reservations for the car trip out West, or his failing to fuss over you when you get sick, that blow up into something utterly out of proportion and nasty because what you're really fighting about, and what's getting you so upset, is the thought that he wouldn't have been (a) so negligent or (b) so uncompassionate IF HE LOVED YOU.

But wait a minute. You may be able to avoid hurling a lot of unpleasant accusations at him if you can recognize that what you are really, *really* fighting about, as is often the case, is differences in style, not lack of love. You may need to recognize, for instance, that although, while you were growing up, your daddy always made hotel reservations and got a million brochures and planned every step of a family trip in advance, some people like to improvise when they travel—that improvisation isn't the same as negligence. You may also need to recognize that although, while you were growing up, a sick person got ten glasses of orange juice and tons of attention and permission to fool around with Mommy's jewelry box, your husband's family was stoic about sickness—that not fussing doesn't have to mean not caring. And once you figure out that the real, real fight has nothing to do with IF HE LOVED YOU, you are more likely to have a clean and constructive fight.

7. *Stick to the point.* If you are having a fight about the way he is handling the children, I promise you that it will not advance your argument if you also note that he is overdrawn at the bank, talks with his mouth full and frequently leaves you the car with no gas in the tank.

8. *Stick to the present.* A sense of history is a wonderful thing. Total recall is certainly impressive. Memory and the long, long view surely contribute to the richness of life. But

reaching back in time for crimes committed in, say, 1967, when you're fighting about a crime committed, say, yesterday, contributes—and I speak from experience—only trouble.

For several years, when fighting with my husband, I displayed my capacity for total recall, providing him with what I rather smugly liked to call "a sense of perspective." I would, for instance, point out to him that not only had he forgotten to pick up my blouse at the cleaners' that afternoon, but that he had also failed in his stop-at-the-cleaners' assignments on the following 14 occasions. I would then list the dates and the garments he hadn't picked up, starting with the beige chiffon dress that—because of his carelessness—I wasn't able to wear to our engagement party.

After a couple of decades of this, however, it began to dawn on me that never once did Milton reply to my historical references with a "Hey, thanks for pointing out this destructive pattern of mine; I sure do appreciate it." Instead he replied with, "Bookkeeper! Scorekeeper!" and other far less charming epithets, and the fighting would deteriorate from there. I now follow—and strongly recommend—the statute of limitations my friends Hank and Gail have established: "No matter how perfectly something proves your point, you can't dredge it up if it's more than six months old."

9. *Never, never attack an Achilles' heel.* If your husband has confessed to you that his cruel high-school classmates nicknamed him "The Hairy Ape," and if, in adulthood, he still has fears about being furrier than most, you can—when you are furious—call him every name in the book, but you can't call him that one. I have a friend who (excuse the mixed metaphor) locates her Achilles' heel in "my fat butt, which I always worry about and which my husband has always assured me he loves." She says that if, in the course of a fight, he told her that he'd never liked her butt, she might never forgive him.

Two Achilles' heels that are mentioned so often that they must be universal are sexual performance and parents. It seems that it is tricky enough, in life's mellowest moments, to discuss sexual dissatisfactions with a mate; but to scream in the heat of battle, as Louise confessed she once did, that "At least my first husband knew where to put it," is a rotten idea. And so is calling your mother-in-law an "old bat," even though her own son—your husband—has used those very words on many occasions. For some reason, we all seem to feel that although we're allowed to criticize our parents, it's dirty pool for our spouses to be doing it.

10. *Don't overstate your injuries.* Don't claim—either directly or indirectly—that he is giving you migraines or destroying you psychologically unless he is. Oh, I know that it is sometimes tempting to score a few points by pressing your fingers to your temples and saying, in the middle of a fight, "Quick, get me my pills, the pain is blinding," or "Maybe I ought to go into psychoanalysis." It is also sometimes tempting to burst into tears—particularly of the "you're so brutal you even make strong women weep," muffled-sob variety. But don't. For overstating your injuries is not just dirty fighting; it is, sooner than you can imagine, ineffective. If you want him to believe that he's gone *too* far when he's gone too far, you've got to try to maintain your credibility.

11. *Don't overstate your threats.* Many people, in the course of a fight, make threats they don't mean, like, "If you don't slow down, I'm getting out and walking," or "If you don't shut up, I'm moving to a hotel," or even "If you don't stop seeing her, I'm getting a divorce." The trouble with these threats is that there is always the risk of being called on them and either actually having to, say, get out and walk or losing a lot of face. Like overstatements of injury, these threats—if not followed through—are subject to the "boy who cried wolf" syndrome. Even worse, I know two women whose "if you don't stop seeing her" ultimatums converted painful marital fights into fierce and fatal power struggles, ending in divorces that neither couple, I am convinced, actually wanted.

12. *Don't just talk—listen.* You needn't go along with a word he says, but shut up long enough to let him say it. And pay attention. For as a lawyer friend likes to point out to her spouse in the midst of a fight: "You can disagree with what I say as long as you can repeat my views to *my* satisfaction."

13. *Give respect to feelings as well as to facts.* You are not allowed to say, when your husband tells you that he is feeling ignored or put down, "That's absurd. You shouldn't feel that way." You may argue that perhaps he is overreacting or misinterpreting, but you have to acknowledge that he feels what he feels.

14. *There needn't be one winner and one loser.* You both could agree to compromise. You both could agree to try harder. You each could understand the other's point of view. You also could lose without treating it as a defeat. You also could win (this really takes class!) without treating it as a victory.

15. *When you've finished fighting, do not continue sniping.* This includes doing take-backs like "I said I'd go but I didn't say I'd enjoy it," or staring bitterly out a window because, as you explain when asked what's wrong, "I guess

READINGS–*continued*

my wounds don't heal as quickly as yours do." Nor, after a fight, is it useful to murmur things like "Why is it always my fault?" or "Why am I the one who makes all the concessions?" or—as in the fight between Milton and me—"Now that you've agreed to buy a new car, I only hope I survive until it gets here."

Though of course we are bound to slip, we at least should try to follow these tips. Let's face it: All is *not* fair in love and war. Clean and constructive fighting is better than down and dirty fighting, that's for sure. And fighting by the rules could help us live happily—although scrappily—ever after.

CHAPTER 15

Family Dysfunctions:
Violence and Abuse

PREVIEW

To gain a sense of what you already know about the material covered in this chapter, answer "true" or "false" to the statements below. You will find the answers as you read the chapter.

1. Twenty-five percent of college-educated Americans condone the use of violence in marriage. True or false?
2. Aggression is generally considered to be a desirable trait in our society. True or false?
3. In a number of states, women are prohibited by law from charging their husbands with sexual assault. True or false?
4. Arrest is not an effective deterrent to domestic violence. True or false?
5. Battered children are often perceived by their parents as different from other children. True or false?
6. Most American children have used some sort of violence against a sibling. True or false?
7. One in six Americans has experienced incest. True or false?
8. Nearly everyone knows an alcoholic. True or false?
9. Teenage drug use is increasing in the 1980s. True or false?
10. Certain family characteristics can "immunize" against drug abuse. True or false?

Outline

Violence and severe disruption within the American family are matters of growing national concern. In this chapter we discuss the prevalence and implications of various forms of family violence including spousal abuse, child abuse and neglect, and the abuse of elderly parents. We then examine our society's most tabooed (and increasingly reported) sexual practice, incest. The abuse of alcohol as it relates to family violence is dealt with, as well as the implications of alcoholism and drug abuse for the individual, the family, and society as a whole.

☐ FAMILY VIOLENCE

Violence and *abuse* are two words that are used repeatedly throughout this chapter. *Violence* may be direct and physical or it may take less obvious, psychological forms such as oppression, exploitation, deprivation, or obstruction. Many feminists today see pornography as violence against women. David Gil (1978) defined violence as "acts and conditions which obstruct the spontaneous unfolding of innate human potential, the inherent human drive toward development and self-actualization." Violence may be seen as a continuum, with abuse at one extreme. We use *abuse* in the sense of "misuse" or "overuse." In discussing abusive violence, it is important to look at the continuum as a whole—to be concerned with "families who shoot and stab each other as well as those who spank and shove, . . . [as] one cannot be understood without considering the other" (Straus et al., 1980).

Research Problems

"When was the last time you threatened your wife with a gun or knife?" seems to be a question ill-designed for eliciting a truthful response; yet this is exactly the kind of question to which researchers in the field of family violence must obtain answers. Because the family is essentially a private institution, direct observation of behavior is usually not possible and family members are often reluctant to discuss personal matters with outsiders (especially if the questions involve sensitive or tabooed subjects).

A number of data collection methods may be employed, including individual interviews; collaborative or conjoint interviews; conflict resolution technique, which asks family members about their use of particular modes of resolving conflict, proceeding from less sensitive to more sensitive areas; and projective techniques such as the Rorschach (ink-blot) Test or Thematic Apperception Test, in which the actual purpose of the research is disguised by asking the subject to respond to abstract shapes or "story" pictures (Gelles, 1978a). Even when data are obtained, it is another matter to put them to practical use. For example, researchers tend to look at a particular phenomenon as an entire "forest," whereas clinicians (doctors, counselors, and so on) are concerned with the individual "trees." When dealing with child abuse in a clinical setting, one researcher-turned-clinician remarked in frustration, "I don't care what I wrote—these people are nuts!" (Gelles, 1982).

The Roots of Violence

Every year millions of Americans are intentionally injured by members of their own families. Those nearest and dearest are also those most slapped, punched, kicked, bitten, burned, stabbed and shot. To better understand violence within the family, we must look at its place in the larger sociocultural environment. Aggression is a trait that our society labels as generally desirable (within limits). Getting ahead at work, asserting ourselves in relationships, and winning at sports are all culturally approved actions. If, however, the permissible limits of aggression are ill-defined (as they often are), and if a person lives in an environment that is economically, socially, or psychologically stressful (as many do), the stage is set for some potentially violent action. This violence is likely to occur in the presence of the following factors: (1) The person has learned an "aggressive" response to stress. (2) Such response is the "culturally recognized script for behavior under stress." (3) The situation is potentially "rewarding" for aggression (Straus et al., 1980; see Gelles, 1983, for a theoretical model of family violence based on exchange and social control). Although domestic violence occurs in all major cultural groups and at all socioeconomic levels, it appears to be higher in the lower economic strata and in families where economic hardship is prevalent (Finkelhor, 1983). War contributes to family abuse (Laufer and Gallops, 1985).

Domestic violence makes the family a source of unhappiness and pain for untold numbers of Americans. It has been cited as one of the causes of all types of assaultive behavior and homicide (including political assassination). Violence can perpetuate itself through generation after generation unless the insidious cycle is interrupted (Straus et al., 1980).

☐ BATTERED WOMEN

No one knows for certain how many battered women there are in the United States, but government figures indicate that battering is probably the most common and must underreported crime in the country. Here are some figures concerning violence against women in the United States (McGrath, 1979; O'Reilly, 1983):

Figure 15–1

The three things most harmful to family life according to a 1980 Gallup survey. [From *White House Conference on Families, Families and Economic Well-Being* (Washington, D.C.: U.S. Government Printing Office), 1980.]

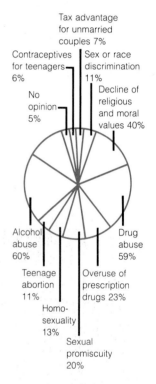

Tax advantage for unmarried couples 7%

Contraceptives for teenagers 6%

Sex or race discrimination 11%

No opinion 5%

Decline of religious and moral values 40%

Alcohol abuse 60%

Drug abuse 59%

Teenage abortion 11%

Overuse of prescription drugs 23%

Homosexuality 13%

Sexual promiscuity 20%

Despite fears to the contrary, it is not a stranger but a so-called loved one who is most likely to assault, rape, or murder us.

RUSSEL AND R. EMERSON DOBASH

One murder makes a villain, millions a hero.

BISHOP BEILBY PORTEUS (1731–1808)

- Every thirty seconds a woman is beaten.
- A National Institute of Mental Health study in 1978 reported that 1.8 million women were beaten by their mates. More recent estimates indicate that nearly six million women may be abused by their husbands or cohabiting lovers each year.
- One-third of female homicide victims were killed by their husbands or lovers.
- According to a Harris poll, 20 percent of all Americans (and 25 percent of college-educated Americans) condone the use of physical violence in marriage.

What Is Battering?

Battering, as used in the literature of family violence, is a catchall term that includes, but is not limited to, the practices of slapping, punching, knocking down, choking, kicking, hitting with objects, threatening with weapons, stabbing, and shooting. (See the reading by Janet Bukovinsky, "The Deadly Rage of a Battered Wife.") Studies have reported that at least one-third of battered women have also been sexually abused by their partners (Finkelhor and Yllo, 1983; O'Reilly, 1983). Although at least seventeen states now have laws permitting the prosecution of husbands for raping their wives, a number of states expressly prohibit women from charging their husbands in these cases. When California adopted a marital rape law, state senator Bob Wilson protested, "If you can't rape your wife, who can you rape?" (O'Reilly, 1983).

The *battered woman syndrome* implies the systematic and repeated use of one or more of the preceding practices against a woman by her husband or lover. The use of physical force against women is certainly not a new phenomenon. It may even be thought of as a time-honored tradition in our culture. The commonly used term *rule of thumb* derives from the legally sanctioned (until the nineteenth century) practice of disciplining one's wife with a switch or rod—provided it was no wider than the disciplinarian's thumb. In recent years the subject of wife battering has gained public notoriety. Whether it is becoming increasingly common or whether the social climate is now permitting freer discussion of it is anybody's guess.

Physical (including sexual) abuse also takes place in dating relationships, especially committed relationships before marriage (Cate et al., 1982; Makepeace, 1981; Roscoe and Benaske, 1985). "Date rape" accounts for about 60 percent of all reported rapes; the actual percentage is probably much higher (Seligman, 1984).

Battered Women and the Law

We have too many high sounding words, and too few actions that correspond with them.

ABIGAIL ADAMS (1744–1818)

Although a gathering trend toward the enforcement of laws against family violence ("domestic disputes") is apparent, in general these situations "have had a police priority somewhere just above that of cats stuck in trees" (McGrath, 1979). The reluctance of police to intervene in these cases may partly reflect the culture's overall approval of a man's "right" to "knock some sense" into "his" woman, but other factors must also be considered. Twenty-two percent of police fatalities and 40 percent of police injuries occur during domestic dispute calls (McGrath, 1979).

Generally, police policy is to smooth over the situation and hope for the best. In most states no arrest is made unless the officer has actually witnessed the assault. In many cases a woman who has brought charges against her mate will subsequently have them dropped—out of fear or love. Also, "all too often . . . state's attorneys

FEATURE

The Mythology of Wife Battering

Here are ten popular myths about battered women in our society. Some of them may apply to some cases, but as generalizations they are not accurate. Usually, these myths are accepted even by the victims of battering, as well as by the batterers themselves.

- The battered woman syndrome affects only a small portion of the population.
- Battered women are masochistic or crazy and are responsible for the violence done to them.
- Battering is mainly restricted to families with low education and low socioeconomic status.

- Minority-group women are more frequently battered than Anglo women.
- Batterers are violent in other relationships.
- Batterers are psychopathic personalities.
- Batterers are not loving partners and parents.
- The police and the law adequately protect battered women.
- A battered woman can always leave home.
- Most of society does not condone domestic violence.

refuse to prosecute and judges refuse to invoke criminal sanctions. In many ways, it is a process that shames women into submission" (Meyer, 1980). The result is a system that has tacitly complied in the injury or death of many of society's female members. One study revealed that in 85 percent of all cases of women murdered by their husbands or lovers, the police had been called on at least one earlier occasion (McGrath, 1979).

In some parts of the country, enlightened law enforcement agencies have recently implemented stricter policies for dealing with offenders in cases of domestic violence. In Minneapolis an experiment in 1981–82 determined that arrest was by far the most effective deterrent to repeated abuse; arrests in domestic violence cases there have tripled. If an officer believes that violence has occurred within four hours before the police arrive on the scene, he or she may make an arrest even if the battered spouse does not wish to press charges. Researcher Lawrence Sherman (quoted in Goodman, 1983) suggested that arrest is a powerful deterrent because generally "the power balance is distorted in favor of the one who has the bigger muscles. When they call the police, women involve the police muscles and even up the power balance."

Profile of a Battered Woman

A typical battered woman probably has a number of the following characteristics (Walker, 1979):

- She has low self-esteem.
- She believes the common myths about battering (see feature, "The Mythology of

Wife Battering," page 455), especially that she is responsible for it. (This is one of the most pervasive and insidious myths—that if a woman is beaten she must deserve it, must have "asked for it," or may possibly even enjoy it.)

- She believes in the traditional home, family, and sex role stereotypes.
- She exhibits physical and psychological symptoms of stress reaction.
- She is manipulative, indirect in approaching problems, and goes to great lengths to keep the peace at home and present a normal façade to the outside world.

"Women are systematically taught that their personal wants, survival, and anatomy do not depend on effective and creative responses to life situations, but rather on their physical beauty and appeal to men. They learn that they have no direct control over the circumstances of their lives" (Walker, 1979). Women who look to their husbands for guidance and approval may become increasingly entrapped by their own *learned helplessness*, especially if their self-esteem is low. If violence is used against them, they may even become desensitized to the accompanying pain and fear. The more it happens, the more helpless they feel and the less they are able to see alternative possibilities.

Profile of a Man Who Batters

A man who systematically inflicts violence on his wife or lover typically has some or all of the following traits (see Edleson et al., 1985 for a literature review):

- He is low in self-esteem (Goldstein and Rosenbaum, 1985).
- He believes the common myths about battering.
- He believes in the traditional home, family, and sex role stereotypes.
- Although usually not in possession of a psychopathic personality, he may be emotionally immature, jealous, and unable to accept responsibility for his actions.
- He may have a Dr.-Jeckyl-and-Mr.-Hyde personality, being capable at times of great charm.
- He uses wife beating and (often) excessive drinking in response to severe stress.
- He may use sex as an act of aggression.
- He believes in the moral rightness of his violent behavior (even though he may "accidentally" go too far).

Sociologist Norman Denzin (1984) defined the violence of batterers as "the attempt to regain, through the use of emotional and physical force, something that has been lost." He wrote:

Men are but children of a larger growth.

JOHN DRYDEN (1631–1700)

The goal of the violent act eludes the man of violence. He is drawn over and over again into the cycle of violence. He can never succeed in establishing his dominance and will over the will of the other. In this sense his violent actions are doomed to failure, yet his very failure destroys the relationship with the one he wishes to control.

The Cycle of Violence

Lenore Walker's (1979) research has revealed a three-phase battering cycle. The duration of each phase may vary, but the cycle goes on . . . and on.

- Phase One: *Tension Building*. Tension is in the air. She tries to do her job well, to be conciliatory. Minor battering incidents may occur. She denies her own rising anger. Tension continues to build.
- Phase Two: *The Explosion*. He loses control. Sometimes she will precipitate the incident to "get it over with." He generally sets out to "teach her a lesson" and goes on from there. This is the shortest phase, usually lasting several hours but sometimes continuing for two or three days or longer.
- Phase Three: *In Love Again*. Tension has now been released and the batterer is contrite, begs forgiveness, and sincerely promises never to do it again. She chooses to believe him and forgives him. This "symbiotic bonding" (interdependence) makes intervention, help, or change unlikely during this phase.

Often the battered woman is surprised by what has touched off the battering incident. It may have been something outside the home—at the husband's job, for example. He may have come home drunk or he may have been drinking steadily at home. Alcohol is implicated in a majority of battering incidents; one study indicated that the husband had been drinking in 74 percent of battering cases (Riggs, n.d.; see Edelson et al., 1985, for a review of conflicting studies about battering and alcohol use). Often battering involves an issue of "women's work"—household duties, child care, pregnancy, and the like. The initial battering incident of a relationship often coincides with the first pregnancy. Miscarriages are five times more common among battered women than among those who are not battered (McGrath, 1979). In a battering relationship not only may the woman suffer physical damage but also she may be seriously harmed by a constant sense of danger and the expectation of violence that weaves a "web of terror" about her (Edelson et al., 1985).

Why Battered Women Stay

All relationships have some degree of mutual dependence, and battering relationships are certainly no different. Women stay in these destructive situations for many reasons. Some common ones are:

- *Economic dependence*. Even if a woman is financially secure, she may not perceive herself as being able to cope with economic matters.
- *Religious pressure*. She may feel that the teachings of her religion require her to keep the family together at all costs, to submit to her husband's will, to try harder.
- *"The children need a father."* She may sincerely believe that even a father who beats the mother is better than no father at all. If the abusing husband also assaults the children, this may be the factor that motivates the woman to seek help (but not always).
- *Fear of being alone*. She may have no meaningful relationships outside her marriage. Her husband may have systematically cut off her ties to other family, friends, and potential support sources. She has nowhere to go and no way to get any real perspective on her situation.
- *Belief in the American dream*. She has accepted without question the "cult of domesticity and beliefs of family harmony and bliss" (Dobash and Dobash, 1979). Even though her existence belies this myth, she continues to believe that is how it should (and can) be.

- *Pity.* She puts her husband's needs ahead of her own.
- *Guilt and shame.* She feels that it is her own fault if her marriage isn't working and that if she left everyone would know she is a failure or her husband might kill himself.
- *Duty and responsibility.* She feels she must keep her marriage vows "till death us do part."
- *Fear for her life.* She believes she may be killed if she tries to escape.
- *Love.* She loves him; he loves her. On her husband's death, one elderly woman (a university professor), spoke of her fifty-three years in a battering relationship (Walker, 1979): "We did everything together. . . . I loved him; you know, even when he was brutal and mean. . . . I'm sorry he's dead, although there were days when I wished he would die. . . . He was my best friend. . . . He beat me right up to the end. . . . It was a good life and I really do miss him."

Alternatives

At the point when a woman finds that she can leave an abusive relationship, even temporarily, she may have any of a number of serious needs. If she is fleeing an attack, she may need immediate medical attention and physical protection. She will need accommodation for herself and possibly her children. She will certainly need access to support, counseling, and various types of assistance—money, food stamps, or other basic survival items for herself and her children. She will need to deal with professionals such as police, doctors, and social workers, who are informed and compassionate.

In recent years the shelter movement has grown to meet the needs of many battered women. The first known safe house was founded in England in 1971 by Erin Pizzey. Her book *Scream Quietly or the Neighbors Will Hear* was largely responsible for drawing public attention to wife battering as a major social problem, both in England and in the United States. The shelter movement here is growing (there were an estimated eight hundred shelters nationwide in 1983), but slowly, hampered by lack of funding and mixed reaction from the public. Yet the need for such shelters is clear; as shelters are established, they are rapidly filled to capacity. Besides offering immediate safe shelter (the locations of safe houses are usually known only to the residents and shelter workers), these refuges let battered women see they are not alone in their misery and help them form supportive networks with one another. Walker's (1979) research indicated that about 50 percent of women who stay longer than a week in shelters will not return to their battering relationships. She further noted that "the percentage rises dramatically if the safe house remains open to those women who return home and then want to come back to the refuge. . . . [The] back and forth process may occur as often as five times before the battered woman is able to leave home permanently." Other means for dealing with the aftermath of family violence and suggestions for its prevention are discussed later in the chapter. Here, however, is a final word on the need for safe houses from family violence researchers Straus, Gelles, and Steinmetz (Straus et al., 1980): "In the United States we spend more money on shelters for dogs and cats than for human beings. If we have effective animal rescue shelters for abused dogs, cats, and bunny rabbits we should be able to spare something for people as well."

A Word About Battered Husbands

There have been speculations about the prevalence of husband abuse. The folklore image of the woman chasing her henpecked mate with a rolling pin illustrates this. Although it is undoubtedly true that some men are injured in attacks by wives or lovers, "husband battering" is probably a misleading term. The overwhelming majority of victims of adult family violence are women (Gelles, 1979). A woman may attempt to inflict damage on a man in self-defense or retaliation, but most women have no hope of prevailing in hand-to-hand combat with a man. A woman may be severely injured simply trying to defend herself, and most find it prudent to submit to a beating and live than to resist and risk being killed. Even if a woman has a fighting chance, her socialization mitigates against taking advantage of it. Self-defense generally is taken to constitute escalation, and escalation ultimately leads to grievous injury or death of one or both parties. Indeed a woman may perceive that the only means of breaking the violence cycle of her existence is the ultimate violent act—suicide or homicide.

☐ VIOLENCE AGAINST CHILDREN

Millions of American children (estimates range from two to six million) are violently abused, molested, or seriously neglected by their parents each year (California Commission . . ., 1981; Gelles, 1978b; Thornton, 1984). Parental violence is a leading cause of death in children under the age of three, and between seven hundred and two thousand children's deaths annually are directly attributable to their parents

Each year millions of children are abused; they, in turn, may abuse their own children in an endless cycle of violence.

(California Commission . . ., 1981). "Spare the rod and spoil the child" was a legacy of our Puritan forebears, and it took a long time for child abuse to be recognized for what it was. In 1874 public attention focused on the plight of a little girl named Mary Ellen whose last and only hope of salvation from abuse came from the Society for the Prevention of Cruelty to Animals. Following that, individuals and humanitarian groups took up the cause of abused children from time to time, but the magnitude and shocking implications of the problem were not brought to the attention of the general public until 1962 with the work of a physician, C. H. Kempe, and his colleagues, who coined the term *battered-baby syndrome* to refer to the clinical condition they observed in physically abused young children (Kempe et al., 1962). By 1967 every state had passed laws mandating that suspected child abuse be reported by medical practitioners, teachers, and others involved in the care of children. Yet such abuse is still grossly underreported, and resources for dealing with it are woefully inadequate (Helberg, 1983; Jason, 1983).

Abuse and *neglect* are both serious problems, but they have different implications. Physically abused children are not necessarily neglected. They may be well-groomed and well-nourished and receive love and attention from their parents. Neglected or emotionally abused children may acquire wounds that are deeper and harder to heal than those inflicted physically (Brody, 1983; California Commission . . ., 1981; Steffen, 1982). Of course, any physical abuse will result in some degree of emotional trauma.

Families at Risk

Parents are the last people on earth who ought to have children.

SAMUEL BUTLER

Research suggests that the following characteristics are likely to be present in families that abuse their children (Straus et al., 1980; also see Turner and Avison, 1985):

- The abusing father was physically punished by his parents, and his father physically abused his mother.
- The parents believe in corporal discipline of children and wives.
- The marital relationship itself may not be valued by the parents. There may be interspousal violence.
- The parents believe that the father should be the dominant authority figure.
- The parents are socially isolated, with few or no close contacts with relatives, friends, and groups.
- Educational level itself is not a significant factor, but low educational attainment combined with low income can create stress that predisposes a family to child abuse.

In addition, parents who batter or seriously neglect their children may (Bourne, 1979):

- Be low in self-esteem.
- Be unrealistic in their expectations of the child.
- Use the child to gratify their own needs rather than vice versa (role reversal).
- Appear unconcerned about the seriousness of a child's injury, responding with "Oh well, accidents happen."

The likelihood of child abuse increases with family size. Parents of two children have a 50 percent higher abuse rate than do parents of a single child. The rate of abuse peaks at five children and declines thereafter (Straus et al., 1980). Also, "considerable, converging evidence [indicates] that child abuse is more frequently found in single (female) parent homes in which the mother is working. . . . [She] experiences considerable stress which is exacerbated by her sense of isolation and separation from any effective social support system" (Zigler, 1979). The overall child abuse rate by mothers is 75 percent higher than by fathers (Straus et al., 1980). Colleen McGrath (1979) wrote, "The structure of power in the family, the emotional tensions of mothering, and the enforced proximity of woman and child all lead to situations where women are likely to abuse their children." But, as David Finkelhor (1983) and others have pointed out, if we "calculate [child] vulnerability to abuse as a function of the amount of time spent in contact with a potential abuser, . . . we . . . see that men and fathers are more likely to abuse." Only 5 to 10 percent of parents who injure their children can be called sociopathic. Most parents do not set out to maim or kill, but feel "on the contrary [that they] have an investment in a living child who must be punished to be once more obedient and satisfactory" (Steele, 1980). (For abuse of parents by adolescents, see Peek et al., 1985.)

Children at Risk

Who are the battered children? Are they any different from other children? Surprisingly, the answer is often yes; they are different in some way or at least perceived by their parents to be so. Brandt Steele (1980) noted that children who are abused are often labeled by their parents as "unsatisfactory." Unsatisfactory may include any of the following:

- A "normal" child who is the product of a difficult or unplanned pregnancy, is of the "wrong" sex, or is born outside of marriage
- An "abnormal" child—premature or low birth weight, possibly with congenital defects or illness
- A "difficult" child—fussy, hyperactive, and so on

Steele also noted that all too often a child's perceived difficulties are a result of abuse and neglect rather than a cause.

The earliest and most fundamental lessons a child learns are taught at home within the family setting. Among the most significant lessons a child needs to learn are how to accept responsibility, make decisions, trust others, acknowledge feelings, and control actions (Helfer, 1980). He or she must also learn how to "get his or her needs met in an acceptable manner and when the most appropriate time is to seek fulfillment." If a child's needs are consistently not met, he or she may develop behaviors for meeting normal needs that are "extreme, inappropriate and maladaptive" (Helfer, 1980). Helfer refers to the environment that fosters these deficiencies in development as the "World of Abnormal Rearing" or WAR. This cyclical WAR continues from generation to generation, depriving children of their right to childhood in perpetuity.

Intervention

Steps toward the prevention of family violence will be discussed later in this chapter. Until we eliminate or drastically reduce the incidence of family violence, we must deal with things as they are—that is, try to protect our society's children and assist

> There was an old woman who lived in a shoe.
> She had so many children she didn't know what to do.
> She gave them some broth without any bread,
> And whipped them all soundly and sent them to bed.
>
> MOTHER GOOSE RHYME

> America has sometimes been described as child-centered; however, any unbiased observer of child life in this nation will find that many millions of children are living and growing up under circumstances of severe social and economic deprivation. . . . Many of these children lack adequate nutrition, medical and dental care, and educational vocational opportunities . . . however high the prevalence of physical abuse of individual children within their families and homes may be, the abuse inflicted upon children collectively by society as a whole is far larger in scope and far more serious in its consequences.
>
> DAVID GIL, *VIOLENCE AGAINST CHILDREN*

462   Part Five: Interiors

FEATURE

Perspectives on the Abuse of Children

The history of children is not particularly happy. At various times and places children have been abandoned to die of exposure in deserts, in forests, and on mountainsides or have simply been murdered at birth if they were deemed too sickly, ugly, of the wrong sex, or just impractical. Male children have been subjected to castration to make them fit for guarding harems or singing soprano in church choirs. These practices (and many others) have all been socially condoned in their time. In the societies where they existed, they would not be recognized as abusive.

Take, for example, the initiation rites of young boys. Among some New Guinea tribes, a boy's entrance to manhood may be marked by beatings, bloodletting, homosexual acts, and humiliation—treatment that we would no doubt classify as cruel. Imagine, too, taking a tiny baby boy, tying him

down, and cutting off the foreskin of his penis, causing him excruciating pain and possibly even putting his life at risk! Although circumcision has been discredited as a medical necessity (Kempe and Helfer, 1980), it is still widely practiced in our culture for reasons of religion, tradition, ritual, fashion, or habit. It is culturally acceptable.

In our society some degree of physical force against children (spankings by mom and dad, swats from the coach) is generally condoned, although most child-care experts currently suggest that parents use alternative disciplinary measures. Psychiatrist Kenneth Kaye (1984) stated that corporal punishment presents violence as an acceptable method of problem solving. He wrote, "Winning your children's respect means getting them to behave as civilized human beings without yourself behaving like a brute." In spite of conflicting opin-

---

There is no crime of which one cannot imagine oneself to be the author.

JOHANN GOETHE

and strengthen their families. Professionals and state agencies provide medical care and counseling and services such as day care, child care education, telephone crisis lines, and temporary foster care. Many of these services are costly, and many of those who require them cannot afford to pay. Since 1981, such services have been drastically reduced by federal budget cuts. Indeed, the federal government has attempted to repeal programs for battered women, battered children, and rape victims ("Federal Budget . . ." 1983); it vigorously opposes gun control (Robbins, 1983). Our system does not currently provide the human and financial resources necessary to deal with these socially destructive problems.

The objective of intervention is to protect the child and strengthen the family as much as possible. Jailing a parent and putting a child in foster care may not be in the child's or the family's best interests. At the same time, no social worker or judge would knowingly place a child in physical jeopardy. Those who must make direct decisions about the future of abused and high-risk children must weigh the question of compassion versus control (Newbergr and Bourne, 1979). The following must be considered (Rosenfeld and Newberger, 1979):

- *Assessment of injury.* Is the injury isolated or part of a recurring pattern?
- *Parents response to incident.* Does the parent feel guilt and concern?
- *Social deviation of parent.* Is alcoholism, criminality, or drug abuse present in the family?
- *Parent's attitude toward child.* Is the child viewed as intrinsically good or bad?

ions on the advisability of corporal punishment, most Americans would express alarm at the thought of children being severely beaten, burned, starved, and so on. Yet these culturally nonacceptable practices are widely prevalent. In a cross-cultural study of child abuse, Jill Korbin (1981) noted that Western nations tend to be low in infant indulgence, to initiate child-training practices at an earlier developmental stage, and to have more stringent expectations of compliance from young children (our toilet-training customs, for example, might be considered highly abusive elsewhere). Western societies are also more highly isolated in nuclear (or single-parent) households and have less support from the large community and less "folk wisdom" to refer to.

Viewing the treatment (and mistreatment) of children from an international perspective, Taylor and Newberger (1983) pointed out that in many countries children are used as soldiers and are victims of wars they do not choose to fight. Close to fifty-two million children (less than age 15) are in the international labor force, forty-two million of them without pay. Corporal punishment is sanctioned in most countries, although it is being reevaluated in light of current concerns. Korbin (1981) stated that the "idiosyncratic [not normally acceptable] child abuse and neglect that we see in the United States and other Western cultures is relatively rare in small-scale non-Western cultures." Other researchers have also indicated that violence and abuse toward children are rare in developing nations (and in Denmark, China, the Soviet Union, Poland, Japan, and Italy) (Gelles and Cornell, 1983). They voice concerns, however, that urbanization and industrialization are breaking down traditional values and family structures, leading to increases in abuse and neglect.

- *Parent's identity with child.* Can the parent see the child as a separate person?
- *Strength of the parent's personality.* Can the parent exercise self-control?

Much intervention in child abuse appears equivalent to putting Band-Aids on a huge malignant tumor of society. Self-help groups such as Parents Anonymous offer nonjudgmental support and are proving to be quite effective. But more research, more commitment, and more caring are needed.

> In every child who is born, under no matter what circumstances, and of no matter what parents, the potentiality of the human race is born again.
>
> JAMES AGEE

☐ OTHER FORMS OF FAMILY VIOLENCE

Abuse of the Elderly

Recent public attention has been focused on yet another type of familial violence: the abuse of elderly parents by their grown children (or in some cases, grandchildren). Popularly referred to as "granny-bashing" in England, this practice has reached alarming proportions in the United States. One researcher (Richard Gelles, in Tiede, 1983) indicated that 2.5 million parents are abused by their children in this country; one million of them are seriously injured. This abuse includes physical assault, verbal harassment, withholding food, theft, threats, and neglect, and it is present at all socioeconomic levels. Another name for this type of maltreatment of parents is the "King Lear syndrome" in reference to Shakespeare's King Lear and his ill-treatment at the hands of his daughters. Much abuse of the elderly goes unnoticed, unrecognized, and unreported. Old people generally don't get out much and are often confined to bed or wheelchair. Many do not report their mistreatment out of fear of institutionalization or other reprisal. Although some research indicates that the abused in many cases were in fact abusing parents (this seems reasonable in view of what we know about the cyclical nature of violence), more knowledge must be gained before we can draw firm conclusions about elder abuse (Gelles and Pedrick-Cornell, 1983).

Violence Between Siblings

Violence between siblings is by far the most common form of family violence (Straus et al., 1980). Much of this type of sibling interaction is simply taken for granted by our culture—"You know how kids are!" Straus, Gelles, and Steinmetz (1980), in a survey that included 733 families with two or more children, found that 82 percent of the children had used some sort of violence against a sibling in the preceding year. The National Association of Child Abuse estimated that twenty-nine million siblings physically harm each other annually (Tiede, 1983). Straus and his colleagues reported these additional findings:

- The rate of sibling violence goes down with the increasing age of the child.
- Boys of all ages are more violent than girls. The highest rates of sibling violence occur in families with only male children.
- Violence between children often reflects what they see their parents doing—to each other and to the children themselves.

The full scope and implications of sibling violence have not been rigorously explored. However, Straus, Gelles, and Steinmetz (1980) did conclude that

conflicts and disputes between children in a family are an inevitable part of life. . . . But the use of physical force as a tactic for resolving their conflicts is by no means inevitable. . . . Human beings learn to be violent. It is possible to provide children with an environment in which nonviolent methods of solving conflicts can be learned. . . . If violence, like charity, begins at home, so does nonviolence.

☐ WHAT CAN BE DONE?

Based on the foregoing evidence, the reader may by now have concluded that the American family is well on its way to extinction as we merrily bash, thrash, chop, bite, shoot, and otherwise wipe ourselves out of existence. Statistically, the safest family homes are those with one or no children in which the husband and wife experience little life stress and in which decisions are made democratically (Straus et al., 1980). By this definition, most of us probably do not live in homes that are particularly safe. What can we do to protect ourselves (and our posterity) from ourselves? The following recommendations are adapted mainly from Straus, Gelles, and Steinmetz (1980; also see Straus, 1983):

- Reduce societal sources of stress such as social inequality, severe unemployment, and inadequate health care.
- Eliminate sexism. Furnish adequate day care, promote educational and employment opportunities equally for men and women. Promote family planning.

FEATURE

Teen Suicide

SUICIDE FACTS

- About 5,000–7,000 teenagers kill themselves every year.
- The suicide rate for 15–24-year-olds has tripled in the past two decades. (It showed a slight decline in 1983, the last year of available statistics.)
- Suicides of white males 15–24 years old show a clear upward trend.
- Teenagers attempting suicide every year number 400,000–500,000.
- Girls attempt suicide three times more frequently than boys; boys succeed four times more frequently.
- Most suicides are committed with guns.

Research shows the following:

- Thirty-four percent of teens have "seriously considered" suicide.
- Thirty-two percent have made plans to commit suicide.
- Fourteen percent have attempted suicide.
- Ninety percent of attempters have known another attempter. (This has been called the "cluster" or "contagion" effect.)

The blame for this seemingly senseless destruction of human potential has been placed variously on parents for neglecting or abusing their children, on schools and on society for promoting unhealthy competition, on television for providing unrealistic and violent models, on drugs, and on the failure of religion. Although casting blame may focus scrutiny on areas where it is needed, more direct methods of prevention are being undertaken. Nationwide, at least 550 crisis centers have been established to provide counseling, information, and in many cases twenty-four-hour telephone hot lines (see Resource Center). Many states have implemented suicide prevention courses as part of their high school curricula (at least four states *require* it). Besides offering peer counseling and other assistance for troubled teens, these courses also teach teens how to recognize presuicidal behavior. Suicide must be viewed as an act of *communication*, a last resort to "make other humans show concern and act accordingly" (Stengel, 1984).

SUICIDE WARNING SIGNS

The following warning signs indicate a possible suicide or suicide attempt (taken from Madison, 1978):

- Mental depression, especially during the time when recovery seems imminent.
- Changes in behavior or personality, especially the discontinuation of habitual activities.
- Making final arrangements, such as giving away prized possessions.
- Suicidal talk, especially direct threats. (Direct threats require direct action. If someone you know threatens suicide, get help!)
- Previous attempt. (Most people who attempt suicide don't repeat it, but some do, and some "succeed").

- Explore means of establishing supportive networks including relatives, friends, and community.
- Break the family cycle of violence. Eliminate corporal punishment and promote education about disciplinary alternatives.
- Eliminate norms that legitimize and glorify violence. For example, legislate gun control, eliminate capital punishment, reduce media violence. (For two views on

the impact of children playing with toy guns, see Marzollo, 1983, and Yarrow, 1983).

A . . . society which promotes the ownership of firearms, women and children; which makes homes men's castles; and which sanctions societal and interpersonal violence in the forms of wars, athletic contests, and mass media fiction (and news) should not be surprised to find violence in its homes.

NORMAN DENZIN

One recent study pointed out the importance of local grass-roots organizations in bringing about change in public policy. Kalmuss and Straus (1983) found that the work of feminist organizations that pressured policy makers was more significant than the availability of funds or a positive social and political climate in establishing domestic violence programs.

Domestic violence has been revealed as a profound and pervasive problem in the United States. It will not be easy to uproot the social and economic sources of this violence, but some government response has been observed. On the federal level, the National Institute of Mental Health is spending close to $1 million annually on research into domestic violence, and the Justice Department has established a family violence task force. On the other hand, according to a survey by the Center for Women Policy Studies, since 1981 nearly every federal program that provides financial or technical support to domestic violence has had its budget eliminated or substantially reduced by the Reagan administration ("Federal Budget . . .," 1983).

☐ INCEST

A near-universal taboo in human societies is the incest taboo. No one knows how it originated, but it has existed with only a few exceptions; the royal families of ancient Egypt, Peru, and Hawaii alone were exempt from this taboo. Apparently, people feel no instinctive aversion to incest; if they did, there would have been no reason to create such adamant rules to prohibit it. It has recently been estimated that one out of every six Americans has been involved in an incestuous relationship (Henry Giarretto, in Thornton, 1984).

Freud considered the Oedipus myth (in which Oedipus killed his father and married his mother) as a prototype of child development. Each child forms strong bonds—including erotic bonds—with the parent of the other sex. So strong are these bonds that the child desires to replace his or her parent of the same sex by marrying the parent of the other sex. This deep sexual competition is repressed through the incest taboo so that it rarely surfaces. Freud called this desire of the child for the parent of the other sex the Oedipus complex. Margaret Mead (1948) pointed out, however, that the taboo is reciprocal. She viewed it as a means of avoiding conflict within the family. It protects children from their parents and parents from their children, avoiding potentially deadly conflict and jealousy. But the taboo goes farther; it is indirectly extended to protect immature children from adults in general.

It was not until Freud's work in the early twentieth century that modern psychiatry began exploring incest. Freud believed that most instances of childhood seduction were actually neurotic fantasies and that actual incest was rare. Most psychiatrists accepted Freud's views on childhood seduction. It was erroneously assumed that court cases on incest reflected its true extent. But in the late 1960s, sexual abuse became reportable under child abuse laws. The various protective care agencies were shocked and alarmed by the large numbers of incest cases that surfaced. At the same time, psychiatrists became increasingly aware of incest among their clients (Rosenfeld, 1977). The extent of incest in the United States is only now being recognized.

Although traditionally we have viewed incest as the result of some kind of character disorder or personality type, it now appears that it is a symptom of severe family dysfunction (Cormier et al., 1962). Valerie and Mohr (1979) found that severe marital conflict had occurred in two-thirds of the incestuous families, spouse abuse in one-fourth, alcoholism in one-third, mental health problems in one-third, and that one or more members had criminal records in one-fifth. Furthermore, more than one-third of the incestuous families had four or more children, whereas only 6.4 percent of the families in the general population had such large families. Incest appears to be one way of holding a dysfunctional family together at any cost. (See the reading by Meredith Maran, "Breaking the Silence.")

Forms of Incest

The most common form of reported incest is father-daughter incest. In such cases the father (or foster father or stepfather) almost always initiates the incest, but often his daughter does not actively resist. These relationships are often long term and usually sexually exploitive. Such relationships usually become known when the daughter becomes angry at her father or decides to end the incest (Weinberg, 1955). The least common form of incest is mother-son, although in myth and in art it is a more common theme, as in Sophocles' *Oedipus Rex*. It is also, as we have seen, a central theme in Freud's theory of psychosexual development and has a compelling hold on the Western imagination. Why this is so is open to speculation.

Another common form of incest is between brother and sister, although it is infrequently reported. Sibling incest usually takes place in early adolescence or earlier, is rarely discovered, and when it is, it is usually not treated seriously. Such incest may be a form of sexual experimentation that occurs when children are given sexual freedom, have little access to sexual partners, or share the same bedroom. If no coercion or exploitation is involved, it may not have a serious impact on the participants (Justice and Justice, 1979).

Predisposing Conditions

Justice and Justice (1979) noted several factors that appear to be prevalent in homes where father-daughter incest occurs. Although these conditions do not cause incest, they may predispose the family to it:

- The father maintains a fantasy of an "all-loving" mother and seeks her in his daughter.
- The father is under severe stress (from job or family changes, moving, and so on). He may increase his drinking.
- Sex ceases between the father and the mother.
- The mother leaves her husband and daughter alone (for example, by working nights or getting sick).
- The daughter is hungry for affection.
- The family's sexual climate is either very lax or very repressive.

Tierney and Corwin (1983) noted that families in which incest occurs are often geographically or socially isolated. The isolated family lacks contact with socially supportive networks and with friends who could validate parental role performance

Lot went out of Zo'ar, and dwelled in the hills with his two daughters, for he was afraid to dwell in Zo'ar. So he dwelled in a cave with his two daughters. Then the first-born said to the other, "Our father is old, and there is not a man on earth to come into us in the manner of men. Let us make our father drink wine and we will lie with him that we may have offspring through our father." So they made their father drink wine that night and his older daughter went in and lay with her father. He did not know when she lay down or when she arose. And then on the next day, the older daughter said to the younger one, "Behold, I lay last night with our father. Let us make him drink wine again tonight, then you go in and lay with him that we may have children by our father." So they gave their father wine that night, and the younger daughter slept with him. He did not know when she lay down or when she arose. Thus both Lot's daughters became great with child by their father.

GENESIS 19:30–36

and exert some social control. Isolation also may lower inhibitions against abuse, as it makes discovery less likely.

Father Profile.   Most incestuous fathers (80 to 85 percent) have "symbiotic personalities" (Justice and Justice, 1979). They crave intimacy but are at a loss as to how to achieve it appropriately. Generally, an incestuous father never identified with his own father and has never freed himself from an excessive attachment to his own mother. He very likely was made the "little man of the house" as a child and was expected to take care of his parents' emotional needs (role reversal). The Justices identify four types of symbiotic father:

- *Introvert.* He feels attacked by the outside world, only leaves home for work, is depressive.
- *Rationalizer.* He views himself as a teacher, protector, or as especially sexually liberated; he may be an "elitist" who considers his daughter his unique and exclusive property.
- *Tyrant.* He is characterized by basic distrust.
- *Alcoholic.* His drinking loosens restraints and is used as an excuse; some degree of drinking is typical of a large number of incest cases.

Daughter Profile.   The incestuous daughter may have many or all of the following characteristics (Justice and Justice, 1979):

- She has a poor (or no) relationship with her mother.
- She has low self-esteem.
- She is seeking attention and affection.
- She develops a seductive manner.
- She is excessively attached to her father.
- She becomes her father's "rescuer"; she may become the "little lady of the house."

Collusive Mothers.   Mothers may collude (sometimes unconsciously) in their husband's sexual exploitation of their daughters (sometimes unconsciously). The collusive mother has usually withdrawn sexually from her husband and may look the other way to avoid confronting the reality of the father-daughter relationship. The mother may be so relieved when her husband stops seeking sex from her that she refuses to upset the equilibrium by asking any questions about a suspected sexual relationship between her husband and daughter. She may, however, be extremely jealous of her daughter's "elevated" status. In many cases, the mother may be unable to face up to the implications of her husband's and daughter's involvement and may talk herself out of her suspicions.

Impact of Incest

The impact of incest is highly subjective and not very predictable (Courtois, 1979). Younger victims may have more severe reactions affecting their personal identities and their subsequent relations to future partners. Sexual molestation is common in the history of women seeking treatment for sexual dysfunctions. These women may be easily orgasmic, but they have little sexual desire, do not like touching or caressing, and frequently feel disgust about sex (McGuire and Wagner, 1978). Seven important

This drawing was made by an adolescent who was impregnated by her father; according to psychologists, it expresses her inability to deal with body images, especially genitalia, and her rejection of her body's violation.

variables appear to affect how a person responds to incest (Courtois, 1979): duration of incident, frequency of incidents, relatedness of the participants, use of force, lack of disclosure, disclosure when no assistance is offered, and passive consent of the victim.

Whether the child gives passive consent or is assaulted is especially important. If the child is assaulted, incest also includes rape. Ordinarily, a child regards his or her home as safe ground and relatives as safe persons. If the child is sexually assaulted at home by a parenting adult, sibling, or other relative, safety, trust, and security are attacked as well. One study of forty-four child victims of incestuous sexual assault found that 78 percent were in their own homes when they were assaulted; eight of them were asleep in their own beds (Burgess et al., 1977). Approximately half of all adolescent runaways are fleeing sexual abuse at home (Graham, 1984).

Incest is an extremely complicated family crisis that affects more than the participants. Incestuous experiences in childhood may lead to lack of trust, fear of intimacy, and sexual dysfunctions in adulthood. Also, incest victims learn victim roles. Furthermore, when children have sexually abusive parents as role models, they are more likely to sexually abuse their own children. Parents United, a self-help group for incestuous families, reports that 80 percent of molesters and mothers of sexually abused children were themselves sexually abused as children (Graham, 1984). The long-term consequences of incest, some of which are still unknown, suggest that therapy is advisable for incest victims (Delson and Clark, 1981).

Intervention

Avoiding Confrontation. Our reluctance to confront incest is reinforced by our reluctance to believe children. Because the molester is a member of the family, to believe a child's report of incest is to create a major family crisis. Despair or fear over what to do about incest leads many to ignore it. As a result, many children live in fear, silence, and self-imposed isolation. They are often tortured by feelings of shame; they may believe they are unfit ever to be loved, to marry, or to become parents.

Schools have traditionally avoided the problem of dealing with children who are the victims of incest. Often psychiatric professionals seek to avoid the issue as well. One psychiatric social worker was discouraged by her supervisor from talking to a twelve-year-old girl who had been molested by her father. She recalled discussing the incident with her supervisor: "I explained that I might help [the child] to understand that her father was the guilty one, and he was the one who ought to be ashamed. But my supervisor would have none of that. The actual event did not shame her, he continued. It was her deep, unconscious, incestuous wish for her father that made her feel guilty" (Rush, 1980).

Education. In the last few years, government at the federal, state, and local levels has begun to respond to the obvious need for research and education about the sexual abuse of children. Television shows, books, articles, and the statements of public figures who were themselves child victims have contributed to growing awareness and greatly increased reporting of abusive incidents. The National Education Association has made a child-abuse education training kit available to teachers. Plays, puppet shows, filmstrips, videotapes, books, and comic books teach children how to identify and avoid potentially abusive situations. They stress that the child is not at fault when such abuse does occur. A number of schools have instituted programs to educate students and their parents as well. The dramatic increase in reported incidents of sexual abuse can be at least partly credited to these efforts.

Disclosure. If an offender is able to gain access to a child, he is likely to continue the activity. Secrecy is crucial for him. Children often help maintain the secret out of fear and guilt, but great tension is usually created. Once the secret is revealed, the offender's power is broken and the tension relieved. Most often the incest is discovered through clues, such as blood on the child's pants, vaginal discharge, noticeable changes in the child's behavior, or unaccountable money or candy. About a third of the time the child will tell someone (Burgess et al., 1977). Once the incest has been discovered, the next decision is whether to keep it a family matter, seek mental health intervention, or turn to the legal authorities.

Family considerations are important when legal action is contemplated. Sometimes removal of the offending adult may cause even more trauma than the incest itself. If the father is imprisoned because of incest with his daughter, the family may lose its means of support, his wife may blame the daughter for initiating the incest, or the daughter may feel guilty because society demands more punishment than she feels is necessary (Valerie and Mohr, 1979). Also, once incest is discovered, family members often experience conflicting loyalties (Burgess et al., 1977):

Should they be loyal to the child victim and treat the offender as they would treat any assailant—thinking of their duty as citizens to bring such an offender before the law? Of should they be loyal to the offender and make an exception for him because he is a family member and let their duty to him as a [family member] prevail? Clearly they cannot honor both expectations. They must choose and the choice may be a difficult one.

Humanistic Treatment. Henry Giarretto (1976), director of a program for the treatment of incestuous families, views incest as one of many possible symptoms of family dysfunctions. He stresses the importance of dealing with the family as an organic system, with emphasis on the quality of the marital relationship. In this humanistic approach it is imperative that a high self-concept be fostered in the parents and thus passed on to the children. Low self-esteem is seen as a promoting factor in destructive behavior; consequently, institutional punishment is not generally encouraged because it simply reinforces low self-esteem and fails to eliminate destructive energy.

Parents United, its auxiliary groups Daughters/Sons United and Adults Molested as Children United, and other self-help groups exist in many parts of the country (see Resource Center). Such programs have shown positive results in low recidivism rates among offenders and high recovery rates for victims (Graham, 1984).

A concept crucial to treatment of incest offenders is the father's acceptance of responsibility. Giarretto (1976) wrote, "No matter the extenuating circumstances, including possible provocative behavior by his daughter, his action betrayed his child and wife and their reliance on him as father and husband."

We are healthy only to the degree that our ideas are humane.

KURT VONNEGUT, JR.

☐ ALCOHOLISM

Ten million Americans—men, women, and children of all socioeconomic strata—are addicted to alcohol (National Institute of Mental Health Study, cited in Leo, 1984). Alcohol addiction is the fourth-ranked cause of death in this country, yet few doctors have the knowledge and training to deal with it. Physical complications associated with alcoholism include suicide, homicide, accidental death or injury, acute and chronic brain syndrome, peripheral neurological defects, and liver and kidney damage. Alcohol abuse by prospective mothers (and fathers) can cause serious fetal damage, resulting in fetal alcohol syndrome, low birth weight, and other impairments (see Chapter 9). Yet alcoholism is not a medical disease in the ordinary sense, nor is alcohol itself the problem: "The person is the problem. Drinking

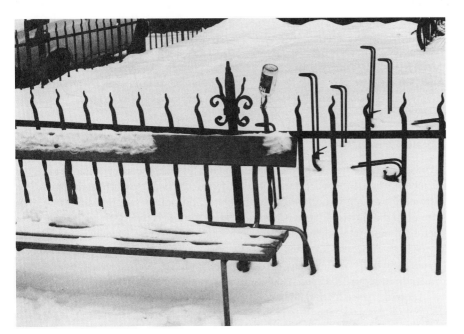

Alcoholics, their families, and their friends typically deny their alcoholism. An alcoholic's family system often unintentionally supports this disorder.

"Don't drink yourself helpless in the beer garden. You speak, and you don't know what you are saying. If you fall down and break your limbs, no one will help you. And your drinking companion will get up and say, 'Away with this drunkard.' "

Thirty-four hundred years before Ann Landers and Miss Manners dispensed advice, the ancient Egyptians wrote an etiquette book called "The Making of Ani" (1500 B.C.). It warned against drunkenness.

excessively is a manifestation of internal stress and uncertainty. Alcohol may be used to allay anxiety, help deny reality, assist one in maintaining social poise, boost one's self-confidence, or ward off intolerable fears and unacceptable temptations" (Verdery, 1973). The abuse of alcohol can be seen as a symptom of a disorder that is emotional and spiritual as well as physical. (See the reading by Ann Ryan, "Love Letter for a Bottle Bobbing Through Rough Tides.")

Although physiological and genetic factors may predispose a person to alcoholism (Blakeslee, 1984), it appears that problem drinking, like ordinary drinking, is a learned behavior. Most people in the United States learn to drink during adolescence; most adolescents have their first drink at home, but do most of their drinking away from home, with their friends. Teenagers drink to celebrate, be social, relieve tension, and practice being grown-up ("anticipatory socialization") (Albrecht, 1973). As with violence, the drinking behavior that children observe at home will greatly influence their own behavior. Many alcoholics have at least one alcoholic parent.

Social Drinking

Drinkers who are not chronic alcoholics may also pose a danger to themselves and society. In the past few decades, social drinking has become an integral part of our cultural life as families drink together at home and women's participation in "American drinking rituals" increases (Gross, 1983). Although the media tend to present a picture of moderate (and harmless) consumption, on closer inspection it appears that as a group American drinkers consume about as much per capita as drinkers in countries with the highest rates of alcohol consumption (Gross, 1983). Even though we drink substantially less distilled liquor than in the past, we consume vast quantities of beer and increasing amounts of wine. Although it is true that the percentage of alcohol in beer and wine is lower than that in distilled liquor, drinkers don't take into account the fact that distilled liquors are generally served diluted in mixed drinks. A

Table 15–1 **Children of Alcoholics Screening Test (C.A.S.T.)**

C.A.S.T. can be used to identify latency age, adolescent, and grown up children of alcoholics.

Please check (√) the answer below that best describes your feelings, behavior, and experiences related to a parent's alcohol use. Take your time and be as accurate as possible. Answer all 30 questions by checking either "yes" or "no."

Sex: Male _____   Female _____   Age: _____

Yes	No	Questions
____	____	1. Have you ever thought that one of your parents had a drinking problem?
____	____	2. Have you ever lost sleep because of a parent's drinking?
____	____	3. Did you ever encourage one of your parents to quit drinking?
____	____	4. Did you ever feel alone, scared, nervous, angry, or frustrated because a parent was not able to stop drinking?
____	____	5. Did you ever argue or fight with a parent when he or she was drinking?
____	____	6. Did you ever threaten to run away from home because of a parent's drinking?
____	____	7. Has a parent ever yelled at or hit you or other family members when drinking?
____	____	8. Have you ever heard your parents fight when one of them was drunk?
____	____	9. Did you ever protect another family member from a parent who was drinking?
____	____	10. Did you ever feel like hiding or emptying a parent's bottle of liquor?
____	____	11. Do many of your thoughts revolve around a problem drinking parent or difficulties that arise because of his or her drinking?
____	____	12. Did you ever wish that a parent would stop drinking?
____	____	13. Did you ever feel responsible for and guilty about a parent's drinking?
____	____	14. Did you ever fear that your parents would get divorced due to alcohol misuse?
____	____	15. Have you ever withdrawn from and avoided outside activities and friends because of embarrassment and shame over a parent's drinking problem?
____	____	16. Did you ever feel caught in the middle of an argument or fight between a problem drinking parent and your other parent?
____	____	17. Did you ever feel that you made a parent drink alcohol?
____	____	18. Have you ever felt that a problem drinking parent did not really love you?
____	____	19. Did you ever resent a parent's drinking?
____	____	20. Have you ever worried about a parent's health because of his or her alcohol use?
____	____	21. Have you ever been blamed for a parent's drinking?
____	____	22. Did you ever think your father was an alcoholic?

(Continued on page 474.)

_____ _____ 23. Did you ever wish your home could be more like the homes of your friends who did not have a parent with a drinking problem?

_____ _____ 24. Did a parent ever make promises to you that he or she did not keep because of drinking?

_____ _____ 25. Did you ever think your mother was an alcoholic?

_____ _____ 26. Did you ever wish that you could talk to someone who could understand and help the alcohol-related problems in your family?

_____ _____ 27. Did you ever fight with your brothers and sisters about a parent's drinking?

_____ _____ 28. Did you ever stay away from home to avoid the drinking parent or your other parent's reaction to the drinking?

_____ _____ 29. Have you ever felt sick, cried, or had a "knot" in your stomach after worrying about a parent's drinking?

_____ _____ 30. Did you ever take over any chores and duties at home that were usually done by a parent before he or she developed a drinking problem?

_____ **TOTAL NUMBER OF "YES" ANSWERS.**

Score of 6 or more means that more than likely this child is a child of an alcoholic parent.

© 1983 by John W. Jones, Ph.D. Family Recovery Press.

five-ounce glass of wine contains as much alcohol as a standard highball. Between 1962 and 1982 beer consumption rose from 15 gallons per person per year to 24.3 gallons; wine and liquor consumption increased from 2.3 gallons to 4.1 gallons over the same time period ("More Alcohol . . .," 1984). (This is the average rate for *all* Americans of drinking age; when you adjust for the nondrinkers and very light drinkers, you can see that the annual rate of consumption for drinkers is much higher.)

The social and economic costs of alcohol abuse are enormous. One of the heaviest costs is the devastation caused by drunk driving. Drivers in the eighteen-to-twenty age group are twice as likely as other drivers to be involved in alcohol-related accidents, and drunken driving is the leading cause of death for teenagers and young adults (Givens, 1985). Increasing concern about this problem has been stimulated by a nationwide crusade against drunken driving by such groups as Mothers Against Drunk Driving (MADD). Their effective lobbying has persuaded Congress to penalize states that don't raise the minimum drinking age to twenty-one years by withholding substantial federal highway funds. It is expected that most states will eventually comply with federal standards. Reflecting this shift in consciousness, alcohol-awareness courses have proliferated on most college campuses. Organizations such as BACCHUS (Boost Alcohol Consciousness Concerning the Health of University Students), which now has more than two hundred campus chapters in forty-six states, are promoting responsible drinking practices and helping students with serious drinking problems to recognize them and seek assistance. Indications are that students are adopting more conservative attitudes toward drinking. One college senior who conducts alcohol-awareness workshops noted that although most of the older fraternity members he counseled resisted the idea of campus restrictions on alcohol consumption, many of the younger ones were in favor of such restrictions (Wolfe, 1985).

Table 15–2 **The Signs of Alcoholism**

Yes	No	Questions
____	____	1. Do you occasionally drink heavily after a disappointment, a quarrel, or when the boss gives you a hard time?
____	____	2. When you have trouble or feel under pressure, do you always drink more heavily than usual?
____	____	3. Have you noticed that you are able to handle more liquor than you did when you were first drinking?
____	____	4. Did you ever wake up on the "morning after" and discover that you could not remember part of the evening before, even though your friends tell you that you did not "pass out"?
____	____	5. When drinking with other people, do you try to have a few extra drinks when others will not know it?
____	____	6. Are there certain occasions when you feel uncomfortable if alcohol is not available?
____	____	7. Have you recently noticed that when you begin drinking you are in more of a hurry to get the first drink than you used to be?
____	____	8. Do you sometimes feel a little guilty about your drinking?
____	____	9. Are you secretly irritated when your family or friends discuss your drinking?
____	____	10. Have you recently noticed an increase in the frequency of your memory "blackouts"?
____	____	11. Do you often find that you wish to continue drinking after your friends say they have had enough?
____	____	12. Do you usually have a reason for the occasions when you drink heavily?
____	____	13. When you are sober, do you often regret things you have done or said while drinking?
____	____	14. Have you tried switching brands or following different plans for controlling your drinking?
____	____	15. Have you often failed to keep the promises you have made to yourself about controlling or cutting down on your drinking?
____	____	16. Have you ever tried to control your drinking by making a change in jobs, or moving to a new location?
____	____	17. Do you try to avoid family or close friends while you are drinking?
____	____	18. Are you having an increasing number of financial and work problems?
____	____	19. Do more people seem to be treating you unfairly without good reason?
____	____	20. Do you eat very little or irregularly when you are drinking?

(Continued on page 476.)

_____ _____ 21. Do you sometimes have the "shakes" in the morning and find that it helps to have a little drink?

_____ _____ 22. Have you recently noticed that you cannot drink as much as you once did?

_____ _____ 23. Do you sometimes stay drunk for several days at a time?

_____ _____ 24. Do you sometimes feel very depressed and wonder whether life is worth living?

_____ _____ 25. Sometimes after periods of drinking, do you see or hear things that aren't there?

_____ _____ 26. Do you get terribly frightened after you have been drinking heavily?

If you have answered "yes" to any of the questions, you have some of the symptoms that may indicate alcoholism.

Questions 1–8 relate to the early stage of alcoholism.
Questions 9–21 relate to the middle stage.
Questions 22–26 mark the beginning of the final stage.

Signs of Alcoholism is published by the National Council on Alcoholism.

Alcohol, the Family, and Violence

Alcoholism is sometimes called a "family disease" because it involves all members of the family in a "complex interactional system" (Krimmel, 1973). The principle of homeostasis—the tendency toward stability in a system—operates in alcoholic families, maintaining established behavior patterns and strengthening resistance to change. Many alcoholic families do not progress through the normal family life-cycle stages, but remain in an unhealthy (yet stable) cycling between "sober and intoxicated interactional states" (Steinglass, 1983). Using an example in which the husband is the alcoholic, Krimmel (1973) described the "pathological complementary relationship" between spouses on the morning after a drinking bout:

[The] wife responds to her husband's plea of physical illness, shame, guilt or remorse with either sympathy and forgiveness or anger and punishment. . . . If the wife is forgiving the husband has learned that forgiveness for being drunk can be obtained, provided he is appropriately remorseful and very sick. If she punishes him . . . his guilt and shame are relieved. . . . In either case the pattern cannot be understood except in terms of the total sequence, as if it were designed to produce forgiveness or punishment or comfortable emotional distance. . . . The spouse may derive considerable gratification from the opportunity to be the forgiver or the punisher.

The effect of parental alcoholism on children can be devastating, especially in families where violence or its threat is also a condition of daily life. Studies indicate that alcohol abuse by one or both spouses or by teenage children is a factor in a majority of incidents of domestic violence (Steffan, 1982). The use of alcohol is strongly linked to homicide, suicide, assaultive behavior in general, and accidents. Alcohol is not necessarily a causative force in these instances, but it is a predisposing factor that lowers inhibitions and self-control (Tinklenburg, 1973). Some researchers have suggested that batterers who drink in conjunction with their acts of violence

UNDERSTANDING YOURSELF

Issues in Your Family

In your family of origin, what, if any, forms of violence occurred among siblings, between parents, or between parents and children? Was this violence condoned by the family? Do you feel it was justified? How has your family's attitude toward violence influenced your own attitudes and behaviors?

Do you consider it violent to spank your child with an open hand on the buttocks if the child is disobedient? To slap your child across the face? To hit your child with a fist? If you spank your small child to teach him or her not to cross a busy street, is that violent? If you spank your child because you are angry, is that violent? If you spank a neighbor child to teach him or her not to cross a busy street, is that violent? Why?

Have you or anyone you know been involved in an incestuous relationship? If so, how was the relationship ended or resolved? Was there disclosure? Legal action? Counseling? Are there still issues that need to be resolved?

Who do you know that seems to have a serious drinking (or drug) problem? Is the person aware of it? Has he or she made an attempt to deal with the problem? Was the attempt successful? Why? What dynamics do you see in this person's family that support the abuser's use of alcohol or drugs? How have family members and close friends responded to the abuser's drinking (or drug) problem?

What resources exist in your community for dealing with domestic violence, incest, and alcohol and drug abuse? If resources are lacking, what could you do to aid in their establishment?

use alcohol as a "disinhibitor," giving themselves "permission" to be violent (Gelles and Cornell, 1983).

Treatment

In one sense alcoholism is not curable. Alcoholics must stay sober to stay well. For most alcoholics this means no more drinking, ever. Although recovery is possible, a major stumbling block exists to motivating the alcoholic to pursue it. *Denial* is used by the alcoholic and his or her family and friends. "I can quit anytime," says the alcoholic, or "It's not my drinking that's the problem, it's . . . (anything else)." The coalcoholic (spouse, parents, lover, and so on) says, "Jane is not *really* like this. She's a wonderful person when she's sober." People often deny the fact of alcoholism because of the social stigma attached to the term "alcoholic." Despite the fact that almost everyone knows a family member, friend, or acquaintance who is afflicted by alcoholism, the popularly perceived image of the "bum in the gutter" prevails.

Treatment for alcoholism is generally not considered possible until the alcoholic makes the conscious choice to become well, although as Riley Regan (1982), of the New Jersey Department of Public Health's Alcoholism Division, said, "There are ways of moving people into systems; we call it voluntary treatment. The judge offers him six months in jail and then he volunteers for treatment." Family support is very important; the best results seem to be obtained when the whole family is treated (Nace et al., 1982; Verdery, 1973). Indeed, for many families it is imperative that the family be treated as a unit as the family's structure and stability may be organized around the existence of alcoholism (Steinglass, 1983). Self-help groups such as Alcoholics Anonymous and Al-Anon (for coalcoholics) have had good success rates. An educated public and enlightened approach by professionals are essential to achieve progress in freeing millions from the destructive grip of alcoholism.

☐ DRUG ABUSE

Although alcohol is the most commonly used and misused substance in the United States, a number of other drugs have achieved widespread popularity among many Americans. There are many kinds of *psychoactive*, or mind-affecting, drugs and many reasons for using them. Some of these drugs are legal and others are not. Instead of discussing whether drug use should be legal or illegal, it may be more useful, as Stanford researcher Richard Blum (1972) has suggested, to look at "how drugs are used, what drugs are used, what condition the user is in, what his family environment is, and what the outcome of that drug use is."

After alcohol, the most commonly used psychoactive drugs include marijuana, hallucinogens (such as LSD, mescaline, and psilocybin), cocaine, phencyclidine (PCP), narcotics ("sleep-inducing" drugs—principally heroin; also other opiates such as morphine and codeine) and inhalants (such as toluene in spray paints and nitrous oxide or "laughing gas"). *Psychotherapeutic* ("mind-healing") drugs such as antidepressants, stimulants, and sedatives are widely used; among the most commonly abused drugs in this group are amphetamines ("speed") and sedative-hypnotics such as methaqualone (Quaaludes), barbiturates (such as Seconol or "reds"), and diazepam (Valium). Drug use is prevalent in virtually all socioeconomic, sociocultural, and age groups (beginning with preteens). What varies is the drug of choice and the usage pattern. Marijuana has been tried by an estimated forty-three million Americans, of which at least twenty million are current, regular users (see Kaufman, 1982). The House Select Committee on Narcotics Abuse and Control reported in 1985 that eight to twenty million people use cocaine regularly ("A Nation . . .," 1985). Approximately half a million heroin addicts account for 90 percent of the narcotic abuse in the United States (White House Conference on Families, 1980b). Psychotherapeutic drugs can be obtained legally through prescriptions and serve legitimate medical functions. (They can also be obtained illegally.) Unfortunately, some of these drugs are among the most addictive and the most dangerous, especially when combined with alcohol.

Pharmaceutical materials do not dispense themselves and the illicit drugs are rarely given away, let alone forced on people. Consequently the menace lies within the person, for there would be no drug without drug attraction.

RICHARD BLUM

The Medicalization of Society

Whether we reach for an aspirin, a birth control pill, a cold tablet, or a cold beer, we are engaging in drug use that is culturally approved and encouraged by the mass media. Television promotes a variety of purported remedies for indigestion, bad breath, colds, coughs, hemorrhoids, and menstrual distress. More than $2 billion a year is spent on drug advertising. Physicians are at risk of being buried alive by avalanches of glossy medical periodicals and advertising circulars that use first-rate photography and third-rate psychology to sell them on the latest uppers, downers, and hormone pills (Jacobs, 1982). (You might ask your doctor if you may see some of this material on your next visit.) This type of drug pushing is part of what has been called the "medicalization of the human condition" (Bernstein and Lennard in Coombs et al., 1976), and its purpose is "to convince the public that human problems, such as anxiety, misbehavior, obesity, insomnia, overpopulation, sadness, rage, marital difficulty, etc., require medical attention. Once a problem is conceived or perceived as a disease, it is natural to think of drugs as a cure" (Coombs et al., 1976).

The availability of drugs also plays an important part in their use and abuse. For many adults, a phone call to the doctor and a trip to the drugstore can produce a bottle of Valium. For adolescents, the process may require a little more time and ingenuity, but the end result will be the same. Drugs are not going to go away. The best defense against their misuse is education—not only about the possible effects but also about the importance of the context of their use—the user and his or her family and social environment.

Drug Use, Adolescents, and Their Families

Many parents today are deeply concerned about the effects of drugs on their children. Public and grass-roots programs have been formed to enable parents to educate themselves and support one another (see Resource Center). The reasons for teenage drug use are many: relaxation, entertainment, sociability, or passing experimentation. Adolescents (or adults for that matter) may use drugs to resolve conflicts, escape stressful situations, express defiance of authority, or elicit sympathy. Drug use may be a symptom of serious disturbance and a threat to health or life. Perhaps partly in response to parental and public concern, the use of alcohol, tobacco, and most drugs by teenagers is beginning to decline. Reported alcohol use by high school seniors declined from 72 percent in 1979 to 67 percent in 1984. "Binge drinking" (five or more drinks in a row during a two-week period) declined from 41 percent in 1983 to 39 percent in 1984. Cigarette smoking by seniors fell in 1984 with 19 percent having smoked a half a pack or more per day. Monthly use of marijuana has fallen steadily in recent years, as has near-daily use, declining from 11 percent in 1978 to 5 percent in 1984. Use of LSD, sedatives, stimulants, and PCP has declined slightly. Teenage use of cocaine, heroin and other opiates has remained fairly stable. In 1984, 16 percent of seniors had used cocaine at least once, 12 percent had used it during the previous year, and 6 percent were at least monthly users (teen drug use statistics from University of Michigan in Ann Arbor study, cited in Bower, 1985). Even though drug use among adolescents does not seem to be increasing, its proportions are still "troublesomely high," according to University of Michigan researcher Lloyd D. Johnson (Bower, 1985).

The White House Conference on Families (1980b) reported that families play a part in substance abuse of all kinds and that they are an especially significant factor in combating such abuse. Blum (1972) found that certain characteristics of what he termed "excellent families" actually did "immunize [those families] against drug risk." The characteristics of these families (essentially the same as those of "successful" families discussed in Chapter 18) included the following:

- The families stressed love and the physical expression of affection. Family members showed mutual concern and interest.
- They showed a tolerance of differences and forgiveness of failings.
- Self-confidence and respect among family members allowed for a variety of self-expression.

- Parents assumed leadership and were strong but not autocratic. They were not afraid to make mistakes or to show emotion.
- They expressed a basic conviction of the goodness of the world and its people.
- Their interaction was characterized by humor and good-natured teasing.
- They communicated clearly and valued honesty and outspokeness.
- The family was a source of joy and happiness to its members.

As in the case of alcoholism, and indeed of psychological health in general, the good health of the family unit promotes the well-being of its individual members.

☐ SUMMARY

- *Violence* may be defined as acts or conditions that obstruct the unfolding of human potential; it may be direct (physical) or indirect (psychological).

- *Abuse* ("misuse" or "overuse") is at the extreme end of the violence continuum.

- Aggression is encouraged in our society; however, its permissible limits are ill-defined.

- The *battered-woman syndrome* is a recently identified phenomenon. Studies suggest that between 1.8 and six million women are battered each year by their mates or lovers.

- A typical profile of a battered woman includes such characteristics as low self-esteem, a belief that she deserves to be beaten, and "learned helplessness."

- A typical profile of a man who batters includes characteristics such as low self-esteem, emotional immaturity, excessive use of alcohol (in many but not all cases), and a belief in the moral rightness of his aggression.

- The typical three-phase *cycle of violence* in battering relationships includes (1) the *tension-building phase*, (2) the *explosive phase*, and (3) the *resolution (love) phase*.

- Women may stay in battering relationships for a number of reasons, including economic dependency, religious pressure or beliefs, the children's need for a father, pity, guilt, a sense of duty, fear, and love.

- Two to six million children are violently abused, molested, or seriously neglected each year. Child *abuse* and *neglect* have differing implications. Neglected or emotionally abused children may suffer the greater long-lasting harm owing to deep psychic injuries.

- Parents who batter their children may have been abused themselves, engage in interspousal violence, believe in the domination of the father and in corporal punishment, and be socially isolated. They may also have low self-esteem, have unrealistic expectations of their children, use their children to meet their own needs, and appear unconcerned with their children's injuries.

- Children at high risk for abuse are perceived by their parents as "unsatisfactory." These children are likely to be abused during times of crisis. Their families lack resources and support, and the parents may be predisposed to be abusive.

- If children's needs are consistently not met, they may develop inappropriate or antisocial behaviors in attempts to meet their needs.

- Some recommendations for reducing violence include: (1) reduce societal stress, (2) eliminate sexism, (3) establish supportive networks, (4) break the family cycle of violence, and (5) eliminate the legitimization and glorification of violence. Pressure from local grass-roots organizations is significant in influencing government policy.

- The extent of incest in the United States is only now being recognized. Father-daughter incest is the most common form. Of incestuous fathers, 80 to 85 percent have "symbiotic personalities"; they crave intimacy but do not know how to achieve it appropriately. Humanistic treatment of incest stresses dealing with the family as an organic system.

- It is estimated that ten million Americans are addicted to alcohol. The abuse of alcohol can be seen as a symptom of an emotional, spiritual, and physical disorder. Social drinking may also be done abusively.

- Alcoholism is sometimes called a "family disease" and involves a system of complex family interactions. Treatment is most successful if it includes the whole family.

- Psychoactive or mind-affecting drugs are widely used by Americans of all socio-economic, sociocultural, and age groups (beginning with preteens). The best defense against the misuse of drugs is education, which must include knowledge of the user and the user's family as well as the effects of the drug itself.

- Typical characteristics of families with low drug abuse rates include the physical expression of love and affection, tolerance and forgiveness, self-confidence and mutual respect, strong but not autocratic parents, humor, and clarity of communication.

READINGS

The Deadly Rage of a Battered Wife
JANET BUKOVINSKY

Although the story of Dorothy Rapp may seem particularly chilling as a story of subjugation and terror, it is in some sense a "classic" case in which many elements of the battered woman syndrome may be recognized. How do you feel about the jury's verdict in the case? What alternatives to killing her husband did Dorothy Rapp have?

Bill Rapp spent a lot of time in his toolshed. He was meticulous about rearranging the tools hanging on the walls and about sharpening his log-splitting wedges and the chain saws he used to cut firewood. He worked as a welder in a Paterson, N.J., foundry.

Back in 1953, he'd moved his wife and baby from Colorado, where he was stationed as a staff sergeant in the Air Force, to New Jersey. They bought a red house in a nice residential neighborhood in Fair Lawn.

On March 26, 1981, Bill and Dorothy Rapp were sitting in their living room in front of the fireplace. Dorothy, a soft-faced woman whose mouth seemed to melt away at its corners, had a cold. She was bundled up in a flannel nightgown and her yellow terrycloth robe. The night was chilly, and their house had no central heating system. The Rapps burned wood to keep warm.

Bill was an alcoholic. He had already put away most of his nightly quart of vodka after dinner. He started picking on Dorothy that night, as usual, berating her because she hadn't brought in another load of wood chips for the fire.

He was drunk. There were plenty of wood chips in the house. Dorothy knew what was coming.

He threw her a punch that landed, hard, in her face, and he started pummeling her. Dorothy steeled herself to the familiar rhythm of his blows, yelling at him to stop, fighting back halfheartedly. When he did, she went into their bedroom, and lay down in the dark on their double bed.

READINGS–*continued*

She was 48. Her life had been this way for 30 years, since she married Bill in Aurora, Col., when she was 18 and he 19. They had rented a little trailer there, and Dorothy soon became pregnant.

Bill's reaction to the news was an awful omen of things to come. It was the first time he beat her. He picked her up and threw her 36 feet—the length of their trailer. She slid on her side into the bedroom.

Bill Rapp's fury as he hurled his 110-pound wife across the trailer shocked her, but it was a kind of excruciating homecoming for Dorothy. At that point, Bill hadn't done anything to his wife that her father hadn't done to her mother.

"That's the way men are," counseled her mother the next day. "You married him for better or worse, until death do you part."

Dorothy returned to the trailer, and her life became one long bout of flinching and screaming.

He followed her into the bedroom, turned on the light and proceeded to drag her from the bed. "You didn't bring in enough wood chips," he screamed. "Go get more." Dorothy didn't argue.

When he threatened her life, as he had with a machete two weeks earlier, she would try to talk him out of his rage.

But tonight she sensed that the path of least resistance was the safest. She put on her slippers and went out into the darkness to fetch more wood chips. Then she went upstairs, where her 25-year-old son, James, was watching television.

He had heard the screams. They were nothing new to him. When the screams grew so agonized that James knew his mother needed help, he'd intervene, grappling with his father.

Tonight, he grimly advised Dorothy to stay out of Bill's way. The two of them heard the back door slam. Bill must have gone outside to his toolshed. She went downstairs, lay back down in their bed and dozed.

Bill was rarely sober now, except at work, and when he was drunk he seemed to prefer beating her to almost any other activity, including sex.

Dorothy spent most of her time in the house. She knew how to drive, but Bill took the car to work. She'd walk to the store or watch soap operas and crochet afghans, which she sold.

On that day in March, nearly one year ago, Dorothy woke for the second time that evening. Bill had come back and was pounding on the back of her head—a favorite spot for abusive men's fists, since hair covers the bruises. He was punching her stomach and back, breaking several of her ribs, she was later to learn.

Dorothy curled her body into a ball, trying to make herself as small as possible. Bill grabbed a handful of her hair and tore it out. His inexplicable wrath was worse than usual.

When he came at her with the machete two weeks earlier, she'd run in terror to a neighbor's house to call the police, who had responded innumerable times to domestic argument calls at the Rapp residence. Bill met them out front, subdued and charming. Just a squabble, he told them.

Dorothy was standing on the sidewalk sobbing. "He's going to kill me!" she screamed. "Can't you just take him down [to the station] and talk to him?" The police advised her to leave and did so themselves.

When Bill ceased his latest round of beating, Dorothy lay, still curled up, with her back to him. She could see him in the mirror.

He took his hunting rifle from under the bed. It was a .30-.30 lever-action Winchester, a relatively lightweight gun and a legal hunting weapon. Dorothy heard a click as Bill pulled down the lever and inserted one bullet. He rested the gun against the wall near the top of the bed, on "his" side. "Your name is on that bullet," he used to tell her when he threatened her with the gun. "Don't you move or breathe until I come back," he seethed. "You're really going to get it." Then he went outside again.

Dorothy soon got out of bed. She picked up the rifle. She walked outside to the small porch. Bill was on his way back to the house. Dorothy couldn't see him well because a shelf on the porch obstructed her view. She stuck the barrel of the rifle through a space in the porch railing, aimed "in front of the sound of his voice" and touched the trigger.

The bullet with Dorothy Rapp's name on it struck Bill Rapp as he was walking toward his house with a chain-saw sharpener in his hand. It entered the front of his body, traveled on a downward path and exited under his left arm. His heart exploded.

Still holding the Winchester, Dorothy went into their bedroom and called the police. "Send somebody, an ambulance. I just shot my husband."

James came downstairs. "What was that?" he asked.

"I just shot Daddy."

At the trial of Dorothy Rapp last November, the prosecution charged that she had committed premeditated manslaughter—that, as a battered wife, she had reason enough to hate Bill and to want to blow him away. Her attorney, Frank Lucianna, characterized her as the archetypal battered wife, paralyzed by fear and guilt. . . .

No socioeconomic group is immune. Connie Francis was a battered wife; so was Doris Day. The 1974 Nobel Peace Prize winner, the late Eisaku Sato, was publicly accused by his wife of abusing her prior to his nomination for the award.

The FBI believes that only one in 10 instances of marital abuse is reported. When the police respond to domestic violence calls, they simply aren't much help.

"Many police officers do not treat assault by a man upon his wife or female companion as a criminal act requiring arrest," said Clyde Allen, chairperson of the N.J. Advisory Committee to the U.S. Commission on Civil Rights.

Dorothy Rapp had found no ally in the police. "There were many times that the police discouraged me," she said. "I wanted to press charges, but they said I shouldn't do that, that I'd be wasting the court's time."

The police never saw Bill Rapp beating his wife. In New Jersey, acts classified as offenses, such as disorderly person charges (most applicable to wife-beating cases) must be witnessed by an officer for an arrest to be made.

At Dorothy Rapp's trial, Frank Lucianna suggested to the jury that the police had been such frequent visitors to the Rapp residence that they had simply stopped filing reports. He was determined to prove that Dorothy had acted in self-defense—that she had fired the shot to prevent Bill from killing her that night.

The fact that Dorothy was so completely subjugated by her husband was also important to her defense, in proving that she didn't have the strength to leave him. Julia Blackman Doron, a professor of psychology at Barnard College and an expert on battered wives, testified. She described Dorothy as a "psychologically cornered" woman, so entrenched in the morass of her marriage that she didn't know how to begin escaping her husband. Bill discouraged her from establishing contact with the outside world. She hadn't worked for years and had no close friends. She was, said Doron, a prisoner in her own home.

The man who beats his wife is often, according to Dr. Arnold Hutschnecker, "a frail boy who did not give his ambition attainable goals in a world of reality. He had no conscious awareness of what it meant to feel secure, to be a man with self-confidence and self-esteem." Hutschnecker, Richard Nixon's former physician, was describing Lee Harvey Oswald, a chronic wife-beater.

The advice that Dorothy received from her mother in 1952, when Bill first beat her, was cited by Lucianna as part of the syndrome that kept her bound to Bill. Her mother viewed divorce as a failure of the most "womanly" role—keeping one's family together.

Had Dorothy been able to look beyond her mother's limited perspective, she might have been able to divorce Bill, though it's difficult to say whether a judge's decree and a piece of paper would have been enough of a deterrent when the urge to beat her washed over him.

Dorothy Rapp was found innocent of manslaughter on November 18. It was the first time that the battered-wife defense was successfully used in a murder trial in New Jersey. The jury of seven men and five women deliberated for less than two hours.

Breaking the Silence
MEREDITH MARAN

As you read the following factual account of an incestuous family, note to what extent the family members resemble the corresponding profiles in the text of the chapter. What reasons does each person give for his or her role in the incest? What is the therapist's role in helping the family to heal?

Jim's shoulders slump as his oldest daughter speaks. "My dad had been molesting me for about 10 years," Rachel begins calmly. "I knew it was wrong because he always said it was our little secret, that he'd go to jail if I told anyone. I loved my dad more than I loved anyone, and I kept thinking about how much my little sisters needed him—but I was afraid that he'd start doing it to them. So I made a deal with him: I wouldn't tell if he promised not to touch my sisters. He swore I was the only one, so I learned to cope. I learned to separate my self from my body—it was just my body lying there on that bed; my dad would never do those things to the real me. At first, I'd be upset for weeks every time he molested me. Near the end I'd gotten to where he'd finish and I'd get up and forget about it within an hour or two."

Sandy's [Rachel's mother] eyes are shut. Rachel glares again at Jim and continues.

"Then one day I heard Lisa crying in her room. I felt like my heart was on fire—I just knew what was wrong. She didn't want to say anything because he'd told her she was the only one. Finally she admitted that Dad had been handling her. When Sarah got home, Lisa and I talked to her. That's when we found out that he'd been molesting all three of us since we were babies.

"Mom wanted to call the police right away. But we told her we'd deny everything if she did. We didn't want to lose our dad, we didn't want our family to fall apart. We just wanted him to stop molesting us."

When Sandy confronted him, Jim cried and swore that it would never happen again, confiding for the first time that

READINGS–*continued*

he'd been molested by his uncle for several years early in his childhood. Succumbing to the pleas of the man she'd loved for 20 years and the daughters she lived her life for, Sandy agreed to keep Jim's crime a secret. The next day, she installed deadbolts on each girl's bedroom door and ordered them to lock themselves in at night. And she swore to her husband that she'd have him arrested if he ever again attempted to have sex with their daughters.

"That next year was terrible for all of us," Sandy remembers. "I was losing my love for Jim, and I was terrified that he'd molest again. I kept asking the girls over and over if he was trying anything, and they kept promising me that everything was fine. I wanted to believe them so I shut out the little voice inside that told me something was wrong. I'd loved that man since I was 15 years old. I'd struggled so long to build the kind of family I thought we had—and I couldn't stand the thought of breaking it up, let alone telling the world that my husband was a child molester!

"Besides, Jim was our breadwinner. My income barely covered the groceries. So I prayed and prayed that somehow things would work out."

Sandy Rand's desperate decision not to report her husband's crime is one many wives of incest perpetrators make. Fear of devastating legal consequences, public humiliation and loss of income has made incest a painfully-guarded secret for untold numbers of victims. But keeping sexual abuse a family secret only allows the abuse to continue. Without treatment, both the perpetrators and the victims may pass their behavior from generation to generation.

Sandy learned this lesson the hard way: Exactly one year after she'd agreed not to report the incest in her family, 12-year-old Sarah came to her in tears. Jim had been begging her for the "special backrubs" that his older daughters now refused to give him.

"When Sandy confronted me the first time," Jim says now, "I knew I was in trouble, that I'd have to convince her to keep it in the family. But when she came to me about Sarah, I knew that I'd go to jail, that I'd never be with my wife and daughters again. Mostly I felt . . . relief. I'd been trying for so long to get Sandy to kick me out—seeing other women, picking fights—because I knew I'd never be able to stop as long as I lived with my daughters. As I watched her dial that phone, all that I could think was, 'It's finally over.' "

The first call Sandy made was to Parents United. The counselor she spoke to explained that if Sandy gave Jim's name, PU would be legally obligated to report him to the police. Things would go better, the counselor said, if Jim turned himself in with the help of a lawyer who worked with PU on such cases. Rachel, Lisa and Sarah didn't want to go to the meeting with the lawyer, but Sandy insisted. "Even after everything that had happened to them, the girls still didn't want Jim to go to jail. I hoped the lawyer would convince them that we were doing the right thing."

It was in the lawyer's office that the history of Jim's sexual abuse of his daughters was told in its entirety for the first time. He admitted everything: How he'd begun fondling Rachel when she was 4; how he'd developed an elaborate system of household chores that always left one daughter available to him; how he'd recently begun begging Rachel to let him penetrate her. He told how frightened he'd become when Sarah had had her first asthma attack while he was molesting her. Hearing his three-hour confession, Jim's victims began to feel the rage they'd been swallowing for so many years.

"Something snapped inside me," Rachel remembers. "Before that, there was no wrong to him. He was my best friend, my wonderful dad. I believed him when he said he molested me because I was so pretty and he loved me so much. But as I was listening to the whole story, I was filled with hate. This man we all worshipped had been hurting us horribly all our lives. We told Mom to go ahead and send him to jail. At that moment, I hoped he'd never get out." She glances at Jim, whose reddened eyes meet hers. "Sometimes I still think he should spend his life in there."

Because Jim pleaded guilty, there was no trial. In January 1983, he was sentenced to one year in Elmwood County Jail. His confession, clean police record and willingness to undergo therapy qualified him for the county Child Sexual Abuse Treatment Program. Jim was placed on work furlough on the condition that he attend weekly counseling sessions and donate weekend labor to Parents United.

"My first night at Elmwood," Jim says, "was when it really hit me. If any other man had done those things to my daughters, I would have taken him apart. But that monster was me." His voice quavers; he swallows hard. "I would have given my life to make up to my daughters for what I'd done." When he was offered an early release after six months, his daughters protested unanimously; they wanted their father to finish his sentence, Jim passed up the release and spent the full year in jail.

Jim's removal from their home provided no respite for his wife and daughters. The girls turned their anger on Sandy, accusing her of not protecting them, of not having sex with Jim often enough, of not loving and understanding them as their father had done. "They called me names I'd never heard from their mouths before," Sandy says, looking down at Sarah. "They wouldn't obey me, they wouldn't listen or talk to me. They refused to go to counseling. Because of the molest, they'd been made wards of the court and I knew if they kept up their acting out I would lose them forever. So I did what I had to do to save what was left of our family."

What Sandy did was write a letter to the judge asking him to order her daughters into individual and family therapy. "At first we fought it, 'cause we were forcd to go," Lisa remembers. 'But then we realized that we couldn't keep our feelings inside forever. Plus, with our dad gone, we needed help dealing with Mom. It was like a war at our house."

Rachel adds quickly, "We still don't get along that well with her. It'll never be like it was with Dad. But at least now Theresa's [the therapist] taught us to communicate."

"I still love my wife deeply," Jim says, his eyes on Sandy. "But I know I've lost her. And my daughters . . . last week when we had our first session with the whole family, they told me they still love me but they hate me, too. I don't blame them one bit. I took the love they were giving me truthfully, I turned it around and abused them as women instead of protecting them as daughters. I knew I had a problem, but I blamed it on everyone else: my uncle who molested me, Sandy, my boss . . . Now I can only blame myself. None of this would have happened if I'd gotten help before it was too late."

"It *is* too late," Sandy says quickly. "I still love this man. But my girls come first with me, and my girls want this marriage to end. So 20 years is dissolved. I've lost more than my husband because of sexual abuse. I lost my father years ago when he abused Rachel. I lost all my friends— they were mostly people Jim and I worked with and I didn't want them to know what we were going through. I lost my job because I fell apart emotionally. The worst thing I lost was my self-esteem: as a wife, a mother, a woman.

"Right now the only thing that gives me hope is the changes I see in myself and in my daughters. We're all more independent now. I just graduated from a nursing program, so I'll never rely financially on anyone again. Rachel's got herself a good job so she can take care of herself, and she's engaged to a fine young man. Lisa—she's always been so quiet—speaks up more now. Sarah's learning not to blame herself for things that have been done to her. In a way, my daughters and I have grown up together through this tragedy. I've learned along with them how I was raised to be a victim, like my mother was before me. I know my daughters won't raise *their* daughters that way! And we've all learned to say no—a word that as females we were taught never to say."

Rachel jerks her head angrily. "You make it sound so

easy, Mom. What about the other things we learned?" She turns to me. "Like not to trust anyone, ever. Like growing up believing that you pay for love with sex. Like having to lie to everyone all your life. I'm *still* lying, trying to explain why I won't let Dad walk me down the aisle on my wedding day. And Lisa's still two grades behind because she was afraid to come home to do her homework. And Sarah's still got her asthma. As long as my sisters and I are suffering because of what he did, I'll *never* forgive him."

"It hurts deep down to face up to what I've done to you," Jim says. He is sobbing now. "I'm so sorry . . ."

Rachel doesn't let him finish. "You should feel sorry—I don't accept your apology. You can sit there and talk about facing up to it. Well, we face up to it whether we want to or not! Do you know that Lisa just lost her babysitting job because the parents found out she was molested? Do you know that Sarah still wakes up screaming almost every night? Do you know that none of us has a single friend who knows the truth about us? You just make me feel guilty with all your damn apologies, and I don't want to hear them anymore."

Sarah begins to wheeze. Sandy sits her up; Lisa digs through Sarah's book bag and pulls out a bronchial inhaler. As Sarah's panting slows, Lisa stares straight at me for a long moment.

"You said you wanted to know our story," she says. "Well, now you see how it is for us. And I want you to write it all down. I want every kid who's being molested right now to know that they shouldn't keep it a secret, that they deserve help and they can get help. And I want every man out there to know what it does to children to be sexually abused."

Tears run down her cheeks. "If we can keep this from happening to just one girl or one boy, maybe all this pain will be worth it."

Love Letter for a Bottle Bobbing Through Rough Tides
ANN RYAN

Alcoholism is one of the most prevalent problems of individual and public concern in our society. In this painful and deeply personal account by the wife of an alcoholic, some typical fears, hopes, angers, regrets, and conflicts are revealed. What are they? What is the nature of Ann Ryan's relationship with her husband? How do you think he views his relationship with her? With their children?

READINGS–*continued*

I do not smash his bottles into the sink anymore. Nor do I cleverly dilute his wine or pour half his cocktail down the drain when he's not looking.

I want to believe that I am too wise to react negatively.

I no longer search out evidence—how many crumpled beer cans in the trash, how many bottles hidden in closets and drawers.

I want to think that I am too intelligent to waste my time.

I know that the illness has him in its clutches; sometimes I can see the invisible fingers uncurling toward him.

I want to be precise and not drawn into analogy.

He comes home in the evening and he wants a drink. Now. Freshly drawn hop-scotch squares on the sidewalk will wait. Little hands smeared with poster-paints will wait. The game of Frisbee in the street will wait, and so will the mail and the poppies that just bloomed today.
I want to believe that I am too experienced to still be disappointed.

I no longer count his drinks when we are in a restaurant, entertaining on our patio, or simply spending a week-night evening at home. I do not complain or nag anymore when he slurs his words, when he cannot remember what was said only hours before. Nor do I accuse him of having a hangover when he says he does not feel well in the morning.

I want to think that I am being tactful.

No matter what I want to think, I feel like an actress.

Alcoholism's perplexing plot structure is a progressive one, and each day becomes a scene for which I devise new techniques.

It has been a long time since I cast myself as the protagonist in a drama that often ended in hysteria. I see those days as frames from an old, memorized movie—title: Alcoholism.

Always it was my dialogue delivered first. If I fantasized that my prepared speech would speed a step toward a possible solution, then my lines bloomed with sincerity and information. Alcoholism, the illness.

If I needed to believe that my disappointments and wounded feelings would make a difference, that my wishes would inspire a change, then my lines were delivered kindly, with direct eye-contact and few tears, his hand clasped gently in mine. Alcoholism, the imposter, the curse.

Most of the time, my dialogue was full of hostility set to the dissonant music of ad-lib shrieks. Alcoholism, the

criminal. Keeper of secrets. Rotter of brains. Alcohol, the hue of old blood, the scent of formaldehyde. Alcoholism, the embezzler of peaceful family evenings, the raper of brilliant minds, the thief of meaningful communications.

Lately, it seems, I have cast myself as a mime, a spectator standing at the misty perimeter of that which confuses me no less now than before, a character wordlessly sorting through the finely tuned dreams of two, trying to make them only mine again.

My role has many faces, but not that of the ingenue. I knew there was a drinking problem when we married. But problems are to be solved; then, I did not believe that there would be stupid, senseless endings.

I will not send my wedding rings spinning through the crossfire of angry words. I have learned that separation results in temporarily controlled drinking, reconciliation, but not the sought-after change. It is my own sense of perspective that I search for now, not changes in drinking patterns, not happy endings or even peaceful ones.

I have watched alcoholism steal others. It weaves through both our families like a corroded strand of beads. Few have been spared. Now, my husband. . . .

No! Not him! He is too beautiful, too talented to be wasted, too important to drown his gifts, too valuable to lose.

I want to think that it is his loss, not mine, his responsibility to himself. Still, I am not yet prepared to write myself out of the script, to make the final exit. There are the sober scenes; they are strewn like bouquets across the stage. Perhaps I am not ready to admit how few the bouquets have become, how quickly they wither. Maybe I think that it will be easier to quit the role of an actress when there are no more sober scenes, and therefore nothing left to love.

It is evening. Now and then a car pulls into one of the driveways across the street; doors shut, groceries are carried into houses. There is a slight breeze stirring and the sounds of children at play; a ball bounces, a skateboard whizzes past, a dog barks and there is laughter. I focus on those sounds and pretend to ignore the background noises inside our house: a wine bottle dragged across the metal rungs of the refrigerator shelf, the pop top of an aluminum can, ice cubes hitting the bottom of a glass.

I will pretend all is silent as I recite these lines to the audience of myself: "God grant me the serenity to accept the things I cannot change, the courage to change the things I can, and the wisdom to know the difference."

PART SIX

Changes

CHAPTER 16

Coming Apart:
Separation and Divorce

PREVIEW

To gain a sense of what you already know about the material covered in this chapter, answer "true" or "false" to the statements below. You will find the answers as you read the chapter.

1. One-third of individuals twenty-nine to thirty-five years of age may divorce by age seventy-five. True or false?
2. Men and women who divorce have similar marital complaints. True or false?
3. There is a fifty-fifty chance that a child born today will be in a single-parent or blended family before he or she reaches age eighteen. True or false?
4. The critical event in a marital breakdown is the separation, not the divorce. True or false?
5. More men than women initiate separation. True or false?
6. Separating individuals often feel attachment to the partner they are leaving. True or false?
7. Generally, only lower-income single mothers use food stamps or welfare to supplement their income. True or false?
8. Adolescents generally keep in contact with their noncustodial parent. True or false?
9. Approximately fifty thousand instances of child snatching by the non-custodial parent occur yearly in the United States. True or false?
10. Joint-custody fathers tend to be more involved with their children than noncustodial fathers. True or false?

Outline

Married people, like any other people, must continue to grow as individuals if they are not to stagnate. . . . That means that no one, at the time of marriage, can know what the spouse is going to become. Moreover, it means that he cannot know what he himself may become.

PAUL BOHANNON, *DIVORCE AND AFTER*

"Divorces are made in heaven," Oscar Wilde drily observed in the nineteenth century. And so it seemed at that time, for divorces were almost impossible to obtain owing to restrictive legal codes. By the turn of the century only slightly more than 11,000 divorces per year were granted in the United States (Gordon, 1978). Restrictive divorce laws helped preserve the ideal of the intact nuclear family. Although desertion and separation split families up as effectively as divorce, marriages remained legally intact. Laws helped preserve the social fiction of the intact family.

But today there is no such social fiction of the eternally lasting marriage. Divorce is an unyielding fact of American marital and family life and one of the most important institutions affecting and changing American lives today (Price-Bonham et al., 1983). Not only does divorce end marriages and break up families but it also creates new forms from the old ones. It creates second marriages (and third and fourth marriages for some). It gives birth to the single-parent family and to blended or stepfamilies. It has produced the world of the formerly married, including a large singles subculture of the divorced, most of whom are on their way to remarriage. But divorce does not create these new forms painlessly. It gives birth to them in pain and travail. There are few easy divorces.

In this chapter we look at divorce trends, the causes of divorce, the changes an individual undergoes when he or she separates, no-fault divorce, custody, and the impact of divorce on children. In the next chapter we examine how people put their lives back together after divorce and how, in doing so, they create new family structures.

☐ DIVORCE TRENDS

A man should not marry a woman with the mental reservation that, after all, he can divorce her.

TALMUD: YEBAMOTH

Before 1974 the majority of marriages ended through death rather than divorce. "Until death do us part" reflected reality. But a surge in divorce rates occurred in the mid-1960s. In 1974 a watershed in American history was reached when more marriages ended through divorce than through death. Today close to 1.25 million divorces take place each year. If the current trend continues, 49 percent of all persons between the ages twenty-nine and thirty-five years will divorce by age seventy-five (Glick, 1984a). (See special issue on divorce in *Journal of Family Issues*, August, 1985.)

Although much of our attention has focused on the divorce rate, another important trend in divorce must be examined. The number of divorces involving children has significantly increased. With the current divorce rate, a 50 percent probability exists that a person will be a member of a blended family (stepfamily) as a child, parent, or stepparent (Furstenberg, 1980; also see Press, 1983). Today 22 percent of America's families are single-parent families (U.S. Census, 1984).

□ CAUSES OF DIVORCE

The trends in divorce are fairly clear, but the causes are not. Sociologists can describe demographic variables that appear to be associated with divorce. Unfortunately, such variables only tell us about groups rather than individuals. Similarly, divorced men and women can tell us what they believe were the causes of their divorces. But human beings do not always know the reasons for their actions; they can deceive themselves, blame others, or remain ignorant of the causes (Burns, 1984). Sometimes marital complaints are culled from long-term marital problems as a justification for the split up (Rasmussen and Ferraro, 1979). Kitson and Sussman (1982) observed that the study of marital complaints as causes of divorce is merely the study of people's perceptions: "It is perhaps an impossibility to determine what 'really' broke up a marriage." (Also see Booth et al., 1985; Menaghan, 1985.)

Because so many factors contribute to divorce, perhaps the best way to determine causes is to look at relationships between marital complaints and demographic factors such as age, class, and religion (Cleek and Pearson, 1985).

Demographic Factors

The demographic factors related to divorce include race, income, education, occupation, age at time of marriage, family background, and region. (See Booth, 1985, for a literature review; also see Spitze and South, 1985.)

Race.   Blacks are more likely than whites to divorce. Combined data from several national surveys taken between 1973 and 1980 indicate that 22.2 percent of white males and 37.2 percent of black males who have ever been married have divorced; the corresponding figure for white females was 23.5 percent and for black females 42.2 percent (Glenn and Supancic, 1984). Blacks are more likely than whites to divorce at all income, educational, and occupational levels (Carter and Glick, 1976).

Income.   The higher the income, the lower the divorce rate for both races. Interestingly, the divorce rate increases for high-income women (Glick and Norton, 1977). Apparently, low-income groups have greater marital instability because of economic pressures. It is not clear why divorce increases for high-income women; perhaps the conflicts between career and homemaker roles take their toll on marriage.

Educational Level.   The higher the educational level for whites, the lower the divorce rate. Divorce rates among blacks are not as strongly affected by educational levels. Men and women with only a high-school education are more likely to divorce than men with a college education (Glick, 1984b).

. . . some people are unhappily married because, for deep-rooted reasons—psychological, biological, or social—they are incapable of happy human relations in any aspect of their lives. Some people, however, are unhappily married not because of any inherent personality defects but because of . . . "team factors." They are quite capable of happiness, including marital happiness, but not with their present partners. And some people, finally, are unhappily married because of a marital history of mistakes in dealing with interactional problems of one kind or another that have deformed the relationship.

JESSIE BERNARD, *REMARRIAGE*

Excuses

Are you leaving me because you are hungry?
Aha! Is your stomach your master?

Are you leaving me to cover yourself?
Have I not a blanket on my bed?

Are you leaving me because you are thirsty?
Then take my breast, it flows over for you.

Blessed is the day of our first meeting.

TRADITIONAL AFRICAN POEM

Occupational Level. Among whites, a higher divorce rate is more characteristic of low-status occupations (such as factory worker) than of high-status occupations (such as executive) (Carter and Glick, 1976; also see Greenstein, 1985).

Age at Time of Marriage. Adolescent marriages are more likely to end in divorce than marriages that take place when people are in their twenties or older. This is true for both whites and blacks. The partners are less likely to be emotionally mature; they are often pressured into marriage because of pregnancy, which is also correlated with a higher divorce rate. After age twenty-six for men and age twenty-three for women, age at marriage seems to make little difference (Glenn and Supancic, 1984). Some scholars (Booth and Edwards, 1985) argue, however, that those who marry in their late twenties and afterward have a higher divorce rate because their habits of independent living and pressure from long-time friends cause stress in their marriages.

Family Background. Both blacks and whites have an increased likelihood of divorce if an individual's family of origin was disrupted by divorce or desertion (see Riley and Spreitzer, 1974). Classic studies (Burgess and Cottrell, 1939; Burgess and Wallin, 1953; Popenoe and Wicks, 1937) indicate that the most important factor predicting marital stability is a person's childhood background.

Geographical Location. The rates of divorce increase from east to west and from north to south. The highest rate is found in California, where currently two divorces occur for every three marriages. The greater likelihood for divorce in the West and Southwest may be caused by the higher rates of residential mobility and a lower level of social integration with extended families, ethnic neighborhoods, and church groups (Glenn and Supancic, 1984; Glenn and Shelton, 1985).

Religion. The frequency with which people attend religious services (not necessarily the depth of their beliefs) tends to lower the divorce rate (Glenn and Supancic, 1984). Among white males, the rate of divorce for those who never attend religious services is three times as high as for those who attend two or three times a month. The lowest divorce rate is for Jews, followed by Catholics and then Protestants.

Marital Complaints

Researchers have found that the complaints of divorced people vary according to sex, class, length of marriage, and rural or urban residence (Goode, 1956; Levinger, 1965; see Bloom et al., 1985).

W. J. Goode (1956) who studied a large group of divorced women in Detroit in 1948, found that the five most common complaints expressed by women about their husbands were, in descending order of frequency, extramarital affairs, authoritarianism, complex complaints (running around, gambling, staying away, and so on), drinking, and personality problems. Goode's study, however, is more than thirty years old, and the state of marriage and divorce has changed significantly since then. Not only is divorce now extremely common and accepted but also the reasons people give for getting divorced are ranked differently and new ones have been added. In a sample weighted to duplicate Goode's, Gay Kitson and Marvin Sussman (1982) found that the reasons women gave in 1974 and 1975 for divorcing were quite different from those their mothers' generation gave. The four most common reasons were, in descending order of frequency, personality problems, home life, authoritarianism, and differing values. Extramarital affairs ranked first in the 1948 study; twenty years later, reflecting the changed values accompanying the sexual revolution, extramarital affairs ranked seventh.

Looking at the same 1974–75 data from a different perspective, the researchers found some indication that stress over changing sex roles may be affecting divorce. The second most frequent complaint that men expressed involved conflict over sex roles; this ranked only eighth for women. Conflict over sex roles involved not only appropriate conduct for the sexes but also complaints that the spouse was too authoritarian, paternal, or maternal. For women, the second most frequent complaint involved sex role conflict about desires for freedom and a life independent of husbands and families. This complaint ranked sixth for men. When responses were combined, 35 percent of the men and 41 percent of the women made complaints about sex roles. Kitson and Sussman (1982) observed:

> The high frequency with which these complaints are mentioned suggests that married couples today are struggling with issues involving the desire for self-growth and the development and allocation of roles within the family. These conflicts, in turn, create dissension within the family when the couple cannot reconcile their differing expectations and desires.

Love, the quest; marriage, the conquest; divorce, the inquest.

HELEN ROWLAND

Marital Cohesiveness

Whatever the demographic or personal reasons we may find for divorce, the ultimate reasons may escape us. Another way to understand divorce is to examine marital cohesiveness. According to Levinger (1965), people remain married because of

Whatever the demographic or personal causes we may find for divorce, the ultimate reasons may escape us.

UNDERSTANDING YOURSELF

Understanding Divorce

Divorce is a common phenomenon these days. But it occurred in other generations as well. If you go back one or two generations and include aunts and uncles as well as parents and grandparents, you will likely find a divorce in the family. In your own family, how many divorces have there been over the last three generations? Who was divorced? What were the reasons? How did your family react to these divorces? What new family relationships (stepcousins, stepuncles, and so on) were created by them? How did you (or your parents) relate to these quasifamily members?

What about your own immediate family (in-

cluding siblings as well as parents)? Have any divorces occurred? If so, how did they affect you and your feelings about having an enduring marriage? What were the stated causes? Do you think the stated causes were the "real" causes?

In today's climate, what factors do you think will have an impact on your marriage (present or future)? For yourself, what do you consider "legitimate" reasons for divorce? Under what circumstances do you think your own marital commitment would erode? What could you do to prevent it?

(1) sources of attraction, (2) barriers against leaving, and (3) sources of alternate attraction. In this model *attraction* refers to positive forces that keep people in a relationship, *barriers* are restraining forces that keep people from leaving a relationship, and *alternative attractions* are other persons, relationships, or activities that compete with the marital relationship. Although Levinger's model is not romantic, it may be realistic. For those who have been ambivalent about ending a long-term relationship, these three factors may seem all too familiar.

It's one thing marrying the wrong person for the wrong reasons: it's another sticking it out with them.

PHILIP ROTH, *LETTING GO*

Attractions.   Attractions include caring for one's partner, the desire for companionship, sexual pleasure, and other affectionate aspects of the relationship. They also include a good standard of living (such as home ownership, family income), similar social values, and educational and occupational status. It is not uncommon for people to stay together because they love their house rather than each other.

Barriers.   Barriers to breaking up include feelings of obligation, moral proscriptions, and external pressures. One of the strongest restraints is a couple's—especially the mother's—deep sense of love and moral obligation to their dependent children (Levinger, 1979). Few things will cut a person deeper than concern over the impact of divorce on his or her children. A recent study, for example, has shown that women with children are significantly less liberal toward divorce than women without children (Jorgensen and Johnson, 1980). The presence of children, however, has little effect on men's attitude toward divorce. The couple may also feel an obligation to the marriage itself, even if they have ceased loving each other. The couple may feel they are morally obliged by their religion not to divorce. Finally, they may feel external pressures not to divorce. (What will our parents say? What will our friends say?) Family pressure and community pressure have been powerful constraints on divorce in the past. But such constraints have weakened in recent years. (For the significance of commitment, see Sabatelli and Cecil-Pigo, 1985; Swenson and Trahaug, 1985.)

Alternatives. The alternatives to marriage may include singlehood and greater independence and self-direction, especially for women who may have felt their potential curtailed in marriage. Also, a person may find (or believe he or she may find) greater happiness with another partner.

Levinger's model of marital cohesiveness is a useful way to look at relationships. J. Richard Udry (1981) conducted a study to see if the existence of marriage alternatives was a significant variable in explaining marital stability. He assumed that we live in a marriage system in which everyone is permanently available as a spouse (Farber, 1964) and is continually comparing his or her current marriage with other potential marriages or with singlehood. If a person's present marital relationship appears strikingly less favorable than the alternatives and the barriers to leaving the marriage do not cancel out the value of the alternatives, then the marriage is more likely to dissolve. Udry found that marriages in which many marriage alternatives were available to both spouses had a high divorce rate. What is striking, however, is that marital alternatives are a better predictor of divorce than marital satisfaction. People often stay in unhappy marriages if they feel they do not have good alternatives. They may also leave relatively satisfactory marriages if they feel their alternatives are better. In a society in which everyone is available, whether married or not, people may have a tendency to see the grass as greener on the other side of the fence. If the fence (barrier) is not too high, people may find themselves abandoning their familiar turf for the greener pastures on the other side. Unfortunately, that grass on the other side may only be Astroturf.

> . . . couples have split up over issues they might well have struggled through. Leaving is more often an avoidance of change than an instrument of change. The pain of parting misleads people into thinking that they have not chosen the easy way out.
>
> DANIEL GOLDSHUE, ET AL., *THE DANCE-AWAY LOVER*

☐ MARITAL BREAKDOWN

Divorce is an increasingly frequent experience for Americans. In 1970, divorced persons represented 4 percent of ever-married persons; in 1984, divorced persons represented 9 percent of the ever-married (U.S. Census, 1985). Most newly separated people do not know what to expect. There are no divorce ceremonies or rituals to mark this major turning point in people's lives. Yet people need to understand divorce to alleviate some of its pain and burden. Except for the death of a spouse, divorce is the greatest stress-producing event in life, even greater than being sent to prison (Holmes and Rahe, 1967).

One study found that women initiated separation more frequently than men (Pettit and Bloom, 1984). These women tended to be less traditional in their marital roles than women whose husbands left them. Women tended to leave when marital problems became more severe; men tended to leave when marital problems were relatively mild but seemed unwilling to terminate the marriage if the difficulties were more severe (but also see Heaton et al., 1985).

The crucial event in a marital breakdown is not the divorce but the act of separating. Divorce is a legal fact that follows the emotional fact of separation (Price-Bonham and Balswick, 1980; Melichar and Chiriboga, 1985). But the changes that take place during separation are crucial because at this point the person's emotions are rawest and most profound. Men and women react differently to this period, although both are more depressed than their married or divorced counterparts (Pearlin and Johnson, 1977). Men have a generally lower sense of well-being than women, yet women undergo greater emotional upheaval (Chiriboga and Cutler, 1978). Marital breakdowns usually begin with isolation, invalidation, and betrayal (Weiss, 1975).

Isolation

As a marriage begins its downward spiral, each partner usually feels isolated from the other. They act as if they were strangers. The silences between them become longer and longer. They grow deaf to each other's needs. For some couples, days may begin with tension, uneasy truces, harsh glances, knifelike words—and end in outright fights. Other couples may be guarded and withdrawn. If the partners do speak, the communication is usually routine, without feeling; or else too much feeling is involved and simple conversations are turned into tense confrontations. Thus conversations tend to become polite and limited to neutral subjects. The real subject underlying the silence—the marriage—is often avoided. The partners may talk about dinner and shopping, the kids, fixing the car, cleaning up the yard—anything but their real feelings—then silence and the sound of the television in the background.

It's not love's going hurts my days
But that it went in little ways.
EDNA ST. VINCENT MILLAY

Invalidation

When a marriage breaks down, the partners may begin a process of mutual invalidation. Whereas once they affirmed each other—gave each other positive reinforcement—they now negate each other. For example, a man comes out of a movie laughing uproariously and his wife turns to him and says, "I don't see what's so funny." Her voice is thick with disapproval and he freezes from its iciness. He stops laughing and probably feels both anger and self-doubt: "Maybe the movie wasn't so funny after all." "Maybe I'm dumb." Or "Maybe I'm driving her up the wall, and she can't enjoy herself around me anymore." So the negativity builds, feeding on itself, creating more bad feelings. Each remains unaffirmed, invalidated, made to feel small, a nobody. "You're a lousy lover." "You're a terrible mother." "You are always spending money." Accusation follows accusation.

By the time such a couple separates, both partners may feel a desperate need for affirmation. Each wants to feel good inside, worthy of being loved. Perhaps such feelings of self-esteem were present earlier in the relationship, but now they have disappeared. The breakdown in their relationship may have shaken their confidence in themselves as human beings.

My wife is unhappy. She is one of those married women who are very, very bored, and lonely, and I don't know what I can make myself do about it (except get a divorce, and make her unhappier still. I was with a married woman not long ago who told me she felt so lonely at times she turned ice cold and was literally afraid she was freezing to death from inside, and I believe I know what she meant).

JOSEPH HELLER, SOMETHING HAPPENED

Betrayal

Trust and loyalty are two key attributes that each partner usually expects of the other in a marital relationship. Each expects that the other will be kind, affirming, and protective. Regardless of what passes between them, each partner counts on the other to be supportive in public, not to start a fight or argument around friends or strangers. But as relationships erode, support is withdrawn. A couple may no longer stand together in disputes with other people. Either partner may side with a friend, relative, or neighbor against his or her own spouse. Little incidents are experienced as betrayals. For most couples, the ultimate betrayal is infidelity, which often leads to a final crisis.

Yet, somehow, many unhappy couples continue to remain together. Their relationship moves from live to dull to dead. Couples generally split up only after "rigor mortis" sets in and there is no longer any hope of resurrecting the marriage. In this sense, despite increasing divorce rates, people do not make the decision to separate very easily. It usually takes a long time after the relationship has lost its meaning to make the break.

☐ ATTACHMENT

How can you miss someone with whom you have been unhappy for years? It seems a strange question, but couples who break up face this contradictory fact again and again. Most people miss their former partner for some time after separation. Yet missing is not the same as loving someone; it is instead an expression of loneliness or attachment (Bohannon, 1971; Weiss, 1975). In a disintegrating marriage, most aspects of love are gradually eroded by the daily tensions of living together. Idealization disappears as partners fail to live up to each other's expectations. The sense of identity and oneness vanishes under the strain of constant differences and conflicts. What remains, however, is attachment. Attachment is what sociologist Robert Weiss (1975) called "a bonding to the other that gives rise to feelings of at-homeness and ease when the other is present, or if not actually present, is felt to be accessible." This sense of attachment can ease loneliness. When a man and woman separate, the attachment for the other lingers on, usually for a considerable period; the only thing that seems to diminish its power is time (see Berman, 1985).

> To free oneself is nothing; it's being free that is hard.
> ANDRÉ GIDE (1869–1951)

Adults associate comfort and security with an "attachment figure" in much the same way that children do. When the attachment figure disappears, Weiss noted, *separation distress* arises, a condition characterized by general stress, anxiety, and anger. These feelings of separation can only be eased when the attachment figure returns. As the separation continues, return is more and more unlikely. Eventually separation distress disappears and is replaced by loneliness.

In most marriages that are breaking down, neither partner is able to let go of his or her attachment to the other; doing so would be too painful. Even more important, marital partners probably could not let go of attachment if they wanted to. Feelings of such great depth are not easily changed, regardless of how desperately the person wants to change them. The heart, in all its wisdom and folly, continues to rule the mind. Weiss (1975) wrote:

> Often individuals in marriages they believe to be hopeless, who recognize the continued attachment to a spouse they feel they must leave, curse themselves for their weakness and dependence. They should not. Attachment can be extraordinarily resistive to dissipation. Even individuals who have been long separated, who believe their marriage to be finished and have found someone new, may discover on meeting the spouse that dormant feelings of attachment are reawakened.

> . . . for four years he kept repeating his love and she would always find a way to reject him without hurting him, for even though she had not succeeded in loving him she could no longer live without him.
> GABRIEL GARCIA MARQUEZ, ONE HUNDRED YEARS OF SOLITUDE

Sometimes the couple may engage in sexual relations again. One study of forty-eight couples found that six had sexual intercourse during their separation (Hetherington et al., 1976). The motivation for these encounters differed, but rarely was it for purposes of reconciliation. Such encounters run a relatively high risk of unintentional pregnancy, since they are usually sudden, highly charged and unplanned. In such circumstances contraception may be neglected and a pregnancy result (Miller, 1973). Approximately 25 percent of the remarried women in the 1970 National Fertility Study had given birth during a period of marital disruption (Rindfuss and Bumpass, 1977). Approximately 11 percent of the women had given birth between separation and divorce, and 14 percent had given birth between divorce and remarriage.

Separation Distress and Loneliness

You will never go wrong in concluding that a man has once loved deeply whatever he hates, and loves it yet, that he once admired and still admires what he scorns, that he once greedily desired what now disgusts him.

GEORG GRODDECK

During separation distress almost all attention is centered on the missing partner and is accompanied by apprehensiveness, anxiety, fear, and often panic. "What am I going to do?" "What is he or she doing?" "I need him . . . I need her . . . I hate him . . . I hate her . . ." Sometimes, however, the immediate effect of separation is not distress but euphoria. Euphoria usually results from the feeling that the former spouse is not necessary, that one can get along better without him or her, that the old fights and the spouse's criticism are gone forever—and that life will now be full of possibilities and excitement. That feeling is soon gone. Almost everyone falls back into separation anxiety (Trafford, 1982, 1983).

As the separation continues, separation distress slowly gives way to loneliness. Eventually, loneliness becomes the most prominent feature of the broken relationship. Psychologist Harry Stack Sullivan (1952) noted that loneliness may make the indi-

When couples break up, each individual usually suffers from separation distress and loneliness.

vidual act in ways that seem alien to him or her. Friends may remark that they hardly know the person any longer. Lonely people may begin frequenting singles bars, change their style of living, become flamboyant where they were once conservative, reckless where they were once cautious, promiscuous where they were once puritanical. Blue jeans may replace skirts, or three-piece suits may replace colorful shirts and patched Levi's. Fantasies and experimental ways of living are more likely to be acted out.

Old friends can sometimes help stabilize a person experiencing a marital breakup, but those who give comfort need to be able to tolerate the other person's loneliness. Sometimes, however, separated people will consider themselves a burden and will turn away from old friends, who seem happy and content. In fact, married friends are generally supportive the first two months, but then their contacts with the separated person rapidly decline (Hetherington et al., 1977), perhaps in part because they related to the person as part of a couple rather than as an individual in his or her own right. Beginning group therapy with other recently divorced people may help. Within such a group, divorced or separated people discover that their loneliness is not strange, they are not going crazy; on the contrary, their responses are quite normal under the circumstances.

Factors Affecting Separation Distress

Separation distress affects people in a variety of ways, depending on whether the person was forewarned, the length of time married, who takes the initiative in leaving, whether someone new is found, the quality of the postmarital relationship, and personal resources.

Forewarning An unexpected separation is probably the most painful kind for the partner. For example, a man who is an "ideal" husband and father may fall in love with someone other than his wife. Keeping his love a secret until all arrangements with the other woman have been made, he may one night read the children stories, say good night to them, tell his wife he loves someone else, and leave. The wife is devastated. How can one person live with another on intimate terms and not know that the marital partner is unhappy or dissatisfied? Weiss (1975) observed that marriage forces each partner to be aware of the other's moods, but does not require each to know the other's plans.

Length of Time Married. Separations that take place during the first two years of marriage are less difficult for the husband and wife to weather. Those who separate after two years find separation more difficult. It seems to take about two years for people to become emotionally and socially integrated into their marriage and their marital roles (Weiss, 1975); after that point additional years of marriage seem to make little difference. Generally, a person married for two years will suffer distress over loss of marital roles as much as one married ten years.

The Leaver and the Left. As anyone might suspect, it makes considerable difference who leaves whom. For one thing, the initiator has a greater sense of personal control over his or her life (Pettit and Bloom, 1984). Yet who leaves whom does not seem to make much difference in the length or intensity of separation distress but rather in the character of the distress. People who do the leaving frequently feel a strong sense of guilt about hurting their partners and may worry about their own capacity to make emotional commitments, since they have broken this major one. The person who is left often experiences a desperate feeling of abandonment—helpless, bewildered, often inadequate. They feel rejected because they have in fact been rejected. They feel powerless because they were unable to prevent the leaving. All they can do is stand by and watch their lives disintegrate. They often feel their fate is undeserved. ("Why did this happen to me? Wasn't I good enough?")

Finding Someone New   Finding someone new helps, but not as much as most people believe. A new relationship reduces much of the distress caused by separation, and it almost entirely prevents the loneliness caused by emotional isolation. It also reinforces a person's sense of self-worth. But it does not entirely eliminate separation distress. It does not end the disruption of intimate personal relations with the former partner, children, friends, and relatives. One woman spent the night with her new lover. At dawn she suddenly felt a great loneliness for her husband. She left her lover early in the morning and drove over to her husband's home. He met her angrily at the door. "What do you want?" he asked. "I still miss you," she said, "I want to be with you." He slammed the door.

Under the stress of loneliness and insecurity, some people form new attachments that in other times they would never have contemplated. In their desperate need for intimacy, they choose an unsuitable person. One woman remarked that her new relationship—in which she was still involved—was even more disillusioning than her marriage, which was rotten. Also, a great deal of emotional turmoil often accompanies relationships with newly separated men and women. Another woman said that she and her friends made a point of not becoming involved with divorced men unless the men had been separated at least a year. She called newly separated men "untouchables," and related her experience with a man who was newly separated. Both he and she were miserable, mostly because she was not his former wife. They broke up shortly afterward.

Quality of the Postmarital Relationship.   After separation the ways that husbands and wives treat each other may range from friendly consideration and care to outright hostility and warfare. Friendly divorces certainly have the most to be said for them, but they are not easy to achieve. It usually takes considerable time for emotions to cool and wounds to heal. It may also require substantial work and insight for the ex-partners to get beyond blame and anger. If former partners do achieve friendly relations, they may feel reassured that the years they spent together were not meaningless.

A friendly divorce will provide a structure of trust: each ex-partner can count on the other within certain limits. This situation is an ideal one and may remain only an ideal for many. For some people the quality of their marriage was so poor that it isn't worth the effort to maintain contact. For others, trying to be friends with an ex-mate is a source of constant frustration. Consider the man who has been separated from his wife for more than a year. They want to be friends with each other. The man says that too often the pain of her having left him prevents anything more than the most superficial interaction. He is afraid of being hurt again. They both fear having a deeper relationship, even though each felt quite close to the other until shortly before their separation.

Resources. The more resources a person has, the better he or she may handle the separation crisis. These resources may be emotional as well as social and financial. Too often people blame themselves for not adjusting better to a marital breakup. They feel depressed and are angry with themselves for feeling depressed. But Weiss (1975) estimated that it takes between two and four years on the average for a person to recover fully from a marital breakup. People who are more resilient and have greater energy and imagination tend to do better than others. Those who have a tendency to withdraw, whose self-confidence is usually low, and who panic or get depressed easily have a harder time recovering. A person who becomes socially isolated following a breakup tends to be susceptible to an emotional or health breakdown (Pilisuk, 1982).

Separation also creates a difficult time socially. Friends often splinter, some remaining friendly to both partners, others being friends only with one or championing one over the other. The old social world breaks up: the relatives of the former spouse generally vanish from the other's life; perhaps the ex-spouses move to different neighborhoods where each is a complete stranger. But having a few friends around helps enormously. One man said he counts as true friends only those who listened to him being miserable day after day. A woman, as she planned to leave her husband, began making a determined effort to establish a network of friends to help cushion the shock.

Finances generally suffer as a result of the separation. Two living places must be found and paid for; often a second car must be purchased and perhaps another television and stereo. This burden generally adds up to financial disaster for most people. Indeed, if the woman has never worked before or has not worked for a considerable time, she may be in a desperate financial situation.

Most women experience dramatic downward mobility when they divorce (Weiss, 1984). For many women their source of income changes from primarily wages during the marriages to wages, private transfers (child support, alimony, help from relatives), and welfare. Private transfers account for 35 percent of the income for lower-income women, 55 percent for middle-income women, and 73 percent for upper-income women. Welfare and food stamps account for 60 percent of the income of lower-income women, 37 percent of middle-income women, and 26 percent of upper-income women.

If there are children, the woman usually retains custody; unfortunately, alimony and child support usually fail to cover child care expesnes (Weiss, 1984). Less than 14 percent of divorcing women are awarded alimony: in 1983, 76.9 percent received the payments awarded them by the courts (Belkin, 1985). In 1983, about 46 percent of divorcing mothers—about 4 million—were awarded child support. Of these mothers, 76 percent received some payment, but only 50 percent received full payment. The average payment was $2341 yearly (Belkin, 1985). Child support was awarded to 67 percent of the white women, 33.7 percent of the black women, and 40.9 of the Hispanic women.

□ LEGAL ASPECTS OF DIVORCE

Most divorces are not contested; between 85 and 90 percent are settled out of court through negotiations between spouses or their lawyers. But divorce, whether it is

DIVORCE SONG

I thought you were good.
I thought you were like silver.
 But you are lead.
Now look at me on the mountain top
As I walk through the sun.
I am sunlight.

TSIMSHIAN TRADITIONAL
SONG

amicable or not, is a complex legal process, involving highly charged feelings about custody and property. Divorce laws are rapidly undergoing change (Press, 1983).

Traditional Legal Grounds

There are several legal grounds for divorce that most people use in legal proceedings, whether they fit the facts or not: adultery, desertion, nonsupport, and cruelty. The law makes two assumptions about these grounds for divorce: (1) that one partner is clearly responsible (translated, "guilty") for the marital breakup and (2) that the cause of the breakup neatly falls into one of the categories recognized by law. Unfortunately, these assumptions fit only legal, not human, realities. To work within the legal framework of divorce means to abandon the human framework and suspend thoughts of the real world. As Joseph Epstein (1975) wrote: "Of course, no one connected with a divorce trial—not the litigants, not the lawyers trying it, not the judge presiding over it—really belives the assumptions that every one of them acts upon." But all act out their parts.

No-Fault Divorce

Since 1970, beginning with California's Family Law Act, forty-eight states have adopted no-fault divorce (while still providing for "legal grounds" divorce when applicable) (Glass, 1984).

Basic Aspects of No-Fault Divorce. No-fault divorce has changed four basic aspects of divorce (Weitzman and Dixon, 1980). First, it has eliminated the idea of fault-based grounds. Under no-fault divorce no one is accused of desertion, cruelty, adultery, impotence, crime, insanity, or the host of other melodramatic acts or omissions. Neither party is found guilty of anything; rather, the marriage is declared unworkable and is dissolved. Husband and wife must agree that they have irreconcilable differences (which they need not describe) and that they feel it is impossible for their marriage to survive the differences. Second, no-fault divorce eliminates the adversary process. The stress and strain of the courtroom are eliminated under the new procedure. Third, the basis for no-fault divorce settlements is equity, equality, and need rather than fault or gender. "Virtue" is no longer financially rewarded, nor is it assumed that women need to be supported by men. Community property is to be divided equally, reflecting the belief that marriage is a partnership with each partner contributing equally, if differently. The criteria for child custody are based on a sex-neutral standard of the "best interests of the child" rather than a preference for the mother. Fourth, no-fault divorce laws are intended to promote sexual equality by redefining the responsibilities of husbands and wives. The husband is no longer considered head of the household but is an equal partner with his wife. The husband is no longer solely responsible for support, nor the wife for care of the children. The limitations placed on alimony assume that a woman will work.

Weitzman and Dixon (1980) contrasted the two visions of justice in traditional and no-fault divorce laws as follows:

The traditional law sought to deliver a moral justice which rewarded the good spouse and punished the bad spouse. . . . The no-fault law ignores both moral character and moral history

---

Nothing proves better the necessity of an indissoluble marriage than the instability of passion.

HONORÉ BALZAC

as a basis for awards. Instead it seeks to deliver a fairness and equity based on the financial *needs* and upon equality of the two parties.

Unanticipated Consequences of No-Fault Divorce.   When California passed the first no-fault divorce law, reformers were optimistic about its results. No-fault has been successful in eliminating much of the sham and acrimony that resulted from traditional divorce law. But Stanford sociologist Lenore Weitzman argued in her landmark work, *The Divorce Revolution* (1985), that no-fault divorce's gender-neutral rules, designed to treat men and women equally, have placed older homemakers and mothers of young children at a disadvantage.

Since a woman's ability to support herself is likely to be impaired during marriage, especially if she is a full-time homemaker and mother she may not be "equal" to her former husband at the point of divorce. Rules that treat her as if she is equal simply serve to deprive her of the financial support she needs.

Husbands typically enhance their earning capacity during marriage. By contrast, wives typically decrease their earning capacity because they either quit or limit their participation in the work force to fulfill family roles. This withdrawal from full participation limits their earning capacity when they reenter the work force. Divorced homemakers reenter the workforce with out-dated experience, few skills, and no seniority. Furthermore, they continue to have the major responsibility and burden of childrearing.

Probably the most damaging unintended consequence of the no-fault divorce laws is that they systematically impoverish divorced women and their children. When women divorce they are often left in great economic hardship. On the average, divorced women and their children suffer a 73 percent decline in their standard of living in the first year after divorce. By contrast, men experience a 42 percent rise in their standard of living because courts typically do not require them to share their salary with their wives or contribute equally to the support of their children. Because about 60 percent of the children born today will live in a single-parent family at some point in their childhood, through no-fault divorce rules "we are sentencing a significant proportion of the next generation of American children to periods of financial hardship" (Weitzman, 1985).

Weitzman argues that a woman's homemaking and child care activities must be considered important contributions to her husband's present and future earnings. If divorce rules don't give a wife a share of her husband's enhanced earning capacity, then the "investment" she made in her spouse's future earnings is discounted. According to Weitzman, alimony and child support awards should be made to divorced women in recognition of the wife's primary childcare responsibilities and her contribution to her husband's work or career. Such awards will raise divorced women and children above the level of poverty to which they have been cast as a result of no-fault divorce's specious equality.

☐ CHILDREN AND DIVORCE

Telling children that their parents are separating is one of the most difficult and unhappy events in life. Whether or not the parents are relieved about the separation, they often feel extreme guilt about their children. Children are generally aware of parental discord (Cantor, 1979) and are upset by the separation of their parents, although their distress may not be apparent. Parental separation and divorce may not be equally disturbing for all children. Several studies (Kurdek et al., 1981; Kurdek and Siesky, 1980) suggest that divorce is not necessarily perceived by children as an overly distressing experience. One study (Hess and Camara, 1979) comparing behavior of children from intact and divorced families found that relationships among family members were more important influences on child behavior than was marital status. A conflict-ridden family was more likely to affect a child than a divorced family was. Other studies found that about 25 percent of children of divorced parents were extremely depressed five years following the divorce (Wallerstein and Kelly, 1980b). (For whether parents should stay together for their children, see Van Meter, 1985, and Gershenfeld, 1985. For "broken home," see Sweetser, 1985.)

The Three Stages of Divorce for Children

Growing numbers of studies have appeared on the impact of divorce on children, but they frequently contradict one another. Part of the problem is a failure to recognize divorce as a process for children rather than a single event. Divorce is a series of events and changes in life circumstances. Many studies focus on only one part of the process and identify that one part with divorce itself. Yet at different points in the process, children are confronted with different tasks and adopt different coping strategies. Furthermore, the diversity of children's responses to divorce is the result, in part, of differences in temperament, sex, age, and past experiences (Hetherington, 1979).

Children experience divorce as a three-stage process, according to Wallerstein and Kelly (1980b). Studying sixty families over a five-year period in California, these researchers found that for children divorce consisted of initial, transition, and restabilized stages. The initial stage, following the decision to separate, was extremely stressful; conflict escalated and unhappiness was endemic. The children's aggressive responses were magnified by the parents' inability to cope because of the crisis in their own lives. The transition stage began about a year after the separation, when the extreme emotional responses of the children had diminished or disappeared. This period was characterized by restructuring of the family and by economic and social changes: living with only one parent and visiting the other, moving, making new friends and losing old ones, financial stress, and so on. The transition period lasted between two and three years for half the families in the study. Finally came the restabilized stage, which the families had reached by the end of five years. Economic and social changes had been incorporated into daily living. The post divorce family—usually a single-parent or blended family—had been formed.

Children's Responses to Divorce

Younger and older children respond differently to divorce, mainly in the way they express—or do not express—their feelings.

Younger Children.   Younger children react to the initial news of parental breakups in many different ways. Feelings range from guilt to anger and from sorrow to relief, often vacillating between all of these. The most significant factor affecting children's responses to the separation is their age. Preadolescent children, who seem to experience a deep sadness and anxiety about the future, are usually the most upset. Some may regress to immature behavior, wetting their beds or becoming excessively possessive. Most children, regardless of their age, are angry because of the separation. Very young children tend to have more temper tantrums. The play patterns of forty-eight preschoolers in one three-year study regressed both cognitively and socially shortly after divorce (Hetherington et al., 1979). A year following the divorce the children showed high rates of dependency, acting out, help seeking, and noncompliant behavior. Slightly older children become aggressive in their play, games, and fantasies; for example, pretending to hit one of their parents. Children of school age may blame one parent and direct their anger toward him or her, believing the other one innocent.

But even here the reactions are varied. If the father moves out of the house, the children may blame the mother for making him go or they may be angry at him for abandoning them, regardless of objective reality. Younger schoolchildren who blame their mother often mix anger with placating behavior, fearing she will leave them. Preschool children often blame themselves, feeling that they drove their parents apart by being naughty or messy. They beg their parents to stay, promising to be better. It is heartbreaking to hear a child say, "Mommy, tell Daddy I'll be good. Tell him to come back. I'll be good. He won't be angry at me any more."

Problems seem to be compounded when there are children of various ages. The parents must deal with a range of responses that can be almost overwhelming. One woman (quoted in Hunt and Hunt, 1977) said:

My fourteen-year-old son was mortified and went to elaborate lengths to keep anyone from knowing. My twelve-year-old daughter had seen it coming; she cried a lot, but in the main she seemed vastly relieved. The eight-year-old blamed herself for all our quarrels and threw up regularly for weeks. The seven-year-old told his father, "We'll get it all fixed up so you can come back, Dad," but he had tantrums, played with matches in his room, and stole money from my purse.

When parents separate, children want to know which one they are going to live with. Feeling strong bonds with the parent who left, they want to know when they can see him or her. If they have brothers or sisters, they want to know if they will remain with their siblings. They especially want to know what will happen to them if the parent they are living with dies. Will they go to their grandparents, their other parent, an aunt or uncle, or an orphanage? These are practical questions, and children have a right to answers. Children need to know what lies ahead for them amidst the turmoil of a family split up so they can prepare for the changes ahead. Some parents report that their children seemed to do better psychologically than they themselves following a splitup (Weiss, 1975). Children often have more strength and inner resources than parents realize. Yet in a study where 560 divorced parents were asked to assess the impact of their divorce on their children two years after it had occurred, the majority felt that their children had been negatively affected (Fulton, 1979).

The outcome of separation for children, Weiss (1975) observed, depended on several factors related to the children's age. Young children needed a competent and loving parent to take care of them and tended to do poorly when a parenting adult became enmeshed in constant turmoil, depression, and worry. With older, preadolescent children, the presence of brothers and sisters helped—the children had others to play with and rely on in addition to the single parent. If they had good friends or did well in school, this contributed to their self-esteem. Regardless of the child's age, it was important that the absent parent continue to play a role in their lives. The children needed to know that they had not been abandoned and that the absent parent still cared (Wallerstein and Kelly, 1980b). They needed continuity and security even if the old parental relationship had radically changed.

The financial impact of divorce appears to have some impact on a child's later adjustment. One study of twenty-five seven- to thirteen-year-olds found that all who were maladjusted came from families that had experienced a 50-percent drop in income (De Simone-Luis et al., 1979). Another study found limited financial resources an important variable in determining stress among children of divorce (Hodges et al., 1979). Economic stress is often an overlooked aspect of American family life. It is particularly acute in divorced families. At a time when government programs assisting families (especially Aid to Families with Dependent Children [AFDC]) are being curtailed, the economic stresses on the children of poor and divorced families may lead to more severe or widespread problems.

Adolescents.   Family life before separation seems to have an impact on how adolescents respond to their parents' divorce. In one study 76 percent of the adolescents reported that there had been conflict in the marriage before separation (McLoughlin and Whitfield, 1984). Sixty percent of the conflict was verbal, but 38 percent was both verbal and physical. In spite of the reported conflict, almost half of this group were surprised that their parents split up. They had come to view conflict as a normal part of marital life. (Also see Glenn and Kramer, 1985.)

Adolescents also find parental separation traumatic. About half the adolescents felt relieved that their parents separated; the other half were troubled. Those who were glad came from homes that had considerable conflict; after the divorce, they tended to believe their parents' divorce was a good idea.

Only about 40 percent of the adolescents continued contact with the noncustodial parent; of these 68 percent saw the parent once a month or more. The 60 percent who did not see their noncustodial parent usually chose not to do so. This was especially true of daughters whose fathers had been involved in an extramarital relationship.

Adolescents tend to protect themselves from the conflict before separation by distancing themselves. Although they usually experience immense turmoil within, they may appear outwardly cool and detached. Unlike younger children, they rarely blame themselves. Rather, they are likely to be angry with both parents, blaming both for upsetting their lives. Adolescents may be particularly bothered by their parents' beginning to date again. Some are shocked to realize that their parents are sexual beings, especially when they see a separated parent kiss someone or bring someone home for the night. The situation may add greater confusion to the emerging sexual life of adolescents. Some may take the attitude that if their mother or father sleeps with a date, why can't they? Others may condemn their parents for acting immorally.

☐ CUSTODY

When the court awards custody, the decision is generally based on one of two standards: the best interests of the child or the least detrimental of the available alternatives (Mussetto, 1981). In practice, however, custody of the children is usually awarded to the mother. Three reasons can be given for this: (1) Women usually prefer

The non-custodial parent often intensely misses his or her children.

custody and men do not. (2) Custody to the mother is traditional. (3) The law reflects a bias that assumes women are naturally better able to care for children.

In recent years increasing numbers of fathers have been gaining custody of their children following divorce (Pearson et al., 1982). Eleven percent of single families are headed by men (U.S. Census, 1984). A child's adjustment to the father as a single parent, according to one study (Santrock, 1979), appears to depend on how well the father parents. Although parenting has been primarily the mother's task, as new parenting roles evolve, increasing numbers of men may have joint or sole custody of their children.

In the last few years, forty-two states have given grandparents the right to request courts to allow them to see their grandchildren after divorce. These laws recognize the role that grandparents play in children's lives as emotional sanctuaries from the stresses of everyday life (Press, 1983).

Types of Custody

The major types of custody are sole, joint, and split. With *sole custody* the child lives with one parent who has sole responsibility for physically raising the child and making all decisions regarding his or her upbringing. Generally, it is the mother who gains sole custody; the father's role is reduced to making support payments and visiting. Approximately 70 percent of all custody is sole custody. Under *joint custody* the children divide their time between both parents and the parents jointly share in decisions about their education, religious training, and general upbringing. Under *split custody* the children are divided between the two parents, the mother usually taking the girls and the father the boys.

Sole custody has been the prevailing practice in the United States. Since women have traditionally remained at home, sole custody by mothers has seemed the closest approximation to the intact nuclear family, especially if the father is given free access (Awad and Parry, 1980). Sole custody by women has been based on three assumptions (Roman and Haddad, 1978): (1) Men are incapable of being good parents. (2) Ex-spouses are unlikely to be able to reconcile differences easily. (3) Sole custody is less likely to cause divided loyalties for the child, and stability and continuity are likely to be increased.

Judith Wallerstein and Joan Kelly (1980b) believe that if one parent is prohibited from sharing important aspects of the children's lives, he or she will withdraw from the children in frustration and grief. Children experience such withdrawal as a rejection and suffer as a result. Generally, it is considered in the best interests of the child for him or her to have easy access to the noncustodial parent. The father's relationship with his child often changes in a positive manner as a result of the divorce, since he has increased opportunity to interact with his child in a conflict-free atmosphere (Friedman, 1980). The relationship between the visiting parent and child may change in unexpected ways. One study showed that the changes for better or worse in the relationship were related to the difficulties and psychological conflicts arising from visitation and divorce, the father's ability to deal with the limitations of his visiting relationship, and the age and sex of the child (Wallerstein and Kelly, 1980a).

Joint custody, in which both parents continue to share important parenting roles, is becoming increasingly important. Wallerstein and Kelly (1980b) argue that such arrangements may work out for the best interests of the child. Joint custody does not necessarily mean that the child's time is evenly divided between the parents but that "two committed parents, in two separate homes [care] for their youngsters in a postdivorce atmosphere of civilized, respectful exchange."

A number of advantages accrue to joint custody. First, it allows both parents to continue their parenting roles. Second, it avoids a sudden termination of a child's relationship with one of his or her parents. Joint custody fathers tend to be more involved with their children, spending time with them and sharing responsibility and decision making (Bowman and Ahrons, 1985). Third, it lessens many of the burdens of constant child care experienced by most single parents by dividing the labor. Joint custody, however, requires considerable energy from both parents in working out the logistics of the arrangement as well as feelings about each other (Abarbanel, 1979). Many parents having joint custody find it difficult, but nevertheless feel that it is satisfactory. The children do not always like joint custody as much. About a third of the children in one study valued the arrangement because it gave them access to both parents but felt overburdened by the demands of two households (Steinman, 1981).

Inevitably, there are benefits and drawbacks to any custody arrangement. Joint custody should be available as an alternative but not automatically awarded (Benedek and Benedek, 1979). Sometimes, although it may be in the best interests of the parents for each of them to continue parenting roles, it may not necessarily be in the best interests of the child. Derdeyn and Scott (1984) noted, "There is a marked disparity between the power of the joint custody movement and the sufficiency of evidence that joint custody can accomplish what we expect of it." For parents who *choose* joint custody, it appears to be satisfactory. But when joint custody is mandated by the courts over the opposition of one or both parents, it may be problematic at best. Joint custody may force two parents to interact ("cooperate" is too benign a word) in instances where they would rather never see each other again.

Table 16–1 Dislocations of the Family Life Cycle, Requiring Additional Steps to Restabilize and Proceed Developmentally

Phase	Emotional Process of Transition Prerequisite Attitude	Developmental Issues
DIVORCE		
1. The decision to divorce	Acceptance of inability to resolve marital tensions sufficiently to continue relationship	Acceptance of one's own part in failure of the marriage
2. Planning the break-up of the system	Supporting viable arrangements for all parts of the system	a. Working cooperatively on problems of custody, visitation, finances b. Dealing with extended family about the divorce
3. Separation	A. Willingness to continue cooperative coparental relationship B. Work on resolution of attachment to spouse	a. Mourning loss of intact family b. Restructuring marital and parent-child relationships; adaptation to living apart c. Realignment of relationships with extended family; staying connected with spouse's extended family
4. The divorce	More work on emotional divorce: overcoming hurt, anger, guilt, etc.	a. Mourning loss of intact family: giving up fantasies of reunion b. Retrieval of hopes, dreams, expectations from the marriage c. Staying connected with extended families
POST-DIVORCE FAMILY		
Single-parent family	Willingness to maintain parental contact with ex-spouse and support contact of children and his family	a. Making flexible visitation arrangements with ex-spouse and his family b. Rebuilding own social network
Single-parent (noncustodial)	Willingness to maintain parental contact with ex-spouse and support custodial parent's relationship with children	a. Finding ways to continue effective parenting relationship with children b. Rebuilding own social network

Source: E. A. Carter and M. McGoldrick (eds.), *The Family Life Cycle: A Framework for Family Therapy* (New York: Gardner Press), 1980. Reprinted by permission.

Child Snatching

In divorce children are often used by parents as pawns against each other. Sometimes parents do this through "child snatching" (Abrahms, 1983). Child snatching can occur when parents are married, divorced, or separated. Parental child snatching is defined by Richard Gelles (1984) as "when a parent physically takes, restrains, or does not return a child under the age of 14 after a visit, and keeps the child concealed so that the other parent does not know where the child is."

Not much is known about the incidence of child snatching, but it is probably more widespread than the current estimates of 100,000 incidents a year, according to Gelles. In a national survey of 3,745 individuals, in a single year (1982), more than 7 percent had personal knowledge of a child-snatching incident in their family or other families. Gelles estimates that in 1982 approximately 1.5 percent of American households were involved in child-snatching incidents. What we don't know, however, is who snatches children, from whom, and under what conditions. We also don't know what the consequences are for the child, the parents, and society. Finally, we don't always know how to prevent child snatching, since often the kidnapping parent has legal grounds for "possessing" the child. As with domestic violence and abuse, the law is unclear and police and courts are reluctant to get involved in "personal" matters between quarreling spouses or ex-spouses.

☐ SUMMARY

- Divorce creates the single-parent family, remarriage, the blended family, and the singles subculture.

- The divorce rate has increased significantly since the 1960s. More marriages end in divorce than in death; there are more divorces than marriages. About 49 percent of men and women between ages twenty-nine and thirty-five will divorce by age seventy-five.

- The demographic variables related to divorce include race, income, educational level, occupational status, age at time of marriage, family background, geographical location, and religion.

- The complaints divorcing couples make vary according to sex, class, length of marriage, and rural or urban residence.

- Levinger's model of marital cohesiveness explains what keeps marriages together in terms of (1) sources of attraction, (2) barriers against leaving, and (3) sources of alternative attraction.

- *Attachment* is the bonding between two people that gives rise to feelings of at-homeness and ease. When the attachment figure disappears, *separation distress* arises, a condition characterized by general stress, anxiety, and anger. Separation distress is usually followed by loneliness.

- Separation distress is affected by (1) whether the person had any forewarning, (2) length of time married, (3) who took the initiative in leaving, and (4) whether someone new is found.

- The more personal, social, and financial resources a person has at the time of separation, the easier the separation generally will be. Women generally experience dramatic downward mobility.

- Most divorces are uncontested. Courts deal with divorce either through a traditional adversary system that seeks to assign blame or through a *no-fault* system that avoids blame and recognizes "irreconcilable differences."

- Children in the divorce process go through three stages: (1) the initial stage, lasting about a year, when turmoil is greatest; (2) the transition stage, lasting up to several years, in which adjustments are being made to new family arrangements, conditions, friends, and social environment; and (3) the restabilized stage, when the changes have been integrated into the children's lives.

- The most significant factor affecting the responses of children to divorce is their age. Young children tend to act out and blame themselves, whereas adolescents tend to remain aloof and angry at both parents for disrupting their lives. Adolescents may be bothered by their parents dating again.

- The outcome of divorce for children depends on several factors, including their own inner resources, contact with the noncustodial parent, economic stability, and, for younger children especially, a nurturing, competent parent.

- Custody is generally based on one of two standards: the best interests of the child or the least detrimental of the available alternatives. Custody is generally awarded to the mother. Recently, however, more fathers have been gaining custody; the child's adjustment to living with the father depends on the father's parenting capabilities, not his gender.

- The major types of custody are *sole, joint,* and *split*. Most custody is sole custody by the mother, who is responsible for all decisions about the upbringing and physical care of the child. Recently, joint custody has become more popular because of men becoming increasingly involved in parenting.

READINGS

Stand By Your Marriage
SARAH CRICHTON, REDBOOK

In this article, Sarah Crichton suggests that marriages may end in divorce for insignificant reasons. They end because "We weren't right for each other," "I just couldn't be happy with her," and due to other vague causes. Do you agree with her that such reasons are not major? Why? Why does the author believe it is difficult for marriages to weather rough times today? What is the author's basic attitude toward divorce? How does it influence her perceptions?

Now, I take pride in being a good friend. I wouldn't dream of avoiding a friend in trouble. When my friends' marriages began splintering, I spent a lot of time making the rounds. The trick to being a good friend is that not only do you have to be willing to listen, but you have to be willing to trade information too. You know: You tell me one dark, intimate fact and I'll put you at ease with one of my own. Toss in enough and you can learn everything about the other person. Toss in enough and you can also reveal more about your life than even *you* want to know.

So my friends would tick off their spouses' flaws and I'd tick off mine. "So he never, in seven years, managed to screw back the top to the shampoo bottle, eh?" Knowing grunt. Derogatory snort. "So he refused to let you drive the car?" Grunt. Snort.

I began to watch my husband secretly, clock his fatal flaws—the flaws that would eventually do us in, lead us to the divorce court. Because when all the marriages around you are crumbling, divorce begins to seem not only a possibility but also an inevitability.

That's what was in the back of my mind when I blurted out that line about divorce. And what did my husband do? He stopped dead for a moment and then he started to laugh. "Crichton," he said, "you're crackers."

I was lucky, really. His laughing derailed the discussion—a discussion I didn't really mean to start, and which could have proved dangerous because, angry as I was, with encouragement I could have blown things way out of proportion.

At Stanford there's a sociologist named William J. Goode, author of *Women in Divorce* (Greenwood Press, 1978), who has found in his studies that the entire divorce process, from quarrels to decree, takes roughly two years. The crucial stage, however, comes during the few months following the first suggestion that a couple split. "Few marriages can survive months of divorce dialogue," warns Dr. Goode. I was relieved when ours didn't begin.

"I just don't understand you people," my 80-year-old grandmother is always saying. "In my day we never thought of divorce. Murder, maybe, but never divorce."

Judy's a good 25 years younger than my grandmother,

but still, married in 1950, hers was not a generation that turned to divorce lightly. And she's glad of it. "If divorce had been so easy in my day, I might have left Bob years ago, which would have been a terrible mistake, because for all the bad years there have been such splendid ones. I can name you the bad years: 1957, a nightmare; 1961, fights, fights, fights. . . . But I can also name the good: 1963, heaven; 1975, bliss. . . . I can go on. It's all cyclical with us, as it is with most couples, I think. And that's what makes it worth sticking it out. The point is this: Divorce just wasn't an option to consider when I got married. By the time it became acceptable, I had learned I didn't need it."

Rita, on the other hand, had the option, and like so many of her crowd, she took it. When she split up with her husband in 1972, divorce had become, in her circles, "almost a fad," she says. "My friends said, 'Rita, you reactionary thing, come on in—the water's fine.' So I took the plunge. What did I find out about myself? That I like living with a man."

If divorce has ever actually been contagious, it was during this early wave of rising divorce rates. Divorce was so newly acceptable, even respectable, that there were those who embraced it with the enthusiasm of religious converts. Because the idea was so new, women, especially, needed assurance that they could fare well on their own—emotionally, socially, financially. The converts were there to assure them they could.

For those of us who became adults during the '70s, divorce is hardly a new phenomenon; and hardly, as it was once considered, a pathological condition. The weaving was done in the '60s and early '70s; now a high divorce rate is part of the fabric of our society. Now divorce is just a stage one passes through on the road to adulthood, an American rite of passage.

Few of my friends' marriages crumbled for major reasons. There was no wife-beating. There were a few affairs, apparently, and in one case somebody ran off with another's spouse (leaving two divorces in their wake). But by and large these were simply cases of "We weren't right for each other"; "I just couldn't be happy with her"; "I couldn't see having children with him"; or the almost bewildering "I don't know—it just seemed like time to move on."

What mystified me was why my friends' marriages all seemed to splinter simultaneously. What made 1982 such a watershed year for them? More than anything, apparently, it was that my friends were (and are) statistically perfect. According to 1979 figures, the average woman is 30.1 years

old when she divorces; the average male, 32.5. My friends, most of them in their early 30s, were just prime divorce material.

Why are we all so vulnerable at that age? In part, says Dr. Roger L. Gould, author of *Transformations: Growth and Change in Adult Life* (Simon & Schuster, 1979), it's because: "During our 20s, we agree to do what is necessary to pursue our dreams. When we accept that contract, we agree to a series of obligations—to be a certain way. Then we wait for the payoff. In our contract, we are looking for self-satisfaction, happiness and contentment; and we are hoping that some undesirable part of us will go away. By the time we reach the end of our 20s, we come to see that the payoffs of our dream of adult life aren't being delivered."

And divorce is the ever-present option. Today if you are dissatisfied with your marriage, you can just end it. Divorce, as University of Pennsylvania sociologist Frank F. Furstenberg, Jr., puts it, "does not necessarily mean that individuals today expect less of marriage. Indeed, it is entirely possible that as marriage has become less binding and inviolable, standards of what constitutes a gratifying and satisfying marriage have risen. . . . Thus the high rates of divorce in our society are not an indication that marriage as an institution is being devalued, but just the opposite. As the cultural importance placed on the personal gratification of marriage grows, the commitment any given couple make to a marriage becomes more conditional, for either partner must be able to exit from the relationship in the event that it does not live up to his or her expectations."

"You'll never catch me getting married again," you may hear again and again, but according to Dr. Furstenberg, "about half of all women and a somewhat greater percentage of men remarry within three years of the date of their divorce decree; eventually three out of four divorced females and four out of five divorced males re-enter wedlock.

It's this persistent desire to remarry that causes Dr. Furstenberg to interpret divorce as "not so much an escape hatch from married life but a recycling mechanism permitting individuals a second (and sometimes a third and a fourth) chance to upgrade their marital situation."

The sad part is, of course, that sometimes people don't find a suitable second (or third or fourth) partner. Sadder still are those who come to believe that divorcing a spouse was, as one 42-year-old woman puts it, "the biggest mistake of my whole life."

It's a refrain that the founder of National Association for Divorced Women, Louise Montague, author of *The Divor-*

READINGS—*continued*

cee's Handbook and *A New Life Plan: A Guide for the Divorced Woman,* keeps picking up on, and it worries her: "I have been hearing from more and more men and women who express genuine regret over ending their marriages. These are the people who divorced by mistake—because they plain made errors of judgment. Many of them say the same thing: "If only I'd tried to solve my problems, instead of using divorce as an out!" . . . I am not suggesting that anyone remain in a dreadful marriage. I am suggesting that we not forget how tough and self-curing marriage can be, and that many problems are still best solved at home."

If there is any way in which divorce may be catching, it is that prevailing attitudes make it tough to weather the rough times in a marriage. It makes one feel almost foolish to persevere during the hard times—as if we were holding on to pipe dreams or were too chicken to try it alone. Especially now, when a psychologically healthy person is viewed as someone in constant evolution, divorce sometimes seems easier than adapting to a partner's changes.

Some couples manage to adapt through openness, or "open communications," as popular psychologists like to call it. Others have found that a little silence can serve that purpose too. In June, Margot will celebrate her 35th wedding anniversary, and celebrate as well the fact that she wed "in those days of silence," as she calls them.

Margot was 20 when she married; her husband was 22. Within ten months of her wedding day, she had a baby girl. Less than a year later, she had a boy. And less than a year after that, her husband ran off with another woman for six weeks. And Margot never told a soul.

"Oh, I know that all the openness of today is extremely important, but people also overlook the equal importance of silence," she says. "Now, if that had happened in 1984, all my friends would have known. But back then we were embarrassed by such things—we told no one something so shameful. The fact is, I wanted him back, and when he returned, he wanted to come back. If I had blabbed the news everywhere, I would have had to leave him—to save face, you know? But leaving him would have been a terrible waste, because he never did it again, and I never would have found anyone else I could have lived with this happily for so long."

None of this is to deny that divorce can have a liberating effect on a person. Dr. Gould, for all his warnings against divorcing too hastily, agrees. "Divorce," he writes, "can also be the result of having worked through to the recognition that there is little basis for a relationship . . . both partners may be able to see the necessity for the divorce

without bitterness; they've grown apart and have become so different that they share only the past. They have no basis for developing a future. Then both partners usually consider the divorce a marvelous release."

Can divorce be catching? Well, it can be tempting, at least, when one sees a friend blossom in its wake. My friend Sybil, 33, is a perfect example. Less than a year after her separation, whole sides of Sybil have begun to emerge. There's a joy to her, a spiritedness, a laser-sharp wit that, for whatever reason—Sybil doesn't know; I don't know; "maybe my analyst knows," she jokes—were squelched during her marriage. The changes are as much a surprise to her as they are to her friends. No one's complaining. But it does make one think. As a mutual friend puts it, "I wonder what's buried in me?"

At the same time, the friends of Sybil have watched her struggle with great pain and loneliness, and her fear that the loneliness will persist for "too long a time." For all the exhilaration of divorce, there's invariably pain, which all of us would rather avoid if we could. The sociologist Robert S. Weiss zeroes in on it: "The increased frequency of marital separation," he writes, "has not reduced the emotional and social upset it produces. In this respect marital separation resembles an auto accident: that it has happened to others does not make it hurt any less."

Of course, the survivors like Sybil make us wonder about our own marriages. But do they communicate divorce fever? I doubt it. But if divorce *is* contagious, for all my husband's flaws, for all his dog-and-wife whistling, I hope neither of us gets the bug.

They Stole Our Childhood
LEE GOLDBERG, *NEWSWEEK ON CAMPUS*

One of the results of divorce, according to Lee Goldberg, who wrote this as a college student, is to make kids into adults. Are the adolescents and young children of divorced parents different from those from intact families? If so, how? Why?

We're the wonderful generation.

We are the kids who are "so adult" when our divorced parents readjusted to the rigors of being suddenly single. We are the kids who discovered sex so early in our lives and were such overachievers in school.

We are looked on by our elders with admiration and awe. And yet, if you wipe away the surface gloss, you will find

READINGS—*continued*

that we are actually victims, casualties of our parents' need for us to grow up fast. That which we are praised for is our biggest problem.

Day-to-day family life for us was a contradiction between what we saw on "The Brady Bunch" and "Courtship of Eddie's Father" and what we were actually living. We were supposed to be thinking about the big dance, playing baseball, getting new handlebars on our bikes, gossiping about our favorite TV stars and, when our parents weren't around, dressing up in their clothes and looking at ourselves in the mirror.

Instead we found ourselves not only dressing up in their clothes, but adopting their state of mind as well. We worried about whether mom would receive her child-support check, whether our parent's date for tonight would become a breakfast guest tomorrow, whether our little sister would ever remember what it was like to have two parents under one roof.

Our parents were always so proud of our capacity to make it on our own, to "be adult." Parents were thinking of us less like children and more like peers. Suddenly we kids weren't being treated like kids anymore.

Part of being adult was not indulging the child in us that hungered for affection. Our generation, it seems, turned to sex for the affection we lacked at home. As we saw it, needing a hug wasn't very adult. Sleeping with someone was. It was an acceptable way to ask for the physical affirmation of self-worth that we weren't getting from our parents, who we saw doing little hugging and a lot of sleeping around.

We found that spending more time at school or work was a welcome alternative to going home in the afternoons. The media had taught us that coming home from school meant milk and cookies, TV and playing with friends, mom or a babysitter in the kitchen, and dad back from work at 6. Suddenly, going home meant confronting dad's new girlfriend, mom's unpaid bills or playing parent to our younger siblings and our parents, too.

It's no wonder so many of us, barely into our 20s, feel as though we've already been married and raised children. In divorce, parents seem to become teen-agers, and the kids become the adults. Many of our younger brothers and sisters see us more as their parents than their real parents. As our parents pursued careers and re-entered the dating

scene, we children coped by forming our own little mini-families, with the older kids parenting for the younger siblings. It was common for single mothers to joke about how their eldest son played doting father, checking out her dates and offering sage advice. Or for parents to find their younger kids wouldn't accept candy from them unless an older sister OK'd it first.

Our parents expected us to understand their problems and frustrations, to grasp the complex machinations of divorce proceedings and the emotional hazards they faced by dating again. More than understanding, they even solicited our advice and guidance in these delicate matters. Our parents sometimes pressured us into becoming participants in their divorce proceedings, encouraging us to take sides. We found ourselves having to withdraw from them just to protect ourselves from the potential pain that could be caused by mixed parental loyalties in the midst of courtroom warfare.

We were rewarded with approval: "My kids are so grown-up," "my kids can handle things," "my kids coped so well," "my kids can make it on their own," "my kids are so together." What we missed was a chance to be childish, immature and unafraid to admit we didn't have it all together.

We pay the price when we need parents to turn to and don't have them—as we toil with our first serious relationships and when our long-suppressed childish side rears its playful head.

Divorce didn't just split up our parents. It stole our childhood.

Our parents are paying, too. They ache for the closeness with us they never had and may never get. They try to grasp memories of our childhood and come up nearly empty. They find themselves separated from their children and wonder how the gap appeared. Some wake up to realize that they know their gas-station attendant better than their children.

The cure is not to curb divorce. We can start by realizing that this generation, which may have it together intellectually, paid with its adolescence. What needs rethinking are the attitudes and expectations of parents. Kids who are mature are fine. Kids who are "so adult" need help.

CHAPTER 17

Coming Together:
New Lives,
New Families

PREVIEW

To gain a sense of what you already know about the material covered in this chapter, answer "true" or "false" to the statements below. You will find the answers as you read the chapter.

1. Divorce does not end relationships; instead, it creates ex-husbands and ex-wives. True or false?
2. Shared parenting tends to be the strongest tie holding ex-spouses together. True or false?
3. The single-parent family—more than the dual-worker or stepfamily—is a radical departure from the traditional family. True or false?
4. The percentage of single-parent families headed by unmarried women is increasing at about twice the rate of single-parent families headed by divorced women. True or false?
5. More than forty percent of children from divorced families have weekly contact with the noncustodial parent. True or false?
6. Children in single-parent families tend to have greater power than those in two-parent families. True or false?
7. People who remarry tend to have the same expectations as those who marry for the first time. True or false?
8. Step-parent roles are ill-defined for both men and women. True or false?
9. Stepmothers often feel that they must disprove the wicked stepmother myth. True or false?
10. When conflict occurs in a stepfamily, the family often divides along kin lines. True or false?

Outline

After divorce a person enters a whole new world. Relationships change. New family forms emerge. A person is single again, but everything seems different than before marriage. Dating has changed because those in the pool of eligibles are older, at different stages in their life cycles, and have had varying experiences. Men and women who become single parents discover they have different relationships with their children. When they remarry their marriages are different; if they have children, they find that blended families involve new possibilities and new problems. Although we feel that our marriages and families will last forever when we begin them, the chances are fairly high that at one point in our lives we will divorce and remarry or live in a blended family either as a child or as a parent.

☐ TASKS FOLLOWING DIVORCE

Creating a New Self

There is no greater sorrow than to recall, in misery, the time when we were happy.

DANTE ALIGHIERI (1215–1321)

The primary task for the newly single person is to create a new identity. Old marital roles end with divorce: the husband or wife role is over, and the parent role is usually severely diminished or over for the father. A man who was actively involved in rearing his children may quite suddenly find himself no longer a father on a day to day basis. His wife is gone. His kids are gone. "Who am I now?" he wonders. "What shall I do?" A woman puts her children to bed, lonely despite their presence, wondering how she is going to care for them by herself. She lies awake trying to figure out how she will support her family. How will she ever make her own life if all she has to look forward to is being a mother and father to her children?

Our married self becomes part of our deepest self. Upon separation and divorce, many people feel as if they have "lost an arm or a leg." This analogy as well as the traditional marriage rite in which men and women are pronounced "one" reveals an important dynamic of marriage: the constant association of both partners makes each almost a physical part of the other. This is true even if two people are locked in conflict; they, too, form their patterns of living around each other.

Somehow divorced people emerge from the confusion (see Trafford, 1982, 1983). The crisis and accompanying pain is an unavoidable part of the transition to a new self. The philosopher Friedrich Nietzsche wrote: "One must first have chaos in himself to give birth to a dancing star." It takes some longer than others to recover because each person experiences the process in his or her own unique way. But most are surprised by how long it does take—they forget they are undergoing a major discontinuity in their lives. Robert Weiss (1975) estimates that it takes between two and four years for a divorced person to establish a new identity, to feel strong and confident. It is probably closer to four years for most people. By anyone's reckoning, that is a long time—especially as it is time marked by mood swings, uncertainty, and questioning.

Transition and Recovery

Weiss believes that a person goes through two distinct phases in establishing a new identity: transition and recovery. The *transition period* begins with the separation and is characterized by separation distress and then loneliness. In its later stages, most people begin functioning in an orderly way again, although they still may experience periods of upset and turmoil. The transition period generally ends within the first year. During this time, individuals have already begun making decisions that provide the framework for new selves. They have entered the role of single parent or absent parent, have found a new place to live, have made important career and financial decisions, have begun to date. Their new lives are taking shape.

The *recovery period* usually begins in the second year and lasts between one and three years. By this time the separated or divorced individual has already created a reasonably stable pattern of life. The marriage is becoming more of a distant memory, and the former spouse does not arouse the intense passions he or she once did. Mood swings are not as extreme and depressed periods are fewer. Yet the individual still has self-doubts that lie just beneath the surface. A sudden reversal, a bad time with the kids, doubts about a romantic involvement can suddenly destroy a divorced person's confidence. By the end of the recovery period, the distress has passed. Those who have a good sense of well-being are more likely to remarry within a few years (Spanier and Furstenberg, 1982).

☐ DATING AGAIN

A first date after years of marriage evokes some of the same emotions experienced by adolescents. Divorced persons who are just beginning to date again may be excited, nervous, worry about how they look, wonder whether or not it is okay to hold hands, kiss, or make love. But there is a significant difference: divorced individuals have been involved in a long-term relationship with deep connections—and there they are, on a date! Dating may seem incongruous with their former selves. They may feel annoyed with themselves for feeling excited and awkward. After all, they are older now, more skilled socially, and sexually experienced.

An even greater problem is how to meet other unmarried people. Most studies indicate that the greatest social problem faced by divorced men and, especially, women is meeting other unmarried persons (Kohen et al., 1979; Spanier and Casto, 1979).

From the moment a goose realizes that the partner is missing, it loses all courage and flees even from the youngest and weakest geese. As its condition quickly becomes known to all the members of the colony, the lonely goose rapidly can become extremely shy, reluctant to approach human beings and to come to the feeding place; the bird also develops a tendency to panic. . . .

KONRAD LORENZ, ON AGGRESSION

What does not destroy me makes me stronger.

FRIEDRICH NIETZSCHE

Only an animal or a god can live alone.

ARISTOTLE

Divorced men have the most active social life (Rashke, 1979). Because of the marriage squeeze, separated and divorced women are at a disadvantage: considerably fewer men are available than women.

Generally, divorced individuals without children have more money to spend and considerably more free time. The problem of meeting others is most acute for single mothers who are full-time parents in the home, since they lack significant opportunities to meet potential partners.

Functions of Dating

Dating fulfills several important functions for divorced people. First, dating is a statement to the world at large (as well as to the former spouse) that the individual is available to become someone else's partner. Second, dating is an opportunity for a new self-evaluation. Free from the stress of an unhappy marriage, dating may lead people to discover, for example, that they are more interesting and charming than either they or their former spouses had imagined. Third, dating initiates the individual into what Morton Hunt (Hunt and Hunt, 1977) calls "the world of the formerly married," a subculture that permits divorced people to experiment with new roles. They must develop their own code of behavior and discover what their body language (a look, a glance, a gesture) means outside the context of marriage. They must understand what a flirtation is and become involved with such issues as who pays for drinks and dinner on a date.

Dating in the Divorced Subculture

Several features of dating in "the world of the formerly married" differ from premarital dating. First, dating may be less spontaneous when the divorced people have children. It is usually the woman who must make arrangements about child care. She may also prefer meeting her date outside the home to prevent his seeing dirty diapers or hearing crying children at departure time. Second, finances are often strained because divorced men may have to pay child support and alimony and divorced women may only have income from part-time jobs while having many child-care expenses. Third, dating does not seem to be a leisurely matter. Divorced people "are too pressed for time, too desperately in search of the 'right' person to waste time on a first date that might not go well" (Hunt and Hunt, 1977). Fourth, the divorced have a different sexual ethic, one that arises from the simple fact that there are few (if any) divorced virgins.

Whether to have sex is one of the most anxiety-ridden questions for newly single people. For years these people have been more or less monogamous. Now what? The Hunts (1977) found that about half of their newly divorced sample were surprised and shocked by the fast-paced, less-inhibited, experimental nature of postmarital sex. A high degree of impersonal, casual sex characterizes the singles world. After participating to a greater or lesser degree, most people find the sexual mores of this world alienating. Men initially tend to enjoy their sexual freedom following divorce, but women generally do not find it as meaningful (Hetherington et al., 1976). After a while, sex becomes a secondary consideration in dating as people look for a deeper, more intimate relationship (Kohen et al., 1979).

☐ SHARED PARENTING

One of the most unique, complex and ambiguous relationships in contemporary America is that between ex-spouses with children. Paul Bohannon (1971) pointed out that divorce does not end a relationship; it creates ex-husbands and ex-wives. If children are involved, divorce is only the beginning of new and often complicated relationships between former spouses (see Furstenberg and Nord, 1985).

Shared parenting keeps former partners in contact with each other. The children are a bond that continues forever. After all, the ex-husband is still the father of the children; the ex-wife is still their mother. This is a simple, irrefutable fact of biology; it is reinforced by culture. Neither time nor distance can change it. So former spouses with children usually have to keep in touch with each other. How they retain contact can greatly influence the quality of their postmarital relationship. Shared parenting is rich soil for conflict, conspiracy, and guilt (see Bloom and Kindle, 1985).

New Parental Relationships

The various ties between former spouses tend to erode except for those that result from shared parenting (Keshet, 1980). Within this new structure of shared parenting, the former spouses relate to each other primarily in their parent roles. The distance between the former spouses tends to increase, since they no longer care for their children in the same place and at the same time. Cooperation between them is no longer motivated by intimacy but by the need to assist the other in his or her childrearing activities. One study suggests that keeping the dialogue on safe ground is the key to cooperation between divorced parents (Irving et al., 1984). The parents share information about their children—how they are doing in school, what illnesses they might have, who their friends are—but they do not share many feelings with each other about the children (Weiss, 1979). Nor do the parents share important symbolic events such as children's birthdays, Christmas, and Thanksgiving. Both parents may attend graduations or weddings, but they tend to celebrate them separately (Hetherington et al., 1977).

When one of the partners remarries, the former spouse will make further adjustments. This is especially true when the primary caretaker remarries. New spouses bring new relationships into the family system. Sometimes the transition is smooth, sometimes difficult. The new stepfather may want to play the total father role against the wishes of the biological father. A new stepmother may intensely dislike the former wife and not want "her" children in the house.

Using Children as Tools

Continued involvement with the children by both parents is important for the children's adjustment (Wallerstein and Kelly, 1980a). The greatest danger is that children may be used as tools by their parents after a divorce. As Myron Harris (1972) pointed out, the recently divorced suffer from a lack of self-esteem and a sense of failure. One means of dealing with the feelings caused by divorce is to blame the other person. To prevent further hurt, divorced partners may try to control each other through their children. Harris wrote:

We have constructed a family system which depends upon fidelity, lifelong monogamy, and the survival of both parents. But we have never made adequate social provision for the security and identity of the children if that marriage is broken . . . We have, in fact, as did the primitive Mundugu-umor, Arapesh and Douan, saddled ourselves with a system that won't work.

MARGARET MEAD

The need to find oneself loved and reassured as to being adequate or exceptional as a parent becomes particularly strong when all else is taken away. Thus, the opportunity for utilizing other individuals in this security-pursuing endeavor beckons most strongly—in fact, more strongly to the unconscious parts of ourselves than to the conscious, for the former are desperate, painfully needful, crying, and often panicked, while the latter have managed somehow to be more reasonable and socially restrained. It is obvious that the presence of children makes them an easily available commodity for use.

Harris suggested that divorced parents who use their children against each other may employ one or more of the following tactics:

1. *Alienating children's affection.* Because one parent feels deprived of the former spouse's affection, he or she may try to deprive the other parent of the children's affection. If a marriage splits up, say, over the wife having an affair, the husband may try to have the wife declared an unfit mother as revenge. She may be a wholly competent, trustworthy mother, but in his rage the husband does not see that. He is so wounded that he wants to hurt her as he has been hurt. The children, of course, are torn by divided loyalties.

2. *Using children to maintain bonds.* Children are sometimes used to continue the attachment between divorced spouses. On the pretext of asking for advice or assistance, a woman may call upon her former husband. "What shall I do about Sally being sick all the time? Do you think it's serious? Do you think I should send her to summer camp?" Although such questions may be legitimate, they can be used to hold on to an ex-spouse, keeping him or her tied to the intimate workings of the family. Some may hope that if they hold on long enough there will be a reconciliation. Here again the child is being manipulated.

3. *Demanding total allegiance.* Each parent may demand the children's total allegiance. The mother may attack the father in front of the children or denigrate him in his absence; the father may similarly attack the mother, telling them what a bad person and parent she is. Harris describes one case in which each divorced partner attempted to turn the children against the other:

   The effort to force them into the position of hostages, held in emotional bondage to the parent with whom they were spending time, was so persisting and unrelenting that the children were forced to alternately deny love to the opposing parent and avow loyalty only to the parent with whom they were currently spending time.

   The children in this case were four and five years old. It is not difficult to imagine their stress and confusion.

4. *Holding children hostage.* Children may be used directly as hostages for money, emotional support, or services. In one divorce agreement, the woman spelled out rigid visitation privileges, and whenever her former husband was late in support payments, late picking up the child, or had to cancel a visit, she would refuse to allow him to see the child next time.

☐ SINGLE PARENTING

The single-parent family, more than the dual-worker family or stepfamily, is a radical departure from the traditional nuclear family. Both the dual-worker family and stepfamily are two-parent families; the single parent family is not. The high incidence of divorce has created an entirely new marriage and family system in the United States (Thompson and Gongla, 1983). (See Figure 17–1.)

Single parenting is difficult, but for many single parents the problems are manageable in contrast to the hopelessness of unhappy marriages. Although most studies emphasize the stress of single parenting, some studies view it as building strength and confidence in many women. Miller (1982) observed:

A significant number of the single women studied have solved many extraordinary problems in the face of formidable obstacles. Their single parenthood has led to personal growth for many. In adulthood they have made major revisions in their roles in life and in their self- and object-representations. Many have become contributors to their community, and their children are often a source of strength rather than difficulty.

The Rise of the Single-Parent Family

In previous generations the life pattern most women experienced was (1) marriage, (2) motherhood, and (3) widowhood. Some single-parent families existed, but they were formed by widowhood rather than divorce. But a new marriage and family pattern has taken root. Its greatest impact is on women and their children. The life pattern many women now experience is (1) marriage, (2) motherhood, (3) divorce, (4) single parenting, (5) remarriage, and (6) widowhood. Divorce is the key factor creating today's single-parent family.

No other family form has increased as rapidly. Between 1970 and 1979 the number of single-parent families increased by 89 percent. About 25 percent of all new households added between 1980 and 1984 are female single-parent families (Rawl-

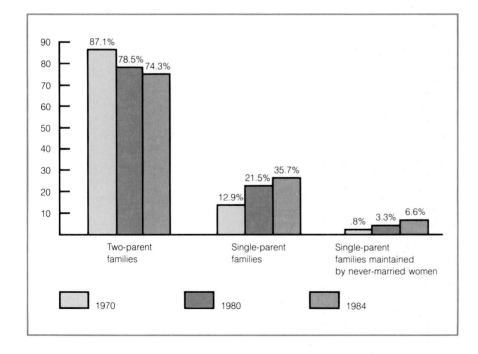

Figure 17–1

Families in Transition, 1970–1984. Source: U.S. Bureau of the Census, 1985.

ings, 1984). More than 60 percent of the people who divorce have children living at home. In 1970, 11 percent of children eighteen years old and under were living in single-parent families. By 1980 the figure rose to 19 percent. One demographer projects that in 1990, 26 percent of all children will live in a single-parent family (Glick, 1984b). As many as 64 percent of white children and 89 percent of black children born in 1980 will spend part of their childhood in a single-parent family (Hofferth, 1985). Nevertheless, single-parent families continue to be suspect because they deviate from our belief in the "correctness" of the traditional intact nuclear family (Thompson and Gongla, 1983).

Characteristics of Single-Parent Families

Single-parent families share a number of characteristics, as described below. As you can see, such families are quite diverse.

Created by Divorce or Births to Unmarried Women.   Single-parent families tend to be created by divorce or births to unmarried women (that is, never-married women) rather than by death (Hoffereth, 1985). In contrast to single parenting by widows, parenting by divorced or unmarried mothers receives less social support. A divorced mother usually receives less assistance from her own kin and considerably less (or none) from her former husband's relatives. Widowed mothers, however, often receive social support from their husband's relatives. Our culture is still ambivalent about divorce and considers single-parent families deviant. (See Leslie and Grady, 1985.)

Single-parent families are increasingly headed by unmarried women. Between 1970 and 1983, single-parent families headed by divorced women increased by 178 percent but such families headed by unmarried women increased by 377 percent; by contrast, there was a 15 percent decrease in families headed by widows (Glick, 1984a). In 1980, 11 percent of white children and 55 percent of black children were born to unmarried women (Hofferth, 1985). The number of single-parent families headed by unmarried women is growing at such a rate that demographers project they will represent nearly a quarter of single-parent households in 1990 (Glick, 1984b).

Unmarried mothers face greater problems than divorced or separated single parents. First, unmarried mothers often receive no assistance from the child's father and family. Second, unmarried mothers receive little social support, and their children may be stigmatized as "illegitimate." The black community, however, is more accepting of unmarried mothers than are whites (Presser, 1980). Third, unmarried mothers are less likely to have stable marriages once they do marry (O'Connell and Rogers, 1984). Fourth, they tend to be economically disadvantaged: they have low levels of employment and hold low-status and low-paying occupations (O'Connell and Rogers, 1984).

Female-Headed.   Ninety percent of single-parent families are headed by women. This has important economic ramifications because of sex discrimination in wages and job opportunities. Single-parent families headed by males make almost twice as much as female-headed ones, averaging around $20,000 (Greif, 1985).

Poverty.   When a woman separates or divorces, she usually experiences a sharp drop in her income. Upper-income women lose about one-half their predivorce income,

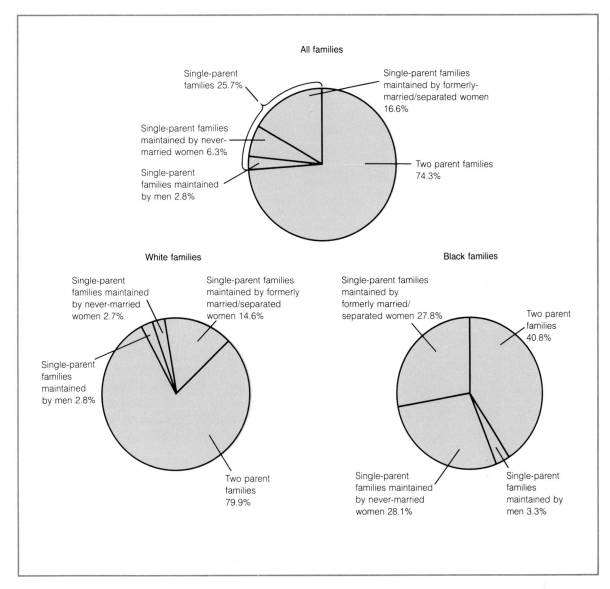

All families

Single-parent families 25.7%

Single-parent families maintained by formerly-married/separated women 16.6%

Single-parent families maintained by never-married women 6.3%

Single-parent families maintained by men 2.8%

Two parent families 74.3%

White families

Single-parent families maintained by never-married women 2.7%

Single-parent families maintained by formerly married/separated women 14.6%

Single-parent families maintained by men 2.8%

Two parent families 79.9%

Black families

Single-parent families maintained by formerly married/separated women 27.8%

Two parent families 40.8%

Single-parent families maintained by never-married women 28.1%

Single-parent families maintained by men 3.3%

Figure 17–2

Two-Parent and One-Parent Families as Proportion of All Family Groups, by Race, 1984. Source: Bureau of the Census. *Current Population Reports.* "Household and Family Characteristics: March, 1984." Series P-20, No. 398. April, 1985, p. 4.

middle-class women about a third, and low-income women about a quarter (Weiss, 1984). Most single-parent families are poor. The average income of single mothers is only 34 percent of that of two-parent families (Johnson, 1980). A U.S. Civil Rights study (cited in Gelman, 1985) found that in 1983 fifty-four percent of single-parent families lived in poverty, compared with eighteen percent of all families with children. Forty-seven percent of female-headed single-parent families were poor compared with 20 percent of male-headed single-parent families (Payton, 1982). Public assistance provides about a third of the income for single mothers less than twenty-five years of age but only about 10 percent of the income for those who are older. Child support and alimony supply only a small amount; only 20 to 30 percent of divorced fathers pay child support, and 53 percent of men under court-order for child support pay nothing (Bohen, 1984). Single parents are unable to do much planning because of their constant financial uncertainty. Economic stress is their only financial constant.

Great Variety.   There are many different kinds of single-parent households. Single-parent families show great flexibility in managing child care and housing problems. In doing so they rely on a variety of household arrangements. Only about 56 percent of single-parent households consist of a single parent with only his or her children (Payton, 1982). Forty-four percent of single parents head other types of family structures. A third live in modified extended families consisting of their own children and another adult who is a relative, a boarder, or a cohabitant.

Significance of Race.   Race in is an important factor affecting the formation of single-parent families. Among families with children in 1983, single-parent families accounted for 51.9 percent of all black families and 17.4 percent of all white families (Rawlings, 1984). Another study found that white single mothers were more likely to be divorced (as opposed to widowed or unmarried) than their black or Hispanic counterparts (50 percent compared with 24 percent of the black mothers and 30 percent of the Hispanic mothers) (Johnson, 1980). Black and Hispanic families are more likely to live below the poverty level, both as single-parent and two-parent families.

Transitional Form.   Single parenting is usually a transitional state between marriages. A single mother has strong motivation to remarry because of cultural expectations, economic stress, role overload, and a need for emotional security and intimacy. Evidence about whether children reduce or enhance the mother's probability of remarrying is conflicting (Koo and Suchindran, 1980).

Children in a Single-Parent Family

More than 60 percent of people who divorce have children living at home. One study indicated that children remain in single-parent homes an average of about six years for whites and 7.5 years for blacks (Hofferth, 1985). Of children born in 1980 who will live in a single-parent family, white children can expect to spend about 31 percent of their childhood in single-parent families; black children, about 59 percent.

Children tend to have little contact with the nonresidential parent. In a study by Furstenberg and Nord (1982), only 16 percent of the children saw their nonresident father as much as once a week; almost 40 percent of the children had had no contact with their father in five years or even knew where he was living. The authors concluded that "marital dissolution involves either a complete cessation of contact between the nonresidential parent and child or a relationship that is tantamount to a ritual form of parenthood."

Stability and Loneliness.   After a divorce, the single parent is usually glad to have the children with him or her (Weiss, 1979). Everything else seems to have fallen apart, but as long as single parents have their children, they retain their parental function. Their children's need for them reassures them of their own importance. The mother's success as a parent becomes even more important to counteract the feelings of low self-esteem that result from divorce. Feeling depressed, she knows she must bounce back for her children. Yet after a short period the mother comes to realize that her children do not fill the void left by her divorce. The children are a chore as well as a pleasure, and she may resent being constantly tied down by their needs. Thus minor incidents with the children—the child's refusal to eat or a temper tantrum—may get blown out of proportion.

A major disappointment for many new single parents is the discovery that they are still lonely. It seems almost paradoxical: How can a person be lonely amid all the noise and bustle and laughing and crying that accompany children? However, children do not ordinarily function as attachment figures; they can never be potential partners. The attempt to make them so is harmful to parent and child. Yet children remain the central figures in the lives of single parents. This situation leads to a second paradox: Although children do not completely fulfill a person, they rank higher in most single mothers' priorities than anything else (Weiss, 1975).

Changed Family Structure.   A single-parent family is not the same as a two-parent family with one parent temporarily absent (Weiss, 1976, 1979). The permanent absence of one parent dramatically changes the way in which the parenting adult relates to the children. Generally, the single-parent mother becomes closer and more responsive to her children. Her authority role changes too. A greater distinction between parents and children exists in two-parent homes. Rules are developed by both mothers and fathers. Parents generally have an implicit understanding to back each other up in childrearing matters and to enforce mutually agreed-on rules.

In the single-parent family no other partner is available to help maintain such agreements; the children may find themselves in a much more egalitarian situation as a result. The children consequently have more power to negotiate rules. They can badger a single parent into getting their way about staying up late, watching a television

In single-parent families children often learn responsibilities earlier than in two-parent families.

program, or going out. They can be more stubborn, cry more often and louder, whine, pout, and throw temper tantrums. Any single parent who has tried to get children to do something they do not want to do knows how soon he or she can be worn down. So single parents are more willing to compromise: "Okay, you can have a *small* box of Cheerios. Put that large one back and promise you won't fuss like this anymore." If both parents were present, such a compromise or capitulation would have been less likely. After a while it is easier for a single parent to ask the children what cereal they want, rather than to try to force them to eat a more nutritional breakfast. In this way children acquire considerable decision-making power in single-parent homes. They gain it through default—the single parent finds it too difficult to argue with them all the time.

Children in single-parent homes may also learn more responsibility. They may learn to help with kitchen chores, to clean up their messes, or to be more considerate. In the single-parent setting the children are encouraged to recognize the work their mother does and the importance of cooperation. One woman related how her husband had always washed the dishes when they were still living together. At that time it had been difficult to get the children to help around the house, particularly with the dishes. Now, she said, the children always do the dishes—and they do vacuuming, and keep their own rooms straightened up too (also see Greif, 1985).

Single Parents and Dating

Single parents are not often a part of the singles world even though they are single. Belonging to the singles world involves more than simply not being married. It requires leisure and money, which single parents generally lack. Children rapidly consume both of these resources. Children structure the life of the single parent from infancy to adolescence, making it impossible for them to participate in the singles world. Single parents must care for their children's physical needs as well as see to their emotional and intellectual development. This requires everything from toilet training, meal preparation, and laundry to soothing hurts and disappointments and sharing joys. It requires time for bedtime rituals, discipline, and play. When two parents are present, some duties may be shared; but in single-parent families there is little relief from the constant demands of childrearing.

Although single parents may wish to find a new partner, their children usually remain the central figures in their lives. This creates a number of problems. First, the single parent's decision to go out at night may lead to guilt feelings about the children. If a single mother works and her children are in day care, should she go out in the evening or stay at home to be with them? Second, a single parent must look at a potential partner as a potential parent as well. A person may be a good companion and confidant, and fun to be with, but if he or she does not want to assume parental responsibilities, then the relationship will often stagnate or be broken off. Too, a single parent's new companion may be interested in assuming parental responsibilities, but the children may regard him or her as an intruder and try to sabotage the new relationship.

A single parent may also have to decide whether to permit a lover to spend the night when the children are present in the home. This is often an important symbolic act. For one thing, it brings the children into the parent's new relationship. If the couple have no commitment, the parent may fear the consequences of the children's emotional involvement with the lover; if they break up, the children may be adversely affected. Single parents are often hesitant to expose their children again to the distress of separation; the memory of the initial parental separation and divorce is often still painful. For another thing, having a lover spend the night reveals to the children that their parent is a sexual being. This may make some single parents feel uncomfortable and may also make the parent vulnerable to moral judgments by his or her children. Single parents are often fearful that their children will lose respect for them under such circumstances. Sometimes children do judge their parents harshly, especially their mothers (they too have learned the double standard of morality). Parents are often deeply disturbed at being condemned by children who do not understand their need for love, companionship, and sexual intimacy. Finally, having someone sleep over may trigger resentment and anger that the children feel toward their parents for splitting up. They may view the lover as a parental replacement and feel deeply threatened. When single parents remarry or cohabit, however, the problem of their children and sexuality generally resolves itself. The commitment to a new partner is made and a new family structure—the blended family—is created. Old problems disappear and new ones arise.

☐ REMARRIAGE

Samuel Johnson described remarriage as "the triumph of hope over experience." In the United States remarriage is more or less standard for divorced persons. About 80 percent of divorced persons remarry, although in recent years the rate has been declining to about 70–75 percent (Glick, 1984a; see Berquist, 1984, for an annotated bibliography on remarriage). Forty-one percent of all marriages in the United States are marriages in which at least one partner has been previously married. Most divorced people not only make a second attempt but they make it fairly quickly, especially if they are younger (Chilman, 1983). For those between twenty-five and thirty-four years of age, the time between first marriage and divorce is about four years; time between divorce and remarriage is about three years.

> Marriage is made in Heaven, but second marriages are arranged by people.
>
> YIDDISH PROVERB

This quickness to remarry is somewhat paradoxical. Many newly divorced men and women express great wariness about marrying again. Yet at the same time they are actively searching for mates. Women often view their divorced time as important for their development as individuals, whereas men, who often complain that they were pressured into marriage before they were ready, become restless as "born-again bachelors" (Furstenberg, 1980).

Characteristics of Remarriage

Remarriage is considerably different from first marriage in a number of ways. First, the new partners get to know each other during a time of significant changes in life relationships, confusion, guilt, stress, and mixed feelings about the past (Keshet, 1980). They have great hope that they will not repeat past mistakes, but usually some fear that the hurts of the previous marriage will come again (McGoldrick and Carter, 1980). The past is still part of the present. A Talmudic scholar once commented, "When a divorced man marries a divorced woman, four go to bed."

About 41 percent of American marriages involve remarriage for at least one of the partners. Remarriage often creates stepfamilies.

1. Bride 2. Groom 3. Groom's daughter from first marriage 4. Bride's mother 5. Bride's mother's current lover 6. Bride's sperm donor father 7.&8. Sperm donor's parents who sued for visitation rights to bride 9. Bride's mother's lover at time of bride's birth 10. Groom's mother 11. Groom's mother's boyfriend 12. Groom's father 13. Groom's stepmother 14. Groom's father's third wife 15. Groom's grandfather 16. Groom's grandfather's lover 17. Groom's first wife

Signe Wilkinson — Mercury News

Remarriages occur later than first marriages. People are at different stages in their life cycles and may have different goals (Furstenberg, 1980). A woman who has already had children may enter a second marriage with strong career goals. In her first marriage, children may have been more important. (See Teachman and Heckert, 1985.) (See Table 17–1 for the remarried family life cycle.)

Divorced people have different expectations of their new marriages. In a study of Pennsylvania second marriages, Furstenberg (1980) discovered that three-fourths of the couples had a different conception of love than couples in their first marriages. Two-thirds believed they were less likely to stay in an unhappy marriage; they had already survived one divorce and knew they could make it through another. Four out of five believed their ideas of marriage had changed. One woman said:

I think second marriages are less idealistic and a little more realistic. You realize that it's going to be tough sometimes but you also know that you have to work them out. You come into a second marriage with a whole new set of responsibilities. It's like coming into a ballgame with the bases loaded. You've got to come through with a hit. Likewise, there's too much riding on the relationship; you've got to make it work and you realize it more after you've been divorced before. You just have to keep working out the rules of the game.

Finally, the majority of remarriages create blended families. Sixty percent of remarriages include a parent with physical custody of one or more children. Another 20 percent include a noncustodial parent (Weingarten, 1980). A single-parent family is generally a transition family leading to a blended family, which has its own unique structure, satisfactions, and problems.

Table 17–1   **Alternative Family Life Cycles**

Family Life Cycle of Those Who Marry Only Once*		Family Life Cycle of Those Who Marry and Divorce*	
Life Stage	Age (Average)	Life Stage	Age (Average)
Marriage	Males: 24 Females: 22	Marriage	Males: 24 Females: 22
First child born	Males: 27 Females: 25	Divorce	Males: 31 Females: 29
Last child born	Males: 33 Females: 31	Remarriage	Males: 34 Females: 33
Last child leaves	Males: 51 Females: 49		
Grandparent	Males: 52 Females: 50		
Widowhood	Females: 70	Widowhood	Females: 70
Death	Males: 70 Females: 78	Death	Males: 70 Females: 78

*Ages are for white males and females and are taken from 1984 U.S. Vital Statistics data.

Source: Knox, David. *Choices In Relationships: An Introduction to Marriage and the Family.* West Publishing Company, 1985.

Marital Happiness and Stability

Marital Happiness.   Remarried people are about as likely to report their second marriages as happy as those who are in their first marriage. Remarried couples "feel particularly fortunate in their second marriages, as if they have been reborn out of the ashes and have managed to snatch victory out of defeat" (Hunt and Hunt, 1977).

Second marriages seem to be better. In a study of remarried men and women, the respondents were asked to compare their second marriages with their first (Albrecht, 1980). Eighty-eight percent said that their second was "much better"; 7 percent rated it "a little better." As Richard Udry (1974) observed:

There are many factors which contribute to the satisfaction which people find in second marriages. . . . The divorced person has probably learned something about marriage from his first failure. If age contributes anything to maturity, he should be able to make a more mature choice the second time. The significance of sex is transformed, since it can be more taken for granted in the second marriage. Second marriages have the advantages of being compared with a marriage which recently ended in bitterness and conflict. The second time around, the first-time loser has probably readjusted his expectations of marriage and is simply easier to please than those without previous marital experience.

Marital Stability.   Although people may feel that their second marriages are happier, there is a substantially higher divorce rate among them. There are three reasons for this higher divorce rate (Udry, 1974). First, the majority who divorce are from the lower and lower-middle class, which generally have a higher divorce rate. When first-marriage divorce rates are compared with second-marriage divorce rates in the same class, little difference appears.

Second, persons who remarry after divorce are more likely to use divorce as a way

A person who has been married many years knows more about marriage than one who has been married many times.

ANONYMOUS

of resolving an unhappy marriage. As Udry (1974) points out, divorced people may differ from those who have never divorced "more in their willingness to divorce than in the unhappiness of the first marriage. . . ."

Third, remarriages may have increased stresses that first marriages don't experience. Remarriages don't receive the same family and kin support as first marriages do; society has not evolved customs and traditions marking second marriages. Perhaps the most important stress is stepparenting, one of the most frequent sources of conflict in remarriages. (For remarriage counseling, see Berstein and Collins, 1985.)

☐ THE BLENDED FAMILY

Remarriages that include children are very different from those that do not. The families that emerge from remarriage with children have often been called stepfamilies, but they are also called *blended, reconstituted,* or *restructured families* by social scientists, names that emphasize their structural differences from other families. They are blends of two previous families. Satirist Art Buchwald, however, calls them "tangled families." He may be close to the truth in many cases (also see Sadler, 1983). We use the terms *blended families* and *stepfamilies* in this book.

Structural Differences

Blended families are significantly different from first-marriage nuclear families (Chilman, 1983). Six structural characteristics make the blended family different from the intact family (Visher and Visher, 1979). Each one is laden with potential difficulties.

The link with death is old and undeniable. All the step-words trace their origin to the Old English steop-, which is linked with words of bereavement. A stepchild was a steop-bearn, an orphan; the stepparent, the new spouse of a widowed parent. The original association, therefore is with the greatest pain a child can experience, the loss of a parent and the loss of the central place in the surviving parent's affections.

BRENDA MADDOX, *THE HALF-PARENT*

In successful families, members experience both a sense of their own individual uniqueness and a sense of family wholeness.

1. In blended families almost all members have lost an important primary relationship. The children may mourn the loss of their parent or parents, and the spouses the loss of their former mates. Anger and hostility may be displaced onto the new stepparent.
2. One biological parent lives outside the current family. He or she may either support or interfere with the new family. Power struggles may occur between the absent parent and the mother or father and there may be jealousy between the absent parent and the stepparent.
3. The relationship between a parent and his or her children predates the relationship between the new partners. Children have often spent considerable time in a single-family structure. They have formed close and different bonds with their parent. A new husband or wife may seem an interloper in the children's special relationship with their parent. A new stepparent may find that he or she must compete with the children for their parent's attention. The stepparent may even be excluded from the parent-child system.
4. Stepparent roles are ill-defined. No one quite knows what he or she is supposed to do as a stepparent. Most stepparents try role after role until they find one that fits.
5. Many children in blended families are also members of the noncustodial parent's household, living in one household and visiting the other. Each home may have differing rules and expectations. When conflict arises, children may try to play one household against the other. Furthermore, as Visher and Visher (1979) observed:

   The lack of clear role definition, the conflict of loyalties that such children experience, the emotional reaction to the altered family pattern, and the loss of closeness with their parent who is now married to another person create inner turmoil and confused and unpredictable outward behavior in many children.

6. Children in stepfamilies have at least one extra pair of grandparents. Children get a new set of stepgrandparents, but the role these new grandparents' are to play is usually not clear. A study by Spanier and Furstenberg (1980) found that grandparents were usually quick to accept their "instant" grandchildren.

Problems of Women and Men in Stepfamilies

Most people go into stepfamily relationships expecting to recreate the traditional nuclear family found in "The Bill Cosby Show" or "Family Ties"; they are full of love, hope, and energy. Perhaps the hardest adjustment they have to make is realizing that stepfamilies are different from traditional nuclear families—and that being different does not make stepfamilies inferior. A nuclear family is neither morally superior to the blended family nor a guarantor of happiness. (See Clingem Peel and Brand, 1985.)

Women in Stepfamilies. To various degrees, women come into stepfamilies with certain feelings and hopes. Mothers and stepmothers generally expect to do the following (Visher and Visher, 1979):

- Make up to the children for the divorce.
- Create a happy, close-knit family and a new nuclear family.

I was a posthumous child. My father's eyes had closed upon the light of this world six months, when mine opened upon it. There is something strange to me, even now, in the reflection that he never saw me, and something stranger yet in the shadowy remembrance that I have of my first childish associations with his white grave-stone in the churchyard, and of the indefinable compassion I used to feel for it lying out alone there in the dark night, when our little parlor was warm and bright with fire and candle, and the doors of our house were—almost cruelly, it seemed to me sometimes—bolted and locked against it.

CHARLES DICKENS, *DAVID COPPERFIELD*

- Keep everyone happy.
- Prove they are not wicked stepmothers.
- Love their stepchild instantly and as much as their own biological children.
- Receive instant love from their stepchildren.

Needless to say, most women are disappointed. Expectations of total love, happiness, and the like would be unrealistic in intact families; in stepfamilies they are impossible. The warmer a woman is to her stepchildren, the more hostile they may become to her because they feel she is trying to replace their "real" mother. If a stepmother tries to meet everyone's needs—especially her stepchildren's, which are often contradictory, excessive, and distancing—she is likely to exhaust herself emotionally and physically. It takes time for her and her children to become emotionally integrated as a family.

Men in Stepfamilies. Different stepfamily expectations are placed on men. Because men are generally less involved in childrearing, they generally have no cruel stepfather myths to counter.

Men entering stepparenting roles may find certain areas particularly difficult at first (Visher and Visher, 1979). A critical factor in a man's stepparenting is whether he has children of his own. If he has children, they are more likely to live with his ex-wife. In this case, the stepfather may experience guilt and confusion in his stepparenting because he feels he should be parenting his own children. When his children visit, he may try to be "superdad," spending all his time with them and taking them to special places; his wife may feel excluded and angry.

A man usually joins an already established, single-parent family. He may find himself having to squeeze into it. The longer a single-parent family has been functioning, the more difficult it usually is to reorganize it. His wife may welcome him, but the children may resent his "interfering" with their relationship with their mother (Wallerstein and Kelly, 1980). His ways of handling the children may be different from his wife's, resulting in conflict.

Working out rules of family behavior is often the area where a stepfamily encounters its first real difficulties. Although the mother consciously wants help with discipline, she often feels protective if the father's style is different from hers. To allow a stepparent to discipline a child requires trust from the natural parent and a willingness to let go. Disciplining often elicits a child's testing response: "You're not my real father. I don't have to do what you tell me." Disciplining establishes legitimacy because only a parent or parent-figure is expected to discipline in our culture. Disciplining may be the first step toward family integration, because it establishes the stepparent's presence and authority in the family.

The new stepfather's expectations are important. Often, however, they are exceedingly unrealistic. "The usual situation," Visher and Visher (1979) noted, "is that he is blind to the complexity of the situation." He believes that "love will conquer all" and that the problems can be easily resolved—usually by his wife. The Vishers continued:

Very often, as tension develops in the stepfamily, the husband looks to his wife to improve the situation. He considers that she is the one responsible for the daily functioning of the family and therefore it is her mismanagement that is causing the upset. Frequently, the wife has the same expectations of herself and tries harder and harder to cope with and alter the situation. The harder she tries the worse things get, and the relationship between the couple usually

---

QUEEN: No, be assur'd you
    shall not find me, daughter.
After the slander of most
    stepmothers,
Evil-ey'd unto you.

IMOGEN: Dissembling cour-
    tesy! How fine this tyrant
Can tickle where she wounds.

SHAKESPEARE, *CYMBELINE*

The Stepfather

doves in the garden
the overly long grass.
seeing him standing there
with ripe pockets
like part of the landscape
one could forget he is a grafted
    limb.

the children let him know
his position is dangerous.
all needs are bargained,
each misreads.
sunsets of silence polish the
    long days.
he leans toward the sun,
the young ones anxious in the
    shade
that he provides.
the woman, pierced by them
    all,
is struck dumb.

his life outside this life is one
of doves in the garden
and long grass.

SUSAN MACDONALD

suffers. The expectation that the wife is responsible for the emotional relationships within the family is unrealistic, for no single person can unravel the complicated stepfamily situation.

Family Solidarity

By the time a parent and his or her children enter a blended family, they have been members of two other family structures: the nuclear family and the single-parent family. (See Table 17–2 for the developmental tasks in forming a remarried family.) Of these two, the nuclear family may be the most significant, but the single-parent family is also important. It is the children's most recent family experience. As we have seen, it has its own particular form of relationships and roles (Weiss, 1979). The single parent and his or her children must make major adjustments in leaving behind the single-parent family (Walker and Messinger, 1979). The most immediate task is to create a new sense of family solidarity. This solidarity inevitably comes at

Table 17–2   **Remarried Family Formation: A Developmental Outline**

Steps	Prerequisite Attitude	Developmental Issues
1. Entering the new relationship	Recovery from loss of first marriage (adequate "emotional divorce")	Recommitment to marriage and to forming a family with readiness to deal with the complexity and ambiguity
2. Conceptualizing and planning new marriage and family	Accepting one's own fears and those of new spouse and children about remarriage and forming a stepfamily	a. Work on openness in the new relationships to avoid pseudomutuality
	Accepting need for time and patience for adjustment to complexity and ambiguity of: 1. Multiple new roles 2. Boundaries: space, time, membership and authority 3. Affective issues: guilt, loyalty conflicts, desire for mutuality, unresolvable past hurts	b. Plan for maintenance of cooperative co-parental relationships with ex-spouses c. Plan to help children deal with fears, loyalty conflicts and membership in two systems d. Realignment of relationships with extended family to include new spouse and children e. Plan maintenance of connections for children with extended family of ex-spouse(s)
3. Remarriage and reconstitution of family	Final resolution of attachment to previous spouse and ideal of "intact" family; acceptance of a different model of family with permeable boundaries	a. Restructuring family boundaries to allow for inclusion of new spouse—stepparent b. Realignment of relationships throughout subsystems to permit interweaving of several systems c. Making room for relationships of all children with biological (noncustodial) parents, grandparents, and other extended family d. Sharing memories and histories to enhance stepfamily integration

Source: E. A. Carter and M. McGoldrick (eds.), *The Family Life Cycle: A Framework for Family Therapy* (New York: Gardner Press), 1980. Reprinted by permission.

the expense of old ties. Remarriage, more than any other single factor, affects the level of contact between children and nonresidential parents. The average level of weekly contact for a single father is double that of a remarried father. If both parents remarry, the level of contact drops 300 percent (Furstenberg and Nord, 1982).

To become families in the emotional and psychological sense, blended families must solve the fundamental problem of solidarity. Solidarity is a sense of oneness, a sharing of common goals. People who feel solidarity will say "We have decided to . . ." rather than "I have decided to . . ." Mutuality and a sense of shared values are present even though each individual will maintain his or her own unique identity.

In biological families this solidarity grows slowly and organically as part of the family process. Biological parents know their children from birth and have bonded with them; in like manner, the children have known their parents from their earliest memories, trusting, loving, and needing them. Their past and day-to-day lives have been intimately intertwined.

Achieving family solidarity in the blended family is a complex task. When a new parent enters the former single-parent family, the family system is thrown off balance (Walker and Messinger, 1979). Where once equilibrium existed, there is now disequilibrium. A period of tension and conflict usually marks the entry of a new person into the family system. (See Chapter 13.) Questions arise about them: Who are they? What are their rights and their limits? Rules change. For example, children may have been permitted to be rowdy in the living room when they lived just with their mother; the new stepfather, however, may object to this behavior. When he objects, he creates tension. To the children, everything seemed fine until he came along. He has disrupted their old pattern. Chaos and confusion will be the norm until a new pattern is established, for it takes time for people to adjust to new roles, demands, limits, and rules. (See, for example, Pink and Wampler, 1985.)

In most small groups—whether clubs, classes, or groups of friends—a new person can readily be identified as an intruder, whose presence can be accepted or rejected (or even cause the group to split up). The same is true of the blended family, with one additional complication: It is sometimes difficult to determine who is intruding on whom. In a sense, both the new parent and the children intrude on each other. The new parent is an intruder into the single-parent family, an outsider who does not belong. But the children too are intruders. The new parent has married for love and adult companionship, not for the purpose of becoming a stepparent. The children are usually considered simply "part of the package" by the new stepparent. The new parent can take control and become dominant but still remain essentially outside, or the family can change and modify itself as each member adapts to the others.

Conflict in Blended Families

Conflict takes place in all families, both biological and blended. If some family members do not like each other, they will bicker, argue, tease, and fight. Sometimes they have no better reason for disruptive behavior than that they are bored or frustrated and want to take it out on someone. These are fundamentally personal conflicts. Other conflicts are about definite issues: dating, use of the car, manners, television, friends. These can be between partners, between parents and children, or among the children themselves. There are certain types of blended-family conflicts, however, whose frequency and intensity distinguish them from conflicts that take place within biological families. Bernard (1955) lists these as conflicts over favoritism, discipline, material goods and services, and values.

Favoritism. Favoritism exists in families of first marriages as well as in blended families. In blended families, however, the favoritism often takes a very different form. Whereas a parent may favor a child in a biological family on the basis of age, sex, or personality, in blended families favoritism tends to run along kinship lines. A child is favored by one or the other parent because he or she is the parent's natural child; or if a new child is born to the remarried couple, they may favor him or her as a child of their joint love. Should a child's rewards be based on merit, need, or kinship? In American culture, where parents are expected to treat children equally, favoritism based on kinship seems particularly unfair.

Discipline. Favoritism is most frequently shown in matters of discipline or allocation of income. Discipline is especially difficult to deal with if the child being disciplined is not the person's biological child. Disciplining a stepchild often gives rise to conflicting feelings within the stepparent. Stepparents may feel they are overreacting to the child's behavior, that their feelings are out of control, that they are being censured by the child's biological parent. Although the discipline applied by the stepparent may be less severe than the biological parent's, both the child and the biological parent may feel it to be excessive or unfair. This feeling may be especially strong if the biological parent has been reluctant—consciously or not—to give the stepparent authority. Compensating for fears of unfairness, the stepparent may become exceedingly tolerant.

When biological children of both parents live in the blended family, the situation becomes even more complicated. What biological parents tolerate in their own children because they are used to it—such as whining, contrariness, or loudness— may become intolerable in stepchildren. In turn, a partner who feels that his or her child is being discriminated against will be resentful. Harmony in the new family requires that each child be rewarded and disciplined on the basis of behavior rather than kinship.

Material Goods and Services. The problem of allocating resources exists in all families, but it often becomes crucial in blended families. Blended families tend to have less money available to them because one parent may be making child-support and alimony payments. Parents must thus be careful to allocate money on the basis of need rather than kinship. For example, if you are a parent in a blended family and your biological child needs dental work but your stepchild needs a new dress, how do you decide where to put the available money? If you do not buy the new dress, your stepchild feels discriminated against, even if she is not. If your child's allowance is greater than your stepchild's, you may be accused of favoritism by the stepchild, even though she is seven and your child is twelve.

These conflicts are often exacerbated when a child enters college (Johnson, 1985). Getting a noncustodial parent to contribute towards a child's education is complicated by the fact that in most states child support stops at age 18 years. Unless parents agreed at the time of divorce who should provide for a child's college education, parents are not obligated to pay except under certain circumstances. By the time a

"Why do you sleep with my mother? My mother sleeps with me," her [the child's] voice quivering.

"You come as well, an' sleep with both of us," he coaxed.

"Mother!" she cried, turning, appealing against him.

"But I must have a husband darling. All women must have a husband."

"And you like to have a father with your mother, don't you?" said Brangwen.

Anna glowered at him. She seemed to cogitate.

"No," she cried fiercely at length, "no, I don't want." And slowly her face puckered, she sobbed bitterly.

He stood and watched her, sorry. But there could be no altering it.

D. H. LAWRENCE, *THE RAINBOW*

child reaches college age, a parent and child may be so estranged that the parent will avoid making any contributions.

As Judith Wallerstein observed (quoted in Johnson, 1985), "Many children of divorced couples are growing up economically and socially disadvantaged. Many children who would otherwise be going to college are not doing so because their parents, in most cases the father, are refusing to pay." Sometimes stepparents pay for their stepchildren's education, putting a strain on their ability to provide support for their biological children.

Parents with two families to support sometimes find themselves in a no-win situation in which they can afford to send only one child to college: Do they send their biological child (whom they perhaps rarely see) or their stepchild with whom they live? Glynnis Walker (quoted in Johnson, 1985), who interviewed a thousand women in second marriages, noted, "Many of these marriages failed because the second wives felt that they were being used. Some second wives decided to remain childless or short-changed their own kids to pay for the college education of their husband's children."

Values. Stepfamilies are less likely to share a value consensus than are intact families. As a result, there may be increased value conflicts between stepparents and stepchildren. Ordinary parent/child conflicts may be exacerbated.

Conflicts over moral values may occur when children are more conservative than adults (Bernard, 1955). Issues of smoking, drinking, or the sexes living together are examples. On the other hand, parental conservatism may come up against children's nontraditional behavior. Strong religious conflicts, for example, may arise between a deeply religious parent and agnostic children. There may be further problems in role definitions. If a new father sees himself as a patriarch but his stepchildren have been raised in an egalitarian fashion by their biological father, the children are liable to resent his style. If, in contrast, the children are used to an authoritarian father, a liberal father may not be respected.

Cleavages in the Blended Family

Conflict in blended families often occurs around shifting personal issues that involve two or three family members. Equity or fairness is often an issue (Nelson and Nelson, 1982). Allegiances shift frequently. Usually coalitions dissolve when a specific issue is settled. But sometimes these coalitions become permanent factions regardless of the issues. The family breaks down into "them" and "us." When this occurs, another divorce may be in the making, or else the family may settle down into a silent (or not so silent) truce.

In first-family marriages, cleavages usually consist of children versus parents, one child against other children, or one child and parent against the other parent. In blended families, the cleavages usually take two forms, both of high intensity: they occur either between the original families along kin lines or between parents and children.

Cleavages Along Kin Lines. We can easily see why splits along kin lines occur. The two original families (which may only consist of a parent and child versus the stepparent) have different histories, values, hopes, feelings, and habits. In such a division, the original single-parent family does not accept the stepparent, who is usually a man. The parent-child system has developed over the years and does not easily admit someone new. A mother may feel that her new partner does not understand the children, that he is not compassionate, that he loses his temper too quickly. She defends her children against what she sees as his unfairness and prevents him from becoming a full member of the family. She intervenes when he tries to discipline her children, undermining his authority. A father-child system may have the same results if the stepmother is excluded. When she intervenes to discipline, she may be viewed as a cruel stepmother (the myth may add fuel to the already fiery situation). Families that divide along kin lines tend to be very fragile because the basic cleavage takes place between the husband and the wife. Such marriages may not survive.

Cleavages Between Parents and Children. A family divided between parents and children has a much better chance of surviving, although such a family too has failed to achieve solidarity. The reason is simple: The parents unite with each other against the children, their common enemy. This is the model of classic folktales: the new mother wins the child's father over to her side. The child is left without protection from anyone save his or her siblings. This may also happen with the stepfather, but it does not occur as frequently. In these situations the stepparent tends to be the aggressor, demanding the loyalty of the biological parent.

☐ SUMMARY

- Following divorce, a person must create a new identity independent of the old one as husband or wife and parent. This period is often chaotic, since the former partner reinforced the old sense of self and provided stability, whether for good or bad.

- A divorced person usually goes through two distinct phases in establishing a new identity: *transition*, characterized by separation distress and loneliness (lasting about a year), and *recovery*, establishing a new identity independent of the marriage (which takes from one to three years).

- Dating again performs important functions for the newly divorced person: it is a statement of independence, provides an opportunity for a new self-evaluation, and initiates the individual into "the world of the formerly married." It differs from premarital dating because of the presence of children, strained finances, a sense of urgency in finding the right mate, and a different sexual ethic among divorced people.

- Relationships with the former spouse continue for some time, perhaps indefinitely if there are children. The postmarital relationship is marked by resiliency and hostility.

- Divorced parents may use their children against each other. Such parents may attempt to (1) deprive the other parent of the children's affection, (2) use the children to maintain bonds with the divorced spouses, (3) demand the children's total allegiance, and (4) use the children directly as hostages for money, emotional support, or services.

- Single parenting is an increasingly significant family form in America. Single-parent families tend to be created by divorce or births to single women, are generally headed by women, are usually poor, involve a wide variety of household types, are predominantly black and Hispanic, and are usually a transitional stage between marriages.

- Relations between the parent and his or her children change after divorce: the single parent generally tends to be closer but to have less authority. Most single parents work; child care is a constant problem. Dating poses unique problems for single parents: they may feel guilty for going out, they must look at potential partners as potential parents, and they must deal with their children's judgments or hostility.

- Remarriage differs from first marriages in several ways: partners get to know each other in the midst of major changes, they remarry later in life, they have different marital expectations, and their marriage often creates a blended family.

- The *blended family* differs from the original family because (1) almost all members have lost an important primary relationship, (2) one biological parent lives outside the current family, (3) the relationship between a parent and his or her children predates the new marital relationship, (4) stepparent roles are ill-defined, (5) many children are members of the noncustodial parent's household, and (6) children have at least one extra pair of grandparents.

- A key issue for blended families is family solidarity—the feeling of oneness with the family. Conflict in blended families is often over favoritism, discipline, material goods and services, and values. Cleavages within the blended family tend to be along kin lines or between parents and children.

READINGS

Single Mothers: Last of the Supermoms
LINDSY VAN GELDER, MS.

Sometimes it seems that a sense of humor is the only thing that can save single parents from insanity. Although her account of single parenting evokes giggles and guffaws, Lindsy Van Gelder has some serious observations to make on the concerns and frustrations of single parenting. What are they? How may they be dealt with?

When I was growing up in the Eisenhower swamplands, children whose parents underwent divorce were said to be "products of a broken home." The phrase was invariably uttered in a pitying stage whisper, and for me it conjured up drastic images of flotsam, jetsam, and kamikaze fighter planes slicing through the roofs of suburban split-levels.

Today such children, mine among them, reside in the far more upbeat-sounding "single-parent family." Divorce is no longer an automatic tragedy, at least among the liberal middle class, but a statistically significant trend, even a

media-sanctioned "lifestyle"—not without a certain amount of pain, surely, but nothing to feel eternally guilty about. Our kids, according to the modern conventional wisdom, would be much worse off in intact households where the resentful adults were only sticking things out "for the sake of the children."

If anything, the single mother (divorced, widowed, or never wed) has been glamorized in recent years as a plucky, option-packed culture hero: Bonnie Franklin's Ann Romano on "One Day at a Time," the lead characters in "Alice Doesn't Live Here Anymore" and "An Unmarried Woman," even Brenda Starr. We apparently combine in many imaginations the independence of the single woman (without the loneliness) and the security of the traditional family woman (without the at-home male-female hassles). We are acknowledged to be thrifty, resourceful, and brave. "I don't know how you do it!" our friends exclaim, and it's true—they probably don't.

Validation is terrific, but meanwhile back in real life,

READINGS–*continued*

most of the single mothers I know do not feel especially razzle-dazzling. What we do feel is tired. And we feel guilty—not for failing as wives necessarily, but for failing to live up to the demands of our *new* roles.

Single motherhood may be, in fact, the last bastion of the Superwoman Syndrome. Whereas our married sisters have increasingly begun to rebel against the pressures of the having-it-all-means-*doing*-it-all juggling routine, and to get genuine coparenting from their husbands, we do not even get that dubious commodity that husbands used to call "help." The buck stops here—as do the bills, the laundry, the report cards, the chicken pox, the "Brady Bunch" reruns, and lots more.

Following, then, are a half-dozen basic minefield areas (culled from my own experience and that of numerous friends and acquaintances) in which single mothers are at a singular disadvantage. There are probably more than six, but I promised one of my kids that I'd fix the broken wheel on her roller skate tonight.

1. *Money.*   Fair or not, I've started to loathe all those demographically desirable folks in the Two-Career Family. Here's why: women make on the average 59 cents for every dollar men make, which means that the Two-Career Family Woman at the next desk has a household income of $1.59 for every 59 cents I make. If I make $5,900 a year, she and her husband presumably make $15,900, and if I make $15,900, they can be expected to bring in $42,849. All other things being equal, the household income of the employed single mother, in other words, is 37 percent of that of the working married couple. (Most single mothers don't receive significant alimony or child support, either.)

There is a particularly nagging guilt attached to the knowledge that if only one could catch (or settle for) a new husband, one's child might be better provided for. To be single in this economy is to be selfish, an unmaternal trait, to say the least. (The mind-set of the Me Generation, alas, has passed us by; most mothers probably interpret "doing our own thing" as spending 10 minutes alone in the bathroom.)

Karen, for example, is the divorced mother of an eight-year-old girl. She is also a public school teacher specializing in work with handicapped children, a woman fiercely dedicated to her job despite comparatively low pay and the frequent threat of layoffs and program cutbacks. Karen recently began advertising in the personals columns for a man who specifically wants to get married. "I don't really want to get married," Karen said. "I don't want to *not* get married, either; it's just that I'm into my job and kid right

now, and I can't support us any more on my salary. If I don't get married, I'm going to have to look for an administrative job, which I really don't want."

2. *Sibling Rivalry.*   Remember all those adorable scenes of Ellen Burstyn's "Alice" and Marsha Mason's "Goodbye Girl" wisecracking and kibitzing with their singleton sons? (Or even those scenes of Dustin Hoffman tenderly tucking his son into bed in "Kramer vs. Kramer"?) Missing from these lineups is the truelife character of The Sibling, poking and interrupting his/her way onto center stage.

Diana recently spent a Saturday afternoon with her seven-year-old daughter when her three-year-old son was at a birthday party. "I felt as though we were out on a *date*," Diana said. "She was just great. She told me all kinds of details about her class and her teacher, the sort of thing I never have time to pursue ordinarily because I'm too busy breaking up fights or just putting them through their bedtime paces. When I was married, I could always assign their father to handle one kid or the other, but now they outnumber me. And unless I can somehow arrange to be with them separately, I can see that I'll be losing out on really knowing them."

On the other hand, Claire, who has only one child and whose ex-husband lives 3,000 miles away, wishes her son had a sibling: "Sometimes it seems that our family is just distressingly small. I'm *it* for him—and I sense that he's desperate for a wider world."

3. *Sons.*   Claire also feels anxious about providing male role models for her seven-year-old son. "He's in a private school with a male teacher, and he's had high school boys for baby-sitters, plus I'm forever dragging in a few male professional acquaintances," she said.

A lesbian who lives in a rural academic community, Claire is bitter about the lack of support she receives from other lesbians and feminists: "Boys are just not welcome at the local women's center. That general attitude is a source of constant friction for me. I *expect* to be put down by the Ronald Reagans of the world, but my angriest times as a mother have been lashing out at my single, feminist, women friends, and that I *didn't* expect."

Another woman remembered that she'd begun her odyssey as an all-alone single parent with the brave notion that *she* hadn't had any terrific feminist role models, so why was her infant son to be pitied?—at least he had her, after all. "But I hadn't counted on all these basic things that happened as he grew older. Like, how the hell do you teach a little boy to pee, and what do you tell him about masturbating? I was practically pulling in strange guys off the streets to deal with that stuff." Even in her son's everyday

READINGS–*continued*

life at school and in the playground, "my advice is often lousy, because I've never been a little boy."

4. *Parent Rivalry*. While the Perfect Feminist Nuclear Family works on its coparenting, some of the rest of us too often engage in what can only be described as counter-parenting: feuding, undercutting, and competing.

"Why is it," one five-year-old asked her mother, "that when we're with Daddy, we go to the circus and the zoo, and when we're with you, we only go to the A&P?" The newly divorced mother retaliated, naturally enough, with tickets to *Peter Pan*. "It went on like that for several weekends, but I couldn't afford to keep it up," she said. "Now I content myself with sort of a mean-spirited begrudging of the kids' good time, followed, of course, by guilt."

5. *Social Life*. My friend Amy calls it the Divorced Woman's Dilemma: "Every guy you meet after your marriage breaks up is either someone who already has kids of his own, and who feels incredibly torn and guilty about relating to yours; or else someone who never wanted kids at all, and who feels incredibly hostile and resentful about relating to yours."

For a lot of us, single motherhood offers all the anxieties of being unattached without any of the freedom. Baby-sitters are expensive, and they have to be reserved in advance. One woman noted that her four-year-old was hardly a social plus: "First of all, he's *there*. For a while, he had this unnerving ability to wake up at the precise instant that I was having an orgasm. It never failed. We seem to be past *that* now, but then there are all these lovely ways that *I've* changed. For example, I've been known to pour grown men's wineglasses one eighth full—you know, so they don't *spill*."

Other complaints were more poignant. A woman who had numerous affairs immediately after her separation said she now felt terrible remorse about her child's "sense of repeated loss. *I* knew that all of these relationships were fleeting but he didn't."

6. *Work*. Once, on my first day at work, my editor gave me an assignment that would have kept me at the office until after midnight. "I'm sorry," I said, "but the day-care center closes at six." The editor turned an interesting shade of puce and bellowed that it had been a horrible mistake to hire me.

He got over it, but the fact remains that the single mother usually cannot participate in a number of activities that can be crucial to one's job or one's advancement: overtime, out-of-town trips, informal after-work drinks with business contacts, night shifts. One's energy levels are also at a disadvantage: "I'm competing with guys who have

women to take care of their creature comforts, and with princessy single women whose biggest decision after five P.M. is whether to have cottage cheese or quiche for dinner," complained one hard-driven businesswoman who seems never to get enough sleep.

I once knew an advertising executive who had three children—but whose company only knew about one of them. (The other two weren't even allowed to answer the phone.) The woman felt that she would never have been hired if her boss had perceived her as someone who was vulnerable to three sets of chicken pox in a row. (How to cope when the children do get sick is, in fact, one of the most obsessive concerns of single mothers. Most of us go to work when we are in the final stages of bubonic plague when we're sick so we can stay home when the kids have the sniffles.)

Another woman confessed that she had come to view her children as a career handicap, like not having a high school diploma. "I have to be that much better than my co-workers who don't have kids," she said. "Probably the biggest consequence is that I never take on work that I'm not positive I can do absolutely perfectly, with my eyes closed and one hand tied behind my back. I base all my career decisions not on what's challenging, or what's on the track for the future, but on what's going to fit in with the demands of motherhood." Once, she said, she turned down a promotion that would have put her on a sure collision course.

"Until my kids are older," she added, "I'm just resigned to being an underachiever."

Children in Stepfamilies: Where Do I Belong?

EMILY VISHER AND JOHN VISHER, EXCERPT FROM *STEPFAMILIES*

Within newly-formed stepfamilies, children often have difficulty figuring out where they belong. What are some of their problems, according to Emily and John Visher? Why do they occur? What can be done to alleviate them?

Mental health professionals find that children's areas of concern keep reappearing and reappearing as though they have never been dealt with. Over and over again a mother may need to reiterate that she and her husband are getting a divorce, and she may need to explain to the children over and over again the general reasons for the dissolution of the marriage.

In the mourning process, after this acute period of denial, there usually come guilt and anger, followed by despair or depression. Individuals have different rates of moving from one stage to another. Many times counselors and therapists can be helpful in assisting both adults and children with this mourning process so that satisfactory reorganization can then take place.

Whether or not stable reorganization has occurred prior to a remarriage, at the time of the remarriage a totally new reorganization needs to occur. Remarriage is the last phase of the disintegration-single-parenting-remarriage process and it also is the beginning of a new phase in the lives of the stepfamilies members. The difficulties for the adults in integrating themselves into a group with previous alliances have been mentioned earlier. For the children a major question becomes "where do I belong?"

For the majority of children their world has been turned upside down. The familiar "givens" are no longer present. An oldest child may no longer be the oldest child or a youngest child the youngest child. An only child may suddenly have two or three siblings; mother or father now needs to give time and attention to three or four children rather than to one child.

Eight-year-old Janet remained with her mother after the divorce. When her mother remarried Janet lived with her mother and stepfather, but things did not go well in the new family. Janet did not see her father very often because he lived in a different city, but after Janet's father remarried she came to live with her father and stepmother. Janet's father and stepmother were very pleased to have Janet join their family, and Janet herself was excited with the prospect of renewing a close relationship with her father. However, the woman Janet's father had married also had a little girl about Janet's age who lived with them. The displacement felt by Janet, as well as the anxiety and insecurity she felt at not knowing just where she was going to fit into the family structure, left her bewildered and depressed. Fortunately, the family sought professional help soon after the formation of this new family group.

For older children the displacement and confusion can be even greater. Imagine a teenage boy who has been the "man of the house" for several years suddenly being asked to relinquish this status to a strange (or even not so strange) male. No longer does the adolescent have the responsibility for cleaning the car, washing the windows, or carrying the heavy loads for his mother. Perhaps he complained bitterly about the tasks at the time, but he did have a recognized status in the home which is now eliminated.

Or take the situation of a 16-year-old girl whose mother had died and who had ben doing the housework and cooking for her father and younger brother for several years. Her father is planning to be remarried to a woman with strong motivation to be a super wife and mother, who is rearranging the kitchen and talking about "her" kitchen and all the delicacies she is going to prepare for the poor motherless family. The stepmother-to-be is full of the very best of intentions, but the daughter who has been running the household feels upstaged, replaced, and crowded in to a very small corner. Where is there going to be a place for her? How can she return to being a child again under the tutelage of an adult when she herself has been the almost-adult female in the household?

If the adults can be helped to see the fears of the children in regards to the family reorganization, attention can be paid to the needs of all the individuals. The concerns can be expressed, the feelings accepted, and a clearer delineation of new roles can be achieved.

The diversity provided by having a membership in two households can eventually give children in remarried families additional role models and a wider variety of experiences from which to learn and grow. Many children, however, do not perceive the back-and-forth trek from one household to another in a positive light. They feel helpless and out of control; they seem to be faced with constant change which feels like complete "culture shock."

The sets of rules in the two homes may be quite different, and unless the children have some help in recognizing that there are many different acceptable patterns of living rather than a "right' and a "wrong" way, they may constantly battle at least one pattern. In doing this they cut themselves off from one parent as well as from a richness of experience that is available to them.

PART SEVEN

Strengths

CHAPTER 18

Marriage and Family Strengths

PREVIEW

To gain a sense of what you already know about the material covered in this chapter, answer "true" or "false" to the statements below. You will find the answers as you read the chapter.

1. The study of healthy families has always been of major interest to psychologists and sociologists. True or false?
2. Researchers agree on the basic components of healthy families. True or false?
3. Among healthy families, family health remains constant over the family life cycle. True or false?
4. A common way of measuring family strength is to see how a family responds to crisis. True or false?
5. The happiness of a couple before marriage is a good indicator of their happiness after they have children. True or false?
6. Although having a perfect family is difficult, it is possible. True or false?
7. Good communication is recognized by the overwhelming majority of researchers as the most important quality for family strength. True or false?
8. Children need to be taught respect and responsibility by their families. True or false?
9. Taking time to play is crucial to family health. True or false?
10. Needing outside help for problems is a sign of unhealthy families. True or false?

Outline

Until recently, families without apparent problems were not studied by family researchers. Although they may have been used as control groups in studies of families with problems, researchers basically dismissed them as being "nonclinical." We have, however, begun to take a closer look at what it is that makes a family "work"—what the actual strengths are in marriages and families. "Nonclinical" families are now being redefined as "healthy," "competent," "successful," "effective," "optimal," or "normal." ("Normal" in this case can denote either a statistical average or an ideal condition.) Families described in these terms are not simply intact units of people that have managed to stick together "in spite of it all." They are growing, changing, interactive systems, and they are doing, to greater or lesser degrees, what we want and expect them to do.

In this chapter we discuss some of the research methods and models used in the study of healthy families and we examine some of their specific strengths.

If we define the family as simply a people-producing factory, we will label all

families that have offspring "successful." Yet we know that a family has other important functions. To evaluate its success, we need to look at these other functions. As you recall from Chapter 1, the basic tasks of the family are (1) reproduction and socialization, (2) economic cooperation, (3) assignment of status and social roles, and (4) intimacy. How well a family is able to accomplish these tasks appears to depend on a number of characteristics and abilities. (See the reading "Of Course You Love Them—But Do You Enjoy Them?" by Anita Shreve.)

☐ MEASURING MARRIAGE AND FAMILY STRENGTHS

Researchers attempt to measure marriage and family strengths in a variety of ways. As discussed in Chapter 2, there are many approaches to research methodology and an equal number of pitfalls. Some researchers prefer to directly observe their subjects; others rely on questionnaires, inventories, and self-reports. All researchers bring their own biases and value judgments with them as they set to work. Nevertheless, when we look at the whole body of work in the area of marriage and family strengths, we note a number of common findings.

Research and the Family Life Cycle

Most family researchers have observed that families function differently at different stages of the family life cycle (discussed in Chapter 10). Families at particular stages or in times of transition typically experience greater stress than during other stages. In measuring family qualities, we need to take the family life cycle into account; we need to look at the family in times of difficulty and times of relative ease to find what strengths it exhibits throughout its life.

Models of Family Functioning

What follows are brief descriptions of three research models used to measure or describe normal family processes. All of these models share certain assumptions about what constitutes healthy functioning within the family (such as good communication), but they also have some notable differences. (For more detailed discussions of these models see Beavers, 1982; Epstein et al., 1982; Lewis et al., 1976; and Olson, 1983). "Crisis models" look at families principally in terms of their coping strategies in times of trouble, whereas "qualitative models" measure family strengths against a predetermined scale of values. Some models allow aspects of both these types to be developed concurrently.

Olson's Circumplex Model. The Circumplex Model of Marital and Family Systems (see page 548), developed by David Olson and his colleagues, classifies families according to three dimensions of family dynamics: cohesiveness, adaptability, and communication, measured across the family life cycle. Cohesion and adaptability are the central dimensions of this model; communication is the facilitating factor. The circumplex model is a typological model. It divides families into three types: Balanced, Mid-Range, and Extreme.

Figure 18–1

Relationship of Satisfaction Scales, Style of Family Life Cycles, and Dimensions of the Circumplex Model. Family members' responses relating to satisfaction with marital and family relationships and quality of life are viewed across the family life cycle. Family response to stress is a significant factor in measuring family strength.

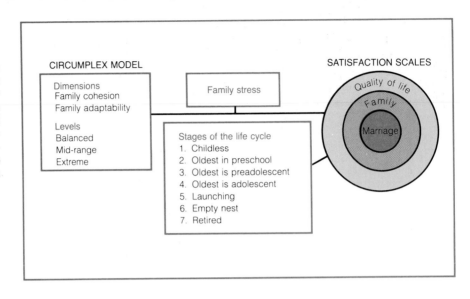

Figure 18–2

The Circumplex Model of Marital and Family Systems. "Balanced" families, those with moderate levels of cohesion and adaptability, are seen as having the greatest marital and family strengths across the family life cycle.

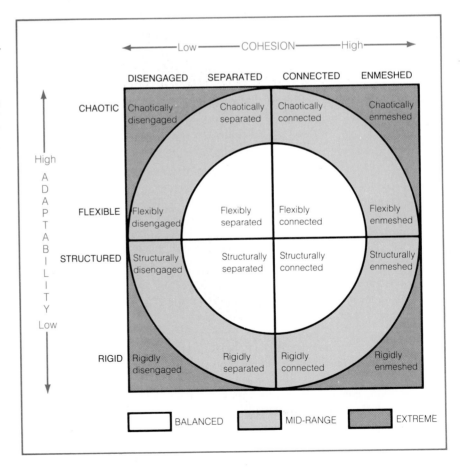

A recent study gathered data from 1,200 "nonclinical" families (Olson et al., 1983). The researchers questioned couples and their adolescent children extensively on different aspects of their family life, such as types of stress, coping strategies, personal health practices, and marital satisfaction and then rated the families' adaptability and cohesion levels accordingly. Looking at Figure 18–2, you can see that the "Balanced" families show moderate levels of cohesion and adaptability (defined according to the model). These "Balanced" families are viewed as exhibiting the greatest marital and family strengths across the family life cycle.

The McMaster Model of Family Functioning   The McMaster Model of Family Functioning, developed at McGill and McMaster Universities, has been used in a number of studies from the late 1950s on. It is based on a family systems approach (see Chapter 13). This model assumes that certain behaviors (represented in the dimensions discussed below) constitute health and "normality," and it uses a wide variety of means to collect and evaluate data, including psychiatric interviews, questionnaires, and a number of psychological inventory tests. These studies focus on three "task" areas: basic (instrumental tasks), developmental (stages of family life), and hazardous (serious crises). The six behavior dimensions measured are problem solving, communication, roles, affective responsiveness, affective involvement, and behavior control. The McMaster Model of Family Functioning has been used to study, among other things, children's emotional health as it relates to the parents' relationship, the effectiveness of placing emotionally disturbed children with parent-therapist families, and problem-solving processes in "normal" families (Epstein et al., 1982).

The Beavers-Timberlawn Approach.   In their book *No Single Thread*, Jerry M. Lewis, W. Robert Beavers, and their colleagues (1976) describe a study they conducted at the Timberlawn Psychiatric Center in Dallas. This study undertook to identify the ways that people in competent families relate to one another; the researchers videotaped volunteer "healthy" families in problem-solving sessions, interviewed these families, and analyzed the collected data. The principal scales used in this study were negotiation, conflict, and closeness. The Beavers-Timberlawn approach is based on a family systems orientation; it also includes the basic assumption (which the other discussed models do not) that power must be evenly distributed between husband and wife for optimally healthy functioning.

All three research models describe similar aspects of family functioning as healthy; they differ in their emphasis and in the complexity of their descriptions (Epstein et al., 1982).

☐ MARITAL STRENGTHS

Marriage has been called a forum for negotiating the balance between the desire for intimacy and the need to maintain one's separate identity. To negotiate this balance successfully, we need to develop what sociologist Nelson Foote (1955) called "interpersonal competence," the ability to share and develop an intimate, growing relationship with another.

Marital Strengths Versus Family Strengths

Many of the traits of healthy marriages are also found in healthy families, discussed later in this chapter. Indeed, marital competence can be viewed as a necessary basis for family success (Epstein et al., 1982; Lewis et al., 1976). It might seem ideal if couples could perfect their interpersonal skills before the arrival of children. Child-free couples generally have more time for each other and significantly less psychological, economic, and physical stress. In reality, however, many of our marital skills probably develop alongside our family skills. Thus, as we improve communication with our spouses, for example, our communication with our children also improves.

It is generally acknowledged that couples are happier together before they have children, and indeed the research on marital satisfaction seems to bear this out (see Chapter 10). There have been hundreds of studies on marital happiness and very few (and those only in the last decade) on *family* happiness. Still, an argument can be made that certain kinds of strengths accrue only to families with children. The relationships of couples with children generally have greater stability than those of childless couples because the emotional cost of a breakup is much greater when children are present. Also, the relationships of parents to their children are rewarding in and of themselves and fulfill much of the need for intimacy. Sometimes the bonds between the individual parent and the children or between the children themselves can sustain a family during times of marital stress. Furthermore, the growing acceptance of singlehood and childfree marriages notwithstanding, society expects its adults to be parents and rewards the attainment of the parental role with approval and respect.

Essential Marital Strengths

Therapist-researcher David Mace (1980) cites the essential aspects of successful marriage as commitment, communication, and the creative use of conflict. The last two elements are discussed at length in Chapter 14. Mace defines commitment in terms of the relationship's potential for growth. He wrote, "There must be a commitment on the part of the couple to ongoing growth in their relationship. . . . there is tremendous potential of loving, for caring, for warmth, for understanding, for support, for affirmation; yet, in so many marriages of today it never gets developed."

Recent research indicates that the strongest predictor of marital success is the effectiveness of communication experienced by the couple before marriage (Goleman, 1985). Classes and workshops are being developed in many communities to help teach these vital marital skills to couples before they commit themselves to marriage.

☐ PRESCRIPTION FOR A HAPPY FAMILY

Of course, it's not really possible to make a marriage or a family healthy by merely prescribing a dose of good communication or a shot of trust. But researchers do observe that certain characteristics tend to exist in the families they view as successful.

A good marriage is that in which each appoints the other guardian of his individuality.

RAINER MARIA RILKE

A Marriage Ring

The ring so worn as you behold
So thin, so pale, is yet of gold;
The passion such it was to prove;
Worn with life's cares, love yet was love.

GEORGE CRABBE

Everything comes of itself at the appointed time. This is the meaning of heaven and earth.

I CHING

Family as Process

"Nobody's perfect," and neither is any family. Perfection in families, as in most other aspects of life, exists as an ideal, not as a reality. Family quality can be seen as a continuum, with a few very healthy or unhealthy families at either end and the rest somewhere in between. Also, as we have noted, family quality varies over the family life cycle. Generally, families experience increased stress during the childbearing and teenager phases of the cycle. The overall cohesiveness of the family is severely tested at these times, and although families often emerge stronger, they may have experienced periods of distrust, disorder, and unhappiness.

Families also are idiosyncratic: Each is different from all the others. Some may function optimally when the children are very young and not so well when they become teenagers, while the reverse may be true for other families. Some families may possess great strengths in certain areas and weaknesses in others. But all families constantly change and grow. The family is a process.

> Our family is not yet so good as to be degenerating.
>
> KURT EWALD

Communication

The role of communication in establishing family strength is paramount. Whatever their differences, all researchers seem to agree that good communication skills are the bedrock of family success. Through communication the family fulfills its roles, especially as socializer of children and provider of intimacy; through communication other significant qualities of family success are generated.

The aspects of healthy communication are discussed in Chapter 14. The communication and conflict resolution skills discussed there apply not only to parents' relationships with each other but also to parent-child and child-child relationships. Among the most significant things a family can teach its children are the value of expressing their feelings effectively and the importance of truly listening to the expressions of others.

Affirmation, Respect, and Trust

Affirmation.   For most of us, the phrase we like best to hear in the world consists of "three little words." "I love you" may be a short sentence, but it can go a long way toward soothing a hurt, drying a tear, restoring a crumbling sense of self-worth, and maintaining a feeling of satisfaction and well-being. Letting others in our family know that we care about them and that we're interested in their projects, problems, feelings, and opinions—and having our family members return our affirmation—is essential to family health.

Respect.   Another way we show that we care about our family members, friends, and fellow human beings is by according them respect for their uniqueness and differences even though we may not necessarily understand or agree with them. Healthy families encourage the development of individuality in their members, even though it may lead to difficulties when the children's views begin to diverge widely from those of their parents—on such subjects, for example, as religion, premarital sex, consumerism, patriotism and childrearing. Criticism, ridicule, and rejection

Successful single-parent and two-parent families give affirmation and a sense of self-worth to their members.

undermine self-esteem and severely restrict individual growth. Families that hamper the expression of their children's attitudes and beliefs tend to send into society children who are unable to respect differences in others. In addition to exhibiting respect for others, a healthy family member also insists on being respected in return.

Trust. The establishment of trust, you will recall, is a child's first developmental stage according to Erik Erikson. Not only must an infant develop trust in his or her parents but also a growing child must continue to feel that other family members can be absolutely relied on. In turn, children learn to act in ways that make their parents trust them. Children in healthy families are allowed to earn trust as deemed appropriate by the parents. Children who know they are trusted are then able to develop self-confidence and a sense of responsibility for themselves and others.

Not only do children need to "earn" the right to be called trustworthy but parents do too. It's important for parents to be realistic in their promises to children and honest about their own mistakes and shortcomings. It's also important for children to see that their parents trust each other.

Role Modeling Many researchers agree that parental role modeling is a crucial factor in the development of qualities that ensure personal psychological health and growth (Epstein et al., 1982; Lewis et al., 1976). A loving relationship between parents, observed a family program administrator, "seems to breed security in the children, and, in turn, fosters the ability to take risks, to reach out to others, to search for their own answers, become independent, and develop a good self-image" (quoted in Curran, 1983). The more children observe their elders in situations that demonstrate mutual trust, respect, and care, the more they are encouraged to incor-

The family you come from isn't as important as the family you're going to have.

RING LARDNER

FEATURE

Family Talk

In her book *Traits of a Health Family*, Dolores Curran (1983) lists some phrases rated as the most and least favorite among family members. The "five big winners" most popular with children are:

"I love you."
"Yes."
"Time to eat."
"You can go."
"You can stay up late."

As children's least favorites, she suggests:

"How many times do I have to tell you. . . ."
"I don't care who says so."
"Don't argue with me."
"Because I say so."
"Ask your father."

The phrases parents least like to hear include:

"Don't ask me."
"Where are my books?"

"I didn't do it."
"It's her turn—I did it last time."
"How come I never get to . . ."
"He started it."
"You never let me do that when I was her age."

Children list the following as things they least like to hear from one another:

"I'm telling."
"Mom says!"
"You think you're so big."
"Just see if I ever let you use my bike again."

Think about your own family: Which of the above phrases strike a familiar chord with you? What words do you like best to hear from your fellow family members? Which are your least favorites? What does your family like to hear from you?

porate these successful and satisfying behaviors into their own lives. In divorced families the continued positive relationship between the parents (if possible) is crucially important to the developing child (Goldsmith, 1982).

Play and Leisure Time

"Lack of time . . . might be the most pervasive enemy the healthy family has" (Curran, 1983). "Stress management," "role overload," and "executive burnout" are concepts that would have been considered strange fifty or so years ago, yet now they are major themes in our everyday life. The fast pace and complex activities of our lives threaten a crucial resource: time. Without time, families lack the opportunity to nurture the basic qualities like communication that ensure their health and growth. Without time, families lack the opportunity to simply *be*. Healthy families realize they need to get away from work and responsibilities and simply enjoy one another and life in general. Quality time together need not be spent on lengthy or expensive vacations; a relaxed meal or a game in which everyone participates can serve the same purpose—a lot more often.

If you're afraid the dark, remember the night rainbow. If you lose the key to your house, throw away the house. And if it's the last dance, you better dance backwards.

PETER VOULKOS

The capacity to enjoy our family, with humor and playfulness and without strict scheduling, seems to come more easily to some than to others. Parents may have difficulty learning to leave a messy desk at work or a sticky kitchen floor at home in order to relax with each other or with their children. They may feel a moral obligation to be a "good provider" or a "perfect housekeeper" that precludes their closing the door on disorder and going for a walk in the park. Yet time taken to play and relax with our loved ones pays off in ways clean desks and shiny floors never can. When we are realistic, we see that the papers will never stop flowing onto the desk and the jam will never stop dripping onto the floor, but our children and our mates will not be as they are now ever again; if we don't take the time now to enjoy our families, we've lost an opportunity forever. Healthy families know this and give play and leisure time high priority.

Responsibility and Morality

One of the family's principal socializing tasks is to teach responsibility—of the individual for his or her own actions—and morality—a code of ethics for dealing with our fellow human beings.

If you have built castles in the air, your work need not be lost; that is where they should be. Now put the foundations under them.

HENRY DAVID THOREAU

Responsibility and Self-Respect. The acquisition of responsibility is rooted in self-respect and an appreciation of the interdependence of people. When we as children develop a sense of our own self-worth, we begin to understand how much difference our own acts can make in the lives of others; this feeling of "making a difference" aids the further growth of self-esteem.

Successful families realize the importance of delegating responsibility (participating in household chores, sharing in family decisions, and so on) and of developing responsible behavior (completing homework, remembering appointments, keeping

Successful families delegate responsibilities to their members.

our word, cleaning up our own mess). Sometimes children may have to accept more responsibility than they want, as when their dual-career or single-parents rely on them for assistance. Although these situations may be detrimental for children in families already suffering severe economic (or other) hardship, in many families children have come to benefit from the added responsibility: they feel a sense of accomplishment and worthiness. Parental acknowledgment for a job well done goes a long way toward building responsibility.

Healthy families also know the importance of allowing children to make their own mistakes and face the consequences. These lessons can be very painful at times, but they are stepping-stones to growth and success.

> Human relationships are always changing. That's in our nature. We always have to keep on trying to become better fathers and mothers, wives and husbands, and children.
>
> THOMAS GORDON

A Moral Code. Along with a sense of responsibility, healthy families help develop their children's ability to discriminate between right and wrong. This morality may be grounded in specific religious principles, but need not be; it is, however, based on a firm conviction that the world and its people must be valued and respected. Some researchers include the development of "transcendent values," such as a belief in God or an ultimate meaning in life, as a significant component of the successful family (Beavers, 1982; Coles, 1979; Stinnett, 1979). Harvard psychologists Robert Coles (1973, 1979) and Jerome Kagan (1984) feel that young children naturally have a basic moral sense; parents need to recognize and nurture that sense from early on. Besides helping children resolve their moral dilemmas, healthy parents take care to be responsible for their own behavior. Parental hypocrisy sets the stage for disrespect, disappointment, and rebellion.

Traditions and Family History

Tradition and Ritual. Through tradition and ritual, families find a link to the past and consequently a hope for the future. There are many varieties of traditions and rituals, from elaborate holiday celebrations to daily or weekly routines. Children's bedtime rituals with blankets, books, bears, or prayers give security and comfort, as do Sunday morning rituals that find the family together in church or in bed with the funny papers. Large and small rituals, if not passed down from preceding generations, can be freshly created and passed *forward*.

Family History. Strong families often have a strong sense of family history. Like family traditions, family memorabilia—scrapbooks, photos, letters, and mementos— are a satisfying link to the past. As discussed in Chapter 3, the family is strengthened by a sense of connection to its roots. When we recall such family tales as the one in which "Grandma was seventeen, and she lost her bloomers on the dance floor," we not only have a good laugh on Grandma but we also identify with her chagrin and her resourcefulness (she kicked them behind a sofa), and perhaps we add to the story an account of an embarrassing moment of our own.

> If you cannot get rid of the family skeleton, you may as well make it dance.
>
> GEORGE BERNARD SHAW

Getting Help

Healthy families are not problem free; they may even have as many problems as unhealthy families. What distinguishes them from their less-successful counterparts

UNDERSTANDING YOURSELF

Your Family Strengths

Think about the strengths in your family of orientation and your family of procreation (if you have one) or other important relationships. What kinds of communication skills exist? What kinds need to be developed? What can you do to facilitate the development of more effective communication. Choose one of those things and do it.

Do you feel loved and supported by your family? Do you feel trusted? How would you like to be treated differently? Tell someone in your family. Do you let your family know that you love them—that you respect and trust them? The next time you see a family member, offer some words of affirmation.

Do you feel that your family has enough time for play and leisure? What can you do about it? Can you give up anything to spend more time with your family? Can you reorder your priorities? Can they? Make a list of things you'd like to do with your family if you had the time. Take the time.

Do you consider yourself to be a responsible person? A moral person? How did you get that way? Do you recall any significant "learning experiences"? Have you had any significant experiences with hypocrisy (yours or someone else's)? How did it feel?

Make a list of your family traditions. Where did they come from? Which are your favorites? Your least favorites? Would you like to create any new ones? Make a list of your daily and weekly family rituals. Note your favorites. Think of some others you'd like to incorporate into your family routine. See "Understanding Yourself" in Chapter 3 for ideas about building your family history.

Does your family seek outside help for problems? How do you feel about asking for help? Make a list of all the resources available to you that you might want to use sometime. Note the ones you've used in the past. The next time you have a family problem, take a look at your list.

Experience is not what happens to a man; it is what a man does with what happens to him.

ALDOUS HUXLEY

is their willingness to face problems head on and to get help when it's needed. Crisis-model approaches to family studies center on this ability to withstand duress; all researchers agree it is significant.

Problems—large and small—beset all of us. Sometimes we don't recognize small problems until they've grown too big to ignore, but healthy families recognize a problem when they see one and are able to take responsibility for it. They know that for many kinds of family problems, they need to look at the entire family system to find solutions (see Chapter 13). Healthy families accept problems as they come along and have developed techniques for dealing with the smaller ones; when the large problems—the true crises—occur, the healthy family knows where to turn for help.

Although some family resources (such as private counseling) can be costly, many low-cost or free services are available. Preventive programs such as parent education classes and marriage enrichment workshops are designed to keep strong families strong. Other resources include support groups that deal with specific problems such as alcoholism, physical disabilities, or loss and grief; family counseling programs; and other programs, workshops and classes offered by schools, churches, hospitals, and community health agencies. (A guide to finding family resources is included in the Resource Center at the end of this book.)

America's families are its greatest resource: they need to be nurtured and protected.

☐ IN CONCLUSION

The main reason researchers study successful families is to figure out how to make more of them. The more we can identify the qualities and dynamics of families that produce involved, caring, and effective members of society, the more we may be able to help society build these kinds of families. Ideas for improving family quality range from incorporating human relationships education courses in all our schools through implementing family therapy and family-life education programs in our communities to improving social and economic conditions in general. As our greatest national resource, the family deserves to be nurtured, strengthened, and preserved.

Here is the test to find whether your mission on earth is finished: If you're alive, it isn't.

RICHARD BACH, *ILLUSIONS*

☐ SUMMARY

- Healthy families have become the objects of psychological and sociological research only in the last decade or so.

- Researchers have developed a number of models and approaches for learning about family strengths. These include the *Olson Circumplex Model of Marital and Family Systems*, which classifies families according to their cohesiveness and adaptability; the *McMaster Model of Family Functioning*, which measures a number of aspects of family and individual health; and the *Beavers-Timberlawn* approach, a family systems-oriented study of the problem-solving abilities of competent families.

- Marital success requires the development of interpersonal competence. Commitment, communication, and the creative use of conflict are the essential aspects of success in marriage.

- The family should be seen as a process and family health looked at over the entire family life cycle.

- Healthy families
  - Develop communication skills.
  - Give affirmation, respect, and trust.
  - Share play and leisure time.
  - Teach responsibility and morality.
  - Preserve tradition and family history.
  - Get help when needed.

READINGS

Of Course You Love Them—But Do You Enjoy Them?

ANITA SHREVE, REDBOOK

This article summarizes Dr. Robert Beavers' five basic components of family success. Think about your own family as you read the article. Do you see areas where the potential for greater enjoyment could be further developed?

Today, with both fathers and mothers in most families working outside the home, children grow up exposed to a large number of authority figures beyond the family—daycare instructors, teachers, baby sitters. Furthermore, contemporary society places great demands on its people to be decision makers and autonomous—to grow up. For these reasons, according to Dr. Robert Beavers, Clinical Professor of Psychiatry at the University of Texas Health Center, in Dallas, and director of the Southwest Family Institute, parents would do well to invite children to be full participants and partners in family life. As for the question "How well does my family function?" Dr. Beavers suggests that the only question you have to ask yourself is: "Am I enjoying my family?" This, he says, is the acid test for a healthy family.

The ability to take pleasure in one's family, and in oneself as a member of that family, is, according to the family specialist, the most important goal worth striving for. If the answer to "Do I like living here?" is yes, parents should relax and not put their families under the microscope. "But if the answer is no," Dr. Beavers says, "ask yourself another question: "What is the thing that would make me enjoy this family more?" You have to ask yourself that because you can't acquire something you can't first imagine."

To help parents get more enjoyment from their families—and in turn make their families healthier—Dr. Beavers outlines five fundamental components of—or

steps toward—family success. When you pay attention to these five components of a healthy family, he believes, family enjoyment will develop as a natural consequence.

1. It Starts with the Marriage

A strong, intimate, sexual, happy marriage in which the parents are truly good friends sets the tone for a happy family life. Research indicates that parents of healthy families share power, have a good sexual relationship and are separate individuals despite strong emotional ties. Most important, they act as a team.

"You have to have an intimate friend," says Dr. Beavers, "someone you can trust and with whom you can talk about the kids. This is absolutely vital. and it's just as important for single parents too. They need to find someone—perhaps an older women who has already had her children—to talk with about raising a family."

As with family success, assessing whether or not you have a good marriage starts with a simple question: "Do I like living with this person?"

"If you're not enjoying your marriage," Dr. Beavers says, "try to identify what it is that you need. Try to complete the sentence 'I want _____ .' Once you actually imagine what it is you need, you can set about trying to get it."

Although a happy marriage is optimal, it is possible to achieve a good family life without one—but only if parents act as a team. "I've seen families in which the parents had a terrible marriage but ran a 'good business,' " says Dr. Beavers. "They could agree on how to run the household even though they didn't have intimacy themselves."

Finally, the psychiatrist warns, it's important for a parent not to team up with a child against the other parent. Such divisiveness leads inevitably to jealousy, anger and a destruction of whole-family intimacy.

READINGS—*continued*

2. Learn to Enjoy Your Children

The scene is a familiar one. During a dinner party at the home of friends of his parents, two-and-a-half-year-old Billy alternately stands on the table, spills his milk, refuses to eat anything that is put in front of him and catapults his peas from his own plate into his hostess's lap with uncanny accuracy. The entire dinner is punctuated with apologies and exclamations of helplessness and dismay. With the possible exception of Billy, everyone is miserable. What has gone wrong?

According to Dr. Beavers, Billy's parents have made themselves martyrs by refusing to lay down basic rules of behavior that would make their own lives easier and would allow them to enjoy their son. "There have to be certain basic rules designed expressly for Mom and Dad's comfort and based on the parents' desire to enjoy themselves. After all, if you don't have rights of your own, you can't very well give them to someone else."

"Thou shalt enjoy thy children" is the first commandment of parenting. Assuming a long-suffering air of martyrdom while the children run wild won't allow parents to take pleasure in them. "In cases in which they haven't set limits, the parents alternate between being 'dutiful' and 'going bananas,' " says Dr. Beavers. "Family rules need to be clear, agreed on and enforced to give parents and children a secure and pleasant home."

3. Lead but Don't Control

Setting basic rules for young children, however, does not mean the same thing as trying to control their thoughts and feelings or ruling like a dictator. Research indicates that although power in healthy families rests securely with the parents, they do not rule as authoritarians. Instead they provide easy leadership, listening to children's opinions and feelings with respect and trying to solve disputes by clarifying issues and negotiating compromises.

Dr. Beavers, who describes himself as a "parent emeritus" and says he has been "consulted" rather than obeyed since his children were small, explains: "Parents cannot—and therefore shouldn't try to—control the thoughts and feelings of their children. Accepting that eliminates two thirds of the problem of parenting."

He gives the example of the child who has bad grades in school: A parent cannot force a child to want to make good grades, but he or she can say, "We're going to have two hours (?) which there will be no distractions." This allows the child to decide for himself to do better in school by using that time to study.

Dr. Beavers believes working together as parents in developing and maintaining family rules is quite different from attempting to control a child's goals. "Efforts at controlling a child's directions, successes, loves and hates are always frustrating to both parent and child," he points out.

The benefits of relaxed leadership are enormous, for it allows the members of the family to be intimate. Or, put another way, you can't have intimacy if one person has power and the other doesn't. This can be seen most easily in a marriage. If all the power in the marriage rests with the husband and the wife is never consulted, respected or allowed to make decisions, there can be no real intimacy between them. The same is true with children. If the parent demands unwavering obedience from the child without ever considering the child's perceptions, the relationship will lack intimacy.

4. Learn How to Negotiate

Over the years, Dr. Beavers has learned to identify a healthy family on the basis of two criteria: (1) Do the members of a family feel good? ("Does it feel good to be around the others and do they have an air of feeling good themselves?"); and (2) Do they know how to negotiate?

"Healthy families know how this is done," he says. "In fact, negotiation may be the single most important factor in developing healthy relationships. Conflict is ever-present. But if a family can dicker its way through these conflicts, it's probably in pretty good shape."

Negotiating starts with an ability to resolve one's own feelings. Each of us has mixed attitudes about many issues. But if we're able to resolve our ambivalence and then communicate clearly these resolved feelings—at the same time allowing other family members to do this too—then there is a fairly sound basis for good negotiating.

An illustration of this is a typical family trying to decide what to do on a free Sunday afternoon. Dad wants to mow the lawn, Michael, who is eight years old, wants the whole family to go bike riding around the lake. Mom wants to go the the lake too, and thinks that two-year-old Jennifer will enjoy riding in the baby seat on the back of her bike. But she's ambivalent because she knows if the lawn doesn't get done, it will be a whole week before Dad can return to it. Mom resolves her ambivalence this way: "I'm torn, but I think a family outing is what we all need right now. Therefore I'll lobby for that." The family begins to negotiate. Dad comes on strong for mowing the lawn. Michael is equally determined to go bike riding. Mom, her feelings resolved, states her position but sees a way to bargain.

READINGS–*continued*

"Let's take a picnic to the lake, eat lunch, ride for half an hour and then come home. By that time, the grass will be dry and Dad can mow the lawn." After a little more discussion, everyone agrees.

Members of healthy families express their feelings— whether they be anger, sadness, love or fear—because the family ambiance is basically one of understanding and warmth. But the idea of totally honest and open communication in a family is a myth, admits Dr. Beavers. "Only when your child is three years old will he or she be completely open and clear—able to say 'I hate you, Mommy' as easily as 'I love you.' Part of being in an intimate relationship is learning to keep certain things to oneself."

5. Learn to Let Go

The usual image of the happy, healthy family is one in which all the family members enjoy doing the same things together—like camping, gardening, or just reading the paper on a rainy Sunday afternoon. But members of healthy families have also learned to be separate individuals, each with an ability to think for himself and to make decisions for himself. The ability to *choose* how to be or how to feel is called *autonomy*, and it is the most treasured asset a parent can give to a child.

Let's take the example of a nine-year-old girl named Jo-anne who has just formed a friendship with a new girl in school. The new friend is of a racial background different from Jo-anne's, and although her parents know better, they can't help but express reservations and concern based on lingering prejudices with which they themselves grew up. Jo-anne's affection for the girl is quite real, however, and the two have discovered they like many of the same activities. Because Jo-anne's parents have fostered in her an ability to think for herself, she feels good about her newly found friendship. If Jo-anne's parents had denied her the ability to think for herself and accept responsibility for her actions, she might have acquiesced to their nameless fears and prejudices and given up the friend—or kept her but felt uncomfortable and guilty about doing so.

"Autonomy *must* be developed," says Dr. Beavers. "One must learn what one feels and thinks and must be able to make decisions and accept responsibility for these decisions. For a parent, the job is to render oneself unnecessary, to see the family as a dissolving unit, leaving the couple with the love ties with which they began but allowing the children to move on. Thus parents have given their children autonomy."

Although it may at first seem strange and uncomfortable to think of the ultimate goal of the family as that of dissolving, this process is necessary in order for the children to grow up to be adults. Parents first need to have a firm sense of their own identity to help the children develop theirs. (Remember that you can't give to someone else what you don't have yourself.) A parent is a person first—and if this is made clear, it allows the child to realize what a grownup can be—a separate individual with unique thoughts and feelings and perspectives. This process can then be facilitated by some of the parenting skills mentioned earlier— setting basic rules, learning how to negotiate, inviting your children into the family as participants and encouraging the expression of feelings.

Being separate does not, however, mean being distant. According to Dr. Beavers, there is more autonomy in close-knit families than in distant ones. "In close-knit families the children feel the roots but know that those roots allow for some breathing space—allow them to say 'I choose.' To be close, you must first learn to be separate. You can't tolerate intimacy if you're not separate, because you fear you'll be swallowed up."

Although following these five steps may help you have a happier family life, it will be obvious to any parent that the steps are interrelated and complex and that family interaction cannot be easily divided into categories. Negotiating, for instance, is dependent on the individual family members' ability to develop autonomy; skill in negotiating with children may be directly related to how well the parents can negotiate and how happy their marriage is; establishing casual leadership probably will work only if everyone in the family already respects the basic family rules.

And certainly no one—especially Dr. Beavers—wants to see a family straining to conform to a rigid system of family life, especially if doing so doesn't make the members happy. In fact, the psychiatrist is the first to suggest that each couple try to find their own way of making a family. "Every marriage is like every new pregnancy," he says. "In the same way that there are infinite possibilities in the unborn, there are also infinite possibilities for a couple to create a family. When two people come together they hold between them the potential to make something unique—a way of being that has never been before. I like to think that instead of conforming to *the* way of making a healthy family, they will say, 'We can do it our way.'"

Resource Center

SELF-HELP RESOURCE DIRECTORY

The information resources listed below include information centers and counseling centers, as well as support groups, prerecorded tape services, and crisis centers. Use them, share the questions that led you to call, and discover new information on numerous health topics.

The directory is easy to use. Each resource is located under a general subject heading. You'll find a description of the service, its hours, and its location by city and state. To call a health resource, follow the code found by the telephone number for each resource:

LD—Long-distance. Many important resources must be dialed at your expense. Dial direct, if you can, and remember the difference in time.

TF—Toll-free. Some numbers listed have toll-free hotlines. The 800 prefix designates that convenience. Telephone these resources at no charge.

C—Collect. A few resources will accept collect calls. If so, place the call using instructions listed in the resource's description.

e.t.—eastern time zone

c.t.— central time zone

p.t.—pacific time zone

Need information on a topic that isn't included? Check your telephone directory for important local resources. If you can't find the information you need, give the National Health Information Clearinghouse a call (9:00 a.m.–5:00 p.m., e.t., at 800-336-4797). Also check at the reference desk at your local public, college, or university library.

Adoption

North American Council on Adoptable Children
LD 202-466-7570

Monday–Friday 9 a.m.–5 p.m., e.t.
1346 Connecticut Ave., N.W., Suite 229
Washington, DC 20036

The Council provides a wealth of information and support services to adoption agencies and parents. Call or write for publications.

OURS, Inc.
LD 612-535-4829

3307 Hwy. 100 North, Suite 203
Minneapolis, MN 55422

OURS is a private, non-profit membership organization which provides problem-solving assistance and information to adoptive and prospective adoptive individuals and families. U.S. membership is $16 yearly and includes subscription to OURS *Magazine*.

You can also contact the appropriate local government agency for adoption information. Check your telephone directory for your city or county's social service, family services, public welfare, child welfare or social welfare department. Check the Yellow Pages under "Adoption."

Aging

National Clearinghouse on Aging
LD 202-245-2158

Monday–Friday   9 a.m.–5 p.m., e.t.
Washington, DC

The Information and Referral Section and the Public Inquiries Section of the Clearinghouse respond to inquiries by referring the caller to an appropriate local agency or by distributing, free of charge, single copy pamphlets on aging. The Statistical Analysis Section responds to inquiries on statistics about the older American.

Medicaid/Medicare
LD 202-245-0923

Monday–Friday   9 a.m. –5 p.m., e.t.
Health Care Financing Administration (HCFA)
Washington, DC

This Consumer Inquiry Office answers questions on child health, social security, and all aspects of Medicaid and Medicare. The Office also provides a referral service which includes listings of local welfare offices.

Project Focus
60 Hudson St., Rm. 9438
New York, NY 10013

Send SASE for information on services to adults who may need protection from abuse.

In addition to the resources above, check your local telephone directory for state or local "Departments of Aging" or "Aging and Adult Services."

AIDS

National Gay Task Force Hotline
TF 800-221-7044

Monday–Friday   3 p.m.–9 p.m., e.t.

U.S. Department of Health and Human Services Hotline
TF 800-342-2437

Monday– Friday   8:30 a.m.–5:30 p.m., e.t.

Alcohol

Alcoholics Anonymous (AA)
LD 212-686-1100

Monday–Friday   9 a.m.–5 p.m., e.t.
New York, NY

AA is a voluntary worldwide fellowship of men and women who meet together to attain and maintain sobriety. There are no dues or fees for membership; the only requirement is a desire to stop drinking. There are over 40,000 groups and more than 1,000,000 members in 92 countries. Information on AA and chapter locations worldwide is available from the General Services Office of Alcoholics Anonymous at the telephone number listed above. Check your telephone directory for local listings.

Al-Anon and Ala-Teen
LD 212-481-6565

Monday–Friday   8:30 a.m.–5 p.m., e.t.
New York, NY

The New York office of Al-Anon, an organization of groups for families and friends of alcoholics, refers callers to one of 17,000 Al-Anon or Ala-Teen groups worldwide. Check your telephone directory for local listings.

National Clearinghouse for Alcohol Information (NCALI)
LD 301-468-2600

Monday–Friday   9 a.m.–5 p.m., e.t.
Rockville, MD

NCALI provides a referral service, answering inquiries on alcohol-related subjects by telephone or mail. The Clearinghouse also gathers and disseminates current information (including books, curriculum guides, directories, and posters) free of charge.

Breastfeeding

La Leche League International
LD 312-455-7730

24 hours a day, 7 days a week

La Leche League provides advice and support for nursing mothers. Also check your telephone directory for local chapters.

Child Abuse

National Center on Child Abuse and Neglect
LD 301-251-5157

Monday–Friday   8:30 a.m.–5 p.m., e.t.
Box 1182
Washington, DC 20013

The National Center on Child Abuse and Neglect provides information on child abuse and neglect to the general public and to professionals involved in the treatment of these problems. Child abuse and neglect cases are referred to State agencies. Write or call for a free copy of the brochure "Child Sexual Abuse Prevention."

National Child Abuse Hotline
TF 800-422-4453

24 hours a day, 7 days a week

Skilled counselors provide information and help locate emergency shelters.

National Committee for Prevention of Child Abuse
332 S. Michigan Ave., Suite 1250
Chicago, IL 60604

Send $2.00 for resource list.

Parents Anonymous (PA)
TF 800-421-0353
TF (California) 800-352-0386

24 hours a day, 7 days a week
22330 Hawthorne Blvd., Suite 208
Torrance, CA

Parents Anonymous has over 1200 local chapters which provide support groups for parents who abuse or fear they may abuse their children. Parents Anonymous also publishes materials on child abuse. There is a small charge for publications.

Disabled

Bureau of Education for the Handicapped
Box 1492
Washington, DC 20013

Write to "Closer Look" at the above address for a complete listing of educational projects for disabled children.

Clearinghouse on the Handicapped
LD 202-472-3796

Monday–Friday   9 a.m.–5 p.m., e.t.
Washington, DC

The Clearinghouse refers disabled individuals and consumers to agencies and educational services able to handle their specific inquiries on disabilities. It also supplies callers with information on the disabled. Single copies of publications are free on request.

Mainstream
LD 202-833-1162
TF 800-424-8089

Monday–Friday   9 a.m.–5 p.m., e.t.
Washington, DC

Mainstream is a hotline service providing clarification on affirmative action for the disabled as legislated in Sections 503 and 504 of the Rehabilitation Act of 1973. The hotline clarifies regulations of this Act and subsequent laws for employers, employees, and consumers. In addition, Mainstream provides other information on affirmative action for the disabled and will make referrals to agencies or State offices. If possible, please call the long-distance number instead of the toll-free number.

Parents Helping Parents
LD 408-272-4774

24 hours a day, leave your name and number and your call will be returned.
San Jose, CA

Parents Helping Parents is a support group for parents of children who are physically and/or mentally disabled. The group provides telephone counseling, in-home visits if possible, and referrals to local agencies that can provide assistance or support. Parents Helping Parents also helps parents set up groups in their own communities.

Drug Abuse

National Clearinghouse for Drug Abuse Information (NCDAI)
LD 301-443-6500

Monday–Friday   9 a.m.–5 p.m., e.t.
Rockville, MD

The NCDAI provides information on drug abuse to the public by answering questions and disseminating free publications on drug abuse.

Phoenix House
LD 212-787-7900

24 hours a day, 7 days a week
New York, NY

Phoenix House, a drug treatment facility with live-in facilities in the New York City area, refers callers in other areas of the country to resources that can help with a drug-related problem.

Family Planning

Check your telephone directory under "Family Planning" or "Planned Parenthood" for the Planned Parenthood office or "Planned Parenthood" for local family planning clinics.

Fatherhood

The Fatherhood Project
LD 212-663-7200

Bank Street College of Education
610 W. 112th Street
New York, NY 10025

A center for field research and literature review and a free resource clearinghouse.

Health Information

Center for Disease Control (CDC)
LD 404-329-3286

Monday–Friday   9 a.m.–5 p.m., e.t.
Atlanta, GA

Inquiries from the public on topics such as preventive medicine, health education, immunization, and communicable diseases can be directed to the Office of Information. The Office will also answer questions on occupational safety and health issues, family planning, and public health problems such as lead-based paint and rodent control. Inquiries are answered directly or referred to an appropriate resource.

National Health Information Clearinghouse (NHIC)
TF 800-336-4797
VA only C 703-522-2590

Monday–Friday   8:30 a.m.–5 p.m., e.t.
Rosslyn, VA

The NHIC is a central referral clearinghouse designed to refer consumers to health information resources. The Clearinghouse has identified many groups and organizations that provide health information to the public. When a consumer contacts the NHIC with a question, the inquiry and referral staff determine which organizations can best provide answers. NHIC staff members then contact the organizations and have them respond directly to the caller. All health-related questions are welcomed, although the NHIC is unable to respond to questions requiring medical advice or diagnosis.

TEL-MED
LD 714-825-6034

Monday–Friday   9 a.m.–9 p.m., p.t.
Colton, CA

TEL-MED is a nonprofit tape library of recorded medical messages. The system is made available as a public service by organizations in 250 communities across the United States. There are over 310 tapes, 3 to 7 minutes in length, on different medical subjects. Titles include "Accidents in the Home," "Heart Attack," "Sleep," "Where Did I Come From, Mama?" and many others. For the name of the TEL-MED system nearest you, call the central California office at the number above or write to:

TEL-MED, 22700 Cooley Drive, Colton, CA 92324

After you've located the nearest TEL-MED system, call or write and ask for a free brochure listing the tapes available at that location.

Herpes

(See **Venereal Disease**)

Incest

Parents United
LD 408-280-5055

Box 952
San Jose, CA 95102

Parents United is a self-help organization for *all* family members affected by sexual abuse.

Infertility

American Fertility Society
1608 13th Ave. South, Suite 10
Birmingham, AL 35205

Send SASE for a list of fertility specialists in your area.

Resolve, Inc.
LD 617-484-2424

Monday–Friday   9 a.m.–4 p.m., e.t.
Belmont, MA

Resolve, a national nonprofit organization focusing on the problem of infertility, refers callers to one of 25 chapters across the nation, provides fact sheets on male and female infertility, and publishes a newsletter and a directory of infertility resources. There is a small charge for publications.

Marriage Enhancement

Worldwide Marriage Encounter
3711 Long Beach Blvd.
Long Beach, CA 90807

Write for information regarding programs in your area.

Mental Health

Counseline
LD 202-462-6610

Monday–Friday   9 a.m.–9 p.m., e.t.
Saturday   9 a.m.–5 p.m., e.t.
Washington, DC

Counseline is a tape library of practical information designed to help the caller understand major life stresses and changes. The library consists of over 50 tapes on issues ranging from divorce to alcohol and drug abuse. A caller asks for a tape by number and the operator plays the request. All calls are confidential. For a brochure listing the tapes, call 202-467-4538 (The Psychiatric Institute of Washington, DC) or 202-462-1122 (The Mental Health Association of the District of Columbia).

Recovery, Inc.
LD 312-263-2292

Monday–Friday   9 a.m.–5 p.m., c.t.
Chicago, IL

Recovery, Inc., a mental health group with over 1,000 chapters, sponsors free weekly group meetings for former mental patients and people with emotional problems (depression, anxiety, etc.) who are 18 years of age or older. The headquarters in Chicago refers callers to local chapters.

Missing Children

The Missing Child Network
TF 800-235-3535

National Center for Missing and Exploited Children
TF 800-THE-LOST (843-5678)
in Washington, DC, 634-9836

If you need to report a missing child or have any information regarding a missing child, call the National Center for Missing and Exploited Children.

Physical Fitness

President's Council on Physical Fitness and Sports
LD 202-755-8131

Monday–Friday   9 a.m.–5 p.m., e.t.
Washington, DC

This office promotes the development of physical fitness by providing information and free publications on fitness programs, fitness testing, recreation, and recreational facilities.

Poison

Poison Control Centers

Poison control centers, located around the country, handle toxic emergency calls on poisonous substances including household and commercial products. Call directory assistance to find the number of the poison control center in your area. Keep the number posted near your telephone.

Pregnancy

Abortion Information Service Clinic
TF 800-321-1682

Monday–Friday   8 a.m.–9 p.m., e.t.
Saturday–Sunday   8 a.m.–7 p.m., e.t.
Cleveland, OH

The Abortion Information Service Clinic provides information and referrals on the abortion procedure. The hotline serves the Eastern United States (Michigan to Georgia and eastward).

Birthright
LD 609-848-1818

Monday– Friday   9:30 a.m.–3 p.m., e.t.
Monday–Thursday   7 p.m.–9 p.m., e.t.
Woodbury, NJ

Birthright is an assistance and counseling service for pregnant women. Services include telephone counseling in any aspect of pregnancy and referral to Birthright chapters and clinics across the nation. The hotline is staffed by volunteers. After hours, a prerecorded tape provides information on Birthright services. Birthright counsels against abortion and does not give out information concerning birth control.

National Abortion Information Hotline
TF 800-523-5350

Monday–Friday   9 p.m. –9 p.m., e.t.
Saturday   9 a.m.–4 p.m., e.t.
Oreland, PA

The Hotline provides telephone information and referrals on contraception and the abortion procedure.

National Pregnancy Information Hotline
TF 800-356-5761

24 hours a day, 7 days a week
Necedah, WI

The Hotline counsels pregnant women, refers them to selected medical clinics, and maintains a resource file.

Pregnancy-Risk Hotline
TF 800-532-3749

When you're living for two, that means being twice as careful. Now, fortunately, pregnant women and health-care professionals seeking the latest information about the effects of drugs and chemicals on unborn babies have a hotline to call.

The California Teratogen (a substance harmful to the fetus) Registry, located at the University of California, San

Diego Medical Center, is the only data-collecting and information center of its kind.

Researchers survey scientific journals to keep abreast of the latest reports on the effects of alcohol, cigarettes, marijuana, Valium, X-rays and pesticides. Pregnant women who have been exposed to suspected teratogens can also participate in a free follow-up program after birth.

Rape

Check your telephone directory for "Rape Crisis Center" or a similar listing to find the local crisis center nearest you; the service is available in almost all cities.

Runaways

National Runaway Switchboard
TF 800-621-4000
IL only TF 800-972-6004

24 hours a day, 7 days a week
Chicago, IL

The National Runaway Switchboard provides toll-free telephone services for young people who have run away from home, those considering leaving home, and parents. The service helps young people define their problems, determines if an emergency exists, and refers callers to programs that provide free or low-cost help. Complete confidentiality is guaranteed. If the caller wants to reestablish communication with his or her family, a message can be taken for delivery within 24 hours.

Safety

Auto Safety Hotline
TF 800-424-9393
DC area only 202-426-0123

Monday–Friday   7:45 a.m.–4:15 p.m., e.t.
Washington, DC

The Auto Safety Hotline provides information on and facilitates the identification of safety defects in motor vehicles and vehicle equipment by providing a call-in service for consumers. If you have a defect or safety problem in your automobile, call the Hotline and report the make, model, and year of the car. An operator will give you information on safety recalls that might affect the car. If you give the operator your name and address, you will receive a postage-paid questionnaire to fill out and return to the Hotline. The information that you provide will assist the technical staff of the National Highway Traffic Safety Administration in their evaluation of the car's safety problem. The Hotline also has recall information on foreign cars, tires, and mobile homes.

Consumer Product Safety Commission (CPSC)
Continental USA only TF 800-638-8326
MD only TF 800-492-8363
AK, HI, VI, PR TF 800-635-8333
TTY for the deaf TF 800-638-8270

Monday–Friday   8:30 a.m.–8:30 p.m., e.t.
Bethesda, MD

The CPSC is involved in the evaluation of the safety of products sold to the public. Commission staff members will answer questions and provide free printed materials on different aspects of consumer product safety. For instance, one area of study concerns the safety of children's toys. Other groups of items studied include household appliances and equipment such as chain saws. The Commission does not answer questions from consumers on drugs, prescriptions, warranties, advertising, repairs, or maintenance.

Food, Drugs and Cosmetics
LD 301-443-3170

Consumer Communications, Food and Drug Administration (FDA)
Monday–Friday   9 a.m.–5 p.m., e.t.
Rockville, MD

The Consumer Inquiry Section acts as a clearinghouse for the Food and Drug Administration, answering inquiries on the safety of food, the effectiveness of drugs, and the proper labeling of cosmetics. Other services include a referral service and the dissemination of free publications.

Occupational Safety and Health Administration (OSHA)
LD 202-523-8151

Monday–Friday   9 a.m.–5 p.m., e.t.
Washington, DC

The OSHA Office of Information provides a referral service on job safety, basic information on job safety, and information on dangers posed by toxic substances in the workplace. There is a charge for some publications.

Sex Education

Check under "Sex Education" in your telephone directory for local sex information hotlines.

Single Parents

National Single Parent Coalition
LD 212-620-0755
10 W. 23rd St.
New York, NY 110010

Parents Without Partners
LD 202-638-1320

7910 Woodman Ave., N.W.
Washington, DC 20014

Write or call for information regarding groups in your area.

Smoking

Office on Smoking and Health
LD 301-443-1575

Monday– Friday   9 a.m.–5 p.m., e.t.
Rockville, MD

The Office on Smoking and Health answers public inquiries on smoking and its consequences and provides, upon request, free, single copies of publications on smoking.

Suicide Prevention

National Save-A-Life League
LD 212-736-6191

24 hours a day, 7 days a week
New York, NY

The League provides a referral service and information on suicide prevention. Although based in New York City, the League will help anyone who calls.

The Samaritans
LD 617-247-0220

24 hours a day, 7 days a week
Boston, MA

The Samaritans is a worldwide, nonreligious organization of trained volunteers who talk with, and listen to, anyone who is suicidal, lonely, or depressed. The confidential service is dedicated to the prevention of suicide and the alleviation of loneliness and depression. Although the service is based in Massachusetts, staffers will help anyone in any area of the country.

Check your telephone directory white pages under "Suicide Prevention" for local listings.

Teenage Pregnancy

Child Welfare League of America
67 Irving Place
New York, NY 10003

Write for a list of agencies in your area that help pregnant teens.

Also see listings under **Pregnancy** on page R5.

Terminal Illness

Hospice
1311A Dolly Madison Ave.
Maclean, VA 22101

Hospice has chapters nationwide which provide support for the terminally ill and bereavement counseling for family members and friends. Check your telephone directory white pages under "Hospice" to locate the chapter nearest you.

Make Today Count
LD 319-753-6521

Monday–Friday   8:30 a.m.–5 p.m., c.t.
Burlington, IA

Make Today Count, a nonprofit organization for terminally ill patients and their families and friends, provides telephone counseling and referrals to local chapters across the country. In addition, the organization publishes free pamphlets on topics such as cancer, chemotherapy, and nutrition.

Venereal Disease

VD Hotline
TF 800-227-8922
TF (California) 800-982-5883

Monday–Friday   8 a.m.–8 p.m., p.t.
Saturday–Sunday   10 a.m.–6 p.m., p.t.
American Social Health Association
Box 100
Palo Alto, CA 94302

The VD Hotline provides information on all aspects of sexually transmitted diseases. Services include Herpes Resource Center. Confidentiality is maintained.

Women

Women USA Hotline
Continental USA TF 800-221-4945
NY only LD 212-344-2531

24 hours a day, 7 days a week
New York, NY

The Women USA Hotline is a tape service providing instant access to information on women's issues such as Equal Rights Amendment, health hazards, and reproductive freedom.

Other Resources

To obtain information on other resources you can write for:

Consumer Information Center

The *Consumer Information Catalog* , issued quarterly, lists selected Federal consumer publications on topics such as children, food and nutrition, health, exercise, and weight control. Many of the publications are free. For a free copy of the catalog, write to the Consumer Information Center, Pueblo, CO 81009.

Family Resource/Referral Center
National Council on Family Relations
1214 University Ave., S.E.
Minneapolis, MN 55415
LD 612-331-2774

Government Printing Office

The *Selected U.S. Government Publications*, issued monthly, lists publications for sale through the Government Printing Office. Publications on health-related topics are always listed. For a free copy, write to the Superintendent of Documents, U.S. Government Printing Office, Washington, DC 20402.

National Self-Help Clearinghouse
33 W. 42nd St., Room 1227
New York, NY 10036
LD 212-840-7606

A nonprofit organization providing information concerning self-help in a vast number of areas, including Parents Without Partners, Debtors Anonymous, Emotions Anonymous, Vegetarians over 50, Fat Pride, and Self-Help for Phobic People. The organization puts people in contact with self-help groups in their particular area of concern.

Office for Families
P.O. Box 1182
Washington, DC 20013
LD 202-472-3853

The Office for Families, Department of Health and Human Services, provides information about current research on families, children, and youth in such areas as education, health, work, and social services. It makes referrals to experts who can provide additional information.

FEDERAL INFORMATION CENTERS

Have you ever tried to find an answer to a simple question about the federal government and ended up on a merry-go-round of referrals? Or, have you ever had a question so confusing that you didn't know where to look for help?

Would you know

- where to get a passport?
- how you can buy surplus government property?
- what office handles Medicare or food stamps?

Every citizen at one time or another, needs information concerning a federal agency or program. All too often, he or she doesn't know where to turn. The Federal Information Centers are a vital part in this effort.

Did you know that this service is close at hand? Centers are located in key cities across the country. Additional metropolitan areas have telephone tielines to the nearest center.

No matter how easy or complex the question you can find help. Get in touch with your local Federal Information Center by telephone, by a visit, or by a letter.

Even if a center or toll-free tieline is not located in your area, a long distance call or letter to the nearest center will be less expensive and time consuming in the long run than several calls or letters to offices without the answers.

The Federal Information Centers offer many added services as well. For non-English speaking persons, a number of centers have specialists who speak foreign languages. And, if you visit a center, you will find several informative government publications on such subjects as consumer information, energy conservation, and leisure activities.

A woman wrote wanting to know how to have a tree planted in one of our national forests as a wedding present. From the U.S. Forest Service, it was learned, that, indeed, she could give such a wedding gift. In fact, tree donations often are given as memorials or as other special remembrances.

One day a consumer purchased a pair of shoes from abroad. Once home, she discovered that the wooden heels on the shoes were infested with insects. She phoned a Federal Information Center and was put in contact with the Animal and Plant Health Inspection Service, U.S. Department of Agriculture, which was pleased to have this evidence brought to its attention.

These inquiries were somewhat extraordinary. But no matter what the question, the Federal Information Center staffs aim to serve everyone. They hope they can serve you soon through one of the tielines or offices listed on the following pages.

Federal Information Centers

Alabama

Birmingham
(205) 322-8591

Mobile
(205) 438-1421

Alaska

Anchorage
(907) 271-3650

Arizona

Phoenix
(602) 261-3313
Federal Building
230 North First Ave. 85025

Arkansas

Little Rock
(501) 378-6177

California

Los Angeles
(213) 688-3800
Federal Building
300 North Los Angeles St. 90012

Sacramento
(916) 440-3344
Federal Building and U.S. Courthouse
650 Capitol Mall 95814

San Diego
(714) 293-6030
Federal Building
880 Front St., Room 1S11 92188

San Francisco
(415) 556-6600
Federal Building and U.S. Courthouse
450 Golden Gate Ave.
P.O. Box 36082 94102

Santa Ana
(714) 836-2386

Colorado

Colorado Springs
(303) 471-9491
Toll-free tieline to Denver

Denver
(303) 837-3602
Federal Building
1961 Stout St. 80294

Pueblo
(303) 544-9523

Connecticut

Hartford
(203) 527-2617

New Haven
(203) 624-4720

Florida

Fort Lauderdale
(305) 522-8531

Jacksonville
(904) 354-4756

Miami
(305) 350-4155
Federal Building
51 Southwest First Ave. 33130

Orlando
(305) 422-1800

St. Petersburg
(813) 893-3495
William C. Cramer Federal Building
144 First Ave., South 33701

Tampa
(813) 229-7911

West Palm Beach
(305) 833-7566

Hawaii

Honolulu
(808) 546-8620
Federal Building
300 Ala Moana Blvd.
P.O. Box 50091 96850

Illinois

Chicago
(312) 353-4242
Everett McKinley Dirksen Building
219 South Dearborn St., Room 250 60604

Indiana

Gary/Hammond
(219) 883-4110

Indianapolis
(317) 269-7373
Federal Building
575 North Pennsylvania 46204

Iowa

From any Iowa location
(800) 532-1556

Kansas

From any Kansas location
(800) 432-2934

Kentucky

Louisville
(502) 582-6261
Federal Building
600 Federal Place 40202

Louisiana

New Orleans
(504) 589-6696
U.S. Postal Service Building
701 Loyola Ave., Room 1210 70113

Maryland

Baltimore
(301) 962-4980
Federal Building
31 Hopkins Plaza 21202

Massachusetts

Boston
(617) 223-7121
J.F.K. Federal Building
Cambridge St., Lobby, 1st Floor 02203

Michigan

Detroit
(313) 226-7016
McNamara Federal Building
477 Michigan Ave., Room 103 48226

Grand Rapids
(616) 451-2628

Minnesota

Minneapolis
(612) 725-2073
Federal Building and U.S. Courthouse
110 South Fourth St. 55401

Missouri

St. Louis
(314) 425-4106
Federal Building
1520 Market St. 63103

From other Missouri locations
(800) 392-7711

Nebraska

Omaha
(402) 221-3353
Federal Building
U.S. Post Office and Courthouse
215 North 17th St. 68102

From other Nebraska locations
(800) 642-8383

New Jersey

Newark
(201) 645-3600
Federal Building
970 Broad St. 07102

Trenton
(609) 396-4400
Toll-free tieline to Newark

New Mexico

Albuquerque
(505) 766-3091
Federal Building and U.S. Courthouse
500 Gold Ave., S.W. 87102

New York

Albany
(518) 463-4421
Toll-free tieline to New York

Buffalo
(716) 846-4010
Federal Building
111 West Huron St. 14202

New York
(212) 264-4464
Federal Building
26 Federal Plaza, Room 1-114 10007

Rochester
(716) 546-5075
Toll-free tieline to Buffalo

Syracuse
(315) 476-8545
Toll-free tieline to Buffalo

North Carolina

Charlotte
(704) 376-3600
Toll-free tieline to Atlanta, Ga.

Ohio

Akron
(216) 375-5638
Toll-free tieline to Cleveland

Cincinnati
(513) 684-2801
Federal Building
550 Main St. 45202

Cleveland
(216) 522-4040
Federal Building
1240 East Ninth St., Room 137 44199

Columbus
(614) 221-1014

Dayton
(513) 223-7377

Toledo
(419) 241-3223

Oklahoma

Oklahoma City
(405) 231-4868
U.S. Post Office and Courthouse
201 Northwest 3rd St. 73102

Tulsa
(918) 584-4193

Oregon

Portland
(503) 221-2222
Federal Building
1220 Southwest Third Ave., Room 109 97204

Pennsylvania

Philadelphia
(215) 597-7042
Federal Building
600 Arch St., Room 1232 19106

Pittsburgh
(412) 644-3456
Federal Building
1000 Liberty Ave. 15222

Rhode Island

Providence
(401) 331-5565

Tennessee

Chattanooga
(615) 265-8231

Memphis
(901) 521-3285
Clifford Davis Federal Building
167 North Main St. 38103

Nashville
(615) 242-5056

Texas

Austin
(512) 472-5494

Dallas
(214) 749-2131

Fort Worth
(817) 334-3624
Fritz Garland Lanham Federal Building
819 Taylor St. 76102

Houston
(713) 226-5711
Federal Building and U.S. Courthouse
515 Rusk Ave. 77002

San Antonio
(512) 224-4471

Utah

Salt Lake City
(801) 524-5353
Federal Building
125 South State St., Room 1205 84138

Virginia

Norfolk
(804) 441-6723
Stanwick Building
3661 East Virginia Beach Blvd., Room 106 23502

Richmond
(804) 643-4928

Roanoke
(703) 982-8591

Washington

Seattle
(206) 442-0570
Federal Building
915 Second Ave. 98174

Tacoma
(206)383-5230

Wisconsin

Milwaukee
(414) 271-2273

SEXUAL LIFE—TAKING CARE OF OUR BODIES *

Contraceptives—Choosing One

Today, many types of contraceptives are available to both men and women. How to choose the best one for yourself, especially for the first time, is not easy. A person needs to ask: "What is most important to me?" Some criteria for the decision might be: Is it really effective? Is it acceptable to my partner too? Do I need a doctor's prescription to get it? A teenager may want a contraceptive that does not require any visits to a doctor so that his or her sexual activity can be hidden from parents. A woman may want an intrauterine device (IUD) because it needs so little attention. A man may prefer wearing a condom so that he can actively share in contraceptive responsibility. A woman may want to switch from a diaphragm to the pill because her partner complains of discomfort.

*See Bryan Strong and Rebecca Reynolds, *Understanding Our Sexuality* (St. Paul, Minn.: West Publishing Co., 1982) for a more detailed discussion of birth control, sexually transmitted disease, and sexual health.

Whatever the criteria may be, it is wise for individuals and couples to consider them in making a choice. Sexual relations are much happier when both people involved feel comfortable about the contraceptive being used. Knowing some facts about the different types available gives a person more freedom of choice, and more security in the decision reached.

In the following material concerning contraceptive effectiveness, *theoretical effectiveness* refers to a method's effectiveness if used consistently and correctly; *user effectiveness* refers to a method's effectiveness in *actual* use (and misuse); actual user effectiveness may be substantially lower than theoretical effectiveness.

Contraceptives Available with a Doctor's Prescription

The Pill—Oral Contraception.   "The pill," as it is popularly called, is actually a series of pills (20, 21, or 28 to a package) containing synthetic hormones that interfere with conception. The hormones released into the woman's body do some or all of the following: inhibit ovulation, thicken the cervical mucus to prevent sperm entry, inhibit implantation of the egg in the uterus if it becomes fertilized, promote early spontaneous abortion if the egg becomes implanted. Basically, the pills produce the same chemical conditions that would exist in the woman if she were already pregnant.

There are several different brands of pills available, each containing different amounts of progesterone and estrogen—the two hormones that regulate egg production and uterine cycles. (Single hormone "mini-pills" are no longer on the market, but may return.) Oral contaceptives must be prescribed by a doctor, but then can be purchased at almost any pharmacy.

With the 20- and 21-day pills, one pill is taken each day until they are all used. Two to five days later the woman should begin her menstrual flow. Commonly, it is quite light. (If the flow does not begin, the woman should start the next series of pills seven days after the end of the last series. If she repeatedly has no flow, she should talk to her doctor.) On the fifth day of her menstrual flow the woman should start the next series of pills.

The 28-day pills are taken continuously. Seven of the pills have no hormones. They are there simply to avoid breaking the routine. Some women prefer them for this reason. They find them easier to remember.

The pill is considered the most effective birth control method available when used correctly. It is not effective when used carelessly. The pills must be taken every day, and even as close to the same time each day as possible. If one is missed, it should be taken as soon as the woman remembers, and the next one taken on schedule. If two are missed, the method cannot be relied on, and another form of contraception should be used in addition for the rest of the cycle.

EFFECTIVENESS The pill is more than 99.3 percent effective theoretically.

ADVANTAGES The pills are easy to take. They are dependable. No applications or interruptions are necessary before or during intercourse. Some women experience side effects that please them, such as more regular or reduced menstrual flow or enlarged breasts.

POSSIBLE PROBLEMS There are many possible side effects that can occur from taking the pill, which may or may not bother the user. Those most often reported are:

    change in menstural flow
    breast tenderness
    nausea or vomiting
    weight gain or loss

Some others are:

    spotty darkening of the skin
    nervousness, dizziness
    loss of scalp hair
    change in appetite
    change in sex drive
    increase of body hair

These side effects can sometimes be eliminated by changing the prescription, but not always. Certain women react unfavorably to the pill because of existing health factors or extra sensitivity to female hormones. Women with heart or kidney diseases, asthma, high blood pressure, diabetes, epilepsy, gall bladder diseases, sickle-cell anemia, or those prone to migraines or mental depression are usually considered poor candidates for the pill.

The pill creates health risks, also, but to what extent is a matter of controversy. There are definitely risks for current users. It is not certain whether the risk of health problems remains after a woman has discontinued taking the pill. All women taking the pill stand a greater chance of problems with circulatory diseases, blood clotting, or heart attack. The health risks are low for the young (about half the number of risks encountered in childbirth), but they increase with age. The risk for heavy smokers, women over 30, and those with other health disorders is about four times as great as childbirth. For women over 40 the risks are very high. Current literature on the pill especially emphasizes the risks for women who smoke.

Other factors might need to be taken into account if you are interested in using oral contraceptives. Young girls who have not finished maturing physically may find development slowed or halted by early use of the pill. And women who wish to breast-feed their infants cannot use oral contraceptives at the same time. The hormones released by the pills will dry their milk supply.

Intrauterine Device (IUD). An IUD is a small plastic or metal device inserted into a woman's uterus. Researchers do not know exactly how the IUD prevents conception. It may be that the presence of the device irritates the lining of the womb so that a fertilized egg has difficulty attaching itself and tends to spontaneously abort. The device must be inserted by a doctor. Once in place it needs almost no attention unless problems arise. A string attached to the IUD protrudes into the vagina. By feeling the string with her fingertips a woman can check that the device is in place.

IUDs come in different shapes and sizes. Most popular now are the Lippes Loop, the Saf-T Coil, the Copper T, the Copper 7, and the hormone-releasing Progestasert. The last three must be replaced periodically because the chemical component that increases their contraceptive effectiveness wears off in time.

EFFECTIVENESS   IUDs are 94 to 99.3 percent effective.

ADVANTAGES   Once inserted IUDs require little care. No mess or apparatus at the time of intercourse.

POSSIBLE PROBLEMS   Insertion is often painful. Heavy cramping usually follows and sometimes persists. Menstrual flow usually increases. The IUD is associated with increased risk of pelvic inflammatory disease (PID). Because of the risk of sterility induced by PID, many physicians recommend that women planning to have children use alternative methods. Up to one-third of the women, especially women who have never been pregnant, expel the device within the first year. This usually happens during menstruation. The IUD can be reinserted, however, and many women retain it the second time.

The IUD cannot be inserted in some women due to physical build. Until recently the IUD was considered difficult to insert and less effective for teenage girls. But newer, smaller IUDs have been found acceptable and good protection even for young teenagers.

Occasionally the device perforates the cervix. This usually happens at the time of insertion, if it happens at all. Removal sometimes requires surgery.

Sometimes pregnancy occurs and is complicated by the presence of the IUD. (The IUD itself does not prevent pregnancy; rather, its function is to cause early spontaneous abortion. Occasionally it fails.) If the IUD is not removed, a tubal pregnancy may result, endangering the woman's life.

Diaphragm.   The diaphragm is a rubber cup with a flexible rim. It is placed in the vagina, over the cervix, to prevent sperm from entering the womb. Different women require different sizes, and a woman may change sizes, especially after a pregnancy. To form an effective barrier it must be fitted by a doctor or nurse-practitioner. Somewhat effective by itself, it is highly effective when used with a contraceptive cream or jelly. (Creams and jellies are considered more effective than foam for use with a diaphragm.) These chemicals will inactivate the sperm deposited in the vagina.

The diaphragm can be put in place up to two hours before intercourse. It should be left in place six to eight hours afterward. A woman should not dislodge it or douche before it is time to remove it. If intercourse is repeated within six hours, the diaphragm should be left in place but more chemical contraceptive should be inserted with an applicator.

Diaphragms need to be replaced about once a year because the rubber deteriorates, losing elasticity and increasing the chance of splitting.

Doctors fit women for diaphragms at their offices, using size rings. They then write a prescription for the proper size. The woman purchases her diaphragm at the pharmacy.

EFFECTIVENESS   When properly used, diaphragms are 96 to 98 percent effective. User effectiveness (actual statistical effectiveness) is in the 80 to 96 percent range.

ADVANTAGES   The diaphragm can be placed well before the time of intercourse. There are no health hazards associated with its use.

POSSIBLE PROBLEMS   Some women dislike handling or placing diaphragms, or the mess or smell of the chemical contraceptives used with them. Some men complain of rubbing or other discomfort caused by the diaphragm. Occasionally a woman is allergic to rubber. Some women become more prone to bladder infections.

Cervical Cap.   The cervical cap is a small barrier device like a diaphragm that can be filled with spermicidal gel and placed over the cervix. It holds to the cervix by suction. Cervical caps come in different sizes and shapes to accommodate the different sizes and shapes of cervices. Proper fit is extremely important, and not everyone can be fitted. After a fitting has been made, the woman is instructed how to place it properly over the cervix. First, she fills it two-thirds full of spermicide. Then she must identify her cervix with her fingertips. Finally she places the cap over the cervix and checks to make sure it is holding.

EFFECTIVENESS   Cervical caps are 85 to 98 percent effective.

ADVANTAGES   The chief advantage of this method is that the cap may be left in place up to seven days without further attention. This means it is less work and interferes less with foreplay than a diaphragm. It does not fill the vagina with foam, creams, or jellies, and so leaves it in a more natural state for oral sex or other foreplay. Another advantage is that it does not interfere with the body physically or hormonally. It simply blocks sperm.

POSSIBLE PROBLEMS   Some users are bothered by an odor that develops from the interaction of the cap's rubber with either vaginal secretions or the spermicide. There is some concern that the cap may contribute to erosion of the cervix. If a woman's partner's penis touches the rim of the cap, it can become displaced during intercourse. Because the cervical cap is still undergoing testing for FDA approval, it is limited in availability.

Contraceptives Available Without a Doctor's Prescription

Condoms.   Condoms are thin sheaths of rubber or sheep's intestine that cover the man's penis during intercourse. They are usually individually packaged, and may be dispensed singly from machines in men's bathrooms or boxed by the dozen or more at a drugstore. The condom is unrolled over the man's erect penis before intercourse. About half an inch of the sheath is left loose at the tip to catch the semen when the man ejaculates. After intercourse the man should hold the sheath at the base of his penis as he withdraws to avoid spilling any semen in the vagina. The condom is then thrown away.

Condoms were originally devised (hundreds of years ago) to protect each partner from passing or catching venereal disease (VD). They are still the most effective protection against VD, short of abstinence.

EFFECTIVENESS   Condoms are 96 to 98 percent effective theoretically. Failures sometimes occur from mishandling the condom, but they are usually the result of not putting it on until after some semen has leaked into the vagina, or simply not putting it on at all.

ADVANTAGES   Condoms are easy to obtain. They are easy for men and women to carry around in a wallet or purse. They help protect against VD. They may help protect against herpes and AIDS.

POSSIBLE PROBLEMS   The chief drawback to a condom is that it must be put on after the man has been aroused but before he enters the woman. This interruption is the major reason for users neglecting or "forgetting" to put them on. Some men complain that sensation is dulled, and (very rarely) cases of allergy to rubber are reported. Both problems can be remedied by the use of animal tissue condoms. These are thinner and conduct heat better.

Contraceptive Foam.   Contraceptive foam is a chemical spermicide sold in aerosol containers. Methods vary with each brand, but usually foam is pushed into the vagina either directly from the container or with an applicator. It should be released as far into the vagina as possible. Inside, it forms a barrier to the uterus and inactivates sperm in the vagina. It is most effective if inserted no more than half an hour before intercourse. Shaking the container before applying the foam will increase its foaminess so that it spreads farther. The foam begins to go flat after about 30 minutes. It must be reapplied when intercourse is repeated.

EFFECTIVENESS   Foam is 96 to 98 percent effective when properly used. User failure brings its effectiveness down to approximately 85 percent. Contrary to popular myth, foam can be quite reliable. User failures tend to come from not applying the foam every single time the couple has intercourse, from relying on foam inserted hours before intercourse, or from relying on foam placed hurriedly or not deeply enough.

ADVANTAGES   There are almost no medical problems associated with the use of foam. Foam provides protection against certain venereal diseases.

POSSIBLE PROBLEMS   Some women dislike applying the foam. Some complain of messiness, leakage, odors, or stinging sensations. Occasionally, a woman or man may have an allergic reaction to the foam.

Contraceptive Sponge.   In 1983 the FDA approved the contraceptive sponge for over-the-counter sales. When inserted into the vagina, the polyurethane sponge blocks the opening of cervix and releases a spermicide. It must be left in place for at least six hours (or as long as twenty-four hours) following intercourse and then disposed of.

EFFECTIVENESS   The sponge has a user-effectiveness rate of about 83 percent.

ADVANTAGES   The sponge's advantages include convenience, safety, effectiveness, and possible prevention of some sexually transmitted diseases. It is easy to obtain.

POSSIBLE PROBLEMS   No long term studies of the sponge's safety have been completed. It is recommended that the sponge *not* be used during menstruation because of the risk of toxic shock syndrome at that time. Some women report an unpleasant odor from the sponge; some report inadvertantly expelling the sponge during a bowel movement.

Creams and Jellies.   These chemical spermicides come in tubes and are inserted with applicators. They can be bought without prescription at most drugstores. They work in a manner similar to foams, but are considered less effective when used alone. Like foam, jellies and creams seem to provide some protection against venereal diseases. This factor makes their use with a diaphragm even more attractive, since it is the only highly effective method that also helps prevent VD. Nothing in the pill or the IUD acts as a deterrent to VD.

Suppositories and Tablets.   These chemical spermacides are inserted into the vagina before intercourse. Body heat and fluids dissolve the contraceptive ingredients, which will inactivate sperm in the vagina after ejaculation. Timing depends on the woman, but they must be inserted early enough to dissolve completely before intercourse.

EFFECTIVENESS   Reports on these methods vary widely. It is suspected that the variations are connected with each user's technique of application. Directions for use that come with these contraceptives are not always clear.

ADVANTAGES   The methods are simple, with virtually no medical problems.

POSSIBLE PROBLEMS   Some people have allergic reactions to the spermicides. Some women dislike the messiness, smells, or necessity of touching their own genitalia. Others complain of irritation or inflammation, especially if the method is used frequently. A few women lack the vaginal lubrication to dissolve the tablets in a reasonable amount of time. And a few women complain of having anxiety about the method's effectiveness during intercourse.

Rhythm Methods

All rhythm methods depend on the "rhythm" of the woman's menstrual cycle. After the egg has been released from the ovary (ovulation), it travels down the fallopian tubes to the uterus (usually in 14 to 16 days). If it is unfertilized, the egg and the uterine lining are expelled by the body (menstruation, 3 to 7 days). Then an ovary prepares a new egg (about 9 days). The egg lives about 24 hours after ovulation. If no sperm meets it in that time, it cannot be fertilized. Since sperm can live for about 3 days, a woman can become pregnant only during 3 to 4 days of her cycle. Rhythm methods of contraception depend on knowing when ovulation occurs and avoiding intercourse on those days.

Basal Body Temperature (BBT) Method. A woman's temperature tends to be slightly lower during menstruation and for about a week afterward. At the time of ovulation it dips and then rises sharply (one-half to one whole degree). It stays high until just before the next menstruation.

A woman practicing this method must record her temperature every morning for 6 to 12 months to have an accurate idea of her lows and highs. When she is quite sure she recognizes the rise in temperature, and can predict about when in her cycle it will happen, she can begin using the method. She will abstain from intercourse for three to four days before the expected rise and for four days after it has taken place. If she limits intercourse to only the time after her temperature has risen, the method is much safer. The method requires high motivation and control. For greater accuracy this method may be combined with the mucus method described below.

EFFECTIVENESS   About 80 to 90 percent; the limited intercourse technique is rated 93 to 99 percent effective.

ADVANTAGES   It is free. There are no applicators or health risks.

POSSIBLE PROBLEMS   It is difficult to use this method if a woman's cycle varies greatly. Some women cannot use the method because they discover that their body temperature continually fluctuates and they cannot make a usable record.

Mucus Method (or Billings Ovulation Method). Since 1964, an Australian husband and wife team has been studying the changes in cervical mucus during the woman's cycle. After menstruation, most women have a dry period, then cloudy, sticky mucus begins being discharged. For a day or two, a clear, jellylike mucus is secreted and then the sticky mucus again, or none at all. Ovulation occurs immediately after the jelly-like mucus secretions. The two

days before and the three days after these secretions are the unsafe days. All other days are safe. The method requires training and high motivation to be successful. Clinics are offered in some cities. (Check with Planned Parenthood.) This method may be combined with the BBT method above.

EFFECTIVENESS   This method is 75 to 99 percent effective.

ADVANTAGES   There are no special health risks.

POSSIBLE PROBLEMS   It is difficult for women whose cycles vary greatly to anticipate the clear mucus change and abstain just before it. Some women find it difficult to distinguish differences in their secretions.

Calendar Method. This method is based on calculating safe days from the length of an average cycle. Only a woman whose cycle is extremely regular year-round should attempt to use it.

A woman usually releases an egg 14 to 16 days before her menstrual period. Women using this method mark off unsafe days on the calendar. Figuring from their usual or average length of a cycle, they count back to the expected day of ovulation and mark off at least 3 days before and 2 days after as the unsafe days.

This method is very risky for women whose cycles vary more than a couple of days. For example, if a woman had a short cycle of 25 days, ovulation would occur between the 9th and 11th days. Because an egg can live for 1 day, and sperm for 3, intercourse would be unsafe between the 6th and the 13th days. If the same woman's next cycle were 31 days, ovulation would happen between the 15th and the 17th days. Intercourse would be unsafe between the 12th and the 19th days. Variations of 5 to 6 days are not uncommon. Furthermore, not every woman ovulates 14 to 16 days before her next period. The woman's only protection is abstinence during her fertile days. Only about one-third of all women (statistically) have cycles regular enough to attempt this method.

Unreliable Methods of Contraception

Withdrawal

A man practices withdrawal by withdrawing his penis from the vagina before he ejaculates. The idea is that no conception can happen if the sperm is not ejaculated inside the vagina. This is the oldest form of contraception known, and it is used by some couples with success. Success may depend on technique, combination with rhythm methods, or on physical characteristics of the partners (such as the tendency toward infertility in one of the partners).

A problem with this method is its riskiness. Secretions from the man's Cowper's glands, which sometimes seep into the vagina before ejaculation, can carry thousands of healthy sperm that may impregnate the woman. Also, the first few drops of ejaculate carry most of the sperm. If the man is slow to withdraw or allows any ejaculate to spill into, or on the outer lips of, the vagina, the woman may get pregnant. About 25 of every 100 women who depend on this method become pregnant.

Douching

To douch, a woman flushes the vagina with liquid. As a contraceptive method it is faulty because after the ejaculation, douching is already too late. By the time a woman can douche, the sperm may already be swimming through the cervix into the uterus. The douche liquid entering may even push the sperm on or into the cervix. Water alone, or with two to three tablespoons of distilled vinegar, is somewhat spermatoxic, but mainly such a mixture is useful only for cleansing the vagina. There is no evidence that soda or other beverages do any good. In fact, douching with any liquid, especially if done often, tends to upset the normal bacterial balance in the vagina and may cause irritation or infection. About 40 of every 100 women who depend on this method get pregnant.

Lactation

When a woman, after giving birth, breastfeeds her child she may not begin to ovulate as long as she continues to nourish her child exclusively by breastfeeding. However, although some women do not ovulate while lactating, others do. Cycles may begin immediately after delivery or in a few months. The woman never knows when she will begin to be fertile. This is considered a method in some other countries, but the success ratings are extremely low. As with douching, about 40 of every 100 women who depend on this for protection will become pregnant.

Mythical Methods of Contraception

There are many myths among young and old about contraception. The young gather many from rumors. Some of the old, who should know better, still carry misconceptions hatched in "the old days" when contraceptive devices were not as easily obtained or as dependable as they are today. (The dependability of condoms, always the most easily purchased device, was greatly improved when the product came under the supervision of the Federal Trade Commission.) Any method is better than no method, but some are practically worthless. Unfortunately, some people still rely on them. Today, when better methods are so easy to obtain, it is senseless for anyone to use risky ones.

Widely known methods that are totally useless include:

1. Standing up after intercourse (too late).
2. Taking a friend's pill the day of, or the day after, intercourse (doesn't work—may even be dangerous).
3. Only having intercourse occasionally (it is when, not how often, that makes a difference; once is enough if you are fertile at that time).
4. Using plastic wrap or plastic bags for condoms (too loose, undependable, and unsanitary).

Effectiveness and Risk

A woman using no contraception has a 60 to 80 percent chance of becoming pregnant, according to figures published by the Food and Drug Administration, or even up to a 90 percent chance, according to Planned Parenthood's literature. Any method having a theoretical effectiveness rating lower than 90 percent is considered a poor one.

The methods of contraception discussed here are those most commonly used in the United States. All device methods are quite effective when properly used. Even abstinence methods can be successful when used carefully. But contraception is not always used properly, carefully, or at all. This "user failure" accounts for the wide range in effectiveness data. Top figures usually represent method failures; low figures, the user failures. Planned Parenthood workers stress that *the best method is the one a person will really use.*

One last word on risks. Although health risks, especially with the pill, have caused a lot of concern, it should be understood that, according to statistics, the health risks associated with pregnancy and childbirth are *twice* as great as those connected with any birth control related hazards.

See the chart on page 218 for an overview of contraceptive methods.

About Teenagers

At this time what some people call an epidemic of teenage pregnancies is occurring. Every year more than a million teenagers get pregnant; 80 percent are unmarried. Each year nearly 30,000 babies are born to girls 15 or under. If the current trend continues, 40 percent of today's 14-year-old girls will be pregnant at least once before they reach the age of 20. Some teenage pregnancies are intended, but most are not. Although most sexually active teenagers understand the basics of how a baby is conceived, their knowledge is sometimes quite vague and adorned with hearsay. Many teenagers are aware of, or even use, some kind of contraception, but they tend to be less faithful than older men and women about using it every time. "Forgetting" is the most common reason given for pregnancies by both teenage girls and boys.

On the other hand, teenage girls reading this should check the problems associated with each type of birth control carefully before choosing one. Due to incomplete development, very young teenage girls especially are more limited than older women in their choices of contraceptives. Pills and IUDs are sometimes unsuitable to young women for health reasons. Doctors will want to prescribe them when they can, however, because they have a better success rating with teenagers than diaphragms, foams, or condoms. Diaphragms are becoming more and more popular, but they cannot be fitted in a woman whose hymen has not been broken. However, virtually all teenagers can use foams and condoms, which provide very good protection and are easily obtained.

Where to Go for Information

Planned Parenthood. Most cities of any size have a Planned Parenthood (PP) organization listed in the telephone directory. PP provides information, counseling, and medical services related to reproduction and sexual health to *anyone* who wants them. No one is denied because of age, social group, or inability to pay. (The so-called "squeal rule," introduced by the Reagan administration, which required federally funded family planning agencies to inform parents of an adolescent obtaining prescription birth control devices, was ruled unconstitutional.) Information can also be obtained through the national office. Write:

Planned Parenthood Federation of America
810 Seventh Avenue
New York, N.Y. 10019

Public Health Departments. Counties throughout the United States, regardless of size, have county health clinics that will provide low-cost family planning services. Some cities also have public health clinics. To locate them one should look up the city or county in the telephone directory, then check under headings such as:

> Department of Health
> Family Planning
> Family Services
> Health
> Public Health Department
> (City or County's name) Health (or Medical) Clinic

Sterilization

Sterilization is the form of birth control most frequently used throughout the world. It is estimated that half again as many people are sterilized as use the pill. In the United States since 1971, over 7 million women and 5,570,000 men have been voluntarily sterilized.

Male Sterilization

Vasectomy. A vasectomy is a simple operation that can be performed in half an hour. A local anesthetic is injected into the scrotum. Small incisions are made on each side, and the two vas deferens (the tubes that carry sperm to the urethra) are tied and severed. There is some pain immediately after the operation, but recovery is rapid. The man may be fertile, however, for several weeks afterward, due to sperm stored in ducts in the abdomen. Another contraceptive technique should be used until laboratory examination shows that the semen is sperm-free. This check is necessary also to ensure that the vasectomy was successful. In a few cases, the tubes have been known to rejoin. Also, rarely, a man may have more than two vas deferens.

Vasectomy does not usually affect a man's sexual performance. He will still have erections and ejaculate semen. There have been some reports of both decrease and increase in sex drive, and many reports of freedom from anxiety about pregnancy after the operation.

Side effects from vasectomy are rare. One side effect concerns the unused sperm, which is absorbed by body tissues. Sometimes, after a vasectomy, a man's body reacts as if it were being attacked by a disease. The body forms sperm-destroying antibodies. This immunological reaction is currently under study. (Sperm antibodies are also being studied as a possible means of birth control for women.) Another possible side effect is sperm granuloma (clumps of sperm in the tubes). At this time, neither of these is considered a serious health problem.

The major problem with vasectomy is its finality. Research on a T-valve that could be inserted in the vas deferens and turned on and off has been going on for some time with positive results, but the device is not considered ready to market.

Research on other types of temporary sterilization include injections of contraceptive hormones or drugs to suppress sperm production or maturation, and ultrasound treatments. In the latter method the temperature in the testicles is increased by ultrasound vibrations to a point where sperm production ceases temporarily. Longer exposure can make the situation permanent. So far it has proved as effective as vasectomy and does not show any side effects.

At the moment, vasectomy is the only approved method for male sterilization besides castration. Most vasectomies are performed on men who have been married ten years or more and have either fathered children or are convinced that they do not want to. This consideration is important because the operation is generally considered to be irreversible. Nevertheless, more men are choosing to have vasectomies every year.
have vasectomies every year.

Voluntary sterilization is legal in every state, but doctors are reluctant to sterilize young men or women or those who have not had children. In the case of married couples, consent of a spouse is not legally required, but most physicians would hesitate to operate without both partners' approval. One should investigate local policies as practices concerning sterilization vary according to locale and physician.

Female Sterilization

Sterilization for women is quite expensive. Surgeon fees are large and hospital visits are not cheap. The new procedures in which the woman returns home on the same day have the advantage of being one-half to one-third as expensive as abdominal surgery, but still may cost several hundred dollars. Many health insurance policies will cover part of the cost of sterilization for both men and women. In some states, Medicaid pays for certain patients. It is worth checking your resources. On the other hand, all expenses for sterilization are tax deductible.

Laparoscopy. Sterilization by laparoscope is now the most common method used in the United States. It requires only a day or two in the hospital or clinic. The woman's abdomen is inflated with gas to make the organs more visible. The surgeon inserts a rodlike instrument with a viewing lens (the laparoscope) through a small incision and locates the fallopian tubes. Through a second small incision, the surgeon inserts another instrument that closes the tubes. The tubes are usually closed by electrocauterization. Special, small forceps that carry an electric current clamp the tubes and cauterize (burn) them. Complications, infections, or painful aftereffects sometimes occur when the hot forceps accidentally burn other tissues in the abdominal cavity. New methods that pull the tubes through a small incision and cauterize them outside the body, eliminating interior burns, are being used now, but are not widespread.

Some laparoscopes have a device for closing the tubes too, so that only one incision is necessary. The procedure is called minilaparoscopy. The incisions leave barely noticeable scars, and a woman can resume sexual relations as soon as she feels like it.

Tubal Ligation. This is the most popular method for sterilizing women. In plain English it is "getting your tubes tied." The operation itself is quite simple. The woman is usually placed under general anesthesia. An incision about two inches long is made in her abdomen. Through this incision the surgeon locates the woman's fallopian tubes (the ducts between the ovaries and the uterus). The surgeon then ties and severs the tubes. Unlike male sterilization, it is considered major surgery and may require a hospital visit of several days. It is, of course, more expensive also. To minimize the cost, women usually have tubal ligation performed at the time of a delivery or some other surgery.

Among women married ten years or more it is the number one means of birth control.

Culdoscopy. The culdoscope is an instrument with a light on the end of it. In this operation, the culdoscope goes through an incision in the back of the vagina. When the tubes are located, they are pulled into view, cauterized, and returned to their former position. Local anesthesia can be used for this procedure, and usually the woman can go home the same day. She may need to recuperate at home for several days. Intercourse is not advised until the vagina has healed completely (several weeks).

Culpotomy. This is essentially the same operation as a culdoscopy, but no viewing instrument is used. The advantage of both vaginal methods is that no visible scar is left on the woman's abdomen. Failure rates for either procedure are less than 2 percent.

Sterilization does not reduce or change a woman's feminine characteristics. It is not the same as menopause and does not hasten the approach of menopause, as some people believe. A woman will still have her menstrual periods until whatever age menopause would naturally occur for her. Her ovaries, uterus, and hormonal system have not been changed. The only difference now is that sperm cannot reach her eggs. (The eggs, which are released every month as before, are reabsorbed by the body.) Sexual enjoyment is not diminished. In fact, a high percentage of women report that they feel more relaxed during intercourse now that anxiety about pregnancy has been eliminated. There do not seem to be any harmful side effects associated with female sterilization. Only the surgery involves risks. Occasionally complications or infection develop after surgery. These can be serious.

Abortion

Most people, when they hear the word "abortion," think of a surgical procedure or operation to end an unwanted pregnancy. But the word carries a wider range of meanings than most people realize. Anytime a growing embryo or fetus is expelled from the uterus, an abortion has taken place. Such expulsion can happen naturally, or it can be made to happen in one of several ways. Many abortions happen spontaneously because the woman wears an IUD, or because she suffers physical shock, or because the fetus is malformed, or, more commonly, because physical conditions within the uterus break down and end the development of the fetus. Approximately one-third of all abortions reported in a year are spontaneous.

Abortions can also be induced in several ways. Methods for early abortions (those performed in the first three months) differ from late abortions (those performed between the third and sixth months).

Vacuum Aspiration (First Trimester Method).   In this method, the cervix is dilated. Then a small tube attached to a vacuum is inserted through the cervix. The uterus is gently vacuumed, which removes the fetus. The patient is given a local anesthetic for this simple procedure, and will recover the same day.

Dilation and Curettage (D & C) (First Trimester Method).   The cervix is dilated and the uterine wall scraped with a small spoon-shaped instrument (the curette). The whole procedure takes only a few minutes. Local anesthesia is given, and the patient recovers the same day.

Saline or Amniotic Fluid Replacement Method (Second Trimester Method).   This method is usually used between the 16th and 20th week of pregnancy. Some amniotic fluid is removed from the sac in which the fetus develops and replaced with a strong saline solution. This induces contractions which begin in twelve to twenty-four hours and cause a miscarriage. In a similar procedure, a hormone is injected into the uterus with similar results. A stay in the hospital may be required.

Dilation and Evacuation (D & E) (Second Trimester Method).   This method is usually performed between the 13th and 20th week of pregnancy. The cervix is slowly dilated and the fetus removed by alternating suction and curettage. The procedure is short, uses local anesthesia, and the patient recovers the same day. The procedure is relatively new and seems to be safer than the saline method for early second trimester abortions.

Hysterotomy (Second Trimester Method).   The fetus is removed through an incision made in the woman's abdomen. This is essentially cesarean section—major surgery requiring four to seven days in the hospital.

Because aborting a fetus purposely interferes with the uterine lining (which can easily become infected), it is important always to have abortions performed by a knowledgeable physician. The advice may seem self-evident, but even though the Supreme Court's decision in 1973 made abortion legal, a sizable number of illegal abortions are reported every year. Some people are ignorant of the risks. Others choose unqualified abortionists who offer a low price in hopes of saving clinic costs. Figures on illegal abortions usually come from clinics and hospitals that have treated women driven in because of infections or other complications resulting from an illegal abortion. But, properly done, early abortion is 6 times safer than childbirth. Second

trimester methods are more dangerous to the mother's health. Amniotic fluid replacement is almost 10 times more dangerous than early abortion. Hysterotomy is about 36 times more dangerous. For health reasons, abortions should always be done as early as possible.

The number of abortions reported each year has increased steadily over the last ten years. About two-thirds of these are performed on single, Caucasian women under 25 years of age. A minor does not need parental consent, and wives do not need the consent of their husbands. The high number of abortions is consistent with the trend toward later and smaller families.

The major obstacles for women today are funds and locale. Fewer than one-half the nation's hospitals perform abortions. Women living outside large, urban areas often need to travel to an urban area to obtain one. This creates difficulty in addition to the added expense. In itself, an abortion may cost a few hundred dollars. Many women cannot raise the initial sum.

In the early 1970s there were several federal and state programs to which a woman could apply for financial aid. The reasoning has been that a woman should be able to control this aspect of her life, and that funding abortion is less costly than supporting a woman and infant on welfare. But in the last decade opinion has turned against this use of tax money, and sources of aid have been cut off. The hardest hit are the young and the poor.

Sexually Transmitted Diseases (STDs)

Many people associate sexually transmitted disease (STD), also known as venereal disease (VD), with "loose" or "unclean" sexual behavior practiced mostly by poor or nonwhite social groups. They assume they will not become infected if they stay away from "those types." This view is totally wrong. Reports of infection come from all economic and education levels, and the total number rises each year. There are an estimated 8.6 to 11.1 million cases of STDs yearly. The National VD Hotling has given these statitics on its callers:

    60% men/40% women
    83% white
    88% heterosexual
    26% married
    55% earn over $15,000
    25% earn over $25,000
    26.5 is mean age
    2 years of college is the mean education level

These figures represent only those who called, but they agree with most other health statistics. Figures from clinics differ somewhat. For instance, some clinics report that the incidence of VD is highest among homosexual males, lowest among lesbian women, highest among both sexes between the ages of 20 and 24, and next highest among 15- to 20-year-olds.

VD and STD are general terms that refer to several different types of diseases closely associated with sexual contact. The most prevalent in the United States today are gonorrhea, chlamydia, genital herpes, and syphilis.

Chlamydia. Chlamydia is the most common venereal disease in America, affecting as many as 3 million persons a year. The symptoms of chlamydia are similar to gonorrhea for both men and women. The man most often has a whitish discharge coming from his urethra; a woman is usually asymptomatic. Chlamydia is a parasite, neither a virus nor a bacterium, which causes a variety of infections. Approximately 55 percent of the urethritis cases in VD clinics are from chlamydia, while the remaining 45 percent are caused by gonorrhea.

The risks of getting chlamydia from an infected partner are less than getting gonorrhea. The use of IUDs, however, is likely to increase the chance of getting chlamydia, gonorrhea and/or PID. It is possible for a person to be infected with both gonorrhea and chlamydia; a treatment for gonorrhea will cure the gonorrhea but not the chlamydia.

Chlamydia is swiftly spreading in part because some physicians mistakenly diagnose it as gonorrhea and prescribe penicillin treatment. Most clinics and physicians do not have the facilities to test for chlamydia. Unfortunately, chlamydia does not respond to penicillin. Therefore, a man with a discharge should insist that a culture be taken to determine whether he is suffering from chlamydia or gonorrhea or both. If he is suffering from chlamydia, then the correct treatment for him and his partner is tetracycline. If the woman is pregnant, however, tetracycline must *not* be used; instead erythromycin should be used, another antibiotic. Since there is a high incidence of persons suffering from both gonorrhea and chlamydia at the same time, tetracycline may become the treatment of choice for uncomplicated gonococcal infections.

Chlamydia is a serious disease although traditionally it has not been treated as an important infection. For men, the serious consequences include sterility; for women, pelvic inflammatory disease (PID) may be a consequence, possibly leading to hospitalization, tubal pregnancies, or sterility. Infected women who deliver may pass their infection on to their babies, causing serious eye infections and pneumonia.

Gonorrhea. This is an old disease, second only to the common cold in age and prevalence around the world. In its early stage a man will usually notice a discharge of fluid from his penis two to seven days after sexual contact, a frequent desire to urinate, and a burning sensation when

he does so. He will usually go to a doctor at this stage and be treated. If untreated, the male commonly suffers various complications, including inflammation of the testes, arthritis, skin infections, urinary disorders, and sterility.

Most women with gonorrhea are asymptomatic, that is, they show no symptoms. For this reason, if her partner discovers that he has gonorrhea, it is imperative that he tell her so that she may be treated. Many cases in women go undetected until secondary symptoms of pain in the lower abdomen develop. This is the stage of pelvic inflammatory disease (PID). By this time the disease has moved into the fallopian tubes and glands surrounding the female organs. The result may be severe damage to tubes or ovaries, with sterility resulting.

The infection can usually be halted in men and women by an injection of penicillin or a tetracycline drug. However, some strains of the gonococcus bacteria are resistant to the usual cures and are thus difficult to treat.

Genital Herpes. Genital herpes is the third most common form of VD in the United States. No cure has been found for the disease, so it has spread rapidly and uncontrollably. Genital herpes is caused by a virus, generally herpes simplex type II (although 15 percent of genital herpes is caused by herpes simplex I, the virus responsible for oral and facial cold sores and fever blisters).

About 2 to 20 days after infection, genital herpes forms blisters on the penis or urethra in men, and the cervix, vagina, or vulva in women. Genital herpes sores may also appear around the mouth if a person engages in oral sex with someone who has this disease. The sores are quite painful, and women may report pain during urination.

Once the disease is contracted, the carrier may experience repeated attacks. Although there is no cure, there are some treatments that reduce the pain and healing time of lesion outbreaks. These also reduce the chance of spreading the disease, which is most contagious during the prodromal (presymptom) stage that precedes blistering by about three days and during the blistering stage. Various ointments also help the lesions to heal quickly. The most effective of these on the market now is acyclovir (this is the generic name; brand names will be different). Acyclovir also minimizes the pain for men, but not for women. Acyclovir is also available as an oral medication. It must be prescribed by a physician. Pregnant women with herpes need to be aware of possible risk to their newborn infants. Informed health practitioners can provide information regarding alternatives.

Syphilis. Syphilis is caused by bacteria that fortunately are easy to identify with a blood test. It can be treated with penicillin or certain other antibiotics. The disease has four distinct stages that are alike for both women and men. The progression of the disease is not painful and is not easily noticed by the victim in its early stage. It is extremely important to arrest the disease in its early stage to avoid irreversible damage to body tissue.

EARLY STAGE   A sore called a chancre (pronounced *shanker*) appears anywhere from ten days to three months after infection at the place of infection. This may be an internal site for a woman. It may look like a pimple, a blister, an ulcer, or a cold sore. It does not hurt. It will heal itself in one to ten weeks.

SECONDARY STAGE   After the chancre heals, the disease spreads to other parts of the body. A rash breaks out (usually on the trunk of the body), but this rash is not painful or itchy. A person may also be bothered with low fever, sore throats, headaches, or other discomforts easily mistaken for ordinary ones. Sometimes lesions form in the mouth during this stage. If so, the mouth will be full of syphilis bacteria and the disease can be passed by kissing.

LATENT STAGE   Beginning six months to two years after infection, the disease becomes latent. During this time the person does not infect others but still tests positive. This stage may continue indefinitely—even until death.

LATE STAGE   The syphilis bacteria sometimes concentrate in certain parts of the body. Then the disease breaks loose. It may be in any part—liver, skin, heart, or central nervous system. Later lesions and ulcers appear. Tissue damage and several disabling diseases can develop. Direct damage, as well as that arising from complications, may prove fatal.

Acquired Immune Deficiency Syndrome (AIDS).   First identified in 1981, acquired immune deficiency syndrome (AIDS) claimed over 16,000 victims by January 1986. Over 8000 of them had died; no one has been cured. The Federal Centers for Disease Control estimated that there would be 15,000 new cases of AIDS in 1986 (Boffey, 1986). The AIDS virus infects cells that normally defend against infection, leaving the body vulnerable to diseases it would ordinarily be able to fight off. The virus is transmitted in bodily fluids, generally through semen or blood, although it has also been discovered in small quantities in saliva and tears. Most AIDS is spread through sexual activity; intravenous drug use and blood transfusions are also implicated.

A blood test to determine the presence AIDS virus has been developed to screen donated blood and blood products. Based on tests administered so far, it is estimated that a million Americans have been exposed to AIDS. Of these, about 10 percent are expected to develop symptoms over the next three to five years. The symptoms of AIDS and ARC (AIDS-related complex) include swollen lymph glands, persistent fatigue, fever, diarrhea, weight loss, and susceptibility to infection.

Although AIDS does not appear to be highly contagious

(only 1 percent of AIDS health workers show any evidence of exposure to it), it does pose a serious threat to certain groups of people. Recipients of blood donations appear to be relatively safe due to the development of effective screening procedures. Intravenous drug users and people who engage in sexual activities with multiple partners should consider themselves at risk. Within the gay community especially (about three-fourths of AIDS victims are gay men), safe sexual practices are being promoted in an effort to control the spread of AIDS. Recommendations for protection against sexually-transmitted AIDS are summarized as follows:

1. Know your partner. Avoid anonymous, multiple sexual contacts.
2. Avoid the transmission or exchange of bodily fluids.
3. Use a condom.

For further information regarding AIDS, contact the organizations listed on page R2 of the Resource Center.

Vaginitis   There are also a variety of urethral and vaginal infections that are considered venereal because they are aggravated or perpetuated by sexual contacts. Sometimes only one partner suffers from the discomfort, while the other seems to be resistant. Partner two acts as a carrier and continually reinfects partner one. These diseases fall under the general category vaginitis and include trichomoniasis, moniliasis (yeast infection), and nonspecific vaginitis.

Here are some hints that may help a woman avoid vaginitis:

Use Good Vaginal Hygiene

- Do not use vaginal deodorants, especially deodorant suppositories or tampons, because they upset the natural chemical balance within the vagina. Use douches rarely and then only for a good reason such as a diagnosed yeast infection. Despite what pharmaceutical companies advertise, the healthy vagina does not have an unpleasant odor. If a vagina does have an unpleasant odor, then something is wrong and you should check with a physician or health practitioner.

Keep the Vaginal Opening Clean

- Regularly wash and rinse the vulva and anus. Be careful about using bubble baths or strongly perfumed soaps since they may cause irritation.
- After a bowel movement, wipe the anus from the front to the back to prevent the spreading of germs from the anus to the vagina.

Avoid Conditions that Might Encourage Bacterial Growth

- Wear cotton underpants or underpants that have a cotton crotch since nylon underpants and pantyhose keep heat and moisture in, encouraging bacterial growth.

- When lubricating the vagina, use only water-soluble lubricants. Despite the mythology of sex and Vaseline, Vaseline is not water-soluble and tends to form a film on the walls of the vagina which keeps heat and moisture in, encouraging infection.

Have Your Male Partner Treated Also

- Vaginitis is often sexually transmitted. Be on the safe side and treat both partners to prevent reinfection.

Prevention of STDs

Apart from abstinence and strict monogamy, there are no certain rules for preventing venereal disease. There are some things you can do, however, to lessen the risks of contracting a sexually transmitted disease if you are sexually active:

- AVOID ANONYMOUS OR CASUAL SEX   Such encounters may run a higher risk of contracting a venereal disease. If your partner does turn out to have a sexually transmitted disease, he or she may be unable to contact you; you yourself may be asymptomatic and spread it to others unknowingly.
- INSPECT YOUR PARTNER'S GENITALS for signs of discharge, sores, blisters, rashes, warts, or anything unusual, prior to coital or oral contact. This may be done while undressing, showering, or pleasuring each other. Unpleasant odors are also a clue. If there are any suspicious signs, do not make love. Remember, though, many venereal infections, especially gonorrhea and chlamydia are often asymptomatic.
- WASH AFTER SEXUAL INTERCOURSE   Using soap and warm water promptly after coitus may provide some benefit. The genitals should be thoroughly washed as soon as possible after intercourse. There is some evidence that washing the genitals before sexual interaction may also provide some protection.
- URINATE AFTER INTERCOURSE   The acid environment of the urine may destroy certain infectious bacteria; urination may also flush out much of the infectious bacteria, especially if the urine is forcefully expelled in a short burst.

- USE CONDOMS, FOAMS, CREAMS, AND JELLIES   Condoms are not only highly effective in preventing pregnancies without any side effects, they are also effective in preventing gonorrhea, syphilis, and chlamydia. They may also help in the prevention of herpes and AIDS. The foams, creams, and jellies used alone or in conjunction with the diaphragm also provide some protection against sexually transmitted diseases, especially gonorrhea, syphilis, trichomoniasis, and possibly herpes.
- ROUTINE MEDICAL EXAMINATIONS SHOULD BE MADE PERIODICALLY, since many venereal diseases are asymptomatic. As many as 80 percent of the women with gonorrhea are asymptomatic and 20 percent of the men. Sexually active individuals should have checkups every three months, or twice a year at the very least.

Getting Help.   Any person who has a venereal infection must assume the responsibility of informing those with whom he or she has had sexual contact that they may be infected. The consequences of undetected infection are potentially so harmful that there is no legitimate excuse for withholding the information. For people who are unwilling to tell their partners directly, there are local public health services that will do so, keeping the informant's identity anonymous if desired.

Most venereal diseases can be cured if they are discovered and treated in their early stages. But for early treatment to be possible, people must familiarize themselves with the symptoms of venereal diseases. If you have even a suspicion that you might be infected, you should immediately consult a doctor or your local public health agency, where diagnosis and treatment are generally free or low cost. Ignoring any sign of trouble, or hoping that it will disappear, is a foolish and dangerous risk. Sometimes a symptom will disappear—such as a chancre sore in the first stage of syphilis—but this does not necessarily mean that the disease is cured.

If you do not know where to go or who to call, contact the VD National Hotline 800-227-8922 (in California call 800-982-5883). These are toll-free numbers.

FOR WOMEN

Make Breast Examination a Health Habit*

Follow these steps to examine your breasts regularly once a month. This examination is best done after the menstrual period.

A. Looking: Stand in front of a mirror with the upper body unclothed. Look for changes in the shape and size of the breast and for dimpling of the skin or "pulling in" of the nipples. Be aware, too, of any discharge from the nipples or scaling of the skin of the nipples. Abnormality in the breast may be accentuated by a change in position of the body and arms.

1. Stand with arms down.
2. Lean forward.
3. Raise arms overhead and press hands behind your head.
4. Place hands on hips and tighten chest and arm muscles by pressing firmly inward.

B. Feeling: Lie flat on your back with a pillow or folded towel under your shoulders and feel each breast with the opposite hand in sequence. With the hand slightly cupped, feel for lumps or any change in the texture of the breast or skin; also, note any discharge from nipples. Avoid compressing the breast between the thumb and fingers as this may give the impression of a lump that is not actually there.

1. Place the left arm overhead. With the right hand, feel the inner half of the left breast from top to bottom and from nipple to breastbone.
2. Feel the outer half from bottom to top and from the nipple to the side of the chest.
3. Pay special attention to the area between the breast and armpit, including the armpit itself.
4. Repeat this same process for the right breast using your left hand to feel.

Feel gently, carefully, and thoroughly. If you find something which you consider abnormal, contact your doctor for an examination. Most breast lumps are not serious, but all should come to the doctor's attention for an expert opinion after appropriate examination. You may have a condition that will require treatment or further study. If necessary, your doctor may recommend laboratory tests or X-rays as part of a more detailed examination. Follow your doctor's advice—as your early recognition of a change in your breast and his or her thoughtful investigation will

*Reprinted from U.S. Department of Health, Education, and Welfare, Publication No. (NH) 76-649.

determine the safest course. Keep up this important health habit even during pregnancy and after menopause.

Practical Hints on Breastfeeding

Most women find that a good nursing bra, one that provides good uplift and that opens easily for nursing, makes nursing easier and more comfortable. Many wear such a bra day and night during the months they are nursing.

Use the first few days, where there is little milk in the breast, to get your nipples used to your baby's nursing. Let him suck for only two minutes at a time at each breast the first day, three minutes the second day, and five minutes the third day. If your nipples get sore at any time later, you can limit nursing time to five minutes at each breast. Even a slow nursing infant gets at least four-fifths of the milk in his first five minutes at breast.

Rest and relax as much as possible during the months that you are breastfeeding, especially at the beginning. Your body is doing a tremendous amount of work and needs extra care.

While nursing, find a position that is comfortable for you and your baby; a foot stool, a pillow and a chair with arms are often helpful.

Touch the baby's cheek with the nipple to start. She will turn her head to grasp the nipple. (If you try to push her to the nipple with a finger touching her other cheek or chin she will turn away from the nipple toward the finger.)

Allow her to grasp the entire darkly colored part of the breast in her mouth. She gets the milk by squeezing it from the nipple, not by actually sucking. Her grasp on your nipple may hurt for the first few seconds, but the pain should disappear once she is nursing in a good rhythm. When you want to remove her mouth from your breast, first break the suction by inserting your finger in the corner of her mouth. This will save sore nipples. If your entire breast becomes sore, you may be able to relieve the painfulness simply by lifting and supporting the breast with one hand during nursing. Hot compresses between nursing sessions may further relieve soreness.

A small amount of milk may come out of your nipples between feedings. A small nursing pad or piece of sanitary napkin inserted in the bra over the nipple will absorb this milk, keeping the bra clean and preventing irritation of the nipple.

If you have difficulty beginning to breastfeed, don't give up! Ask friends, women's centers, clinics, or the local La Leche League chapter for help. Don't worry about not having enough milk; the more your baby nurses, the more you'll produce. If you notice a spot of tenderness or redness on your breast or nipple that persists for more than two feedings be sure to seek advice from your breastfeeding support group or physician promptly.

For further information, we recommend Sheila Kitzinger's *The Experience of Breastfeeding* (Penguin Books, 1982) and *The Womanly Art of Breastfeeding* by La Leche League International (Plume, 1981).

Gynecological Checklist*

Regular physical checkups are important for us so that we can catch any problems before they become too serious. For women, a regular gynecological ("gyn") exam is particularly necessary. . . . This checklist can help in our effort to achieve higher quality health care.

Suggestions for Use of this Checklist

- Read it thoroughly and write down any questions you have.
- Be prepared to discuss your exam with the doctor. This might include requesting a particular test or exam, as well as asking for clear explanations of procedures, treatments, etc.
- All of the following procedures are standard parts of a complete gyn exam. Don't let the doctor intimidate you by making you feel that you're asking for something extra.
- You're entitled to have a friend or "patient advocate" with you throughout the exam. This person can help you remember your questions, the health worker's answers, and generally give you support during the entire visit.

What To Do Before Your Visit.   Here are some things to do before your gyn exam in order to (1) prepare yourself better and (2) help you get the most out of your visit.

- Be clear on the purpose of your visit. For example, it is for a routine annual exam, diagnosis and treatment of a problem you are having, contraceptives, etc.
- Be clear on what you want to get out of the exam. For example, do you want to learn more about the various types of cancer, or to have your questions answered about a particular pelvic pain, etc.
- Do some research on the various elements of the exam or on any particular problem you might be having.
- List all the questions you want answered during your exam and put them in order of priorities in case you are rushed through the visit.

*Adapted from the Santa Cruz Women's Health Center.

- Write down the answers to the questions to be covered in the health history (see below).
- Find out what the charges for the visit are likely to be and, if applicable, whether or not health insurance, Medicaid, etc., will be accepted.
- Find a friend or patient advocate to accompany you during the visit.

The History.   Before the exam, you should discuss with your health worker a complete history of your own and your family's health. Here are the main topics you should cover.

- Preliminary data: your age and how many times pregnant and the outcomes of those pregnancies.
- Chief complaint: reason for the visit.
- Present illness.
- Menstrual history.
- History of contraceptives used.
- History of other gynecological problems.
- General medical history: include parents, grandparents, sisters, brothers, etc.
- Hospitalizations and operations: please explain regarding the year (date), type, length of confinement, nature of operation, etc.
- Drugs currently taking: obviously your answer may depend on how well you trust your health worker, but you should know that your health problems and treatments are closely related to any drugs you may be taking; in particular, if a drug is prescribed for you, you should make sure that it does not interact with any other drugs you are taking. Also include alcohol, cigarettes, coffee, etc.
- Drugs taken in the past and reactions.
- DES daughter.

The Examination.   The following should be included in a complete gyn exam.

- *Your height, weight, temperature, and blood pressure* should be measured and recorded.
- *Breast Exam*: you should be shown how to do one. Your health worker should also examine your breasts thoroughly.
- If you are taking or want to take birth control pills or estrogen therapy, your heart and lungs should be listened to and percussed (tapped).

The following exams should be done, although not necessarily in this order.

- *External Genitalia Visual Exam* A check of the labia, pubic area, clitoral area, anus and urethra for coloring, lumps, sores, growths, lice or discharges.
- *Palpation* (feeling) of Bartholin's glands (near vaginal opening) and Skene's glands (behind urinary opening or urethra).

- *Internal Vaginal Visual Exam* A metal or plastic speculum is used to open the vagina so that vaginal walls and cervix can be seen. You can learn to do a speculum exam yourself . . . , and you can ask your health worker for a mirror if you want to see what the inside of your vagina looks like. There should be a check for any abnormal situations. Usually tests such as Pap smear and gonorrhea culture and any other vaginal tests are taken at this point (see section on tests).
- *Internal Bimanual Exam* ("two hands exam") With a glove on, your health worker inserts two fingers into your vagina and places the other hand on your abdomen. This is a check for the position, size, firmness, mobility, and any abnormalities of your uterus. You can find out if your uterus is anteverted or anteflexed (tipped forward), midline (straight up and down), or retroverted or retroflexed (tipped backwards). This should also be a check of the fallopian tubes and the ovaries, and for any lumps or growths inside your vagina. You will also be asked to push downward (as in having a bowel movement) to check for relaxed muscles or a prolapsed uterus. The bimanual may be somewhat uncomfortable, with slight twinges of pain; if you have any substantial pain or tenderness you should tell your health worker.
- *Recto-Vaginal Exam* This is done if your health worker feels that the bimanual was not sufficient. One lubricated finger is inserted in the vagina while another is inserted in the rectum. Some pelvic organs can be better felt in this manner. This exam may feel strange or uncomfortable, but it usually lasts only a few seconds. You should be told before being given this exam so that you aren't taken by surprise.
- *Rectal Exam* This exam is similar to the recto-vaginal exam, without a finger in the vagina. It is important as a check for growths or other abnormal conditions in the rectum.

Tests. The following tests should be included either routinely or as indicated.

"Routine":

PAP SMEAR:

1. Pap smears are important because they can detect cancer before there are symptoms, before it has spread and while it is still totally curable.
2. Every woman should have a Pap smear at least once a year except for women under 18 who are not sexually active.
3. A Pap smear is a scraping of cells taken from the surface of the cervix to tell if you have cervical cancer. It can also detect changes in cells due to irritation, infection or a hormonal imbalance.

4. The test usually does not hurt unless you have an inflamed or tender cervix or a very small one.

ROUTINE CHECK FOR GONORRHEA:

1. This is very important, even if you think there is no chance you could have it because 80% of all gonorrhea in women (20% in men) has no symptoms.
2. A gonorrhea test is done by inserting the tip of a cotton swab in your cervix (it shouldn't hurt) and smearing the discharge on a culture plate and then letting it incubate for 24–48 hours.
3. You can catch VD from men or women, if you are gay or straight, from oral or genital and anal sex, therefore if you have oral or anal sex, make sure an appropriate culture is taken.

"As indicated":

SYPHILIS TEST (VDRL):   Syphilis can also exist undetected in your body for many years without noticeable symptoms. Unlike gonorrhea, syphilis immediately enters your bloodstream; therefore a blood test is necessary to diagnose it.

VAGINITIS: If you have symptoms of vaginal infection, e.g., itching, burning, foul smelling or unusual discharge, then a smear and/or culture with your vaginal secretions should be taken and examined microscopically to determine what type of infection it is.

The 3 most common types are yeast (monilia), trichomonas and hemophilus (nonspecific vaginitis).

ENDOMETRIOSIS: The *endometrium* is the tissue which lines the uterus. Abnormal growth of endometrial tissue— on the ovaries, fallopian tubes, and so on—is called endometriosis. It is often chronic, painful, and difficult to treat. Its causes are obscure. Symptoms involve pelvic pain, painful intercourse, mid-menstrual cycle pain and severe menstrual cramps. Physicians can sometimes diagnose endometriosis by pelvic examination, but usually laparoscopy, a surgical procedure, must be performed for a definitive diagnosis. If endometriosis is suspected, you will need to undergo further testing or be referred elsewhere. Hormonal therapy and surgery are possible treatments. Information and support for women with endometriosis may be obtained from the Endometriosis Association, % Bread and Roses Women's Health Center, 238 W. Wisconsin Avenue, #700, Milwaukee, WI 53203.

PELVIC INFLAMMATORY DISEASE (PID):   Pelvic inflammatory disease is a general term for infections of the fallopian tubes, ovaries, or uterus. It is primarily caused by sexually transmitted diseases; it may also be acquired during IUD insertion, abortion, childbirth, and surgery. Pain is the primary symptom, although there may be others, including fever, urinary difficulties, vaginal discharge, irregular bleeding, and nausea. Complications (which include impaired fertility) can be very serious, so PID should be treated as soon as it is suspected, even before test results are in. Experts disagree strongly about PID testing and treatment. Since any of a number of organisms may be involved, many tests may be necessary; furthermore, their results may not be accurate as these organisms are difficult to culture. Rest is a necessity. Occasionally hospitalization is required. *Both* partners must be treated with antibiotics to avoid reinfection.

OTHER TESTS: If you have any other problems, tests should be done for them or else you should be referred elsewhere.

After the Exam. This is a list of things to do after your exam but before you leave the doctor's office, to make sure you got what you wanted and you know what to do next.

- If you have a problem or infection that needs treatment, *discuss with your health worker* what to do about it, how it could be prevented.
- *You should be told the information that diagnosis is based on.*
- *You should be told your options for treatment* including different drugs or therapeutic procedures, natural healing methods, home remedies, herbs, nutrition, or doing nothing. Remember, it is *your choice* which option to take.
- If you receive any drugs, *you should be told about all possible side effects* and how you should take the drug so it will be most effective.
- *Find out if the health worker is available for consultation.*
- *Find out when the results of any tests that are sent out will be back.*
- Ask yourself if you got what you came for.
- Ask any other questions you may have *now*.

The Alternatives in Unwed Pregnancy*

If a single woman becomes unintentionally pregnant, she has four alternatives: marriage, single parenthood, adoption, or abortion. Each choice involves many considerations, some of which are suggested in what follows. (See listings under **Pregnancy** on page R5 for resources to help with decision-making in unplanned pregnancy.)

Marriage

You can continue the pregnancy and marry. Your parents may want you to do this. Or the man may want you to marry him. But be sure it is what you want. Does a marriage to this man fit into your future as you see it? THE WAY YOU FEEL IS IMPORTANT.

*Source: "Problem Pregnancy Alternatives," Planned Parenthood of Minnesota.

Are you and the man you are considering marrying good friends as well as lovers? Do you see yourself as the mother of a child and the man as the father? You'll want to explore your feelings about your relationship.

You may feel that more education is important to you, or you may want to continue working. Then you will need to talk with your man about ways to provide childcare while you are in school or working.

You may think that if your marriage doesn't work out you can get a divorce, and you can. But you will have a child to consider in that decision. And divorce can be an emotionally difficult process for everyone involved.

You've probably been asking yourself many of these questions. Marriage is an alternative that may solve an immediate problem of your pregnancy—or it may create additional problems in your future.

Single Parenthood

Many women today decide to raise a child without help from the man involved. It is more socially acceptable for women to do this now than it has been previously. But it is still hard work. Babies need continual attention and care. And raising a child costs money.

There are agencies in your community to help you in single parenthood. A counselor can give you information about pre-natal care, childbirth arrangements and financial aid. Payments may be available to you through the Aid to Families with Dependent Children (AFDC) program if it is not possible to obtain financial support from the father of the child.

You and the man involved may want to raise the baby together but not marry. Is your commitment to each other deep enough that you can raise a child without being married? Do you feel that it will be a problem for your child to have unmarried parents? As you can see, there are many questions to think about, lots of feelings about yourself and your relationships to sort out.

Adoption

If you decide to continue your pregnancy, but feel that you cannot raise a child at this time, you may be thinking about placing your baby for adoption. Recently there have been more families wanting to adopt children, and fewer children to adopt. So you can be sure that there is a family who really wants to adopt your child.

Counseling on adoption is available to you at community agencies. If you decide that adoption is the best alternative for you, you can talk to the counselor at an adoption agency about the kind of home and family you would like for your child.

Sometimes a woman is unable to make the decision about

placing her baby for adoption before childbirth. She may find it difficult to accept the idea of being separated from her child, even though she may feel that another family could offer her child more. This decision does not need to be made until after the baby is born. It is possible to place the baby in a foster home until you decide. However, it is best for the child if you don't wait too long.

The father of the baby has a legal right to present his views at a hearing before the baby can be placed for adoption.

Abortion

If you feel that you cannot continue the pregnancy and have a child at this time in your life, abortion is an alternative you can choose.

Abortions performed up to 24 weeks from the first day of the last menstrual period are now legal in the United States. The Supreme Court ruled in 1973 that women have a constitutional right to terminate their pregnancies by abortion if the procedure is performed by a doctor.

Now that abortion is legal it is a safe medical procedure. However, the risks increase as the pregnancy lengthens so it is important for you to make a decision early in the pregnancy.

When you are making the decision about a problem pregnancy, your own feelings are the most important factor. Some people feel that abortion is not moral—others feel that it is more moral to have an abortion than to have an unwanted child. You can explore your feelings with a pregnancy counselor to help you make the decision that fits best with your values.

What to Do in Case of Rape*

This Can't Be Happening to Me . . .

There are no hard and fast rules to prevent a rape once you are attacked. Only you know what will work in your case. There are a number of ways to protect yourself that may work in some cases. However, you should be aware of their pitfalls as well as their merits.

Screaming (and Noise). Before you start screaming, consider what the rapist's reaction might be. He may be scared off, but he might feel forced to shut you up. Screaming and noise (whistles and air horns) can work effectively if you're sure help is near, sure that it will arrive in time, and that it will be enough when it does.

Struggling It may rebuff him, but it can work against you. It could wear you out, make you angry, or sexually

*This information was prepared for the "Rape Awareness" program in Clackamas County, Oregon.

arouse him. Ask yourself if you're willing to seriously hurt him to stop him; you may have to. If your natural reaction would be to fight, then make sure you know how. Take a class in martial arts and keep up with it.

Weapons. You probably carry all your so-called weapons in your purse . . . the first thing you're going to drop if attacked. Also, a weapon can be taken away and used against you. Finally, it may be illegal for you to carry certain weapons such as guns and knives.

Running This will work if you're sure you can get to safety. He will probably try to stop you.

Surrender. Letting your attacker think you're surrendering can be used as a stall to buy time and think.

Psychological Warfare. Communicate with your attacker. Use words, gestures, or whatever, but get him talking to you. Don't be afraid to let him see you're afraid. Try to talk him out of it with any argument you can think of: "I'm pregnant," "I've got VD," or "I'm only 16," or "How would you feel if this was your sister?" Make it believable or it won't work.

There are some physical techniques with which you can turn off an attacker, too. Vomiting on him is a good example. Use your head—it can be your best weapon.

Whatever method you choose, if it gets you home alive, it was the right one. Too many women suffer from the "what-ifs" (What if I had done this or that) unnecessarily. If you survive your attack, if you make it home safely, your technique worked. Your life was interrupted by a rape, instead of death.

If You Are Raped

If, in spite of your efforts, you are raped, try not to panic. Concentrate on the attacker's identity. Remember his exact description, any peculiar marks, scars, defects, or identifying traits. Remember his vehicle and anything inside of it. Call the police as soon as you can. Your cooperation with them may ensure that someone else will not have to suffer the same experience. Do not bathe or shower. Do not apply medication. Do not throw away your clothes or wash them. All of these are natural reactions after an assault, but they destroy important evidence.

What Happens Next

When the police arrive, they will take you to the hospital for a medical examination. The police will have to interview you as to the details of the crime and as to your assailant. They are not interested in past sexual activity except that which may affect the evidence just gathered at the hospital. If you decide to prosecute, the trial will not be easy. But remember, there is no shame in what has happened to you. The shame would be if the attacker went free.

Reactions to Rape

A victim has many feelings after a rape. Confusion about what happened and confusion as to what to do are normal. There may be a feeling of being degraded or abused, or fear of further violence from the rapist. Feelings of hurt and anger are common; in fact, anger is a healthy reaction. There may be a loss of self-respect, a feeling of isolation and some distrust of everyone. Support by a victim's family and friends is essential at this point to re-establish her feelings of normalcy. The problem may be compounded by their feelings which may be those of betrayal, confusion or guilt. All of these are normal and can be worked through. If the feelings become overwhelming, counseling is available.

Rapists do not have a special look. Therefore, it is important to recognize potentially dangerous situations to protect yourself. Here are some common-sense suggestions toward that end.

At Home

1. Have your keys in hand as you approach the door. Always keep entrances well lit.
2. When you move to a new place or lose your keys, change the locks.
3. Install single cylinder deadbolt locks, or if there's glass in the door or a window nearby, a double cylinder deadbolt.
4. Keep doors and windows secured, even if you leave for just a few minutes.
5. Drill and pin all windows and sliding glass doors.

6. Don't let a stranger in to use the phone; make the call yourself.
7. Demand identification from any stranger. If you have doubts, call his company.
8. If you live alone, use initials in the phone book, on the mailbox, and on mail.
9. Vary your routine each day. Remember most rapes in the victim's home are planned.

Walking

1. Try not to go anywhere alone.
2. Let someone know where you're going and when you're due back.
3. Walk on well-lit, well-traveled familiar streets.
4. Walk close to the road, avoiding houses and hedges.
5. Walk facing traffic so you can see any autos approaching you.
6. Be constantly aware of who and what is around you. If you are unaware, an attacker has a better chance.

In the Car

1. Have your keys in hand when you approach the car. Check the back seat before entering the vehicle.
2. Always keep the doors locked and the windows rolled up.
3. Check your gas gauge before each excursion. Keep your car in good running order. Know how to change a flat tire.
4. If you suspect someone is following you or trying to run you off the road, do something to attract attention. Keep your car operable as long as you can. If you have to stop, leave the engine running and in gear. Wait until the pursuer gets out of his car, then drive away as fast as you can. Don't drive home. Go to a fire or police station or any place there will be people.

FAMILY MATTERS

Marriage Laws by State

State	Age Marriage Can Be Contracted Without Parental Consent MALE	Age FEMALE	Age Marriage Can Be Contracted With Parental Consent MALE	Age FEMALE	MAXIMUM PERIOD BETWEEN EXAM & ISSUANCE OF LICENSE (DAYS)	Common Law Marriage MAY BE CONTRACTED BUT NOT VALID IF ATTEMPTED AFTER DATE SHOWN	RECOGNIZED IF VALID AT TIME & PLACE WHERE CONTRACTED
Alabama	18	18	17	14	30	Yes	Yes
Alaska	18	18	16	16	30	1/1/64	Yes
Arizona	18	18	16	16	30	No	Yes
Arkansas	18	18	17	16	30	No	Yes
California	18	18	18	16	30	1895	Yes
Colorado	18	18	16	16	30	Yes	Yes
Connecticut	18	18	16	16	35	No	†
Delaware	18	18	18	16	30	No	Yes
Dist. of Columbia	18	18	16	16	30	Yes	Yes
Florida	18	18	18	16	30	1/1/68	Yes
Georgia	18	18	16	16	30	Yes	Yes
Hawaii	18	18	16	16	30	No	Yes
Idaho	18	18	16	16	—	Yes	Yes
Illinois	18	18	16	16	15	6/30/05	†
Indiana	18	18	17	17	30	1/1/58	†
Iowa	18	18	16	16	20	Yes	Yes
Kansas	18	18	18	18	30	Yes	Yes
Kentucky	18	18	none	none	15	No	Yes
Louisiana	18	18	18	16	10	No	†
Maine	18	18	16	16	60	†	†
Maryland	18	18	16	16	—	No	Yes
Massachusetts	18	18	18	18	30	No	Yes
Michigan	18	18	16	16	30	1/1/57	Yes
Minnesota	18	18	18	16	—	4/26/41	†
Mississippi	21	21	17	15	30	4/5/56	†
Missouri	18	18	15	15	15	3/3/21	†
Montana	18	18	18	18	20	Yes	Yes
Nebraska	19	19	17	17	30	1923	Yes
Nevada	18	18	16	16	—	3/29/43	Yes
New Hampshire	18	18	14	13	30	No	Yes
New Jersey	18	18	18	16	30	1/12/39	Yes
New Mexico	18	18	16	16	30	No	Yes
New York	18	18	16	14	30	4/29/33	Yes
North Carolina	18	18	16	16	30	No	Yes
North Dakota	18	18	16	16	30	No	Yes
Ohio	18	18	18	16	30	Yes	Yes
Oklahoma	18	18	16	16	30	Yes	Yes
Oregon	18	18	17	17	30	No	Yes
Pennsylvania	18	18	16	16	30	Yes	Yes

†Legal status unclear.

Source: Department of Labor, Women's Bureau.

State	Age Marriage Can Be Contracted Without Parental Consent MALE	Age FEMALE	Age Marriage Can Be Contracted With Parental Consent MALE	Age FEMALE	MAXIMUM PERIOD BETWEEN EXAM & ISSUANCE OF LICENSE (DAYS)	Common Law Marriage MAY BE CONTRACTED BUT NOT VALID IF ATTEMPTED AFTER DATE SHOWN	RECOGNIZED IF VALID AT TIME & PLACE WHERE CONTRACTED
Rhode Island	18	18	18	16	40	Yes	†
South Carolina	18	18	16	14	—	Yes	Yes
South Dakota	18	18	16	16	20	7/1/59	†
Tennessee	18	18	16	16	30	No	Yes
Texas	18	18	14	14	21	Yes	Yes
Utah	18	18	16	14	30	No	Yes
Vermont	18	18	16	16	30	No	†
Virginia	18	18	16	16	30	No	Yes
Washington	18	18	17	17	—	No	Yes
West Virginia	18	18	none	none	30	No	Yes
Wisconsin	18	18	16	16	20	1913	†
Wyoming	19	19	17	16	30	No	Yes

†Legal status unclear.

Divorce Laws by State

State	"No-fault" Divorce* Break-down	Separation	Cruelty	Desertion	Non-support	Alcohol/ Drugs	Felony	Impotency	Insanity
AL	X	2 yrs.	X	X	X	X	X	X	X
AK	X		X	X		X	X	X	X
AZ	X								
AR		3 yrs.	X	X	X	X	X	X	
CA	X								X
CO	X								
CT	X	18 mos.	X	X	X	X	X		X
DE	X	6 mos.							
DC		6 mos.-1 yr.							
FL	X								X
GA	X		X	X		X	X	X	X
HI	X	2 yrs.							
ID	X	5 yrs.	X	X	X	X	X		X
IL			X	X		X	X	X	
IN	X						X	X	X
IA	X								
KS	X								
KY	X	1 yr.							
LA		1 yr.	X	X	X	X	X		
ME	X		X	X	X	X		X	X
MD		1-3 yrs.	X	X			X	X	X
MA	X	6 mos.-1 yr.	X	X	X	X	X	X	
MI	X								
MN	X								
MS	X		X	X		X	X	X	X
MO	X								
MT	X								
NB	X								

(Continued on page R32.)

Divorce Laws by State—continued

State	"No-fault" Divorce* Break-down	Separation	Cruelty	Desertion	Non-support	Alcohol/ Drugs	Felony	Impotency	Insanity
NV	X	1 yr.							X
NH	X	2 yrs.	X	X	X	X	X	X	
NJ		18 mos.	X	X		X	X		X
NM	X		X	X					
NY		1 yr.	X	X			X		
NC		1 yr.						X	X
ND	X		X	X	X	X	X	X	X
OH	X	2 yrs.	X	X		X	X	X	X
OK	X		X	X	X	X	X	X	X
OR	X								
PA	X	3 yrs.	X	X			X	X	X
RI	X	3 yrs.	X	X	X	X	X	X	
SC		1 yr.	X	X		X			
SD			X	X	X	X	X		
TN	X		X	X	X	X	X	X	
TX	X	3 yrs.	X	X			X		X
UT			X	X	X	X	X	X	X
VT		6 mos.	X	X	X		X		X
VA		6 mos.-1 yr.	X	X			X		
WA	X								
WV	X	1 yr.	X	X		X	X		X
WI	X	1 yr.							X
WY	X	2 yrs.							X

*"No-fault" includes all proceedings where no proof for divorce is needed. Not called "no-fault" in all states. Grounds in "no-fault" divorce may be "breakdown" (or "incompatibility") or separation.
Source: U.S. Department of Labor, Women's Bureau (1982).

Genetic Counseling

About 2 to 4 percent of American children are born with birth defects. Each year, 1 to 2 million infants, children, and adults are hospitalized for treatment of birth defects. These birth defects involve abnormalities of body structure or function, which may be genetically caused, the result of environmental influence on the fetus, or both. About 20 percent are inherited; 20 percent are caused by environmental influences on the fetus (such as smoking, drinking, diet, drugs, or exposure to toxic chemicals); and the remainder result from heredity and the environment interacting with each other.

Hereditary defects result from the interaction of the mother's and father's genes. Not all genes have an equal effect. Some genes are dominant over other genes, which are called recessive. The odds that a child will inherit a particular trait and the degree to which that trait will appear depend on many interrelated factors. These include: (1) whether the trait is dominant or recessive, (2) the degree to which either parent has the trait, (3) the child's sex, and (4) the overall genetic makeup of the parents.

Individuals with hereditary defects are at significant risk in passing their disorder on to their children. Others are healthy themselves but carry a recessive abnormal gene; if they mate with another carrier of the same abnormal gene, there is a 25 percent risk in each pregnancy of having a child with that particular birth defect. (Each of us probably carries two to eight abnormal recessive genes.) Finally, there are some female carriers of sex-linked recessive traits who themselves are healthy but will pass the abnormal gene to half their children. Half their sons will inherit the defect (such as hemophilia), while half their daughters will be carriers (Kaye, 1981).

While any couple may have a child with a birth defect or hereditary disease, some individuals or couples are at high risk. Some can be identified during routine medical examination. Women over 35 years, persons with congenital defects or hereditary diseases, and women who have had multiple miscarriages are all at high risk. Others can be identified by a careful review of their family medical history. Each person should obtain a family medical history from his or her parents and keep it as part of his or her permanent records.

Factors and risks that indicate the need for genetic counseling include the following (adapted from Kaye, 1981):

Factor	Risk
Maternal age 35 years	Chromosomal anomaly
Previous child with chromosomal abnormality	Chromosomal anomaly
Adult with congenital abnormality	Occurrence in child
Previous child with congenital abnormality	Occurrence in child
Previous child with autosomal recessive gene or sex-linked condition	Occurrence in child
Family history of sex-linked condition	Occurrence in child
Adult with known hereditary syndrome	Occurrence in child
Ashkenazi Jew	Tay-Sachs disease
Black	Sickle cell anemia
Mediterranean ethnic group	Thalassemia
Infertility or multiple miscarriages	Chromosomal abnormality
Parent taking teratogen	Child with multiple congenital abnormalities
Family history of diabetes mellitus	Child with congenital malformation; diabetes mellitus
Deafness	Deafness
Psychosis	Psychosis

In genetic counseling, persons or couples who are at high risk are given lengthy examinations to determine whether they are potential carriers of birth defects to their unborn children. After the diagnosis is made, the meaning of the disorder, its prognosis, and its treatment are explained. Finally the genetic etiology of the disorder is determined, along with an estimate of the risks of passing on a birth defect. If the disorder can be detected prenatally, the risks and benefits of amniocentesis and other techniques are explained; the couple's feelings about abortion are discussed so that they can make an informed and appropriate (for them) decision in the event that the fetus is defective (Kaye, 1981). Genetic counseling may be long and involved, but for those at risk it improves the chances of giving birth to healthy children.

How to Choose Daycare

Daycare refers to any formal arrangement in which someone who is not a child's parent takes care of that child during the day. Traditionally, a child spent time with a parent—usually the mother—during the day. Now, this is not always possible.

Some families depend on daycare to make life liveable. Single-parent families as well as families with both parents working usually need to find some sort of daycare for their children. If the children are school-aged, especially in the upper grades, the parent may ask a friend, neighbor, or relative to watch the child until after work. This arrangement might be quite informal. Sometimes such convenience is impossible. Then a parent must make formal arrangements. The varieties of childcare possibilities are unending, but daycare arrangements usually fall into one of the general categories listed here.

Neighborhood Childcare Cooperatives. These work under the principle that each person involved will watch other peoples' children for a certain amount of time in exchange for someone else watching theirs. Each cooperative has its own rules. Generally, neighborhood cooperatives are only suitable for people who work part-time or for people who have definite periods of time available and a suitable home to offer the group. An advantage is that cooperatives may take very young children, even infants. It depends on the group. There usually is no exchange of money.

Freelance or Licensed Babysitters. People who like to babysit in their homes can always be found. They may sit for one or many children. They charge. Some states require sitters, especially those who take in more than one child, to be licensed. Sitters also may take very young children and infants. It depends on the sitter. Cost depends on the sitter's rate.

Daycare Centers. These are organizations that provide daycare, usually from 7:30 or 8 A.M. to 6 P.M., for a fee, at a particular site. They are often located in churches or community centers. Most require children to be toilet trained before joining. The age of the oldest children allowed varies. Generally, daycare centers tend to serve either the two-to-six age group or the five-to-nine age group. Costs vary, and always go up with inflation and more respectable salaries for the staff. Currently, monthly costs range between $200 and $500 per child for full-time care. Some centers are partial cooperatives, requiring parental participation in some way. Some have scholarship funds. Most are acceptable institutions to the government, which may provide daycare assistance to some low-income families.

The demand for daycare today is greater than the spaces available. The best sources usually fill their lists for fall by June or midsummer. It is wise to check the possibilities well before your personal needs arise. Nothing is as informative as a visit to the daycare facility or home.

Here is a checklist of questions to help you judge each place:

What is the ratio of adults to children?

How large are the grounds?

What kinds of toys, games, or playground equipment are provided?

What activities, if any, are led (music, dance, pottery)?

Do they have nap time? Is it required?

Do they have pets?

Does it meet your standards of cleanliness?

Is it run cooperatively?

Will parents be asked to provide snacks or participate in work weekends? If so, how often?

What food is served?

Do the sitter, staff, or members of the cooperative seem generally to hold your values?

Do you trust the judgment of the adult(s) running the show?

When do half days end/start?

Can they accommodate irregular hours (if you need to work an extra or different shift, can they keep your child on short notice)?

What do they do when faced with medical emergencies?

What funds might be available to children attending (city, county, state, federal, or other)?

Parental Stress and Child Abuse

Virtually all parents experience stress, inability to cope, anger, or hostility toward their children from time to time during the demanding period of childrearing. The feelings are not unnatural, but behavior stemming from them can be cruel and uncontrolled. This is the realm of child abuse. Figures on child abuse cases that have come to the attention of state or county authorities run to the hundreds of thousands. Milder cases of physical abuse or neglect, most cases of emotional torment, and many cases of sexual mistreat-

ment are never reported to officials. It is suspected that several million children suffer abuse of some sort every year.

What is being done to develop effective methods of treatment? Because disclosure of an abuse problem can result in loss of custody of their child and social ostracism, parents have been fearful of seeking help through the traditional mental health resources. Total community involvement is needed to help these families. Teachers, doctors, counselors, and neighbors can all lend support. Some areas have a Parental Stress Hotline listed in the telephone directory. Parents Anonymous is a national group offering assistance. The following is from their flyer "Losing Your Cool With Your Kids?"

1. Are you a troubled or nervous parent who has no place to get help?
2. When you are ready to blow up is it you and the children who bear the brunt of it?
3. Do you feel confused, guilty, and frightened about your parental behavior and feelings?
4. Do you believe that you were treated indifferently or cruelly as a child and that now you're repeating some of the "past"?
5. When you hear the words "abuse" or "neglect" do you end up thinking about your childhood or the parenting you're doing now?
6. Are you physically or emotionally abusing or neglecting one or more of your children?
7. Do you want your relationship with your children to be different . . . your family life more fulfilling . . . less explosive and tense . . . more loving?

Thousands of parents have become members of Parents Anonymous because their answers were yes to one or more of these seven questions. P.A. provides them with a program where they can finally develop a meaningful involvement that helps them overcome the crushing inner turmoil. A place where they can sort through the hurting and painful experiences of the past . . . relieve the confusion, fear and dread of what's happening now . . . and not have to live with the anger, frustration and loneliness that can build up when it appears that nobody cares . . . enough to help.

P.A. members find that the once-a-week P.A. chapter meeting is helpful; at the meeting they get together with other parents who have similar difficulties. Chapter members select a member to provide the active leadership. This member is then the chapter chairperson. To further enhance and strengthen the chairperson's role, the chairperson is aided and "backed up" by a sponsor, who is a professional person in one of the mental health fields. Together, as a group, they support and encourage each other in searching out positive alternatives to the abusive behavior in their lives.

Members also share phone numbers and, occasionally,

addresses so that during the week, should a crisis arise, they can call or visit one another for direct help. They also call other group members and share their successes in preventing a crisis or abusive incident.

P.A. is anonymous and no one needs to use other than their first name, although some members choose to use their full names. There are no membership fees, dues or other costs. No one has to openly "admit" their parenting problems, although many members do, and most find that "getting it off one's chest" is a great relief.

P.A. is not a religious or spiritual belief program, therefore P.A. asks none of its members to change their individual religious or spiritual beliefs, or to believe in anything other than the human capacity for change and growth.

P.A. has no "magic cures or answers" nor does P.A. believe that any "magic answers" are available. Members do have a common purpose, a unity in goals and a sincere interest in helping each other. In its own way, one might say that people helping people has its own touch of "magic."

The address and phone numbers for Parents Anonymous are listed on page R3. Check your telephone directory for local chapter.

Your Rights as a Disabled Person*

Is Your Disability Covered?

In its section 504 regulation, HEW identifies a handicapped person as anyone with a physical or mental disability that substantially impairs or restricts one or more of such major life activities as walking, seeing, hearing, speaking, working, or learning. A history of such disability, or the belief on the part of others that a person has such a disability, whether it is so or not, also is recognized as a hand-

*U.S. Department of Health, Education, and Welfare.

icap by the regulation. Handicapping conditions include, but are not limited to:

Alcoholism**

Cancer

Cerebral palsy

Deafness or hearing impairment

Diabetes

Drug addiction**

Epilepsy

Heart disease

Mental or emotional illness

Mental retardation

Multiple sclerosis

Muscular dystrophy

Orthopedic, speech, or visual impairment

Perceptual handicaps such as dyslexia, minimal brain dysfunction, and developmental aphasia.

What You Can Do

If you feel that your rights have been violated by a business, hospital, physician, school, college, or any other institution receiving HEW assistance, because of your disability or your child's disability, write, giving details to:

Office for Civil Rights, Dept. of Health, Education, and Welfare in *your* region.

**The U.S. Attorney General has ruled that alcoholism and drug addiction are physical or mental impairments that are handicapping conditions if they limit one or more of life's major activities.

NUTRITION

The Major Nutrients*

Protein.   After water and possibly fat, protein is the most plentiful substance in the body. The substances, called enzymes, which control the processs that keep the body working are made of protein. Protein is also part of the hemoglobin molecule in red blood cells that carries oxygen

*U.S. Department of Agriculture and U.S. Department of Health, Education, and Welfare (in cooperation with the Grocery Manufacturers of America and the Advertising Council).

into the system. And the antibodies in the bloodstream that fight off disease and infection are also protein. Another important use of protein in the body is to build the muscle tissue which holds the bone structure together and provides the strength to move and work. Most Americans get more than enough protein.

Where is protein found? Meat, poultry, fish, milk, cheese, and eggs provide good quantities of it. Bread and cereal are also important sources.

And such vegetables as soybeans, chickpeas, dry beans, and peanuts are also good sources of protein. You do not have to load up on meat, poultry, or eggs to get enough in your diet.

Combining cereal or vegetable foods with a little milk, cheese, or other animal protein can provide good protein in your diet.

For example, eat cereal with milk, rice with fish, spaghetti and meat balls, or simply drink a glass of milk during a meal. All these combinations provide the high quality protein the body needs.

Fats.   Fats provide energy and add flavor and variety to foods. They make meals more satisfying. Fats carry vitamins A, D, E, and K and are essential parts of the structure of the cells which make up the body's tissues.

Our body fat protects vital organs by providing a cushion around them.

Fats are plentiful in butter, margarine, shortening, salad oils, cream, most cheeses, mayonnaise, salad dressing, nuts, and bacon.

Carbohydrates.   These are starches and sugars found in cereal grains, fruits, vegetables, and sugar added to foods for sweetening.

Carbohydrates are the major source of energy in the diet. Wheat, oats, corn and rice—and the foods made from them, such as bread, sphaghetti, macaroni, noodles or grits—provide starch along with other important nutrients. So, too, do potatoes, sweet potatoes, and vegetables such as peas, dry beans, peanuts and soybeans.

Most of the other other vegetables contain smaller amounts of carbohydrates.

In vegetables they are usually in the form of starch; in fruits they occur as sugar. And, of course, candies, jams, molasses and syrups are primarily sugar.

Water.   Water is a most important nutrient. Water stands next to air in importance to life. You can get along for days, even weeks, without food but only a few days without water.

Water is necessary for all the processes of digestion.

Nutrients are dissolved in water so they may pass through the intestinal wall and into the bloodstream for use throughout the body. Water carries waste out of the body and water also helps to regulate body temperature.

The body's most obvious source of water is the water a person drinks, but some is produced by the body's burning of food for energy. Coffee and tea are mostly water, and so are fruit juices and milk.

Soup is a water source and so are many fruits and vegetables. Even meat can be up to 80 percent water.

Minerals

CALCIUM   The most abundant mineral in the body is calcium and, except for iron, it is the most likely to be inadequate in the diets of many age groups.

(From the age of 9, the diets of girls and women may lack as much as 25 to 30 percent of the calcium they need.)

Almost all calcium, and most phosphorus, which works closely with calcium in the body, is in bones and teeth.

The rest plays a vital role in tissue and body fluids. Soft tissue, or muscle, especially has a high phosphorus content. Calcium is required for blood to clot and for the heart to function normally. The nervous system does not work properly when calcium levels in the blood are below normal.

Most people who buy from the milk counter are stocking up on calcium supplies.

In the U.S. we rely on milk as a basic source of calcium, and two cups of milk, or an equivalent amount of cheese or other dairy products except butter, go a long way toward supplying all the calcium needed for the day.

But milk is not the only source. Dark green leafy vegetables like collards, mustard greens or turnip greens provide some calcium, and salmon and sardines supply useful amounts of it if the very tiny bones are eaten.

IRON   Iron is another essential mineral. Women of childbearing age require more iron than men. The diets of infants and pregnant women may need special attention to see that they contain the iron needed.

Unfortunately, only a few foods provide iron in very useful amounts. However, liver, heart, kidney and most lean meats are generously supplied with it. So are shellfish, particularly oysters. Whole grain and enriched breads and cereals can provide 20 to 25 percent of the daily iron need.

Dark green leafy vegetables are also sources of iron.

IODINE   The most important fact about iodine is that a deficiency of it can cause goiter—a swelling of the thyroid gland. The most practical ways to be sure of getting enough iodine are to use iodized salt regularly and add seafood to the diet whenever possible.

OTHER ESSENTIAL ELEMENTS   Calcium, iron and iodine are not the only minerals you need. Most of the others—zinc, copper, sodium, potassium, magnesium and phosphorus—are widely available in so many foods that a little variety in making your choice at the grocery store takes care of them easily. Magnesium, for example, abounds in nuts, whole grain products, dry beans and dark green vegetables.

Phosphorus shows up in the same goods that supply you with protein and calcium, although leafy vegetables contain little phosphorus.

FLUORINE   Fluorine—an element that helps protect teeth from decay—is not so readily found in food. Many metropolitan areas add minute amounts of fluorine to local sources of drinking water.

Vitamins.   Scientists know of a dozen or more vitamins that you must have to enjoy good health. Ordinarily, you can get them from a well-chosen assortment of everyday foods.

A few of these vitamins are of great importance and you should know what foods provide them.

VITAMIN A   This vitamin plays a very important role in eye function, and in keeping the skin and mucous membranes resistant to infection. Although vitamin A occurs only in foods of animal origin, the deep yellow and dark green vegetables and fruits supply a material—carotene—which your body can turn into vitamin A.

Produce can easily supply all the vitamin A you need. Such items as collards, turnip greens, kale, carrots, squash, and sweet potatoes can more than take care of daily needs; yellow peaches, apricots, cantaloupe and papayas also help. Many people, however, do not regularly eat these foods.

Liver is an outstanding source of vitamin A. A two-ounce serving of cooked beef liver provides more than 30,000 international units of the vitamin. That's six times more vitamin A than you would need during the day. Kidney is also an excellent source of vitamin A.

There are plenty of other sources of vitamin A. Whole milk is a source, but skim milk doesn't have any vitamin A unless it is fortified, that is, unless vitamin A has been added to it.

Cheese made from whole milk, or margarine enriched with vitamin A, both supply this vitamin.

THE B VITAMINS   Three of the best known vitamins—riboflavin, thiamin and niacin—release the energy in food. They also have a role in the nervous system, keep the digestive system working calmly, and help maintain a healthy skin.

Vitamin B_2 (riboflavin) is easy to find and extremely important to your diet. It is plentifully supplied by meats, milk, whole grain or enriched breads and cereals.

Organ meats (liver, kidney, etc.) also supply this vitamin.

A lack of thiamin (vitamin B_1) causes beri-beri. Fortunately, this disease is now almost nonexistent in the U.S., although it is still seen in some alcoholics.

Thiamin is abundant in only a few foods. Lean pork is one. Dry beans and peas, some of the organ meats, and some nuts supply some thiamin.

Whole grain and enriched cereals and breads are also dependable sources of the vitamin. Niacin can be found in whole grain and enriched cereals, meat and meat products, and peas and beans.

Other B vitamins such as B_6, B_{12}, and folacin are needed to maintain normal hemoglobin, the substance in blood which carries oxygen to the tissues. B_{12} occurs in foods of animal origin.

Strict vegetarians run a risk of developing the symptoms of B_{12} deficiency; these include soreness of the mouth and tongue, numbness and tingling in the hands and legs, anemia and loss of coordination.

Folacin is available in many foods but in small quantities.

VITAMIN C   Vitamin C, ascorbic acid, is not completely understood, but it is considered important in helping to maintain the cementing material that holds body cells together.

The citrus fruit juice you may have for breakfast can give you over half of the vitamin C needed for the day.

In fact, unless good foods are consciously avoided, the rest of the fruit and vegetables eaten during the day will help to provide the vitamin C required.

Potatoes and sweet potatoes provide helpful amounts of vitamin C and so do tomatoes and peppers. In addition, the green vegetables such as broccoli, turnip greens, raw cabbage and collards make a contribution of vitamin C.

VITAMIN D   Although few foods contain vitamin D, it is readily available in milk fortified with it. Sunlight enables the body to produce vitamin D if it shines directly on the skin.

Vitamin D is important in building strong bones and teeth and is needed through the growth period.

Without it the body cannot absorb the calcium supplied by food and for this reason milk is often fortified with vitamin D. Adults rarely need more vitamin D than they get in food and from the sun, but infants and young children sometimes do not get enough. A disease called rickets results from a lack of vitamin D. Children who suffer from this disease have absorbed too little calcium, their bodies cannot form strong and rigid bones and consequently they may have enlarged joints, bowed legs, knock knees or beaded ribs.

On the other hand, too much vitamin D can be dangerous. This causes a calcium overload in the blood and tissues. Infants given too much vitamin D may develop calcium deposits in the kidneys and other organs and end up with kidney damage.

VITAMIN E   Vitamin E is known to be essential but its exact role in the body is not fully understood. Vitamin E is abundant in vegetable oils and margarine and contained in such foods as wheat germ and lettuce.

If a diet regularly includes fruits, vegetables, vegetable oil, milk, meat and eggs, it is not lacking in vitamin E.

VITAMIN K   Vitamin K is essential for the manufacture of a substance that helps blood to clot. Vitamin K is widely distributed in a variety of foods such as the green and leafy vegetables, tomatoes, cauliflower, egg yolks, soybean oil and any kind of liver.

Basic Foods You Need Each Day During Pregnancy

	Under 18 Years		Over 18 Years		
	BEFORE AND DURING FIRST THREE MONTHS OF PREGNANCY	LAST SIX MONTHS OF PREGNANCY	BEFORE AND DURING FIRST THREE MONTHS OF PREGNANCY	LAST SIX MONTHS OF PREGNANCY	Count as One Serving
Meat, fish, poultry, eggs or alternates	2–3 Servings	3 Servings	2–3 Servings	3 Servings	2 to 3 ounces cooked lean meat, fish or poultry without bone; 2 medium eggs, 4 tablespoons peanut butter; 1 cup cooked dried beans or peas; 1½ cups split pea or bean soup; 2 or 3 ounces cheddar type cheese; ½ to ¾ cup cottage cheese; ¼ to ½ cup nuts or seeds.
Milk and milk products	3–4 Cups	4–5 Cups	3 Cups	4 Cups	1 cup (8 fluid ounces) of skim, whole, buttermilk or diluted evaporated milk. The following foods provide as much calcium as a cup of whole milk: 1½ ounces cheddar type cheese; 1 cup plain yogurt; 3 tablespoons regular nonfat dry milk; 6 tablespoons instant nonfat dry milk solids; 1½ cups cottage cheese; 1 cup custard or puddings made with milk; 1½ to 2 cups soup made or diluted with milk.
Fruits and vegetables (Vitamin C rich)	1 Serving	1–2 Servings	1 Serving	1–2 Servings	½ cup citrus juice or 1 medium orange; ½ grapefruit; ½ cantaloupe; ½ cup strawberries; ½ cup broccoli; ½ green pepper. You will need to eat 2 servings of food which are fair sources of vitamin C. These foods include tomatoes, tomato juice, tangerines, tangerine juice, asparagus tips, raw cabbage, Brussel sprouts, watermelon, and dark leafy greens.

Nutrients and Energy. Almost all foods provide energy—some more than others.

This energy is measured in calories. Foods rich in fats, starches or sugars contain large amounts of calories—or energy.

Fat is the most concentrated source of energy. Ounce for ounce, it provides more than twice as much energy as protein or the carbohydrates.

Foods that contain a lot of water, like watermelon and cucumbers, have few calories because water, which makes up most of their weight, provides no calories and so no energy. When you eat a diet that furnishes more energy—or calories—than you need, the excess is stored in the body as fat.

And when you continue to overeat you become overweight or fat. When you eat fewer calories than the body uses, you lose weight.

How It All Works Together. The body can pick and choose what it needs from the nutrients in the diet, and see to it that each organ or part of the body gets exactly the right amounts of nutrients—not more and not less. But, if the diet lacks some of the needed nutrients, the body has no way to get them.

The body keeps busy, working twenty-four hours a day, always building itself up, repairing itself, and discarding waste products.

It needs a constant supply of nutrients to do its job and

| | Under 18 Years | | Over 18 Years | | |
	BEFORE AND DURING FIRST THREE MONTHS OF PREGNANCY	LAST SIX MONTHS OF PREGNANCY	BEFORE AND DURING FIRST THREE MONTHS OF PREGNANCY	LAST SIX MONTHS OF PREGNANCY	*Count as One Serving*
Fruits and vegetables (Vitamin A rich)	1 Serving	2 Servings	1 Serving	2 Servings	½ cup deep yellow fruits and vegetables such as apricots, cantaloupe, carrots, pumpkins, sweet potatoes, winter squash; ½ to ¾ cup dark green leafy vegetables such as collard greens, mustard greens, chard, kale, turnip tops, spinach, broccoli, watercress. In addition to vitamin A, dark green leafy vegetables supply folacin, magnesium and iron.
Other fruits and vegetables	2 Servings	1 Serving	2 Servings	1 Serving	½ cup of other fruits and vegetables such as green beans, wax beans, celery, corn, mushrooms, cauliflower, green peas, cucumbers, potatoes, lettuce, beets, pears, apples, bananas, pineapple, prunes, cherries, etc.
Breads and cereals (whole grain, enriched or restored)	4 Servings	5–6 Servings	4 Servings	4–5 Servings	1 slice bread; 1 muffin; 1 hamburger or hot dog roll, 4 to 5 saltine crackers; ½ to ¾ cup cooked cereals, rice, macaroni, noodles, spaghetti, and other pastas; ¾ cup (1 ounce) ready-to-eat cereal. Read labels and select whole grain or fortified breads and cereals. Avoid presweetened cereals.

Fats and Sweets   These energy foods supply mostly calories. Eat them in amounts to meet your energy needs.

when it receives the nutrients it applies them where they are needed. . . .

No single nutrient can function properly alone. It takes calcium to build strong bones but that is just the beginning.

Without vitamin D, the calcium is not absorbed from the intestines.

Protein is needed for the framework of the bone and to form part of every cell and all the fluids that circulate in and around the cells.

It takes vitamin C to help produce the materials between cells.

This is why nutritionists suggest eating appropriate quantities of a wide variety of foods—including milk products, meat or an alternate, fruits and vegetables, bread and cereal—in order to provide diets with all the needed nutrients.

The more varied your diet the better off you will be—tomorrow as well as today. . . .

The Value of Processed Foods.   Fresh or frozen? Canned or dried? Instant or from scratch? Which foods have the nutrients? Which do not? They all do. All foods have their place.

And virtually all food in its place is good food. Some foods are safer to use when they are processed. Some are more appealing when fresh.

Packaged, pasteurized, fortified milk has been around so long no one thinks of it anymore as a processed food, but it is.

Whole grain breads and cereals retain the germ and outer

layers of grain where the B vitamins concentrate. Milling wheat to white flour refines them out.

Since many people seem to prefer white bread, it is wise to choose the enriched product because of added nutrients.

Brown rice has food value that unenriched polished white rice does not; enriched, parboiled or converted rice retains most, though not all, of the nutrients.

Buy the mix or do it yourself? It is all the same nutritionally if the ingredients listed on the label are used in the same amounts and are the same as the ingredients you would use doing it yourself.

Foods in the frozen food case offer as much food value as those in the produce section of the store. It just depends on which foods one prefers and the cost factor.

Any loss of vitamin C in frozen fruits is negligible. The blanching process does, however, reduce slightly the vitamin C and some of the other water-soluble vitamins and minerals in frozen vegetables.

A Good Diet During Pregnancy

The baby that you are carrying gets its food from you. You need to eat the right kinds of food to keep healthy and to help your baby grow. If you did not eat the right kinds of foods before pregnancy, NOW is the time to begin good eating habits.

The chart on R38–39 will help you select foods that provide the nutrients needed for good nutrition during pregnancy.

MONEY

Budget

Some people have a natural talent for money management. If you are one of these, you can skip this section. Most young adults, however have only a sketchy idea of how to manage their own money when setting up house for themselves: How much money is reasonable to spend on a place to live? How can you decide?

There are two ways to approach family budgeting. One can set guidelines according to public statistics, or one can take an inventory of personal priorities and work from there. These figures (U.S. Department of Labor, Bureau of Labor Statistics) show what percent of income the average urban family of four, living at an intermediate income level, spends for different needs.

Lower-income families (those earning $10 to $12,000 a year) tend to spend significantly more of their income on food (31 percent) and medical care (9 percent) and a lower percentage on housing (20 percent) and taxes (14 percent). High-income families ($27,000 + per year) spend about 23 percent of their income on housing, about 25 percent on taxes, about 21 percent on food. Don't forget that these figures are percentages. A high-income family will spend more dollars on medical care than a low-income family, but those dollars (say, $1,000) only represent 4 to 5 percent of their total income as opposed to 9 to 10 percent for the lower-income family.

If you want to use norms as guidelines for budgeting, you would allot a certain percentage of your income to each category—25 percent of this, 8 percent for that—and make sure you stay within your budget. Leftover money could be saved for emergencies or special purchases or vacations.

The second method of budgeting is to itemize carefully all your expenditures each month for two or three months

Needs	Percent (%)
Food	24.8
Housing	22.5
Taxes	20.5
Other*	9.5
Transportation	8.5
Clothing	6.5
Medical Care	5.7
Personal Care	2.2

*Includes reading, movies, recreation, tobacco, alcohol, etc.

and then see where you stand. You might use a form such as the "Monthly Budget" you see on R41 or make up your own.

After recording your typical expenditures you can round off dollar amounts and how much you spend for which items. If you are continually in trouble in some area or wish to save money, you now have an idea of where you can make adjustments. Or if you have a job with a flexible income (commission or temporary, part-time jobs) you can figure what you need for a minimum monthly income before you start "living it up." ("I need at least $550. If I make $700 I can buy that bicycle and some clothes.")

Dealing with Unemployment*

Step 1: Take Time to Talk. Come right out and let your family know what's happened. Layoff? Plant closing? Depressed economy? Business down? Explain what happened. Break down the big words so that everyone understands. Especially the kids.

*Source: WDIV/TV 4 A Post-Newsweek Station.

Monthly Budget

Income

take-home pay   _____   dividends   _____

repaid loans   _____   other   _____

                                                        Total cash available   _____

Expenses

FIXED

mortgage or rent   _____   amount paid or reserved for

daycare   _____   taxes   _____

loan payments   _____   medical insurance   _____

childrens' allowances   _____   life insurance   _____

other   _____   car insurance   _____

                                                   home insurance   _____

                                                   other   _____

                                                        Total fixed expenses   _____

FLEXIBLE

water   _____   household expenses   _____

gas/electricity   _____   personal care   _____

telephone   _____   clothing   _____

food   _____   recreation (eating out, movies,   _____

automobile   records, trips, etc.)

    gasoline   _____   extra childcare   _____

    repairs   _____   other bills   _____

other transportation   _____   other expenditures   _____

medical services   _____

    medication   _____

                                                   Total flexible expenses   _____

                                                   Total expenses   _____

Total cash available − total expenses = balance*   _____

*If your figure is less than zero you are in debt, over zero you have something to save or spend on extras.

Fill in everyone at a family meeting or on a one-to-one basis. The important thing is don't leave anyone in the dark. If a family meeting seems out of the question, take time to talk when:

cleaning up after meals
cutting or raking the lawn
taking trips to the store

Don't "sugar-coat" the facts or tell "fairytales." Living with less money will force your family to make hard changes. Yet, let your kids know that even though there's less money, they can still count on a loving family. Maybe more loving than ever.

Step 2: Take Time to Listen. Let everyone have their say about what these changes mean to them. Especially now, kids should be seen *and* heard.

Listen to words *and* actions. Is someone suddenly:

having a lot of crying spells
sleeping in late all the time
acting mean
drinking heavily
withdrawing
abusing drugs
complaining of stomach pains

Step 3: Find Out Who's Hurting. Let everyone say what he or she is *really* feeling from time to time.

Just repeat whatever you hear, right when it's said. Then look for a nod to see if you heard it right. Is someone feeling:

helpless	sad
unloved	confused
worried	frightened
angry	like a burden to the family

Try not to say, "you shouldn't feel that way" because someone may be in real pain. The best you can do is let your loved ones have their say and get it off their chest.

Step 4: Let Your Feelings Out, Together or Alone. Give everyone in your family a space and time to let deep feelings out. Don't bottle them up, or hide them from yourself. If you're not comfortable showing others how you feel or fear you may strike someone who's dear to you, consider:

getting out of the house for a run or a brisk walk

having a good cry, alone

hitting a cushion or pillow

going to your room, shutting the door, and screaming

all of the above

Step 5: Solve Problems Together. Every week, look at the changes taking place in your household and work out ways to deal with them. Working together as a team, your family can do *more* than survive. It can grow together and come through stronger.

Decide together things like:

what we can't afford now

what things we can do for family fun that don't cost a lot of money

who will do what chores around the house

how we'll all get by with less

If your discussions break down, go back to Step 1.

If you have a lot of trouble going through these steps, professional help may be what you need. Call and make an appointment with the family service agency nearest you. Whether you have money or not to pay for the services, the agency will do its best to help your family. Remember, you're not alone.

Sources of Help in Financial Crises

Aid to Families with Dependent Children (AFDC)

You may be entitled to AFDC if you have dependent children up to age 20 living with you who are your own or who are related to you. The program provides money and services to needy families with children until the families become self-supporting. The money for this program comes from federal, state, and county governments. The program is governed by federal and state laws but is administered through the county welfare department. Each state has different eligibility regulations and they constantly change. Contact your local county welfare office to find out if your family qualifies.

Food Stamps. You may be eligible for Food Stamps that will help stretch your food dollar. Eligibility is based on the household's net monthly income and your assets. If you live in your own home, its value is not included in your assets. If you qualify for food stamps, your allotment will be based on the number of people in your family, current or expected income, costs of shelter and dependent care, as well as other factors. These regulations are constantly changing, so check with your county welfare office.

Emergency Needs Program. Any person may apply for emergency help under the Emergency Needs programs administered by the Department of Social Services in some states. Emergency needs for food, clothing, rent, house payments, shelter, utility payments, taxes, security deposits, home repairs, appliances, furniture, transportation, and certain other necessities are considered under this program.

General Assistance (GA).   The General Assistance Program is available in some states to those in need who do not qualify for other public aid. The program offers financial help and out-patient medical care. You can be working or receiving disability insurance or other compensation as long as you meet certain income requirements. Incomes of all your family members are considered when your eligibility is being determined.

Medical Assistance.   Some states have Medical Assistance programs to help needy persons pay for a variety of medical services.

Your eligibility for medical assistance is determined according to your particular situation and income. You may still be eligible if you own certain types of property. You may be allowed to have (1) a homestead; (2) household items; (3) any tangible personal item you use in earning money; and (4) one passenger car per family. However, you usually cannot claim exemptions for intangible property such as securities, bonds, or cash that's invested or deposited in a savings account if their value is more than certain limited amounts.

Unemployment Insurance.   You will probably qualify for unemployment insurance, which is paid through a payroll tax by your employer, if you have been laid off or lost your job. Also, you may qualify if you are a veteran or a retiree. Unemployment benefits, however, usually do not last longer than six months to a year, depending on state and federal policies.

Mortgage Arrangements.   If you are unable to make your mortgage payment because of unemployment, an extended strike, illness, or other circumstances beyond your control, you should contact your mortgage lender *immediately* to discuss your situation. It is best to talk in person with your lender if you can. You may be able to make special arrangements during the period that your income is reduced. If you cannot make such arrangements, you may be able to get other help as suggested below.

If you have an FHA-insured mortgage, ask your mortgage lender to refer you to a HUD-approved home ownership counseling agency. The agency will discuss your problem with you and try to find solutions. If you have a VA mortgage or land contract, contact the VA Loan Service and Claims Section.

You may find that other bills are falling behind in addition to your mortgage payments. If so, credit counseling can help you.

Credit Counseling   If you are worried about past due bills, wage garnishment, repossessions, or mortgage foreclosure, help is available. Nonprofit family financial counseling services can help you work out your financial problems and help you get back on your feet with dignity and a minimum of confusion. They will assist you in working out a budget and a debt repayment schedule. Also, they provide professional counseling on money management, family budgeting, and wise use of credit. If needed, they will provide debt management services in which they negotiate with your creditors and forward your payments to them.

Counseling services are often free. For debt management services, fees are based on your ability to pay. No one is refused service because of inability to pay a fee. For referral to the office nearest you, call your local family services or consumer affairs offices.

Utility Assistance.   You may qualify for help with your utility bills if you are having trouble paying them or are threatened with a shut-off. There are programs in many states that help those on a limited income to meet their utility payments. Also, assistance in weatherizing homes is available to keep utility costs down. To see if you are eligible for such assistance, contact your local department of social services.

The Federal government offers a Residential Energy Tax Credit. If you have added insulation or certain other energy-conserving measures to your home since April, 1977, you should apply for this credit on your Federal income tax return. For further information call this toll-free number: 800-462-0830.

Utility Shut-Offs (Gas, Electric, Telephone).   In most states, companies must allow you 14–21 days to pay your bills. If your bill is not paid within this period, you may receive a shut-off notice and ten additional days to pay or to register a complaint. If there is a valid medical emergency in your home, the companies may be prevented temporarily from shutting off your service. They may be able to only shut off service between the hours of 8 A.M. and 4 P.M., and not before a day when reconnection cannot be made. You have a right to challenge your bills if you think they are too high or incorrect. Ask for a hearing before the company's hearing examiner. If you are not satisfied with the examiner's decision, you can usually appeal it.

On any question or complaint you have about a utility bill, or if you cannot make full payment on any of your utilities, be sure to call the company's local office before your bill is due and ask for credit arrangements for partial payments. Approval of such a request usually depends on your payment history.

Legal Services.   Persons with limited incomes can get legal counseling by contacting Legal Aid offices. Check in the Yellow Pages under "Attorneys."

CONSUMER INFORMATION

Shopping for Goods and Services

There are many criteria that you as a consumer can use to choose any product. The first step to take is to decide what your needs are. Is the purchase necessary at all? If the answer is "yes," you can form a clearer idea of your choice by listing your criteria before looking at the market.

For example, suppose you are choosing a blanket for your child's bed.

Necessary?	Yes, complains of cold
Size?	Twin (single bed)
Long life?	Yes, she's young (10 to 15 years)
Color?	Anything but white
Dry-clean?	No
Warmth?	Very warm
Resale possibilities?	Not important

Equipped with these decisions you can buy the quality you need and avoid features you do not need. Sometimes comparative shopping is not reasonable. If your car is sputtering, for example, immediate necessity has the strongest claim and you are likely to pull into the nearest gas station, not the cheapest. But for many purchases, especially the larger ones (rugs, appliances, automobiles, house paint), comparative shopping is worth the time and effort it requires. Telephoning two or three stores for price checks will usually give you an idea of high and low prices, and it only takes ten minutes.

Many people are unsure of the quality or special features of merchandise they are considering. Brand name advertising and store clerks' sales pitches are not necessarily reliable sources of information. In our example, how would you know what the warmest, longest lasting, machine washable blanket on the market might be? The publications of the Consumers Union and Consumers Research, Inc. are a good source of this type of information. These two non-profit organizations for consumer protection and enlightenment test products at random and publish their findings. They are mostly testing for safety and efficiency. If you are basically interested in economy or style, your opinions may differ.

The *Consumer Reports Buying Guide and Consumers Research Annual Guide*, although they sometimes list brand names that have gone off the market during the year, have a wealth of information on a wide range of goods. You can receive a free copy of "Consumer's Resource Handbook" by writing to: U.S. Consumer Information Center, Dept. 579L, Pueblo, CO 81009.

Secondhand Goods. Many durable goods (as opposed to foods or services) can be purchased secondhand and serve your need just as happily and more economically. A rake, a rug, a bicycle, a car would be some examples of this sort of purchase. Many people discard goods before they have worn out. If newness is not a major criterion, you can save many dollars by buying used items.

It is also wise to be cautious in making these purchases. Some people get carried away by the prospect of picking up something for almost nothing. Are you getting your money's worth? Many items—a rake or a bed frame, say—most people can judge themselves. But if the item requires repair or involves mechanical or electrical equipment, you can only judge well according to how much you know about that item. Ask yourself: Do you want to spend six hours and several dollars repainting that chest of drawers? Or, if you know nothing about cars, it is wise to consult or bring someone you trust with you to judge the car before you buy it. Buying second-hand goods you are unable to judge can be a way of throwing away money.

Newspaper want-ads, garage sales, and secondhand stores are the most common sources for finding secondhand goods.

Buying Services. In the matter of buying services—insurance, gardening, hauling, plumbing—there is nothing like shopping around. Services are almost always competitive. There may be a going rate in the area for a particular service, but there is usually some company that hopes to get business by being cheaper. And for many services the price range varies widely. This may or may not reflect the quality of the service you will get. It is wise to ask lots of questions:

Will repairpeople make housecalls?
Will the garden clippings be hauled away?
What does the insurance cover exactly?

Companies are used to getting these calls. You may run into some grouches, but most businesspeople will be happy to answer your questions. They are offering a service. You are paying. You have the right to know how your money will be spent.

Consumer Complaints. What do you do when you are tricked, gypped, or robbed? What do you do when the service is not provided or the item is no good?

The first step is to call or write the place of business. State the problem and state what you want (I want the item replaced. I want my money back. I expect you to do the work this week.) If you write you should make sure the letter has your address, is dated, and you should make a copy of it to keep. Often the problem is unintentional. The storekeeper is happy to replace the item; the businessperson happy to provide the service. If you cannot get prompt, courteous service from an employee, contact the manager. If the manager does not provide satisfaction, write directly to the president of the company or corporation, describing the problem. Letters to the president often produce quick action. Send a copy to the person with whom you were dealing.

You usually want to avoid calling in a third party. It always means time and trouble on your part. However, if you feel that you have been treated unfairly or that the provider does not respond to your complaint, you should tell the company that you intend to call in a consumer agency, and then do it.

Every state and most counties across the United States have a consumer affairs agency listed in the phone book under the name of the county you live in. This is the best place to start. Tell the person at the agency what sort of complaint you have. You will probably be referred to another number. There are many branches of consumer protection. These agencies usually carry weight with businesspeople. They are your "big stick." Often their intervention will produce the results you want if you can prove your case. However, it may be months before this happens. Sometimes, though, they can do nothing (if the company has gone bankrupt, for instance). This possibility must be accepted.

Buying on Credit

Credit buying is how most people purchase houses, automobiles, and other large consumer goods. This term also refers to some credit card buying. Buying on credit is always more expensive than purchasing with cash. Besides paying for the item, you are paying to use someone's money. This raises the price of the purchase considerably. Why does anyone do it then? Why not wait until you have the cash to buy?

Buying on credit gives a person the advantage of using something he or she does not have the money to buy at the moment. If you buy a car on credit and your payments are $200 a month, you have the use of a car for about $6 a day for several years. And at the end of those years you own it.

How to Obtain Credit. Remember that credit is something like rented money. You want to rent it from the person who will charge you the least for borrowing. The lender wants to have some assurance that you will pay back the loan plus a little something for letting you use the money in the first place. Some lenders can be quite mercenary

about the "little something." This is why you want to know your options.

THE LENDER'S QUESTIONS The lender will want to know how able or likely you are to pay back the debt.

What your yearly income is

How long you have worked at the same job

How long you have lived where you live now

What your normal expenses are per month

How much will be available to pay a loan with

What your past record for repaying loans shows (called a credit rating*)

What assets (called collateral) you have that can cover the debt if you cannot repay. Assets include real estate (land, houses), savings accounts, stocks, cars, and other material goods

THE BORROWER'S RIGHTS The 1968 Truth-in-Lending Act, which applies to loans of $25,000 or less from most regular institutions, requires the lender to tell the borrower exactly how much interest is being charged on the loan. Ask.

The 1975 Equal Credit Opportunity Act prohibits discrimination in lending on the basis of sex, age, or marital status. It is now illegal for lenders to demand that a person provide their spouse's name, salary, or job description when the person wants credit in his or her own name. A parent or spouse's co-signature cannot be required if the loan does not involve them. Alimony and child support payments must be considered regular income. Young couples do not need to divulge their methods of birth control or their intentions to bear children. And a lender cannot change the terms of credit because of a borrower's change in marital status, age, or job status.

The Equal Credit Opportunity Act was chiefly designed to end unfair practices against women. Banks and other lenders advise women to establish their own credit histories to avoid problems when borrowing. This can be done by obtaining credit cards in one's own name (Janet Doe not Mrs. John Doe) or by taking out and repaying a small loan.

Where to Get Money. The cheapest way to borrow money is from yourself (if you can).

SAVINGS If you have a savings account you can use it as collateral for a loan. You might be able to borrow up to 95 percent of the value of the account. If the loan is at 16 percent and your account makes 6 percent, the net interest on the loan is 10 percent.

---

*Paying your bills on time does not give you a good credit rating—you must prove you are capable of repaying *loans*.

LIFE INSURANCE   Certain life insurance policies have a pool of money—the cash value—from which you can borrow. It is your money, so you cannot be turned down for the loan. If you do not or cannot repay, the debt is repaid from your insurance policy.

CREDIT UNIONS   Credit Unions are cooperatives so you must belong to use one. They are very attractive however. The average interest on loans runs two to three percent less than commercial banks. If the cooperative has a good year, you will also get some money back at the end.

Other Sources of Credit

COMMERCIAL BANKS   The usual source for many business and personal loans, especially for cars and homes.

SALES FINANCE COMPANIES   These companies buy installment contracts, and their risks, from retail merchants. Most car loans that are not paid to commercial banks are paid to finance companies. About one-third of all personal loans also come from these finance companies.

CONSUMER FINANCE COMPANIES   These companies make small loans to consumers usually at a very high interest rate. The loans are usually made for items other than the "biggies" (cars, homes, stereos), for furniture, perhaps. The companies usually advertise their loan consolidation services on the TV and radio—that is, paying several small loans with one bigger one.

Credit Cards.   Credit cards issued by retail stores or national companies can be used in two ways. If you use your card only for purchases within your budget, you can always pay your credit card bill in full on time. No finance charge is made and no extra charges. You have used it like a check or like cash. It has the advantage of delaying cash payment, since it may take a month or more for a purchase to show on the bill. But you are not paying to borrow money, only for the item. Credit cards can also be used to buy items on credit—hence, the name. You can buy $200 speakers today and pay $20 plus finance charges for the next ten months. And use the speakers. Many credit card holders receive various "enhancements" along with their cards, such as travel and health insurance, emergency cash, airline tickets, travel discounts, and bonus merchandise programs.

The pitfalls of credit card buying is that they are easy to use but the finance charges are high, usually equivalent to 18 or 19.8 percent interest. Also, late charges are added if payments are not made within a certain number of days. Many people buy items on credit that are not worth the high price of the money they are using. Many people also overbuy without considering their income, and so find themselves continually in debt. Only one-third of credit card users pay their bills before incurring finance charges (that is, interest).

There is an ominous aspect to credit cards that has nothing at all to do with credit. Credit cards are required as a form of identification in many stores—especially chain stores—in order to purchase goods by check. Thus, people who do not believe in using credit cards are forced to have at least one major credit card in order to use their personal checks in buying goods.

Another aspect of credit cards that has nothing to do with personal credit per se is that banks charge stores approximately five percent service fees when their customers use credit. Thus, when a customer buys a cup for $1.00 using a credit card, the store sends the credit slip to the bank. The bank then returns 95¢ to the store. The store's profit is therefore cut by five percent. In order to make up the loss, the store may increase the price of the cup to $1.05.

The indirect result of a store accepting credit cards is twofold. First, credit cards tend to raise consumer prices. Second, credit cards penalize those who do not use them because nonusers are forced to pay higher prices as a result of other people using credit cards. Thus, some stores refuse to accept credit cards, and others will give a discount if goods are bought with cash. Still others impose a service charge on those who use credit cards.

Comparing Costs.   Credit card charge accounts are also called "revolving charge plans." These are open-ended. There is a top limit, but purchases are added as they are made without a new agreement being written. Finance charges average 19.8 percent annually. A credit card's top limit, however, is usually no more than several thousand dollars. Most large purchases must be financed differently.

Under the closed-end plans you ordinarily sign a promissory note, if you are borrowing cash, or a retail installment contract, if you are using sales credit. You agree in advance on the specific amount to borrow, the number and size of weekly or monthly payments, and a due date.

When Financing Search for the Lowest Annual Percentage Rate (APR).   If you need to make a purchase on credit, check with banks, saving and loan associations, finance companies, your credit union, your life insurance company and possibly the company from which you are making the purchase to determine which one offers the lowest APR.

Buying a Home*

What Can You Afford?

You've probably heard various ways to estimate what you can afford to spend on a home. These methods can be useful in arriving at approximate figures, but they overlook the variables that can affect your financial capability.

Generally, the ideal monthly payment should equal about 25% of your gross monthly income, minus any outstanding debts. But you may be able to manage a montly payment up to 40% of your gross monthly income, depending on other factors. For example, you may be willing to cut back on other, nonessential costs, or you may be at the start of a promising career.

To figure what you can spend on a home, you need to make two basic calculations: How much can you pay each month for the long-term expenses of owning a home? How much cash can you spend for the initial costs of buying a home?

Monthly Housing Costs.   You can calculate how much you have to spend by preparing a personal financial statement that details total income and expenses. You'll also need this information when you apply for a loan. Begin preparing your statement by listing monthly income after taxes and other deductions. You should include your income and the income of anyone else participating in the purchase. Use an average figure if the income varies from month to month or year to year, and exclude any irregular income.

Next, estimate your average monthly expenses for all nonhousing items—food, clothing, savings, debts, and so on—and subtract them from your monthly net income. What's left is the maximum amount you can pay each month for all long-term home ownership costs.

Remember, in addition to loan payments, your monthly costs also will include payments for taxes and assessments, insurance, maintenance, and utilities. Unless you're willing to stick to a very strict budget, you'll probably be more comfortable with a home loan payment that's less than the maximum amount you can afford. When you find a home in which you're interested, get estimates of monthly costs for the following:

HOME LOAN PAYMENTS   You'll probably take out a loan to pay a major part of the purchase price, so it's a good idea to shop for a loan before you look for a home. Talk to several lenders about your eligibility for a loan, the maximum amount you can reasonably expect, their current loan terms, and the monthly payments for different loan amounts, repayment periods, and interest rates.

*Reprinted by permission of Bank of America CIRcular® Consumer Information Reports.

PROPERTY TAXES [Laws vary by state.] Improving the home can affect its tax valuation.

PROPERTY INSURANCE   The cost of insuring a home varies with the home's age, type of construction, and location. As a general estimate, the annual insurance premium is one-third of one percent of the home's price. For a more accurate figure, call several local insurance agents, describe the home, and ask what you must pay to insure it. Lenders usually require you to carry enough insurance to cover the amount of your loan, but you may consider getting more, based on the cost of replacing your home.

REPAIR AND UTILITIES   These costs vary with the home's age, size, design, and condition.

TAX CONSIDERATIONS   At the present time, you can deduct your property taxes, the interest payments on your home, and the loan origination fee you pay your lender on your federal income tax returns. [State laws may vary.]

Cash Needed.   To calculate how much you have available to spend on a home, add up savings (other than an emergency reserve) and investments you might cash in. You'll need money for the following costs:

PROFESSIONALS' FEES   You might hire professionals such as a housing inspector and an attorney during the home-buying process. Ask them for fee estimates first.

CLOSING COSTS   These are fees for services, including those performed by the lender, escrow agent, and title company. Closing costs can range from several hundred to several thousand dollars. Federal law requires the lender to send you an estimate of the closing costs within three days after you've applied for the loan. Although local custom usually determines who—you or the seller—pays for what costs, you may be able to negotiate some of the fees. Include the results of any negotiations in your written purchase contract.

For a full explanation of various closing fees, read the booklet on settlement costs prepared by the U.S. Department of Housing and Urban Development (HUD). It's available free from lenders and HUD offices.

DOWN PAYMENT   The usual down payment required by many lenders is 20% of the home's total cost. The actual amount depends on the type of loan, your lender's policy, and current economic conditions. Typically, for down payments of less than 20%, the lender will require that the buyer purchase *private mortgage insurance* (PMI). PMI protects the lender against loss if you don't pay as agreed.

It is possible to reduce or eliminate your need for down payment cash. For instance, you can:

- Apply for a Federal Housing Administration [or a] Veterans Administration loan, which require relatively low down payments. . . .
- Lease a home with an option to buy it at a later date for an agreed-upon price. Usually, some or all of the rent you pay is credited against the purchase price. The buyer may have to pay an added charge for this option.

Select an Area

The area you choose can greatly affect your pocketbook as well as your personal happiness. For instance, you should consider how far the home is from your job and what distance you're willing to commute each day. Drive around and note the neighborhoods that appeal to you. Ask city officials, real estate agents, local businesspeople, and your prospective neighbors about the following points:

Public Services. How close is the fire station? Where is the nearest hospital? Is reliable public transportation available? Are good schools nearby? And can your children safely and easily walk or take transportation to get to them?

Public Safety. Get crime statistics from the local police. Ask for a report or map indicating the crime rates for various areas.

Zoning and Taxes. Contact the city or county planning department about plans for your area. Are there plans to widen the streets or add new buildings nearby? Ask the local tax assessor about *assessments*—charges for local public improvements such as paving, street lighting, and public transit. Have they been rising sharply, and are they likely to continue doing so? Find out about any local homeowner's tax exemptions or other tax credits you may be entitled to receive.

Environmental Conditions. City or county planning officials can tell you about such problems as flooding, erosion, smog, fire hazards, and earthquake fault lines that are present in your area.

Look for Homes

Begin looking for houses that best meet your needs. Consider the following:

Type of Ownership. Do you want to live in a single- or multiple-family residence? Or are you interested in a condominium or a planned unit development (PUD)? With a condominium or PUD, you and the other owners share rights to some parts of the property—called *common areas*. Usually, you'll also have to pay homeowner's dues.

Length of Use. Many people stay in their homes longer than they originally planned. Look ahead at least five years and try to anticipate changes—such as family size—that might affect your housing needs.

Space. Measure your present home's rooms, storage areas, and work surfaces, noting which spaces are large enough and which aren't. Then look for houses that are designed to meet your needs.

Where to Look. Find out about homes for sale by reading newspaper ads and by consulting real estate agents recommended by your friends, other agents, or the local real estate board. Pick up buyers' guides from realty and builders' associations, lenders, and stores. And ask friends living in the area to watch for home sales.

Inspect the Home

Inspect thoroughly any home you're interested in buying. Read books on homes and consult knowledgeable friends to learn how to inspect a home and judge the quality of the workmanship, materials, and design.

Professional Inspectors. It's generally a wise investment to hire a housing inspector to confirm your own judgment about the home. A housing inspector—unlike an appraiser, who judges the dollar value of a home—provides a detailed, written evaluation of the home's condition. Fees typically range from $100 to $200. Before hiring an inspector, make sure he or she is licensed and bonded. Find out whether the inspector's work is guaranteed and, if so, for how long.

You also should have a licensed pest control inspector check the home whether or not the lender requires such an inspection. The seller usually pays the cost.

Warranties. The seller may provide a *home protection contract* (home warranty). Or you can purchase one from a home protection company. A typical new-home warranty, whose term may range from one to ten years, covers the home's structure, its major systems (plumbing, heating, and electrical), and any appliances sold with the home. On an existing home, the warranty typically covers the major systems and appliances for one year.

Make an Offer

Consider making your first offer for less than the asking price if you think the home is overpriced for the market or the circumstances are favorable—for example, if the seller seems eager to close the sale.

The Purchase Contract.   When you decide what price to offer, you draw up a contract stating the sale terms. You submit your offer to the seller, who either accepts it as is or makes changes and sends it back to you. The contract goes back and forth as many times as necessary to reach an agreement. You should sign the contract only when both of you are satisfied.

According to state law, no agreement for the sale of real estate can be enforced unless it's in writing. Look over the contract carefully—with your legal adviser if possible—to make sure it covers all the sale conditions you want included. Following are some points you may wish to cover:

- The conditions under which the contract may be canceled without penalty—for instance, if you can't get the financing you want or if the home doesn't pass professional inspection.
- The closing costs you'll pay and those the seller will pay.
- An itemized list describing furnishings, appliances, and other personal property the sale includes and excludes.
- The date on which you'll check the home's condition before the sale is final.
- The date you get possession of the home.

The Deposit.   At the time you sign the contract, you'll be asked for a deposit, sometimes referred to as *earnest money*. The amount can range from hundreds to thousands of dollars, depending on what you're willing to give and what the seller is willing to accept. The deposit usually is applied to the down payment or to your share of the closing costs. If the sale falls through, the deposit either will be kept by the seller or returned to you, according to the terms of your purchase contract.

Escrow.   Once you and the seller have signed a purchase agreement, you're ready to begin *escrow*—a procedure in which your deposit and any other pertinent documents are placed in the keeping of a neutral third party called the *escrow agent*. You and the seller must agree on the agent, who may be from a title insurance company, an escrow company, or the lender's own escrow department.

Escrow can begin before or after you've arranged financing. You and the seller negotiate and sign a set of escrow instructions listing the conditions (including financing) that must be met before the sale is finalized. The escrow agent distributes the money and documents according to the escrow instructions.

Compare Loan Terms.   Before you choose a loan, it's critical that you compare the following loan terms for similar types of loans:

DOWN PAYMENT AND LOAN FEES   These vary with the lender and type of loan.

INTEREST RATE   This is the cost of borrowing the money, usually a percentage of the loan amount. A small variation in the interest rate can add up to thousands of dollars in the total loan payment amount.

The lender is required to tell you the *annual percentage rate* (APR). This is the cost of the loan per year including interest and additional finance charges, such as loan origination and certain closing fees. The APR expresses these charges as a percentage.

REPAYMENT PERIOD   With a fixed-rate loan, the longer the repayment period, the higher the total cost of the loan; but, a shorter repayment period generally means a larger monthly payment. With an adjustable rate loan, the total cost and the monthly payment are affected by interest rate changes as well as by the repayment period. If your loan rate isn't fixed, you'll want to know whether you can extend the repayment period to reduce any increase in your monthly payment.

PREPAYMENT   A lender may reserve the right to charge a fee—called a *prepayment premium*—if you pay back all or part of your loan early. Your *promissory note* (loan contract) usually will contain a clause describing under what conditions you must pay this premium. If the promissory note isn't specific, ask what these conditions are.

Other Financing   Instead of—or in addition to—getting a new loan from a lender, you may be able to obtain financing in one of the following ways:

ASSUMPTIONS   Federal law permits lenders to make most loans non-assumable. To find out whether you can *assume* (take over) the seller's loan, check with the seller's lender. If the loan is assumable, you may be able to pay the seller the difference between the amount still owed on the loan and the purchase price and take over payments where the seller left off.

You make payments either to the seller or directly to the seller's lender. In the latter case, you may have to pay any loan fees and provide whatever credit information the lender requires.

An assumption can be a good arrangement if you can take over the loan at a lower-than-current interest rate. Some lenders, however, may require you to assume the loan at the current rate.

You may need more financing to make up the difference between the purchase price and the amount assumed. The seller often may *carry the loan*—grant you credit—for a short time (usually three to five years). This way, depending on the amount and the credit terms, you could have a large balloon payment. If you're thinking about having the seller carry the loan, consider whether you'll be able to meet the credit terms and make any balloon payment when it comes due. You'll also need to determine whether refinancing will be available, and, if not, whether the seller will extend the term of the financing agreement.

As an alternative to assuming the seller's loan, you might negotiate with the seller's lender to give you a loan for the difference between the purchase price of the home and the down payment. In many cases, you can obtain an interest rate that's between the rate on the seller's original loan and the current rate.

BUY DOWNS   With a buy-down arrangement, the seller pays the lending institution an amount to lower the interest rate on your loan. Usually, the term is for a specified period of time—typically one to five years. After that, you pay the rate the lender was charging at the time you took out the loan.

EQUITY SHARING   Consider arranging for other investors to pay part of the loan, the down payment, or closing costs in exchange for part of the equity in your home. Many real estate agents, and some states and local government agencies, offer this kind of financing arrangement—sometimes called a *shared-appreciation program*.

In addition to all these financing alternatives, the seller may offer a variety of other arrangements. When considering any type of loan, be sure to get professional legal, tax, and real estate advice.

Close the Deal

Closing—also called *settlement* or *closing escrow*—is the final step. Before the sale is finalized, you must deposit in escrow all of the down payment and your closing costs. At the close of escrow, the agent will give your deposit and loan funds to the seller and have the deed recorded. After the recording, you'll receive the deed by mail in about 30 days.

Credit Bureaus and Debt Collectors

Credit bureaus are computerized operations that accumulate and record your credit history. A company considering you for a loan may request your file and use its contents to decide whether or not to grant the loan. According to the Fair Credit Reporting Act (operative since 1971), the company should let you know they are sending for your file.

Denial of Credit

If you are denied credit you must be told if the decision was based at all on your file. If so, the company must give you the name and address of the credit bureau that supplied your file. If you request to see your file within thirty days of the incident, the bureau *must* show and explain it to you

free of charge. (At any other time you can request to see it for a fee.) Except for individual names (of neighbors, for instance) and certain medical information, all the contents must be divulged.

If the credit bureau has inaccurate information in the file you can demand that it be rechecked and deleted. You can also have deleted any derogatory information over seven years old, except bankruptcy. You can insert your own version of any unclear incidences that sound derogatory. Last of all, if the credit bureau violates the law by neglecting to add or correct information, and that causes you to lose a job or credit opportunity, you can sue it for damages.

Complaints/Information.   Write or call:

Equal Credit Opportunity
Federal Trade Commission
Washington, DC 20850

Telephone 202-523-3727
(Bureau of Consumer Protection)

The Fair Debt Collection Practices Act*

As of March 20, 1978, Federal law prohibits abusive, deceptive, and unfair debt collection practices by debt collectors. What does this mean to the consumer? What is the law designed to do? Its purpose is to see that people are treated fairly by debt collectors. The law will not permit debt collectors to use unjust means while attempting to collect a debt. But, the law does not cancel genuine debts which consumers owe.

Many people never come in contact with a debt collector. For those who do, under the new law, you have new rights.

What Debts Are Covered?   Personal, family, and household debts are covered, like money owed for the purchase of a car, for medical care, or for charge accounts.

Who Is a Debt Collector?   A debt collector is anyone, other than the creditor or his or her attorney, who regularly collects debts for others.

How May a Debt Collector Contact You?   A debt collector may contact you in person, by mail, telephone, or telegram. However, it can't be at inconvenient or unusual times or places, such as before 8:00 A.M. or after 9:00 P.M., unless you agree.

A debt collector may *not* contact you at work if your employer disapproves.

*From the Federal Trade Commission

Can You Stop a Debt Collector from Contacting You?
Yes, you may stop a debt collector from contacting you by saying so in writing. Once you tell a debt collector not to contact you, the debt collector can no longer do so, *except* to tell you that there will be no further contact. Also the debt collector may notify you that some specific action may be taken, but only if the debt collector or the creditor usually takes such action.

May a Debt Collector Contact Any Other Person Concerning Your Debt? A debt collector may contact any person to locate you. However, the debt collector must:

- Only tell people that the purpose is to try to contact you.
- Only contact your attorney if you have an attorney.

The debt collector must not:

- Tell anybody else that you owe money.
- In most cases, talk to any person more than *once*.
- Use a postcard.
- Put anything on an envelope or in a letter that identifies the writer as a debt collector.

What Is the Debt Collector Required to Tell You about the Debt? Within 5 days after you are first contacted, the debt collector must send you a *written notice* telling you—

- the amount of money you owe;
- the name of the creditor to whom you owe the money; and
- what to do if you feel you do not owe the money.

If You Feel You Do Not Owe the Money, May a Debt Collector Continue to Contact You? The debt collector must not contact you if you send a letter within thirty days after you are first contacted saying you do not owe the money. However, a debt collector can begin collection activities again if you are sent proof of the debt, such as a copy of the bill.

What Types of Debt Collection Practices Are Prohibited? A debt collector may not harass, oppress or abuse any person. For example, a debt collector cannot:

- Use threats of violence to harm anyone or anyone's property or reputation.
- Publish a list of persons who alledgedly refuse to pay their debts (except for a credit bureau).
- Use obscene or profane language.
- Repeatedly use the telephone to annoy anyone.
- Telephone any person without identifying the caller.
- Advertise your debt.

A debt collector may *not* use any false statements when collecting any debt. For example, the debt collector cannot:

- Falsely imply that the debt collector represents the United States government or any state government.
- Falsely imply that the debt collector is an attorney.
- Falsely imply that *you* committed any crime.
- Falsely represent that the debt collector operates or works for a credit bureau.
- Misrepresent the amount of the debt.
- Represent that papers being sent are legal forms, such as a summons, when they are not.
- Represent that papers being sent are *not* legal forms when they *are*.

Also, a debt collector may not say:

- That you will be arrested or imprisoned if you do not pay your debt.
- That he or she will seize, garnish, attach or sell your property or wages, unless the debt collector or the creditor intends to do so and it is legal.
- That any action will be taken against you that cannot legally be taken.

A debt collector may not:

- Give false credit information about you to anyone. Send you anything that looks like an official document that might be sent by any court or agency of the United States or any state or local government.
- Use any false name.

A debt collector must *not* be *unfair* in attempting to collect any debt. For example, the debt collector cannot:

- Collect *any amount* greater than the amount of your debt, unless allowed by law.
- Deposit any postdated check before the date on that check.
- Make you accept collect calls or pay for telegrams.
- Take or threaten to take your property unless there is a present right to do so.
- Contact you by postcard.
- Put anything on an envelope other than the debt collector's address and name. Even the name cannot be used if it shows that the communication is about the collection of a debt.

What Control Do You Have Over Specific Debts? If you owe several debts, any payment you make must be applied as you choose. And, a debt collector cannot apply a payment to any debt you feel you do not owe.

What Can You Do If the Debt Collector Breaks the Law? You have the right to sue a debt collector in a state or federal court within 1 year from the date the law was violated. You may recover money for the damage you suffered. Court costs and attorney's fees can also be recovered.

A group of persons may sue a debt collector and recover money for damages up to $500,000.

Who Can You Tell if the Debt Collector Breaks the Law? You should contact the proper federal government enforcement agency. The agencies use complaints to decide which companies to investigate. Many states also have debt collection laws of their own. Check with your state attorney general's office to determine your rights under state law.

Bibliography

ACOG. *See* American College of Obstetricians and Gynecologists.

Abarbanel, Alice. "Shared Parenting after Separation and Divorce: a Study of Joint Custody." *American Journal of Orthopsychiatry* 49(2) (April 1979):320–329.

Abbott, Douglas, and Gene Brody. "The Relation of Child Age, Gender, and Number of Children to the Marital Adjustment of Wives." *Journal of Marriage and the Family* 47(1) (February 1985):77–84.

Abbott, Douglas, and James Walters. "Parenthood Is a Question of Free Choice, and There Should Be No Societal Pressure." In Harold Feldman and Margaret Feldman, eds., *Current Controversies in Marriage and the Family*. Beverly Hills, Calif.: Sage, 1985.

Adams, Bert. "The Family: Problems and Solutions." *Journal of Marriage and the Family* 47(3) (August 1985):525–529.

Adams, J. K. "The Hidden Taboo on Love." In Herbert Otto, ed., *Love Today*. New York: Association Press, 1972.

Adams, John, and Alice Kasakoff. "Migration and the Family in Colonial New England." *Journal of Family History* 9(1) (Spring 1984):24–42.

Adams, Virginia. "Getting at the Heart of Jealous Love." *Psychology Today* 13(2) (May 1980):38–47.

Adler, Jerry, et al. "The Joy of Gardening." *Newsweek* (July 26, 1982).

Al-Anon Family Groups. *The Dilemma of the Alcoholic Marriage*, 1977.

Albrecht, Gary L. "The Alcoholism Process: A Social Learning Viewpoint." In Peter G. Bourne and Ruth Fox, eds., *Alcoholism: Progress in Research and Treatment*. New York: Academic Press, 1973.

Alcott, William. *Courtship and Marriage*. Boston: Cowan, 1868.

———. *The Young Wife*. Boston: Cowan, 1849.

Aldous, Joan. *Family Careers: Developmental Change in Families*. New York: Wiley, 1978.

———, ed. *Two Paychecks*. Beverly Hills, Calif.: Sage, 1982.

Allgeier, A. R. "Sexuality and Gender Roles in Middle-Aged and Elderly Persons." In Elizabeth Allgeier and Naomi McCormick, eds., *Gender Roles and Sexual Behavior*. Palo Alto, Calif.: Mayfield, 1982.

Allgeier, Elizabeth. "Reproductive Processes and Outcomes: Whose Responsibility?" In Elizabeth Allgeier and Naomi McCormick, eds., *Gender Roles and Sexual Behavior*. Palo Alto, Calif.: Mayfield, 1982.

Allgeier, Elizabeth, and Naomi McCormick, eds. *Gender Roles and Sexual Behavior*. Palo Alto, Calif.: Mayfield, 1982.

Altman, Meryl. "Everything They Always Wanted You to Know: The Ideology of Popular Sex Literature." In Carole Vance, ed., *Pleasure and Danger: Exploring Female Sexuality*. Boston: Routledge and Kegan Paul, 1984.

Alwin, Duane, et al. "Living Arrangements and Social Integration." *Journal of Marriage and the Family* 47(2) (May 1985):319–334.

American College of Obstetricians and Gynecologists (ACOG). "Infertility: Causes and Treatment." Chicago, 1978.

Andelin, Helen. *Fascinating Womanhood*. New York: Bantam Books, 1974.

Anderson, John, ed. *Psychological Aspects of Aging*. Washington, D.C.: American Psychological Association, 1956. In Nick Stinnett et al., eds., *Family Strengths 4: Positive Support Systems*. Lincoln: University of Nebraska Press, 1982.

Anderson, Kurt. "Private Violence." *Time* (September 5, 1983):18–19.

Andre, Rae. *The Homemakers: The Forgotten Workers*. Chicago: University of Chicago Press, 1981.

Andrews, Lori. *New Conceptions*. New York: St. Martin's Press, 1984.

———. "Laws on Private Adoption." *Parents* 58(2) (February 1983):70–71.

Annas, George. "Fathers Anonymous: Beyond the Best Interests of the Sperm Donor." *Child Welfare* 50(3) (March 1981):119–123.

Archer, Sally. "Career and/or Family: The Identity Process for Adolescent Girls." *Youth and Society* 16(3) (1985):289–314.

Arehart-Treichel, Joan. "Pets: The Health Benefits." *Science News* 121 (March 27, 1982):220–223.

Aries, Philippe. *Centuries of Childhood*. New York: Vintage Books, 1962.

———. *The Hour of Our Death*. New York: Knopf, 1981.

———. *Western Attitudes Toward Death*. New York: Knopf, 1974.

———. "The Sentimental Revolution." *Wilson Quarterly* 6(4) (1982):46–53.

Askham, J. "Identity and Stability Within the Marriage Relationship." *Journal of Marriage and the Family* 38 (1976):535–547.

Atchley, Robert. "Retirement: Leaving the World of Work." *Annals of the American Academy of Political and Social Science* 464 (November 1982):120–131.

Atkinson, Maxine, and Jacqueline Boles. "WASP (Wives as Senior Partners)." *Journal of Marriage and the Family* 46(3) (November 1984):861–870.

Atkinson, Maxine, and Becky Glass. "Marital Age Heterogamy and Homogamy, 1900 to 1980." *Journal of Marriage and the Family* 47(3) (August 1985):685–691.

Atwater, Lynn. "Long-Term Cohabitation Without a Legal Ceremony Is Equally Valid and Desirable." In Harold Feldman and Margaret Feldman, eds., *Current Controversies in Marriage and the Family*. Beverly Hills, Calif.: Sage, 1985.

Auletta, Ken. *The Underclass*. New York: Random House, 1982.

Avioli, Paula. "The Labor-force Participation of Married Mothers of Infants." *Journal of Marriage and the Family* 47(3) (August 1985):739–745.

Awad, George, and Ruth Parry. "Access Following Marital Separation." *Canadian Journal of Psychiatry* 25(5) (August 1980):357–365.

Bach, George R., and Peter Wyden. *The Intimate Enemy*. New York: Avon Books, 1968.

Bachrach, Christine. "Contraceptive Practice Among American Women, 1973–1982." *Family Planning Perspectives* 16(6) (November/December, 1984):253–258.

Bahr, Stephen. "The Economics of Family Life: An Overview." *Journal of Family Issues* 3(2) (June 1982a):139–146.

———. "Effects on Power and Division of Labor in the Family." In Lois Hoffman and Ivan Nye, eds., *Working Mothers*. San Francisco, Calif.: Jossey-Bass, 1974.

———, ed. *Economics of the Family*. Lexington, Mass.: Lexington Books, 1980.

———. "The Economics of Family Life." Special issue, *Journal of Family Issues* 3(2) (June 1982b).

Baird, Donna, and Allen Wilcox. "Cigarette Smoking Associated with Delayed Conception." *Journal of the American Medical Association* 253(20) (1985):2979–2983.

Balis, Andrea. "Only the Pregnant Woman Should Have the Right To Decide." In Harold Feldman and Margaret Feldman, eds., *Current Controversies in Marriage and the Family*. Beverly Hills, Calif.: Sage, 1985.

Balkwell, C. "Transition to Widowhood: A Review of the Literature." *Family Relations* 30 (1981):117–127.

Balswick, Judith. "Explaining Inexpressive Males: A Reply to L'Abate." *Family Relations* 29 (1980):231–233.

Bane, Mary Jo. *Here to Stay: American Families in the Twentieth Century*. New York: Basic Books, 1976.

Bane, Mary Jo, and Robert S. Weiss. "Alone Together: The World of Single-Parent Families." *American Demographics* 2(5) (1980):11–15, 48.

Bank, Stephen, and Michael Kahn. *The Sibling Bond*. New York: Basic Books, 1982.

Barbach, Lonnie. *For Each Other: Sharing Sexual Intimacy*. Garden City, N.Y.: Doubleday, 1982.

Barclay, Andrew. "The Effect of Hostility on Physiological and Fantasy Responses." *Journal of Personality* 37(4) (December 1969):651–667.

Bardwick, Judith. *The Psychology of Women*. Belmont, Calif.: Wadsworth, 1970.

Barranti, Chrystal C. Ramirez. "The Grandparent/Grandchild Relationship: Family Resource in an Era of Voluntary Bonds." *Family Relations* 34(3) (July 1985):343–352.

Barros, Ricardo. *Sexual Fantasies*. London: Luxor Press, 1970.

Barrow, Georgia, and Patricia Smith. *Aging, Ageism, and Society*. St. Paul, Minn.: West, 1979.

Bart, Pauline. "Depression in Middle-Aged Women." In Vivian Gornick and B. K. Moran, eds., *Women in Sexist Society*. New York: The New American Library, 1972.

Baruch, Grace, et al. *Lifeprints: New Patterns of Love and Work for Today's Women*. New York: McGraw-Hill, 1983.

Bass, Ellen, and Louise Thornton, eds. *I Never Told Anyone: Stories and Poems by Survivors of Child Sexual Abuse*. New York: Harper & Row, 1983.

Bassoff, Evelyn. "Relationship of Sex-Role Characteristics and Psychological Adjustment in New Mothers." *Journal of Marriage and the Family* 46(2) (May 1984):449–454.

Bassuk, Ellen. "The Homeless Problem." *Scientific American* 25:1 (July, 1984):40–45.

Bate, Barbara, and Lois Self. "The Rhetoric of Career Success Books for Women." *Journal of Communication* 33(2) (Spring 1983):149–165.

Bateson, Gregory, et al. "Towards a Theory of Schizophrenia." In Gerald Handel, ed., *The Psychosocial Interior of the Family*. Chicago: University of Chicago Press, 1967.

Baum, Andrew, et al. "Stress and Environment." *Journal of Social Issues* 37(1)(1981):4–35.

Baumrind, Diana. "Authoritarian Versus Authoritative Parental Control." *Adolescence* 3 (1968):255–272.

———. "Current Patterns of Parental Authority." *Developmental Psychology Monographs* 4(1) (1971):1–102.

Beale, Ross. "In Search of the Historical Child." *William and Mary Quarterly* 20 (1975):379–398.

Beard, Doris, and Francille Firebaugh. "Morphostatic and Morphogenic Planning Behavior in Families: Development of a Measuring Instrument." *Home Economics Research Journal* 6(3) (1978):192–205.

Beauvoir, Simone de. *The Coming of Age*. New York: Putnam's, 1972.

———. *The Second Sex*. New York: Knopf, 1948 and 1952.

Beavers, W. Robert. "Healthy, Midrange, and Severely Dysfunctional Families." In Froma Walsh, ed., *Normal Family Processes*. New York: Guilford Press, 1982.

Beck, Melinda. "Women's Work—and Wages." *Newsweek* (July 9, 1984):22–23.

Becker, David. "Persons Should Find Dating Partners Only in the Traditional Ways—Church Groups, School, Neighborhood, or Workplace." In Harold Feldman and Margaret Feldman, eds., *Current Controversies in Marriage and the Family*. Beverly Hills, Calif.: Sage, 1985.

Bell, Alan, and Martin Weinberg. *Homosexualities: A Study of Diversities among Men*. New York: Simon & Schuster, 1978.

Bell, Alan, et al. *Sexual Preference: Its Development in Men and Women*. Bloomington: Indiana University Press, 1981.

Bell, Colleen, et al. "Normative Stress and Young Families: Adaptation and Development." *Family Relations* 29(4)(1980):453–458.

Bell, David, et al. "Marital Conflict Resolution." *Journal of Family Issues* 3(1) (March 1982):111–132.

Beller, Andrea. "Occupational Segregation and the Earnings Gap." In U.S. Commission on Civil Rights, *Comparable Worth: Issue for the 80's*. Vol. 1. Washington, D.C., 1984.

———. "Occupational Segregation by Sex: Determinants and Changes." *Journal of Human Resources* 17 (Summer 1982):371–392.

Belsky, Jay. "Early Human Experience: A Family Perspective." *Developmental Psychology* 17(1) (January 1981):3–23.

———. "Exploring Individual Differences in Marital Change Across the Transition to Parenthood: The Role of Violated Expectations." *Journal of Marriage and the Family* 47(4) (November 1985):1037–1044.

———, et al. *The Child in the Family*. Reading, Mass.: Addison-Wesley, 1984.

———. "Stability and Change in Marriage Across the Transition to Parenthood: A Second Study." *Journal of Marriage and the Family* 47(4) (November 1985):855–865.

———. "The Work–Family Interface and Marital Change Across the Transition to Parenthood." *Journal of Family Issues* 6 (June 1985):205–220.

Bem, Sandra. "Androgyny vs. the Tight Little Lives of Fluffy Women and Chesty Men." *Psychology Today* 9(4) (September 1975):58–59ff.

———. "Gender Schema Theory: A Cognitive Account of Sex Typing." *Psychological Review* 88 (1981):354–364.

———. "Gender Schema Theory and Its Implications for Child Development: Raising Gender-Aschematic Children in a Gender Schematic Society." *Signs* 8(4) (Summer 1983):598–616.

———. "The Measurement of Psychological Androgyny." *Journal of Consulting and Clinical Psychology* 42 (1974):155–162.

———. "Sex Role Adaptability: One Consequence of Psychological Androgyny." *Journal of Personality and Social Psychology* 31(4) (1975):634–643.

Bem, Sandra, and J. Bem. "Training Woman to Know Her Place." In Sue Cox, ed., *Female Psychology*. Chicago: Science Research Associates, 1976.

Benedek, Elissa, and Richard Benedek. "Joint Custody: Solution or Illusion?" *American Journal of Psychiatry* 136(12) (December 1979):1540–1544.

Benin, Mary, and Barbara Nienstedt. "Happiness, Job Satisfaction, and Life Cycle." *Journal of Marriage and the Family* 47(4) (November 1985):975–984.

Berardo, Donna. "Divorce and Remarriage at Middle Age and Beyond." *Annals of the American Academy* 464 (November 1982):132–139.

Berardo, Felix. "Widowhood Status in the United States." *Family Coordinator* (July 1968):191–203.

———, ed. "Middle and Late Life Transitions." Special issue, *Annals of the American Academy of Political and Social Science* 464 (November 1982).

Berardo, Felix, and Constance Sheehan. "Family Scholarship: A Reflection of the Changing Family?" 5(4) (December 1984):577–598.

Berelson, Bernard. "The Value of Children: A Taxonomical Essay." In Nathan B. Talbot, ed., *Raising Children in Modern America*. Boston: Little, Brown, 1976.

Berger, Bennett. *Working-Class Suburbs*. Berkeley: University of California Press, 1960.

Bergmann, Barbara. "'Comparable Worth' for Professors." *Academe: Bulletin of the American Association of University Professors*. 71(4) (July/August 1985):8–10.

Bergquist, Beatrice. "The Remarried Family: An Annotated Bibliography, 1979–1982." *Family Process* 23 (1984):107–119.

Berman, Claire. "Raising the Adopted Child." *Parents* 58(2) (February 1983):67–74.

Berman, William. "Continued Attachment After Legal Divorce." *Journal of Family Issues* 6(3) (September 1985):375–392.

Bernard, Jessie. *The Future of Marriage*. New York: Bantam, 1972.

———. *Remarriage*. New York: Dryden Press, 1955.

———. "Between Two Worlds: The Housewife." In Phyllis Stewart and Muriel Cantor, eds., *Varieties of Work*. Beverly Hills, Calif.: Sage, 1982.

———. "Jealousy in Marriage." *Medical Aspects of Human Sexuality* 5 (1971):200–215.

———. "Remarriage—Afterward." *Journal of Family Issues* 1(4) (December 1980):566–571.

Bernstein, Arnold, and Henry Lennard. "Drugs, Doctors, and Junkies." *Society* 10(3) (May/June 1973):14–25.

Berscheid, Ellen, and J. Frei. "Romantic Love and Sexual Jealousy." In Gordon Clanton and Lynn Smith, eds., *Jealousy*. Englewood Cliffs, N.J.: Prentice-Hall, 1977.

Berscheid, Ellen, and Elaine Walster. "A Little Bit About Love." In T. L. Huston, ed., *Foundations of Interpersonal Attraction*. New York: Academic Press, 1974.

Berstein, Barton, and Sheila K. Collins. "Remarriage Counseling: Lawyer and Therapist's Help with the Second Time Around." *Family Relations* 34(3) (July 1985):387–391.

Bibring, Grete. "Some Specific Psychological Tasks in Pregnancy and Motherhood." In S. Hammer, ed., *Women: Body and Culture*. New York: Harper & Row, 1975.

Bielby, William, and James Baron. "Woman's Place Is With Other Women: Sex Segregation in the Workplace." Unpublished paper, National Research Council, Workshop on Job Segregation by Sex, 1982.

Bienvenu, M. J., Sr. "Measurement of Marital Communication." *Family Coordinator* 19(1) (1970):26–31.

"Big Erosion in Welfare Check." *Washington Post*. Reprinted in *San Francisco Chronicle*, March 25, 1985.

Bigner, Jerry J. *Parent-Child Relations: An Introduction to Parenting*. New York: Macmillan, 1979.

Bird, Caroline. *The 2-Paycheck Marriage*. New York: Pocket Books, 1979.

Bird, Gerald, and Gloria Bird. "Determinants of Mobility in Two-Earner Families: Does the Wife's Income Count?" *Journal of Marriage and the Family* 47(3) (August 1985):753–758.

Blakeslee, Sandra. "Scientists Find Key Biological Causes of Alcoholism." *New York Times*, August 14, 1984:19ff.

Blassingame, John. *The Slave Community*. New York: Oxford University Press, 1972.

Blood, Robert, and D. M. Wolfe. *Husbands and Wives: The Dynamics of Married Living*. New York: Free Press, 1960.

Bloom, Bernard, and Konnie Kindle. "Demographic Factors in the Continuing Relationship Between Former Spouses." *Family Relations* 34(3) (July 1985):375–381.

Bloom, Bernard, et al. "Sources of Marital Dissatisfaction Among Newly Separated Persons." *Journal of Family Issues* 6(3) (September 1985):359–373.

Blum, Richard H., et al. *Horatio Alger's Children*. San Francisco: Jossey-Bass, 1972.

———. *Society and Drugs*. San Francisco: Jossey-Bass, 1969.

Blumstein, Philip. "Identity Bargaining and Self-Conception." *Social Forces* 53(3) (1975):476–485.

Blumstein, Philip, and Pepper Schwartz. *American Couples*. New York: McGraw-Hill, 1983.

Boffey, Philip. "AIDS in the Future: Experts Say Deaths Will Climb Sharply." *New York Times*. January 14, 1986:17, 21.

Boggs, Carol. "An Analysis of Selected Christian Child-Rearing Manuals." *Family Relations* 32(1) (January 1983):73–80.

Bohannon, Paul. *Divorce and After*. New York: Doubleday, 1971.

Boken, Halcyone. "Gender Equality in Work and Family." *Journal of Family Issues* 5(2) (June 1984):254–272.

Boken, Halcyone, and Anamarie Viveros-Long. *Balancing Jobs and Family Life: Do Flexible Work Schedules Work?* Philadelphia: Temple University Press, 1981.

Bollinger, Richard. "Unspoken Marital Contracts." *Medical Aspects of Human Sexuality* 17(3) (April 1983):74–93.

Booth, Alan. "Who Divorces and Why: A Review." *Journal of Family Issues* 6(3) (September 1985):255–293.

———. "Wife's Employment and Husband's Stress: A Replication

and Refutation." *Journal of Marriage and the Family* 39 (1977):645–650.

———, ed. Special Issue of *Journal of Family Issues*. 6(3) (September 1985).

Booth, Alan, and John Edwards. "Age at Marriage and Marital Instability." *Journal of Marriage and the Family* 47(2) (February 1985):67–74.

Booth, Alan, et al. "Predicting Divorce and Permanent Separation." *Journal of Family Issues* 6(3) (September 1985):331–346.

Borland, Dolores. "A Cohort Analysis Approach to the Empty-nest Syndrome Among Three Ethnic Groups of Women: A Theoretical Position." *Journal of Marriage and the Family* 44 (February 1982):117–129.

Boss, Pauline. "Normative Family Stress: Family Boundary Changes across the Life-Span." *Family Relations* 29(4) (1980):445–450.

Bossard, James. "Residential Propinquity as a Factor in Marriage Selection." *American Journal of Sociology* 38 (September 1932):219–244.

Bossard, James, and E. Boll. *The Larger Family System*. Philadelphia: University of Pennsylvania Press, 1956.

Boston Women's Health Book Collective. *The New Our Bodies, Ourselves*. New York: Simon & Schuster, 1984.

———. *Our Bodies, Ourselves*. Boston: Little, Brown, 1978.

———. *Ourselves and Our Children*. New York: Random House, 1978.

Boswell, John. *Christianity, Social Tolerance, and Homosexuality*. Chicago, Ill.: University of Chicago Press, 1980.

Botkin, B. A., ed. *Lay My Burden Down: A Folk History of Slavery*. Chicago: University of Chicago Press, 1945.

Bott, Elizabeth. *Family and Social Network*. London: Tavistock Publications, 1957.

Bourne, Peter G., and Ruth Fox, eds. *Alcoholism: Progress in Research and Treatment*. New York: Academy Press, 1973.

Bourne, Richard. "Child Abuse and Neglect: An Overview." In Richard Bourne and Eli Newberger, eds., *Critical Perspectives on Child Abuse*. Lexington, Mass.: Lexington Books, 1979.

Bourne, Richard, and Eli Newberger, eds. *Critical Perspectives on Child Abuse*. Lexington, Mass.: Lexington Books, 1979.

Bowen, Ezra. "Facing Up to Sex Abuse." *New York Times*, April 1, 1984:8.

Bowman, Madonna, and Constance Ahrons. "Impact of Legal Custody Status on Father's Parenting Post-divorce'. *Journal of Marriage and the Family* 47(2) (May 1985):481–485.

Bradford, William. *History of Plymouth Plantation*. Cambridge, Mass.: Harvard University Press, 1945.

Bradley, Buff, et al. *Single: Living Your Own Way*. Reading, Mass.: Addison-Wesley, 1977.

Breiner, Sander. "Sequential Chronological Stress in the Family." *Family Therapy* 7(3) (1980):247–254.

Brenner, Harvey. *Mental Illness and the Economy*. Cambridge, Mass.: Harvard University Press, 1973.

———. "Influence of the Social Environment on Psychopathology: The Historic Perspective." In James Barrett et al., eds., *Stress and Mental Disorder*. New York: Raven, 1979.

Brenton, Myron. *Sex Talk*. New York: Stein and Day, 1972.

Breskin, David. "Dear Mom and Dad." *Rolling Stone* (November 8, 1984):26–35ff.

"Bringing Up a Child Now Costs $80,000." *New York Times*, May 26, 1985.

Bristor, Martha Wingerd. "The Birth of a Handicapped Child—A Holistic Model for Grieving." *Family Relations* 33(1) (January, 1984):25–32.

Broderick, Carlfred. "Both Males and Females Should Be Virgins at the Time of Marriage." In Harold Feldman and Margaret Feldman, eds., *Current Controversies in Marriage and the Family*. Beverly Hills, Calif.: Sage, 1985.

Broderick, Carlfred, and James Smith. "The General Systems Approach to the Family." In Wesley Burr, et al., eds., *Contemporary Theories About the Family: General Theories/Theoretical Orientations*. New York: Free Press, 1979.

Brody, Jane. "Emotional Deprivation Seen as Devastating Form of Child Abuse." *New York Times*, December 20, 1983:21–22.

———. "Infertility: Not Uncommon Male Problem but Often Treatable." *New York Times*, March 20, 1985:21.

———. "Licking the Trauma of Unemployment." *San Francisco Chronicle*, January 5, 1983:I:34–35.

———. "Why a Dog on the Couch May be Worth Two Psychoanalysts." *Redbook* 160(4) (February 1983):54, 56.

Bronfenbrenner, Uri. *The Ecology of Human Development*. Cambridge, Mass.: Harvard University Press, 1980.

Brown, Lynne H., and Jeannie Kidwell. "Methodology in Family Studies: The Other Side of Caring." *Journal of Marriage and the Family* 44(4) (November 1982):833–840.

———, eds. "Methodology in Family Studies." Special issue, *Journal of Marriage and the Family* 44(4) (November 1982):829–1054.

Brownmiller, Susan. *Against Our Will: Men, Women, and Rape*. New York: Simon & Schuster, 1975.

———. *Femininity*. New York: Fawcett Columbine, 1983.

Bumpass, Larry. "Bigger Isn't Necessarily Better: A Comment on Hofferth's 'Updating Children's Life Course.'" *Journal of Marriage and the Family* 47(3) (August 1985):797–798.

Bumpass, Larry, and James Sweet. "Differentials in Marital Stability." *Sociological Review* 37 (1972):754–766.

Burgess, Ann, et al. "Child Sex Initiation Rings." *American Journal of Orthopsychiatry* 51(1) (January 1981):110–119.

———, et al. "Child Sexual Assault by a Family Member: Decisions Following Disclosure." *Victimology: An International Journal* 2(2) (1977):236–250.

Burgess, Ernest. "The Family as a Unity of Interacting Personalities." *The Family* 7(1) (March 1926):3–9. Reprinted in Jerold Heiss, ed., *Family Roles and Interaction*. Chicago: Rand McNally, 1968.

Burgess, E. W., and L. S. Cottrell. *Predicting Success or Failure in Marriage*. Englewood Cliffs, N.J.: Prentice-Hall, 1939.

Burgess, E. W., and Paul Wallin. *Engagement and Marriage*. Philadelphia: Lippincott, 1953.

Burke, R. J., and T. Weir. "Relationship of Wives' Employment Status to Husband, Wife and Pair Satisfaction and Performance." *Journal of Marriage and the Family* 38 (1976):279–287.

Burns, Scott. *The Household Economy*. New York: Harper & Row, 1972.

Burr, Wesley, et al. *Contemporary Theories About the Family*. 2 vols. New York: Free Press, 1979.

Burroughs, Louise, et al. "Careers, Contingencies, and Locus of Control Among White College Women." *Sex Roles* 11(3/4) (1984):289–302.

Buunk, Bram. "Strategies of Jealousy: Styles of Coping with Extramarital Involvement of the Spouse." *Family Relations* 31 (January 1982):13–18.

Byrne, Donn. *The Attraction Paradigm.* New York: Academic Press, 1971.

———. "A Pregnant Pause in the Sexual Revolution." *Psychology Today* 13(2) (July 1977):64–69.

———. "Social Psychology and the Study of Sexual Behavior." *Personality and Social Psychology Bulletin* 3 (1977):3–30.

Caine, Lynn. *Widow.* New York: Bantam, 1974.

Caldwell, Marie Coles, and Adrian Solomon. "The Putative Father Should Have Equal Rights To Decide." In Harold Feldman and Margaret Feldman, eds., *Current Controversies in Marriage and the Family.* Beverly Hills, Calif.: Sage, 1985.

Calhoun, Arthur. *A Social History of the American Family.* Cleveland, Ohio: Ames, 1919.

California Commission on Crime Control and Violence Prevention. "An Ounce of Prevention: Toward an Understanding of the Causes of Domestic Violence." Sacramento, Calif., 1981.

Callan, Victor. "Perceptions of Parents, the Voluntarily and Involuntarily Childless: A Multidimensional Scaling Analysis." *Journal of Marriage and the Family* 47(4) (November 1985):1045–1050.

Campbell, A. *The Sense of Well-Being in America.* New York: McGraw-Hill, 1981.

Cantor, Dorothy. "Divorce: A View from the Children." *Journal of Divorce* 22(4) (Summer 1979):357–361.

Carey, John. "The Comforts of Home." *Newsweek* (November 26, 1984):96–98.

Cargan, Leonard, and Matthew Melko. *Singles: Myths and Realities.* Beverly Hills, Calif.: Sage, 1982.

Carter, Elizabeth, and McGoldrick, Marcia, eds. *The Family Life Cycle.* New York: Gardner Press, 1980.

Carter, Hugh, and Paul Glick. *Marriage and Divorce: A Social and Economic Study.* Cambridge, Mass.: Harvard University Press, 1976.

Cartwright, D., ed. *Studies in Social Power.* Ann Arbor, Mich.: University of Michigan Press, 1959.

Cass, Vivienne. "Homosexual Identity: A Concept in Need of Definition." *Journal of Homosexuality* 9(2/3) (Winter 1983/Spring 1984):105–125.

Castleman, Michael. "Sperm Crisis." *Medical Self-Care* (Spring 1981):26–27.

Cate, Rodney. "Premarital Abuse: A Social Psychological Perspective." *Journal of Family Issues* 3(1) (March 1982):79–90.

Chaback, Elaine, and Pat Fortunato. "When You're Home Alone: A Kid's Survival Checklist." *Parents* 58(2) (February 1983):134–136.

Chafetz, Morris. "How Parents Can Help Prevent Children from Developing Destructive Drinking Habits." *Medical Aspects of Human Sexuality* 16(12) (December 1982):54.

Chaze, William. "New, Nationwide Drive to Curb Child Abuse." *U.S. News and World Report* (October 1, 1984).

Cherlin, Andrew. *Marriage, Divorce, and Remarriage.* Cambridge, Mass.: Harvard University Press, 1981.

———, ed. Special issue on Family Policy. *Journal of Family Issues* (June 1984).

Chess, Stella, and Alexander Thomas. "Infant Bonding: Mystique and Reality." *American Journal of Orthopsychiatry* 52(2) (April 1982):213–222.

Chesser, Barbara Jo. "Analysis of Wedding Rituals: An Attempt to Make Weddings More Meaningful." *Family Relations* (April 1980).

Chilman, Catherine. *Adolescent Sexuality in a Changing American Society: Social and Psychological Perspectives.* Washington, D.C.: U.S. Department of Health, Education, and Welfare, 1980.

———. "Parental Satisfactions, Concerns, and Goals for Their Children." *Family Relations* 29 (July 1980):339–345.

———. "Remarriage and Stepfamilies." In Eleanor Macklin and Roger Rubin, eds., *Contemporary Families and Alternative Lifestyles: Handbook on Research and Theory.* Beverly Hills, Calif.: Sage, 1983.

Chiriboga, D. A., and L. Cutler. "Stress Responses Among Divorcing Men and Women." *Journal of Divorce* 1 (Winter 1978):95–106.

Clanton, Gordon, and Lynn Smith, eds. *Jealousy.* Englewood Cliffs, N.J.: Prentice-Hall, 1977.

Clark, Ann, ed. *Culture and Childrearing.* Philadelphia: F. A. Davis, 1981.

Clark, Matt. "Still Too Many Caesareans?" *Newsweek* (December 31, 1984):70.

———, et al. "Infertility: New Hopes, New Cures." *Newsweek* (December 6, 1982):102–110.

Clarke, Juanne. "Becoming Fascinating." *Alternative Lifestyles* 4(1) (February 1981):75–89.

Cleek, Margaret, and T. Allan Pearson. "Perceived Causes of Divorce: An Analysis of Interrelationships." *Journal of Marriage and the Family* 47(2) (February 1985):179–191.

Clemens, Audra, and Leland Axelson. "The Not-so-empty-nest: The Return of the Fledgling Adult." *Family Relations* 34 (April 1985):259–264.

Clemes, Harris, and Reynold Bean. *How to Raise Children's Self-Esteem.* San Jose, Calif.: Enrich, 1983.

Clingempeel, W. Glenn, and Eulalee Brand. "Quasi-kin Relationships, Structural Complexity, and Marital Quality in Stepfamilies: A Replication, Extension, and Clinical Implications." *Family Relations* 34(3) (July 1985):401–409.

Clore, G. L., and David Byrne. "A Reinforcement–Affect Model of Attraction." In T. L. Huston, ed., *Foundations of Interpersonal Attraction.* New York: Academic Press, 1974.

Coggle, Frances, and Grace Tasker. "Children and Housework." *Family Relations* 31 (July 1982):395–399.

Cohler, Bertram, and Scott Geyer. "Psychological Autonomy and Interdependence within the Family." In Froma Walsh, ed., *Normal Family Processes.* New York: Guilford Press, 1982.

Cohn, Richard M. "The Effect of Employment Status Change on Self-Attitudes." *Social Psychology Quarterly* 41 (1978):81–93.

Colamosca, Ann. "International Adoption: Considering *All* the Families." *Ms.* 11(7) (January 1983):96–98.

Cole, Charles, and Anna Cole. "Husbands and Wives Should Have an Equal Share in Making the Marriage Work." In Harold Feldman and Margaret Feldman, eds., *Current Controversies in Marriage and the Family.* Beverly Hills, Calif.: Sage, 1985.

Collier, Betty, and Louis Williams. "Towards a Bilateral Model of Sexism." *Human Relations: Studies Toward the Integration of the Social Sciences* 34(34) (February 1981):127–140.

Collins, Glenn. "The Gray Horizon." *New York Times.* Reprinted in *San Jose Mercury,* January 4, 1985.

———. "U.S. Day-Care Guidelines Rekindle Controversy." *New York Times,* February 4, 1985:20.

Colman, Arthur, and Libby Colman. *Pregnancy: The Psychological Experience*. New York: Seabury Press, 1972.

Condron, John, and Jerry Bode. "Rashomon, Working Wives, and Family Division of Labor: Middletown, 1980." *Journal of Marriage and the Family* 44(2) (May 1982):421–426.

Condry, J., and S. Condry. "The Development of Sex Differences: A Study of the Eye of the Beholder." *Child Development* 47(4) (1976):812–819.

"Confusion Over Herpes." *Time* (January 16, 1984):73.

Congressional Budget Office. *Reducing Poverty Among Children*. The Congress of the United States. Washington, D.C., 1985.

Conway, Colleen. "Psychophysical Preparations for Childbirth." In Leota McNall, ed., *Contemporary Obstetric and Gynecological Nursing*. St. Louis, Mo.: C. V. Mosby, 1980.

Cook, Alicia, et al. "Changes in Attitudes Toward Parenting Among College Women: 1972 and 1979 Samples." *Family Relations* 31 (January 1982):109–113.

Cook, Mark, ed., *The Bases of Human Sexual Attraction*. New York: Academic Press, 1981.

Coombs, Robert, et al. *Socialization in Drug Abuse*. Cambridge, Mass.: Schenkman, 1976.

Corby, Nan, and Judy Zarit. "Old and Alone: The Unmarried in Later Life." In Ruth Weg, ed., *Sexuality in the Later Years: Roles and Behavior*. New York: Academic Press, 1983.

Cormier, B., et al. "Psychodynamics of Father–Daughter Incest." *Canadian Psychiatric Association Journal* 7(2) (1962):203–217.

Corsaro, Maria, and Carole Korzeniowsky. *STD: A Common Sense Guide*. New York: St. Martin's Press, 1980.

Cosby, Bill. "The Regular Way." *Playboy* (December 1968):288–289.

Coser, Lewis. *The Function of Social Conflict*. New York: Free Press, 1967.

Coser, Lewis, and Bernard Rosenberg, eds. *Sociological Theory*. New York: Macmillan, 1957.

Coulanges, Fustel de. *The Ancient City*. 1867. Reprint. New York: Anchor Books, 1960.

Courtois, Christine. "The Incest Experience and Its Aftermath." *Victimology: An International Journal* 4(4) (1979):337–347.

Cowan, Ruth. "Two Washes in the Morning and a Bridge Party at Night." *Women's Studies* 3 (Fall 1976):147–172.

Cozby, P. C. "Self-Disclosure: A Literature Review." *Psychological Bulletin* 79(2) (1973):73–91.

Crandell, Barbara, et al. "Follow-up of 2000 Second-Trimester Amniocenteses." *Obstetrics and Gynecology* 56 (November 1980):625–628.

Cretcher, Dorothy. *Steering Clear: Helping Your Child Through the High Risk Drug Years*. Minneapolis: Winston Press, 1982.

Croby, Nan, and Judy Zarit. "Old and Alone: The Unmarried in Later Life." In Ruth Weg, ed., *Sexuality in the Later Years: Roles and Behavior*. New York: Academic Press, 1983.

Cromwell, Ronald, and David Olson, eds. *Power in Families*. New York: Halstead Press, 1975.

Crull, Peggy. "Stress Effects of Sexual Harassment on the Job: Implications for Counselling." *American Journal of Orthopsychiatry* 52(3) (July 1982):539–544.

Cuber, John. "Adultery: Reality vs. Stereotype." In Gerhard Neubeck, ed., *Extramarital Relations*. Englewood Cliffs, N.J.: Prentice-Hall, 1969.

Cuber, John, and Peggy Haroff. *Sex and the Significant Americans*. Baltimore: Penguin Books, 1965.

Culp, R. E., et al. "A Comparison of Observed and Reported Adult-Infant Interactions: Effects of Perceived Sex." *Sex Roles* 9 (1983):475–479.

Culverwell, Melissa. "New Hope for Infertile Couples." *Mother Earth News* 85 (January/February 1984):142–143.

Curie-Cohen, M., et al. "Current Practice of Artificial Insemination by Donor in the United States." *New England Journal of Medicine* 300(11) (March 15, 1979):585–590.

Curran, Dolores. *Traits of a Healthy Family*. New York: Ballantine Books, 1983.

Daniluk, Judith, and Al Herman. "Parenthood Decision-Making." *Family Relations* 33 (October 1984):607–612.

David, Deborah, and Robert Brannon. *The 49% Majority: The Male Sex Role*. Reading, Mass.: Addison-Wesley, 1976.

Davis, Clive, ed. *Challenges in Sexual Science: Current Theoretical and Research Advances*. Philadelphia: Society for the Scientific Study of Sex, 1983.

Davis, Keith. "Near and Dear: Friendship and Love Compared." *Psychology Today* 19(2) (February 1985):22–30.

De Cecco, John, and Michael Shively. "From Sexual Identity to Sexual Relationships: A Conceptual Shift." *Journal of Homosexuality* 9(2/3) (Winter 1983/Spring 1984):1–26.

De Simone-Luis, Judith, et al. "Children of Separation and Divorce: Factors Influencing Adjustment." *Journal of Divorce* 3(1) (Fall 1979):37–42.

DeMaris, Alfred, and Gerald Leslie. "Cohabitation with the Future Spouse: Its Influence Upon Marital Satisfaction and Communication." *Journal of Marriage and the Family* 46(1) (February 1984):77–84.

DeVries, Hilary. "Teen Suicide." *Christian Science Monitor*, February 7, 1985:23ff.

Degler, Carl. *At Odds*. New York: Oxford University Press, 1980.

Delamater, J.D., and P. MacCorquodale. *Premarital Sexuality: Attitudes, Relationships, Behavior*. Madison: University of Wisconsin Press, 1979.

Delson, Niki, and Margaret Clark. "Group Therapy with Sexually Molested Children." *Child Welfare* 50(3) (March 1981):161–174.

Demos, John. *A Little Commonwealth*. New York: Oxford University Press, 1970.

Denzin, Norman. "Toward a Phenomenology of Domestic, Family Violence." *American Journal of Sociology* 90(30) (1984):483–513.

Department of Health and Human Services. *Let's Talk About Drug Abuse*. Rockville, Md.: National Institute on Drug Abuse, 1980.

Derdeyn, A. and E. Scott. "Joint Custody: A Critical Analysis and Appraisal." *American Journal of Orthopsychiatry* 54 (April 1984):199–209.

Derrick, Frederick, and Alan Lehfeld. "The Family Life Cycle: An Alternative Approach." *Journal of Consumer Research* 7(2) (September 1980):214–217.

Dick-Read, Grantly. *Childbirth Without Fear*. New York: Harper & Row, 1972, 4/e.

Dion, Karen. "Physical Attractiveness, Sex Roles, and Heterosexual Attraction." In Mark Cook, ed., *The Bases of Human Sexual Attraction*. New York: Academic Press, 1981.

————, et al. "What Is Beautiful Is Good." *Journal of Personality and Social Psychology* 24 (1972):285–290.

Doan, Michael, and Jeannye Thornton. "Parents Live It Up After Kids Leave Home." *U.S. News and World Report* (September 26, 1983):59–60.

Dobash, R. Emerson, and Russell Dobash. *Violence Against Wives: A Case Against the Patriarchy.* New York: Free Press, 1979.

Donahue, C., Jr. "The Canon Law on the Formation of Marriage and Social Practice in the Later Middle Ages." *Journal of Family History* 8(2) (Summer 1983):144–158.

Douthewaite, Graham. *Unmarried Couples and the Law.* Indianapolis: Allen Smith, 1979.

Downs, William. "Alcoholism as a Developing Family Crisis." *Family Relations* 31 (January 1982):5–12.

Dreikurs, Rudolf. *Children: The Challenge.* New York: Hawthorne Books, 1964.

Druly, Dawn. "Thomas Gordon: The Effective Parent." *Parents* (December 1980).

Duncan, Greg, et al. *Years of Poverty, Years of Plenty.* Ann Arbor: Survey Research Center, Institute for Social Research, Univ. of Michigan, 1985.

Dunham, Richard, and Jeannie S. Kidwell. "One Should Marry on the Basis of Love and Compatability of Intellect and Personality, Regardless of Background." In Harold Feldman and Margaret Feldman, eds., *Current Controversies in Marriage and the Family.* Beverly Hills, Calif.: Sage, 1985.

Dutton, Donald, and Arthur Aron. "Some Evidence for Heightened Sexual Attraction under Conditions of High Anxiety." *Journal of Personality and Social Psychology* 30(4) (October 1974):510–517.

Duvall, Evelyn. *In-Laws: Pro and Con.* New York: Association Press, 1954.

Edleson, Jeffrey, et al. "Men Who Batter Women." *Journal of Family Issues* 6(2) (June 1985):229–247.

Edmonds, V. H. "Marriage Conventionalization: Definition and Measurement." *Journal of Marriage and the Family* 29 (November 1967):681–688.

Eekelar, John, and Sanford Katz, eds. *Family Violence.* Toronto: Buttersworth, 1978.

Ehrenreich, Barbara, and Deirdre English. *For Her Own Good: 150 Years of the Experts' Advice to Women.* Garden City, N.Y.: Anchor, 1979.

Elder, Glen H., Jr. *Children of the Great Depression.* Chicago: University of Chicago Press, 1974.

Elder, Glen, and Jeffrey Liker. "Hard Times in Women's Lives: Historical Influences Across Forty Years." *American Journal of Sociology* 88(2) (September 1982):241–269.

Ellis, Godfrey, ed. Special issue on Media and the Family. *Journal of Family Issues* (June, 1983).

Ellis, Havelock. *Studies in the Psychology of Sex.* New York: Random House, 1936.

Ephron, Nora. *Crazy Salad.* New York: Alfred Knopf, 1975.

Epstein, Joseph. *Divorced in America.* Baltimore: Penguin Books, 1975.

Epstein, Nathan B., et al. "McMaster Model of Family Functioning: A View of the Normal Family." In Froma Walsh, ed., *Normal Family Processes.* New York: Guilford Press, 1982.

Erikson, Erik. *Childhood and Society.* New York: Norton, 1963.

————. *Identity, Youth and Crisis.* New York: Norton, 1968.

Erkut, Sumru. "Exploring Sex-Differences in Expectancy, Attribution, and Academic Achievement." *Sex Roles* 9(2) (1983):217–231.

Eshleman, J. Ross. "One Should Marry a Person of the Same Religion, Race, Ethnicity, and Social Class." In Harold Feldman and Margaret Feldman, eds., *Current Controversies in Marriage and the Family.* Beverly Hills, Calif.: Sage, 1985.

Espenshade, T. J. "The Economic Consequences of Divorce." *Journal of Marriage and the Family* 41 (1979):615–625.

Etaugh, Claire, and Barbara Petroski. "Perceptions of Women: Effects of Employment Status and Marital Status." *Sex Roles* 12 (1985):329–339.

Evans, H. L., et al. "Sperm Abnormalities and Cigarette Smoking." *Lancet 1* no. 8221 (March 21, 1981):627–629.

Faller, Kathleen, ed. *Social Work with Abused and Neglected Children.* New York: Free Press, 1981.

Family Economics Review 3 (1982). Special issue, 'Household Production.'

Featherstone, Helen. *A Difference in the Family.* New York: Basic Books, 1980.

"Federal Budget Cuts Jeopardize Domestic Violence Programs." *Response to Violence in the Family and Sexual Assault.* 6(3) (May/June 1983).

Federal Trade Commission. *FTC Staff Report on Television Advertising to Children.* Washington, D.C.: Government Printing Office, 1978.

Fein, Robert. "Research on Fathering." In Arlene Skolnick and Jerome Skolnick, eds., *The Family in Transition.* Boston: Little, Brown, 1980.

Feirstein, Bruce. *Real Men Don't Eat Quiche.* New York: Pocket Books, 1982.

Feldman, Harold, and Margaret Feldman. "The Family Life Cycle: Some Suggestions for Recycling." *Journal of Marriage and the Family* 37 (May 1975):277–284.

————, eds. *Current Controversies in Marriage and the Family.* Beverly Hills, Calif.: Sage, 1985.

Feldman, Philip. "Extramarital Sex as a Substitute for Communication." *Medical Aspects of Human Sexuality* (April 1981):52J–52X.

Feldman, Shirley and Sharon Churnin. "The Transition from Expectancy to Parenthood." *Sex Roles* 11(1/2) (1984):61–78.

Feldman, Shirley, et al. "Fluctuations of Sex-related Self-attributions as a Function of Stage of Family Life Cycle." *Developmental Psychology* 17(1) (January 1981):24–35.

Felton, Barbara. "The Coping Function of Sex-role Attitudes During Marital Disruption." *Journal of Health and Social Behavior* 21(3) (September 1980):240–248.

Ferber, Marianne, and Bonnie Birnbaum. "Economics of the Family: Who Maximizes What?" *Family Economics Review* (Summer–Fall, 1980):13–16.

Ferman, Lawrence. "After the Shutdown: The Social and Psychological Costs of Job Displacement." *Industrial and Labor Relations Report* 18(2) (1981):22–26.

Ferree, Myra. "The Confused American Housewife." *Psychology Today* 10(4) (September 1976):76–80.

Findlay, Steven. "Active Dads See Rewards and Snags." *USA Today*, November 7, 1984:3D.

Finkelhor, David. *Sexually Victimized Children*. New York: Free Press, 1979.

———. "Common Features of Family Abuse." In David Finkelhor et al., eds., *The Dark Side of Families*. Beverly Hills, Calif.: Sage, 1983.

Finkelhor, David, and Kersti Yllo. "Forced Sex in Marriage: A Preliminary Research Report." Unpublished study. National Institute of Mental Health, 1980.

———. "Rape in Marriage." In David Finkelhor et al., eds., *The Dark Side of Families*. Beverly Hills, Calif.: Sage, 1983.

Finkelhor, David, et al. *The Dark Side of Families*. Beverly Hills, Calif.: Sage, 1983.

Finklestein, Barbara, and Remi Clignet. "The Family as Inferno: The Dour Visions of Four Family Historians." *Journal of Psychohistory* 9(1) (1981):135–141.

Firestone, Shulamith. *The Dialectic of Sex*. New York: Morrow, 1970.

Fischer, Claude. *To Dwell Among Friends: Personal Networks in Town and City*. Chicago: University of Chicago Press, 1982.

———. "The Friendship Cure-all." *Psychology Today* 17(1) (January 1983):74, 78.

Fischer, David Hackett. *Old Age in America*. Boston: Little, Brown, 1978.

Fisher, William, and Donn Byrne. "Social Background, Attitudes, and Sexual Attraction." In Mark Cook, ed., *The Bases of Human Sexual Attraction*. New York: Academic Press, 1981.

Flanzer, Jerry. "Alcohol and Family Violence." In Jerry Flanzer, ed., *The Many Faces of Family Violence*. Springfield, Ill.: Charles C Thomas, 1982.

———, ed. *The Many Faces of Family Violence*. Springfield, Ill.: Charles C Thomas, 1982.

Floge, Liliane. "The Dynamics of Child-Care Use and Some Implications for Women's Employment." *Journal of Marriage and the Family* 47(1) (February 1985):143–154.

Fontana, V. J. *The Maltreated Child*. Springfield, Ill.: Thomas, 1964.

Foote, Nelson, and Leonard Cottrell. *Identity and Interpersonal Competence*. Chicago, Ill.: University of Chicago Press, 1955.

Forsstrom-Cohen, Barbara, and Alan Rosenbaum. "The Effects of Parental Marital Violence on Young Adults." *Journal of Marriage and the Family* 47(2) (May 1985):467–472.

Forward, Susan, and Craig Buck. *The Betrayal of Innocence: Incest and Its Devastation*. New York: Penguin Books, 1979.

Foucault, Michael. *The History of Sexuality*. New York: Pantheon Books, 1979.

Fox, Vivian. "Is Adolescence a Phenomenon of Modern Times?" *Journal of Psychohistory* 5 (1977):271–290.

Francke, Linda Bird, et al. "Childless By Choice." *Newsweek* (January 14, 1980):96.

Fraser, Antonia. *The Weaker Vessel*. New York: Alfred Knopf, 1984.

Freedman, Estelle, and Barrie Thorne. "Introduction to 'The Feminist Sexuality Debates.'" *Signs: Journal of Women in Culture and Society* 10(1) (1984):102–105.

Freeman, Ellen. "Adolescent Contraceptive Use." *American Journal of Public Health* 70 (August 1980):790–797.

Freeman, Jo. "Social Construction of the Second Sex." In Sue Cox, ed., *Female Psychology*. Chicago: Science Research Associates, 1976.

Freeman, M. D. *Violence in the Home*. Westmean, England: Saxon House, 1979.

French, J. P., and Bertram Raven. "The Bases of Social Power." In I. Cartwright, ed., *Studies in Social Power*. Ann Arbor, Mich.: University of Michigan Press, 1959.

Freud, Sigmund. *New Introductory Lectures on Psychoanalysis*. New York: Doubleday, 1933.

Friday, Nancy. *Men in Love*. New York: Delacorte Press, 1980.

———. *My Mother Myself*. New York: Delacorte Press, 1978.

———. *My Secret Garden*. New York: Delacorte Press, 1972.

Fried, Marc. "Endemic Stress: The Psychology of Resignation and the Politics of Scarcity." *American Journal of Orthopsychiatry* 52(1) (January 1982):4–19.

Friedan, Betty. *The Feminine Mystique*. New York: Norton, 1963.

———. *The Second Wave*. New York: Norton, 1980.

Friedman, Henry. "The Father's Parenting Experience in Divorce." *American Journal of Psychiatry* 137(10) (October 1980):1177–1182.

Friedrich, Otto. "The American Way of Debt." *Time* (May 31, 1982):45–49.

———. "A Legal, Moral, Social Nightmare." *Time* (September 10, 1984):54–56.

Friend, Richard. "GAYging: Adjustment and the Older Gay Male." *Alternative Lifestyles* 3(2) (May 1980):231–248.

Frieze, Irene, et al. *Women and Sex Roles: A Social Psychology Perspective*. New York: Norton, 1978.

Fromer, Margot. *Ethical Issues in Sexuality and Reproduction*. St. Louis, Mo: C. V. Mosby, 1983.

Fromm, Erich. *The Sane Society*. New York: Holt, Rinehart, 1955.

Fulton, Julie. "Parental Reports of Children's Post-Divorce Adjustment." *Journal of Social Issues* 35(4) (1979):126–139.

Furstenberg, Frank K., Jr. "Recycling the Family: Perspectives for a Neglected Family Form." *Marriage and Family Review* 2(3) (1979):12–22.

———. "Reflections on Remarriage." *Journal of Family Issues* 1(4) (1980):443–453.

Furstenberg, Frank Jr., and Christine Nord. "Parenting Apart: Patterns of Childrearing after Marital Disruption." *Journal of Marriage and the Family* 47(4) (November 1985):893–904.

———. "The Life Course of Children of Divorce: Marital Disruption and Parental Contact." Paper presented at the annual meeting of the Population Association of America, San Diego, April 29–May 1, 1982.

Furstenberg, F. K., et al., eds. *Teenage Sexuality, Pregnancy, and Childbearing*. Philadelphia: University of Pennsylvania Press, 1980. 37 (February 1975):121–128.

Gaesser, David, and Susan Whitbourne. "Work Identity and Marital Adjustment in Blue-collar Men." *Journal of Marriage and the Family* 47(3) (August 1985):747–751.

Gagnon, John. *Human Sexualities*. New York: Scott, Foresman, 1977.

Gagnon, John, and Cathy Greenblat. *Life Designs*. New York: Scott, Foresman, 1977.

Gagnon, John, and William Simon. *Sexual Conduct: The Social Sources of Human Sexuality*. Chicago: Aldine, 1973.

Gallardo, Florence. "Till Death Do Us Part: The Marriage of Abraham Lincoln and Mary Todd." *Lincoln Herald* 1 (1984):3–10.

Galligan, Richard. "Innovative Techniques (in studying marriage and the family): Siren or Rose?" *Journal of Marriage and the Family* 44(4) (November 1982):875–888.

Gaylin, Ned. "Legal Marriage Is the Most Satisfying Method of Pairing Couples with a Long-Term Commitment to Each Other." In Harold Feldman and Margaret Feldman, eds., *Current Controversies in Marriage and the Family*. Beverly Hills, Calif.: Sage, 1985.

———. "Rediscovering Family." In Nick Stinnett et al., eds., *Family Strengths*. Lincoln: University of Nebraska Press, 1980.

Gebhard, Paul. "The Acquisition of Basic Sex Information." *Journal of Sex Research* 13(3) (August 1977):148–169.

Gelles, Richard. "An Exchange/Social Control Theory." In David Finkelhor et al., eds., *The Dark Side of Families*. Beverly Hills, Calif.: Sage, 1983.

———. "Applying Research on Family Violence to Clinical Practice." *Journal of Marriage and the Family* 44 (February 1982):9–20.

———. "Methods for Studying Sensitive Family Topics." *American Journal of Orthopsychiatry* 48(3) (July 1978a):408–423.

———. "The Myth of Battered Husbands." *Ms.* (October, 1979).

———. "Parental Child Snatching: A Preliminary Estimate of the National Incidence." *Journal of Marriage and the Family* 46(3) (August 1984):735–739.

———. "Violence Toward Children in the United States." *American Journal of Orthopsychiatry* 8 (October 1978b):580–592.

Gelles, Richard J., and Claire Cornell, eds. *International Perspectives on Family Violence*. Lexington, Mass.: D.C. Heath, 1983.

Gelman, David. "Playing Both Father and Mother." *Newsweek* (July 15, 1985):42–50.

———, et al. "Who's Taking Care of Our Parents?" *Newsweek* (May 6, 1985):61–70.

Genovese, Eugene. *Roll, Jordan, Roll*. New York: Harper & Row, 1976.

George Levinger and H. Rausch, eds. *Close Relations*. Amherst, Mass.: University of Massachussetts Press, 1977.

George, Linda. "Models of Transition in Middle and Later Life." *Annals of the American Academy* 464 (November 1982):22–37.

Gershenfeld, Matti. "Couples Have a Right to Divorce Even If They Have Children." In Harold Feldman and Margaret Feldman, eds., *Current Controversies in Marriage and the Family*. Beverly Hills, Calif.: Sage, 1985.

Gerstein, Dean. "Can Anything Be Done to Curb Drug Abuse?" *Los Angeles Times*, December 29, 1982:II:5.

Giarretto, Henry. "Humanistic Treatment of Father-Daughter Incest." In Ray Helfer, and Henry C. Kempe, eds., *Child Abuse and Neglect: The Family and the Community*. Cambridge, Mass.: Ballinger, 1976.

Gibson, Rose. "Blacks at Middle and Late Life: Resources and Coping." *Annals of the American Academy* 464 (November 1982):79–90.

Gil, David. *Violence Against Children*. Cambridge, Mass.: Harvard University Press, 1970.

———. "Societal Violence and Violence in Families." In John Eekelar, and Sanford Katz, eds., *Family Violence*. Toronto: Buttersworth, 1978.

Gilbert, Lucia, et al. "Perceptions of Parental Role Responsibilities: Differences Between Mothers and Fathers." *Family Relations* 31 (April 1982):261–269.

Gilbert, S. J. "Self-Disclosure, Intimacy, and Communication in Families." *Family Coordinator* 25(3) (1976):221–231.

Ginott, Haim G. *Between Parent and Child*. New York: Avon Books, 1965.

Gitlow, Stanley E. "Alcoholism: A Disease." In Peter Bourne and Ruth Fox, eds., *Alcoholism: Progress in Research and Treatment*. New York: Academic Press, 1973.

Givens, Ron. "A New Prohibition." *Newsweek On Campus* (April 1985):7–13.

Glenn, Norval, and Michael Supancic. "The Social and Demographic Correlates of Divorce and Separation in the United States: An Update and Reconsideration." *Journal of Marriage and the Family* 46 (August 1984):563–575.

Glass, B. L. "No-Fault Divorce Law: Impact on Judge and Client." *Journal of Family Issues* 5 (1984):47–69

Glazer-Malbin, Nona, ed. *Old Family/New Family*. New York: Van Nostrand, 1975.

Glenn, Norval. "Interreligious Marriage in the United States: Patterns and Recent Trends." *Journal of Marriage and the Family* 44(3) (August 1982):555–566.

Glenn, Norval, and Kathryn Kramer. "The Psychological Well-being of Adult Children of Divorce." *Journal of Marriage and the Family* 47(4) (November 1985):905–912.

Glenn, Norval, and Sara McLanahan. "Children and Marital Happiness: A Further Specification of the Relationship." *Journal of Marriage and the Family* 43(1) (February 1982):63–72.

Glenn, Norval, and Beth Ann Shelton. "Regional Differences in Divorce in the United States." *Journal of Marriage and the Family* 47(3) (August 1985):641–652.

Glick, Paul. "American Household Structure in Transition." *Family Planning Perspectives* 16(5) (September/October 1984):205–211.

———. "Marriage, Divorce, and Living Arrangements: Prospective Changes." *Journal of Family Issues* 5(1) (March 1984):7–26.

———. "Marriage Experiences of Family Life Specialists." *Family Relations* 29(1) (January 1980a):111–118.

———. "Remarriage: Some Recent Changes and Variations." *Journal of Family Issues* 1(4) (1980b):455–478.

———. "Updating the Life Cycle of the Family." *Journal of Marriage and the Family* 39(1) (February 1977a):5–14.

Glick, Paul, and Arthur Norton. "Marrying, Divorcing, and Living Together in the U.S. Today." *Population Bulletin* 32(5) (October 1977):2–39.

Gnezda, Therese. "The Effects of Unemployment on Family Functioning." Prepared statement presented to the Select Committee on Children, Youth and Families. House of Representatives. Hearings on the New Unemployed. Detroit, Michigan, March 4, 1984. 35–714O. U.S. Government Printing Office. Washington, D.C.: 1984.

Goebel, Karen. "Time Use and Family Life." *Family Economics Review* (Summer 1981):20–25.

Goetting, Ann. "Divorce Outcome Research." *Journal of Family Issues* 2(3) (September 1981):350–378.

———. "The Six Stages of Remarriage: Developmental Tasks of Remarriage After Divorce." *Family Relations* 31 (April 1982):213–222.

Goffman, Erving. *The Presentation of Self in Everyday Life*. New York: Doubleday, 1959.

Goldberg, Martin. "How to Prevent Marital Sexual Estrangement." *Medical Aspects of Human Sexuality* 17:2 (February 1983):69, 76–84ff.

Goldman, Noreen, et al. "Demography of the Marriage Market in the United States." *Population Index* 50(1) (Spring 1984):5–25.

Goldman, Sara. "Tilting into Old." *California Living* (May 23, 1976).

Goldsmith, Jean. "The Postdivorce Family." In Froma Walsh, ed., *Normal Family Processes*. New York: Guilford Press, 1982.

Goldsmith, Marsha. "Possible Herpes Virus Role in Abortion Studied." *Journal of the American Medical Association* 251(23) (1984):3067–3070.

Goldstein, David, and Alan Rosenbaum. "An Evaluation of the Self-Esteem of Maritally Violent Men." *Family Relations* 34(3) (July 1985):425–428.

Goldstein, Joseph, Anna Freud, and Albert Solnit. *Beyond the Best Interests of the Child*. New York: Free Press, 1973.

Goleman, Daniel. "Marriage: Research Reveals Ingredients of Happiness." *New York Times*, April 16, 1985:19–20.

———. "Spacing of Siblings Strongly Linked to Success in Life." *New York Times*, May 28, 1985:17–18.

Goode, William J. *After Divorce*. Glencoe, Ill.: Free Press, 1956.

———. *World Revolution and Family Patterns*. New York: Free Press, 1963.

———. "Force and Violence in the Family." *Journal of Marriage and the Family* 33 (November 1971):624–636.

———. "The Theoretical Importance of Love." *American Sociological Review* 24 (February 1959):38–47.

Goodman, Ellen. "Long Arm of the Law Replaces Rule of Thumb." *San Jose Mercury*, April 19, 1983.

Goodman, Walter. "Equal Pay for 'Comparable Worth' Growing as Job Discrimination Issue." *New York Times*, September 4, 1984.

Gordon, Margaret, and Stephanie Riger. "Fear and Avoidance: A Link Between Attitudes and Behavior." *Victimology: An International Journal* 4(4) (1979):395–402.

Gordon, Michael. *The American Family: Past, Present, and Future*. New York: Random House, 1978.

Gordon, Sol, et al. *The Sexual Adolescent*. North Scituate, Mass.: Duxbury Press, 1979.

Gordon, Thomas. *P.E.T. in Action*. New York: Bantam Books, 1978.

Gottman, J. M. *Marital Interactions: Experimental Investigations*. New York: Academic Press, 1979.

Gough, Kathleen. "Is the Family Universal: The Nayar Case." In Norman Bell and Ezra Vogel, eds., *A Modern Introduction to the Family*. New York: Free Press, 1968.

Graham, Meredith Maran. "Breaking the Silence." *West Magazine*, *San Jose Mercury* (May 20, 1984):17ff.

Graham-Combrinck, Lee. "A Developmental Model for Family Systems." *Family Process* 24(2) (June 1985):139–150.

Granvold, Donald, and Roxanne Tarrant. "Structured Marital Separation as a Marital Treatment Method." *Journal of Marital and Family Therapy* (1983).

Green, A. W. "The Middle-Class Male Child and Neurosis." *American Sociological Review* 11 (1946):31–41.

Green, Maurice, ed. *Violence and the Family*. Boulder, Colo.: Westview Press, 1980.

Greenberg, Dan, and Marsha Jacobs. *How to Make Yourself Miserable*. New York: Random House, 1966.

Greenstein, Robert. "The Bottom Line on Poverty." *Los Angeles Times*, April 29, 1984.

Greenstein, Theodore. "Occupation and Divorce." *Journal of Family Issues* 6(3) (September 1985):347–357.

Greer, Germaine. *Sex and Destiny*. New York: Harper & Row, 1984.

Greif, Geoffrey. "Children and Housework in the Single Father Family." *Family Relations* 34(3) (July 1985):353–357.

———. "Single Fathers Rearing Children." *Journal of Marriage and the Family* 47(1) (February 1985):185–191.

Greven, Philip. *The Protestant Temperament: Patterns of Child-Rearing, Religious Experience, and the Self in Early America*. New York: Knopf, 1977.

Gross, Leonard. *How Much Is Too Much?* New York: Random House, 1983.

Grosskopf, D. *Sex and the Married Woman*. New York: Wallaby, 1983.

Grossman, Allyson. "Working Mothers and Their Children." *Monthly Labor Review* 104(5) (1981):49–54. U.S. Department of Labor, Bureau of Labor Statistics.

Grossman, Frances, et al. *Pregnancy, Birth and Parenthood: Adaptations of Mothers, Fathers, and Infants*. San Francisco: Jossey-Bass, 1980.

Groth, Nicholas. *Men Who Rape: The Psychology of the Offender*. New York: Plenum Press, 1980.

Groth, Nicholas, and H. Jean Birnbaum. "Adult Sexual Orientation and Attraction to Underage Persons." *Archives of Sexual Behavior* 7(3) (May 1978):175–181.

Grover, Kelly, et al. "Mate Selection Processes and Marital Satisfaction." *Family Relations* 34(3) (July, 1985):383–386.

"Growing Numbers of Young Catholics Are Staying Single." *New York Times*. Reprinted in *San Jose Mercury*, March 10, 1985.

Gruson, Lindsey. "Groups Play Matchmaker to Preserve Judaism." *New York Times*, April 1, 1985.

Gubrium, Jaber, ed. *Late Life: Communities and Environmental Policies*. Springfield, Ill.: Thomas, 1974.

———. Special issue on Institutionalization and the Family. *Journal of Family Issues* (December 1983).

Guest, Felicia, et al. *My Body, My Health: The Concerned Woman's Guide to Gynecology*. New York: Irvington, 1979.

Guidubaldi, John. "The Status Report Extended: Further Elaborations on the American Family." *School Psychology Review* 9(4) (Fall 1980):374–379.

Guttentag, M., et al. *Mental Health of Women: Fact and Fiction*. New York: Academic Press, 1980.

Guttmacher, Alan. *The Black Family in Slavery and Freedom: 1750–1925*. New York: Harper & Row, 1976.

Haas, Linda. "Parental Sharing of Childcare Tasks in Sweden." *Journal of Family Issues* 3 (September 1982):389–412.

Haley, Alex. *Roots*. Garden City, New York: Doubleday, 1976.

Hall, G. Stanley. *Adolescence*. 2 vols. New York: Appleton's, 1909.

Hareven, Tamara. *Transitions: The Family and the Life Course in Historical Perspective*. New York: Academy Press, 1978.

Haring-Hidore, Marilyn, et al. "Marital Status and Subjective Well-being: A Research Synthesis." *Journal of Marriage and the Family* 47(4) (November 1985):947–953.

Harmon, D., and O. Brim. *Learning to be Parents: Principles, Programs, and Methods*. Beverly Hills, Calif.: Sage, 1980.

Harriman, Lynda. "Personal and Marital Changes Accompanying Parenthood." *Family Relations* 32 (July 1983):387–394.

Harris, Barbara. "Male Power and the Women's Movement." In Sue Cox, ed., *Female Psychology*. Chicago: SRA Press, 1976.

Harris, Myron. "Children as Hostages." In Stuart Irving, ed., *Children of Separation and Divorce*. New York: Grossman, 1972.

Harris, Sandra. "The Family and the Autistic Child." *Family Relations* 33(1) (January 1984):67–77.

Harry, J. "Gay Male and Lesbian Relationships." In E. Macklin and R. Ruben, eds., *Contemporary Families and Alternative Lifestyles: Handbook on Research and Theory*. Beverly Hills, Calif.: Sage, 1983.

Hass, Aaron. *Teenage Sexuality: A Survey of Teenage Sexual Behavior*. New York: Macmillan, 1979.

Hassett, J. "But That Would Be Wrong." *Psychology Today* (December 1981):34–53.

Heatherington, E. Mavis. "Divorce: A Child's Perspective." *American Psychologist* 34(10) (October 1979):851–858.

Heaton, Tim, et al. "The Timing of Divorce." *Journal of Marriage and the Family* 47(3) (August 1985):631–639.

Hechinger, Fred. "Child Care Facing Greater Scrutiny Amid New Demands." *New York Times*, February 26, 1985:19.

Heckman, N. A., et al., eds. "Problems of Professional Couples: A Content Analysis." *Journal of Marriage and the Family* 39 (1977):323–330.

Heer, D. M. "The Prevalence of Black-White Marriage in the United States, 1960 and 1970." *Journal of Marriage and the Family* 36 (1974):246–259.

Hefferan, Colleen. "Family Financial Planning—Research." *Family Economics Review* (Spring 1981):14–19.

———. "New Methods for Studying Household Production." *Family Economics Review* 3 (1982a):16–25.

———. "Workload of Married Women." *Family Economics Review* 3 (1982b):10–15.

Heffernan, Virginia. "The Model for Marriage Contracts Is Found in the Bible." In Harold Feldman and Margaret Feldman, eds., *Current Controversies in Marriage and the Family*. Beverly Hills, Calif.: Sage, 1985.

Heilbrun, Carolyn. *Toward a Recognition of Androgyny*. New York: Norton, 1982.

Heins, M. "Medicine and Motherhood." *Journal of the American Medical Association* 249 (January 14, 1983):209–210.

Helberg, June. "Documentation in Child Abuse." *American Journal of Nursing* 83(2) (February 1983):236–239.

Helfer, Ray. "Developmental Deficits Which Limit Interpersonal Skills." In Henry Kempe and Ray Helfer, eds., *The Battered Child*. Chicago: University of Chicago Press, 1980.

Helitzer, Marvin, and Carl Heyl, *The Youth Market*. New York: Media, 1970.

Hennon, Charles, and Charles Cole. "Role Strain and Stress in Split-shift Relationships." *Alternative Life Styles* 4(2) (May 1981):142–145.

Herek, Gregory. "Beyond 'Homophobia': A Social Psychological Perspective on Attitudes Toward Lesbians and Gay Men." *Journal of Homosexuality* 10(1/2) (Fall 1984):1–21.

Herndon, W. H., and J. W. Weik. *Herndon's Lincoln*. New York: Harpers, 1920.

Herold, Edward, and Leslie Way. "Oral-Genital Sexual Behavior in a Sample of University Females." *Journal of Sex Research* 19(4)

(November 1983):327–338.

Hess, Robert, and Kathleen Camara. "Post-Divorce Relationships as Mediating Factors in the Consequences of Divorce for Children." *Journal of Social Issues* 35(4) (1979):79–96.

Hessellund, H. "Masturbation and Sexual Fantasies in Married Couples." *Archives of Sexual Behavior* 5 (1976):133–147.

Hetherington, E. M., et al. "The Aftermath of Divorce." In J. J. Stevens, Jr., and M. Matthews, eds., *Mother-Child, Father-Child Relations*. Washington, D.C.: NAEYC, 1977.

———. "The Development of Children in Mother-headed Families." In David Reiss and Howard Hoffman, eds., *The American Family: Dying or Developing?* New York: Plenum Press, 1979a.

———. "Divorced Fathers." *Family Coordinator* 25 (1976):417–428.

———. "Play and Social Interaction in Children Following Divorce." *Journal of Social Issues* 35(4) (1979b):26–49.

Hicks, Mary. "Dual-Career/Dual Worker Families: A Systems Approach." In Eleanor Macklin and Roger Rubin, eds., *Contemporary Families and Alternative Lifestyles*. Beverly Hills, Calif.: Sage, 1983.

Hicks, Mary, and Marilyn Platt. "Marital Happiness and Stability: A Review of the Research in the Sixties." *Journal of Marriage and the Family* 32 (1970):553–574.

Hill, Elizabeth, and Lorraine Dorfman. "Reaction of Housewives to the Retirement of Their Husbands." *Family Coordinator* (April 1982):195–200.

Hill, Martha. "The Changing Nature of Poverty." *Annals of the American Academy of Political Science* 479 (May 1985):31–37.

Hill, Reuben. "Whither Family Research in the 1980's: Continuities, Emergents, Constraints, and New Horizons." *Journal of Marriage and the Family* 43(2) (May 1981):255–257.

Hiller, Dana, and William Philliber. "Predicting Marital and Career Success Among Dual-worker Families." *Journal of Marriage and the Family* 44 (February 1982):53–62.

Hiltz, Roxanne. "Widowhood: A Roleless Role." *Marriage and Family Review* 1(6) (November/December 1978).

Hirschman, Charles, and Marilyn Butler. "Trends and Differentials in Breast Feeding: An Update." *Demography* 18(18) (February 1981):39–54.

Hite, Shere. *The Hite Report*. New York: Macmillan, 1976.

———. *The Hite Report on Male Sexuality*. New York: Knopf, 1981.

Hodges, William, et al. "Divorce and the Preschool Child." *Journal of Divorce* 3(1) (Fall 1979):55–67.

Hoelter, J. W. "Factoral Invariance and Self-Esteem—Reassessing Race and Sex Differences." *Social Forces* 61(3) (March 1983):834–846.

Hofferith, Sandra. "Updating Children's Life Course." *Journal of Marriage and the Family* 47(1) (February 1985):93–115.

Hoffman, L. W., and J. D. Manis. "Influences of Children on Marital Interaction and Parental Satisfactions and Dissatisfactions." In R. M. Lerner and G. B. Spanier, eds., *Child Influences on Marital and Family Interaction*. New York: Academic Press, 1978.

Holmes, T., and R. Rahe. "The Social Readjustment Rating Scale." *Journal of Psychosomatic Medicine* 11 (1967):213–218.

Holmstrom, Linda. *The Two Career Family*. Cambridge, Mass.: Harvard University Press, 1972.

Hood, J., and S. Golden. "Beating Time/Making Time: The Impact of Work Scheduling on Men's Family Roles." *Family Coordinator*

28 (October 1979):572–582.

Hook, Ernest. "Spontaneous Deaths of Fetuses with Chromosomal Abnormalities Diagnosed Prenatally." *New England Journal of Medicine* 299(19) (November 9, 1978):1036–1038.

Horner, M. "Femininity and Successful Achievement: A Basic Inconsistency." In Judith Bardwick et al., eds., *Feminine Personality and Conflict*. Belmont, Calif.: Wadsworth, 1970.

Houseknecht, Sharon. "Achievement of Women Outside the Home is the Phantom Factor in Marital Breakdown." In Harold Feldman and Margaret Feldman, eds., *Current Controversies in Marriage and the Family*. Beverly Hills, Calif.: Sage, 1985.

———. "Childlessness and Marital Adjustment." In Jeffry Rosenfeld, ed., *Relationships: The Marriage and Family Reader*. Glencoe, Ill.: Scott, Foresman, 1982.

———. "Some Promising Research Developments in the Area of Nonnormative Family Sizes." *Journal of Family Issues* 3(4) (December 1982):419–430.

———. "Voluntary Childlessness: Toward a Theoretical Integration." *Journal of Family Issues* 3(4) (December 1982):459–471.

———, ed. "Childlessness and One-Child Families." Special issue, *Journal of Family Issues* (December 1982).

"How Much Drinking Is Safe During Pregnancy?" *American Journal of Nursing* 85(20) (February 1985):175.

"How to Judge Money-Market Funds." *Consumer Reports* (January 1983):30–34.

Howard, Elizabeth. "Overcoming Rape Trauma." *Ms.* (November 1980):35.

Howell, Mary. *Helping Ourselves: Families and the Human Network*. Boston: Beacon Press, 1975.

Hunt, Morton. *The Divorce Experience*. New York: World, 1978.

———. *Sexual Behavior in the 1970's*. Chicago: Playboy Press, 1974.

Hunt, Morton, and Beatrice Hunt. *The Divorce Experience*. New York: McGraw-Hill, 1977.

Huston, Ted, and Elliot Robins. "Conceptual and Methodological Issues in Studying Close Relationships." *Journal of Marriage and the Family* 44(4) (November 1982):901–926.

Indvik, Julie, and Mary Fitzpatrick. " 'If You Could Read My Mind, Love...,': Understanding and Misunderstanding in the Marital Dyad." *Family Relations* 31 (January 1982):43–51.

Irving, Howard, et al. "Shared Parenting: An Empirical Analysis Utilizing a Large Data Base." *Family Process* 23 (1984):561–569.

Istvan, Joseph, and William Griffith. "Effects of Sexual Experience on Dating Desirability and Marriage Desirability." *Journal of Marriage and the Family* 42 (May 1980):377–385.

JAMA. See *Journal of the American Medical Association*.

Jacoby, Arthur, and John Williams. "Effects of Premarital Sexual Standards and Behavior on Dating and Marriage Desirability." *Journal of Marriage and the Family* 47(4) (November 1985):1059–1065.

Jacques, Jeffrey, and Karen Chason. "Cohabitation: Its Impact on Marital Success." *Family Coordinator* 28(1) (1979):35–39.

Jeffords, Charles, and R. Thomas Dull. "Demographic Variations in Attitudes Toward Marital Rape Immunity." *Journal of Marriage and the Family* 44(3) (August 1982):755–762.

Jeffrey, Kirk. "The Family as Utopian Retreat from the City." *Soundings* 55 (1972):21–41.

Jelliffe, Derrick, and E. F. Patrice Jelliffe. *Human Milk in the Modern World*. New York: Oxford University Press, 1978.

Jencks, Christopher. "Divorced Mothers Unite!" *Psychology Today* 16(11) (November 1982):73–75.

Jenkins, C. "Psychological and Social Precursors of Coronary Heart Disease." *New England Journal of Medicine* 284 (1971):244–255.

Jennings-Walstedt, Joyce, et al. "Influence of Television Commercials on Women's Self-confidence and Independent Judgment." *Journal of Personality and Social Psychology* 38(2) (February 1980):203–210.

Jensen, Michael. "Adolescent Suicide: A Tragedy of Our Times." *Family Life Educator* (Summer 1984).

Jeter, Kris, and Marvin Sussman. "Each Couple Should Develop a Marriage Contract Suitable to Themselves." In Harold Feldman and Margaret Feldman, eds., *Current Controversies in Marriage and the Family*. Beverly Hills, Calif.: Sage, 1985.

Johnson, Beverly. "Single Parent Families." *Family Economics Review* (Summer–Fall, 1980):22–27.

Johnson, Carolyn, and Sharon Price-Bonham. "Women and Retirement: A Study and Implications." *Family Relations* (July 1980): 381–385.

Johnson, G. Timothy, and Stephen Goldfinger, eds. *The Harvard Medical School Health Letter Book*. Cambridge, Mass.: Harvard University Press, 1981.

Johnson, Sharon. "In Broken Families, Paying for College." *New York Times*, August 1, 1985.

Johnston, Lloyd. *Drugs and American Youth*. Ann Arbor, Mich.: University of Michigan Institute for Drug Research, 1973.

Jones, Jacqueline. *Labor of Love, Labor of Sorrow: Black Women, Work, and the Family from Slave to the Present*. New York: Basic Books, 1985.

Jones, Landon. *Great Expectations: America and the Baby Boom Generation*. New York: Coward, McCann, and Geoghegan, 1980.

Jong, Erica. *Fear of Flying*. New York: Holt, Rinehart, 1975.

Jorgensen, Stephen R., and J. C. Gaudy. "Self-disclosure and Satisfaction in Marriage: The Relation Examined." *Family Relations* 29(3) (1980):281–287.

Jorgensen, S. R., and A. C. Johnson. "Correlates of Divorce Liberality." *Journal of Marriage and the Family* 42 (1980):617–622.

Jourard, Sidney. *The Transparent Self*. New York: Van Nostrand, 1964.

Julian, Valerie, and Cynthia Mohr. "Father-Daughter Incest: Profile of the Offender." *Victimology* 4 (1979):348–360.

Justice, Blair, and Rita Justice. *The Broken Taboo: Incest*. New York: Human Sciences Press, 1979.

Kach, Julie, and Paul McGee. "Adjustment to Early Parenthood." *Journal of Family Issues* 3(3) (September 1982):375–388.

Kagan, Jerome. *The Growth of the Child*. New York: Norton, 1978.

———. *The Nature of the Child*. New York: Basic Books, 1984.

———. "The Child in the Family." *Daedalus* (Spring 1977):33–56.

———. "The Psychological Requirements for Human Development." In Nathan Talbot, ed., *Raising Children in Modern America*. Boston: Little, Brown, 1976.

Kagan, Jerome, and Robert Coles, eds. *Twelve to Sixteen: Early Adolescence*. New York: Norton, 1972.

Kalish, Richard. "Death and Survivorship: The Final Transition."

Annals of the American Academy of Political and Social Science 464 (November 1982):163–173.

Kalmuss, Debra. "The Intergenerational Transmission of Marital Aggression." *Journal of Marriage and the Family* 46(1) (February 1984):11–20.

Kalmuss, Debra, and Murray Straus. "Feminist, Political, and Economic Determinants of Wife Abuse Services." In David Finkelhor et al., eds., *The Dark Side of Families.* Beverly Hills, Calif.: Sage, 1983.

———. "Wife's Marital Dependency and Wife Abuse." *Journal of Marriage and the Family* 44(2) (May 1982):277–286.

Kanter, R. *Work and Family in the United States: A Critical Review and Agenda for Research and Policy.* New York: Russell Sage, 1977.

Kanter, Rosabeth. "Why Bosses Turn Bitchy." *Psychology Today* 9(12) (May 1976):56–59.

Kantor, David, and William Lehr. *Inside Families.* San Francisco, Calif.: Jossey-Bass, 1975.

Kaplan, Helen Singer. *Disorders of Desire.* New York: Simon & Schuster, 1979.

———. *The New Sex Therapy.* New York: Bruner/Mazel, 1974.

Karlen, Neal, "Homeless Kids: Forgotten Faces." *Newsweek.* (January 6, 1986):20.

Kasl, Stanislav. "Changes in Mental Health Status Associated with Job Loss and Retirement." In James E. Barrett, et al., eds., *Stress and Mental Disorder.* New York: Raven, 1979.

Katz, Alvin, and Reuben Hill. "Residential Propinquity and Marital Selection: A Review of Theory, Method, and Fact." *Marriage and Family Living* 20 (February 1958):27–35.

Kaye, Celia. "Genetic Counselling." *Medical Aspects of Human Sexuality* 15(3) (March 1981):164–180.

Kaye, Kenneth. *Family Rules.* Walker, 1984.

Keith, Pat, et al. "Older Men in Employed and Retired Families." *Alternative Lifestyles* 4(2) (May 1981):228–241.

Kelley, Robert. "The Family and the Urban Underclass: An Integrative Framework." *Journal of Family Issues* 6 (June 1985):159–184.

Kelley, Robert, and Patricia Voydanoff. "Work/Family Role Strain Among Employed Parents." *Family Relations* 34(3) (July 1985):367–374.

Kelly, Susan. "Changing Parent-Child Relationships: An Outcome of Mother Returning to College." *Family Relations* 31 (April 1982):287–294.

Kempe, C. Henry, and Ray Helfer, eds. *The Battered Child.* Chicago: University of Chicago Press, 1980.

Kempe, C. Henry, et al. "The Battered Child." *Journal of the American Medical Association* (July 7, 1962).

Kempler, Hyman. "Extended Kinship Ties and Some Modern Alternatives." *Family Coordinator* (April 1976):143–149.

Keniston, Kenneth. "The Future of the American Family." *Parents* (August 1978):38–40.

Kennedy, David. *Birth Control in America.* New Haven: Yale University Press, 1970.

Kennedy, Donald. "Why Adoptions Get Harder Every Year." *U.S. News and World Report* (September 20, 1982).

Keppel, Bruce. "Sexual Segregation Prevails in Business." *Los Angeles Times,* August 22, 1982:VI:3ff.

Keshet, Jamie. "From Separation to Stepfamily." *Journal of Family Issues* 1(4) (December 1980):517–532.

Kessler-Harris, Alice. *A History of Wage-earning Women in America.*

New York: Oxford University Press, 1982.

———. *Women Have Always Worked: A Historical Overview.* New York: McGraw-Hill, 1981.

Kett, Joseph. *Rites of Passage: Adolescence in America, 1790 to the Present.* New York: Basic Books, 1977.

Kilpatrick, Allie. "Job Change in Dual-Career Families: Danger or Opportunity?" *Family Relations* 31 (July 1982):363–368.

Kingston, Paul, and Stephen Nock. "Consequences of the Family Work Day." *Journal of Marriage and the Family* 47(3) (August 1985):619–629.

Kinsey, Alfred, et al. *Sexual Behavior in the Human Female.* Philadelphia: Saunders, 1953.

———, et al. *Sexual Behavior in the Human Male.* Philadelphia: Saunders, 1948.

Kitson, Gay, and Marvin Sussman. "Marital Complaints, Demographic Characteristics, and Symptoms of Mental Distress in Divorce." *Journal of Marriage and the Family* 44(1) (1982):87–101.

Kitson, Gay, et al. "Sampling Issues in Family Research." *Journal of Marriage and the Family* 44(4) (November 1982):965–981.

Kitzinger, Sheila. *The Experience of Childbirth.* Baltimore: Penguin Books, 1974.

———. *Women As Mothers: How They See Themselves in Different Cultures.* New York: Vintage Books, 1979.

Klagsbrun, Francine. *Too Young to Die.* New York: Pocket Books, 1981.

Klein, Carole. *How It Feels to Be a Child.* New York: Harper Colophon Books, 1977.

Klein, David, and William Smith. "Historical Trends in the Marriage and Family Textbook Literature." *Family Relations* 34 (April 1985):211–219.

Klemmack, David, and Lucinda Roth. "Heterosexual Alternatives to Marriage: Appropriateness for Older Persons." *Alternative Lifestyles* 3(2) (May 1980):137–148.

Klemsrud, Judy. "Mothers Who Shift Back From Jobs to Homemaking." *New York Times,* January 19, 1983:13,16.

Klinman, Deborah, and Carol Vukelich. "Mothers and Fathers: Expectations for Infants." *Family Relations* 34(3) (July 1985):305–313.

Klinman, Deborah, et al. *Fatherhood, USA: The First National Guide to Programs, Services, and Resources for and about Fathers.* New York: Garland Publishing Co., 1984.

Knapp, Mark, et al. "Compliments: A Descriptive Taxonomy." *Journal of Communication* 34(4) (Autumn 1984):12–31.

Knitzer, Jane. "Children's Rights in the Family and Society: Dilemmas and Realities." *American Journal of Orthopsychiatry* 52(3) (July 1982):481–495.

Knox, David. *Choices in Relationships.* St. Paul, Minn.: West, 1985.

Knox, Melvin. "Social Class and Parental Values." *American Journal of Sociology* 64 (1959):337–351.

Knox, Richard. "A Lonely Heart Can Hurt Health." *Los Angeles Times,* February 14, 1982:VI:23.

Kohen, J. A., et al. "Divorced Mothers: The Costs and Benefits of Female Family Control." In G. Levinger and O. C. Moles, eds., *Separation and Divorce.* New York: Basic Books, 1979.

Kohlberg, Lawrence. "The Cognitive-Development Approach to Socialization." In A. Goslin, ed., *Handbook of Socialization Theory and Research.* Chicago: Rand McNally, 1969.

———. "Stage and Sequence: The Cognitive-Developmental Approach to Socialization." In D. A. Goslin, ed., *Handbook of Socialization Theory and Practice*. Chicago: Rand McNally, 1969.

Kolata, Gina. "Early Warnings and Latent Cures for Infertility." *Ms.* (May 1979):86–89.

Kolodny, Robert, et al. *Textbook of Sexual Medicine*. Boston: Little, Brown, 1979.

Komarovsky, Mirra. *Blue-Collar Marriage*. New York: Vintage Books, 1967.

———. *Dilemmas of Masculinity: A Study of College Youth*. New York: Norton, 1976.

———. *Women in College*. New York: Basic Books, 1985.

———. "Cultural Contradictions and Sex Roles: The Masculine Case." *American Journal of Sociology* (January 1973):873–884.

Koo, Helen, and C. M. Suchindran. "Effects of Children on Women's Remarriage Prospects." *Journal of Family Issues* 1(4) (December 1980):497–515.

Korbin, Jill, ed. *Child Abuse and Neglect: Cross-Cultural Perspectives*. Berkeley: University of California Press, 1981.

Korpivaara, Ari. "Can Sex Survive AIDS?" *Playboy* (February 1986):48–49.

Kretchmer, Arthur. "Can Sex Survive AIDS?" *Playboy* (February 1986):48–49.

Krimmel, Herman. "The Alcoholic and His Family." In Peter Bourne and Ruth Fox, eds., *Alcoholism: Progress in Research and Treatment*. New York: Academic Press, 1973.

Krogh, Kathryn. "Women's Motives to Achieve and Nurture in Different Life Stages." *Sex Roles* 12(1/2):75–84.

Kubler-Ross, Elisabeth. *On Death and Dying*. New York: Macmillan, 1969.

———. *Working it Through*. New York: Macmillan, 1982.

Kupersmid, Joel, and Donald Wonderly. "Moral Maturity and Behavior: Failure to Find a Link." *Journal of Youth and Adolescence* 9 (June 1980):249–261.

Kurdek, Lawrence, and Albert Siesky. "Children's Perceptions of their Parents' Divorce." *Journal of Divorce* 3(4) (Summer 1980):339–378.

———. "An Interview Study of Parents' Perceptions of Their Children's Reactions and Adjustments to Divorce." *Journal of Divorce* 3(1) (Fall 1979):5–17.

Kurdek, Lawrence, et al. "Correlates of Children's Long-Term Adjustment to Their Parents' Divorce." *Developmental Psychology* 17(5) (September 1981):565–579.

LaRossa, Ralph, and Jane Wolf. "On Qualitative Family Research." *Journal of Marriage and the Family* 47(3) (August 1985):531–541.

Laing, R. D. *The Politics of Experience*. New York: Random House, 1967.

———. *The Politics of the Family and Other Essays*. New York: Random House, 1972.

———. *Self and Others*. Baltimore, Md.: Penguin Books, 1969.

Lainson, Suzanne. "Breast-Feeding: The Erotic Factor." *Ms.* 11(8) (February 1983):66ff.

Lamaze, Fernand. *Painless Childbirth*. Chicago: H. Regnery, 1970; 1956.

Lamb, Michael. "Why Swedish Fathers Aren't Liberated." *Psychology Today* 16(10) (October 1982):74–77.

Landau, Erika, and Benjamin Maoz. "Continuity of Self-Actualization: Womanhood in the Climacterium and Old Age." In Ruth

Weg, ed., *Sexuality in the Later Years: Roles and Behavior*. New York: Academic Press, 1983.

Langdon, Philip. "Design Notebook." *New York Times*, January 6, 1983:24.

Langway, Lynn, et al. "Unveiling a Family Secret." *Newsweek* (February 18, 1980):104.

Lantz, Herman. "Family and Kin as Revealed in the Narratives of Ex-Slaves." *Social Science Quarterly* 60(4) (March 1980):667–674.

———. "Romantic Love in the Premodern Period." *Journal of Social History* 15(3) (Spring 1982):349–370.

Larkin, Ralph. *Suburban Youth in Cultural Crisis*. New York: Oxford University Press, 1979.

Lasch, Christopher. *Haven in a Heartless World*. New York: Harper Colphon Books, 1978.

Laufer, Robert, and M. S. Gallops. "Life-course Effects of Vietnam Combat and Abusive Violence: Marital Patterns." *Journal of Marriage and the Family* 47(4) (November 1985):839–853.

Lawrence, D. H. *Women in Love*. New York: Penguin Books, 1950.

Lawson, Carol. "Women in State Jobs Gain in Pay Equity." *New York Times*, May 20, 1985.

LeMasters, E. E. *Blue-Collar Aristocrats: Lifestyles at a Working-Class Tavern*. Madison, WI.: University of Wisconsin Press, 1975.

———. *Parents in Modern America*. Homewood, Ill.: Dorsey Press, 1974.

Leach, Barry. "Does Alcoholics Anonymous Really Work?" In Peter Bourne and Ruth Fox, eds., *Alcoholism: Progress in Research and Treatment*. New York: Academic Press, 1973.

Leboyer, Frederic. *Birth Without Violence*. New York: Knopf, 1975.

Lederer, William, and Don Jackson. *Mirages of Marriage*. New York: Norton, 1968.

Lee, Gary. "Effects of Social Networks on the Family." In Wesley Burr, ed., *Contemporary Theories of the Family*. 2 vols. New York: Free Press, 1979.

Lee, John. *The Colors of Love*. Toronto, Canada: New Press, 1973.

Leites, Edmund. "The Duty to Desire: Love, Friendship, and Sexuality in Some Puritan Theories of Marriage." *Journal of Social History* 15(3) (Spring 1982):383–408.

Leo, Jacqueline. *The New Woman's Guide to Getting Married*. New York: Bantam, 1982.

Leo, John. "Lessons in Bringing Up Baby." *Time* (October 22, 1984):97.

———. "Polling for Mental Health." *Time* (October 15, 1984):80.

Lerner, Richard M., and Graham Spanier, eds. *Child Influences on Marital and Family Interaction*. New York: Academic Press, 1978.

Leslie, Gerald. *The Family in Social Context*. New York: Oxford University Press, 1976.

Leslie, Leigh, and Katherine Grady. "Changes in Mothers' Social Networks and Social Support Following Divorce." *Journal of Marriage and the Family* 47(3) (August 1985):663–673.

Levi-Strauss, Claude. "The Family." In Harry Shapiro, ed., *Man, Culture, and Society*. New York: Oxford University Press, 1956.

———. "Reciprocity: The Essence of Social Life." In Lewis Coser and Bernard Rosenberg, eds., *Sociological Theory*. New York: Macmillan, 1957.

Levine, Linda, and Lonnie Barbach. *The Intimate Male*. New York: Signet Books, 1985.

Levine, Martin. "The Sociology of Male Homosexuality and Lesbianism: An Introductory (Annotated) Bibliography." *Journal of*

Homosexuality 5(3) (Spring 1980):249–275.

Levinger, George. "Marital Cohesiveness and Dissolution: An Integrative Review." *Journal of Marriage and the Family* 27 (1965):19–28.

———. "A Social Psychological Perspective on Marital Dissolution." In George Levinger and O. C. Moles, eds., *Divorce and Separation: Context, Causes, and Consequences.* New York: Basic Books, 1979.

———. "Sources of Marital Dissatisfaction Among Applicants for Divorce." *American Journal of Orthopsychiatry* 36 (October 1966):803–807.

Levinger, George, and O. C. Moles, eds. *Divorce and Separation: Context, Causes, and Consequences.* New York: Basic Books, 1979.

Levinson, Arnold. "Home Birth: Joy or Jeopardy?" *Medical Self-Care* (Fall 1980):42–46.

Levinson, Daniel J. *The Seasons of a Man's Life.* New York: Ballantine Books, 1977.

Levitan, Sar, and R. Belows. *What's Happening to the American Family.* Baltimore: Johns Hopkins University Press, 1981.

Lewin, Bo. "Unmarried Cohabitation: A Marriage Form in a Changing Society." *Journal of Marriage and the Family* 44(3) (August 1982):763–773.

Lewis, Jerry M. *How's Your Family? A Guide to Identifying Your Family's Strengths and Weaknesses.* New York: Brunner/Mazel, 1979.

Lewis, Jerry M., et al. *No Single Thread.* New York: Brunner/Mazel, 1976.

Lewis, R. A., and B. Berns. *Three Out of Four Wives: Widowhood in America.* New York: Macmillan, 1975.

Lewis, Robert, et al. "Commitment in Same-Sex Love Relationships." *Alternative Lifestyles* 4(1) (February 1981):22–42.

Licata, Salvatore, and Robert Peterson, eds. *Historical Perspectives on Homosexuality.* New York: Haworth Press, 1982.

Liem, Ramsay, and J. Liem. "Social Support and Stress: Some General Issues and Their Application to the Problem of Unemployment." In L. Ferman and J. Gordus, eds., *Mental Health and the Economy.* Kalamazoo, Mich.: Upjohn Institute, 1979.

Liem, Ramsay, and Paula Rayman. "Health and Social Costs of Unemployment." *American Psychologist* 37(10) (October 1982):1116–1123.

Lifton, Betty Jean. *Lost and Found.* New York: Dial Press, 1979.

———. *Twice Born.* New York: McGraw-Hill, 1975.

Lindsey, Karen. *Friends as Family.* Boston: Beacon Press, 1982.

Lingren, Herbert, et al. "Enhancing Marriage and Family Competencies through Adult Life Development." In Nick Stinnet et al., eds., *Family Strengths 4: Positive Support Systems.* Lincoln: University of Nebraska Press, 1982.

Lipkin, Mack, and Gerri Lamb. "The Couvade Syndrome: An Epidemiologic Study." *Annals of Internal Medicine* 96(4) (April 1982):509–511.

Lipnack, Jessica, and Jeffrey Stamps. *Networking: People Connecting with People, Linking Ideas and Resources.* New York: Doubleday, 1982.

Loevinger, Jane. "Patterns of Child Rearing as Theories of Learning." *Journal of Abnormal and Social Psychology* 59 (1959):148–150.

Lombardo, W. K., et al. "Fer Cryin' Out Loud—There Is a Sex Difference." *Sex Roles* 9 (1983):987–995.

Lopata, Helena. *Occupation: Housewife.* New York: Oxford University Press, 1972.

———. *Women As Widows: Support Systems.* New York: Elsevier, 1979.

———. "Contributions of Extended Families to the Support Systems of Metropolitan Area Widows: Limitations of the Modified Kin Network." *Journal of Marriage and the Family* 40(2) (May 1978):355–364.

———. "Couple-Companionate Relationships in Marriage." In Nona Glazer-Malbin, ed., *Old Family, New Family.* New York: Van Nostrand, 1975.

———, ed. *Widowhood in an American City.* Cambridge, Mass.: Schenkman, 1973.

Luker, Kristin. *Taking Chances.* Berkeley: University of California Press, 1975.

Lunde, Donald. *Murder and Madness.* San Francisco: San Francisco Book Co., 1976.

Luria, Zella. "Psychosocial Determinants of Gender Identity, Role, and Orientation." In Herant Katchadourian, ed., *Human Sexuality: A Comparative and Developmental Perspective.* Berkeley: University of California Press, 1979.

Lurie, G. E. "Sex and Stage Differences in Perceptions of Marital and Family Relationships." *Journal of Marriage and the Family* 36 (May 1974):209–269.

Lustig, Noel, et al. "Incest: A Family Group Survival Program." *Archives of General Psychiatry* 14(1) (1966):31–40.

Lynch, James. *The Broken Heart: The Medical Consequences of Loneliness.* New York: Basic Books, 1977.

MacCorquodale, Patricia, and John DeLameter. "Self-Image and Premarital Sexuality." *Journal of Marriage and the Family* (May 1979):327–339.

Maccoby, Eleanor, and Carol Jacklin. *The Psychology of Sex Differences.* Stanford, Calif.: Stanford University Press, 1974.

Mace, David, and Vera Mace. "Enriching Marriage." In Nick Stinnet, et al., eds., *Family Strengths.* Lincoln: University of Nebraska Press, 1979.

———. "Enriching Marriages: The Foundation Stone of Family Strength." In Nick Stinnet, et al., *Family Strengths: Positive Models for Family Life.* Lincoln: University of Nebraska Press, 1980.

———. "Lifetime Monogamy Is the Preferred Form of Marital Relationship." In Harold Feldman and Margaret Feldman, eds., *Current Controversies in Marriage and the Family.* Beverly Hills, Calif.: Sage, 1985.

Macklin, Eleanor. "Heterosexual Cohabitation Among Unmarried College Students." *Family Coordinator* 21 (1972):463–472.

———. "Nonmarital Heterosexual Cohabitation." *Marriage and Family Review* 1 (March/April 1978):1–12.

———. "Non-traditional Family Forms: A Decade of Research." *Journal of Marriage and the Family* 42 (1980):175–192.

Macklin, Eleanor, and Roger Rubin, eds. *Contemporary Families and Alternative Lifestyles: Handbook on Research and Theory.* Beverly Hills, Calif.: Sage, 1983.

Madison, Arnold. *Suicide and Young People.* New York: Clarion Books, 1978.

Magnuson, Ed. "Child Abuse: The Ultimate Betrayal." *Time* (September 5, 1983):23–26.

Makepeace, James. "Courtship Violence Among College Students." *Family Relations* 30(1) (January 1981):97–102.

Mander, Jerry. *Four Arguments for the Elimination of Television.* New York: Morrow, 1978.

Maneker, Jerry, and Robert Rankin. "Education, Age at Marriage, and Marital Duration: Is There a Relationship." *Journal of Marriage and the Family* 47(3) (August 1985):675–683.

Marano, Cynthia, et al. "Displaced Homemakers: Critical Needs and Trends." *Family Economics Review* (Summer/Fall 1980):17–21.

Marciano, Teresa Donati. "Homosexual Marriage and Parenthood Should Not Be Allowed." In Harold Feldman and Margaret Feldman, eds., *Current Controversies in Marriage and the Family.* Beverly Hills, Calif.: Sage, 1985.

Maret, Elizabeth, and Barbara Finlay. "The Distribution of Household Labor Among Women in Dual-earner Families." *Journal of Marriage and the Family* 46(2) (May 1984):357–364.

Margolis, Maxine. *Mothers and Such: Views of American Women and Why They Changed.* Berkeley, Calif.: University of California Press, 1984.

Marmor, Judd, ed. *Homosexual Behavior.* New York: Basic Books, 1980.

Marshner, Connaught. "Once Conceived, A Child Has the Right To Be Born." In Harold Feldman and Margaret Feldman, eds., *Current Controversies in Marriage and the Family.* Beverly Hills, Calif.: Sage, 1985.

Martin, Del. *Battered Wives.* San Francisco: New Glide, 1981.

Martin, Michael, and James Walters. "Familial Correlates of Selected Types of Child Abuse and Neglect." *Journal of Marriage and the Family* 44(2) (May 1982):267–276.

Marzollo, Jean. "My Pistol-Packing Kids." *Parents* 58(1) (January 1983):53–55.

Maslow, Abraham. *Toward a Psychology of Being.* New York: Van Nostrand, 1968.

Masnick, George, and Mary Jo Bane. *The Nation's Families: 1960–1990.* Cambridge: Harvard University Press, 1980.

Mason, M. L. *Human Sexuality: A Bibliography and Critical Evaluation of Recent Texts.* Westport, CT: Greenwood Press, 1983.

Masters, William, and Virginia Johnson. *Homosexuality in Perspective.* Boston: Little, Brown, 1979.

———. *Human Sexual Inadequacy.* Boston: Little, Brown, 1970.

———. *Human Sexual Response.* Boston: Little, Brown, 1966.

Matthaei, Julie. *An Economic History of Women in America.* New York; Schocken Books, 1982.

Mauk, Susan. "Breast-Feeding and Work." *Working Woman* 9(4) (April 1984):43–44.

Mazor, Miriam. "Barren Couples." *Psychology Today* 12(12) (May 1979):101–108, 112.

McBee, Susanna. "Heroes Are Back." *U.S. News and World Report* (April 22, 1985):44–48.

McCormick, Naomi, and Clint Jesser. "The Courtship Game: Power in Sexual Encounters." In Elizabeth Allgeier, ed., *Sex Roles and Sexual Behavior.* Palo Alto, Calif.: Mayfield, 1982.

McCormick, Naomi, et al. "Social Desirability in the Bedroom: Role of Approval Motivation in Sexual Relationships." *Sex Roles* 11(3/4) (1984):303–314.

McGhee, P. E., and T. Frueth. "Television Viewing and the Learning of Sex-Role Stereotypes." *Sex Roles* 6 (1980):179–188.

McGoldrich, Monica, and Elizabeth Carter. "The Family Life Cycle." In Froma Walsh, ed., *Normal Family Processes.* New York: Guilford Press, 1982.

———. "Forming a Remarried Family." In E. Carter and M. McGoldrich, eds., *The Family Life Cycle.* New York: Garner Press, 1980.

McGuire, L., and N. Wagner. "Sexual Dysfunction in Women who Were Molested as Children." *Sex and Marriage* 4(1) (1978):11–15.

McIntyre, Jennie. "The Structural-Functional Approach to Family Study." In F. Ivan Nye, and Felix Berardo, eds., *Emerging Conceptual Frameworks in Family Analysis.* New York: Praeger, 1981, 2/e.

McLanahan, Sara, et al. "Network Structure, Social Support, and Psychological Well-Being." *Journal of Marriage and the Family* 43 (August 1981):601–612.

McLoughlin, David, and Richard Whitfield. "Adolescents and Their Experience of Parental Divorce." *Journal of Adolescence* 7 (1984):155–170.

McNab, Warren. "Advocating Elementary Sex Education." *Health Education* 12(5) (September/October 1981):22–25.

McNamara, Mary, and Howard Bahr. "The Dimensionality of Marital Role Satisfaction." *Journal of Marriage and the Family* 42(1) (February 1980):45–55.

Mead, Margaret. *Male and Female.* New York: Morrow, 1948, 1968.

———. "Jealousy: Primitive and Civilised." In S. D. Schmalhausen and V. F. Calverton, eds., *Woman's Coming of Age.* New York: Liveright, 1931.

Meckel, Richard. "Childhood and the Historians: A Review Essay." *Journal of Family History* 9(4) (Winter 1984):415–424.

Mehl, Louis. "Research on Alternatives in Childbirth: What Can It Tell Us About Hospital Practice?" *Twenty-first Century Obstetrics Now!* New York: NAPSAC, 1977.

Mehren, Elizabeth. "A Real Man: He's a Put-On Who's Starting to Take Off." *Los Angeles Times,* May 4, 1982:V:1, 8.

Meiselman, Karen. *Incest.* San Francisco: Jossey-Bass, 1978.

Melichar, Joseph, and David Chiriboga. "Timetables in the Divorce Process." *Journal of Marriage and the Family* 47(3) (August 1985):701–708.

Melito, Richard. "Adaptation in Family Systems: A Developmental Perspective." *Family Processes* 24 (1985):89–100.

Melody, William. *Children's Television: The Economics of Exploitation.* New Haven: Yale University Press, 1973.

Melton, Gary. "Children's Rights: Where Are the Children?" *American Journal of Orthopsychiatry* 52(3) (July 1982):530–538.

Menaghan, Elizabeth. "Depressive Affect and Subsequent Divorce." *Journal of Family Issues* 6(3) (September 1985):295–306.

Menard, Russell. "The Maryland Slave Population, 1658 to 1730." *William and Mary Quarterly* 32 (January 1975):29–54.

Menning, Barbara. *Infertility: A Guide for Childless Couples.* Englewood Cliffs, N.J.: Prentice-Hall, 1977.

Merkel, William, and John Rudisill. "Educational Strategies for Teaching Basic Family Dynamics to Non-Family Therapists." *Family Relations* 34(3) (July 1985):393–399.

Meyers-Walls, Judith. "Balancing Multiple Role Responsibilities During the Transition to Parenthood." *Family Relations* 33 (April 1984):267–271.

Miller, Brent C., and D. L. Sollie. "Normal Stresses During the Transition to Parenthood." *Family Relations* 29 (1980):459–466.

Miller, Brent C., et al. "On Methods of Studying Marriages and Families." *Journal of Marriage and the Family* 44 (November 1982):851–873.

Miller, I. W., and W. H. Norman. "Learned Helplessness in Humans: A Review and Attribution Theory Model." *Psychological Bulletin* 86 (1979):93–118.

Miller, Jean B. "Psychological Recovery in Low-Income Single Parents." *American Journal of Orthopsychiatry* 52(2) (April 1982):346–352.

Miller, John. *The First Frontier.* New York: Dell, 1966, 1975.

Miller, S. M. "The American Lower Classes." In Paul H. Glasser and Lois Glasser, eds., *Families in Crisis.* New York: Harper & Row, 1970.

Miller, Warren. "Psychological Vulnerability to Unwanted Pregnancy." In Frank Furstenberg, et al., eds., *Teenage Sexuality, Pregnancy, and Childbearing.* Philadelphia: University of Pennsylvania Press, 1981.

Minuchin, Salvadore. *Families and Family Therapy.* Cambridge, Mass.: Harvard University Press, 1974.

———. *The Family Kaleidoscope.* Cambridge, Mass.: Harvard University Press, 1984.

———. *Family Therapy Techniques.* Cambridge, Mass.: Harvard University Press, 1981.

Modell, John, and Tamara Hareven. "Urbanization and the Malleable Household: An Examination of Boarding and Lodging in American Families." *Journal of Marriage and the Family* 35 (August 1973):467–479.

Moen, P. "Unemployment, Public Policy, and Families: Forecasts for the 1980's." *Journal of Marriage and the Family* (November 1983):751–760.

Mohr, James. *Abortion in America: The Origin and Evolution of National Policy, 1800–1900.* New York: Oxford University Press, 1978.

Monahan, Thomas. "Are Interracial Marriages Really Less Stable?" *Social Forces* 48 (1970):461–473.

Money, John. *Love and Lovesickness.* Baltimore: Johns Hopkins University Press, 1980.

Montagu, Ashley. *Touching.* New York: Columbia University Press, 1971.

Montgomery, Jason. *Family Crisis as Process.* Washington, D.C.: University Press of America, 1981.

Moody, Kate. *Growing Up on Television.* New York: Times Books, 1980.

Moore, Kristin, and Isabel Sawhill. "Implications of Women's Employment for Home and Family Life." In Juanita Kreps, ed., *Women and the American Economy.* Englewood Cliffs, N.J.: Prentice-Hall, 1976.

"More Alcohol, Less Milk in U.S. Consumers' Diet." *New York Times,* November 27, 1984.

Morgan, Edmund. *The Puritan Family.* New York: Harper & Row, 1966; 1st ed., 1944.

———. *Viginians at Home.* Williamsburg, Va.: Colonial Williamsburg Foundation, 1956.

Mosher, Donald. "Sex Guilt and Sex Myths in College Men and Women." *Journal of Sex Research* 15(3) (August 1979):224–234.

Mosher, William, and Christine Bachrach. "Childlessness in the United States: Estimates from the National Survey of Family Growth." *Journal of Family Issues* 3(4) (December 1982):517–544.

Mott, P. E., et al. *Shift Work: The Social, Psychological, and Physical Consequences.* Ann Arbor, Mich.: University of Michigan Press, 1975.

Murdock, George. *Social Structure.* New York: Free Press, 1965; 1st ed., 1949.

———. "World Ethnographic Sample." *American Anthropologist* 59 (1957):664–687.

Musetto, Andrew. "Standards for Deciding Contested Child Custody." *Journal of Clinical Child Psychology* 10(1) (Spring 1981):51–55.

Myers, J. K., et al. "Six-Month Prevalence of Psychiatric Disorders in Three Communities." *Archives of General Psychiatry* 41(10) (October 1984):954–970.

Nace, Edgar, et al. "Treatment Priorities in a Family-Oriented Alcoholism Program." *Journal of Marital and Family Therapy,* January 1982:143–150.

Napier, Augustus, and Carl Whitaker. *The Family Crucible.* New York: Harper & Row, 1978.

Nasaw, David. *Children of the City: At Work and Play.* New York: Basic Books, 1985.

National Committee for the Prevention of Child Abuse. "Prevent Child Abuse." Chicago, 1976.

National Institute of Mental Health. *Television and Behavior: Ten Years of Scientific Progress and Implications for the Eighties.* Washington, D.C.: Government Printing Office, 1982.

Nelson, Bryce. "Etan Patz Case Puts New Focus on a Sexual Disorder, Pedophilia." *New York Times,* January 4, 1983.

Nelson, Margaret, and Gordon Nelson. "Problems of Equity in the Reconstituted Family: A Social Exchange Analysis." *Family Relations* 31 (April 1982):223–231.

"Neonatal Herpes Is Preventable." *USA Today,* 112, February 1984:8–9.

Neugarten, Bernice. "Personality and the Aging Process." *Gerontologist* 12 (Spring 1972):9–15.

———. "Time, Age, and the Life Cycle." *Annals of the American Academy of Political and Social Science* (September 1974): 187–198.

Neugarten, Bernice, and Gunhild Hagestad. "Aging and the Life Course." In R. H. Binstock and Ethel Shanas, eds., *Handbook of Aging and the Social Sciences.* New York: Van Nostrand Reinhold, 1976.

Neugarten, Bernice, et al. "Sociological Perspectives on the Life Cycle." In Paul Baltes and K. Warner Schaie, eds., *Life-Span Developmental Psychology: Personality and Socialization.* New York: Academy Press, 1973.

Nevid, Jeffrey. "Sex Differences in Factors of Romantic Attraction." *Sex Roles* 11(5/6) (1984):401–411.

Newberger, Eli, and Richard Bourne. "The Medicalization and Legalization of Child Abuse." In Richard Bourne and Eli Newberger, eds., *Critical Perspectives on Child Abuse.* Lexington, Mass.: Lexington Books, 1979.

Newberger, Eli, and James Hyde. "Child Abuse: Principles and Implications of Current Pediatric Practice." In Richard Bourne and Eli Newberger, eds., *Critical Perspectives on Child Abuse.* Lexington, Mass.: Lexington Books, 1979.

Newcomb, Michael. "Cohabitation in America: An Assessment of Consequences." *Journal of Marriage and the Family* (August 1979):597–603.

Newcomb, Michael, and Peter Bentler. "Assessment of Personality and Demographic Aspects of Cohabitation and Marital Success." *Journal of Personality Development* 4(1) (1980):11–24.

Newman, Philip R. "Successful Marriages are Primarily the Job of the Man." In Harold Feldman and Margaret Feldman, eds., *Current Controversies in Marriage and the Family*. Beverly Hills, Calif.: Sage, 1985.

Newton, Niles. *Maternal Emotions*. New York: Basic Books, 1955.

Nguyen, Tuan, et al. "The Meaning of Touch: Sex Differences." *Journal of Communications* 25 (1975):92–103.

NiCarthy, Ginny. *Getting Free: A Handbook for Women in Abusive Relationships*. Seattle, Wash.: Seal Press, 1982.

Nichols, Sharon, and Edward Metzen. "Impact of Wife's Employment upon Husband's Housework." *Journal of Family Issues* 3(2) (June 1982):199–216.

Noller, Patricia. *Nonverbal Communication and Marital Interaction*. Oxford, England: Pergamon Press, 1984.

Norton, A. J. "Family Life Cycle: 1980." *Journal of Marriage and the Family* 45 (1983): 267–275.

Norton, Arthur, and Paul Glick. "Marital Instability: Past, Present, and Future." *Journal of Social Issues* 32 (1976):5–20.

Notarius, Clifford, and Jennifer Johnson. "Emotional Expression in Husbands and Wives." *Journal of Marriage and the Family* 44(2) (May 1982):483–489.

Notman, M. "Adult Life Cycles." In Jacquelyn Parsons, ed., *The Psychobiology of Sex Differences and Sex Roles*. Washington, D.C.: Hemisphere, 1980.

Nye, F. Ivan. *Role Structure and Analysis of the Family*. Beverly Hills, Calif.: Sage, 1976.

Nye, F. Ivan, and Felix Berardo. *The Family: Its Structure and Interaction*. New York: Macmillan, 1973.

————, eds. *Emerging Conceptual Frameworks in Family Analysis*. 2 vols. New York: Praeger, 1981.

Nyquist, Linda, et al. "Household Responsibilities in Middle-Class Couples: The Contribution of Demographic and Personality Variables." *Sex Roles* 12(1/2) (1985):15–34.

O'Connell, Martin, and Carolyn Rogers. "Out-of-Wedlock Births, Premarital Pregnancies, and Their Effect on Family Formation and Dissolution." *Family Planning Perspectives* 16(4) (July/August 1984):157–162.

O'Neil, William. *Divorce in the Progressive Era*. New Haven: Yale University Press, 1967.

O'Reilly, Jane. "Wife Beating: The Silent Crime." *Time* (September 5, 1983).

Oakley, Ann. *The Captured Womb: A History of the Medical Care of Pregnant Women*. Oxford, England: Blackwell, 1984.

————. *Sex, Gender, and Society*. New York: Harper & Row, 1972.

————. *Sociology of Housework*. New York: Pantheon Books, 1974.

Odent, Michel. *Birth Reborn*. New York: Pantheon, 1984.

Offit, Avodah. *Night Thoughts: Reflections of a Sex Therapist*. New York: Congdon and Lattis, 1981.

Okun, B. F., and L. J. Rappaport. *Working with Families: An Introduction to Family Therapy*. North Scituate, Mass.: Duxbury Press, 1980.

Olson, David. "Insiders' and Outsiders' Views of Relationships: Research Studies." In George Levinger and H. Rausch, eds., *Close Relations*. Amherst, Mass.: University of Massachusetts Press, 1977.

Olson, David, and Herbert Laube. "How Different Types of Marital Interaction Affect Sexual Functioning." *Medical Aspects of Human Sexuality* 16(5) (May 1982):64–76.

Olson, David H., et al. *Families*. Beverly Hills, Calif.: Sage, 1983.

Paley, Grace. "Child Molesting—Why Parents Won't Listen." *Ms.* (January 1981):39–40.

Pallow-Fleury, Angie. "Your Hospital Birth: Questions to Ask." *Mothering* (Winter 1983):82–85.

Paloma, Margaret. "Role Conflict and the Married Professional Woman." In C. Safilios-Rothschild, ed., *Toward a Sociology of Women*. Lexington, Mass.: Xerox, 1972.

————, et al. "Reconsidering the Dual Career Marriage." In Joan Aldous, ed., *Two Paychecks*. Beverly Hills, Calif.: Sage, 1982.

Papp, Peggy. *The Process of Change*. New York: Guilford Press, 1983.

Parish, Thomas, and James Taylor. "The Impact of Divorce and Subsequent Father-Absences on Children's and Adolescents' Self-Concepts." *Journal of Youth and Adolescence* 8(4) (December 1979):427–432.

Parker, Dorothy. "The Waltz." In Dorothy Parker, *The Portable Dorothy Parker*. New York: Viking Press, 1972:47–51.

Parrot, Andrea, and Michael Ellis. "Homosexuals Should Be Allowed to Marry and Adopt or Rear Children." In Harold Feldman and Margaret Feldman, eds., *Current Controversies in Marriage and the Family*. Beverly Hills, Calif.: Sage, 1985.

Parsons, Jacqueline. "Sexual Socialization and Gender Roles in Childhood." In Elizabeth Allgeier and Naomi McCormick, eds., *Gender Roles and Sexual Behavior*. Palo Alto, Calif.: Mayfield, 1982.

————, ed. *The Psychobiology of Sex Differences and Sex Roles*. Washington, D.C.: Hemisphere, 1980.

Parsons, Talcott, and R. F. Bales. *Family Socialization and Interaction Processes*. Glencoe, Ill.: Free Press, 1955.

Patterson, G. *Families: Applications of Social Learning to Family Life*. Champaign, Ill.: Research Press, 1971.

Paul, Jude. "The Emotional Side of Amniocentesis." *Mothering* (Winter 1983):80–82.

Payne, Jaynann. "The Traditional Family with the Woman as Homemaker and the Man as Breadwinner Is Best for Most Families and for Society." In Harold Feldman and Margaret Feldman, eds., *Current Controversies in Marriage and the Family*. Beverly Hills, Calif.: Sage, 1985.

Payton, Isabelle. "Single-Parent Households: An Alternative Approach." *Family Economics Review* (Winter 1982):11–16.

Pear, Robert. "47% of Households Receive Federal Benefits." *New York Times*, April 17, 1985.

————. "What Causes the High U.S. Rate of Infant Deaths?" *New York Times*, March 20, 1985:19.

Pearlin, L. I. "Status Inequality and Stress in Marriage." *American Sociological Review* 40 (1975):344–357.

Pearlin, L. I., and J. S. Johnson. "Marital Status, Life Strains, and Depression." *American Sociological Review* 42 (1977):704–715.

Pearson, Jessica, et al. "Legal Change and Child Custody Awards." *Journal of Family Issues* 3(3) (March 1982): 5–24.

Peck, Robert. "Psychological Developments in the Second Half of Life." In John Anderson, ed., *Psychological Aspects of Aging*. Washington, D.C.: American Psychological Association, 1956.

Pedrick-Cornell, Claire, and Richard Gelles. "Elder Abuse: The Status of Current Knowledge." *Family Relations* 31 (July 1982):457–465.

Peek, Charles, et al. "Teenage Violence Toward Parents: A Neglected

Dimension in Family Violence." *Journal of Marriage and the Family* 47(4) (November 1985):1051–1058.

Peplau, Letitia. "What Homosexuals Want." *Psychology Today* 15(3) (March 1981):28–38.

Peplau, Letitia, and Steven Gordon. "The Intimate Relationships of Lesbians and Gay Men." In Elizabeth Allgeier and Naomi McCormick, eds., *Gender Roles and Sexual Behavior*. Palo Alto, Calif.: Mayfield, 1982.

Peplau, Letitia, et al. "Sexual Intimacy in Dating Relationships." *Journal of Social Issues* 33(2) (Spring 1977):86–109.

Peskin, Janice. "Measuring Household Production for the GNP." *Family Economics Review* 3 (1982):16–25.

Peterson, J. R., et al. "The *Playboy* Reader's Sex Survey." *Playboy* (March, 1983).

Pettit, Ellen, and Bernard Bloom. "Whose Decision Was It? The Effect of Initiator Status on Adjustment to Marital Disruption." *Journal of Marriage and the Family* 46(3) (August 1984):587–595.

Phillips, Celeste, and Joseph Anzalone. *Fathering: Participation in Labor and Delivery*. St. Louis: C. V. Mosby, 1978.

Pilisuk, Marc. "The Delivery of Social Support: The Social Inno-culation." *American Journal of Orthopsychiatry* 52(1) (January 1982):20–31.

Pines, A., and E. Aronson. "Antecedents, Correlates, and Conse-quences of Sexual Jealousy." *Journal of Personality* 51 (1983):108ff.

Pink, Jo Ellen, and Karen Smith Wampler. "Problem Areas in Stepfamilies: Cohesion, Adaptability, and the Stepfather-Adoles-cent Relationship." *Family Relations* 34(3) (July 1985):327–335.

Pitt, Leonard. *We Americans*. Glenview, Ill.: Scott, Foresman, 1976.

Pizzey, Erin. *Scream Quietly or the Neighbors Will Hear*. Short Hills, N.J.: R. Enslow, 1977.

Plato. *The Collected Dialogues of Plato*. Edith Hamiliton, ed. New York: Pantheon Books, 1961.

Pleck, Elizabeth. "Wife Beating in the 19th Century." *Victimology: An International Journal* 4(1) (1979):60–74.

Pleck, Joseph. *The Myth of Masculinity*. New York: Norton, 1981.

———, et al. "Conflicts Between Work and Family Life." *Monthly Labor Review* 103(3) (1980):29–32. U.S. Department of Labor, Bureau of Labor Statistics.

Pogrebin, Letty Cottin. *Family Politics*. New York, N.Y.: McGraw-Hill, 1983.

———. *Growing Up Free: Raising Your Child in the 1980's*. New York: McGraw-Hill, 1980.

———. "Are Men Discovering the Joys of Fatherhood?" *Ms.* (Feb-ruary 1982b):41–46.

———. "A Feminist in Sweden." *Ms.* (April 1982a):82–88.

Pohlman, E. H. *The Psychology of Birth Planning*. Cambridge, Mass.: Schenkman, 1969.

Poindexter, Joseph. "Shaping the Consumer." *Psychology Today* 17(5) (May 1983):64–68.

Polit-O'Hara, Denis, and Janet Kahn. "Communication and Con-traceptive Practices In Adolescent Couples." *Adolescence* 20(77) (Spring 1985):33–43.

Polk, Barbara. "Male Power and the Women's Movement." In Sue Cox, ed., *Female Psychology*. Chicago: Science Research Asso-ciates, 1976.

Pollis, Carole. "Value Judgments and World Views in Sexuality Education." *Family Relations* 34 (April 1985):285–290.

Pollitt, Katha. "The Parent Trap." *Mother Jones* 8(1) (January 1983):57–58.

Pollner, Melvin, and Lynn Wikler. "The Social Construction of Unreality." *Family Process* 24(2) (June 1985):241–254.

Polonko, Karen, et al. "Childlessness and Marital Satisfaction: Fur-ther Assessment." *Journal of Family Issues* 3(4) (December 1982):545–574.

Powell, D. H., and P. F. Driscoll. "Middle-Class Professionals Face Unemployment." *Society* (January/February 1973):14–19.

Powers, Mary, and Joseph Salvo. "Fertility and Child Care Arrange-ments as Mechanisms of Status Articulation." *Journal of Marriage and the Family* 44 (February 1982):21–33.

President's Commission on an Agenda for the Eighties. *The Quality of American Life*. Washington, D.C.: Government Printing Of-fice, 1980.

Press, Aric. "Divorce American Style." *Newsweek* (January 10, 1983):42–43.

Press, Robert. "Hunger in America." *Christian Science Monitor*, February 15, 1985:18–19.

Presser, Harriet. "Sally's Corner: Coping with Unmarried Mother-hood." *Journal of Social Issues* 36(1) (1980):107–129.

Price, Jane. "Who Waits to Have Children? And Why?" In Jeffrey Rosenfeld, ed., *Relationships: The Marriage and Family Reader*. Glenview, Ill.: Scott, Foresman, 1982.

Price-Bonham, S., and J. O. Balswick. "The Noninstitutions: Di-vorce, Desertion, and Remarriage." *Journal of Marriage and the Family* 42 (1980):959–972.

Price-Bonham, S., et al. "Divorce." In Eleanor Macklin and Roger Rubin, eds., *Contemporary Families and Alternative Lifestyles: Handbook on Research and Theory*. Beverly Hills, Calif.: Sage, 1983.

Proxmire, William. "Should the Congressional Ban on Credit Card Surcharges Be Extended?" *New York Times*, February 19 1984.

Puglisi, J. T., and D. W. Jackson. "Sex Role Identity and Self-Esteem in Adulthood." *Journal of Aging and Human Development* 12 (1981):129–138.

Radloff, Lenore. "Depression and the Empty Nest." *Sex Roles* 6(6) (December 1980):775–782.

Rados, Bill. "Herpes." *FDA Consumer* 19(3) (April 1985):4–7.

Rapoport, Rhona, and Robert Rapoport. "New Light on the Hon-eymoon." *Human Relations* 17 (February 1964):33–56.

Rapoport, Rhona, et al. *Fathers, Mothers, and Society*. New York: Vintage Books, 1977.

Rashke, Helen. "Family Conflict and Children's Self-Concepts: A Comparison of Intact and Single–Parent Families." *Journal of Marriage and the Family* 41(2) (May 1979):367–374.

———. "The Role of Social Participation in Post-Separation and Post Divorce Adjustment." *Journal of Divorce* 1 (1977):129–140.

Rasmussen, P. K., and K. J. Ferraro. "The Divorce Process." *Alter-native Lifestyles* 2(4) (1979):443–460.

Raven, Bertram, et al. "The Bases of Conjugal Power." In Ronald Cromwell and David Olson, eds., *Power in Families*. New York: Halstead Press, 1975.

Rawlings, Steve. "Families Maintained by Female Householders, 1970–1979." *Current Population Reports*. Special Studies, Series P23, No. 107. U.S. Department of Commerce, Bureau of the Census, 1980.

———. "Household and Family Characteristics: March 1983." *Cur-rent Population Reports* Bureau of the Census. Series P–20, No. 388. May 1984.

Rebelsky, F., and C. Hanks. "Fathers' Verbal Interaction with Infants in the First Three Months of Life." *Child Development* 42 (1971):63–68.

Regan, Mary, and Helen Roland. "Rearranging Family and Career Priorities: Professional Women and Men of the Eighties." *Journal of Marriage and the Family* 47(4) (November 1985):985–992.

Regan, Riley. "Alcohol Problems and Family Violence." In Jerry Flanzer, ed., *The Many Faces of Family Violence.* Springfield, Ill.: Charles C Thomas, 1982.

Reiger, D. A., et al. "The NIMH Epidemiologic Catchment Area Program." *Archives of General Psychiatry* 41(10) (October 1984):934–941.

Reiss, David. *The Family's Construction of Reality.* Cambridge, Mass.: Harvard University Press, 1981.

———. "Commentary: The Social Construction of Reality—The Passion Within Us All." *Family Process* 24(2) (June 1985):254–257.

Reiss, David, and Ellen Oliveri. "The Family Paradigm and Family Coping: A Proposal for Linking the Family's Intrinsic Adaptive Capacities to Its Responses to Stress." *Family Relations* 29(4) (1980):431–444.

Reiss, David, and Howard Hoffman, eds. *The American Family: Dying or Developing?* New York: Plenum Press, 1979.

Reiss, Ira. *Family Systems in America.* New York: Holt, Rinehart, and Winston, 1980, 3/e.

———. *The Social Context of Premarital Sexual Permissiveness.* New York: Irvington, 1967.

———. "Premarital Contraceptive Use." *Journal of Marriage and the Family* 37 (August 1975):619–630.

———, et al. "A Multivariate Model of the Determinants of Extramarital Sexual Permissiveness." *Journal of Marriage and the Family* 42 (May 1980):395–411.

Renne, Karen. "Correlates of Dissatisfaction in Marriage." *Journal of Marriage and the Family* 32 (February 1970):54–67.

Rettig, K. D., and M. M. Bubolz. "Interpersonal Resource Exchanges as Indicators of Quality of Marriage." *Journal of Marriage and the Family* 45 (1983):497–510.

Rexroat, Cynthia. "Women's Work Expectations and Labor-Market Experiences in Early and Middle Life-Cycle Stages. *Journal of Marriage and the Family* 47(1) (February 1985):131–142.

Riben, Marsha. "Adoption: A Circle of Love." *Mothering* (Winter 1983):20–23.

Rich, Adrienne. *Of Woman Born.* New York: Norton, 1976.

———. "Compulsory Heterosexuality and Lesbian Existence." In Ann Snitow, et al., eds., *Powers of Desire: The Politics of Sexuality.* New York: Monthly Review Press, 1983.

Richardson, J. G. "Wife Occupational Superiority and Marital Troubles: An Examination of the Hypothesis." *Journal of Marriage and the Family* 41 (1979):63–72.

Ridley, C. A. "Exploring the Impact of Work Satisfaction and Involvement on Marital Interaction When Both Partners Are Employed." *Journal of Marriage and the Family* 41 (1973):229–237.

Riegle, Donald. "The Psychological and Social Effects of Unemployment." *American Psychologist* 37(10) (October 1982):1113–1115.

Rierdon, Jill, and Elissa Leoff. "Representation of the Female Body by Early and Late Adolescent Girls." *Journal of Youth and Adolescence* 9 (August 1980):339–346.

Riggs, Kathryn. "The Battered Woman: What Makes Her Tick?" Unpublished paper, Women's Crisis Support and Shelter Services of Santa Cruz County, n.d.

Riley, David and Moncrieff Cochran. "Naturally Occurring Childrearing Advice for Fathers." *Journal of Marriage and the Family* 47(2) (May 1985):275–286.

Riley, L. E., and E. A. Spreitzer. "A Model for the Analysis of Lifetime Marriage Patterns." *Journal of Marriage and the Family* 36 (1974):64–70.

Rindfuss, Ronald, and Larry Bumpass. "Fertility During Marital Disruption." *Journal of Marriage and the Family* 39 (August 1977):517–528.

Robbins, Anthony. "Editorial: Can Reagan Be Indicted for Betraying Public Health?" *American Journal of Public Health* 73(1) (January 1983):12–13.

Roberts, Elizabeth. "Childhood Sexual Learning: The Unwritten Curriculum." In Clive M. Davis, ed., *Challenges in Sexual Science.* Philadelphia: Society for the Scientific Study of Sex, 1983.

———. "Television and Sexual Learning in Childhood." In National Institute of Mental Health, *Television and Behavior.* Washington, D.C.: Government Printing Office, 1982:209–223.

Robertson, J. "Interaction in Three Generation Families." *International Journal of Aging and Human Development* 6(2) (1975):103–110.

Robins, L. N., et al. "Lifetime Prevalence of Specific Psychiatric Disorders in Three Sites." *Archives of General Psychiatry* 41(10) (October 1984):949–958.

Robinson, Bryan, et al. "Gay Men's and Women's Perceptions of Early Family Life and Their Relationships with Parents." *Family Relations* 31 (January 1982):79–83.

Robinson, Donald. "How Can We Protect Our Elderly?" *Parade* (February 17, 1985):3–7.

Robinson, Paul. *The Modernization of Sex.* New York: Harper & Row, 1976.

Robinson, Pauline. "The Sociological Perspective." In Ruth Weg, ed., *Sexuality in the Later Years: Roles and Behavior.* New York: Academic Press, 1983.

Rollins, B. C., and K. L. Cannon. "Marital Satisfaction over the Family Life Cycle: A Reevaluation." *Journal of Marriage and the Family* 36 (May 1974):271–282.

Rollins, B. C., and H. Feldman. "Marital Satisfaction over the Family Life Cycle." *Journal of Marriage and the Marriage and the Family* 32 (February 1970):20–28.

Roman, Mel, and William Haddad. *The Case for Joint Custody.* New York: Holt, Rinehart, and Winston, 1978.

Roscoe, Bruce, and Nancy Benaske. "Courtship Violence Experienced by Abused Wives: Similarities in Pattens of Abuse." *Family Relations* 34(3) (July 1985):419–424.

Rosenblatt, Paul, and Roxanne Anderson. "Human Sexuality in Cross-Cultural Perspective." In Mark Cook, ed., *The Bases of Human Sexual Attraction.* New York: Academic Press, 1981.

Rosenfeld, Alvin. "Sexual Misuse and the Family." *Victimology: An International Journal* 2(2) (Summer 1977):226–235.

Rosenfeld, Alvin, and Eli Newberger. "Compassion vs. Control: Conceptual and Practical Pitfalls in the Broadened Definition of Child Abuse." In Richard Bourne and Eli Newberger, eds., *Critical Perspectives on Child Abuse.* Lexington, Mass.: Lexington Books, 1979.

Rosenthal, Carolyn. "Kinkeeping in the Familial Division of Labor."

Journal of Marriage and the Family 47(4) (November 1985):965–974.

Rosenthal, K., and H. F. Keshet. *Fathers Without Partners: A Study of Divorced Fathers and Their Families.* Totowa, N.J.: Rowman and Littlefield, 1980.

Ross, L., et al. "Television Viewing and Adult Sex-Role Attitudes." *Sex Roles* 8 (1982):589–592.

Rossi, Alice. "Transition to Parenthood." *Journal of Marriage and the Family* 30 (February 1968):26–39.

Ruben, Harvey. *Crises Intervention.* New York: Popular Library, 1976.

Rubenstein, C. "Wellness Is All." *Psychology Today* (October 1982):27–37.

Rubin, Lillian. *Intimate Strangers.* New York: Harper & Row, 1983.

———. *Women of a Certain Age.* New York: Harper Colophon, 1982.

———. *Worlds of Pain.* New York: Basic Books, 1976.

Rubin, Roger. "It Is Important that Both Men and Women Have Premarital Sex, Especially with the Person They Are Considering for Marriage." In Harold Feldman and Margaret Feldman, eds., *Current Controversies in Marriage and the Family.* Beverly Hills, Calif.: Sage, 1985.

Rubin, Zick. *Liking and Loving: An Invitation to Social Psychology.* New York: Holt, Rinehart, and Winston, 1973.

———, et al. "The Eye of the Beholder: Parents' View of Sex of Newborn." *American Journal of Orthopsychiatry* 44 (Fall 1974):512–519.

———. "Loving and Leaving: Sex Differences in Romantic Attachments." *Sex Roles* 7 (1981):821–835.

———. "Self Disclosure in Dating Couples: Sex Roles and the Ethic of Openness." *Journal of Marriage and the Family* 42 (1980):305–317.

Runyan, William. "In Defense of the Case Study Method." *American Journal of Orthopsychiatry* 52(3) (July 1982):440–446.

Rush, Florence. *The Best Kept Secret: Sexual Abuse of Children.* Englewood Cliffs, N.J.: Prentice-Hall, 1980.

Russell, Diana. *Rape in Marriage.* New York: Macmillan, 1982.

Ryder, R. G. "Compatability in Marriage." *Psychological Reports* 20 (1967):807–813.

———. "Longitudinal Data Relating Marriage Satisfaction and Having a Child." *Journal of Marriage and the Family* 35 (November 1973):604–606.

Sabatelli, Ronald, and Erin Cecil-Pigo. "Relational Interdependence and Commitment in Marriage." *Journal of Marriage and the Family* 47(4) (November 1985):931–938.

Sadler, Judith. "Stepfamilies: An Annotated Bibliography." *Family Relations* 32(1) (January 1983):149–152.

Safilios-Rothschild, Constantina. *Love, Sex, and Sex Roles.* Englewood Cliffs, N.J.: Prentice-Hall, 1977.

———. "Family Sociology or Wives' Sociology? A Cross-Cultural Examination of Decisionmaking." *Journal of Marriage and the Family* 31 (May 1969):290–301.

———. "A Macro- and Micro-Examination of Family Power and Love: An Exchange Model." *Journal of Marriage and the Family* 38 (1976):355–362.

———. "The Study of the Family Power Structure." *Journal of Marriage and the Family* 32 (November 1970): 539–543.

———, ed. *Toward a Sociology of Women.* Lexington, Mass.: Xerox, 1972.

Saghir, Marcel, and Eli Robins. *Male and Female Homosexuality.* Baltimore: Williams and Wilkins, 1973.

Sampson, Ronald. *The Psychology of Power.* New York: Pantheon Books, 1966.

Sanday, Peggy. "Margaret Mead's View of Sex Roles in Her Own and Other Societies." *American Anthropologist* 82(2) (June 1980):340–348.

Sanoff, Alvin. "When Wives Earn More Than Their Husbands." *U.S. News and World Report* (January 23, 1984):69–70.

Santrock, John. *Life-Span Development.* Duboque, Iowa: William C. Brown, 1983.

Santrock, John, and Richard Warsack. "Father Custody and Social Development in Boys and Girls." *Journal of Social Issues* 35(4) (1979):112–125.

Sarrel, Lorna, and Philip Sarrel. *Sexual Turning Points: The Seven Stages of Adult Sexuality.* New York: MacMillan, 1984.

Satir, Virginia. *Conjoint Family Therapy.* Palo Alto, Calif.: Science and Behavior Books, 1967.

———. *Peoplemaking.* Palo Alto, Calif.: Science and Behavior Books, 1972.

Scanzoni, John. *Sexual Bargaining.* Englewood Cliffs, NJ: Prentice-Hall, Inc., 1980, 2/e.

———. *Shaping Tomorrow's Families.* Beverly Hills, Calif.: Sage, 1983.

———. "Reconsidering Family Policy: Status Quo or Force for Change?" *Journal of Family Issues* 3(3) (September 1982):277–300.

———. "Social Processes and Power in Families." In W. Burr et al., eds., *Contemporary Theories about the Family* Vol. 1. New York: Free Press, 1979.

Scanzoni, John, and G. L. Fox. "Sex Roles, Family and Society: The Seventies and Beyond." *Journal of Marriage and the Family* 42 (November 1980):743–756.

Scarf, Maggie. *Unfinished Business.* New York: Doubleday, 1980.

Schafer, Robert, and Patricia Keith. "A Causal Analysis of the Relationship Between the Self-Concept and Marital Quality." *Journal of Marriage and the Family* 46(3) (November 1984):909–914.

———. "Equity in Marital Roles Across the Family Life Cycle. *Journal of Marriage and the Family* 43(2) (May 1981):359–367.

Schaffer, H. R. *The Growth of Sociability.* Baltimore: Penguin, 1971.

Schneider, David. *American Kinship: A Cultural Account.* Chicago: University of Chicago Press, 1980, 2/e.

Schooler, Carmi, et al. "Work for the Household: Its Nature and Consequences for Husbands and Wives." *American Journal of Sociology* 90(1) (July 1984):97–124.

Schorr, Lisbeth. "How We Can Ease the Pain of Youth in America." *San Jose Mercury,* April 7, 1985.

Schumm, Walter. "Marriage and Parenthood Are Necessary for a Happy Life for Both Men and Women." In Harold Feldman and Margaret Feldman, eds., *Current Controversies in Marriage and the Family.* Beverly Hills, Calif.: Sage, 1985.

———, et al. "His and Her Marriage Revisited." *Journal of Family Issues* 6 (June 1985):221–227.

Schvaneveldt, Jay. "The Interactional Framework in the Study of the Family." In F. Ivan Nye, and Felix Berardo, eds., *Emerging Conceptual Frameworks in Family Analysis.* New York: Praeger, 1981,

2/e.

Scott, David, and Bernard Wishy, eds. *America's Families: A Documentary History*. New York: Harper & Row, 1982.

Scott, Hilda. *Sweden's 'Right to be Human' Sex Role Equality: The Goal and the Reality*. Armonk, N.Y.: M. E. Sharp, 1982.

Sears, Robert. "Sex Typing, Object Choice, and Child Rearing." In Herant Katchadourian, ed., *Human Sexuality: A Comparative and Developmental Perspective*. Berkeley: University of California Press, 1979.

Sears, Robert, et al. *Patterns of Child Rearing*. Stanford, Calif.: Stanford University Press, 1976.

Seidenberg, Robert. "Advertising and Drug Acculturation." In Robert Coombs et al., *Socialization in Drug Abuse*. Cambridge, Mass.: Schenkman, 1976.

Select Committee on Children, Youth and Families, U.S. House of Representatives. *Families and Child Care: Improving the Options*. Report 98–1180. 98th Congress; 2nd Session. Washington, D.C.: U.S. Government Printing Office, 1985.

Seligmann, Jean. "The Dates Who Rape." *Newsweek* (April 9, 1984):91–92.

Seligson, Marcia. *The Eternal Bliss Machine*. New York: Bantam Books, 1973.

Shanas, Ethel. "Family-Kin Networks and Aging in Cross-Cultural Perspective." In P. J. Stein et al., eds., *The Family*. Reading, Mass.: Addison-Wesley, 1977.

Sharpley, C. F., and D. G. Cross. "A Psychometric Evaluation of the Spanier Dyadic Adjustment Scale." *Journal of Marriage and the Family* 44(3) (August 1982):739–742.

Sheehy, Gail. *Passages*. New York: Dutton, 1975.

———. "Are You Ready to Listen?" *Parade* (July 29, 1984):4–6.

Sherman, Beth. "Spanking: Experts Say No." *San Jose Mercury*, June 24, 1985.

Shipman, Gordon. *Handbook for Family Analysis*. Lexington, Mass.: D. C. Heath, 1982.

Shneidman, Edwin, ed. *Death: Current Perspectives*. Palo Alto, Calif.: Mayfield, 1984.

Shornack, L., and E. Shornack. "The New Sex Education and the Sexual Revolution." *Family Relations* 31 (1982):531–544.

Sidorowicz, Laura, and G. Sparks Lunney. "Baby X Revisited." *Sex Roles* 6(1) (February 1980):67–73.

Silverman, I. "Physical Attractiveness and Courtship." *Sexual Behavior* (September 1971):22–25.

Simenauer, Jacqueline, and David Carroll. *Singles: The New Americans*. New York: Simon & Schuster, 1982.

Simmel, Georg. *The Sociology of Georg Simmel*. Edited by K. Wolff. New York: Free Press, 1950.

Simon, William, and John Gagnon. *Sexual Conduct*. Chicago: Aldine Press, 1973.

Singh, B. K. "Trends in Attitudes Toward Premarital Sexual Relationships." *Journal of Marriage and the Family* 42 (May 1980):387–393.

Sitower, Curtis. "A Society Mobilizes Against Teen Suicide." *Christian Science Monitor*, February 7, 1985:23ff.

Skinner, Denise. "Dual-career Family Stress and Coping: A Literature Review." *Family Relations* 29(4) (October 1980).

Skolnick, Arlene. *The Intimate Environment*. Boston: Little, Brown, 1978.

Skolnick, Arlene, and Jerome Skolnick, eds. *Family in Transition*. Boston: LIttle, Brown, 1973 and 1980.

Slater, Philip. "On Social Regression." *American Journal of Sociology* 28 (1963):339–364.

Sluzki, C. E., and V. Eliseo. "The Double Bind as a Universal Pathogenic Situation." *Family Process* 10 (1971):397–410.

Smart, Laura. "It Is Equally Acceptable to Meet Others in Less Conventional Ways—Advertising, Computer Dating, Singles Parties, and the Like." In Harold Feldman and Margaret Feldman, eds., *Current Controversies in Marriage and the Family*. Beverly Hills, Calif.: Sage, 1985.

Smelser, Neil, and Erik Erikson, eds. *Themes of Work and Love in Adulthood*. Cambridge, Mass.: Harvard University Press, 1980.

Smith, Daniel, and Michael Hindus. "Premarital Pregnancy in America: 1640–1971." *Journal of Interdisciplinary History* 4 (Spring 1975):537–570.

Smith, Page. *Daughters of the Promised Land*. Boston: Little, Brown, 1968.

Smith, William. *The Stepchild*. Chicago: University of Chicago Press, 1952.

Snitow, Ann, et al., eds. *Powers of Desire: The Politics of Sexuality*. New York: Monthly Review Press, 1983.

"Soaking the Poor." *San Jose Mercury*, April 11, 1984.

Sollie, Donna. "Transition to Parenthood." In Nick Stinnett et al., eds., *Family Strengths*. Lincoln: University of Nebraska Press, 1980.

Sommerville, John. *The Rise and Fall of Childhood*. Beverly Hills, Calif.: Sage, 1982.

Sontag, Susan. "The Double Standard of Aging." *Saturday Review* 55 (September 1972):29–38.

Sorenson, Robert. *Adolescent Sexuality in Contemporary America*. New York: World, 1973.

Spanier, Graham. "Improve, Refine, Recast, Expand, Clarify—But Don't Abandon." *Journal of Marriage and the Family* 47(4) (November 1985):1073–1074.

———. "Married and Unmarried Cohabitation in the United States: 1980." Paper presented at the annual meeting of the Population Association of America, San Diego, April 29–May 1, 1982.

———. "Measuring Dyadic Adjustment." *Journal of Marriage and the Family* 38 (February 1976):15–28.

Spanier, G. B., and E. A. Anderson. "The Impact of the Legal System on Adjustment to Marital Separation." *Journal of Marriage and the Family* 41 (1979):605–613.

Spanier, G. B., and R. Casto. "Adjustment to Separation and Divorce: A Qualitative Analysis." In G. Levinger and O. C. Moles, eds., *Separation and Divorce*. New York: Basic Books, 1979.

Spanier, G. B., and Frank Furstenberg. "Remarriage After Divorce: A Longitudinal Analysis of Well-Being." *Journal of Marriage and the Family* 44(3) (August 1982):709–720.

Spanier, G. B., and Robert Lewis. "Marital Quality: A Review of the Seventies." *Journal of Marriage and the Family* 42(4) (November 1980):825–840.

Spanier, G. B., and R. L. Margolis. "Marital Separation and Extramarital Sexual Behavior." *Journal of Sex Research* 19 (1983):23–48.

Spanier, G. B., and Linda Thompson. "A Confirmatory Analysis of the Dyadic Adjustment Scale." *Journal of Marriage and the Family* 44(3) (August 1982):731–738.

Spanier, G. B., et al. "Marital Adjustment over the Family Life Cycle: The Issue of Curvilinearity." *Journal of Marriage and the Family* 37 (May 1975):263–275.

————, et al. "Marital Trajectories of American Women: Variations in the Life Course." *Journal of Marriage and the Family* 47(4) (November 1985):993–1003.

Spence, Janet, et al. "Ratings of Self and Peers on Sex Role Attributes and their Relation to Self-Esteem and Conceptions of Masculinity and Femininity." *Journal of Personality and Social Psychology* 32 (1975):29–39.

Spitze, Glenna, and Scott South. "Women's Employment, Time Expenditure, and Divorce." *Journal of Family Issues* 6(3) (September 1985):307–329.

Spock, Benjamin. *Baby and Child Care.* New York: Pocket Books, 1945, 1968, and 1976.

Spock, Benjamin, and Michael Rothenberg. *Dr. Spock's Baby and Child Care.* New York: Pocket Books, 1985.

Sprecher, Susan. "Sex Differences in Bases of Power in Dating Relationships." *Sex Roles* 12(3/4) (1985):449–462.

Sprey, Jetse, and Sarah Matthews. "Contemporary Grandparenthood." *Annals of the American Academy* 464 (November 1982):91–103.

Stacey, Barrie. "Infant-Mother Attachment: A Social Psychological Perspective." *Social Behavior and Personality* 8(1) (1980):33–40.

Stake, Jayne. "Women's Self-estimates of Competence and the Resolution of the Career/Home Conflict." *Journal of Vocational Behavior* 14(1) (February 1979):33–42.

Stampp, Kenneth. *The Peculiar Institution.* New York: Vintage Books, 1956.

Stanton, M. Colleen. "The Fetus: A Growing Member of the Family'. *Family Relations* 34(3) (July 1985):321–326.

Stanyon, Mary. "Getting Back to Wedding Basics." *San Francisco Examiner*, April 11, 1982.

Steele, B. F. "Parental Abuse of Infants and Small Children." In E. J. Anthony and T. Bendeck, eds., *Parenthood: Its Psychology and Psychopathology.* Boston: Little, Brown, 1970.

————. "Psychodynamic Factors in Child Abuse." In C. Henry Kempe and Ray Helfer, eds., *The Battered Child.* Chicago: University of Chicago Press, 1980.

Steele, B. F., and C. B. Pollock. "A Psychiatric Study of Parents Who Abuse Infants and Small Children." In Ray Helfer and C. Henry Kempe, eds., *The Battered Child.* Chicago: University of Chicago Press, 1976.

Steffen, John. "Social Competence, Family Violence, and Problem Drinking." In Jerry Flanzer, ed., *The Many Faces of Family Violence.* Springfield, Ill.: Charles C Thomas, 1982.

Stein, Peter. *Single.* Englewood Cliffs, N.J.: Prentice-Hall, 1976.

————. "The Lifestyles and Life Chances of the Never-Married." *Marriage and Family Review* 1 (July/August 1978):1–11.

————, ed. *The Single Life.* New York: St. Martin's Press, 1981.

Stein, Peter, and Meryl Fingrutd. "The Single Life Has More Potential for Happpiness than Marriage and Parenthood for Both Men and Women." In Harold Feldman and Margaret Feldman, eds., *Current Controversies in Marriage and the Family.* Beverly Hills, Calif.: Sage, 1985.

Steinglass, Peter. "A Life History Model of the Alcoholic Family." In David Olson and Brent Miller, eds., *Family Studies Review Yearbook.* Vol. 1. Beverly Hills, Calif.: Sage, 1983.

Steinman, Susan. "The Experience of Children in a Joint-Custody Arrangement: A Report of a Study." *American Journal of Orthopsychiatry* 51(3) (July 1981):403–414.

Steinmetz, Suzanne, and Sarah Foulke. "Marriage and Family Periodicals." *Behavioral and Social Sciences Librarian.* 1(3) (Spring 1980):225–243.

Stengel, Edwin. "The Suicide Attempt." In Edwin Shneidman, ed., *Death: Current Perspectives.* Palo Alto, Calif.: Mayfield, 1984.

Stephen, Beverly. "How Today's Woman Plans Her Wedding." *San Francisco Chronicle*, April 19, 1982.

Stephen, Timothy. "Fixed-sequence and Circular-causal Models of Relationship Development: Divergent Views on the Role of Communication in Intimacy." *Journal of Marriage and the Family* 47(4) (November 1985):955–963.

Stephen, Timothy, and Teresa Harrison. "A Longitudinal Comparison of Couples with Sex-Typical and Non-Sex-Typical Orientations to Intimacy." *Sex Roles* 12(1/2) (1985):195–205.

Stewart, Phyllis, and Muriel Cantor, eds. *Varieties of Work.* Beverly Hills, Calif.: Sage, 1982.

Stinnet, Nick. "In Search of Strong Families." In Nick Stinnet et al., eds., *Building Family Strengths.* Lincoln: University of Nebraska Press, 1979.

————, et al., eds. *Building Family Strengths.* Lincoln: University of Nebraska Press, 1979.

————. *Family Strengths 4.* Lincoln: University of Nebraska Press, 1982.

Stockard, Jean, and Miriam Johnson. "The Social Origin of Male Dominance." *Sex Roles* 5(2) (April 1980):199–218.

Stone, Elizabeth. "Breast-Feeding: A Feminist Fad?" *Ms.* 11(8) (February 1983):68ff.

Strasser, Susan. *Never Done: A History of American Housework.* New York: Pantheon Books, 1982.

Straus, R. "Alcoholism and Problem Drinking." In R. K. Merton and R. Nisbet, eds., *Contemporary Social Problems.* New York: Harcourt Brace Jovanovich, 1976.

Strauss, Murray. "Preventing Violence and Strengthening the Family." In Nick Stinnett, et al., *Family Strengths 4.* Lincoln: University of Nebraska Press, 1980.

————, et al. *Behind Closed Doors.* Garden City, N.Y.: Anchor Books, 1980.

Strong, Bryan. "Sex, Character, and Reform: Sexual Attitudes in America, 1820–1920." Unpublished doctoral dissertation, Stanford University, 1972.

————. "Sex and Incest in the 19th Century: Toward a History of the Experiential Family." *Journal of Marriage and the Family* 34 (August 1973):457–466.

Strong, Bryan, and Christine DeVault. "Inside America's New Families." *Family Life Educator* 1(3) (Spring 1983):9–11.

Strong, Bryan, and Rebecca Reynolds. *Understanding Our Sexuality.* St. Paul, Minn.: West, 1982.

Strong, Bryan, et al. *The Marriage and Family Experience.* St. Paul, Minn.: West, 1979.

Strout, Richard. "Census Bureau Figures Show Fewer Traditional Families, More Poverty." *Christian Science Monitor*, August 10, 1982:5.

Strube, Michael J., and Linda Barbour. "Factors Related to the Decision to Leave an Abusive Relationship." *Journal of Marriage and the Family* 46(4) (November 1984):837–844.

Stuckert, R. P. "Role Perception and Marital Satisfaction." *Marriage and Family Living* 334 (February 1973):415–419.

Suid, Murray, et al. *Marriage, Etc.* Reading, Mass.: Addison-Wesley, 1976.

Sullivan, Harry Stack. *The Collected Works of Harry Stack Sullivan.*

New York: Norton, 1952.

Sunoff, Alvin. "A Conversation with Jerome Kagan." *U.S. News and World Report* (March 25, 1985):63–64.

Sussman, Marvin. "Relationships of Adult Children with their Parents." In Ethel Shanas and G. F. Streib, eds., *Social Structure and the Family*. Englewood Cliffs, N.J.: Prentice-Hall, 1965.

Sweetser, Dorrian Apple. "Broken Homes: Stable Risk, Changing Reasons, Changing Forms." *Journal of Marriage and the Family* 47(3) (August 1985):709–715.

Swenson, Clifford, and Geir Trahaug. "Commitment and the Long-Term Marriage Relationship." *Journal of Marriage and the Family* 47(4) (November 1985):939–945.

Symons, Donald. *The Evolution of Human Sexuality*. New York: Oxford University Press, 1979.

"TLC for DWMs and SWFs." *Time* (January 10, 1983):65.

Talbot, Nathan, ed. *Raising Children in Modern America*. Boston: Little, Brown, 1976.

Tamashiro, R. J. "Developmental Stages in the Conceptualization of Marriage." *Family Coordinator* 28 (1978):237–244.

Tavris, Carol, and Susan Sadd. *The Redbook Report on Female Sexuality*. New York: Dell, 1977.

Tavris, Carol, and Carole Wade. *The Longest War: Sex Differences in Perspective*. New York: Harcourt Brace Jovanovich, 1984, 2/e.

Taylor, Leslie, and Eli Newberger. "Child Abuse in the International Year of the Child." In Richard Gelles and Clair Cornell, eds., *International Perspectives on Family Violence*. Lexington, Mass.: Lexington Books, 1983.

Teachman, Jay, and Alex Heckert. "The Impact of Age and Children on Remarriage." *Journal of Family Issues* 6 (June 1985):185–203.

Teachman, Jay, and Karen Polonko. "Timing of the Transition to Parenthood: A Multidimensional Birth-interval Approach." *Journal of Marriage and the Family* 47(4) (November 1985):867–879.

Teevan, James. "Reference Groups and Premarital Sexual Behavior." *Journal of Marriage and the Family* (May 1972):283–291.

Tesser, Abraham, and Richard Reardon. "Perceptual and Cognitive Mechanisms in Human Sexual Attraction." In Mark Cook, ed., *The Bases of Human Sexual Attraction*. New York: Academic Press, 1981.

Teyber, Edward. "Structural Family Relations: A Review." *Family Therapy* 8(1) (1981):39–48.

Thoen, Gail. "Only Qualified Persons Should Be Parents." In Harold Feldman and Margaret Feldman, eds., *Current Controversies in Marriage and the Family*. Beverly Hills, Calif.: Sage, 1985.

Thompson, Anthony. "Emotional and Sexual Components of Extramarital Relations." *Journal of Marriage and the Family* 46(1) (February, 1984):35–42.

———. "Extramarital Sex: A Review of the Research Literature." *Journal of Sex Research* 19(1) (February 1983):1–22.

Thompson, Edward, Jr., and Patricia Gongla. "Single-Parent Families: In the Mainstream of American Society." In Eleanor Macklin and Roger Rubin, eds., *Contemporary Families and Alternative Life Styles*. Beverly Hills, Calif.: Sage, 1983.

Thompson, Linda, et al. "Developmental Stage and Perceptions of Intergenerational Continuity." *Journal of Marriage and the Family* 47(4) (November 1985):913–920.

———. "Do Parents Know Their Children: The Ability of Mothers and Fathers to Gauge the Attitudes of Their Young Adult Children." *Family Relations* 34(3) (July 1985):315–320.

Thompson, Roger. "Adolescent Culture in Colonial Massachussetts." *Journal of Family History* 9(2) (Summer 1984):127–144.

Thomson, Elizabeth, and Richard Williams. "Beyond Wive's Sociology: A Method for Analyzing Couple Data." *Journal of Marriage and the Family* 44(4) (November 1982):999–1008.

Thomson, Keith. "Research on Human Embryos: Where to Draw the Line." *American Scientist* 73(2) (March–April 1985):187–189.

Thorman, George. *Family Violence*. Springfield, Ill.: Charles C Thomas, 1980.

Thornton, Jeannye. "Behind a Surge in Suicides of Young People." *U.S. News and World Report* (June 20, 1983):66.

———. "Family Violence Emerges from the Shadows." *U.S. News and World Report* (January 23, 1984):66.

Tierney, Kathleen, and David Corwin. "Exploring Intrafamilial Child Sexual Abuse." In David Finkelhor et al., eds., *The Dark Side of Families*. Beverly Hills, Calif.: Sage, 1983.

Tinklenberg, Jared. "Alcohol and Violence." In Peter Bourne and Ruth Fox, eds., *Alcoholism: Progress in Research and Treatment*. New York: Academic Press, 1973.

Tolchin, Martin. "Librarians Rally the Troops to Battle U.S. on Information." *New York Times*, April 8, 1985.

Tolstoy, Leo. "Family Happiness." In Leo Tolstoy, *The Death of Ivan Illych and Other Stories*. New York: Signet Books, 1972.

Tooth, Geoffrey. "Why Children's TV Turns Off So Many Parents." *U.S. News & World Report* (February 18, 1985):65.

Trafford, Abigail. *Crazy Time*. New York: Harper & Row, 1982.

———. "Crazy Time: The Aftermath of Divorce." *Cosmopolitan* (January 1983):177–179, 197ff.

———. "Medical Science Discovers the Baby." *U.S. News and World Report* (November 10, 1980):59–62.

Treas, Judith, and Vern L. Bengtson. "The Demography of Mid- and Late-Life Transitions." *Annals of the American Academy* 464 (November 1982):11–21.

Trethowan, W. H. "The Couvade Syndrome." In J. Howells, ed., *Modern Perspectives in Psycho-Obstetrics*. New York: Bruner/Mazel, 1972.

———. "The Couvade Syndrome: Some Further Observations." *Journal of Psychosomatic Research* 12 (1968):107–115.

Troiden, Richard, and Erich Goode. "Variables Related to the Acquisition of a Gay Identity." *Journal of Homosexuality* 5 (Summer 1980):383–392.

Troll, Lillian E. "The Family of Later Life: A Decade Review." *Journal of Marriage and the Family* 33 (1971):263–290.

———. "Family Life in Middle and Old Age." *Annals of the American Academy* 464 (November 1982):38–46.

Trost, Jan. "Abandon Adjustment!" *Journal of Marriage and the Family* 47(4) (November 1985):1072–1073.

Trotter, Robert. "Born Too Soon." *Science News* 118 (October 11, 1980):234–235.

Tufte, Virginia, and Barbara Myerhoff, eds. *Changing Images of the Family*. New Haven: Yale University Press, 1980.

Turk, James, and Norman Bell. "Measuring Power in Families." *Journal of Marriage and the Family* 34 (May 1976):215–222.

Turner, R. Jay, and William R. Avison. "Assessing Risk Factors for Problem Parenting: The Significance of Social Support." *Journal of Marriage and the Family* 47(4) (November 1985):881–892.

U.S. Bureau of the Census. "Household and Family Characteristics: March 1983." *Current Population Reports.* Population Characteristics. Series P–20; No. 388. (May 1984).

U.S. Bureau of the Census. "Household, Families, Marital Status, and Living Arrangements: March 1984 (Advanced Report)." *Current Population Reports.* Population Characteristics. Series P–20, No. 391. (August 1984).

U.S. Bureau of the Census. "Marital Status and Living Arrangements: March, 1984." *Current Population Reports.* Population Characteristics. Series P–20, No. 399. (July 1985).

U.S. Commission on Civil Rights. *Child Care and Equal Opportunity for Women.* Clearinghouse Publication No. 67, June 1981.

U.S. Commission on Civil Rights. *The Federal Response to Domestic Violence.* January 1982.

U.S. Commission on Civil Rights. *Under the Rule of Thumb: Battered Women and the Administration of Justice.* January 1982.

U.S. Department of Labor, Women's Bureau. "Twenty Facts on Women Workers." Washington, D.C.: U.S. Government Printing Office, 1984.

Udry, J. Richard. *The Social Context of Marriage.* Philadelphia: Lippincott, 1974.

———. "Marriage Alternatives and Marital Disruption." *Journal of Marriage and the Family* 43 (November 1981):889–897.

Valentine, Deborah. "The Experience of Pregnancy: A Developmental Process." *Family Relations* 31 (April 1982):243–248.

Van Gelder, Lindsy, and Carry Carmichael. "But What About Our Sons?" *Ms.* 4 (October 1975):24–26.

Van Meter, Mary Jane. "Couples Who Have Children Should Stay Together Even If They Are Unhappy With Each Other." In Harold Feldman and Margaret Feldman, eds., *Current Controversies in Marriage and the Family.* Beverly Hills, Calif.: Sage, 1985.

Vance, Carole. "Gender Systems, Ideology, and Sex Research." In Ann Snitow et al., eds., *Powers of Desire: The Politics of Sexuality.* New York: Monthly Review Press, 1983.

———, ed. *Pleasure and Danger: Exploring Female Sexuality.* Boston: Routledge and Kegan Paul, 1984.

Vandell, Deborah, and Mary Anne Corasaniti. "After School Care: Choices and Outcome for Third Graders." Paper presented to Association for the Advancement of Science, May 27, 1985.

Vanek, Joann. "Time Spent in Housework." *Scientific American* 231 (1974):116–120.

Vann, Richard. "The Youth of *Centuries of Childhood.*" *History and Theory* 21(2) (1982):279–297.

Veevers, J. E. "Voluntary Childlessness." *Family Coordinator* 22 (April 1973):199–206.

Velsor, Ellen, and Angela O'Rand. "Family Life Cycle, Work Career Patterns, and Women's Wages at Midlife." *Journal of Marriage and the Family* 46(2) (May 1984):365–373.

Vera, Hernan, et al. "Age Heterogamy in Marriage." *Journal of Marriage and the Family* 47(3) (August 1985):553–566.

Verbrugge, Lois. "Marital Status and Health." *Journal of Marriage and the Family* 41 (May 1979):267–285.

Verdery, E. Augustus. "Treatment of the Alcoholic by the Nonphysician. In Peter Bourne and Ruth Fox, eds., *Alcoholism: Progress in Research and Treatment.* New York: Academic Press, 1973.

Verzaro-Lawrence, Marce. "Shared Childrearing: A Challenging Alternative Lifestyle." *Alternative Lifestyles* 4(2) (May 1981):205–217.

Vicinus, Martha. "Sexuality and Power: A Review of Current Work in the History of Sexuality." *Feminist Studies* 8(1) (1982):133–156.

Visher, E. B., and J. Visher. *Stepfamilies: A Guide to Working with Stepparents and Stepchildren,* New York: Brunner/Mazel, 1979.

Voeller, Bruce. "Society and the Gay Movement." In Judd Marmor, ed., *Homosexual Behavior.* New York: Basic Books, 1980.

Voydanoff, Patricia. "Work Roles as Stressors in Corporate Families." *Family Relations* 29(4) (1980):489–494.

Voydanoff, Patricia, and Robert Kelly. "Determinants of Work-Related Family Problems Among Employed Parents." *Journal of Marriage and the Family* 46(4) (November 1984):881–892.

Vrazo, Fawn. "Anti-Abuse Books Geared to Children." *San Jose Mercury,* October 28, 1984:3L.

Waite, Linda. "Working Wives and the Family Life Cycle." *American Journal of Sociology* 86(2) (September 1980):272–294.

Wald, Esther. *The Remarried Family: Challenge and Promise.* New York: Family Service Association of America, 1981.

Waldman, Elizabeth. "Today's Girls in Tomorrow's Labor Force: Projecting Their Participation and Occupations." *Youth and Society* 16(3) (March 1985):375–392.

Waletzky, Lucy. "Husbands' Problems with Breastfeeding." *American Journal of Orthopsychiatry* 49(2) (April 1979):349–352.

Walker, Alexis J. "Reconceptualizing Family Stress." *Journal of Marriage and the Family* 47(4) (November 1985):827–837.

Walker, Alexis, and Linda Thompson. "Feminism and Family Studies." *Journal of Family Issues* 5(4) (December 1984):545–570.

Walker, Kathryn. "At Home: Organizing Eases the Load." *U.S. News and World Report* (January 25, 1982).

Walker, Kathryn, and Margaret Woods. *Time Use: A Measure of Household Production of Family Goods and Services.* Washington, D.C.: The Center for the Family, American Home Economics Association, 1976.

Walker, Kenneth Nevada, and Lillian Messinger. "Remarriage after Divorce: Dissolution and the Reconstitution of Family Boundaries." *Family Process* 18(2) (June 1979):185–192.

Walker, Lenore. *The Battered Woman.* New York: Harper Colophon, 1979.

———. "Battered Women: Sex Roles and Clinical Issues." *Professional Psychology* 12(1) (February 1981):81–91.

Waller, Willard. "The Rating and Dating Complex." *American Sociological Review* 2 (1937):727–734.

Waller, Willard, and Reuben Hill. *The Family: A Dynamic Interpretation.* New York: Dryden Press, 1951.

Wallerstein, Judith, and Joan Kelly. *Surviving the Breakup: How Children and Parents Cope With Divorce.* New York: Basic Books, 1980b.

———. "Effects of Divorce on the Visiting Father-Child Relationship." *American Journal of Psychiatry* 137(12) (December 1980a):1534–1539.

Wallis, Claudia. "The New Origins of Life." *Time* (September 10, 1984):46–53.

Walsh, Froma, ed. *Normal Family Processes.* New York: Guilford Press, 1982.

Walster, Elaine, and G. William Walster. *A New Look at Love.* Reading, Mass.: Addison-Wesley, 1978.

Warren, Carol. *Identity and Community in the Gay World.* New York: Wiley, 1974.

Warshaw, Robin. "The American Way of Birth." *Ms.* (September 1984):45ff.

Watkins, Harriet, and Marilyn Bradbard. "Child Maltreatment: An Overview with Suggestions for Intervention and Research." *Family Relations* 31 (July 1982):323–333.

Watson, Russell. "A Hidden Epidemic." *Newsweek* (May 14, 1984):30–36.

———. "What Price Day Care?" *Newsweek* (September 10, 1984):14–21.

Weber, Timothy, et al. "A Beginner's Guide to the Problem Oriented First Family Interview." *Family Process* 24(3) (September 1985):356–364.

Wedemeyer, Nancy, and Harold Grotevant. "Mapping the Family System: A Technique for Teaching Family Systems Theory Concepts." *Family Relations* 31 (April 1982):185–193.

Weeks, M. O'Neal, and Bruce Gage. "A Comparison of the Marriage-Role Expectations of College Women Enrolled in a Functional Marriage Course in 1961, 1972, and 1978." *Sex Roles* 11(5/6) (1984):377–388.

Weg, Ruth. "Introduction: Beyond Intercourse and Orgasm." *Sexuality in the Later Years: Roles and Behavior.* New York: Academic Press, 1983b.

———. "The Physiological Perspective." In Ruth Weg, ed., *Sexuality in the Later Years: Roles and Behavior.* New York: Academic Press, 1983c.

———, ed. *Sexuality in the Later Years: Roles and Behavior.* New York: Academic Press, 1983a.

Weideger, Paul. *Menstruation and Menopause.* New York: Knopf, 1975.

Weinberg, Daniel. "Measuring Poverty." *Family Economics Review* 2 (1985):9–13.

Weinberg, Martin, and Colin Williams. *Male Homosexuals: Their Problems and Adaptations.* New York: Oxford University Press, 1974.

Weinberg, S. K. *Incest Behavior.* New York: Citadel Press, 1955.

Weingarten, Helen. "Marital Status and Well–being: A National Study Comparing First-Married, Currently Divorced, and Remarried Adults." *Journal of Marriage and the Family* 47(3) (August 1985):653–662.

———. "Remarriage and Well-Being." *Journal of Family Issues* 1(4) (December 1980):533–559.

Weis, David, and Joan Jurich. "Size of Community as a Predictor of Attitudes toward Extramarital Sexual Relations." *Journal of Marriage and the Family* 47(1) (February 1985):173–178.

Weiss, Robert. *Going It Alone.* New York: Basic Books, 1979.

———. *Marital Separation.* New York: Basic Books, 1976.

———. "The Fund of Sociability." *Transactions* (July/August 1969):36–43.

———. "The Impact of Marital Dissolution on Income and Consumption of Single-Parent Households." *Journal of Marriage and the Family* 46(1) (February 1984):115–127.

———. "Men and the Family." *Family Processes* 24 (1985):49–58.

———. "The Study of Loneliness." In Peter Stein, ed., *The Single Life.* New York: St. Martin's Press, 1981.

Weitzman, Lenore. *The Divorce Revolution: The Unexpected Social and Economic Consequences for Women and Children in America.* New York: The Free Press, 1985.

———. *The Marriage Contract.* Englewood Cliffs, N.J.: Prentice-Hall, 1978.

Weitzman, Lenore, and Ruth Dixon. "The Transformation of Legal Marriage through No-Fault Divorce." In Arlene Skolnick and Jerome Skolnick, eds., *Family in Transition.* Boston: Little, Brown, 1980.

Welch, Mary, and Dorothy Herman. "Why Miscarriage Is So Misunderstood." *Ms.* (February 1980):14–22.

"The Welfare State in America," Special Issue of *Annals of the American Academy* 479 (May 1985).

Wertheimer, Barbara. *We Were There: The Story of Working Women in America.* New York: Pantheon Books, 1979.

Wharton, Donald. "Adverse Reproductive Outcomes: The Occupational Health Issue of the 1980's." *American Journal of Public Health.* 73(1) (January 1983):15–16.

Whelan, Elizabeth. *Boy or Girl?* New York: Pocket Books, 1978.

White House Conference on Families. *Families and Economic Well-being.* Washington, D.C.: U.S. Government Printing Office, 1980a.

White House Conference on Families. *Families and Major Institutions.* Washington, D.C.: U.S. Government Printing Office, 1980b.

White, Gregory. "Inducing Jealousy: A Power Perspective." *Personality and Social Psychology Bulletin* 6(2) (June 1980a):222–227.

———. "Jealousy and Partner's Perceived Motives for Attraction to a Rival." *Social Psychology Quarterly* 44(1) (March 1981):24–30.

———. "Physical Attractiveness and Courtship Progress." *Journal of Personality and Social Psychology* 39(4) (October 1980b):660–668.

White, K. L., and P. Bulloch. *Health of Populations.* New York: Rockefeller, 1980.

White, Susan. "Sexuality and Pregnancy." *Archives of Sexual Behavior* 11(5) (October 1982):429–444.

Whitehurst, Robert. "There Are a Number of Equally Valid Forms of Marriage, Such as Multiple Marriage, Swinging, Adultery, and Open Marriage." In Harold Feldman and Margaret Feldman, eds., *Current Controversies in Marriage and the Family.* Beverly Hills, Calif.: Sage, 1985.

Williams, Juanita. "Middle Age and Aging." In Juanita Williams, ed., *Women: Behavior in a Biosocial Context.* New York: Norton, 1977.

———. "Sexuality in Marriage." In Benjamin Wolman and John Money, eds., *Handbook of Human Sexuality.* Englewood Cliffs, N.J.: Prentice-Hall, 1980.

Wilson, Glenn. *The Secrets of Sexual Fantasy.* London: J. M. Dent, 1978.

Winch, Robert. *Mate-Selection: A Study of Complementary Needs.* New York: Harper & Row, 1958.

Winick, Marianne, and Charles Winick. *The Television Experience: What Children See.* Beverly Hills, Calif.: Sage, 1979.

Winn, Marie. *The Plug-In Drug.* New York: Bantam Books, 1978.

Winn, Rhoda, and Niles Newton. "Sexuality and Aging: A Study of 106 Cultures." *Archives of Sexual Behavior* 11(4) (August 1982):283–298.

Wirtz, Richard, and Dorothy Wirtz. *Lying-In: A History of Child-*

birth in America. New York: Harper & Row, 1978.

Wishy, Bernard. *The Child and the Republic.* Philadelphia: Lippincott, 1968.

Wolfe, Linda. *The Cosmo Report.* New York: Bantam, 1982.

Wolfe, Lisa. "Colleges Are Taking New Steps to Reduce Drinking on Campus." *New York Times,* March 8, 1985:1ff.

Wolfron, Jill. "Have You Hugged a Kid Today?" *San Jose Mercury,* October 28, 1984:1L–2L.

Wolkind, Stephen, and Eva Zajicek, eds. *Pregnancy: A Psychological and Social Study.* New York: Grune and Stratton, 1981.

Wootan, George. "An Update on Breast-Feeding." *Mother Earth News* 91 (January/February 1985):84–85.

"Work Interruptions and Earnings." *Family Economics Review* 2 (1985):30–31.

Wynne, Lyman, et al. "Pseudo-Mutuality in the Family Relationships of Schizophrenics." *Psychiatry* 21 (1958):205–220.

Yankelovich, Daniel. *New Rules.* New York: Random House, 1981.

Yarber, William. "Student Perceptions of Need for Family Life and Sex Education." *Education* 101(3) (Spring 1981):279–284.

Yarrow, Leah. "Should Children Play With Guns?" *Parents* (January 1983):51–53.

Ybarra, Lea. "When Wives Work: The Impact on the Chicano Family." *Journal of Marriage and the Family* (February 1982):169–178.

Yeager, Anne. "Infections and Pregnancy." *The Helper* 1(2) (October 1979):1–2.

Yogev, Sara, and Janne Brett. "Perceptions of the Division of Housework and Child Care and Marital Satisfaction." *Journal of Marriage and the Family* 47(3) (August 1985):609–618.

Youngs, David, and Anke Erhardt, eds. *Psychosomatic Obstetrics.* New York: Appleton-Century-Crofts, 1980.

Youngs, David, and Mary Jane Lucas. "Postpartum Depression: Hormonal vs. Alternative Perspectives." In David Youngs and Anke Erhardt, eds., *Psychosomatic Obstetrics.* New York: Appleton-Century-Crofts, 1980.

Zajicek, Eva. "The Experience of Being Pregnant." In Stephen Wolkind and Eva Zajicek, eds., *Pregnancy: A Psychological and Social Study.* New York: Grune and Stratton, 1981.

Zaslow, Martha, et al. "Depressed Mood In New Fathers." Unpublished paper presented to the Society for Research in Child Development. Boston, April 1981.

Zawada, Mary. "Displaced Homemaker: Unresolved Issues." *Personnel and Guidance Journal* 59(2) (October 1980):110–112.

Zelizer, Viviana. *Pricing the Priceless Child: The Changing Social Value of Children.* New York: Basic Books, 1985.

Zellman, Gail, and Jacqueline Goodchilds. "Becoming Sexual in Adolescence." In Elizabeth Allgeier and Naomi McCormick, eds., *Gender Roles and Sexual Behavior.* Palo Alto, Calif.: Mayfield, 1982.

Zelnick, Melvin. "Sex Education and Knowledge of Pregnancy Risk Among United States Teenage Women." *Family Planning Perspectives* 11 (November/December 1979):335.

Zelnik, Melvin, and Farida Shaw. "First Intercourse Among Young Adults." *Family Planning Perspectives* 15 (1983):64–70.

Zigler, Edward. "Controlling Child Abuse in America: An Effort Doomed to Failure?" In Peter Bourne and Eli Newberger, eds., *Critical Perspectives on Child Abuse.* Lexington, Mass.: Lexington Books, 1979.

Zigler, Edward, and Kirby Heller. "Strengthening the Family by Strengthening Social Policy in Behalf of Children and Families." In Nick Stinnett et al., eds., *Family Strengths.* Lincoln: University of Nebraska Press, 1980.

Zilbergeld, Bernie. *Male Sexuality.* New York: Bantam Books, 1979.

Zimmerman, Shirley. "Alternatives in Human Reproduction for Involuntarily Childless Couples." *Family Relations* 31 (April 1982):233–241.

Zolla, Elemire. *The Androgyne.* New York: Crossroads Publishers, 1981.

Index

Acknowledgments (*continued*)

Newsweek, Inc. All rights reserved. Reprinted by permission.; **121** From: *Family Systems in America*, 3rd ed. by Ira Reiss. Copyright © 1980 by Holt, Rinehart and Winston. Reprinted by permission of CBS College Publishing.; **137** Copyright © 1984 by The New York Times Company. Reprinted by permission.; **140** From *Sexual Bargaining*, 2nd ed., by John Scanzoni, © 1982. Published by The University of Chicago Press.; **141** "Jealousy," by Gordon Clanton and Lynn Smith, Copyright © 1977, Prentice-Hall, Inc.; **148** "Cathy" by Cathy Guisewite. Copyright, 1984, Universal Press Syndicate. Reprinted with permission. All rights reserved.; **173** Courtesy of Compatability Plus; **174** Reprinted from *U.S. News & World Report*, Issue of 1/11/82. Copyright, 1982, U.S. News & World Report, Inc.; **177** "Variations in Life-Style," *The Family Coordinator*, Vol. 24, No. 4, October, 1975, by Peter J. Stein. Reprinted by permission of National Council on Family Relations.; **208** © Copyright National Broadcasting Company, Inc., 1976; **210** Copyright © 1984, Sara Jennifer Malcolm. Published in *Ms.*, October 1984.; **234** Abridged from pp. 206, 208, 209–213 in *American Couples* by Philip Blumstein, Ph.D. and Pepper Schwartz, Ph.D. Copyright © 1983 by Philip Blumstein and Pepper W. Schwartz. Reprinted by permission of William Morrow & Company.; **236** Reprinted with permission from *Family Planning Perspectives*, Vol. 16, No. 3, 1984.; **256** Illustrations courtesy of Carnation Company.; **273** Reprinted by permission of The Sterling Lord Agency, Inc. Copyright © 1985 by James Webb.; **269 and 271** Copyright, 1984, Janet Isaacs Ashford. Published by The Crossing Press, Box 640, Trumansburg, NY 14886.; **288** "Changing Family Roles and Interactions," M. Szinovacz, *The Marriage and Family Review*, Vol. 7, No. 3/4, 1984. Published by The Haworth Press, Inc., New York, NY.; **306** Drawing by Koren; © 1977 The New Yorker Magazine, Inc.; **314** "Succeeding in the Union" by Jean Marzollo. Copyright, 1985. Reprinted with permission from the San Jose Mercury News.; **316** © Philip Zwerling; **316** This first appeared in the *Los Angeles Times*.; **317** Reprinted by permission: Tribune Media Services; **350** Excerpts reprinted from Pat Mainardi, "The Politics of Housework," *Discrimination Against Women*, Hearings Before the Special Subcommittee on Education of the Committee on Education and Labor, House of Representatives, 91st Congress, second session, Part I (Washington: U.S. Government Printing Office, Committee on Education and Labor, 1970) pp. 265–268.; **351** Reprinted with permission from the San Jose Mercury News.; **366** "Doonesbury" by Garry Trudeau. Copyright, 1985, Universal Press Syndicate. Reprinted with permission. All rights reserved.; **370** Drawing by Weber; © 1966 The New Yorker Magazine, Inc.; **380** From p. 18 in *The Myth of the Happy Child* by Carole Klein. Copyright © 1975 by Carole Klein. Reprinted by permission of Harper & Row, Publishers, Inc.; **386** "Warning! Keep Out! No Children Allowed," by Linda Lee. Copyright © 1984. Published in *Redbook*.; **387** Reprinted by permission of the San Jose Mercury News.; **388** Reprinted by permission from *Growing Up Free* by Letty Cottin Pogrebin, © 1980. Published by McGraw-Hill, Inc.; **411** Courtesy of Mell Lazarus and News America Syndicate.; **416** From pp. 83–87 in *The Family Crucible* by Augustus Y. Napier with Carl A. Whitaker. Copyright © 1978 Augustus Y. Napier and Carl A. Whitaker. Reprinted by permission of Harper & Row, Publishers, Inc.; **419** "Inside the Family," by David Kantor and William Lehr. Copyright © 1975. Published by Jossey-Bass Publishers.; **428** © 1966 by Helen Thurber from *Thurber & Company* published by Harper & Row.; **446** *Body Politics: Power, Sex and Nonverbal Communication*, by Nancy M. Henley. Copyright © 1977 by Prentice-Hall, Inc., Englewood Cliffs, NJ 07632. Reprinted by permission of the publisher.; **447** Copyright © 1984 by Judith Viorst. Originally appeared in *Redbook*.; **469** Reprinted by permission; Sexual Abuse Diagnostic Center, Children's Institute International.; **481** © Janet Bukovinsky/New Jersey Monthly, 1982.; **483** Copyright 1984, Meredith Maran, excerpted from *West Magazine*, May 20, 1984.; **485** This first appeared in the *Los Angeles Times*.; **511** "Stand By Your Marriage," by Sarah Crichton. Copyright © 1984. Originally appeared in *Redbook*.; **513** Copyright 1983, by Newsweek, Inc. All rights reserved. Reprinted by permission.; **528** © Signe Wilkinson: San Jose Mercury News.; **538** "Single Mothers: Last of the Supermoms," by Lindsy Van Gelder, *Ms.*, April 1981, reprinted by permission.; **540** *Stepfamilies* © 1978/Emily Visher and John Visher; Bruner/Mazel, Inc. Reprinted by permission.; **548** (top and bottom) David Olson et al., "Marital and Family Satisfaction," Figure 10.1/p. 172; "Circumplex Models in Families," Figure 4.1/p. 50, in *Families*. Copyright © 1983 by Sage Publications, Inc. Reprinted by permission of Sage Publications, Inc.; **558** Copyright © 1983 by Anita Shreve. All rights reserved. Reprinted by permission of the Author.

Photo Credits

5 Laurie DeVault; **9** Courtesy of George Gold; **11** Courtesy of the Library of Congress; **14** Louise Thornton; **33** Laurie DeVault; **40** Karen Rosenthal, Stock, Boston, Inc.; **63** Abby Aldrich Rockefeller Folk Art Center, Williamsburg, Virginia; **72–73** Bryan Strong and Christine DeVault; **76** Courtesy of the Library of Congress; **93** (left) Laurie DeVault; **93** (right) Christine DeVault; **96** The Bettmann Archive; **98** Laurie DeVault; **104** (left and right) Christine DeVault; **120** Nancy Durrell McKenna, from *Woman's Experience of Sex* by Sheila Kitzinger; **122** Fredrik D. Bodin, Stock, Boston, Inc.; **127** Laurie DeVault; **131** P. François Gérard, *Cupid and Psyche*, Musée National du Louvre—Alinari/Art Resource, N.Y.; **162** (top and bottom) Laurie DeVault; **169** Laurie DeVault; **189** Laurie DeVault; **197** Allan Burgis; **219** Peter Behrens, *The Kiss* (1898)

Photo Credits (*continued*)

.